International Directory of
COMPANY
HISTORIES

International Directory of

COMPANY

HISTORIES

VOLUME 24

Editor

J. Pederson

St. James Press

AN IMPRINT OF GALE

DETROIT • NEW YORK

STAFF

Jay P. Pederson, *Editor*

Miranda H. Ferrara, *Project Manager*

Joann Cerrito, David J. Collins, Nicolet V. Elert, Kristin Hart,
Margaret Mazurkiewicz, Michael J. Tyrkus, *Contributing Editors*

Peter M. Gareffa, *Managing Editor, St. James Press*

Library of Congress Catalog Number: 89-190943

British Library Cataloguing in Publication Data

International directory of company histories. Vol. 24
I. Jay P. Pederson
338.7409

ISBN 1-55862-365-5

Printed in the United States of America
Published simultaneously in the United Kingdom

St. James Press is an imprint of Gale

Cover photograph: The Philadelphia Stock Exchange, Philadelphia, Pennsylvania
(courtesy Philadelphia Stock Exchange)

10 9 8 7 6 5 4 3 2 1

CONTENTS _____

Company Histories

PREFACE

The St. James Press series *The International Directory of Company Histories (IDCH)* is intended for reference use by students, business people, librarians, historians, economists, investors, job candidates, and others who seek to learn more about the historical development of the world's most important companies. To date, *IDCH* has covered over 3,400 companies in 24 volumes.

Inclusion Criteria

Most companies chosen for inclusion in *IDCH* have achieved a minimum of US$100 million in annual sales and are leading influences in their industries or geographical locations. Companies may be publicly held, private, or non-profit. State-owned companies that are important in their industries and that may operate much like public or private companies also are included. Wholly owned subsidiaries and divisions are profiled if they meet the requirements for inclusion. Entries on companies that have had major changes since they were last profiled may be selected for updating.

The *IDCH* series highlights 10% private and non-profit companies, and features updated entries on approximately 35 companies per volume.

Entry Format

Each entry begins with the company's legal name, the address of its headquarters, its telephone, toll-free, and fax numbers, and its web site. A statement of public, private, state, or parent ownership follows. A company with a legal name in both English and the language of its headquarters country is listed by the English name, with the native-language name in parentheses.

The company's founding or earliest incorporation date, the number of employees, and the most recent sales figures available follow. Sales figures are given in local currencies with equivalents in U.S. dollars. For some private companies, sales figures are estimates. The entry lists the exchanges on which a company's stock is traded and its ticker symbol, as well as the company's principal Standard Industrial Classification codes.

Entries generally contain a *Company Perspectives* box which provides a short summary of the company's mission, goals, and ideals, a list of *Principal Subsidiaries*, *Principal Divisions*, *Principal Operating Units*, and articles for *Further Reading*.

American spelling is used throughout *IDCH*, and the word "billion" is used in its U.S. sense of one thousand million.

Sources

Entries have been compiled from publicly accessible sources both in print and on the Internet such as general and academic periodicals, books, annual reports, and material supplied by the companies themselves.

Cumulative Indexes

IDCH contains two indexes: the **Index to Companies**, which provides an alphabetical index to companies discussed in the text as well as companies profiled, and the **Index to Industries**, which allows researchers to locate companies by their principal industry. Both indexes are cumulative and specific instructions for using them are found immediately preceding each index.

Suggestions Welcome

Comments and suggestions from users of *IDCH* on any aspect of the product as well as suggestions for companies to be included or updated are cordially invited. Please write:

The Editor
International Directory of Company Histories
St. James Press
27500 Drake Rd.
Farmington Hills, Michigan 48331-3535

ABBREVIATIONS FOR FORMS OF COMPANY INCORPORATION

A.B.	Aktiebolaget (Sweden)
A.G.	Aktiengesellschaft (Germany, Switzerland)
A.S.	Atieselskab (Denmark)
A.S.	Aksjeselskap (Denmark, Norway)
A.Ş.	Anomin Şirket (Turkey)
B.V.	Besloten Vennootschap met beperkte, Aansprakelijkheid (The Netherlands)
Co.	Company (United Kingdom, United States)
Corp.	Corporation (United States)
G.I.E.	Groupement d'Intérêt Economique (France)
GmbH	Gesellschaft mit beschränkter Haftung (Germany)
H.B.	Handelsbolaget (Sweden)
Inc.	Incorporated (United States)
KGaA	Kommanditgesellschaft auf Aktien (Germany)
K.K.	Kabushiki Kaisha (Japan)
LLC	Limited Liability Company (Middle East)
Ltd.	Limited (Canada, Japan, United Kingdom, United States)
N.V.	Naamloze Vennootschap (The Netherlands)
OY	Osakeyhtiöt (Finland)
PLC	Public Limited Company (United Kingdom)
PTY.	Proprietary (Australia, Hong Kong, South Africa)
S.A.	Société Anonyme (Belgium, France, Switzerland)
SpA	Società per Azioni (Italy)

ABBREVIATIONS FOR CURRENCY

DA	Algerian dinar		M$	Malaysian ringgit
A$	Australian dollar		Dfl	Netherlands florin
Sch	Austrian schilling		Nfl	Netherlands florin
BFr	Belgian franc		NZ$	New Zealand dollar
Cr	Brazilian cruzado		N	Nigerian naira
C$	Canadian dollar		NKr	Norwegian krone
RMB	Chinese renminbi		RO	Omani rial
DKr	Danish krone		P	Philippine peso
E£	Egyptian pound		Esc	Portuguese escudo
Fmk	Finnish markka		SRls	Saudi Arabian riyal
FFr	French franc		S$	Singapore dollar
DM	German mark		R	South African rand
HK$	Hong Kong dollar		W	South Korean won
HUF	Hungarian forint		Pta	Spanish peseta
Rs	Indian rupee		SKr	Swedish krona
Rp	Indonesian rupiah		SFr	Swiss franc
IR£	Irish pound		NT$	Taiwanese dollar
L	Italian lira		B	Thai baht
¥	Japanese yen		£	United Kingdom pound
W	Korean won		$	United States dollar
KD	Kuwaiti dinar		B	Venezuelan bolivar
LuxFr	Luxembourgian franc		K	Zambian kwacha

International Directory of

COMPANY
HISTORIES

Acclaim Entertainment Inc.

1 Acclaim Plaza
Glen Cove, New York 11542
U.S.A.
(516) 656-5000
Fax: (516) 656-2040
Web site: http://www.acclaimnation.com

Public Company
Incorporated: 1986
Stock Exchanges: NASDAQ
Ticker Symbol: AKLM
Employees: 680
Sales: $165.4 million (1997)
SICs: 7372 Prepackaged Software

Acclaim Entertainment Inc. is a worldwide independent manufacturer of entertainment software for PCs, and video game cartridges for Nintendo, SEGA, and Sony systems, targeted mostly at teens. Its Acclaim Distribution Company (ADI) subsidiary sells and distributes various entertainment software publishers' products. Acclaim Comics publishes comic books under numerous imprints. Acclaim also operates motion capture studios, creating movie special effects and, until 1998, developed coin-operated arcade video games.

As part of its development and marketing strategy, Acclaim maintains relationships with Fox, The Major League Baseball Players Association, The National Basketball Association, The National Football League, Warner Bros., and The World Wrestling Federation, among others.

Acclaim went from a shoestring budget and one-room office in Oyster Bay, to a two-story brick structure, millions in net income, and offices in France, Germany, Japan, Spain, and the United Kingdom. Some of Acclaim's top gaming competitors include The 3DO Company, Activision Inc., Broderbund Software Company, Electronic Arts Inc., The Learning Company, Macromedia Inc., MicroProse Inc., Sierra On-Line, Software Toolworks, and Toy Headquarters; allies include Nintendo

Company Ltd. and Sega Enterprises Ltd. Some of Acclaim's competitors in comics include DC, Marvel, Dark Horse, and Image.

Getting Started, 1986–92

Founded in 1986 by three former Activision executives, CEO/Co-chairman Gregory Fischbach, Executive Vice-President/Co-Chairman James Scoroposki, and President/COO Robert Holmes, Acclaim Entertainment Inc. was the first independent company in the United States to publish software for the Nintendo Entertainment System (NES), launching several of the best-selling products in the entertainment software industry's history, debuting with *Star Voyager* in August 1987. Acclaim went public via a reverse merger with Gamma Capital Corp. that year.

Acclaim was incorporated in Colorado in June 1988 and, the following month, the videogame market was booming again. Acclaim made its mark selling games like *Rambo*, *Wizards & Warriors*, and *WrestleMania* for Nintendo.

Acclaim was reincorporated in Delaware in May 1989. In October, Acclaim established a Tokyo-based subsidiary—Acclaim Japan Ltd.—to distribute products in Asia and Europe. Revenue for 1989 reached $109.3 million, with net income of $12.3 million.

In the late 1980s, a barrier faced dedicated home video systems because of the proliferation of home computers like Amiga, Apple, Atari, and Commodore, which had greater market penetration and could play games from floppy disks. Early software titles for the NES and Sega 8-bit "Master System" were not sufficiently advanced over PC games for consumers to buy new hardware. From 1990 to 1992, that changed. Cost reductions in ROM chips for cartridges led to vast improvements in game graphics for NES and Master System, Sega's Genesis/Megadrive system was successful, Nintendo's Super NES (SNES) grew faster than 8-bit systems, and GameBoy—Nintendo's portable video game player, debuting in 1989—had high market penetration.

Company Perspectives:

Acclaim Entertainment Inc. is a developer, publisher and mass marketer of interactive entertainment software for use with dedicated interactive entertainment hardware platforms and multimedia personal computer (PC) systems. The company operates its own software design studios and a motion capture studio, and markets and distributes its software in the major territories throughout the world. The company's operating strategy is to develop software for the entertainment platforms and multimedia PCs that dominate the interactive entertainment market at a given time or which the company perceives as having the potential for achieving mass market acceptance. The company's strategy is to emphasize sports simulation and arcade-style titles for entertainment platforms, and fantasy role-playing, adventure, and sports simulation titles for multimedia PCs. The company intends to continue to support its existing key brands with the introduction of new titles supporting those brands and to develop one or more additional key brands each year based on its original and licensed properties, which may then be featured on an annual basis in successive titles.

From 1987 to 1991, most of Acclaim's revenue came from video game cartridge sales, like *Double Dragon II: The Revenge*—licensed for use with the 8-bit NES—and *Kwirk*, Acclaim's first GameBoy product.

In April 1990, Acclaim acquired LJN Toys Ltd. from MCA Inc. for $13.75 million in cash and stock. The acquisition of the toy manufacturing company increased the number of Acclaim's Nintendo "slots." (Nintendo's restricting the number of titles its licensees could introduce annually made acquiring slots from other companies the only way licensees could accelerate their game-release rate.) In September, Acclaim sold the Entertech Division of LJN for $1.7 million. Acclaim also entered GameBoy's compact video system software market with three titles under the Acclaim/LJN labels, and introduced new games for the NES, a line of Super-Play hand-held electronic games, and a dual wireless-remote controller system.

In June, Acclaim created the Acclaim Entertainment Canada Ltd. subsidiary to distribute products in Mexico, and a subsidiary in Europe to support its increased growth overseas.

In October, Acclaim, inspired by its own *Masters of the Game* newsletter, entered an exclusive marketing agreement with Sears to promote products through Sears' *Wish Book* catalog, reaching over 12 million consumers nationwide, with a *Video Game Magic* insert featuring information, playing hints, and tips on Acclaim/LJN products, marking Acclaim's largest direct-mail venture, and a first for Sears with a Nintendo licensee.

From 1986 to 1990, NES hardware sales grew, triggering concurrent demand for game cartridges. By Christmas 1990, retailers were swamped with hundreds of NES titles, and Acclaim posted revenues of $140.7 million, with net income of $6.9 million.

During 1991, 8-bit NES sales fell, along with demand for cartridges. In February, Acclaim released *Bart Versus the Space Mutants*—based on the popular animated TV show "The Simpsons"—and *WWF Wrestlemania Challenge*. Nintendo introduced its 16-bit SNES in late August, including a *Super Mario World* cartridge and two controllers, and Sega's Genesis, introduced in 1989, with a huge library of titles, was gaining market share rapidly.

In December, Acclaim agreed to distribute software for Sega's 16-bit Genesis and GameGear units. Retail sales reached $142.2 million. But, as obsolete inventory built up, Acclaim's first SNES title—*Populous*—sold poorly, costs rose, and product returns cut into gross profits, Acclaim posted a six-figure loss. The company to catch was Electronic Arts, considered the best developer/marketer of interactive entertainment software.

In January 1992, Acclaim acquired Mirrorsoft Ltd., including U.S. subsidiary Arena Entertainment Inc., from Robert Maxwell's empire, for $231,250 and a waiver of $1 million in debt. At The Consumer Electronics Show (CES) that month, and again in June, Nintendo and Sega slashed prices on hardware, making the machines more accessible to recession-battered consumers. By the end of 1992, video hardware sales were strong, demand for games increased, and Acclaim had hot arcade titles like *Double Dragon*, *NARC*, and *Smash TV*.

In March, Acclaim became the first American company to publish 16-bit Nintendo Super Famicom software in Japan when it introduced *WWF Super Wrestlemania*. Acclaim also created a subsidiary called Flying Edge, debuting at CES with Genesis' 16-bit titles *Krusty's Fun House* (based on *The Simpsons*), *Ferrari Grand Prix*, and arcade-successful *Arch Rivals*.

In November, Acclaim reached agreements with Nintendo of America, Sony Corporation, and Sega of Japan to publish CD-ROM software for CD-ROM hardware systems, and signed an exclusive agreement with Ardent Studios and Biomechanics Corporation of America, experts in motion study and biomechanical, medical, and sports analysis for motion capture techniques leading to development of synthetic actors as models for videogame characters.

That year, Acclaim took a $3.1 million write-off for its remaining investment in *Video Power*, a 30-minute syndicated television show featuring characters from Acclaim games, but managed to post revenue of nearly $250 million, with net income of $17.1 million. By year's end, Acclaim was developing software titles like *The Simpsons: Bart's Nightmare*, *George Foreman's Knockout Boxing*, and *Trog*. LJN released *Roger Clemens's MVP Baseball*, *NBA Super All-Star Challenge*, *The Amazing Spiderman & Uncanny X-Men: Arcade's Revenge*, *Terminator 2: Judgment Day*, *Aliens 3*, *Bill and Ted's Excellent Adventure*, *Wolverine*, *Thrilla's Surfari*, *The Amazing Spider-Man*, *The Amazing Spider-Man 2*, *Crash Dummies*, *WWF Superstars*, *NBA All-Star Challenge 2*, and *Beetlejuice*, for nearly a dozen hardware platforms, compared to three in 1991.

Controversy Brings Revenue, 1993–94

Until May 1992 virtually all Acclaim's revenue was derived from Nintendo's platform. Beginning in 1993, Acclaim intensified efforts to develop entertainment software for Sega's platform. In June, concurrent with Nintendo's purchasing major European distributor Bandai, Acclaim established ADI to service retailers, including Toys-R-Us, Wal-Mart, Kmart, Sears, Target, Electronic Boutique, Kay-Bee Toys, and Babbage's/Software Etc. Additionally, Acclaim became one of the first entertainment software companies to establish direct distribution in Europe, creating sales offices in the United Kingdom, France, Germany, the Benelux countries, plus Canada and Japan, and initiated distribution relationships with Phillips Electronics and Sony's Columbia TriStar Home Video Distribution.

In July, Acclaim received the rights to develop video game software titles to the first 15 films produced by director James Cameron's film company Lightstorm Entertainment, beginning with Arnold Schwarzenegger's *True Lies*. Acclaim also signed an agreement with video game software developer Hi Tech Expressions allowing the latter to distribute PC-based versions of *Mortal Kombat, Smash TV, WWF Super WrestleMania*, and others throughout North America.

By August, Acclaim had two of the top-selling arcade titles: *Mortal Kombat*—which competed with Capcom's *Street Fighter II*—and *NBA Jam* (hitting number one and number two, respectively). *Mortal Kombat* was launched on "Mortal Monday" (September 13) following a $10 million advertising blitz—more than any independent producer had spent marketing a game—selling two million units across the four major software formats for Sega and Nintendo (something no other game maker had done) in the first few weeks, and finishing the year as the top-selling video game. Additional titles released in 1993 included *WWF Royal Rumble* and *Championship Soccer*.

Also that month, Acclaim signed with London-based Probe Entertainment Ltd.—a manufacturer of games, including *Lemmings, SimCity*, and *Dracula*—to jointly develop several hardware and software platforms.

In September, *Mortal Kombat* created controversy for its violence and explicit graphics (including ripping out opponents' hearts or spines, with gushing blood). Although some stores refused to carry it, the game did not slump in the retail market, selling over six million copies. The controversy reached the U.S. Congress, which exerted pressure on the video and computer game industries, warning that a mandatory federal ratings system was forthcoming unless they created an acceptable system. The video game industry, dominated by Nintendo and Sega, responded by forming The Interactive Digital Software Association (IDSA) which, in June 1994, reluctantly organized a ratings system before the holidays, so parents would have a superficial guide to game content, like the familiar G/PG-13/R/NC-17/X ratings for movies. But the effort divided video game and computer game developers. The Software Publishers Association (SPA)—primary representative of computer software developers—resisted Congressional pressure to join IDSA because of the $500 required by developers for each game rated (by a panel of parents and educators), wanting a self-administered system where developers would review predetermined ratings criteria and make its own decisions on ratings, something The Senate Government Affairs Subcommittee on Regulation and Government Information, led by Senators Herb Kohl and Joseph Lieberman, found unacceptable.

The debate raged into 1994, with SPA forming another group, The Recreational Software Advisory Council (RSAC), which pledged to create an independent board providing ratings. Then, confusing matters more, Sega adopted a self-administered rating system in late 1993, with three symbols: "GA" (general audiences), "MA-13" (mature audiences), and "MA-17" (adults only) before switching to IDSA ratings in 1994. 3DO also released a self-administered system early in 1994, with four ratings: "E" (everyone), "12" (suggesting guidance for players under 12), "17" (suggesting guidance for those under 17), and "AO" (adults only).

Also in 1993, Acclaim signed through 1995 with WMS Industries under which it had first right of refusal to convert any of WMS's arcade games to the Sega or Nintendo game formats for three years after their release. Acclaim also released *Terminator 2: The Arcade Game* with an infrared game controller under its Arena label, and signed development agreements with content provider Park Place Entertainment, as well as distribution agreements with Virgin Games. By year's end, in an industry estimated at nearly $4 billion, sales for Acclaim jumped to $327.1 million, with net income of $28.2 million.

By early 1994, 16-bit software sales slowed, and 8-bit software sales continued to slide as consumers lost interest in low-graphics capability, turning their eyes toward the new technology of CD-ROM. Acclaim entered that technology with CD-ROM editions of *Mortal Kombat II* (arcade game of the year), *Corpse Killer, Slam City with Scottie Pippen, Kids on Site, What's My Story?, Supreme Warrior, World Federation Raw* (Acclaim's first 24-Meg video game), and two games based on Itchy and Scratchy, cartoon characters from "The Simpsons."

In April, Sega joined with Acclaim to develop games using Acclaim's motion capture technology and Sega's proprietary Titan architecture video game system technology, based on Hitachi RISC chips similar to those at the heart of the Saturn and Super 32X advanced systems, which allowed easy transfer of arcade versions to home formats. Acclaim was the first U.S. publisher to take advantage of the Titan system. In May, Acclaim entered the coin-operated game business with *Batman Forever*, based on the hit movie.

In June, consolidations in the computer software and service industries continued, with Computer Associates International Inc. buying ASK Group Inc. and Novell Inc. acquiring WordPerfect Corp. and part of Borland International Inc. Acclaim followed suit in July, buying Voyager Communications Inc. (renamed Acclaim Comics Inc.) for $65 million in cash and stock. Voyager, founded in 1990, possibly the third largest comic book publisher in the United States with 16 monthly series under its "Valiant" imprint; plus proprietary comics for KFC, Kraft Foods, MCA, Metropolitan Life, Nintendo, and others; also licensed properties for trading cards and other merchandise. In September, Acclaim acquired a minority interest in Digital Pictures Inc.—a publisher and developer of

CD-based software—for $4 million, and Digital became the first independent label distributed worldwide by ADI.

In July, Acclaim extended its agreement with Marvel Comics, giving Acclaim exclusive worldwide rights to sell and distribute products under the Marvel Software brand. In September, *Red City*, a short ''film'' directed by Chelsea Pictures/ Redwing Film Company's David Anderson, showed in movie theaters and on television to spot Acclaim's game *Maximum Carnage*, based on the villainous Marvel character. In October, Tele-Communications Inc. (TCI) invested $80 million for 10 percent of Acclaim, and formed a joint-venture company to develop and acquire entertainment and gaming software. TCI's acquisition gave the telecommunications giant the ability to send interactive video games via its cable TV infrastructure.

In December, Acclaim introduced its new product development facilities—including blue screen studio, motion capture studio, and post-production facilities—for developing and publishing technologically advanced interactive software for 16- (Genesis/SNES), 32-, and 64-bit entertainment systems (32X/ Saturn/Ultra 64/PlayStation) and PCs. The blue screen studio was created to film character close-ups for transport into video games in the same process used in movie and television production. The motion capture studio—the first dedicated solely to digital motion capture—was created for Acclaim's software development and for leasing to special effects companies and movie studios (i.e., Warner, who used it for *Batman Forever* and *Forsaken*). The motion capture process involves filming the motion of an individual wearing a special suit containing motion sensors; digitizing the video data into computer-legible format; processing the data using Acclaim's proprietary software, which performs algorithmic computations needed to transpose the data into a skeletal structure; rendering the skeletal structure with such third-party software as *Wavefront*, *Alias*, or *SoftImage*; and placing fully rendered 3D characters into digital background sets.

Also that year, Acclaim purchased a 70,000-square-foot corporate headquarters building in Glen Cove, New York. Total revenue and net income both soared to a record $480.8 million and $45.1 million, respectively.

Regrouping, 1995-Date

Acclaim continued acquiring in January 1995, purchasing Iguana Entertainment Inc. for $7.4 million; receiving most all of struggling Lazer-Tron Corporation in a stock swap in August, changing the name to Acclaim Redemption Games; and, in October, acquiring both Probe and Sculptured Software Inc.— leading independent entertainment software developers— bringing 250 programmers, musicians, graphic artists, and engineers to Acclaim.

In February, Acclaim was the first company known to use the closed-captioning feature required in all 13 + " TV sets for promotional purposes, embedding special player codes for *NBA Jam: Tournament Edition* in commercials.

By July, Acclaim had distribution deals with Sunsoft and Interplay, and joined WB, DC Comics, and America Online (AOL) in an interactive promotion offering gamers a free sneak preview of *Batman Forever* (featuring full-motion video of the

making of the game, movie trailers, art and sound bites, and AOL's startup kit). Major promotional tie-ins included specially produced holographic trading cards featuring game tips in packages of Fleer's *Ultra '95 Batman Forever* trading cards, and a special video game version featured in the final round of Blockbuster Video's World Championship.

In August, attempting to boost its affiliated label program, ADI agreed with Sound Source Interactive (SSI), a leading developer of PC-based edutainment and entertainment products, to resell SSI's titles. In September, Acclaim's first PlayStation titles, *NBA Jam: Tournament Edition* (successor to the original game that sold more than three million cartridges) and *Street Fighter: The Movie*, sold out in retail stores in about a month. In October, Acclaim began jointly publishing, with WB Interactive Entertainment, software based on several WB films; and agreed with Taito Ltd. that Acclaim would received first option on Taito products for all leading home interactive entertainment systems for the Western hemisphere. The first Acclaim-Taito titles—*Jupiter Strike* and *Galactic Attack*— debuted in December.

By the end of 1995, sales on Acclaim's top titles began sagging, but revenues reached an all-time record high of $566.7 million, and netted $44.8 million, a mark from which it would fall precipitously.

In 1996, the dedicated platform industry underwent a hardware transition from 16-bit cartridge to 32- and 64-bit CD-ROM, and Acclaim was hit hard, with revenues dropping nearly 75 percent to $161.9 million, leading to a massive loss of $221.4 million. Nonetheless, the company persevered with a flurry of new introductions and joint ventures and began regaining lost ground.

In February, ADI entered distribution agreements with Take 2 Interactive—releasing *Ripper* (starring Christopher Walken), *Star Crusader*, and *Hell: A Cyberpunk Thriller*—and Domark. In March, Acclaim joined Tiger Electronics and Sega as licensees for live-action/animated film *Space Jam*, starring Michael Jordan and WB's Looney Tunes characters. In July, Acclaim released *D*, a very graphic 3-D blood-and-guts mystery/action-adventure game. Other 1996 releases included *Rise II: Resurrection* (soundtrack by Queen guitarist Brian May), *College Slam*, *Cutthroat Island* (from the Geena Davis film), *WWF Wrestlemania*, *NFL Quarterback Club '96*, *Venom/ Spiderman: Separation Anxiety*, and *Frank Thomas Big Hurt Baseball*.

Acclaim entered the book business early in 1997 by reintroducing the ''Classics Illustrated'' line of comics, including Shakespeare, Dickens, Twain, and Poe. The company also jumped on the football bandwagon with NFL Quarterback Club '97, joining Sierra's *Front Page Sports Football Pro '97* and Electronic Arts' *Madden '97* and, in March, unloaded most of Lazer-Tron for $6,000.

In April, Acclaim entered the 6- to 11-year-old children's book market by creating Acclaim Young Readers, agreeing with Disney, Fox Kids Network, and Saban Entertainment to develop ''visual storybooks'' based on their characters, with distribution through Penguin Books, including *Hercules*, ''Disney's Enchanting Stories'' (featuring *Beauty and the Beast* and

101 Dalmatians), "Disney's Action Club" (including *Toy Story* and *The Lion King*), "Fox Funhouse" (featuring *The Tick* and *Life with Louie*), and "Saban Powerhouse" (with *Power Rangers* and *Masked Rider*).

In May, Acclaim released *Magic: The Gathering—Battlemage,* based on Wizards of the Coast's staggeringly successful card game, and July saw *The Crow: City of Angels.* Also early that year, Acclaim released *Turok: Dinosaur Hunter* (the top-selling third-party N64 title), *NFL Quarterback Club '98* (featuring veteran sports announcer Marv Albert, hired prior to his guilty plea in his highly publicized sex case), and *Extreme-G.* Other 1997 products included *Constructor* and *NHL Breakaway Hockey '98,* and Acclaim Publishing released its first strategy guide, *Extreme-G Official Game Secrets.*

N64 hardware sales grew to eight to ten million worldwide in 1997, with PlayStation reaching another eight to nine million consumers. Key titles released for Christmas 1997 included *Quarterback Club '99* and *NHL Hockey '99.* Revenue rebounded slightly to $165.4 million, but net losses, at $97 million, were still painful.

Early in 1998, Acclaim Coin-Operated Entertainment introduced the *Magic: The Gathering* video game but, by March, Acclaim had closed the division, reallocating its resources to Acclaim Studios, and focusing on core competencies of developing, publishing, and marketing home entertainment software. Other early 1998 releases included *Riven, Batman and Robin, Bust-A-Move, Extreme G2, Iron & Blood, Major League Baseball, NBA Jam '99, Recking Balls, Shadowman, WWF Warzone,* and *X-Men COTA.*

In March, TCI divested its 4.3 million shares of Acclaim for $19 million, months before AT&T purchased TCI. In June, Acclaim landed two nominations in the Post-E3 Show Awards with *Turok 2* (Best Video Game) and *All-Star Baseball '99* (Best Sports Game), and *Supercross '98* was displayed, with Jeremy McGrath making a guest appearance to promote the release. Although profitability had become a cause for concern, Acclaim appeared firmly on the comeback trail, posting revenues of $315 million by third quarter's end, and heading for renewed success.

Principal Subsidiaries

ACA Holdings Inc.; Acclaim Cable Holdings Inc.; Acclaim Character Animation LP; Acclaim Coin-Operated Entertainment Inc.; Acclaim Comics Inc.; Acclaim Distribution Inc.; Acclaim Entertainment Inc.; Acclaim Corporate Center I Inc.; Acclaim Entertainment Canada Ltd.; Acclaim Entertainment Espana SA (Spain); Acclaim Entertainment GmbH (Germany); Acclaim Entertainment Ltd.; Acclaim Entertainment SA (France); Acclaim Interactive Software Division; Acclaim Japan Ltd.; Acclaim Redemption Games Inc.; ACTC LP; Iguana Entertainment Inc.; Iguana Entertainment Ltd.; Lazer-Tron Limited; LJN Toys Ltd.; Oyster Bay Warehouse Corp.; Probe Entertainment Limited; Sculptured Software Inc.

Further Reading

"Acclaim Account Moved Out of Grey, London," *ADWEEK Eastern Edition,* September 11, 1995, p. 15.

"Acclaim Adds 2 Titles," *HFD—The Weekly Home Furnishings Newspaper,* March 16, 1992, p. 113.

"Acclaim Agrees to Market, Distribute Sega Software," *HFD—The Weekly Home Furnishings Newspaper,* December 2, 1991, p. 6.

"Acclaim and Lazer-Tron," *Television Digest,* August 7, 1995, p. 16.

"Acclaim Buys Voyager," *HFD—The Weekly Home Furnishings Newspaper,* August 15, 1994, p. 86.

"Acclaim Closes a Game Division," *Wall Street Journal,* March 9, 1998, p. A6(W)/B8(E).

"Acclaim Donating Games to Troops," *Crain's New York Business,* December 3, 1990, p. 29.

"Acclaim Drops 16-Bit Games," *Television Digest,* April 22, 1996, p. 21.

"Acclaim Entertainment," *Billboard,* February 7, 1998, p. 65.

"Acclaim Entertainment Completed 4.6 Million Share Public Offering at $4.25 Per Share," *Television Digest,* December 30, 1991, p. 11.

"Acclaim Entertainment Has Acquired 'Certain Assets' of Mirrorsoft," *Television Digest,* January 20, 1992, p. 14.

"Acclaim Entertainment Inc.," *New York Times,* April 7, 1998, p. C7(N)/D7(L).

"Acclaim Entertainment Signed," *Television Digest,* November 16, 1992, p. 13.

"Acclaim Entertainment, Tiger Electronics," *HFN: The Weekly Newspaper for the Home Furnishing Network,* March 4, 1996, p. 48.

"Acclaim in Pact with Nintendo, Sony, Sega," *HFD—The Weekly Home Furnishings Newspaper,* November 16, 1992, p. 111.

"Acclaim Jams $10M into NBA Videogame Push," *Advertising Age,* February 14, 1994, p. 2.

"Acclaim Lays Off 115," *Television Digest,* May 26, 1997, p. 17.

"Acclaim: Loss of $6.8 Million for Quarter," *HFD—The Weekly Home Furnishings Newspaper,* August 5, 1991, p. 90.

"Acclaim Reaches Agreement to Distribute Utility Software," *HFN: The Weekly Newspaper for the Home Furnishing Network,* August 14, 1995, p. 86.

"Acclaim Releasing 50 Titles Backed by $10M Campaign," *HFN: The Weekly Newspaper for the Home Furnishing Network,* December 18, 1995, p. 87.

"Acclaim Reports Loss Widened in Quarter on Sales Drop, Charge," *Wall Street Journal,* July 14, 1997, p. B2(W)/B2(E).

"Acclaim Said It Will 'Terminate,' " *Television Digest,* July 24, 1995, p. 19.

"Acclaim Slates Diversification," *Television Digest,* April 11, 1994, p. 16.

"Acclaim to Dismiss 15% of Its Employees," *New York Times,* May 2, 1997, p. C13(N)/D13(L).

"Acclaim, Warner Bros. Enter Entertainment Alliance," *Broadcasting & Cable,* October 16, 1995, p. 55.

"Acclaim Will Ship Its First Title for 16-Bit Super Nintendo Entertainment System," *Television Digest,* August 19, 1991, p. 14.

Alaimo, Dan, "Rental Volume Strong Despite 'Kombat' Battle," *Supermarket News,* September 27, 1993, p. 29.

"Anthony Williams," *Television Digest,* October 26, 1992, p. 17.

"As Part of An Overall Cost-Management Measure, Interactive-Developer Acclaim Entertainment Has Cut Its Work Force," *HFN: The Weekly Newspaper for the Home Furnishing Network,* September 30, 1996, p. 94.

Autry, Ret, "Acclaim Entertainment," *Fortune,* December 31, 1990, p. 98.

Avalos, George, "Shareholders at California's Lazer-Tron Approve Merger with Acclaim," *Knight-Ridder/Tribune Business News,* September 1, 1995, p. 9010045.

"Barry Taylor," *Television Digest,* October 26, 1992, p. 17.

Berniker, Mark, "TCI Goes Gaming, Buys 10% of Acclaim Entertainment," *Broadcasting & Cable,* October 24, 1994, p. 64.

"Boys' Life Is Where Acclaim and Its Subsidiary, LJN, Go to Turn Video Game Software into Hard Sales," *MEDIAWEEK,* March 1, 1993, p. CM37.

Brandt, Richard, "Video Games: Is All That Gore Really Child's Play?" *Business Week*, June 14, 1993, p. 38.

Byrd, Veronica, "Is There Life After Mortal Kombat?: Game Maker Acclaim Must Overcome the Loss of Key Contract," *Business Week*, May 16, 1994, p. 76.

Cochran, Thomas N., "No Acclaim: Restatement, Auditor's Filing Bash Software Firm's Stock," *Barron's*, December 11, 1995, p. 13.

"Communique," *HFD—The Weekly Home Furnishings Newspaper*, October 31, 1994, p. 95.

"Continuing Diversification," *Television Digest*, March 20, 1995, p. 17.

"The Crow: City of Angels," *PC Magazine*, July 1997, p. 422.

DeSalvo, Kathy, "Dir. David Anderson Sees Red for Maximum Carnage," *SHOOT*, September 2, 1994, p. 11.

"Digital Pictures," *Television Digest*, October 17, 1994, p. 15.

"Entrepreneur of the Year Award Winner, Gregory Fischbach, Acclaim Entertainment," *LI Business News*, July 9, 1990, p. 6.

"Federal Judge Dismissed Copyright Suit," *Television Digest*, September 5, 1994, p. 15.

Fitzgerald, Kate, "Nintendo Software TV Blitz Planned," *Advertising Age*, November 13, 1989, p. 4.

Gault, Ylonda, "Less Joy As Acclaim Sticks to Margins," *Crain's New York Business*, January 21, 1991, p. 21.

Gourlay, Richard, "Mortal Kombat Game Creator Makes Killing," *Financial Times*, October 14, 1995, p. 20.

"Grass Roots," *PC Week*, October 7, 1996, p. A8.

Greenman, Catherine, "Acclaim Buys Talent, Acquires Two More Game Developers," *HFN: The Weekly Newspaper for the Home Furnishing Network*, October 16, 1995, p. 99.

Gross, Neil, "Dino-Mite!" *Business Week*, March 10, 1997, p. 40.

"In First Known Example of Promotional Use of Closed-Captioning," *Television Digest*, February 20, 1995, p. 18.

"James DeRose," *Television Digest*, June 23, 1997, p. 24.

"James DeRose Jr. Has Been Named President of Acclaim Interactive Software," *HFN: The Weekly Newspaper for the Home Furnishing Network*, October 16, 1995, p. 90.

Jeffrey, Don, "Acclaim Claims Higher Sales," *Billboard*, July 25, 1992, p. 49.

LaFemina, Lorraine, "Visionary Companies Are Us," *LI Business News*, January 23, 1995, p. 24T.

Kontzamanys, Gregory, "New Acclaim Unit Will be Relocating to LI," *LI Business News*, April 30, 1990, p. 11.

Langberg, Mike, "Game Ratings Reinforce a Dispute Between Video, Computer Game Developers," *Knight-Ridder/Tribune Business News*, July 25, 1994, p. 07250035.

"Mark Hattendorf," *Television Digest*, October 20, 1997, p. 15.

McConville, James A., "Video Game Players Plan Their Moves," *HFD—The Weekly Home Furnishings Newspaper*, June 20, 1994, p. 82.

McDonald, T. Liam, "Smoke and Mirrors," *PC Magazine*, May 6, 1997, p. 370.

Meeks, Fleming, "Captain Video," *Forbes*, July 11, 1988, p. 137.

Milliot, Jim, "Acclaim Books Launches Young Readers Line," *Publishers Weekly*, April 14, 1997, p. 19.

"NFL Quarterback Club '97," *PC Magazine*, December 3, 1996, p. 505

"Nintendo Took Advantage," *Television Digest*, September 20, 1993, p. 19.

"On the Eve of CES," *Billboard*, July 16, 1994, p. 60.

"Out of Cabbage Patch," *PC Week*, October 16, 1995, p. A8.

Palmeri, Christopher, "Kombat Marketing," *Forbes*, February 28, 1994, p. 102.

"PC Software Selection Changing," *Television Digest*, July 7, 1997, p. 12.

"Quarterly Deficit Exceeds the Forecasts of Analysts," *Wall Street Journal*, November 6, 1997, p. B15(W)/B4(E).

"Quarterly Profit Is Posted; Revenue Increases by 73%," *Wall Street Journal*, January 13, 1998, p. B20(W)/A4(E).

Ryan, Michael E., "Deep-Thinking Puzzlers for the Adventurous Gamer," *PC Magazine*, July 1996, p. 458.

Saia, Rick, "CD-ROM Super Bowl Simulations Show Cheeseheads Rule," *Computerworld*, January 20, 1997, p. 105.

Schuman, Michael, "Levitating," *Forbes*, February 15, 1993, p. 240.

Seavy, Mark, "That's Entertainment for Acclaim," *HFD—The Weekly Home Furnishings Newspaper*, January 14, 1991, p. 92.

"Sega Enterprises Ltd.," *HFD—The Weekly Home Furnishings Newspaper*, April 18, 1994, p. 210.

"Sega Licensed Acclaim Entertainment to Publish and Market Software," *Television Digest*, November 11, 1991, p. 16.

"Shigekazu (Kaz) Hayashi," *Television Digest*, December 1, 1997, p. 20.

"Software Downturn," *Television Digest*, December 11, 1995, p. 17.

Sreenivasan, Sreenath, "Can Marv Albert's Voice Lift Acclaim's Fortunes?" *New York Times*, November 17, 1997, p. C5(N)/D5(L).

"Take 2 Joins Forces with Acclaim," *HFN: The Weekly Newspaper for the Home Furnishing Network*, February 5, 1996, p. 80.

Talley, Karen, "LI Index Plunges on More Bad News," *LI Business News*, October 22, 1990, p. 4.

"TCI Sold Stake," *Television Digest*, March 2, 1998, p. 8.

"TCI Takes 10% Stake in Acclaim," *Advertising Age*, October 24, 1994, p. 40.

"Toy Firm Disputing Price of Acquisition," *Crain's New York Business*, July 16, 1990, p. 22.

Trachtenburg, Jeffrey A., "TCI Buys 10% Stake in Acclaim, Announces New Venture in Games," *Wall Street Journal, Europe*, October 24, 1994, p. 8.

"Turok Garners Acclaim," *HFN: The Weekly Newspaper for the Home Furnishing Network*, April 7, 1997, p. 147.

"Video-Games Maker Acclaim Socked on Its Bottom Line," *Wall Street Journal, Europe*, December 18, 1996, p. 3.

Williams, Norman D., "Toys R Us Pulls Violent Video Game from Shelves," *Knight-Ridder/Tribune Business News*, December 15, 1993, p. 12150034.

—Daryl F. Mallett

Alamo Rent A Car, Inc.

Republic Tower
110 Southeast 6th Street
Fort Lauderdale, Florida 33301
U.S.A.
(305) 522-0000
(800) GO-ALAMO (462-5266)
Fax: (305) 527-6589
Web site: http://www.goalamo.com

Wholly Owned Subsidiary of Republic Industries, Inc.
Incorporated: 1974
Employees: 7,000
Sales: $1.6 billion
SICs: 7514 Passenger Car Rentals

Alamo Rent A Car, Inc. is the third largest car rental company in the United States with a fleet of more than 150,000 cars servicing 15 million travelers annually. Alamo has 148 locations in the United States and Canada and 275 international locations in Belgium, the Czech Republic, Germany, Greece, Ireland, Malta, Mexico, the Netherlands, Portugal, Slovakia, Switzerland, and the United Kingdom (serviced through its London-based affiliate, Alamo Rent A Car [U.K.] Limited). Alamo established itself as an inexpensive, off-airport car rental agency catering to leisure travelers, but has sought out business travelers as well to become a viable competitor of the larger industry leaders.

In the Beginning, 1974–83

Alamo began operations in 1974 with 1,000 cars at four Florida locations. Its name had been chosen for the position it would command in classified telephone directories, rather than for any historical reference. From the beginning, the company pursued a discount strategy, charging up to 20 percent less than its much larger competitors, offering free mileage, and using cheaper, off-airport sales locations.

In the mid-1970s Michael S. Egan left Florida-based Olins Rent-a-Car to join Alamo as the Miami-area manager for its owner, insurance billionaire John MacArthur. In 1978, after MacArthur died, Egan and several others bought the firm and began turning attention to markets overlooked by the more established car rental companies, starting with the vacation traveler. Alamo courted travel agents and paid them commissions for referrals. Sales in 1979—the first full year under the Egan group's ownership—reached $30 million, and the company grew to 11 locations.

Just prior to this time, the Federal Trade Commission (FTC) sued the industry's Big Three—Hertz, Avis, and National Car Rental—accusing them of rigging bids for airport sales counters and fixing prices at 10 to 40 percent higher than those charged by smaller competitors such as Alamo. The FTC discovered airports had joined in on pricing smaller companies out of space; in some cases airports had even forbidden airport advertising by off-airport companies. After the suit was settled, the end to such price-fixing led to considerable expansion into airports by the smaller car rental companies, most notably Budget Rent A Car. Alamo, however, did not immediately follow other rental companies to airport locations. Egan reasoned that deregulated air passenger service would increase opportunities for travel by budget-minded vacationers. In order to exploit this market, Alamo chose to remain at less expensive, off-airport locations and concentrate on serving vacationers, not business customers, at lower prices.

In 1980 Alamo expanded beyond Florida, entering two major leisure markets by purchasing the California company Trans Rent-A-Car and gaining operating rights in Hawaii. Alamo also opened a marketing and sales office in London. In 1981 Alamo made a tentative move to commercial sales, experimenting with an on-airport facility in Atlanta, Georgia. By the end of that year Alamo had 17,000 cars and 600 employees; by 1983 it had 1,300 employees. During this time, Alamo also expanded to such western cities as Denver, Seattle, and Phoenix, and moved eastward into the Boston market, all without a loss in profits. Still appealing heavily to leisure travelers, Alamo ran advertisements promising that "at Alamo, mileage is priceless. Zero cents a mile."

Company Perspectives:

Alamo Rent A Car principally targets leisure travelers and cost-conscious business travelers. Alamo's objective is to be the low-cost provider of quality vehicle rental service and to increase customer satisfaction and retention by developing innovative, time-saving options for customers and other quality services based on the customer's specific needs.

Gaining and Keeping Market Share, 1984–87

Over the years Alamo's sales practices came under periodic government review and censure. In June 1984 the Florida attorney general charged Alamo with using "bait and switch" tactics and charging customers for unnecessary insurance. The Florida charges were dropped when Alamo agreed to obey the law concerning these matters and to reimburse customers who had legitimate complaints. A later investigation of industry pricing and advertising was conducted by the National Association of Attorneys General, which resulted in Alamo agreeing to mention extra charges—gas, insurance, etc.—in its advertisements.

In 1984 Alamo moved more decisively into the business market, which accounted for 65 percent of the $4.4-billion-a-year car rental market. Alamo was generating $125 million a year in business and was projecting $175 million for 1984. It was prepared to target the small-business customer, to whom savings would matter more than amenities such as airport location. Egan decided to make a run for the new market, in part because of his confidence in Alamo employees—who, coming mostly from outside the industry, were not overly specialized. Alamo had more than quintupled sales in five years with managers recruited from stock brokerage, retail sales, airline management, the U.S. Navy, and even the medical profession. The Alamo recruit was chosen for "iron-willed determination," Egan told *Inc.* magazine in November 1984. "We're not smarter than our competitors, so we have to outwork them."

Alamo employees were "gung ho, like Marines," said industrial psychologist George Dunlevy, who tested new hires. Alamo employees had "almost a work sickness, a drive to succeed," said Elizabeth Smith, a former naval officer and Alamo executive and company director. In hiring for Alamo, Smith looked for people with "a certain steel in the back," she told *Inc.* Egan viewed the work environment as a new, somewhat controversial "centering force" in people's lives, to replace religion, community, and extended families.

By 1985 Alamo had 43 locations in 12 states and was ranked a distant ninth among United States car rental companies, behind other mostly off-airport companies such as Thrifty Rent-A-Car, American International, Ajax, and General Rent A Car. But Alamo was quickly advancing; *Fortune* writer Edward Boyer labeled the agency "the fastest-growing rental car company in the United States." Alamo seemed not to suffer from such singular policies as charging $9.95 for the half tank of gas it supplied and its refusal to reimburse the customer for what was left when the car was returned (a policy later declared optional, mostly because of business travelers' objections). Al-

amo was now serving airports in Dallas-Fort Worth and Washington, D.C., among its other numerous locations.

Alamo's service became even more appealing when on-airport locations started to become less attractive. Rental car lots for the larger companies had been moved farther from terminals, so off-airport companies, requiring less space for their smaller fleets, were sometimes closer than on-airport ones. In addition, limited counter space for airport rental agencies caused lines and delays, making Alamo service more inviting. Adding to the company's success was a shift in the market. In Alamo's first ten years of operation, Hertz and Avis's combined share of airport business had dropped 13 points to 58 percent, with National, Budget, Alamo, and others picking up the difference. Alamo's revenues did not suffer during this time, because industry revenues rose 14 percent a year. In the mid-1980s, though, price wars cut into the leaders' profits, due in part to pressure from companies like Alamo, whose fleet had risen from 7,900 to 30,000 cars in six years and who had expanded into the business market from its leisure travel niche.

Alamo's rapid growth continued and by August 1986 it had more than 50,000 cars in 57 cities and 2,500 employees or "family members," as they were known within the company. Sales topped the $300 million mark, and Alamo passed other small companies to reach fifth place. In addition, it had 100,000 customer companies enrolled in its corporate-rate program. The price wars had also ceased earlier that year, and industry revenues jumped accordingly more than 20 percent to $6.5 billion. Profits increased most notably for Hertz and Budget, the latter now one of the Big Four. Alamo and other second-tier companies—Dollar Rent A Car, Thrifty Rent-A-Car, and General Rent A Car chief among them—took advantage of the increased prices, raising theirs only slightly and thereby cutting deeper into the business travelers market. Alamo's rates stood at $28 to $35 a day, about 30 percent lower than Hertz's. The next year, 1987, Egan boasted to *Business Week* that Alamo offered "free unlimited mileage in every U.S. city we serve." Alamo had 60,000 vehicles in 65 U.S. locations, compared to Dollar's 46,000 in 450 locations, Thrifty's 24,000 in 360 locations, and General's 20,000 in 33 locations.

A Major Competitor, 1988–92

Hertz and Avis fought back by matching Alamo's free mileage, seeking to capture more of the leisure market, worth an estimated $2.3 billion a year in the late 1980s and growing two to three times as fast as the business market. Alamo responded by extending its free mileage offer beyond weekly rentals and aggressively advertising the difference. Alamo's share of the entire airport car rental market—both leisure and business—was an estimated seven percent, compared with Hertz's 25 percent, Avis's 22 percent, and Budget's and National's 15 percent each.

Alamo had grown "dramatically over the past few years at the expense of its big four competitors," industry analyst Charles Finnie told Ira Teinowitz in *Advertising Age*; Teinowitz noted Alamo had "carved out a niche as the leading off-airport renter of cars to leisure travelers." In 1988 Alamo opened rental facilities in London, and the next year in Glasgow, Scotland, as well as additional American cities. Within two years, Alamo expanded its presence further with the acquisition of a British company, Guy Salmon Service, Ltd., which offered luxury car rental and chauffeur services throughout the United Kingdom. As Alamo Rent A Car (U.K.) Limited, this firm consolidated Alamo's operations in Scotland and England.

In 1989 Alamo's revenues were more than $500 million a year. It had now possessed more than eight percent of the airport market, and profit margins ranged from three to five percent. Alamo management was ''one of the smartest, most aggressive managements in the industry,'' Finnie told *Forbes*. Its proven strategy was not only to rent cars at the busiest and cheapest locations, but, according to various government agencies, went further to pressure customers into renting larger, higher-rate cars and taking expensive collision insurance. Perhaps due in part to this latter practice, Alamo received the lowest customer satisfaction rating among 11 companies reviewed by *Consumer Reports* magazine. Sales growth, however, was still high at 14 percent, partly because of business rentals, which were producing 30 percent of its revenues.

Clearly Alamo was not notably damaged by negative press; nonetheless, it started to retrain its 4,000 employees to emphasize courtesy (''Make your customers your best friends,'' admonished Egan) and sent a corps of ''phantom shoppers'' into the field to check up on service and sales practices. Complaints dropped and reservations rose sharply. Alamo's collision-damage surcharge, though, was a more difficult matter for the company—for it netted around 20 percent of Alamo's customers, and Egan was reluctant to give it up. Alamo developed a new waiver program offering price and coverage options costing $3 to $9 a day. There were also complaints about collision-repair charges billed to drivers. In July 1991 Alamo agreed to refund $3 million to customers overcharged for repairs in the 1980s as federal prosecutors had found a pattern of such overcharging from 1983 through 1989.

By 1991 Alamo had 100,000 cars at or near 92 of the busiest U.S. airports. Among them were 10,000 at its Orlando, Florida, car rental plaza, the world's biggest with 52 counter positions, and new locations including Chicago, Fresno, Albany, Sacramento, and Dayton. Alamo gained five points of market share in the last half of the 1980s while the Big Four lost 20 points as a group. Alamo was grossing $600 million a year, with profit margins of around four percent better than Hertz and almost as good as Avis.

Alamo continued its course of head-to-head price competition with Hertz and the other big companies; in April 1992 it cut prices nationwide for several months, dropping its economy-car rate to a uniform $15 a day in all 102 U.S. locations, including 45 on-airport locations, while also offering discounts on midsize cars and Cadillacs. Hertz immediately responded with a similar announcement of reductions. Alamo's intent in sweeping the country with this type of offer, a spokesperson told Michael J. McCarthy in the *Wall Street Journal*, was to fix itself in the business traveler's mind as a national operation as the car rental industry now had annual domestic revenues of $11.4 billion. Alamo's declaring nationwide rates, as opposed to locally structured ones, was described by a travel industry specialist as both ''interesting'' and ''definitely innovative,'' in the *New York Times*. Two weeks later Hertz, along with Alamo,

again unveiled price cuts, this time for the small-business customer. The reasoning went that recent airline fare discounts were bringing small-business airline passengers back, so it was time to woo them with car-rental savings as well. Discounts in each case called for presentation of an airline ticket by the renter. Hertz required three days notice on the reservation, while Alamo required only one.

More Than Price Wars, 1993–95

In 1993 Alamo added a strategic location in Los Angeles, considered the world's largest rental car market, along with several other on-airport locations in Palm Springs, San Francisco, Dallas, and Jackson Hole, Wyoming, and metro locations in Atlanta, Chicago, and Minneapolis. Overseas, Alamo established three new on-airport sites in Ireland, and one in Amsterdam. According to the *Automotive Fleet Factbook*, industry figures for leased or rented automobiles hit 4.86 million for 1993, with business and corporate leasing as the top form of auto renting/leasing with 44.6 percent of the market. Alamo's slice of the pie was growing with $1.1 billion in revenues, which ranked it as the fifth largest private company in Florida, according to *Florida Trend* magazine.

As in previous years, Alamo continued to add locations throughout the world—new on-airport stations in Belgium, England, and Germany came on line in 1994, while in the United States, Alamo conquered its 42nd state by opening a plaza in Rhode Island. Towards the end of the year Alamo acquired a majority stake in Autohansa Autovermietung, bolstering its European presence. Year-end figures climbed to $1.3 billion in systemwide revenues, behind Hertz ($4.8 billion), Avis ($3 billion), Budget ($2.3 billion), and Enterprise ($2 billion), but ahead of National ($1 billion), who would play a significant role in Alamo's future.

By 1995 Alamo had opened in another major venue, Chicago's O'Hare airport (the company already had a station at Midway), while expanding globally into Greece, Portugal, and the Czech Republic, and adding more sites in the Netherlands and Switzerland. Back in North America, Alamo finally tapped its neighbor, Canada, by opening several locations in Montreal. In a *Wall Street Journal* ranking of the top Car-Rental Agencies in the Airport Market, Alamo's fleet of 150,000 vehicles came in at number three, just under Avis's 165,000 and Hertz's 215,000. Yet behind the glare of competition, each of the top car rental companies was experiencing trouble in an industry-wide slump. Both Budget and Alamo had been forced to lay off workers and announced losses, for Alamo, its first ever. In a shuffle to shore up the company, Egan relinquished his CEO duties to D. Keith Cobb, who shared vice-chairman duties with Roger H. Ballou, who joined the company in May from American Express Travel Related Services. Part of Alamo's financial woes was the climb in fleet costs, which had doubled in the past three years, a cost that could not be offset by increasing car rental rates when competition remained so fierce. Alamo was also smarting from an attempt to buy National Rental System Inc. from General Motors; it may have lost that particular battle, but circumstances later gave Alamo an upper hand in the war.

A New Era, 1996 and Beyond

In the late 1990s, the national car rental industry was rife with ''merger mania,'' as Avis was bought by HFS in 1996, and Ford Motor Company was interested in selling Budget Rent A Car. Alamo, too, fell into the fray by becoming a wholly owned subsidiary of Republic Industries, Inc., a diversified conglomerate of automotive, solid waste, electronic, and media segments with revenues of just under $6.1 billion for the year. The merger complimented both companies, since Republic's automotive division included hundreds of new and used-car dealers under the AutoNation USA banner (the largest in the U.S. industry), and auto parts and insurance services.

Republic was on the prowl in 1997, consolidating its automotive rental division with five strategic additions: National Car Rental System Inc., one of Alamo's nemeses, in February; Spirit Rent-A-Car in April and Snappy Rent A Car in July, which both specialized in insurance replacement rentals and were soon operating under the CarTemps USA name; Value Rent-A-Car in June; and two months later, EuroDollar Rent A Car, the second largest renter in the United Kingdom. Yet, partnering the power of Alamo in the leisure market and National in the business market was Republic's diamond in the rough—by merging two of the top five car rental giants, Republic was able to topple Avis from its berth of second largest national auto rental chain. Alamo and National's combined fleet topped 225,000 and the duo were expected to generate revenues of $2.7 billion for 1997.

In 1998 Alamo promotions included a national television advertising campaign from Foote, Cone & Belding New York called ''Drive Happy'' to the tune of Bobby McFerrin's ''Don't Worry, Be Happy,'' with a tie-in to a merchandise giveaway. There were also a myriad of discounts for Alamo customers including merchandise from Bloomingdale's, airline mileage tie-ins, and special programs for leisure travelers from Latin America and the Caribbean. Although Alamo was still smaller than major competition, like Hertz and Avis, having National as a complementary sibling not only helped position both of them for the future, but put each on firm ground to some day wrest control of the nearly $15 billion car rental industry. With the power of Republic Industries vast automotive holdings behind Alamo, the company had the freedom to pay less attention to its bottom line and concentrate more fully on competing with Hertz and Avis. In addition, with access to Republic's new car dealerships, Alamo could slash its biggest expense—fleet costs—and continue to move forward with aggressive expansion.

Principal Subsidiaries

Alamo Rent A Car (U.K.) Limited.

Further Reading

Boyer, Edward, ''Airport Rent-A-Car Bargains,'' *Fortune,* February 4, 1985.

Brannigan, Martha, ''Corporate Focus: Rocky Road—Alamo Maps a Turnaround,'' *Wall Street Journal,* August 14, 1995.

——, ''Travel: Why the Cost of a Car Rental Is Likely to Rise,'' *Wall Street Journal,* December 27, 1995, p. 13.

Bryant, Adam, ''Alamo Rent A Car Offering Uniform Rates Nationwide,'' *New York Times,* April 21, 1992.

Croghan, Lore, ''Positioning Alamo As a Low-Price, Quality Rental,'' *Adweek,* September 11, 1986.

Ellis, James E., ''Small Fry Start Nipping at the Whales of Auto Rental,'' *Business Week,* August 31, 1987.

''Hertz, Alamo Aim New Rate Plans at Small Businesses,'' *Wall Street Journal,* May 5, 1992.

''Hit 'em First,'' *Forbes,* July 30, 1984.

Kolton, Ellen, ''No Experience Required,'' *Inc.,* November 1984.

Loomis, Carol J., ''The Rumble in Rental Cars,'' *Fortune,* March 7, 1983.

McCarthy, Michael J., ''Alamo Slashes Car-Rental Rates; Hertz Responds with Limited Cuts,'' *Wall Street Journal,* April 21, 1992.

Petzinger, Thomas, Jr., ''The Front Lines: Chip Burgess Plots Holiday Coup to Make Hertz No. 1 in Florida,'' *Wall Street Journal,* December 22, 1995, p. B1.

Poole, Claire, ''Born to Hustle,'' *Forbes,* May 28, 1990.

Santora, Joyce E., ''Alamo's Drive for Customer Service,'' *Personnel Journal,* April 1991.

Simison, Robert L., ''Alamo Leads in Bidding for National,'' *Wall Street Journal,* March 27, 1995, p. A3.

Simmons, Jacqueline, ''Rental-Car Firms, Beset by Troubles, Are Trying Again to Boost Their Prices,'' *Wall Street Journal,* July 26, 1995, p. A3.

Sullivan, Robert E., Jr., ''Michael Egan Shrugs Off the H-word,'' *Condé Nast Traveler,* March 1991.

Teinowitz, Ira, ''Alamo's Fighting Mad on Mileage,'' *Advertising Age,* March 26, 1990.

''Trying Too Hard?,'' *Time,* June 23, 1975.

—Jim Bowman
—updated by Taryn Benbow-Pfalzgraf

Algo Group Inc.

225 Chabanel Street West, Suite 1100
Montreal, Quebec H2N 2C9
Canada
(514) 382-1240
Fax: (514) 382-4436

Public Company
Incorporated: 1942
Employees: 500
Sales: C$202.14 million (1996)
Stock Exchanges: Toronto Montreal
Ticker Symbol: AO.A
SICs: 2337 Women's, Misses', & Juniors' Suits, Skirts, & Coats; 2321 Men's & Boys' Shirts, Except Work Shirts; 2325 Men's & Boys' Separate Trousers & Slacks; 2329 Men's & Boys' Clothing, Not Elsewhere Classified; 2331 Women's, Misses', & Juniors' Blouses & Shirts; 2335 Women's, Misses', & Juniors' Dresses; 2339 Women's, Misses', & Juniors' Outerwear, Not Elsewhere Classified; 2361 Girls', Children's, & Infants' Blouses & Shirts; 2369 Girls', Children's, & Infants' Outerwear, Not Elsewhere Classified; 2221 Broadwoven Fabric Mills-Manmade

Founded in 1942 as a small dress manufacturer, Algo Group Inc. has grown to become Canada's leading apparel company. The company's 16 divisions have a presence in four segments of the apparel industry: ladieswear, children's wear, sportswear, and textiles. Algo's product lines are oriented towards the mid-market consumer and are made up of such well-known licenses as Bugle Boy, Ocean Pacific, and Hank Player as well as the company's own brands, including S.O.S., Badge, Green Jeans, and Robin. The company's textile division, operating under the banner of the Hamil Group, is a leading international textile converter that caters to a broad client base including moderate to designer sportswear, activewear, weekend wear, children's wear, and lingerie. Operated out of divisional centers in Toronto, Montreal, Vancouver, New York, Los Angeles, Dal-las, Osaka, and Seoul, Algo derives about 40 percent of its C$200 million in sales from outside of Canada.

Company Origins in the 1940s

Algo Group Inc. was founded in 1942 by two brothers, Joseph and Ben Schaffer, whose family had emigrated from Poland to Montreal, Canada, in the 1930s when the brothers were children. By the 1940s Montreal had become the center of a burgeoning Canadian fashion industry and, searching for a business venture, the young Schaffer brothers rented a small office on Peel Street in downtown Montreal and began to manufacture ladies' dresses designed to sell for under C$10. The Schaffer brothers' business prospered, and soon they were able to move the company's headquarters to Chabanel Street in the heart of Montreal's famous garment district.

Over the next two decades, Algo became a leading Canadian manufacturer of moderate to higher-priced ladies' dresses and related apparel. Algo's dresses, produced by the company's Algo and Lori Ann divisions, appeared at major social occasions across Canada. As the emphasis in the fashion industry moved towards less formal apparel, Algo entered the ladies' sportswear and casual wear segments with the opening of a number of new divisions.

From the start, Algo's program of expansion was characterized by a unique approach to company management. Convinced that a good work ethic springs from a commitment to the company, the Schaffers hand-picked division managers and then gave them up to a 30 percent share in the subsidiary's ownership. These highly motivated management teams were granted a great deal of autonomy in terms of production, sales, marketing, and shipping, with the Algo Group working as an umbrella company to provide accounting, administration, and other corporate management services. Reflecting on this approach to expansion in a 1989 interview with *Bobbin*, Joe Schaffer commented, "It's true I put in all the money, but they give me 70 percent. I don't give them 30 percent . . . I am able to have all these companies, whereas by myself I could run only one—at best, two. I didn't give; I got."

Company Perspectives:

Algo Group's mission is to be a recognized leader in the fashion industry in Canada, the United States and Europe. We will strive to create strategic alliances with our customers and to consistently meet their expectations with respect to product design, value, and timely and responsive service and support. We will foster an environment that encourages teamwork among our employees and supports their creativity. We will provide them with the training and technology that enable them to build challenging and rewarding careers. Consistent with this mission, we will conduct ourselves at all times in a fair and ethical manner with our employees, customers, suppliers and the community at large. We believe that the successful pursuit of these goals will enable Algo Group to achieve growth, profitability and above average returns for our shareholders.

In addition to diversifying its product line through the careful building of subsidiaries, Algo minimized the risks inherent in the volatile fashion industry by contracting out most of the company's manufacturing, thereby reducing the need for huge investments in plants and inventory. In this way, Algo became essentially a fashion supplier, with design teams to capitalize on fashion trends but without the expense or risks of production.

Expansion and an IPO in the 1970s and 1980s

As Algo entered the last quarter of the century, the company had become one of the leading suppliers of ladies' dresses in Canada, but with annual sales of only about C$10 million the company was poised for further growth. According to company lore it was Joseph Schaffer's son-in-law, Elliot Lifson, who was in large part responsible for the program of expansion undertaken by Algo Group through the 1970s and 1980s. Lifson, a practicing attorney, had decided to go back to school to earn an M.B.A. and chose Algo as the subject of his master's thesis. After intensive study of the company's operations, Lifson's thesis recommended that Algo should "expand and grow," advice that was taken seriously by the Schaffer brothers. Over the following decade Algo Group made a major thrust into the U.S. and international markets, as well as further diversifying its product line.

One major new venture for the Algo Group during these years began as a temporary solution to a supply problem. Hamil Textiles Ltd., the company's main textile company, was founded as a clearing house for the excess fabric that Algo companies had bought but that, for one reason or another, they were unable to use. "We thought it would be most advisable for us to open up an area where we could sell our mistakes, to retailers and to manufacturers, and get as close to cost and better if we could. This proved so successful that it became a business and I was left without a cellar of mistakes," Schaffer explained to *Bobbin*.

Although in the early days of Algo's operations manufacturing was concentrated in the Montreal area, as Canadian labor costs escalated production was moved increasingly to Asia. In the mid-1970s the company opened an office in Hong-Kong to oversee Asian supply, a demanding task because of the system of import quotas imposed by the Canadian government. "If one supplier's quota is used up, it's our job to find another," Allan Zeeman, Algo's chief operating officer and head of the Asian office, told the *Globe and Mail* in 1987. By the mid-1980s Asian imports accounted for a full 60 percent of Algo's North American sales.

By 1986 Algo's expansion into men's, women's, and children's sportswear, as well as a gradual penetration into the U.S. market, saw profits reach C$11.5 million on sales of C$190 million. With 13 subsidiaries and 20 percent of sales derived from the United States, the company prepared itself for a major push towards new levels of growth. The first step in this new phase of expansion was an IPO of two million shares on the Montreal and Toronto stock exchanges which netted C$17 million. About C$4 million of this new capital was to be dedicated to expand U.S. sales and C$9 million was targeted to the development of a new line of children's wear in Canada. The ever-optimistic Joe Schaffer predicted that by 1990 total sales volume would be divided equally between the United States and Canada and might even reach the C$1 billion mark.

Schaffer's optimism appeared well-founded when, in 1987, sales for Algo's first major entry into the U.S. market, Tangiers International, increased by over 30 percent in a single year. The Algo subsidiary, which marketed a line of women's sportswear, had been spun off from the company's Canadian Tangerine division two years earlier in order to take the division's Tangerine and Tangiers sportswear line into the United States. In its first week of operation the subsidiary signed up seven of the leading department stores in the New York area, including Macy's, Bloomingdale's, Lord and Taylor, and Gimbel's. Over the next two years the Tangiers line swept through the American market, capturing sales in all 50 states by 1987. Tangiers International opened nine sales offices across the country, establishing an apparent U.S. beachhead for parent Algo. In spite of the initial dramatic success of Tangiers International, the volatility of the fashion industry and the recession of the late 1980s caused an equally dramatic drop-off in sales, and Algo was forced to retract its U.S. presence. By 1990 U.S. sales had shrunk to only about 15 percent of total revenues, and losses from the company's U.S. operations mounted to over C$1 million. "We thought we had discovered America," Joe Schaffer told *Bobbin* in 1989. "[But] we moved too quickly and we had to cut back."

In addition to Algo's U.S. thrust, the company sought to expand in the 1980s through a program of acquisitions. In 1988 Algo Group made a significant break with its traditional role as a wholesaler with the purchase of two struggling retail chains; One Plus One, a women's specialty chain carrying higher-priced fashion merchandise, and La Vie En Rose, which sold upscale lingerie. The chains, which had been owned by Harry and Rosemary Kaner, had combined sales of C$25 million in 1987, but both had been forced to file for bankruptcy protection after overexpanding during the tough retail environment of the late 1980s.

In fulfillment of the firm's objective to expand its presence in the children's apparel segment, Algo made the largest acquisition in its history with the 1988 purchase of Robin International Inc. for about C$30 million. Robin International, itself a 59-year-old company, specialized in children's outerwear but also marketed a line of children's sportswear. In accord with Schaffer's policy of maintaining strong, independent management teams for his subsidiaries, Robin International's senior management were retained after the acquisition. The new subsidiary was expected to add C$65 million in sales to Algo's total revenues.

Losses and Retrenchment in the 1990s

As the Algo Group entered the 1990s, the company and its subsidiaries appeared to have weathered the recession of the late 1980s. When other Canadian garment companies were struggling or folding, Algo's sales had risen to a record C$305 million in 1989, and income had remained steady at about C$7 million. The Canadian retail industry, however, trailed the rest of the economy in the financial recovery, and in the early 1990s retail bankruptcies forced Algo to write off millions in bad debt. While sales stayed relatively steady, profits dropped to only C$1.5 million in 1990 and then shrunk to an almost nonexistent C$418,000 and C$74,000 in 1991 and 1992, respectively.

Algo responded to the problems in the Canadian apparel industry, which had been exacerbated by the new Canadian Goods and Services Tax (GST) and cross-border shopping, by attempting to expand their U.S. and international sales. In 1992 the company purchased two divisions of the California-based Roam Corp., which were expected to add about C$20 million to Algo's U.S. sales. The company's U.S. business became one of the few bright spots in Algo's financial picture as sales rebounded to about 30 percent of the company's total, and U.S. operations returned to profitability in 1993. The company's Tangerine division also began an intensive marketing campaign in Russia, opening a small office in Moscow that was expected to bring in about C$5 million in sales in 1993.

In spite of small gains in the U.S. and international markets, Algo's financial position worsened as the Canadian retail industry continued to undergo a major restructuring into the mid-1990s. To make matters worse for Algo, the Montreal garment industry, once the center of the fashion business in Canada, had been slowly deteriorating as uncertainty about the political future of Quebec drove business out of the city to the more stable centers of Toronto and Vancouver. In 1993 the company closed eight of its 29 divisions in an attempt to stem growing losses, but in 1994 Algo nevertheless suffered a disastrous net loss of C$11 million on sales of C$280 million, the first red ink in the company's 53-year history.

After recording a second straight loss in 1995, and faced with shareholder grumbling, Algo Group began to make a serious effort to revitalize the management of the half-century-old firm. One of the company's two retail chains, One Plus One Fashions, was closed after filing for bankruptcy, and the other, La Vie en Rose, was sold, ending Algo's venture into retail trade. New directors were also appointed, and, most significantly, in 1996 75-year-old company founder Joseph Schaffer stepped down as Algo president, being replaced by longtime administrator Jack Wiltzer. Along with Ben Schaffer's death a few months earlier, Joe Schaffer's resignation ended an era for the Montreal company.

Nearing the end of the century, the pared-down company was once again in the black with a modest net income of C$2 million on sales of C$202 million in fiscal 1996. With only 16 divisions and 500 employees, as compared to the 1,300 people that worked for the company's 29 divisions in the late 1980s, Algo prepared to regroup and to reassess the Canadian and world fashion markets. A number of "shop in shop" boutiques, selling the company's Lori Ann and JS Collections lines, were opened in The Bay stores. The Bay was one of Canada's oldest and largest department store chains and the new boutiques were seen as an attempt to rebuild consumer interest in shopping at these traditional outlets. If successful, the company planned to extend the in-store boutique concept to the U.S. department store chains with which it did business. In a 1997 speech to shareholders, Algo President Jack Wiltzer emphasized that the company's new approach to marketing was now to be "narrow in product, wide in market." By narrowing its focus to women's apparel, sportswear, children's outerwear, and textiles, Algo hoped to rebuild its reputation as one of the leaders of the Canadian fashion industry.

Principal Subsidiaries

Algo Industries Ltd.; Robin International Ltd.; Hamil Textiles Ltd.; Jeric Fashions Group Inc.; Take Two Textiles Inc.; Hamil America Inc.; Hamil Textiles (U.S.A); J.S. Group USA, Ltd.; Robin International (U.S.A.) Inc.

Further Reading

Aarsteinsen, Barbara, "Algo Acquiring Two Chains in Expansion into Retail Area," *Globe and Mail,* June 21, 1988, p. B23.

——, "Algo Group Makes Takeover Bid for Robin International, *Globe and Mail,* May 7, 1988, p. B7.

——, "Sportswear Maker Establishes U.S. Beachhead," *Globe and Mail,* May 6, 1987, p. B12.

Cherney, Elena, "Struggling Algo's Patriarch Retires After 54 Years," *Montreal Gazette,* August 16, 1996, p. D6.

Colgate, Ann Imperato, "The House That Joe Built," *Bobbin,* August 1989, pp. 37–42.

Delean, Paul, "Algo Cuts Losses to $6.3 Million," *Montreal Gazette,* June 22, 1996, p. G3.

French, Paul, "Algo Has Its Eye on Shops in U.S. Stores," *Women's Wear Daily,* October 21, 1997, p. 13.

Gibbens, Robert, "Algo Building Momentum in Its Thrust into the U.S.," *Globe and Mail,* May 26, 1987, p. B5.

——, "Algo Group Is Planning an Aggressive U.S. Thrust," March 12, 1987, p. B3.

Gibbon, Ann, "Algo Ready to Go Global," *Globe and Mail,* June 19, 1991, p. B4.

Hadekel, Peter, "Apparel Company Algo Group Pins Hopes on Rebound in Shirt-and-Pants Index," *Montreal Gazette,* June 18, 1993, p. D1.

Ravensbergen, Jan, "Algo Says Clothing Stores It Supplies Have Seen 20 Percent Upturn in Sales," *Montreal Gazette,* June 17, 1992, p. F3.

Shalom, François, "Algo Closing Five Divisions," *Montreal Gazette,* November 19, 1994, p. C1.

——, "Algo Vows to Get Back on Track," *Montreal Gazette,* June 22, 1995, p. C8.

——, "Clothing Firm Seeks Protection," *Montreal Gazette,* February 14, 1996, p. F1.

——, "Narrow in Product, Wide in Market: Algo Chairman States Aims After Clothier Reports Dip in Profits," *Montreal Gazette,* June 19, 1997, p. C1.

Toomey, Craig, "Tailor-Made Deal; Algo Group's Venture in Russia Is Taking Off," *Montreal Gazette,* March 4, 1993, p. F1.

Wilton, Katherine, "Feel for Fabric; Algo Says Up Is the Only Way the Economy Can Go," *Montreal Gazette,* August 11, 1993, p. F1.

—Hilary Gopnik

Allied Healthcare Products, Inc.

720 Sublette Avenue
St. Louis, Missouri 63110-1927
U.S.A.
(314) 771-2400
Fax: (314) 771-0650

Public Company
Incorporated: 1980
Employees: 884
Sales: $118.11 million (1997)
Stock Exchanges: NASDAQ
Ticker Symbol: AHPI
SICs: 3841 Surgical & Medical Instruments; 3842
   Surgical Appliances & Supplies

Allied Healthcare Products, Inc. is a leading manufacturer of respiratory products used in hospitals, ambulances, and patients' homes. The company's business can be divided into three broad lines: respiratory therapy equipment, such as critical care ventilators, humidifiers, and monitoring systems, which in 1997 accounted for 54 percent of its sales; medical gas equipment, including in-wall medical gas system components, pumps, and compressors, amounting to 36 percent of sales; and emergency medical products, such as trauma burn kits, spine immobilization products, portable resuscitation systems, and bag masks, which represented the remaining 10 percent of sales. Although by the mid-1990s consolidation in the U.S. healthcare industry led to a reduction in Allied's domestic sales, its international sales boomed during the same period. The company marketed and distributed its products under a variety of brand names, such as Chemetron, Gomco, Timeter, Oxequip, and Life Support Products.

Early History

Allied Healthcare's origins date back to the Great Depression and a St. Louis company called Stilecraft. Carl Sciuto and his four brothers founded that company in their hometown to manufacture wooden blinds. Stilecraft diversified over the years

and eventually focused on the production of medical care equipment. In 1971 Sciuto sold the firm to Chemetron, which at the time concentrated on chemicals, metals, and electronics. Chemetron developed Stilecraft into its distinct medical products division, and four years after Chemetron's 1976 merger with the massive conglomerate Allegheny International, Inc., the medical division was renamed Allied Healthcare Products, Inc. Allied manufactured medical gas equipment, such as valves, vacuum pumps, and air compressors, as well as a range of patient care products, including gauges, regulators, and humidifiers.

Harbour Group, a St. Louis-based holding company, acquired Allied in 1985 when Allegheny underwent a corporate restructuring. At the time, Harbour Group focused exclusively on stable manufacturing companies with proven financial success. Sam Fox, who founded and led Harbour Group, summed up the philosophy of his acquisitions in the January 15, 1995 issue of the *St. Louis Post-Dispatch.* "We don't traffic in companies. We build companies. We covet our companies. They are not a piece of meat." Not passive investors, Harbour Group and Fox played an influential role in Allied's development. Although Allied's management remained autonomous, Harbour Group actively assisted Allied in managing budgets and creating corporate strategies.

Growth and Diversification in the Mid-to-Late 1980s

Harbour Group and Fox charted a course of aggressive expansion for Allied. In a June 1985 *St. Louis Business Journal* article, Fox and B. H. Ware, Allied's president, outlined what would lie ahead. "We now are looking at companies that will mix with Allied. We'll expand in the industry both via Allied product expansions and acquisitions." In 1986 Allied began to fulfill this agenda with the acquisition of Oxequip Health Industries. Oxequip manufactured medical gas control panels, outlets, valves, compressors, pumps, and alarms, which strengthened Allied's position in the medical gas industry. Allied continued its growth with the 1988 purchase of Architectural Medical Products, which made modular medical walls and service columns for hospital construction and remodeling. In July of that year Allied grew again, buying Timeter Instrument

Corporation, a market leader in the production of flowmeters, regulators, and air compressors used in the distribution and control of medical gases. Thanks to these strategic acquisitions, Allied became "one of the largest domestic suppliers of capital equipment for medical gas pipeline systems, suction equipment, and related accessories for hospitals," according to a company press release. By 1988 more than 50 percent of hospitals in the United States were served by Allied's medical gas delivery systems. Sales for the year reached $50 million.

To finance its acquisitions, Allied assumed a great deal of debt. But its performance in the late 1980s and early 1990s sufficiently impressed potential investors that Allied was able to go public in January 1992 with an initial stock offering of 1.2 million shares. The effort was a success, and Allied emerged from the sale free of debt. Although after the stock offering Harbour Group no longer directly controlled Allied, the former parent company continued to exert considerable influence. Even after the stock sale, Harbour Group and Fox retained a 67 percent share in Allied. In a January 1992 *St. Louis Post-Dispatch* article, Earl R. Refsland, the newly appointed president and chief executive officer of Allied, stressed the "fine relationship between Allied and the Harbour Group," although he did assert that "this company is totally managed by [Refsland's] team." Refsland had no plans to alter the successful strategy initiated by Harbour Group. Speaking in December to the *St. Louis Post-Dispatch*, he reiterated Allied's commitment to expanding existing market shares and to "acquiring smaller medical firms whose products fit with Allied's existing lines."

Throughout 1992 and 1993 Allied continued to develop its core markets within the healthcare industry. Bolstered by technical advances—such as the Trio Headwall System, an innovative "3-in-1" gas outlet that allowed healthcare facilities to switch quickly between air, oxygen, and vacuum services—Allied's hospital construction and renovation products sold well. Its inpatient respiratory therapies were also strong performers. At the same time, the company recognized the exciting potential of the home healthcare market for its respiratory equipment. An aging population was coming to prefer home medical care over hospital treatment, a development that fueled a higher demand for home respiratory therapy products. The introduction of such products as Allied's FDA-approved oxygen concentrator, a device that converted room air to nearly pure oxygen, increased the company's presence in the home care market. Allied's sales of home care health products rose 30 percent in 1993 alone. Total sales for the year soared to $61 million.

In 1993 the leadership of Allied changed hands. Earl Refsland, citing personal reasons, resigned as president and

chief executive officer in July and was replaced by James Janning, who had served both as a director of Allied and as the president and chief executive officer of Harbour Group. Although Janning was appointed only as an interim chief executive officer, he headed the company for over a year and presided over two important Allied acquisitions—Life Support Products, Inc. and Hospital Systems, Inc.

The purchase of Life Support Products in December 1993 further diversified Allied's product lines, maneuvering the company into the emergency medical field. Life Support Products manufactured emergency medical equipment with an emphasis on ventilators and trauma care products. Meanwhile, the acquisition of Hospital Systems in March 1994 reinforced Allied's hospital construction line. The headwall products (prefabricated wall units that housed medical gas, electrical outlets, and fixtures for monitoring equipment) made by Hospital Systems were used in the renovation of hospitals. According to the August 5, 1994 issue of the *St. Louis Post-Dispatch*, the revenues generated from these two companies boosted Allied's sales 11.5 percent, and *Forbes*, in its November 6, 1995 issue, recognized Allied as a "steady performer." The magazine stated, "There is no one special technology that distinguishes Allied from its many competitors. Rather Allied's strength is in its comprehensive product line."

At the same time that Allied expanded into the home healthcare and emergency medical markets, the company substantially increased its international presence. By 1994 Allied had opened sales offices in Mexico City, Singapore, London, and Paris and employed a fleet of representatives to sell the company's diverse array of products abroad. Allied's growing international sales contributed to its overall strong sales performance. In 1993 alone Allied's international sales rose 31 percent.

Changes in the 1990s

The pace of Allied's expansion only accelerated when David LaRusso took the helm of the company. After he was appointed president and chief executive officer in August 1994, LaRusso directed Allied through five major acquisitions in 16 months at a total cost to the company of $61.7 million. The revenues generated by these strategic acquisitions contributed to Allied's trend of record sales that began in 1992, the year it went public, and ended in 1996.

In September 1994 Allied purchased B&F Medical Products, Inc., a manufacturer of home healthcare respiratory products, such as tubing, kits and masks, aspirators, oxygen concentrators, and oxygen regulators. This takeover moved Allied further into the home healthcare respiratory equipment field, especially with the addition of B&F's Shuco nebulizer to Allied's product line. The nebulizer converted liquid medication into an aerosol, which was especially useful for chronic lung disease patients with airway problems. Buoyed by the B&F purchase, Allied's 1994 sales surpassed $74 million.

LaRusso next engineered Allied's January 1995 acquisition of Bear Medical Systems, Inc., the producer of the market-leading Bear 1000 adult ventilator. In addition to its line of acute, sub-acute, and home care ventilators, Bear Medical Systems provided Allied with its first high-tech manufacturing facility. In the January 24, 1995 issue of the *Press-Enterprise,* LaRusso acknowledged the significance of this aspect of the deal. "The [facility] acquisition will complement Allied's existing research and development efforts, and clearly will position Allied as a medical device company, and not just a manufacturer of medical hardware."

Allied then purchased BiCore Monitoring Systems in June 1995. BiCore manufactured and marketed respiratory assessment systems, equipment designed to monitor the breathing of critically ill patients in order to allow them to spend less time on ventilators. On top of its significant domestic sales, BiCore also marketed its products to intensive care units in Western Europe, the Far East, and the Middle East. BiCore's distribution channels allowed Allied to further expand its international marketing efforts.

With its July 1995 acquisition of Design Principles, Inc., Allied continued to position itself as a key player in the emergency medical products market. Design Principles developed, manufactured, and marketed specialized products used in the transportation of patients with spine and neck injuries (including the Life and Lite Emergency Stretchers, an extremely durable yet X-ray translucent transport device). In December 1995 Allied completed its buying spree with the purchase of Omni-Tech Medical, Inc., another manufacturer of ventilation products. All these acquisitions had a powerful effect on Allied's sales, which in 1995 totaled over $111 million.

Allied's booming sales, however, masked underlying structural problems. The string of acquisitions had left the company saddled with substantial debt, which a September 1995 stock offering had been unable to eliminate. Although Allied's 1996 net sales increased to $120 million, the company's costs rose dramatically, leaving Allied with a profit of only $1.8 million, down 80 percent from 1995. Allied's sales actually declined in 1997, and the company operated at a net loss for the year. Allied's diminishing profitability reflected the company's growing pains as it sought to integrate its numerous acquisitions. In a September 1996 press release, Allied's president underscored the complexities of assimilating its diverse companies: "[M]aking the necessary additional investments to enhance [the acquisitions'] value and adapting their management systems and controls has turned out to be more difficult than originally anticipated." He explained that the "investments required in new product development, international expansion, manufacturing equipment, and operating systems contributed to earning problems." Allied's stock price plummeted in response.

Political issues were also a factor in Allied's financial woes. Proposed changes in Medicare and Medicaid reimbursement policy had an impact on hospitals' routine purchases of medical products and equipment. In addition, as the *Financial Post* noted in January 1996, the U.S. Congress's budget impasse of that year detracted from earnings across the entire healthcare industry. Allied also fell prey to evolutionary changes within the healthcare industry. Increasingly frequent hospital consolidations and the rise of managed care contributed to steady decreases in domestic orders for medical equipment and hospital construction products. For a business such as Allied, which had relied on its medical gas devices for 40 percent of its 1995

sales, the slackening pace of hospital construction and renovation was devastating. Allied's domestic sales flattened.

In an effort to emerge from its slump, Allied instituted a program to improve operational efficiencies and to reduce costs. In November 1996 it invested $1.8 million in its Toledo, Ohio, manufacturing plant and $1.5 million in the St. Louis plant. The company installed new computer-controlled machining centers in St. Louis and modernized the injection mold equipment in Toledo. Management consolidated the sales force and sought to decrease redundancies. In a bold move Allied's board of directors removed LaRusso from his position as president in May 1996. Six months later, after Janning served once more as interim president, Uma Aggarwal was appointed to the post.

Despite its domestic troubles, Allied's international markets remained a bright spot for the company, generating continually rising sales. This trend was due to the fact that a core element in Allied's product line—medical gas systems—remained in high demand abroad. While hospital construction in the United States had slowed substantially, developing countries continued to carry out large hospital building and modernization projects. As Janning told the *St. Louis Post-Dispatch* in November 1996, "[O]ur products are things countries use early in their process of developing modern health-care systems." Allied's international sales grew from 18 percent of total sales in 1994 to 26 percent in 1996.

Under the leadership of Aggarwal, Allied continued to address its falling profits. After suffering setbacks from a machinist strike at the St. Louis plant in June 1997, the company refinanced its debt through a new $46 million credit facility. This arrangement allowed Allied to repay some outstanding debt and provided additional liquidity. In November 1997 Allied shed two of its recent acquisitions, Bear River Medical Systems and BiCore, in a sale to Thermo Electron Company. The proceeds from the sale were used to pay off all of Allied's subordinated debt and some term notes and also provided Allied with the opportunity to shift its focus. As Aggarwal explained at the time in a press release, the sale of the two companies "allow[ed] Allied to focus on its medical gas equipment and home care business." Allied's return to its core competencies also allowed it to achieve profitability by April 1998. That year, in February, Harbour Group and Allied Healthcare finally parted ways when Sam Fox sold or donated almost all of his Allied stock.

Further Reading

"Allied Healthcare Acquires Timeter Instruments," *PR Newswire,* July 29, 1988.

"Allied Healthcare Earnings Up," *St. Louis Post-Dispatch,* August 5, 1994.

"Allied Healthcare Expects Poor Results," *Financial Post,* January 16, 1996.

"Allied Healthcare Products Anticipates Lower Fourth-Quarter and Year End Results," *PR Newswire,* July 23, 1996.

"Allied Healthcare Products Reports First Quarter Results," *PR Newswire,* November 10, 1997.

"Allied Healthcare Products Reports Third Quarter Results," *PR Newswire,* April 28, 1998.

Flannery, William, "Good Medicine One Year After Going Public, Allied Healthcare Is Thriving," *St. Louis Post-Dispatch,* December 14, 1992.

Gianturco, Michael, "Technology Without the Volatility," *Forbes,* November 6, 1995.

Goodman, Adam, "Self-Made Sam Fox Makes a Fortune Buying and Building Companies," *St. Louis Post-Dispatch,* January 15, 1995.

Manning, Margie, "Allied Turns Overseas to Offset Weak Domestic Market," *St. Louis Business Journal,* November 1, 1996.

McAuliffe, Don, "Allied Healthcare to Acquire Bear Medical; Expansion May Occur After Merger," *Press-Enterprise,* January 24, 1995

Melnick, Robert, ""Harbour Group Diversifies," *St. Louis Business Journal,* June 24, 1985.

Norman, Nancy Lee, "Aerosol Medication Therapy," *Independent Living,* November 1, 1994.

Steyer, Robert, "How Allied, Harbour Group Fared in Stock Offering," *St. Louis Post-Dispatch,* January 20, 1992.

—Rebecca Stanfel

Aloha Airlines, Incorporated

P.O. Box 30028
Honolulu, Hawaii 96820
U.S.A.
(808) 484-1111
Web site: http://www.alohaair.com

Wholly Owned Subsidiary of Aloha Airgroup, Inc.
Incorporated: 1946 as Trans-Pacific Airlines
Employees: 2,200
Sales: $248.3 million (1996)
SICs: 4512 Air Transportation, Scheduled

Aloha Airlines, Incorporated occupies a special place in the sun. One of the legion of postwar start-ups that has survived, Aloha has overshadowed its rival Hawaiian Airlines in the inter-island market by specializing and concentrating on customer service. Although it flies five and a half million passengers a year, the carrier often tallies the smallest number of customer complaints. A new generation of management aims to keep the company "flexible and focused."

A Bird of Paradise Takes Wing, 1946

The surplus of military aircraft and pilots after World War II gave rise to many postwar start-up airlines across the world. Trans-Pacific Airways (TPA) began its flying life using the ubiquitous Douglas DC-3 (or C-47) and two former Naval aviators, Al Olson and Louis Lucas. The three planes only cost about $25,000 a piece. The maiden flight for paying passengers took place on July 26, 1946—a perfect day, according to Lucas, for flying between Oahu, Maui, and the Big Island of Hawaii. In spite of a spartan, military-style atmosphere all around, including cargo and baggage lashed into the cabin and deafening engine noise, the passengers were treated to bounteous views of unspoiled scenery. The first flights carried a full capacity of 21 passengers (to be increased by seven after reconfiguring the seating), but cash for payroll and other expenses would remain in short supply.

The venture was put together by publisher Ruddy Tongg, a shrewd Honolulu businessman of Chinese ancestry. Asian Americans (including future U.S. Senator Daniel K. Inouye and U.S. Representative Pat Saiki) also made up a great deal of the TPA staff. The enterprise was a symbol of cultural progress, therefore, as opportunity in the Hawaiian business community had been owned by the *haole* descendants of New England missionaries that controlled the "Big Five" companies and the sugar plantations—then comprising Hawaii's leading industry. Ironically, thanks to aviation, tourism would soon supplant agriculture in importance.

Former Navy pilot Richard "Dick" King, marketing chief at TPA during its first 25 years, orchestrated the airline's promotions, which pitched Hawaii itself. The planes themselves were dubbed "Alohaliners." Flight attendants served not only pineapple juice, but hula and ukulele music. Celebrities began to pour aboard, from Frank Sinatra to Leonard Bernstein.

A dock strike in 1949 stymied the whole Hawaiian economy. There were other difficulties. To compete with Inter-Island Airlines (a subsidiary of Inter-Island Steam Navigation Co., later to become Hawaiian Airlines), TPA needed permission to operate scheduled flights, not just charters. The incumbent used the legal process to inflict devastating delays upon the upstart airline, but TPA was allowed to fly scheduled routes in February 1949. The order had to be signed by President Truman since Hawaii was a territory at the time. TPA also fought for a U.S. mail contract, hotly contested, but finally won in 1951.

In spite of the shortages imposed by the Korean War, the carrier, then calling itself TPA Aloha Airlines, was managing to trim its losses and posted its first profit, $36,000, in 1952. It had grown its share of the inter-island air market from 10 to 30 percent.

Flower Power in the Jet Age, 1950s-70s

Tongg had brought Dave Benz in to manage the airline early on. In 1957, Hung Wo Ching was named CEO and president while Benz returned to Tongg's publishing operations. Ching immediately shortened the company's name to simply "Aloha Airlines." He also arranged for millions of dollars in new

Company Perspectives:

Whether you seek the lush serenity of Kaua'i or the unrivaled excitement of Waikiki, Aloha Airlines will take you there. With a unique spirit of service that has consistently placed us among the leading carriers in the nation for customer satisfaction, Aloha Airlines has an all-jet Boeing-737 fleet for fast, comfortable travel between O'ahu, Maui, Kaua'i and the Big Island of Hawai'i. Best of all, with over 180 flights daily, there's always a jet leaving soon.

In fact, combined with our sister airline, Island Air, no one offers more flights to more places in the islands. For those seeking the truly "hidden Hawai'i," Island Air offers daily scheduled flights to Moloka'i and Kalaupapa, and the resort destinations of Lana'i City, Hana, and Kapalua with DeHavilland Dash-6 and Dash-8 jetprop service.

But we're more than just reliable transportation. Aloha is the only airline in Hawai'i to offer first class seating and service. For business passengers, our modern Suite 737 lounge offers complimentary beverages and a variety of business amenities. And no one matches Aloha Airlines for truly innovative service—we're the only airline in the world to offer Drive-Thru Check-In that allows passengers to drop off baggage and check-in from the comfort of their car.

So when your travels bring you to the magnificent islands of Hawai'i, see for yourself why we're Hawai'i's Favorite Airline.

financing and ordered Fairchild F-27 propjets to compete with Hawaiian Airlines' piston-engined but still modern Convair fleet. The F-27 aircraft proved instantly successful and helped Aloha capture a 40 percent market share. They were introduced the year Hawaii became a state, 1959.

Another propjet, the Vickers Viscount, was introduced in 1963. But it did not work as well in Hawaii as it had elsewhere in the world, and it was promptly replaced with the BAC-111 jet. It also had limitations, however, particularly taking off from short runways. Meanwhile, Hawaiian had begun flying DC-9 jets. The answer came in one of the most popular airliners of all time, the Boeing 737.

Aloha decorated the new jets with kitschy yellow and orange flowers, celebrating the "flower power" motif of the day, and called them "Funbirds," much to the chagrin of Boeing representatives. But their introduction was not all sunny. Delays in deliveries resulted in business lost to Hawaiian's DC-9s, so that Aloha posted a loss in 1968.

It was not the aircraft of the inter-island carriers, however, that boosted tourism the most. United Airlines, TWA, and American Airlines began sending jet airliners to the islands, cutting flying time in half. Unfortunately, this service also was delayed as the newly installed Nixon administration reviewed the route awards. This new service did not start until September 1969, overflying the summer tourist season.

The sum of these delays put Aloha on the ropes. Hawaiian Airlines, a past suitor of the company, made yet another overture of a merger. This time the two parties agreed. Aloha canceled orders for new 737s, incurring stiff penalties; yet, as journalist Bill Wood recounts in *Fifty Years of Aloha*, Hawaiian CEO John Magoon was having second thoughts. Why merge when Aloha was going out of business anyway? "In 1971 Magoon walked away from the merger and left Aloha to die. But it didn't," reports Wood, although the airline was $7 million in debt and had lost $2.4 million in 1970. "In fact, Aloha rebounded to a banner year in 1972." Further, Aloha sued Hawaiian for antitrust violations and eventually won.

All indicators pointed up in 1972. Not only did incoming passenger traffic pick up, but Mainland airlines had contracted to include inter-island flights in their package deals. The Vietnam War had ended. The local economy was booming. On top of all this, Aloha's market share rose to 40 percent. It earned a profit of $1.4 million—most impressive for a carrier nearly bankrupt the year before.

The 1973 Arab oil embargo put an end to that growth. In spite of record load factors—the number of seats sold per flight—fuel costs had risen to the point (they doubled) that it was nearly impossible to break even. They further depressed the islands' economy and kept tourists at home.

Stuart T. K. Ho became director in the mid-1970s. The company's 30th anniversary and the U.S. bicentennial gave cause to celebrate. Aloha had been steadily garnering recognition for its superior service. It attracted the attention of a California-based company, International Air Service Co., which mounted a weak takeover attempt in 1976.

Deregulated Flight, 1980s-90s

The aviation industry after deregulation became one of extremely low margins and fierce competition. The number of carriers was reduced eventually, although the volume of traffic grew by leaps.

One spawn of deregulation was Mid Pacific Airlines, which was launched into the inter-island market in 1981. It relied on old planes and cheap labor to undercut Hawaiian and Aloha. The upstart quickly grabbed a fifth of the recessionary market and Aloha, faced with dwindling market share, again posted a loss in 1982. The company called on executives and employees for concessions to stay in the air. Still, the struggling carrier led the country in fewest customer complaints. The Mid Pacific threat was met by matching fares—but not on all seats.

Joseph O'Gorman, a former United Airlines executive, was called in to lead Aloha for two critical years. Among other accomplishments, he made meeting customers' expectations—particularly relating to on-time service—a top priority. He also joined Aloha Airlines with United's frequent flyer program.

Seeing expansion as the only way to survive in the free-for-all atmosphere of deregulation, O'Gorman initiated the company's first international service, to Taiwan via Guam. The venture, dubbed Aloha Pacific, proved troublesome and was terminated within six months. Aloha posted a loss of $1.9 million in 1984. Using a leased jet, the company lost less money than it could have, though, and tempered its expansion plans while rival Hawaiian Airlines went gung ho into the overseas market. As Hawaiian's fortunes fell, the price of Hawaiian's sprawling Pacific network appeared to be that of surrender on the home front.

Maurice Myers succeeded O'Gorman. Aloha began offering jet cargo transport to the islands via dual-purpose 737 jets and the company soon owned the market, achieving up to a 90 percent market share. Myers also initiated the AlohaPass frequent flyer program and premium service, culminating in the Alii Club.

The company's stock price soared in 1986 when it became the apparent target of a leveraged buyout led by Norman Seigal of Dallas. Aloha Airline's principals managed to buy back the 16 percent share the group accumulated within the year, repulsing the takeover attempt and keeping the company operating and in local hands. At the end of the ordeal, Aloha's owners took the company shares off the public market. They created the holding company Aloha Airgroup, Inc. and bought a commuter airline called Princeville Airlines, whose propjet fleet could reach places Aloha's big jets could not. It was later renamed Island Air.

Aloha was having a great business year in spite of the threat to its existence. The Hawaiian economy was booming; the number of visitors increased by 15 percent in one year. Aloha built up its fleet to 12 737s while losing a competitor, Mid Pacific, due to cash flow problems. The worst day in the company's history, however, was soon to come.

On April 28, 1988, part of the roof of Flight 243 flying from Hilo to Honolulu peeled off, killing a flight attendant. The accident, which occurred in an older 737, brought the issue of metal fatigue to national attention, leading to new inspection standards.

An economic downturn was also on the horizon. The wave of Japanese speculation in Hawaii finally slowed, diminishing the volume of air traffic. The early 1990s, which saw the Persian Gulf War, were slow for airlines worldwide.

In spite of all this, Aloha Airlines fared relatively well. Its air cargo operations continued to thrive, and it had finally established leadership in the inter-island passenger market—a 60 percent share, while rival Hawaiian Airlines was busy losing $111 million in one year, 1992, forcing it into bankruptcy. Aloha dressed its jets with a smart new design, resplendent with an elegant bird of paradise flower on a navy tail. Still, Aloha was not immune to misfortune in 1992. In September, Hurricane Iniki ravaged the island of Kauai, sweeping away with it a quarter of Aloha's market as well as its profits.

These factors postponed a planned initial public offering. Nevertheless, Aloha soon recovered, while Hawaiian continued to flounder. Yet another entrant, Mahalo Air, emerged to compete with low fares. Aloha stayed on the offensive, entering into a code-sharing agreement with United Airlines in 1993 and installing what it billed as the world's very first drive-through check-in service.

Focusing on the Horizon

Glenn Zander, a former TWA executive, emerged as the successor to Maury Myers. Zander had more of a financial focus than Myers. He brought the company to a new level of corporate sophistication. Interestingly, he furthered standardization by trimming the fleet to include only 737-200 series aircraft, cutting out the larger variants bought to meet an anticipated rise in demand. The smaller aircraft's passenger compartments were reconfigured to hold an equivalent number of seats. Although this cost $12 million to perform, the measures trimmed roughly $10 million per year from operating expenses. The company lost $6.9 million in 1995, not including the cost of reconfiguring the fleet, but the next year (the company's silver anniversary) saw a strong performance and net profits of $4.8 million, in spite of rising fuel costs.

Aloha's freight business was estimated to be worth $30 million per year, and in 1997 the carrier was able to devote a dedicated 737 to cargo flights. UPS implemented plans to enter the inter-island market itself, however. It had originally subcontracted these parcels to various lines before settling on Aloha in 1987. Aloha also carried parcels for Federal Express.

Several factors boded well for Aloha Airlines in the new millennium. Tourism was expected to increase and Hawaii was expected to continue to reap the benefits of its position at the economic center of the Pacific Rim. Honolulu appeared to supplant Hong Kong as the region's premier retail outlet thanks to the phenomenon of tourist shopping. The opening of the city's new convention center and a statewide moratorium on landing fees late in 1997 did not hurt, either.

Further Reading

Gomes, Andrew, ''Aloha Airlines Celebrates Fiftieth,'' *Pacific Business News,* July 29, 1996.
——, ''Aviators Question Intentions of Aloha's Earnings Release,'' *Pacific Business News,* March 24, 1997.
——, ''Code-Sharing Not Vital, But Definitely Beneficial to Hawaii's Airlines,'' *Pacific Business News,* September 1, 1997.
——, ''Hawaiian Steps Up to Aloha with Drive-Thru Check-In,'' *Pacific Business News,* April 20, 1998.
——, ''Labor Negotiations Spur UPS to Add Cargo Flights,'' *Pacific Business News,* May 19, 1997.
Shapiro, Walter, Botticelli, Ann, and Reingold, Edwin M., ''The Plane Was Disintegrating,'' *Time,* May 9, 1988.
Wood, Bill, *Fifty Years of Aloha: The Story of Aloha Airlines,* Honolulu: Aloha Airlines, Incorporated, 1996.

—Frederick C. Ingram

The American Cancer Society

1599 Clifton Road, NE
Atlanta, Georgia 30329-4251
U.S.A.
(404) 320-3333
(800) ACS-2345 (227-2345)
Fax: (404) 325-0230
Web site: http://www.cancer.org

Nonprofit Company
Incorporated: 1913 as American Society for the Control
    of Cancer
Employees: 4,700
Sales: $538 million
SICs: 8099 Health & Allied Services, Not Elsewhere
    Classified

The American Cancer Society (ACS) is a not-for-profit organization whose mission is to eliminate cancer. With a highly professional staff comprised of not-for-profit administrators and fundraisers, and personnel from the medical healthcare field including doctors, nurses, and technicians, plus more than two million volunteers at community locations throughout the United States, the American Cancer Society is one of the most effective organizations in the fight against the disease. The ACS designs and supports a number of educational programs for both the medical professional and general public, provides large amounts of money for cancer research, and also offers direct patient services such as transportation for treatment, assistance in obtaining home medical needs such as wheelchairs, and emotional support for newly diagnosed cancer patients. The ACS has recently decided to add a new component to its activities by becoming an advocate for public policy initiatives that directly affect the prevention of cancer and the welfare of cancer patients.

Early History

The roots of the American Cancer Society can be traced back to 1912. In that year, the American Gynecological Society met in Washington, D.C., and discussed how a greater control of cancer could be achieved through a campaign to educate the general public. A committee was appointed to draft a plan for the implementation of a comprehensive cancer education program, which was endorsed at the Society's meeting one year later. Having endorsed the establishment of a national society to prevent cancer through education, an organizational meeting was held in May 1913 at the Harvard Club in New York City, and the American Society for the Control of Cancer was formed. With a budget of $10,000, the Society helped place the first article on cancer published in a popular woman's magazine, the *Ladies' Home Journal.*

From the middle of the decade onward, the organizers of the American Society for the Control of Cancer engaged in a concerted effort to inform the general public about the disease. Mrs. Robert G. Mead, the Chair of the Ways and Means Committee of the Society, was instrumental in coordinating this highly successful effort. Public meetings about the danger of cancer were held in Chicago, New York, St. Louis, Boston, and New Orleans. In 1914, the Society began to print pamphlets on cancer and one in particular, entitled "Facts About Cancer," was mailed to approximately 14,000 people. Posters, exhibits, lantern slides, and newspaper articles on cancer began to appear regularly, and doctors reported that as a consequence patients were showing up earlier for diagnostic assessments.

At the same time, the Society began to focus specifically on educational programs for women, and enlisted the support of the *Ladies's Home Journal* for disseminating a host of information on the warning signs and possible treatments for the disease. When the United States entered World War I in 1917, the Society reached an agreement with the National Safety Council to circulate more than six million bulletins on cancer to working men and women throughout the country. By the end of the decade, the Society had helped to establish a National Cancer Week, had started publishing pamphlets in foreign languages at the request of the League of Red Cross Societies, and had been instrumental in convincing the U.S. government to publish its first pamphlet on cancer, more than 250,000 copies of which were distributed in 1919 alone.

By 1922, the Society had grown so large that its budget was increased to $60,000. Nearly 700 cancer committees had been formed throughout the United States, and the organization estimated that half the country's population was aware of cancer and its dangers. In 1924, while continuing to educate, the American Society also established cancer clinics to provide early diagnosis and treatment for patients, and to fight fraudulent cancer cures. During the decade, "What Everyone Should Know About Cancer," a pamphlet published by the organization, had grown to become one of the most popular and widely circulated medical handbooks in the country. The not-for-profit agency was growing at a dizzying rate, and generous people throughout America opened up their pocketbooks to help the cause. John D. Rockefeller contributed the sum of $125,000 in 1926, substantially helping the Society toward its goal of $1 million for an endowment campaign. Not surprisingly, the goal was reached just one year later. In 1929, the organization published one of its most influential booklets, "What Every Woman Should Know About Cancer," while an earlier released pamphlet, the "Danger Signals of Cancer," had become so popular that it was being published in 22 languages.

The Great Depression and World War II

When the stock market crashed in the fall of 1929, every institution within the United States was affected. Businesses went bankrupt, banks closed their doors forever, and many people found themselves standing in bread lines for something to eat. The American Society for the Control of Cancer was also hit hard by the depression, with a dramatic drop in contributions which led to extensive salary reductions and staff layoffs. Doctors were compelled to augment the wages they received from medical practice with other work, and consequently had less time for volunteer activities associated with the Society. In addition, all the plans that had been laid for new cancer clinics around the country had to be indefinitely postponed.

To take the place of diminishing contributions from both the general public and private enterprise, many people within the organization began to look toward the government for help. In 1937, the National Cancer Institute Act was signed by President Roosevelt, stating as its intention to "provide for and to foster the continuous study of the cause, the prevention, the diagnosis and the treatment of cancer." On its six member National Advisory Council, there sat four of the Society's directors. But many doctors interpreted the Society's alliance with the government as a harbinger of its support for socialized medicine, and thus became suspicious of its intentions for educating the public. As a result, donations from many doctors who had given in the past also began to trickle away

With its donor base shrinking, and more staff cuts inevitable, the Society focused on what it could reasonably expect to fund, namely, bringing the message of cancer control to doctors throughout America. During the entire decade of the 1930s, the Society focused on professional education, including publishing professional literature, sending speakers to professional meetings, and arranging for lectures to be given at medical schools. This effort allayed the fears of doctors that the Society was advocating socialized medicine, and convinced them that a more comprehensive and intensive program to educate the public about cancer was necessary.

The turning point for the Society, both in terms of heightened publicity and financial stability, occurred during the years of World War II. In 1943 Mary Lasker, the wife of Albert Lasker, who was the president of the renowned advertising firm of Lord & Thomas, was informed that her housekeeper had been diagnosed with cancer. Shocked when the doctors told her nothing could be done, Mrs. Lasker was appalled that there was practically no research conducted on the disease. When she called the American Society on Cancer Control, Mrs. Lasker learned that the Society had no money for research. She then asked her husband to help the Society make public the need for cancer research funds, and her husband delegated one of his younger associates, Emerson Foote, the man who became one of the famous founders of Foote, Cone & Belding Advertising Agency, to create a publicity and fund-raising campaign. Foote immediately suggested a name change for the organization, to the American Cancer Society (ACS), and embarked upon a comprehensive advertising strategy to raise funds for cancer research, including appeals for money on early radio shows such as "Bob Hope," and "Fibber McGee and Molly." The first fund-raising campaign conducted by the American Cancer Society in 1945 garnered more than $4 million, of which 25 percent was set aside for research. Since the federal government was only spending a total of $750,000 for cancer research during the same year, the amount raised by the ACS was significant. A director of research was hired at the national office, and from that time forward the ACS designated 25 percent of all funds raised annually to be used for cancer research.

The Postwar Era

During the late 1940s, the American Cancer Society began to share, with other national health organizations in such countries as England and Sweden, accumulated evidence regarding the relation between tobacco smoking and cancer. Spurred on by this evidence, the ACS funded a case-control study of lung-cancer patients and patients without lung cancer at the Washington School of Medicine in St. Louis, Missouri. The study found that 94 percent of the patients diagnosed with lung cancer were smokers of cigarettes. Following up on the conclusions to this study, a more comprehensive investigation was conducted during the early 1950s involving over 200,000 interviews, questionnaires, and clinical research. On June 21, 1954, a representative of the ACS told the American Medical Association convention in San Francisco that those people who smoked two packs of cigarettes a day were 25 times more likely to get lung cancer than nonsmokers and, in addition, that smokers were twice as likely to have a heart attack as nonsmokers.

The report created front page news not only across the United States but in Asia and Europe as well. Cigarette sales dropped precipitously. The tobacco companies responded by developing and marketing a safer product, namely, filter-tipped cigarettes. But the die had been cast, so to speak, and the ACS and tobacco firms began the fight that lasts to this day. In 1959, the Society tried to use its influence to persuade the U.S. Surgeon General to warn smokers about the risk of cancer, but bureaucratic red tape prevented a statement from being given, and two years later a version which was summarily ignored appeared in the *Journal of the American Medical Association.* The ACS would not give up, however, and was instrumental in the Surgeon General's Report that was published in 1964, which stated that "cigarette smoking is a health hazard." As its influence began to spread around the world, the ACS was active in promoting government campaigns against smoking in England, Sweden, and Norway. In 1965, the ACS won a hard-fought battle in convincing the U.S. Congress to pass the first law regulating the labeling of cigarettes, including the now ubiquitous warning: "Caution: Cigarette smoking may be hazardous to your health." By 1971, Congress was persuaded to prohibit all cigarette advertising on both radio and television.

Saving Lives in the 1970s and 1980s

During the 1970s and 1980s, the ACS was involved in researching and teaching the public about many other forms of cancer as well. Bladder cancer, gastric cancer, mouth, colon, and kidney cancers were studied and the results developed into major breakthroughs for the medical professions' understanding and treatment of the diseases. Perhaps the two most researched types of cancers during the 1970s and 1980s, in addition to lung cancer caused by tobacco, were cervical cancer and breast cancer. During the 1950s, the ACS had implemented a comprehensive public awareness campaign to encourage women to ask their doctor for a pap smear. In 1960, only 30 percent of American women had been given a pap smear, but by the mid-1970s the number had increased to over 50 percent, and by 1980 the figures had jumped to 80 percent. Early diagnosis was necessary for avoiding death from the disease, and the pap smear was overwhelmingly successful. In fact, this was widely regarded as the American Cancer Society's first mass cancer-prevention program, and the Society could justifiably claim that the death rate among women with an early diagnosis was substantially reduced.

During the 1970s, the ACS had issued a formal statement in favor of annual mammography screening for women over 35 in order to diagnose breast cancer. However, the ACS was intensely criticized for its position due to the discovery that radiation used in the mammography x-rays were found to cause cancer or result in adverse side effects. The ACS revised its position in 1980 and advocated annual mammography screenings only for women over 50, and continued to work with experts to lower the radiation dosages and sharpen the x-ray images. As the criticism subsided, by the end of the decade the ACS claimed that mammography screenings were one of the most important diagnostic tools in the treatment of breast cancer.

In addition to its focus on the diagnosis and treatment of both cervical cancer and breast cancer, during the 1970s and 1980s the ACS initiated numerous programs which were meant to reduce or avoid known carcinogens. The most prominent of these programs was the one against cigarette smoking, well known as the most dangerous cause of lung cancer. Other programs concentrated on carcinogens confined to the workplace, including asbestos, uranium, aromatic amines used in the dye industry, and a variety of chemicals used in the production of artificial rubber and plastics. The public awareness campaigns of the ACS were significant factors in convincing the American government to enact legislation that protected employees from carcinogens found in the workplace.

The 1990s and Beyond

The ACS has led the fight against cancer in the decade of the 1990s by engaging in extensive research projects in the fields of cancer genetics, cancer vaccines, monoclinal antibodies, rational drug design, angiogenesis inhibitors, oncolytic viruses, chemotherapy, and cancer survivorship. In 1997, the ACS received $488 million from the American public for its cancer control programs. The most important development for the organization during the 1990s, however, has been its focus on advocacy, especially regarding the legislative proposals and tobacco settlement debated in the U.S. Congress. Positioning itself as a third-party watchdog, the ACS has actively and aggressively lobbied key policymakers in the White House and Congress to prevent the tobacco industry from marketing its products to children and to enact comprehensive national policies that will reduce the number of deaths caused by the use of tobacco. The ACS strongly advocates that the U.S. Food and Drug Administration (FDA) be given the unfettered power to regulate nicotine and require tobacco firms to stop marketing cigarettes to teenagers.

With a budget of over $500 million, the ACS is well-positioned to advocate public policy initiatives affecting the welfare of cancer patients, the protection of the public from cancer risks, access to healthcare, and also engage in cutting-edge research into the cause and treatment of the many forms of the disease. Undoubtedly, though, the ACS views its most important role to be played in the heated debate surrounding tobacco control, and will use every resource at its disposal to fight the tobacco industry.

Further Reading

Brewster, Elizabeth, "Battle of the Binge: New Diet Guidelines Streamline Healthy Eating Advice," *Food Processing,* December 1996, p. 98.

Brooks, Warren T., "The Wasteful Pursuit of Zero Risk," *Forbes,* April 30, 1990, p. 161.

"Cancer Society's Deal to Sell Its Name Sparks Protests," *Marketing News,* September 23, 1996, p. 5.

Carey, John, "So Many Chemicals, So Few Answers," *Business Week,* March 13, 1995, p. 98.

"Estrogen and Cancer," *Time,* June 14, 1976, p. 65.

Gross, Neil, "Quiet Strides in the War on Cancer," *Business Week,* February 6, 1995, p. 150.

Nash, Madeleine, "Stopping Cancer," *Time,* April 25, 1994, p. 54.

"A Potential Tool Against Cancer," *Business Week,* May 18, 1981, p. 154.

Ross, Walter, *Crusade: The Official History of the American Cancer Society,* New York: Arbor House, 1987.

—Thomas Derdak

American Eagle Outfitters, Inc.

150 Thorn Hill Drive
Warrendale, Pennsylvania 15086-7528
U.S.A.
(412) 776-4857
Fax: (412) 779-5585
Web site: http://www.ae-outfitters.com

Public Company
Incorporated: 1993
Employees: 5,441
Sales: $405.7 million (1997)
Stock Exchanges: NASDAQ
Ticker Symbol: AEOS
SICs: 5699 Miscellaneous Apparel & Accessory Stores

American Eagle Outfitters, Inc. is a specialty retail chain offering casual, ''outdoor-inspired'' fashion apparel, footwear, and accessories for men and women ages 16–34. There are more than 330 American Eagle Outfitters stores located in 40 states, primarily those east of the Rockies; nearly all the units are in regional shopping malls. The stores average about 4,200 square feet in size. Approximately 98 percent of the chain's sales are generated from private label brands—American Eagle Outfitters, AE, and AE Supply; this focus on private-label merchandise was launched through a 1992 repositioning and was intended to differentiate American Eagle from its mall competitors, such as The Limited, The Gap, and Abercrombie & Fitch. To keep up with the latest fashion trends, the company employs an in-house design team, whose merchandise designs are then manufactured to specification by outside vendors or by American Eagle's manufacturing subsidiary, Prophecy Ltd. This private-label/in-house design system enables American Eagle to keep tight control of quality and hold prices down; for example, its clothes typically cost from 15 to 30 percent less than comparable clothes at The Gap. Nearly half of the chain's sales are for ''ladieswear,'' while ''menswear'' accounts for about 35 percent of sales and outdoorwear/accessories/footwear for about 17 percent. Customer credit is offered through an American Eagle Outfitters credit card. Approximately 60 percent of the company's stock is owned by the Schottenstein family, whose Schottenstein Stores Corp. is a large privately held company based in Columbus, Ohio, with numerous retail holdings.

1977 Debut

When American Eagle Outfitters was launched in 1977, it was part of Silvermans Menswear, Inc., a retailing company whose flagship was the Silvermans chain, which sold young men's apparel and accessories and was founded in McKees Rocks, Pennsylvania (near Pittsburgh), in 1904. The Silverman family owned and operated Silvermans Menswear, and by the mid-1970s two brothers—in the third generation of Silvermans in the family business—were running things: Jerry Silverman, president and CEO, and Mark Silverman, executive vice-president and COO. The Silverman brothers believed that they needed more than one concept to continue growing their company—that the addition of other chains would then enable them to operate more than one store in the same mall. They thus opened the first American Eagle Outfitters store in 1977, positioning it as a seller of brand-name leisure apparel, footwear, and accessories for men and women, with an emphasis on merchandise geared toward outdoor sports, such as hiking, mountain climbing, and camping. American Eagle quickly established itself as a mall store able to attract an unusually wide array of shoppers, although its ''rugged'' offerings were geared more toward men. And with a nationally distributed mail-order catalog supporting the retail units, the new chain quickly became a key competitor not only to such established retailers as The Gap but also to such venerable catalogers as L.L. Bean and Lands End.

In 1980 Silvermans Menswear changed its name to Retail Ventures, Inc. (RVI). That same year, the Silvermans ran into some financial difficulties and sold a 50 percent stake in RVI to the Schottenstein family. The Schottensteins owned Schottenstein Stores, a retailing giant based in Columbus, Ohio. Schottenstein Stores was founded in the early 20th century by E. L. Schottenstein when he opened the first Value City Department Store, a discount department store chain which by the early

1990s included 93 stores in 15 states generating about $1 billion in sales annually.

Became Focus of RVI in Mid-1990s

In 1985 RVI launched three more new chains: His Place and Go Places, concepts similar to that of Silvermans, and Help-Ur-Self, a bulk food store. The following year the company spent $8 million to expand its headquarters, adding 25,000 square feet to its office space and 146,000 square feet to its 119,000-square-foot distribution center. Also in 1986 RVI added 34 new stores to its existing 200. Many of these were American Eagle units, as the company began that year to concentrate more of its resources on American Eagle, which was achieving rapid sales growth, than on Silvermans, whose sales were being hurt from increasing competition, particularly from discount chains.

This shift in emphasis culminated in early 1989 when RVI announced a major restructuring in which it sold its Silvermans, His Place, and Go Places chains—a total of 125 stores—to Merry-Go-Round Enterprises Inc., a Towson, Maryland-based operator of 430 mall-based clothing stores, including Merry-Go-Round, Cignal, and Attivo. RVI also spun off to the Silverman family the 11-store Help-Ur-Self chain, which had performed reasonably well but was not considered synergistic with American Eagle. RVI was thus left with American Eagle Outfitters—now with 137 stores in 36 states and sales of $125 million—as its single focus. The company planned to aggressively expand its sole remaining chain by as many as 120 stores over the following three years. It began to implement this plan but only after The Gap had approached RVI in early 1989 about buying American Eagle and after negotiations to do so had fallen through.

Sold to Schottensteins and Repositioned in Early 1990s

By mid-1991 American Eagle had grown to 153 stores—not nearly the expansion rate envisioned two years earlier—and sales had stagnated. For the fiscal year ending in July 1991, sales were $144.3 million, a minuscule increase over the $142.4 million of the previous year. The chain also posted a net loss of $8.9 million for the year. In a deal designed to position American Eagle for renewed growth, the Schottenstein family bought the 50 percent of RVI owned by the Silverman family, giving the Schottensteins full control of the company and its only chain. Jay L. Schottenstein became the new chairman and CEO of RVI, replacing Mark Silverman, while Sam Forman was brought in to become president and COO. Forman had been CEO of Kuppenheimer Clothiers.

In the midst of the recessionary early 1990s, American Eagle's difficulties could be traced in part to its line of branded merchandise. With brand-name apparel increasingly being offered by various clothing chains and discounters, American Eagle was facing increasing competition. Under its new ownership and leadership, the chain was repositioned in 1992 to focus on private-label casual apparel for men and women, while retaining the outdoor-oriented look for which it was best known. The private label strategy was intended to position American Eagle merchandise as value priced. The company also began opening American Eagle outlet stores to reduce its inventory of out-of-season clothing items.

Went Public in 1994

American Eagle's 1994 fiscal year was its best year ever, evidence that the repositioning was working. Sales for the year were $199.7 million, while net income was a healthy $11.9 million. In the midst of this successful year, RVI announced that it would go public through an initial public offering. In November 1993 an American Eagle Outfitters, Inc. subsidiary was established and it was under this name that RVI and the American Eagle chain emerged in April 1994, with a listing on the NASDAQ stock exchange and with the Schottenstein family maintaining roughly a 60 percent stake in the new company and Forman about ten percent. American Eagle went public as a 167-store chain with nine outlet stores and locations in 34 states.

Much of the approximate $37 million raised through the IPO was almost immediately poured back into the company for an aggressive program of expansion and renovation. From July through December of 1994 alone, 55 new stores were opened. At the one-year anniversary of the IPO, nearly 90 new stores had been added. Unfortunately, several of these new locations were unprofitable from the time they opened their doors, and it became apparent that the chain had expanded too rapidly.

Adding to the confusion at this time was a rapid succession of management changes. In early 1995 Forman was named vice-chairman, with Robert G. Lynn, a one-time president and CEO of F.W. Woolworth Co., becoming vice-chairman and COO and Roger S. Markfield, who had served as executive vice-president of merchandising, being promoted to president and chief merchandising officer. Lynn, however, left the company in December 1995 over reported management differences. Later that same month, George Kolber took over Lynn's vice-chairman and COO spots.

Forman, meanwhile, sold his ten percent stake in American Eagle in early 1995, then in late 1995 resigned from his position as vice-chairman following his purchase of 32 American Eagle outlet stores in 18 states for between $14 million and $16 million. The company had decided to divest the outlets in order to concentrate on its mall locations, and it subsequently closed its remaining seven outlet stores. Forman signed a licensing agreement with American Eagle, whereby the outlets he purchased would operate under the American Eagle Outlets name and would sell merchandise made specifically for the outlets. Through all of these changes, Jay Schottenstein continued in his role of chairman and CEO.

Repositioned Again in 1996

The year 1996 was a transitional one for American Eagle as it cut back drastically on its expansion plans in order to reposition the chain once again. In search of higher-margin merchandise to offer, Markfield and Kolber determined that the chain had to sell more women's apparel, which is typically more profitable. The leaders also decided to completely divorce American Eagle of its once-eclectic range of customers and target the lucrative youth market—ages 16 to 34—through a younger and hipper feel to the clothing and in the chain's marketing. Finally, American Eagle would strongly emphasize value pricing through a commitment to private label merchandise. Remaining at the chain's core was its venerable rugged, outdoorsy style.

For fiscal 1996 (the first year of the company's new fiscal year, which now ended at the end of January), about 98 percent of the company's sales were generated from its private label brands, American Eagle Outfitters, AE, and AE Supply. Women's clothing, meantime, which in fiscal 1995 had accounted for only 30 percent of sales, accounted for 47 percent of sales in fiscal 1996.

If 1996 was a transitional year for American Eagle, then the transition went exceedingly well, as 1997 turned into a breakout year. For the year, sales increased 24.3 percent to a record $405.7 million, while net income more than tripled, going from $5.9 million in 1996 to $19.5 million in 1997. Comparable store sales were very strong, increasing 15.1 percent in 1997 compared to the previous year.

In addition to opening 32 new stores in 1997, American Eagle that year also for the first time began manufacturing its own clothing through the acquisition of Prophecy Ltd., a New York-based contract apparel maker which had been majority owned by the Schottenstein family. This move toward further vertical integration was in keeping with the chain's desire to control costs and maintain quality. The terms of the purchase were $900,000 in cash plus a contingency payment of up to $700,000.

Early 1998 was a busy period for American Eagle as it introduced the AE Clear Card, the first clear credit card; announced plans to start selling merchandise from its web site, a move that would fit in well with the chain's youth-oriented customer base (American Eagle's mail-order catalog had been discontinued some years prior); and said it would open new units outside of enclosed malls, in airports, strip malls, and other locales. The renewed strength of American Eagle was also evident in two separate three-for-two stock splits, which occurred during the first five months of 1998. The company also announced that over the next several years it would expand its store count 15 to 20 percent each year; the largely untapped West Coast was likely to be a prime area of expansion. Also planned was an increase in average store size from 4,200 square feet to 5,000. And with its new youthful format that emphasized women's clothing, American Eagle was beginning to revamp many of its older stores whose designs were very "masculine." All of these developments pointed toward a bright future for a company that seemed destined to outfit Americans for years to come.

Principal Subsidiaries

Prophecy Ltd.

Further Reading

Benson, Betsy, "Retail Ventures Plans Restructuring: New Focus on American Eagle Outfitters Unit," *Pittsburgh Business,* February 27, 1989.

Fitzpatrick, Dan, "New Lines Pace American Eagle Comeback Bid," *Pittsburgh Business Times,* December 30, 1996, pp. 1+.

Gallagher, Jim, "Gap Won't Buy American Eagle," *Pittsburgh Post Gazette,* March 18, 1989.

Much, Marilyn, "Retailer Moves into New Venues, Cyberspace," *Investor's Business Daily,* January 30, 1998, p. A3.

Phillips, Jeff, "Schottensteins Buy 153 Stores," *Business First of Columbus,* June 3, 1991, pp. 1+.

Walters, Rebecca, "American Eagle Going Public," *Business First of Columbus,* March 21, 1994.

—David E. Salamie

American Power Conversion Corporation

132 Fairgrounds Road
West Kingston, Rhode Island 02892
U.S.A.
(401) 789-5735
(800) 788-2208
Fax: (401) 788-2710
Web site: http://www.apcc.com

Public Company
Incorporated: 1981
Employees: 2,650
Sales: $706.9 million (1996)
Stock Exchanges: NASDAQ Pacific
Ticker Symbols: APCC; ACC
SICs: 3679 Electronic Components, Not Elsewhere
Classified

Named one of *Fortune* magazine's "100 Fastest Growing Companies" in 1996, American Power Conversion Corporation (APC) is the world's leading supplier of power protection solutions.

Start Up, 1981

Founded as a Massachusetts corporation on March 11, 1981, the company manufactures products that improve the reliability and productivity of computer systems worldwide by protecting hardware and data from the ongoing threat of power disturbances through its line of electrical surge protection devices, uninterruptible power supply (UPS) products, power conditioning products, and associated software and accessories for use with computer and computer-related equipment. Protected applications include Internet usage, wide-area networks (WANs), local-area networks (LANs), mid-range computers, home and office workstations, file servers, Integrated Services Digital Network (ISDN) equipment, a variety of consumer electronics, as well as data, network, serial, coaxial (CATV), and telephone lines, and other electronic devices which rely on electric utility power.

The variation or interruption of power to sensitive parts of a computer system may damage or destroy important data or the computer's set of operating instructions. The company's UPS products provide protection from disturbances in the smooth flow of power while utility power is available and provide automatic, virtually instantaneous backup power in the event of a loss of utility power, lasting from five minutes to several hours, allowing the user to continue computer operations or conduct an orderly shutdown of the protected equipment and preserve data.

The company markets its products to business users around the world through a variety of distribution channels, including computer distributors and dealers, mass merchandisers, catalog merchandisers, and private label accounts. Major customers include Ingram Micro Corporation, Constellation Energy Corporation (the ninth largest utility company in the United States), Entex Information Services, St. Mary's Parish School Board (Louisiana), General Motors, and Deloitte & Touche. The company ranks as one of five domestic businesses providing a full range of UPS products and services worldwide in the 0-5 kVA UPS market. The company's principal competitors in the United States include Exide Electronics Group Inc.; Best Power; a business unit of General Signal Corporation; and Trippe Manufacturing Company. The company also competes with a number of other companies which offer UPS products similar to the company's products, including Exabyte, Fujitsu, Hewlett-Packard, Lexmark, NEC, Seagate, and Viewsonic.

Located in West Kingston, Rhode Island, the company's corporate offices are housed in a 166,000-square-foot facility, some of which is also given over to manufacturing capabilities. The company also leases four other facilities in that state: a 95,000-square-foot warehouse in North Kingston, a 334,000-square-foot warehouse in West Warwick, a 75,000-square-foot warehouse and manufacturing facility in Cranston, and a 116,000-square-foot warehouse and manufacturing facility in East Providence. An additional 151,000 square feet of manufacturing and warehouse space is split between two facilities located in Fort Myers, Florida, and the company's research and development facility located in Billerica, Massachusetts. The company's primary manufacturing operations outside the

United States are located in Galway, Ireland, and in the Philippines. Other major facilities are located in Lognes, France (through the company's subsidiary American Power Conversion Europe S.A.R.L., this facility provides sales and marketing support to customers in Europe, the Middle East, the former Soviet Union, and Africa and its revenues are in the form of commissions from the Galway operations), and Tokyo, Japan, and the company utilizes third-party warehouse facilities in Australia, Japan, Canada, Singapore, The Netherlands, South Africa, and Uruguay for distribution into its international markets and has sales offices throughout the world.

Products

The company's growth reflects a similar growth in the UPS industry, itself a result of the rapid proliferation of microprocessor-based equipment and related systems in the corporate marketplace, as well as in small businesses and home environments. Personal computers (PCs) have become an integral part of the overall business strategy of many organizations and are now the workstation of choice in most office environments, as well as in many technical and manufacturing settings. As businesses continue to change their computer configurations from mainframe and remote terminals to linked PCs in LANs, PCs will continue to become increasingly important and it will become even more necessary to ensure that the data stored in, and operating instructions for, PCs are protected from fluctuations in utility power. Businesses are also becoming aware of the need to protect devices such as hubs, routers, bridges, and other "smart" devices that manage and interconnect networks. In addition to the demand that traditional server-based networks create for UPSs, the growth opportunities from the proliferation of peer-to-peer networks (where intelligence is distributed among all the devices in the network, rather than a single server) and wide-area networks (such as the Internet) will further stimulate UPS demand.

The company believes that the increasing awareness of the costs associated with poor power quality has increased demand for power protection products. Complete failures ("blackouts"), surges ("spikes"), or sags ("brownouts") in the electrical power supplied by a utility can cause computers and electronic systems to malfunction, resulting in costly downtime, damaged or lost data files, and damaged hardware. The company's strategy has been to design and manufacture products which incorporate high-performance and quality at competitive prices.

The company manufactures over 140 standard domestic and international UPS models designed for different applications. The principal differences among the products are the amount of power which can be supplied during an outage, the length of time for which battery power can be supplied, the level of intelligent network interfacing capability, and the number of brownout and overvoltage correction features. The company's present line of UPS products ranges from 200 volt-amps (suitable for a small desktop PC) to 5,000 volt-amps (suitable for a minicomputer or a file server cluster). The products can also support work groups utilizing either a LAN or a multi-user system consisting of a host computer and linked terminals.

Growth, 1993-Present

National Quality Assurance granted the company its ISO 9000 quality seal in 1993 and the West Kingston, Cranston, and Galway facilities have been audited to the even more stringent ISO 9002 standards. Gross revenue for 1993 was $250.3 million, up from $157.5 million in 1992.

In 1994, the company established operations in Galway through a subsidiary, American Power Conversion Corporation B.V. The Ireland facility, a 280,000-square-foot plant at Ballybrit Industrial Estate, provides manufacturing and technical support to better service the company's markets in Europe, the Middle East, Africa, and the countries of the former Soviet Union. A warehouse facility in Limerick, Ireland, is also used for storage of raw materials.

That year also saw the company expanding its Smart-UPS and Back-UPS families of products. The Back-UPS Pro series of products provide enhanced Back-UPS power protection for advanced workstations. The Smart-UPS v/s products are designed to provide power protection for small business and departmental LANs. In addition, the company developed new Smart-UPS products in the 700, 1000, 1400, 2200, and 3000 volt-amp category. The company also introduced data line surge protection with its ProtectNet product line. Software development achievements resulted in the introduction of new and enhanced versions of the company's software applications by adding to the number of operating systems with which the company's software applications were compatible. Gross revenue for 1994 was $378.3 million.

In April 1995, the company purchased a 41,000-square-foot facility in Billerica, Massachusetts, for $1.2 million, which was then renovated to accommodate growing research and development operations. That same year saw the company introduce 155 new products, including a major transition of its flagship product line, the Smart-UPS, from its five-year-old design to a new third-generation product feature set, including automatic voltage regulation and adjustment, a user-replaceable battery replacement system, and an internal accessory option slot. The company also introduced its Back-UPS Pro product, which was the first UPS product to be "plug & play" compatible with Windows 95, and the Smart-UPS v/s products, a line of UPS products for departmental server applications. Software product introductions included the company's first advanced UPS/ Power Management software package tailored specifically for the IBM AS/400 environment. The company also reorganized its domestic sales force in 1995 in order to provide a much closer focus on the customer by creating customer units dedicated to specific customer groups. Gross revenue for 1995 was $515.3 million.

Continuing to investigate potential sites for manufacturing expansion in international locations, the company, in June 1996, established a manufacturing operation in the Philippines. The company purchased and upgraded a 70,000-square-foot facility located in a designated "economic zone" for $1.5 million. This facility manufactures some of the company's Back-UPS products to be sold in the domestic (American) market. In this year, the company's new product offerings included the Back-UPS Office, which was introduced in the second quarter. This product was designed to be solution-specific to the end user, especially those using the Internet. The company also added additional products which strengthened the company's position as an overall network solution provider. These products included web management capability with PowerChute plus software, a network manageable power distribution unit, and Masterswitch, which enabled a network manager to control attached loads independent of each other.

The company's commitment to enhance the overall productivity of its manufacturing facilities led to a reorganization in 1996 of its West Kingston, Rhode Island; Galway; and Philippines locations to move toward leaner, cell-based manufacturing processes in order to increase efficiency, decrease work in process, and improve the overall quality of the company's manufacturing processes. The company also adopted a "Focused Factories" philosophy aimed at reducing the number of products built in any given location in order to increase efficiency and overall quality.

The company was feted with awards and recognition in 1996, receiving nearly 40, including six for Back-UPS Office, four for Smart-UPS, three for Back-UPS Pro 280, three for Smart-UPS 2200, two for Back-UPS Pro PNP, and two for Smart-UPS 1000.

Major trends which affected the company's business in 1996 included growth of the Internet and associated web servers, the growth of networking and PCs in international geographies and emerging markets, and the onset of electronic commerce and the commoditization of the server market. Gross revenue for 1996 was $706.9 million, a 37 percent increase over 1996.

In January 1997, the company purchased a second facility in the Philippines for approximately $3 million. Also in 1997, the company entered the above-5kVA power protection market with the Symmetra Power Array. February of the same year saw the company complete its acquisition of Acquired Systems Enhancement Corporation. The seven-year-old privately held St. Louis, Missouri-based manufacturer of power management software and accessories for the UPS market was purchased in a $12.6 million stock swap. That year also saw more awards heaped upon the company, including *ComputerWorld*'s "Reseller's Choice" Award, *Computer Shopper*'s "Best UPS" Award, *PC Bulgaria*'s "Editor's Choice" Award, and, for the sixth year in a row, the company was named "Best to Sell" by *The Var* magazine in the United Kingdom, bringing the total number of awards the company has received to over 100, more than all other UPS vendors combined.

A Look Ahead

As the computer industry continued to grow rapidly during the late 1990s, the company remained in a choice position to grow with it. In pursuit of this potential continued growth, the company continued to build new and enhance existing relationships with many leading technology vendors, including, in 1997, beginning the ProtectMe! with APC marketing campaign with Dell Computer Corporation, Gateway 2000, and Quantex Microsystems Inc., and a new sales and marketing relationship with Acer Sertek in Taiwan. The company also targeted the Small Office/Home Office market, which it identified as a growth opportunity for the future, and continued to target industries that were becoming more dependent on electronic systems, such as the telecommunications industry. The company also planned to continue to expand its international marketing efforts and manufacturing operations with a full line of internationally positioned products already available.

Principal Subsidiaries

Acquired System Enhancements; American Power Conversion Corporation B.V. (Ireland); American Power Conversion Europe S.A.R.L. (France).

Further Reading

Abelson, Alan, "Up & Down Wall Street," *Barron's,* August 30, 1993, p. 1.
"American Power Conversion," *ComputerWorld,* December 2, 1996, p. 74.
"American Power Conversion Hits 52-Week Low As Analyst Slams Firm," *Knight-Ridder/Tribune Business News,* October 2, 1995, p. 10020202.
"APC Surges Ahead with Symmetra Power Array," *PC Week,* March 17, 1997, p. 111.
Autrey, Ret, "American Power Conversion," *Fortune,* May 6, 1991, p. 100.
"Being There," *New England Business,* October 1991, p. 46.
Berinato, Scott, "Liebert, APC Broaden Lineup of UPSes to Fend Off Surges," *PC Week,* May 19, 1997, p. 120.
——, "UPS Upgrade Adds Web Management," *PC Week,* November 4, 1996, p. 14.
——, "Vendors Gear Up to Release UPSs, Software for Management Platforms," *PC Week,* May 19, 1997, p. 48.
Bulkeley, William M., "American Power Conversion Fans Fear to Win Customers," *Wall Street Journal, Europe,* November 25, 1994, p. 4.
Ellis, Junius, "A Top Manager Names Stocks Poised to Gain 25% or More," *Money,* July 1992, p. 161.
Gotschall, Mary G., "America's Powerhouse of Growth Companies," *Fortune,* May 12, 1997.
Kistner, Toni, "Absolute Power," *PC Magazine,* May 27, 1997, p. 37.
Mamis, Robert A., "The *Inc.* 100: The 12th Annual Ranking of America's Fastest-Growing Small Public Companies," *Inc.* May 1990, p. 32.
"Power Strip Sparks Surge of Affection," *Windows Magazine,* October 1996.
Serwer, Evan, "To Find Tomorrow's Hot Stocks, Go Where the Big Boys Aren't," *Fortune,* February 27, 1989, p. 29.
"UPS for Multiple Servers," *Byte,* June 1997, p. 172.
Zipser, Andy, "Potent Power Surge," *Barron's,* June 10, 1991, p. 32.

—Daryl F. Mallett

◢Amfac

Amfac/JMB Hawaii L.L.C.

900 North Michigan Avenue
Chicago, Illinois 60611
U.S.A.
(312) 915-2420
Fax: (312) 915-2409

Wholly Owned Subsidiary of Northbrook Corporation
Incorporated: 1918 as American Factors, Ltd.
Employees: 2,500
Sales: $86.4 million (1997)
SICs: 0133 Sugarcane & Sugar Beet Production; 2061
Cane Sugar, Except Refining; 4941 Water Supply;
4971 Irrigation Systems; 6519 Lessors of Real
Property, Not Elsewhere Classified; 6552 Land
Subdividers & Developers, Except Cemeteries; 6799
Investors, Not Elsewhere Classified; 7992 Public Golf
Courses

Chicago-based but exclusively Hawaiian in activity, Amfac/
JMB Hawaii L.L.C. is a subsidiary of Northbrook Corporation,
which is itself a subsidiary of Chicago-based real estate giant
JMB Realty Corporation. Amfac/JMB is the main successor
company to Amfac Inc., which was bought by JMB Realty in
1988. Amfac/JMB's principal activities are land development
and sales, golf course management, and agriculture. The company owns about 43,000 acres of land on the Hawaiian islands
of Oahu, Maui, Kauai, and Hawaii. Among its real estate
ventures are several commercial, residential, and resort developments. The company manages three 18-hole golf courses. In
agriculture, Amfac/JMB is involved in the cultivation, processing, and sale of sugar cane and coffee. The company also
controls—primarily for the purpose of irrigating sugar cane—
the rights to more than 100 million gallons of water per day.

Early History

In 1849 a German ship captain named Heinrich Hackfeld
docked his 156-ton boat *Wilhelmine* in Hawaii after a 238-day
journey from Bremen, Germany. After deciding to become a
permanent resident, Hackfeld opened a general store which
became very popular with the imported laborers who worked on
the islands' isolated plantations. Hackfeld's small venture
quickly expanded into other lines of business, including
boardinghouses and real estate. Hackfeld later opened a trading
house, exporting Hawaii's primary agricultural product, sugar,
and importing building materials. Hackfeld's company became
one of the largest in Hawaii, operating retail stores and hotels,
trading a wider variety of products, and purchasing thousands of
acres of property. Several years later Hackfeld died and ownership of the company passed to his family.

In July 1918, soon after the United States became involved
in World War I, the American Alien Property Custodian
confiscated H. Hackfeld & Company on the grounds that it was
owned by "enemy aliens." All of the company's assets were
taken over by a group of competitors, including Castle &
Cooke, Alexander & Baldwin, and C. Brewer. The company
was incorporated and its name was changed to American Factors (a factor is a commissioned agent), and its chain of B.F.
Ehlers retailing outlets was renamed "Liberty House." Under
the new management American Factors became more involved
in sugar production. Demand for sugar remained high during
the Great Depression and World War II, which kept American
Factors profitable and allowed it to continue paying dividends
to stockholders.

Although it continued to diversify during the 1950s, American Factors remained primarily involved with the production of
sugar. However, in 1959, the same year Hawaii was made a
state, airline companies acquired long-range passenger jetliners
which made Hawaii suddenly more accessible to the American
vacationer. Just as suddenly, demand for hotel space and land
began to increase. As a major landowner, American Factors
recognized this as an opportunity to exploit its hotel and lodging
interests. Many of its existing properties were improved, additional facilities were constructed, and several parcels of undeveloped land were sold to developers at a sizable profit.

Despite its increased involvement in the Hawaiian tourist
industry, a great deal of American Factors' business remained in
sugar production. The sugar market had always been cyclical,

alternating between periods of strong demand and oversupply. Yet during the 1950s increased competition lowered profit margins, even when markets were strong. In 1964 low demand for sugar and molasses forced the company's operating profits to decline by 43 percent (it still paid a dividend, however). The first of many changes at American Factors occurred on April 30, 1966. The company's name was changed to Amfac Inc., which was shorter, easier to remember, and more "corporate-sounding."

Began to Diversify and Expand Geographically in Late 1960s

Henry A. Walker, Jr., a native Hawaiian whose father had served for many years as president of American Factors, was himself named president of Amfac in 1967. The board of directors gave Walker three instructions: enlarge the company, decrease the company's dependence on sugar, and geographically diversify its operations. In 1968 Amfac purchased the Fred Harvey hotel chain and later acquired the Island Holiday group on Hawaii. Amfac's Liberty House retail department stores were introduced to the American mainland along with its wholesale distribution network of electrical, medical, industrial, and agricultural products. Amfac acquired the family-run Joseph Magnin retail chain for $31 million in 1969. Walker directed the company to sell additional parcels of Hawaiian real estate to help finance acquisitions on the American mainland, which included Pacific Pearl, Wakefield Seafoods, and the 1971 purchase of Lamb-Weston, a potato and vegetable processor responsible for a substantial share of American's frozen french fry and mushroom production.

In 1974 the Federal Trade Commission accused Amfac and other suppliers to the C&H sugar consortium of price fixing. The settlement that resulted cost Amfac several million dollars. Although sugar prices that year were high, it was the last time that Amfac would report a profit on its sugar operations for several years; Congress failed to renew the Sugar Act of 1948, which guaranteed a broader degree of price stability by limiting sugar imports.

After several years of poor performance all 48 stores in Amfac's Joseph Magnin chain were sold to the Ross Hall Corporation for $35 million. Although Amfac added 18 stores to the chain, increasing sales from $50 million to $83 million, expected profits failed to materialize. Henry Walker told *Business Week,* "We're getting out of the women's apparel business because we find we're not very good at it." Amfac did, however, retain its 55 highly profitable Liberty House stores, 23 of which were located in Hawaii.

Amfac's earnings declined every year until 1978. Losses until that time were due primarily to non-operating factors, such as the continued write-off of the Joseph Magnin chain and the company's switch to a uniform "last in, first out" (LIFO) accounting method, which tends to show lower profits, but also provides the company with taxation benefits.

Fended Off 1970s Hostile Takeovers

During the period that its profits were depressed Amfac became a takeover target for a number of hostile acquisitions. The takeover attempts failed because Amfac was protected by Gulf + Western, a New York conglomerate which owned 20 percent of the company's stock. Henry Walker, who incidentally was a Gulf + Western board member, told *Financial World,* "A number of people have tried to acquire Amfac, but they couldn't without first getting control of G&W's block." Gulf + Western was committed to Amfac's independence, maintaining that its substantial interest in Amfac was strictly for "investment purposes." Any hostile bid for the company would almost certainly have encountered strong opposition from Gulf + Western.

Amfac was not, however, protected from a different kind of corporate raid. Sid, Ed, Robert, and Lee Bass, four Stanford and Yale-educated brothers from Fort Worth, Texas, announced in 1982 that they had acquired 11 percent of Amfac's stock, and had filed a "13-D" financial disclosure form with the Securities and Exchange Commission. The Bass brothers did not intend to take over Amfac, but their sudden interest in the company concerned stockholders, particularly Gulf + Western, which at the time owned just under 25 percent of Amfac's stock. Amfac's management arranged a complex joint venture with the brothers called Fort Associates. The joint venture gave the Bass brothers interests in several hotels and real estate in Texas and Hawaii, in addition to $52 million in cash, while it retrieved half of the Basses' ownership of Amfac's stock. Fort Associates was set up to give the Bass brothers an early return on their investment and Amfac a later return with tax advantages. While the venture remained profitable, Amfac stated that it would rather have resolved the situation differently.

In the meantime, sugar prices began to recover after Congress included sugar in its 1981 Farm Act. Although Amfac was making money on sugar again, Walker continued to reduce the company's exposure to the volatile commodity through a process of continued diversification. Amfac had acquired over 50 companies since 1967, most of which were located on the mainland.

Myron Du Bain, a former chairman and president of Fireman's Fund Insurance, was named president of Amfac on January 1, 1983. Du Bain, who had no previous experience with sugar, directed Amfac's operations from the San Francisco office. Du Bain was hired to "tighten the screws" at Amfac, deciding which businesses should be emphasized and which should be scaled down or sold. Henry Walker remained in Hawaii, where he continued to serve as chairman of the board, managing Amfac's sugar operations.

During Du Bain's first year Amfac sold 12 percent of its assets for $177 million, but still posted a $68 million loss. In addition, Gulf + Western sold all its stock in Amfac, although with little consequence. The company recovered during 1984, yet lost almost $29 million in the final quarter when its Hotels and Resorts Group was restructured. As a result, Amfac was forced to withhold its quarterly dividend for the first time in 66 years. Amfac sold its commercial nurseries, seafood fisheries, Hawaiian tour business, and its Liberty House outlets in California. By 1985 Du Bain had reduced Amfac's debt by $120 million to $400 million. Du Bain left Amfac in September of that year, taking an early retirement to pursue community and civic activities. He was replaced by Ralph Van Orsdel for an interim period lasting until the following May when Ronald

Sloan, who had been with Amfac for 25 years, was named president and chief executive officer.

Aborted Restructuring Led to JMB Acquisition in 1988

Amfac lost $66.6 million in 1986 on sales of $2 billion, the third year in four in which it posted a large loss. A restructuring was clearly in order, and in late 1987 Sloan advocated the sale or spinoff of the company's Hawaiian assets—particularly its 50,000 acres of land—in order to take advantage of a significant run-up in land prices in Hawaii that had taken place over the previous year. But in November 1987 Amfac's board, still largely dominated by Walker, balked at this idea and fired Sloan when he refused to resign. In December the board approved a far different restructuring plan, one that aimed to divest all U.S. mainland operations (including wholesale distribution, food, and resorts), find a joint venture partner for its Hawaiian landholdings, and return the net proceeds from the restructuring to shareholders.

Subsequently, Amfac sold Lamb-Weston for $276 million and Monterey Mushrooms for $30 million in early 1988. But the restructuring plan came to a halt in May 1988 when a management group led by new president and CEO Richard L. Griffith proposed a $41/share, $800 million buyout. The offer set off weeks of speculation about competing takeover bids, and finally JMB Realty Corporation made a $49/share, $920 million offer which was accepted in July and finalized in November 1988. At the time, privately held, Chicago-based JMB Realty was the largest real estate syndicator in the United States with $20 billion of property under management. The company was founded in 1969 when three Chicago accountants—Bob Juddelson, Judd Malkin, and Neil Bluhm—pooled $5,000 to invest in real estate.

Following the takeover, JMB split Amfac into several separate subsidiaries. The main successor to Amfac operated under the name Amfac/JMB Hawaii, Inc. This company was responsible for all of Amfac's activities in Hawaii, as well as Liberty House. Operating separately within the JMB umbrella were Amfac Distribution and Amfac Resorts (on the mainland). Amfac/JMB essentially had three main operations: property development, agriculture, and Liberty House. But in 1990 JMB decided to separate Liberty House from Amfac/JMB, and formally divided the company into two divisions: property development and agriculture (the latter consisted principally of sugar and coffee).

Amfac/JMB was immensely smaller than the old Amfac, with annual revenues in the 1990s averaging about $117 million (compared to the $2.1 billion posted by Amfac in 1987). The company was also consistently in the red, losing $13 million in 1994, $34.2 million in 1996, and $25.6 million in 1997. Recessions in Japan and the United States (especially in California) severely depressed the once sky-high Hawaiian real estate market. Significant events in the early 1990s were the closure of a money-losing sugar plantation on Oahu and the completion of the Waikele master-planned community on the island of Oahu. The Waikele development included 2,700 residential units, a retail commercial center, and the Waikele golf course, which Amfac/ JMB also managed. By early 1994 the development had brought more than $275 million in gross revenues to Amfac/JMB.

In March 1997 the company restructured its operations into six separate operating divisions: sugar farming, coffee farming, water, golf, land, and property development. The sugar, coffee, and water divisions were part of the old agriculture division, with water consisting of the company's control of the rights to 300 million gallons of water per day, which was primarily used to irrigate sugar cane. The golf division managed three golf courses in Kaanapali and Waikele. The land division was responsible for selling or leasing the company's nonstrategic landholdings. It seemed likely that Amfac Property Development Corp. was the most important division of the future Amfac/JMB and that some of the other divisions may be jettisoned. The company stated that it planned to focus its future development activities on its Maui land parcels. Already under development there were a 280-unit timeshare resort and a 1,700-unit affordable-housing project. Gary Grottke served as president in the later 1990s. In March 1998 Amfac/JMB was converted into Amfac/JMB Hawaii L.L.C. in order to change the company from a corporation to a limited liability company.

Principal Subsidiaries

Amfac Land Company Limited; Amfac Property Development Corp.; Amfac Property Investment Corp.; H. Hackfeld & Co., Ltd.; Kaanapali Estate Coffee, Inc.; Kaanapali Water Corporation; Kekaha Sugar Company, Limited; The Lihue Plantation Company, Limited; Oahu Sugar Company, Limited; Pioneer Mill Company, Limited; Puna Sugar Company, Limited; Waiahole Irrigation Company, Limited; Waikele Golf Club, Inc.

Principal Divisions

Amfac Golf Division; Amfac Sugar Division; Kaanapali Estate Coffee Inc.; Amfac Water Division; Amfac Land Co.; Amfac Property Development Corp.

Further Reading

Bagamery, Anne, "What Makes Myron Run?," *Forbes,* January 28, 1985, pp. 37+.

Carey, David, "Amfac Betting on the Come," *Financial World,* November 17, 1987, p. 14.

Cooper, George, *Land and Power in Hawaii: The Democratic Years,* Honolulu: Benchmark Books, 1985, 518 p.

Dawson, Donne, "Amfac: New and Improved?," *Island Business,* August 1997, pp. 17–22.

Ellis, James E., and Jonathan B. Levine, "Lock, Stock—and Beachfront," *Business Week,* August 8, 1988, p. 28.

Jokiel, Lucy, "Amfac's Intentions," *Hawaii Business,* July 1990, pp. 10+.

Levine, Jonathan B., "A Boardroom Drama As Time Ran Out for Amfac's CEO," *Business Week,* December 7, 1987, p. 59.

Markrich, Mike, "Reality Check," *Hawaii Business,* February 1994, pp. 28+.

Miller, James P., "Amfac Board Approves Broad Revamp; U.S. Mainland Operations to Be Shed," *Wall Street Journal,* December 14, 1987, p. 7.

——, "Amfac Inc. to Sell Lamb-Weston Unit for $276 Million," *Wall Street Journal,* April 4, 1988, p. 6.

——, ''Amfac Ousts Sloan As President, Chief, Plans to Pursue 'Prudent Restructuring,' '' *Wall Street Journal,* November 23, 1987, p. 7.

——, ''Group Proposes Amfac Buy-Out for $800 Million,'' *Wall Street Journal,* May 20, 1988, p. 14.

Parker, Wayne, ''The Amfac Diet,'' *Hawaii Business,* August 1997, pp. 31+.

Schmitt, Richard B., and Roger Lowenstein, ''Amfac Accepts JMB Realty's $49-a-Share Bid,'' *Wall Street Journal,* July 27, 1988, p. 36.

Simpich, Frederick, Jr., *Dynasty in the Pacific,* New York: McGraw-Hill, 1974, 270 p.

Smith, Kit, ''Amfac: Losses Biggest Factor in Decision to Close,'' *Honolulu Advertiser,* August 5, 1993.

——, ''Amfac Splits into Ag/Realty Divisions,'' *Honolulu Advertiser,* November 6, 1993.

TenBruggencate, Jan, ''Amfac/JMB Seeks to Tighten Sugar Operation,'' *Honolulu Advertiser,* October 2, 1994.

—updated by David E. Salamie

Anchor Gaming

815 Pilot Road, Suite G
Las Vegas, Nevada 89119
U.S.A.
(702) 896-7568
Fax: (702) 896-6221
Web site: http://www.anchorgaming.com

Public Company
Incorporated: 1993
Employees: 869
Sales: $153.8 million (1997)
Stock Exchanges: NASDAQ
Ticker Symbol: SLOT
SICs: 7993 Coin-Operated Amusement Devices

Anchor Gaming is an industry-leading diversified gaming company with experience as an operator and developer of gaming machines and casinos. The three business segments in which Anchor does business are: a slot machine route in Nevada; casinos in Colorado and Canada; and proprietary games. CEO Stanley E. Fulton and his family owned approximately 37 percent of the company in 1998, and the corporate headquarters were located in Las Vegas, Nevada.

Slot Machine Route

Anchor Gaming operates a slot machine route in the state of Nevada, in which slot machines are placed at taverns, grocery stores, and convenience stores. The slot machines are regularly serviced by Anchor in exchange for a split of the revenues, or for a fixed-fee payment. The company's Anchor Coin subsidiary operates one of the largest gaming machine routes in the state of Nevada, with more than 800 video poker machines and slot machine units at retail stores and taverns. It is not the largest slot route in the state, but it is the most profitable. Las Vegas, one of the fastest-growing cities in the United States, provides a strong demographic base for slot machine routes. Anchor's largest customer is the Smith's Food and Drug Centers chain, where the company has exclusive location contracts locked in until 2010.

The company's deal with Smith's ıs a space-lease agreement, so any upside in slot revenues goes to Anchor rather than being divided with the store. Anchor's major competitors in the route business are Alliance Gaming and Jackpot Enterprises.

Casinos

Anchor Gaming operates what may be the most profitable casino in the state of Colorado. Limited stakes gambling was made legal in three historic mining towns in the Rocky Mountains of Colorado in November 1990, and Anchor was quick to jump at the opportunity.

The Colorado market in which Anchor participates is both unique to North American gaming and important to the continued growth of Anchor Gaming for a number of reasons. First of all, gaming in Colorado is limited stakes, which means $5 is the maximum permissible wager. Unlike Missouri, however, there is no limit on the amount one patron can lose. The main effect of this maximum bet is that the casinos focus more on gaming machines than on table games. Second, casinos in Colorado are on a much smaller scale than most other U.S. markets (such as the obvious cities of Las Vegas and Atlantic City), for several reasons: Each town's ordinances state that all casinos must be built in the historical style of the town's architecture. Because of this, most of the casinos in Colorado are in already-existing buildings and, consequently, are rather small. Additionally, the downtown location of these already existing buildings, combined with the mountainous terrain, limits available parking space as well as any expansion space a casino might want to undertake in the future. In fact, most casinos in Colorado offer little or no parking space for their patrons, and few, if any, amenities, such as restaurants, hotel rooms, or bars (only Harvey's Casino in Central City offered hotel rooms as of 1997).

Due to the building, space, parking, and growth restrictions, major casino operators have stayed away from the Colorado market, so Anchor has not experienced significant competition. In fact, the only other major operators in the cities of Black Hawk and Central City are Harvey's Wagon Wheel, the Gilpin Hotel & Casino, Promus, Lady Luck, and Fitzgeralds; the remainder are operated as small "Mom & Pop" businesses.

Company Perspectives:

Anchor Gaming is a diversified gaming company that seeks to capitalize on its experience as an operator and developer of gaming machines and casinos by developing gaming oriented businesses. Anchor develops and distributes unique proprietary games, currently operates two casinos in Colorado, and operates one of the largest gaming machine routes in Nevada.

The Colorado Central Station Casino, located in the city of Black Hawk (approximately 40 miles from Denver), however, did not occupy an already existing building. It was built to specifications and features an exterior design resembling a 19th-century railroad station. Colorado Central Station is the larger of the two Anchor facilities, generating more revenue than the smaller Colorado Grande Casino, located in Cripple Creek, which features primarily slot machines, with blackjack and poker tables mixed in. Colorado Central Station, which opened its doors on Christmas Day in 1993, is situated on approximately 1.8 acres of land at the south end of Black Hawk, near Main Street and Colorado State Highway 119, considered by many to be the best location in Black Hawk/Central City, since it is the first casino encountered on the road from Denver and Interstate Highway 70 and the first stop on the shuttle bus from the Black Hawk/Central City public parking lot, which most casino patrons use. Colorado Central Station has more than 680 gaming machines, 19 table games, and a food court restaurant area. The Colorado Central Station building has approximately 49,000 square feet of floor space, with 16,637 square feet of gaming area spread over three floors. The casino has more than 770 parking spaces and is the first shuttle stop from Black Hawk's 3,000-space public facility. Colorado Central Station generates more than $15 million in annual pretax income and dominates the Colorado market, with 6.5 percent of the state's casino capacity generating 17 percent of the state's $420 million casino revenues.

The second casino is The Colorado Grande Casino, located 45 miles from Colorado Springs and 75 miles from Pueblo, Colorado. The facility, which is leased, occupies 15,000 square feet of a commercial facility, of which 3,125 square feet are devoted to gaming. The Colorado Grande is located at one of the principal intersections in Cripple Creek; the casino features more than 210 gaming machines, a full service restaurant, and bar.

Anchor and Revenue Properties, a Canadian company, entered a joint venture to manage seven charitable casinos in Ontario, Canada. The seven casinos are relatively small, capped at 40 table games and 150 gaming machines per location. The Ontario Gaming Control Commission gave Anchor and Revenue an eight-year lease and the companies will be responsible for casino buildout at existing sites such as racetracks, shopping centers, and hotels. The company will receive ten percent of gaming machine revenue, five percent of table game and food and beverage revenue, and ten percent of operating income.

Proprietary Games

The fastest-growing segment of Anchor Gaming's business is its proprietary games division, which has grown at an 87 percent compound rate over the past three years. The company does not actually manufacture the games. Instead, it creates ideas for novelty slot and video games, develops the game concepts, and then incorporates those concepts into existing game formats from suppliers such as International Game Technology (IGT), Bally Gaming, and Universal, then places the games in casinos throughout the United States. Proprietary games include Double Down Stud video poker, Clear Winner (a transparent slot machine), the highly-successful Wheel of Gold slot machine, the Wheel of Fortune progressive slot machine (developed in conjunction with IGT), Totem Pole (a nine-reel, eight-foot-high slot machine), and Silver Strike (a slot machine that pays out an encased souvenir silver token on a winning combination). Although Anchor initially began developing proprietary games as a complement to its own gaming machine operations, since February 1993 the company has been actively marketing its proprietary games to unaffiliated casinos; rather than selling its games to casino operators, Anchor places them on the casino floor for free in exchange for a share of the revenues. Anchor also controls games such as Cash Ball, Road Rally, and Cash Fire.

According to Anchor's joint venture agreement with IGT, the latter company has the right to take any or all of Anchor's games and place them in its wide area progressive systems (WAPs). The WAP systems link these slot machines and create large jackpots that are popular with players. Anchor continues to place its games as freestanding units in addition to the WAP units placed by the joint venture; therefore, most casino floors in the U.S. have a mix of Anchor's freestanding units and Anchor/IGT WAP units. In addition to Canada, Colorado, and Nevada, Anchor also is or has been licensed in Arizona, Connecticut, Illinois, Indiana, Iowa, Mississippi, Missouri, New Jersey, and South Dakota.

Entering the Game, 1993

Anchor Gaming was incorporated in Nevada on July 28, 1993 by Stanley E. Fulton, a man who had been involved in the gaming equipment business since the early 1970s. In 1976, he founded Fortune Coin, a company which introduced the first video poker game in 1977. One year later, he sold Fortune Coin, which eventually evolved into International Game Technology, ironically later becoming one of Anchor's primary business partners.

Fulton then went on to work at Gaming and Technology Inc., where he helped build one of the largest gaming routes in Nevada, eventually becoming chairman of that company, now known as Alliance Gaming Corporation.

Fulton founded Anchor Gaming's predecessor, Anchor Coin, in 1991, building another large gaming route, and eventually creating Anchor Gaming.

Also in 1993, Colorado Grande Casino outperformed the average Cripple Creek casino, generating an average of $73 in daily revenue from each of its 186 slot machines and card tables during its second year of operation (ended September 30, 1993), compared to the citywide average of $50 during the same period.

By 1994, the company operated 629 slot machines leased in 45 locations (primarily Albertson's grocery stores and Smith's) throughout the Las Vegas area. In February of that year, The Colorado Grande Gaming Parlor became the second Cripple Creek casino to be owned by a publicly traded company when Anchor Gaming raised $30.7 million in an initial stock offering of 2.75 million shares. Cripple Creek-based Alpine Gaming Inc.—which owns The Long Branch Saloon & Casino, and was making plans to merge with Denver-based Century Casinos Management Inc.—is the only other publicly traded company to own one of the city's 23 casinos. The public offering came just as the Cripple Creek economy was beginning to feel the hurt by the December closing of a tunnel on Colorado Highway 67, forcing gamblers to take long detours from the principal route to the town. Most of the money from the offering was used to pay off $17.5 million in debts, including $11.2 million to repay loans from Anchor CEO Stanley Fulton and his six children; another $1.8 million was used to buy 163,789 shares from minority shareholders in the Colorado Grande.

The following month, the company used $900,000 in cash from the public offering, and some 1.3 million shares to acquire ownership of Global Gaming Products LLC, and certain related assets from Global Gaming Distributors Inc., which leased slot machines that paid out silver tokens and serviced Anchor's leases in northern Nevada. The acquisition also gave Anchor the rights to the game Silver Strike.

October of the same year saw the company consolidate its Las Vegas offices into a new headquarters facility, expanding to 17,000 square feet of office space and 30,000 square feet of sub-assembly and warehouse space, all of which is leased. Revenues for 1994 reached $54.8 million, with a net income of $10.5 million. Revenues for the following year jumped to $97.4 million, with net income also rising, to $16 million.

In April 1996, the company completed a second successful public offering, raising nearly $54 million. The following month, *Business Week* ran an article featuring Anchor Gaming among the six "Hot Growth Companies," along with Encad Inc. and Remedy Corp., two high-tech firms, as well as Logan's Roadhouse Inc., HPR Inc., and MedCath Inc. In November, Anchor announced the suspension of a planned $60 million addition of 144,000 square feet of space directly across the street from the existing facility, connected by an enclosed walkway, adding 120 hotel rooms, 36,000 square feet of gaming space, 600 gaming machines, 12 table games, a full-service restaurant, a fast-food restaurant, and 720 additional parking spaces. Revenues for 1996 reached $116.5 million, with net income of $22.3 million.

In the fall of 1997, Anchor Gaming and a Canadian joint venture partner were awarded licenses to operate seven charitable casinos in Ontario, Canada. Poor weather in late October of that year caused the company some worry, but the Colorado casino operations posted record revenues and profits for the quarter. Revenues for the year reached $153.7 million, with net income of $35.7 million. Later that year, Fulton sold 1.8 million shares (at $91 each) to "diversify" his holdings, but some analysts believed the major shareholder was cashing out just in case things went poorly.

In 1998, the company began shipping a stand-alone slot machine game it created, called The Totem Pole. Two other products released in 1998 included Crazy Joker and Wheel Winner Poker, both aimed at the distinct video poker market, an area that Anchor has not really focused on in the past. A third product, called Cash Ball, which features a pinball-type secondary game manufactured by WMS Industries, the world's leading pinball manufacturer, and Bally Gaming, was introduced on field trial in the Bahamas in 1998, and a fourth product, Pinball Wizard, began shipping as well.

Anchor Gaming and IGT, the largest games manufacturer in the industry, signed a joint venture agreement in September 1996 to market the Wheel of Fortune game. Starting out initially with 650 units in early 1998, by mid-year, over 4,000 units were in use in the Native American, Nevada, New Jersey, Mississippi, and Missouri markets, making it the most successful slot ever introduced on the casino floor. Also part of the joint venture were the Totem Pole progressive slot, Pinball Wizard, and Keno Bucks. But, the joint venture was not without its downside. Revenues generated from the company's Wheel of Gold game began to decline with the release of Wheel of Fortune.

Additionally, fierce competition from other companies' games, such as Bally's Roll the Dice game and IGT's Jeopardy and Vision Series games, began to squeeze out Anchor's previously unchallenged games, and analysts at the recent gaming manufacturers conference came away "unimpressed" by Anchor's Cash Ball, Wheel Winner Poker, and Big Bucks Bingo offerings, but highly touted IGT's Vision Series (a traditional fitted with an LCD screen, with "bonusing," i.e., giving the player another chance to win). By the end of fiscal 1998, though, the company should have entered new markets such as Illinois, Louisiana, and Indiana. Anchor's strong floor presence and previously unchallenged near-monopoly, track record with previous games, and aggressive marketing strategy would likely continue to carry it as an industry leader well into the 21st century.

Principal Subsidiaries

C. G. Investments Inc.; Colorado Grande Enterprises Inc.; DD Stud Inc.; Anchor Coin; Green Mountain Enterprises Inc.

Further Reading

"Anchor Gaming," Moody's Investors Service, February 21, 1998.
"Anchor Gaming," *New York Times*, October 13, 1997, p. C10(N)/D10(L).
"Anchor Gaming," *New York Times*, May 18, 1998, p. C10(N)/D10(L).
"Anchor Gaming," *Wall Street Journal*, April 20, 1998, p. C15(W).
"Anchor Gaming—Company Report," Institutional Shareholder Services, November 24, 1997.
"Anchor Gaming Group Gets Clearance to Open Seven Ontario Casinos," *Wall Street Journal*, September 29, 1997, p. C25(W)/B2(E).
"Anchor Gaming—History & Debt," Moody's Investors Service, March 14, 1998.

"Anchor Gaming Inc.," *Wall Street Journal*, October 14, 1997, p. C25(W)/C27(E).

"Anchor Gaming Says Finance Chief Resigned," *Wall Street Journal*, June 17, 1997, p. B8(W)/B8(E).

Bannon, Lisa, "Anchor Gaming to Record Change, Warns on Profit," *Wall Street Journal*, December 4, 1997, p. B2(W)/B6(E).

Barrett, Amy, et al, "Hot Growth Companies: Corporate America Is Slowing? Don't Tell These Dynamos," *Business Week*, May 27, 1996, p. 110.

Davila, D., et al, "Anchor Gaming—Company Report," Rodman & Renshaw, Inc./ABACO, October 23, 1997.

Heilman, Wayne, "Second Colorado Casino Goes Public, with $30.7 Million Offering," *Knight-Ridder/Tribune Business News*, February 2, 1994, p. 02020029.

Jordan, T. D., et al, "Anchor Gaming—Company Report," Raymond James & Associates Inc., May 12, 1997.

Linde, S., "Anchor Gaming—Company Report," Gerard Klauer Mattison & Co., March 14, 1995.

MacDonald, Elizabeth, and Bridget O'Brian, "Anchor CEO and Family Reduce Stake," *Wall Street Journal*, December 3, 1997, p. C1(W)/C1(E).

Murren, J. J., et al, "Anchor Gaming—Company Report," Deutsche Morgan Grenfell Inc., August 4, 1997.

Ryan, T. M., et al, "Anchor Gaming—Company Report," BT Alex Brown, January 15, 1998.

—Daryl F. Mallett

Apollo Group, Inc.

4615 E. Elwood Street
Phoenix, Arizona 85040
U.S.A.
(602) 966-5394
(800) 990-APOL (990-2765)
Fax: (602) 968-1159
Web site: http://www.apollogrp.com

Public Company
Incorporated: 1981
Employees: 5,319
Sales: $283.5 million (1996)
Stock Exchanges: NASDAQ
Ticker Symbol: APOL
SICs: 8221 Colleges, Universities & Professional
    Schools; 6719 Offices of Holding Companies, Not
    Elsewhere Classified

Apollo Group, Inc. is one of the largest providers of higher education programs for working adults in the United States. Through its wholly owned subsidiaries the University of Phoenix, the Institute for Professional Development, and Western International University, the Apollo Group teaching/learning model by 1998 had been successfully replicated at 110 campuses and learning centers in 32 states, Puerto Rico, and London. The company cooperates and interacts with businesses and governmental agencies in offering programs designed to meet their specific needs either by modifying existing programs or, in some cases, by developing customized programs which are held at the employers' offices or on-site at military bases. Some education partnerships have included companies such as AT&T and Ingram Micro.

Founded for Working Adults: The 1970s

Apollo Group, Inc. was founded in 1973 in response to a gradual shift in higher education demographics from a student population dominated by youth to one in which approximately half the students are adults and over 80 percent of whom work full-time.

The University of Phoenix (UOP) was founded in 1976 by Dr. John G. Sperling, now chairman and CEO of Apollo Group, as the first accredited for-profit university in the United States with the sole mission of identifying and meeting the educational needs of working adult students. The idea for UOP started earlier than that though. Sperling received his undergraduate degree from Reed College and a doctorate in economic history from Kings College at Cambridge University before becoming a fully tenured humanities professor at San Jose State University in the early 1970s with a grant to study a means by which to deal with delinquency rates in one of San Jose's rougher neighborhoods. In his interactions with the police department and other public officials, Sperling discovered that they wanted educational programs which would help them do their jobs better, improve their skills, and give them new skills for advancement. He approached his university, San Jose State, with a request to support an adult degree program. When they refused, he quit to start his own for-profit business offering adult, degree-granting programs at colleges and universities.

Sperling received his first contract from the University of San Francisco and signed up 500 students in 1973, his first year of operation. By his third year, he had added two more colleges and 2,000 students, earning over $200,000 on revenues of nearly $2 million. The existing education bureaucracy was apparently put out by the competition. The Western Association of Schools and Colleges was outraged that a for-profit entity was so successfully cutting into the markets of competing colleges and universities. Shortly thereafter, the accrediting association told Sperling's three schools that they could either end their contracts with him or lose their accreditation and suddenly Sperling was without clients.

Fed up with the political maintenance of dealing with other schools, Sperling leased office space in downtown Phoenix, Arizona, in 1976 and decided to start his own university. The North Central Association of Colleges and Schools, Arizona's regional accreditor, inspected Sperling's operation and accredited the program. UOP opened in 1976 with a class of eight students and celebrated its 20th anniversary in 1996 with an enrollment of more than 38,000 students. By then it was boasting a net income estimated at $30 million on revenues of $282 million; was the second largest regionally accredited private institution of higher education in the United States; had one of the nation's largest business schools; offered bachelor's and master's degree programs in business, management, computer information systems, education, and health care; and had 51 campuses and learning centers located in Arizona, California, Colorado, Florida, Hawaii, Louisiana, Michigan, Nevada, New Mexico, Utah, and Puerto Rico.

Established in 1973, the Institute for Professional Development (IPD) assists colleges and universities in the design, development, implementation, and continuing administration of higher education programs designed specifically for working adults. IPD's higher education management consulting services enable traditional colleges to establish viable and profitable programs serving working adults. Nineteen ninety-six saw more than 12,000 students enrolled in IPD-assisted programs at 18 regionally accredited private colleges and universities throughout the United States at 38 campuses and learning centers in 20 states from Texas to Massachusetts and was primarily in the Midwest, South, and East, including a new opening in Stamford, Connecticut, in 1997.

Shift Towards Off-Campus Learning, 1990s

While most students utilize the classroom setting for their educational experience, the demand and need for flexibility and alternatives in educational delivery exists so, in 1989, the company began distance learning modality by offering its educational programs throughout the world via UOP's Distance and Online Education and CPEInternet, their computerized educational delivery system, joining the growing trend of distance learning. As late as 1993, less than 93 "cyberschools" existed. However, by 1997, according to an Arizona-based company called InterEd, there were some 762 cyberschools and approximately half of the over 2,000 four-year colleges and universities in the United States had online classes available, including Washington State University, Pullman; California State University, Dominguez Hills, and Duke University's Fuqua School of Business's Global Executive M.B.A. Program, and vocational schools such as National Technological University (Fort Collins, Colorado); New York Institute of Technology's On-Line Campus (Central Islip, New York), and New School for Social Research (New York, New York). Also in 1997, it was estimated that over one million students took classes online, compared to 13 million who attended on-campus classes and that this number would triple in the next few years. The University of Phoenix Center for Distance Education (CDE) is able to deliver degree programs to students anywhere in the world if they have access to phone, fax, or postal communications through Directed Study. Course work is completed through independent study while interacting with the instructor via fax, phone, e-mail, or their fax/voice messaging.

From September 1991 through August 1996, UOP opened 26 campuses and learning centers and IPD established 13 campuses and learning centers with its client institutions. The company also adopted a plan in March 1992 to discontinue the operations of its technical training schools and these operations were phased out from March 1992 through 1993.

In September 1995, Apollo Group acquired certain assets of Western International University. Western International University was created as a private nonprofit educational institution and was accredited by The North Central Association of Colleges and Schools and was also incorporated in 1978. Apollo Group created a new wholly owned subsidiary called Western International University (WIU). By 1996, WIU had 1,200 working adult students at campuses and learning centers in Arizona and London; a large portion of their students came from more than 40 different countries to learn English as a Second Language and continue on to pursue a degree in higher education. WIU's mission was to provide the educational foundation needed to prepare its students to achieve their full potential in a dynamic and complex global marketplace; the university offered undergraduate and graduate degree programs at four campuses and learning centers in Phoenix, Fort Huachuca, and Douglas, Arizona; and London, England.

Starting with 68 campuses and learning centers in August 1995, Apollo Group grew to 85 one year later and enrollment more than doubled from 21,163 to 46,935, with campuses from San Diego to New Orleans, Honolulu to Guaynabo, Puerto Rico. The Institute for Professional Development increased the number of contracts it held with private universities from 15 to 18, with 83 percent of these contracts extending beyond the year 2000.

1997 and Beyond

By mid-1997, the company opened nine new UOP learning centers in Los Alamos, New Mexico; Phoenix; the 32nd Street Naval Base in San Diego; Rancho Bernardo, Stockton, Ontario, Pleasanton, and Pasadena, California; and Las Vegas; IPD opened a new learning center for Albertus Magnus College in Stanford, Connecticut; and the company had plans to open several additional campuses and learning centers and to expand its product offerings to address increased market demands.

In April 1998 the company authorized a three-for-two split of its common stock. Two months later, Apollo announced that it would open—through its University of Phoenix subsidiary—two new campuses in Oklahoma as well as one in Vancouver, British Columbia. In addition, the company gained state licensure in Maryland and was pursuing approval from the North Central Association of Colleges and Schools prior to opening a location in that state. Such expansion augured well for Apollo, which by then was serving some 66,000 degree-seeking students and continually positioning itself as a leading provider of higher education for working adults.

Principal Subsidiaries

Institute for Professional Development (IPD); University of Phoenix (UOP); Western International University (WIU); College for Financial Planning.

Further Reading

Gabele, Bob, "Apollo Group Inc.—APOL," *CDA-Investnet Insiders' Chronicle,* March 3, 1997, p. 1.

Gonzales, Angela, "Apollo Group to Expand with Public Sale," *Business Journal* (Phoenix), July 28, 1995, p. 31.

——, "Apollo Execs Take Home $7 Million Stock Profits," *Business Journal* (Phoenix), January 31, 1997, p. 7.

Reagor, Catherine, "University of Phoenix Goes Public," *Business Journal* (Phoenix), September 23, 1994, p. 1.

Rolwing, Rebecca, "Apollo CEO to Sell $37M in Stock," *Business Journal* (Phoenix), January 5, 1996, p. 1.

Schonfeld, Erick, "Back to School," *Fortune,* September 4, 1994, p. 137.

—Daryl F. Mallett

Applause Inc.

6101 Variel Avenue
P.O. Box 4183
Woodland Hills, California 91365-4183
U.S.A.
(818) 992-6000
(800) 777-6990
Fax: (818) 595-2823

Private Company
Incorporated: 1966 as The Wallace Berrie Company
Employees: 600
Sales: $280 million (1996)
SICs: 3942 Dolls & Stuffed Toys; 5092 Toys & Hobby
    Goods & Supplies

Applause Inc. is a leader in design innovation, marketing year-round gift products for consumers of all ages. The company specializes in plush toys, figurines, and collectibles and is known worldwide for its high-quality, emotionally appealing product lines, featuring the most popular classic, promotional, and collectible characters in the marketplace.

Licenses have included characters from Mickey for Kids and Mickey Unlimited; Looney Tunes; Jim Henson's Muppets; *Sesame Street*; Raggedy Ann and Andy; Peanuts; Precious Moments; Disney's *Winnie the Pooh, The Little Mermaid,* and *Mu-Lan*; LucasFilm's *Star Wars*; Twentieth Century Fox's *Anastasia*; Nickelodeon's "Rugrats"; New Line Cinema's "Lost in Space"; as well as proprietary plush designs under the Dakin brand name, including new and classic plush, puppets, infant products, and seasonal merchandise, and Dakin's own licenses of Benji; Garfield and Odie; Fido Dido; Chip & Cookie; the Beast from Disney's *Beauty and the Beast*; Clifford the Big Red Dog; Snoopy; The Pink Panther; The Animaniacs; Cuddles Bear; Lamb Chop; Looney Tunes Lovables; Barney the dinosaur; The Flintstones; Betty Boop; and the 1996 Olympic mascot, Izzy, among others.

Larger competitors have included Hasbro Inc., Tyco/Matchbox, Mattel, Milton Bradley, Kenner, Parker Bros., Playskool, Playmobil, Playmates, and Galoob.

From the Start to the Smurf Boom, 1966–86

The company was founded in 1966 by Wallace Berrie, a successful manufacturer of drugstore novelty items, as The Wallace Berrie Company. Early growth was slow until 1979, when a package arrived containing little blue characters about "three apples tall."

Unaware that other companies had turned down the property, Berrie obtained worldwide rights to the little-known characters otherwise known as The Smurfs, created in 1958 by a European artist named Peyo. "The Smurfs Song" was recorded for Decca in 1977 by the "characters" and Dutch singer Vader Abraham, followed in 1978 by two other singles, "Dippety Day" and "Christmas in Smurfland," all of which became hits in Europe. A Belgian company called IMPS was marketing the little blue characters, including a hit television series, product merchandising, and even a theme park in Lorraine, France.

Berrie's company released the little blue figures in 1979 at $1.50 each, compared to the industry's standard $.29 and $.39 little stuffed figures. By 1982, the diminutive blue Smurfs had joined Steven Spielberg's alien E.T., a fat orange cat named Garfield, a doll named Strawberry Shortcake, everyone's favorite dog Snoopy, and G.I. Joe and Barbie dolls among the best-selling toys of 1982, ultimately going on to become a leader in the licensing industry, selling more than $1 billion in merchandise throughout the world and appearing on everything from apparel and home decor to sleepwear and bedding, from novelties and Halloween costumes to plush toys and lunch pails. By 1983, the company had doubled its sales every year, climbing to $700 million in sales from its nearly 100 licensees, plus another $100 million from its own Smurf products. By 1984, NBC led the network war with "The Smurfs," a reign which continued through 1986.

Sales for the company were bolstered by more recordings featuring songs like "Macarena" and Fool's Garden's "Lemon Tree" on follow-up albums like *Smurfenhits* (1996) and

Company Perspectives:

Applause Inc. specializes in the design, manufacturing, and distribution of high-quality, innovative plush, collectibles, and novelty gift items for children of all ages, featuring America's favorite licensed and non-licensed brands.

Smurfenholiday (1997) which featured Smurfs singing tracks by such artists as The Spice Girls and Coolio.

Operations, 1982–95

In a feeding frenzy for finances, a licensing boom occurred in 1982, with everyone marketing every product they possibly could think of, from toys and posters to plushies and figurines, from trading cards and resin kits to models and mugs, from action figures and lunch pails to shot glasses and cigarette lighters. During that year, Berrie acquired the Applause division from Knickerbocker Toys and, with the acquisition, inherited a number of classic licenses such as Disney, Sesame Street, and Raggedy Ann and Andy.

The stuffed animal industry enjoyed slow growth from $740 million in 1984 to $796 million in 1985. In 1986, the company changed its name to Applause Inc. and released The California Raisins items, which went on, like The Smurfs, to become another one of the most incredible licensing success stories in history. In 1987, for toddlers and tiny tots, the company released Bundles, a loveable stork, and was one of the only licensing opportunities featuring a stork.

By 1988, the stuffed toy category plummeted to about $934 million from highs of $1.4 billion in 1986 and $1.6 billion in 1987 as electronic stuffed toys and other fad-oriented stuffed toys—such as Cabbage Patch dolls and the Teddy Ruxpin talking bear—entered the marketplace.

In 1992, Applause released The Magic Trolls Babies, the first product from the company's newly created Toy Division. Magic Trolls Play Friends and Play Sets accessories came next, soon followed by "The Magic Trolls" animated TV special, which debuted during Thanksgiving week 1992. A second license introduced in 1992 was the Magic Glow Friends line, the first-ever plush products to feature a unique glow-in-the-dark design.

By 1993, the Smurfs and Applause were being pressured by other toys. Hasbro Inc. took the number one position with their Battle Trolls. Sunday morning purple PBS dinosaur Barney brought in second place, primarily with Dakin Inc.'s plushies. Others in the top ten included Mattel, Davis Grabowski's Thomas the Tank Engine line, the Belle doll from Disney's *Beauty and the Beast,* the EZ Squeeze Mix 'N Spin, and Gak.

In May, however, Design Licensing Group, the North American licensing representative for Viva La Wombat!, signed a multiyear licensing agreement with Applause, allowing the company to use the contemporary artwork on a wide range of decorative accessory products in conjunction with Springs In-

dustries and Terragrafics, who would market novelty bedding and picture frames, respectively, under the Viva La Wombat! label.

In 1994, the company further explored direct marketing, establishing Applause Express, a program which created products in prepackaged sets offered either retail or via phone order.

Merger with Dakin, 1995

Late in 1995, Applause, the gift-market leader in classic and film licensed merchandise, merged with fellow Woodland Hills, California company, Dakin Inc., the most widely recognized brand name in stuffed animals.

By this time, Applause's portfolio included film and television licenses for stuffed toys, candles and figurines featuring classic Looney Tunes and Sesame Street characters, as well as characters from *The Lion King, Star Wars, Star Trek, Gargoyles, The Mask,* the California Raisins ads, Budweiser's Spuds Mackenzie commercial spots, and "The Smurfs."

Dakin had undergone a tumultuous ride in its long history. Founded in 1955 by Richard Dakin as an import business, the company pioneered the marketing of stuffed animals as impulse gifts during the 1960s. In 1963, Dakin, experiencing an increased market demand for its popular stuffed toy line, contracted Stafford Enterprises Inc. to serve as its East Coast warehousing and distribution arm, and the company was growing rapidly. But, in December 1966, tragedy struck the family and the company as Richard Dakin and his wife, their son Roger, his wife, and four of their five children were killed in an air accident. Harold Nizamian was elected president and Chief Executive Officer, and the company continued to manufacture stuffed animals, puppets, and baby products such as crib decorations and musical gifts.

As the mini-recession of the stuffed animal industry struck in 1988, Dakin Inc. introduced the Garfield "Stuck on You" stuffed toys, which were hot sellers and soon seen in car windows everywhere. By 1989, Dakin was enjoying sales of $200 million. That same year, Korea lost its "duty free" GSP status as a "most favored nation" and, by December 1990, Dakin, who outsourced nearly all of its manufacturing to the Far East, shifted much of its plush business from Korea to Thailand to escape unfavorable exchange rates and rising labor costs. Nonetheless, 1990 sales for the plushie giant dropped to $75 million.

Early in 1990, as competition in the stuffed animal market increased due to department stores and other retailers across the country starting massive give-away programs of stuffed animals as part of their promotions, Kansas City-based Hallmark Cards Inc., long considered one of the best companies in the nation to work for, expressed that it had been interested in purchasing Dakin for over ten years. The two companies signed an agreement in principle for Hallmark to purchase Dakin, which would operate as an independent subsidiary of the $2.5 billion company. The acquisition was called off in April; at the same time other companies, including Applause, expressed interest in purchasing Dakin.

Bob Solomon took over as CEO of Dakin in 1992, instituting a new strategy which balanced stuffed animals, seasonal gifts, and licensed character merchandise. The company also began seeking out new licensing. That year, Dakin launched its spring line with the addition of the Big Top line to its classic, branded plush.

In the plush category, joining licensed characters Benji, Garfield and Odie, Fido Dido, Chip & Cookie, and the Beast from Disney's *Beauty and the Beast* film, Dakin's Cuddles Bear appeared in six new styles, including Mama & Baby and a Limited Edition Carnival Bear wearing yellow and purple satin, a Mardi Gras mask, ruffled smock, and a commemorative brass medallion. A new 50-inch Garfield was released with especially long arms and legs designed in nylon parachute material and the Garfield Stuck On You Window Decoration reappeared with the message "I'm baa-aack."

In 1993, Patricof & Company bought a 30 percent interest in the primarily plush products giant. The following year, as every other company in the industry was downsizing, Dakin doubled its number of employees early in 1994 when it offered all its independent sales representatives positions as permanent employees.

By the time the merger with Applause occurred in 1995, Dakin had licenses featuring Snoopy, The Pink Panther, The Animaniacs, Cuddles Bear, Lamb Chop, Looney Tunes Lovables, Barney the dinosaur, The Flintstones, Betty Boop, the Coca-Cola polar bears and seals, and the 1996 Olympic mascot, Izzy, among others.

Both lines were maintained separately in the merged company and the sales force grew to 250 people serving more than 50,000 accounts throughout the world. The company would obtain licenses to characters from four popular films of 1995: *Pocahontas, Casper, Congo,* and *Batman Forever.*

The merger was in keeping with other consolidations in the industry at the time, including Tyco's purchase of Matchbox. But, since Applause and Dakin both manufactured stuffed animals and children's products sold to the gift retail business, and served mainly upscale retailers such as F.A.O. Schwarz, department stores, and specialty stores like Hallmark card shops, their products, which competed in the children's gift market, were not in direct competition with Mattel and Hasbro toys, distributed mainly through Wal-Mart and Toys "R" Us stores. The merger, however, did accelerate expansion into new and existing markets such as premiums (McDonald's Happy Meal toys, for example) and direct-marketing.

Applause created a Strategic Alliances Group to establish and oversee large, low-margin, food-related, premium-based programs for several major accounts, including Taco Bell, KFC, Kellogg's, General Mills, Pillsbury, and ConAgra's Kid's Cuisine Division, and the company had previously manufactured a Pocahontas locket for a South American firm. The company's revenues for 1995 were estimated at $150 million.

From Dakin On, 1996-Date

In 1996, the company received numerous awards and accolades for its innovative in-store merchandising displays and high-quality product design, including the prestigious Gold Popai Award for a Taco Bell Merchandising Display and the Bronze Popai Award for a Looney Tunes permanent floor unit. The company also received The National Parenting Center's Seal of Approval on the Disney's 101 Dalmatians Barking Body Puppet and the Kermit the Frog Body Puppet. Additionally, *Family Fun* magazine named Applause's Kermit the Frog Body Puppet a finalist for the 1996 Toy of the Year Award in the Stuffed Animals for Kids Aged 8–10 category. Annual revenue for 1996 was estimated at $280 million.

In September 1997, Applause Enterprises was acquired by a holding company formed by a management group and Frontenac Co., but retained its name. That same year, the company was honored with The President's Award at the annual Warner Bros. Worldwide Licensing Conference for innovation, partnering to grow the business, successful programs, and commitment to Warner Bros. Additionally, Applause received *Family Fun*'s Toy of the Year Award for Sad Sam Huggable Plush, and Applause's Raggedy Ann Dance with Me Doll was included in *Parents* magazine's Top Toys of 1997 list.

In 1998, the company continued to maintain its classic licenses while picking up new ones, including those for characters from Disney's 1998 animated films *A Bug's Life* and *Mu-Lan*. Seemingly assured of an endless succession of such prominent character tie-ins, Applause's future appeared bright indeed.

Principal Subsidiaries

Dakin Inc.; International Tropic-Cal Inc.

Further Reading

"Applause, a Novelty Maker, Sold to Management Group," *New York Times,* September 26, 1997, p. C4(N)/D4(L).

Bozman, Jean S., "New, Tougher Garfield Emerges," *Computerworld,* February 17, 1992, p. 53.

Cuneo, Alice Z., "Hot Raisins; It's Licensed Products That Bring Big Bucks," *Advertising Age,* May 16, 1988, p. 30.

"Custom Warehousing, Distributor Services Pay; Dakin, Stafford Make a Winning Combination," *Playthings,* May 31, 1989, p. 10.

"Dakin to Nearly Double Employee Count," *Playthings,* March 1994, p. 6.

"Design Licensing Group," *HFD-The Weekly Home Furnishings Newspaper,* May 3, 1993, p. 104.

Dishman, Phyllis, "E.T., Smurfs Pace Licensing Boom," *Playthings,* November 1982, p. 23.

"E.T., Smurfs Top Bestseller List; 60% of Respondents Report Sales Increases Despite Economic Malaise," *Playthings,* February 1983, p. 86.

Fix, John, "Snoopy Gives Smurfs a Run for the Money," *Playthings,* November 1982, p. 22.

Foreman, Liza, "Teutonic Tykes Tune to Toons," *Variety,* November 17, 1997, p. 40.

"Ginny Doll Additions, Mister Rogers Puppets Top Dakin Entries," *Playthings,* March 1992, p. 42.

Greene, Richard, and Ellyn Spragins, "Smurfy to the Max," *Forbes,* November 8, 1982, p. 67.

Harrison, Joan, "Forming a Power in Toys and Gifts," *Mergers & Acquisitions,* September/October 1995, p. 43.

"How They Keep Smurfs Under Control," *Sales & Marketing Management,* December 5, 1983, p. 63.

"Licensing Pioneer Applause Is Still Blazing New Trails," *Playthings,* June 1992, p. 50.

Maes, Marc, "Smurfs Have the Last Laugh: 'Little Blue Men' Sell 8 Million in Europe," *Billboard,* October 11, 1997, p. 57.

"Merger of Applause, Dakin Is Likely As Prelude to IPO," *Wall Street Journal, Europe,* June 19, 1995, p. 5.

Muller, E. J., "Santa's (Real) Helpers," *Chilton's Distribution,* December 1990, p. 32.

Rakstis, Ted J., "Chicago: Barney, Thomas Are Still Ringing Up Sales," *Playthings,* March 1993, p. 23.

Reysen, Frank, Jr., "Retailers Exploit Licensing Boom," *Playthings,* August 1982, p. 36.

Roberts, Irving, "G.I. Joe Vies with Smurfs, E.T., Masters," *Playthings,* December 1982, p. 20.

Schwimmer, Anne, "Patricof Runs with the Dinosaurs," *Pensions & Investments,* July 26, 1993, p. 10.

Shaw, Jan, "Dakin's Sale Allows Family to Diversify," *San Francisco Business Times,* January 15, 1990, p. 4.

Shiver, Jube, "Child's Play: NBC Vice President Phyllis Tucker Vinson Employs the Smurfs and Savvy Programming to Push the Network to the Top of the Ratings," *Black Enterprise,* August 1986, p. 30.

Storm, Bill, "Smurfs Stand Out in Spotty Market," *Playthings,* June 1982, p. 26.

——, "Smurfs Still Hot in Many Stores," *Playthings,* December 1982, p. 18.

——, "TV Blitz Focuses Attention on Smurfs," *Playthings,* May 5, 1982, p. 28.

Tyson, Salinda, "Hallmark Calls Off Purchase of Dakin," *San Francisco Business Times,* April 9, 1990, p. 13.

Wanderer, Robert, "San Francisco: Battle Trolls Taking Charge," *Playthings,* March 1993, p. 20.

"With Strong Upfront Market Behind Them, ABC and CBS Take Aim at NBC and the Smurfs," *Television-Radio Age,* August 20, 1984, p. 38.

—Daryl F. Mallett

Ascend Communications, Inc.

1 Ascend Plaza, 1701 Harbor Bay Parkway
Alameda, California 94502-3002
U.S.A.
(510) 769-6001
(800) ASCEND-4
Fax: (510) 747-2300
Web site: http://www.ascend.com

Public Company
Incorporated: 1989 as Aria Communications, Inc.
Employees: 1,800
Sales: $1.16 billion (1997)
Stock Exchanges: NASDAQ
Ticker Symbol: ASND
SICs: 3577 Computer Peripheral Equipment, Not
    Elsewhere Classified; 3669 Communications
    Equipment, Not Elsewhere Classified; 7371 Computer
    Programming Services; 7372 Prepackaged Software;
    7373 Computer Integrated Systems Design; 8711
    Engineering Services

Ascend Communications, Inc. is a leading developer, manufacturer and marketer of high-speed digital remote-networking access technology and equipment solutions for telecommunications (telco) companies and corporate customers worldwide. Since its inception, Ascend has quickly gained extensive experience manufacturing comprehensive product families necessary to build high-performance, cost-effective public and private network infrastructures from end-to-end, whether a wide area network (WAN), local area network (LAN), carrier, or ISP network.

The products are termed ''bandwidth-on-demand'' because they establish high-speed switched digital connections with adjustable bandwidth, duration, and destination configurable to application needs. They support existing digital and analog networks, and are used for videoconferencing remote access, Internet access, bulk-file transfer, and imaging and integrated voice, video, and data access. Bandwidth-on-demand is also utilized for automatic emergency backup and bandwidth capacity for peak-period overflow to complement private-leased line, frame relay, and Asynchronous Transfer Mode (ATM)—a high-bandwidth, cell-switching technology enabling reliable, ultra-high-speed transmission for voice, video and data service—networks. Some products include: The MAX products, designed as a concentration layer for the Internet, Corporate Remote Access (CRA), and Carrier Infrastructure (CI) markets, combine the functionality of a router, modem bank, terminal server, ISDN switch and frame relay concentrator in a single hardware platform.

The GRF (Goes Real Fast) line, designed as a backbone layer for the Internet, CRA and CI markets, are high-performance devices providing scalable, high-bandwidth Layer-3 IP (Internet Protocol) switching for remote access.

The award-winning Pipeline and NetWarp families, designed as an access layer for the Telecommuting/SOHO and CRA markets, provide remote access for the Internet, remote offices, home offices and telecommuters. NetWarp products provide PC users with plug-and-play solutions for implementing high-speed digital links.

The Secure Access family, designed for access, concentration and backbone layers to the Internet, Telecommuting/SOHO, CI and CRA markets, are integrated into all MAX and Pipeline products, bringing industrial-strength security to remote networks.

As of 1998, most leading international post and telephone companies, global carriers, and network service providers offered Internet access using Ascend equipment, and Ascend had installed over 3.5 million access concentrator ports at ISP, carrier and corporate enterprise sites worldwide.

The Beginnings, 1989–94

Armed with $3 million in venture capital, four employees at Hayes Micro's ISDN research facility—Robert Ryan, Jennette Symons, Jay Duncanson, and Steven Speckenbach—

incorporated Aria Communications, Inc. in California in February 1989.

Aria's early products targeted the ISDN aggregator market when ISDN was poised to explode. Telco systems vendors were pushing it as the wave of the future but, as one industry analyst noted, "the early introduction of ISDN in North America was a spectacular non-event." Aria changed its name to Ascend Communications, Inc. in May 1990.

In 1991, Ascend shifted directions, introducing the Multiband line. Designed as an access layer to the Videoconferencing/Multimedia Access market, the inverse multiplexer established high-quality desktop, room, and multi-point videoconferencing operations. A less-expensive version, Multiband Plus, was introduced in 1992. Net sales for 1991 reached $3.2 million, with a net loss of $2.4 million; in 1992, net sales reached $7.2 million, with $3.8 million in losses.

From 1993 to 1996, Ascend entered the datacentric Remote Access Server (RAS) market with its central site and Customer Premise Equipment (CPE) MAX and Pipeline products. Net income for Ascend in 1993 reached $16.2 million, with a net income of $1.4 million.

Ascend was reincorporated in Delaware in May 1994, with its initial public offering netting $25.2 million in proceeds. Concurrently, Ascend formulated a hybrid distribution channel strategy. Revenues for 1994 were $39.3 million, with net income at $8.7 million.

Transitioning in 1995

In 1995, Ascend moved further from a singular focus on the videoconferencing access market (where it had long held the lead) to a broader focus on multiple expanding market segments (Internet access and infrastructure, CRA, Telecommuting/SOHO access and multimedia access).

New products released included the Multiband VSX, which supported scalable bandwidths for single-session videoconferencing, letting users construct economical multimedia-access networks for videoconferencing, distance learning, electronic banking or publishing and telemedicine; the MAX 4000 WAN access switch, which aggregated simultaneous incoming calls from analog, ISDN and frame relay circuits onto a single high-speed digital line; the MAX 1800, which provided the functionality of larger MAX products on a smaller scale; and user-friendly MAXLink software, which turned remote PCs into nodes on an enterprise network connecting to any MAX product.

In June, Ascend introduced the Pipeline 25, an ISDN remote-access bridge/router for Telecommuting/SOHO applications. New EtherFrame products included a low-cost Pipeline frame relay access router, plus software that added frame relay concentration capabilities to Pipeline and MAX products.

Acquisitions and Partnerships

Ascend developed a strategy to acquire technologies which enhanced its core product capabilities. In September 1995, Ascend made its first acquisition, buying from Dayna Communications, Inc. technology and related assets of the DaynaLINK prod-

uct family for approximately $3 million. The acquisition expanded the MAX line and, a month later, the MAX 200, offering dial-up network connectivity for small and remote offices, was introduced.

In the third quarter of 1995, Ascend completed another successful public offering, providing capital resources needed to meet its growth objectives, and the stock split two-for-one three times between May 1995 and January 1996.

Ascend also began partnering with other industry leaders, establishing alliances with several Regional Bell Operating Companies and their subsidiaries, including Bell South Network Solutions, Pacific Bell, Pacific Bell Internet Services and Southwestern Bell Telephone Company. Ascend created a service agreement with AT&T Paradyne's Customer Support Organization; expanded its resale alliance with AT&T Global Business Communications Systems; and GTE Telephone Operations, the largest U.S.-based local telco company, began reselling Ascend products. Ascend also expanded existing relationships with leading independent ISPs like PSINet and UUNET.

Ascend also began implementing its distribution strategy in North America, establishing a two-tier structure which used national distributors to supply products to more value-added resellers than Ascend could handle directly. Merisel Inc. and Tech Data, two leading worldwide computer and network products distributors, and Sprint/North Supply, a leading national distributor of videoconferencing equipment, participated in the program.

Fueled by the growth of Internet access services and expansion of CRA networking, the remote-access equipment market jumped 146 percent from 1994 to $1 billion in 1995. Revenues for Ascend in 1995 reached $149.6 million, with net income at $30.6 million.

Continuing with New Products in 1996

New products for 1996 included the Pipeline 130 family of remote-access routers in January, which provided unparalleled hardware integration and software support, and combined ISDN and frame relay technology for maximum flexibility; the MAX 200Plus in February; and the Pipeline 25-Fx, Pipeline 25-Px and Pipeline 75, and bundled options into the Multiband Plus and Multiband VSX systems in April. June saw the Secure Access Firewall and Secure Access Manager products released.

In September, Ascend launched the high-density MAX TNT—a central site carrier-class WAN access switch that delivered unprecedented network capacity and supported more services in one system (including analog, ISDN, frame relay and digital subscriber line (DSL)) than any other WAN access switch on the carrier and ISP markets at the time. The NetWarp product family for the SOHO market followed in October, and a Java-based configurator was bundled with all Pipeline products in December.

The Telecommunications Act

The passage of The Telecommunications Act of 1996 changed restrictions on the industry, altering the structure and markets for local, long-distance, cable and other telco companies. A violent shake-up was on the horizon for technologically related fields and experts predicted a plethora of mergers and consolidations in the telco, ISP and database industries. In order to stay at the forefront of changing remote networking requirements Ascend, which had already proven itself adept at adapting to market trends and changes, formed even more alliances to extend and enhance access to Internet and intranet functions.

In January, Ascend teamed up with telco giant MCI to demonstrate wireless remote LAN access. March saw Ascend ally with Microsoft to create new technology allowing users to create secure, multi-protocol virtual private networks (VPNs) over the Internet for global data communications without the need for long-distance connections, and Bell Atlantic selected Ascend's Pipeline products for its residential ISDN remote LAN access.

In April, Ascend entered a strategic alliance with Panasonic for improved Videoconferencing/Multimedia Access capabilities, and PictureTel began reselling Multiband products. In June, Lucent Technologies, a premier global provider of networking software and systems, selected the Ascend RAS platform as a component for their Access Gateway product.

In July, ZipLink standardized its network on Ascend's MAX platform and North American Internet upgraded its network with MAX products. The following month, Ascend entered a multi-phase development and marketing alliance with NetManage Inc., the leading provider of standards-based intranet and Internet software applications to the corporate marketplace, and UUNET Technologies, one of the nation's leading ISPs, certified the Pipeline 130 family of integrated ISDN, frame relay and leased-line remote-access routers for resale to its corporate customers.

Ascend entered a joint development agreement with Rockwell Semiconductor Systems in November to create a fully integrated central-site modem solution supporting 56Kbps transmission speeds. Ascend and 27 other leaders from segments of the communications and computer industries, joined forces to create the Open 56K Forum, an industry-wide coalition dedicated to achieving widespread implementation of 56Kbps analog modem technology. In December, Ascend allied with Alcatel, a telco systems integrator, to further carrier-class Internet services, and U.S. West's !NTERPRISE Networking Services organization chose Ascend's IDSL product to provide high-speed Internet access for their customers.

Ascend was honored in 1996 with numerous awards, including *Network World*'s "World Class Award" for the MAX 1800, and *PC/Computing* magazine's MVP Award for the Pipeline 50. The Secure Access Firewall Control Protocol (FCP) received certification from the National Computer Security Association, and eight leading security vendors endorsed it.

Acquisitions in 1996

In March 1996, Ascend acquired Morning Star Technologies Inc. for approximately 440,000 shares of stock. Morning Star's industry-leading firewall security technology was integrated across Ascend's remote networking MAX and Pipeline families, providing the only remote networking products with reliable, cost-effective built-in security.

NetStar Inc. was acquired in August for approximately $300 million in stock. By applying NetStar's high-speed switching technology, Ascend was able to deliver the next generation of IP switching products. A month later, the GRF 400 high-speed hybrid IP Switch/Router, the first product to utilize the technology acquired from NetStar, was released, bringing Ascend equipment into the backbone layer of the remote networking infrastructure, delivering throughput capabilities that were orders of magnitude larger and faster than then-conventional backbone routers, and marking an aggressive entry into the carrier-based switching/routing market dominated by Cisco. By integrating the GRF 400 with the MAX TNT, Ascend created the first MegaPOP solution, designed to alleviate increasingly critical congestion problems on carrier and Internet networks.

Subspace Communications, Inc. was also acquired in August. Subspace products extended Ascend's offerings for the SOHO market, providing cost-effective performance optimizations and advanced ease-of-use features to enhance Internet access, remote LAN access and telecommuting capabilities for PC users.

December saw Ascend acquiring StonyBrook Services Inc. for nearly 480,000 shares of stock. StonyBrook's acquisition strengthened Ascend's sophisticated network management software, which was incorporated into all Ascend products, creating a total end-to-end network solution, easily manageable using a single network management platform.

New distributors for 1996 included Tech Data, ALLTEL Supply and Ingram Micro; Martin Lee Schoffstall, cofounder of the world's first commercial ISP, PSINet, and one of four coauthors of SNMP, an industry standard for network management, was named to the Board of Directors in June; two Technical Assistance Centers were opened––in Japan to serve the Pacific Rim, and in France to serve Europe, the Middle East and Africa; the number of employees jumped from 304 to 721; construction was completed on a 250,000 square-foot, four-building campus in Alameda, California, which included principal administrative, engineering, manufacturing, marketing and sales facilities; sales offices were established in Belgium, Italy, Korea, Malaysia, Singapore and Sweden; and Ascend's net sales grew 260 percent to $549.3 million, and net income rose 311 percent to $113.1 million.

New Products for 1997

In January 1997, Ascend launched a line of bandwidth-on-demand Multiband MAX controllers to provide software to support multimedia applications and a migration path for future upgrading to remote access. Ascend also continued making remote access more cost-effective for telecommuters and home users with the MAX 4048 WAN Access Switch, Pipeline 15 External Terminal Adapter, with dynamic bandwidth allocation and integrated analog/digital support providing high-speed dial-up access to a corporate headquarters intranet or the Internet.

Other releases included a MAX and Series56 Digital Modem for central site customers so corporations and network service providers could offer users the ability to download data from the Internet or a corporate network at almost twice the speed of their old modems. As of mid-1997, MAX products accounted for over 50 percent of the worldwide market share in access concentrator analog ports, 62 percent of access concentrator ISDN PRI ports and 33 percent of access concentrator TI DSOs, and supported over 30 million Internet connections daily.

In February, Ascend released the ISDN DSL (IDSL), an innovative solution developed with one of Ascend's customers, MFS Communications, and its subsidiary, UUNET Technologies, reflecting Ascend's long-standing tradition of delivering custom, state-of-the-art products. Ascend also expanded its Net-Warp family with the NetWarp Pro ISDN Terminal Adapter, featuring a single analog port providing plain-old telephone services with full-ring and dial-tone generation capabilities, letting users connect a phone, fax or answering machine to NetWarp Pro and simultaneously surf the Internet and make analog calls over a single ISDN BRI line.

Growth continued when Ascend acquired Whitetree Inc., a privately held provider of high-speed switching products, for approximately 1.1 million shares of stock. Ascend also acquired substantially all the outstanding stock of InterCon Systems Corporation for approximately $12 million in cash and the assumption of nearly $9 million in liabilities.

In March, Ascend was strengthened by the acquisition of competitor Cascade Communications, Inc. for approximately $3.7 billion in stock. Besides having numerous mutual customers, the companies had each established dominant positions in the ISP and carrier markets. With the acquisition, Ascend became the leading provider of frame relay and ATM equipment to ISPs worldwide, with over 40 percent of frame relay WAN switch connections and 20 percent of ATM WAN switch connections, creating a huge disparity between Ascend and its competitors.

Following the acquisition, Ascend reorganized into four business units. The Core Switching Systems Unit, under Cascade CEO Dan Smith, focused on the Cascade frame relay and ATM switches and the Ascend IP switch/router; The Access and Concentrator Products Unit, on the remote-access concentrator product lines (MAX, MAX TNT; Cascade's AX 800/1600); The Remote Products Unit, on SOHO connectivity products (Pipeline, NetWarp products); and The Multimedia Access Products Unit, to leverage existing leadership in videoconferencing access and to pioneer the design and marketing of innovative multimedia access products.

Also in March, Ascend began shipping SDSL Line Cards for the MAX TNT and DSLPipe-S for remote users accessing SDSL services. These products offered support for high-speed services and unsurpassed speeds over the local loop. Ascend surpassed its own performance benchmark with the GRF 1600, the only IP switch capable of delivering 10 million packets per second throughput with a fully-loaded 16-slot configuration of high-speed media cards.

When GTE acquired BBN Corp., primary systems integrator for AOL and a large Ascend customer, in May 1997, there was some excitement in the industry because GTE agreed to start using Cisco gear on its own network and reselling Cisco hardware to its customers. But, with Newbridge acquiring UB Networks, 3Com picking up U.S. Robotics, and Cisco buying

Stratacom, it was merely par for the course for market consolidation following the passage of the Telecommunications Act.

In July, PSINet Inc.—a worldwide leading provider of turnkey corporate Internet and intranet access, wholesale access services to telco and ISP companies, electronic commerce solutions and Web-hosting services, which managed one of the world's largest, most advanced fast-packet networks—announced the deployment of MAX TNT WAN access switches, expanding the ISP's capacity by 40,000 ports, adding them to its base of MAX 4000 WAN access switches and GRF 400 high-performance routers which supported over 21,000 customers through 350 POPs worldwide.

In August, Ascend joined Bay Networks and Cisco to support AimQuest Corp.'s GRIC-Ready Program. The alliance gave Ascend access to 150 of the world's largest ISPs and telcos—including Chungwha Telecom, Cybernet AG, DTI Mitsubishi, Finland Telecom, FranceNet, Fujitsu, Hong Kong Telecom, Hyundai, KDD, Korea PC Telecom, Malaysia Telecom, NEC, NETCOM, Prodigy, Samsung, Singapore Telecom, and Telstra—to deploy value-added global Internet communication services throughout the GRIC network, which extended throughout 150 countries, over 1,300 POPs and served more than 13 million dial-up subscribers and 20 million corporate users.

VPNet Technologies Inc.—the first company formed with a singular focus on VPNs, dedicated to developing and marketing cost-effective products and technologies for implementing high-performance VPNs—released new hardware for high-performance site-to-site connectivity and remote access, which supported RADIUS authentication technology, including Ascend's Access Control implementation.

Electric Lightwave Inc.—a telco company offering local and long-distance telephone, videoconferencing and data and Internet access services, and prepaid debit cards—in a major upgrade to its broadband network infrastructure, selected Ascend's CBX 500 switches for ATM backbone support for various network services and ATM-based services. ELI would use the switches with its installed base of Ascend B-STDX 9000 Frame Relay multiservice switches and the CascadeView network management system to manage the switches as a single network from one management platform. This gave Ascend access to ELI's parent company, Citizens, a full-service telco company, and its subsidiaries, Citizens Communications, the United States' 15th largest independent telco company; Centennial Cellular Corp.; and Hungarian Telephone and Cable Corp.

Ascend also introduced the Ascend Certified Technical Expert Program to test internetworking expertise to ensure quality and proficiency levels requiring standardized testing for anyone wishing recognition as an Ascend networking expert.

August continued to be busy, as Ascend released the Pipeline 220, the first router capable of delivering Secure Access dynamic firewall technology, IP Layer Security Protocol-compliant encryption, a draft standard which defines encryption, packet authentication, and key management services for VPNs, multi-protocol routing and bridging, and VPN tunneling capabilities from a single device; and the Pipeline 85 CPE dial-up router, created to address the SOHO market's need for an economical, all-in-one solution for LAN-to-LAN and Internet connectivity.

By mid-1998, with surging demand for increased bandwidth being fueled by rapid growth of the Internet and the urgency to upgrade corporate networks, Ascend was the unquestioned market leader. Cicso made a stab at Ascend when it released its Gigabit Switch Router at Networld+Interop in Las Vegas in mid-1997, but no one could compete with Ascend for speed and product density, the TNT was without competition in the marketplace, and the competition, excepting 3Com Corporation, was far behind in remote-access technology and market thrusts. With the Internet, CRA, Telecommuting/SOHO and Videoconferencing/Multimedia Access markets all expanding, Ascend showed no sign of stopping to provide integrated remote networking solutions.

Principal Subsidiaries

Ascend Communications Europe Ltd.; Ascend Communications GmbH; Ascend Credit Corp.; Ascend Foreign Sales Corp.; InterCon Systems Corp.; Morning Star Technologies Inc.; Whitetree Inc.

Principal Divisions

C3I Systems Division; High Performance Networking Division.

Principal Operating Units

Core Switching Systems; Access and Concentrator Products; Remote Products; Multimedia Access Products.

Further Reading

"Ascend Asked by U.S. for Additional Data on Cascade Proposal," *Wall Street Journal,* May 16, 1997, p. A9(W)/B12(E).

"Ascend, Bay, Digital Roll Out Switch Hardware," *PC Week,* February 10, 1997, p. 3.

"Ascend Extends MAX with 56K-bps Modems," *PC Week,* May 5, 1997, p. 126.

"Ascend ISDN Switch Boasts 8 BRI Connections," *PC Week,* December 4, 1995, p. 57.

"Ascend Protocol, Spec Fill Firewall Holes," *PC Week,* October 28, 1996, p. 8.

"Ascend Shares Slide on a Delay in Product Shipments," *New York Times,* June 11, 1997, p. C4(N)/D4(L).

Capell, Kerry, "The Good, the Bad, and the Unspeakable: In 1995, Many Ate Caviar, Some Ate Crow, and a Few Had to Settle for Humble Pie," *Business Week,* December 25, 1995, p. 126.

Carter, Wayne, "Ascend Bulks Up to Battle Cisco," *Telephony,* April 7, 1997, p. 10.

"Cascade and Ascend Hook New Acquisitions," *PC Week,* January 6, 1997, p. 3.

Cohen, Sarah, "Ascend, Cascade to Merge," *Electronic News,* April 7, 1997, p. 1.

Gomes, Lee, and Jon G. Auerbach, "Ascend Deal Puts Firm on Heels of Cisco; Cascade Purchase Expected to Heat Up Rivalry; Investors See the Risks," *Wall Street Journal,* April 1, 1997, p. A3(W)/A3(E).

Lavilla, Stacy, and Scott Berinato, "Modem Makers Bond for Higher Data Rates," *PC Week,* May 26, 1997, p. 136.

Leonhardt, David, "Good Things in Small Packages," *Business Week,* March 25, 1996, p. 94.

"Loss of $48.8 Million Posted After Merger-Related Costs," *Wall Street Journal,* July 16, 1997, p. B14(N)/B4(L).

Schonfield, Erick, "Cisco and the Kids: Are They As Scary As They Look?" *Fortune,* April 14, 1997, p. 200.

"Whitetree Accepts $72 Million Bid from Ascend," *New York Times,* February 19, 1997, p. C4(N)/D4(L).

Young, Jeffrey, "Follow the Internet," *Forbes,* September 25, 1995, p. 196.

—Daryl F. Mallett

CUDIO KING®

Audio King Corporation

3501 South Highway 100
Minneapolis, Minnesota 55416
U.S.A.
(612) 920-0505
Fax: (612) 920-0940

Division of Ultimate Electronics, Inc.
Founded: 1953
Sales: $65.6 million (fiscal year ending June 30, 1996, as
 Audio King Corporation)
SICs: 5731 Radio, TV & Electronics Stores; 7699 Repair
 Shops & Related Services, Not Elsewhere Classified

Audio King Corporation, which operated high-end consumer electronics specialty stores and the Midwest's largest independent audio/video electronics repair service, was purchased by Ultimate Electronics, Inc. in 1997. The two regional marketers merged to keep a footing in the $70 billion industry which was dominated by giant mass merchandisers Best Buy Company and Circuit City Stores. Ultimate Electronics, Inc. operates businesses under the names Ultimate Electronics, SoundTrack, and Audio King.

Hi-Fi Company Branches Out: 1950s-80s

Audio King, founded in 1953 by Albert C. Kempf, initially sold cameras as well as audio products. Operating from a single Minneapolis location, the business went on to build a reputation among audiophiles and other seekers of high fidelity equipment. Sales grew to around $1.6 million by the mid-1970s. When Randel S. Carlock became a partner in the company in 1977, he pushed for a broader range of products and additional stores. By the time Carlock bought out Kempf in 1985, Audio King was a chain of seven stores. The company further expanded its business with the purchase of an audio service center in early 1986. Sales for fiscal 1986 were about $10.4 million.

Image Retailing Group, Inc., a holding company formed in 1985, acquired Audio King for about $2 million in September 1986. The company planned to add similar consumer electronics specialty stores and open additional Audio King outlets. In rapid order, Audio King expanded outside the Twin Cities metropolitan area, opening stores in Rochester and Mankato, Minnesota, and Sioux Falls, South Dakota.

Audio King lured "discriminating" home electronics customers with its limited distribution, brand name products, and professional service. Its principal vendors included Alpine Electronics of America, Inc., Bang & Olufsen of America, Inc., and Yamaha Electronics Corporation. Through its Audio Video Environments unit, the company offered custom design and installation of home entertainment systems. Audio systems, burglar alarms, and cellular phones for automobiles and recreational vehicles were sold and installed at two service locations. A merchandise clearance center sold trade-ins and floor samples, and customer insurance claims were handled by an insurance replacement division.

In May 1987, the privately held company announced plans for a public stock offering. At the time of the sale, Carlock held 25 percent of Image Retailing stock and served as president and chief executive officer. Image Retailing secured $3.2 million through the sale of 800,000 common shares, but the offering brought in less capital than the company had expected. The consumer electronics industry, which had been experiencing rapid growth, began to slow down about the time Image Retailing took the company public. The stock dropped to $3.50 per share and then fell to $1 per share when the stock market crashed in October.

The consumer electronics market was hit by plummeting sales growth in the late-1980s. Audio King had opened another store in November 1987, but flat industry sales forced the company to hold back on further expansions plans. Sales were up by 33.4 percent to $15.9 million in 1988, but net income fell by 90.5 percent to only $8,000. The company improved its 1989 numbers by drawing in more first-time customers with the addition of popular brand name products such as Sony televisions. Audio Video Environments' custom design service and the Fast Trak unit repair service also helped boost performance. Net income rebounded to $122,000.

Top consumer electronics specialty retailers were luring in customers with the promise of exciting and entertaining shopping environments. Image Retailing planned to exploit that tactic by renovating and enlarging some of its existing stores. In 1989, a prototype Audio King was introduced. The store featured a BMW equipped with a $7,000 car stereo and alarm system, a home theater demonstration room with an array of large screen televisions and speakers, and listening rooms with state-of-the-art audio equipment.

Continuing Pressure on Retailers: Early 1990s

In March 1990, Audio King President H. G. (Gary) Thorne succeeded Randel Carlock as president and chief executive officer of Image Retailing. Carlock moved to the newly created position of chairman of the board. The company was nearing the completion of its $2 million store remodeling program, but the depressed retail environment hurt profitability and net income slumped again in fiscal 1990. On a brighter note, Audio King was named one of the country's top 10 audio/video retailers by *AudioVideo International* magazine, and the company had added another store, bringing the number of retail stores to 11.

Michigan-based Highland Superstores, Inc. pulled out of Audio King's primary market area in 1991. Highland's 1990 Twin Cities-area sales were approximately $45 million, while its chief competitor, Bloomington, Minnesota-based Best Buy, Inc., had area sales of about $140 million. By contrast, Audio King's total sales for 1990 were $22.3 million. According to an article by Dan Wascoe, Jr., Best Buy, Montgomery Ward's Electric Avenue, Sears' Brand Central, Dayton's electronics departments, and Audio King would be among those competing for Highland's former customers.

A crucial part of Image Retailing's plan to remain competitive in the consumer electronics market was to acquire other high-end specialty stores. In May 1991, Image Retailing announced a proposed merger with Sound Advice, Inc. The 18-store Florida retailer of middle-to high-end electronics had average store sales of $5.4 million or more than double that of Audio King, which had average store sales of $1.9 million. According to a May 1991 article by Sally Apgar, Carlock saw the merger as an opportunity for Audio King to increase its financial and marketing strength, while continuing to distinguish itself from the discounters. But the merger failed to materialize, and Audio King continued to be Image Retailing's only chain of stores.

The company's master plan was faltering. According to a 1992 article by Marc Hequet, not only had consumer electronics acquisition opportunities dried up, but Audio King had failed to build ample sales growth from its traditional customer base. Under a new plan, the "promoting specialist strategy," Audio King continued to emphasize professional service but modified its high-end image via increased advertising, expanded mid-priced product lines, and more revamped stores. To accommodate increased inventory, the company upgraded its warehouse and ordering systems.

Image Retailing Group, Inc. changed its name to Audio King Corporation in 1992. CEO Gary Thorne said in a March 7 *Star Tribune* article, "We have operated our stores for 39 years with the Audio King name, and we believe that name awareness will help our stock in the public market." The stock had been trading around the $2 mark.

In fiscal 1992 the company expanded one store. Three stores which had either provided excess market coverage as other stores were expanded or could not be expanded themselves had been closed. The total number of Audio King stores was down to nine. A private stock sale brought in more funds for the expansion and remodeling of existing stores. Audio King began reaping some success from its efforts: net income nearly doubled, and its stock price rose by 213 percent during the calendar year.

Competition Heats Up: Mid-1990s

Audio King continued to switch existing stores to the larger format, expand its product offerings, and increase advertising expenditures. The company launched its first television ads in 1993 in anticipation of the entry of Circuit City Stores, Inc. into the Twin Cities market. The Richmond, Virginia-based retailer had been adding about 60 stores per year to its chain, while Best Buy was adding about 45. The Audio King showroom opened in Des Moines, Iowa, in 1994, was the first new store added in several years.

Circuit City differentiated itself from other consumer electronics discounters by promoting the quality of its product and service in addition to pricing. Tony Carideo wrote in April 1994 that this positioned the company directly against the much smaller Audio King: "Thorne does, in fact, anticipate some margin squeeze, estimating that about 20 percent of the company's mix—primarily in its Sony and RCA lines—is vulnerable to competition. These products represent about 15 percent of sales, he said, and 10 percent of earnings."

Audio King marked its fourth consecutive year of growth in 1994: net sales were up to $45.8 million, and net income was $637,000. In 1995, the company opened another new store in Iowa and announced plans to replace its oldest store, in Edina, Minnesota, with its largest store to date. Sally Apgar wrote, "This will be the flagship of the chain's 11 stores and will feature interactive displays ranging from a home theater demonstration to cars rigged with the latest audio and security products." Audio King had been using these marketing tools from the beginning of the decade, but discounters had begun to add similar displays.

Sales continued to rise, but net income held about even in 1995. The situation worsened in 1996 when the company reported losses of $251,000 on revenue of $65.6 million. Audio King contributed the losses to lower than expected sales and gross margins in the expanded stores. A drop in electronics prices, a dearth of new products, increased competition, and decreased consumer spending added to the stress on the company's profits.

Audio components and systems, which continued to be sold primarily on a limited distribution basis, contributed 31 percent of net sales for fiscal 1996. Automobile audio products, which were sold on both a limited and broad distribution basis, brought in 24 percent. Video products—color televisions, big screen televisions, video cassette recorders, camcorders, and digital satellite systems—which competed directly with department and chain stores as well as electronics superstores, produced 35 percent of net sales. Customer service and repair accounted for the remaining

10 percent. Nine of the 11 Audio King stores had been converted to the new format by fiscal 1996.

Audio King, faced with sliding consumer electronics prices, cut its workforce from 400 to 360 to lower costs. However, the company continued to struggle with flat sales, falling earnings, and a depressed stock price during the first half of its 1997 fiscal year. Thorne predicted better days for the company and the industry with the introduction of new products such as Digital Video Disc (DVD) players. Audio King was among the first to begin selling the high-priced technology which produced top-notch sound and images.

New Ownership for the Future

In March 1997, the company announced that it had agreed to be acquired by Colorado-based Ultimate Electronics, Inc., a 1,200-employee, home entertainment and consumer electronics retailer operating 18 high-end stores and six service centers in six western states. The merger talks had actually begun nearly a year earlier, in May 1996, when William J. Pearse, Ultimate chairman and CEO, contacted Carlock. A wave of consolidations had hit the consumer electronics industry as smaller specialty retailers were banded together in an effort to survive in the highly competitive market.

Pearse and his wife, Barbara, began the business as a Team Electronics franchise operation in 1968. In 1974, they changed the name to SoundTrack and opened additional audio specialty stores in Colorado. They added products and capitalized on the surge in sales of VCRs and CD players in the 1980s. In 1993, the company went public under the name Ultimate Electronics, Inc. The inflow of cash allowed Ultimate to open a new generation of stores called Ultimate Electronics and extend the business outside Colorado.

Ultimate then moved to expand existing outlets. "We've had phenomenal success with the new [larger] stores," said Pearse in a June 1997 *Star Tribune* article by Janet Moore. "Basically, the new stores were designed to be upscale electronics superstores with a large selection of audio and video, including computers." Ultimate planned to bump the Audio King outlets up to the larger format.

As a regional retailer, Ultimate faced the same market woes as Audio King. Giant competitors and slow industry sales contributed to a drop in earnings in 1997. While sales climbed to $261 million, income fell to $0.8 million from $2.8 million the previous year. According to the Moore article, analysts said that to survive the new company would have to continue appealing to consumers seeking the newest products while drawing a larger consumer base with competitive pricing. In line with that philosophy, Pearse had years earlier founded the Progressive Retailers Organization (PRO), a group of upscale companies which joined together to boost their buying power.

The merger, valued at about $5 million in cash and stocks, was completed in June 1997. Pearse, named chair and CEO, held about 40 percent of the stock. Top Audio King executives relinquished their management posts. The newly combined company operated 30 stores in nine central region states and had annual sales of $306.3 million in the fiscal year ended January 31, 1998. Six Audio King stores were remodeled during the year. Two of the six, those located in Iowa, reopened as Ultimate Electronics stores.

Further Reading

Apgar, Sally, "Audio King Plans Merger with Florida's Sound Advice," *Star Tribune* (Minneapolis), May 31, 1991, p. 1D.
——, "Audio King Plans to Open Biggest-Ever Store In Edina," *Star Tribune* (Minneapolis), July 6, 1995, p. 1D.
"Audio King Buys Audiophile Center," *Star Tribune* (Minneapolis), March 27, 1986, p. M1.
"Audio King Turns Up the Volume," *Corporate Report Minnesota*, June 1992, p. 24.
"Audio King-Ultimate Merger Closer," *Television Digest*, June 23, 1997, p. 22.
Borger, Judith Yates, "Denver Firm to Buy Audio King," *St. Paul Pioneer Press Dispatch*, March 5, 1997, p. 1B.
"Business Briefs," *Star Tribune* (Minneapolis), March 7, 1992, p. 2D.
Carideo, Tony, "Audio King Is Confident There's a Market for its Style of Retail Electronics," *Star Tribune* (Minneapolis), March 19, 1992, p. 2D.
——, "Circuit City Is Arriving Soon to Do Battle with Best Buy and Audio King," *Star Tribune* (Minneapolis), April 14, 1994, p. 2D.
——, "A Spiffed-Up, Energized Audio King Says It Has Iowa Expansion Plans," *Star Tribune* (Minneapolis), February 15, 1994, p. 2D.
Covett, Collin, "Digital Video Disc Players Are Here," *Star Tribune* (Minneapolis), February 15, 1997, p. 2E.
Forster, Julie, "Mercy Killing," *Corporate Report Minnesota*, April 1997, pp. 46–47.
Foster, Jim, "Image Retailing Calls Off Merger," *Star Tribune* (Minneapolis), July 17, 1991, p. 3D.
Feyder, Susan, "Denver Firm to Acquire Audio King in Deal Valued at about $5.7 Million," *Star Tribune* (Minneapolis), March 5, 1997, p. 1D.
Hequet, Marc, "Building a Company—the Second Time Around," *Minnesota Ventures*, November/December 1992, pp. 64–66.
Howatt, Glenn, "Stocks of State Companies Finish Year with Gains," *Star Tribune* (Minneapolis), January 1, 1993, p. 3D.
"Image Retailing Completes IPO," *Star Tribune* (Minneapolis), July 7, 1987, p. 8B.
"Image Retailing Group, Inc.," *Corporate Report Minnesota*, April 1989, p. 102.
Lambert, Brian, "High-End Audio-Visual Store Set to Handle Lots of Volume," *St. Paul Pioneer Press Dispatch*, October 10, 1989.
Lieber, Ed, "More Consolidation: Ultimate & Audio King," *HFN The Weekly Newspaper for the Home Furnishing Network*, March 10, 1997, p. 4.
McCartney, Jim, "Audio King Parent Plans to Sell Shares," *St. Paul Pioneer Press Dispatch*, May 19, 1987.
Merrill, Ann, "Audio King Expands in Suburbs," *St. Paul Pioneer Press Dispatch*, September 16, 1992.
"Monday's People," *Star Tribune* (Minneapolis), March 26, 1990, p. 2D.
Moore, Janet, "Audio King Completes Merger with Colorado Electronics Firm," *Star Tribune* (Minneapolis), June 28, 1997, p. 4D.
——, "The Ultimate Merger," *Star Tribune* (Minneapolis), June 4, 1997, p. 1D.
Randle, Wilma, "Electronics Downturn Hurts Image Retailing," *St. Paul Pioneer Press Dispatch*, May 23, 1988.
"Ultimate Electronics/Audio King Regional Office," *Corporate Report Fact Book 1998*, p. 709.
Wascoe, Dan, Jr., "Highland Closing Its Six 'Superstores,'" *Star Tribune* (Minneapolis), April 4, 1991, p. 1A.
Waters, Jennifer, "Audio King Seeks Volume," *Minneapolis/St. Paul CityBusiness*, April 19, 1996.
"A Winning New Store Prototype," *AudioVideo International*, December 1995.

—Kathleen Peippo

Aveda Corporation

4000 Pheasant Ridge Drive
Blaine, Minnesota 55449
U.S.A.
(612) 783-4000
(800) AVEDA-24
Fax: (612) 783-4110
Web site: http://www.aveda.com

*Wholly Owned Subsidiary of Estée Lauder Companies
    Inc.*
Incorporated: 1978
Employees: 500
Sales: $120 million (1996 est.)
SICs: 2844 Perfumes, Cosmetics, & Other Toilet
    Preparations; 7231 Beauty Shops

Aveda Corporation develops and manufactures hair, skin, makeup, perfumes, and lifestyle products from the essential oils of flowers and plants gathered from around the world. Brands such as Shampure, Pure-Fume, and All-Sensitive are sold primarily in professional hair salons and in Aveda Environmental Lifestyle stores which feature a range of products from natural fragrances to clothing. Founder Horst Rechelbacher sold the privately held Minnesota-based company to Estée Lauder Companies Inc. in 1997.

The Salon Years: 1960s-70s

Horst Rechelbacher grew up in Nazi-occupied Austria, where his father worked as a shoemaker and his mother as an herbalist. Poverty brought Rechelbacher's formal education to an end after the fourth grade, but at 14 years of age he apprenticed as a hairdresser. When he was 17 he left Austria and moved on to Rome and London. He worked in some of the best salons, styled hair for magazine photo layouts, and tested products for companies such as L'Oréal. On the European hairdressing circuit, he cultivated his technique and won styling awards.

Rechelbacher went to New York in 1963—he was 22—for his first American hairstyling exhibition. During his hairstyling tours in the United States he became known by his first name, Horst. A 1965 automobile accident in Minneapolis saddled him with thousands of dollars in hospital bills. To pay off his debt, Horst took a job at a top Minneapolis salon, the Golden Door in the Sheraton Ritz. His styling technique and charm quickly earned him regular clients, one of whom loaned him $4,000 to start his own shop. He continued doing weekend hair demonstrations for manufacturers and opened additional shops in the upscale areas of the Twin Cities. Marriage to a Minneapolis woman and the birth of their two children further cemented his ties to the area.

Horst's reputation grew in scope: he became a well-known figure in the local nightclub scene. But burning out from the fast-paced life, Horst turned to meditation and other Eastern philosophies. After hearing the Swami Rama speak at the University of Minnesota, Horst followed him to India and stayed for six months. There Horst studied the use of herbs and other plants to promote health and longevity. When he returned to the United States he began developing products for his salons using the essential oils derived from plants.

New Territory: 1980s

Horst entered another aspect of the haircare business in 1977. He established a cosmetology school to counter the loss of personnel from his shops: people he trained often ended up as competitors.

In 1986, with about 200 students paying $4,500 for a 9-month training program, he expanded the school. Horst spent $2.5 million to renovate a five-story building, a former Masonic temple, complete with stages and auditoriums, into a beauty/fashion/wellness institute. Estimated 1986 sales of Horst & Friends salons and the Horst International Education Center were $5 million. Another $11 million in sales were from Aveda Corporation products which were sold through 41 U.S. distributors.

Aveda Corporation—a name inspired by Horst's India experience—was founded in 1978. Horst had formulated the first product, a clove shampoo, in his kitchen sink. In the early

1980s, about the time other well-known hair stylists were introducing their own haircare products, Horst began marketing his shampoos and conditioners to other salons.

According to a 1991 *Corporate Report Minnesota* article by Eric J. Wieffering, National Beauty Supply Inc. helped Horst get his products in salons in North Dakota, South Dakota, Iowa, Wisconsin, and Minnesota. By 1988, product sales in the five-state area exceeded $1 million. Horst then instituted an exclusive distribution system. Distributors were expected to carry only Aveda products: an uncommon move in the industry.

Horst distinguished his body-care products from others in two significant ways. First, he popularized the concept of aromatherapy. New scientific evidence increased the credibility of the older theories to which he ascribed that linked the sense of smell to health and well-being. A new line of Aveda products, wrote Bob Ehlert in a 1986 *Star Tribune* article, "called 'Body Rituals,' are seven different formulas whose very names seem to suggest their applications: Motivation, Attraction, Equipoise, Fulfillment, Creative, Intuition and Bliss." He was also a vocal supporter of environmental causes and incorporated his beliefs into the marketing of his products. "From the beginning, he's been opposed to the use of synthetic, petroleum-based or animal-tested products," wrote Georgann Koelln in a 1990 *St. Paul Pioneer Press* article.

Like many entrepreneurs, Horst was pushed to hire professional managers to run his growing products company. He brought on former Tonka Toys marketing executive Joseph Garcia as president in 1987. Garcia, according to the Wieffering article, helped the company increase its credit line, thus opening the way for in-house production. But disagreements with Horst, including one regarding Aveda's entry into the makeup and perfume business, led to his departure within a year. Horst's son Peter, a college sophomore at the time, was recruited to replace Garcia as president, but he left the day-to-day management of the business after 18 months.

Entrepreneurial Spirit Continues: 1990s

The innovative Horst continued to expand the range of his business. The New York Madison Avenue salon, wrote Connie Nelson in an August 1989 *Star Tribune* article, "will be converted to an 'esthetique,' selling more than 75 original perfumes that can be used to custom scent Aveda products." A state-of-the-art spa in Osceola, Wisconsin, a farming community of 2,000 people about 45 miles northeast of the Twin Cities, opened in 1990. Horst renovated an early 20th century, prairie-style mansion on an 80-acre estate on the St. Croix River and equipped it with a hair and makeup salon, workout rooms, an Aveda Esthetique, and offered services such as body massage, hydrotherapy or water jet massage, and self-improvement seminars. All the meals were made from organically grown food.

Horst was ahead of the pack in the early 1980s when he began marketing the environmental aspects of his products—plant-based formulas and recycled packaging—but competition had grown. More and more companies in the beauty care industry were touting their own use of natural ingredients and ban on animal testing of their products. Body Shop International PLC of the United Kingdom was opening stores in the United States, and Estée Lauder Inc. had begun offering a natural product line.

The giant companies, such as Estée Lauder with $1.4 billion in sales and the Revlon Group with $2.7 billion in sales, distributed their products by way of drug and department stores. Aveda, which sold its products only in salons, was considered part of the professional market. Redken Laboratories Inc. was the leader with sales of $130 million followed by John Paul Mitchell Systems, which had sales of $100 million. Horst felt that Aveda's rapid growth—beauty product revenues had been increasing by about 40 percent a year—could push sales to the $1 billion mark by 1995.

But detractors said Aveda produced too many different products for a company of its size. The sheer number and variety would tax both the production and distribution systems. John Paul Mitchell Systems—a company begun by another well-known stylist—had limited itself to haircare products and racked up twice the revenues of Aveda. In 1991, Aveda was bringing in about $50 million in revenues, but 85 to 90 percent of all profits were derived from ten haircare products.

Aveda headquarters and manufacturing operations moved to a facility in Blaine, Minnesota, just north of the Twin Cities, in 1991. The Aveda Institute continued to operate out of the Minneapolis site, which housed the well-known school, a salon, an Esthetique, and an organic restaurant. The five Horst Salons were sold to David Wagner, president and chief executive office of Horst Salons Inc., in 1992. The upscale salons, which had been operated as a separate entity from Aveda Corporation, brought in about $7 million a year in revenue.

In line with the company's commitment to all things environmental, Horst planned to begin selling organically grown coffee and tea, as well as dish, laundry, and house cleansers. And daughter Nicole Rechelbacher introduced a line of clothes made from recycled materials. But Aveda's high-profile environmental activities also drew criticism from some local activists.

Aveda Corporation revenues were an estimated $70 million in 1994. Sales had been expanded to 25,000 salons worldwide: 1,600 were concept salons selling only Aveda products. Fifty-six Aveda Environmental Lifestyle stores—the Esthetique concept—sold a broad range of Aveda products.

In mid-1996, Horst told his employees he would be stepping back from the daily operations of the company. Based on his previous unwillingness to let go of control of the company he was greeted with some skepticism by outsiders. "But some observers say there's more reason to take Rechelbacher at face value this time around. While the company continues to expand its product lines and stores, it may have grown as far as Rechelbacher, an Austrian-born former hairdresser, can take it, they suggest," wrote Peter Kafka in a July 1996 *Minneapolis/St. Paul CityBusiness* article.

New Look for the Future

At year-end 1997, Horst sold Aveda Corporation to Estée Lauder for $300 million in cash—Horst and his children were sole owners. While publicly held, Estée Lauder, with $3.4 billion in sales, was nearly 80 percent owned by the Lauder family. The idea for the deal was sparked earlier in the year when Horst met CEO Leonard Lauder and his wife at the Aveda spa. Estée Lauder, which claimed almost 45 percent of the U.S. department store prestige cosmetics, skin care, and fragrance market, had been in an expansion mode since the latter half of 1995.

The Aveda purchase moved the giant manufacturer into the rapidly growing professional salon segment of the $15 billion haircare market. Sassaby Inc. and its Jane line brought on board earlier in the year gave Estée Lauder entry into the mass market segment, and the addition of a licensing deal with Donna Karan advanced the cosmetic and fragrance areas.

The Aveda purchase included the Blaine manufacturing plant and Aveda Institute. The corporate headquarters would remain in Minnesota with Horst as chairman of the new Estée Lauder business unit. Horst had rejected an earlier offer from L'Oréal which included only the businesses. According to a November 1997 *Star Tribune* article by Susan Feyder, the sale to Estée Lauder gave Horst the access to greater resources and the opportunity to continue what he enjoyed most: developing products.

A November 1997 *Women's Wear Daily* article by Soren Larson said the industry estimated Aveda would produce wholesale volume of between $175 million and $200 million for 1997. And Lauder said, "The company is profitable; it's actually very profitable." He also praised the company for its tight distribution system and trademark protection. Aveda's growth rate, which had been 20 percent compounded over the past five years, was expected to improve as Estée Lauder expanded international sales. About half of Estée Lauder's sales came from overseas markets compared with only eight percent for Aveda.

Further Reading

"Aveda Corporation," *Corporate Report Fact Book 1998*, Minneapolis: Corporate Report, Inc., 1998, p. 537.

Covert, Colin, "Horst Rechelbacher: A Grass-Roots Entrepreneur Who Hit It Big," *Star Tribune* (Minneapolis), November 20, 1997, p. 14.

Ehlert, Bob, "How Can You Travel the Road to Physical and Spiritual Nirvana?" *Star Tribune* (Minneapolis), December 14, 1986, p. 6SM.

Feyder, Susan, "Essence of the Deal: Estée lauder Will Buy Aveda for $300 Million," *Star Tribune* (Minneapolis), November 20, 1997, p. 1.

Grow, Doug, "Picket Says Aveda Is Concerned About a Different 'Green,'" *Star Tribune* (Minneapolis), June 29, 1993, p. 3B.

Kafka, Peter, "Will Horst Wash Aveda Out of His Hair?" July 12–18, 1996, *Minneapolis/St. Paul CityBusiness*, pp. 1, 10.

Kahn, Aron, and Georgann Koelln, "Estée Lauder Buys Minnesota-Grown Aveda," *St. Paul Pioneer Press*, November 20, 1997. p. 1A.

Koelln, Georgann, "Horst World," *St. Paul Pioneer Press*, June 24, 1990, pp. 1E, 6E.

Larson, Soren, "Lauder in Deal for Aveda," *Women's Wear Daily*, November 20, 1997, p. 4.

Maler, Kevin, "Horst Plans to Sell Salons to Firm Insider," *Minneapolis/St. Paul CityBusiness*, September 18, 1992, pp. 1, 27.

Marcotty, Josephine, "Alternative Therapies," *Star Tribune* (Minneapolis), October 17, 1995, p. 1D.

"Recycling Makes It to the Runway," *Star Tribune* (Minneapolis), October 21, 1992, p. 3E.

Souder, William, "The Man Who Fell to Earth," *Minneapolis/St. Paul*, November 1996, pp. 56–61, 130–39.

Nelson, Connie, "Horst's Style of Business Earns Him Raves As an Entrepreneur," *Star Tribune* (Minneapolis), August 7, 1989, p. 2D.

Wieffering, Eric J., "New Age, Old Story," *Corporate Report Minnesota*, April 1991, pp. 27–32.

Wilner, Richard, "Estée Lauder Buys Aveda Hair Products for $300 Million," *New York Post*, November 20, 1997.

—Kathleen Peippo

Aviacionny Nauchno-Tehnicheskii Komplex im. A.N. Tupoleva (Tupolev Aviation and Scientific Technical Complex)

17 Naberezhnaya Akademika Tupoleva
Moscow
Russia
111250
7 (095) 267 25 08
Fax: 7 (095) 261 71 41

State-Owned Company
Incorporated: 1933 as A.N. Tupolev Experimental
Design Bureau
Employees: 15,000
SICs: 3721 Aircraft

Although it has designed everything from sleighs to spacecraft, Aviacionny Nauchno-Tehnicheskii Komplex im. A.N. Tupoleva (ANTK Tupolev, or Tupolev) is best known for its large airplanes. If you add ''bigger'' to ''higher, faster, farther,'' you have a good operating philosophy for the company. Tupolev aircraft also have a reputation for durability. According to aviation writer Bill Gunston, ''The name Tupolev. . . deserves to be the *most* famous in the whole history of aircraft design.''

Birth of Flight

Andrei Nikolayevich Tupolev grew up in a well-educated, liberal family of modest means that worked a small farm in the Tver region of Russia. He discovered a passion for physics at an early age and was introduced to gliders at the illustrious Imperial Moscow Higher Technical Institute, where he began studying under the pioneer Russian aviator N. Zhukovsky. Tupolev built a wind tunnel for the school and assembled a detailed model airplane, earning his place as Zhukovsky's protegé.

In 1911, Tupolev was expelled from the Technical Institute for his part in organizing student strikes. He spent the following year working the family farm in Pustomazovo and diligently educating himself. Upon returning to Moscow, Tupolev busied himself not only with formal studies but with various aviation projects, such as studying hydroplanes (the subject of his academic thesis) for the Duks Factory. In 1916, his mentor invited him to join the country's first design bureau. He would retain Zhukovsky's emphasis on heavy aviation—large bombers and transports—throughout his life.

After the October Revolution in 1917, Tupolev and most of his colleagues threw their lots with the ''new forces'' of Soviet power. World War I proved the military power of aviation and these scientists encouraged the Soviet government to establish the Central Aero-Hydronamics Institute (TsAGI). A bout with tuberculosis took Tupolev out of commission in 1919.

Tupolev's first design, a sleek monoplane with wings free of World War I-style braces and struts, was constructed mostly of an aluminum alloy reverse-engineered from German airframes. Dubbed the ANT-1 after Tupolev's initials, the ''Little Bird'' (its motor was only rated at 35 horsepower) first flew in 1922. A second design, the 100-horsepower ANT-2, followed in 1924. Although only five of the latter were built, the small passenger plane confirmed the viability of all-metal construction.

The Air Force then commissioned the ANT-3 (or R-3) reconnaissance plane. Tupolev made it a biplane to give it the required maneuverability. The ANT-4 and ANT-5 monoplane bombers compared favorably with the most modern foreign designs, further cementing Tupolev's reputation. In addition, several of his associates, including Pavel Sukhoi, would eventually become esteemed general designers in their own right.

In the 1930s, Tupolev built the world's largest plane, the monstrous, eight-engined ANT-20 passenger aircraft. Other notable creations included the ANT-25, which set a world distance record, and the ANT-40 "SB" light bomber, which was widely used by the Red Air force at the outbreak of World War II. The TsAGI was reorganized in 1933 and a section designated the A.N. Tupolev Experimental Design Bureau. Tupolev also served as chief engineer of the Aviation Industry Administration, working to build large aircraft factories.

Reign of Terror

In spite of his stature (including winning the Order of Lenin, the U.S.S.R.'s top honor), Tupolev could not escape Stalin's paranoia and in October 1937 he was imprisoned for allegedly supplying Germany with the design for the Messerschmitt Bf 110 fighter-bomber. He was allowed to resume his design work behind bars after about a year, for a period returning to his former offices, now themselves converted to a prison. Among his new comrades: Sergei Korolyev, who would lead the Soviet space program. The incarcerated team completed the Tu-2, a fast, capable, light bomber, which, like the Bf 110, sported twin engines and twin tails. Tupolev was freed in July 1941, but continued to work with the "special prison workshop," which in the fall was transported to Siberia to avoid advancing German forces.

Though he would describe Tupolev as energetic and affable in his memoirs, another, younger aircraft designer, Aleksandr Yakovlev, criticized the poor performance of Tupolev's planes against Messerschmitt fighters in the Spanish Civil War. Yakovlev was Stalin's aviation advisor and also questioned Tupolev's "conscientiousness," according to a *samizdat* account of the period. Yakovlev's interventions consistently frustrated Tupolev's efforts to build winning designs.

Cold War

Stalin had long desired a long-range strategic bomber, and the Japanese theater gave the Soviet Union a chance to develop one. Three American B-29 Superfortresses, short of fuel, made emergency landings in Vladivostok in 1944 and Tupolev was ordered to reverse engineer a copy (known as the Tu-4) of the complex, state-of-the-art aircraft.

After World War II, Tupolev's firm constructed a handful of long-range bombers incorporating technology originally gleaned from the Boeing B-29. The highly successful Tu-16, code-named "Badger" by NATO forces, incorporated swept wings and jet engines. The Tu-95 "Bear" used the ingenious configuration of contra-facing propellers mounted on jet turbines to achieve both high speed and intercontinental range. It reportedly stayed in production longer than any other aircraft except for the Piper Cherokee. Its passenger version, the Tu-114, became a mainstay of the Aeroflot fleet. One of them flew Nikolai Khrushchev to the United States in 1956.

Conflicts in Southeast Asia spurred the development of ground attack aircraft and supersonic fighters and bombers. Aeroflot's requirements produced the Tu-124, ubiquitous throughout the 1960s, and its successor, the three-engined Tu-154, introduced in 1968. New versions of the latter were continually developed, and the plane continued to serve with the

airlines of various republics well after the breakup of the Soviet Union. It was also exported to 17 foreign countries.

The Tu-144 supersonic transport (SST) was created to compete with the Anglo-French Concorde and the American Boeing SST projects, and it edged out the others to the make the first SST flight on December 31, 1968. It did not reach production until a few years later. The aircraft's fortunes fell due to a lethal accident at the 1973 Paris Air Show and dwindling interest from Aeroflot. This was Andrei Tupolev's last program; he died in December 1972. His son, Alexei, who had been placed in charge of the Tu-144, was appointed to lead the design bureau a few years later.

Department "R" was created in the early 1970s in order to develop cruise missiles. The Tupolev Design Bureau also worked on high speed bombers with variable sweep wings in the 1970s. The pinnacle of this was the Tu-160, the most powerful military aircraft ever and reportedly the most aerodynamically efficient supersonic aircraft. The long-range, high payload bomber was similar in mission and appearance to the American B-1, which was canceled by President Carter in 1977.

The company continued to innovate in the 1980s, researching low-pollution cryogenic fuels such as liquefied natural gas, methane, and hydrogen. This work continued in the 1990s in collaboration with Daimler-Benz Aerospace.

A New World Order

The Tupolev Design Bureau was reorganized as an "Aviation Scientific-Technical Complex" (ANTK) in 1990. Defense orders fell dramatically after the breakup of the Soviet Union, quite a blow for the company, which had previously spent 85 percent of its time working on bombers. Tupolev subsequently focused more attention on the civil marketplace. Development projects ranged from cropdusters to business jets to a Tupolev mainstay, commercial transports.

A more practical design, the Tu-204, was introduced to replace the previous generation of Soviet airliners. It also provided the hope of a salable product in the Western market. Like most other former Soviet airframe makers, Tupolev offered the option of ordering these planes with more efficient Western engines as well as avionics. The Aerostar (then known as Aviastar) plant in Ul'yanovsk and London investment banker Robert Fleming teamed with Tupolev to form the Bravia (British-Russian aviation) marketing alliance.

The Tu-204, like fellow Russian firm Ilyushin's Il-96 program, was plagued with delays. Nevertheless, the project eventually began to attract supporters. Airbus Industrie agreed in August 1997 to help the Tu-204 obtain European Joint Aviation Authorities (JAA) certification. A leasing company, Sirocco Aerospace, ordered 30 of the airliners, worth about $38 million each, equipped with Rolls-Royce engines. Kato Group, an Egyptian firm, made an initial order of 13 similarly equipped models. Tupolev also tapped General Electric Aircraft Engines for a new line of smaller, regional airliners and business jets. Financing proved a final, considerable hurdle in delivering these planes.

Aeroflot desperately needed new airliners to update its massive, aging fleet. However, it ordered 10 Boeing 737s in September 1996, a blow to Russian aerospace industry morale. This provided yet another stimulus for workers, who often went months without being paid, to strike. At the time, only one in 20 jets bought by Russian airlines were Russian-made. The prices of the planes rose sharply after 1990. In 1994, a Tu-154 was priced at $3 million; however, Western jets, even used ones, were so much more fuel-efficient that they proved far more profitable to operate over time.

Valentin Klimov became general director in 1992, four years after Andrei Tupolev's son Andrei was named to the post. He was succeeded by Igor Shevchuk.

Tupolev 2000

Although ANTK Tupolev faced grave financial challenges, its proven engineering expertise earned it a unique role in shaping the future of aviation. Several ambitious projects were underway at the end of the century: a huge, 1,000-passenger capacity flying wing powered by six engines with 12 counter-rotating propellers (similar to those on the Tu-95 "Bear" bomber); a giant supersonic airliner; the Tu-2000 research vehicle, designed to fly at the edge of the atmosphere.

One of the Tu-144 supersonic transports was used by NASA in the mid-1990s to study high speed flight. In 1996, Boeing, McDonnell Douglas, Rockwell, Pratt and Whitney, and General Electric co-sponsored a series of flights using the Tu-144 to develop technologies for the next generation of supersonic airliners.

In June 1997, production subsidiaries, the joint stock companies Aviakor and Aviastar, proposed merging with Tupolev ANTK to form Tupolev Corporation. Several other design firms, such as Ilyushin and Yakovlev, contemplated forming similar structures.

The company's most advanced plans may seem futuristic, but Tupolev has designed the future of aviation before. Russia's oldest design bureau, the firm celebrated 75 years of design in October 1997.

Further Reading

Banks, Howard, "Is That a Tupolev on Boeing's Horizon?" *Forbes,* March 18, 1991, pp. 38–40.

Covault, Craig, "Aerospatiale Eyes Tupolev Production," *Aviation Week and Space Technology,* September 6, 1993, p. 59.

Duffy, Paul, "Design and Production: Finding Common Ground," *Air Transport World,* August 1993, pp. 81–84.

"Eastward, Ho!" *Air Transport World,* August 1991, pp. 18–21.

Godsmark, Chris, "Rolls-Royce Wins Pounds 290M Russian Engine Order," *Independent,* August 30, 1996.

Gunston, Bill, *Tupolev Aircraft Since 1922,* Annapolis: Naval Institute Press, 1995.

Kerber, L. L. [A. Sharagin, pseud.], *Stalin's Aviation Gulag: A Memoir of Andrei Tupolev and the Purge Era,* edited by Von Hardesty, Washington and London: Smithsonian Institution Press, 1996. Originally published as *Tupolevskaya sharaga* (Tupolev's special prison workshop), Druck: Possev-Verlag, V. Gorachek KG, Frankfurt/M., 1971.

——, *Tu—Chelovek i samolet* (Tupolev: the man and the aircraft), Moscow: Sovetskaya Rossiya, 1973.

Melloan, George, "Aerospace Hybrids Tackle a Shrinking Market," *Wall Street Journal,* June 21, 1993, p. A11.

Novichkov, Nicolay, "Russia's Tu-144LL Readied for Supersonic Research," *Aviation Week and Space Technology,* March 25, 1996, pp. 32–33.

Rigmant, Vladimir, "Pod znakami "ANT" i "Tu" (Under the names of ANT- and Tu-), *75-letiyu Kb i.m. Tupoleva posvyashchaetsya* (Dedicated to the 75th anniversary of the Tupolev Design Bureau), 1997.

Rybak, Boris, and Jeffrey M. Lenorovitz, "Most NIS Transports Past Service Life," *Aviation Week and Space Technology,* August 1, 1994, pp. 31–32.

Smith, Bruce A., "Funding Key Challenge for CIS Joint Ventures," *Aviation Week and Space Technology,* August 14, 1995.

Taverna, Michael A., "Civil Aircraft Outlook Improving in Russia," *Aviation Week and Space Technology,* September 8, 1997, pp. 54–55.

Verchere, Ian, and Peter Conradi, "Fund Halts Financing for Anglo-Russian Jet," *The European,* November 25, 1994, p. 17.

Williams, Carol, "Clipped Wings: Aeroflot's Order for 10 Boeing Planes Sent a Message to Russia's Aerospace Companies: Modernize or Else," *Los Angeles Times,* November 10, 1996.

—Frederick C. Ingram

Baccarat

20 rue Cristalleries
54120 Baccarat
France
(33) 3.83.76.60.06
Fax: (33) 3.83.76.60.04
Web site: http://www.baccarat.fr

Public Company
Incorporated: 1824 as Société de Cristallerie de
     Vonêche-Baccarat
Employees: 1,870
Sales: FFr 544.3 million (US$100 million) (1996)
Stock Exchanges: Paris
SICs: 3231 Products of Purchased Glass; 3229 Pressed &
     Blown Glass, Not Elsewhere Classified; 5999
     Miscellaneous Retail Stores, Not Elsewhere
     Classified; 3911 Jewelry & Precious Metal

The name Baccarat has become nearly synonymous with luxury. For more than 200 years, this company has produced and distributed some of the world's finest luxury crystal. With a catalog spanning some 2,500 items, Baccarat produces full-lead crystal tableware, jewelry, lamps, vases, carafes, decorative pieces, and home fittings, sold through its own retail stores and through third-party retailers. Among crystal manufacturers, Baccarat has pioneered the incorporation of computer-aided design and manufacturing techniques, as well as modernized production systems, without relinquishing its tradition of hand-crafted quality. Baccarat's artisans, who undergo an eight-year apprenticeship, have won numerous awards throughout the company's history. Beyond luxury goods, Baccarat also produces glass for mining lamps for the coal mining operations of Charbonnages de France.

Baccarat operates retail stores in Paris, New York, and Tokyo. In the mid-1990s, the company has begun expanding its retail activities, including opening new outlets—such as its minority position in a partnership with a private investor operat-ing a Baccarat store in Lyon, France—with the goal of doubling its revenues by the year 2000. The company has also created a new subsidiary, Baccarat Pacific Limited, in Hong Kong, with the intent of entering the growing Chinese market. This subsid-iary has opened the first Baccarat retail outlet in Peking.

The recession in the United States in the early 1990s, the lengthy financial crisis in Europe, and continuing economic troubles in Japan and other Asian countries in the late 1990s have combined to cripple the demand for luxury goods and to slow Baccarat's growth; however, after a number of years of losses, the company, led by its resurgent U.S. subsidiary, has returned to profitability, posting earnings of FFr 11.2 million on revenues of FFr 544.3 million in 1996. In that year, the com-pany added 400 new products to its catalog. Vases and decora-tive pieces represented some 45 percent of Baccarat's sales; glasses and carafes added another 33 percent of sales, while lamps and furnishings provided 12 percent of the company's revenues. Since the mid-1990s, the Louvre group has been Baccarat's majority shareholder.

200 Years of Tradition

While much of Europe, including France, was engaged in the Seven Years War (1759–63), chiefly for control of the North American territories, the costs of the war were being felt closer to home. France's involvement in a succession of wars under the reign of Louis XV had left its economy devastated; by the middle of the Seven Years War, joblessness was rampant, particularly among the woodcutters and other craftsmen in the forest-rich northeast region centered around the city of Metz and bordered by the Meuse and Moselle rivers. At the same time, a number of notables had become concerned about the lack of glassworks in France, and especially French artisans capable of producing decorative crystal glass that could rival that of Bohemia—then, even more so than Venice and England, the chief center of fine crystal in Europe.

At that time in France, the existing glassworks operations were the province of the nobility; yet, while these operations attempted to mimic the qualities of Bohemia glass, the true Bohemian product remained the preferred choice for glass tableware, windows, and objects. By the end of the Seven Years War, however, the bishop of Metz, Monseigneur de Montmorency-Laval, had become convinced that his region, with the beech forests (for potash) and plentiful pure quartz of the Vosges mountains, as well as a ready supply of artisans, contained the raw materials needed to create a glassworks to rival the Bohemian, Venetian, and English masters. Apart from the need to provide work for the region, the bishop of Metz was also motivated by a degree of protectionism—with the French treasury depleted by the Seven Years War, the importation of Bohemian crystal, and the resulting exportation of French money, had become a burden to France. Montmorency-Laval petitioned Louis XV on behalf of Antoine Renaut to found a glassworks. Renaut's works would become the first glassworks in France operated by a non-nobleman.

The Verrerie Renaut et Cie was created in 1764 in the small village of Baccarat. Providing housing for some seventy artisans and their families, the factory restricted its initial production to flat glass for windowpanes and mirrors, and to the production of white glass à la Bohême. While the Renaut works provided a French alternative to the Bohemian imports, another famed French glassworks, Saint-Louis (founded in 1767 and still in existence in the 1990s), was bringing the production of a relatively new type of glass, lead crystal, to France. Modern lead crystal originated in England toward the end of the 17th century. The depletion of the English forests—in part to feed the furnaces of the kingdom's glassworks—had led to a ban, in 1615, on the use of wood as fuel. Coal was substituted; however, coal produced lower temperatures than wood, lengthening the fusion of the materials used to create crystal glass. This problem found a solution in the 1670s, when George Ravenscroft discovered that, by replacing the calcium oxide traditionally used in glassmaking, as well as some of the silica (sand) derived from quartz, with lead oxide, the resulting glass not only melted at lower temperatures, but also proved easier to cut and engrave, while producing a clearer, more luminous finished product. While 20th-century analysis would lead to the discovery that lead oxide had been an ingredient in glass pieces from the ancient Babylonian and later Chinese Han Dynasty eras, Ravenscroft continued to be credited with the inauguration of the modern lead crystal era.

Lead crystal only gradually imposed itself on the glass market over the next century. The glassworks at Baccarat continued to cling to the production of windowpanes and Bohemian-style white glass—responding to the need for the former and the consumer preference for the latter. By the beginning of the 19th century, however, lead crystal had supplanted the crystal glass of Bohemia and Venice as the glass of choice. At the same time, the French Revolution, the rise of Napoleon, and a fresh series of wars, combined not only to ruin the Bohemian glass production abroad, but to threaten the existence of the Baccarat glassworks. In 1816, the factory was bought by Aime-Gabriel D'Artigues. Formerly director of the Saint-Louis glassworks (which had already begun lead crystal production in the early 1780s), D'Artigues had left France for Belgium, then under French rule, operating the Cristallerie de Vonêche. With Napoleon Bonaparte's defeat at the Battle of Waterloo in 1815, and the resulting Belgium independence, D'Artigues was forced to return to France. Installing his glassworks at the Baccarat plant, which was renamed the Verrerie de Vonêche à Baccarat, D'Artigues converted production entirely to lead crystal. The Baccarat glassworks began crafting crystal tableware and *objets d'art*, while adding a level of design that would bring the company to international fame. Already in 1819, the company's clientele featured among the European royalty.

The Baccarat glassworks would achieve a reputation not only for its design excellence, but also for its continued refinement of lead crystal materials and techniques. Under D'Artigues, the glassworks had rapidly caught up with the level of quality produced by the prominent lead crystal makers in England, as well as by Saint-Louis. After D'Artigues sold the glassworks to his partners, the factory, especially under Pierre Antoine Godard, began a pursuit of "perfection" that would raise Baccarat to the peak of the craft. The glassworks name was changed to Société de Cristallerie de Vonêche-Baccarat in 1824; soon after, the name was changed again, to Compagnie des Cristalleries de Baccarat—which the company would keep until 1994, until the name was changed simply to Baccarat. Over the previous 150 years, the name Baccarat had become synonymous with crystal.

19th-Century Success

By the middle of the 19th century, Baccarat was already one of the most celebrated names in lead crystal. This success was due to several factors, but rooted in the Godard's desire to achieve "perfection." The company ceased its other glass-making activities to focus solely on lead crystal—so-called premium or full lead crystal, defined as containing a lead content of not less than 24 percent. Baccarat also set out to improve the quality of its crystal, starting with the raw materials. Looking beyond its own region, the company began importing the highest grade sand, red lead, and potash, from as far away as the United States. The company was also quick to adopt new techniques and tools, including the use of "decalcomania" (the use of decals) and impression techniques, and, later in the 19th century, photoengraving, mechanical cutting, and improved furnace designs.

If in the early years of the century, Baccarat adopted easily a number of classic crystal and glass types—among the company's first successes were its opaline glassware, a translucent glass meant to mimic the look of opal; around the same time, Baccarat also began producing agate glass, a specialty of the Bohemian glass-makers—the company also proved adept at creating the fashion, rather than merely following others in the craft. In the late 1830s, Baccarat pioneered the use of colored glass, adding various materials to its crystal formula to achieve layered color effects. In the 1840s, Baccarat introduced a new crystal, dubbed "dichroic crystal"—the addition of uranium oxide gave this glass the appearance of changing colors, depending on the light. The company also popularized another new name, a green-colored, opaque crystal, called chrysoprase, after the variety of quartz.

Another key element of Baccarat's success was its innovative relationship with its employees. The company set rigorous standards for its employees, including an eight-year apprenticeship. But from the beginning, Baccarat proved a model of social enlightenment. Already at the glassworks's formation, the company's artisans and workers were given housing within the factory's confines. In 1827, Baccarat began adding benefits far in advance for its era, including medical assistance for its employees and opening a school for its employees' children. In 1830, the company began offering pensions to certain of its workers; the following year, employees were offered a savings account, with a five percent annual interest rate. In 1850, Baccarat established a retirement fund for all of its employees, paying in one percent of workers' annual salaries. A second retirement fund was established at the end of that decade for the company's engravers. In 1890, lastly, the company established an unemployment benefits fund for its employees.

Yet, while its employees and its technical improvements formed the raw materials of Baccarat's work, its excellence in design would provide the company its fame. Among the company's early design triumphs was its Harcourt design of table service, first produced in 1828. The Harcourt design would prove lastingly popular—a set of the service produced in 1841 continues to be used by the President of France during official receptions. Another glass design, the St. Remy tulip-shaped glass, became a mainstay of champagne drinkers. The company's designs quickly became the favorites of European royalty. In the mid-century, Baccarat began branching out beyond tableware. In 1846, the company began producing paperweights, starting with the Italian-inspired millefiori style, but quickly extending the range to include sulfide paperweights featuring real flowers, insects, and other objects enclosed in glass. Toward the end of the century, Baccarat paperweights often featured cameo portraits of its famous customers.

Baccarat also began producing vases, urns, and other objects. But by the mid-19th century, the company was working on a larger scale as well, producing elaborate interior furnishings, such as chandeliers, candelabra, oil lamps, and large vases. Two Baccarat triumphs were unveiled at the 1855 Paris World's Fair: a 17-foot-tall candelabra and a 23-foot-tall crystal water fountain.

The Modern Years

While the 20th century brought mass-production techniques to manufacturing, Baccarat maintained its tradition of hand-crafted elegance and excellence. The dwindling numbers of nobility were replaced by a new breed of customers, including wealthy industrialists and heads of state. The rise of the United States as a world economic power was recognized by the company when it opened its first subsidiary, Baccarat and Porthault Inc., operating a Baccarat store in Manhattan in 1949. Another of the company's design triumphs followed three year later, when French artist Georges Chevalier created the famed Stag's Head design.

In the 1960s, Baccarat began modernizing its factory. A new furnace was installed in 1962. In 1967, the company installed the industry's first continuous-melting tank, which enabled Baccarat to create larger, single-piece crystal designs. One such design was the company's 200 pound "De la Terre à la Lune," a representation of the earth and moon displayed at the Lisbon fair in 1972; this piece was the largest crystal object ever made. On the financial front, Baccarat went public in 1978, reserving 11 percent of the company's shares for its employees.

The economic boom—and the high-flying atmosphere—of the 1980s led Baccarat to further expansion. In 1984, the company created another subsidiary, Baccarat Pacific KK, to tap the surging Japanese market. The following year, Baccarat launched a German subsidiary, based in Frankfurt. In that same year, Baccarat added computer-aided manufacturing and design techniques to its production process. The bulk of the company's work, however, remained the province of its craftsmen.

If Baccarat had ridden high on the 1980s, the start of the 1990s would prove more sobering. The reunification of Germany in 1989 led to an extended economic crisis in that country, forcing Baccarat to end its German subsidiary's operations. The war in the Persian Gulf, and the economic recession of the early 1990s would soon lead to Baccarat's own financial crisis. From revenues of FFr 488 million in 1991, the company's sales slipped to FFr 437 million the following year. The company was also struggling to maintain profitability, aided principally by the booming economies among the Asian countries. Despite the United States' recovery from the recession, the luxury mood of the previous decade had become tempered. Falling sales in the United States led the company to post a loss in 1994 of FFr 28 million on revenues of FFr 473 million.

Sales rebounded in 1995, however, limiting the company's losses to just FFr 1 million on sales of FFr 524 million. Baccarat was forced to reorganize, a move which included the laying off of a number of its workers. The reorganization proved successful in bringing the company back into profitability in 1996, when, on sales of FFr 544 million, the company posted a net profit of FFr 11.2 million. In that year, the company moved to expand its Asian presence, forming a Hong Kong-based subsidiary, Baccarat Pacific Limited. The new subsidiary's chief market was China; in that year the company opened a new magazine, in the shopping area of a Peking Hotel.

Baccarat, led by CEO Marc Leclerc, continued to maintain its tradition of hand-crafted excellence, while eyeing a doubling of its sales for the year 2000—an optimistic forecast given the free-falling economies of many Asian countries, including Japan, in 1997. Yet the slow European recovery from its extended economic crisis, and the booming U.S. economy of the late 1990s, offered at least short-term hope. For the long-term, Baccarat remained at the forefront of its craft and a name synonymous with luxury and elegance.

Principal Subsidiaries

Baccarat Inc. (U.S.); Baccarat Pacific KK (Japan); Baccarat Pacific Limited (Hong Kong).

Further Reading

Baccarat, Compagnie des Cristalleries de Baccarat: Baccarat, France, 1987.

"Baccarat: déficit chronique," *Offrir Revue des Industries d'Art*, June 1995, p. 29.

Barois, Roland, and Jacques Mouclier, *Le Cristal*, Armand Colin: Paris, 1994.

Boyer, Dean, "Baccarat," *Encyclopedia of Consumer Brands,* vol. 3, Detroit: St. James Press, 1994, pp. 25–26.

Moritz, Yves, and Pierre Warnia, "Baccarat: s'adapter à la transformation du marché," *Offrir Revue des Industries d'Art*, May 1996, p. 31.

—M. L. Cohen

Bechtel Group, Inc.

50 Beale Street
San Francisco, California 94105-1895
U.S.A.
(415) 768-1234
Fax: (415) 768-9038
Web site: http://www.bechtel.com

Private Company
Incorporated: 1925 as W. A. Bechtel Company
Employees: 29,000
Operating Revenues: $11.33 billion (1997)
SICs: 1542 General Contractors-Non-Residential
   Buildings; 1611 Highway & Street Construction,
   Except Elevated Highway; 1622 Bridge, Tunnel &
   Elevated Highway Construction; 1623 Water, Sewer,
   Power Line, Pipeline & Communications
   Construction; 1629 Heavy Construction, Not
   Elsewhere Classified; 8711 Engineering Services;
   8713 Surveying Services; 8741 Management Services;
   8742 Management Consulting Services; 8999
   Services, Not Elsewhere Classified

Bechtel Group, Inc. is one of the leading construction and engineering firms in the world, building everything from roads and bridges, to dams and pipelines, to power plants, and even entire cities. One industry analyst has noted that Bechtel's more than 19,000 projects over the course of a century have reshaped more of the earth's landscape than virtually any other human effort in history. As a private and predominantly family-controlled company, Bechtel has long been averse to publicity, an attitude which has sometimes been problematic in light of the firm's numerous links to prominent U.S. government officials.

Early History

In 1884 when he was 12 years old, Warren A. Bechtel moved with his family from a farm in Illinois to the frontier area of Peabody, Kansas. After graduating from high school, Bechtel ventured unsuccessfully into a music career. When "The Ladies Band" failed, Bechtel's father wired return fare to the stranded slide trombonist. The disappointed musician went back to work on the family farm. Some years later, poor farming conditions left Bechtel virtually without any possessions other than a team of 14 healthy mules. When the Chicago Rock Island and Peoria Railway Company pushed westward in 1889, Bechtel gathered up his mule team and worked his way across the continent grading railbed for frontier train lines.

Bechtel eventually sold his mule team, but he continued working for the rail industry in a variety of manual-labor positions. He managed to accumulate a small fortune and formed the W. A. Bechtel Company with his three sons and his brother. The young company began many new ventures, including construction of the Northern California Highway and the Bowman Dam, which was at the time the second largest rock-fill dam in the world. By the time the company was incorporated in 1925, Bechtel was the largest construction firm in the western United States. When a six-company consortium received the $49 million contract for construction of the Hoover Dam, Warren Bechtel became president of the group. Work on the enormous dam lasted from 1931 to 1936. Warren Bechtel did not live to see the project completed, however; he died suddenly in 1933 at age 61.

Stephen Bechtel, one of the founder's three sons, took over the presidency in 1935. He had previously been a vice-president. The young executive directed the company to new financial and industrial heights, supervising completion of the Hoover Dam as well as work on the San Francisco-Oakland Bay Bridge, a hydrogeneration plant, and the Mene Grande Pipeline in Venezuela.

As the United States entered World War II, an already established partnership between Bechtel and John McCone, a steel salesman, grew to encompass a syndicate of companies participating in the construction of large shipyards. McCone and Stephen Bechtel had met at the University of California and had become business associates during work on the Hoover Dam. As an employee of Consolidated Steel, McCone secured the supply of necessary support structures for Bechtel. The business association proved so successful that after the dam was finished the former classmates formed a partnership. By 1940 McCone secured contracts for the partnership to build ships and tankers, and to modify aircraft for the war effort. Later the partnership developed the syndicate that built the Calship and Marinship yards in California, as well as a total of 500 ships. When McCone took a postwar position as undersecretary of defense, it was revealed that the directors of Calship earned 440 times their initial investment of $100,000—a profit of $44 million.

Pipeline and Nuclear Power Plants Highlighted Postwar Years

Bechtel's operations continued to expand in the years following the war. The 1,100-mile Trans-Arabian Pipeline, completed in 1947, is regarded as the first major structure of its kind. The South Korean Power Project effectively doubled that nation's energy output. In 1951 the pioneering company developed the first electricity-generating nuclear power plant, in Arco, Idaho. Later the company built a nuclear fuel reprocessing plant there. By the end of the 1950s Bechtel had construction and engineering projects on six continents and was ready to take advantage of the emerging market for nuclear power.

In 1960 Stephen Bechtel became chairman of the board, and Stephen, Jr., a Stanford Business School graduate and grandson of the founder, stepped into the chief executive officer post. A 1978 estimate suggested that the two men controlled at least 40 percent of company stock. In the likely event of the younger Stephen one day inheriting his father's wealth, it was estimated that he could become the richest person in the United States. The other 60 percent of Bechtel stock was held by some 60 top executives who agreed to sell back their shares when they left the company or died.

With a new generation of leadership in place, the company sought to gain hegemony in the emerging nuclear power industry. In 1960 Bechtel completed the nation's first commercial nuclear station in Dresden, Illinois. Two years later the company built Canada's first nuclear power plant. Construction in foreign markets began to increase almost immediately thereafter. Although the nuclear power industry subsequently ran into difficulties such as cost overruns, questions about environmental safety, and stiff regulatory measures, Bechtel continued to promote nuclear energy as a necessary option to conventionally generated power.

Bechtel's construction projects in the 1960s and 1970s included the San Francisco Bay Area Rapid Transit system (BART), the subway transit system in-and-around Washington, D.C., a slurry pipe in Brazil, and an innovative tar sands project in Alberta, Canada.

In the 1970s two former Nixon cabinet members took executive posts at the company. Later both men, George Shultz and Caspar Weinberger, would leave Bechtel for positions in the Reagan Administration. Bechtel has actively cultivated its ties to the federal government, and employs several former high officials—a fact that has led to criticism of the company.

Plan to Build Jubail Industrial City Unveiled in 1976

In 1976 Bechtel unveiled plans for its Jubail Project, the largest undertaking ever attempted by a construction company. The company spent more than 20 years building a futuristic industrial community on the site of an ancient fishing village on Saudi Arabia's Persian Gulf coast, at an estimated cost of more than $40 billion. The new city became the home of Saudi Arabia's integrated petrochemical industry. A 1973 meeting between Stephen Bechtel, Jr., and King Faisal was the catalyst for the project, which hauled off about 370 million cubic meters of sand and built a modern city complete with a five-million-gallon desalination plant, a national airport, a hospital and clinics, modular homes, mosques, a sex-segregated swimming marina, and a number of factories.

Due in part to a broad-based political effort to halt the use of nuclear power in the United States, in the 1970s and early 1980s Bechtel turned away from nuclear energy to less controversial markets. Nevertheless, problems in the nuclear power industry persisted. A 1978 lawsuit concerning malfunctions at the Palisades nuclear generator in Michigan cost Bechtel $14 million in settlement fees. In addition, a 1984 *Mother Jones* magazine article suggested that the company's use of irregular payments in attempting to secure nuclear power contracts in South Korea may have violated the 1977 Foreign Corrupt Practices Act. The article also argued that certain Bechtel executives, who later became top U.S. government officials, may have known the payments warranted investigations by the Federal Bureau of Investigation and the Justice Department but said nothing. The company issued a point-by-point rebuttal of the article to its employees.

The company was the subject of negative publicity several times during the 1970s. A 1972 class-action suit alleging sex discrimination at Bechtel was settled out of court for $1.4 million. A bribery scheme involving construction of a New Jersey pipeline led to convictions for four Bechtel employees. Further unwanted publicity arose from the revelation that Bechtel had installed a 420-ton nuclear-reactor vessel backward. Finally, in 1975 the U.S. Justice Department sued Bechtel for allegedly participating in an Arab boycott of Israel, a charge the company denied.

The decade was also a turning point for Bechtel's traditional business in construction and engineering. Prompted by increased government regulation and changing economic conditions, Bechtel embarked on a new program of financing and operational services. Soon after they began, the new divisions contributed 66 percent of total revenues. To defray increasing construction costs, Bechtel began securing financing for its customers, in some cases even putting up the company's own money. Bechtel's diversification program also included acquiring a 15 percent share of the Peabody Coal Company and a major interest in the prestigious Dillon, Read & Company investment firm. By 1982 over half of the company's business involved overseas markets.

During the Reagan presidency Bechtel's ties to the federal government increased considerably. Shultz left the presidency of Bechtel Corporation to become Secretary of State after Alexander Haig, former chairman of United Technologies, left the post in 1982. Weinberger, previously the Bechtel general counsel, was Secretary of Defense for the first seven years of the Reagan administration. By 1984 Bechtel's connections in Washington also included CIA director William Casey, Middle East special envoy Philip Habib, and former CIA director Richard Helms, all of whom had worked for the company either as employees or as consultants in the past.

Lack of Big Projects in the Mid-1980s

By the mid-1980s, Stephen Bechtel, Jr., was chairman of the board. Alden P. Yates, who was Bechtel's president, led the firm into numerous projects previously regarded as too small for Bechtel. These included finishing jobs abandoned by the company's competitors and actively seeking contracts, even those as small as $2 million. Furthermore, remodification and modernization efforts at existing plants offset the lack of contracts for new construction. Finally, the company's operating services division kept skilled experts at work in their fields, mostly in ongoing maintenance of existing facilities.

Despite measures to locate new sources of income, Bechtel had to cut its workforce in 1984 to 35,000 (from 45,000 in 1982). The smaller projects that the company had been forced to take on were no replacement for the megaprojects of the past. The dearth of large projects stemmed from multiple developments. The U.S. nuclear power industry was virtually at a standstill in terms of new plants. In the Middle East, a traditional Bechtel area of strength, big construction projects were no longer the norm, thanks largely to significantly lower oil prices; in fact, the company suffered a severe blow when Saudi Arabia suddenly halted construction on a $1 billion refinery being built by Bechtel in Qasim. Bechtel and other American engineering companies also faced increasing competition from European, South Korean, and Japanese construction firms. U.S. companies saw their share of the world's large construction projects fall from 50 percent in 1980 to 25 percent in 1988.

Bechtel's revenue fell from $14.13 billion in 1983 to $6.55 billion in 1986. New orders, meanwhile, dropped from $13.05 billion to $3.54 billion over the same period. One of the company's responses to this crisis was to reorganize into a more decentralized structure. In July 1986, its two main operating companies, Bechtel Power Corp. and Bechtel Inc., were restructured into five new units: Bechtel Western Power Corp., Bechtel Eastern Power Corp., Bechtel Civil Inc. (civil engineering projects), Bechtel Inc. (petroleum and mineral activities), and Bechtel National Inc. (advanced technical and research areas). At the same time, a separate Bechtel Inc. subsidiary was created, called Bechtel Ltd., which took over the company's British-based activities. These included one of the company's major projects of the later 1980s, the construction of the Channel Tunnel connecting England and France that began in 1986.

By early 1988 continuing difficulties forced the company to further slash its workforce to less than 18,000. That year Bechtel was once again the subject of negative news coverage after it was revealed that in 1984 and 1985 the company had been involved in an abortive effort to build a $1 billion pipeline from oil fields in northern Iraq through Jordan to the Red Sea. Although the pipeline project had been scuttled when the Iraqi government began construction on an alternative pipeline, the special prosecutor investigating Attorney General Edwin Meese looked into an allegation that individuals acting on Bechtel's behalf tried to bribe Israeli officials into promising not to bomb the pipeline. Although no charges were ever filed against Bechtel in the case, this was another instance of unwelcome publicity for the company.

In 1989 Riley P. Bechtel, son of Stephen Bechtel, Jr., became president of Bechtel Group. That year also saw work begin on a major project in downtown Boston, the Boston Central Artery/Tunnel, which was the largest urban highway redevelopment effort in U.S. history. The project was a joint venture between Bechtel and Parsons Brinckerhoff.

Rebound in the 1990s

Bechtel rebounded strongly during the 1990s under the direction of Riley Bechtel, who became chairman and CEO following Stephen Bechtel's retirement in 1991. After the Gulf War, Bechtel led the effort to restore the oil fields of Kuwait, putting out 650 oil-well fires and rebuilding the country's upstream oil and gas installations. Work on airports was significant in the 1990s as the company provided project management services for a $20 billion airport in Hong Kong and worked on the King Fahd International Airport in Saudi Arabia. From 1990 to 1993 Bechtel expanded a natural-gas pipeline in the western United States owned by Pacific Gas Transmission Company. The end of the Cold War brought work to Bechtel in the form of the demilitarization of weapons for Russia. In 1993 the company began providing management, engineering, and support services for the $2.8 billion Athens Metro subway system.

Bechtel was also boosted in the 1990s by emerging markets in Asia, particularly China. In 1995 Bechtel became the first U.S. company to be granted a construction license by the Chinese government. The company had been active in the country since 1978 through a joint venture with the government-controlled China International Trust & Investment Corp. Among the venture's achievements was the building of a manufacturing complex for Motorola in Tianjin, China, which was due to open in 1999. Also in the mid-1990s, Bechtel helped to raise the funds for, and began supervision of, construction on a 430-kilometer toll road in China, the Greater Beijing Regional Expressway. In May 1998 the government of Ukraine selected a Bechtel-led consortium to stabilize a concrete shelter covering the damaged Unit 4 reactor of the Chernobyl nuclear power plant. Other consortium partners for the $760 million project were Electricité de France and the Battelle Memorial Institute.

From 1993 to 1996, annual revenues for Bechtel were no lower than $7.34 billion and no higher than $8.5 billion. After this steady performance, 1997 was perhaps a breakthrough year with revenues surging to $11.33 billion. New orders remained very strong as well, with $12.25 billion booked in 1997, following figures of $11.32 billion in 1996 and $12.47 billion in 1995. It appeared that Bechtel would continue to maintain an impressive presence within the international construction industry.

Principal Subsidiaries

Bechtel Civil, Inc.; Bechtel Enterprises, Inc.; Bechtel Financing Services, Inc.; Bechtel National, Inc.; Bechtel Petroleum, Chemical & Industrial Co.; Bechtel Power Corporation; Bechtel Savannah River; Bechtel Construction Company, Inc.; The Fremont Group; Coldwell Banker Corporation.

Further Reading

"Bechtel Group Inc. Will Reorganize into Five Concerns," *Wall Street Journal,* May 28, 1996, p. 26.

The Bechtel Story: Seventy Years of Accomplishment in Engineering and Construction, San Francisco: Bechtel Group, Inc., 1968.
Building a Century: Bechtel, 1898–1998, San Francisco: Bechtel Group, Inc., 1997.
Crow, Robert Thomas, "The Business Economist at Work: The Bechtel Group," *Business Economics,* January 1994, p. 46.
Dwyer, Paula, et al, "Bechtel's Iraqi Pipe Dream Could Land It in Hot Water," *Business Week,* February 22, 1988, pp. 33–34.
Kahn, Joseph, "Bechtel Tests Waters for Big Jobs in China: Financing Arrangements for Projects May Be Model," *Wall Street Journal,* May 1, 1995, p. A10.
Labaton, Stephen, "Bechtel Faces Lack of Big Projects," *New York Times,* February 24, 1988, pp. D1, D4.
McCartney, Laton, *Friends in High Places: The Bechtel Story: The Most Secret Corporation and How It Engineered the World,* New York: Simon and Schuster, 1988.
Shao, Maria, "A Bonanza for Bechtel? Well . . .," *Business Week,* May 6, 1991, p. 36.
Zachary, G. Pascal, and Susan C. Faludi, "New Blueprint: Bechtel, Hurt by Slide in Heavy Construction, Re-Engineers Itself," *Wall Street Journal,* May 28, 1991, pp. A1, A16.

—updated by David E. Salamie

Bon Secours Health System, Inc.

1505 Marriottsville Road
Marriottsville, Maryland 21104
U.S.A.
(410) 442-5511
Fax: (410) 442-1082
Web site: http://www.bshsi.com

Nonprofit Company
Founded: 1824 as Sisters of Bon Secours of Paris
Incorporated: 1979 as Sisters of Bon Secours Health
    Corporation
Employees: 20,000
Operating Revenue: $1.1 billion (1997)
SICs: 5912 Drug Stores & Proprietary Stores; 6512
    Operators of Nonresidential Buildings; 6513 Operators
    of Apartment Buildings; 6732 Educational, Religious
    & Charitable Trusts; 7352 Medical Equipment Rental
    & Leasing; 8011 General & Specialized Physician
    Practices; 8021 Total Dental Practice Revenues; 8049
    Offices & Clinics of Health Practitioners, Nothing
    Else; 8051 Skilled Nursing Facilities; 8059 Nursing &
    Personal Care Facilities; 8062 General Medical &
    Surgical Hospitals; 8063 Psychiatric Hospitals; 8071
    Reference Laboratory Outside of Acute Care; 8082
    Home Health Care Services; 8092 Kidney Dialysis
    Centers; 8093 Specialty Outpatient Facilities, Not
    Elsewhere Classified; 8099 Health & Allied Services,
    Not Elsewhere Classified; 8741 Management Services

Bon Secours Health System, Inc. (BSHSI), headquartered in Marriottsville, Maryland, was founded in 1983 to fulfill the healthcare mission of the Sisters of Bon Secours USA. Without regard for race, creed or color, BSHSI strives to alleviate all types of human suffering, especially that of the poor, the sick, and the dying. In the United States, BSHSI's activities radiate in, and from, a wide variety of healthcare facilities that include 14 acute-care hospitals, one psychiatric hospital, five assisted-living facilities, seven long-term care facilities, and numerous ambulatory and community health services. BSHSI is committed to pastoral and home healthcare as well as a wide variety of other professional services, such as nursing, rehabilitation of children and of adults, mobile primary care of the poor, and many other outreach programs. Bon Secours is an active member of the New Covenant Steering Committee, the Catholic Health Association, the American Hospital Association, and Premier Inc. BSHSI President/CEO Christopher M. Carney is a board member of Consolidated Catholic HealthCare Association and Bon Secours Sister Patricia A. Eck—Chairperson of the BSHSI Board—is also secretary/treasurer of Partners for Catholic Health Ministry Leadership. Bon Secours facilities are located in Florida, Maryland, Michigan, Pennsylvania, South Carolina, and Virginia. According to *Modern Healthcare's* May 1997 listing of healthcare systems ranked by net patient revenue, BSHSI ranks 20th among Catholic not-for-profit healthcare systems and 50th among the top 192 national healthcare systems.

Historical Background: 17th to 19th Centuries

According to M. Adelaide Nutting and Lavinia L. Dock's *History of Nursing,* during the latter part of the 17th century and until the middle of the 19th century, nursing was undergoing a "Dark Period." Hospitals were overcrowded, disease-ridden and unsanitary: "The hospitals of cities were like prisons, with bare, undecorated walls and little dark rooms, small windows where no sun could enter, and dismal wards where 50 or 100 patients were crowded together, deprived of all comforts and even of necessities. The rich did not want to put up with the frightful, deplorable conditions in hospitals and the poor sought hospitals only as a last resort. It was during this dire period in the wake of the French Revolution, specifically in 1824, that the Sisters of Bon Secours were founded in Paris. They committed themselves to nursing and, when necessary, to living in the homes of the sick—rich and poor alike. Thus began the world's first-recorded formal home-healthcare service. In 1827 the French government recognized the Congregation of the Sisters of Bon Secours of Paris as the first sisterhood established in France exclusively for nursing the sick.

Company Perspectives:

Bon Secours Health System, Inc. is a body of people who share the healing ministry of the Sisters of Bon Secours and the Catholic Church. Our mission is to provide healthcare services to those in need, especially the poor and dying, for the purpose of alleviating human suffering and affirming human meaning in the midst of pain and loss. Recognizing the dignity of all persons, we provide compassionate healthcare services contributing to the physical, social, emotional and spiritual well-being of those we serve. We commit ourselves to help bring people to wholeness by understanding and responding to healthcare needs (especially unmet needs); by developing the potential of those who serve with us; by advocating a just and equitable public-health policy; and by modeling justice in the workplace. Guided by our values and our responsibility to the communities we serve, we will achieve planned growth in response to community need while continually improving our systems and services so as to become ever more faithful to our mission.

The Sisters went wherever their services were needed. For example, they tended the sick in their homes and very often lived with the family; they cared for the wounded on the 1870 battlefields of the Franco-Prussian War and, during the cholera epidemic that followed, housed the sick in their convents and even in their motherhouse. Healthcare of this nature was considered a radical innovation: traditionally, women religious were expected to be in their convents at least by nightfall. Other women joined the Sisters, expanded their compassionate nursing throughout France and soon reached out to the sick in Ireland (1861), Great Britain (1871), the United States (1881), and Scotland (1948).

Early Years in the United States: 1881–1983

The first Americans to come into contact with these nursing sisters—as recorded by Bon Secours Sister Mary Cecilia O'Sullivan in *A Century of Caring*—were Mr. and Mrs. Whedbe during their honeymoon in Paris. When Mrs. Whedbe became seriously ill, her husband asked the doctor for an English-speaking nurse. Irish-born Sister Matilda, C.B.S. was sent to nurse Mrs. Whedbe in her hotel room—and restored her to health. Upon their return to America the Whedbes told a family friend, Bishop Gibbons (later elevated to Archbishop of Baltimore), and several doctors about the Bon Secours care and kindness they had experienced in Paris. They urged Archbishop Gibbons to obtain Bon Secours Sisters for his archdiocese. On his way to Rome in 1880, the Archbishop visited the Bon Secours Sisters in Paris and requested a foundation of the Congregation in Baltimore.

Three Sisters of Bon Secours arrived in Baltimore in 1881. As was the case in many other large cities where numerous immigrants lived together in very unsanitary conditions, Baltimore was disease-ridden: typhoid fever, diphtheria, and scarlet fever ran rampant. Mindful of their commitment to a ministry of "zeal and charity for the relief of the body and especially for the

salvation of souls," the Sister became a familiar sight in the streets of Baltimore as they went about bringing "good help" (the English translation of *Bon Secours*) wherever it was needed. According to *A Century of Caring*, "The Sisters of Bon Secours were the first society of visiting nurses in the United States. They preceded by 15 years visiting nursing in Baltimore and by six years visiting nurses in Philadelphia and Boston. They antedated all forms of public-health nursing as well as organized private-duty nursing in the homes of patients."

In answer to increasing demands for Bon Secours care, more Sisters came from France and Ireland. A convent was opened in Washington, D.C., in 1905 and still another in Detroit in 1909. Sensitive to the needs of Baltimore's working mothers, whose only choice when working away from home was to place their children in orphanages, in 1907 the Sisters founded the first day-care facility to be opened in Baltimore: St. Martin's Day Nursery, which functioned according to its original purpose until 1958.

The Sisters nursed the sick in their own homes, without distinction of creed or class. In the early 1900s Baltimore citizens and physicians had asked the Sisters to extend their personalized nursing care to institutionalized settings. The Sisters were well aware of the need to nurse the sick outside the home setting; they had cared for them in the guest rooms of their convent! In 1919 generous donors brought about the opening of Bon Secours Hospital where, according to Sr. Mary Cecilia's history of the Congregation of Bon Secours, people came from far and near to "get not only the best medical and surgical attention, splendid care, and the ever present unselfish, and watchful nursing from the Sisters but, in addition, the feeling that one was in a true hospital, not an institution."

The Sisters cared for hundreds of poor patients, especially during the economic depression that followed the stock market crash of 1929. According to archived annual reports, in 1932 the Sisters—without financial help from city or state—gave hospital care to 420 nonpaying patients and distributed 98,945 lunches to unemployed men. Furthermore, even during these hard times, in 1933 the Sisters opened a three-story wing to the hospital in order to enlarge the hospital's maternity department, which at that time could accommodate only about 10 patients. With this new maternity building, the hospital added the number of beds required for official recognition by the American Medical Association for the training of interns and residents and received full AMA approval in 1934. An obstetrical clinic opened in 1934 continued to serve the needy: poor mothers were "taken in freely in this department and given the best of care together with their newborn," according to the minutes of a 1934 meeting of the hospital's board of trustees.

By 1979 the Sisters of Bon Secours sponsored or staffed other facilities: a hospital in Grosse Pointe, Michigan; one in Methuen, Massachusetts; another in Richmond, Virginia; and still another in Portsmouth, Virginia. A rehabilitation hospital was set up in Miami, Florida, and a residential home for the handicapped in Rosemont, Pennsylvania. All these institutions functioned autonomously; each one reported to the Congregation's Provincial Council. In 1979 all the Bon Secours facilities were formally incorporated into one system: the Sisters of Bon Secours Health Corporation. After a few years it became obvious that still more centralization of management was needed and Bon Secours Health System, Inc. was established for that purpose in 1983.

Expanding the Dimensions of Caring: 1983–98

BSHSI operated as a hierarchical structure under the governance of Bon Secours, Inc. (BSI), which represented the civic incorporation of the healthcare mission of the Sisters of Bon Secours. The only BSI subsidiary was BSHSI which operated, in part, through regional holding corporations at the locales of some of the larger healthcare facilities. In 1996, exploding growth of the system occasioned the grouping of all BSHSI facilities into four regions, namely, the Northeast Region, the Richmond Region, the Hampton Roads Region, and the Southeast Region.

BSHSI set leadership in its field as a goal to be reached by a four-point strategy centered on development of people, advocacy, active pursuit of growth, and of new partnerships with organizations committed to the same value system as Bon Secours. Implementation of the Continual Development System prepared employees to respond to the rapid changes occurring in the business, social, and healthcare environments. In all Bon Secours communities, special emphasis was placed on deepening the education, skills, and training of care-givers for the terminally ill and their families. As a major corporate entity, in its communities BSHSI advocated to protect human dignity and human rights by promoting economic and/or public policy at local, state, and federal levels and advocated against legislation that threatened the common good of the community, especially that of the marginalized.

BSHSI sought to cooperate with congregations of other women religious in the healthcare field. For instance, a joint venture with the Bernardine Sisters of the Third Order of St. Francis for the operation of Mary Immaculate Hospital and of St. Francis Nursing Care Center in Newport News, Virginia; co-sponsorship with the Sisters of the Holy Family of Nazareth for the operation of Bon Secours-Holy Family Regional Health System in Altoona, Pennsylvania; and co-sponsorship with the Felician Sisters for the operation of Bon Secours-St. Joseph Health Care Group in Port Charlotte, Florida.

In fact, by collaborating with public and private organizations and other groups dedicated to solving problems at neighborhood, municipal, and regional levels, BSHSI served as a catalyst for positive change. For example, Bon Secours worked with pastors of churches in Detroit, Michigan, to initiate the *Parish Nurse Program,* which established Health Cabinets of parishioners concerned about the healing ministry of their churches. Community educational activities included health seminars, safety fairs, screenings, and the pairing of active parishioners with home-bound church members.

Bon Secours-St. Joseph Health Care Group in 1993 introduced the Care A Van program in southwest Florida. This program, affiliated with the University of South Florida Medical and Nursing Schools, was the only federally certified mobile rural health clinic in Florida and one of only a few in America. The program focused on both episodic illness and preventive healthcare, including physical examinations in public schools

and daycare centers, immunization of children, early pregnancy testing, prenatal care, STD (sexually transmitted diseases) screenings, and health education. By 1998 the Care A Van program had served some 12,000 patients in southwest Florida—including about 8,000 children. Many of these patients were migrant workers and/or among the rural poor in Charlotte, Hardee, Highlands, DeSoto, and Glade counties. In Richmond, Bon Secours joined forces with local health departments, the Virginia Health Care Foundation, and Aetna Life Insurance to establish the *Care A Van* community program. By year-end 1998, more than 4,500 immunizations had been given to children in the city's low-income neighborhoods.

In Norfolk, the *Call a Friend* project helped some 50 patients ("friends") who lived alone and were not often in touch with family members. Volunteers contributed to the emotional, social, and spiritual needs of these people by weekly calls or visits and donations of food. In Newport News, Virginia, three *Family Focus* programs operated as a joint venture of BSHSI, Mary Immaculate Hospital, and Colonial Service Board. The programs, created to reduce the risk of child abuse, helped parents to raise their children from birth to age five; a variety of services—including parent education classes, play groups, and support groups—drew over 17,000 family members into these *Family Focus* programs. Another venture in the state of Virginia was the *Jeremiah Project*, organized by BSHSI and 40 pastors of racially, economically, and culturally diverse congregations in Portsmouth. These congregations, in collaboration with local government and private agencies, developed and coordinated action plans to address issues facing welfare families, namely, literacy, transportation, mentoring, and child care.

The brief descriptions of the projects mentioned above are but a sampling of how BSHSI exercised its creative leadership in the 1980s and early 1990s. Furthermore, a special fund was created to assure the continuing development of holistic health and well-being in these communities and to help other communities face their healthcare needs. Thus, the *Mission Fund* promoted research and development of health and human services geared to improving quality of life, particularly for groups of disenfranchised and marginalized people.

Toward the 21st Century

BSHSI, ever conscious that treatment of disease and infirmity did not suffice for a person's total well-being, found new ways of directing its traditional energy for creative healthcare services focused on the impact of the environment, genetics, and lifestyle. Bon Secours, in order to provide quality care while holding down operational costs—among other goals—intensified a strategic program for acquisitions, mergers, and joint ventures. In 1996, for example, Bon Secours established a continuing-care division in Richmond to oversee the senior services of its Richmond community. "We now have our financial incentives aligned to make sure patients are moving through the continuum in the most cost-effective way," said Vice-President Kathryn A. Beall, in an interview reported in the June 16, 1997 issue of *Modern Healthcare*. The new division included home healthcare and subacute services for seniors, a retirement condominium village, a senior health center, a health-information membership program. Here, in 1997, BSHSI became part of a joint venture between Bon Secours Richmond and Richmond-based Manorhouse Retirement Centers to open the national system's first assisted-living facility: the Bon Secours Retirement Community at Ironbridge. Beall commented that BSHSI planned to open additional assisted-living facilities in its other markets; assisted living "is a natural in the development of our continuum of care," said she.

Additionally, in West Baltimore, Bon Secours initiated a comprehensive multi-agency partnership, titled *Operation ReachOut,* to revitalize a deteriorating neighborhood glutted with boarded-up houses and reeling from a bevy of social problems. Participants in this 1997 program transformed 30 abandoned row houses into 60 apartments for low-income families. The Bon Secours Community Support Center distributed food and provided healthcare services. Furthermore, the Center offered counseling, training in parenting, activities for early-childhood development, child care, adult education, classes to prepare for graduate equivalency diplomas (GEDs), computer training, and enrollment in Women and Infant Children (WIC) classes.

"We are redefining our mission; it's not only to take care of the sick but to partner with others to build a healthy community," commented Bon Secours Sister Nancy Glynn, in "Building Bridges to Health," a story published in the Feb. 11, 1997 issue of the *Baltimore Sun*. Indeed, the biggest challenge for Bon Secours, Sister Patricia Eck pointed out in an interview reported in the October 5, 1997 issue of *Hospitals & Health Networks*, consisted in creating "a successful future that focuses on compassionate care for those in need. While we must maintain our competitive posture, we have a clear advantage with our employees: most of them are here because they want to give care. There's no confusion about our vision. . . . By contrast, when you mix in the profit motive, you really risk confusing your organization's vision," emphasized this chairperson of the BSHSI board.

In short, as a new millennium drew near, Bon Secours Health Systems, Inc. had found innovative ways of providing "good help to those in need." It was going beyond the walls of traditional nursing to meet the immediate and long-range holistic health and related social/economic needs of the communities it served. To this end BSHSI was continuing to develop, coordinate, and implement the array of services, processes, and delivery mechanisms required to assure a *continuum of care*— compassionate care from the cradle to the grave—for the poor, the sick, and the dying.

Principal Subsidiaries

Bon Secours Healthcare System, Inc. is structured as 15 Bon Secours subsidiaries/affiliates that, in turn, include nine parent corporations to which are related 126 other subsidiary/affiliated entities. The nine parent corporations are: Bon Secours of Michigan Health Care System, Inc.; Mary Immaculate Hospital, Incorporated; Bon Secours-Richmond Health Corporation; Bon Secours Holy Family Regional Health System; Bon Secours-Venice Healthcare Corporation; Bon Secours-Maryview Health Corporation; Bon Secours-St. Joseph HealthCare Group, Inc.; Bon Secours-St. Francis Xavier Hospital; and Bon Secours-Baltimore Health Corporation.

Further Reading

Appleby, Chuck, "More a Calling Than a Job," *Hospitals & Health Networks*, Oct. 5, 1997, p. 90.
"Bon Secours Enjoying Rapid Growth in Virginia," *Catholic Health World*, Feb. 15, 1997, pp. 1, 4.
A Century of Caring, Bon Secours Hospital: Mariottsville, Md., 1983.
"Healthcare Systems Ranked by Net Patient Revenue," *Modern Healthcare,* May 26, 1997. pp. 64–68.
Karibo, Joeann, "Granting Authority to a New Policy: A Community Benefit Services Policy Becomes Part of the General Business Strategy," *Health Progress*, May 1994, pp. 32–35.
Lazarus, Jeremy M., "Clinic Closing; Hospital Expanding," *Richmond Free Press*, January 29–31, 1998, p. A5.
McCreaven, Marilyn, "Building Bridges to Health," *Baltimore Sun*, February 11, 1997, pp. B1, B5.
Moore, Don, "Hospital Wins Heart Surgery Center," *Venice Gondolier*, January 10–11, 1998, pp. 1, 15.
Nutting, M. Adelaide, and Lavinia L. Dock, *A History of Nursing: The Evolution of Nursing Systems from the Earliest Times to the Foundation of the First English and American Training Schools for Nurses*, New York: G.P. Putnam's Sons, 1935, vol. 1, p. 500.
O'Sullivan, Mary Cecilia, C.B.S., *A Century of Caring: The Sisters of Bon Secours in the United States, 1881–1981*, 320 p.
Peck, Jeanne, "Delivering Health Care: Nonprofit Hospital System Expanding," *Daily Press*, Oct. 20, 1996, pp. E1, E4.
Reed, Stephen G., "Venice Lands Heart Unit," *Sarasota Herald-Tribune*, January 10, 1998, pp. A1, A13.
Salganik, M. William, "Joining for Wellness: Liberty, Bon Secours Seeking Healthy Futures Together," *Baltimore Sun*, November 3, 1996, pp. D1, D8.
Snow, Charlotte, "Senior Services," *Modern Healthcare*, June 16, 1997, p. 31.

—Gloria A. Lemieux

THE BOOTS COMPANY

The Boots Company PLC

One Thane Road West
Nottingham NG2 3AA
United Kingdom
44-1-159-506111
Fax: 44-1-159-592727
Web site: http://www.boots.co.uk

Public Company
Incorporated: 1883 as Boot and Company Limited
Employees: 73,758
Sales:£4.58 billion (US$7.48 billion) (1997)
Stock Exchanges: London
Ticker Symbol: BOOOY
SICs: 2834 Pharmaceutical Preparations; 2844 Perfumes,
    Cosmetics & Other Toilet Preparations; 5122 Drugs,
    Drug Proprietaries & Sundries; 5149 Grocers &
    Related Products, Not Elsewhere Classified; 5251
    Hardware Stores; 5531 Auto & Home Supply Stores;
    5912 Drug Stores & Proprietary Stores; 5995 Optical
    Goods Stores

The Boots Company PLC is one of the leading retailers in the United Kingdom, in addition to being a major manufacturer and marketer of cosmetics, toiletries, and nonprescription drugs. Of the company's seven principal operating units, Boots The Chemists (BTC)—the company flagship—is by far the largest, accounting for about two-thirds of the company's total sales. BTC is the United Kingdom's leading drugstore chain, with more than 2,250 locations retailing a wide range of health and beauty products, toiletries, baby products, gifts, and film (as well as film processing). The company's second largest unit is Halfords (responsible for about eight percent of sales), the leading car parts and servicing chain in the United Kingdom, with more than 400 units. Do It All (six percent of sales) is one of the three largest do-it-yourself (DIY) home improvement chains in the United Kingdom, with more than 160 stores. The company's fourth retail chain is Boots Opticians (three percent of sales), a major U.K. optician with about 275 locations offer-

ing a full examination and dispensing service. Boots Contract Manufacturing (five percent of sales) was created in 1991 and is the largest contract manufacturer (with more than 4,000 products and over 420 million units per year) in Europe of medicines, cosmetics, and toiletries—most of which are private-label Boots branded; this unit has eight factories and one major development lab. Also created in 1991 was Boots Healthcare International (BHI; five percent of sales), which sells over-the-counter analgesics (pain relievers), cough and throat remedies, and skincare products; three-quarters of BHI's business is generated outside the United Kingdom, in more than 130 countries. Boots Properties (two percent of sales) is one of the U.K.'s largest owners of shopping centers. Although The Boots Company has been steadily expanding abroad, mainly through acquisition, more than 95 percent of overall sales are still generated at home.

Jesse Boot, Founding Father

Jesse Boot, the founder of the company, was born in Nottingham in 1850, the first child and only son of John Boot and his second wife, Mary. An agricultural laborer by trade, John Boot was much influenced by the ideas of popular medicine then current among nonconformists, particularly those of the disciples of the American Samuel Thompson, whose remedies, based on medical botany, were then enjoying considerable success in Britain. After John Boot's health broke down, he opened a small shop in 1849 in Goosegate, Nottingham, selling his own herbal and botanical medicines. His death in 1860 left his widow and her two children dependent on the shop for their livelihood, and Mary Boot continued to run the business with the help of her 10-year-old son. Three years later Jesse Boot left school to work full time in the business, and over the next few years he took charge of it.

In the 1870s, rising real incomes allowed the working class to purchase the patent and proprietary medicines of the kind manufactured and sold by Thomas Holloway and Thomas Beecham, displacing the remedies of medical botany. Although the shop in Goosegate continued to sell herbal medicines, young Jesse Boot started to expand the business, first by adding a range of household goods, including groceries, sold at cut prices; an

Company Perspectives:

The Boots Company embraces businesses operating principally in retailing, the manufacture and marketing of health and personal care products throughout the world and the development and management of retail property.

Our objective is to maximise the value of the company for the benefit of its shareholders. We will do so by investing in our businesses to generate strong cash flows and superior long term returns.

While vigorously pursuing our commercial interests, we will, at all times, seek to enhance our reputation as a well managed, ethical and socially responsible company.

advertisement of the early 1870s claimed more than 2,000 articles in stock. He decided in 1874 to enter the business of retailing proprietary medicines; as he recalled in 1904, he thought that "if he could afford to sell proprietary articles at prices lower than were being charged by the ordinary chemists, there would be a large future before him." Jesse Boot's commercial strategy, the basis on which he built his large and successful business, was to buy in large quantities from wholesalers and to sell at prices well below those prevailing in the town. It won for him the enduring hostility of the established chemists, first in Nottingham, and later in other towns and cities where he opened branches.

Although at first Boot had difficulties both in persuading the wholesalers to supply him with such large quantities and in finding the money to pay them, he secured the support of a number of influential businessmen and professional men in Nottingham, and, following an extensive advertising campaign in the local press, his business grew rapidly. By the autumn of 1877 his turnover had reached £100 a week, far surpassing his own original target of £20 a week. In the following year he opened a new and larger shop, also in Goosegate, and five years later he extended, refurbished, and refitted it.

In July 1883 Boot incorporated his business as Boot and Company Limited, with a nominal capital of £10,000 of which almost a half was fully subscribed, most of it by Boot himself. Incorporation with limited liability could have opened the way for external investment in the business, but Boot chose to keep control in his own hands, offering shares only to a few close friends and associates in the 1880s; for the time being, he continued to rely on the banks for financial backing, and a decade later, when he started to encourage investors, he sold only preference, nonvoting shares. Some of these shares were offered to customers, through the shops, and some to employees, for the cooperative ideal attracted the nonconformist and liberal side of Jesse Boot's character, although at the same time he was determined to keep control of his business.

Began Dispensing Prescriptions in 1880s

More significantly at the time, incorporation opened up a new area of business for Boot's shop, that of dispensing prescriptions. In a test case brought by the Pharmaceutical Society in 1880 against the London and Provincial Supply Association, the House of Lords decided, much to the chagrin of the society, that limited liability companies had the right to employ qualified pharmacists or chemists to dispense prescriptions. In 1883 Boot recruited Edward Waring as the company's first pharmacist in the Nottingham store and, with dispensing at half-price, the prescription section was off to a good start.

Expansion of the business continued with the opening in 1884 of branches in Lincoln and Sheffield and the start of small-scale manufacturing behind the shop in Goosegate. By 1885 Boot's annual turnover had reached £40,000, but in that year his health deteriorated, and he briefly contemplated selling the business. He recovered, and while recuperating on holiday in Jersey he met Florence Rowe, daughter of a bookshop owner. In August 1886 they were married.

The 1890s saw an ambitious plan of expansion implemented. New shops were opened to extend the company's coverage of England and Wales, and Boot also bought, where he could, small chains of chemists' shops. By the end of 1893, according to *The Chemist and Druggist,* Boots was then the largest of the company-chemist chains.

Boots and Company was reconstituted in 1888 as Boots Pure Drug Company Limited, which became the holding company for a number of subsidiary companies such as Boots Cash Chemists (Lancs) Ltd., 1899. The size of the company—there were 180 shops by the end of the century—was enhanced when in 1901 Boot bought the Southern Drug Company and the Metropolitan Drug Company, which together formed a chain of more than 60 shops, the largest in the metropolitan area. Between 1901 and 1914 more new shops were opened, bringing the total to 560 in 1914, including prestigious sites in Princes Street, Edinburgh, in 1911 and Regent Street, London, in 1912.

While pharmaceuticals and dispensing remained the core of the business, the range of merchandise retailed also widened, particularly in the larger shops, which were closer to department stores, and as the company tried to widen its appeal to attract middle-class customers. Florence Boot's experience of retailing in her father's bookshop gave her a direct interest in the business, resulting in the introduction of departments offering stationery, books, artists' materials, and gifts that proved popular and successful and remained in her charge. Around the turn of the century, Boots Booklovers Libraries were established and cafés or tearooms were installed in some of the larger stores; both these innovations proved a success in terms of customer appeal.

By 1892 manufacturing, which had started in a small way behind the shop, occupied the whole of a former cotton mill in Nottingham, and the interest always taken by Jesse Boot in the design, fitting, and appearance of the shops led to the establishment and growth of a building and shopfitting department. A printing department to serve the company's needs opened in 1890. The continued growth of the business was reflected in its rising sales, which passed the £2 million mark in 1911 and reached £2.5 million in 1913.

Manufacture of Pharmaceuticals Began During World War I

World War I brought new opportunities that Jesse Boot—who was knighted in 1909—was quick to seize. Despite being increasingly disabled by arthritis, he continued to control the company. In the last two decades of the 19th century, the German fine-chemical industry had discovered, developed, and patented a number of pharmaceuticals—aspirin and phenacetin for example—that it exported to the United Kingdom. The outbreak of war left Boots and the country without a supply of these and other essential fine chemicals, and Boot soon decided to start to manufacture them. He recruited research chemists from Burroughs Wellcome, and production at the new plant started in 1915. In addition to fine chemicals, the company also started to manufacture saccharin during the war. Sales increased at this time, reaching £5 million in 1918.

Jesse Boot, who was awarded baronetcy in 1916 as a reward for contributions to the Liberal Party, was 70 in 1920. Fearing the effects of the postwar slump on business, which was becoming increasingly burdensome to him to run but which he did not want to hand over to his son John, Boot negotiated privately the sale of his controlling interest to American Louis K. Liggett and his Rexall group of U.S. drugstores. Liggett paid £2.27 million for Boots. Jesse, who remained titular chairman of Boots until 1926 and was made Lord Trent in 1929, gave large amounts of the money to his home city, particularly to University College, Nottingham, which used the money to fund the construction of buildings on the city's outskirts. After the sale of the business, he retired to Jersey where he died in 1931.

Boots was part of the Liggett group from 1920 to 1933, although in 1923 John Boot, vice-chairman of the company, who had disliked his father's transaction with Liggett, persuaded Liggett to sell 25 percent of its shareholding in Britain; thus, for the first time, Boots shares became publicly held, and the company was quoted on the London Stock Exchange. In 1928 the L.K. Liggett Company became part of a much larger U.S. combine, Drug Inc., which, faced with the effects of the American Depression, decided to sell Boots. The money required for the purchase, between £6 million and £7 million, was raised by a group led by Sir Hugo Cunliffe-Owen and Reginald McKenna.

During the 13 years of U.S. ownership there were some major organizational changes, which lasted beyond that time. Two committees—later merged into one—composed of Boots's senior managers and American representatives, were designated in 1920 to run the company. Nine territorial general managers were appointed to control the 600 shops, and senior managers were sent to the United States to be trained. Stricter control of stock and better accounting systems were introduced, for although sales had continued to rise, profitability had slipped.

As Britain emerged from the worst of the postwar slump, Boots became prosperous again. John Boot, joint managing director, gradually asserted his control over the business, and in 1927 work started on a long-planned new factory at Beeston, just outside Nottingham, which opened in 1933.

From 1933 until 1953 John Boot, now the second Lord Trent and chairman and managing director as his father had been

before him, ruled Boots as autocratically as his predecessor. In the years immediately before World War II, expansion was steady—the 1,000th shop opened in Scotland, at Galashiels in 1933, and in 1936 the first shop in New Zealand was opened.

Slow Recovery Following World War II

Between 1939 and 1945, like most of the British industry, Boots's manufacturing capacity was directed to the war effort, and the production of pharmaceuticals such as mepacrine, for the treatment of malaria, took priority. Many of the company's shops and some of its manufacturing sites were destroyed or severely damaged by the bombing. Recovery after the war was slow, not least because of the shortage of building materials and skills. The manufacture of new pharmaceutical products increased as Boots started to make antibiotics and, in 1953, cortisone products. The immediate postwar years also saw the start of businesses in Kenya, South Africa, Singapore, Australia, and Pakistan. At home, however, the company had an increasingly old-fashioned image as consumer tastes started to change and shoppers expected a wider range of products.

The second Lord Trent retired in 1954 and died in 1956; his successor as chairman was his former chief assistant, J. P. Savage, who had then been with the company for more than 40 years. When Savage retired in 1961, the offices of chairman and managing director were separated, with W. R. Norman, the second Lord Trent's son-in-law, becoming chairman and F. A. Cockfield, who had joined the company in 1952 from the Board of the Inland Revenue in order to introduce cost accounting methods, being named managing director.

Acquired Timothy Whites in 1967

A reorganization of the company took place in 1967 and included establishment of a divisional structure. In 1968 Boots bought—it was described at the time as a merger, a face-saving formula to preserve corporate pride—the business of Timothy Whites, a long-standing competitor holding more than 600 retail branches, most of them drugstores selling other consumer goods, and more than 100 shops selling housewares merchandise only. The Timothy Whites business had been founded in Portsmouth in 1848 and had followed a pattern of growth similar to that of Boots. In 1935 it had merged with Taylors Drug Company Ltd., a longtime competitor of Boots. The drugstores were integrated immediately with Boots, but the Timothy Whites Houseware branches continued to operate as such until 1983.

In 1971 the purchase of Crookes Laboratories Ltd. and Crookes Anestan Ltd. brought more pharmaceutical business to Boots, and a merger proposed in the following year would have given Boots greater presence in that field. In 1972 the Beecham Company made an unwelcome bid for Glaxo, which instead turned to Boots and a hastily arranged defensive merger. Both arrangements, however, were reported to the Monopolies Commission and in July of that year the commission ruled that neither should take place.

Anxious for expansion in Europe, Boots tried in 1973 to take over the House of Fraser, which already had some department stores in Europe. The bid was referred to the Monopolies Commission again, but even before their adverse recommendation was made, the oil crisis of that year and its effect on stock market prices made it impossible for the two to agree on price.

Several Acquisitions Marked Late 1970s and 1980s

Instead Boots turned its attention to the United States, where in 1977 it acquired Rucker Pharmacol (renamed Boots Pharmaceuticals Inc.), and in 1986 it added to the company's U.S. operations with the £377 million purchase of the Flint Division of Baxter Travenol. Also across the Atlantic, Boots bought in 1977 and 1978 two chains of drugstores in Canada, and in 1978 it also bought 60 percent of Hercules Agrochemical in the United States. This was merged with Fisons agrochemical interests in 1980, and the joint venture was sold to Schering in 1983. In Europe Boots acquired 50 percent of the Spanish company Laboratorios Liade S.A. in 1979, and 95 percent of the West German company Kanoldt in 1984. New branches of the Sephora shops in France were opened. In 1982 the parent company was renamed The Boots Company PLC.

The acquisition of consumer eye products manufacturer Optrex in 1983, for £9 million, led to the opening of optical services departments, and sometimes separate shops, augmented by the purchase of opticians' chains, including Clement Clarke in 1986, Curry & Paxton in 1987, and Miller and Santhouse in 1989; these moves led to the formation of the Boots Opticians chain. Boots bought Farleys Health Products, maker of baby food and adult nutrition products, in 1986 to add to its manufacturing base. In 1987 Boots launched Children's World, a new retail chain selling clothing, toys, and other items for babies and children under 12. The following year, the company divested its loss-making Canadian drugstore chain. Domestic drugstore operations were increased with the acquisition of Underwoods Chemists in 1989. That same year, the £900 million purchase—in a bitterly fought takeover battle—of the Ward White group brought into Boots the Halfords auto parts chain, the Payless do-it-yourself (DIY) home-improvement chain, and A. G. Stanley, operator of the FADS DIY home-decorating chain (Ward White's U.S. operations were soon sold off).

The Ward White acquisition was largely attributed to chief executive James Blyth (later Lord Blyth of Rowington), who had taken over the position only in 1987. Blyth also engineered a 1989 restructuring, whereby the company's activities were divided into four operating units: Boots The Chemists, the largest unit, consisting of the BTC chain of drugstores; a retail division, which primarily included Boots Opticians, Children's World, Halfords, A.G. Stanley, and Payless; Boots Pharmaceuticals, developer and marketer of prescription and over-the-counter medicines and healthcare products, cosmetics, and toiletries; and a newly created property division, later known as Boots Properties, which managed the company's property portfolio in the United Kingdom, including a large assortment of shopping centers.

Tumultuous 1990s

Blyth's attempt to diversify Boots into other areas of retailing quickly turned sour. In 1990 the Payless chain was merged into the Do It All chain, a 50-50 joint venture with W.H. Smith. Unfortunately, the U.K. housing market plunged into a five-year depression, which severely cut into DIY sales, thereby turning both Do It All and FADS into loss-makers. Boots was also hurt in the early 1990s by the high debt it had to incur to acquire Ward White. On the plus side, Halfords was consistently profitable in the 1990s.

The company's Boots Pharmaceuticals unit also faced difficulties, largely because its small size made it difficult to compete in the drug industry. In 1991 Boots created two new operating units out of Boots Pharmaceuticals: Boots Healthcare International (BHI), which assumed the over-the-counter drugs business; and Boots Contract Manufacturing (BCM), which became the company's maker of mostly private label health and beauty products. Boots Pharmaceuticals thus became a prescription-drugs-only unit. In 1993 this unit failed in an attempt to create a breakthrough drug to keep itself viable, when development of its Manoplax heart treatment drug had to be abandoned because of side effects. Boots quickly decided to divest the unit, and in early 1995 did so in selling Boots Pharmaceuticals to BASF for about £850 million, thus ending the company's 80 years in the prescription drugs business.

Meanwhile, Michael Angus, chairman of Whitbread, had been serving as Boots's chairman, with Blyth taking on the additional role of deputy chairman. Also in 1994 Boots sold the Farleys group to H. J. Heinz for £94 million; Farleys had been part of BHI but did not fit into the core over-the-counter categories the unit decided to specialize in, notably pain relievers, cough and throat remedies, and skincare products. In 1995 the BCM unit was bolstered through the acquisition of Croda International PLC's private label cosmetics and toiletries manufacturing businesses in France and Germany.

As the 1990s progressed, Boots began to pull back from its diversified retail operations. During the 1993–94 fiscal year, the Sephora retail chain in France was sold. In 1996 Children's World was sold to Storehouse PLC. Later that same year, the company bought W. H. Smith's 50 percent share of Do It All for £63.5 million, taking complete ownership of the troubled chain. Although Do It All was approaching profitability by late 1997, speculation that Boots would divest itself of this albatross was rife. The company did jettison one of its loss-making Ward White businesses in late 1997 when it sold A. G. Stanley to Alchemy Partners, a private venture-capital group, for a nominal amount. By early 1998, Boots's remaining non-drugstore retail operations—Boots Opticians, Halfords, and Do It All—were each operating as separate units, providing the company with a seven-unit structure (including BTC, BHI, BCM, and Boots Properties).

Meanwhile, the flagship Boots The Chemists chain continued to keep the company profitable. In its first moves outside the United Kingdom since its failed Canadian venture, BTC announced in late 1996 plans to expand the chain on a pilot basis into Thailand (where six stores opened in 1997) and the Netherlands (where three stores opened in 1997). In the fall of 1996 BTC opened its first unit in Ireland, and had seven stores there by the end of 1997. In January 1998 Boots acquired the Hayes Conyngham & Robinson drugstore chain, the largest such chain in Ireland with 15 stores. In April 1998 BTC expanded in both the United Kingdom and Ireland through the £18 million purchase of Connors Holdings Ltd., a privately owned pharmacy chain with 25 stores in Northern Ireland, five in the Republic of Ireland, three in England, and one in Wales.

Boots Healthcare International was also bolstered in 1997 through the £173.6 million (US$275.6 million) acquisition of Hermal Kurt Herrmann, the leading manufacture of skincare products in Germany, from Merck. The purchase added Germany to BHI's European operations, which already included the United Kingdom, France, and Italy.

More than 95 percent of Boots's sales were still being generated in the United Kingdom in the late 1990s. With the rapid expansion of BHI and BCM in the 1990s and the potential for overseas growth of the BTC chain, it appeared that Boots would become a much more international company in the 21st century. It also seemed that the success of BHI and BCM could pave the way for the divestment of Do It All and even Halfords—neither of which provided much synergy with the company's other units. It could nonetheless be said with some certainty that Boots's healthcare, retailing, and manufacturing operations faced a very bright future indeed.

Principal Operating Units

Boots The Chemists; Halfords; Boots Opticians; Do It All; Boots Healthcare International; Boots Contract Manufacturing; Boots Properties.

Further Reading

Britton, Noelle, "Boots Treads Carefully," *Marketing,* May 26, 1988, p. 22.

Buckley, Neil, "Divide and Thrive at Boots," *Financial Times,* July 4, 1994, p. 12.

Buckley, Neil, and David Blackwell, "Boots to Expand Health and Beauty Division," *Financial Times,* June 29, 1995, p. 18.

Chapman, S., *Jesse Boot of Boots the Chemists,* London: Hodder & Stoughton, 1974.

——, "Strategy and Structure at Boots the Chemists," in Hannah, Leslie, ed., *Management Strategy and Business Development,* London: Macmillan, 1976, 267 p.

Green, Daniel, "BASF in £850m Deal to Acquire Boots' Drugs-Making Business," *Financial Times,* November 15, 1994, pp. 1, 20.

Greenwood, J. E., *A Cap for Boots: An Autobiography,* London: Hutchinson, 1977, 254 p.

Hollinger, Peggy, "Boots Back on International Stage," *Financial Times,* October 11, 1996, p. 24.

——, "Slow Waking from a Nightmare," *Financial Times,* August 29, 1997, p. 16.

——, "Trying to Lay a £900m Spectre," *Financial Times,* November 6, 1997, p. 29.

Hollinger, Peggy, and Graham Bowley, "Boots Expands into Germany," *Financial Times,* September 11, 1997, p. 31.

Humes, Christopher Brown, "DIY, Disillusionment and Divorce," *Financial Times,* August 22, 1996, p. 21.

Jackson, Tony, "Registering the Value of Cash," *Financial Times,* January 19, 1998, p. 14.

Monopolies and Mergers Commission, *The Boots Company Limited and the House of Fraser Limited: A Report on the Proposed Merger,* London: HMSO, 1974, 44 p.

Weir, Christopher, *Jesse Boot of Nottingham: Founder of the Boots Company,* Nottingham: The Boots Company PLC, 1994.

Weyer, Martin Vander, "Good Value at Boots," *Management Today,* September 1995, pp. 42+.

—Judy Slinn
—updated by David E. Salamie

Bouygues S.A.

1, avenue Eugène Freyssinet
78061 Saint-Quentin
Yvelines Cedex
France
(1) 30-60-23-11
Fax: (1) 30-60-48-61
Web site: http://www.bouygues.fr

Public Company
Incorporated: 1952
Employees: 101,000
Sales: FFr91.07 billion (US$18.21 billion) (1997)
Stock Exchanges: Paris
SICs: 1541 General Contractors-Industrial Buildings &
  Warehouses; 1542 General Contractors-Non-
  Residential Buildings; 1611 Highway & Street
  Construction, Except Elevated Highway; 1622 Bridge,
  Tunnel & Elevated Highway Construction; 1629
  Heavy Construction, Not Elsewhere Classified; 2041
  Flour & Other Grain Mill Products; 4812 Radio
  Telephone Communications; 4813 Telephone
  Communications, Except Radio Telephone; 4833
  Television Broadcasting Stations; 4841 Cable & Other
  Pay Television Services; 4899 Communication
  Services, Not Elsewhere Classified; 4941 Water
  Supply; 4952 Sewerage Systems; 7812 Motion Picture
  & Video Tape Production; 7822 Motion Picture &
  Video Tape Distribution; 8711 Engineering Services

Bouygues S.A. is a diversified group with two main operating sectors: construction and services. The construction sector is the business upon which the company was founded and includes buildings, oil-related and maritime works, public works, roads, and property. Starting in the 1980s, founder Francis Bouygues (pronounced ''Bweeg'') developed the services sector, which includes management of public utilities as well as media and telecommunications interests. The company is active in about 80 countries, and generates about 35 percent of its revenues outside of France.

Early History

Prior to 1952, Francis Bouygues worked alongside Eugène Freyssinet, a construction pioneer who revolutionized the industry through the introduction of prestressed concrete. With a sense of vision inspired by the works of Freyssinet, and an entrepreneurial spirit that would become his trademark, the young engineer used a US$1,700 loan acquired from his family to set up a small firm which operated from his apartment.

Much of Bouygues's work lacked the glamour of his future achievements. Yet Bouygues immersed himself in every aspect of his business, from driving a truck to managing construction sites. His first construction jobs included the renovation of old factories and predawn repair work at the Lido cabaret.

It was not long before Bouygues had made a name for himself; positive trends in the industry afforded Bouygues many opportunities to demonstrate his business acumen. To ensure the ready identification of the company's projects, Bouygues became one of the first firms to paint its equipment uniformly in one color, ''minimum orange.''

As the construction industry expanded during the 1950s and 1960s, due mainly to large public works projects, the rate of employee turnover became problematic. Competition among companies to hire workers was so acute that employees of Bouygues worked an average of only six months. In order to halt this trend, Bouygues created an elite corps of workers in 1963 called the *Compagnons du Min-orange*. Identified by the company color, this cadre of membership-only employees displayed greater dedication to the company, were less likely to leave Bouygues, and asked for fewer salary increases.

Membership in the *Compagnons* required nomination by a site manager and approval by a committee of *Compagnons*. Only one in ten nominees gained admittance. Members of the corps wore uniforms with badges or stars indicating rank. Although membership assured job security, members could be demoted, if they proved unworthy of their rank. *Compagnons* were rewarded with long weekend holidays to such vacation spots as Sardinia, Istanbul, and Dubrovnik. Bouygues's plan worked well; employee turnover decreased noticeably.

With a force of committed workers in place, Bouygues proceeded to make impressive gains in the industry. During the 1950s and 1960s the company erected several subsidized housing projects in Paris. The company's first large-scale project was the Parc des Princes soccer stadium, awarded to Bouygues in 1969. While the contract marked Bouygues's entrance to the higher ranks of the industry, Francis Bouygues's enthusiasm failed to conceal a certain degree of inexperience.

An extremely complex design, combined with the need for custom-made precast concrete, threatened the project from the start. When the first column erected began to slide, a school near the construction site was evacuated. With his reputation at stake, Bouygues quickly assumed personal control of the project and instituted corrective measures. When the project was completed (ahead of schedule), Bouygues's profit from the job was negligible. Nevertheless, Bouygues earned great respect for its efforts, and soon new orders began to accumulate.

Unlike industry competitors, Francis Bouygues insisted on complete control of his projects. And even though he was compelled to form partnerships on several occasions, he nevertheless avoided these arrangements as much as possible. In one instance, a joint highway contract placed Bouygues at one end of a road and the company's partner at the other end. Joint work commenced only when the two roads were connected.

Another example of Francis Bouygues's management style was shown by his decision to create a company union in 1968. This came at a time when the industry was plagued with labor disagreement and strikes. As members of a separate union, Bouygues employees never joined these strikes. Bouygues later encouraged his employees to gain affiliation with the Force Ouvrière, a politically conservative nationwide union, largely opposed to the more militant Confédération Générale du Travail. Force Ouvrière organized many of Bouygues's employees, although as late as 1982, 70 percent elected to remain exclusively with the company union. Even more significant than its lack of union organization, Bouygues employees had very few grievances; all were generally well-paid.

Domestic and Overseas Expansion Started in the Mid-1970s

Bouygues went public on the Paris Stock Exchange in 1970. The company's successes in and around Paris continued to grow as Bouygues completed power plants, an airport passenger terminal, a conference center, and numerous skyscrapers. In 1974 the company established Bouygues Offshore, a constructor of offshore oil rigs, barges, and other oil-related and maritime works. By the mid-1970s Bouygues announced plans to expand on two fronts: in the remainder of France, and overseas. Domestic operations centered on the private home building industry. The Maison Bouygues division built homes to satisfy individual tastes at inexpensive prices. By the early 1980s Bouygues had become the largest home builder in France.

The company's late entrance into overseas markets compelled Bouygues to bid lower than its competitors for an Iranian

contract to build the 1974 Asian Games stadium in Teheran. Bouygues's price was 30 to 40 percent less than those of larger industry veterans such as Bechtel Group, Inc. Bouygues won the contract. This project led to further contracts to build residences in Iran and to perform repairs on the Shah's palace. Using the revolutionary concrete truss design of the Asian Games stadium, Bouygues went on to complete the 1.5-mile Bubiyan Bridge in Kuwait in 1983. Business expanded to Iraq, where the company constructed a nuclear power plant (destroyed by Israeli bombing in 1984). In addition, Bouygues constructed a mosque in Jeddah, Saudi Arabia. Outside the Middle East, the company secured contracts to build power plants and universities in West Africa.

As eager as it was to enter foreign markets, Bouygues was prevented from doing so by strict financial policies which were intended to protect the company from losses in unstable countries. Francis Bouygues refused to work on credit in these high-risk markets, and always remained ready to leave them on short notice; during the Iranian revolution in 1978, Bouygues moved out without incurring any losses.

One exception to Bouygues's reluctance to work with partners came in the late 1970s, when the Saudi Arabian government opened bidding for the construction of the University of Riyadh. Bouygues's desire to maintain his independence was overridden by his ambition; when the Saudi government informed Bouygues that his company was too small to win the contract alone, he formed a partnership with Alabama-based Blount, Inc. Still, Bouygues insisted on a 55 percent controlling interest in the partnership, which gave him the final approval in all decisions. The 40-month deadline set by the Saudis for the completion of the project discouraged most bidders. By the time the US$2 billion contract was to be awarded, all but two contenders had dropped out of the competition. When the contract was finally awarded to the Bouygues-Blount partnership in 1981, it was the largest fixed-price construction agreement ever. Because the two companies stood to lose money if the construction fell behind schedule, Bouygues and Blount completed the project on time and collected an additional US$50 million windfall.

Bouygues entered the 1980s with impressive financial credentials and great prestige. Yet changes in both the French and world economies forced the company to change its business strategy. High interest rates, falling oil prices, and a shrinking construction market forced Bouygues to reduce its workforce. President François Mitterand's social policies reduced the amount of government funds available for large public works projects. To compensate for the changing economic conditions, Bouygues was also forced to alter its financing methods for overseas projects; the Nigerian government paid the company four months late for a US$620 million power plant.

Began Diversifying in the 1980s

Bouygues initiated a program of diversification in order to mitigate the effects of the beleaguered construction market. An attempt to purchase Druout, a French insurance company, was thwarted when that company's former owners sued to halt the takeover. Later, Bouygues acquired a 55 percent share of Amrep S.A., an oil services company. In an attempt to broaden its presence in the United States, Bouygues purchased a number of engineering firms and reorganized them as an Omaha-based consortium called HDR, Inc. A larger holding company, called the Centerra Corporation, was also formed to perform work in design, engineering, financing, and construction. Centerra's first large project was construction of the New World Center in Seattle.

Among other acquisitions, the more significant long-term were Saur (water treatment and supply), ETDE (electrical power and communications networks), and Smac Acieroïd (waterproofing). However, the largest of all Bouygues's purchases of this period was in the area of construction. France's second largest construction group, Screg, accumulated a massive debt which made it vulnerable to a takeover; Bouygues thereby acquired Screg Group in 1986. With the addition of Screg, Bouygues's revenues increased to nearly US$7 billion. Through three Screg Group companies—Colas, Screg, and Sacer—Bouygues became involved in the road construction industry. Bouygues also added another construction company in 1986, Dragages et Travaux Publics, which specialized in public works.

In 1987 the company failed to take over Spie-Batignolles, a large French contractor in which Bouygues claimed it had an original 10 percent interest. Not only was the attempted takeover particularly acrimonious, it resulted in an inquiry in which Bouygues was accused of failing to declare a major corporate interest. (French law required investors to declare any corporate interest in excess of 10 percent.) The Commission des Operations de Bourse, the French stock market regulatory committee, later charged Bouygues with failing to declare a 24 percent interest in Spie-Batignolles.

Bouygues continued to diversify in the late 1980s. In April 1987 Bouygues and a consortium of private investors acquired a controlling interest in TF1, the leading French national television network. In 1989 the company acquired Grands Moulines de Paris, the leading flour-milling concern in France. Bouygues's construction side also completed several prestigious construction projects in the late 1990s: the Île de Ré Bridge in western France in 1988; the Grande Arche de La Défense, which was Paris's main monument to the bicentennial of the French Revolution, in 1989; and the Hassan II Mosque in Casablanca, also in 1989. In 1988 the company also moved into its impressive new headquarters, called Challenger, located in Saint-Quentin-en-Yvelines, northeast of Paris.

But perhaps the most noteworthy event of the late 1980s was the change in leadership at Bouygues. That year, Martin Bouygues, 37-year-old son of the company founder, was appointed group chairman and CEO. Francis Bouygues remained involved in the company's media activities, not only TF1 but also the 1990 launch of a start-up film production company, Ciby 2000. As chairman of Ciby 2000, Francis Bouygues helped to develop a movie company that produced such award-winning films as *The Piano* (1993), *Underground* (1995), and *Secrets and Lies* (1996). Bouygues, however, died of a heart attack at age 71 on July 24, 1993, after suffering from a long illness. He did not survive to see Ciby 2000 become profitable by 1997, at which time it had the rights to 80 films.

But also by that time, Bouygues (the company) decided to put the nascent production company up for sale.

1990s and Beyond

Meanwhile, under Martin Bouygues's leadership, Bouygues completed several noteworthy construction projects in the 1990s, several through partnerships: the Library of France in 1992; the Channel Tunnel, which connected England and France, and the Normandy Bridge, the longest cable-stayed structure in the world, both in 1994; the Sydney metro in 1995; the Central Railway Station in Kuala Lumpur, Malaysia, in 1997; and the Stade de France, a stadium finished in time for the 1998 World Cup (of soccer) held in France. The company also continued to expand its nonconstruction operations. In 1991 Saur entered the power supply business. In 1994 the company increased its stake in TF1 from 25 percent to 37.5 percent. Forming partnerships became increasingly common at Bouygues in the 1990s, and in 1994 the company joined with French and international partners in winning a license for the third French mobile telephone network. A mobile service was subsequently launched by Bouygues Telecom on May 29, 1996. Bouygues in May 1994 entered into a strategic alliance with French power utility EDF to develop joint operations internationally in the area of public utilities management. In 1997 Bouygues purchased another French utilities company, Cise, and merged it with Saur to create the third largest public utilities management group in France.

While this expansion continued, problems were cropping up. In 1995 Bouygues posted a net loss of US$593 million resulting from writeoffs taken for losses in its property business and for start-up costs associated with Bouygues Telecom and the development of a paging service called Kobby. Several senior executives, including Martin Bouygues, were under formal investigation during 1997 for "misuse of corporate funds." And the company faced pressure from one of its largest shareholders—French financier Vincent Bolloré, who purchased about 10 percent of Bouygues through the open market in late 1997 and early 1998—to divest its money-losing telecommunications businesses. But it appeared that Bouygues had no intention to do so, and in fact announced in December 1997 that it had formed a joint venture called 9 Telecom with Telecom Italia and Veba Telecom of Germany to develop a fixed-line telephone service in France. This latest move was made in anticipation of Europe's telecommunications markets being opened to competition at the beginning of 1998. Meantime, Bouygues had improved its financial position through the late 1996 initial public offering of 40 percent of Bouygues Offshore.

Bouygues returned to profitability for both 1996 and 1997. Revenues reached US$15.34 billion by 1997, more than double the level of ten years earlier. Construction remained by far Bouygues's largest sector, accounting for more than two-thirds of overall revenue. About 15 percent came from public utilities operations, 11 percent from media, and only 4.7 percent from telecommunications. Bouygues neared the 21st century running strong operations in construction and public utilities, with a more uncertain future in media and telecommunications.

Principal Subsidiaries

Bouygues BTP; Bouygues Offshore S.A. (60%); Bouygues Immobilier; Colas (57%); Saur (84.7%); TF1 (40%); Bouygues Telecom (55%); Grands Moulins de Paris.

Further Reading

Barbanel, Alain, and Jean Menanteau, *Bouygues: L'empire moderne,* Paris: Ramsay, 1987.

"Bouygues Offshore Building Future Offshore Business While Diversifying into Onshore, Maritime, and Maintenance," *Offshore,* April 1992, pp. 71+.

Campagnac, Elisabeth, and Vincent Nouzille, *Citizen Bouygues, ou, L'histoire secrete d'un grand patron,* Paris: P. Belfond, 1988, 511 p.

Cane, Alan, "Bouygues Leads New Telecoms Venture," *Financial Times,* December 10, 1997, p. 34.

Cane, Alan, David Owen, and Robert Graham, "Stet Joins Bouygues in French Telecoms Move," *Financial Times,* October 11, 1996, p. 24.

Carson-Parker, John, "Francis Bouygues Reshapes Europe," *Chief Executive,* July/August 1989, pp. 34–37.

Cohen, Norma, "Lehman and Bouygues Plan East European Malls," *Financial Times,* March 13, 1998, p. 21.

Crabbe, Matthew, "A Good M&A Vintage in Prospect," *Euromoney,* January 1987, pp. 35+.

Hurtado, Robert, "The Rising Tide of Oil Strikes Lifts a Floating-Platform Maker," *New York Times,* August 21, 1997, p. D8.

Owen, David, "Bouygues Quiet on Possible Revamp," *Financial Times,* April 1, 1998, p. 28.

——, "Bouygues Seeks Transatlantic Link," *Financial Times,* April 7, 1998, p. 30.

——, "Bouygues Under Pressure," *Financial Times,* April 6, 1998, p. 24.

——, "French Businessmen in Probe," *Financial Times,* February 28, 1997, p. 2.

——, "Lines to Profit Still Open as Bouygues Enters French Mobile Market," *Financial Times,* June 19, 1996, p. 31.

Ridding, John, "Bouygues-Led Consortium Wins Mobile Net License," *Financial Times,* October 5, 19 94, p. 30.

Schenker, Jennifer L., "Stet and Bouygues Team Up to Create French Phone Firm," *Financial Times,* October 11, 1996, p. A7F.

Schuman, Joseph, "Bouygues Bid Boldest," *Variety,* November 27, 1995, p. 76.

Tully, Shawn, "France's Master Builder Is on the March," *Fortune,* May 2, 1983, pp. 210+.

Tutt, Nigel, "An Effective Performer," *Financial Times,* November 19, 1997, p. FTS6.

—updated by David E. Salamie

BRIO AB

BRIOgaten 1
SE-283 83, Osby
Sweden
(464) 791-9000
Fax: (464) 791-4724
Web site: http://www.brio.se

Public Company
Incorporated: 1884
Employees: 1,052
Sales: SEK 1.41 billion (1997)
Stock Exchanges: Stockholm
SICs: 5092 Toys & Hobby Goods & Supplies; 3944
    Games, Toys & Children's Vehicles; 5945 Hobby,
    Toy & Game Shops

BRIO AB is a century-old toy company based in Osby, Sweden, with subsidiaries in North America and Europe. The family-run company operates in several child-related business areas. BRIO is best known for its line of wooden trains and preschool toys which are sold by 14,000 stores in 34 countries. With a market share of about 40 percent, BRIO is the largest supplier of wooden toys in the world. In the Nordic region (Sweden, Norway, Finland, and Denmark), BRIO is the leading toy wholesaler, distributing both its own BRIO brand toys and a wide range of imports including products from such large American toy manufacturers as Hasbro, Tyco, Mattel, and Fisher-Price. The company also manufactures a line of baby carriages and high-chairs that are marketed primarily in the Nordic region. BRIO's Lek & Lär division, operating in Sweden, Norway, and Finland, distributes daycare and school equipment through a mail-order catalogue. Other ventures include the manufacture and sale of Alga games, a toy wholesaling business in Poland, and a promotional toy licensing company.

Company Origins at the Turn of the Century

The roots of the BRIO organization are traced back to 1878 when 17-year-old Ivar Bengtsson invested his savings of 77 riksdaler (the Swedish currency of the time) in the purchase of woven slatted baskets to sell in neighboring Denmark. The youthful venture was a success, and by 1884 Bengtsson and his wife, Sissa, were operating a small basket factory out of their cottage in Boalt, just outside Osby, Sweden. By 1902 the basket company required larger facilities, and the company was moved to Osby, an expanding community in the province of Skåne. Osby's position on the main railway line in the country made it an excellent location for the growing wholesaling concern because it allowed Bengtsson to distribute his products across the region.

With its new location and facilities, the Ivar Bengtsson Basket Company was able to greatly expand its product line. The 1907 catalogue lists more than 170 articles available for order. Among these items was the Göinge Horse, a traditional wooden pull toy. This small, painted horse on wheels marked BRIO's first entry into the wooden toy business that would become the company's hallmark product line.

In 1908, at the age of 47, Bengtsson decided to turn his business over to his sons, Viktor, Anton, and Emil Ivarsson. Although the three boys were still young, Bengtsson hoped that by giving them the management of the company they would be dissuaded from joining the waves of Swedish youths who were then immigrating to the United States. His ploy worked. The boys stayed in Sweden, and the company name was changed to BRIO for Bröderna Ivarsson of Osby (Ivarsson Brothers of Osby). The company continued to expand its range of product offerings so that by 1914 the BRIO catalogue offered 6,000 items for sale by mail-order and traveling salesmen. Product types included toys, ceramics, glass, and porcelain among other diverse merchandise. BRIO also opened a small retail shop, called the "15-öre Bazaar," to sell the company's products directly to Osby consumers.

BRIO Brands and Barbie, 1930–70

BRIO opened a new phase in its history in 1930 when the bold BRIO trademark was painted onto the side of two wooden cars distributed by the company. The development of the BRIO brand would become key to the growth and development of the company over the next 70 years. Some five years later the company lent its name to a line of baby carriages manufactured by another Osby firm but distributed by BRIO. By the mid-1930s, when BRIO was officially incorporated as a limited liability corporation, the company was employing 150 people and had achieved annual sales of SEK 4.3 million. BRIO's product line had begun to focus on the wooden toys and baby carriages that would become the core of the company's business.

Although BRIO had been placing its brand name on products distributed by the company since the 1930s, it was only after World War II that BRIO began its own manufacturing concern with the opening of a baby carriage factory in 1947. By the late 1950s the postwar baby boom had come into full swing and BRIO baby carriages became one of the best-selling brands in the country. This success was cemented in 1959 with the introduction of the Sylvana model, the first baby carriage in the world to be equipped with a fully-welded collapsible frame.

BRIO toys received worldwide recognition with the introduction of the BRIO Labyrint in 1946. The wooden maze toy, with its distinctive tilting box, was distributed throughout the world during the 1950s and 1960s and was largely responsible for the original dissemination of the BRIO brand name. Following the success of Labyrint, BRIO began to expand its line of wooden toys for the domestic and international markets. The 1950s saw the introduction of Bygg-BRIO, a wooden construction toy that was the predecessor to BRIO MEC, and, most significantly, the BRIO Wooden Railway, which was to become the best-selling wooden railway in the world and BRIO's most popular toy ever.

The 1960s were marked by growth in BRIO's importing and wholesaling business, which increased dramatically in 1963 when BRIO obtained the Scandinavian distribution rights to a new American fashion doll, Barbie. The attraction of this small plastic doll to little girls was apparently universal as total sales for BRIO jumped by over 30 percent in a single year thanks to the Barbie phenomenon. In 1964 the company set up new subsidiaries in Denmark and Finland, followed six years later by a Norwegian subsidiary, largely in order to distribute the fashion doll. Although sales for Barbie tapered off in following years, the doll remained a substantial part of the BRIO import unit through the 1970s and a factor in the company's sales in Norway through the 1990s.

BRIO Wooden Toys for the Export Market, 1970–90

While in the domestic and Nordic markets the center of BRIO's business was toy wholesaling and baby carriages, beginning in the 1970s the export of BRIO brand wooden trains, construction toys, and preschool toys to the rest of Europe and North America became a substantial contributor to total revenues. Previously, BRIO toys had been exported via distribution agreements with toy wholesalers but in 1974 small subsidiaries were opened in the United Kingdom and Germany mainly in order to market the company's wooden toys.

It was the opening of the American subsidiary BRIO Corp. in 1977, however, that changed the nature of BRIO's toy business. BRIO Corp. was largely the product of its president, Peter Reynolds, and his determination to create a market for the company's high-quality toys. Reynolds began his career as a salesman for a variety of British food distributors but had moved to Milwaukee when he was hired by a British jigsaw puzzle company that was one of the five agents for BRIO products in the United States. When that company went bankrupt in 1975, Reynolds persuaded BRIO to let him use the Milwaukee warehouse to establish a U.S. subsidiary.

From the start, Reynolds had his own approach to the marketing of BRIO's wooden toys, believing that they would sell only because they were truly good toys and that his job consisted of convincing parents that good toys were important to their children's development. Key to Reynolds's marketing philosophy was his insistence that the small retail stores that had traditionally sold the wooden toys were the best venue for promoting good play value. Even after sales of BRIO toys started to take off in the United States, Reynolds refused to market his product to the large superstores like Toys "R" Us that were taking over the American toy retail industry. This strategy allowed BRIO Corp. to maintain a close relationship with the owners of small toy boutiques who did not have to worry about price undercutting by the big chains.

The relationship with small toy stores was crucial to the marketing of BRIO toys because it permitted Reynolds to run educational campaigns instructing salespeople about the benefits of the products. "We need people who'll tell the story, not just show [the product]." Reynolds told the *Seattle Times*. The story that Reynolds wanted told was that BRIO toys promote good play by catering to the "whole" child which includes the child's physical, social, and intellectual development. Reynolds's campaigns also stressed the value of the high-priced BRIO toys. "BRIO-trained retailers are able to educate customers about the concepts of open-ended toys and playthings as an investment. For example, a $50 set of wooden blocks is both open-ended and an investment because it captures the child's attention and imagination in different ways over the years. Such a toy, if played with for five years, costs only $10 a year—a wise, long-term purchase," Reynolds wrote in a column in *Playthings*.

Reynolds had to convince not only store owners and parents about the importance of good play but his bosses in Sweden as well. "They didn't really understand the importance of play. Consequently, they didn't understand the value of their toys," he explained to the *Milwaukee Journal*. If Reynolds's philosophy had not sold the parent company on the merits of his approach, his results would have. When Reynolds started the U.S. subsidiary, sales of BRIO toys in the United States were under $4 million and accounted for only a negligible percentage of BRIO's total sales. By 1991, U.S. sales had mounted to $14.6 million and represented over 50 percent of BRIO wooden toys sold worldwide. Reynolds's approach to marketing was adopted wholeheartedly by BRIO AB, which began to actively promote the "good play" value of the company's wooden toys.

In 1985 a Canadian subsidiary, BRIO Scanditoy, was opened to further grow North American sales. Under the direction of Kate Baldwin, BRIO Scanditoy adopted the same approach to marketing that had spelled such a success for BRIO Corp., emphasizing the company's relationship to the toy boutiques that sold BRIO products. Canadian sales reached about five percent of BRIO's wooden toy sales by the 1990s.

Domestic Growth in the 1980s-90s

In addition to growth in the export of BRIO's wooden toys, in the Nordic region the company's toy and baby carriage business continued to expand. In the early 1980s BRIO AB won the distribution rights to the American board game Monopoly from Sweden's leading game company, Alga, and then proceeded to buy the Alga subsidiary from the Bonniers Company outright. In the mid-1980s BRIO obtained the rights to a number of very successful promotional toys, including Trivial Pursuit and My Little Pony, as well as reaching a distribution agreement with General Mills toys. The combined sales of these products caused the company's total income to rise to a record SEK 68.3 million on sales of SEK 1.008 billion in 1987.

The management and ownership of BRIO AB had remained in the Ivarsson family throughout the century. In 1985 the balance of ownership changed somewhat when the company issued an IPO of shares on the OTC market of the Stockholm Stock Exchange. This offering came in conjunction with a share offering to employees that saw 60 percent of BRIO employees buying a stake in the company.

In the 1990s a number of new BRIO brand product introductions, including plush toys, bath toys, and child-sized gardening tools, along with a 1992 distribution agreement with Hasbro,

created record income of SEK 85 million on sales of SEK 1.52 billion in 1994.

After the impressive results of the early 1990s, the company suffered a decline in sales towards the mid-1990s. A sharp drop in the Swedish birthrate coupled with the loss of the Hasbro license damaged the company's baby carriage and wholesale business in the Nordic region, and in 1997 BRIO suffered a net loss of SEK 28 million, the largest loss in the company's history. Restructuring costs involved with the purchase of Plasto Bambola, a maker of high-quality plastic toys, also added to the company's financial difficulties. By 1998 it appeared likely that the general restructuring of the worldwide toy industry, which was undergoing dramatic consolidation, would force BRIO to make changes in the company's toy wholesaling business. The timelessness of the BRIO brand wooden toys, however, virtually guaranteed the viability of the company into the next century.

Principal Subsidiaries

BRIO Leksaker; BRIO Toy; Alga; BRIO Barnvagnar; BRIO Lek & Lär; BRIO A/S (Denmark); BRIO OY (Finland); BRIO AS (Norway); BRIO Ltd. (U.K.); BRIO Wonderland Ltd. (U.K.); BRIO Corp. (U.S.); BRIO Scanditoy Inc. (Canada); BRIO SA (France).

Further Reading

"BRIO Beefs Up Three Major Toy Lines," *Playthings,* February 1993, p. 117.
Foster, Janine, and Otte Rosenkrantz, "Child's Play," *London Business Monthly Magazine,* June 1997, pp. 18–22.
Israelson, David, "Little Engines of Wood Scale Heights in Toy Trade," *Toronto Star,* February 6, 1996, p. D1.
Newhouse, David, "Beanie Babies Cross Toyland's Great Divide," *Seattle Times,* December 21, 1997, p. E1.
Reynolds, Peter, " 'Children First' Focus Helps Specialty Retails," *Playthings,* February 1989, p. 278.
Schmelz, Abigail, "Swedish Toy Maker Says Business Not Child's Play," *Journal of Commerce,* December 23, 1996, p. A5.
Sharma-Jensen, Geeta, "The Mantra of Mr. Brio," *Milwaukee Journal,* December 19, 1993, pp. D1–D2.

—Hilary Gopnik

British Aerospace plc

Warwick House
Farnborough Aerospace Centre
Farnborough
Hampshire GU14 6YU
United Kingdom
(01252) 373-232
Fax: (01252) 383-000
Web site: http://www.bae.co.uk/html/home.htm

Public Company
Incorporated: 1978
Employees: 75,823
Sales: £8.55 billion (1997)
Stock Exchanges: London
Ticker Symbol: BTASF
SICs: 1522 General Contractors, Other Than Single-
   Family Houses; 1541 General Contractors—Industrial
   Buildings & Warehouses; 1542 General Contractors—
   Non-Residential Buildings; 1622 Bridge, Tunnel &
   Elevated Highway Construction; 1629 Heavy
   Construction, Not Elsewhere Classified; 3482 Small
   Arms Ammunition; 3483 Ammunition, Except Small
   Arms, Not Elsewhere Classified; 3484 Small Arms;
   3489 Ordnance & Accessories, Not Elsewhere
   Classified; 3663 Radio & TV Broadcasting &
   Communications Equipment; 3721 Aircraft; 3764
   Guided Missile & Space Vehicle Propulsion Units &
   Propulsion Unit Parts; 8711 Engineering Services;
   8741 Management Services

British Aerospace plc (BAe) is the largest defense contractor in Europe, as well as being a leading aerospace company. The company's defense operations include military aircraft, missiles, small arms and ammunition, warships, and combat command systems. In aerospace, BAe holds a 20 percent interest in Airbus Industrie, the European plane-making consortium, provides a variety of services, and makes various equipment. The largest exporter in the United Kingdom, BAe generates more than 80 percent of its revenues overseas. In addition to its defense and aerospace operations, British Aerospace also has a property development unit called Arlington Securities plc, which is a leading developer of business parks in the United Kingdom.

Many of BAe's activities are conducted through international joint ventures and consortia, with more than 30 partners linked to the company. In addition to Airbus Industrie, other notable BAe-involved ventures include Eurofighter Jagdflugzeug GmbH, which is 33 percent owned by BAe and is developing the next-generation Eurofighter 2000 military aircraft; Euromissile Dynamics Group, which is developing the Trigat third-generation antitank missile and is owned by three equal partners: BAe, Aérospatiale S.A. of France, and Daimler-Benz Aerospace AG (DASA) of Germany; Matra-BAe Dynamics, which is 50-50 owned by BAe and Lagardère Groupe SCA of France and specializes in guided missile systems; Panavia Aircraft GmbH, a three-nation consortium, 42.5 percent owned by BAe, which produces the Tornado military aircraft; and Saab-BAe Gripen AB, which makes the Gripen combat aircraft and is 50-50 owned by BAe and Saab Aircraft AB of Sweden. British Aerospace also holds a 35 percent stake in Saab AB, the parent of Saab Aircraft.

Predecessors Consolidated in the 1960s

In the years after World War II the British aircraft industry was overpopulated with manufacturers who had an increasingly difficult time competing not only with each other but with larger American manufacturers such as Boeing, Douglas (later McDonnell Douglas), and Lockheed. British companies were victimized by small orders from a government that was divesting itself of most of its empire and thus had greatly reduced military needs. Noting that the British aircraft industry was three times larger than France's, "with no obvious justification for being so," the *Economist* asked the critical question, "Does Britain need an aircraft industry?" Throughout the 1950s the health of British aviation was a major political issue and was the subject of many Parliamentary debates. Finally, in 1960, after intense lobbying from the Minister of Aviation, Duncan Sandys, Parliament passed a bill that called for a "rationalization" of the British aircraft industry through the merger of several existing companies that were facing closure.

The purpose of the rationalization was to combine the talent and resources of about 20 companies and limit overall production, while avoiding the politically sensitive issue of creating unemployment or allowing the British aeronautics industry to fall victim to external economic pressures. It was hoped that the program would raise the intensity of technological development to a level equal to that of the Americans. It was also noted that British aeronautic companies were diversifying themselves out of aircraft production, a trend that could have left Britain without an aircraft industry of any kind.

Early in 1960 Vickers-Armstrong, Ltd., which was originally founded in 1928, merged with English Electric (founded in 1918) and Bristol Aeroplane (founded in 1910) to form the British Aircraft Corporation (BAC). The three companies continued to operate as divisions of BAC, with Vickers and English Electric each accounting for 40 percent of the consortium's capital and the remaining 20 percent coming from Bristol. In May 1960 BAC acquired a controlling interest in another British company, Hunting Aircraft.

At the time of the British Aircraft Corporation merger, a second group of British aircraft companies were amalgamated to form the Hawker-Siddeley Aviation Company. Like BAC, Hawker-Siddeley's constituent companies, Armstrong Whitworth (founded in 1921), A.V. Roe & Company (1910), Folland Aircraft (1935), Gloster Aircraft (1915), and Hawker Aircraft (1920), were operated as subsidiaries. Each brought an area of expertise to the new company. Armstrong produced large cargo airplanes, Avro built smaller passenger liners, and Folland, Gloster, and Hawker were known for their Gnat, Javelin, and Hunter jetfighters. Hawker-Siddeley also acquired a controlling interest in de Havilland Holdings, Ltd. and The Blackburn Group, as well as a 50 percent share of Bristol-Siddeley, Ltd., the airplane engine manufacturer.

The amalgamation that created British Aircraft Corporation and Hawker-Siddeley also made Westland Aircraft Britain's primary helicopter and hovercraft manufacturer. Rolls-Royce

(which received most of its publicity from its manufacture of automobiles but most of its profits from aircraft engine production) and Bristol-Siddeley, Ltd. became Britain's leading engine manufacturers. Handley Page, Short Brothers, Scottish Aviation, and British Executive and General Aviation were the only British companies that were not a part of the government's rationalization program.

During the 1960s BAC continued to manufacture English Electric's Lightning and Hunting's Jet Provost fighters in addition to Vickers's four-engine VC10 jetliner. The company also built a new twin-engine jetliner called the BAC-111. In 1962 BAC entered a coproduction agreement with Aérospatiale of France to build the Concorde supersonic passenger transport.

Hawker-Siddeley was divided into two divisions: Aircraft, for aircraft production, and Dynamics, for missiles and rockets. The aircraft division took over production of the HS-125 executive twin-jet from de Havilland and the HS-748 turboprop airliner from Avro. In 1964 it introduced the Trident, a three-engine jetliner intended to compete against the BAC-111, Douglas DC-9, and Boeing 727. In the military field, Hawker-Siddeley assumed production of Blackburn's Buccaneer fighter and developed the HS-1182 Hawk trainer as well as a military patrol version of the de Havilland Comet called the Nimrod. The unique product of Hawker-Siddeley during the 1960s was the Harrier fighter jet.

The Harrier featured thrust nozzles that the pilot could aim either straight backward or toward the ground. When the nozzles were pointed backward the Harrier could take off on a runway like a conventional jet. When the nozzles were pointed down it could take off vertically like a helicopter. The Harrier was built in two configurations, one for the Royal Air Force and one for Royal Navy aircraft carriers.

Hawker-Siddeley Dynamics produced the Seaslug, Firestreak, and Red Top missiles. BAC also operated a missile division that manufactured the Vigilant, Blue Water, Thunderbird, and Bloodhound missiles. The Bloodhound was a particularly effective weapon, but created a scandal when details of BAC's high profits from the project were made public.

The success of the rationalization program was, however, limited, and by 1965 Britain's aerospace industry was again unable to compete with foreign competitors. Lord Plowden headed a special Parliamentary committee that recommended a second major restructuring of the aircraft industry. The Plowden Report proposed that Rolls-Royce and Bristol-Siddeley merge to form a single company that manufactured aircraft engines. This merger, which included the sale of Hawker-Siddeley's 50 percent interest in Bristol-Siddeley to Rolls-Royce, was carried out in 1966. The second proposal, a merger of BAC and Hawker-Siddeley, was abandoned.

In February 1969 the governments of France and West Germany concluded an agreement that established a consortium called Airbus Industrie to manufacture a new passenger jetliner designated the A-300. The British government was invited to join Airbus as a full partner, but declined when it decided the project was doomed to failure. In its opinion, there was simply too little room in the commercial airliner market (already dominated by Boeing, McDonnell Douglas, and Lockheed) to support another competitor. Hawker-Siddeley, however, agreed to produce wings for the A-300 as an Airbus subcontractor. Because of intense competition, BAC and Hawker-Siddeley made no plans to develop successors to the BAC-11 and Trident. Even British Overseas Airways (BOAC), Britain's state-owned international air carrier, was ordering the more advanced American-made jetliners. In addition, the American aircraft companies had extremely profitable military divisions that enabled them to devote large sums of money to the development of new commercial aircraft. BAC and Hawker-Siddeley had excellent military divisions, but the requirements of the domestic military establishment were small. At the same time, the international arms market was dominated by the American and Soviet manufacturers. American arms import restrictions prevented Hawker-Siddeley from selling its Harrier to the United States, despite interest in the jet from the Pentagon.

More Financial Difficulties Led to 1977 Creation of BAe

British Aircraft Corporation, Messerschmitt-Bölkow-Blohm (MBB) of Germany, and Aeritalia of Italy created the Panavia partnership to develop the Tornado Interdictor Strike fighter. Separately, BAC and Breguet of France created another consortium called SEPECAT (Société Européenne de Production de L'avion E.C.A.T.) to develop the Jaguar jet fighter. Both of these programs were a financial drain on BAC, despite substantial contributions from the British government. Finally, it became apparent that BAC was unlikely to realize a profit from its costly coproduction of the Concorde with Aérospatiale. Only 16 were built (seven each for British Airways and Air France, with two remaining unsold), the first of which did not enter service until 1976. Once again the two largest British aerospace companies were in financial trouble and facing bankruptcy.

Engineers at Hawker-Siddeley designed a new short-haul 80-passenger jetliner called the HS-146. Convinced of the aircraft's commercial potential and the need for Hawker-Siddeley to remain in the commercial aircraft market, the British government pledged to share the development costs for the HS-146. To generate capital, the company's chairman, Sir Arnold Hall, authorized the sale of de Havilland of Canada to the Canadian government for $38 million. Similarly, BAC sold assembly rights for the BAC-111 to the government of Romania.

While the HS-146 was being developed, poor economic conditions and intense competition from the Americans eroded the already tenuous position of the British aerospace industry. In 1975 the Plowden merger proposal for BAC and Hawker-Siddeley had been resurrected in the form of an Aircraft and Shipping Industries Bill. The following year BAC and Hawker-Siddeley were nationalized, less in an attempt to protect their finances than to force a merger upon them. In 1977, after once being rejected in the House of Lords and defeated in the Commons, the Industries Bill was successfully ushered through Parliament.

The Aircraft and Shipping Industries Bill merged the Aircraft and Dynamics divisions of Hawker-Siddeley with the British Aircraft Corporation and Scottish Aviation, Ltd. The new company, called British Aerospace (BAe), continued to be operated by the British government as a state-owned corporation. British Aerospace was divided into two divisions: Aircraft, based at the Hawker-Siddeley facility in Kingston, and Dynamics, headquartered at the BAC Guided Weapons plant in Stevenage.

Scottish Aviation, the third and smallest member of the BAe group, was established in 1935 to create employment opportunities in aviation in Scotland. Scottish Aviation built the international airport in Prestwick, which later became the forward traffic control base for flights between London and North America. Later, Scottish Aviation manufactured a series of propeller-driven general purpose aircraft.

Joined Airbus Consortium in 1979

In 1978 British Aerospace considered partnership with foreign companies to produce a new large passenger airliner. Even in its new form British Aerospace lacked the resources to develop a commercial jetliner any larger than the HS-146 (renamed BAe-146). Airbus, for which BAe was still building A-300 wings, was a candidate, as was Boeing, which was beginning work on its next generation of commercial aircraft. To join Boeing would have been politically inexpedient since Boeing was the primary source of the British aerospace industry's decline. In addition, British officials expressed concern over Boeing's size and aggressive corporate personality. Joining Airbus, on the other hand, would require a substantial entry fee for development costs already incurred by the Airbus partners.

Eventually Boeing lost interest in a partnership with BAe. On January 1, 1979, British Aerospace purchased a 20 percent share of Airbus, pledging $500 million through 1983 for incurred costs and development of a new aircraft designated the A-310.

In 1979 Sir Keith Joseph, industry secretary for the Conservative government of Prime Minister Margaret Thatcher, announced the government's intention to privatize (or sell to the public) most of Britain's state-owned corporations, including British Aerospace. At first this announcement alarmed officials, including BAe Chairman Lord Beswick, who had worked hard to reform the nation's aerospace industry. They feared that private investors would divide the company and indiscriminately sell the more profitable divisions, possibly to foreigners.

The privatization program moved slowly because of political opposition and the government's desire to offer shares only when market conditions were most favorable. In the meantime, BAe appointed a new chairman to succeed Lord Beswick. The man they chose was the chairman of Esso Petroleum, Austin Pearce. Pearce was faced with the dual task of guiding British Aerospace through the privatization while ensuring that the company's orders were being filled. The increased military budget of the Conservative government contributed to the company's backlog of orders.

Became Public Company in 1981

The unconventional method in which British Aerospace was privatized established the form of future privatizations. On December 31, 1979, British Aerospace became a private limited company with authorized capital of £7 divided into seven shares, each with a par value of £1. All seven shares were held by nominees of the Secretary of State for Industry. On January 2, 1981, pursuant to the British Aerospace Act of 1980, the seven shares were split into 14, each with a value of 50p, and an additional 79,999,986 shares were created, raising the company's share capital to £40 million. On the same day, BAe adopted new Articles of Association and was registered as a public limited company. By February 4, 1981, British Aerospace's share capital was increased to 200 million shares, 50 million of which were made available to the public.

In its first year as a substantially public company, British Aerospace registered a pretax profit of £71 million. This was £6 million more than had been predicted, despite £50 million in development costs for the BAe-146 and A-310. The Panavia Tornado was past its development stages and in full production. The West German Panavia partner MBB prevented the consortium from realizing a substantial profit from the Tornado project, however, by not allowing exports of the fighter to countries outside of NATO, such as Saudi Arabia.

Management at British Aerospace was reorganized on January 1, 1983. Admiral Sir Raymond Lygo was appointed to the newly created position of managing director. Under the new system all group executives were to report to Sir Raymond. This enabled the board chairman, Pearce, to handle matters such as company finances more easily. One such external matter was British Aerospace's involvement in the Airbus A-320 project.

The A-320 was designed to carry 150 passengers and featured advanced "fly-by-wire" electronic control and navigation systems. BAe persuaded the other partners to allow it a 26 percent share of the A-320. The British government supported the company's involvement in the new Airbus project by making a £250 million line of credit available on favorable repayment terms. Under the terms of the agreement British Aerospace produced wings for the A-320.

Rejected Mid-1980s Takeover Bids

As a public company, BAe enjoyed greater independence in its policy making. But like other public companies it also risked becoming a takeover target. On May 15, 1984, the chairman of Thorn EMI, Peter Laister, announced his company's intention to merge with BAe. Thorn EMI was a profitable electronics and leisure conglomerate, whose assets included everything from production rights for video recorders to performance rights to Placido Domingo and the rock group Duran Duran. British Aerospace, described as a company that earned money making missiles and lost it building airliners, was also profitable but involved in an entirely different line of business. The London financial community reacted to Laister's announcement with amazement. In Parliament the Labour Party asked: "Is it sensible to allow a firm which has been successful in the fields of color television, videos and the marketing of pop groups to have the responsibility of looking after the development of Britain's largest company in civil and military aviation, in missile technology and space satellites?"

The announcement also invited criticism from the managing director of Britain's General Electric Company (GEC), Lord Weinstock: On two previous occasions when GEC expressed an interest in purchasing all or part of British Aerospace, it was privately rebuffed by the government, which was concerned that GEC would become too dominant a force in the British defense industry. GEC, which was a principal owner of BAC before 1977, was fully prepared to exceed any bid submitted by Thorn EMI.

In June 1984 British Aerospace rejected Thorn EMI's takeover proposal, and the following month did the same with GEC, citing a lack of any specific proposals. The government was satisfied with the takeover rejections because it ensured that British Aerospace would remain under British ownership and that it would continue to be a part of the Airbus group.

In 1985, confident about the company's position, the British government sold its 48 percent of British Aerospace, retaining, however, a special £1 share to ensure that BAe would stay under U.K. control. The £550 million offer was tightly restricted to institutional investors. The company also was reorganized into eight functional divisions during the year, a move that was intended to economize utilization of engineering teams by having them specialize in the development of products in specific fields. BAe was also the prime contractor on a lucrative contract known as Al Yamamah, which was signed with Saudi Arabia in 1985. Under Al Yamamah, the largest defense export contract in British history, BAe supplied Tornado fighter-bombers and other military aircraft to Saudi Arabia. By the early 1990s, the company's contracts with Saudi Arabia accounted for about half of its defense business.

In 1986 the Lockheed Corporation reached an agreement with BAe to develop new versions of the BAe-146 for military and cargo applications. Coproduction agreements with American companies were nothing new to British Aerospace, whose Harrier fighter jet had been built in the United States in conjunction with McDonnell Douglas since the mid-1970s.

Spate of Late 1980s and Early 1990s Acquisitions

In April 1987 British Aerospace acquired Royal Ordnance plc, a state-owned maker of small arms ammunition, for £190 million. Shortly thereafter, Pearce stepped down as chairman. Instead of Lygo replacing him, however, an outsider was brought in: Roland Smith, a professor of marketing who had been chairman of a number of other U.K. firms. Under Smith's leadership—which followed the predominant trend of the period—BAe diversified in the late 1980s and early 1990s through a spate of acquisitions, some of which resulted from additional British government privatizations. In 1987 the company acquired Steinheil Optronik GmbH, a German manufacturer of optical equipment, for £17 million, and Ballast Nedam Group, a Dutch construction concern, for £47 million. BAe also bought stakes that year in Reflectone Inc., a U.S.-based maker of flight simulators and other training devices, and System Designers plc, which specialized in computer software and systems and was renamed SD-Scicon plc (the latter stake was sold in July 1991). In 1988 Smith made his biggest—and farthest afield—purchase when BAe acquired The Rover Group plc, an automobile maker, from the British government for £150 million (US $255 million), a sum considered to be a steal. The following year British Aerospace continued to diversify by spending £278 million for Arlington Securities Plc, a major developer of business parks in the United Kingdom. BAe already had a large property portfolio, including substantial holdings gained with Royal Ordnance and with Rover, and the rationale for purchasing Arlington was that through streamlining and plant closings BAe would have additional property to develop and could generate profits by doing so.

Smith's last significant acquisitions were a 76 percent stake in Liverpool Airport in May 1990 and all of Heckler & Koch GmbH, a German small arms, machine tool, and general engineering company, in March 1991. By the time of the latter purchase, BAe was near collapse. A recession had severely impacted the automobile and real estate sectors, turning the acquisitions of Rover and Arlington sour. The economic downturn also wreaked havoc with the company's already troubled regional and corporate aircraft operations. Smith approached first Trafalgar House (a construction engineering and property group) and then GEC about a merger. When the BAe board found out about the talks with GEC, they ordered that the discussions be terminated. In September 1991 the company's dire straits forced Smith to attempt to raise £432 million (US $755 million) through a stock offering. When current shareholders revolted, the board ousted Smith, replacing him temporarily with Graham Day, who had been chairman of Rover. During Day's brief six-month tenure, he succeeded in turning away yet another attempt by GEC to acquire BAe. He also restructured the company's defense operations, placing them under a single umbrella subsidiary called British Aerospace Defence Limited.

Restructuring Began in 1992

In April 1992 John Cahill, former chief executive of BTR PLC, was brought in as the new chairman. By this time, thanks in large part to Smith, British Aerospace had evolved into a quite unwieldy conglomerate, with seven core activities: defense, Rover, Airbus, commercial property development, corporate aircraft, regional aircraft, and satellite communications. Under Cahill, BAe began a major restructuring aimed at concentrating the company's efforts on the first four of these seven areas. In late 1992 the company took a £1 billion writeoff to close a plant belonging to its troubled regional aircraft unit and to lay off 3,000 workers. For the year, BAe posted an after-tax loss of £970 million. The company attempted to spin off the regional aircraft unit into a joint venture with Taiwan Aerospace Corporation but the deal fell through. BAe proceeded, however, to sell its corporate jet unit to Raytheon Co. in June 1993. Earlier that year, in January, the company had secured a second-stage Al Yamamah contract with Saudi Arabia totaling US $7.5 billion.

Meanwhile, behind the scenes, Cahill had approached GEC yet again about a merger, this time of the two companies' defense units. When word leaked out in mid-1993 about the discussions, the BAe board once again quickly moved to scuttle the talks. Nevertheless, British Aerospace remained in financial trouble and it was expected that merger talks would soon revive. But within a matter of months, BAe's financial picture improved dramatically following a spate of divestments, which exceeded the initial bounds of Cahill's restructuring. In December 1993 Ballast Nedam was sold to a consortium of Hochtief

AG, Internationale Nederlanden Group, and the Ballast Nedam Pension Fund. In March 1994 Rover, which was gobbling up cash and whose acquisition was proving to be a huge blunder, was sold to BMW AG, with BAe netting £529 million in the process. And in July of that same year the company's satellite communications unit was sold to Matra Marconi Space for £56 million. Around this same time, yet another boardroom coup resulted in the ouster of Cahill, who was replaced by Bob Bauman, former CEO of U.S. pharmaceutical giant SmithKline Beecham.

Mid-1990s European Aerospace/ Defense Consolidation

While BAe had been busy cleaning up its balance sheet and trying to stay independent, dramatic changes in the world scene brought new threats. Following the breakup of the Soviet Union and the concomitant end of the Cold War, the defense industry in the United States quickly consolidated into three giant firms—Boeing, Lockheed Martin, and Raytheon. In Europe, however, consolidation did not come nearly so quickly, and European companies were increasingly at a competitive disadvantage in comparison with U.S. firms. In response, a healthier BAe began to seek out strategic acquisitions and, perhaps more importantly, to create numerous links with other European defense and aerospace firms in what were likely the first moves toward a Europe-wide consolidation.

In June 1995 BAe lost out—to GEC—in a bid for VSEL, a U.K. maker of submarines. That same month, however, British Aerospace formed a joint venture, Saab-BAe Gripen AB, with Saab AB's Saab Military Aircraft to manufacture and sell the Gripen combat aircraft. In January 1996 the company shifted its troubled regional aircraft operations into a three-way consortium, Aero International (Regional) SAS, with Aérospatiale of France and Alania of Italy. This venture was dissolved in mid-1998, however, following disagreements among the partners. BAe in April 1996 expanded into the Australian defense market with the acquisition of AWA Defence Industries (AWADI, later renamed British Aerospace Defence Industries) for A $50 million. Following more than three years of negotiations, BAe and Lagardère's defense arm, Matra, merged their guided missile businesses into a £1 billion joint venture called Matra-BAe Dynamics. In October 1997 the company announced that it would bolster its defense electronics sector through the £320 million (US $536.5 million) purchase from Siemens AG of Siemens Plessey businesses in the United Kingdom and Australia. One of BAe's longer-standing joint ventures, the one that had spent years developing the next-generation Eurofighter military jet, received a huge boost in December 1997 when Britain, Germany, Italy, and Spain signed a $40 billion deal to build the jet, ordering more than 600 of them. Also in 1997 BAe announced that it would cease manufacturing its Jetstream turboprop regional aircraft, further distancing the company from this troubled sector.

In April 1998 BAe announced that it would buy a 35 percent stake in Saab AB, furthering the consolidation of European defense. With this link, the two companies planned to cooperate more closely and on more projects. Around this same time, the company was contemplating the purchase of a stake in Construcciones Aeronautics S.A. (CASA), a defense and aerospace firm owned by the Spanish state and a partner of BAe's in Airbus (CASA held a 4.2 percent stake). British Aerospace was eager to join with other European companies to form a pan-European defense and aerospace firm, and the four Airbus partners (BAe, CASA, Aérospatiale of France, and DASA of Germany) had issued a report—following a request from their respective governments—in March 1998 saying that they wanted to merge, though no timetable for doing so was set. A major sticking point to such a merger was that Aérospatiale was owned by the French government. Both BAe and DASA insisted that the French firm had to be privatized for a merger to work, but the French government was opposed to doing so. BAe, meantime, had ruffled some feathers of its own in November 1997 when it signed a multimillion-dollar deal with Boeing—Airbus's arch-rival—to make wing parts for the next generation of 737 jets.

British Aerospace continued to divest itself of noncore assets in 1998, most notably selling 16.1 percent of its 21.1 percent stake in Orange PLC, an operator of mobile telephones, for £763.8 million (US $1.28 billion), netting £368 million (US $616.7 million) in the process. The possibility that Arlington Securities would be divested became very real around this time. In the event of such an occurrence, BAe would have come full circle, returning by and large to its defense and aerospace roots. Starting in May 1998, a new management team would see the steadily improving company—which in 1997 had posted profits before taxes and exceptional items of £596 million, a 31 percent gain over 1996—into whatever the future might have in store. Replacing Bauman in the chairman's seat that month was Richard Evans, who had been chief executive of the company since 1990, while John Weston, who had been in charge of BAe's defense operations, took over the chief executive slot. The two executives faced perhaps the biggest challenge in British Aerospace's chronically challenging history—merging or transforming the company into "European Aerospace."

Principal Subsidiaries

Arlington Securities plc; BAeSEMA Ltd. (50%); British Aerospace Aerostructures Ltd.; British Aerospace Airbus Ltd.; British Aerospace (Aviation Services) Ltd.; British Aerospace (Consultancy Services) Ltd.; British Aerospace Finance Ltd.; British Aerospace Flight Training (UK) Ltd.; British Aerospace (Insurance) Ltd.; British Aerospace (International) Ltd; British Aerospace (Operations) Ltd.; British Aerospace Properties Ltd.; British Aerospace (Systems & Equipment) Ltd.; Lee Valley Developments Ltd. (50%); Liverpool Airport plc (76%); Orange plc (5%); Reflectone UK Ltd. (48%); Royal Ordnance plc; Spectrum Technologies Ltd. (20%); British Aerospace Australia (Holdings) Ltd.; British Aerospace Australia Ltd.; British Aerospace Flight Training (Australia) Pty. Ltd.; British Aerospace (France) SAS; Airbus Industrie (France; 20%); Euromissile Dynamics Group (France; 33.3%); Matra BAe Dynamics SAS (France; 50%); SEPECAT S.A. (France; 50%); British Aerospace Deutschland GmbH (Germany); Cityline Simulator und Training GmbH (Germany; 50%); Competence Center Informatik GmbH (Germany; 30%); Eurofighter Jagdflugzeug GmbH (Germany; 33%); Heckler and Koch GmbH (Germany); Panavia Aircraft GmbH (Germany; 42.5%); BAeHal Software Ltd. (India; 40%); Muiden Chemie International BV (Nether-lands); Asia Pacific Training and Simulation Pte. Ltd. (Singapore; 63%); Singapore British Engineering Pte. Ltd. (51%); Saab AB (Sweden; 35%); Saab-BAe Gripen AB (Sweden; 50%); Asia Pacific Space and Communications Inc. (U.S.A.; 17%); British Aerospace Holdings, Inc. (U.S.A.); Reflectone Inc. (U.S.A.; 48%).

Further Reading

Betts, Paul, "BAe Benefits As It Brings Its Head Out of the Clouds," *Financial Times,* June 14, 1993, p. 17.

Betts, Paul, and Jackson, Tony, "Defence May Be the Best Attack," *Financial Times,* February 5, 1994, p. 6.

——, "A Flight Back to Basics," *Financial Times,* August 3, 1992, p. 10.

Buchan, David, and Gray, Bernard, "BAe, Matra in £1bn Missiles Merger Move," *Financial Times,* May 14, 1996, pp. 1, 20.

Cohen, Norma, "Cash Is the Stumbling Block in Property Separation," *Financial Times,* April 7, 1998, p. 27.

Cook, Nick, "BAe Sees United Europe As Only Way Forward," *Interavia Business & Technology,* April 1996, pp. 18+.

Davidson, Andrew, "Sir Richard Evans," *Management Today,* January 1997, pp. 38–41.

"The Defence Industry Jettisons Its Excess Baggage," *Economist,* August 8, 1992, pp. 57+.

Dwyer, Paula, "Triage for Battered British Aerospace," *Business Week,* October 5, 1992, pp. 109–10.

Elliott, Simon, "The Drive to Survive," *Flight International,* December 25, 1991, p. 17.

"Europe's Defence Companies Join the Modern World," *Economist,* December 10, 1988, pp. 67–68.

Feldman, Elliot J., *Concorde and Dissent: Explaining High Technology Project Failures in Britain and France,* Cambridge: Cambridge University Press, 1985.

"Fly Off with Me," *Economist,* October 5, 1991, pp. 70, 72–73.

"Getting Together," *Economist,* August 10, 1996, pp. 46, 48.

Goldsmith, Charles, "Airbus Prepares for Unique Restructuring," *Wall Street Journal,* August 30, 1996, p. A6.

——, "British Aerospace in Enviable Turnaround," *Wall Street Journal,* March 1, 1996, p. A10.

——, "British Aerospace Opts to Team with Lockheed on U.S. Jet Bid," *Wall Street Journal,* June 19, 1997, p. B4.

——, "Re-Engineering: After Trailing Boeing for Years, Airbus Aims for 50% of the Market," *Wall Street Journal,* March 16, 1998, pp. A1, A10.

——, "Report on Defense Restructuring in Europe Is Short on Details," *Wall Street Journal,* March 30, 1998, p. A14.

Gray, Bernard, "BAe Lands Behind Barricades in the UK," *Financial Times,* June 22, 1995, p. 23.

——, "BAe Pulls Out of £835m Bid Battle for VSEL," *Financial Times,* June 22, 1995, p. 1.

——, "An Elusive Moving Target," *Financial Times,* May 14, 1996, p. 19.

——, "How BAe Pulled Back from the Brink," *Financial Times,* December 18, 1995, p. 7.

——, "Time to Seek a Grand Alliance," *Financial Times,* December 19, 1995, p. 7.

Hayward, Keith, *International Collaboration in Civil Aerospace,* New York: St. Martin's Press, 1986.

Levine, Jonathan B., and Dwyer, Paula, "Europe's Weapons Makers Start Linking Arms," *Business Week,* May 24, 1993, p. 130A.

Lorenz, Andrew, "Up in the Air at British Aerospace," *Management Today,* February 1995, pp. 32–36.

"Making Rover Fly," *Economist,* December 9, 1989, pp. 61–62.

"Men of Property," *Economist,* October 22, 1988, p. 62.

Monopolies and Mergers Commission, *British Aerospace Public Limited Company and VSEL plc: A Report on the Proposed Merger,* London: HMSO, 1995.

Nelms, Douglas W., "Sea Change for Ship of State: Like a Giant Oil Tanker, British Aerospace Is Slowly, Ponderously Altering Course," *Air Transport World,* December 1993, pp. 64–69.

Nicoll, Alexander, "BAe, Dasa Win Siemens Arm," *Financial Times,* October 31, 1997, p. 25.

——, "Re-Arming for the Battlespace As a Competitive All-Rounder," *Financial Times,* April 15, 1998, p. 26.

——, "Siemens' Sale Creates Fresh Fighters," *Financial Times,* October 31, 1997, p. 27.

O'Toole, Kevin, "BAe's Brave New World," *Flight International,* March 22, 1995, pp. 28+.

"Rescued by Rover," *Economist,* February 22, 1992, pp. 62+.

Skapinker, Michael, "Aerospace Groups Back Merger," *Financial Times,* March 28, 1998, p. 2.

——, "BAe Reshuffles for Wider Role," *Financial Times,* April 3, 1998, p. 25.

Wood, Derek, "BAe Foresees Major Changes in Europe," *Interavia Aerospace World,* May 1993, pp. 30–31.

—updated by David E. Salamie

BWAY Corporation

8607 Roberts Drive, Suite 250
Atlanta, Georgia 30350
U.S.A.
(770) 587-0888
Fax: (770) 587-0186
Web site: http://www.bwaycorp.com

Public Company
Incorporated: 1989 as Brockway Standard Holdings
   Corporation
Employees: 2,086
Sales: $402.2 million (1997)
Stock Exchanges: New York
Ticker Symbol: BY
SICs: 3411 Metal Cans; 3089 Plastics Products, Not
   Elsewhere Classified; 2796 Platemaking & Related
   Services; 3479 Coating, Engraving, and Allied
   Services, Not Elsewhere Classified

BWAY Corporation is a holding company whose principal subsidiaries are leading manufacturers of steel containers for the general line segment of the North American steel industry. The metal container industry is divided broadly into three segments: beverage, food, and general line (which includes containers for such products as aerosol, automotive products, and paint and varnish). Few companies compete in all three segments and most of the companies serving the beverage and food segments do not compete in the general line segment. This includes BWAY, as the company does not manufacture beverage containers.

Approximately 75 percent of the company's business is derived from the general line segment of the metal container industry. The company's principal products in this segment include a wide variety of steel cans and pails used for packaging paint and related products, lubricants, cleaners, roof and driveway sealants, charcoal lighter fluid, and household and personal care products. These items include round cans with rings and plugs (such as those found on a typical paint can) and range from one-quarter pint to one gallon; oblong or "F" style cans (used for packaging paint thinner, lacquer thinner, turpentine, deglossers, and other paint-related products, charcoal lighter fluid, and waterproofing products, ranging from three ounce to one imperial gallon capacity); specialty cans (including small screw-top cans which typically have an applicator or brush attached to a screw cap and are used for PVC pipe cleaner, PVC cement, and rubber cement; and cone-top cans usually used for packaging specialty oils and automotive after-market products like brake fluid, gasoline additives, and radiator flushes); aerosol cans (typically used for packaging various household and industrial products including paint and related products, personal care products, lubricants, and insecticides); and pails (typically used for packaging paint and related products, roof and driveway sealants, marine coatings, vegetable oil, and water repellant, ranging in size from two to seven gallons and in either "closed head," for easy-pouring products, or "open head," for more viscous products).

The three major players in the general line segment of the industry are BWAY; U.S. Can, and Crown, Cork & Seal. In the aerosol can market, Crown and U.S. Can are the two largest manufacturers, with BWAY third. BWAY holds the largest market share in the paint can, oblong can, and steel pail segments, followed by U.S. Can, Cleveland Steel, and Van Leer. In food cans, the company's major competition is Crown, Stilgan, and General Foods.

About 20 percent of the company's manufacturing is in the food products segment. The company produces cans for coffee, vegetable oil, and vegetable shortening, with coffee cans accounting for a majority of sales and ranging in size from one pound to three pounds, with various smaller specialty sizes and shapes.

Approximately five percent of the company's manufacturing is in the ammunition box segment, with containers providing a hermetic seal, coated with a corrosion-resistant finish and used to package small arms and other ordnance products. A major customer is the U.S. Department of Defense, and the company also sells these products to other major domestic and foreign producers of ordnance.

Company Perspectives:

BWAY Corporation is a leading manufacturer of steel containers for the general line segment of the North American metal container industry. The Company's principal products include a wide variety of steel cans and pails used for packaging paint and related products, lubricants, cleaners, roof and driveway sealants, food and consumer products.

Major customers also include paintmakers Sherwin-Williams and Benjamin Moore, waxmaker Thompson Mini-wax, Pratt & Lambert, and consumer products giant Proctor & Gamble Company and Folgers Coffee Company (itself a wholly owned subsidiary of Proctor & Gamble).

Background and Getting Started, 1989

In January 1989, Brockway Standard Holdings Corporation (BSHC) was created when current Chairman and CEO of BWAY Warren J. Hayford (formerly President, COO, and Vice-Chairman of Gaylord Container Corporation) and Marvin Pomerantz—partners who owned a business that included an Arkansas-based paper mill and bag plant they purchased from Weyerhauser in 1985 and the brown paper assets of Crown Zellerbach in 1986—purchased the Brockway Standard Can Division of Owens-Illinois Corporation. The two, who both formerly worked for Gaylord Container Corporation, obtained 100 percent of the outstanding stock and assets of the metal and plastic container business of Owens-Illinois, including a manufacturing facility in Homerville, Georgia, and BSHC set up a subsidiary called Brockway Standard, Inc. (BSI). John T. Stirrup, who has been president and COO since 1985, has also been a director of the company since 1989.

BSI is an acknowledged leader in the markets it serves. The wholly owned subsidiary of BWAY traces its roots back to 1875 when a family-owned company in Brooklyn, New York, began manufacturing cans and other products from triplated steel. Later called Standard Container, and located in New Jersey, the company moved to southern Georgia in the 1950s and was acquired by Brockway Glass in the late 1970s. Owens-Illinois eventually purchased Brockway Glass before being purchased itself by Kohlberg Kravis Roberts & Co. (KKR) in late 1988. KKR began shedding its non-core assets and BSHC acquired the metal container division.

BSI manufactures tinplate containers ranging from three ounce to five-gallon capacity for paint, coatings, cleaners, chemicals, oils and lubricants, and other dry or liquid products for the automotive and specialty markets and also for food products such as coffee, tea, vegetable oils, nuts, shortening, snack foods, and fresh-pack fish products; cold rolled and black plate steel for pails from three- to seven-gallon capacity for paint, coatings, sealants, chemicals, and other industrial products; and steel munitions boxes for conventional and high-tech armaments. All of the containers manufactured by BSI have either plain or decorated exteriors and may be internally lined with sophisticated coatings to protect hard-to-hold products.

1990-Date

In April 1990, the U.S. Department of Justice (DOJ) commenced an investigation into allegations of price fixing in the metal container industry. BSHC was called into the investigation from 1990 to 1994 and company employees were involved in grand jury testimony during that time, though the company denied any wrongdoing in connection with the investigation. Two of the company's competitors pleaded guilty to fixing prices with other manufacturers of steel pails. As of the end of 1995, the company had received no further contact from the DOJ and had no knowledge of any continuing investigation.

In 1991, Richard E. Jakubecy, formerly an area manager for Continental Beverage Packing, was hired as vice-president of sales & marketing. Net revenue reached $132.1 million and net income was $5 million, jumping the following year to $134.3 million in revenue, with a net income of $3.4 million.

In March 1993, BSI acquired certain equipment, intellectual property, and other assets related to the Monotop business of Ellisco, Inc. for $1.5 million. The following month, BSI acquired all of the stock of Armstrong Containers, Inc. (formerly known as Armstrong Industries, Inc.) for $46.5 million. In May, BSI acquired substantially all of the assets of DK Container, Inc. for $997,000. Net revenue for the year reached $181 million with net income at $5.2 million.

In January 1994, Perry H. Schwartz, formerly senior vice-president of finance and CFO of Heekin Can, Inc., was hired as executive vice-president and CFO. October of that year saw the U.S. Department of Transportation creating new, stricter regulations for pails containing certain volatile materials. The regulations, which were adopted from United Nations mandates, required containers to pass certain performance test criteria, including drop and vapor pressure tests. The company quickly developed and patented a lightweight steel pail, called "The U.N. Pail," which was the first to conform to these new standards and, as of August 1997, was the only can of its type on the market. The company also developed the "powder striping" process for coating the interior of its containers at the weld point to improve the container's performance. By doing so, the company was able to increase the number of units sold in 1994 and 1995. Net revenue for the year reached $224.7 million, with net income dropping slightly to $5 million.

In June 1995, the company completed an initial public offering of its common stock. Also that year, the Homerville, Georgia, facility received ISO 9002 certification and the Mira Loma, California-based DK Container and Santa Fe Springs, California-based Armstrong Container facilities were consolidated into one facility in Fontana, California. Net revenue for 1995 increased 10 percent to close at $247.5 million, and net income jumped 75 percent over 1994 to reach $8.8 million.

In February 1996, the company changed its name from Brockway Standard Holdings Corporation to BWAY Corporation. The company also spent $5.3 million on renovation and moved into a new 75,000 square-foot facility in Memphis, creating 14 new jobs in the process, with an average salary of $18,000 per year.

May saw the company acquire all the outstanding stock of Milton Can Company Inc., a metal container manufacturer producing similar products founded in 1988, for $29 million in cash and stock. The subsidiary changed its name after the acquisition to Brockway Standard (New Jersey), Inc. This acquisition brought the company three facilities, one in Peabody, Massachusetts, and two in Elizabeth, New Jersey, and allowed the company to expand its geographic presence in the northeastern United States.

The following month, the BSI subsidiary offered to purchase substantially all of the assets of the Davies Can Division of the Van Dorn Company, itself a wholly owned subsidiary of Crown, Cork & Seal Company, Inc. for $41.7 million in cash. Upon completion of the deal, the company acquired three facilities located in Covington, Georgia; Solon, Ohio; and York, Pennsylvania. BWAY also created a strategic alliance with Crown Cork & Seal Canada Inc. in which the latter would begin offering BWAY products in Canada and BWAY would supply paint, oblong, and specialty containers produced by Crown Canada to its customers in the United States.

In October the company created a new subsidiary called the Milton Can Company Inc., reusing the name of the previously acquired company, to acquire the assets of Cincinnati, Ohio-based Ball Aerosol, the aerosol can business of Ball Metal Food Container Corporation for $42.4 million. Ball Aerosol was itself purchased by Ball Corporation in 1993 when that company acquired Heekin Can, Inc. The purchase gave the company a $50 million-per-year entrance into the estimated $600 million-per-year aerosol can market, with the potential for the company to reach $150 million in sales before even beginning to run into competition with the two larger companies in that market (U.S. Can and Crown, Cork & Seal). The subsidiary was renamed Brockway Standard (Ohio), Inc. and proceeded to acquire Peabody, Massachusetts-based Eagle Can Co., which was founded in 1926.

About the same time, the company also acquired, in a separate transaction, Plate Masters Inc., a lithography trade shop business located in Chicago, Illinois, improving the company's overall material centers growth strategy. A month later, in November, the company switched from the NASDAQ to begin trading on the New York Stock Exchange. By the end of fiscal 1996, the company owned facilities in Chicago, Illinois; Homerville, Georgia; Solon, Ohio; York, Pennsylvania; Cincinnati, Ohio; and two in Dallas, Texas, and leased facilities in Fontana, California; Franklin Park and Elk Grove, Illinois; Garland, Texas; Memphis, Tennessee; Picayune, Mississippi; Peabody, Massachusetts; and two in Elizabeth, New Jersey, as well as the company's corporate headquarters in Atlanta, Geor-

gia, with a total of over 1.2 million square feet of facilities. Net income for 1996 reached $283.1 million, a 14.4 percent increase over 1995, with net income dropping to $1.2 million.

In the first quarter of 1997, the company closed its Peabody, Massachusetts facility, incorporating its operations into other facilities. The company also relocated its Memphis, Tennessee operations to a larger facility in that city. Early in May, approximately half of the Cincinnati-based Milton Can Company subsidiary's workforce went on strike. The facility remained open and the strike was resolved early in June. August saw the company's stock split three-for-two. In September, David P. Hull, formerly vice-president of operations for Imperial Wallcovering Inc., was hired as president of BSI, replacing John T. Stirrup, who will remain president, CEO, and a director of BWAY Corporation. Revenues for 1997 reached $402.2 million, a 42 percent increase over 1996 sales, with a net income of $13.1 million, compared to $1.2 million the previous year.

With precisely targeted acquisitions and the company's tried and true "3R" strategy of *r*ationalizing plant location and customer needs, *re*-engineering streamlined operating and business processes, and *re*capitalizing investment in new technology, the company remained poised to continue to grow in certain segments of the markets it serves.

Principal Subsidiaries

Brockway Standard, Inc.; Armstrong Containers, Inc.; Brockway Standard (Ohio), Inc.; Brockway Standard (New Jersey), Inc.; Brockway Standard Metal Decorating Division; Milton Can Company, Inc.; Eagle Can Company.

Further Reading

"Broadway Buying Crown Cork Unit," *American Metal Market,* May 1, 1996, p. 4.

"BWAY Corporation Reports Sales and Earnings for the Fourth Quarter and Fiscal Year Ended September 28, 1997," *PR Newswire,* November 18, 1997, p. 1118ATTU004.

"BWAY Corporation to Continue Purchasing Shares," *PR Newswire,* November 24, 1997, p. 1124ATM016.

Chamberlin, Gary, "Energy-Storage System Bridges Power Disturbances," *Design News,* September 8, 1997, p. 13.

Franklin, Richard, "BWAY Corporation," *Wall Street Corporate Reporter,* March 17–23, 1997.

Scott, Jonathan, "Three Firms Adding About 75 Positions with New Projects," *Memphis Business Journal,* December 16, 1996, p. 1.

"Small Players Have Advantages," *Directors & Boards,* Fall 1991, p. 37.

—Daryl F. Mallett

Caribiner International, Inc.

16 West 61st Street
New York, New York 10023
U.S.A.
(212) 541-5300
Fax: (212) 541-5384
Web site: http://www.caribiner.com

Public Company
Incorporated: 1989 as Ingleby Enterprises Inc.
Employees: 3,680
Sales: $342.26 million (1997)
Stock Exchanges: New York
Ticker Symbol: CWC
SICs: 7359 Business Services

Caribiner International, Inc. is a global, fully integrated business-to-business communications company. Caribiner offers a wide range of business-communications services, including conceptualization, planning, and production of corporate meetings and events. Caribiner also creates interactive trade show exhibits, providing all the required audio-visual equipment. The company develops training and educational materials related to new job skills, products, systems, organizational processes, and internal corporate communications. The company's services can be delivered in any configuration of media, including film, interactive technologies, videotape, slides, computer graphics/animation, print, or multimedia. Furthermore, Caribiner offers a full spectrum of state-of-the-art presentation technologies for sale or short-term rental. For rental needs, more than 200,000 pieces of presentation equipment can be tracked in some 500 inventory locations ready for immediate delivery by 350 delivery vehicles.

The company has offices throughout North America as well as in Australia, Hong Kong, England, and New Zealand. Caribiner's client list covers a number of industry sectors, including automotive, consumer products, information technologies, insurance, pharmaceuticals, financial services, fast-food, government, insurance, lodging, petroleum, and telecommunica-

tions. Typical clients are among the world's largest companies in need of ongoing communication with sizable internal and external constituencies. Among Caribiner's clients are American Airlines, ARAMARK, Dow Chemical, Eastman Kodak Corporation, Ford Motor Co., Holiday Inn Worldwide, IBM, McDonald's Corporation, Parke-Davis, Sears, Shell Oil Company, Shering-Plough, and State Farm Group. The company's revenues grew from $21.76 million in 1992 to $342.26 million in 1997.

Founding a Business-Services Company: 1989–95

The roots of Caribiner International, Inc. are in northern England where, in 1985, Raymond S. Ingleby was chairman of an advertising company engaged in the installation of advertising display units in hotels. He rapidly acquired other companies and was soon the owner of one of the United Kingdom's most successful media sales companies. Three years later, Ingleby sold his company and, having agreed not to compete with the new owner, immigrated to the United States in search of a company he could eventually take public. In 1989, in New York City, he founded Ingleby Enterprises Inc. and began to build a new empire by acquiring Ray Simon, a business-event company.

In the early 1990s providers of business-communications services were part of a young and still very fragmented industry that consisted mainly of mom-and-pop operations. A slowing down of the economy caused many businesses to "cut back on all their corporate events—ranging from small meetings for sales people to major new product announcements for clients and suppliers," according to Emily Denitto in a 1997 article in *Crain's New York Business.* "Dozens of event producers went out of business, and the few that survived brought in much money," wrote Denitto.

Tough times notwithstanding, in June 1992 Ingleby obtained financial backing from Warburg, Pincus Investors, L.P., for the acquisition of Caribiner Inc.—a rival firm founded in 1970 in New York City to provide staging and production resources for corporate events. Ingleby changed the name of his company to Business Communications Group, Inc. He then carved out an industry niche distinct from firms that helped businesses to

94

Company Perspectives:

The mission of Caribiner International, Inc. is simple but powerful: to help a company achieve its business objectives by using the power of communications to connect more effectively with its key constituencies.

communicate with, or through, the news media. His company was also unlike advertising agencies that created advertising and marketing campaigns to reach out to consumers.

Caribiner zeroed in on the large-scale events and programs vital to a company's communication of corporate information to its constituencies. The unique skills needed to develop, produce, and stage such events were not usually part of a company's core businesses. Since large corporate events tended to occur sporadically, depending on the timing of product introductions, changing competitive environments, and shifts in corporate strategy, it was relatively costly for companies to maintain the internal resources required for effective corporate communications. Caribiner astutely capitalized on the fact that many companies had to compensate for the lack of these skills by engaging outside firms. ''Major companies will always need to communicate with their employees and their clients. But there are big savings to outsourcing the work to an operation like ours,'' Ingleby told Denitto in 1997.

Caribiner focused on increased penetration of existing accounts; the development of new large accounts; diversification into areas of training, education, and corporate communications; the acquisition of other companies offering business-communications services; and the opening of new offices. Sales and marketing activities targeted ''million-dollar clients'' with significant recurring needs for business communications services. When Caribiner recognized notable opportunities to expand relationships with potentially large accounts, it increased resources devoted to the servicing of these accounts.

From 1993 to 1995 the number of Caribiner's clients grew from nine to 12. Ford Motor Co. and IBM accounted for approximately 34 percent and 16 percent, respectively, of Caribiner's revenues in 1995. For Ford Motor Co., Caribiner executed more than 175 projects of various sizes for 13 Ford business units. Caribiner also obtained agreements from several key accounts, including Ford Motor Co., Holiday Inn Worldwide, and ARAMARK, for a variety of business-communications services. The company, whose fiscal year ended on September 30, had seven such agreements in place with clients by the end of fiscal 1995, compared to two agreements of this kind in 1994, and none in 1993.

Caribiner broadened its product portfolio by offering services sold in conjunction with, and separately from, its meetings business. This included the training and education of employees and programs for corporate communication. Revenues from the ''non-meetings'' business increased from a relatively insignificant amount in 1993 to about $18 million, or 22 percent of total revenues in 1995. Caribiner also implemented its growth strat-

egy by taking advantage of the fragmented nature of the business-communications industry. From 1992 to 1995, Caribiner acquired five other companies related to its services. These acquisitions expanded the company's existing client base, brought in additional large-account clients and experienced personnel, and allowed for the opening of offices in Los Angeles, Dallas, and Houston.

During the early 1990s, despite the faltering economy, Caribiner's revenues increased from $21.76 million in 1992 to $81.13 million in 1995. Increased sales to the Ford Motor Co. accounted for approximately two-thirds of the revenue growth in 1995. Additional clients in the information technology sector contributed about 25 percent of the increase.

Continued Domestic and International Expansion, 1995–97

Caribiner was listed on the New York Stock Exchange in 1996, trading under the symbol CWC. The company wanted to tap opportunities for growth in the emerging international market for business communications, especially because of the global marketing approach undertaken by many of its clients. Caribiner planned not only to pursue opportunities for the acquisition of foreign-based providers of business-communications services but also to open foreign offices.

To this end, Caribiner acquired Spectrum Communications Holdings International Limited; Wavelength Corporate Communications Pty Limited; WCT Live Communication Limited; and Consumer Access Limited. Ownership of Wavelength, a leading provider of business-communications services in Australia and New Zealand, enabled Caribiner to extend its ''relationships with a number of existing clients while inheriting new relationships with several multi-national companies. . . . We are now particularly well-positioned to serve Asian markets due to the combined resources of our existing Hong Kong offices and the addition of Wavelength's operations,'' commented Raymond Ingleby, Caribiner's chairman and chief executive officer. WCT Live, a 20-year-old business engaged in creating, producing, and consulting for live media events, reinforced Caribiner's presence in Europe and expanded the capabilities of Caribiner's London operations, initiated in June 1996. Through the acquisition of Spectrum, the operations of Hong Kong-based Consumer Access Limited were integrated into Caribiner's office in that city.

On the domestic front, in 1996 Caribiner acquired Atlanta-based Koors Perry & Associates, Inc.—a regional provider of business communications services—and integrated that company into Caribiner's Atlanta office, which became a base for marketing in the southeastern United States. With the purchase of Lighthouse, Ltd., Caribiner established a relationship with Motorola, Inc., among other clients. The company integrated its Chicago office with Lighthouse's headquarters in Rolling Meadows, Illinois, which became a base for operations in the Midwest. With the purchase of Total Audio Visual Services (TAVS), a leading provider of hotel audiovisual outsourcing services as well as of audiovisual equipment staging services, Caribiner no longer had to rely on third-party vendors to obtain its audiovisual equipment and services. The acquisition of San Francisco-based Rome Network, Inc. expanded Caribiner's presence in new geographic areas and strengthened ties with various corporate clients, including Charles Schwab & Co., Inc., SAP America, and Sun Microsystems, Inc.

In 1997 acquisitions of seven other domestic companies further extended Caribiner's reach in the national market, added new clients, and strengthened the company's ability to serve clients more efficiently by operating in regional offices closer to clients. These acquisitions included Projexions Video Supply, Inc.; Blumberg Communications Inc.; D&D Enterprises, Inc.; Watts/Silverstein, Inc.; Bauer Audio Visual, Inc.; Envision Corporation; and Spectrum Data Systems, Inc. The operations of Projexions, Blumberg, D&D, Bauer, and Spectrum were integrated with those of TAVS to provide more comprehensive service to the southeastern, Midwestern, and southern United States. The Bauer acquisition allowed Caribiner to enter several new markets, including Mexico. The purchase of Watts/Silverstein resulted in the establishment of a digital-media group within Caribiner. Watts was integrated into the company's Communications division and served to expand operations on the West Coast as well as to bring in new clients. Envision was integrated into Caribiner's Boston office, strengthening the company's resources and giving it access to a new group of clients.

In 1995 Caribiner designed and developed a series of training tools for Key Pharmaceuticals' UNI-DUR product launch. Training tools included computer-based learning modules, a series of video presentations, and a continuous computer-based learning competition that required the sales representatives to demonstrate their mastery of the UNI-DUR product platform. In another market sector, Caribiner designed the structure and all visual elements for Philip Morris's exhibit at the 1995 American Wholesale Markets Association's trade show. An oversized booth featured light-boxes, motion message signs, a video wall, and interactive kiosks.

Caribiner personnel worked closely for eight months with Ford Motor's management and product teams to prepare the automobile maker's message to its dealers about the complete line of 1996 Fords. For the introductory show, 8,000 dealers met in San Antonio, Texas, for a three-week period in August 1995. Caribiner designed and constructed all sets and stage layouts, drafted corporate speeches made by Ford's management, composed several original songs, choreographed the unveiling of the new 1996 vehicles, produced several audiovisual presentations, and arranged for live entertainment. Caribiner also designed and developed a glove box video for each of the 1997 Ford Expeditions, Mercury Mountaineers, and Lincoln Mark VIIIs. The video accompanied the sale of each new vehicle and demonstrated the features, advantages, and benefits of the vehicle.

Caribiner served ARAMARK on site at its corporate headquarters in Philadelphia. Work produced for ARAMARK included trade-show design, training, application of interactive technology, video production, brochure design and printing, and ongoing communication services. Caribiner also became the preferred in-house provider of rentals for audiovisual equipment in some 475 hotel properties, including hotel chains, such as Westin, Doubletree, Holiday Inn, Hyatt, Red Lion, and Sheraton, located throughout the United States, Mexico, and the

Caribbean. Additionally, Caribiner struck agreements with the Westin Hotel Company and the Doubletree Hotels Corporation pursuant to which these companies would promote Caribiner's audiovisual operations to hotels operated or franchised under their respective flags. Caribiner also secured an agreement with Starwood Lodging Corporation that allowed TAVS to become the preferred in-house provider of audiovisual services to various hotels owned by Starwood. The company also supplied audiovisual equipment and services to other business-communications companies for use at meetings, events, presentations, and training programs.

Caribiner differentiated itself from other providers of services for business-communications and corporate meetings by the quality of its customer service, its breadth of creative and technical expertise, its ability to execute programs successfully with complete backup system technology, and its established expertise in producing a broad range of projects of all sizes across a number of industries. Caribiner benefitted from having a full range of business-communications services, a sound reputation for continuous investment in new technology and equipment, organizational breadth, and an international presence.

Since its inception in 1989, Caribiner sought to be "a dynamically different kind of company." The degree to which Caribiner succeeded in reaching that goal was borne out, in part, by its financial success and the growth in the number of clients serviced by the company. In 1993, Caribiner revenues stood at $50.1 million and reached $342.26 million in 1997. Through continued acquisitions and internal growth, revenues for 1997 increased 130 percent over 1996 revenues of $148.33 million. The integration of recent acquisitions in the meetings and events, audiovisual equipment rental, and exhibition services industries, as well as improved cross-promotion and operating efficiencies across these businesses, led to increases of 138 percent and 160 percent in 1997 gross profit and earnings, respectively. The company, which ended fiscal 1993 with 65 accounts, had more than 300 accounts by the end of fiscal 1997.

Toward the 21st Century: 1998 and Beyond

In 1998, Caribiner remained committed to growth through acquisitions, consolidation, and internal expansion. In November 1997 the company acquired Visual Action Holdings plc, one of the largest providers of audiovisual equipment rental and exhibition-support services in the United Kingdom and the United States, thereby adding considerable support to Caribiner's marketing position in the United States, the United Kingdom, and Southeast Asia. In January 1998 the company purchased Right Source, Inc., a marketing support and training services company that focused on product launches for the information technology industry.

In March 1998 Caribiner signed a five-year contract with Inter-Continental Hotels Corporation to be the preferred provider of in-house audiovisual equipment rentals and related services to the corporation's managed hotels in the United States and Canada. Caribiner chairman and CEO Ingleby commented that the company is "very pleased to form a relationship with Inter-Continental, one of the world's premiere global hotel companies . . . . The partnership will form the foundation of

Caribiner's international expansion in hotel audiovisual outsourcing.''

In the same month, Caribiner also announced that its Hotel Services Group would provide computer workstations, referred to as the Nomad system, to select hotels and resorts in 19 cities across the country. The Nomad system was a portable workstation that could be wheeled into a hotel room, enabling business travelers to have an in-room office on a daily- or hourly-rental basis. Nomad users received on-site technical support from Caribiner's hotel-property representatives and could use a toll-free number to call Hewlett Packard for solutions to hardware and software problems. Caribiner planned to have more than 100 four- and five-star hotels offering the Nomad service by year-end 1998.

As Caribiner prepared itself for the 21st century, the business-communications industry was very competitive. Caribiner's revenues had grown significantly through internal growth and acquisitions, and the company had become a global leader of services for business communications. The company's growth strategy was on track and remained focused on building an infrastructure capable of supporting the geographic diversity of a dynamic business.

Further Reading

''Caribiner International, Inc.,'' *New York Times,* December 21, 1996, p. 39.
Denitto, Emily, ''Meeting the Street: Little-Known Planning Firm's IPO Stars,'' *Crain's New York Business,* April 14, 1997, pp. 3–4.

—Gloria A. Lemieux

CATELLUS

Catellus Development Corporation

201 Mission Street
San Francisco, California 94105
U.S.A.
(415) 974-4500
Fax: (415) 974-4613
Web site: http://www.catellus.com

Public Company
Incorporated: 1990 as Catellus Development Corporation
Employees: 304
Sales: $183.3 million (1996)
Stock Exchanges: New York
Ticker Symbol: CDX
SICs: 6552 Subdividers & Developers, Not Elsewhere
Classified

The largest private landowner in California, Catellus Development Corporation is a diversified real estate operating company supported by a large portfolio of income-producing properties and land awaiting development. Catellus was formed in 1984 as an indirect subsidiary of Santa Fe Pacific Corporation to oversee its parent company's non-railroad real estate activities. Catellus gained its name and its independence when it was spun off from its parent company in 1990. During the late 1990s, the company's portfolio of industrial, residential, retail, and office projects were located in major markets in California and 10 other states. Of Catellus's total property, 76 percent of its industrial property, 65 percent of its office property, and 85 percent of its retail property were located in California. The balance of the company's properties was located primarily in Texas, Illinois, and Arizona.

1990 Spinoff

Catellus began life on its own in 1990, although the assets of the company—its vast real estate holdings—had roots stretching back to the 19th century-predecessors of the Santa Fe Pacific Railroad. Until 1990, Catellus operated as Santa Fe Pacific Realty Corp., the massive real estate development arm of the Chicago-based railroad company. Financial difficulties during the late 1980s prompted the railroad company to spin off its real estate businesses to shareholders, creating a new, independent company that emerged from the expansive corporate umbrella of Santa Fe Pacific Corp. as Catellus Development Corporation. Although the separation cut the ties that linked the two businesses, Catellus made its debut saddled with a significant burden, the inheritance from its parent company. In the years leading up to the 1990 spinoff of Catellus, Santa Fe Pacific Corp. was reeling from debilitative debt. The railroad was carrying more than $2.5 billion of debt, an astronomical amount that forced management to rethink its corporate strategy and implement sweeping changes. As the conglomerate prepared to enter the 1990s, it resolved to focus on its core transportation business and shed businesses deemed inconsistent with its new, sharpened focus. The decision signaled the end of the company's involvement in real estate, which primarily had consisted of divesting its considerable land holdings, and transferred an estimated $800 million of its debt into the hands of the rechristened Catellus Development Corporation.

Catellus embarked on its own facing several fundamental challenges. The company was rich in land holdings, owning 1.5 million acres of land, but needed to develop its properties to realize the full financial potential of its assets. It also was hobbled by the heavy debt load it inherited from Santa Fe Pacific Corp., which made the difficult and costly task of financing its development projects that much harder. Further, the company broke free from the starting blocks at the outset of a pernicious economic recession. The early 1990s were tenuous years for many businesses, particularly for those companies like Catellus: positioned in a real estate market weakened significantly by an anemic economy. The boom years of the 1980s, when the California real estate market grew energetically, were over, leaving Catellus in the unenviable position of having to contend with nearly $1 billion of debt while it tried to develop mammoth industrial and commercial projects in a market stripped of its vitality. Against this backdrop, the company steeled itself for the difficult challenges ahead.

From Catellus's starting point in 1990, conditions worsened before they improved. One month before the company's debut on the New York Stock Exchange, San Francisco voters dealt Catellus a serious blow, stalling the company's efforts to develop what was regarded as the prime property within its portfolio. On the site of an old Santa Fe railyard, Catellus owned 166.9 acres of a 313-acre site adjacent to downtown San Francisco called Mission Bay. Undeveloped, the property was not worth much, at least in comparison to its potential value if the site, by all accounts an industrial wasteland, was developed into a residential and commercial property. The decision to develop the property, however, was not strictly up to Catellus. In the business of real estate development on the scale that Catellus operated, politics played a major, and a frequently decisive, role in determining whether development projects could break ground. In November 1990, San Francisco voters contributed their part in the decision-making process concerning the Mission Bay project by narrowly defeating Proposition I, which would have exempted Mission Bay from growth limits. It was the first stumbling block of many that slowed the company's progress during its first several years of business; ahead were further obstacles.

As the company's management scrambled to discover alternative means to turn Mission Bay into a revenue-generating property, Catellus began trading as a public company, making its debut in December 1990. Shortly thereafter, in early 1991, the company announced a new Mission Bay development plan, declaring its intention to transform the property into a residential and commercial neighborhood that would include five million square feet of new office space. As the national economic

recession deepened, however, the redevelopment project was put on hold. Critics contended the project drew its strength from the halcyon days of the 1980s, when the fertile real estate market gave birth to one major development after another. In the bleaker economic climate of the early 1990s, the project withered on the vine.

Meanwhile, the company moved forward in other areas. As a subsidiary operating within Santa Fe Pacific Corp., Catellus's predecessor had directed much of its efforts toward selling off parcels of property. Catellus, on the other hand, was looking to develop properties rather than liquidate its assets. Under the leadership of its president and chief executive officer, Vernon Schwartz, the company pushed ahead with smaller development projects, but the heavy burden of its inheritance from Santa Fe Pacific Corp. was making appreciable progress elusive. Not so for Santa Fe Pacific, whose stock value nearly doubled over the course of two years after shedding the $800 million debt load relegated to Catellus. Catellus, in contrast, suffered profoundly. Its stock value plunged between 1990 and 1992, dropping nearly in half. By 1992, the company's debt towered at $925 million with $225 million of the total due in 1994. As the company looked ahead, it appeared as if the next two years would determine its fate, a period in which Catellus needed to realize a substantial portion of its potential or else succumb to the economic realities of the conditions surrounding it.

New Management, New Focus in 1994

Catellus's stock, which had peaked in the mid-$30s, fell precipitously as the company moved forward into 1993 and early 1994, cascading downward to around $6 per share. At the end of 1993, there was little to point to for encouragement. The year had resulted in a numbing $53 million loss, and the road ahead loomed threateningly. Then new management arrived, led by a former college football player named Nelson C. Rising who was intent on turning Catellus's ephemeral potential into a financial reality. With him, Rising brought an extensive background in politics, which would prove instrumental in the art of convincing county, city, state, and federal officials to ally themselves with Catellus's cause. He also brought a wealth of experience in developing real estate property, a background that made him well aware of the potential value of Catellus's acreage, which ranked the company as the largest private landowner in California. ''When Catellus approached me about the job,'' Rising recalled, ''I was not terribly interested because of what I was doing at Maguire Thomas. When I started reading and poking around, I discovered the potential of Catellus. I felt California had been greatly discounted by those east of the California border. I saw a very diverse and far-flung portfolio. I was seduced by the opportunity and challenge.''

Rising was a lineman on a University of California—Los Angeles (UCLA) football scholarship in the late 1950s when an injury in his sophomore season sidelined him and directed all of his energies toward his studies. He graduated with honors and entered the car leasing business for a year with a football teammate before being admitted to UCLA's law school. Again, Rising matriculated with honors, which enabled him to secure a job at a prestigious Los Angeles law firm called O'Melveny & Myers in 1967. At the law firm, Rising's mentor was Warren Christopher, later secretary of state in the Clinton Administration, whom Rising followed in 1970 when he was selected as campaign chairman for John Tunney's run for the Senate. With Rising serving as campaign manager, Tunney won the election.

After working as associate producer and technical adviser on Robert Redford's *The Candidate,* Rising entered the real estate business, becoming president of Coto de Caza, which for decades ranked as Orange County's largest residential project. Once that project was completed in 1977, Rising entered the political scene again, managing Tom Bradley's successful Los Angeles mayoralty campaign. Next, Rising established his own real estate company and developed 3,000 acres in Tampa, Florida. After a five-year stint devoted exclusively to real estate, Rising took time out to serve as campaign chairman for Bradley's run for California governor in 1982. After Bradley lost the race, Rising sold his real estate company and joined Maguire Thomas Partners, a Los Angeles real estate firm where Rising worked on major downtown Los Angeles high-rise projects. After more than a decade at Maguire Thomas Partners, Rising joined Catellus in September 1994 and quickly lent his dual passions of politics and real estate to righting the floundering Catellus Development Corporation.

What Rising had seen when he began studying Catellus was a portfolio that included nearly one million acres of land and 15 million square feet of buildings scattered around the country. In between Los Angeles and Las Vegas, Catellus owned 786,000 acres of arid land, primarily in the Mojave Desert. Among the company's California land holdings were the Mission Bay property, which was anticipated to be a 4.8-million-square-foot, mixed development, and 840 acres in Fremont, California, the largest vacant site in Silicon Valley. These and other properties were the opportunities that seduced Rising; the challenges that attracted Rising were successfully developing these properties and curing the company's threatening financial ills.

Mid-1990s Reorganization

Rising addressed himself to putting Catellus on a firm financial foundation first, and quickly implemented bold and pervasive cost-cutting measures. Coming off 1993's $53 million loss, Rising decided to reorganize and restructure the company's operations before beginning to tap into the potential that had attracted him to Catellus initially. Shortly after walking into Catellus's corporate offices for the first time as its CEO, Rising laid off 40 percent of the company's staff. Next, he consolidated the company's corporate offices into smaller and more inexpensive confines and obtained a new line of construction credit from the financial community. All told, Rising introduced $10 million in cost reductions between the end of 1994 and 1995.

Before moving forward on Catellus's numerous development fronts, Rising took time to assess the company's property holdings and its financial position. With this information, he devised a new corporate strategy for the company to pursue, but it took roughly a year-and-a-half for the new strategy to manifest itself in Catellus's actions. When the new strategy did emerge in early 1996, its emphasis was on the residential segment of the construction industry, as opposed to the commercial segment that had previously been Catellus's forte. As 1996 got underway, Catellus was striving to become one of the largest home builders in California, where the residential market had

wrested free from the effects of the early 1990s recession and was beginning to show demonstrable signs of growth. The company took an important step toward strengthening its involvement in the residential segment by acquiring The Akins Companies, a major residential housing company with much of its activities concentrated in Orange County. The chief benefit of the acquisition was the expertise gained in developing residential housing. Akins management, led by Bruce Akins, the son of the company's founder, joined forces with Catellus's senior officers and provided valuable assistance in orchestrating residential development projects. "Catellus did not have core competencies in residential construction," Rising explained, referring to the rationale behind the Akins merger. "Rather than take time to develop these types of core competencies, we wanted to get in the current cycle."

As the company's new strategy took shape, Rising continued to try to resolve Catellus's perennial difficulties in developing its prized Mission Bay property. To invigorate the proposed development with new life, Rising applied his skills in the art of political persuasion and his talents in the real estate business, combining a bold vision of what could be erected on the 300-acre site and a thorough understanding that approval from political officials was required to make his vision a reality. Between 1993 and 1997, Catellus contributed an estimated $140,000 to state and local politicians and political causes, part of the company's ongoing efforts to ingratiate itself to the political powers who were intrinsically important to the company's development projects. Efforts to curry favor from the political sector also led Rising to donate 29 acres of land to the University of California at San Francisco for a biotech research campus, which became part of the company's Mission Bay development project as it existed in the late 1990s. On the 300-acre site, Rising was proposing to develop five million square feet of office space, 850,000 square feet of retail space for stores and move theaters, 6,000 condominiums and apartments, a 500-room hotel, and the university's 2.65-million-square-foot research campus. Rising was envisioning $3 billion worth of construction.

With the company's Mission Bay project awaiting approval, Catellus broke ground on its Pacific Commons development in January 1997. Situated on an 880-acre site in Fremont, California, formerly owned by Santa Fe, the Pacific Commons project called for an 8.4-million-square-foot business park featuring corporate campuses, a retail center, and light-industrial and warehouse facilities. As this project was underway, Catellus reached an agreement with the City of San Francisco for the development of a 65-acre portion of the Mission Bay site. The agreement called for the development of up to 3,000 residential units, a combination retail-entertainment complex measuring 350,000 square feet, and an additional retail complex measuring 250,000 square feet. As the company prepared for the remainder of the late 1990s, it was awaiting the conclusion of the entitlement process for its Mission Bay development, which was expected to carry on into 1998. Although the agreement with the City of San Francisco did not guarantee the company's proposed development would be approved, expectations were high that in the years ahead Catellus could begin reaping the rewards of its potentially lucrative asset.

Principal Subsidiaries

Santa Fe Towers Land Company; Seabridge Properties, Inc.; Harbor Drive Company; SF Pacific Properties Inc.; Westada Corporation; Catellus Management Corporation; Collinsville Property Corporation; Catellus Union Station, Inc.; Catellus Residential Group, Inc.; Dallas International, Ltd. (25.21%); New Orleans International Hotel (14.5%); International Rivercenter (25.16%); New Orleans Rivercenter (38.75%); Desman Road Partners (37.82%); Gilman Property Corporation.

Further Reading

Freeman, Michael, "Catellus Spun Off as Unit, As Voters Slow Mission Bay," *San Francisco Business Times,* December 21, 1990, p. 12.

Ginsberg, Steve, "Catellus Tries to Catch a Rising Star for Its Turnaround," *San Francisco Business Times,* March 3, 1995, p. 2A.

Greim, Lisa, "Catellus Stock Skyrockets in Heavy Trading," *San Francisco Business Times,* March 8, 1991, p. 4.

Grover, Mary Beth, "Placating Tadpoles, Buttering Up Mayors," *Forbes,* November 3, 1997, p. 58.

Harman, Liz, "Two Developers Vie for Oceanfront Hotel in Oceanside," *San Diego Business Journal,* October 20, 1997, p. 4.

Hemmila, Donna, "Catellus Set to Turn Oil Refinery into Houses," *San Francisco Business Times,* August 1, 1997, p. 1.

McLeister, Dan, "With 854,000 Acres, Catellus Becomes a Big Player in California Real Estate," *Professional Builder,* September 1996, p. 22.

Rudnitsky, Howard, "Contrarians' Delight?," *Forbes,* October 26, 1992, p. 46.

Shaw, Jan, "Catellus Takes New Tack on Mission Bay," *San Francisco Business Times,* December 7, 1990, p. 3.

Staton, Tracy, "Catellus Unveiled," *Dallas Business Journal,* June 4, 1990, p. 11.

—Jeffrey L. Covell

Catholic Order of Foresters

355 Shuman Boulevard
P.O. 3012
Naperville, Illinois 60566-7012
U.S.A.
(630) 983-4900
(800) 552-0145
Fax: (630) 983-4057
Web site: http://www.catholicforester.com

Nonprofit Company
Incorporated: 1883
Employees: 350
Sales: $208.76 million (1997)
SICs: 6411 Insurance; 6311 Life Insurance
   (Underwriters); 8399 Nonprofit Organizations; 8611
   Associations; 8641 Fraternal Organizations (pre-1988)

Catholic Order of Foresters (COF), headquartered in Naperville, Illinois, was founded in 1883 as a fraternal benefit society. The name of the society connotes the care that true foresters have for woodlands and other natural resources. Therefore, by connotation, COF members are Foresters who care for each other. More than 134,000 members in 30 states and the District of Columbia are organized in over 600 local branches, henceforth referred to as *courts,* that sponsor social, educational, religious, and benevolent activities, such as raising money for school, parish, community, and humanitarian needs. Membership in the organization requires purchase of at least one financial product—a life insurance policy, disability insurance, long-term care insurance, or an annuity. As members Foresters share in an organized way of living as "neighbors helping neighbors." The Order, with assets in excess of $380 million and a surplus of $51 million, ranks among the top 10 fraternal benefit societies in the United States.

The Early Years: 1883-1920

During the latter part of the 19th century, the United States (then composed of 38 states) was still recovering from the Civil War and the financial panics of the 1870s. Railroads had connected the Eastern states with the Western states, which were rapidly being populated by people taking advantage of liberal homestead laws. Impoverished immigrants from Europe were streaming into this country; many were settling in large cities like Chicago, where common problems and hardships bound them in mutual dependence. Rich with dreams but poor in financial resources, these immigrants were devastated when death struck. The time was ripe for the establishment of fraternal benefit societies that operated for the mutual benefit of their members by providing insurance coverage and a structure to involve members in charitable, educational, patriotic and, very often, religious activities within their own communities.

In 1883, when Chicago was celebrating its half-century mark, Irish immigrant Thomas Taylor set about realizing his dream of founding a Catholic benevolent society. Accompanied by two Jesuit priests of Chicago's Holy Family Parish, Taylor presented his plan for "Fraternalism in Action" to 42 men gathered in the parish hall. Each man paid dues of $1 to become a charter member of a society of that nature. According to Julius A. Coller's *A Century of Fraternalism,* seven of these pioneer members applied to the state of Illinois for a charter to establish an association for "the promotion of fraternity, unity, and true Christian charity; the establishment of a fund for the relief of the sick and the distressed members" and of a widow-and-orphans' benefit fund for the surviving dependents of a deceased parent.

Upon receipt of certification in 1883, the Illinois Catholic Order of Foresters was launched on the insurance world. Seventy-four members established Holy Family Court Number One; in a relatively short time other courts (branches) sprang up in Chicago and throughout Illinois. When a court was organized in Milwaukee in 1887, the Order dropped the word *Illinois* from its name. COF opened in many other states and grouped them into State Courts bearing the name of each state. In 1888 COF received a charter to open a court in Canada.

COF had expanded rapidly. By the turn of the century the Order had 79,895 members. Initially, dues consisted of a per-capita assessment collected upon the death of a Forester. This system of replenishing the treasury, however, soon became

cumbersome for the expanding business of the Order. In 1896 a
graded-assessment system was adopted: each Forester was as-
sessed a fixed monthly payment (determined by his age at the
time of entry) that would remain the same throughout his lifetime. To maintain the Order's financial stability, a reserve fund
was established in 1899. Between May 13, 1883 and January 1,
1901, COF disbursed $3.5 million to beneficiaries of deceased
Foresters. And, although no provision had been made for payment of insurance if death occurred because of war or any
related incident, during the last three months of 1918 COF paid
out $1.1 million in death claims, an amount that included
$354,250 of war claims.

Peak, Decline, and Regrouping: 1921–33

Catholic Order of Foresters continued its phenomenal
growth: membership peaked at 163,248 in 1921. As early as
1905 there had been heated discussions about the need to
readjust assessment rates but no action had been taken. In 1922,
however, at the insistence of the Illinois Insurance Department,
delegates to a special COF session voted to upgrade insurance
rates in order to keep the society financially sound. They
adopted the four percent American Experience Mortality Table
for all Foresters (as of their attained age) but allowed exceptions
for members enrolled under the National Fraternal Congress
Rates; for other members over 61 years of age, a maximum rate
of $4.80 per thousand was established. Bitter reaction to this
change of rates had an adverse effect on membership. Although
the majority of Foresters remained committed to the organization, many others surrendered their insurance policies; some
members remained in the society but took no part in its activities; and still others stayed on but were harshly critical of almost
everyone and everything. By year-end 1923, COF membership
was down to 127,461.

Dedicated officers and members journeyed from court to
court and meeting to meeting to explain the change of rates and
to emphasize the advantages of remaining Foresters. At first
COF had been open only to men but in 1928 it offered boys a
$600 ''juvenile policy'' carrying a fixed annual fee of $3 from
birth to age 16. The Order weathered the time of discontent and,
although membership losses continued for several years, paid
all claims in full and continued its fraternal activities, including
large donations, such as $50,000 for the Shrine of the Immacu-
late Conception in Washington, D.C., and $25,000 toward the

building of the Seminary of St. Mary of the Lake, an institution
for training Catholic priests.

At its golden anniversary in 1933, Catholic Order of Foresters had 135,000 members in courts located in 28 states and in
all the provinces of Canada. The Order had set up a Juvenile
Division for Boy Rangers, the name given to boys insured from
birth to age 16. To men between the ages of 16 and 60, the
Order offered eight forms of insurance policies ranging from
term- and whole-life insurance to endowments. After three
years, all policies acquired a reserve value. COF also provided
total disability benefits, premium loan privileges, old-age cash
surrender benefits, and paid-up insurance benefits. The maximum insurance any Forester could carry was raised to $10,000.
From 1923 to 1933, annual dividends remained at approximately 8 ⅓ percent of premiums. Dating from the founding of
the Order in 1883, a total of $52.2 million was paid to widows,
orphans, and other beneficiaries. The initial treasury of $42
grew to invested reserves of over $28 million—an amount more
than 25 percent above the society's total insurance liability.

Completing a Centenary of Fraternalism: 1934–83

For everyone, the years after the Great Depression were a
time of long, uphill struggle against unemployment. Financial
insecurity and social unrest ran rampant. Historian Coller wrote
that ''this was an era when Fraternalism was sorely tried and not
found wanting'' and quoted Past High Chief Ranger Richard T.
Tobin as saying that during these adverse circumstances ''the
practice of Fraternalism brought brilliance where there was
darkness.'' When the Foresters met for the 1940 Convention,
harmony again reigned in the Order and drives to increase
membership were under way.

Then came the 1941 attack on Pearl Harbor and the Foresters
added another dimension to their activities: promotion of investment in War Savings Bonds and Stamps. By November
1945 a total of $10.55 million in Victory Bonds had been
purchased by the COF High Court, its employees, and other
COF members. The U.S. Treasury Department sent a special
representative to present an official commendation to COF employees and a Silver Award, the Treasury's highest award for
volunteer patriotic service, to Thomas H. Cannon and Thomas
R. Heaney for their outstanding leadership in the bond program.

At the end of all hostilities a total of 13 million American
men and women had served in the war; 11,185 of these people
were Foresters. As stated above, during World War I the Order
had not included a war clause in its Constitution. Nonetheless,
COF had paid war-related claims amounting to $362,000 by
implementing a patriotic assessment of $1 per member. During
World War II the Order was in such excellent financial position
that it paid war claims from the Reserve Fund. Also, COF
donated $25,000 to the Chicago archdiocesan seminary, St.
Mary of the Lake in Mundelein.

An amendment to the COF Constitution in 1952 gave the
Foresters a new look: membership was opened to women and
girls. Two new all-women courts were formed but, for the
most part, women and girls joined existing courts and held
important offices not only in these subordinate courts but also in
the State Courts. Another innovation occurred in 1965 when the

Catholic Central Union, a Czech ethnic fraternal society organized in 1877, merged its entire membership into Catholic Order of Foresters, thereby adding 3,383 adults and 850 youths as members to the Foresters. The adopted members received all the Forester benefits, including cash dividends on insurance certificates.

Another significant event was the 1967 establishment of the COF Scholarship Program. From then on, the Order awarded annual scholarships of $2,000 ($500 for each of four years at college) to Forester children. The total amount of the scholarships was increased to $4,000 in 1980 and then to $5,000 in 1996. A committee of educators, basing their evaluation on grades and extra-curricular activities, selected the winners of the scholarships.

Review of the COF operation in Canada brought about another change. When the 1922 rate adjustment became effective, Canadian membership—which had peaked at 22,156—immediately began to decline. Attrition continued steadily; by 1973 total Canadian membership had fallen to 3,118. Operating in Canada had always been expensive because Canadian law required that a Canadian COF agent maintain complete membership files in that country. Since the COF Home Office in the United States had to keep all records for the entire Order, Canadian requirements necessitated duplication of all Canadian files.

Furthermore, in 1964 Canada made a radical revision of its tax laws, removed all tax exemptions from fraternal organizations, subjected them to income taxes and to the rates applicable to for-profit insurance corporations. In 1971 COF, with no net gain from its Canadian business, had to pay taxes amounting to $20,532. Separation from the Canadian operation became financially necessary. To take care of its remaining Canadian members, COF made reinsurance arrangements for them with the Artisan Life Insurance Cooperative, a Montreal-based Catholic fraternal society similar to Catholic Order of Foresters. This transfer ended COF's function as an international society.

During the first years of its existence COF moved its home office several times, going from a single room in 1883 to office suites in various Chicago office buildings until it relocated in its own four-story building in 1952. By 1975 the ever-increasing cost of transportation became a serious problem for COF employees of the Home Office; furthermore, the COF building was soon to be dwarfed by skyscrapers. In 1981 the Order accepted an offer for its property (now worth 4 ½ times book value), stipulated right of occupancy for a flexible period not to exceed four years, and began to look for a new location.

As COF's first 100 years came to a close, the Order was competing with banks, savings and loan organizations, money-market funds, retail and mail-order companies—to name but a few rivals for dollars. Nevertheless, the Order's financial results for 1982 broke all records. Assets totalled $178.2 million; dividends paid to members reached an all-time high of $7.3 million, that is, Foresters received 55 cents for every dollar they had put into the Order; and there was a net surplus of $32.1 million. Insurance in force, one of the criteria by which the size of a life insurance company is measured, totaled $627.65 million.

Nurturing Fraternalism into the 21st Century

COF bought land and built its new headquarters in Naperville, Illinois, a site about 30 miles west of Chicago. The 1984 relocation came after 100 years of COF's founding, explosive expansion, and decline and resurgence of membership. Throughout those years the Order never reneged on its commitment to the financial security of its members, or the support of their spiritual growth and involvement in civic, social, educational, and humanitarian needs.

Over the years, COF gradually increased its operating efficiency by taking advantage of developing technologies; for instance, COF implemented a computerized membership database, direct billing, and the mailing of premium notices. However social changes—for example, the weakening of family units as a result of divorce and of having both parents in the work force—left less time for supporting the kind of local-court activities defined by an earlier generation.

The Order responded by strengthening its Youth Courts through the offer of financial incentives, such as college scholarships, educational awards, and federal student bank loans to young adults who became members with the purchase of a low-cost whole-life insurance policy. COF also set up new programs, such as recognition dinners and awards to members involved in civic, social, athletic, and humanitarian activities. Membership in the Adult Courts was stimulated by updating and expanding existing programs and by reaching out with new financial products, such as loans to churches and other Catholic organizations; a Matching Funds Program for Catholic and community causes; a Newborn Infant Benefit; an Orphan Benefit Program; and an Accelerated Death Benefit Rider for eligible COF policies. This Rider allowed members diagnosed with a terminal illness to receive advance payments of up to 75 percent of their insurance proceeds.

COF assured continuing financial stability, by adhering to a strategic business plan based on conservative investments and business practices. To absorb fluctuations in market values of investments, insurance companies—unlike other businesses—were required to keep a reserve for asset valuation and another reserve for interest maintenance. At year-end 1997, the COF total reserved for this requirement was $6.05 million, a sum that—when added to surplus funds—amounted to an adjusted surplus of $51.08 million and indicated a new level of financial strength for the Order. Total COF assets amounted to $381.57 million and insurance in force stood at $1.97 billion.

At the end of the 20th century, Catholic Order of Foresters continued to build on its foundation of success. The Order met evolving needs without compromising the financial security of its members, remained focused on fraternal caring, and entered the 21st century still totally committed to operating an insurance organization based on Christian values and ethics.

Further Reading

Cannon, Thomas H., "Confidence Reborn," *Catholic Forester*, April 1933, p. 3.

Ciesla, Robert, "Sharing Our Successes: Building on Our Foundation," *Catholic Forester*, March/April, 1997, pp. 6–9.

"COF Cash Dividend Equal to 8⅓% of Annual Premium," *Catholic Forester*, June 1933, cover page and p. 9.

Coller, Julius A., II, *A Century of Fraternalism*, Chicago, Ill.: circa 1984, pp. 4–6, 44.

"Did You Know That COF Has a War Memorial in Washington, D.C.?" *Catholic Forester*, January/February, 1983, pp. 22–25.

Gorski, John A., "1982 Annual Report," *Catholic Forester*, March/April, 1983, pp. 4–5.

Heaney, Thomas R., "A Half Century of Catholic Forestry," *Catholic Forester*, May 1933, p. 2.

Wimmer, Don H., "Modernizing Fraternal Accounting," *Catholic Forester*, July 1933, p. 9.

—Gloria A. Lemieux

Chancellor Media Corporation

Consolidation of radio station ownership accelerated dramatically following the passage of the Telecommunications Act of 1996 in February of that year. The 1996 Act amended the Communications Act of 1934, which established the Federal Communications Commission (FCC) and set forth the FCC's authority. Among other things, the 1996 Act significantly changed the rules of station ownership. It eliminated national ownership caps, which under the 1934 Act limited national ownership to 20 FM stations and 20 AM stations.

The 1996 Act also increased local ownership limits. Prior to the 1996 Act, a single owner was limited to owning two FM and two AM stations in a single large radio market. In smaller markets single ownership was limited to three stations. The 1996 Act increased local ownership limits significantly: in markets with 45 or more stations, ownership was limited to eight stations, no more than five of which could be in the same service (FM or AM); in markets with 30 to 44 stations, ownership was limited to seven stations, with no more than four in the same service; in markets with 15 to 29 stations, ownership was limited to six stations, with no more than four in the same service; and in markets with 14 or fewer stations, ownership was limited to no more than half of the market's total with no more than three stations in the same service.

As a result of these relaxed federal regulations on station ownership, the radio industry experienced an intense period of mergers and acquisitions in 1996 and 1997. The largest collection of radio stations was formed in December 1996, when Westinghouse Electric Corporation paid $5 billion for Infinity Broadcasting Corporation to become the United States' largest broadcast company. That was just a little more than a year after Westinghouse acquired CBS Inc. The Infinity acquisition made Westinghouse the number one radio group in terms both of number of stations and annual station revenue.

The second largest radio group in terms of annual station revenue was formed in 1997 when Evergreen Media Corporation merged with the Chancellor Broadcasting Company to form Chancellor Media Corporation. The merger, announced in February and completed in September, was valued at $2.0 billion. At the same time, it was announced that the new Chancellor Media Corporation would acquire the Viacom Radio Group from Viacom Inc. for $1.075 billion.

Chancellor Broadcasting Company Formed in 1993

Chancellor Broadcasting was formed in Dallas, Texas, in August 1993 by radio veteran Steven Dinetz with financial backing from investment firm Hicks, Muse, Tate & Furst, Inc. Hicks, Muse was one of the most active investment firms in the United States. During the period 1990–95 it completed or had pending 39 acquisitions with an aggregate value of approximately $5 billion. Dinetz was chosen to build Chancellor Broadcasting into a major force in the radio industry. His first purchase involved two Sacramento radio stations (KFBK and KGBY: Y92) from Group W Broadcasting, a unit of the Westinghouse Electric Corporation, for $48 million.

Chancellor Broadcasting grew through a series of acquisitions targeting the top 40 radio markets in the United States. In 1994 the company acquired 11 radio stations of the American Media Station Group, owned by MBD Broadcasting of Dallas, including a third station in Sacramento (KHYL: Cool 101), for $150 million. For 1994 Chancellor Broadcasting, a privately held company, reported a double-digit growth in broadcast cash flow and revenue. The company's stations generated broadcast cash flow of $22.7 million in 1994, compared with $16.8 million in 1993. Net revenues increased 13.3 percent from $49.1 million in 1993 to $55.7 million in 1994. The company's 13 stations were located in Minneapolis-St. Paul, Cincinnati, Long Island, Riverside-San Bernardino, and Sacramento. Approximately 90 percent of the company was owned by investment firm Hicks, Muse, Tate & Furst.

Attempted to Acquire SFX Broadcasting Inc., 1995

In March 1995 Chancellor Broadcasting failed in its attempt to buy SFX Broadcasting Inc., which was based in Austin, Texas, and owned 12 radio stations. At the time Chancellor owned 13 stations and was in the process of acquiring its 14th station. On March 15, Chancellor offered $160 million to acquire all of the publicly owned SFX Broadcasting's outstanding common stock. But the next day, SFX's board of directors rejected the offer, noting that it had recently received a similar offer from another interested party and that the company was not for sale.

Acquired Shamrock Broadcasting Inc. in 1995

Chancellor Broadcasting acquired Shamrock Broadcasting Inc. in August 1995 for $395 million. The acquisition added 19 radio stations to Chancellor's portfolio. Shamrock was a private company owned by Roy Disney, nephew of Walt Disney, that had been in business since 1979. The purchase was billed as the largest radio transaction in history, according to the *Los Angeles Times.* However, it would soon be overshadowed by Walt Disney Co.'s acquisition of Capital Cities/ABC Inc. and Westinghouse Electric Corporations' purchase of CBS Inc., both of which were announced at the same time.

The Shamrock acquisition was financed with $145 million of bank debt, a $100 million equity contribution by Hicks, Muse, and the remainder through corporate bonds sold to the public. Most of Shamrock's stations were located west of the Mississippi River and included two Los Angeles stations, KZLA-FM (country) and KLAC-AM (oldies), which broadcast the Los Angeles Lakers' basketball games. Shamrock's headquarters were in Burbank, California.

Dinetz and Thomas O. Hicks, chairman and CEO of Hicks, Muse, told the *Los Angeles Times* they anticipated few layoffs, since the Shamrock stations were "not overstaffed." Dinetz said, "If anything, we'll probably increase the size of the advertising sales staff." Chancellor had been successful in boosting the profitability of its stations by focusing on local ad sales.

Consolidation in the radio industry was being fueled by a strong advertising market, the prospect of relaxed federal regulations regarding station ownership, and the economies of scale

that came with size. As a result, radio stations were selling for historically high prices. According to the *Los Angeles Times,* "The key to making a deal work is controlling costs and pumping up ad sales—all in the service of higher profit margins." Clifford Miller, managing director of Shamrock Broadcasting, said of radio acquisitions in general, "I think at least in the radio market, the cycle is either peaking or has peaked."

The $395 million price tag on Shamrock was calculated to be 11 times the cash flow of the stations purchased. Tom Taylor, editor of *Inside Radio,* told the *Sacramento Business Journal* that similar deals in the past year had ranged from seven to 11 times cash flow. "Now we're clearly pushing that toward 12." At this time federal regulations established limits on multiple-station ownership in each market. For a market the size of Sacramento, one company could not own more than two AM and two FM stations, provided that they did not collectively account for more than 25 percent of the market's radio listeners.

Chancellor's acquisition of Shamrock's 19 radio stations prompted speculation that the privately owned Chancellor would soon go public. The purchase increased Chancellor's holdings to 33 radio stations with a combined revenue of $165 million based on 1994 figures. That made Chancellor the third largest radio-only media company in the United States. Although there were no plans to take Chancellor public after the Shamrock deal was approved, Dinetz told the *Sacramento Business Journal,* "With the group of assets [and] the type of cash flows we expect in the coming two years, it certainly makes sense for us to tap into public markets if the window remains open." From mid-1993 to mid-1995, Chancellor had grown from zero to $700 million worth of investments in radio properties.

The Shamrock acquisition gave Chancellor at least three stations in each of six markets and dual AM/FM combinations in four markets. In California, Chancellor would now have four San Francisco stations, plus two in Los Angeles. It also owned three Sacramento stations and had an AM/FM combination in Riverside.

Outside of California, the Shamrock acquisition added 13 stations in markets such as New York, Detroit, Houston, Atlanta, Minneapolis, Pittsburgh, Phoenix, and Denver. These would be added to the family of Chancellor stations in Long Island, New York, Minneapolis, Cincinnati, and Orlando.

Other Stations Acquired in 1996 as Radio Industry Consolidated Ownership

In another acquisition deal, Chancellor acquired 12 more radio stations, including three in the Washington, D.C., area, for $365 million from Washington's Rales family in mid-1996. In July the company acquired two more radio stations on Long Island, New York, from SFX Broadcasting. Chancellor already owned WALK-AM/FM, the top-rated station, there. To its top-rated station it added WBAB, the number two station, and the number three station, WBLI. As part of the deal Chancellor also took control of WGBB-AM and WHFM, which simulcast the WBAB signal. In exchange, Chancellor gave up two stations in Jacksonville, Florida, and $11 million in cash to SFX Broadcasting.

At the time the deal was announced, rumors were flying that the Walt Disney Co. was negotiating to acquire Chancellor. Disney had just become the fifth largest operator of radio stations with its 1995 acquisition of Cap Cities/ABC. If Disney were to acquire Chancellor's 33 radio stations, it would become the United States' second largest radio operator.

Indicative of the rapid rate of change in the radio industry was the fact that Chancellor did not yet have full ownership of the two Jacksonville radio stations it traded to SFX Broadcasting. Chancellor was in the process of acquiring the stations from the Los Angeles-based OmniAmerica Communications Co. In another deal, Chancellor acquired its fourth Sacramento radio station when it purchased KSTE-AM from Boston-based American Radio Systems Corporation.

Consolidation in the radio industry was continuing to occur, fueled by federal legislation passed earlier in 1996 that allowed companies to own as many as eight radio stations in major markets, but no more than five FM or five AM stations. In December 1996, just a little more than a year after it acquired CBS Inc., Westinghouse Electric Corporation paid $5 billion for Infinity Broadcasting Corporation to become the United States' largest broadcast company.

Chancellor Media Corporation Formed in 1997

Then, in February 1997, Chancellor, Evergreen Media Corporation, and Viacom Inc. entered into a three-way deal that created the nation's second largest radio empire. With simultaneous announcements, Evergreen Media said it would pay $1.5 billion in debt and stock to acquire Chancellor, merging with it to form a new company to be called Chancellor Media Corporation. The new company would then purchase the Viacom Radio Group from Viacom Inc. for $1.075 billion. As a result, Chancellor Media Corporation would then own 103 stations, including 10 previously owned by Viacom, 51 owned by Chancellor Broadcasting, and 42 owned by Evergreen. However, some of the stations would likely have to be divested to comply with current federal regulations governing multiple-station ownership.

Chancellor Media's 103 stations would operate in 21 markets and have an estimated annual revenue of $810 million, or about twice as much as the revenue of the nation's second largest radio group, Jacor Communications Inc. However, Jacor would retain its number two ranking in terms of number of stations, since it owned 122 stations in 26 markets, most of them medium-sized. Westinghouse, with its recent acquisition of Infinity, would remain the number one radio group in terms both of number of stations and annual station revenue.

According to the *Cincinnati Enquirer,* Evergreen paid about 11 times Chancellor's estimated 1998 broadcast cash flow of $130 million and about 15 times the cash flow of Viacom's stations. Viacom said that it sold its radio group to strengthen its balance sheet and focus on its core business units, which included Blockbuster, MTV Networks, Paramount Parks, Paramount Pictures, Showtime Networks, Simon & Schuster, and other entertainment and publishing properties. Viacom's 10 radio stations operated in five major markets and included FM duopolies in New York, Los Angeles, and Washington, D.C.

Chancellor Media would be headed by Scott Ginsburg, Evergreen's chairman and chief executive officer, and Thomas Hicks, chairman of Chancellor Broadcasting and of Hicks, Muse, Tate & Furst. Ginsburg became Chancellor's CEO and president while Hicks was named chairman. After the merger, Evergreen's shareholders would own about two-thirds of Chancellor Media's shares, while Chancellor Broadcasting shareholders would own the other one-third.

Stations Sold to Comply with Federal Regulations

Following the merger, Chancellor owned eight stations in Detroit; seven FM and three AM stations in San Francisco; six FM and five AM stations in Washington, D.C.; seven FM and two AM stations in Chicago; one AM and six FM stations in Philadelphia; and four FM stations in New York City. In some of these cities Chancellor would have to sell off some stations to comply with federal regulations that permitted ownership of a maximum of eight stations in the largest markets, but no more than five FM or five AM stations.

In April 1997, Chancellor Media sold stations in some of those markets for $418 million, including stations in Chicago, Philadelphia, and San Francisco. WDRQ-FM in Detroit and WJZW-FM in Washington, D.C., were sold to The Walt Disney Company for $105 million in cash. WDRQ and WJZW were previously owned by Viacom. Three smaller stations in Washington, D.C., and San Francisco were sold in May by Evergreen to a small private company called Douglas Broadcasting/Personal Achievement Radio for $18 million. Following the sell-offs, Chancellor Media owned 96 stations.

Katz Acquisition Announced in July 1997

With the merger between Evergreen Media and Chancellor Broadcasting still pending, the two companies, along with investment firm Hicks, Muse, Tate & Furst, Inc., announced they would acquire Katz Media Group Inc. for approximately $373 million. Katz Media, with a sales force of some 1,500 people, was the only full-service media representation firm in the United States that served several types of electronic media, including radio and television stations, cable television systems, and Internet media outlets. It was a recognized leader in the industry and allowed its clients, of which Chancellor Media was the largest, access to a growing base of national advertisers.

Battle with Westinghouse for Top Spot in New York City

By late 1997, Chancellor Media owned five radio stations in New York City, three of which ranked among the city's top ten radio stations. Its main competitor was Westinghouse, which owned six stations in New York City and took in nearly twice as much advertising revenue as Chancellor. To improve its stations' ratings and advertising revenues, Chancellor did its research and changed its stations' formats as needed.

Chancellor's biggest success in the New York market was WYNY-FM, which it transformed from a country music station ranked 21st in the market into a reborn WKTU-FM, a dance station that quickly rose to the number four spot. Cross-dressing personality RuPaul was brought in as a morning host to give the station an identity, and special promotions were held, including reopening Studio 54 for a night. Chancellor expected the station's revenue to grow to $35 million in 1997, up from $19 million in 1996.

In another move, Chancellor acquired New York's 105.1 FM (The Buzz) when that station attempted to challenge Chancellor's 106.7 Lite FM, the number one station in the market, by changing from a modern rock format to an easy listening format. Chancellor remade 105.1 into Big 105 FM and brought in Danny Bonaduce to host the station's morning show. Bonaduce, a child star of "Partridge Family" fame, had made a name for himself as a radio personality in Chicago and Detroit before coming to New York. To attract attention, the station held an open casting call at Caroline's Comedy Nation for the on-air roles of Sidekick, News Anchor, Traffic Person, Weather Person, and a "Make Your Own Job" position. It attracted 1,000 candidates, from which nine New York area residents were selected for additional consideration.

U.S. Justice Department Challenged Acquisition of Two Long Island Radio Stations, 1997

In an unprecedented move, the U.S. Justice Department challenged Chancellor's acquisition of WBAB-FM and WBLI-FM from SFX Broadcasting. It was the first time the agency had gone to court to challenge a radio industry merger since the new communications act was passed in February 1996. According to the Justice Department, the acquisition, which also included WHFM-FM in Southampton and WGBB-AM in Freeport, would give Chancellor more than 65 percent of radio advertising sales in Suffolk County. According to one statement issued by the Justice Department, "Allowing Chancellor to buy a dominant position in this concentrated market will result in higher radio advertising prices for Suffolk County businesses that rely on radio to sell their products and services." Pending Justice Department approval of the acquisition, Chancellor had been operating the stations under an agreement with SFX Broadcasting.

More Acquisitions, Public Offering Slated for 1998

SFX Broadcasting, meanwhile, was in the process of being acquired by Capstar Broadcasting, which was based in Austin, Texas, for $2.1 billion. In February 1998 Chancellor and Capstar reached an agreement whereby Chancellor would give Capstar an undisclosed number of stations in smaller markets in exchange for 11 SFX stations in four major markets. Capstar, the third largest radio group in terms of revenue, specialized in medium and small markets, while Chancellor was focused on major markets. Among the stations involved in the swap were two stations in the Dallas-Forth Worth area, which would give Chancellor a total of six stations in that market. The other stations involved in the trade were located in Houston, Pittsburgh, and San Diego. Hicks, Muse, a substantial shareholder in Chancellor, also controlled Capstar, and certain of Chancellor's directors were also directors and/or executive officers of Capstar and/or Hicks, Muse.

Also in February, Chancellor announced it would acquire two Washington, D.C., radio stations, WWDC-FM and WWDC-AM, from Capitol Broadcasting Company for $72

million. The acquisition gave Chancellor five FM and three AM stations in Washington, D.C., the nation's eighth largest radio revenue market. According to Scott Ginsburg, Chancellor's president and CEO, "Chancellor Media Corporation will be established as the leading radio station group in Washington, D.C., ranked first in both audience and revenue share in the market. Additionally, we will own a full complement of radio stations in the nation's capitol—five FM and three AM radio stations—as specified in the Telecom Act of 1996." He went on to note that Chancellor ranked first or second in revenues in eight of the nation's top ten radio revenue markets. He said, "We intend to pursue additional acquisitions that will further strengthen our position in the nation's largest radio markets."

The AMFM Radio Networks Was Formed in September 1997

With such a broad listener base, it was logical that Chancellor would become involved in programming and product development. It launched a new division, The AMFM Radio Networks, in September 1997, and in March 1998 the company announced it had signed radio and television veteran Casey Kasem. Kasem's well-known popular music countdown show would be syndicated over The AMFM Radio Networks as part of his multiyear contract. In making the announcement, Ginsburg also indicated that The AMFM Radio Networks would be announcing new products throughout the year.

To provide additional financing and help with its balance sheet, Chancellor announced in January 1998 that it would make a public offering of 16 million shares of common stock. The company expected to use the proceeds from the sale to reduce borrowings under its senior credit facility. However, it also noted that it could reborrow those funds for general corporate purposes, including further acquisitions and the repurchase of the company's preferred stock.

Chancellor Media Poised to Maintain Its Active Acquisitions Program

In 1997 Chancellor Media completed its merger with Evergreen Media, which added 52 radio stations to the company's portfolio, for approximately $2 billion. It also acquired 23 radio stations for a net purchase price of approximately $1.5 billion. It exchanged seven stations for five stations and $6 million in cash, and it sold or otherwise disposed of 10 radio stations for $269.3 million in cash and a promissory note for $18 million. It also acquired Katz Media Group for approximately $379.1 million. Chancellor also had pending agreements to purchase an additional 13 radio stations in exchange for two stations and $656.5 million in cash and, in another transaction, to swap three of its stations and $60.0 million in cash for three other stations.

With its senior management team having extensive experience in acquiring and operating large market radio station groups, Chancellor Media will continue to pursue its business strategy of assembling and operating radio station clusters in order to maximize broadcast cash flow. As part of this strategy, Chancellor Media will seek to own and operate the leading superduopoly in the largest markets in the United States while maximizing their revenue growth and expense savings. Superduopolies became permissible with the passage of the Telecommunications Act of 1996.

In terms of station operation, Chancellor Media's strategy called for establishing strong listener loyalty and maintaining strict cost controls. During the period 1995–97, the company was able to achieve broadcast cash flow margins of 40 percent or more as a result of its cost control measures.

Finally, Chancellor Media expected to leverage its radio expertise by expanding into related industries and complementary media businesses. As part of this strategy it acquired Katz Media Group, a full-service media representation firm, and formed a national radio network, The AMFM Radio Networks.

Principal Subsidiaries

The AMFM Radio Networks; Katz Media Group Inc.; 97 radio stations.

Further Reading

"AMFM Radio Networks Signs Casey Kasem," *PR Newswire*, March 2, 1998.

Berkowitz, Harry, "Feds Sue to Block LI Radio Buy," *Newsday*, November 7, 1997, p. A63.

Bernstein, James, "$2.6B Radio Merger Announced," *Newsday*, February 19, 1997, p. A43.

"Big 105 FM Reports Preliminary Results of Auditions for the Danny Bonaduce in the Morning Show," *Entertainment Wire*, February 17, 1998.

Block, Valerie, "Chancellor, CBS Retune FM Losers in Radio Face-Off," *Crain's New York Business*, January 26, 1998, p. 3.

——, "Radio Powerhouse Pumping up Volume," *Crain's New York Business*, November 10, 1997, p. 3.

"Capstar and Chancellor to Divide SFX Broadcasting Assets," *Business Wire*, February 23, 1998.

"Chancellor Media Agrees to Acquire WWDC-FM and WWDC-AM," *Business Wire*, February 18, 1998.

"Chancellor Media Corporation Files Prospectus Supplement Regarding Sixteen Million Share Public Offering of Common Stock," *Business Wire*, February 23, 1998.

DePass, Dee, "Chancellor Broadcasting, Evergreen Media to Merge," *Minneapolis Star-Tribune*, February 19, 1997, p. D1.

Devine, Matthew E., "Evergreen Media and Chancellor Broadcasting Agree to Sell 107.7 FM Frequency in San Francisco for $44 Million," *Business Wire*, April 9, 1997.

——, "Evergreen Media and Chancellor Broadcasting Sell Two Radio Stations to Disney's ABC Radio for $105 Million," *Business Wire*, April 14, 1997.

——, "Evergreen Media and Chancellor Broadcasting to Acquire Katz Media Group," *Business Wire*, July 14, 1997.

Folta, Carl, "Viacom Signs Agreement to Sell Its Radio Stations Group," *Business Wire*, February 18, 1997.

Furman, Phyllis, "Chancellor Radio Muscles into NY with Big Merger," *Crain's New York Business*, February 24, 1997, p. 1.

Harrington, Jeff, "$2.58B Radio Mega-Merger Knocks Jacor to 3rd-Largest," *Cincinnati Enquirer*, February 19, 1997, p. B10.

Hofmeister, Sallie, "$2.7-Billion Deal Would Create No. 2 Radio Group in U.S.," *Los Angeles Times*, February 19., 1997, p. D1.

Joshi, Pradnya, "Radio Daze," *Newsday*, March 3, 1997, p. C6.

Kaplan, Peter, "Evergreen to Clear Merger by Selling Small D.C. Stations," *Washington Times*, May 21, 1997, p. B7.

——, "Three-Way Deal to Forge Radio Giant," *Washington Times*, February 19, 1997, p. B7.

——, "Wave of Megamergers Signals Changes Across Radio Dial," *Washington Times*, August 4, 1997, p. D12.

Kirkpatrick, John, "Chancellor, Capstar Swap Radio Stations," *Dallas Morning News*, February 24, 1998, p. 4D.

——, "Justice Department Sues Chancellor; Irving-Based Media Giant Says Purchase of NY Radio Stations Isn't Anti-Competitive," *Dallas Morning News*, November 7, 1997, p. 10D.

Larson, Mark, "Chancellor Rebuffed by N.Y. Radio Chain," *Sacramento Business Journal*, March 20, 1995, p. 10.

——, "Deal by KFBK Parent May Foreshadow Public Offering," *Sacramento Business Journal*, August 14, 1995, p. 2.

——, "Waived Rules Start Rush to Rule Airwaves," *Sacramento Business Journal*, August 12, 1996, p. 6.

Mulligan, Thomas S., "It's Radio's Turn: Chancellor to Buy 19 Shamrock Stations," *Los Angeles Times*, August 4, 1995, p. 1.

Otter, Jack, "Dallas Company Locks in LI Dial," *Newsday*, July 2, 1996, p. A35.

Paeth, Greg, "Radio Giants Draw Battle Lines for Listeners," *Cincinnati Post*, February 19, 1997, p. C1.

Windle, Rickie, "Investor Sues Austin's SFX over Rejected Buyout Offer," *Austin Business Journal*, March 24, 1995, p. 1.

Winnick, Roy, "Chancellor Broadcasting Company Announces 1994 Results," *Business Wire*, April 4, 1995.

—David Bianco

C. H. Heist Corporation

810 North Belcher Road
Clearwater, Florida 34625-2103
U.S.A.
(813) 461-5656
Fax: (813) 447-1146
Web site: http://www.heist.com

Public Company
Incorporated: 1949
Employees: 3,700
Sales: $106.52 million (1996)
Stock Exchanges: American
Ticker Symbol: HST
SICs: 7349 Building Maintenance Services, Not
    Elsewhere Classified; 7363 Help Supply Services;
    1742 Plastering, Drywall, Acoustical, & Insulation

C. H. Heist Corporation offers U.S. businesses an array of industrial services using specialized, state-of-the-art equipment. Services include high-pressure water maintenance cleaning of industrial and chemical equipment and facilities; sandblasting; industrial painting; wet and dry vacuuming of industrial waste; exchanger extraction and insertion; shell side cleaning; tube cleaning; heat exchanger field service repairs; and insulation for commercial applications. Heist's customers consist of oil refineries; the petrochemical industry; chemical plants; ferrous and nonferrous metal facilities; mining installations; government authorities; nuclear, fossil fuel, and electrical generating plants; and pulp and paper mills. Its largest client—E. I. DuPont De Nemours and Company—accounted for eight percent of Heist's total sales in 1996.

Heist's Canadian subsidiary extends similar industrial services to businesses in that country. Another wholly owned Heist subsidiary—Ablest Service Corporation—provides professional and industrial temporary staff to companies in the eastern United States.

Partnering in 1949

One Charles H. Heist founded a painting and sandblasting company, which he named after himself, in 1949. He built the company around the principle of partnering with his clients, decades before the concept was in vogue. "Partnering is not a new concept for Heist," explained the founder's son, C. H. Heist, in a corporate brochure. "Today, through partnering," he continued, "Heist has become a permanent part of the day-to-day functions of many Fortune 500 companies. . . . Partnering allows us to provide our customers with better service through better employees. It helps us create stability in the work force with a stronger work ethic, better customer service attitudes, and a safer working environment."

Throughout the 1950s, Heist researched the specific needs of his target customers, then established long-term, mutually beneficial arrangements to serve those same clients. According to son C. H. Heist, "No job was too messy, too dirty, too hot, or too cold. That was the secret of Heist's market strategy then, as now."

The senior Heist relied on communications with customers and resource sharing, including labor and equipment, to perform his early painting and sandblasting contracts. He concentrated on selecting the proper materials, carefully adhering to all specifications, and taking every necessary safety precaution for each job.

Coatings and Abrasive Blastings

Heist specialized in protective coatings and abrasive blasting. Clients contracted with the company to protect equipment or facilities from corrosion. Since its inception, Heist used technologically advanced methods of abrasive blasting. For example, the company utilized self-contained mobile sandblasting units from the beginning of its operations. Not only did such devices lower costs for customers, the mobile sandblasting units also were fast and offered quick response times, so they were ready on short notice or for emergency situations.

The company also provided its customers with clean, healthy methods for abrasive blasting or for applying protective coatings. Heist offered businesses and industries environmentally friendly

Company Perspectives:

At Heist, we like to create "partnering" relationships with our customers. Partnering is a long-term, mutually beneficial arrangement between two companies in which labor, equipment and other resources are often shared. And communication is closely maintained between management for maximum teamwork efforts.

Within a strong partnering context, we can adapt quickly to our customers' changing situations and provide them with the kind of personal attention we feel they deserve.

alternatives for painting or abrasive blasting operations. The company also maintained high standards for safety among its operatives. Heist workers received extensive safety training in the areas of respiratory protection, hazardous communication, confined-space entry, first aid, and hazardous response.

As the industrial services business evolved, Heist expanded into high-performance coatings such as flame spray metals and plastics. Then the company extended services further to vacuuming and hydrocleaning.

Vacuuming and Hydrocleaning

Heist developed expertise in both wet and dry vacuuming. The company maintained a mobile fleet of wet-vacuum trucks, with capacities between 3,000 and 4,000 gallons. The trucks' hydraulic dumping mechanisms allowed for the clean up of liquid wastes and contaminants. High-powered vacuum units collected dust, debris, and other dry wastes. Heist vacuuming operations serviced utility plants, steel plants, cement plants, roofing projects, construction sites, refineries, and chemical complexes.

Heist went on to develop a safe and effective industrial system devoid of chemicals. Heist's hydrocleaning services offered the high-pressure cleaning of chemical and petrochemical process equipment using water instead of chemicals. "We wash away the dirt, grime, and mess, not our customers' property," the company revealed in *On Stream with Heist.* "Hydrocleaning is even safe for intricate process equipment that could be damaged by other cleaning methods."

A variety of industries utilized Heist's hydrocleaning services, including steel, power, chemical, marine, petroleum refining, and pulp and paper enterprises. Despite the diversity, each client received customized service because Heist engineers designed equipment to handle each customer's job efficiently, inexpensively, and safely. "While several industrial service companies have some of the tools with which to do significant general mechanical turnaround and maintenance projects," noted a "Business Update" in *BIC,* "Heist owns the toolbox."

Passing the Torch

Heist changed leadership in 1983 when the company's founder died. Heist received a restated certificate of incorporation that year, and internal practices and policies continued to evolve throughout the decade. The son of the founder (also named C. H. Heist), a director of the company since 1978, assumed control as president and chief executive officer in 1988.

Throughout its history, Heist grew through acquisitions. For example, Pipe & Boiler Insulation, Inc. (PBI) of Charlotte, North Carolina, became a division of Heist. Serving the southeastern United States predominantly, PBI installed and distributed commercial and industrial insulation to nuclear and fossil fuel power plants; chemical, tobacco, textile, and food processing industries; airports and airlines; hospitals; schools; the military; and government installations. The division's crews and fleets of trucks operated 365 days a year and offered products from all major manufacturers—fiberglass, calcium silicate, mineral wool, fabricated materials, mastics, jacketing materials, air handling insulation, and accessories.

Ablest Service Corporation

Heist's subsidiary Ablest Service Corporation conducted the company's second line of business: temporary staffing. Under the direction of W. David Foster since 1986, Ablest broke sales records and performed well financially throughout the decades. Ablest specialized in providing clerical, light industrial, and information technology (IT) staff to a variety of employers. Ablest maintained company-owned offices throughout the midwestern and southeastern United States, expanding to more than 30 offices by the 1990s.

Like its industrial services counterpart, Ablest relied on dedication to customer service to retain its position in the marketplace. As Foster explained in the 1996 annual report, "We look for clients who want value-added services and a supplier they can partner with. Our major competitive strength is our ability to empower local management to react as owners of the company and have the motivation to satisfy their customers' expectations. These local offices have the backing of a larger company, providing human resources support and IT systems, but they have the autonomy to operate as a local company which can meet the needs of their customers."

Growth Through Acquisitions

In 1993, Heist acquired the assets of Ohmstede Mechanical Services, Inc., of Baytown, Texas. Ohmstede Mechanical expanded the industrial services offered by Heist to refineries and the petrochemical industry. The Texas company provided onsite exchanger repair and maintenance; exchanger cleaning; and bundle extraction.

Three years later, Heist revised its operating structure. Looking to reduce costs, the company outsourced some support functions and closed an industrial maintenance and repair facility in Buffalo, New York. Heist also initiated its Economic Value Added (EVA) process in 1996. The company launched this long-term strategy to monitor and measure its systems for financial reporting and incentive compensation. Though long-term in nature, the EVA program elicited some short-term gains. As Charles H. Heist explained in the company's 1996 annual report, "We fully anticipate definitive long-term benefits from our EVA program. While our intentions and strategies with regard to EVA have indeed been long term, we've also enjoyed some immediate improvements. By improving inventory turnover and reducing inventory size—through implementation of just-in-time deliveries or having vendors stock inventory—we have reduced investment in inventory by $400,000.''

Spinning Off Ablest

In 1996, Heist announced the planned spinoff and initial public offering of its wholly owned subsidiary Ablest Service Corporation. In part, the move was a response to the trend toward consolidation in the commercial staffing sector. ''We want to complete the spinoff and IPO to make Ablest a 'pure-play' company,'' explained Foster in the 1996 annual report, ''so it is easier for us to participate in the consolidation movement by making acquisitions. The spinoff and IPO will enable us to assemble more creative purchase plans and buyout offers. Our intention is to become one of the consolidators.'' Acquisition activity would bring the goal of $200 million in annual sales by the year 2000 within the subsidiary's reach. Shortly thereafter, in September 1996, Ablest purchased Tech Resources, Inc., an Atlanta-based company active in the area of information technology staffing. Ablest established a new division—Tech Resource Group—dedicated to information technology staffing after the acquisition.

Despite the company's plans, conditions in the stock market were unfavorable for an initial public offering at the beginning of 1997, so Heist postponed the spinoff of Ablest. President C. H. Heist remarked in a January press release that ''Ablest will continue to aggressively pursue acquisitions and open new offices in strategic markets where the company currently does not have a presence. . . . This should provide the critical mass necessary to complete an initial public offering on the terms originally contemplated.''

During the second quarter of 1997, Ablest acquired Solution Source, Inc. This growth—with Ablest's strong financial performance—reinforced Heist's board of directors commitment to the subsidiary's spinoff and IPO later in the year. By June, Ablest purchased yet another company to expand its services in information technology staffing. Ablest's Tech Resource Group absorbed the Kelton Group of Raleigh, North Carolina, which provided information technology staffing and documentation services. ''Raleigh was a market area we had planned to open leveraging our existing traditional staffing operation. This gives us immediate revenues and profitability compared to an organic set-up,'' Foster explained in a June 1997 press release.

By August 1997, Ablest operated 37 offices, but conditions never became suitable for the planned spinoff of the subsidiary. ''By keeping the companies together,'' president and chief executive officer C. H. Heist revealed, ''we can better utilize the financial strength and leverage of the combined entities to aggressively pursue acquisitions and open new offices in strategic markets.''

Future Plans in 1997

Ablest's plans at the end of 1997 included new offices and acquisitions. ''Our acquisition strategy remains aggressive and strong,'' reported President and CEO C. H. Heist in an August 1997 press release. ''Staffing firms, especially those that specialize in information technology staffing, that are accretive to earnings, are compatible with our corporate culture and fit into our geographic expansion plans will be strong candidates and carefully considered.'' Heist's plans for its industrial cleaning and maintenance services involved refocusing on chemical cleaning and introducing new services such as dewatering, which utilized mobile filter presses to remove liquids from industrial wastes. ''This year,'' remarked C. H. Heist, ''we've brought new capabilities on line that allow our industrial maintenance segment to provide additional services to existing customers, as well as provide new services to new markets.''

Principal Subsidiaries

C. H. Heist Ltd. (Canada); PLP Corporation; Inpro Industries Inc.; Ablest Service Corporation; Ablest Personnel Services Ltd.

Further Reading

''C. H. Heist: Chemical Cleaning and Contamination Services,'' *BIC*, September 1997, p. 62.
''C. H. Heist: Specialty Services Second to None,'' *BIC*, May 1997, p. 32.
''C. H. Heist: The Field Machining Experts,'' *BIC*, July 1997, p. 41.
''C. H. Heist: The Indoor-Air-Quality Professionals,'' *BIC*, August 1997, p. 23.
''C. H. Heist Corporation,'' *Tampa Bay Business Journal*, September 17, 1993, p. S9.
''C. H. Heist Corporation,'' *Oil and Gas Journal*, August 30, 1993, p. 94.
''Earnings and Announcements . . . C. H. Heist Corporation, HCO Energy, Unit Corporation,'' *Energy Alert*, February 21, 1996.
On Stream with Heist, Clearwater, Fla.: C. H. Heist Corporation, n.d.

—Charity Anne Dorgan

Chicken of the Sea International

4510 Executive Drive, Suite 300
San Diego, California 92121-3029
U.S.A.
(619) 558-9662
Fax: (619) 597-4568
Web site: http://www.chickenofthesea.com

Private Company
Founded: 1914 as Van Camp Seafood Company, Inc.
Employees: 2,900
Sales: $297 million (1997 est.)
SICs: 2091 Canned & Cured Fish & Seafoods

Chicken of the Sea International is one of the leading canned seafood companies in the world and one of the largest in the United States. The company specializes in tuna products, but also markets more than a dozen varieties of high-quality fish and shellfish products. By 1998, tuna was the largest per capita consumption of all seafood products. Some of the company's product lines have included: Dolphin-safe and kosher-certified albacore tuna products like Solid White Albacore Packed in Spring Water; Chunk White Albacore Packed in Spring Water; Solid White Albacore Packed in Saturated Fat-Free Canola Oil; Very Low Sodium Albacore; and Low Sodium Albacore. Lightmeat tuna products from prime skipjack and yellowfin tuna, like Chunk Light in Spring Water; Chunk Light Tuna in Saturated Fat-Free Canola Oil; Solid Light in Olive Oil; Low Sodium Yellowfin Packed in Spring Water; and 50% Less Salt Chunk Light with Added Vegetable Broth. Other products include: Traditional Red Salmon and Traditional Pink Salmon; Skinless/Boneless Pink Salmon; crabmeat in an assortment of white, fancy, and lump styles; a variety of shrimp products, from tiny to small, medium, and regular domestic and international shrimp, both veined and deveined; mackerel; oval and tall sardines in an assortment of sauces and spring water; clams offered in minced, chopped, or whole styles; and oysters available in boiled and smoked-pack styles.

Out of the Blue: History, 1914–75

Van Camp Seafood Company, Inc. was founded back in the spring of 1914 when Frank Van Camp and his son, Gilbert, bought the California Tunny Canning Company to can albacore. Three years later, Van Camp Seafood Company became the first cannery to commercially pack yellowfin tuna. In the 1930s, Van Camp acquired its first two fishing vessels.

But the company did not attain household recognition until the late 1950s, when the company created the famous commercial jingle that goes, ''Ask any mermaid you happen to see, who's the best tuna? Chicken of the Sea.'' The company created the mermaid as its mascot at the same time, and she has remained to this day as a food industry icon, along with the likes of The Pillsbury Doughboy, The Green Giant, and colleague Charlie Tuna.

In 1963, the company was sold to Missouri-based Ralston Purina, known primarily as a producer of processed foods, pet food, and livestock and poultry feeds. Ralston Purina built a cannery in San Diego, California, in 1975, following the closing of a plant in Los Angeles County.

During the three decades following World War II, southern California (including San Diego, Terminal Island, and Long Beach) became the world center for tuna, albacore, and bluefin processing and canning. By 1975, with The U.S. Tuna Foundation, Van Camp Seafood Co., Bumble Bee Seafoods, Pan Pacific Fisheries, and Mitsubishi Foods, among others, maintaining as many as 16 bustling canneries, employing more than 10,000 workers ranging from fishermen and cannery workers to administrators and dock workers, tuna sandwiches, tuna salads, and tuna casseroles became commonplace. By 1994, the number of industry workers in southern California had dropped to a mere 500. By 1976, the company was operating canneries in San Diego and Terminal Island, California, American Samoa (in the South Pacific), and Ponce, Puerto Rico.

Tuna is processed through a number of steps. First, fresh-caught tuna is frozen on the boat in brine at temperatures as low as 10 degrees Fahrenheit. Once at the cannery, the frozen tuna is

Company Perspectives:

Chicken of the Sea International is committed to leading the industry with safe, wholesome, nutritious and delicious products, including its well-known and extensive tuna product line and more than a dozen varieties of high-quality fish and shellfish.

thawed, which takes an hour or two. Next, it is butchered and gutted to remove the entrails. The gutted parts are ground up and used to make organic fertilizer. The butchered fish is steam cooked and then cooled. In the packing room, it is deboned. The head, tail, and fins are removed, as are its bones. The skin and red meat are also removed. The red meat is used to manufacture pet food, while the bony parts are ground up to make fish meal animal feed and fertilizer. What remains is a loin, or large, dressed piece of tuna, and flakes of tuna that have come off in the cleaning process. They are packed by an automatic filling machine into cans. The loin portions are used to pack chunk, or solid, tuna, while the flakes are used for lower grades of canned tuna. Salt and water or oil are added to the can. The can is sealed with lids in a vacuum process, then washed. The tuna is pasteurized and the can is heated with steam to kill bacteria, giving the can a shelf life of about five years. Finally, the cooled can is labeled and shipped.

A Fishy Situation: Fleeing from the West Coast, 1980s

In 1984, Ralston Purina gutted Van Camp's San Diego facilities, closing the cannery facility and moving it to the distant shores of American Samoa, in order to access the more inexpensive labor pool, and also to be closer to one of the richest fishing grounds in the world. Ralston Purina also moved Van Camp's main offices to St. Louis, Missouri.

It was only the beginning of a time of shake-up for the industry as, the following year, San Francisco-based Castle & Cooke Inc. sold its Bumble Bee Seafoods salmon and tuna cannery operations on Harbor Drive in San Diego to the division's four top managers for $73 million. Bumble Bee, one of Van Camp Seafood's primary competitors, eventually found its way into Thai hands, and reported revenues of $450 million in 1997 and, by then, maintained processing plants in Thailand, Puerto Rico, and Ecuador, as well as returning to southern California, with another facility in the city of Santa Fe Springs (which originally was a Bumble Bee facility owned by Unicord of Thailand).

In 1988, a group of private investors from Indonesia, called P. T. Mantrust Corporation, purchased Van Camp's from Ralston Purina in a highly leveraged transaction. The new owners planned to leverage their fishing fleet and expanded canning operation in Indonesia with Van Camp's American Samoa cannery and brand name to execute a fully integrated approach to supplying canned tuna to the United States. But, due to high interest rates in Indonesia, and its overly leveraged structure,

P. T. Mantrust experienced cash flow difficulties and the primary creditor, The Prudential Life Insurance Company of America, became the majority owner.

Boycott for Dolphins, Early 1990s

In April 1990, the tuna industry was faced with a growing consumer boycott of canned tuna products when the public was made aware that over 100,000 dolphins died per year when they were caught by purse-seine methods, in which fishermen cast a large net around a school of tuna and then pull it taut like the drawstring of a purse. In response, the three largest sellers of canned tuna in the United States made a decision that they would no longer sell tuna caught by methods harmful to dolphins. Star-Kist Seafood, the world's largest tuna canner at the time, owned by food giant H. J. Heinz, led the way, followed by the two other major canners, Bumble Bee Seafoods and Van Camp Seafood.

In October of that year, Van Camp Seafood Co. moved its corporate headquarters and 115-member staff from St. Louis back to its home city of San Diego, into a 33,362-square-foot building in Chancellor Park, an office complex located in an area known as "The Golden Triangle."

Two years later, in December 1992, much of the company's senior hierarchy moved up. Dennis Mussell, who formerly worked for companies such as Ocean Garden Products and Mitsubishi Foods, was promoted to chief operating officer; J. Douglas Hines was promoted to senior vice-president of sales and marketing; and Don George was made senior vice-president for the newly formed logistics department.

In the summer of 1995, Pan Pacific Fisheries filed for bankruptcy, leaving more than $15 million in debts and nearly 700 people without jobs. The desperate move also meant the closing of the last full-service tuna processing plant in the continental United States, as it shut down operations at the last canning facility on Terminal Island. By this time, Star-Kist had moved their headquarters from its southern California location in Long Beach to distant Pennsylvania.

In 1996, consumer research group Leo J. Shapiro & Associates listed the Chicken of the Sea brand name as one of the top 10 consumer packaged goods in the United States.

Early that same year, Tri-Marine International Inc. of San Pedro, California, bought the half-century-old former Pan Pacific Fisheries plant on Cannery Street on Terminal Island, for $7.3 million, spending another $5 million to renovate the 10-acre complex and renaming the cannery Tri-Union Seafoods LLC. The facility was reopened in June of that year, and Tri-Union rehired nearly 300 of the old Pan Pacific workers, and another 400 workers were hired a few months later when the renovations were completed. A canning facility in the United States was back in business again. Thailand's Unicord also sold the Bumble Bee product line back to a group of U.S. investors and the canning facilities of Bumble Bee to Star-Kist. Meanwhile, total annual revenue for Van Camp in 1996 reached $440 million.

In October 1997, in a $97 million deal, Van Camp Seafood was saved from Chapter 11 bankruptcy as Tri-Union Seafoods LLC purchased the venerable canned seafood company, the third time it changed hands in its long history.

Tri-Union Seafoods LLC by that time was a conglomeration of several companies located throughout the world. The first, Bangkok-based Thai Union International Inc. [also known as Thai Union Frozen Products Public Co. Ltd., itself made up of Thai Union Frozen Products PCL, Songkla Canning PCL, and Thai Union Manufacturing Co. Ltd. (established in 1977)] was, at the time, the largest tuna packer in Asia and second largest in the world, with total annual sales exceeding $500 million in 1996, and 10,000 employees worldwide, producing over 600 metric tons of canned tuna, pouched tuna, frozen tuna loin, frozen shrimp, canned pet food, canned seafood, and canned salmon per day. The second, Tri-Marine International Inc., was one of the largest tuna traders in the world, with offices and subsidiaries in Europe, Japan, Singapore, the Solomon Islands, Taiwan, Thailand, South America, and the United States. Established in 1972, it had 1996 sales of $342 million on over 300,000 tons of products per year, including raw tuna, swordfish, salmon, shrimp, and squid. And the third was Ed Gann, a Rancho Santa Fe, California resident with more than 40 years experience in the fishing industry, and one of the world's most respected purse-seine tuna boat operators and owner of a company called Caribbean Marine, whose fleet consisted at the time of five fishing vessels with a total holding capacity of nearly 6,500 tons, producing an annual catch of nearly 40,000 tons of dolphin-safe tuna distributed to the United States, Central America, South America, Puerto Rico, and Europe. He had, at that point in his career, operated or owned more than 50 fishing vessels (Van Camp Seafood itself already contracted nine vessels).

Tri-Union Seafoods changed the name of Van Camp Seafood Co. Inc. to Chicken of the Sea International, adopting its brand name for the company, to help avoid confusion with Van de Kamp's Inc., located in St. Louis, best-known for their pork and beans, but who also manufactured a line of frozen breaded fish sticks. Chicken of the Sea International, under the direction of its new leadership, began aggressive marketing of its Chicken of the Sea family of products in retail, food service, and club stores. The new owners also left the Chicken of the Sea International main offices, and the staff of 2,200 people, located in San Diego.

Around the same time, Bumble Bee Seafoods Inc., yet another of the canned seafood companies which also had filed for Chapter 11, was acquired by International Home Foods Inc. for $163 million in cash and stock.

Also in 1997, Chicken of the Sea International launched its web site to respond to consumer inquiries about dolphin-safe tuna, overfished species, and requests for tuna recipes as well as allowing vendors to place orders via the site. The company also began a program attempting to increase sales of its non-tuna canned products such as shrimp, crab, clams, oysters, and sardines, since nearly 80 percent of the company's business was canned tuna. Total revenue for the company in 1997 reached $297 million.

By 1998, the company was the Port of San Diego's largest container customer, importing more than 700,000 cases of canned-food products monthly, sorted at Chicken of the Sea's 100,000-square-foot central warehouse facility at the 10th Avenue Marine Terminal, and the company's main markets were the United States and Israel, but it was looking to the Pacific Rim for expansion. At the same time, the tuna industry as a whole was searching for a "Got Milk?" type of campaign to help promote all tuna products.

Early that year, Chicken of the Sea International and Tri-Union International LLC merged into one company, still called Chicken of the Sea International. The company, which by this time operated canneries located in American Samoa and San Pedro, California, added additional processing capacity, allowing Chicken of the Sea to be a significant strategic partner by offering private label brands to selected customers, offering complete canned seafood selections (both branded and private label) to the retail, foodservice, club store, mass merchandiser, and the pharmaceutical trade customers, as well as a high grade, gourmet quality canned catfood for U.S. and export markets. As the 20th century drew to a close, Chicken of the Sea was running strong in the industry again.

Further Reading

Green, Frank, "Global Factors Shrivel San Diego's Tuna-Processing Business," *Knight-Ridder/Tribune Business News*, August 2, 1994, p. 08020006.

Siedsma, Andrea, "Chicken of the Sea Rises from the Depths," *San Diego Business Journal*, October 20, 1997, p. 1.

"Thai Companies to Buy Chicken of the Sea," *New York Times*, July 17, 1992, p. C3(N)/D3(L).

"Tri-Union Adds VP Position," *Supermarket News*, January 20, 1997, p. 48.

"Tuna Without the Guilt: Canners Aim to Make the Seas Safer for Cetaceans," *Time*, April 23, 1990, p. 63.

Utumporn, Pichayaporn, "Thai Exporters Ride Tide," *Asian Wall Street Journal*, February 9, 1998, p. 20.

"Van Camp Becomes Chicken of the Sea," *Nation's Restaurant News*, August 25, 1997, p. 43.

"Van Camp Moves Its Staff Back to San Diego," *San Diego Business Journal*, October 1, 1990, p. 16.

"Van Camp Unveils Corporate Restructuring," *Nation's Restaurant News*, December 21, 1992, p. 90.

Wong, Art, "Tuna Cannery Makes Comeback on Southern California's Terminal Island," *Knight-Ridder/Tribune Business News*, July 29, 1996, p. 7290274.

—Daryl F. Mallett

Coach USA, Inc.

One Riverway, Suite 600
Houston, Texas 77056-1903
U.S.A.
(713) 888-0104
Fax: 713-888-0218

Public Company
Incorporated: 1995
Employees: 4,100
Sales: $542.8 million (1997)
Stock Exchanges: New York
Ticker Symbol: CUI
SICs: 4141 Local Bus Charter Service

Coach USA, Inc. is the largest provider of motorcoach charter, tour, and sightseeing services in the United States. The company ranks as one of the five largest private sector providers of commuter and transit motorcoach services in Canada and the United States. Additionally, Coach USA provides airport ground transportation, paratransit, taxi, and other related passenger ground transportation services.

Founded As a Rollup, 1995

Founded in September 1995, Coach USA was the creation of a merchant banking firm, Notre Capital Ventures II, L.P. (Notre) a Houston, Texas-based organization recognized for its successful "roll-ups," in which several choice smaller companies within a growth industry are identified and then combined to form one large company. Major funding is then established through the sale of stock. For a decade or more, principals at Notre had worked at various accounting and acquisition functions related to the waste industry, which had undergone extensive consolidation. That successful model was applied to roll-up ventures in other industries. The Notre group was responsible for the public offerings of U.S. Delivery Systems, Physicians Resource Group, Allwaste, Sanifill, and American Medical Response. They focused on industries that were very large, very fragmented, with businesses that were stable from a non-cyclical and profit margin

standpoint. The criteria utilized by Notre for selecting individual companies within various industries has included profitability, sizable operations, a long track record, and demonstrated leadership and entrepreneurial management.

By the mid-1990s, the Notre management team identified the motorcoach industry as "ripe for consolidation," according to Larry Plachno of the *National Bus Trader.* Within the United States the motorcoach industry primarily offered three types of services: recreation and excursion (charter, tour and sightseeing); commuter and transit; and regularly scheduled intercity service. In 1996 the highly fragmented industry accounted for approximately 5,000 motorcoach operators, which collectively generated roughly $20 billion in annual revenues. With the U.S. travel and tourism industry growing substantially, the targeting of large organizations such as AAA, AARP, and convention organizers by chartering companies—and growing numbers of tourists from Europe and Asia, in particular, the motorcoach industry was viewed by the investors as a potentially lucrative market.

Notre management first opted to concentrate on motorcoach businesses that specialized in the charter and tour market, and privatized transit and commuter service, rather than companies in the scheduled intercity bus service market. Also, they anticipated future expansion due to declining transit funding of capital intensive operations by state and local governments, which would eventually steer transit agencies to the more competitive privatized companies. Management forecast a scenario where sizable federal funding available for subsidizing commuter, transit, and ancillary services, such as paratransit services required under the Americans with Disabilities Act, would diminish. By merging a number of companies they could benefit by the large scale of their operations, qualifying them for lower equipment and insurance costs, financing costs, and other cost advantages.

Going Public, 1996

Coach USA went public in May 1996, with an initial offering of 3,600,000 shares priced at $14 per share. Coach USA was formed with six initial "founding companies" which were well

Company Perspectives:

Our Corporate Strategy is straightforward: to create a national company that meets passengers' diverse ground transportation needs, particularly focusing on services for domestic and international tourists and conventioneers. To this end, Coach USA builds by acquiring motorcoach tour and charter companies headquartered in gateway cities and convention centers. Operations in these key locations provide the infrastructure from which we can expand our other services, including transit, privatization and outsourcing contracts, regular route operations, airport shuttles and other ground transportation services.

established in the motorcoach industry: Suburban Transit Corp. of New Brunswick, New Jersey; Gray Line of San Francisco, California; Leisure Time Tours in Mahway, New Jersey; Community Bus Lines in Passaic, New Jersey; Adventure Trails in Atlantic City, New Jersey; and Arrow Stage Line in Phoenix, Arizona. The acquisitions were valued at $88.4 million. Forty million passengers were accommodated annually by these companies equipped with a combined force of 760 coaches. Owners of the merging companies exchanged their corporate stock for stock in Coach USA, which gave the company ownership of equipment as well as the individual businesses. Coach USA espoused a decentralized management philosophy. Their arrangement allowed previous owners to continue as presidents of the acquired companies so that the new consolidated company gained from experienced management in localized operations. Almost half of the stock holdings were held by the founding companies following the consolidation. The individual companies, including most of the later acquisitions, were restructured as subsidiaries of Coach USA, retaining their original identities and operating practices.

Using Notre Capital's effective management model the team was split into an operational management team and an acquisition management team. Heading the operations team, John Mercandante—industry veteran and prior owner of Adventure Trails—became the first Coach USA president and chief operating officer. Local operators continued to identify candidates for corporate management, who focused on the acquisition program and coordinated equipment sharing among the various companies, set safety standards, and conducted financing procedures and vendor contacts. This arrangement allowed entrepreneurs at the acquired companies to continue to deal with day-to-day operations, including customer relationships, equipment utilization, and local pricing. Former Arthur Anderson partner Richard H. Kristinik was named chairman and chief executive officer of the company, responsible for leading strategic initiatives and coordinating acquisition activities and negotiations. The company's executive management team consisted of eight professionals, including CFO Larry King, Senior Vice-President and Corporate Development Officer Frank Gallagher, and Senior Vice-President and General Counsel Doug Cerney.

Kristinik told John O'Hanlon of the *Wall Street Corporate Reporter* that ''We think our decentralized management philos-

ophy is one of the keys to our success. It is a key for Coach USA being able to attract new companies to become part of Coach USA. . . he (the owner-operator) can sell his company, enjoy the benefit of selling his company at capital gains rates, and continue to be president of his company.'' Kristinik also stated that the decentralized management philosophy was also important in remaining close to the customer by keeping the ''former owner-operator entrepreneur in his own backyard, serving the customer and growing the business.''

In an effort to begin strengthening Coach USA's geographical position a second stock offering was made in November 1996, followed by the addition of six companies which were merged into Coach USA, including American Bus Lines Inc. of Miami; Gray Line and Texas Bus Lines of Houston; KT Contract Services of Las Vegas; and California Charter Inc. of Los Angeles and San Diego. The Yellow Cab Service companies of Houston and Austin, Texas, and Colorado Springs, Colorado, were also acquired during this time period.

Acquisitions Ensue

Two months after the 3.1 million shares of common stock were sold at $25 a share, another round of acquisitions followed. Four new companies were added in December 1996. Their aggregate annualized revenues totaled $52 million, bringing Coach USA within the range of their projected $73 million of acquired revenue for 1997. By this time the company, with a fleet of approximately 1,700 coaches, was rivaling the Greyhound lines. The addition of Gray Line of Anaheim, California, which operated mainly in per capita sightseeing and tour and charter services in and around Disneyland, had given Coach USA a strong presence in California. The acquisition of Powder River Transportation opened up an entirely new area for the company, with substantial contract operations including use of transit buses to accommodate the attractive employee shuttle business, as well as tour and charter business to major national parks in and around Wyoming and the Rocky Mountains, including Mt. Rushmore and Yellowstone. Another transit contract company, Progressive Transportation of New York, was added, offering commuter and transit services for small and medium-sized municipalities. The company acquired the Gray Line of Montreal and Quebec City, its first expansion outside the continental United States. As the premiere motorcoach and tour and charter company in the Montreal area, the Gray Line focused on per capita sightseeing and airport shuttle services, in addition to offering equipment repair and maintenance services to companies that offer tours and charters into Montreal and Quebec.

The company used a network of hotel lobby ticket counters, hotel concierges, and travel agents to sell sightseeing tours. Charter and tour services were provided on a fixed daily rate, based on mileage and hours of operation. Coach USA's charter and tour fleet vehicles were designed for comfort, featuring plush interiors with televisions and VCRs. Customers traveling in the San Francisco area could comfortably enjoy the sites while touring the Napa Valley wine country, the Monterey Peninsula tour, or the San Francisco city tour. Businesses, schools, and social organizations chartered Coach USA motorcoaches to visit sporting venues, ski resorts, and historical sites. International groups book trips from Niagara Falls to the

Rocky Mountains among the various other attractions. Large events serviced by the company have included the Super Bowl, Rose Bowl, the massive COMDEX trade show in Las Vegas, the Home Builders Association, Houston Livestock and Rodeo, Phoenix Open Golf Tournament, and the Arizona State Fair. In 1997, Coach's tour and charter businesses comprised 47 percent of company revenues. The company also provided special services to regions not served by airports or ground transportation, as in service from Colorado Springs to Denver, or other ski destinations, where customers travel from airline to coach without having to claim their bags. Additionally, the company provided service from airports in Atlantic City, Houston, Las Vegas, Los Angeles, Miami, and Philadelphia, transporting customers to casinos, hotels, cruise ships, and convention sites.

Due to the company's diverse operations, Coach USA can rotate its equipment according to specific need requirements. For example, a motorcoach used for the tour and charter business, where a customer may spend a week or more, should be a newer, more luxurious vehicle. When that same motorcoach was four or five years old it might be used in a commuter and transit operation where its customers were simply going back and forth to work. When that same motorcoach was eight or nine years old, it might be effectively used in an airport shuttle operation, according to industry analyst Anthony Gallo, interviewed in the *Wall Street Corporate Reporter*. Coaches on commuter routes could be used on mid-day routes nearby, at times when commuter bussing was not needed. Coach USA has increased profits by closely considering the logistics of optimizing its equipment.

By 1997 the company claimed approximately 52 percent of the U.S. industry's commuter and transit business. They boasted operations in Seattle, Houston, Los Angeles, New York, and San Francisco. For the most part the company had fixed routes serviced on a daily basis. Some of Coach USA's commuter service motorcoaches were owned by a state or municipal transit authority and provided to the company at a nominal rent, or sometimes even given to the company. Contracts to provide these services were generally won through a bidding process which challenged companies to demonstrate significant guaranteed cost savings. Typically, a contract was structured so that the municipality carried the risk of delivering ridership levels, while the service provider was responsible for its own costs. In the highly competitive municipal transit market, average savings from these privatized operations ran in the 30 percent range.

Two of Coach's major transit contract competitors are Laidlaw and Ryder. The three companies also compete for contracts that provide accessible transportation to the disabled (paratransit services), in addition to competing for potential acquisitions. Within the United States Laidlaw's annual revenues from non-school bus operations average $300 million. Their tour and charter business generates about $40 million annually, compared to Coach USA's revenues of approximately $200 million in that sector. Ryder has neither tour nor charter services but accounts for approximately $150 million of transit

dollars annually. Ryder has not been as aggressive in its acquisitions as the other two major competing companies. Estimates indicate that Coach's acquisition program could result in 20 to 30 properties being added annually, with aggregate annual revenues of $200 to $250 million, according to a 1997 financial report by investment banking firm Donaldson, Lufkin & Jenrette.

A Look Back and a Look Forward

By early 1998 Coach USA had completed 53 acquisitions since its IPO in May 1996, and the company continued to show strong internal growth. Management reported progress in infrastructure development, and indicated that further expansion efforts would occur through the implementation of strategies to acquire platform operations in key convention and gateway entertainment cities. A long list of possible merger partners were being considered, and no real competition loomed on the horizon.

Principal Subsidiaries

Greater Austin Transportation Company; Yellow Cab Service Corporation; Colorado Springs Airport & Transportation Company; Gulf Coast Transportation; American Bus Lines, Inc.; Kerrville Bus Company, Inc.; Bayou City Coaches, Inc.; Arrow Stage Lines, Inc.; K-T Contract Services, Inc.; California Charter; Texas Bus Lines; PCSTC, Inc.; Antelope Valley Bus, Inc.; Grosvenor Bus Lines, Inc.; Powder River Transportation Services, Inc.; International Express Corporation; Progressive Services, Inc.; Red & Tan Enterprises, Inc.; Leisure Line, Inc.; Suburban Trails, Inc.; Community Coach; Cape Transit Corporation.

Further Reading

Brooks, George, "If You Could Love Only One. . .," *Equities*, December 7, 1997, pp. 11–12.

"Coach USA, Inc.," *Business Journal,* June 28, 1996, p. 124 (B).

"Coach USA, Inc., Creating Value Through Consolidation" (investment report), Baltimore, Alex. Brown & Sons, January 31, 1997.

"Coach USA to Add 8 Ground Transportation Companies," *New York Times,* December 10, 1997, p. C4.

Gannon, Joyce, "Coach USA of Texas to Buy Yellow Cab of Pittsburgh, Sister Firm," *Knight-Ridder/Tribune Business News,* December 10, 1997, p. 1210B0948.

O'Hanlon, John, "Consolidating the Industry," *Wall Street Corporate Reporter*, October 6, 1997, pp. 1–4.

Plachno, Larry, "Coach USA," *National Bus Trader,* April 1997, pp. 1–4.

Robertshaw, Nicky, "Browder Tours Gets New Ride; Texas-Based Coach USA Buys and Expands Local Firm," *Memphis Business Journal,* November 10, 1997, p. 3.

Svaldi, Aldo, "Cab Companies Pass Hurdle in Merger," *Denver Business Journal,* November 7, 1997, p. 3A.

"Tour Company Acquires Four Transport Businesses," *Wall Street Journal,* June 1, 1997, p. A3.

—Terri Mozzone

Comcast Corporation

1500 Market Street
Philadelphia, Pennsylvania 19102
U.S.A.
(215) 665-1700
Fax: (215) 981-7790
Web site: http://www.comcast.com

Public Company
Incorporated: 1969
Employees: 17,600
Sales: $4.91 billion (1997)
Stock Exchanges: NASDAQ
Ticker Symbol: CMCSK
SICs: 4812 Radio Telephone Communications; 4813
  Telephone Communications, Except Radio Telephone;
  4841 Cable & Other Pay Television Services; 4899
  Communication Services, Not Elsewhere Classified;
  6512 Operators of Nonresidential Buildings; 7941
  Professional Sports Clubs & Promoters; 7999
  Amusement & Recreation Services, Not Elsewhere
  Classified

Comcast Corporation is a leading cable, telecommunications, and entertainment firm. The company's earliest roots are in cable television, and Comcast Cable is now the fourth largest cable company in the United States, with 4.4 million customers in 21 states. Comcast Cellular serves 783,000 cellular telephone customers in Pennsylvania, New Jersey, and Delaware. Comcast also is a partner with Sprint Corp., Tele-Communications Inc., and Cox Communications Inc. in the Sprint PCS digital wireless telephone joint venture. In content, which provides the most revenue of the company's three sectors, Comcast holds a 57 percent stake in QVC, Inc., the leading cable television shopping channel; has a controlling interest with the Walt Disney Company in E! Entertainment Television, a cable channel devoted to entertainment and celebrity programming; and holds a majority interest in the Philadelphia 76ers NBA basketball team, the Philadelphia Flyers NHL hockey team, the Phila-

delphia Phantoms minor league hockey team, two indoor sports arenas, and Comcast-Sports Net, a 24-hour regional sports network serving the Philadelphia area. The company also holds stakes in a number of other content providers. Controlled by the Roberts family of Philadelphia, Comcast also has the powerful backing of Microsoft Corp., which owns 11.5 percent of the company.

Originated with Tupelo Cable System

Comcast has its origin in the early 1960s with American Cable Systems, Inc., a small cable operation serving Tupelo, Mississippi. At the time, American was one of only a few community antenna television (CATV) services in the nation. The CATV business was predicated on the fact that rural areas were underserved by commercial television stations which catered to large metropolitan areas. Without CATVs huge antennas that pulled in distant signals, consumers in these areas had little use for television. Although required to pay for CATV, customers considered the benefits worth the cost.

In 1963 Ralph J. Roberts and his brother Joe sold their interest in Pioneer Industries, a men's accessories business in Philadelphia, and were looking to invest the proceeds in a new industry. After some research, they learned that the Jerrold Electronics Company, the owner of American Cable Systems, wished to sell the CATV concern. The Roberts brothers enlisted a young CPA named Julian Brodsky, who had helped them liquidate Pioneer Industries, and Daniel Aaron, a former system director at Jerrold Electronics, to help them evaluate the opportunity. The four agreed that while the system carried only five channels and served only 1,500 customers, the investment had great potential. Ralph Roberts bought American Cable Systems and later asked Brodsky and Aaron to join him in managing the company.

Growth within Tupelo was difficult, however. At times, the three were forced to serve as door-to-door salesmen. By 1964 they decided to buy additional franchises in Meridian, Laurel, and West Point, in eastern Mississippi. The following year, American acquired more franchises in Okolona and Baldwyn, Mississippi. While these acquisitions succeeded in increasing subscribership, they failed to have much effect on penetration; there remained an insufficient number of subscribers to deliver a high return given the cost of setting up a local system.

Expanded Aggressively in the Late 1960s and 1970s

Roberts turned his attention to the bigger potential market of Philadelphia. In 1966 he bid successfully for cable franchises in Abington, Cheltenham, and Upper Darby, all northern suburbs of Philadelphia. He then purchased the Westmoreland cable system that served four other communities in western Pennsylvania. To achieve better economies of scale, Roberts dovetailed Westmoreland's operations with those of his other franchises. After establishing a strong foothold in suburban Philadelphia, Roberts extended his company's presence into six additional local communities.

Highly leveraged from this acquisition binge, but eager for more opportunities, Roberts enlisted the *Philadelphia Bulletin* newspaper for a joint venture to build additional cable systems serving Sarasota and Venice, Florida. As part of a limited diversification in 1968, Ralph Roberts joined his brother Joe— by then a minor partner in American but also an executive vice-president of Muzak Corporation—in purchasing a large franchise to provide the subscription "elevator music" service in Orlando, Florida.

Having decided that the name American Cable Systems sounded too generic for his growing company, Roberts decided in 1969 to change its name. In an effort to build a more technological identity, he took portions of the words "communication" and "broadcast," creating Comcast Corporation and reincorporating the company in Pennsylvania.

Comcast reorganized its operations somewhat in 1970, selling off its Florida operations to Storer Communications and forming a limited partnership to purchase Multiview Cable, a local franchise serving Hartford County in Maryland. Limited partnerships enabled Comcast to finance growth with a minimal use of operating funds and were used to finance subsequent acquisitions. Predicting growth in the Muzak business, Comcast also acquired a franchise in 1970 for the service in Denver. The company later purchased Muzak franchises in Dallas, San Diego, Detroit, and Hartford, Connecticut.

Boasting 40,000 customers, but hampered by a continued stagnation in subscriber penetration rates, Comcast still needed funds to finance further expansion. In 1972 Roberts decided to take the company public, offering shares on the OTC market. In 1974 Comcast purchased a cable franchise for Paducah, Kentucky, and in 1976 acquired systems in Flint, Hillsdale, and Jonesville, Michigan. The following year, Comcast bought out its partners' interest in Multiview.

Cable by this time had become much more than an antenna service. For several years, cable operators included local access and special programming channels, as well as programming from large independent stations such as WGN in Chicago and WTBS in Atlanta. The government restricted what programming a cable operator could offer, often blocking access to programs that customers clearly wanted. Dan Aaron, a manager with Comcast was active in the National Cable Television Association (NCTA), lobbying effectively for the relaxation of programming and other restrictions. In 1977, as chairman of the NCTA, Aaron brought many of the industry's efforts to fruition. As the cable industry was allowed to mature, additional cable-only stations were added, making the service viable within metropolitan areas that were well served by broadcasters.

With this added strength in the company's product offerings, Comcast was able to win franchises to serve parts of northern New Jersey in 1978, as well as Lower Merion, Pennsylvania, and Warren and Clinton, Michigan, in 1979. Through limited partnerships, the company later won franchises for Sterling Heights and St. Clair Shores, Michigan, and Corinth, Mississippi. By 1983 Comcast had purchased Muzak franchises in Indianapolis, Buffalo, Scranton, Pennsylvania, and Peoria, Illinois.

Expanded into the United Kingdom in 1983

The company made an important move in 1983 when, in partnership with a British gambling and entertainment enterprise, Ladbroke, it won a license to establish a cable television system in the residential suburbs of London. Most cable licenses in the United States had been taken, and those that remained were expensive or only marginally profitable. But the industry was still in its infancy in the United Kingdom. In addition, British viewers would appreciate cable's selection; Britain had only about five stations, offering mostly government-supported programming.

In 1984, as Comcast added a cable partnership in Baltimore County and a Muzak franchise for Tyler, Texas, an important change took place in another industry. After a half century of antitrust litigation, the U.S. government broke up the Bell System. As a result, AT&T and its long distance operations were separated from 22 local Bell companies. Each of these Bell companies was organized into one of seven companies that saw cable television as the next logical course of progression for their telephone networks. The U.S. Congress, however, had already enacted legislation that would prevent telephone companies from taking over the still fragile cable industry. The Cable Act, which was written primarily to guarantee fair pole attachment rates to cable companies, had the effect of locking telephone companies out of the cable business.

Free for the moment from the ominous threat of competition from any of these multibillion-dollar companies, Comcast proceeded with growth through acquisitions. In 1985, after purchasing cable operations in Pontiac/Waterford, Michigan, Fort Wayne, Indiana, and Jones County, Mississippi, Comcast won a plum: the right to serve the densely populated northeast Philadelphia area. In 1986 Comcast took over a cable system serving Indianapolis and purchased a 26 percent share in Group W, one of the country's largest cable companies. This brought the company's subscribership to more than one million customers. The following year, Comcast acquired a cable system in northwest Philadelphia from Heritage Communications, thus cementing its position in suburban Philadelphia.

Turning more toward investments in other cable companies than in actual franchises, Comcast purchased a 20 percent share of Heritage Communications and a 50 percent share of Storer Communications in 1988. The Storer acquisition brought subscribership to more than two million customers and elevated Comcast to the fifth largest cable company in the United States. Consolidating its partnerships, the company took full control of its Maryland Limited Partnership, Comcast Cablevision of Indiana, and Comcast Cable Investors, a venture capital subsidiary.

Moved into Cellular Service in 1988

Also in 1988, Comcast turned an important strategic corner regarding telephone companies when it purchased American Cellular Network, or Amcell, a cellular telephone business serving New Jersey. For the first time, cable and telephone companies, prevented from competition in landline services, were facing each other in the cellular telephone business. And for the first time, a cable company was able to offer telephone customers an alternative to the telephone company.

In 1990, a year after relocating the corporate offices from Bala Cynwyd, Pennsylvania, to Philadelphia, Ralph Roberts shocked the company and the industry by naming his 30-year-old son Brian to succeed him as president of the company, while Ralph Roberts remained as chairman. Brian Roberts, who had impeccable academic credentials, silenced critics by proving to be a highly effective manager. In addition, having begun work in the company at the age of seven, he had 23 years seniority, more than virtually anyone but his father.

Also in 1990, after having purchased an interest in an additional franchise serving suburban London, the company's newly formed international unit won more British franchises, allowing the company to serve Cambridge and Birmingham. Comcast now counted more than one million customers in Britain alone. Increasingly, however, Comcast's smaller companies, such as Amcell, were beginning to experience slower growth. Rather than allow Amcell to be swallowed up later by a larger suitor, Comcast struck a deal in 1991 with the Metromedia Company, in which it purchased that company's Metrophone cellular unit for $1.1 billion. The new joint company, established in 1992, quadrupled Comcast's potential market to more than 7.3 million customers.

Later that year, the company's offices at One Meridian Plaza in Philadelphia were destroyed by a fire that took 19 hours to put out. Only eight days later, the company set up shop four blocks away at 1234 Market Street. While officially a temporary location, the company's 250 employees were once again in business.

In September 1992, Comcast staged a five-way international telephone call using the Comcast network and a long-distance carrier. The purpose was to demonstrate that the company could handle telephone calls and completely bypass the local telephone network. While the demonstration was intended to raise investor interest in such bypass operations, it also succeeded in scaring telephone companies sufficiently to argue for permission to offer cable television services. The company continued

to bolster its position in the bypass business in 1992, when it gained a 20 percent interest (later reduced to 15 percent) in Teleport Communications Corporation, operator of a fiber-optic-based bypass telecommunications network which by the mid-1990s was serving more than 50 major markets nationwide.

Late in 1992, Comcast took over 50 percent of Storer Communications, dividing the assets of that company with Denver-based Tele-Communications, another leading cable firm. Storer was forced into dissolution by heavy debt carried at high interest. The proceeds from the sale enabled Storer's parent company, SCI Holdings, to retire much of that debt.

Aggressive Moves into Content Highlighted Mid-1990s

The mid-1990s saw a frenzy of activity throughout the cable and telecommunications industries, as deregulation increasingly brought cable and telephone companies into competition with each other, as well as into partnerships. The period also saw a flurry of acquisitions, mergers, and system swaps in the cable industry as companies sought to build networks of contiguous systems to improve efficiencies. Comcast was at the center of all of this activity, and also made aggressive moves into the area of programming content.

As early as 1992, Comcast had begun testing a forerunner of what eventually became known as the Sprint PCS (personal communications services) digital cellular technology, which delivered crisper sound and more security than analog cellular phone technology. In 1994 Comcast entered into an alliance that formed the Sprint Telecommunications Venture, renamed Sprint Spectrum LP in 1995. The alliance partners were Sprint Corp., owning 40 percent of the venture; Tele-Communications Inc., 30 percent; and Comcast and Cox Communications Inc., 15 percent each. In the early 1995 Federal Communications Commission (FCC) auction of PCS licenses, Sprint Spectrum was the biggest winner, gaining the rights to wireless licenses in 31 major U.S. markets, covering a population of 156 million. The venture was soon renamed Sprint PCS and the four partners spent millions of dollars building a wireless network. In 1997 Comcast's cellular operations in Pennsylvania, New Jersey, and Delaware were converted to the digital technology, but by then the company considered Sprint PCS—which faced tough competition from cellular veterans such as AT&T Corp.—a drag on earnings. In May 1998 the Sprint PCS partners announced that they planned to sell 10 percent of the venture to the public through a public offering, with Sprint PCS set up as a tracking stock under Sprint's corporate domain (shareholders of tracking stocks have very limited voting rights). This move was considered the first step toward the possible exit of Comcast, Cox, and TCI from the joint venture. Meanwhile, in January 1998, Comcast acquired GlobalCom Telecommunications, a regional long-distance service provider. Along with the company's other operations, the addition of GlobalCom—renamed Comcast Telecommunications—enabled Comcast to offer a full range of telecommunications services.

In cable, Comcast in 1994 acquired Maclean Hunter's U.S. cable operations for $1.27 billion, gaining an additional 550,000 customers. In November 1996 Comcast acquired the cable properties of E. W. Scripps Co in a $1.575 billion stock swap. Scripps's 800,000 customers brought Comcast's cable holdings to more than 4.3 million customers in 21 states, the fourth largest cable system in the United States. In February 1998 the company agreed to sell its underperforming U.K. cable operations to NTL Inc. for $600 million in stock plus the assumption of $397 million in debt. Three months later, Comcast announced that it would spend $500 million over the next several years to take over the 30 percent interest in Jones Intercable Inc. held by the Canada-based BCI Telecom Holding Inc. Jones had a technologically advanced, one-million-customer cable system, much of which was in the suburbs of Washington, D.C., strategically contiguous to some of Comcast's main markets.

Comcast's aggressive moves to become a major provider of entertainment content were perhaps the company's most dramatic actions of this period. Already holding a 13 percent stake in QVC, Inc., the number one cable-based shopping channel, Comcast in July 1994 scuttled at the last minute a planned merger between QVC and CBS Inc. by offering to pay $2.2 billion for a controlling interest in QVC. CBS, refusing to engage in a bidding war, immediately retreated, leaving Comcast to increase its QVC interest to 57 percent. In early 1996 Comcast paid $250 million to acquire a 66 percent stake in a new venture, Comcast-Spectacor, L.P. Most of the remaining ownership interest was held by Spectacor, which owned the Philadelphia Flyers NHL hockey team and two sports arenas in Philadelphia. Comcast-Spectacor was set up to own and operate the Flyers, the Philadelphia 76ers NBA basketball team, and the two arenas. Comcast then leveraged these ownership interests into establishing Comcast SportsNet, a 24-hour regional cable sports channel, which debuted in the fall of 1997 and featured telecasts of Flyers, 76ers, and Philadelphia Phillies (major league baseball) games, in addition to other sports programming. In March 1997 Comcast partnered with the Walt Disney Company to acquire a majority interest in E! Entertainment Television, a 24-hour cable network devoted exclusively to entertainment and celebrity programming. E! was available in more than 45 million homes in more than 120 countries around the world.

In June 1997 Microsoft Corp. announced that it would invest $1 billion in Comcast in return for an 11.5 percent nonvoting interest. Microsoft wanted a cable partner for testing interactive television and high-speed computer services, and chose Comcast because its cable system was one of the most technologically advanced in the country. By the end of 1997, Comcast had converted about 70 percent of its customers to a new hybrid fiber-coaxial technology, which was more reliable, offered improved signal quality, and had the capacity to deliver more services. The company was also a partner—with a 12 percent interest—in At Home Corporation. Comcast@Home was launched in December 1996, offering high-speed interactive services, including 24-hour unlimited Internet access, through a cable modem to customers in Baltimore County, Maryland, and Sarasota, Florida. Additional markets were soon added.

In 1987 Comcast Corporation was almost exclusively a cable television company. Just ten years later, cable was no longer even the company's largest unit. Out of 1997 revenues of $4.91 billion, $2.083 billion (or 42.4 percent) came from the company's content operations, $2.073 billion (42.2 percent)

came from cable, and $444.9 million (9.1 percent) came from cellular. Clearly, Comcast was not a firm that rested on its laurels. And with the partnership with Microsoft promising involvement in additional innovative technologies and services, Comcast seemed certain to be a central player in the high-tech world of the 21st century.

Principal Subsidiaries

Comcast Cable Communications, Inc.; Garden State Cablevision L.P. (50%); Primestar Partners, L.P. (10%); Comcast Cellular Communications, Inc.; QVC, Inc. (57.45%); Comcast Spectacor, L.P. (66%); E! Entertainment Television, Inc. (79.2%); At Home Corporation (12%); Sprint Spectrum Holdings Company, L.P. (15%).

Further Reading

Brown, Rich, "Brian Roberts: Stretching Comcast's Reach Through New Technology," *Broadcasting & Cable,* August 2, 1993, p. 29.
——, "Comcast Bid Derails CBS-QVC," *Broadcasting & Cable,* July 18, 1994, p. 6.
——, "Comcast Buying Scripps System for $1.6 Billion," *Broadcasting & Cable,* November 6, 1995, p. 98.
"Cable/Cellular/CAP Combo Demos Competition for LECS," *Telephony,* September 14, 1992.
Cauley, Leslie, "Sprint, Partners Consider Issuing Shares in PCS," *Wall Street Journal,* April 21, 1998, p. B4.
Cohen, Warren, "Scrambled Signals in the TV World: Comcast Scuttles the Vaunted CBS-QVC Deal," *U.S. News & World Report,* July 25, 1994, p. 43.
Colman, Price, "Comcast Closes on Scripps Howard," *Broadcasting & Cable,* November 18, 1996, p. 65.
"Comcast Corporation, a Historical Perspective," *Metrophonelines* (company publication), March 1992.
Fabrikant, Geraldine, "The Heir Is Clearly Apparent at Comcast," *New York Times,* June 22, 1997, sec. 3, pp. 1, 12.
Fairclough, Gordon, and Leslie Cauley, "BCI to Sell Comcast a 30% Interest in Jones Intercable," *Wall Street Journal,* May 26, 1998, p. C20.
"Friend of Bill: He Is a Young Cable Tycoon, Much Loved by Microsoft. What Can Brian Roberts Possibly Worry About?," *Economist,* November 1, 1997, p. 69.
Hazelton, Lynette, "Comcast Online Makes Its Debut," *Philadelphia Business Journal,* July 18, 1997, p. 10.
Higgins, John M., "Brian Roberts in Charge at Comcast," *Broadcasting & Cable,* November 3, 1997, p. 54.
Higgins, John M., and Richard Tedesco, "PC/TV a la Bills Gates: Comcast Deal Is the Latest Evidence of Microsoft's Quest to Grab a Large Piece of TV Action," *Broadcasting & Cable,* June 16, 1997, p. 6.
Keller, John J., "Comcast Agrees to Buy Metromedia's Cellular Operations in $1.1 Billion Deal," *Wall Street Journal,* May 8, 1991, p. A3.
Kupfer, Andrew, "How Hot Is Cable, Really?," *Fortune,* February 16, 1998, p. 70.
Landler, Mark, Ronald Grover, and Joseph Weber, "Comcast Plays Spoiler," *Business Week,* July 25, 1994, pp. 28–30.
Landro, Laura, "Comcast Names Brian Roberts President, Extending Family's Hold on Cable Firm," *Wall Street Journal,* February 8, 1990, p. B6.
"Making a Point Long Distance," *Philadelphia Inquirer,* September 11, 1992.
McGraw, Dan, "No Ordinary Cable Guys," *U.S. News & World Report,* July 8, 1996, p. 44.

Platt, Larry, "Robert Rules," *Philadelphia Magazine,* November 1997, p. 29.

Rose, Matthew, "NTL Deal to Buy Comcast Unit Spurs U.K. Cable Stocks," *Wall Street Journal,* February 6, 1998, p. A19.

Rudnitsky, Howard, "Curtains for the Video Stores," *Forbes,* April 12, 1993, pp. 54–55.

Samuels, Gary, "In for a Pound, in for a Penny," *Forbes,* December 18, 1995, p. 108.

Sandomir, Richard, "Another Media Concern Dashes into Professional Sports," *New York Times,* March 20, 1996, p. D4.

"Sprint, TCI, Cox, and Comcast Team Up," *Television Digest,* October 31, 1994, p. 1.

Webber, Maura, "Microsoft Investment Attests to Appeal of Comcast," *Philadelphia Business Journal,* June 13, 1997, p. 1.

Weber, Joseph, "Comcast Plays Hard to Get," *Business Week,* November 29, 1993, pp. 82–83.

——, "Please Hold, Mr. Roberts Will Connect You," *Business Week,* October 26, 1992, p. 94.

—John Simley
—updated by David E. Salamie

Consolidated Delivery & Logistics, Inc.

380 Allwood Road
Clifton, New Jersey 07012
U.S.A.
(973) 471-1005
Fax: (973) 471-5519
Web site: http://www.dsii.com

Public Company
Founded: 1994
Employees: 2,900
Sales: $171.5 million (1997)
Stock Exchanges: NASDAQ
Ticker Symbol: CDLI
SICs: 4215 Courier Services Except By Air; 4513 Air
    Courier Services

Consolidated Delivery & Logistics, Inc. is one of the largest full-service, same-day ground and air delivery companies in the United States. Operating 24 hours a day, seven days a week, the company provides one-, two-, and four-hour rush pickup and delivery of material for customers such as hospitals, lawyers, advertising and travel agencies, and commercial and industrial companies. The sorting, routing, and delivery of time-sensitive materials are also made on a more scheduled basis for deliveries such as large shipments from pharmaceutical suppliers to pharmacies and the distribution of financial documents, payroll data, and other documents between branches of insurance companies, banks, and other financial institutions. CD&L also provides home delivery services for customers including catalog marketers, large cosmetic companies, and other direct sales firms. For air delivery, the company offers next-flight-out (rush) and scheduled air services both domestically and internationally. In addition to its delivery services, the company provides mailroom management services (including providing and supervising personnel) for companies and professional firms.

As of February 1998, the company operated 60 offices in 23 states and the District of Columbia. Its ground delivery services were concentrated on the East Coast, with some operations in the Midwest and on the West Coast. CD&L's air delivery services operated throughout the United States and to major cities around the world.

The Combination: 1994–95

Consolidated Delivery and Logistics, Inc. was founded in June 1994, by John Mattei and Joseph Wojak to consolidate localized operations that provided same-day delivery and logistics services into a national company. Mattei was president of JKM Associates, a consulting firm specializing in mergers and acquisitions, and became chairman and CEO of CD&L. Wojak, a financial and management consultant, became executive vice-president and CFO.

The ground and air delivery industry was essentially divided into three segments. The next-day and two-day delivery markets were dominated by national companies such as Federal Express and United Parcel Service. The same-day delivery market was completely different, being composed of some 10,000 companies. While that market generated over $15 billion in 1994, it was very segmented. The majority of the companies were very small and operated on a local basis to provide messenger and courier services or other ground delivery. Even those services were further segmented into companies specializing in rush/on-demand delivery or in scheduled and routed delivery. Completely different companies specialized in distribution or air courier/air freight or warehousing for just-in-time delivery. And the complexity of the business created the demand for other companies that specialized in logistics, coordinating all the steps involved in getting a product where it was supposed to go.

Several factors led Mattei and Wojak to establish CD&L. First, many of the larger companies that used same-day delivery and logistics services were outsourcing these activities as part of their cost-control efforts. Second, these and other customers were increasingly looking for a single source to provide a full range of delivery and logistic services that included responsive customer services such as tracking, storage, or customized billing. Finally, the growth in catalog sales, in-home medical care, and home shopping offered substantial growth opportunities in the home delivery area.

Company Perspectives:

Businesses that are outsourcing their transportation needs are looking for a single-source vendor that can meet their expedited delivery needs from multiple points around the country. These businesses are also looking for a vendor that can offer a broad range of services, from time-critical ground delivery and overnight transportation to timely logistics distribution support both domestically and internationally at the local, regional and national level and globally. CD&L's ability to meet this constellation of needs will enable it to broaden its sales and marketing reach.

The company actually began operating on November 27, 1995, the date CD&L completed its initial public offering and, at the same time, acquired 11 existing companies (the founding companies). The IPO raised approximately $33.2 million (after expenses) from the sale of 3.2 million shares of common stock at a price of $13 per share. Most of the proceeds, approximately $29.6 million, were used to pay the cash portion of the purchase prices of the 11 founding companies. The total price of the combined mergers was $67.8 million, including 2.9 million shares. The company also used money from the offering to pay off $2.3 million in debt.

The 11 companies had been operating independently in the same-day delivery market for an average of 15 years. American Courier Express, Inc., a six-year old company based in Edison, New Jersey, specialized in rush/demand delivery and also offered distribution services and air courier/air freight. CD&L paid $536,000 in cash and 102,485 shares of stock for the merger. Click Messenger Service, Inc., of Cranford, New Jersey, had more than 35 years experience in the market. Click operated in New Jersey, upstate New York, and New York City, specializing in scheduled and routed delivery and also offering distribution, rush/demand, warehousing, and contract logistics. The merger with Click and related companies cost CD&L $1.77 million in cash and $177,212 shares. Court Courier Systems, Inc., also based in New Jersey, had been in business for over 16 years and provided scheduled and routed delivery in Hartford, Connecticut; Augusta, Maine; New Jersey, and upstate New York. Court also offered distribution services, rush/on-demand delivery, contract logistics, and warehousing. CD&L paid $1.75 million in cash and 175,362 shares for Court and a related company. Crown Courier Systems, Inc. and Bestway Distribution Services, Inc. (Crown-Bestway) was headquartered in Miami, Florida, and had operations throughout central and south Florida. In addition to its distribution services, the 20-year-old operation provided rush/demand and scheduled delivery, air courier/air freight, contract logistics, and warehousing. The price for Crown-Bestway was $1.9 million in cash and 192,063 shares. Distribution Solutions International, Inc. (DSI) was based in Michigan with another location in Philadelphia, and had been providing logistics services for over five years. DSI's price was $1.37 million and 137,239 shares. One of the biggest of the founding companies, Clayton/National Courier Systems, Inc. was a same-day ground and air delivery service based in St. Louis, Missouri, with additional operations in San Francisco

and Seattle. National also offered distribution, contract logistics, and facilities management services. CD&L paid $3.15 million in cash and 290,357 shares for 23-year-old National and a related company.

New York City-based Olympic Courier Systems, Inc. had been providing rush/on-demand delivery, air courier/air freight, and warehousing services in New York City and Long Island City for 12 years. CD&L paid $1.17 million in cash and 116,644 shares for Olympic and a related company. Orbit/Lightspeed Courier Systems, Inc. was also based in New York City, and had been providing rush/on-demand delivery, facilities management, and warehousing in New York City and Bayonne, New Jersey, for five years. The merger with Orbit/Lightspeed and related companies cost $1.89 million in cash and 194,000 shares. Securities Courier Corporation was another of the largest of the founding companies. Headquartered in South Hackensack, New Jersey, it had locations throughout New Jersey and New York City for its scheduled and routed delivery business. CD&L paid $3.74 million in cash and 357,301 in shares for the 22-year-old operation plus 16,667 shares for Liberty Transfer Corporation, a Securities Courier contractor. Six-year-old Silver Star Express, Inc. was headquartered in Miami, Florida. Primarily a distribution business, the company also offered scheduled and routed delivery and warehousing services, and operated in select cities in Florida, Georgia, Indiana, Louisiana, Maryland, New Jersey, Ohio, and Tennessee. The merger with Silver Star and related companies cost $3.34 million in cash and 307,327 shares. The biggest of the founding companies, SureWay Air Traffic Corporation was headquartered in Long Island City, New York. SureWay had been providing same-day air delivery services for 20 years, with additional operations in Los Angeles, Chicago, New Jersey, North Carolina, and Washington, D.C. SureWay also had sales agents across the United States. CD&L paid $8.96 million in cash and 968,045 shares for SureWay and a related company.

Upon completion of the "Combination," the president or CEO of each of the founding companies was named to CD&L's board of directors. The board was a large one, with 18 members, 12 of them from the original companies. John Mattei remained chairman of the board and CEO, while Wojak continued as executive vice-president and CFO. William Brannan, who had 23 years of experience in the transportation and logistics industry, was named president and COO. As CD&L began operations, it employed over 2,800 people, most as drivers, operated 64 leased facilities (not counting SureWay's sales agent locations), and owned or leased 506 cars and 278 trucks. It also had contracts with some 770 independent owner/operators.

CD&L established its headquarters in Paramus, New Jersey. The companies kept their individual names initially, with plans to add "Consolidated Delivery & Logistics." The new company ended the year with sales of $150.4 million, an increase of over nine percent from combined sales in 1994. Profits increased 7.7 percent to $45.5 million from $42.2 million.

Building a National Company: 1996

CD&L's strategy for becoming the leading provider of same-day delivery and logistics services focused on three areas. To begin with, the company expected to realize internal growth opportunities. This would be accomplished by offering existing customers a wider range of services and expanded geographic coverage, by having the original companies purchase services from each other rather than from outside delivery companies, and by offering customers a single source for meeting national and multi-regional delivery and logistics needs.

The company also expected to grow by making its operations more efficient. This meant consolidating operations as well as achieving savings in areas such as insurance coverage and vehicle costs as a result of its size and purchasing power. Finally, CD&L planned to grow by buying additional companies in existing markets as well as in new regions.

CD&L moved quickly to add new companies, spending some $3.3 million in cash and shares during 1996 to buy five smaller businesses whose annual revenues approached $15.6 million. The purchases were International Courier Services, Inc.; Celadon Express, Inc.; Interim Personnel, Inc.; HurryWagon, Inc.; and W.I. Services, Inc., and included three ground delivery services in the Northeast and two air courier companies, which expanded the New York to Los Angeles air route.

At the same time, CD&L worked to bring all the original companies under a single common management and began merging and rationalizing operations. For its delivery activities it initially established four divisions. The Manhattan Region combined Olympic, Orbit/Lightspeed, and the Manhattan operations of Click. The Northeast Region combined Court, American, and the rest of Click. Silver Star and Crown-Bestway combined to form the Southeast Region. The company's fourth delivery division was SureWay Air Courier, providing air delivery services. Distribution Solutions International (DSI) handled the company's contract logistics services.

But the anticipated cost savings did not occur as quickly as planned. After three quarters of improved earnings, the company lost money in the fourth quarter. As the company's 1996 annual report acknowledged, "the melding of 11 original companies, overlaid by the acquisitions we did complete—meshing diverse systems, personalities and capabilities into a unified whole—proved much more difficult than originally anticipated, slowing the pace of consolidation cost savings." According to Thom Albrecht, an analyst at A.G. Edwards, although the Southeast and SureWay divisions were profitable, problems developed in the Northeast and Manhattan, largely due to "jealous managers, infighting, poor customer service, and imprudent facility consolidation." However, the biggest contributor to the loss was Distribution Solutions International.

Causing further problems, CD&L's stock price dropped after the initial offering and remained lower than expected, and the company lost $3.5 million in business when several long-term customers canceled or did not renew their logistic services contracts.

In September, Chairman and CEO John Mattei announced that he would leave the company at the beginning of 1997. Albert Van Ness, Jr., a director of the company, was named to replace him. The company also reduced the size of the board, from 18 to 13, buying out several of the original owners. Because of the problems in the logistic services business, the board decided to sell Distribution Solutions International, its contract logistics subsidiary.

In its first full year of operation, the company increased its revenues by 13.7 percent to $171 million, with sales growth in all areas except contract logistics. However, in the fourth quarter the company registered a loss of $1.7 million due to severance costs and charges related to consolidation, and a net loss for the year of $683,000. The financial situation caused the company to reexamine and alter its business strategy, deciding to curtail acquisitions and to focus on internal growth. The new strategy included 1) putting into place a new management incentive system that linked compensation to results in each region, and 2) eliminating underperforming subsidiaries and management.

As CD&L was working to build a national organization, the same-day delivery market segment was continuing to undergo changes. By September 1996, Colorado-based Corporate Express Corporation had become the largest operator in the market after buying up the number one and two operations. In March it acquired industry leader U.S. Delivery Systems of Houston for $500 million. Like CD&L, USDS was created in 1994 by consolidating a number of same-day delivery operations, though it initially concentrated on ground services and did not include air courier and air freight services. A few months later, Corporate Express paid $138 million for United TransNet, Inc. of Roswell, Georgia. As a result of these acquisitions, CD&L suddenly found itself in the number two position in the same-day delivery market.

1997 and Beyond

At the beginning of 1997, Albert Van Ness took over from John Mattei as chairman and CEO, and the company sold DSI to its former owner in exchange for 137,239 shares of CD&L common stock, worth approximately $601,107. CD&L continued its internal reorganization by further reducing the size of its board of directors to nine, with five outside directors, cut interest payments by restructuring its debt, and moved corporate headquarters from a Paramus, New Jersey, office park to an existing company facility in Clifton, New Jersey.

By the second quarter of the year, the financial picture had improved, and that situation continued through the end of the year. CD&L sold its fulfillment and direct mail business for $850,000 in cash and notes, further concentrating on its core delivery operations. Revenue for 1997 increased to $171.5 million. And even with the loss of $1.7 million in business when two of the company's largest banking customers merged and closed branches, ground delivery revenue (70 percent of total sales) increased by 7.4 percent as a result of the 1996 acquisitions and several new contracts. Revenue from air courier services (30 percent of sales) increased 9.1 percent due to growth of existing accounts and the 1996 acquisitions. Net income for the year was $459,000, compared to a net loss of $638,000 the year before. Earnings per share reached 25¢ for the year, up from a 13¢ loss in 1996.

For 1998, Van Ness announced that the company would examine selective acquisitions, implement a profit improvement plan for the air courier division, and continue to increase customer service standards.

Principal Subsidiaries

American Courier, Inc.; Clayton/National Courier Systems, Inc.; Click Messenger Service, Inc.; Click Messenger Service of NY, Inc.; Court Courier Systems, Inc.; National Express Company, Inc.; Olympic Courier Systems, Inc.; Securities Courier Corporation; Silver Star Express, Inc.; SureWay Air Traffic Corporation; SureWay Logistics Corporation.

Further Reading

Albrecht, Thom S., "Consolidated Delivery & Logistics," *A.G. Edwards Investment Opinion*, April 25, 1997.
"Consolidated Delivery & Logistics, Inc. Announces Sale of Discontinued Operation," *PR Newswire*, January 26, 1998.
"Consolidated Delivery & Logistics, Inc. Records Nearly $4.2 Million Operating Improvements From Continuing Operations for the Full Year 1997," *PR Newswire*, February 25, 1998.
"The New America: Dynamex Inc.," *Investor's Business Daily*, October 4, 1996.

—Ellen D. Wernick

Cuisinart Corporation

---

1 Cummings Point Road
Stamford, Connecticut 06904
U.S.A.
(203) 975-4600
(800) 726-0190
Fax: (203) 975-4660

Wholly Owned Subsidiary of Conair Corporation
Incorporated: 1973
SICs: 3634 Electric Housewares & Fans

Cuisinart Corporation is a well-known manufacturer of small kitchen appliances. Best known for its food processors, Cuisinart established this home appliance as a market segment in its own right. The company eventually expanded its product line to include coffee makers, hand blenders, hand mixers, and toasters, among other housewares. Whatever the kitchen convenience, the Cuisinart brand has been equated with quality construction and top-of-the-line pricing.

Starting Out

Cuisinart was founded by Carl and Shirley Sontheimer. Trained at the Massachusetts Institute of Technology as an engineer and physicist, Carl Sontheimer owned and operated Amzac Electronics until he sold the company in 1967. Rather than face retirement, he opted for a livelihood that combined his expertise in electronics with cooking, his favorite hobby.

The Sontheimers first saw restaurant food preparation machines manufactured by Robot-Coupe while visiting a housewares show in France in 1971. Certain that they could create a home version of the device, the Sontheimers launched their own housewares business—Cuisinart. At first, the couple allocated $20,000 to import and resell top-of-the-line cookware from Europe to Americans. The Sontheimers also obtained the sole U.S. distribution rights for three prototype food preparation machines purchased from the inventor of Robot-Coupe's restaurant food processors.

Building a Better Food Processor

In 1972, Sontheimer engineered the redesign of these restaurant food processors for home use. He improved and refined the machines, lengthening the feed tubes and enhancing the disks and blades. Sontheimer also initiated safety features that brought the device in line with U.S. codes and standards. Sontheimer then asked Robot-Coupe to manufacture his design, and within a year he introduced his food processor at the 1973 National Housewares Exposition in Chicago, Illinois.

Sontheimer continued refining his food processor design throughout 1974. His improvements to the device's blades and disks made it possible to chop a pound of meat in less than 60 seconds or to mix puff shell dough in just 15 seconds. Sontheimer's refinements not only decreased food preparation time dramatically, but also made cleanup easier.

Gaining Acceptance

Though professional chefs long had been using food preparation machines for slicing and shredding, the device largely was unknown to the American public before its debut in Chicago. Sontheimer's timing was perfect for introducing U.S. consumers to the food processor, for during the early 1970s Americans were preparing more elaborate foods at home and their interests in kitchen gadgets was at its peak. Yet initially Sontheimer's device sold poorly. Marketed to department and food stores, the Cuisinart food processor appeared to retailers and consumers to be nothing more than a high-priced, revved-up blender.

To gain acceptance, Sontheimer showed his food processor to James Beard, Julia Child, and other notable culinary experts. Their endorsements—as well as favorable articles in *Gourmet* magazine and the *New York Times*—likened Sontheimer's Cuisinart food processor to landmark inventions such as the cotton gin and the steamboat.

Not surprisingly, sales accelerated in 1975, making Cuisinart first in the market it created. Eva Pomice, writing in *Forbes,* explained: ''With marketing savvy and a credible product, [the Sontheimers] were able to dominate the upper end of

Company Perspectives:

Cuisinart has been perfecting the art of great cooking for over 25 years. Now we've translated everything we know into a complete kitchen of easy-to-use appliances that makes cooking a pleasure.

the food processor business against such top competitors as Moulinex and Robot-Coupe. Sontheimer did it by making the Cuisinart name synonymous with top quality and price.''

At the time, industry analysts suspected that Cuisinart went from selling a few food processors monthly to moving between 150,000 to 250,000 of the devices in 1976, although no company statistics were available to confirm the estimates. By 1977, however, Cuisinart's sales totaled $50 million. With its product firmly established, the company suspended its contracting of Robot-Coupe as the manufacturer of its food processors. A Japanese firm assumed the production of Cuisinart models instead.

Competition Heats Up

Other well-known kitchen appliance manufacturers—Sunbeam and Hamilton Beach, for example—began to enter the food processor market around 1977. By the end of that year, consumers could choose from more than 30 models of food processors, varying in price from $30 to $400. Though smaller, lower-priced food processors became the industry norm, Cuisinart would not bend in its quality standards or pricing. The company introduced a larger, more powerful, and more expensive model in 1978. Despite the proliferation of cheaper models by other name brand manufacturers, Cuisinart remained in control of the market, establishing a new level of price points for kitchen appliances. Owning a Cuisinart, Pomice observed, ''was tantamount to wearing a pair of Calvin Klein jeans. You could hardly boast of a gourmet kitchen if you didn't own one of these.''

Without its contract to manufacture and distribute Cuisinart's food processors, Robot-Coupe launched its own model in 1978. The French company formed its own U.S. subsidiary and issued ads with pictures of food processors above captions reading, ''It used to be pronounced Cuisinart.'' Irked, Cuisinart retorted through brochures suggesting that Robot-Coupe lost its position as a manufacturer and distributor of the company's food processors because of inferior workmanship.

Legal Troubles Follow

Such promotional battles waged into the 1980s. Both companies placed ads in the *New York Times* during 1980 and 1981. Cuisinart asked consumers: ''Are you as easily fooled as they hope you are?'' Robot-Coupe ads responded: ''Whose fooling whom?'' Eventually, a lawsuit ensued. Robot-Coupe, the losing party, was ordered to stop producing ads implying that Cuisinart had changed its name or claiming that it manufactured Cuisinart food processors.

Though Cuisinart emerged from this litigation victoriously, the company was less successful later in 1980 when a grand jury accused it of price fixing. Retailers who sold Cuisinart food processors between 1974 and 1979 claimed that they experienced smaller supplies or were threatened with decreased supplies of Cuisinart food processors if they sold the products below the company's ''suggested'' retail prices. The courts fined Cuisinart $250,000 and prohibited the company from suggesting retail prices for one year. In addition, Cuisinart was required to clarify for retailers that compliance with any suggested pricing was purely voluntary.

New Models for the 1980s

Despite its legal troubles, Cuisinart was able to introduce six new food processor models by 1982. The new designs were larger and more expensive than earlier models and proved to be the company's testament to product diversity. These models featured more powerful motors, more blades, more attachments, and higher prices. In fact, one model sold for $600.

Nevertheless, Cuisinart's critics warned that this was not the type of diversity of product needed: They wanted a variety of kitchen appliances manufactured by Cuisinart, not just a variety of food processors. Kerry Hannon, for one, told *Forbes:* ''Sontheimer's market blindness . . . kept him from capitalizing on the quality of image that the Cuisinart name conveyed. He introduced a line of high-priced cookware into a jam-packed and fading market. But more natural line extensions like blenders, for example, eluded him.''

The Impact of Competition

Around 1983, Kitchen Aid introduced a direct competitor to the Cuisinart food processor—a high-priced food processor manufactured by Robot-Coupe. In response, Cuisinart instituted a trade-in allowance on its food processors to encourage existing food processor owners to upgrade their equipment. Consumers were allowed up to $66 in credit toward the purchase of a newer, more advanced Cuisinart model when they returned their older models. Soon the company accepted any brand of food processor for credit when upgrading to a new Cuisinart model.

The following year, Sunbeam debuted the Oskar food processor. At half the size of a Cuisinart, the little machine cost a mere $60, about $165 less than a Cuisinart. By 1985, Sunbeam sold 700,000 Oskars, commanding 25 percent of the market. (The previous year, Cuisinart controlled 20 percent of the market.)

In 1984 and 1985, Cuisinart began promoting culinary education and awareness through cookbooks and other media. Anne Greer's *American Southwest,* published by Cuisinart, won the Tastemaker Award presented by the R.T. French Company as the best American cuisine cookbook of 1984. The following year, Cuisinart began a cooking videotape series to enhance the culinary education of consumers.

The trend of downsized, lower-cost food processors—food processors for the mass market—continued in 1986. At first Cuisinart refrained from entering the foray because Sontheimer did not believe that he could manufacture a better product than already existed. He explained his thinking in *Forbes:* "We could put pebbles in a can, and if we put the Cuisinart name on it, it would sell. But after that, the name would be absolutely worthless. If we don't feel we can make a better product, we don't enter the market."

Overcoming Sontheimer's reticence, Cuisinart introduced the Mini-Mate, a chopper and grinder with a reversible, patented blade, in the fall of 1986. At $40 the device was less expensive than competing products and was introduced through a glossy magazine ad campaign created by Geers Gross. Promotions emphasized the Mini-Mate's use in preparing common recipes such as tacos. The next year, Cuisinart followed the Mini-Mate with the Little Pro, a similar product in the $75 range.

Selling the Company

In 1988, the Sontheimers sold Cuisinart to a group of investors for $60 million. The time was right for the sale. Cuisinart showed good cash flow, and—with 85 percent of its revenue from food processors—the company's line of extensions was ready for development. The new owners—a leveraged buyout group headed by former E. F. Hutton chair Robert Fomon—renamed the company Cuisinart, Inc., and readied itself for the upcoming decade.

Still, the company's sales slid in 1988. Consumers liked—and purchased—competitors' smaller and cheaper machines. They complained that Cuisinart models were too big and bulky to keep on kitchen counters. Frequently stored in closets, Cuisinart food processors had to be lugged out of hiding, which made their use inconvenient. Consumers also found Cuisinart hard to learn. Six to eight blades often overwhelmed the average cook, who saw uses for maybe one or two blades.

By 1989, Cuisinart controlled 12 percent of the market, and its revenues fell to about $50 million. Though Cuisinart maintained its image as a high-priced product for serious cooks, consumers more and more perceived its products as too heavy, too complicated, and too expensive in an arena with too much competition. Highly leveraged, the company filed for Chapter 11 bankruptcy, with $43 million in debts and $35 million in assets. In December the current owners sold the company to Conair Corporation, a national manufacturer of home appliances and personal care products based in Stamford, Connecticut.

Conair renamed the company Cuisinart Corporation and instituted a new marketing program for its products. With more advertising and product demonstrations, the new owners hoped to improve relations between Cuisinart and department stores, as well as become a presence in the bridal market.

New Product Development

In 1990, Cuisinart launched the Food Preparation Center. This device was a food processor with a feed tube large enough to hold whole tomatoes and a whisk attachment so that it could handle operations of a standard mixer. In 1991, planning for the brand extension of upscale products began in earnest. In the meantime, Cuisinart introduced the Mini Prep, a smaller version of its food processor, and offered a newsletter and coupon

incentives to Cuisinart buyers. The company also established new accounts with gourmet specialty stores.

The following year Cuisinart continued to plan for a product line beyond food processors. In 1993, Cuisinart introduced its first hand-held and countertop blenders. The company also launched an innovative pasta maker. The Cuisinart Deluxe Pasta Maker debuted at the Gourmet Products Show. With a three-pound capacity and heavy-duty induction motor, the machine made a lot of pasta at once—and quickly (in about 20 minutes). Unused pasta could be stored for use at a later date. The pasta maker directly answered consumers requests for kitchen appliances that supported more health-conscious lifestyles and more consumers staying at home.

Cuisinart also began developing coffee makers around 1994. By 1995, the home appliance market needed a revolutionary new product to lift it from the doldrums. As Lewis Mendelson, an executive vice-president of Dazey, explained in the *Discount Store News:* "There's a lack of innovation, and that's not because nobody's trying. The problem is that there's a finite number of things people do in the kitchen and a finite number of solutions."

Nonetheless Cuisinart impressed the industry with a line of coffee makers introduced at the 1995 Gourmet Products Show. These coffee makers reduced the acidity common to many home models. In addition, Cuisinart models responded to consumers' tangible needs such as color and design. Moderately priced coffee makers started to look like Euro-styled top-of-the-line models.

Cuisinart also excited the high-end appliance sector with hand-mixers and toasters. In particular, the company introduced a long, extra wide slot toaster in 1996 that was one of eight preferred toasters *Good Housekeeping* magazine selected from a field of 25. Chosen the toaster for bagel lovers, the Cuisinart two-slice model was applauded for wide slots able to accommodate a whole, unsliced bagel, for a motorized raising and lowering system, and for a setting to defrost without toasting.

After 25 Years

The year 1996 marked Cuisinart's 25th anniversary in culinary appliances. To commemorate the occasion, the company adopted "Your Kitchen Resource" as a new advertising tag line. At this point in its history, Cuisinart had products in 70 percent of all small appliance categories.

In October 1997, Cuisinart debuted the industry's first iced cappuccino and hot espresso machine within its Coffee Bar line. A company press release explained: "The professional quality results achieved with Cuisinart's Iced Cappuccino and Hot Espresso Maker answer the growing consumer demand for great tasting specialty coffee at home. And with the number of cappuccino drinkers steadily increasing in America, Cuisinart's new culinary appliance has a definite place in today's kitchens."

The next year, Cuisinart entered two new market categories: The first foray, into kitchen textiles, expanded the company's kitchen accessories line, which until that time included kitchen utensils, scales, and prep boards. Now Cuisinart offered towels, aprons, oven mitts, and potholders as well. Cuisinart also entered the hard anodized non-stick cookware market in March 1998. Previously the company offered only non-stick and stainless steel lines. With the addition of a hard anodized non-stick cookware line, Cuisinart gained a presence in every major cookware category.

Cuisinart continued to add to its product line in 1998 with a cordless percolator in the Coffee Bar line and a new electronic hand mixer. The SmartPower CountUp Hand Mixer featured the lowest mixing speeds available and came equipped with a digital timer.

In the Future

Cuisinart planned to continue developing innovative culinary tools and devices beyond 1998. The company expected to promote culinary education; for example, by underwriting the public television series *Cooking Secrets of the CIA*[Culinary Institute of America], by publishing booklets and other materials, and by supporting promotional activities for brides and home chefs. Cuisinart sought to maintain its upscale image through marketing to fine department and gourmet stores, thus serving cooking hobbyist and professionals alike. As the company's promotional material revealed: ''People who love cooking can find comfort in the fact that Cuisinart has the financial strength and resources to provide ongoing support to consumers and to the culinary industry. . . . [T]he company is dedicated to building worldwide recognition for all Cuisinart products. . . . Reaching cooking enthusiasts everywhere is our lifelong goal.''

Further Reading

Dobrian, Joseph, ''Gourmet Show Sizzles with Ideas, Surprises; Manufacturers Will Be Emphasizing Higher-End Product Features to Help Raise Sales and Profits in Housewares,'' *Discount Stores News,* May 1, 1995, p. 50.

Hannon, Kerry, ''Diced and Sliced,'' *Forbes,* October 2, 1989, p. 68.

Pomice, Eva, ''Losing the Cutting Edge,'' *Forbes,* October 6, 1986, p. 162.

Ratliff, Duke, ''Health Eating Seen Pushing Pasta Makers,'' *HFD— The Weekly Home Furnishings Newspaper,* May 3, 1993, p. 120.

''Toasters: The Best of the New Ones, from Basic to Bagel-Ready; Some Even Have Bun Warmers and More,'' *Good Housekeeping,* March 1996, p. 38.

Troester, Maura, ''Cuisinart,'' *Encyclopedia of Consumer Brands,* vol. 3, Detroit: St. James Press, 1992, pp. 92–94.

''Your Kitchen Resource,'' Stamford, Conn.: Cuisinart Corporation, 1996.

—Charity Anne Dorgan

DHL Worldwide Express

333 Twin Dolphin Dr.
Redwood City, California 94065
U.S.A.
(415) 593-7474
(800) CALL-DHL (225-5345)
Fax: (415) 593-1689
Web site: http://www.dhl.com

Private Company
Incorporated: 1969
Employees: 50,000
Sales: $4 billion (1996 est.)
SICs: 4513 Air Courier Services

DHL Worldwide Express, a privately held worldwide delivery service comprised of DHL Airways and DHL International, is the world's oldest and largest international air-express company. Since 1969 when it began as an air-courier service from California to Hawaii, the firm has grown phenomenally and dominates the global express marketplace, delivering to over 70,000 destinations in 227 countries. DHL delivers both small and heavyweight parcels to destinations from the Middle East and Pacific Rim countries to throughout Europe and the United States. DHL's ever-expanding international presence prompted such stateside competitors as Federal Express and United Parcel Service, as well as the United States Postal Service, to join the fray of global express delivery.

Three Men and a Purpose, 1969–79

DHL was founded by three young shipping executives—Adrian Dalsey, Larry Hillblom, and Robert Lynn—who were casting about for a way to increase turnaround speed for ships at ports. They reasoned that if the shipping documents could be flown from port to port, they could be examined and processed before the ships arrived, and speeding up the process would decrease port costs for shippers. With this in mind, the trio combined the first letters of their last names to form the acro-

nym DHL, thus beginning an air-courier company that revolutionized the delivery industry.

DHL rapidly developed into an express delivery service between California and Hawaii, then quickly expanded to points east. The company's primary customer was the Bank of America, which needed a single company to carry its letters of credit and other documents. DHL branched into the international market in the early 1970s when it began flying routes to the Far East. In addition, while competitor Federal Express was developing its domestic overnight delivery network, DHL focused on further developing its international service.

In 1972, the three original investors recruited Po Chung, a Hong Kong entrepreneur, to help them build a global network. Chung started DHL's sister company, DHL International Ltd., headquartered in Brussels, Belgium. Since that date DHL Worldwide has functioned as two separate companies, DHL Airways, Inc. based in Redwood City, California, and DHL International. While each company acted as the exclusive agent for the other, by 1983 DHL International had grown to be five times larger than its domestic counterpart. DHL International's rapid expansion continued throughout the 1970s, adding destinations in Europe in 1974, the Middle East in 1976, Latin America in 1977, and Africa in 1978.

FedEx and UPS Up the Ante, 1980–88

The 1980s would bring the firm increased growth as well as greater competition. During this time DHL continued to expand, by turns cooperating with competitors and warring with them. The company also sought new outlets for service, working out an arrangement with Hilton International Co. in 1980, agreeing to provide daily pickup of documents at 49 Hilton Hotels, arranging for international delivery—its couriers moving the packages through customs—then delivering them locally. It was a win-win situation as Hilton was able to offer its patrons a high-class delivery service and DHL was guaranteed new outlets for its business. The next year, 1981, DHL flew 10 million shipments between 268 cities and had approximately $100 million in sales. The following year, Lawrence Roberts, who had founded Telenet Communications Corp. and headed GTE, joined DHL Corp. as president.

Although DHL had a strong international presence, business was occasionally made difficult because it was necessary for the company to negotiate with foreign governments. In 1982, for example, the French post office sought to reassert a monopoly dating back to the 15th century, and DHL—possessing 80 percent of the French market—was ordered to halt operations outside Paris. What could have been a potential crisis for the company was, however, favorably resolved.

DHL continued to expand its horizons, though, adding Eastern bloc nations in 1983. Prior to 1983, DHL had not pursued much business in the United States, leaving the field to Federal Express and United Parcel Service (UPS). Despite counting 97 percent of the nation's 500 largest companies among its customers, DHL still held only a minuscule share of the overall domestic market. To bolster its share of the American market, DHL installed two major hubs at airports in Cincinnati and Salt Lake City, and added nine mini-hubs in major cities across the country. The company also bought three Boeing 727s and seven Learjets, as well as new sorting equipment. In addition, in 1983 DHL Worldwide started using helicopters in New York and Houston to expedite documents during rush hour and the following year initiated helicopter service in Los Angeles as well.

Once the hubs had been installed, DHL Airways began offering point-to-point overnight service between 126 American cities. Still, for the year ending in 1983, DHL reached only two or three percent of the domestic market—yet had more than 5,000 employees with 400 offices in over 90 countries. As in its earliest days, banks accounted for a large portion of its business; other common shipments consisted of computer tapes, spare parts, and shipping papers. That year, DHL estimated it carried 80 percent of the bank material traveling by courier from Europe to the U.S. and revenues were approximated at $600 million. In 1984, as former courier-driver Joseph Waechter became president of DHL Airways, DHL provided service to more than 125 countries, and its 500 stations were handling 15 million international and domestic shipments annually.

But just as DHL was looking to cut into the business of its domestic competitors, those same companies were aiming to siphon off portions of DHL's international business. In 1985 both Federal Express and UPS entered the international express market. As competition became more intense, DHL increasingly began to cooperate with businesses in similar areas. The company teamed up with Western Union to deliver documents generated on Western Union's EasyLink electronic mails, allowing people to send documents via courier without having to hand-deliver material to the courier's office. The next year, 1986, as DHL International formed its first joint venture with the People's Republic of China, known as DHL Sinotrans, Charles A. Lynch was named chairman and chief executive of DHL Airways, replacing Roberts. Lynch remained with the company just two years and was replaced by Patrick Foley, the former chairman of Hyatt Hotels. Meanwhile, FedEx and UPS were eroding DHL's market share, which fell from 54 percent in 1985 to 50 percent in 1987. However, an important competitive battleground existed in Japan, and while FedEx and UPS gained

footholds in that country in the 1980s, by 1988 DHL still controlled 80 percent of the Japanese overseas market.

As the world economy boomed in the 1980s, DHL followed suit, even breaking new ground in the Communist-bloc countries. The company had first cracked the eastern bloc in 1983, when it began delivering packages to Hungary, East Germany, and several other countries. DHL Airways was not slouching either, reporting that between 1986 and 1987 alone, its volume rose 34 percent; in 1987 it was the 318th largest private company in the United States, with 5,000 employees and estimated sales of $375 million. Revenues for the entire DHL network, in 1988, were calculated to be between $1.2 and $1.5 billion, helped in part by another joint venture with a Hungarian company to create DHL Budapest Ltd. That year, DHL controlled 91 percent of the packages bound for Eastern Europe from the West and 98 percent of all outbound shipments.

Holding and Increasing Market Share, 1989–93

In 1989, DHL Worldwide was the 84th largest company in the United States with 18,000 employees, more than 50 million shipments, and service to 184 countries. However, though DHL's international success was becoming firmly established, the company was not making the headway it had planned in the United States. As of 1989, DHL had only five percent of the domestic market. To bolster its name recognition in the United States, the company turned to innovative advertising techniques, including the use of humor. Cartoonist Gary Larson, creator of the wildly popular comic "The Far Side," was employed to draw cartoons for use in DHL advertising, and in 1990 the company introduced a campaign featuring flying DHL vans whizzing past competitors' planes. DHL also took an unusual approach to air delivery. Although the company used its own fleet of planes within Europe and on some major routes, DHL often used scheduled airlines to carry its shipments. Federal Express, in contrast, maintained its own fleet and seldom used other airlines. Rather than purchase its own planes, DHL chose instead to invest its capital in technology and ground-handling equipment, spending some $250 million on those areas in 1990 and 1991 alone.

In 1990, in order to infuse the company with fresh capital and take advantage of the resources of larger airlines, DHL International sold parts of its business to three companies. Japan Air Lines and the German airline Lufthansa each purchased five percent, while Nissho Iwai, a Japanese trading company, purchased 2.5 percent. Each firm also had the option of buying greater shares. In addition, the three companies also own a combined stake of 2.5 percent in the U.S-based DHL Airways. The sale of these closely held interests brought $500 million in capital into the firm. The same year, despite a 60 percent share of the international overnight delivery market, the company began to expand into new areas of business. To keep up in an increasingly competitive industry, DHL Worldwide entered the freight services industry and began carrying heavier cargo. In the company's 20-year history of carrying small packages— generally under 70 pounds—this was DHL's first major departure from its core business. In 1991, DHL Worldwide had revenues of $2.3 billion, and was the 59th largest private company in the U.S., its 21,000 employees handling more than 80 million shipments.

In June 1992, all three of DHL's major shareholders exercised their option to increase their shares in DHL International; Japan Air Lines and Lufthansa each increased their stake to 25 percent, while Nissho Iwai's holdings grew to 7.5 percent. This was also the year DHL began service to Albania, Estonia, Latvia, and Greenland, and reestablished ties with Kuwait. In addition, in an unusual move DHL signed an agreement to share transatlantic and European aircraft operations with one of its competitors, Emery Worldwide. The economic recession and an overcrowded North Atlantic airway were cited as the reasons behind these cooperative measures, which would allow greater operating efficiency and expanded service. The arrangement represented the first of several alliances between integrated carriers, due to increasing pressure from other competitors, including Airborne Express and TNT. In 1993 as revenues hit $3 billion, DHL commenced a four-year $1.25 billion capital spending program to step up its technological capabilities, automation, and communications.

Towards a New Century, 1994 Onward

By 1994, DHL Worldwide's 25-year anniversary, the company controlled 52 percent of the Asian express shipment marketplace, with FedEx and UPS garnering a 24 percent slice each. The next year, DHL poured over $700 million into expansion of its Pacific Rim operations. DHL was not only shoring up facilities in Hong Kong and Australia, but venturing into 16 new cities in China, India, and Vietnam. A new $60 million hub at Manila's Ninoy Aquino International Airport was scheduled to open in late 1995, with additional facilities slated for Bangkok, Tokyo, Auckland, and Sydney. In the midst of its ambitious expansion, DHL was rocked by the news of founder and majority shareholder Larry Lee Hillblom's death. Known as an avid though reckless pilot (he had survived a previous crash and had his pilot's license suspended), Hillblom, who had withdrawn from DHL's daily operations in 1980, was killed in a seaplane accident near Saipan where he lived.

The management at DHL was soon embroiled in an ugly controversy after Hillblom's 1982 will was released, as a spate of paternity claims and lawsuits were filed. Lurid details of Hillblom's penchant for young island girls reached the press, including an in-depth exposé in the generally staid *Wall Street Journal*. Since Hillblom had retained a mighty 60 percent of DHL Airways and 23 percent of DHL International (valued conservatively at the time at around $300 million), the company's officers scrambled to exercise an option to repurchase his shares. Yet financing and a host of complications held up the buyback and soon the entire estate was a miasma of lawsuits, bad judgement calls, and island politics.

Yet 1995 was still a good year for DHL Worldwide, as the company debuted its web site (www.dhl.com) and experienced an overall 23 percent growth in revenue to $3.8 billion, with an incredible 40 percent surge in volume in its Middle East operations. In response to the encouraging numbers, DHL broke ground on a new $4 million state-of-the-art express facility at the Dubai International Airport in the United Arab Emirates in 1996. The new 42,000-square-foot hub was to complement DHL's existing facilities in Bahrain. Over on the Asian continent, DHL broke with its longstanding tradition of leasing planes to buy its own cargo fleet. Though DHL International's

previous strategy of leasing out cargo space had proved both successful and prudent, Chairman and CEO Foley told the *San Francisco Business Times* the company needed to control its own destiny, and having its own fleet would help alleviate the space limitations and scheduling snafus of commercial flights.

In 1996, DHL was looking to the future again by announcing plans for a $100 million hub in the Midwest to carry the company through the next two decades. While its Cincinnati "superhub" handled around 45 incoming flights every night, and sorted over 135,000 pieces at a rate of 60,000 per hour—DHL believed its growth would soon outpace the facility. The same was true for the San Francisco area, where Silicon Valley shipments represented 40 percent of DHL Airways' business in the Bay Area. Internationally, DHL was still growing at the speed of sound with expansion in the former Soviet Union to 37 branches, a new facility at Ferihegy Airport in Budapest, and the acquisition of Shigur Express in Israel. Though DHL had worked with Shigur for years, the $3.5 million purchase gave DHL a firmer presence in the country's emerging market. By 1998, DHL served 227 countries with 2,381 stations in cities from Paris and Prague to Bombay and Bangkok with over 53,200 employees. Stateside, however, DHL Airways still represented less than two percent of the market, though the California-based company got a boost from the Teamsters' strike against UPS.

As the 1990s came to a close, DHL International announced its intention to sell a 22.5 percent stake in the company to Deutsche Post AG, for an infusion of funds and to strengthen its presence in Germany. With the air cargo industry projected to grow at an annual rate of 6.7 percent for the next dozen or so years, DHL International continued to stave off competitors and dominated global express shipments with over 40 percent of the market. Its U.S.-based sibling, DHL Airways, maintained a healthy bottom line and was positioned to carve away at the market share of FedEx and UPS.

Principal Subsidiaries

DHL International Ltd.; DHL Airways, Inc.

Further Reading

"Air-Express Firms Battle for Turf in Japan," *Wall Street Journal*, December 27, 1988.

"The Battle of Zaventem," *Forbes*, April 29, 1991.

Blackmon, Douglas A , "Transportation: Federal Express, UPS Battle for a Foothold in Asia," *Wall Street Journal*, January 22, 1997, p. B1.

Bole, Kristin, "DHL Gets Its Wings: Plans to Buy Own Jets in Asia Marks Change in Strategy," *San Francisco Business Times*, May 10, 1996, p. 1.

Brady, Diane, "Delivery Giants Race to Set Up Hubs for Overnight Service to Asian Cities," *Wall Street Journal*, August 7, 1997, p. B6.

"Clal Trading Sells Shigur Express to DHL," *Israel Business Today*, February 28, 1997, p. 15.

"DHL Expands Its Domestic Operations," *H&SM*, July 1983.

"DHL International Stake to Be Bought by Three Concerns," *Wall Street Journal*, May 30, 1990.

"DHL International Will Sell 22.5% Stake to Deutsche Post AG," *Wall Street Journal*, March 27, 1998.

"DHL Ties Up East Europe Package," *Advertising Age,* August 29, 1988.

"DHL Worldwide Express Network Statistics," DHL Network, http://www.dhl.com/info/glopres.htm.

"An International Courier Takes on Federal Express," *Business Week,* May 9, 1983.

"Larson's Humor Flies for DHL," *Industry Week,* April 3, 1989.

Nelms, Douglas W., "Holding Its Own: A Massive Global Expansion Is Keeping DHL Well Ahead of Growing U.S. Competition," *Air Transport World,* June 1996, p. 151.

Ott, James, "Heavy-Weight Expansion Propels DHL Hub Growth," *Aviation Week & Space Technology,* March 4, 1997, p. 37.

Schwartz, Judith D., "DHL Puts Its Foot to the Floor As FedEx and UPS Pick Up Speed," *Adweek's Marketing Week,* January 1, 1990.

Solomon, Mark, "DHL, Japan Air and Lufthansa Seek to Reshape Express Sector," *Traffic World,* May 21, 1990.

Tausz, Andrew, "DHL Is Delivering on Courier Challenges," *Distribution,* September 1997, p. 22.

Waldman, Peter, "Heir Freight: How the Strange Life of a DHL Founder Left His Estate a Mess," *Wall Street Journal,* May 15, 1996, p. A1.

"We Go Anywhere," *Financial World,* January 25, 1984.

—Daniel Gross
—updated by Taryn Benbow-Pfalzgraf

DIAGEO

Diageo plc

8 Henrietta Place
London W1M 9AG
United Kingdom
(0171) 927-5200
Fax: (0171) 927-4600
Web site: http://www.diageo.com

Public Company
Incorporated: 1997
Employees: 85,000
Sales:£12.87 billion (1997)
Stock Exchanges: London
Ticker Symbol: DEO
SICs: 2024 Ice Cream & Frozen Desserts; 2033 Canned
   Fruits, Vegetables, Preserves, Jams & Jellies; 2037
   Frozen Fruits, Fruit Juices & Vegetables; 2045
   Prepared Flour Mixes & Doughs; 2051 Bread &
   Bakery Products, Except Cookies & Crackers; 2082
   Malt Beverages; 2084 Wines, Brandy & Brandy
   Spirits; 2085 Distilled & Blended Liquors; 2099 Food
   Preparations, Not Elsewhere Classified; 5812 Eating
   Places

Diageo plc is a world leader in branded food and drinks. The company was formed from the December 1997 merger of liquor and beer giant Guinness PLC and alcohol and food power Grand Metropolitan plc. Diageo (pronounced dee-AH-zhay-oh) consists of four main businesses. United Distillers & Vintners (UDV) is the world's leading spirits and wines company with such brands as Smirnoff vodka, Johnnie Walker and J&B whiskey, Gordon's and Gilbey's gin, and Baileys liqueurs—in all, a full quarter of the top 60 international liquor brands. Pillsbury is a global food giant boasting four megabrands: Pillsbury dough, baking, and baked products; Häagen-Dazs ice cream and frozen yogurt; Green Giant vegetables; and Old El Paso mexican food products. Guinness is one of the largest brewers in the world. Led by the flagship Guinness brand—the world's number one stout beer—the brewer's other brands include Harp lager, Kilkenny Irish Beer, and Kaliber alcohol-free lager. Diageo's fourth business is Burger King, the second largest hamburger chain in the world (after McDonald's). Among the company's smaller operations is Guinness Publishing, which puts out the renowned *Guinness Book of Records.* Diageo also holds a 34 percent stake in the Moët Hennessy champagne and cognac division of LVMH Moët Hennessy Louis Vuitton S.A., a French luxury-goods and drinks giant. In turn, LVMH owns 11 percent of Diageo.

Early History of Guinness PLC

Diageo's history begins with the formation of the Guinness empire. In 1759 Arthur Guinness, an experienced brewer, leased an old brewery at James Gate in Dublin. Besides renting the brewery Guinness signed an unusual 9,000-year lease for a mill, storehouse, stable, house, and two malthouses. As it turned out, in just four years significant quantities of ale and table beer were emerging from the new workplace.

Soon after the brewery was in full operation, Arthur Guinness began to establish a reputation in both business and civic affairs. The company secured an active trade with pubs in towns surrounding Dublin and also became one of the largest employers in the city. As a vocal participant in public life, Guinness supported such diverse issues as penal reform, parliamentary reform, and the discouragement of dueling. Furthermore, although a Protestant, he strongly supported the claims of the Irish Catholic majority for equality.

The business nearly came to an abrupt end in 1775 when a dispute over water rights erupted into a heated exchange between Guinness and the mayor's emissaries. The argument centered around the City Corporation's decision to fill in the channel that provided the brewery with water. When the sheriff's men appeared at James Gate, Guinness grabbed a pickaxe from a workman and with a good deal of ''improper language'' ordered them to leave. For fear of escalating violence, the parties to the dispute finally settled by means of a tenant agreement.

In 1761 Arthur Guinness married Olivia Whitmore; of the 21 children born to them only 10 survived. Since the eldest son became a clergyman, the thriving company was passed on to the second son, Arthur, after the founder's death in 1803. Like his father, Arthur soon became active in both civic and political affairs. He served in the Farming Society of Ireland, the Dublin Society, the Meath Hospital, and the Dublin Chamber of Commerce. Most importantly, as an elected director in the Bank of Ireland, he played a significant role in settling currency issues. In politics, Arthur adhered to his father's beliefs by advocating the claims of the religious majority.

From the very beginning of his career, it appears that Arthur's main concern was not so much in managing the company as in pursuing his banking interests. Nonetheless, brewery records indicate that from the end of the Napoleonic Wars to the end of the Great Famine in 1850, the company's production output increased by 50 percent. For this reason, Arthur is often credited with making the Guinness fortune.

A great deal of that success, of course, can be attributed to Arthur Guinness's decision to shift most of the firm's trade from Ireland to England. Yet the growth of Guinness was a result not only of management's business acumen and the firm's financial strength but also of the myths surrounding the beverage: from its earliest days Guinness stout—a dark and creamy brew—was considered a nutritional beverage and promoter of virility. Although the company was once accused of mashing Protestant Bibles and Methodist hymn books into the brew in order to force ingestion of anti-Papal doctrine, Britain's leading medical journal during the mid-19th century claimed the drink was "one of the best cordials not included in the pharmacopeia." This notion formed the basis of the company's advertisement campaign of 1929, which suggested that drinking Guinness could lead to the development of "strong muscles," "enriched blood," and the alleviation of "exhausted nerves." Somewhat surprisingly, this tradition continued in Britain into the late 20th century, when the national health insurance system was underwriting the purchase of Guinness for nursing mothers.

When Arthur died in 1855, his son, Benjamin Lee, assumed control of the company. Fifty-seven at the time, he had already worked for nearly 30 years at the brewery. During his tenure as head of the firm, the James Gate facility became the preeminent porter brewery in the world. Following the tradition of his family, he was also intimately involved in civic affairs. He was awarded a baronetcy in 1867 for his contributions to the restoration of St. Patrick's Cathedral and other services. He died a year later.

Although in his will Benjamin Lee Guinness divided the responsibility for running the firm equally between his two sons, Edward Cecil and Arthur Edward, Edward soon emerged

as the more astute of the two. The younger of the brothers, he was said to be an energetic yet excitable man. His decisions were controversial and, apparently, overwhelming: after eight years Arthur decided to leave the brewing business, and the partnership between brothers was dissolved.

In the tradition of his family, Edward became a leading figure in both civic affairs and in English social life. After his marriage to his cousin Adelaide, he seems to have "arrived," and the young couple circulated freely in elite circles. Among the many dignitaries entertained at their opulent 23,000-acre estate in Suffolk was King Edward VII.

Edward Guinness's wealth, prestige, influence, and philanthropic work eventually earned him the title of Lord Iveagh. He drew heavily from the family fortune to contribute to worthy causes; he established the Iveagh Trust to provide basic necessities for 950 indigent families and donated money for the continuing restoration of St. Patricks' Cathedral. He was, as well, recognized as an enlightened employer, ahead of his time in providing pension plans, health services, and housing for his employees.

Guinness Became Public Company in 1886

In 1886 Guinness became a public company (under the name Guinness PLC), its shares traded on the London exchange (Dublin, at that time lacked its own exchange). The company raised six million pounds on its shares, and embarked on an ambitious period of expansion in Ireland, England, and abroad. Guinness's unique brewing process ensured that the quality of the product would not be impaired by long voyages to foreign markets. By the 1920s Guinness had reached the shores of East and West Africa and the Caribbean.

In 1927 leadership of the company passed to the next generation. The second Lord Iveagh is recognized primarily for his role in creating a modern brewery at Park Royal in London, built to service the company's growing business in southeast England. The facility became operational in 1936, and it is there that Guinness Extra and Draught Guinness were first brewed for the British market. By 1974 production at this plant exceeded that at James Gate by 100 percent.

Construction of the Park Royal facility was completed under the supervision of a civil engineer named Hugh E. C. Beaver. He formed a close association with managing director C. J. Newbold yet turned down Newbold's invitation to join the Guinness board of directors. After World War II Lord Iveagh personally asked Beaver to join the company as assistant managing director—and this time Beaver accepted. When Newbold died in the late 1940s, Beaver assumed the position of managing director. He is credited with modernizing the company's operations, introducing new management and research policies, increasing exports, and diversifying the company's product base. On his initiative the company was officially divided into Guinness Ireland and Guinness U.K. (control of both concerns remained with a central board of directors).

Harp and Guinness Book of Records Introduced in the 1950s

Beaver was also a strong advocate of generating new ideas through brainstorming sessions. One now-famous product to emerge from these meetings was Harp lager. When Britons began taking their holidays abroad during the 1950s, they returned home with a new taste for chilled lager. Beaver sensed this changing preference, and during one intensive company meeting, executives decided that Guinness should become the first local firm to market its own lager. Named for the harp on Guinness's traditional label, Harp lager soon became the most successful product in the growing British lager market.

Beaver is also recognized as the founder of the extraordinarily successful publication *Guinness Book of Records*. Initially created as something of a lark, the book was such a success throughout the world, that it became a company tradition. By the late 1980s the *Guinness Book of Records* was selling some five million copies in 13 different languages.

Guinness Diversified Widely in the 1960s and 1970s

Beaver, now Sir Hugh, retired in 1960, but throughout the next decade Guinness continued to expand—notably abroad, in countries with warm climates. Consistent with this strategy, the company constructed new breweries in Nigeria and Malaysia—then a second and third brewery in Nigeria as well as breweries in Cameroon, Ghana, and Jamaica. Guinness also developed a new product during this period, Irish Ale, which was exported to France and Britain. To offset the declining market for stout, the company began to diversify into pharmaceuticals, confectionery, and plastics, as well as other beverages.

Although both sales and earnings per share had doubled between 1965 and 1971, Guinness entered the 1970s confronting a number of problems. Compared to those of its competitors, the company's shares sold at modest prices, largely because Guinness operated outside the tiedhouse system (the five largest brewers owned and operated most of the country's 100,000 pubs), and investors felt the other breweries had the advantage for growth. The London financial community reasoned that Guinness was at a disadvantage because the company had to absorb the added costs of retailing.

There were also problems at the James Gate brewery. The Park Royal facility continued to outproduce the older Dublin site, and the company and its employees' union reached an agreement whereby the James Gate workforce would be reduced by nearly one half. This solution temporarily solved the problem of decreasing profits at the James Gate facility and allowed operations to continue at the highly esteemed landmark facility. By 1976, however, the cost-cutting plan was seen to have achieved less than had been expected.

Diversification efforts during this period were also less than stellar; the company had gone on a purchasing spree in which 270 companies, producing a wide variety of products from baby bibs to car polish, had been acquired, and many of these companies were operating at a deficit.

Even in the base brewing business, Guinness had its share of troubles. The company's witty advertisements appealed to the middle class but ignored the working class that provided the bulk of Guinness's customers. A new product, designed to combine the tastes of stout and ale, was a £3 million mistake. The Guinness share price continued to decline.

Saunders Era Brought Scandal to Guinness, 1980–87

To remedy the company's problems, Guinness executives called in the first non-family professional manager to take over leadership of the company. The sixth Lord Iveagh, as well as numerous Guinness relations, remained on the board, but Ernest Saunders, a former executive at J. Walter Thompson and Nestlé, stepped in as chief executive in 1980.

Saunders saw his first task as reducing the company's disparate holdings. He sold 160 companies, retaining only some retail businesses. He then reduced the workforce and brought in a new management team to develop and market the company's products in addition to investing in increased and more eclectic advertising. He also made canny acquisitions in specialty foods, publishing, and retailing (including the 7-Eleven convenience stores). Brewing, according to Saunders, would in the future comprise only half of Guinness's total volume. Financial analysts, and the City of London in general, were pleased with Saunders's efforts. The Guinness share price began noticeably to climb.

By mid-1985 Saunders seemed to have conquered. During his tenure the company's profits had tripled, and its share price increased fourfold. He had accomplished a dazzling takeover of Distillers Company, gaining such liquor brands as Gordon's and Tanqueray gin and Johnnie Walker whiskey. That Guinness could—and would—pay £2.5 billion (US$4.6 billion) for a company twice its size surprised many industry analysts, yet Saunders's wish to create a multinational company on the scale of Nestlé seemed to justify the expense. There were rumors that Saunders might be honored with a knighthood.

Within a matter of months, however, there were other kinds of rumors in the City—rumors concerning Saunders's methods in pursuing the Distillers acquisition. In order to make the takeover possible, Saunders with two of his fellow directors, allegedly had orchestrated an international scheme to provoke the sale of Guinness shares and thereby raise their value. Outside investors were indemnified in various ways against any losses incurred in purchasing huge numbers of Guinness shares. Bank Leu in Switzerland purchased Guinness shares with the understanding that the company would eventually buy them back. In return, Guinness deposited $75 million (in a non-interest-earning account) with the bank. The bank's chairman happened to be Saunders's ex-boss at Nestlé and a Guinness board member. Ivan F. Boesky, the American arbitrageur who later admitted to insider trading in numerous deals, was cited as the primary source of information about the Distillers takeover. It was believed that Boesky himself played a large role in the takeover; Guinness made a $100 million investment in a limited partnership run by Boesky only one month after Boesky had made significant purchases of Guinness shares. Further investigation revealed that Boesky was seemingly only one of many international investors who bought Guinness shares in an effort to increase their value. The company's auditors discovered some $38 million worth of invoices for "services" rendered by various international investors during the takeover.

In December 1986 the British Trade and Industry Department instigated an investigation of Guinness. In January 1987 the Guinness board of directors asked for Saunders's resignation, and subsequently, in March, brought legal action against Saunders and one of his fellow directors, John Ward. In May the British government brought charges of fraud against Saunders: the claim was that Saunders knowingly destroyed evidence during the Trade and Industry Department investigation. Throughout these events, Saunders continued to deny all charges brought against him. In 1990, however, he was convicted of fraud and sentenced to two years in jail. Nine months into his incarceration he was released on the basis of a medical report claiming that he might be in the early stages of Alzheimer's disease. Subsequently, he twice tried and failed to have his conviction overturned on appeal. In December 1996 the European Court of Human Rights ruled that Saunders's rights had been violated during his trial, but it did not clear his name.

Guinness Focused on Brewing and Distilling in the Late 1980s and 1990s

Meanwhile, the survival of Guinness as an independent company was in peril. The company's share price tumbled as a result of the continuing scandal. To prevent any further decline, Anthony Tennant, Guinness's new chief executive, refocused the company on two core areas—brewing and distilling—jettisoning the bulk of the businesses outside these areas (a notable exception to all of the company's various purges of the later 20th century was the *Guinness Book of Records*). Tennant—along with Tony Greener, managing director of distilling operations—overhauled the unit, which was eventually renamed United Distillers, getting rid of numerous marginal brands and centralizing operations that had been organized into numerous separate companies. Distillers was also bolstered by the September 1987, US$555 million acquisition of Schenley Industries Inc., which held the U.S. rights to Dewar's and Gordon's gin. Guinness further tightened its grip on the all-important distribution side of the liquor business through joint ventures, most notably a 1987 agreement with LVMH Moët Hennessy Louis Vuitton S.A., a French drinks and luxury-goods manufacturer. By 1989 each company had gained a 24 percent stake in the other, although Guinness's holding in LVMH was indirect.

In 1990 Guinness's brewing unit was beefed up through the acquisition of La Cruz Del Campo, the largest brewer in Spain, for £518 million. Two years later, Greener succeeded the retiring Tennant as chief executive. The company's alliance with LVMH was restructured in 1994 so that Guinness held a direct 34 percent stake in LVMH's Moët Hennessy champagne and cognac division, while LVMH's stake in Guinness was reduced to 20 percent (and by 1997 to about 14 percent). The following year Guinness sold 37 U.S. domestic liquor brands and two production facilities to Barton Inc., a division of Canandaigua Wine Company, for £111 million (US$171 million), as part of an effort to concentrate on premium high-priced brands. Back on the brewing side, the early to mid-1990s saw Guinness build its flagship brand by helping investors around the world open up Irish-style pubs. The company did not own any of these houses, but encouraging their establishment helped to create a growing market for the quintessentially Irish Guinness stout.

In July 1996 Guinness denied that it was planning a takeover of Grand Metropolitan or considering divesting its brewing unit. Less than a year later, however, the two companies announced the merger that in late 1997 would create Diageo plc. In 1996, Guinness posted revenue of £4.73 billion and record profits before tax and exceptionals of £975 million.

Grand Metropolitan Was Focused on Food and Drinks by the Mid-1990s

Much like Guinness, Grand Metropolitan (GrandMet) had diversified widely in the 1970s and 1980s, before settling on a portfolio of food and beverage brands by the late 1980s. The company's roots extended to the early 1930s with founder Maxwell Joseph's investments in real estate. GrandMet eventually developed into a powerful European hotel firm; however, the last of the company's hotels were sold in the late 1980s. In the 1970s branded food businesses, restaurants and pubs, breweries, and distilling operations were acquired. The breweries were divested in 1991, while the restaurants and pubs were sold off piecemeal from 1989 to 1995. Other peripheral businesses acquired along the way included the U.S.-based Pearl Vision chain of optical shops, which were sold to Cole National Corp. in November 1996.

Under the leadership of Allen Sheppard, who became chief executive in 1987, and his eventual successor George J. Bull, GrandMet made three significant acquisitions of U.S.-based firms from 1987 through 1995. The brands and businesses gained thereby formed the very heart of the company that merged with Guinness. In 1987 GrandMet bolstered its liquor unit—International Distillers & Vintners—by acquiring Heublein Inc. from RJR Nabisco for £800 million (US$1.3 billion), gaining such brands as Smirnoff vodka, Arrow liqueurs, and Harvey's Bristol Cream sherry in the process. Two years later, GrandMet completed a £3.2 billion (US$5.68 billion) hostile takeover of Pillsbury Company, which featured the Pillsbury baked goods brand, the Green Giant vegetables brand, the Häagen-Dazs ice cream brand, and the Burger King hamburger chain, which Pillsbury had acquired in 1967. GrandMet in 1995 paid £1.8 billion (US$2.6 billion) for Pet, Inc., which produced most notably the line of Old El Paso Mexican-food products, as well as Progresso soups.

By early 1997—when Bull was serving as chairman and John McGrath as chief executive—GrandMet had narrowed its packaged-food focus to four core international brands: Pillsbury, Green Giant, Häagen-Dazs, and Old El Paso. The company had by that time completed the sale of its various European-branded food businesses. For fiscal 1996, Grand Metropolitan posted revenues of £8.73 billion and profits before tax and exceptionals of £965 million.

Diageo Formed in December 1997

In May 1997 Guinness and Grand Metropolitan announced that they would merge to form a new company, tentatively called GMG Brands. Seven months later the £12 billion (US$19 billion) merger—the largest in U.K. history to that point—had been finalized, but not before a five-month battle with LVMH had ended peacefully. LVMH agreed to drop its opposition to the merger in return for receipt of £250 million upon the merger's consummation; the merged entity would retain Guinness's 34 percent stake in LVMH's Moët Hennessy champagne and cognac division, while LVMH would hold about 11 percent of the new company. Guinness and GrandMet also had to agree to divest the Dewar's Scotch whiskey and Bombay gin brands in order to gain approval from U.S. and European regulators. In late March 1998, the merged company, now named Diageo plc, announced an agreement to sell these brands to Bermuda-based Bacardi Ltd. for £1.15 billion (US$1.94 billion) in cash. The name "Diageo" had been derived from the Latin "dia" (day) and the Greek "geo" (world). The company explained that the name was supposed to convey that "every day, all around the world, millions of people enjoy our brands."

Diageo was centered on brands. At its founding, the company had four main businesses: United Distillers & Vintners (UDV), Pillsbury, Guinness, and Burger King. UDV (which generated about 45 percent of overall revenue) was a combination of the numerous leading liquor brands of Guinness's United Distillers unit and GrandMet's International Distillers & Vintners unit; UDV became the world's number one distiller upon its formation. Pillsbury (29 percent) retained GrandMet's four packaged-food megabrands: Pillsbury, Green Giant, Häagen-Dazs, and Old El Paso. Guinness (18 percent) included such stellar brewing brands as Guinness, Harp, Kilkenny, Cruzcampo of Spain, Red Stripe, and Kaliber. Burger King (eight percent) trailed only McDonald's among the world's hamburger chains. Bull and Greener were named cochairmen of Diageo, while McGrath became Diageo's first chief executive. Prospects for Diageo appeared bright, although almost immediately upon its creation the company faced the impact of the financial crisis in Asia, where about 12 percent of the company's gross profits were generated.

Principal Operating Units

United Distillers & Vintners; Pillsbury; Guinness; Burger King.

Further Reading

Banks, Howard, "We'll Provide the Shillelaghs," *Forbes,* April 8, 1996, p. 68.

Beck, Ernest, "Bacardi to Buy Dewar's Label, Bombay Gin," *Wall Street Journal,* March 31, 1998, p. A18.

——, "Liquor Giants Brew New Name in Greek, Latin," *Wall Street Journal,* October 30, 1997, pp. B1, B11.

Beck, Ernest, Tara Parker Pope, and Elizabeth Jensen, "GrandMet, Guinness to Form Liquor Colossus," *Wall Street Journal,* May 13, 1997, pp. B1, B8.

Blackwell, David, "Guinness Sells US Brands and Plants in $171m Deal," *Financial Times,* August 30, 1995, p. 17.

Brady, Rosemary, "Beyond the Froth," *Forbes,* March 28, 1983, p. 171.

Donlon, J. P., "Blithe Spirits," *Chief Executive,* April 1992, p. 34.

Flynn, Julia, and Laura Zinn, "Absolut Pandemonium: As Liquor Sales Fall, Companies Are Battling for Premium Brands," *Business Week,* November 8, 1993, pp. 58–59.

Frank, Robert, "European Moguls Slug It Out U.S. Style," *Wall Street Journal,* August 4, 1997, p. A14.

Goldsmith, Charles, "Prefab Irish Pubs Sell Pints World-Wide," *Wall Street Journal,* October 25, 1996, pp. B1, B8.

Guinness, Jonathan, *Requiem for a Family Business,* London: Macmillan, 1997.

Heller, Robert, "Guinness's 'Brand New' Strategy," *Management Today,* December 1996, p. 25.

Jack, Andrew, "Adieu As Burger King Goes Off Menu in France," *Financial Times,* July 30, 1997, p. 1.

Jackson, Tony, "A New Spirit Is Brought into the World," *Financial Times,* May 13, 1997, p. 25.

Jackson, Tony, and John Ridding, "Heady Cocktail with Lots of Fizz," *Financial Times,* January 21, 1994, p. 17.

Kirkland, Richard I., Jr., "Britain's Own Boesky Case," *Fortune,* February 16, 1987, p. 85.

Lee, Peter, "Bending the Rules Till They Break," *Euromoney,* February 1987, p. 120.

Marcom, John, Jr., "The House of Guinness," *Forbes,* June 12, 1989, p. 85.

Maremont, Mark, and Amy Dunkin, "Guinness: A Lesson in Dealing with Drier Times," *Business Week,* June 27, 1988, pp. 52–54.

Mason, John, and Robert Rice, "Way Cleared for Saunders to Fight On," *Financial Times,* December 18, 1996, p. 10.

"Master of the Bar: Grand Metropolitan and Guinness," *Economist,* May 17, 1997, p. 70.

Moss, Nicholas, and Charles Masters, "Merger on the Rocks," *European,* July 31, 1997, p. 8.

Murphy, Chris, "GrandMet Tries to Regain Its Concentration," *Marketing,* July 11, 1996, p. 16.

Oram, Roderick, "Finn's Tune Takes Time to Strike the Right Chord," *Financial Times,* November 9, 1995, p. 29.

——, "GrandMet Focuses on Core Brands," *Financial Times,* September 6, 1996, p. 17.

——, "Guinness Rules Out GrandMet Bid and Option for Demerger," *Financial Times,* July 8, 1996, p. 1.

——, "Resisting the Calls for a Flash of Pure Genius," *Financial Times,* July 8, 1996, p. 19.

——, "Sweeping the Shelves Clean," *Financial Times,* September 6, 1996, p. 19.

——, "An Unfinished Masterpiece," *Financial Times,* February 19, 1996, p. 17.

Palmer, Jay, "Stout Fellow: A New Head Man Brews Up a Recovery at Guinness," *Barron's,* March 4, 1991, pp. 12–13.

Rawstorne, Philip, "Guinness Restructures Alliance with LVMH," *Financial Times,* January 12, 1994, pp. 1, 18.

——, "Pure Genius Needed to Maintain Growth," *Financial Times,* December 12, 1992, p. 12.

Reier, Sharon, "Getting Scotch Off the Rocks," *Financial World,* August 6, 1991, p. 25.

Rice, Robert, "Success by Stealth," *Financial Times,* January 13, 1998, p. 12.

Seneker, Harold, "Watch Out, Seagram," *Forbes,* May 19, 1986, p. 200.

Sherrid, Pamela, "Britain's Business Elite Takes a Fall," *U.S. News & World Report,* February 2, 1987, p. 47.

"Stout Fellows," *Economist,* June 9, 1990, pp. 66, 68.

Syedain, Hashi, "Spirits Are Good for You: Guinness Has Now Emerged from Some Very Dark Times in the Company's History to Enjoy a More Golden Age," *Management Today,* October 1990, p.64.

——, "Tony Greener," *Management Today,* September 1993, p. 48.

Wilke, John R., "Grand Met and Guinness to Shed Lines," *Wall Street Journal,* December 3, 1997, pp. A3, A6.

Willman, John, "Adversaries Toast Outbreak of Peace," *Financial Times,* October 14, 1997, p. 24.

——, "Diageo Tops Global Spirits League Table," *Financial Times,* February 18, 1998, p. 36.

——, "Remarkably Relaxed and in Control of His Destiny," *Financial Times,* December 17, 1997, p. 25.

Willman, John, Andrew Jack, and Emma Tucker, "LVMH Chairman Drops Opposition to Drinks Link-Up," *Financial Times,* October 14, 1997, pp. 1, 22.

—updated by David E. Salamie

Dofasco Inc.

1330 Burlington Street East
Post Office Box 2460
Hamilton, Ontario L8N 3J5
Canada
(905) 544-3761
Fax: (905) 548-3236
Web site: http://www.dofasco.ca

Public Company
Incorporated: 1912 as Dominion Steel Castings
    Company, Ltd.
Employees: 7,200
Sales: C$3.07 billion (1997)
Stock Exchanges: Toronto Montreal
SICs: 1011 Iron Ores Mining; 3312 Steel Works & Blast
    Furnaces; 3316 Cold Rolled Steel Sheet, Strip &
    Bars; 3317 Steel Pipe & Tubes; 3325 Steel Foundries,
    Not Elsewhere Classified; 3479 Coating, Engraving &
    Allied Services, Not Elsewhere Classified

Dofasco Inc. is one of Canada's largest steelmakers. The company and its subsidiaries and joint ventures in Canada and the United States manufacture hot and cold rolled steel, galvanized steel, chromium-coated and flat-rolled prepainted steels, tinplate, and tubular products. Dofasco also has iron ore mining operations. It sells its steel products to a wide variety of customers, including those in the automotive, construction, energy, manufacturing, pipe and tube, appliance, container, and steel distribution industries.

Founded on Steel Castings in 1912

Clifton W. Sherman built the foundry that served as the cornerstone for Dofasco in Hamilton, Ontario, in 1912. Then known as the Dominion Steel Castings Company, Ltd., the foundry initially made steel castings for Canada's expanding railway system. The original plant covered five acres. In 1913 Domin-

ion merged with Hamilton Malleable Iron Company, and took a new name, Dominion Steel Foundry Company (Dominion).

In 1914 Frank A. Sherman, brother of the founder, joined the firm. Production for war goods began to roll. As World War I progressed, orders for stirrups, bridles, and clevises were replaced with orders for munitions, marine forgings, and steel plate, reflecting changes in the nature of warfare. In 1917 a plate mill was purchased, and a new forging plant began churning out shell forgings. The company's name changed again that year, to Dominion Foundries and Steel, Limited, even then known as Dofasco. When the war drew to a close in 1918, Dofasco had 11 open hearth furnaces producing about 750 tons of steel per day. The plant had sprawled to 26 acres, and about 2,280 workers were on the payroll, nearly ten times the number just four years prior.

The 1920s was a difficult decade for the Canadian steelmaker. Following the end of the war, demand for steel dropped off drastically. To make matters worse, low tariffs allowed U.S. steel producers to control a sizable chunk of the Canadian steel market. Dofasco operated Canada's only heavy plate mill capable of producing six- to 42-inch universal steel plate. It was completed in 1921, but tough foreign competition kept the mill working below capacity for most of the decade. The foundry, however, picked up the slack for the mill during the 1920s, and the company's expertise in steel castings improved accordingly. By 1928 the market for Canadian steel plate improved, and in 1929 a second shift was operating at the universal plate mill.

In 1930 Dofasco's foundry poured a 95,000-pound casting for a hydroelectric development in Quebec. It was the largest such casting ever produced in Canada. During the Great Depression demand for steel was up and down. Canada's rail system continued to expand, and it provided sporadic orders for Dofasco. Sometimes the foundry was overbooked; at other times it was virtually idle.

The second half of the decade saw many improvements at Dofasco. In 1935 a 20-inch cold reducing mill was brought on line, and the company began producing the first Canadian tin plate. Dofascolite, the name under which the company's tin plate was marketed, was a tremendously successful product. In

1937 a 42-inch cold mill was built, enabling the company to produce 100 tons of cold-rolled steel per day.

By the late 1930s the menace of war once again loomed on the horizon. Dominion Foundries and Steel geared up to meet Canada's war demands. Between 1935 and 1940, the company spent $5.8 million on new facilities. Three-quarters of all steel and one-third of all tin produced in Canada came from Dofasco. In 1941 the company became Canada's only domestic producer of armor plate, supplying the Canadian armed forces until the end of World War II.

Postwar Growth

After the war the company continued to produce at record levels. In August 1951 Dofasco ignited its first blast furnace. Three years later it became the first North American company to produce basic oxygen steel. This new process resulted in higher quality steel at reduced costs. Also in 1954, Dominion Foundries and Steel acquired the galvanized sheet division of Lysaght's Canada, Limited.

In 1955 the company began operating a 56-inch cold mill with a continuous galvanizing line. In 1956 a second blast furnace began operations. Substantial replacement of facilities was made during the next five years. Between 1950 and 1959 Dofasco had invested $120 million in new plant facilities.

Dofasco's postwar growth continued into the next decade. In 1960 a second galvanizing line was installed. Steel production potential was up to one million tons per year. Dofasco next branched out through acquisition. In 1961 a joint venture to run the Wabush Iron Company was initiated. In 1962 National Steel Car Corporation, a leading manufacturer of railroad cars, was purchased. Another purchase was the Temagami property, destined to become the Sherman mine. The Sherman mine delivered its first iron ore pellets to the Hamilton plant in 1968. In 1970 the company expanded its iron ore capacity when it bought the Adams mine in northern Ontario.

Capital investments continued throughout the 1960s. When industrial impact on the environment became a growing concern in the late 1960s, Dominion Foundries and Steel reacted. In 1968 the company installed pollution-control equipment to improve the quality of water returned to Lake Ontario from the plant.

Steady demand for steel kept the facilities at Dofasco humming through the late 1960s and early 1970s. In March 1973 Dofasco bought the BeachviLime Ltd. quarry, ensuring a steady supply of lime. A month later, pipe manufacturer Prudential Steel was acquired.

In the mid-1970s massive construction was under way to double steel output within 20 years. A second five-stand cold mill was built in 1974. While the world economy was in recession, Dofasco spent several million dollars on environmental controls and renovated its foundry. By 1976 sales rebounded from the recessionary trough, reaching record levels in some areas.

In 1978 the company launched what was at that time its largest single construction project, a second melt shop. It also purchased Guelph Dolime that year, a lime quarry to be operated as a part of the BeachviLime unit. As the 1970s drew to a close, Dofasco announced its plans to build a fourth galvanizing line and a second hot strip mill.

Became Dofasco in 1980

In October 1980 Dominion Foundries and Steel, Limited officially changed its name to Dofasco Inc. A severe recession struck Canada in the second half of 1980, causing a plant shutdown for part of July. The steel industry was hit hard, but Dofasco continued with new plant construction on schedule. As the recession deepened, however, Dofasco had to take cost-cutting measures. Demand for steel was low. In November 1982 the company laid off 2,100 employees. Net income in 1982 dropped to $63.8 million from $169.3 million the previous year.

In 1983 production levels improved, and laid-off employees were called back. Demand for higher-quality steel prompted Dofasco's conversion in 1984 of its number-one galvanizing line to production of a new corrosion-resistant steel, Galvalume. In 1985 a $750 million cast slab expansion, Dofasco's most expensive project ever, was begun. The new facilities enabled Dofasco to produce new and higher-quality steel products.

Several major acquisitions helped Dofasco's sales jump from $1.9 billion in 1985 to $3.9 billion in 1989. In December 1986 Dofasco acquired the Whittar Steel Strip Company of Detroit. Whittar specialized in strip products used in the automotive industry. In August 1988 Dofasco purchased the Algoma Steel Corporation of Sault Sainte Marie, Ontario, for C$713 million, thereby becoming Canada's largest steelmaker.

Early 1990s Troubles Led to Restructuring

The purchase of Algoma, a fully integrated steel manufacturer, turned out to be a major blunder for Dofasco. Algoma ran into serious difficulties in 1990, suffering a C$702 million loss that year, in part as a result of a lengthy strike. It also had run up a huge debt of C$800 million and was able to stave off bankruptcy only through a bridge loan from the government of Ontario. As Algoma reorganized itself, Dofasco cut its losses first by writing off its entire investment in Algoma in 1991, then by giving up ownership of Algoma in 1992.

The Algoma debacle exacerbated Dofasco's own troubled situation, which was caused in large measure by economic forces. Demand for durable consumer goods was weak during the early 1990s, and as a result Dofasco's major customers—the automotive, appliance, and construction industries—cut orders. All told, the company suffered three straight years of net losses: C$679.2 million in 1990, C$25 million in 1991, and C$207.1 million in 1992.

To rebound from its troubles, Dofasco began restructuring its operations. From the mid-1980s to the mid-1990s, the company cut its workforce nearly 45 percent, from 12,700 to 7,000 workers. Most of the reductions were achieved through voluntary retirement programs and attrition. Dofasco also divested a number of noncore businesses in an effort to focus more on higher-end steelmaking. In 1991 the company sold Whittar Steel Strip (acquired only five years earlier) to Samuel, Son &

Co. Ltd. of Mississauga, Ontario. The following year, Dofasco sold its Steel Castings division, the unit upon which it was founded, to Atchison Castings Corp.; its National Steel Car railway car manufacturer to TMB Industries of Chicago; and its BeachviLime lime-quarrying unit to Calcitherm Group, a holding company based in Holland. Also jettisoned in the mid-1990s were the pipe and tubular steel maker Prudential Steel and the company's 50 percent interest in Ferrum Inc., also a producer of pipe and tubular products.

Meanwhile, the company joined a general trend in the steel industry toward joint ventures—which combatted overcapacity problems—and high-tech, low-labor-cost minimills. In 1990 Dofasco entered into a joint venture with NKK Corporation of Japan and National Steel Corporation of the United States to build a plant in Windsor, Ontario, to make hot-dip, galvanized, flat-rolled steel. The venture, called DNN Galvanizing Limited Partnership and 50 percent owned by Dofasco, was the first steel industry joint venture involving companies from three countries. The plant was completed in 1993, producing its high-margin galvanized steel primarily for the automobile industry.

Also in 1993, Dofasco formed another joint venture, Gallatin Steel Company, 50-50 owned by Dofasco and Toronto-based Co-Steel Inc. Gallatin was created to build a C$400 million minimill in Gallatin County, Kentucky, to produce hot-rolled, thin-slab steel. The venture took advantage of the two companies' bases of experience: Co-Steel's in minimills and Dofasco's in flat-rolled steel. Minimills—which were typically nonunion, used state-of-the-art equipment, and required only a few hundred workers—were designed to produce lower-cost steel, compared with traditional integrated steel plants. The Gallatin plant began production in July 1995; in 1997 it shipped more than one million tons of hot-rolled steel and was profitable for the first time.

In 1996 Dofasco completed installation of a new electric-arc furnace and slab caster at its Hamilton facilities; this new technology enabled the plant to reduce its consumption of purchased semi-finished steel. The following year, a new 140,000-metric-ton-per-year tube mill began production at the Hamilton plant, with the resulting products designed specifically to help automakers build stronger and lighter vehicles. In December 1997 Dofasco entered into another joint venture, this one with Sollac, a division of French steelmaker Usinor. Eighty percent owned by Dofasco and utilizing technology developed by Sol-

lac, the venture was created to build a 400,000-metric-ton-per-year, 72-inch-wide hot-dip line to make corrosion-resistant galvanized steel primarily for automotive body panels. The line was slated to be operational by mid-1999. In early 1998 Dofasco issued a statement denying rumors that the company was negotiating with fellow Canadian steelmaker Stelco Inc. about a merger or alliance.

Through its successful restructuring—particularly its use of joint ventures, its emphasis on higher-margin specialized products, and its use of the latest technology—Dofasco was consistently profitable in the mid- to late 1990s. Sales in 1997 were C$3.07 billion, with net income a respectable C$193.2 million. By continuing to react quickly to changes in the steel market, Dofasco assured itself of a bright future.

Principal Subsidiaries

Iron Ore Company of Canada (6.9%); Quebec Cartier Mining Company (50%); Wabush Mines (24.3%); Baycoat (50%); DNN Galvanizing Limited Partnership (50%); Sorevco and Company Limited (50%); Dofasco USA Inc.; Gallatin Steel Company (U.S.A.; 50%).

Further Reading

Beirne, Mike, "Canadians Set Mini-Mill in US," *American Metal Market,* March 12, 1993, pp. 1+.

Davie, Michael, "Paternal Tradition at Dofasco Appears to Ebb," *American Metal Market,* April 20, 1994, p. 6.

Dofasco 75: 1912–1987, Hamilton, Ontario: Dofasco Inc., 1987.

Freedman, David H., "Steel Edge: Steelmaking Is Low Tech; So Why Is Gallatin Steel Crammed with Rocket Scientists and Computer Power?," *Forbes* (ASAP), October 6, 1997, pp. S46+.

"Out to Survive, Grow to Succeed," *American Metal Market,* July 3, 1997, p. 10.

Ritt, Adam, "Streamlining Steelmaking on Lake Ontario," *New Steel,* January 1995, pp. 18+.

Schriefer, John, "Spending Less to Increase Capacity," *New Steel,* September 1996, pp. 58+.

Scolieri, Peter, "Dofasco to Shut Castings Unit," *American Metal Market,* April 23, 1992, pp. 2+.

Viani, Laura, "Algoma Steel's Cord Is Cut," *American Metal Market,* May 2, 1991, pp. 3+.

—Thomas M. Tucker
—updated by David E. Salamie

The Dress Barn, Inc.

30 Dunnigan Dr.
Suffern, New York 10901
U.S.A.
(914) 369-4500
Fax: (914) 369-4829
Web site: http://www.dress-barn.com

Public Company
Incorporated: 1962
Employees: 7,000
Sales: $554.8 million (1997)
Stock Exchanges: NASDAQ
Ticker Symbol: DBRN
SICs: 5621 Women's Clothing Stores

The Dress Barn, Inc. is the owner and operator of around 700 stores throughout the United States that offer specialty apparel for women at discounted prices. The chain caters to career-oriented women in the middle-range income bracket, Still operated by its original founders, The Dress Barn has store units positioned throughout 43 states under the names Dress Barn, Dress Barn Woman (specializing in women's plus-sized apparel), and Westport Woman.

The Early Years

The beginnings of The Dress Barn can be traced to 1962, when Elliot Jaffe was working as a merchandising manager for Macy's Department Store in Connecticut. He approached his wife, Roslyn, with an idea for a women's discounted apparel store, and the two decided to begin planning a test store. Knowing that they needed a reliable source of income to support their children, Jaffe retained his job at Macy's as he and Roslyn worked after-hours to open the first Dress Barn store later that year in Stamford, Connecticut.

According to Jaffe, the first store was marked by numerous retail errors, such as the lack of convenient parking nearby, the lack of dressing rooms for customers, and the existence of stairs that customers had to climb in order to access the store. Despite these shortfalls, however, the new store was an immediate success. In fact, it was so successful that less than a year after its grand opening, Jaffe was able to leave his job at Macy's to focus solely on the operations of their new enterprise. Meanwhile, Roslyn had begun planning the preparation and introduction of a second store nearby. In March 1963, the second store unit was opened, and The Dress Barn store chain was born.

Increased sales demands at the two Dress Barn stores soon prompted the Jaffes to begin searching for another store location and a new warehouse in the Stamford area. Previously, The Dress Barn's warehousing, receiving, and distribution operations had been done from the first store's basement, which could only be accessed using a narrow flight of stairs. After searching the area for a new location that would lend itself to more efficient operations, the Jaffes chose an old barn in Stamford, a choice well-suited to the company's name. This barn was renovated to become the company's third store as well as its distribution center.

In mid-1966, the company's holdings were incorporated as Dress Barn, Inc. Throughout the rest of the decade, the company experienced calculated and planned growth under the watchful eye of Jaffe and his expanding management team. They made sure that the business was not expanded too quickly, in order to maintain available capital and avoid sinking all resources into the company at once. Meanwhile, stores were added to the chain sporadically at a rate consistent with the company's increase in earnings.

Rapid Growth in the 1970s and 1980s

By the 1970s, after almost a decade of steady growth and expansion, The Dress Barn, Inc. was composed of almost 20 store units. The company was large enough to have gained the buying power to bring in products from big-name designers, such as Liz Claiborne, Calvin Klein, and Jones New York. Dress Barn continued to focus on selling this apparel to career-oriented women at discounted prices—usually 20 to 50 percent lower than those of its department store competition. Meanwhile, the chain continued to expand through the opening of new stores and the acquisition of other chains, such as Pants Corral and Off the Rax.

On May 3, 1983, Dress Barn went public, offering its stock for $23 per share. Half of the shares were sold in the public

---

Company Perspectives:

Dress Barn is America's leading discount retailer of women's business apparel and accessories. Founded in 1962, we now have over 700 locations nationwide. We offer our current, name brand apparel and 20–50% off department store prices. Most of our locations are located in or around major metro areas nationwide.

---

domain, while the other half were retained by management insiders. The money earned through the public offering gave Dress Barn added capital with which to expand and grow, and also provided added responsibility for the company to perform well for all of its new owners.

By July of the following year, Dress Barn owned and operated 100 stores throughout the United States, holdings which marked a 30 percent increase from the year before. By the end of 1984, the company possessed 157 stores, after the acquisition of 46 Off the Rax stores, eight stores from The Gap, and the addition of three new Dress Barn stores.

The year 1985 saw the company begin to earn national recognition, as *Forbes* magazine ranked Dress Barn number 42 out of the Top-200 Small Companies in the United States. The following year, *Business Week* listed Dress Barn as number 26 of the country's Top-200 Hot Growth Companies. By that point in time, the company was operating over 200 stores throughout the United States, with high concentrations in the Atlantic Northeast, the Midwest, and California.

Two years later, Dress Barn's store count had increased almost 50 percent to 307, spread throughout 26 states. The company was clearly achieving success in the discount women's apparel niche that it had created for itself, and decided to build on that by entering the market for plus-sized women's clothing. In 1989, Dress Barn Woman was introduced, targeting plus-sized women from the same basic demographic segment as the original Dress Barn stores. Most new Dress Barn Woman store units were placed in areas nearby existing Dress Barn stores, so as to capitalize on Dress Barn's name recognition factor.

The 1990s and Beyond

At the beginning of the decade, Dress Barn received further recognition of its achievements in the retail market when it was awarded the High-Performance Retailer Award from Management Horizons, a division of Price Waterhouse. The award was based on four consecutive years of performance highs for the company. Also in 1990, Dress Barn purchased JRL Consulting Corporation for $2.56 million.

The 1990s saw the company continue to enter new markets in the United States through the opening of new stores and the acquisition of existing chains. In 1993, Dress Barn added 21 new women's apparel stores when it purchased them from

Country Miss. At that point in time, the company was operating hundreds of Dress Barn and Dress Barn Woman stores, as well as numerous combination units.

Dress Barn, which had traditionally marketed its women's apparel at discounted prices, suffered a hit to its earnings potential in the early 1990s when many department stores began to introduce their own moderately priced private-label clothing lines. Dress Barn's sales advantage was diminished by the move, which was reflected by the company's annual profit margins. Another detriment to Dress Barn's sales potential was the fact that a few of its own suppliers, such as Jones Apparel Group, also moved into the discounted apparel market through the introduction of their own factory outlet stores.

Despite its hardships, however, Dress Barn continued to achieve increased sales figures each year in the first half of the 1990s. Its continued growth prompted the company to begin searching for a larger and more advanced headquarters and distribution location. In 1994, the company moved into a new facility in Suffern, New York. The state-of-the-art facility handled all distribution and warehousing needs, while also housing the company's executive offices. Also in 1994, Dress Barn issued its own credit card to the public, and soon thereafter over half a million cards were in circulation.

From 1995 through 1996 the company opened an impressive number of new stores, 136 in all. The chain eventually peaked at some 775 stores, but this number dropped to near 700 by the end of 1997 due to closures of poorly performing stores. Approaching the end of the century, Dress Barn was exploring new expansion ideas with the introduction of shoe and petite departments at its existing stores across the United States. The company was continuing its efforts to enter new markets and capitalize on consumers' desire for reasonably priced and yet fashionable apparel. Most new stores being introduced were combination Dress Barn/Dress Barn Woman stores, a decision which allowed the company to reach both target groups while using less space and capital. If past success was any indication of future growth potential, then Dress Barn appeared to enter the end of the decade well-positioned for further retail success.

Principal Subsidiaries

D.B.R., Inc.; JRL Consulting Corp.; D.B.X. Inc.

Further Reading

Brammer, Rhonda, ''Recovery in Store: Sizing Up Small Caps,'' *Barron's,* August 1, 1994, p. 19.
Coletti, Richard J., ''Spaghetti Straps: How a Top Niche Player in the Rag Trade Is Coping with the Campeau Crunch,'' *Financial World,* March 20, 1990, p. 56.
Dress Barn 35th Anniversary Video, Suffern, N.Y.: Dress Barn, Inc., 1997.
Reda, Susan, ''Dress Barn: Opens Doors in New Markets, New Formats,'' *Stores,* August 1992, p. 19.

—Laura E. Whiteley

Duckwall-ALCO Stores, Inc.

401 Cottage Street
Abilene, Kansas 67410
U.S.A.
(913) 263-3350
Fax: (913) 263-7531

Public Company
Incorporated: 1901 as The Racket Store
Employees: 4,850
Sales: $323.3 million (1998)
Stock Exchanges: NASDAQ
Ticker Symbol: DUCK
SICs: 5331 Variety Stores

A regional discount retailer, Duckwall-ALCO Stores, Inc. operates more than 200 stores in an 18-state region surrounding the central United States. Duckwall-ALCO's stores operate under two names, Duckwall and ALCO, but all of the company's retail outlets share the distinction of operating in small rural communities. Of the company's two formats, ALCO represents the dominant force. There were 152 ALCO stores in operation in 1998, each stocking roughly 35,000 items, including automotive supplies, candy, crafts, electronics, fabrics, furniture, hardware, jewelry, health and beauty aids, and housewares. The company's Duckwall variety stores, similar to the typical five-and-dime store popular during the first half of the 20th century, offer a more limited selection of merchandise. In 1998 there were 60 Duckwall stores in operation. Duckwall-ALCO's strategy focused on tapping consumer demand in small rural towns with populations lower than 5,000 and in markets comprising fewer than 16,000 residents. By adhering to this strategy, the company operated in communities frequently ignored by other discount retailers.

Early 20th-Century Origins

Duckwall-ALCO traced its roots to humble and rural beginnings, back to the first store opened by the company's entrepreneurial founder, A. L. Duckwall, Sr. Duckwall laid the foundation for an enterprise that would endure for more than a century when he spent $400 in 1901 to establish The Racket Store. A variety merchandise store, Duckwall's first retail creation "offered a little bit of everything," according to its owner, presenting the store's farmland customers with an array of goods from which they had rarely had the luxury to choose. This premise set the theme for subsequent stores established in the following decades. The generations of leadership that followed in Duckwall's wake continued to target rural communities deprived of the diversity of merchandise to which their urban counterparts had become accustomed. In the decades following the success of The Racket Store, a steady stream of variety stores were established in rural communities, each operating under the Duckwall banner. The concept, and the series of new stores that presented the concept to eager rural customers, proved to be an encouraging success, able to surmount the economic vagaries of the first half of the 20th century and adapt to the changing consumer tastes of the years. By the end of the 1960s, after six decades of tapping rural demand for a potpourri of goods, there were 100 Duckwall variety stores situated in the Midwest, positioned in rural towns with populations ranging between 2,000 and 10,000.

The late 1960s marked a signal turning point in the business established by A. L. Duckwall, Sr., a defining transition that was overseen by his son, A. L. Duckwall, Jr. By 1968 the company had opened its first ALCO discount store. Although the opening of the first discount-oriented store did not drastically alter the heart of the company's strategic philosophy of catering to rural customers, it did represent a decided shift toward a new merchandising strategy. The success of the first ALCO store heralded the birth of a new, stronger retail breed and sounded the death knell for Duckwall's variety store concept. During the seven decades separating the beginning of the 1970s and the era in which Duckwall had opened his first store, the dynamics of operating a retail business in a rural setting had changed considerably. The modern rural customer had become accustomed to a broad selection of merchandise as large national chains moved into smaller communities. Accordingly, price became the leverage point for any retail business hoping to succeed against much larger competition. Duckwall-ALCO, operating under its new corporate name, had changed with the times.

1980s Acquisitions

By the early 1980s the number of Duckwall variety stores operated by the company, which had peaked at 100 units ten years earlier, had been winnowed down to 34. In their stead, a slew of ALCO discount stores had emerged, stores that by this point bore the burden of driving the company's financial growth. Of the roughly $200 million Duckwall-ALCO was collecting in sales during the early 1980s, the 34 Duckwall variety stores contributed a mere $10 million. A changing of the guard had taken place at the company's Abilene, Kansas, headquarters, and all hopes were pinned to the vitality of the ALCO chain. For those executives who awaited strident financial growth, however, the early 1980s were remembered as a tortuous time.

During the early 1980s Duckwall-ALCO was best known as a rurally oriented retail chain based in the birthplace of President Dwight D. Eisenhower. It was also known—and quickly disregarded by those on Wall Street—as a company suffering from anemic financial performance. In 1981, for instance, sales increased a paltry one percent, as profits slid precipitously by 24 percent. As one analyst noted at the time, in reference to Duckwall-ALCO's regard among investors, ''It was an ignored stock for a long, long time.'' Caught in the grip of pernicious economic recession, Duckwall-ALCO executives were grappling to find a solution and end the trauma. Their salvation was found through an important acquisition, completed just as the company's financial standing was becoming precarious.

In May 1983, in a deal brokered with a handshake in February, Duckwall-ALCO acquired Sterling Stores Co. Inc., the parent company of a 48-store discount chain based in Little Rock, Arkansas, that operated under the name Magic Mart. Its inclusion within Duckwall-ALCO's fold was the remedy for which company executives were searching, quickly effecting an about-turn in Duckwall-ALCO's financial performance. The Magic Mart chain, which generated $111.6 million in revenues in 1982, was credited for the robust increase in Duckwall-ALCO's financial totals, arresting what threatened to be a damaging slide and restoring to its new owner the solid financial state it historically had enjoyed. Less than two years after watching profits sink 24 percent, Duckwall-ALCO's stock price more than tripled. In 1983 sales swelled to $317 million, up nearly 50 percent from the previous year's total. The company's profits accomplished an even more dramatic leap, nearly doubling to $8.6 million. By all measures, the company once again stood as a solid performer, piquing the interest of Wall Street and earning the respect of other similarly sized retailers competing for the business of rural consumers.

Buoyed by the resurgence realized from the Sterling/Magic Mart acquisition, Duckwall-ALCO made another move on the acquisition front a short time later. In January 1984 the company purchased four discount stores in Wichita, Kansas, operating under the David's banner. One year later Duckwall-ALCO completed another acquisition, acquiring nine stores from the Illinois-based Hornsby chain. The acquisitions were indicative of the optimism pervading Duckwall-ALCO's corporate offices, the same optimism that prompted a management-led leveraged buyout of the company in 1985. A. L. Duckwall, Jr., the last member of the founding family to head the business, had decided to retire at roughly the same time an investment firm,

E.F. Hutton LBO, approached Duckwall-ALCO's president, Robert Soelter, about initiating the buyout. Planning to include as many as 57 ALCO managers in the buyout group, Soelter pushed ahead with the deal, completing the purchase of the company in September 1985. At this point there were 127 ALCO discount department stores in operation in 14 states, complemented by 33 Duckwall variety stores operating in a four-state territory. The strength of the company resided in its ALCO units, which served as one-stop-shopping destinations situated in markets too small to support specialty stores.

Troubles in the Late 1980s

Slightly less than three years after the management-led buyout, Soelter retired, paving the way for the promotion of Glen Shank, a Duckwall-ALCO employee since 1973 and merchandising vice-president for the previous eight years. To Shank, who would guide the company through the 1990s, fell the unenviable responsibility of announcing Duckwall-ALCO's most devastating news in its nearly 90-year history. In May 1989 Duckwall-ALCO, the promising and vibrant discount retailer of the early and mid-1980s, filed for Chapter 11 protection, a last-ditch effort to stave off deleterious financial losses. Duckwall-ALCO's darkest hour had not arrived suddenly. Between 1986 and early 1989 the company had closed 20 stores, as poor profit performance at a number of the stores forced closures. By 1989 the piecemeal elimination of unprofitable stores was no longer an option. The financial losses racked up by dozens of stores had become too severe. Wholesale changes were desperately needed, and Shank, who barely had time to settle into his new position at Duckwall-ALCO, was the central figure responsible for devising what those sweeping changes needed to be.

The root of the problem, ironically, was the source of Duckwall-ALCO's strident growth during the early and mid-1980s. The three acquisitions the company had completed between May 1983 and January 1985 had done much to revitalize Duckwall-ALCO's financial health, but the absorption of the acquired stores had also created serious problems. Magic Mart, the greatest savior of the three acquisitions, also ranked as the biggest culprit, bringing the company in close competition with giant national discount chains such as Arkansas-based Wal-Mart. Prior to the acquisition of the Magic Mart chain, Duckwall-ALCO had competed directly against Wal-Mart in six of its markets; after the acquisition, Duckwall-ALCO was positioned in close proximity to Wal-Mart in 40 new markets. The results were disastrous. Duckwall-ALCO could not compete effectively against the far more financially powerful Wal-Mart, as consumers flocked to the larger stores operated by the behemoth Arkansas retailer.

By the time the company filed for Chapter 11, it had identified 52 of its worst-performing stores, units that registered $10 million in losses in 1988 alone. The stores were scattered throughout a ten-state territory and included many of the units acquired from Magic Mart, David's, and Hornsby. On May 15, 1989, all 52 of the stores were closed, stripping the company of one-third of its store count. Next began the arduous task of developing a reorganization plan, as Shank labored to find a solution that would appease creditors and enable Duckwall-ALCO to emerge from under the protective umbrella of Chapter

11. For two years the reorganization process dragged on until at last Duckwall-ALCO received approval to begin anew in 1991.

The road back to a healthy and promising future was a difficult course to travel, and it did not progress quickly. After Chapter 11, it took roughly two years before company officials could point to anything that suggested a return to consistent prosperity. The first solid sign arrived in 1993, when Duckwall-ALCO posted a heartening $2.3 million in earnings. The next positive development occurred in the fall of 1994, when the company completed a successful initial public offering of stock. (Throughout its history the company had vacillated between public and private ownership.) With the proceeds gained from the company's stock offering, it entered 1995 with the best opportunity it had seen in years for a full revival. Optimism had returned to the company's headquarters in Abilene.

As proof of the bright outlook Duckwall-ALCO officials embraced, the company announced it would open 20 stores a year as it entered 1995. Planning to open three ALCO discount stores for every two Duckwall variety stores it opened, the company was employing the strategy it had devised to compete against larger discounters and to protect itself from the profit erosion that had signaled its near collapse in 1989. Duckwall-ALCO executives resolved to establish new stores in the smallest of rural communities, reducing its maximum population base for a store to fewer than 16,000 residents in a particular market and fewer than 5,000 residents in a targeted town. The plan placed a new emphasis on the once-forsaken Duckwall format. Further, it was a preemptive expansion strategy predicated on avoiding competition rather than meeting other regional discounters head on. By opening a store in a location that met the company's population criteria, Duckwall-ALCO established a presence that discouraged other, similarly sized discount retailers from encroachment and positioned it in markets largely ignored by heavyweights such as Wal-Mart. The operating strategy developed by A. L. Duckwall, Sr., in 1901 had been fine-tuned for the 1990s.

To the relief of anxious Duckwall-ALCO executives, the strategy worked. Financial health returned to the company, with a consistency and strength that suggested a complete turnaround from the troubled late 1980s and early 1990s. Moreover, optimistic expectations for the future were buttressed by the identification of more than 100 locations that were "understored" in markets matching the company's demographic criteria. Accordingly, expansion pushed ahead as the company moved into the late 1990s and neared its centennial.

In September 1996 Duckwall-ALCO acquired 14 retail locations from New Castle, Indiana-based Val Corp., which added stores located in eastern Indiana and western Ohio. The acquired stores were remodeled as ALCO units and reopened in early 1997, accelerating the company's previously announced expansion pace. In November 1997 Duckwall-ALCO acquired 18 stores located in Texas and New Mexico from Perry Brothers, Inc., which debuted as Duckwall units in early 1998. On this note, with the pace of expansion exceeding expectations and the company's financial growth pointing to a healthy enterprise, Duckwall-ALCO prepared for the century ahead and the coming celebration of its 100th year of business. As it had been since 1901, Duckwall-ALCO was firmly rooted in the rural communities of America.

Principal Subsidiaries

SPD Truck Line, Inc.

Further Reading

Diennor, Richard, "Duckwall Gets OK on Disclosure," *Daily News Record,* April 10, 1991, p. 11.
"Duckwall-ALCO Inks Deal to Acquire 14 Locations," *Daily News Record,* September 19, 1996, p. 10.
"Duckwall-ALCO Stores, Inc. Continues Aggressive Expansion Through New Store Openings," *Business Wire,* March 12, 1998, p. 1.
Gilman, Hank, "Duckwall-ALCO: Gold in Those Small-Town Hills," *Chain Store Age—General Merchandise Edition,* March 1984, p. 28.
Kelly, Mary Ellen, "ALCO Files for Chapter 11; To Close 52 Units in 10 States," *Discount Store News,* May 22, 1989, p. 2.
——, "ALCO Names Shank Prez; Fortifies Merchandising Staff," *Discount Store News,* July 4, 1988, p. 3.
Mammarella, James, "Duckwall-ALCO Bounces Back," *Discount Store News,* February 20, 1995, p. 23.
"New Stores Push Up Sales, Profits; Duckwall-ALCO," *Chain Store Age–-General Merchandise Edition,* June 1984, p. 96.
"Strong Duckwall-ALCO Growth Prompts $150M Buyout Bid," *Discount Store News,* February 4, 1985.

—Jeffrey L. Covell

Eljer

Eljer Industries, Inc.

17120 Dallas Parkway
Dallas, Texas 75248
U.S.A.
(972) 560-2000
Fax: (972) 407-2696

Wholly Owned Subsidiary of Zurn Industries, Inc.
Founded: 1904
Employees: 3,700
Sales: $397.4 million (1996)
SICs: 3432 Plumbing Fittings & Brass Goods; 3431
    Enameled Iron & Metal Sanitary Ware; 3585
    Refrigeration & Heating Equipment; 3429 Hardware,
    Not Elsewhere Classified

Eljer Industries, Inc. is a leading manufacturer of plumbing and heating, ventilating, and air conditioning (HVAC) products to wholesale, retail, commercial, and institutional markets. Eljer services residential and commercial construction and repair and remodeling markets in particular. Specifically, Eljer makes and sells plumbing and HVAC products in the United States and Canada and HVAC products in Europe. The company is one of North America's three leading suppliers of bath and kitchen fixtures, faucets, registers, grills, and venting systems and one of Europe's leading manufacturers of prefabricated chimneys and venting systems. For the most part, Eljer markets its products through wholesale distribution channels. In North America, it also markets to building product retailers. In January 1997 Eljer was acquired by Dallas, Texas-based Zurn Industries, Inc. A further consolidation occurred in June 1998, when U.S. Industries, Inc. and Zurn agreed to merge. It was expected that the Eljer business and name would continue to thrive under the new ownership.

The Origin and Growth of Eljer, 1900s–90s

Although little information is available for the early years of the company's history, it is known that Eljer was originally the name of a plumbing supply manufacturer that started operations in 1904. In 1925 the company expanded into the HVAC products business. The business manufactured and sold plumbing fixtures for residential and commercial applications. Some of its products have come to include vitreous china toilets, enameled cast-iron tubs, whirlpools, and vitreous china and enameled cast-iron lavatories. The Eljer name is the company's trademark for cast-iron and vitreous china fixtures. Eljer has also come to be known for its manufacture of bathroom and kitchen fixtures for use in new construction or remodeling.

Over the years, Eljer's product line, colors, and styles changed to reflect design trends and demands of consumers. In the mid-1990s the company introduced three new ceramic pedestal lavatories—the Savannah, the Senora, and the Darrow—each with a unique style to fit the design of different bathrooms. Introduced about the same time, Eljer's Hi-Low Undermount cast-iron kitchen sink was designed to be installed under kitchen countertops.

Similarly, Eljer's commercial products underwent changes through the years. For example, the company redesigned its lavatories to be compliant with the Americans With Disabilities Act (ADA). It also introduced products to reflect the changing lifestyles of consumers. With the growth of daycare centers and preschools, the company introduced a two-piece toilet especially for youngsters. Just ten inches from floor to rim, Eljer's Kindergarten model made using a commode safer for small children to use, which contributed to this learner's model being very attractive to daycare institutions.

Despite its efforts to offer new and unique products, in 1993 Eljer was sued by Kohler, its major competitor, for patent infringement. Kohler accused Eljer of "pirating" its designs for toilets, lavatories, and kitchen and bar sinks, among other products. The competitor also cited Eljer for copying its marketing materials. The products in question represented only a small percentage of Eljer's sales and were not recent releases to the marketplace, which prompted Eljer to wonder at the motives behind the lawsuit. "Eljer is investigating whether this aggressive action is an attempt by Kohler to interface with our revitalization as a supplier of choice in this very competitive industry which Kohler dominates," Scott G. Arbuckle, Eljer Industries'

Company Perspectives:

Eljer Industries is a company with quality building products and well-trained, dedicated people who serve our customers' needs, equipped with effective manufacturing facilities that ensure our company remains competitive—both in value and in product for changing markets. Eljer is noted for its innovation with 1.6 gallon toilets, suites designed to meet the interior designer's needs, and an expanded gas fireplace product line, innovative new faucets, and in particular, in Europe, a wide range of chimney and venting products to meet the needs of different industries' markets and the design standards of each country. With this product mix, combined with cost-effective manufacturing and strong sales and marketing, Eljer is a leader with the total capability needed to make a difference in the marketplace.

president and chief executive officer, told *Contractor* magazine in 1993.

Technological Improvements

In 1995 the company spent $14 million in capital improvements to its North American plants. With one of the industry's best fill rates, Eljer pursued innovations to increase production and reduce costs at its plants. The foundry for manufacturing enameled cast-iron products—located in Salem, Ohio—received some of the new technology. The addition of robotic enameling stations there allowed Eljer to utilize a more effective process for manufacturing sinks, lavatories, and tubs. Robotics not only proved more efficient, but produced products with smoother, more uniform finishes. Eljer's 477,000-square-foot plant in Tupelo, Mississippi, also benefited from technological improvements. The company installed a cutting-edge pressure cast system in the plant for the manufacture of china products. Eljer also enhanced the material handling system and kilns at the facility, resulting in higher-quality products produced more quickly with reduced energy costs.

U.S. Brass

Besides manufacturing and marketing its own products, Eljer also marketed faucets manufactured by U.S. Brass. U.S. Brass became a plumbing company in 1962. The company manufactured and marketed faucets, plumbing supplies, connectors, and flexible plumbing systems for residential and commercial construction, remodeling, and do-it-yourselfers. Trademarks of the company included Valley, Valley Plus, Eastman, and Qest, and each product line offered its specific consumers a range of items. Valley and Valley Plus brands, for example, offered residential or commercial construction buyers modestly priced as well as luxury bathroom and kitchen faucets. Valley's novel Leisure Personal Shower, on the other hand, was designed for the remodeling market since the shower installed to an existing shower or bath-and-shower faucet. Its adjustable slide bar allowed the height of sprayer to be adjusted to the size of bather, making the shower equipment more convenient and safer for children, the physically challenged, and the odd-sized

individual. Another innovative product offered through the commercial construction market, Valley's Regulator, even protected bathers and showers from scalding water. In addition to its own products, U.S. Brass also manufactured private label faucets for large retailers.

U.S. Brass's plumbing supplies—supply tubes, valves, fittings, air gaps, and flexible gas and water connectors—were manufactured under the Eastman trademark. U.S. Brass's plumbing systems were designed under the Qest trade name. Known for their easy installation, tolerance of cold, and lower cost, Qest systems were installed by builders and plumbing contractors extensively from 1975 through 1990. In particular, Qest systems were used in residential site-built installations from 1979 through 1986. Qest products were made with polybutylene pipe and metal connective fittings, which made the system the subject of serious litigation in the early 1990s. Homeowners initiated a class action suit based on the grounds that the plumbing system did not tolerate chlorine well and, thus, leaked profusely, causing significant property damage. U.S. Brass discontinued the Qest polybutylene plumbing system in 1995 when Shell Chemical, its supplier of polybutylene, stopped selling the resin for plumbing applications. In 1996, U.S. Brass introduced QestPEX plumbing systems that used pipe extruded from cross-linked polyethylene resin instead of polybutylene.

This litigation—which began shortly after legal proceedings that ended with a California state court ordering U.S. Brass to pay $3.6 million in damages because of a defective plumbing device in 1993—prompted U.S. Brass to file for reorganization under Chapter 11 of the Federal Bankruptcy Code in 1994. Shell Chemical and Hoechst Celanese, as the developers of raw material for polybutylene systems, offered a $950 million settlement to repair plumbing systems and pay for property damage to those consumers adversely affected by polybutylene plumbing systems. As the largest manufacturer of these systems, U.S. Brass agreed to contribute to the settlement as well. (A resolution of the U.S. Brass bankruptcy was completed in fiscal 1998, under Zurn ownership.)

To accommodate the production of the QestPEX line, U.S. Brass added production capacity to its plants. The Abilene, Texas, manufacturing facility—where faucets were made—enhanced its operating systems and invested in capital to ensure sufficient production capacity for QestPEX products.

Other North American Divisions

Selkirk Mesbestos and Dry Manufacturing, two other divisions of Eljer, were considered the North American leaders in registers, grilles, and venting systems. Each division made and sold HVAC products—notably registers, grilles, venting systems, prefabricated chimneys, air diffusers, and fireplaces—under the brand names of Metalbestos, Airmate, P.S. Chimney, and Sel-Vent. Their venting systems in residential, commercial, and industrial construction provided for venting discharges from furnaces, appliances, boilers, or diesel engines. The companies' plants in Winters and Coleman, Texas, manufactured registers, grilles, fireplaces, diffusers, and gas vents, while plants in Logan, Ohio, and Nampa, Idaho, made gas vents and chimney systems.

Selkirk/Dry, based in Canada, manufactured products—sold in the United States as Airmate and Selaire brands—for new residential and commercial construction. The company marketed these products in Canada under the Lloydaire trade name and in the retail market under the Showcase trademark. Selkirk/Dry also made specialty products such as gas and woodburning fireplaces. The company's plant in Brockville, Ontario, Canada, manufactured fireplaces and chimney systems, and the plant in Mississauga, Ontario, Canada, produced registers and grilles.

International Operations

Eljer began its European operations in 1964. With subsidiaries in the United Kingdom and Germany, Selkirk Europe made and sold prefabricated chimneys and venting systems. The company provided commercial, industrial, and residential markets with products for new construction, repair and replacement, and energy conversion. The company ranked as a market leader in energy conversion in Europe—especially in Eastern Europe—as it converted to natural gas. Projections suggested this as a strong market for the future. The company's European brands included Selkirk, Nova, Supra, and Europa trademarks. Selkirk Europe maintained plants in Barnstaple, England, and in Mullicott Cross, England, for the manufacture of gas vents, chimney systems, and venting and specialty products. Selkirk Europe also sold beyond Europe. According to the company's 1996 annual report, "Eljer Industries recognizes the acceleration and integration of the global economies and continues to implement its strategies to grow on a worldwide basis. Our markets include not only North America, but also Europe, South America, and the Far East. . . . Eljer sees growth opportunities in South America and continues to grow its presence in the Pacific Rim countries, designing products to fit this market's needs. Our presence has also increased in the Middle East, where the rebuilding process continues to bring significant opportunities for specifying our product. Selkirk Europe's new product introductions have enhanced its penetration of the European markets. The result has been significant improvement in the eastern and southern European markets."

Another subsidiary with international scope, Industrias Eljer de Mexico, S.A. de C.V., was formed under Mexican laws in Ojinaga, Chihuahua, Mexico, in 1995. This subsidiary maintained responsibilities for assembly and packaging operations.

Spinoffs and Mergers, 1980s–90s

Household International acquired the enterprises that comprise Eljer Industries during the 1980s. On January 26, 1989, Eljer Industries incorporated itself in Delaware as a wholly owned subsidiary of Household International. On April 14 of that year, all outstanding shares of Eljer common stock were distributed to holders of Household International's common stock, and Eljer became a publicly held corporation. In 1993 Eljer lost a fraud and misrepresentation case to a former partner of Household. Arbitration in that case called for Eljer to pay $12.2 million to the company. Eljer initiated plans to spin off from Household two years later.

Late in 1996 Eljer announced its plans to merge with Zurn Industries, Inc. All outstanding shares of Eljer common stock were sold at $24 per share. Like Eljer, Zurn manufactured and marketed plumbing products, in addition to providing water resource construction services and fire protection systems. Zurn was attracted to Eljer as it sought to expand its plumbing products business. The merger was expected to establish a new forerunner in the plumbing products and HVAC markets.

Then in June 1998, it was announced that U.S. Industries, formerly part of Hanson PLC, would merge with Zurn in an all-stock transaction. At the time, Zurn had annualized sales of $634 million, while U.S. Industries—whose other holdings included Ertl toys, Jacuzzi, EJ Footwear, and Lighting Corporation of America—had posted revenues of $2.3 billion. A few weeks prior to the announcement, Zurn reported $28.1 million in net income for the fiscal year ended March 31, 1998, a 28 percent increase over 1997. A significant percentage of the increase was attributed to the Eljer business and its "operating synergies" with Zurn. Presumably, this strong alliance would continue under the guidance of U.S. Industries.

Principal Subsidiaries

Eljer Plumbingware; U.S. Brass; Selkirk Metalbestos and Dry Manufacturing; Selkirk/Dry (Canada); Selkirk Europe (U.K.); Eljer de Mexico, S.A. de C.V.

Further Reading

"Eljer Foundry Lowers Belt Splicing Costs," *Foundry Management & Technology,* January 1996, p. F3.

"Eljer Industries Reports Court Ruling in U.S. Brass Bankruptcy," *Business Wire,* May 17, 1995, p. 5171151.

"Eljer Industries Reports It Is Participant in Proposed Polybutylene Settlement—Eljer Agreement Subject to Confirmation of Reorganization Plan Providing Complete Relief to Eljer and U.S. Brass Unit," *Business Wire,* November 9, 1995, p. 11091151.

"Eljer Industries Reports Strike at Salem, Ohio, Plant," *Business Wire,* March 6, 1996, p. 3061271.

"Eljer Provides Update on U.S. Brass Bankruptcy," *Business Wire,* April 15, 1996, p. 4151231.

"Eljer Reports on U.S. Brass Bankruptcy; Receives Favorable Ruling in Direct Claims Case; Reports Ruling in Suit Against Household International," *Business Wire,* June 26, 1995, p.6261087.

"Kohler Sues Eljer; Says Styles, Colors, Marketing Copied," *Contractor,* May 1993, p. 63.

"Patent Suit Adds to Eljer's Legal Problems," *Chilton's Hardware Age,* June 1993, p. 32.

Schmitt, Richard B., and Carlos Tejada, "Judge Approves $950 Million Settlement of Suit over Polybutylene Plumbing," *Wall Street Journal* (eastern edition), November 10, 1995, p. A4.

"United States Brass Corporation Files Third Amended Plan of Reorganization," *Business Wire,* December 2, 1996, p. 12021076.

"U.S. Industries and Zurn Industries Complete Merger," Dallas, Zurn Industries, Inc., June 11, 1998.

"Zurn Industries, Inc., to Buy Eljer Industries, Inc.," *Business Wire,* December 16, 1996, p. 12161093.

"Zurn Reports Strong Operating Performance for Fourth Quarter and 1998 Fiscal Year," Dallas, Zurn Industries, Inc. May 27, 1998.

—Charity Anne Dorgan

Essence Communications, Inc.

1500 Broadway
New York, New York 10036
U.S.A.
(212) 642-0600
(800) ESSENCE (377-3623)
Fax: (212) 921-5173
Web site: http://www.essence.com

Private Company
Incorporated: 1969 as Hollingsworth Group
Employees: 150
Sales: $92.8 million (1996)
SICs: 2721 Periodicals; 2741 Miscellaneous Publishing;
7999 Amusement & Recreational Services, Not
Elsewhere Classified

Essence Communications, Inc. is the publisher of *Essence,* a magazine catering to the contemporary African-American woman that, in 1997, was reaching an estimated five million readers each month, 30 percent of them male. The company also publishes two other magazines and a mail-order catalogue and has an entertainment division hosting an annual televised award ceremony and four-day music festival in New Orleans.

A Voice for Black Women: 1969–85

Essence Communications grew out of a conference for aspiring African-American entrepreneurs attended by, among others, Edward Lewis, a First National City Bank executive trainee, and Clarence O. Smith, a Prudential insurance salesman. The company that would become Essence was founded in 1969 as the Hollingsworth Group by Lewis, Smith, Cecil Hollingsworth, a graphics consultant, and Jonathan Blount, an advertising salesman, in order to publish the first general-interest magazine aimed at African-American women. Blount was the original publisher; Gordon Parks, a noted photographer and writer and later a filmmaker, was the editorial director.

"It was really Nixon and his talk about black enterprise that helped us get started," Lewis later said, recalling the need felt for action following the urban riots in the wake of the assassination of Martin Luther King, Jr. "Had it not been for a minority bank here in New York City, Freedom National Bank, which lent us $13,000, we may not be here now," Lewis added in 1995. Other money, he said, came from "family, friends, credit cards." The lion's share of funds, however, came from First National City Bank, Chase Manhattan Bank, and several minority venture-capital concerns, which provided a total of $130,000 in start-up money.

Several months later, the initial investors and new ones, including Bancap Inc. and Equitable life Assurance Society of the U.S., invested about $1.87 million, mostly in loans, to get *Essence* up and running. Playboy Enterprises Inc. later added $250,000. The first issue of the monthly magazine appeared in 1970, featuring a cover photo of a female model with her hair styled in an Afro as well as a promise to "delight and to celebrate the beauty, pride, strength, and uniqueness of all Black women." There were only 13 pages of advertising out of a total of about 100 pages in the first issue of *Essence.* About 50,000 copies were sold at 60 cents apiece from a press run of 150,000 to 175,000. The second and third issues each had only five pages of advertising.

In the first four years, Hollingsworth, Blount, and Parks all left the enterprise—renamed Essence Communications—because of differing views, leaving Lewis as chairman and publisher and Smith as president. The other founders filed suit in 1977, initiating a three-year-long attempt to take over the company that nearly bankrupted it and ended only after an investor agreed to buy out Hollingsworth. This struggle cost the company much of the $2 million it had borrowed and which it was unable to pay back until 1985. Moreover, Smith later acknowledged, "We had to learn about the business of magazines; we didn't know anything."

Editorially, the fledgling enterprise also was in disarray. During its first year three editors-in-chief came and went in rapid order. "One of the greatest hurdles back in the 1970s," Smith later conceded, "was the lack of professional black magazine talent. Most of the people we had to hire had little experience in the jobs for which they were hired.'' In 1971, however, Marcia Ann Gillespie began a successful nine-year tenure as editor-in-chief.

Fashion, beauty, food, health, childcare, and other staples of women's service magazines were covered from a distinctly African-American perspective. *Essence* offered career advice before some other women's publications took up the subject. The magazine also extended its reach to such topics as the criminal-justice system and political crimes. Another controversial stance was the magazine's condemnation, in its first issue, of men who ''talk black and sleep white.'' ''Politics, war, religion, sex, you name it, *Essence* talked about it,'' Gillespie later recalled, adding, ''In retrospective, I think we used too heavy a hand.''

Essence also offered its readers original fiction by such black writers as Maya Angelou, Amiri Baraka, Nikki Giovanni, Toni Morrison, Gloria Naylor, Ishmael Reed, Ntozake Shange, and Alice Walker. Their frankness in language and subject matter inspired some angry letters and threats of canceled subscriptions, but the editorial policy remained, ''If the word fits, use it.''

Susan L. Taylor, who joined the magazine in its first year as the part-time beauty editor and later became fashion editor as well, had the job of creating layouts from a uniquely African-American perspective, without regard to ''white standards'' of beauty. She made a point of using some models who had strongly African features, displaying, as she said, the ''whole range of black beauty—from ebony to ivory.'' Moreover, some of *Essence*'s models exceeded the fashion industry's weight standards, and the clothing they wore was affordable as well as attractive.

After becoming editor-in-chief in 1981, Taylor reached out to male readers by introducing an annual issue on men and a monthly column by men titled ''Say, Brother.'' In addition to editing the magazine and writing a monthly column, Taylor also, in 1983, became host and executive producer of a half-hour television program that eventually was syndicated to 60 American television markets as well as several Caribbean and African countries. This program, which featured celebrity guests and discussions about black culture and social issues, was the first nationally syndicated African-American magazine program on television and ran for five years.

During speaking engagements at colleges, churches, and seminars, as well as in her column, Taylor conveyed an inspirational message. ''The mission of *Essence*,'' Taylor told a *New York Times* reporter in 1995, ''is to inspire, inform, and uplift black women, to help our sisters move their lives forward so that they can spread the word and thereby hopefully uplift our race.'' In the office, Taylor put her philosophy into practice by allowing most editorial decisions to be made collectively through a participatory process in which each staff member was heard. Maya Angelou told a *New York Times* reporter in 1995, ''Her spirituality deepens the mission of the magazine. . . . I don't know any nonreligious magazine that addresses spiritual health as *Essence* does.''

Broadening Its Base: 1985–97

By 1975 *Essence* had a circulation of 450,000. Annual advertising pages increased from 455 in 1974 to 884 in 1979, when circulation reached about 600,000. The magazine became profitable during 1975–76 and its parent company saw profits around 1980, according to Lewis. When rival publisher John M. Johnson (founder of *Ebony* and other magazines) took a 20 percent stake in Essence Communications in 1985, Lewis and Smith were faced with having to match his price in buying stock from other selling investors in order to assure themselves majority control of the enterprise. Another investor, Pioneer Capital Corp., raised its interest to 20 percent at that time.

Essence Communications, which had sales of nearly $25 million in 1985 (compared to $14 million in 1980), invested in the company that purchased Buffalo television station WKBW that year, making it the largest black-owned television station in the nation. By 1984 Essence Communications was also producing a mail-order catalogue in collaboration with Hanover House, Inc. The catalogue featured moderately priced apparel, other soft goods, jewelry, and art objects. The company also created a licensing division in 1984, lending the Essence name to intimate apparel, eyeglasses, hosiery, and a collection of sewing patterns by Butterick Co. In 1987 Essence Communications purchased part of Amistad Press, a black-owned publisher.

Advertising support remained a major challenge to the prosperity of *Essence*. To make a sales pitch, the magazine's representatives had to persuade prospective space buyers to overlook the low household income of the typical reader. ''A $20,000 household income doesn't stop a black woman from spending $40 on a fragrance,'' Smith insisted. Avon, a longtime advertiser, confirmed that black women spent relatively more for beauty products than white women, yet for most cosmetic companies, Smith told the *Wall Street Journal*, ''it's as if black women don't count as consumers.''

Some companies also were reluctant to commit time and money to create advertising for a publication like *Essence*, which preferred that models used in its ads be black. Certain advertising executives privately admitted that they were afraid a product identified with black consumers would do poorly among white consumers. One company that proved ready to engage African-American models, however, was Estée Lauder. When that company began advertising in the magazine for the first time in 1993, some of its ads were tailored for the magazine and cited the benefits of the product for women of color. A marketing executive for Estée Lauder said in 1995 that when one of her company's products was advertised in *Essence* ''we can really see the results because we see consumers with a page of the magazine coming in to ask for it.''

By 1990 *Essence* was exploring some creative endeavors to raise its advertising base. In what was said to be the first program of its kind among minority publications, thousands of readers were to sit in focus groups and provide detailed survey results to the magazine's clients. The research results were expected to validate the publication's argument that advertisers would do better in the $250 billion black consumer market with specially created and positioned advertising. And readers of *Essence*'s 20th anniversary issue were subjected to the publication's first commercial use of ink-jet messaging, in which Coca-Cola sent personalized messages detailing a sweepstakes promotion to all readers. Subscribers were singled out by name, while newsstand copies were labeled "Dear *Essence* Reader."

Essence also was raising its profile in the mid-1990s by hosting free mall tours around the country, offering information, sample products supplied by co-sponsoring advertisers, and discussions about fitness, health, beauty, and spirituality. Most of these events were attended by Taylor.

In 1992, Essence Communications acquired *Income Opportunities,* a magazine with a circulation of 400,000 aimed at people who had been let go from their jobs and wanted to start their own businesses. The company's revenues reached $77 million in 1994, the year the circulation of *Essence* passed one million. Also by 1994 a subsidiary, Essence Television Productions, Inc., was producing an annual prime-network special hosted by Taylor; the Essence Awards honored achievements of African-Americans.

In 1995 the parent company, along with Alegre Enterprises, launched *Latina,* a magazine aimed at Hispanic women 18 to 45 years old. Also that year, *Essence* joined with Golden Books to establish a line of children's books featuring characters created by African-American authors and illustrators. The first dozen appeared in a variety of formats, among them hardcover storybooks, paperback activity books, Golden Naptime Tales, and Golden Super Shape Books.

Essence celebrated its 25th anniversary in 1995 with a 300-page May issue featuring Oprah Winfrey on the cover. The company capped its anniversary party with a three-day music festival in New Orleans, over the Fourth of July weekend, that was described by *USA Today* as the largest gathering of black performers ever. This event—which included appearances by such entertainers as Bill Cosby, Aretha Franklin, Luther Vandross, Patti LaBelle, and Boyz II Men and was attended by more than 150,000 people—contributed an estimated $75 million to the city's tourist industry. As part of the admission price, visitors also had the opportunity to attend empowerment seminars during the day.

Plans to make the Essence Music Festival an annual event in New Orleans almost foundered when Louisiana Governor Mike Foster issued an executive order the following year banning affirmative action in state government (although the state had no such program). Essence was planning to pull out in protest until Foster agreed to issue a new executive order announcing a program to help disadvantaged businesses, under which the state could consider race and gender as criteria for awarding contracts and other benefits. By 1997 the annual festival, being held in the Louisiana Superdome, had expanded to four days.

Essence appeared in 1997 with a comprehensive redesign that added several sections and increased beauty, fashion, and home coverage; introduced a flat-spine binding for more advertiser inserts and coupons; and made four-color advertisements available throughout the magazine. The newsstand price rose from $2.50 to $2.75. Also that year, Essence Communications and Time Inc. were considering a joint venture to produce a black lifestyle magazine to be called *Savoy.*

Principal Subsidiaries

Essence Television Productions, Inc.

Further Reading

Agins, Teri, and Udayan Gupta, "Black Women Enjoy Vogue, But Essence Is a Magazine for Them," *Wall Street Journal,* December 11, 1986, pp. 1, 20.

Alonzo, Vincent, "Soul Search," *Incentive,* December 1995, pp. 22–26.

"Black Venture," *Time,* May 4, 1970, pp. 79–80.

Britt, Donna, "Behind the Spirit of Essence," *Washington Post,* May 5, 1990, pp. G1, G10.

"Broadcasting Lures Founder of Essence," *New York Times,* August 13, 1985, p. D2.

Carmody, Deirdre, "An Enduring Voice for Black Women," *New York Times,* January 23, 1995, pp. D1, D8.

Chambers, Veronica, "The Essence of *Essence,*" *New York Times Magazine,* June 18, 1995, pp. 24–27.

Donahue, Deirdre, "A Magazine Showcase for Sisterhood," *USA Today,* April 2, 1990, pp. 1D-2D.

Dougherty, Philip H., "Essence Is Continuing to Gain," *New York Times,* April 11, 1973, p. 52.

Dullea, Georgia, "Essence Marks 15 Years of Serving Black Women," *New York Times,* April 5, 1985, p. B6.

George, Lynell, "In Touch, in Style," *Los Angeles Times,* May 8, 1995, pp. E1, E4.

Masterson, John, "*Essence* Signs on 9,157 Product Experts," *Folio,* November 1, 1990.

"Meaningful Images," *Newsweek,* May 11, 1970, p. 74.

Pogebrin, Robin, "Success and the Black Magazine," *New York Times,* October 25, 1997, pp. D1, D3.

Verton, Stewart, "Straight Talking Defused Crisis," *New Orleans Times-Picayune,* February 18, 1996, pp. A1 +.

Willen, Janet L., "Not for Women Only," *Nation's Business,* September 1994, p. 16.

—Robert Halasz

FARAH®

Farah Incorporated

8889 Gateway West
El Paso, Texas 79925-6584
U.S.A.
(915) 496-7000
Fax: (915) 496-7188
Web site: http://www.savane.com

Public Company
Incorporated: 1947 as Farah Manufacturing Co., Inc.
Employees: 3,950
Sales: $273.7 million (1997)
Stock Exchanges: New York
Ticker Symbol: FRA
SICs: 2321 Men's & Boys' Shirts; 2325 Men's & Boys'
Trousers & Slacks; 2331 Women's, Misses & Juniors'
Blouses & Shirts; 2337 Women's, Misses & Juniors'
Suits, Skirts & Coats; 5699 Miscellaneous Apparel &
Accessory Stores

Farah Incorporated is a leading manufacturer and marketer of medium-priced men's and boys' apparel, with a particular emphasis on casual and dress slacks but also production of shirts, shorts, sports coats, and suit separates (matching slacks and sports coats). It also introduced a line of women's shirts, skirts, shorts, and slacks in 1996. In addition, the company has factory outlet stores that market its excess or slow-moving products as well as apparel from third-party vendors.

Early Development and Growth: 1920–71

Mansour Farah, a Lebanese immigrant, came to El Paso, Texas, from Canada as a hay and dry-goods merchant. He and his wife, Hana, started making shirts in 1920 and expanded their line in the 1930s to bib overalls, denim pants, and similar work clothes. James Farah, the elder son, took over the administrative duties of the operation upon Mansour's death in 1937, while younger son William took charge of production. Sales increased every year from the company's incorporation in 1947 as Farah

grew from an anonymous contractor to the military and big mail-order chains to a brand-name manufacturer and wholesaler. In the early 1960s the brothers developed their signature product—inexpensive, durable, permanently pressed slacks.

After James Farah died in 1964, William took over the helm. At this time, The company was making dress slacks for men and boys sold exclusively under the Farah label. In fiscal 1962 the company had net income of $1.5 million on net sales of $26.7 million. Under William Farah's direction it grew rapidly, and in 1967, the year the company went public, raising $5.9 million, it had net sales of $73.9 million and net income of nearly $4 million. The Farah family and relatives retained about 56 percent of the outstanding common stock.

All of Farah's products in 1968 were being designed in-house and manufactured in four highly automated production facilities in El Paso and San Antonio. Fabrics procured from domestic textile manufacturers were cut into components using patterns prepared by the company. Sewing-machine operators assembled the components and affixed items such as zippers, pockets, and trim. The clothing was then pressed and heat-treated, emerging wrinkle-free with permanently pressed creases. Farah's own trucks delivered the goods to about 150 independent contractors and returned to the plant with materials from textile mills. The contractors were selling Farah slacks and jeans to more than 9,000 department and specialty stores throughout the country.

By offering a quality product in mass volume at very competitive prices, Farah continued to grow rapidly and by 1972 was the world's largest manufacturer of men's and boys' slacks, turning out 30 million pairs a year. Sales reached $164.5 million in fiscal 1971 although profits slumped from the record $8.3 million the previous year as the company was caught off-guard by a shift in fashion from woven to knit fabrics. William Farah, a hands-on manager who invented a machine that could sew zippers, pockets, and belt loops and another that could press a jacket shoulder with one movement, often rode a bicycle through the aisles of his sewing rooms, monitoring productivity. A factory in Belgium was opened in 1971, bringing the company total to 11.

The Turbulent and Unprofitable 1970s

The company's growth came to a halt in the spring of 1972, when at least 2,000 workers in Farah's seven plants, most of them Mexican-Americans, went out on strike, seeking higher wages, greater job security, and the right to be represented by the Amalgamated Clothing Workers of America. In July 1972 the AFL-CIO authorized a nationwide boycott of all Farah products, only the third time in its history that the labor federation had initiated such an effort. The strike also had the backing of El Paso's Roman Catholic bishop and Senator George McGovern, the Democratic Party's presidential candidate. In many ways Farah was a paternalistic employer, paying typical wages for semi-skilled work in the El Paso area, treating plant workers in company medical clinics, subsidizing hot lunches, and transporting them to work in company buses, but its hiring and promotion policies were arbitrary, and a number of union supporters were fired.

In fiscal 1972 Farah's sales slumped by $8 million and it lost $8.3 million because of a $20.8 million writedown of unsold inventory. Farah's stock price dropped from a high of $49.25 a share in 1971 to $3.38 a share at the end of 1973. The company earned a meager $43,000 in net income on sales of $132 million in fiscal 1973 and closed four of its plants late in the calendar year. Moreover, the company's dividend was suspended and not resumed until 1983. In February 1974 a settlement was reached whereby Farah agreed to recognize the union as its workers' bargaining agent and to rehire the 2,000 remaining strikers "as needed." The company and the union agreed on a three-year contract with pay raises and an improvement in fringe benefits.

But Farah's troubles were just beginning. The company made its first real profit in four years in fiscal 1975 by committing more than a quarter of its production to leisure suits. When that market collapsed in 1976, however, Farah missed the shift to demand for jeans and lost $24.4 million on sales of only $137.3 million in the fiscal year. The company had to reduce the number of its domestic plants to three and cut its labor force to only 4,000. Farah's bank creditors sought and obtained William Farah's resignation as president and chief executive officer. He remained chairman, however, and in March 1977 pushed out his successor. This action angered the bankers, who accepted the new management team but forced Farah to resign as chairman and CEO.

Farah's new president refinanced the company's bank loans and closed five plants during 1976–77, including the two-year-old El Paso fabric plant, the remaining San Antonio facility, and the Belgian factory. Nevertheless, Farah lost another $17.8 million in fiscal 1977. William Farah, in April 1978, again used his control of about 40 percent of the company stock to overturn its management, firing not only the president and seven vice-presidents but also their secretaries, directing armed guards to escort all of them off company property. He resumed his position as CEO, refinanced bank loans through a new lineup of lenders, and brought out a line of coordinate jackets to supplement the company's slacks, jeans, and walking shorts. In fiscal 1979 Farah, after three losing years, was profitable again.

More Turmoil, More Red Ink in the 1980s

The following year Farah introduced a women's line of casual slacks and jackets (dropped in 1987) and an upscale W.F.F. de-signer line featuring an $85 suede jacket. In 1981 the company opened two new plants in Ireland, soon thereafter establishing facilities in Costa Rica and Mexico. During fiscal 1982 Farah began manufacturing and marketing, under license, men's slacks, jeans, shorts, blazers, and sports coats and jackets bearing the John Henry label. For fiscal 1983 the company reported record net income of $21 million on sales of $206 million.

This period of peace and prosperity was not to last, however. William Farah's relations with company president Ray W. Williams deteriorated in 1984, because Farah wanted to deviate from its traditional market and concentrate its sales on upper-tier specialty stores. Accordingly, the company purchased Generra Sportswear and introduced four new fashion-oriented labels. Williams, who had been credited with the company's resurgence, resigned and was succeeded by Farah's son Jimmy. However, Jimmy also opposed his father's drive for higher output, which included introduction of the E. Joven, N.P.W., and Savane labels. By 1987, the year the company's name was shortened to Farah Incorporated, Jimmy Farah and his two brothers had been forced out of their positions.

Once again, Farah fell into deep trouble. In his drive for further growth, William Farah had allowed product quality to slip, shipments to fall behind schedule, and inventories to grow out of control. The company had record sales of $386.1 million in 1986, when it paid its last dividend, but net income was only $4.1 million. It lost money for the next six years, the worst of which was 1989, when it finished $13.7 million in the red and, in order to avoid bankruptcy, sold Generra Sportswear for less than it had paid. Sales dropped to only $139.6 million in 1990, compared to $339.2 million in 1988. William Farah accepted a payment to resign as president and chief executive officer in June 1989 and was succeeded by Richard C. Allender.

Predictably, however, Farah was soon at odds with the new managers, who ousted him as chairman of the board in 1990. In a lawsuit, the company asked court permission to prevent its former leader, who retained an office at headquarters, from "interfering in the day-to-day management of the company" and added that the present board believed he "bears substantial responsibility" for $40.7 million in cumulative operative losses by its domestic unit since 1985. In a 1990 settlement Farah, who still held 15 percent of the company's common stock, agreed to stop criticizing the company and to stay off its property without authorization. In return, the company extended a financial settlement that allowed him to avoid personal bankruptcy. Farah sold his stake in the company in 1992.

Repositioning the Company in the 1990s

In order to return to solvency, Farah cut back on operations and expenses, secured $32 million in new bank financing, and established a chain of factory outlet stores called Value Slacks, mainly to sell its excess Farah U.S.A. products. The company earned a razor-thin profit of $132,000 in 1993. Marciano Investments, Inc., an investment group representing two of the brothers who owned the jeansmaker Guess, Inc., took a 37 percent stake in the company during this period, reaping big capital gains in 1994 after Farah continued its resurgence with a new all-cotton, wrinkle-free line of the Savane shorts and casual slacks that it had introduced in 1989. The company also licensed its wrinkle-free processes to Oxford Industries Inc. for its shirts in 1994 and earned $10.8 million that year.

In 1995 Farah opened an 85,000-square-foot finishing plant at the Piedras Negras, Mexico, complex where the company had, since 1979, established four sewing plants. The new facility featured a laundry system designed to wash and dry 25,000 pairs of pants in each eight- or nine-hour shift as part of Farah's Process 2000, the company's treatment to generate soft, wrinkle-resistant, and shrink-resistant apparel. A similar operation opened in Costa Rica the same year for sports coat production, and a new cutting room and distribution center was established in El Paso.

By this time, however, the company was back in the red, having lost its hold on the wrinkle-free slacks market to such aggressive competitors as Haggar Corp. and Levi Strauss & Co.'s Dockers line. The company lost $12.9 million in fiscal 1995. Accordingly, Farah sold its Costa Rica facility in 1995 and the Piedras Negras complex for about $22.3 million in 1996. During 1997 the company closed one of its Irish manufacturing facilities and sold the other one. It was planning to close or sell its finishing facility in Cartago, Costa Rica, during fiscal 1998 and to reduce production significantly at its remaining Costa Rican manufacturing plant. The company also was significantly reducing its U.S. production work force as it shifted all sewing and finishing processes to independent contractors abroad to take advantage of lower costs.

Farah also cut back on its Value Slacks stores. By the end of fiscal 1995 all the Puerto Rican stores were closed, with the remaining 36 all in the mainland United States. Because of competition from discount retailers and other men's apparel manufacturers in this market, Farah in 1996 began to shift its retail focus to offer a line of first-quality products. Accordingly, Value Slacks was renamed Savane Direct and given a more fashionable appearance with upscale fixturing and displays.

Farah USA broke into the women's market in 1996 with two styles of cotton twill pants and one style of shorts for women in black, natural, and khaki. This merchandise carried the Savane label. This Farah division, however, mainly saw its future in wrinkle-free private-label sales to such big retailers as Wal-Mart, The Gap, Dillard's, and Federated Department Stores. Private label business was accounting for 22 percent of the company's output.

A gain of $10 million from the sale of assets enabled Farah to report net income of $6.8 million in fiscal 1996 despite only a marginal increase in sales. Sales grew significantly in 1997, but despite a $5.1 million credit for termination of foreign operations, the company earned only $270,000. The company's long-term debt was $13.8 million at the end of fiscal 1997.

Farah in 1997

As it approached a new century, Farah was selling men's casual and dress slacks under the Farah label, with the dress products made from blended fabrics and the casual products mainly all-cotton. This label was repositioned in 1996 from department store sales to marketing through a single mass-market distributor. The Savane label was for men's and boys'

casual pants and shorts in cotton and a cotton-lycra blend; men's cotton and polyester/cotton shirts; men's dress slacks, coats, and suit separates, mainly in blends of polyester/wool and polyester/wool/lycra; and women's casual cotton slacks, shorts, shirts, and skirts. Savane-label goods were being sold primarily in department stores. The John Henry label was primarily for dress slacks, suit separates, and sports coats produced from blended fabrics and was being sold to Sears. Farah also was producing casual and dress wear, women's wear, and boys' clothing for various retailers under their own labels.

Although Farah U.S.A. was shifting its production activities from company-owned facilities to third-party contractors, it was still, in 1997, operating a cutting facility in El Paso and sewing and finishing services in Chihuahua and Ciudad Juarez, Mexico, and San Jose and Cartago, Costa Rica. This division's distribution center was in El Paso. Farah International was selling apparel primarily in the United Kingdom, Australia, and New Zealand. With the termination of manufacturing operations in Ireland, this division entered into an agreement with the new owners for supplying the United Kingdom's needs. Two factories in Fiji in which Farah had a half-interest were supplying the Australian and New Zealand markets. In fiscal 1997 Farah U.S.A. accounted for 76 percent of company sales, Farah International for 18 percent, and Savane Direct for six percent.

Principal Subsidiaries

Farah (Far East) Limited (Hong Kong); Farah Clothing Company, Inc.; Farah International, Inc.; Farah U.S.A., Inc.; Savane Direct Incorporated.

Further Reading

Barmash, Isadore, "Ex-Farah Head Battles for Old Job," *New York Times,* July 29, 1990, pp. 29, 31.

Corchado, Alfredo, "Patriarch of Farah Inc. Loses His Company—And His Children, Too," *Wall Street Journal,* August 10, 1990, pp. A1, A12.

"The Family Is Tightening Its Grip on Farah," *Business Week,* November 12, 1984, p. 46.

Haber, Holly, "Farah Enters Women's," *Women's Wear Daily,* January 3, 1996, p. 10.

Lawson, Robert, "Farah Manufacturing Company, Inc.," *Wall Street Transcript,* June 24, 1968, pp. 13,684.

Mack, Toni, "A Painful Lesson," *Forbes,* January 19, 1981, pp. 51–52.

Malley, Deborah DeWitt, "How the Union Beat Willie Farah," *Fortune,* August 1974, pp. 165–167, 238, 240.

Poole, Claire, " 'We Did What We Had to Do,' " *Forbes,* December 9, 1991, pp. 148–50.

Rabon, Lisa C., "Farah Finishes First in Post Sew," *Bobbin,* September 1995, pp. 52+.

Rutberg, Sidney, "Farah, Inc. Settles Battle with Willie," *Daily News Record,* February 7, 1991, p. 7.

Simison, Robert L., " 'Willie' Farah, Leading Farah Mfg. Again, Stirs Debate Over Prospects," *Wall Street Journal,* June 5, 1978, pp. 1, 16.

Vargo, Julie, "Farah Out to Prove WR Critics Are All Wet," *Daily News Record/DNR,* March 27, 1995, pp. 8–9.

"Willie Farah's Special Incentive," *Financial World,* December 1–5, 1982, pp. 25–26.

—Robert Halasz

FinishMaster, Inc.

54 Monument Circle, 7th Floor
Indianapolis, Indiana 46204
U.S.A.
(317) 237-3678
Fax: (317) 237-2150

Public Subsidiary of Lacy Diversified Industries, Ltd.
Incorporated: 1968
Employees: 1,660
Sales: $130.2 million (1997)
Stock Exchanges: NASDAQ
Ticker Symbol: FMST
SICs: 5198 Paints, Varnishes, & Supplies

FinishMaster, Inc. has grown from a single outlet in Michigan in 1968 to become the leading automotive paint distributor in the United States. As of December 31, 1997, it owned 143 outlets in 22 states and had sales of $130.2 million. For all but its first five years, the company was a subsidiary of a parent company that provided financing for expansion through acquisitions. From 1973 to 1996, it was a subsidiary of Maxco, Inc., a diversified holding company based in Lansing, Michigan. In 1996 it was acquired by Lacy Diversified Industries, Ltd. of Indianapolis, Indiana. By the end of 1997 FinishMaster had acquired its largest competitor to become the industry leader in automotive paint distribution.

Founded in 1968 by James White

FinishMaster was founded by James White in 1968 with a single outlet in Grand Rapids, Michigan. He ran the business independently until 1973. It served as an intermediary between automotive paint manufacturers and body shops that repaired cars, including automobile dealerships. "From the outset, my idea was to start a paint business and follow the lines of automotive parts divisions, like NAPA has," White told the *Grand Rapids Business Journal.*

In 1973 White sold the company to Maxco, Inc., which was based in Lansing, Michigan, to finance its growth. FinishMaster became a wholly owned subsidiary of Maxco, Inc. Maxco allowed White to remain as president and acted as a silent partner. White told the *Grand Rapids Business Journal,* "They allowed me to build it the way I wanted and provided the financing." In 1975 White began acquiring stores, spreading throughout Michigan and eventually into Chicago and Indiana.

Opened New Corporate Headquarters, 1990

In 1990 FinishMaster moved from its headquarters in Wyoming, Michigan, to new facilities in Kentwood, Michigan. The company owned and operated 15 stores in Michigan and Illinois. It leased its former headquarters, but now it would own its new facility, a 40,000-square-foot building with 8,000 square feet of office space on four acres.

The new distribution facility and corporate headquarters in Kentwood was a sign of the company's growth and expansion. It planned to open two new stores per year over the next five years. Three stores were opened in the Chicago area in 1989 and 1990. When looking for new outlets to acquire, the company would typically survey markets within a 250- to 300-mile radius of its warehouse. Its customers were primarily body shops and automobile dealerships.

Acquired Master Glass & Color in Indianapolis, 1993

In February 1993 FinishMaster announced it would acquire certain assets related to the refinishing business of Master Glass & Color in Indianapolis. Max A. Coon, chairman of Maxco, Inc., the parent company of FinishMaster, said, "The Indianapolis location fits into our plan of expanding the company's domination of the Great Lakes area within a radius of the Grand Rapids, Michigan, distribution facility. About 40 percent of FinishMaster's sales volume now comes from Wisconsin, Illinois, and Indiana, markets we entered beginning in late 1989."

Coon noted that FinishMaster had long dominated the Michigan market. Expansion into other geographic markets was accomplished through the acquisition of existing locations. These acquisitions were backed up by "FinishMaster's purchasing power, the strong management organization, and emphasis on service and training," said Coon.

FinishMaster's strategy was to consolidate within the Great Lakes region. According to Coon, "Auto paint distribution is a fragmented industry." Master Glass & Color was one of the largest auto paint jobbers in Indianapolis, so FinishMaster was entering the market in a strong position.

Maxco was a diversified holding company that owned several distribution and manufacturing businesses. Its construction supplies group, consisting of Ersco and Wisconsin Wire and Steel, marketed commercial and highway construction materials. Its manufacturing businesses were Wright Plastics, Pak Sak Industries, and Akemi.

Reported Record Sales and Earnings for 1994 and 1995

For FinishMaster's fiscal year 1994 (ending March 31), the company reported earnings of $2.1 million on net sales of $64.7 million, up from earnings of $1.4 million on net sales of $50.6 million in 1993. Two new outlets acquired in March and April 1993 accounted for $7.6 million of the increase, with the remainder coming from sales growth from existing outlets.

For 1995, FinishMaster again reported record sales and earnings levels. The company had net income of $3.5 million on sales of $79.4 million. The regional expansion strategy was paying off. The company enjoyed double-digit growth among its existing outlets in Indiana, Illinois, and Wisconsin. Within Michigan, outlet sales increased by about five percent. Overall, same outlet sales increased by 10.9 percent for the year.

During 1995, FinishMaster expanded into Ohio with acquisitions in two of the largest markets in that state. The company also established a new Southwest region with the acquisition of seven outlets in the Dallas-Fort Worth area of Texas. A total of five acquisitions were completed during the year, accounting for a sales volume of $18 million. On April 1, 1995, the company completed the acquisition of another Texas distributor with annual sales of $5 million.

FinishMaster Went Public in February 1995

FinishMaster became a publicly owned company when it floated its initial public offering (IPO) on February 14, 1995. The IPO sold 1.7 million shares of common stock at $10.50 per share, generating net proceeds of $16.6 million to the company. The funds enabled FinishMaster to build two new stores and to grow from a regional company to a national one with acquisitions in the East and Southwest.

At the time of the IPO there were 46 FinishMaster outlets in operation. In the following six months, FinishMaster acquired nine additional outlets. Bob Johnson, FinishMaster's marketing manager, told the *Grand Rapids Business Journal,* "There are a lot of different competitors in different market areas, but there isn't one force in all the markets that we are in." He noted that a West Coast company, Thompson PBE, "does the same type of business, but geographically we have not run into each other yet."

FinishMaster Acquired by Lacy Diversified Industries, 1996

In July 1996 FinishMaster was acquired by Lacy Diversified Industries, Ltd. (LDI), a privately held holding company based in Indianapolis. LDI purchased Maxco's 67 percent stake in FinishMaster for $63 million. Just a few weeks earlier, LDI had acquired Florida-based Steego Auto Paints, an automotive paint distributor with annual sales of $12 million. The two acquisitions vaulted LDI into a leadership position in the automotive paint distribution business. Its main competitor was Thompson PBE Inc., a California-based firm that was the only other public company in the industry. The rest of the industry consisted primarily of smaller, privately owned companies. Thompson PBE reported annual sales of $132 million in 1995. At the time of the acquisition, FinishMaster owned and operated 56 stores in 12 states.

Ronald White, son of company founder James White, resigned as FinishMaster's president, and Thomas Young was appointed by the new board of directors to the position of president and chief operating officer (COO). Andre B. Lacy became FinishMaster's new chairman and CEO. Lacy was also chairman, president, and CEO of LDI Management Inc.

Financially, 1996 was a difficult year for FinishMaster. After changing the end of its fiscal year to December 31, the company reported net income of $662,000 on net sales of $125.8 million for the year ending December 31, 1996. Sales were flat in the industry for several reasons, including fewer OEM (original equipment manufacturer) paint warranty issues, fewer repairable accidents, and more efficient products and equipment. In addition, FinishMaster experienced more intense competition from the increased sales and marketing efforts by overseas paint companies.

Acquired Its Main Competitor, Thompson PBE Inc., in November 1997

In a move to achieve an even stronger leadership position in the automotive paint distribution business, FinishMaster announced it would acquire and merge with its primary competitor, Thompson PBE Inc., in October 1997. Through a tender offer that was completed in November, FinishMaster acquired

97.9 percent of the outstanding shares of Thompson PBE for $8 per share. The tender price represented a 73 percent premium over Thompson's current stock price and was equal to Thompson's 52-week high closing price. Although Thompson was experiencing sales growth, its stock had fallen from $19.50 per share in June 1995 to $2.75 in April 1997 before rebounding to $7 per share. The overall cost of the acquisition to FinishMaster was $73.4 million, including acquisition costs, plus the refinancing of some $34.5 million of Thompson's outstanding indebtedness.

Together, the two companies would own 143 distribution outlets in 22 states. Combined revenues were projected to be $320 million for 1998. There was minimal geographic overlap between the two companies, making the new merged company truly national in scope. As a result, little restructuring was expected following the merger.

Once the merger was completed, FinishMaster would begin competing head on with some 4,000 small firms in the industry. Lacy told the *Indianapolis Business Journal,* "That battle will be fought customer by customer. Being big isn't important. We've got to appear to our customers as the enterprise that gives the greatest value at the lowest cost. There are some very good small companies out there who have longstanding personal relationships with their customers and do very well."

For 1997, FinishMaster reported flat net income of $656,000 on slightly higher sales of $130.2 million. Only one month of Thompson's sales contributed to FinishMaster's results for the year, which offset soft same-outlet sales for the company. The company's volume purchasing strategies, however, helped to increase its gross profit as a percentage of sales.

Reorganization, New Corporate Headquarters Positioned FinishMaster for Future Growth

FinishMaster was now organized into four regional divisions. The Midwest Division included Michigan and northern Indiana. The Central Division covered Wisconsin, Illinois, southern Indiana, and Ohio. The Southwest Division consisted of Texas and Oklahoma. The Eastern Division took in outlets in Pennsylvania, New Jersey, Maryland, and Virginia. Each regional division was headed by a vice-president, general manager. The new regional organization of the company was designed to rebuild the localized nature of the sales outlets and provide for greater accountability. As company management noted in its annual report, "In our business, market share is won or lost at the local level by providing top-notch service and building relationships with customers at body shops and dealerships."

As of March 1, 1998, FinishMaster relocated its corporate headquarters to newly renovated office space in Indianapolis. It was felt that Indianapolis represented a major metropolitan city and was more central to the company's national distribution strategies. The Kentwood location remained a divisional office and distribution facility.

Continuing to expand its outlets through acquisitions, FinishMaster announced in February 1998 that it would acquire LDI AutoPaints, Inc., in consideration for the issuance of approximately 1.5 million additional shares of common stock. LDI AutoPaints had 16 distribution outlets in Florida and was owned by Lacy Diversified. The all-stock transaction would increase Lacy Diversified's ownership of FinishMaster from 67 percent to approximately 75 percent. The transaction would be presented to FinishMaster's shareholders for approval at the company's 1998 annual meeting.

Principal Divisions

Midwest Division; Southwest Division; Central Division; Eastern Division.

Further Reading

Coon, Max, "Maxco's FinishMaster, Inc. Announces Acquisition, Expands Midwest Operations," *PR Newswire,* February 3, 1993.

"FinishMaster Agrees to Acquire Florida Distributor LDI AutoPaints," *Business Wire,* February 20, 1998.

"FinishMaster Announces Year-End 1997 Results," *Business Wire,* April 2, 1998.

"FinishMaster, Inc. Accepts 97.9% of Thompson PBE, Inc. Shares in Tender Offer," *Business Wire,* November 19, 1997.

"FinishMaster Reports First-Quarter Results," *Business Wire,* April 27, 1998.

Lacy, Andre B., "Thomas Young Named President and COO of FinishMaster," *Business Wire,* July 25, 1996.

Luymes, Robin, "FinishMaster Is Showing Growth," *Grand Rapids Business Journal,* July 2, 1990, p. 5.

Pletz, John, "Buyout May Make LDI a $1 Billion Company," *Indianapolis Business Journal,* October 20, 1997, p. 4.

Schneider, A. J., "Buying Binge Lifts LDI," *Indianapolis Business Journal,* June 10, 1996, p. 1.

VanderVeen, Don, "Flourishing Company Forges New Frontier," *Grand Rapids Business Journal,* September 11, 1995, p. 11.

White, Ronald P., "FinishMaster Reports Record Earnings for Year," *Business Wire,* May 2, 1994.

——, "FinishMaster Reports Results for Fourth Quarter and Record Sales and Earnings for Fiscal Year Ended March 31, 1995," *Business Wire,* May 3, 1995.

Young, Thomas, "FinishMaster to Acquire Thompson PBE for $8.00 per Share in Cash Tender Offer," *Business Wire,* October 15, 1997.

—David Bianco

(F) Fisher Scientific

Fisher Scientific International Inc.

One Liberty Lane
Hampton, New Hampshire 03842
U.S.A.
(603) 926-5911
Fax: (603) 926-5661
Web site: http://www.fishersci.com

Public Company
Incorporated: 1902 as Scientific Materials Company
Employees: 7,000
Sales: $2.18 billion
Stock Exchanges: New York
Ticker Symbol: FSH
SICs: 5049 Laboratory Equipment

Fisher Scientific International Inc. is the world leader in serving science. Reaching out to some 150,000 customers worldwide, Fisher operates as a one-stop source for the scientific and laboratory needs of its customers in research, healthcare, industry, education, and governments around the world. The company offers more than 245,000 products from 3,200 manufacturers and leading brands of scientific instruments, research chemicals, diagnostics, and laboratory supplies. Fisher manufactures many of the products it distributes and offers services ranging from an Internet mall and high-performance transaction-processing software to the design, construction and equipping of turnkey laboratories. The company also provides integrated-supply services for procurement of MRO products. Self-manufactured and proprietary products account for about 40 percent of Fisher's sales. The company's three largest markets are those of scientific research, U.S. clinical-laboratory testing, and safety. In 1992 Fisher Scientific International Inc. became the first American producer of reagents and fine chemicals to have its facilities ISO-9000 certified. Ranked by sales, Fisher is the second largest public corporation in New Hampshire, according to a 1997 *N.H. Business Review* survey.

Founding and Early Years: 1902–50

At the beginning of the 20th century, the United States was becoming an industrial nation. In Pittsburgh, Pennsylvania, Chester G. Fisher—a 20-year-old engineering graduate of Western University of Pennsylvania, recognized the need for a company that would supply scientific tools for the city's many industries, especially the burgeoning steel business. He bought the stockroom of the Pittsburgh Testing Laboratories, which served as Western Pennsylvania's only source of laboratory supplies. Fisher dreamed of realizing the ideal expressed by French scientist Louis Pasteur: "Take interest in these sacred dwellings which we call laboratories. There it is that humanity grows greater, stronger, better." In 1902, the young engineer founded the Scientific Materials Company, the first commercial source of equipment and reagents for the region's laboratories. In the early 1900s, laboratory work consisted mainly of simple volumetric and gravimetric analysis; since very little instrumentation was available, chemists depended primarily on their eyes for analysis. Fisher's earliest products, such as microscopes, burets, pipettes, litmus, balances, and colorimeters, allowed for better visual analysis. These tools were state-of-the-art in those days and, though relatively crude by contemporary standards, were the foundation for Fisher Scientific International Inc.'s technical leadership in serving science.

In 1904 Chester Fisher published the 400-page *Scientific Materials Co. Catalog of Laboratory Apparatus & Supplies,* illustrated with handmade woodcuts and featuring standard laboratory supplies as well as dissecting sets encased in Moroccan leather and anatomical models of the eye, the ear, and the heart. Later this catalog evolved into the *Fisher Catalog,* the company's most famous marketing tool. This biennial product reference became the industry standard as both a buying guide and a source of product specifications and technical information. The electronic edition available on the company's web site was the industry's most comprehensive source for laboratory equipment and supplies, including apparatus, instrumentation, disposable lab supplies, glassware, chemicals, safety supplies, laboratory workstations, and specialized products for biotechnological, clinical, chromatographical, and environmental applications.

When World War I cut the company off from its European suppliers, Scientific Materials set up its own research, development, and manufacturing capabilities. The company's earliest manufactured products proved to be superior to those formerly imported from Europe. For example, Scientific Materials' electric-combustion furnace and combustion train for analyzing carbon levels in steel was the first of its kind, as was the electrically heated and thermostatically controlled bacteriological incubator that replaced the erratic gas-flame German incubator.

Furthermore, when the United States entered World War I, Chester Fisher made his company the first home of the U.S. Chemical Warfare Service and rushed an entire American Expeditionary Force Research Laboratory to the front lines in France to help the Allies defend themselves against gas warfare. Another landmark event was the invention of the Fisher Burner, which Ernest Child, in his book titled *Tools of the Chemist: Their Ancestry and American Evolution,* hailed as "the most significant development in burners since the original Bunsen burner." Other early inventions included a unitized system for gas analysis and an electromagnetic instrument for rapid determinations of carbon in steel. Then, in 1925, the company transcended its regional markets by purchasing Montreal-based Scientific Supplies, Limited. In 1926 Chester Fisher renamed his company Fisher Scientific Company to differentiate it from new companies with "generic" names.

In 1940 Fisher acquired Eimer & Amend (a New York-based chemical company for which Scientific Materials had once been an agent), and took over its laboratory-supply business and manufacturing of fine chemicals. Fisher Scientific established a sound reputation for its quality chemicals. It supplied chemicals used in the U.S. government's top-secret Manhattan Project for producing the world's first atomic bomb. According to company archives, in 1947 Chester Fisher was given the Award of the American Chemical Society by its Pittsburgh Section. His contributions were summarized in this way: "The nation and much of the world owe a debt to C. G. Fisher .... A bit of C. G. is in most of the world's steel. The aluminum wings of man carry their loads more effectively because of him. Our foods are safeguarded . . . our farm soils maintained . . . our hospitals work more effectively . . . virtually no phase of modern life exists that has not been influenced or touched by some product of the Fisher Company." Chester Fisher served 47 years as company president before he became

chairman in 1949 and was succeeded by his son Aiken W. Fisher.

Inventions, Acquisitions, and Restructuring: 1951–91

As a manufacturer, Fisher set a new industry standard in 1954 when it introduced volumetric packaging, that is, the packaging of liquid chemicals based on volume rather than on weight. This method of packaging resulted in better use of storeroom space, easier ordering, and cost savings. Volumetric packaging was quickly adopted by other chemical manufacturers. As a quality supplier to the medical market, Fisher provided the reagents used by Dr. Jonas Salk to develop the polio vaccine introduced in 1955. By 1961 the incidence of polio had dropped by 95 percent. Company acquisitions continued apace with the 1957 purchase of New York-based E. Machlett & Sons, which specialized in medical apparatus and supported critical medical research, including early cancer investigations.

Then Fisher Scientific established the Instrument Division to manufacture laboratory supplies ranging from complex optical-electronic instrumentation and automatic freeze-dryers to precision-scaled atom models. In 1965 the company introduced the Differential Thermalyzer, an automatically programmed system for conducting differential thermal analysis. According to the company's web site, *Chemical & Engineering News*—the official publication of the American Chemical Society—called the product "a real price breakthrough," noting that this $950 Fisher product replaced instruments typically selling for $4,000 to $8,000. And the industry magazine *Industrial Research* named the Differential Thermalyzer one of the 100 most significant new technical products of the year. Another significant event was the 1962 installation of an IBM computer system to record and track inventory levels for more than 40,000 items. By June 1970 all U.S. Fisher branches were linked to this system, thereby providing immediate control of inventory information.

In 1965 Chester G. Fisher died and was succeeded by his son Aiken as chairman of Fisher Scientific; another son, Benjamin, became the company's president. Chester had seen his company grow from a regional laboratory supply company, staffed by six employees in a Pittsburgh warehouse, to a leading position in manufacturing and distribution of scientific products and supplies, with $58 million in sales and close to a million customer transactions. The company went public in 1965 and was listed on the New York Stock Exchange in 1968.

With the acquisition of Pfeiffer Glass, Inc. in 1966, Fisher added the capability of mass producing accurate pipets for many laboratory applications. Fisher pipets became—and remained—the industry standard. That same year Fisher's Photometric Titralyzer helped to change the way scientists did their jobs: it could analyze 15 successive samples and print out the results. The industry journal *Industrial Research* cited the Photometric Titralyzer as one of the 100 most significant new technical products of 1966. A similar honor went to the company's 1968 Hem-alyzer, which provided printed information about a patient's hemoglobin content, as well as red and white blood-cell counts, in 96 seconds. Then, following the 1968 purchase of Massachusetts-based Jarrell-Ash Company, Fisher was able to design and manufacture sophisticated optical instrumentation—particularly in the fields of emission and atomic absorption spectroscopy.

Fisher Scientific entered the educational marketplace in 1967 with the acquisition of Stansi Scientific Company, a Chicago manufacturer and distributor of equipment for teaching science in elementary and secondary schools, colleges, and universities. Nine years later, the Nigerian Ministry of Education chose Fisher Scientific from among 40 different organizations around the world to support education programs for life and physical sciences. Fisher, chosen for its competitive prices, complete product lines, and ability to fill the total order in just nine months, sent 16 chartered cargo jets carrying nearly 100,000 pieces of teaching equipment to Nigeria. At $8.75 million, this was a record-setting order in Fisher's 74-year history. Years later, Fisher shipped a large quantity of scientific supplies to Kuwait to re-equip 80 laboratories of colleges and institutes ravaged by the Persian Gulf War.

During the 1970s, *Industrial Research* magazine placed two other Fisher inventions among the top 100 most important technical products of the year: the Autotensiomat, a fully automated surface-tension-measuring instrument that could be used on most liquids; and the Model 750 AtomComp, a computer-controlled, direct-reading spectrometer that was the first commercially available instrument of this type. To ensure that its millions of instruments in the field worked at peak efficiency, in 1976 Fisher Scientific established an Instrument Service Division having 11 service centers across the nation; the division installed new equipment and trained laboratory personnel in its use.

For 73 years Chester Fisher's scientific company was headed by either himself or one of his sons. In 1975 Aiken retired as the company's chairman and was replaced by his brother, Benjamin Fisher. Edward Perkins became the first non-family member to be named president and chief executive officer. He held that position until the company was acquired by Allied Corporation in 1981.

For the next decade, the company operated as a subsidiary of Allied Corporation, successor AlliedSignal Inc., and The Henley Group—an Allied Signal spinoff. In 1982 Fisher chemicals were an integral component of the in-flight battery power system for the Columbia space shuttle, which was launched for its fourth mission June 27. Fisher provided 55-gallon drums of chemicals for the 1984 development of Nova, the world's largest and most powerful laser, housed in four rooms of the Lawrence Livermore National Laboratory in Livermore, California. To meet the growing needs of scientists in biotechnology, biochemistry, and related fields, in 1985 Fisher established a Biotechnology Division. With unique products—such as Promega molecular biologicals and Mediatech bacteriological culture media—Fisher BioTech sales grew more than 30 percent annually for the next eight years. In 1988 Fisher patented its Code-On technology, a spectacular new use of automation in molecular histopathology; during that year more than 150 Code-On units were installed in laboratories throughout North America. At year-end 1991 The Henley Group sold a 57 percent interest in Fisher through a public stock offering. The public entity emerged as Fisher Scientific International Inc., based in

Hampton, New Hampshire. Fisher Scientific Company remained in Pittsburgh as an operating subsidiary.

Worldwide Expansion and Electronic Commerce: 1992 and Beyond

Henley President Paul M. Montrone became president and chief executive officer of Fisher Scientific International in 1991 and chairman in 1998. David T. Della Penta became president and chief operating officer in 1998. Fisher, in 1992, became the first American producer of reagents and fine chemicals to have its facilities ISO-9000 certified by the Geneva, Switzerland-based International Standards Organization, which based certification on a common set of manufacturing, trade, and communication standards. ISO-9000 Certification is the worldwide standard measurement of total quality management. Fisher won a seven-year, $150 million contract with the University of California; research centers on nine of the university's campuses were linked directly to Fisher via some 50 remote-order stations and advanced electronic data systems.

Throughout the 1990s Fisher experienced dramatic growth both nationally and internationally through strategic acquisitions and mergers, joint ventures and alliances, expansion of current lines, additions to its product portfolio, and the development of its global distribution network. For instance, the purchase of Hamilton, the premier American designer and manufacturer of laboratory workstations, led to the merger of Fisher's existing laboratory-furniture capability with Hamilton to form Fisher Hamilton Inc., the world's largest manufacturer and supplier of laboratory workstations, even providing experts for design, budgeting, and project coordination.

In 1993 and 1995 Fisher completed two major laboratory-renovation projects in Russia in collaboration with one of the company's dealers, Intertech Corporation of Atkinson, New Hampshire. In early 1997 Fisher received a $400,000 grant from the U.S. Trade and Development Agency as partial funding to conduct a feasibility study for the development of a $10 million state-of-the-art laboratory in Moscow. The laboratory, the first of its kind in Russia, was to test and certify pharmaceuticals for the Russian Federation's Ministry of Health and Medical Industry, which is similar to the U.S. Food and Drug Administration. Fisher worked with personnel of the Food and Drug Administration and sent a team of engineers, architects, and designers to Moscow to evaluate the proposed site of the laboratory. Both the United States and Russian governments were expected to provide financial support for implementation of the project.

The acquisition of the organic-chemicals business of Eastman Kodak Company and of Belgium-based, industry-leader Janssen Chimica allowed Fisher to add a strong new component to its international chemical operations by merging the two product lines to form Acros Organics. Curtin Matheson Scientific, a leading supplier of diagnostic instruments, tests and related products, was integrated into Fisher's clinical-laboratory operations to form CMS/Fisher HealthCare. And a strategic alliance with Bedford, Massachusetts-based Millipore Corporation allowed Fisher to distribute Millipore laboratory filtration products in the United States, Puerto Rico, and Canada.

Aiken Fisher, the company's second president and chairman of the board, died in 1996. During his 50-year career at Fisher, he had seen the company become a leading supplier of scientific and laboratory products. His contemporaries attributed his effective leadership to a deep understanding of the business, common sense, unfailing civility, and commitment to continuing innovation.

The acquisition of Kühn + Bayer—a leading German provider of scientific equipment and supplies to more than 4,000 customers from Central Europe to Moscow—represented Fisher's first equity investment in Europe. This company was later merged with another Fisher subsidiary, Udo Fleischhacker GmbH & Co. KG, to form Fisher Scientific GmbH, which served as an automated distribution center and sales operation in Germany. Similarly, in the Netherlands two Fisher subsidiaries were combined to form Fisher Scientific of the Netherlands B.V., and in the United Kingdom, two other Fisher subsidiaries were consolidated as Fisher Scientific UK, the largest Fisher subsidiary in Europe. Other acquisitions included Singapore-based Fisher General Scientific Pte Ltd and Malaysia-based Fisher Scientific Holdings (M), which exported to China, India, Thailand, Vietnam, Brunei, and other Asian markets.

Global Electronic Commerce: Toward a New Millennium

Chester Fisher's company pioneered as a distributor of scientific supplies. As early as 1904 he published an illustrated catalog to facilitate ordering of the company's laboratory apparatus and supplies. In 1962 an IBM computer recorded and tracked inventory levels for some 40,000 items; by mid-1970 all the U.S. company's branches were linked to Fisher ''Fastback,'' the industry's first real-time computer system. In 1978 Fisher installed computer terminals at its major customers' sites, enabling them to place orders directly and to receive immediate order verification printouts, as well as information on their past purchases and account status.

During the 1990s, Fisher established itself as an industry leader in electronic commerce by extending the company's historical technology in inventory management and procurement systems. Search, retrieval, order-management and transaction-processing functions were added to Fisher's Internet site. CornerStone software allowed buyers and suppliers to create public or private Web sites to support their business-to-business transactions. ProcureNet, a public mall owned and operated by Fisher, gave the general commercial community access to Fisher electronic catalogs and those of other suppliers. In 1997 the Internet & Electronic Commerce Conference, organized by The Gartner Group, recognized ProcureNet as ''the first public electronic mall for business-to-business transactions'' and awarded Fisher Scientific the iEC Award for the Best Internet Infrastructure.

The company's distribution network comprised 32 locations in the United States, including a national distribution center in Somerville, New Jersey, four regional centers (New Jersey, California, Illinois, and Georgia), and 27 local facilities throughout the United States. Fisher Scientific also had two centers in Canada, and one each in Germany, France, England, Belgium, Singapore, Korea, Malaysia, Mexico, and Australia.

The company distributed an average of 20,000 items every business day, with products accounting for more than 90 percent of total 1997 sales shipped to customers within 24 hours of being ordered. By year-end 1997, Fisher Scientific's sales had increased to $2.18 billion, compared with $757.7 million in 1991, the year Fisher Scientific International Inc. became a public company. Sales had increased every year since 1954, when revenues were only $2.1 million.

In January 1998, Fisher Management and an investor group led by Thomas H. Lee Company completed a $1.4 billion recapitalization of Fisher Scientific. According to Elisabeth Kirschner's story in *Chemical & Engineering News*, this action followed an unsolicited 1997 proposal from the company's former largest shareholders, the Bass brothers of Texas, who were seeking to recapitalize or take over Fisher. In an introduction to Fisher's 1997 annual report, President Paul M. Montrone wrote that 1997 was a challenging time for the company, ''which did not sustain the sales and income trends of previous years.'' He pointed out that continuing costs associated with consolidation and restructuring, market dynamics, and the 16-day strike against United Parcel Service (responsible for over 60 percent of Fisher's domestic deliveries) affected results.

Although ''total results in 1997 were not strong,'' wrote President Montrone, ''a number of business units performed well.'' Fisher Hamilton, the manufacturer of laboratory workstations and fume hoods, registered significant growth with new products and the initiation of buying alliances with major pharmaceutical customers. Fisher Safety, one of the fastest-growing units, won a multimillion-dollar contract for clean-room supplies and services at Texas Instruments Inc. Fisher Laboratory Products posted strong gains and successfully launched a new line of pH meters that are programmable in any language; and Fisher Technology gained strong partners in electronic commerce through new marketing agreements with IBM Corporation and Oracle Corporation. Furthermore, since its initial public offering in 1991, the company increased shareholder value over 22 percent per year and demand remained strong for Fisher-manufactured products.

In short, as the 21st century drew near, it seemed possible to affirm that Fisher Scientific International Inc. would remain a driving force in the service of science and keep as its trademark the words founder Chester Fisher had gleaned from Louis Pasteur: ''Take interest in these dwellings which we call laboratories. There it is that humanity grows greater, stronger, better.''

Principal Subsidiaries

Acros Organics N.V. (Belgium); Fisher Chimica N.V. (Belgium); Fisher Hamilton Inc.; Fisher Scientific B.V. (Netherlands); Fisher Scientific Company L.L.C.; Fisher Scientific GmbH (Germany); Fisher Scientific Holding Company; Fisher Scientific Holdings, S.A. (France); Fisher Scientific Holding U.K. Limited; Fisher Scientific Limited (Canada); Fisher Scientific of the Netherlands B.V.; Fisher Scientific S.A. (France); Fisher Scientific U.K., Limited; Fisher Scientific Worldwide Inc.; Fisher Technology Group Inc.; Kühn + Bayer GmbH (Germany); Orme Scientific Limited (U.K.); Resco Trade N.V.; Strategic Procurement Services Holdings Inc.

Principal Divisions

CMS/Fisher HealthCare; Fisher Products Group; Fisher Research; Fisher Safety; Logistics and Operations.

Further Reading

Child, Ernest, *Tools of the Chemist: Their Ancestry and American Evolution*, New York: Reinhold Publishing Corporation, 1940, 220 p.

"Fisher Catalog Updated," *Chemical Market Reporter*, February 23, 1998, p. 37.

"Fisher Expects Little Change," *Union Leader*, January 20, 1998, p. 1.

"Fisher Scientific Venture Taps Japanese Market," *Pittsburgh Business Times*, January 8, 1996.

"Friendly Investors Buy Fisher Scientific for $1.48," *Boston Business Journal*, August 8–14, 1997, p. 3.

"Gone Fisherin': Investor Group Pays $1.4 Billion for Fisher Scientific," *New Hampshire Business Review*, September 1–11, 1997, p. 34.

Hussey, A. F., "Scientific Boasts Growing Stake in Laboratory Supply Field," *Barron's*, May 2, 1977, p. 41.

Jaffe, Thomas, "Fisher Redux," *Forbes*, March 2, 1992, p. 130.

Kirschner, Elisabeth, "Fisher Scientific Going Private," *Chemical & Engineering News*, August 18, 1997, p. 10.

"Top N.H.-Based Public Companies," *New Hampshire Business Review*, December 19, 1997, p. 146.

"UPS Strike Fails to Dry Supply Channel," *Health Industry Today*, September 1997, p. 5.

—Gloria A. Lemieux

Footstar, Incorporated

933 MacArthur Blvd.
Mahwah, New Jersey 07430
U.S.A.
(201) 934-2000
Fax: (201) 934-0398
Web site: http://www.footaction.com

Public Company
Incorporated: 1996
Employees: 15,200
Sales: $1.79 billion (1997)
Stock Exchanges: New York
Ticker Symbol: FTS
SICs: 5661 Shoe Stores, Retail; 6719 Holding
   Companies, Not Elsewhere Classified; 5699
   Miscellaneous Apparel & Accessory Stores

Footstar, Incorporated is a holding company whose two subsidiaries, Footaction and Meldisco, are leading shoe retailers of their types. Since Footstar was created as a spinoff of the Melville Corporation in 1996, Footaction, a mall-based chain of over 550 athletic shoe stores, has shown strong sales growth, with significant numbers of new stores added each year. Meldisco, operator of over 2,500 discount shoe outlets, primarily in leased space in Kmart stores, has been the backbone of Footstar's business, generating about twice the annual revenue of Footaction, though growth has been slower. Together, these chains cover much of the spectrum of the retail shoe market, which tends to favor either the low or high ends of the price range. Having combined distribution operations since the spinoff, and with plans to acquire a third, complementary shoe retailer, Footstar appears likely to maintain its position as one of the largest shoe retailing companies in the United States.

Roots Date to 1893

Footstar's history could be said to begin in 1893, with the founding in New Jersey of the Melville Corporation, a shoe manufacturer. In 1922, the Thom McAn chain of stores was purchased by Melville, becoming the company's first retail division. The year 1952 saw the acquisition of another shoe retailer, Miles Shoes. In 1960, Miles established a division called Meldisco, whose name was a contraction of ''Melville Discount Corporation.'' Meldisco did not have its own stores, but rather leased space to sell its shoes in department or other large stores. Its first Kmart-based outlet, in Greenville, North Carolina, was opened a year later, and in 1962 Meldisco signed an agreement to act as Kmart's exclusive shoe retailer. Years of steady growth followed, as both Meldisco and the Michigan-based Kmart expanded. By the early 1980s, Meldisco had become one of the largest shoe retailers in the United States, with annual sales topping the $1 billion mark in 1985. Over 95 percent of Meldisco's outlets were located in Kmart stores, though a few were in grocery stores and drugstores. Meldisco also had a scattering of locations overseas, from Mexico and Puerto Rico to Czechoslovakia and Hungary.

The Melville Corporation started another chain of shoe stores in the 1980s called FanClub. This operation was geared more toward younger customers looking for athletic shoes, in line with the exploding sales of that segment of the shoe market at the time. In 1991, Melville purchased a privately owned Dallas, Texas-based chain of 128 athletic shoe stores called Footaction, and converted the 129 FanClub stores into Footaction stores, creating the third largest chain of athletic shoe specialty stores in the nation. Melville, which had largely become a conglomerate of retail chains by this time (it had stopped manufacturing shoes in the mid-1980s), now had three large shoe store chains in Thom McAn, Footaction, and Meldisco. The company also owned about a dozen other retail chains, including CVS drugstores, Kay-Bee Toys, Chess King men's apparel stores, and Linens 'N Things home furnishings.

Melville's new acquisition, Footaction, had been founded in 1976 by Charles Cristol. Cristol, then 57 years old, had been a World War II Air Force pilot and later worked in a variety of jobs, ultimately spending over 20 years in various positions related to the shoe business. He had risen to the level of president of a western-style clothing company by the mid-1970s, but Cristol sensed the possibilities for retailing athletic shoes, and decided to strike out on his own. With several partners he opened a store in Wichita Falls, Texas, called Footaction. Cristol initially gave his business the corporate name of Webmit, which stood for ''We Better Make It,'' but it was later changed to Footaction when it appeared that they had indeed ''made it.'' Cristol's goal from the beginning was expansion, and over the next 15 years he added locations in 17 states, primarily in shopping malls. A related chain of stores, Footaction for Kids, was also started. These were typically located adjacent to existing Footaction locations, enabling the company to use stockroom space and some personnel for both stores. By 1990, Footaction had opened its 100th store, and annual sales were estimated at over $50 million. That year, the company also bought Marvin's Sports City, a Baltimore, Maryland-based chain of nine sporting goods stores. The following year, when Footaction was sold to Melville, founder Cristol stepped down as CEO and was replaced by Chief Operating Officer Ralph T. Parks.

The Early 1990s: Tough Times for Thom McAn

Though Melville Corporation's Thom McAn business had had a long and successful history, and had achieved the coveted position of becoming a household name, its sales had begun declining by the early 1980s. Its reliance on its own shoes, rather than those of well-advertised, trendy brandnames, was one reason, as was the shifting marketplace, which had moved away from McAn's more conservatively styled, low- to mid-priced shoes. Tennis or athletic shoes had broken fashion barriers and were now much more acceptable wear off the court or field, and the wild success of several lines of athletic shoes, particularly those of Nike, left the ''old-fashioned'' shoes of McAn hurting. In the early 1980s the chain had over 1,100 stores, but the numbers were shrinking, with a particularly large drop coming in late 1992 when Melville announced the closing of 350 of the 740 remaining McAn outlets, some being shuttered and a few converted to other Melville Corp. stores. Within the next several years McAn continued to falter, and additional stores were closed. The early-to-mid-1990s was in fact a tough period for all discount shoe retailers, with an estimated 1,500 such stores closing during 1995.

Over the years, Melville Corporation had evolved from a manufacturer into a conglomerate of unrelated retail operations. By the mid-1990s, however, many corporations were refocusing on single areas of business and getting rid of distractions and sidelines. In this climate, Melville, which had originally been a shoe company, decided to concentrate on its chain of CVS drug stores, announcing in the fall of 1995 that it would sell off its other retailing operations. The Kay-Bee Toys chain and the shoe companies would be first, with an apparel chain

called Bob's and the Linens 'n Things housewares stores coming last. After it had completed selling off these subsidiaries, the corporate name would be changed to CVS.

1996: Footstar Created

When Melville decided to divest itself of its shoe retailing operations, a long, hard look was taken at Thom McAn, and it was decided that there was little hope for turning around the steady decline which the company had suffered. Less than 300 stores were left, and many of these were only marginally profitable. It was decided that most of the McAn stores would be closed; those that had viable locations would be converted into Footaction outlets. Over the next several years close to 100 conversions were planned. The newly named Footstar, Incorporated would thus solely consist of the Meldisco and Footaction shoe businesses. The new CEO, chairman, and president of Footstar was J. M. ''Mickey'' Robinson, who had previously held those positions with Meldisco. Stock was offered on the New York Stock Exchange in October 1996. At this time Footaction consisted of 444 stores, and was the third largest athletic shoe specialty chain, behind Foot Locker and Athlete's Foot. Annual sales were reported at $423 million. Meldisco had over 2,100 leased outlets in Kmart stores, with a few additional ones in other locations. Its annual sales were $1.2 billion in 1995. The two companies combined employed some 12,600 persons.

The business of selling shoes, as with many other things, had been changing a great deal by the 1990s, and Footaction and Meldisco both responded to the challenge to keep up with the times. Footaction had begun converting some of its locations into larger, more inviting ''Superstores'' in 1993. These outlets, some newly opened and some expansions, were two to five times larger than the 2,200 square feet of the company's average store. There was a wall of video screens and a ''walk of fame'' with bronze stars embedded in the floor featuring the names of prominent athletes who were associated with its shoes, such as Shaquille O'Neill and Michael Jordan. The idea was to make the store a fun place to go for the target audience of 12- to 24-year-old, largely male shoppers. Products were also redisplayed together in ways that improved the sales of accessories. In the industry this was known as a ''hookup,'' for example selling a customer a pair of shoes, a t-shirt, a baseball cap and a warm-up suit all with the Nike ''swoosh'' logo for a package price. Footaction had been selling these accessory items along with its shoes for years, but sales had always been unremarkable. The company also worked with vendors to ensure that it had exclusive versions of their products to feature. This might involve getting Reebok or Adidas to create a special edition of a particular line of shoes, with colors or details only available on the shoes found at Footaction. These ''Exclusives'' constituted up to half of all sales. Other methods of attracting business included advertising campaigns which strongly stressed the identity of the Footaction chain, rather than the specific products it carried, and a magazine-cum-catalog launched in 1997 which featured interviews with athletes and information about products. This was mailed out to customers who had signed up for a preferred-customer ''Star Card.'' Data taken when the cards were issued enabled the company to compile a detailed database about its customers. Footaction also started a web site, www.footaction.com, designed to appeal to its target audience. The chain had been involved since 1993 in sponsoring a competition called the ''NFL Quarterback Challenge,'' for high school seniors, which culminated in a championship match at a professional sports facility. National Football League quarterbacks made personal appearances in cities where the competitions were held, and the final matches received national television coverage.

For Meldisco, the response to the changing retail environment was largely under the control of Kmart. That company's market share had been slipping for some time, and in the early 1990s it was forced to close a number of stores. In an effort to reverse this slide, Kmart inaugurated its Big K concept. This entailed offering more ''branded'' merchandise, and, later, placing a special emphasis on products that shoppers needed to buy on a frequent basis, such as household cleaning products and paper goods. The stores were also redesigned, and relative placement of the different departments was shifted. Meldisco's Shoemart outlets, as they were officially known in Kmart stores, were given a higher-traffic spot near men's and ladies' apparel. With its early test sites showing significant sales improvements, Kmart Corporation announced plans to upgrade all its stores by the end of the year 2000. Meldisco also introduced several new lines of shoes in association with its vendors, such as the Cobbie Cuddlers line from NineWest, which contributed to increased sales.

Continuing to Move Forward in the Late 1990s

Footstar's first year following its stock offering was a profitable one, with sales of more than $1.6 billion, an increase of 3.5 percent over the previous year. Meldisco's improving fortunes with Kmart, and Footaction's growing sales and aggressive expansion, kept the company in the black—in fact it had no long-term debt whatsoever. By the end of this first year 35 new Footaction stores were open, some of which were conversions of Thom McAn locations, with a number of other stores expanded to Superstore size. The company had now enjoyed 30 consecutive months of same-store sales increases. Footaction's success, however, was largely tied to that of shoe giant Nike, which had shown phenomenal annual growth for several years running. In the spring of 1997, reports from both Nike and Footstar that athletic shoe sales were leveling off caused a brief investor panic, with the company's stock plunging by over 25 percent. Fortunately, this had no lasting impact, as Footstar had already begun planning to cut costs, and was soon announcing the imminent consolidation of Footaction and Meldisco distribution operations, with a similar consolidation of accounting activities to follow. In November 1997, Meldisco stores began selling a new line of shoes with a familiar brand name—Thom McAn. Footstar had retained the name and now successfully played on its history and recognition value.

The end of 1997 saw further gains, as Footaction stores had grown in number to 550, with a total of 669 anticipated by the turn of the century. Meldisco now had over 2,500 outlets, and was seeing modest sales growth, compared to the slight decline of the previous year, as Kmart's turnaround continued to bring business back to the chain. In early 1998, Footstar announced that it was planning on finding a third shoe store format by year's end, with acquisition or internal development both under consideration. In March, a consulting firm was retained to help with the process.

As it approached the end of the 1990s, Footstar was on solid ground, with its backbone business of Meldisco rebounding due to the improved fortunes of Kmart Corporation. Meldisco's sales accounted for 16 percent of the United States discount shoe market. Footaction, the third largest specialty athletic shoe chain in the country, was continuing to grow, both in sales and in the expanding number of store locations. Footstar's plans to add a third shoe business met with the approval of industry analysts, who observed that such an operation would be able to take advantage of the corporation's infrastructure and its strong relationships with key vendors. Selling a product that was always in demand also seemed to be a basic part of Footstar's success.

Principal Subsidiaries

Footaction; Meldisco.

Further Reading

Baldwin, Pat, ''Footaction Agrees to Buyout Deal,'' *Dallas Morning News*, October 3, 1991, p. 2D.

Dimeo, Jean, ''On Solid Footing: Shoe Seller's Chief Keeps Foes on Toes,'' *Dallas Times Herald*, October 11, 1990, p. 1.

Feitelberg, Rosemary, ''Hookups Reeling in Shoppers,'' *WWD*, September 26, 1996, p. 15.

Fitzgerald, Beth, ''Footstar Opens Public Stock Trading,'' *Newark Star-Ledger*, October 15, 1996, p. F4.

''Footstar Seeks New Format,'' *Footwear News*, May 18, 1998, p. 4.

Gerena-Morales, Rafael, ''Mahwah-Based Footstar Is Making Great Strides,'' *Northern New Jersey Record*, May 21, 1997, p. B1.

Gilligan, Gregory, ''Footaction Chain Offers Mall Store with Wide Range of Merchandise,'' *Richmond Times-Dispatch*, September 4, 1994, p. D3.

Golden, Ed, ''Changes Afoot,'' *Las Vegas Review-Journal*, July 11, 1996, p. 8D.

Lefton, Terry, ''Footaction Extends QB Challenge into NFL Market High Schools,'' *Brandweek*, October 21, 1996, p. 12.

MacDonald, Laurie, ''Malling It Over: The Athlete's Foot & Footaction Stand Their Ground,'' *Footwear News*, January 23, 1995, p. S18.

Markowitz, Michael, ''Melville Spins Off Shoe Business—Footstar Steps into the NYSE,'' *Northern New Jersey Record*, October 15, 1996, p. B1.

McGee, Bob, ''Louder Than Words,'' *SportStyle*, January 31, 1994, p. 95.

Narayan, Chandrika, ''New York Firm Buys Shoe Chain,'' *Dallas Times Herald*, October 3, 1991, p. 1.

Quick, Rebecca, ''Footwear Industry Shares Stub Toes on Footstar Caveat,'' *Wall Street Journal*, April 18, 1997, p. B4.

Ricketts, Chip, ''Footaction USA Buys Baltimore Sporting Goods Chain,'' *Dallas Business Journal*, October 9, 1989, p. 5.

——, ''Footaction USA Sprints Forward with Growth Plans,'' *Dallas Business Journal*, November 27, 1989, p. 4.

Ryan, Thomas, ''Melville Will Close 350 Units of Thom McAn in Realignment,'' *Footwear News*, December 28, 1992, p. 4.

Scott, Dave, ''Footaction Sprints for Growth,'' *Dallas Business Journal*, November 27, 1992, p. 1.

''Specialty Retail Parent Melville to Split into 3 Public Companies,'' *Dallas Morning News*, October 25, 1995, p. 1D.

Strauss, Gary, ''Melville Moves to Make Itself Known,'' *USA Today*, August 25, 1988, p. 3B.

Strope, Leigh, ''Stepping Out: Footaction USA Being Spun Off by Melville,'' *Fort Worth Star-Telegram*, September 10, 1996, p. 1.

Zimmerman, Martin, ''Footaction USA at Home in Irving,'' *Dallas Morning News*, August 25, 1996, p. 1T.

—Frank Uhle

Fox Family Worldwide, Inc.

10960 Wilshire Boulevard
Los Angeles, California 90024
U.S.A.
(310) 235-5100
Fax: (310) 235-5102
Web site: http://www.foxkids.com

Private Company
Incorporated: 1996 as Fox Kids Worldwide, Inc.
Employees: 505
Sales: $307.8 million (1997)
SICs: 4833 Television Broadcasting Stations

A leading broadcaster to a global audience, Fox Family Worldwide, Inc. is a family-oriented entertainment company that develops, acquires, produces, broadcasts, and distributes television programming and motion pictures. Originally the Fox Children's Network, which debuted in 1990, Fox Family Worldwide blossomed into a multifaceted, broadly based broadcasting network during the 1990s under the guidance of Margaret Loesch and Haim Saban. Part of Rupert Murdoch's labyrinthine media empire, Fox Family Worldwide comprised the Fox Family Channel, the Fox Kids Network, Saban Entertainment, and Fox Kids International.

Origins

Although few outside observers believed it could be done, Australian media mogul Rupert Murdoch created a successful fourth television network in the United States, which at last broke the grip held by the country's three national heavyweights, American Broadcasting Corporation (ABC), National Broadcasting Corporation (NBC), and Columbia Broadcasting Station (CBS). Murdoch's success with Fox Broadcasting Company set the stage for his bold forays into all facets of the commercial and cable television industry, all of which were governed by The News Corporation Limited, the company Murdoch presided over as chairman of the board. From within the vast media empire superintended by The News Corporation

Limited, emerged a new television broadcasting entity in 1990, a network christened the Fox Children's Network, which proved to be the foundation upon which Fox Family Worldwide, Inc. was built. Fox Children's Network, organized by Murdoch's maverick Fox Broadcasting Company and most of the network's member stations, set out to provide television programming targeted at children, beginning with a broadcast schedule consisting of 5.5 hours of programming that aired on weekdays and Saturday mornings. Both the range of Fox Children's operations and the number of hours of programming it offered increased in the ensuing years, as the fledgling effort to tap into the market for children's television shows blossomed into Fox Kids Worldwide, Inc.

The leader of Fox's entry into children's programming and its recognized founder was Margaret Loesch, who demonstrated considerable skill in transforming the network into a market share contender. The task assigned to Loesch was similar to the objective pursued by Fox Broadcasting Company: entice viewers away from the entrenched broadcast networks. Toward this goal, the subsidiary emulated its parent, stealing away enough viewers to legitimize itself as a formidable force in its industry. Once the network had gained a foothold and established itself as a genuine player in its market, the next objective was to secure a ratings winner that would enable the network to charge top advertising rates. For roughly two years, the network searched for the program that would lift it to the top of its market, and scored its coup with the 1992 debut of "X-Men," an animated program produced by Saban Entertainment, Inc. In February 1993, during the month-long "sweeps" rating period when advertising rates were determined, "X-Men" ranked as the winner, giving Loesch and Fox Children's Network their first ratings crown and breaking the stranglehold held by the major networks on Saturday mornings. Once the network rose to its dominant position, it never looked back. Shortly after "X-Men" captured the hearts of young viewers, Loesch aired another new children's program that obliterated every record in children's television history. The program ignited a powerful trend that could rightly be termed a phenomenon, making Fox Children's Network the preeminent children's broadcaster in the country.

On August 28, 1993, the ''Mighty Morphin Power Rangers'' debuted on the Fox Children's Network, quickly sparking incredible popularity among young viewers that led to unprecedented ratings and an armada of merchandising paraphernalia. Within several weeks after its debut, the half-hour ''live-action cartoon'' became the most popular children's television show in the country. Among viewers between two and 11 years old, the ''Power Rangers'' earned a record-setting 73 share. During one week in October 1994, the program averaged a previously unfathomable 91 share among boys aged six to 11. Once the program demonstrated its dominance in the United States, the ''Power Rangers'' frenzy swept into foreign markets, ascending to the number one ranking among children's television series in a host of countries, including France, Canada, Italy, Germany, and Israel. The popularity of the show was staggering, establishing a new benchmark for other networks to pursue, but the ratings earned by the television program represented only a portion of its power.

Aside from attracting legions of loyal viewers, the ''Power Rangers'' represented a mighty revenue-generating engine capable of producing cash outside the realm of television. The Power Ranger characters were cultural icons, selected as the national teen ambassadors of D.A.R.E., the United States' largest anti-drug and anti-violence program, which targeted children in thousands of schools throughout the nation. The popularity of the show's heroes spawned a line of toys that represented more than $1 billion worth of merchandise available to consumers worldwide. A $3 million live stage production called ''Mighty Morphin Power Rangers Live'' was put on tour, eclipsing all-time box office records for family entertainment by grossing nearly $30 million in 82 North American shows between 1994 and 1995. As plans were being developed for a follow-up tour of the stage production that would include shows in Mexico and Australia, *Mighty Morphin Power Rangers: The Movie* debuted under distribution by 20th Century Fox, grossing nearly $40 million during its first month.

Mid-1990s Alliance with Saban

''Power Rangers'' became a legendary television program, and like ''X-Men,'' the show was produced by Saban Entertainment, a broadly based entertainment organization that had helped Loesch carve a lasting place for Fox Children's Network on the airwaves. The ties between Saban Entertainment and Loesch's network were strengthened considerably when the two organizations formed a strategic alliance in 1995. A short time later, Saban Entertainment and Fox Children's Network consolidated, which gave rise to the formation of Fox Kids Worldwide, Inc., the immediate predecessor to Fox Family Worldwide. The central personality behind Saban Entertainment was its founder and most senior executive, Haim Saban. Saban's growing influence over Fox Children's Network and its parent company, Fox Kids Worldwide, Inc., engendered controversy and tumult during the late 1990s, changing the face of Fox's children's television network.

Saban, an Israeli born in Egypt, displayed his entrepreneurial bent early in life, employing a crew of boys to clean barns near the agricultural school he attended as a 14-year-old. Later, when he was in his early 20s, Saban joined a band, then put away his musical instrument to become the band's manager.

Saban's passion for music and his penchant for the business world led to a quick rise in his country's music industry. By the age of 25—three years after he had joined a local band—Saban was the leading music promoter and manager in Israel, holding sway as the head of his own company, Saban/Tait Productions. Through his company, Saban managed several well-known bands and arranged concert dates in Israel for such popular U.S. music artists as Jose Feliciano and Blood, Sweat, and Tears. Fast on the rise, Saban appeared headed for considerable fame and fortune as an Israeli music mogul, but the Yom Kippur War in 1973 cut short his promising career. Saban tried to promote several special music events in the wake of hostilities, but all were disappointing ventures. Unable to rekindle the success he had enjoyed earlier, Saban left Israel with $1,500 in his pocket and resettled in France.

Shortly after arriving in France, Saban convinced a backer to finance the production of a record featuring a nine-year-old boy named Noam Kaniel, who sang in French. The record went platinum, selling two million copies, which gave Paris-based Saban Records an encouraging start in the business world. For Saban, success bred further success, making Saban Records the leading independent recording company in France seven years after it was started. Within that period, Saban Records had produced 15 gold and platinum records, but the ambitious Saban wanted more. One year after forming Saban Records, he showed his skill in other business areas by diversifying into television soundtrack recordings. His company's first recording was the soundtrack to the Japanese animated television series ''Goldorak,'' which sold more than 3.5 million copies.

Saban registered further success by creating foreign soundtracks to popular American television shows such as ''Dallas,'' ''Starsky & Hutch,'' and ''Hart to Hart,'' selling different versions for French, Spanish, and Latin American broadcasters. Next, he began producing soundtracks for children's animated television programs in the United States, selling the soundtracks to international markets. By the beginning of the 1980s, a Saban empire was taking shape, particularly after the 1980 formation of Los Angeles-based Saban Entertainment, which began producing music for U.S. television series. Another petal to the blossoming empire was added when Saban began producing television programs. In 1985, he sold his first in-house production to NBC, a program titled ''Kidd Video'' that mixed live action with animation. ''Kidd Video'' proved to be an unequivocal success in the United States and ultimately was syndicated in more than 70 countries.

Such were the antecedents to Saban Entertainment's production of ''X-Men'' and the ''Mighty Morphin Power Rangers.'' The partnership between Saban Entertainment and Fox Children's Network in 1995, however, augured a new era for Saban, one that would include the stewardship of a television network, which represented a meaningful leap from his previous role as a supplier of programming to television networks. One year after the alliance between Saban Entertainment and Fox Children's Network was cemented, the two companies consolidated and Fox Kids Worldwide, Inc. was created, its mission to oversee the operation of both Saban Entertainment and Fox Children's Network.

Owned equally by Murdoch's The News Corporation Limited and Saban Entertainment, the newly created Fox Kids Worldwide sent a reverberating shockwave throughout the U.S. television industry with its June 1997 announcement that it was acquiring International Family Entertainment. The acquisition, valued at nearly $2 billion, included International Family Entertainment's principal asset, cable television's widely popular The Family Channel, which provided family-oriented programming to more than 72 million U.S. television homes. The transaction, completed in September 1997, caused a considerable stir at Fox Kids Worldwide well before any final papers were signed. In July 1997, a management shakeup occurred that included Loesch. She was promoted to vice-chairman, but common consensus both within and outside the company pointed to the exact opposite of a promotion. With no staff responsible for reporting to her and with the ephemeral duties of the company's "global strategist," Loesch had effectively been removed from all operations. She was "blindsided," according to one colleague, and many inside the company did not expect her to return from a month-long vacation. Saban, along with top executives at Murdoch's The News Corporation, apparently had decided to move toward the future without the help of Loesch.

Critics and proponents alike explained Loesch's "promotion" by noting that despite the popularity of the shows she had aired, she had never delivered a big hit with merchandising opportunities that the company owned. Her ouster, these same sources reasoned, was signaled by the inclusion of Saban as a partner and the billions of dollars at stake in the International Family Entertainment acquisition. Senior executives close to Murdoch were anxious about the mega-acquisition, desirous of a "business-first" leader, and Saban was renowned for running "his own ship" and bestowing little authority to his second-in-command. Other Fox Kids Worldwide executives were shown the exit door in July 1997, but Loesch was the most prominent personality to suffer from the company's ambitious moves in the late 1990s.

1997 Acquisition of The Family Channel Spawns New Company

The assimilation of International Family Entertainment's The Family Channel into Fox Kids Worldwide's operations, led to a significant corporate name change in May 1998 when Fox Kids Worldwide changed its name to Fox Family Worldwide, Inc. Beneath the corporate umbrella of Fox Family Worldwide were a number of different operating companies, including the Fox Family Channel, Fox Kids Network, Saban International, and Fox Kids International, which comprised dedicated cable and satellite channels that broadcasted programming to 30 countries. Saban, chairman and chief executive officer of the newly named company, explained the reasoning behind the name change, noting in a press release, "By embracing the 'Family' designation in our corporate name and broadening the demographics, we are more accurately acknowledging our target audience and business objectives." Saban added, "We are creating media for kids, their teenage siblings as well as their parents and grandparents—consumers of all ages." With this lofty objective directing the company's future as it prepared for the beginning of the 21st century, Fox Family Worldwide moved forward, striving to offer enticing television programming to, quite simply, everyone.

Principal Subsidiaries

Fox Family Channel; Fox Kids Network; Saban Entertainment; Fox Kids International.

Further Reading

Schmuckler, Eric, "Tough Times for Fox Kids: with Saban Now in Charge, Company Faces Pressure on Several Fronts," *MEDIAWEEK*, August 18, 1997, p. 8.

—Jeffrey L. Covell

Gart Sports Company

1000 Broadway
Denver, Colorado 80122
U.S.A.
(303) 861-1122
Fax: (303) 829-1511
Web site: http://www.gartsports.com

Public Company
Incorporated: 1946 as Gart Bros. Sporting Goods Co.
Employees: 2,391
Sales: $717 million (1997 est.)
Stock Exchanges: NASDAQ
Ticker Symbol: GRTS
SICs: 5941 Sporting Goods & Bicycle Shops

Appropriately headquartered in the recreation haven of Colorado, Gart Sports Company is the second largest sporting goods retailer in the United States, trailing only The Sports Authority. Thanks to its early 1998 merger with Sportmart, Inc., Gart includes more than 120 stores in its chain, which are located in 16 states in the West and Midwest and average around 35,000 square feet. About half of the stores operate under the Gart Sports name, in Colorado, New Mexico, Wyoming, Utah, Idaho, Montana, Washington, and Nevada; the other half use the Sportmart name, including stores in Illinois, Minnesota, Wisconsin, Iowa, Ohio, California, Oregon, and Washington. The Western-located Gart stores tend to generate a large percentage of their sales from winter sports equipment, rentals, and apparel. By comparison, Sportmarts are primarily located in major metropolitan areas where many customers seek the latest athletic shoes and fashionable sporting apparel. This contrast provides Gart Sports with some protection against the cyclicality of sporting goods sales. Approximately 60 percent of the company's stock is held by Leonard Green & Partners LP, a Los Angeles-based private merchant banking firm.

Founded in 1928

The founding father of Gart Sports was Nathan Gart, the son of a house painter who had emigrated from Russia. Gart started out selling newspapers in downtown Denver, then used his profits to begin buying and selling rings and watches from his customers as a sort of alternative pawn shop. By 1928 he had saved enough money to buy a 12- by 17-foot store at 1643 Larimer Street in Denver for $500. Among the other stores on Larimer at the time were a hamburger stand, a fish and oyster house, and a saddle shop. With $33 in fishing equipment as his inventory and high hopes, he opened Gart Bros., a family sporting goods store specializing in hunting, fishing, and camping supplies. Gart was creative in his use of the cramped store; he, for example, lined boxes of ammunition on the floor, thereby creating both storage space and a new floor at the same time. His first sale was a pocket knife.

The store soon became a family store in another sense when Nathan was joined by his brother George in 1932, his brother Kibby in 1934, and his brother Melvin in 1946. The brothers then incorporated the company as Gart Bros. Sporting Goods Co. in 1946.

"Sniagrab" Debuted in 1954

Meanwhile, during the Great Depression, skiing was slowly turning into a commercial recreational activity in Colorado. The first truly commercial ski resort in Colorado was in place at Winter Park by the late 1930s. Aspen, Breckenridge, and a host of other resorts soon followed. The state's burgeoning ski industry—which really took off in the 1960s—created a huge demand for equipment and apparel, which Gart Bros. quickly stepped in to meet.

In 1954 Gart Bros. held its first annual "Sniagrab" Ski Sale ("Sniagrab" is "bargains" spelled backwards), a preseason sale of ski equipment which became an annual Gart—and Denver—tradition and by the mid-1990s was being touted as the "world's largest ski sale." Company lore has it that the sales event originated during a marketing meeting when Nathan's son Jerry Gart, who had only joined the firm earlier in the year, wrote "bargains" on a paper napkin and, upon turning the napkin over, saw marketing potential in the word "sniagrab." This event eventually became Denver's largest annual sales event. Over the years, Gart also began to offer ski equipment rentals.

Sports Castle Opened in 1971

Under Nathan Gart's continued leadership, Gart Bros. expanded the original store several times over the years so that the initial 12-foot frontage was 100 feet by 1971. By that time, the company had opened four other Gart outlets in the Denver area, including suburban locations in Aurora and Englewood. In 1971, however, the Larimer store was replaced by what became known as the Gart Bros. Sports Castle, a pioneering superstore located at 1000 Broadway in downtown Denver. Built in 1925 by Walter Chrysler for an auto dealership, the building was modeled on a French castle, complete with stone, parapets, and a turret. Gart purchased the building and turned it into a seven-floor, 100,000-square-foot sporting goods superstore featuring a wide range of brand-name merchandise; until the late 1980s, this was the largest sporting goods retail store in the world. The headquarters of Gart Bros. was also set up in this building. The Sports Castle would eventually include an indoor ski ramp and basketball and tennis courts on its roof.

In 1976 the company formed a new division, Gart Bros. Sports Country Stores, for expansion outside of the Denver area. The first non-Denver store was soon open in Fort Collins, a city in Colorado north of Denver. In 1981 Nathan Gart died, leaving a company that had grown to 12 stores. By that time, Jerry Gart was largely running the business, having assumed the presidency some years prior.

Purchased by Thrifty Corp. in 1986

In December 1986 Thrifty Corp.—a Los Angeles-based retailer and a subsidiary of California utility company Pacific Lighting Corp. (soon to be known as Pacific Enterprises Inc.)—bought Gart Bros. for approximately $20 million, with the Gart family slated to continue to run the company. By this time, Gart was a 16-store chain with annual sales estimated at between $25 and $30 million. Jerry Gart needed a cash infusion in order to pursue an aggressive expansion strategy, including taking the company outside its home state for the first time. He did just that the following year, with a 65,000-square-foot ''sports castle'' superstore opening in Salt Lake City; five other smaller Gart stores opened in Utah as well, all in 1987.

Utah, however, was just the beginning of a Gart spending spree. In mid-1987 the company bought three Hagan Sports stores in Denver. In early 1988 Gart bought Dave Cook Sporting Goods Co. for about $20 million. Dave Cook was a longtime rival to Gart and the number two sporting goods retailer in Denver at the time of its purchase by Gart. While the first Dave Cook store had opened in 1932, there were 21 by 1988, all located in Colorado, except for a single store in Casper, Wyoming. Gart and Cook had been bitter competitors

for 60 years, frequently engaging in price wars, but were now joined together in a 48-store regional sporting goods empire. Herb Cook, son of founder Dave Cook, initially joined Gart Bros. following the sale, but resigned—along with other Cook family members—in early 1989. Although at first Gart continued to use the Hagan and Dave Cook names on its acquired stores, by the early 1990s a gradual conversion had resulted in all the stores bearing the Gart name.

In 1988 Gart also bought Casey's Sports Stores, a 49-year-old, 12-store chain based in St. Louis. Following the purchase, six more Casey's were soon opened in Kansas City. By the recessionary early 1990s, however, Gart executives had decided to return to the company's Rocky Mountain base. In June 1991, therefore, they sold their St. Louis and Kansas City stores to MC Sports of Grand Rapids, Michigan. By 1991 Gart had 13 stores in Utah and had entered Idaho for the first time with a store in Boise. Annual sales of Gart Bros. for 1990 were estimated at more than $140 million.

New Owner, Resignation of Garts in 1992

In February 1992 Pacific Enterprises put up for sale Thrifty Corp., including its Gart Bros. subsidiary as well as two other sporting goods chains and three drugstore chains. In September Leonard Green & Partners LP, a Los Angeles-based investor group experienced in the retail sector, paid $275 million for Thrifty. The following month the Gart family attempted to repurchase Gart Bros. through a management buyout but were unable to reach an agreement with Leonard Green. In November six members of the Gart family who held senior management positions at the company resigned, ending 64 years of Gart family management. The Garts subsequently entered the real estate business, building and selling condominiums, before returning to the sporting goods business in January 1994 when they began purchasing smaller specialty sporting goods retailers, including Grand West Outfitters, Colorado Ski & Golf, and Boulder Ski Deals. Jerry Gart died on October 12, 1996, following a series of strokes.

Upon the resignations of the Gart family members, John Chase was named president and CEO of Gart Bros. Chase was a 27-year retailing veteran, with stints as president of Home Base, Fotomat Corporation, and Child World/Children's Palace. With the departure of the Garts, the company's new owners felt that a name change was appropriate. A new holding company called Gart Sports Company was created, with Gart Bros. Sporting Goods Co. becoming its operating subsidiary.

Superstore and Geographic Expansion in the Mid-1990s

By the beginning of 1993 the number of units in the Gart Sports chain still stood at 48 as the company had concentrated on assimilating its late 1980s acquisitions. In mid-1993, however, growth was back on the front burner, evidenced by the purchase of 10 stores from the bankrupt Herman's World of Sporting Goods chain. Five of the stores were in Utah, bringing the total there to 17, while the other five joined two existing stores in Idaho. Gart Sports had clearly become the top sporting goods retailer in the Rocky Mountain region. In 1994 the company expanded into Montana and the following year into New Mexico, while the states of Washington and Nevada became Gart territory in 1997.

At the same time that it was expanding geographically, Gart Sports joined the trend toward larger stores. Although the company had been a pioneer in large-format stores with its Sports Castle, many of the stores in its chain were either shopping mall locations averaging 11,500 square feet or freestanding/strip center stores—typically located in smaller markets—averaging 15,000 square feet. In the mid-1990s, Gart Sports opened several "superstores" ranging from 45,000 to 60,000 square feet and intended to be "category killers." The move was in part a defensive one, as the company was facing increasing pressure from such large-format chains as JumboSports and REI. In 1993 Gart opened its first suburban superstore in Aurora, Colorado, while three more superstores debuted the following year, including one in Billings, Montana. In 1996 four superstores opened for business, two in Salt Lake City, one in Colorado Springs, and one in Missoula, Montana.

Meanwhile, in September 1993 Gart announced plans to sell 15 percent of the company to the public. Less than two months later, however, Leonard Green called off the IPO because of complications resulting from Green's purchase of PayLess Drug Stores Northwest Inc. In May 1995 Chase resigned as head of Gart Sports. Doug Morton was named the new president, CEO, and chairman. Morton had joined the company in 1986 as manager of the Utah division, eventually rising to the position of executive vice-president of operations and advertising in 1995.

1998 Acquisition of Sportmart

By the middle of 1997, Gart Sports had 61 stores in seven states. Seeking to fund further expansion, company officials once again began to plan an initial public offering. But an opportunity to expand rapidly through a huge acquisition presented itself in the form of Sportmart, Inc. [for Sportmart's history, see *IDCH* 15], scuttling this IPO as well. Ironically, the first Sportmart had opened in 1971, the year the Gart Sports Castle debuted. Sportmart, based in Wheeling, Illinois, was the first category killer to enter the sporting goods market. By 1997 it had 59 stores in seven states—Illinois, Minnesota, Iowa, Ohio, California, Oregon, and Washington—and posted sales of $514.6 million but a loss of $27.1 million for fiscal 1997. Sportmarts—averaging 40,000 square feet apiece—were larger on average than Gart stores and they were concentrated more heavily in large metropolitan areas than Gart's more scattered stores.

In a deal completed in January 1998, Sportmart agreed to merge into Gart Sports' Gart Bros. subsidiary, with Gart Sports Company emerging through a stock split as a public company on the NASDAQ exchange. Adding Gart's approximate revenue of $202 million to the $514.6 million pushed the new Gart Sports into the number two position in sporting goods in the United States, behind The Sports Authority and its approximate revenues of $1.7 billion. Gart Sports now had 120 stores in 16 states, compared to Sports Authority's 174. Leonard Green & Partners controlled about 60 percent of the company's stock following the acquisition. Morton was named chairman, CEO, and president of Gart Sports, while Andrew Hochberg, who had headed up Sportmart, served as a consultant.

The merger seemed to be a good marriage between two chains that overlapped very little geographically—with the exception of Washington state. In part for this reason, no imme-

diate plans were announced to change store names, so the company operated both Gart Sports and Sportmart units. The match also seemed promising because Gart stores were largely located in the mountain states, while Sportmart's category killers had landed mainly in large metropolitan areas. This mixture held hope for countering some of the cyclicality of sporting goods sales, as the Gart units generated almost a quarter of their revenue from winter sports, while Sportmarts generated a large proportion of their sales from athletic shoes and apparel—20 percent from Nike-brand products alone (only eight percent of Gart sales were for Nike wear). Although issues of integration were likely to predominate for a few years following the merger, another opportunity presented therein was that of further growth through purchases of smaller chains struggling in the highly competitive sporting goods market or through moving into any number of additional markets not yet served by either Gart or Sportmart.

Principal Subsidiaries

Gart Bros. Sporting Goods Company; Colorado Wholesale Sporting Goods Company; Sportmart, Inc.; Sportdepot Stores Inc.; Thaxton Corporation.

Further Reading

Accola, John, "Gart Bros. Owner Hunts for a Buyer," *Rocky Mountain News,* February 6, 1992, pp. 33, 37.

Bernstein, Andy, "Gart Takes Two-Spot with Sportmart Buy," *Sporting Goods Business,* October 14, 1997, p. 8.

Bronikowski, Lynn, "Parent of Gart Bros. Chain Sold in $275 Million Deal," *Rocky Mountain News,* May 23, 1992, pp. 71, 76.

Bunn, Dina, "Gart Becomes a Big Player," *Rocky Mountain News,* September 30, 1997, pp. 1B, 8B.

"Gart Focuses on Communication and Customization," *Discount Store News,* February 9, 1998, pp. 40+.

George, Melissa, "The World According to Gart: Sportmart Deal Only the Start," *Crain's Chicago Business,* February 2, 1998, pp. 4+.

Graham, Judith, "Garts Walk Off the Sporting Goods Field," *Denver Post,* November 10, 1992, pp. 1A, 10A.

Mayer, Kimberly, "Gart Buys St. Louis Firm, Plans Midwest Expansion," *Rocky Mountain News,* March 17, 1988, p. 70.

——, "Los Angeles Company Buys Gart Bros., Enabling Growth," *Rocky Mountain News,* January 1, 1987, p. 77.

——, "Public Won't See Changes in Stores, Say Gart, Cook," *Rocky Mountain News,* March 21, 1988, pp. 63, 65.

McEvoy, Chris, "Doug Morton," *Sporting Goods Business,* December 15, 1997, pp. 28+.

Parker, Penny, "Gart Now a Sports Giant," *Denver Post,* September 30, 1997, pp. 1C, 9C.

——, "Merger of Sportmart, Gart Expected," *Denver Post,* January 9, 1998, p. 3C.

Raabe, Steve, "Wall Street Player, Larimer Street Roots," *Denver Post,* September 30, 1997, pp. 1C, 9C.

Rebchook, John, "Gart to Acquire Sportmart," *Rocky Mountain News,* September 29, 1997, pp. 4A, 20A.

Troy, Mike, "Gart Grows to No. 2," *Discount Store News,* February 9, 1998, pp. 39+.

——, "Sporting Goods Chains Target Southern California Customers," *Discount Store News,* February 23, 1998, pp. 6, 42.

Wiscombe, Janet, "Garts Vs. Cooks," *Denver Magazine,* February 1987, pp. 72–77.

—David E. Salamie

General Re Corporation

Financial Centre
695 East Main Street
Stamford, Connecticut 06904-2351
U.S.A.
(203) 328-5000
Fax: (203) 328-6423
Web site: http://www.genre.com

Public Company
Incorporated: 1921 as General Casualty and Surety
Reinsurance Corporation
Employees: 3,737
Total Assets: $8.25 billion (1997)
Stock Exchanges: New York
Ticker Symbol: GRN
SICs: 6331 Fire, Marine & Casualty Insurance; 6351
Surety Insurance; 6411 Insurance Agents, Brokers &
Services; 6719 Offices of Holding Companies, Not
Elsewhere Classified

General Re Corporation is a holding company for General Reinsurance Corporation and National Reinsurance Corporation, which together comprise the largest U.S.-based property/casualty reinsurance group. Reinsurance is a means by which an insurance company is able to dilute its total liability by ceding a percentage of its policies to another insurer, who is therefore said to provide "reinsurance." Such a practice was frowned upon in the early history of insurance as little more than gambling, but with the growth of insurance coverage in the 20th century, reinsurance has become a widespread, profitable, and even prestigious business. General Re also holds a 78 percent stake in the oldest reinsurance company in the world, Cologne Re, which is active in nearly 150 countries; the combined operations of General Re and Cologne Re rank as the world's third largest reinsurance business. Among the company's other operations are Herbert Clough Inc., provider of reinsurance brokerage services; United States Aviation Underwriters, Inc., a manager of aviation insurance risks; and Ardent Risk Services, Inc., a business development consultant and reinsurance intermediary.

Formed Through 1921 Merger

General Casualty and Surety Reinsurance Corporation was formed by the 1921 merger of Norwegian Globe and Norwegian Assurance, two insurance companies under the direction of Robert Iberstein. The new company, with Iberstein as president, began operations in New York with a capital fund of $800,000. As reinsurance was not yet widely practiced in the United States, General Casualty and Surety had few domestic competitors, and even overseas only a handful of European firms were actively pursuing reinsurance clients. In 1923 Iberstein and his board of directors resigned and James White, an engineer of some renown and a business consultant, took over the company's leadership. White then renamed the company General Reinsurance Corporation.

An excellent national economy allowed General Reinsurance to expand rapidly until the Great Depression struck in 1929. President White assembled a board of directors that included Edgar H. Boles, a lawyer formerly associated with the Lehigh Railroad. In 1930 Boles became president of General Reinsurance. The company had assets of approximately $12.3 million at the time. As the Depression lengthened, General Reinsurance not only struggled with the generally poor economic conditions but also sustained a number of heavy losses as an insurer. The experience and sagacity of Edgar Boles is widely credited with saving the company.

During these early years, General Reinsurance concentrated primarily on fire and casualty reinsurance, forming agreements with its primary insurance customers that called for General Reinsurance to assume a fixed proportion of the primary insurer's total liability. An alternative type of reinsurance, known as facultative reinsurance and often used for large, well-defined risks, requires that the two insurers negotiate a separate premium for each new policy written. Because it was nearly alone in the domestic U.S. reinsurance market, General Reinsurance early discovered that it could charge a healthy fee for its services without losing significant amounts of business. The company's assets rose steadily, and despite the setbacks of the 1930s, General Reinsurance built a reputation as a solid, blue-chip firm.

Merged with Mellon Indemnity in 1945

Increased international competition during and immediately after World War II forced General Reinsurance to seek additional sources of capital. In 1945 the company found a suitable partner in Mellon Indemnity Corporation, a somewhat smaller insurance company owned by the Mellon family of Pittsburgh, Pennsylvania. Mellon Indemnity actually wrote little insurance, serving mainly as an investment vehicle for the Mellons, but its strong balance sheet was attractive to General Reinsurance. In November 1945 a stock swap merged the two companies, which together boasted $38 million in assets and wrote $18 million worth of premiums in the following year. Edgar Boles remained as president of the new company, 40 percent of which was owned by the Mellon family.

In 1946 Edgar Boles retired after 16 years as the head of General Reinsurance. His replacement, Edward Lowry, served from 1950 to 1960, and played an important role in formulating General Reinsurance's business philosophy for the coming decades. Under Lowry, the board decided that General Reinsurance could best make use of its leadership position and strong assets by adopting a conservative posture. General Reinsurance would accept only those policies that met its standards for safety and premium level, thereby assuring itself of a net profit from its underwriting business alone. In addition, General Reinsurance decided to make only the most prudent investments, chiefly in bonds; to maintain unusually large reserves against the threat of multiple catastrophes; and to pay out a dividend smaller than the industry norm. Bolstered by the Mellons' financial security and golden name, General Reinsurance set out to become not only the largest and most profitable of U.S. reinsurers but also the industry's most distinguished player.

This policy succeeded in every respect. Under the leadership of James Cathcart and Robert Braddock, two members of the management team put together by Edward Lowry, General Reinsurance enjoyed several decades of remarkable financial health. The firm stuck to its high-priced premiums, demanding and getting the kind of fees that allowed it to earn a consistent profit on its underwriting business. A standard measure of underwriting success is the "combined ratio," which matches operating losses and expenses against annual underwriting income. If that figure comes out about even—expressed as 100 percent—the company's underwriting division is breaking even, and the firm can anticipate earning good money on its extensive investments. At General Reinsurance, the combined ratio hovered at a low 97 percent during the 30 years following the 1946 merger with Mellon—a good indication that General Reinsurance was not only highly profitable but also building unusually large reserves against potential future losses.

Recorded as assets, these reserves increased over the years. From the $38 million recorded in 1946, General Reinsurance's assets rose to approximately $175 million in 1960 and to four times that amount a decade later. Part of this capital was used to open branches in Canada and Brazil, as well as an additional half-dozen locations in the United States, but most of General Reinsurance's growing wealth was simply reinvested in secure, low-tax bonds. This expanding portfolio supplied the lion's share of General Reinsurance's profit, which showed an enviable 16 percent annual compounded growth rate from 1959 to 1969. Such sustained profitability, in turn, allowed the company to further strengthen its asset base and continue its tough premium pricing.

Faced Increased Competition in the 1970s and 1980s

As profit growth increased at an even greater rate in the early 1970s, General Reinsurance's extraordinary record began to attract attention. The Reinsurance business looked more appealing when it was accompanied by a 22 percent annual increase in profit, as General Reinsurance's was during the decade of the 1970s, and the once exclusive club of reinsurers was soon crowded with new competitors. Prudential and Sears' Allstate formed reinsurance divisions, followed by newcomers to the entire insurance field like Ford, Armco, and Gulf Oil. The many large companies that had recently formed "captive" insurance units to handle their own risk management were also soon chasing the apparently easy money in reinsurance.

General Reinsurance responded to the suddenly competitive market conditions by doing nothing. It chose not to compete at a depressed premium level and issued a number of dire warnings about the danger of doing business with reinsurance firms lacking the experience and capital reserves sufficient to meet the next nationwide catastrophe. True to its philosophy, General Reinsurance accepted only those policies for which it could charge high premiums, and as a result its underwriting premiums dropped in 1979 for the first time in corporate history. Chairman Harold Hudson, Jr., was also faced with the departure of a number of key executives and a growing perception in the industry that General Reinsurance's patrician style of reinsurance was out-of-date. In response, Hudson initiated a few changes, most notably the 1980 organization of General Re Corporation, which acquired General Reinsurance Corporation and its subsidiaries. The formation of the holding company followed General Reinsurance's acquisition of its first primary insurance subsidiary, and both moves signaled a new competitiveness at General Re. The company, however, reiterated its conviction that reinsurance was no place for fast-moving profit hounds and that survival was the real measure of success in a business that in a sense depends on disaster.

As events unfolded, it appeared that Hudson and his conservative colleagues at General Re were correct. After enduring a few nervous years as a probable takeover target and a brief mid-1980s profit dip, General Re turned around its underwriting slump and continued its traditionally steady growth. Despite the onslaught of competitors, General Re remained the dominant factor in U.S. reinsurance, writing some 10 percent of all U.S. polices, while its field of challengers thinned after only a few years. As the company always maintained, reinsurance is a business for those with deep pockets, and General Re's portfolio of $8.8 billion in invested insurance assets in 1989 amply met even its conservative definition of adequate reserves.

More Aggressive Stance in the 1990s

The 1990s brought a host of new challenges to reinsurance companies, including ever fiercer competition, a rapidly changing financial services industry, and globalization. In response, General Re took a more aggressive posture to protect its leading position, seeking out acquisitions and establishing new lines of business.

With lines between traditional reinsurance, financial derivatives, and securities blurring, General Re in 1990 took the preemptive action of establishing General Re Financial Products Corporation, a global derivative products dealer offering interest rate, currency, equity swaps and options, and other derivative products to help clients manage financial risks. Two other new subsidiaries were formed in the 1990s to expand General Re's range of services. In 1993 General Re Asset Management was established to provide investment management and advisory services to the insurance and healthcare industries (this unit was later known as General Re-New England Asset Management, Inc.). In late 1997 General Re formed Ardent Risk Services, Inc., a business development consulting firm and reinsurance intermediary.

In the early 1990s only about 10 percent of General Re's premiums came from overseas. General Re sought to join the globalization trend in financial services, although its first major attempt failed. The company in April 1991 agreed in principle to purchase an 80 percent stake in Royal Reinsurance Co. Ltd. of the United Kingdom, but a few months later the deal fell apart. Over the next few years the company made two small international acquisitions and opened offices or operations in Cologne, Milan, Singapore, Buenos Aires, and Copenhagen. But it was in late 1994 that General Re seriously stepped up its international presence through the purchase of a 75 percent stake in Germany-based Kölnische Rückversicherungs-Gesellschaft AG (Cologne Re), the world's oldest reinsurance company, having been founded in 1846. Cologne Re handled property-casualty, life/health, and financial reinsurance in nearly 150 countries through 37 offices in 27 countries. Combining General Re's number four position in reinsurance worldwide with Cologne Re's number five position created the third largest reinsurer in the world. About 45 percent of General Re's premiums now came from outside the United States.

General Re also used an acquisition to boost its domestic operations, when it bought National Reinsurance Corporation for about $940 million in October 1996. National Re was the 17th largest U.S. reinsurer with net premiums booked of $334.4 million in 1995 (General Re booked $2.96 billion in North American premiums that year). The addition of National Re,

which was also headquartered in Stamford, Connecticut, was considered to be particularly strategic in that the acquired firm was likewise a conservatively run reinsurer with one of the lowest combined ratios in the industry. National Re's clients, however, were mainly regional and small, niches that General Re had not been able to fully penetrate.

Overall, General Re fared well in the challenging years of the 1990s, despite some difficulties. The entire property-casualty industry was hurt by record disasters in 1992, leading General Re to post a combined ratio of 108.4. For the overall ten-year period ending in 1997, however, the company posted an average combined ratio for its North American operations of 100.7, which, while not the best results in company history, was much better than its competitors' during the same period. Net premiums written of $6.55 billion and invested insurance assets of $24.58 billion in 1997 provided additional support for the strength of America's number one reinsurer.

Principal Subsidiaries

General Reinsurance Corporation; Kölnische Rückversicherungs-Gesellschaft AG (Cologne Re) (Germany; 78%); General Star Management Company; Herbert Clough, Inc.; Genesis Underwriting Management Company; Ardent Risk Services, Inc.; General Re Financial Products Corporation; General Re-New England Asset Management, Inc.; United States Aviation Underwriters, Inc.

Further Reading

Andresky, Jill, "General Re: Dark Before Dawn," *Financial World*, February 21, 1989, p. 18.

"General Re: Number One and Planning to Stay There," *Institutional Investor*, August 1994, p. S7.

Greenwald, Judy, "General Re Consolidates Its Lead: Acquisition of National Re Seen As Strategic Move and a Good Fit for Reinsurer," *Business Insurance*, July 8, 1996, pp. 1, 22.

Jennings, John, "Gen Re Deal with Colonia a 'Home Run,'" *National Underwriter Property & Casualty-Risk & Benefits Management*, July 11, 1994, p. 3.

——, "Gen Re Still Way Out in Front of the Pack," *National Underwriter Property & Casualty-Risk & Benefits Management*, July 1, 1991, p. S18.

Maxey, Brigitte, "General Re Beginning to Recover from Underwriting Profit Slump," *Journal of Commerce*, August 7, 1992, pp. 1A, 3A.

McLeod, Douglas, "Gen Re, Berkley to Combine Units: Proposed Joint Venture to Operate North Star Re, Signet," *Business Insurance*, February 22, 1993, pp. 2, 16.

Pitt, William, "General Re Drops Plans to Purchase Royal Re," *Journal of Commerce*, July 1, 1991, p. 9A.

Rumely, Paul, *The History of General Re: 65 Years in Reinsurance*, Stamford, Connecticut: General Re Corporation, 1986.

Scism, Leslie, "General Re Agrees to Buy National Re in Deal Valued at About $940 Million," *Wall Street Journal*, July 2, 1996, p. A4.

Starkman, Dean, and Leslie Scism, "General Re's USAU Is Ordered to Pay Fine of $20.5 Million in Fraud Case," *Wall Street Journal*, June 27, 1997, p. B9.

—Jonathan Martin
—updated by David E. Salamie

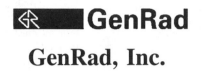

GenRad, Inc.

300 Baker Avenue
Concord, Massachusetts 01742-2174
U.S.A.
(508) 287-7541
Fax: (508) 287-2002
Web site: http://www.genrad.com

Public Company
Incorporated: 1978
Employees: 1,239
Sales: $183.6 million (1996)
Stock Exchanges: New York
Ticker Symbol: GEN
SICs: 3829 Measuring & Controlling Devices, Not
  Elsewhere Classified; 7371 Computer Programming
  Services; 7372 Prepackaged Software; 7373 Computer
  Integrated System Design; 3825 Instruments for
  Measuring & Testing of Electricity & Electrical
  Signals

GenRad, Inc. is a worldwide leader in providing after-market service solutions—supplying manufacturers, OEMs, and their customers with hardware, software, and services to optimize manufacturing and after-market service productivity through increased yields and lower life cycle costs—for the in-line testing of printed circuit boards (PCBs), primarily in the networking, computer, communications, transportation, and automotive industries.

In 1997, the company had sales offices in Fremont, Irvine, and San Jose, California; Altamonte Springs, Florida; Arlington Heights, Illinois; Frederick, Maryland; Concord and Westford, Massachusetts; Novi, Michigan; Portland, Oregon; and Plano, Texas in the United States, and in Cedex, France; Ismaning and Munich, Germany; Milan, Italy; Science Park, Singapore; Zurich, Switzerland; and Maidenhead, Manchester, and Windsor, United Kingdom.

Major customers include personal computer (PC) board fabricators Avex Electronics Inc., Jabil Circuit Inc., and Solectron; computer and telecommunications equipment manufacturers Acer, Alcatel, Cabletron Systems, Compaq, Dell, Digital Equipment Corp., IBM Corp., Lucent Technologies, Motorola, Nokia, SCI Systems, Seagate Technology Inc., and U.S. Robotics; and transportation manufacturers Aston-Martin, BMW AG Motorcycle Group, British Airways, Chrysler Corp., Claas, Ford Motor Co., Jaguar, and Saab AB of Sweden; as well as the U.S. Marine Corps. and an Asian military manufacturer. Major competitors include Hewlett-Packard Co., Siemens AG, and Teradyne.

The company has three major divisions: Advanced Diagnostic Solutions (ADS), Electronic Manufacturing Systems (EMS), and Integrated Customer Services (ICS). Complementing each other, the three divisions give the company unprecedented breadth of testing solutions to the electronics manufacturing markets.

The Manchester, England-based Advanced Diagnostic Solutions division focuses on providing comprehensive diagnostic solutions to transportation manufacturers, especially in the automotive industry. The ADS division brought in approximately 23 percent of total 1996 revenues for the company.

The Concord-Massachusetts-based Electronic Manufacturing Systems division, formerly known as Concord Products, which includes circuit testing, functional testing, and the Mitron product line, was responsible for approximately 73 percent of revenues for 1996. Circuit testing attempts to determine whether integrated circuit parts are physically connected to the PCB. Functional testing—comprised mainly of the company's "GENEVA" (GenRad's Extended VXI Architecture) product line, a family of integrated, open, standards-based test systems, designed to operate on the manufacturing line and featuring integrated scanning techniques with the capability for performing design, parametric, and compliance tests—verifies that the PCB does what it is supposed to do. The Mitron product line

---

---

consists of software which integrates not only the board and circuit testing machines, but other testing devices in a manufacturing line.

The Integrated Customer Services division was created by the acquisition of several companies in 1996. The ICS division focuses on custom test programming and test fixture integration to manufacturers of electronic products. Every PCB manufactured and tested requires a program to be written and loaded into the tester to tell the machine how to test the board. Every time a new type of board is tested, a new program must be written. The programming industry that services this area has traditionally been fragmented by region. With the creation of this division in 1996, the company became the largest market share holder in this industry.

The Clapp-Eastham Company, 1906–15

GenRad, which may be the oldest company in the world with the word "radio" in it, traces its roots back to 1906, when Melville Eastham cofounded The Clapp, Eddy and Eastham Company. Located at 100 Boylston Street in Boston, it was started to manufacture x-ray machines. In 1907 Eddy left and the firm was renamed The Clapp-Eastham Company.

Eastham found that the high-voltage spark coils used to excite x-ray tubes were becoming popular with radio amateurs, called "ham radio operators" or "hams," for their transmitters. The company began to manufacture heavy-current keys, tuning coils, spark gaps, crystal detectors, and many other components used by professional radio operators and hams. As the radio segment of the business grew and the x-ray segment diminished, Clapp, whose interests lay mostly in x-ray equipment, sold his portion of the business in 1910 to O. Kerro Luscomb. That same year, the company moved to a larger facility at Kendall Square in Cambridge, across the river from its old location. By now the company was a staple of the radio industry; its customers included such radio pioneers as E. H. Armstrong, K. A. Fessenden, John Hays Hammond, Jr., G. W. Pickard, G. W. Pierce, and John Stone.

Faced with an increase in commercial competition, and chafed by new restrictions beginning to hamper the company in the manufacture of communications equipment as the industry flourished, Eastham recognized an emerging need for instrumentation in the developing radio field. In 1915, he withdrew from active participation in Clapp-Eastham, leaving Luscomb as manager, and founded the General Radio Company, though Luscomb was interested in Eastham's new company.

General Radio Company, 1915–World War I

Needing finance capital, the two agreed to contribute patents, ideas, and their individual skills for 25 percent interest apiece. Ralph C. Emery, Ralph C. Watrous, and Cyrus P. Brown, three individual investors, put up $9,000 for the other 50 percent. Eastham rented an office on the third floor of a small building (that was still standing in 1997) at the corner of Massachusetts Avenue and Windsor Street in Cambridge. Eastham brought machinist Knut Johnson from Clapp-Eastham, where he had been employed for the previous two years; Johnson remained with the company until he retired in 1945.

Eastham immediately began designing new instruments and landed a commission to build a nine-phase, synchronous, commutator-type rectifier for the American Telephone and Telegraph Company (AT&T). This rectifier played a part in the early history of the radio-telephone. In 1915, AT&T had successfully made the first transcontinental telephone call via land lines. AT&T, and business partner Bureau des Postes, Telegraphes et Telephones in France, was worried that World War I would interrupt communications between the two continents, and wanted to see if radio could be utilized to extend telephone communications across the Atlantic. The Bureau des Postes installed a receiver on the Eiffel Tower, AT&T erected a transmitter in Arlington, Virginia, using 500 15-watt vacuum tubes connected in parallel, and General Radio's synchronous rectifier supplied the high voltage required. Though a historic occasion, the experiment was not quite successful, and it would be many years before a practical, reliable transatlantic telephone would arrive.

General Radio continued research and development and, in 1916, published its first instrument catalog. Some of the products listed included a Precision Variable Air Condenser ($25), a Decade Resistance Box ($19), a Precision Variable Inductance ($24), and an Absorption Wavemeter ($60). Besides AT&T, other early customers included The General Electric Company and The National Bureau of Standards.

The following year, when the U.S. entered World War I, General Radio got caught up in the national effort and found demand for its products increasing. In addition to meeting immediate orders for catalog instruments, the company began manufacturing large amounts of portable wavemeters and crystal sets for trench-warfare communications. The company expanded almost overnight from 24 employees to over 200.

At this time, another General Radio part played a small role in another historic radio event. Some of the first instruments shipped for use in the war were a number of precision air capacitors or "condensers," one of which landed in an Army laboratory in France, where Lieutenant E. H. Armstrong was experimenting with a new circuit to improve the performance of radio receivers. Armstrong quickly appropriated and incorporated the capacitor, his new circuit was successful, and one of General Radio's first products tuned the first super-heterodyne receiver. Today, the same super-heterodyne circuit is used in virtually every television, radar, and communication receiver worldwide.

World War I brought Henry Southworth Shaw to the company. Shaw, a ham operator who had met Eastham when purchasing the company's products, approached Eastham late in 1917 to ask what he could do to help. Eastham hired him on the spot as an instrument designer, but Shaw, the son of a textile-mill treasurer and a liberal arts graduate of Harvard, soon ended up as bookkeeper and office manager. Errol H. Locke joined the company in 1918 via Harvard and, in 1919, Harold B. Richmond arrived via Massachusetts Institute of Technology (MIT) and a wartime lieutenancy in the coast artillery. Locke, Richmond, Eastham, and Shaw would form the nucleus of the company and guide it for the next 30 years.

When the war ended in 1918 and military contracts were canceled, Eastham wanted to manufacture high-quality measuring instruments, but his partners Brown, Emery, and Watrous, wanted to mass-produce radio components. The dispute was resolved when Shaw bought the three out in 1919 for $32,000, which was the last outside financing the company ever needed through at least 1965. Eastham and Shaw now each held 50 percent interest and served as directors, with Lawrence Mayo, Shaw's uncle, brought on to replace Emery and Watrous as a third director.

The company spun off a number of important people in the electronics manufacturing industries, including Homer E. Rawson, who joined the company in 1917, eventually becoming vice-president, and Superintendent Ashley C. Zwicker, a former Clapp-Eastham employee who was General Radio's first foreman. Rawson left in 1919 to join Arthur J. Lush in cofounding Rawson Instrument Company, a manufacturer of sensitive direct-current meters, and Zwicker left in 1920 to found The Acme Apparatus Company, a manufacturer of transformers, rectifiers, and battery eliminators. Later renamed The Delta Manufacturing Company, Zwicker's brainchild eventually became a part of The Raytheon Corporation.

Between World War I and World War II

In 1920, The Westinghouse Electric Company pioneered broadcasting, airing the results of the Harding-Cox Presidential election over the air on KDKA, Pittsburgh. The dramatic success of this first program stimulated the construction of broadcast stations around the country and soon about 30 were on the air. There were, however, almost no receivers except those built by radio hams, known as "ham shacks," which quickly became popular neighborhood rendezvous. Practically overnight, the home-built receiver craze developed, as everyone decided that they could do it, too. General Radio, which had been supplying hams with high-quality components for years, now found itself swamped with tens of thousands of orders. The demand persisted for approximately three years, when complete sets became available at reasonable prices, and the do-it-yourself fad died as quickly as it was born.

The following year, the company contracted with the U.S. Navy to manufacture hydrophones, developed by Professor G. W. Pierce of Harvard to detect underwater sounds. The company added two engineers—assistants of Pierce's at Harvard—H. W. Lamson and P. K. McElroy, to its staff of 135 for the project.

In 1924, General Radio launched into the measurement business in earnest, and began developing and commercializing its long line of instruments, so many of which were firsts in the field. Arthur E. Thiessen, formerly with Bell Telephone Laboratories and Johns Hopkins University, joined the company in 1928 as a development engineer, eventually moving on to marketing, and becoming vice-president of sales in 1944, and a director shortly thereafter.

By 1932, the company was shipping products all over the world, with about 18 percent of all shipments being exported. By 1937, with the lagging European radio industry catching up and the company's reputation established, exports reached 39 percent of total sales, with products being shipped to the U.S.S.R., England, France, Holland, and Belgium.

As the electronics industry rapidly grew, General Radio published a famous advertisement in 1941 captioned, "We Don't Want to Grow Too Large." This may have hurt the company a little. As the threat of another war loomed in the late 1930s, television broadcasting had begun in Great Britain and was approaching commercial form in the United States. Ten years previously, the company pioneered the cathode-ray oscilloscope, with imported tubes from Germany. As satisfactory American tubes reached the market, and demand for oscilloscopes developed, lower-priced competition appeared. Believing that oscilloscopes could be better supplied by others, the company dropped out of the business. In the 1930s, new techniques underlying television and radar rekindled interest, and the company developed, in 1938, a wide-band oscilloscope. The instrument was ahead of its time and was never produced because it was deemed too expensive and complicated. In the 1960s, oscilloscopes far more sophisticated and expensive created a market many times larger than the total instrument market in the 1930s—but General Radio did not make them.

The company entered World War II with two products that played important parts in the war effort—the "Variac" continuously adjustable autotransformer, and the "Strobotac" short-flash light source. The Variac, patented in 1934, is used to efficiently control electrical power (It was another General Radio first which has created an industry that now supports four major competitors.) The Strobotac, created as a result of research by Dr. Harold E. Edgerton and Dr. Kenneth J. Germeshausen at MIT, was the progenitor of electronic-flash units used by photographers, and makes possible the observation, in slow motion, of cyclically recurring events.

Known for its good reputation and solid product line, the company was awash with orders when World War II's industrial mobilization started. Everyone at General Radio threw themselves into the fervor of technological development. Eastham became an early member of MIT's famous Radiation Laboratory, where he was responsible for the development of the Loran system of navigation; Richmond became Chief of "Division 5" of The National Defense Research Council, in charge of the development of guided missiles; W. Norris Tuttle pioneered operations research with the Eighth Air Force in Great Britain; their contributions won them, respectively, two Presidential Medals of Merit, and the Medal of Freedom. Other employees became involved in communications, radar, and radar countermeasures at the company and as members of the Radiation Laboratory and the Radio Research Laboratory at Harvard.

Although materials were in short supply, The War Production Board, which established the priority system allocating scarce materials, felt General Radio's production was important to the war effort and materials flowed in quantities adequate to win the company five Army-Navy "E" awards for excellence in the production of war materials.

Workers were also scarce. The New England Confectionery Company, "Necco" for short, a neighbor completely put out of business by the wartime sugar shortage, came to the rescue. A deal with Necco for use of their workforce, in their factory, solved problems for both companies. General Radio had enough simple, repetitive assembly operations to perform to warrant training and using Necco's girls, who made substantial and useful contributions. Since General Radio had traditionally been an all-male preserve in the production departments, it was hard for the men to accept help from women. When a small group of girls was trained to do inspection jobs in the factory, the acronym GRIEF (General Radio Inspection Emergency Force), was promptly adopted to designate them.

The problem of adequate space was also eased by the Necco arrangement, but permanent additions were needed. The neighboring building, which had been an automobile showroom and garage, became available, adding 39,000 square feet of office space to the company, making 125,000 square feet total. The company's revenues jumped from $1.4 million in 1939 to $6.1 million in 1942, and back down to $2.6 million in 1945.

World War II to 1993

After World War II, with the explosion of scientific knowledge, General Radio, formerly a lone wolf struggling to create a market for quantitative measuring equipment, found itself suddenly with dozens of small new companies, short on capital but long on ideas and enthusiasm. From almost a monopoly position, the company moved to one of participation in a hotly competitive industry.

As electronics companies went public in the great stock market surge of the 1950s and 1960s, General Radio continued to quietly expand its ownership among its own employees. But the grand old men of the company were beginning to leave.

In 1950, Eastham, president and chief engineer since the start, retired. He was succeeded as chief engineer by Donald B. Sinclair, who had been with the company since 1934 as a part-time employee while getting his doctorate in science from MIT. Locke retired in 1955 and was replaced as president by Charles C. Carey, formerly vice-president of manufacturing. Richmond retired in 1960 and was replaced as chairman by Thiessen.

Around the same time, the Cambridge facilities were becoming cramped. In 1948, the company found an 83-acre tract in West Concord, with access by road and rail and, in 1952, General Radio's first suburban building was operating, when the initial wing of a four-wing building was completed. In 1959, when the remaining three wings were built, the Cambridge building was sold, the agreement with Necco was terminated, and General Radio moved into the new building.

The company went public in 1978 and performed well through the 1980s as a tester of PCBs, but ran into trouble in the 1970s when it entered the chip side of the testing market. This move, combined with a lack of focus on the mainstay board-testing business, eventually brought about a financial crisis. In 1992, the company's total revenues reached $144.2 million, but net loss was $7.7 million. The following year, though the company's net sales were $158.7 million, a net loss of $43.8 million was incurred.

1993 to Date

James F. Lyons, formerly president and CEO of Harry Gray Associates, was hired as president and CEO in July 1993 and immediately began to turn the company around. Two divisions were sold, huge amounts of debt were written off, and Lyons redirected the company at its board-testing core.

The following year, the company created an internal research and development (R&D) team to create new software and hardware with in-process inspection capabilities and the company turned its first profit in several years, reaching total revenues of $147.9 million and net income of $4.5 million. In 1995, total revenue increased to $158.8 million, with a net income of $12.3 million.

In June 1996, the company acquired Mitron Inc., a manufacturing software company. The acquisition of the Portland, Oregon-based manufacturer of software products, built on the industry standard "CIMBridge" architecture to analyze and report on data gathered from all points on the manufacturing line, gave the company an immediate competitive position in the industry. Concurrently, the company acquired Milpitas, California-based Test Technology Associates, Inc. (TTA) in January and Hudson, Massachusetts-based Testware, Inc. in November, two test programming service companies. The acquisitions gave the company the largest foothold in the test programming industry. The price for the three companies was approximately $5 million and 1,176,000 shares of stock. Additionally, the company purchased the TRACS software product line from Field Oriented Engineering AG, which provided manufacturers of electronic products real-time data collection, analysis, reporting, and paperless repair for improved manufacturing processes and control.

Also in 1996, the R&D team introduced an inspection management tool suite called "InPro," for use with standard Windows-NT operating platforms. Concurrently, the company unveiled a new inspection system called "The Viper Electrical System," geared toward consumer markets where low-cost testing is key due to more-simplified PCBs. Revenues for 1996 reached $183.6 million, net income jumped to $27.3 million, and the company ranked in the top 25 corporations on the New York Stock Exchange in terms of price performance for the year.

In 1997, the R&D team released another breakthrough system called "Viper Vision," with the ability to optically inspect PCBs at various points in the manufacturing line. That same year, the company landed its largest contract ever when it replaced Hewlett-Packard and beat out Siemens to become the supplier of automotive diagnostic systems for Ford's estimated 20,000 Aston-Martin, Ford, Jaguar, Lincoln-Mercury, and Mazda car dealers worldwide. As part of the $200-$400 million deal, the company planned to build a new facility in Dearborn,

Michigan, near Ford's headquarters, and hire about 150 additional people, plus another 100 employees in Manchester, England. The company already held a similar contract with Saab.

In April 1997, the board of directors authorized a stock repurchase of up to two million shares and K-TEC Electronics selected the company as a partner for manufacturing optimization and information management solutions. In May, the company signed a distribution agreement with Interro Systems. In June, the corporate headquarters moved from Concord to Westford, Massachusetts, and the company announced an agreement, estimated at $10 million in revenues, with Cabletron—a leader in providing high-performance intranet and Internet solutions, including local area network (LAN) and wide area network (WAN) switches, remote access products, and network and systems management software—wherein the company would provide GENEVA Functional Test and Measurement Systems, including "ENCOMPASS" Test Data Management Software and services. December saw the company's Mitron subsidiary selected by Jabil to provide advanced EMS services.

With the PCB manufacturing market estimated at approximately $600 million annually, with GenRad being the only company focusing entirely on vertical integration of testing functions, and with continuing strategic alliances, partnerships, and contracts, the company was in excellent position to grow.

Principal Subsidiaries

Advanced Diagnostic Solutions (U.K.); Electronic Manufacturing Systems; GenRad Benelux B.V. (Netherlands); GenRad Europe Limited (U.K.); GenRad GmbH (Germany); GenRad Holdings Limited (U.K.); GenRad Limited (U.K.); GenRad SA (France); GenRad Securities Corporation; Integrated Customer Services, Inc.; Mitron Corporation; Test Technology Associates.

Principal Divisions

Advanced Diagnostic Solutions; Electronic Manufacturing Systems; Integrated Customer Services.

Further Reading

Andrews, Walter, "GenRad Finds $4 Million in Used Equipment Sales," *Electronic News,* April 11, 1994, p. 48.
Berger, Jeffrey, "Analysts Hear of GenRad's Future," *Electronic News,* October 9, 1995, p. 52.
Dunn, Peter, "After Shakeup, GenRad Plots Next Move," *Electronic News,* April 12, 1993, p. 10.
Earls, Alan R., "GenRad Rejuvenates," *Electronic Business Today,* February 1997, p. 67.
Elliott, Stuart, "GenRad Inc.," *New York Times,* October 22, 1996, p. C7(N)/D13(L).
"GenRad Buys Test Technology Associates," *Electronic News,* January 22, 1996, p. 65.
"GenRad Stock Drops by 24% on Rumors of Weak Earnings," *Wall Street Journal,* March 11, 1997, p. B3(W)/B5(E).
Glass, John, "Six Years Later, Still Losing Money," *Boston Business Journal,* June 10, 1991, p. 1.
"Mitron Buy, Rev. Gains Spur GenRad Results," *Electronic News,* February 3, 1997, p. 56.
Rosenberg, Ronald, "GenRad in Pact with 20,000 Ford Dealers," *Boston Globe,* July 15, 1997, p. E2.

—Daryl F. Mallett

Gleason

Gleason Corporation

1000 University Avenue
P.O. Box 22970
Rochester, New York 14692-2970
U.S.A.
(716) 473-1000
Fax: (716) 461-4092
Web site: http://www.gleasoncorp.com

Public Company
Incorporated: 1903 as The Gleason Works
Employees: 1,543
Sales: $248.1 million (1996)
Stock Exchanges: New York
Ticker Symbol: GLE
SICs: 3541 Machine Tools, Metal Cutting Types; 3829
  Measuring & Controlling Devices, Not Elsewhere
  Classified

With a history stretching over 130 years, Gleason Corporation is the world's most comprehensive resource for the development and manufacture of technologically advanced gear production machinery and tooling. The company is also an acknowledged leader in the theory of gear design and in the application, testing, and analysis of prototype and production gears, with a worldwide reputation for high-quality products.

The Early Years of The Gleason Works, 1836 to 1900

Born on April 4, 1836, William Gleason traveled to the United States from Borrisokane, County Tipperary, Ireland, with his mother and brother when he was 15 years old. After receiving training as a mechanic through a series of apprenticeships at the Rochester, New York machine shops of Asa R. Swift and I. Angell & Sons, Gleason worked during the Civil War at Colt's Armory located in Hartford, Connecticut. Gleason's wife claimed Susan B. Anthony as a friend.

In 1865, Gleason returned to Rochester and began working in his own machine shop located on Brown's Race (now known as the High Falls Historical District), which overlooked the Genesee River. Gleason's tiny shop began manufacturing a general line of metalworking tools and machines, with special emphasis on engine lathes and planers. The company eventually evolved into The Gleason Works, a name by which it is sometimes still referred. Almost a decade later, in 1874, Gleason invented the first bevel gear planer, which proved to be the start of a brand-new industry, the bevel gear industry, and created incredible new opportunities for the transmission of motive power.

All four of Gleason's children worked with him in the early days of the company. Gleason's son, Tom, worked as his personal assistant, but died in 1877.

Tom's half-sister, Kate Gleason, after overhearing her father bemoaning the loss and wondering what to do, came to the rescue and began working at the age of 11, helping her father with the company's bookkeeping tasks. In a time when women were not normally engaged in industrial jobs, and the suffragette movement was still 40 years away, this was the start of a career which would propel Gleason Works to the top rung in its industry and would take Kate to a position where she would be hailed by some as The First Lady of the gear industry.

In 1884, Kate became the first woman to ever study engineering at Cornell University but, before she could graduate and take her degree, Gleason called her back to Rochester to help run the company. Although expressing disappointment at the time, Kate was later to remark that it had been a blessing in disguise, since it allowed her the opportunity to learn the machine tool business from top to bottom. By 1884, Kate, at 22, was traveling to Ohio on business trips. Three years later, she was the company's chief salesperson. In 1890, she became the company's Secretary-Treasurer, a position in which she served until 1913. In 1914, she was the first woman to be elected to full membership in the American Society of Mechanical Engineers and, two years later, was one of the first women elected to the Rochester Chamber of Commerce.

Company Perspectives:

For more than 130 years, Gleason Corporation has focused all of its efforts on serving the precision gear industry and optimizing both bevel and cylindrical (spur and helical) gear-making processes.

In 1893, at the age of 27, Kate traveled to Europe alone and, in one of the first moves by an American company to establish overseas markets, secured orders for Gleason machines from prestigious companies in England, Scotland, France, and Germany, a move which would help the company soar to the top, as even in 1997, two-thirds or more of the company's sales came from outside of the United States. She had a letter of introduction from Henry Sharpe of Brown & Sharpe, which helped her immeasurably. In an attempt to thank him, Kate allegedly sent Sharpe half of the money she earned from the trip, but he gallantly returned it to her. In 1913, she resigned from the company amidst tensions between her and her two brothers, partly because she was so visible, gregarious, and well-liked by everyone, including Henry Ford.

In 1914, Kate went on to reorganize Ingle Machine Company, located in East Rochester, New York. In just under two years, she managed to turn Ingle from a company having $140,000 in debt into a company worth over a million dollars. When the president of First National Bank of East Rochester went away to fight in World War I, Kate was named acting president, the first woman in the United States to hold such a position. Following the war, Kate founded eight new businesses in the East Rochester area, including the Concrest community, a subdivision of 100 low-cost, poured-concrete, six-room houses, with a country club, golf course, and park. Her second career in real estate made her millions and she moved to Berkeley, California in 1924 and became an advisor to the city following a disastrous fire. She went on to build homes in Sausalito, California, and some of the land she owned is where the northern end of the Golden Gate Bridge is now located. She also owned land in Beaufort, South Carolina, and Septmonts, France. She died in 1933 while building an artists and writers colony on her South Carolina property.

James E. and Andrew C. Gleason followed their sister to Cornell University and into the company. Andrew, whose primary interest lay in the gear design and manufacturing phase of the business, served as vice-president of the company until his retirement in 1934. James focused his energies upon machine design and production and later became president, improving types of bevel gear machines, manufacturing techniques, and industrial relations, which were, in large part, responsible for the company's preeminent position in the industry in the 1990s. Truly devoted to his father's company, James died in his office, while working, at the age of 94.

The Gleason Works was incorporated in New York in 1903. The following year, The Gleason Works acquired a second site, the new one located on University Avenue, where the company headquarters remained. The first building was constructed there

in 1905. By 1911, the activities of the company had outgrown the facilities at Brown's Race, and all the operations were moved to the site on University Avenue.

Going Public, 1984-Date

Little information, unfortunately, is available regarding the years leading up to the company's eventual reincorporation in Delaware in 1984 as the Gleason Corporation.

Since that time, the company has spawned an extensive product line under The Gleason Works, Pfauter, Pfauter-Maag Cutting Tools, and Gleason-Hurth names, including machinery for the production, finishing, and testing of bevel gears, used to transmit mechanical power at right angles, such as from a drive shaft to the rear axle of a vehicle; and of cylindrical gears, used to transmit power in a straight line. The company's ever-developing generations of advanced computer-numerically controlled (CNC) Phoenix-brand gear machinery have been recognized as being among the most flexible and productive manufacturing equipment on the market. The company also manufactures a complete line of tooling and software products for cutting, grinding, lapping, and inspection of bevel gears; and for hobbing (dry or wet), shaping, saving, honing, grinding, chamfering/deburring, and inspection of cylindrical gears. Gleason also produces workholding equipment, as well as spare parts, field service, and gear design software.

In 1997, the company owned or leased manufacturing facilities located in Rochester, New York; Loves Park, Illinois; Plymouth, England; Ludwigsburg and Munich, Germany; Bologna and Porretta, Italy; Biel, Switzerland; and Bangalore, India; and had sales and service offices in Indiana, Michigan, New York, South Carolina, and Wisconsin in the United States, as well as in England, France, Germany, Italy, Spain, Sweden, Australia, India, and The People's Republic of China.

With approximately a 75 percent share of the bevel gear equipment market in 1996, at that time estimated to be worth nearly $175 million, and an expanding share of the larger cylindrical gear equipment market, the company served customers in over 50 countries worldwide. Two-thirds of the company's sales typically came from outside the United States. Major customers have included leading companies in the aerospace, aircraft, recreational vehicle, power tool production, contract gear producing, construction, farm, and marine industries, with approximately 65 percent of the company's sales coming from the passenger car, light truck, and heavy truck industries, to companies such as BMW, Chrysler, Daimler-Benz, Dana, Ford, General Motors, and Toyota, as well as The Black & Decker Corporation in the non-automotive segment. The company also offered complete support, from design to inspection, to gear manufacturers throughout the world, including application development services, PC-based gear processing software, training programs, engineering support, machine rebuild and upgrade services, and weekly hob pickup and express delivery service.

In 1989, the company put its Components Group, made up of four subsidiaries that manufactured industrial products, including powder metal parts, metal stampings, and precision plastic parts, up for sale. In December of that same year, the company introduced the Phoenix 250HC, the first gear production machine in its new Phoenix product line, which incorporated state-of-the-art, full CNC design for the production of bevel and hypoid gears. Some of the features of the Phoenix line included the elimination of manual setups, which permitted a significant reduction in the overall cost of manufacturing spiral bevel and hypoid gears; superior operating flexibility, including the ability to change over jobs in seconds; the ability to perform closed-loop inspection; and to achieve precise degrees of accuracy and repeatability. With an estimated worldwide installed base of more than 15,000 Gleason Corporation bevel gear machines having an average age in excess of 25 years, many of the company's longtime customers, by 1997, had indicated their intention to make the transition to the more productive and modern Phoenix line of machines.

The 1990s

In the 1990s, corporate management, led by Chairman of the Board and President James S. Gleason, grandson of Andrew, aggressively focused the company on its core business and on improving its long-term profitability by introducing a record number of new products, modernizing and consolidating manufacturing capacity, reducing operating costs, and pursuing strategic acquisitions.

In December 1991, the company sold all of the stock of Pennsylvania Pressed Metals, Inc., the largest of its four Components Group companies, to a group of investors. The following year, the company sold its Alliance Precision Plastics and Alliance Carolina Tool and Mold subsidiaries, two more of the Components Group companies, for a total of $6.1 million in cash and another $2.2 million in notes receivable. Revenues for 1992 reached $147.3 million, with a net loss of $61.2 million.

In 1993, the company began shipping its first Phoenix 125GH gear hobbing machines for the parallel axis market, targeted at automotive applications, the largest single segment of the precision cylindrical gear market. Another product introduced in 1993 was the Phoenix 175 bevel gear cutting machine. The company also entered into a joint agreement to build the Gleason TAG 400 spur and helical gear grinder, the first product that would come out of a joint venture with Okamoto Machine Tool Works Ltd. of Japan. The company also entered into a joint agreement with the China National Automobile Industry Corporation, an agency that works with vehicle producers in China, providing service and training to companies associated with China's transportation industries.

Late in 1993, the company sold its Belgian manufacturing operation for $2.3 million. Revenues for 1993 dropped to $103.9 million, with a net loss of $2.9 million.

In 1994, the company acquired a 20 percent interest in OGA Corporation, its exclusive sales and service representative in Japan and Taiwan, in order to strengthen the company's presence and enhance growth in that region of the world. The company also ceased operations that year at the fourth and final company in the Components Group, Alliance Metal Stamping and Fabricating, selling the machinery and equipment for approximately $3.6 million.

As the American automotive industry had higher sales and improved profitability, revenues for the company in 1994 reached $128.5 million, with a net income of $7.3 million. In July 1995, the company acquired the operations of Munich, Germany-based Hurth Maschinen und Werkzeuge GmbH, a leading manufacturer of precision shaving and honing equipment used in cylindrical gear production and finishing. With Gleason's annual sales reaching between $60 million to $70 million, the acquisition of Hurth's products complemented the company's existing offerings and gave the company another step toward sustained growth in that market.

Late in 1995, the company formed a wholly owned subsidiary in India which began limited production of bevel gear cutting tools the following year. The company's presence in the emerging market there was estimated to result in near-term gains for its cutting tooling sales in that market, and a better position for long-term growth for the company's machine products in that region. That year, the company also released the Phoenix 400 gear hobber, which produced gears ranging from 200 to 400 millimeters in diameter. The company's revenues for 1995 were $197.1 million, with a net income of $30.8 million.

In 1996, the company introduced the Phoenix 450HC, a machine which extended the capabilities of the 250HC, the original Phoenix machine introduced in 1989. Revenues for the year reached a record high of $248.1 million, a 26 percent jump over 1995 revenues, and net income was $19.7 million.

In July 1997, the company acquired all the operations of The Hermann Pfauter Group, headquartered in Ludwigsburg, Germany, and with additional facilities located in Italy and the United States, for approximately $34.8 million. A leader in cylindrical gear production equipment, with 1996 sales of about $178 million, the acquisition of Pfauter also brought the company a machine-manufacturing subsidiary, called American Pfauter, a cutting tool-manufacturing subsidiary called Pfauter-Maag Cutting Tools, both located in Loves Park, Illinois; Hermann Pfauter GmbH & Co.; and 1,050 new employees. The combined acquisition of Pfauter and Hurth moved the company into the number one worldwide position in overall gear production equipment and related technology, and significantly expanded the company's volume and breadth in cylindrical gear machinery and tooling, jumping sales to approximately 66 percent of total sales in 1997, compared to less than 10 percent of sales in 1993. The following month, the company's common stock split two-for-one, increasing the number of common shares outstanding to approximately 10 million.

In September, the company ranked 41st on *Fortune* magazine's top 100 list of fastest-growing companies in the United States, with an earnings per share annual growth rate of 95 percent. The following month, the company signed an OEM contract with Saikuni Manufacturing Co., Ltd. in Japan in which Gleason would maintain and sell Saikuni's Spiral Cutter Sharpener machines throughout the world. Also in October, the British-American Chamber of Commerce, at a transatlantic awards dinner, honored James Gleason, among others, for strengthening trade ties, his entrepreneurial spirit, and for his company's achievements in furthering the growth of business between the United Kingdom and the United States.

Looking Ahead

Described in a *Fortune* magazine article as "an outfit in overdrive," the company has steadily been increasing sales to the Asian and European marketplaces. In late 1997, the company turned its corporate eye toward South America and potential expansion in that market. Riding a crest of increasing sales and income, the company remained in a position to continue being a leader in the industry it served.

Principal Subsidiaries

OGA Corporation (Japan, Taiwan; 20%).

Further Reading

"America's Fastest-Growing Companies: The Top 100," *Fortune*, September 29, 1997.

"Gleason Corp.," *Wall Street Journal*, October 17, 1994, p. C20.

"Gleason Corp.," *Wall Street Journal*, July 1, 1997, p. C18(W).

"Gleason Corp.," *Wall Street Journal*, December 5, 1997, p. C13(W)/ B21(E).

"Gleason Declares Stock Split," *Wall Street Journal*, August 29, 1997, p. C14(E).

"Gleason Plans to Acquire Hermann Pfauter Group," *New York Times*, August 29, 1996, p. D3.

"Gleason to Resume Buyback," *Wall Street Journal*, January 26, 1995, p. C14.

Hardy, Eric S., "The *Forbes*/Barra Wall Street Review," *Forbes*, August 15, 1994, p. 137.

"Net Income Increases 58% on 87% Jump in Revenue," *Wall Street Journal*, April 17, 1996, p. C12.

Vasilash, Gary S., "Meeting the Future Head-On," *Production*, July 1993, p. 50.

—Daryl F. Mallett

GOULDS PUMPS
ITT Industries

Goulds Pumps Inc.

240 Fall St.
Seneca Falls, New York 13148
U.S.A.
(315) 568-2811
Fax: (315) 568-2418
Web site: http://www.goulds.com

Wholly Owned Subsidiary of ITT Industries, Inc.
Founded: 1848 as Downs, Mynderse and Co.
Employees: 5,200
Sales: $774 million (1996)
SICs: 3561 Pumps & Pumping Equipment; 3594 Fluid
Power Pumps & Motors; 3714 Motor Vehicle Parts &
Accessories

Goulds Pumps Inc. began in the mid-19th century as the world's first manufacturer of iron pumps and has grown to become the world's largest manufacturer of industrial, agricultural, and consumer pumps. The company is organized into two main groups: Water Technologies, which serves municipal water systems, the agricultural market, and the residential market; and Industrial Products, which serves several markets, including the chemical industry, the petroleum industry, and the pulp-and-paper industry. Like other companies in the fluid technology business, Goulds Pumps' sales and earnings are dependent on overall economic conditions. A downturn in the economy or in one of Goulds' markets can result in reduced orders and flat earnings. After a period of ups and downs in the 1980s and 1990s, Goulds Pumps was acquired in 1997 by ITT Industries, Inc., a global diversified manufacturing company based in White Plains, New York. Goulds Pumps continues to operate as a wholly owned subsidiary of ITT Industries as part of its fluid technology segment.

Early History

Although Goulds Pumps dates its corporate anniversary from 1848, the company's roots began in 1840, when Abel Downs began manufacturing wooden pumps in a former cotton factory in Seneca Falls, New York. Downs teamed with John

Wheeler, and the two were joined in 1846 by Edward Mynderse, who owned a large amount of property in the area, to form a company that became Downs, Mynderse and Co. in 1848, the official founding of Goulds Pumps.

Seabury S. Gould was also working on pumps in his shop in Seneca Falls, and in the mid-1840s oversaw the casting and assembling of the world's first all-metal pump. Gould served as president of Downs, Mynderse and Co. from 1848 to 1872. He bought out Mynderse and H. C. Silsby, another co-owner, in 1851, and the company's name was changed to Downs and Company. Downs and Company constructed a new plant in 1853, and in 1864 the company was incorporated in the state of New York. In 1869, the name Goulds Manufacturing Company was adopted.

Seabury Gould probably could not envision all the uses to which his all-metal pumps would be put. At that time they solved a problem associated with trains and their need for water. They were served by windmill-driven pumps, which often caused trains to be delayed for up to a day. Eventually, the problem was solved by steam-powered pumps that were developed in Gould's shops.

Seabury Gould was succeeded by his son, James H. Gould, who served as president from 1872 to 1896. With the nation rapidly expanding westward, it was a period of great activity in the pump business. Proliferating agriculture, ranching, lumbering, mining, and manufacturing were growing markets for a wide range of pumps. Suction pumps, lift pumps, and power, steam, and piston pumps were introduced to meet their needs.

In 1900 a second plant was constructed in Seneca Falls to produce Goulds' "Triplex" pumps, under the presidency of Seabury S. Gould II (1896–1908), He was followed by Norman Judd Gould, who served as president from 1908 to 1964. The company's present name, Goulds Pumps Inc., was adopted in March 1926.

In 1944 Goulds Pumps received the Army-Navy "E" Award for outstanding production of war material. Sales in that year reached $10 million. In 1945 Goulds Pumps produced its largest pump to date. To be used on a petroleum pipeline, the horizontal pump had a 36-inch stroke and required three railroad flat cars to ship. After World War II, Goulds Pumps developed new pump lines for water systems and general industry. The company expanded by making acquisitions and opening branch offices in the United States. It gradually expanded operations throughout the world.

With the death of Norman Judd Gould in 1964, control of the company passed from the Gould family. Most of the company's stock was now owned by the general public and by employees of the company. The company grew from sales of $15.9 million in 1960 to $45 million in 1969. It acquired U.S. Pumps, Inc., with plants in Los Angeles and Lubbock, Texas; Goyne Pump Co. of Ashland, Pennsylvania; and Morris Pump Co. of Baldwinsville, New York. It also entered into a joint venture with Oil Dynamics, Inc., to manufacture submersible pump units for oil wells.

Recent History

Although the 1970s began with an economic recession, pump sales reached record levels during the decade and continued at record levels in the early 1980s. Goulds sales rose from $48.8 million in 1970 to $239 million in 1980. Expectations in the fluid technology industry were unreasonably high. Pump companies could not keep up with the demand, as major projects were being built in the Middle East, oil shortages were projected, and a lot of money was being spent on new projects. Eventually the bubble burst, and pump manufacturers were caught with excess capacity and had to fight for survival. As a result, Goulds and other pump companies had to reduce their workforces to remain competitive.

In 1981, Goulds' sales were $308.7 million and falling. In late 1981 Goulds suffered through a bitter labor strike that was marked by vandalism and harassment of non-striking workers. Two years later sales stood at $275.3 million.

Stephen Ardia Became CEO, 1985

By 1985 the company needed to be revitalized after its poor financial performance and labor troubles. Stephen Ardia was named CEO of Goulds Pumps. He introduced a commitment to quality and participatory management. He was able to focus the company's culture on "looking for opportunities to improve how we're doing and what we're doing; much greater involvement of our people; and a greater openness to ideas and ways that other people do things," he told the *Rochester Business Journal.*

Ardia had risen through the ranks at Goulds, starting at the company in 1965 as an applications engineer. The two areas he focused on were participatory management and total quality. Under his leadership, CATS (Competitive Advantage Through

Simplification) was introduced to update and cut through the company's 140-year accumulation of procedures. CATS was designed to reduce the costs of entering, handling, and billing orders. Other systems were revamped and updated under the CATS program, with savings estimated at $7.5 million over four years.

However, the company's future was still uncertain. Declining oil prices had slowed exploration and production, and the pump market was dependent on a growing petroleum business. However, Goulds had already begun negotiating its entry into the Chinese market. By early 1988, the company had completed talks to establish a joint venture with the Nanjing Deep Well Company of China. The venture was expected to produce some 600 pump units for four petrochemical plants in China. Production on units for two of the four plants had already begun in March 1987 at Goulds' Seneca Falls facility.

Goulds began building its export business around 1980. By 1988 it had offices in Singapore, South Korea, Hong Kong, and Jakarta, and a representative in Beijing. Goulds' Industrial Products group already had an established presence in China, where it manufactured industrial pumps for sale in the United States. According to Juergen Schulz, Goulds' director of international sales, it was the company's presence in China that initially "allowed us the opportunity to make inroads to sell products made here in the United States." Goulds was also acquiring companies in other countries. In 1985 it acquired a company in Lowara, Italy, for $19.8 million, which grew from about $30 million in sales to more than $100 million by 1991.

Ardia Achieved Record Sales After Five Years in 1990

By 1990 Goulds Pumps had more than 1,900 employees in New York and more than 3,000 in North America. Sales rose to $554.7 million, a nine percent increase over the 1989 figure. Net income from continuing operations increased six percent to $30.6 million. Goulds Pumps continued to grow globally. It marketed its products in more than 90 countries and was expanding its production facilities into other countries. International sales of $192 million accounted for 35 percent of the company's total revenues. Overall, the Industrial Products group represented 62 percent of sales, with the remaining 38 percent coming from Water Technologies.

The next year net sales reached $566.6 million, and earnings inched up to $30.7 million in a year of economic recession. The company was named to the Covenant 200, an honor roll of the most responsible big corporations in the United States. "Our diversification comes through the many markets we serve," Ardia told the *Rochester Business Journal.* "We're not dependent upon any single industry. We serve the water systems market, the chemical industry, the petroleum industry, the pulp-and-paper industry, and we serve markets outside the United States." Other factors contributing to Goulds' rebound from its 1980s slump included improving service to its customers, increasing market share, introducing new products, and enhancing productivity.

The company was organized into two main groups, Water Technologies and Industrial Products. Water Technologies over the past ten years had increased its market share from 15 percent to 25 percent. About half of its business was produced in the United States and half outside the U.S. Industrial Products held about 20 percent of the industrial market share in the United States, up from about 15 percent in 1986. Of $350 million in industrial business, $95 million came from export sales. The company did not have a large manufacturing facility overseas. Global market share for industrial products was estimated at eight to 10 percent.

Globalization was perceived as an opportunity for growth. International sales accounted for about 40 percent of Goulds Pumps' business in the early 1990s. Key areas for growth were the Asia-Pacific area and Latin America. International expansion occurred in Venezuela, where the company acquired the remaining 80 percent of its investment in 1991 to become the largest pump company in that country. Another company in Mexico was wholly owned. In 1992 the company opened a manufacturing facility in Korea.

Period of Flat Sales in Difficult Economic Times, Early 1990s

Sales were flat from 1990 to 1993, hovering around $555 million. The period 1992–93 was seen as a cyclical low point. There was a recession, and the whole process industry was down. Goulds reduced its U.S. workforce from 3,100 to 2,746 in January 1992, mostly through early retirement incentives and attrition.

In October 1993 Goulds acquired Environamics, Inc., a privately owned company in New Hampshire. A start-up company, Environamics had developed and patented hermetically sealed pump technology that Goulds could use in its pumps for the chemical processing industry. After recording pre-tax losses of approximately $3 million in 1994 and 1995, ownership of Environamics was transferred back to two senior managers at Environamics.

New President and CEO in 1994

Thomas McDermott, a former president and chief operating officer of Bausch & Lomb Inc., replaced Stephen Ardia as president and CEO in July 1994. He had been a member of Goulds' board of directors since 1988. In May 1995 he was also named chairman of the board.

Under Ardia, Goulds had been beset by lackluster performance in the 1990s. Sales hovered around $555 million, but net earnings from continuing operations (before extraordinary charges and cumulative effects of accounting changes) fell from $31.3 million in 1991 to $21.8 million in 1992, then recovered in 1993 to $23.5 million. In 1994 the company reported net sales of $585.5 million and net earnings of $18.2 million.

Ardia was credited with solving Goulds' labor problems by instituting participatory management and total quality management programs, and he brought sagging sales and earnings up to respectable levels. However, as earnings drifted lower, the company began to experience other problems. It had environmental problems with a consumer pump in California. A lawsuit over alleged health risks from the pump caused the company's stock price to dip by 20 percent. Then it was hit with a shareholder suit that claimed Ardia hid the problem to prevent

Goulds' stock price from falling. In mid-1995 Goulds agreed to a $300,000 out-of-court settlement.

McDermott kept Goulds' management team in place as he introduced a sweeping five-point plan that closely followed Ardia's agenda: cut costs; increase inventory turnover; expand global business; grow through acquiring related businesses and expanding market share; and change the corporate culture. He eventually created a new top management team, hiring or promoting 15 executives to upper-level posts.

In the first several months of McDermott's tenure, the company acquired an Austrian pump company and sold its 50 percent interest in Oil Dynamics Inc., a Tulsa, Oklahoma-based pump manufacturer for oil rigs. These moves were indicative of McDermott's desire to build global market share and refocus the company's domestic business. Pumpenfabrik Ernest Vogel AG was the leading pump manufacturer in Austria with 1993 sales of $60 million. The acquisition was valued at approximately $51 million, including the assumption of some $34 million in debt.

Corporate Headquarters Moved in 1995

In 1995 McDermott separated the company's corporate offices from its manufacturing operations and moved the company's headquarters from Seneca Falls to Fairport, near Rochester. He believed managers were too close to the company's operations; with added distance, he thought they would be able to better focus on strategic rather than operational issues. It was a move to spur change in the company's corporate culture.

Sales jumped in 1995 to $718.8 million, but earnings were flat at $18.1 million. However, the company was performing well under McDermott. Before restructuring charges, earnings per share were up 41 percent over 1994 and operating earnings rose more than 26 percent. The company took a pre-tax restructuring charge of $18.5 million in connection with its divestiture of Environamics and the closing of its manufacturing facilities in Venezuela. The operation in Venezuela had resulted in losses in almost every year since Goulds assumed ownership in 1990. Goulds would continue to maintain sales offices in Venezuela and make shipments there from its manufacturing facilities in the United States.

In 1996 Goulds reported revenues of $774 million and had more than 5,200 employees throughout the world. It was a major supplier to engineering contractors around the world. It was also the world's leading manufacturer of residential well-water pump systems.

Goulds Acquired in 1997

In April 1997 ITT Industries, Inc., a global diversified manufacturing company based in White Plains, New York, announced it had reached an agreement with Goulds Pumps to acquire the company for approximately $815 million in cash plus the assumption of $119 million of Goulds' debt. The acquisition would be accomplished through a tender offer to Goulds' shareholders at $37 a share, which was completed in May.

According to Travis Engen, chairman, president, and CEO of ITT Industries, "This combination will create the world's largest pump producer and contribute significant efficiencies for both growth and cost improvement.'' With the addition of Goulds Pumps, ITT Industries' fluid technology business would represent more than 20 percent of the company's sales and contribute more than 25 percent of its operating income. Fluid technology was one of ITT Industries' ''most profitable and fastest-growing business segments,'' said Engen.

The fit between Goulds and ITT Industries was expected to be a good one. On the one hand, Goulds was a leading producer of pumps for the industrial sector, while ITT Industries was a world leader in submersible pumps for municipal water treatment systems. In addition to cost efficiencies, ITT Industries noted there were important geographic efficiencies in the combination. Taking the Pacific Rim as an example, ITT Industries had distribution points in Australia, New Zealand, Vietnam, and several Central Asian republics, while Goulds had distribution facilities in The Philippines, Korea, and Thailand. Both companies had operations in China, Taiwan, Singapore, Malaysia, and Indonesia. In Latin America, Goulds' presence in Venezuela and Mexico complemented ITT Industries' operations in Chile, Argentina, and Brazil.

The two companies together would serve more than 130 nations. Engen noted, ''The industry's growth and profit potential is most promising in the developing world, where the combined company will have access to the full range of infrastructure-related and industrial markets.''

ITT Industries' fluid technology business specialized in the manufacture of pumps, valves, heat exchangers, and related equipment used to move, measure, and control fluids. The company's fluid technology segment had 1996 sales of $1.3 billion. Its markets included wastewater treatment, chemical processing, construction, bio-pharmaceutical, aerospace, and general industry.

With the acquisition of Goulds, ITT Industries' fluid technology business increased 34.9 percent in 1997 to $1.8 billion. Operating income, excluding special charges, was $156.7 million, a 38.4 percent increase over 1996. Overall, ITT Industries had 1996 sales of $8.72 billion and was active in three primary business segments: fluid technology, automotive, and defense and electronics. In 1997 ITT Industries' sales increased $59 million to $8.78 billion.

The takeover was a friendly one, with ITT Industries' offer of $37 a share giving Goulds shareholders more value. The company's stock was underperforming in spite of 20 percent increases in net earnings for the past two years. As part of ITT Industries, Goulds would keep its own name and operate as a wholly owned subsidiary. At first McDermott was undecided if he would stay on as head of Goulds, even though ITT Industries wanted him to. Then, in May 1997, the *Rochester Business Journal* reported that McDermott would leave Goulds once the buyout was completed.

Goulds Pumps Returned to Seneca Falls in 1998

It was announced that Goulds would move its corporate headquarters back to Seneca Falls by January 1, 1998. ITT Industries wanted to reintegrate Goulds' corporate managers with the company's production operations in Seneca Falls. McDermott and much of the top management team he had assembled had left Goulds. It was originally McDermott's idea to separate top management from operations as a way to improve efficiency. Under McDermott's leadership, Goulds' bottom line and prospects improved significantly. Although ITT Industries tried to convince McDermott to stay on, he told the *Rochester Business Journal*, ''I'm at a point where I don't think I could work for somebody else.'' Approximately half of McDermott's management team left when he did.

Principal Subsidiaries

Eight wholly owned subsidiaries in the United States and 31 in other countries.

Principal Divisions

Water Technologies; Industrial Products.

Further Reading

Astor, Will, ''Drawing Goulds Pumps' New Blueprint,'' *Rochester Business Journal,* March 31, 1995, p. 10.
——, ''Goulds CEO to Leave Firm After Buyout,'' *Rochester Business Journal,* May 23, 1997, p. 1.
——, ''Goulds Ends Era of Ups, Downs by Agreeing to Sale,'' *Rochester Business Journal,* April 25, 1997, p. 1.
——, ''Goulds Pumps Moving Offices to Main Facility,'' *Rochester Business Journal,* October 3, 1997, p. 1.
——, ''Goulds Pumps Readies for Upswing in Demand,'' *Rochester Business Journal,* December 10, 1993, p. 4.
——, ''New Goulds Pumps CEO Targets Fundamentals,'' *Rochester Business Journal,* July 1, 1994, p. 1.
Bruce, Caryn, ''Goulds Pumps, Inc.,'' *Central New York Business Journal,* July 1, 1991, p. 13.
Ericson, Paul, ''Matters of Survival: A Quality Strategy Revived Goulds Pumps, Inc., But Stephen Ardia Says the War's Never Won,'' *Rochester Business Journal,* July 17, 1992, p. 2.
Johnston, Phil, ''Priming the Pump of Goulds' Prosperity,'' *Rochester Business Journal,* August 21, 1989, p. 10.
Kurty, Diana, ''Goulds Pumps Acquires Innovative Environmental Pump Company,'' *PR Newswire,* October 27, 1993.
Lambertsen, Mary Ann, ''Goulds Pumps Names McDermott President and CEO,'' *PR Newswire,* June 27, 1994.
''Manufacturing—Special Report: Goulds Pumps,'' *Syracuse Business,* March 1993, p. 6.
Martin, Thomas R., ''ITT Industries and Goulds Pumps Inc. Agree to $815 million Cash Merger,'' *PR Newswire,* April 21, 1997.
Morphy, John, ''Goulds Pumps Announces Full Year and Fourth Quarter Results,'' *PR Newswire,* January 27, 1993.
Murphy, Sean, ''Goulds Pumps Announces Record Fourth Quarter Orders and Financial Results at Expected Level,'' *PR Newswire,* January 26, 1994.
——, ''Goulds Pumps Completes Acquisition of Leading Pump Manufacturer in Austria,'' *PR Newswire,* December 5, 1994.
Segelken, Jane Baker, ''Seeing Red Puts This Company in the Black,'' *Central New York Business Journal,* February 1988, p. 18.

—David Bianco

Granada Group PLC

Stornoway House
13 Cleveland Row
London SW1A 1GG
United Kingdom
(0171) 451-3000
Fax: (0171) 451-3023
Web site: http://www.granada.co.uk

Public Company
Incorporated: 1934 as Granada Theatres Limited
Employees: 70,538
Sales: £4.09 billion (US $6.61 billion) (1997)
Stock Exchanges: London
Ticker Symbol: GAA
SICs: 4833 Television Broadcasting Stations; 4841 Cable
& Other Pay Television Stations; 5541 Gasoline
Service Stations; 5812 Eating Places; 7011 Hotels &
Motels; 7299 Miscellaneous Personal Services, Not
Elsewhere Classified; 7389 Business Services, Not
Elsewhere Classified; 7922 Theatrical Producers
(Except Motion Picture) & Miscellaneous Theatrical
Services

Granada Group PLC is a leading U.K. player in media and hospitality. The company's media operations include broadcast licenses in London and northern England for the Independent Television Network; a television production unit that is the largest commercial television production company in the United Kingdom (the state-owned British Broadcasting Corporation is number one overall); various channels available through satellite and digital broadcasting; and part ownership of pay television joint ventures Granada Sky Broadcasting and British Sky Broadcasting (both satellite-based) and British Digital Broadcasting, a digital terrestrial television operation. Through its hospitality operations, Granada maintains 42 motorway service areas offering fuel, catering, retail, and budget accommodations; a chain of 400 Little Chef roadside family restaurants; the second largest contract catering business in the United Kingdom; and the U.K.

market-leading hotel group, consisting of 162 Travelodge budget hotels throughout the country, 18 hotels in London, 147 Posthouse and Heritage hotels outside of London, and 88 hotels overseas. In addition to its two core areas, Granada owns nearly 500 shops that rent and sell consumer electronics and maintains a commercial rental operation that supplies television and communications products.

Founded As Small Theater Operator in the Early 20th Century

Granada traces its roots to the early 1900s when, shortly after the turn of the century, Alexander Bernstein opened the Edmonton Empire music hall. During the 1920s his sons Sidney and Cecil started up a chain of movie theaters. The Bernstein brothers approached their business with an innovative spirit and a desire to bring their deep appreciation of cinema to larger audiences. They actively promoted many kinds of films, conducted surveys to determine the kinds of films people most wanted to see, and initiated children's matinees.

The theater chain adopted the name Granada in 1930. The name was chosen by the well-traveled Sidney Bernstein, who felt that its exotic connotation fit with the image he wanted for the theaters. Following the formation of Granada Theatres Limited in 1934, which consolidated all activities into one group, the company made its first public stock offering in 1935 on the London Stock Exchange.

Over the next three years, Granada opened a new theater almost every three months, including "super cinemas" with seating capacity for as many as 3,000 patrons. Created by leading architects, artists, and theatrical designers of the period, the super cinemas offered live programming as well as films in elegantly appointed surroundings. As theatergoing habits changed with the times, however, Granada gradually phased out this concept in favor of theaters with either single or multiple screens and converted others into bingo and social clubs. The firm moved cautiously into bingo, even though it was lucrative, maintaining a low profile until the 1968 Gaming Act legalized bingo and permitted the company to feel more comfortable about its business involvement and the longevity of the game's consumer appeal.

Turned to Television in Late 1940s

By the late 1940s, Granada's attention gradually had turned away from theatrical entertainment toward the fledgling television industry. After requesting a license to operate an independent television station in 1948, the company finally received the contract in 1954 to broadcast five days a week in all of northern England, becoming one of the four founders of Britain's Independent Television Network. Granada subsequently made its first black-and-white transmission on May 3, 1956, with a program called "Meet the People." This development was particularly well-timed, since it offered Granada a new growth area to offset continuing declines in its theatrical operation. In November 1956 the company introduced a new show, "What the Papers Say," which later became the country's longest-running weekly program on current events. Two years later, Granada became the first network to provide live coverage of a local election, despite strong official opposition, and later it pioneered broadcasts of the annual meetings of the country's major political parties and trade unions.

As the first television company in the country to construct its own studio rather than to use existing facilities built for other purposes, Granada also brought widely acclaimed plays to audiences who had never before had such viewing opportunities. Another program, "Coronation Street," whose characters captured the regional flavor of northern England, began production in 1960 and continues as one of the country's longest-running series.

To reflect its evolving focus, the company changed its name in 1957 to Granada Group Limited. Management remained under the tight control of the Bernstein family, with Sidney's eye for opportunities and insistence on quality and creativity to drive the company's business operations.

Entered Television Rental in the Early 1960s

One of Granada's major areas of growth in the early 1960s was the television rental business. Granada first opened showrooms under the name Red Arrow to handle rentals of televisions and other merchandise such as record players, washing machines, refrigerators, and vacuum cleaners. Granada also expanded into book publishing, in 1961, as an extension of its involvement in the visual media. This business was sold eventually to William Collins & Sons in 1983, since it no longer fit the company's business focus.

In 1963 Granada Television introduced "World in Action," a weekly program that broke with broadcasting tradition by addressing the subject of current events without a host or moderator. Later that year, the company expanded its activities into furniture rental with the formation of Black Arrow Leasing, a business that was sold in 1971.

In 1964 Granada began to export television programming through Granada Overseas Limited (later changed to Granada Television International and then to British Independent Television Enterprises Ltd. [BRITE] in 1995). That year Granada also acquired Barranquilla Investments, a real estate developer, and formed Granada Motorway Services to sell food and fuel to highway travelers across Britain. This business stood in marked contrast to Granada's other ventures in the media area and almost folded within its first six years because of high leasing costs and low profits.

Seven years after the introduction of its domestic television rental business, Granada expanded into the West German market under the name Telerent Europe. Additional showrooms were opened in France, Spain, Italy, Sweden, Switzerland, and North America as Granada looked to establish a television rental market in areas where the concept had never before been introduced.

Granada Group Services also was formed in 1968, initially to provide computerized support to the firm's own businesses, but later to develop systems for outside clients as well. In the meantime, Granada Television continued to prosper and grow technologically. Having been awarded a new seven-days-a-week contract for Great Britain's northwest region, the company began broadcasting programming in color for the first time in September 1969.

The 1970s brought two additional businesses into the Granada fold. Novello and Company, a music publisher founded in 1811, and L'Etoile, a 70-year-old Belgian insurance company, were acquired in 1973 and 1974, respectively, followed by the 1981 purchase of a second Belgian insurance company, Eurobel, which was merged with L'Etoile. The insurance business was sold a decade later after incurring consistent losses; Novello was sold in 1988 because it no longer fit with the company's core businesses.

In 1979 Sidney Bernstein retired as chairman of Granada and turned over leadership of the company to his nephew Alex. Alex Bernstein inherited an organization whose television rental operation had grown to represent more than 60 percent of the company's profits by 1979, but was now threatened by a marked decline in business. The company's overall long-range planning system was erratic and informal at best. He gradually instituted a more decentralized management structure to give Granada's subsidiaries greater operating autonomy.

Continued expansion in the motorway services business in the early 1980s was accompanied by similar success in the television production area. Granada's programming franchise was renewed in 1982 for another eight years—it was the only independent TV contractor in Great Britain to hold onto its license. Its critically acclaimed dramatic series "Brideshead Revisited" was broadcast with resounding success in the United States, and Granada Cable and Satellite was formed in 1983 to capitalize on new broadcasting technology.

Continued Diversification in the 1980s

The firm also embarked upon another new venture in 1983, Granada Microcomputer Services, to market computer hardware to businesses through retail outlets. Granada Microcomputer Services began with a single store and from the start met heavy competition from a number of other retailers, making the undertaking less lucrative than it first promised. Granada decided to reposition its shops as business centers that could package microcomputer hardware and software programs into customized systems for small businesses. This operation, however, was sold in 1987 as Granada reorganized and shifted away from computer retailing toward providing computer maintenance services for businesses through Granada Computer Services.

In 1984 Granada made a major move to consolidate its position in the rental business with the acquisition of Rediffusion, a major rental competitor. Although the television rental market had been declining for several years, the Rediffusion purchase increased Granada's cash flow, market share, and profits and also gave it a stronger position in VCR and movie rentals. After the Rediffusion outlets had been consolidated and integrated with its own, Granada made a second major decision: to begin selling TVs and video recorders to offset declines in the rental area. That same year Granada Television scored a major programming success in the production area with the premiere of the award-winning series "The Jewel in the Crown."

In February 1986 Granada received an unwelcome merger offer from the Rank Organisation, a British company with similar interests in the television, entertainment, and leisure industries. At the time, Granada had broken off merger negotiations with the Ladbroke Group because of a difference in opinion over Granada's net worth. The Independent Broadcasting Authority, Britain's regulator of broadcasting licenses, blocked the takeover, much to Granada's relief, by ruling that Rank's offer would illegally shift ownership of Granada's television franchise. Rank withdrew its bid a month later, after exhausting its legal appeals.

This incident appeared to sharpen the company's outlook on the future. Shortly thereafter, Granada began refining its planning systems with an eye toward growing in several directions at the same time. This approach contrasted with the Bernsteins' original managerial style, which had focused on personal pet projects, whether or not they fit with the company's strengths and resources.

The new strategy backfired to a certain degree in July 1986 when Granada's plan to acquire Comet, an electrical appliance retailer, fell through. This purchase was part of an intricate arrangement in which Dixons Group sought to acquire Woolworth Holdings and then sell Woolworth's Comet subsidiary to Granada. When the Dixons takeover attempt failed, Granada was prevented from making a major move into electrical retailing.

Granada overcame this setback the following year, when it made the largest single acquisition in its history. In November 1987 Granada launched and successfully completed a $450 million bid for Electronic Rentals Group PLC. This purchase gave Granada a stronger presence in the consumer rental and retail markets in the United Kingdom, with two chains, and also served as a springboard for renewed growth in the European rental business. The 1987 acquisitions of NASA in France and Kapy in Spain provided additional retailing strength in those countries. The Granada Hospital Group also was formed during the year to oversee the company's television rentals to hospitals in Canada and the United States.

Granada made another significant purchase in June 1988 when it bought DPCE, a European-based computer mainte-

nance company. Integrated with the company's existing maintenance businesses under the Granada Computer Services International umbrella, DPCE gave the company a larger customer base and a wider range of services to make it a more competitive player in the industry.

By the late 1980s, Granada defined its overall business in terms of four major areas: rental and retail, television, computer services, and leisure. This latter area encompassed not only the original motorway services operation and bingo clubs, but also bowling centers, travel and tour activities, and theme parks and holiday villages managed by Park Hall Leisure, a 1986 acquisition.

Transformed into Media and Hospitality Group in the 1990s

The 1990s brought a host of changes to Granada, dramatically transforming it once more. The decade began inauspiciously with the company in dire straits largely because of the expansion into computer maintenance. This unit was losing money and its growth through acquisition had burdened Granada with a heavy debt load. The company was forced to make a £163 million stock offering in May 1991 to stay afloat. Granada also sold its bingo clubs to Bass PLC for £147 million. To mollify its stockholders, the company forced Derek Lewis out as chief executive. In October 1991 Gerry Robinson, who had been chief executive of catering specialist Compass Group, was brought in to replace Lewis. Robinson, who has been credited in large part with the quick turnaround that followed his appointment, brought with him from Compass his right-hand man, Charles Allen, to run Granada's television and leisure sectors— the two sectors that within a matter of a few years would become the company's core areas. In March 1996, Alex Bernstein retired as chairman, Robinson replaced him, and Allen took over the chief executive slot.

During the 1990s Granada's television sector continued to develop its satellite pay television operations through the company's involvement in Granada Sky Broadcasting and British Sky Broadcasting. The company was also in the forefront of the nascent digital television industry, through British Digital Broadcasting plc (BDB), a 50-50 joint venture of Granada and Carlton Communications. BDB launched a digital television service in late 1998 requiring only a set-top box and receiving digital signals for a maximum of 30 channels through existing television antennae. Meanwhile, in August 1997 the company's independent television and television programming operations received a boost through the acquisition of Yorkshire-Tyne Tees Television (YTT) for about £700 million. The addition of YTT's independent television licenses gave Granada a dominant position in independent television in northern England, while YTT's programming arm bolstered Granada's standing as the largest commercial television production company in the United Kingdom.

By the time of this acquisition, Granada had made some critical divestments. The company's near-disastrous foray into computer services came to an end when that unit was jettisoned through an £89 million management buyout. In rental, Granada during fiscal 1997 decided to focus its resources on its core U.K. operation, and thereby sold off its North American and German (Telerent) rental businesses.

But it was Granada's leisure sector that underwent the most dramatic transformation of all in the 1990s. By mid-decade the core of this sector was the motorway service areas (the market leader in the United Kingdom), a chain of Granada Lodges with a total of 1,400 rooms, and a contract catering operation (the bowling centers and travel unit having been divested in 1995). In January 1996 Granada boldly paid £3.9 billion (US $6 billion) for Forte PLC, the second largest hotel group in Europe, in a fierce hostile takeover. Gained thereby were the Travelodge chain of budget hotels in the United Kingdom (to which were added the Granada Lodges, converted to the new brand); 147 "provincial" hotels located outside of London, under the business-traveler-oriented Posthouse and the more historic Heritage brands; 17 London "trophy" hotels in the Savoy Hotel group, in which Granada now owned a 68 percent stake; and 103 Meridien and Exclusive luxury hotels, mainly located overseas. Also added through the Forte purchase were a chain of 400 Little Chef roadside family restaurants and 21 Welcome Break motorway service areas in the United Kingdom, which were sold for antitrust reasons in February 1997 for £473 million to Investcorp, a Bahrain-based investment group. In December 1997 Granada sold the French motorway service areas, also included in Forte, for FFr 820 million (£83 million) to Autogrill, an Italian roadside restaurant chain. In April 1998 Blackstone Hotel Acquisition Co., a U.S. investment company, agreed to buy the Savoy Group for £520 million (US $866.5 million).

The Exclusive hotels were also divested, leaving Granada with four core lodging brands: Travelodge, Posthouse, Heritage, and Meridien. With such a strong presence in what was now called the hospitality sector (instead of leisure), Granada in mid-1997 considered demerging its media operations, but decided not to for the time being. Such a move likely would have led also to the divestment of the rental operation. In any case, Robinson and Allen had changed Granada into a company that in fiscal 1997 generated only 17 percent of its revenues and 21 percent of its profits from media, while hospitality operations generated 69 percent of revenues and 64 percent of profits (with rental responsible for nearly all of the remaining 14 percent of revenues and 15 percent of profits). Having already progressed through its history from film to television to rental, Granada Group had now clearly staked its future to hospitality.

Principal Subsidiaries

Granada Media Group Ltd.; Granada Television Ltd.; LWT (Holdings) Ltd.; London Weekend Television Ltd.; Yorkshire-Tyne Television Holdings plc; Forte (UK) Ltd.; Granada Food Services Ltd.; Granada Hospitality Ltd; Granada Purchasing Ltd.; Granada Services Group Ltd.; Granada Entertainments Ltd.; Forte France S.A.; Forte Hotels (Deutschland) GmbH (Germany); Forte USA Inc.; Forte Hotels (UK) Ltd.; Forte Holdings Ireland Ltd.; Forte International B.V. (Netherlands); Forte Italia S.p.A. (Italy); Granada Travel PLC; Heritage Hotels Ltd.; Lusotel Industria Hoteleira Ltda. (Portugal); Meridien Hotels Ltd.; Posthouse Hotels Ltd.; Société des Hotels Méridien S.A. (France); Granada UK Rental and Retail Ltd.; UK Consumer Electronics Ltd.; UK Retail Ltd.; GIL Insurance Ltd.; Direct Vision Rentals Ltd.; AFI Hotels Ltd. (Italy; 50%); British Digital Broadcasting plc (50%); Granada Sky Broadcasting Ltd. (50.5%).

Further Reading

Cassell, Michael, "Serving Up a Recipe for Revival," *Financial Times,* July 27, 1996, p. 6.

Daneshkhu, Scheherazade, "Hotel Investors Find a Little Room for Improvement," *Financial Times,* October 3, 1997, p. 25.

Daneshkhu, Scheherazade, and Raymond Snoddy, "Granada Finds That Good News Isn't Enough," *Financial Times,* June 14, 1997, p. WFT5.

Davidson, Andrew, "The Davidson Interview: Gerry Robinson," *Management Today,* June 1995, pp. 48–50, 55.

"Fortissimo?," *Economist,* November 25, 1995, pp. 59+.

Gapper, John, "Vision of the Future Is Down to Earth," *Financial Times,* November 25, 1997, p. 35.

Gapper, John, and Scheherazade Daneshkhu, "Granada Prepares to Sell Its £870m Stake in BSkyB," *Financial Times,* November 21, 1997, p. 19.

Goldsmith, Charles, "Blackstone to Buy Savoy Hotel Group for $866.5 Million," *Wall Street Journal,* April 8, 1998, p. C20.

"Hotels and Planes," *Economist,* January 27, 1996, p. 17.

Jackson, Tony, "Stand and Deliver," *Financial Times,* August 21, 1997, p. 12.

Lorenz, Andrew, "Worth More Together . . . or Apart?," *Management Today,* November 1997, pp. 56+.

Plender, John, "A Risk of Indigestion," *Financial Times,* December 7, 1995, p. 25.

Price, Christopher, "Granada Sells Welcome Break in £473m Deal," *Financial Times,* February 19, 1997, p. 25.

"Report to Staff: 1934–1984 Special Golden Jubilee Edition," London: Granada Group, 1985.

Snoddy, Raymond, "Bernsteins Take Final Bow from Granada," *Financial Times,* October 4, 1995, p. 21.

——, "Granada Rules Out TV Demerger," *Financial Times,* May 23, 1997, p. 23.

——, "YTT Board Backs Granada Deal," *Financial Times,* June 14, 1997, p. 18.

—Sandy Schusteff
—updated by David E. Salamie

GRAY

Gray Communications Systems, Inc.

126 N. Washington St.
Albany, Georgia 31701
U.S.A.
(912) 888-9390
Fax: (912) 888-9374

Public Company
Incorporated: 1946
Employees: 1,020
Sales: $103.5 million (1997)
Stock Exchanges: New York
Ticker Symbol: GCS
SICs: 4833 Television Broadcasting Stations; 2711
   Newspapers, Publishing & Printing; 2741
   Miscellaneous Publishing; 4812 Radiotelephone
   Communications; 4899 Communications Services, Not
   Elsewhere Classified

Established in 1946 by James H. Gray, a native New Englander who relocated to southeast Georgia, Gray Communications Systems, Inc. has grown since 1993 into a modern communications company through a series of acquisitions. For many years James Gray and his company embodied small-town power in Albany, Georgia, where he controlled the town's only newspaper and television station. He also served as the town's mayor for more than ten years. After Gray died in 1986, the terms of his will threw the company into turmoil, and his heirs were unable to maintain control of the company. Finally, a major new investor emerged in 1993, and the company began to acquire television stations and newspaper properties in the southeastern United States. At the beginning of 1998 Gray Communications owned eight network-affiliated television stations in medium-size markets in the southeastern United States and was in the process of adding three more stations. More than half of its 1,020 employees were employed in television, with the remaining in newspapers and paging.

Established in 1946 with the Purchase of the Albany Herald

James H. Gray's newspaper career began with writing for the *Hartford (Connecticut) Courant* and later the *New York Herald Tribune.* Gray was born into New England society, the son of a Massachusetts lawyer, and attended Dartmouth College in New Hampshire. Gray became interested in Albany, Georgia, through his first wife, Dorothy Ellis. Her father was a wealthy Massachusetts businessman who owned a plantation in Albany and spent four months of the year there.

Gray had his eye on the *Albany Herald* in the early 1940s, but his plans to purchase the newspaper were delayed by the onset of World War II. Gray served in Europe as a paratrooper during the war after taking basic training at Fort Benning, Georgia. After serving in World War II, he moved his family to Albany and purchased the *Albany Herald.* Albany was the largest city in southwest Georgia, and the *Herald* was a monopoly newspaper.

Gray Started Albany's Television Station in 1954

In 1954 Gray started his television station, WALB, in Albany. It was only the second television station in the state after Atlanta's WSB. WALB became an NBC affiliate, broadcasting with a VHF signal (channels 2 through 13 on the dial at that time) that was stronger than UHF signals. WALB's signal could be picked up as far away as Jacksonville, Florida. Gray later bought television stations in Louisiana and Florida, first purchasing WJHG in Panama City, Florida, in 1960, and then KTVE serving El Dorado, Arkansas-Monroe, Louisiana, in the late 1960s.

Throughout the 1960s, 1970s, and the first half of the 1980s, Gray Communications and James Gray personified small-town power in the South. He not only controlled Albany's only television station and newspaper, he also served as the city's mayor for 13 years. He was president of the local chamber of commerce five times. For a long while he served as chairman of the Albany Water, Gas and Light Commission, which took in twice as much money as the city government and in some ways

Company Perspectives:

Gray Communications Systems, Inc. owns and operates businesses in three media segments: broadcasting, publishing and paging. Gray's broadcasting division includes seven network-affiliated television stations in medium size markets in the southeastern United States, of which six are ranked number one in their respective markets. The broadcasting division also owns and operates two satellite uplink businesses. Gray's publishing division consists of three daily newspapers and two weekly, advertising only publications. Gray's paging division owns and operates a paging company which serves three southern states with approximately 56,000 pagers in operation. Significant operating advantages and cost saving synergies are realized through the size of Gray's television station group and the regional focus of its television, publishing and paging operations. These advantages and synergies include (i) sharing television production facilities, equipment and regionally oriented programming, (ii) the ability to purchase television programming for the group as a whole, (iii) negotiating network affiliation agreements on a group basis and (iv) purchasing newsprint and other supplies in bulk. In addition, Gray's focus can provide advertisers with an efficient network through which to advertise in the fast-growing Southeast.

was more powerful. Some citizens called him ''Lord Jim'' and ''Citizen Gray.''

In the 1980s he was dedicated to reviving Albany's decaying urban center. He spearheaded the building of Albany's new $15 million, 10,000-seat civic center, which was named for him. At the time of his death in 1986, he was putting $3 million of his own money into the Central Square project to revive the city's ailing downtown district.

James Gray's Death in 1986 Affected the Company's Ownership, Fortunes

In September 1986, while recovering from surgery to correct a circulatory problem in his leg, James H. Gray died of a heart attack at the age of 70. At the time of his death, his 50.5 percent of Gray Communication's stock was worth an estimated $50 million. Since 1977 the stock had climbed from around $10 per share to $130 per share in December 1985, giving the company an estimated market value of about $65 million. Traded in the over-the-counter market, the company's stock rose from $140 to $200 per share in the months following Gray's death.

The company was in good financial shape when Gray died. It had $4 million in cash, only $600,000 in debt, and a strong record of profitability. It earned $3.5 million in 1986, a 13 percent return on equity. After the company's stock rose from around $60 to above $130, the *Atlanta Business Chronicle* named Gray Communications ''Public Company of the Year.''

Gray rewrote his will in 1974 when he married his second wife, Cleair Ranger Gray. He put his 50.5 percent of the company stock into a trust to be divided among his children: James Gray, Jr., Geoffrey Gray, and his daughter Constance (Connie) Greene. Under the terms of the will, the heirs were forced to either work together, sell their stock to each other, or sell out together. No one heir could sell his or her portion of the stock without approval from the others. The will also named Terry P. McKenna, Gray's longtime corporate and personal attorney, as executor of Gray's estate, keeper of the trust, and president of Gray Communications.

For two years McKenna worked to reach a settlement between the estate and Gray's second wife, Cleair Gray, who contested the will that originally left her only $20,000 a year. She claimed the elder Gray had promised her stock in the company in exchange for her promise not to divorce. In 1988, she accepted a settlement worth $750,000, plus $10,000 a month for life and two houses.

Following the settlement, disputes between the three siblings began. The will had the effect of forcing the three children to remain in the business together or to get out of it together. Geoffrey and Connie wanted to get out of the business. They accused their older brother of not being able to raise enough financing to purchase their stock. None of the siblings could sell their stock to outsiders without permission from the others. As a result, all three had to borrow heavily to pay inheritance taxes.

In August 1990 the company's board rejected James Gray, Jr.'s latest offer as inadequate. It was his second offer to buy the company from his siblings. They accused him and his advisers of being greedy. James Gray, Jr., was portrayed in the media and around town as a driven man with ''an inherited role to play.'' He was named by *Georgia Trend* magazine as one of the state's 100 most powerful people. Some thought his stature and public achievements, which included taking over Albany's civic development and becoming editor of the newspaper, were bitterly resented by his younger siblings.

In April 1991 James Gray, Jr., filed two lawsuits to remove Terry P. McKenna from the estate, charging that he was blocking the sale of the estate. The suits asked that the stock owned by the estate either be sold to an outsider or equally distributed among the three heirs. The suits were canceled at the last minute, though, as McKenna and the Gray family sought to repay a $21 million bank loan that was coming due.

In an attempt to end the Gray's majority interest in the company, the board of directors voted in August 1991 to buy 25 percent of the Gray stock for a fair-market price of $17.50 per share, or $30 million. The heirs would retain a 26 percent interest in the company. Like many other media companies, Gray Communications had lost considerable value over the previous five years. Revenues had fallen from $52 million in 1986 to $27.5 million in 1991. Then in the spring of 1992 Gray Communications' stock opened on NASDAQ's small-cap market and bottomed at $8 per share, causing concern among other shareholders over the price paid for the Gray family stock in 1991.

New Investor Emerged in 1993

Toward the end of 1992 the board announced it would consider offers for all or part of the assets of the company. It received about 40 offers, of which one director said there were a half-dozen serious offers. Then in March 1993 Robert Prather, president and CEO of Bull Run Corporation of Atlanta, Georgia, bypassed the board and approached the Grays directly. He offered them $17 a share for their remaining 25.8 percent interest in the company. As part of the deal, the Grays and Connie's husband would resign from the board of directors. Bull Run's investors included J. Mack Robinson, an Atlanta businessman whom *Forbes* magazine had included on its list of the 400 wealthiest Americans.

John Williams, formerly with the Texas-based newspaper company Harte-Hanks Communications, Inc., was named president and CEO to replace McKenna. Williams focused on transforming the *Albany Herald* from an afternoon to a morning newspaper. Among the improvements he made were installing new electronic hardware for the paper's newsroom, advertising, and circulation departments, doubling the size of the news staff, and hiring a new management team. That included hiring new general managers for the company's three television stations and bringing in a new publisher for the *Albany Herald*.

In August 1993 the Grays prepared to sell their remaining 25.8 percent interest in Gray Communications to Robert Prather's Atlanta-based investment group for $13.5 million. The sale was subject to approval by the Federal Communications Commission (FCC), because Gray owned both a television station and a newspaper in Albany, an arrangement that was no longer permitted under federal regulations but that was grandfathered in under Gray ownership.

Prather intended to acquire additional newspapers in the Southeast. The company adopted a plan to grow through strategic acquisitions. The driving forces behind Gray's acquisition strategy were Prather and Williams. They intended to make Gray a regional media company, with ''regional'' defined as the Southeast, not just Georgia.

Gray Communications Began to Grow Through Acquisitions, 1993

Gray Communications began implementing its strategy of growth through acquisitions in October 1993, when it submitted the highest bids for two television stations in Kentucky that were owned by the failed Kentucky Central Life Insurance Co. The stations were WKYT-TV of Lexington and WYMT of Hazard, Kentucky. The sale to Gray was subject to the approval of Kentucky's Insurance Commissioner Don Stephens, because the state had taken control of the troubled Kentucky Central in February 1993.

CEO and President John Williams said, ''Stations of the quality of these two very seldom come on the market. The only reason that these came on the market was because of Kentucky Central's troubles.'' He told the [Louisville] *Courier-Journal* that the two stations would be the ''crown jewels'' of Gray Communications. WKYT had been the dominant local news station in Lexington for many years. The company expected to keep WKYT's general manager, Ralph Gabbard, because the station was doing well.

However, the acquisition was challenged by the heirs to Garvie Kincaid, who built Kentucky Central into the state's second largest insurance company in 1976. They maintained that Kentucky's insurance commissioner did not have the right to sell off the business's non-insurance properties. Gray petitioned the FCC to dismiss the challenge, and in September 1994 a court ruling allowed Gray to complete its acquisition of WKYT and WYMT. WKYT in Lexington, the nation's 69th largest market, gave Gray its first top 100 station. The two stations would increase Gray's annual revenues from around $27 million to more than $40 million. Gray paid $38 million for the stations in its winning bid.

Acquired Second Newspaper in 1994

On May 31, 1994, Gray acquired its second newspaper, the *Rockdale Citizen,* based in Conyers, Georgia, a suburb of Atlanta. While the total price was not disclosed, Gray issued 150,000 shares of stock with a current market value of $2 million as part of the purchase price of $4.8 million. With a circulation of 10,600, the Monday-through-Friday suburban newspaper added only about $2.5 million in annual gross income. More importantly it gave Gray a presence in the Atlanta suburban newspaper market.

Joe Cunningham was brought in to be the *Rockdale Citizen*'s publisher. He was formerly circulation manager for the *Gwinnett Daily News,* which was shut down in 1992 by its parent, the New York Times Co., after attempting to wage a circulation war with the *Atlanta Journal Constitution.* Cunningham told the *Atlanta Constitution,* ''I have a one-word marketing campaign when it comes to competing with *The Atlanta Journal Constitution,* and that is don't.'' Corporate executives viewed Rockdale County as a small market in its own right rather than as an Atlanta suburb. For fiscal 1994, Gray Communications reported net income of $2.8 million on revenues of $36.5 million.

In January 1995 Gray acquired its third newspaper, the *Gwinnett Post-Tribune,* for $3.7 million. Later in the year Gray announced it would change the newspaper's name to the *Gwinnett Daily Post* and expand its distribution schedule from three times a week and make it a daily published every Tuesday through Saturday. The newspaper's circulation was 14,100. Gwinnett was the fourth largest county in metropolitan Atlanta. It was served by the *Gwinnett Daily News* until that newspaper was shut down in 1992. Its competitor, the *Gwinnett Extra,* was published every weekday by the *Atlanta Journal Constitution* and had a circulation of 62,774.

Gray's goal was to increase the *Gwinnett Daily Post*'s circulation to 20,000 over the course of the year. In addition to increasing the newspaper's frequency, Gray doubled the size of its newsroom staff to 19 and added comics and national news briefs. *Journal Constitution* publisher Dennis Berry said, ''I have a lot of respect for the Gray Communications company. They are well-financed. They are ambitious, and they are a competitor to watch.'' Gray's major stockholder was J. Mack Robinson, a wealthy Atlanta businessman and principal financier of Bull Run Corporation. Directly and indirectly through Bull Run, Robinson had increased his ownership of Gray Communications to 44 percent of the outstanding shares.

For fiscal 1995, Gray Communications reported net income of $930,969 on revenues of $58.6 million. During the year Gray's stock was listed for the first time on the New York Stock Exchange. Gray was placing more emphasis on its television holdings and less on its newspapers. John Williams, Gray's newspaper-trained president, resigned in late 1995. Just three months after expanding the staff of the *Gwinnett Daily Post,* the company laid off one-third of the staff there. In January 1996, Gray laid off 29 of the *Albany Herald*'s 200 employees. Further problems in the newspaper segment became apparent when the *Rockdale Citizen*'s editor, Barry King, and publisher, Joe Cunningham, left.

In 1995 the company's broadcast division's profit margins were rising as those of the publishing division were falling. Newly named president Ralph Gabbard, who continued to work out of Lexington, told the *Atlanta Constitution* that Gray's publishing unit has been profitable, "but it wasn't anywhere near where it should be." In addition to its three newspapers, Gray's publishing division included seven advertising weeklies in south Georgia and north Florida.

More Television Stations Were Acquired in 1996

In January 1996 Gray acquired WRDW-TV, the CBS affiliate in Augusta, Georgia, for $37.2 million. It became Gray's sixth television station and was the top-rated station in the Augusta market. Gray now owned three NBC-affiliated and three CBS-affiliated television stations in the Southeast.

In February 1996, the *Atlanta Constitution* observed the transformation taking place at Gray Communications. With three newspapers and eight television stations, "It took Albany-based Gray Communications [two years] to explode its image as a sleepy family-led south Georgia newspaper publisher and become a hot southeastern media player." In October *Fortune* magazine ranked Gray Communications as the nation's 81st fastest growing company with an annual growth rate of 48 percent.

In its single largest acquisition to date, Gray had also made an offer to First American Media, Inc., of Tallahassee, Florida, for WCTV-TV, the CBS affiliate in Tallahassee, Florida/ Thomasville, Florida; WVLT-TV, the CBS affiliate in Knoxville, Tennessee; Satellite and Production Business Services based in Tallahassee; and PortaPhone, a communications and paging business in the Southeast. The purchase price was $183.9 million, and the deal closed in September 1996.

Gray sold KTVE serving Monroe, Louisiana-El Dorado, Arkansas, on August 20, 1996, for $9.5 million in cash plus approximately $829,000 worth of accounts receivable. In addition to closing the deal with First American in September, which marked its entry into the paging business, Gray completed a public offering of its Class B common stock and 10.5 percent senior subordinated notes, resulting in net proceeds to Gray of more than $200 million. The company also issued $200 million worth of preferred stock and entered into a new bank credit facility of $125 million. These actions were taken as part of a financing plan to increase liquidity and improve operating and financial flexibility. For fiscal 1996, Gray Communications reported net income of $2.5 million on revenue of $79.3 million.

The company also underwent a change in leadership. In September 1996, newly named president and CEO Ralph Gabbard died unexpectedly at the age of 50 of a heart attack. Gabbard was credited with giving Gray a national presence in the broadcast industry by serving as chairman of the National Association of Broadcasters' Television Board and as chairman of the CBS Affiliates Advisory Board. J. Mack Robinson, chairman of the board of Bull Run Corporation, was named Gray's interim president and CEO. Prather, who was also president and CEO of Bull Run, became Gray's interim executive vice-president—acquisitions.

Acquisitions Continued in 1997

In January 1997 Gray announced its intention to purchase Gulflink Communications, Inc., a transportable satellite uplink business based in Baton Rouge, Louisiana. The acquisition was completed in April. The acquisition complemented the company's existing satellite transmission and production services business, Lynqx Communications.

In February 1997 Gray continued with its strategy of acquiring broadcast properties in fast-growing markets in the Southeast by entering into an agreement to purchase WITN-TV from Raycom-US, Inc., who was in the process of acquiring the station from AFLAC Broadcast Group, Inc. Raycom had to sell the station, because under current FCC regulations Raycom also owned WECT-TV in Wilmington, North Carolina. WITN-TV served the Greenville-Washington-New Bern, North Carolina area, which included 236,000 television households and East Carolina University. The acquisition was completed on August 1, 1997.

During 1997 Gray boosted the circulation of the *Gwinnett Daily Post* by entering into agreements to provide copies of the daily paper to cable television subscribers. In one such agreement, the *Daily Post* provided newspapers to 20,000 metro Atlanta subscribers of Genesis Cable Communications LLC, which purchased the papers from the *Daily Post.*

Gray Began Looking for Acquisitions Outside the Southeast in 1998

In its first move into broadcast markets outside of the southeastern United States, Gray announced in January 1998 that it had entered into an agreement to acquire the assets of Busse Broadcasting Corporation, a Michigan-based company that owned three midwest television stations: KOLN-TV, the CBS affiliate in Lincoln, Nebraska; KGIN-TV in Grand Island, Nebraska; and WEAU-TV, the NBC affiliate in Eau Claire, Wisconsin. All three stations served fast-growing markets. They were the number one rated stations and local news leaders in their markets. The acquisition would bring to 11 the number of television stations owned by Gray Communications. The purchase price was approximately $112 million.

It appeared that, in order to comply with FCC regulations governing common ownership of television stations with overlapping service areas, Gray Communications would be forced to divest itself of WALB-TV in Albany, Georgia, and WJHG-TV in Panama City, Florida. However, the company received an extension from the FCC while the commission reviewed its rulemaking in this area.

At the beginning of 1998 Gray Communications owned eight network-affiliated television stations in medium-size markets in the southeastern United States. Five of the eight were affiliated with the CBS Television Network, and three were affiliated with the NBC Television Network. It was in the process of adding three more stations in the pending acquisition of Busse Broadcasting. It also owned three daily newspapers, two weekly advertising-only publications, a paging business, and satellite transmission and production services companies. For the future, it appeared that Gray Communications would continue to pursue its strategy of growth through selective acquisitions.

Further Reading

Earle, Joe, "Words to Grow on in Rockdale," *Atlanta Constitution,* September 29, 1994.

Fielder, Bill, "Gray Communications Announces Letter of Intent for Acquisition of Television Station," *PR Newswire,* February 13, 1997.

"Georgia Earnings: Gray Communications," *Atlanta Constitution,* August 3, 1994.

"Gray Communications Systems, Inc. Announces Signing of Definitive Purchase Agreement to Acquire Three Television Stations," *PR Newswire,* February 17, 1998.

Haddad, Charles, "Gray Buying Three Midwest TV Stations," *Atlanta Constitution,* January 16, 1998.

——, "Gray Family Races to Settle Media Empire Fight," *Atlanta Constitution,* April 26, 1991.

——, "Gray Files Suit to Gain Control of Media Company," *Atlanta Constitution,* April 3, 1991.

——, "Gwinnett Paper Strikes Deal to Hike Circulation," *Atlanta Constitution,* November 1, 1997.

——, "Victory Eludes Media Scion in Battle for Company," *Atlanta Constitution,* February 3, 1991.

Hayes, Katheryn, "The Mystery of James Gray," *Georgia Trend,* March 1987.

Heath, David, "Big Changes Not Expected at Insurer's TV Stations," *Courier-Journal,* October 8, 1993.

——, "Winners Chosen in Bidding for Insurer's Stations," *Courier-Journal,* October 6, 1993.

Kamuf, Rachael, "FCC Asked to Dismiss Challenge to Station Sale," *Business First-Louisville,* February 7, 1994.

——, "Kincaid Heirs Seek to Block Sale of Television Stations," *Business First-Louisville,* January 24, 1994.

Kempner, Matt, "Gray Communications CEO Dies Unexpectedly," *Atlanta Constitution,* September 11, 1996.

——, "Gray Communications to Expand Gwinnett Newspaper," *Atlanta Constitution,* August 24, 1995.

——, "Gray Glows Bright on Media Scene," *Atlanta Constitution,* February 14, 1996.

McGinty, David, "Stations Owned by Insurer Are Sold," *Courier-Journal,* September 3, 1994.

Pousner, Michael, "Gray Communications Redefines Small-Town Power," *Atlanta Business Chronicle,* May 5, 1986.

Reece, Chuck, "Family Feud: The Grays of Albany," *Georgia Trend,* March 1991.

Sharpe, Anita, "Gray's Stock Price Surges This Month," *Atlanta Business Chronicle,* December 16, 1985.

Shipp, Bill, "Gray Moves into Atlanta Market," *Georgia Trend,* July 1994.

Wilkinson, Bruce, "Albany Standoff Ends, Gray Heirs Sell Newspaper," *Georgia Trend,* August 1993.

Williams, John, "Gray Communications Systems Reports Fourth Quarter Results," *PR Newswire,* August 21, 1992.

——, "Gray Communications Systems Reports Results," *PR Newswire,* January 14, 1993.

——, "Gray Communications Systems Reports Results," *PR Newswire,* August 27, 1993.

—David Bianco

Hadco Corporation

12A Manor Parkway
Salem, New Hampshire 03079
U.S.A.
(603) 898-8000
Fax: (603) 898-6227
Web site: http://www.hadco.com

Public Company
Incorporated: 1966 as Hadco Printed Circuits, Inc.
Employees: 8,000
Sales: $648.7 million (1997)
Stock Exchanges: NASDAQ
Ticker Symbol: HDCO
SICs: 3672 Printed Circuit Boards; 3679 Electronic
    Components, Not Elsewhere Classified; 3678
    Electronic Connectors

For over two decades, Hadco Corporation has been a leader in the development and manufacture of electronic packaging solutions. With the acquisition of Santa Clara, California-based competitor Zycon in 1996, with major customers such as Solectron, Cabletron, Sun Microsystems, Northern Telecom, AT&T Technologies, Intel, and Compaq, and with mounting sales, Hadco has become the largest manufacturer of high-density double-sided and complex multilayer printed circuits and backplate assemblies for the telecommunications, computer, and industrial automation industries in North America among the approximately 700 independent printed circuit board manufacturers in the United States alone, outselling such competitors as Altron, Elexsys International, Merix, and Sanmina.

The company got its start in Massachusetts in 1966 as Hadco Printed Circuits, Inc. Founder Harold Irvine named the company Hadco after himself and two other partners, using the initial of each of their first names for ''Had,'' with the ''co'' standing for ''Company.'' They began by manufacturing traditional single-sided printed circuits.

In 1969, Hadco built its first manufacturing facility in Derry, New Hampshire. A second facility was acquired in Owego, New York, in 1979. The company has not stopped growing since its early days.

Growth Since the 1980s

The company operated under the original moniker until 1982, when it changed its name to Hadco Corporation. That same year, the company acquired Lamination Technology, Inc. (LTI), a manufacturer of printed circuit materials, and Systems Corp. In 1983, Circuit Image Industries, Inc. (Hudson, New Hampshire), an inner layer PCB manufacturer, was obtained. Another inner layer facility was built at Owego in 1991.

In 1985, the Lamination Technology division was sold, but the company picked up a 49 percent interest in SA Comelim, paying just over $2.5 million. Two years later saw the formation of Hadco Limited as a wholly owned subsidiary. During that year, the company also built a plant in Ireland in order to better service its customers in the European market.

A hazardous waste spill at the company's New Hampshire facility ended up in city storm drains and earned Hadco a lawsuit which was settled in 1994 for $157,000. In the early 1990s, many of Hadco's competitors ramped up their value-added manufacturing capabilities. Hadco did not follow suit for several years. When Andrew E. Lietz, COO, was promoted to president and CEO of the company in 1995, replacing the retiring Patrick Sweeney, the company began selling off some of its backlog, accomplished quick turnaround of its product, and began meeting the demand for time-to-volume requirements of its customers.

In late 1996, the company acquired competitor Zycon Corporation for $205 million. Zycon had previously been negotiating with a Hicks, Muse, Tate and Furst affiliate for a $180 million buyout. With the purchase of Zycon, Hadco became the largest manufacturer of advanced electronic interconnect products in North America, with nine facilities. The tenth facility, a state-of-the-art offshore manufacturing plant in Kuching, the state capital of Sarawak, Malaysia, was acquired as part of

---

Company Perspectives:

HADCO Corporation is one of the world's largest developers and suppliers of advanced electronic interconnect solutions. We serve OEM's and contract manufacturers in the computing, data communications, telecommunications, and industrial automation markets across the globe.

Our wide range of products and services provide an integrated solution to the electronic industry's accelerating technology and time-to-market requirements.

HADCO offers extensive circuit design and engineering services, dedicated quick-turn, prototype and development fabrication, complex advanced technology volume production, and complete backplane assembly devices.

Zycon and made Hadco the first American offshore multilayer printed circuit board manufacturer. In company materials, Lietz said, "Overall, the integration of Hadco and Zycon and the joint efforts of the employees of the company have led to record financial results."

New Technologies

Hadco has been a leader in the development of new technologies in the electronics industry. The company has a two-pronged approach to this development, something called "Evolution and Revolution in Increasing Board Density." Hadco defines "Evolution" as "the ongoing, continuous process of enhancing current technologies by increasing board densities while lowering overall costs." These changes have successfully brought Hadco finer line and space geometries into volume production than were imaginable just a few years ago.

"Revolution" is defined as "looking at PCB and interconnect issues from new, creative and sometimes radical technological perspectives. Revolutionary change means bringing entirely new processes, materials and technologies to the table." Because Hadco anticipates that standard component I/O requirements should be above 800 by the year 2000, with line and space geometries ranging to .002/.002, it is exploring revolutionary methods of meeting these future needs, actively investigating alternative interconnect strategies and forming partnerships with companies that bring new and creative processes, materials, and ways of thinking to the table, including IBM, Hewlett-Packard, Aesop, and Cosen. Some of the specific revolutionary technologies that Hadco continued to explore during the 1990s included photo-defined vias, conductive inks, conductive adhesives, and alternative surface finishes (including organic coatings, nickel, gold, and palladium).

One of the technologies created by Hadco is called Buried Capacitance, or BC. This technology utilizes ZBC-2000 Laminate (originally developed and patented by Zycon) and is a board manufacturing technique in which distributed decoupling capacitance is achieved by embedding thin dielectric layers within the board. This technique allows for the removal of discrete decoupling capacitors, clearing board space and en-

abling designers to design boards that have greater functionality and/or reduced overall size. This new technology was the winner of *Surface Mount Technology* magazine's 1992 Vision Award and the 1993 Milton S. Kiver Grand Award for Excellence in Electronic Packaging and Production. EmCap was developed in 1997 and was the next generation of Buried Capacitance. EmCap, which combines ferro-electric material and epoxy to make a pliable pw-board laminate, is projected to have five times the capacitance value of ZBC-2000, allowing the removal of even more surface discrete capacitors. A similar technology developed by Hadco allows for the removal of surface resistors as well as capacitors.

During 1996 and 1997 Hadco introduced another new technology: a resistive, conductive ink, called ResistAIR. This ink can be screened onto a core material, replacing the traditional metal circuit paths. Also associated with ResistAIR are Embedded Capacitance and Embedded Resistance. Hadco removed discrete resistors and capacitors from the surface of printed circuit boards and embedded them inside a multilayer printed circuit. This process made room for more active components, allowing an overall reduction in size and an improvement in electrical performance. It also eliminated placement, soldering, inspection and testing associated with surface components.

President and CEO Lietz stated that Hadco's objective "is to take a leadership position in the world interconnect market." As the demand for more complex, higher layer count circuit boards and backplates continued to rise, and as the company continued to upgrade and expand its facilities, Hadco appeared in a very good position to fulfill that objective. In a mid-1998 press release, Lietz reiterated: "We already have the best people, equipment and technology in our industry and I am confident that we will execute our strategy to ensure our long-term success."

Principal Subsidiaries

Zycon Corporation.

Further Reading

Derman, Glenda, " 'Integral' Passives to Spur Products," *EETimes,* March 31, 1997, p. 156.

Guinther, Fred, "Zycon Sold—Twice in One Week," *Electronic News,* December 9, 1996, p. 1.

"Hadco Agrees to Deal for Rival Maker of Circuit Boards," *New York Times,* December 6, 1996, p. C3(N)/D3(L). "Hadco Corp.," *CDA-Investnet Insiders' Chronicle,* April 22, 1996, p. 3.

"Hadco Corp.—Company Report," *Moody's Investor Service,* March 26, 1997.

"Hadco Corporation Files Amendment to Registration Statement to Change Securities Offering," *PR Newswire,* May 13, 1997, p. 513NETU019.

"Hadco Corporation Organizational Announcement," Salem, N.H.: Hadco Corporation, May 20, 1998.

"Hadco Corporation Reports Second Quarter Results," *PR Newswire,* May 8, 1997, p. 508NETH036.

"Hadco Displaces Hicks Muse in Pact to Acquire Zycon," *Wall Street Journal,* December 6, 1996, p. B2(W)/B5(E).

"Orbotech Wins Major Orders from Hadco," *Israel Business Today,* November 20, 1996, p. 23.

"Subsidiary's Tender Offer for Zycon Is Completed," *Wall Street Journal,* January 13, 1997, p. B7(W)/B6(E).

Wood, Craig H., Allen Kaufman, and Michael Merenda, "How Hadco Became a Problem-Solving Supplier," *Sloan Management Review,* Winter 1996, p. 77.

"Zycon Corp.—Company Report," *Moody's Investor Service,* January 10, 1997.

"Zycon Corp.—Company Report," Prudential Securities Inc., January 10, 1996.

—Daryl F. Mallett

Hahn Automotive Warehouse, Inc.

415 West Main Street
Rochester, New York 14608
U.S.A.
(716) 235-1595
Fax: (716) 235-7134

Public Company
Incorporated: 1958
Employees: 1,100
Sales: $142.2 million (1997)
Stock Exchanges: NASDAQ
Ticker Symbol: HAHN
SICs: 5013: Motor Vehicle Supplies & New Parts

Hahn Automotive Warehouse, Inc. is a distributor of automotive aftermarket parts to the East Coast and the Midwest. The company obtains the parts directly from manufacturers and sells them to both wholesale and retail establishments, such as independent jobbers, car dealerships, repair shops, and government agencies. Hahn's products include replacement and repair parts—such as exhaust systems, chassis parts, and ignition systems—and maintenance items and accessories, including oil, antifreeze, and transmission and brake fluid. Hahn also owns Advantage Auto Stores, a chain of jobber outlets. Hahn is the largest company participating in Auto Value, a nationwide auto parts program through which Hahn provides supportive marketing programs and operational assistance to both its own stores and its customers.

The Beginning of the Road: The 1950s

In 1952 Michael Futerman, the company's founder, traveled to the United States from his home in Israel. The 25-year-old visited a relative in Cleveland, Ohio, who owned an auto parts store. During his stay Futerman worked at the store and began to learn and like the business. He then traveled to Erie, Pennsylvania, where he worked for another auto parts store, this one also owned by a relative. While in Pennsylvania, he met his future

wife, Sara, and began to search for an opportunity to launch his own auto parts business.

Futerman's goal became a reality in 1958 with his purchase of an existing auto supply business, Hahn Tire and Battery, in Rochester, New York. Two years later, in 1960, Futerman was able to expand beyond this small, redistributing jobber store. He convinced vendors to sell directly to Hahn Tire and Battery, in the process establishing his business as a wholesale distributor. This accomplishment marked Futerman's true entrance into the automotive aftermarket. In recognition of this fact, he renamed the company Hahn Automotive Warehouse, Inc. In its first year, Hahn did approximately $200,000 worth of business. In part because of this early success, Hahn would post increased earnings in 34 of its first 35 years.

Growth Through Acquisitions: 1969 to the 1980s

Over the next three decades Hahn grew steadily as it strategically acquired failing automotive parts businesses and successfully integrated them into the company. In 1969 Hahn made its first acquisition, F.A. Crossman, an automotive aftermarket warehouse distributor based in Syracuse, New York. With this purchase Hahn extended its sales region into central New York. Beginning in the early 1970s Hahn also expanded its network of wholesale outlets by purchasing small, independent auto parts stores. A milestone for Hahn was its 1982 acquisition of United Consolidated Industries, an auto aftermarket company on the East Coast. United Consolidated provided Hahn with seven additional distribution facilities, as well as four new company-owned jobber stores. With this purchase Hahn not only expanded its sales region but also established itself as a force along the entire eastern seaboard. United Consolidated's warehouses and outlets ranged along the Atlantic coast from Newburgh, New York, to Richmond, Virginia. In 1983 Hahn acquired another auto parts distribution center, Alco Standard Warehouse, located in Buffalo, New York.

In 1988 the company acquired the assets of a division of AI Automotive, an auto parts distributor based in Dayton, Ohio. It was the largest acquisition Hahn had carried out, and it provided Futerman's enterprise with four additional distribution centers and 23 new stores. More significant, however, was the fact that this takeover afforded Hahn access to the Midwestern auto parts market. Hahn's sales region now spread along the East Coast and stretched west to Indiana. Throughout the late 1980s Hahn also established its Advantage Auto Stores, at the time a chain of 51 commercial jobber outlets. These stores supported Hahn's rapidly growing warehouse distribution centers.

In the 1980s Hahn also sought to maximize its operational capacities. During this period the company became the first wholesaler to provide its jobbers with computer terminals. These terminals, equipped with modems, tracked the sales at each jobber store. This sales information was then sent electronically to the warehouse, which enabled Hahn easily to monitor and replenish its inventory. Hahn would thereafter continue to upgrade its computer system, most notably with the 1988 installation of an advanced system specifically designed for the auto aftermarket parts industry.

A New Path: Acquisitions of the Early 1990s

In January 1993 Hahn Automotive became a publicly held company with an initial stock offering of 1,610,000 shares at $12.50 per share. Trading on the NASDAQ stock exchange, shares rose quickly in price. Analysts were impressed with Hahn's moves into key segments of the aftermarket auto parts industry. Despite its new status as a publicly held company, however, Hahn remained a family-run operation. Futerman's son, Eli, had worked at Hahn from an early age, and he had gained a great deal of experience with various aspects of his father's business. In 1980 he had been made vice-president of the company, and he was appointed president in 1992. At the same time, Michael Futerman became the company's chief executive officer. The father and son team planned to continue Hahn's successful strategy of identifying underperforming warehouse distributors and parts stores. After acquiring them, the company would integrate them into Hahn's corporate structure and seek to return these new assets to profitability.

Hahn carried out an important acquisition in November 1993, when it spent $13 million to buy the faltering AUTOWORKS Holdings, Inc., of Phoenix, Arizona, from the Northern Automotive Holdings Corporation. This purchase marked the first time that Hahn had ventured into the retail market. At the time, AUTOWORKS consisted of 159 retail stores, as well as a warehouse distribution center in Ohio. The AUTOWORKS stores carried a range of automobile replacement parts, maintenance items, and accessories for the ''do it yourself'' customer. With the addition of AUTOWORKS,

Hahn's revenues soared 50 percent. Moreover, the acquisition tripled the number of stores owned by Hahn and extended the company's sales region into 13 states, including Illinois, West Virginia, Missouri, and Kentucky. Sales for 1993 totaled $119 million.

Hahn continued to expand with its September 1994 acquisition of both Meisenzahl Auto Parts, Inc. and its subsidiary Regional Parts, Inc. Hahn kept the name of Meisenzahl and incorporated the company into a new division, which it named Professional Auto Warehouse. With the Meisenzahl acquisition, Hahn moved into the last segment of the automotive aftermarket industry it had not touched—direct distribution. In this new, ''two-step'' distribution, Hahn sold directly to professional installers, fleet operators, vehicle dealerships, government agencies, and do-it-yourselfers. In this way Hahn eliminated a distribution step and attained a greater margin of profit than in the traditional ''three-step'' distribution method. The acquisition of Meisenzahl was a successful one. By the end of 1994, Hahn posted net sales of $215 million. The AUTOWORKS retail stores contributed 43 percent of sales, while Advantage Auto wholesale outlets provided 24.5 percent. Sales to independent commercial customers accounted for the remaining 32.5 percent of the total.

Despite its strong sales volume, the AUTOWORKS acquisition was not a resounding success for Hahn. Although Hahn's corporate strategy was to revitalize underperforming operations, the problems with AUTOWORKS were too great for its parent to cure. After more than four years of operating losses, the AUTOWORKS subsidiary did not prove to be a viable entity for the company. The subsidiary filed for bankruptcy in the Bankruptcy Court for the Western District of New York on July 24, 1997. The liquidation of AUTOWORKS was completed in November of that year. The proceeds of the liquidation sale were used to pay down portions of AUTOWORKS' outstanding loans. As a result of the bankruptcy filing, an Official Creditors Committee was established to evaluate potential claims against Hahn. In February 1998 an agreement was reached with the committee, and the company resolved approximately $6.5 million in claims against it. In this settlement Hahn was to pay $1.6 million in five equal annual installments. Eli Futerman stressed the positive aspects of the settlement. In an April 22, 1998, press release, he emphasized that ''this resolution permits Hahn to direct its total focus to the operation of its existing business.''

Developments from the Mid-1990s

Hahn continued to explore new opportunities for expansion. In June 1995 Hahn became the first American company to enter the Israeli auto parts market. It did so by embarking on a joint venture with Pinros Automotive Spare Parts, Ltd., an Israeli distributor, and Federal-Mogul Corporation, an American producer and distributor of auto parts. Because the Israeli market was thought to be fragmented, Hahn saw potential for its own growth in the area.

In September 1996 Hahn's Professional Warehouse division was chosen by the state of New York to be the exclusive supplier of replacement parts for all state-owned vehicles. The agreement—which covered 17 different product groups, including lighting, rubber products, fuel systems, electrical components, and bearings and seals—increased Hahn's opportunities to obtain further government contracts. The next month Hahn acquired Nu-Way Auto Parts, Inc., a group of direct distribution centers located in Rochester, New York. As with Meisenzahl, Hahn maintained the Nu-Way name but integrated the company into its Professional Auto Warehouse division. In 1997 Hahn acquired Finn Auto Parts of Canandaigua, Inc. This company became an Advantage Auto Store within Hahn's wholesale division.

By the late 1990s the company stocked more than 156,000 name-brand and private-label products, which it purchased from approximately 320 manufacturers. Hahn also maintained valuable relationships with many of its manufacturers dating back to the early years of the company. Hahn delivered these products to its 85 company-owned Advantage Auto Stores and more than 1,400 independent jobbers through strategically located distribution centers. It also serviced car dealerships, independent repair facilities, government agencies, independent fleets, and retail consumers. During this period, moreover, Hahn was benefiting from changes in vehicle ownership. Nationwide the number of vehicles was growing, and the percentage of cars on the road more than ten years old had tripled between 1972 and 1995. These older cars required more frequent repair and as a result more aftermarket parts.

Principal Subsidiaries

Meisenzahl Auto Parts, Inc.

Further Reading

Astor, Will, "Fragmented Israeli Market Creates Opening for Hahn," *Rochester Business Journal*, June 18, 1995.

Galarza, Pablo, "Providing Parts to Keep Cars Driving Longer," *Investors' Business Daily*, August 19, 1994.

"Industry Veteran Hired to Fix Hahn Subsidiary," *Rochester Business Journal*, November 17, 1995.

"Monro, Hahn Struggle Through Industry Slump," *Rochester Business Journal*, September 22, 1995.

"Strong Move into Retail by Hahn Wows Analysts," *Rochester Business Journal*, August 19, 1994.

—Leslie-Anne Skolnik and Rebecca Stanfel

Harbison-Walker Refractories Company

600 Grant St., Suite 50
Pittsburgh, Pennsylvania 15219-2703
U.S.A.
(412) 562-6200
Fax: (412) 562-6209
Web site: http://www.hwr.com

*Wholly Owned Subsidiary of Global Industrial
    Technologies, Inc.*
Incorporated: 1865 as Star Fire Brick Company
Employees: 1,750
Sales: $335.5 million (1997)
SICs: 3255 Clay Refractories; 3297 Nonclay Refractories

Harbison-Walker Refractories Company (Harbison) is the world's leading supplier of refractory technology, products and services (refractories are nonmetallic materials suitable for use at high temperatures in furnace construction). The company manufactures more than 300 refractory brands, and mines and processes ores for both internal use and for sale to third parties. Harbison's worldwide presence of affiliates, licensees, and international sales agents enables Harbison to directly service the pyro-processing industry globally. The company controls over 65 percent of the raw materials it consumes, making it virtually invulnerable to worldwide supply fluctuations.

The refractories industry was born with the advent of the steel-producing Bessemer Converter served by blast furnaces capable of melting metal. The Bessemer process was an early method for making steel by blowing air through molten pig iron, whereby most of the carbon and impurities are removed by oxidation. Prior to the Industrial Revolution, European companies began manufacturing firebrick for the construction of walls for blast furnaces, kilns, crucibles, and ladles. The Industrial Revolution ignited a manufacturing boom in America for the production of machinery, glass, and forged metals, giving rise to the need for massive quantities of firebrick. Emerging technology industries created new markets for specialized refractories. Seizing upon the opportunities of the time, the founders of

Harbison determined to develop products that would accommodate the growing marketplace.

A Post-Civil War Venture

The Harbison-Walker Refractories Company (Harbison) was organized in 1865 by J. K. Lemon and originally operated under the name of the Star Fire Brick Company. With a capitalization of $8,000 the venture was financed by ten partners who had no knowledge of brickmaking. The first plant utilized raw materials from clay mines at Bolivar, Pennsylvania, which went into the making of Star brand fireclay brick. In 1875 the original partnership became known as Harbison and Walker, and was later reorganized into the Harbison-Walker Refractories Company in 1902, led by Samuel P. Harbison and Hay Walker. At the outset Samuel Harbison had been hired as company secretary but soon assumed responsibilities for organizing a systematic investigation of fire clays and their suitability for refractory brick uses. Walker was the other remaining original partner and functioned as bookkeeper as well as the person responsible for the study of plant efficiencies and kiln records that chronicled each kiln's reject loss in burning. Between 1909 and 1910 the Harbison-Walker Research Department was formally established, with studies conducted at the company's Hays Lab on the Monongahela River. Their research contributed to the development of super-duty silica refractories largely useful in the steel industry, special fireclay and super-duty fireclay blast furnace refractories, forsterite refractories for glass and other industries, new types of basic refractories especially adapted for the lining of rotary kilns, open-hearth steel furnaces, copper converters, and many other furnaces.

Dawn of the 20th Century: Supplying U.S. Steel

Refractories were made in the form of bricks of various sizes, but mortars and special shapes were also important in company product lines. Refractories are usually a light, buff color and are distinguished from ordinary building bricks by their composition of high silica and alumina clays and by being fired at much higher temperatures. These products are resistant to thermal stress and chemical abrasion, and play a fundamental role in many kinds of industrial production, particularly within the steelmaking industry. The company's primary customer was Andrew Carnegie's iron mills, and Harbison's development shadowed his. According to Kim Wallace in *Brickyard Towns, A History of Refractories Industry Communities in South-Central Pennsylvania*, "In 1902, one year after the merger of Carnegie's holdings into the U.S. Steel Corporation, the Harbison and Walker Company orchestrated a merger that brought its holdings to thirty-three plants and thousands of acres of clay mines."

In 1905 the company began using steel molds instead of wooden molds in the making of byproduct coke ovens and other shapes. It became the first U.S. company of its type to use and develop the continuous tunnel kiln for the burning of silica brick, when it erected its East Chicago, Indiana, kiln in 1927. Harbison held the license on the discovery that steel or iron sheets heated between magnesite bricks would oxidize and bond the brick together into a solid structure. The company developed this process until it came out with its "H-W Matalkase," which produced the first chemically bonded magnesite-chrome refractory.

In further expansion developments, Harbison assumed ownership of the Northwest Magnesite Company in 1923, selling off 40 percent of that venture three years later. Harbison expanded into Canada and became that country's largest refractory producer when it combined the assets of three magnesite producing companies, and organized them into Canadian Refractories Ltd. in 1933.

World War II-Era Fostered Expansion Explosion

Entering a new market, the company began producing kiln devices for the pottery industry and other applications with the purchase of the Loughan Manufacturing Company of Ohio in 1947. Another milestone was the company's contract to supply materials for the construction of the world's largest blast furnace at the Zug Island Plant of the Great Lakes Steel Corporation in 1955. Throughout the decade the company and its subdivisions grew to operate 33 plants in 12 states and Canada, producing refractories of silica, fire clay, super duty high alumina, magnesite, chrome, forsterite, plastic fire brick, castables,

insulating refractories, mortars, and ramming materials. During this period Harbison initiated a program of modernization and new construction, including the construction of 32 continuous tunnels and a renewed emphasis on quality control.

By the mid-20th century, the south-central Pennsylvania refractories business was dominated by three companies which had grown through a series of mergers. Harbison emerged as the company with the largest holdings. From 1955 to 1965 the company established its first overseas manufacturing subsidiary in Lima, Peru, called Rafractarios Peruanos, S.A. Their principal products were fireclay, silica, and basic refractories. Within the year, Harbison added Frabrica de Ladrillos Industriales, S.A. in Monterrey, Mexico, to their operations, naming the venture Harbison-Walker-Flir. Six years later a Venezuelan affiliate company, Cermica Carabobo, C.A. was added to the company's production facilities. Harbison invested $73 million in expansion during this time period, including a $2 million modern Garber Research Center located in Pittsburgh. Harbison also signed a joint-venture agreement with the Carborundum Company of Niagara Falls, New York, in 1960, and in 1966 the Tanner Plating Company of New Castle, Pennsylvania, was acquired, adding the services of complete industrial hard chrome plating, grinding, and honing. A further South American development included the addition of a Chilean affiliate, Refractarios Chilenos, S.A. Moving into Australia the following year, the company acquired a subsidiary in Unaderra, New South Wales, Harbison-A.C.I. PTY. Ltd.

Continued Overseas Expansion in the 1960s

In 1967 Harbison merged with and became a division of Dresser Industries of Dallas, Texas, a company that principally catered to the oil service industry. The acquisition offered the needed diversity to buffer the company during slack growth periods, and also accelerated the company's move into non-steel related industries. A new company was formed four years later when Dresser signed a joint venture refractory products manufacturing agreement with a West German company, Martin & Pagenstecher GMBH. The new company, named Magnesital-Feuerfest, was stationed in the Ruhr district in a newly constructed $10 million plant. The Harbison facilities were operating at full capacity during this period, and managed to cope with energy shortages and shortages of many of the raw materials needed for production. The company supplied refractory products and high purity fused grains to the electronics, chemical, fiberglass, and foundry industries. They sold improved high-alumina products to the non-ferrous industry and resin bonded magnesia-carbon brick for basic oxygen converters and electric furnaces and special magnesite refractory products. The company continuously improved upon technological means of producing more and more specialized products for the changing steel industry.

Downsizing in the 1980s

In 1973 Dresser expanded into Iran, establishing a new company, Iran Refractories Company (IREFCO), centered in the hub of the Iranian steelmaking industry. Their newly constructed $5.5 million plant began operating in 1976. After peaking in its cycle of capital spending, Harbison experienced a time of declining production that lasted into the 1980s, shadowing an overall industry decline. Changes in production technology affected the major industries that used refractories, challenging Harbison to completely restructure its facilities. Harbison acquired a fused silica production facility in Calhoun, Georgia, in 1976, which enabled the company to diversify into a new product line.

In 1992 the INDRESCO Company Inc. was created as an independent public company in a spinoff to shareholders by Dresser Industries, Inc. INDRESCO raised $92 million by reducing partnership in a joint venture with Komatsu and selling its European compressor business, with a plan to develop a new enterprise with a new growth strategy. The top refractory producer in Mexico was acquired, resulting in enhanced capability in processing and recycling. The remainder of the Komatsu joint venture was liquidated and a leading Chilean refractory producer was acquired while the company began showing increased sales and expansion. Concentrating on overseas expansion in 1995, INDRESCO created an International unit within the refractories division. The following year a new parent company was formed, structured as a holding company named Global Industrial Technologies, Inc.

Harbison entered the 1990s as a worldwide leader in new technology refractory products and service. The company was honored with the receipt of the "E" Award, in recognition of excellence in exports and the introduction of a new generation of magnesite-carbon, ultra high-alumina brick, and specialty products. Two marketing arms, the Iron and Steel Marketing Group and the Industrial Marketing Group, meet the refractory needs of these diverse segments separately. Other company delineations accommodated the specialized areas involved in researching and understanding a new generation of refractories of heat processing industries, which grew to include waste incineration, recycling, the conversion of steam to energy, carbon black for automobile tires, cement, and virtually every other process related to industrial boilers or furnaces.

The mining and minerals unit primarily produced high-purity magnesite, which was used in the manufacture of premium refractory items. Although the unit was formed with the intention of supplying Harbison's business, the company also began selling raw materials to refractory manufacturers worldwide. With just 20 producers of these supplies worldwide, the company sold about 11 percent of the world's total high-purity magnesite (approximately 1.5 tons).

1996 and Beyond: Aggressive Capital Spending

In 1996 Harbison booked the largest project sales order in its history, a $25 million contract to provide refractory products for 268 new coke ovens being constructed in Indiana. The Sun Coal and Coke project at Indiana Harbor in East Chicago, Indiana, required 73,000 metric tons of Harbison's premium silica and fireclay based refractory products. Also in that year export sales reached $25 million, with shipments to 53 countries. New sales offices were established in Singapore and Milan to facilitate progress in penetrating markets in southeast Asia and Europe. Over 25 percent of refractory sales for the year were from products less than five years old, confirming the commitment to an aggressive new capital spending plan of more than $24 million for research and development for the following year.

Global Technologies revised its businesses into five segments: Refractory Products, Minerals, Industrial Tool, Specialty Equipment Products, and Forged Products. In March 1997 Harbison entered into a joint venture agreement with the Siam Cement Group to develop, build, and operate refractory plants throughout southeast Asia. In addition, the company began negotiating the formation of a joint venture in the People's Republic of China to manufacture refractories for use in China's coal gasification industry, which was scheduled to begin in 1998. Additionally, the parent company purchased the Refractarios Lota-Green Limitada and refractory related assets of Concepcion, Chile, for $13.6 million. Combined with its other existing Refractarios Chilenos S.A. business in Santiago, Chile, the two companies became known as RECSA-LOTA and gave Harbison a significant market share in Chile. The alignment helped RECSA to win its largest contract in history: an agreement to supply $27 million of refractory products for Compania Siderurgica Huachipato, the country's largest steel producer. RECSA-LOTA was positioned to penetrate the Southern Cone Common Market, particularly in the copper industry markets. Harbison continued to evaluate potential regional opportunities in response to the Latin American growth and industry privatizations.

Harbison revenues hit an all-time high in 1997, reaching $333.5 million with an increase of 12 percent over the previous year. A large-scale cost reduction program had been initiated domestically and was partly accountable for profit increases. The cement business had also improved as a result of a strong U.S. economy and mild weather in the North for the year. Harbison's response to the decline in the availability of skilled bricklayers, which was driving up costs, involved a plan to move customers to monolithics (a furnace lining without joints), which were cheaper to install because they were less labor-intensive and required reduced furnace downtime. Looking ahead, the company planned to distance itself from the strong competition by moving away from being "only a product supplier to being a solution supplier," according to company statements. Plans were focused not only on providing refractory products but extended to include the removal of old and the installation of new products as well.

Principal Operating Units

Minerals & Mining; Harbison-Walker U.S./Canada; Harbison Walker International; Technology Group; REFMEX (Mexico); RECSA-LOTA (Chile).

Further Reading

Leasure, Robert R., *History of the Harbison-Walker Refractories Company*, Pittsburgh: Harbison-Walker Refractories Company, 1987, pp. 1–8.

MacCloskey, James E., Jr., *The History of The Harbison-Walker Refractories*, Pittsburgh: Harbison-Walker Refractories Company, 1952, 129 p.

Wallace, Kim E., *Brickyard Towns: A History of Refractories Industry Communities in South-Central Pennsylvania*, Washington, D.C.: National Park Service, 1993, 188 p.

—Terri Mozzone

Hayes Corporation

5835 Peachtree Corners East
Norcross, Georgia 30092
U.S.A.
(770) 840-9200
Fax: (770) 441-1213
Web site: http://www.hayes.com

Public Company
Incorporated: 1997
Employees: 1,100
Sales: $199.6 million (1997)
Stock Exchanges: NASDAQ
Ticker Symbol: HAYZ
SICs: 3577 Computer Peripheral Equipment, Not
    Elsewhere Classified; 3661 Telephone & Telegraph
    Apparatus

Hayes Corporation is a leading manufacturer in the personal computer (PC) modem industry. Just as IBM set the standard by which all other PCs are judged, Hayes did the same for modems. The company, however, has endured a less than glorious history, marked during the 1990s by fierce infighting at the executive level and a Chapter 11 bankruptcy, from which the company eventually emerged and reorganized itself through consolidation with Access Beyond Inc.

Beginnings, 1977–85

One of two boys of G. C. (a Southern Bell cable repairman) and Sadie (a telephone operator), Dennis Carl Hayes was described by Sadie as a ''bookish boy . . . drawn to high-technology'' and won a school science fair award with a laser-operated device.

In the 1970s, Hayes worked at Financial Data Sciences (FDS), a Florida-based producer of savings and loans automated teller machines (ATMs), modified from bank ATMs. ''They had a targeted market and a very specific product for that market,'' Hayes said in a February 1990 interview. The strategy appealed to Hayes because FDS competed with larger corporations by targeting a niche market. Hayes adopted the strategy.

Hayes, then 27, left Georgia Tech after five years to start Hayes Microcomputer Products with Dale Heatherington. As the first microcomputers and PCs were introduced, they capitalized on simultaneous business opportunities. Feeling the market would be ignored long enough to get started, they were among the first to develop modems (modulator/demodulators, devices which translate analog telephone signals into digital signals computers can understand), as their company's product. Less investment capital was required, too, compared to diskdrives or printers. They literally invented the modem industry and created the standards for PC modems.

Hayes and Heatherington built their first product, the 80-103A, operating at 300 baud (bits per second) and connecting to the MITS Altair's S-100 bus, on Hayes's dining room table in Spartanburg, South Carolina. With friends, they built a handful of modems daily, releasing the product in April 1977. Hayes subcontracted assembly work from larger computer companies to pay his group and raise equity. They peddled modems from their cars to hobby computer dealers, persuading them to carry the product as kit-computer enhancements, selling $125,000 their first year, and attracting 20 competitors.

A second product shipped in 1978. The Micromodem II for the Apple II was the first modem to directly connect into the telephone network. Demand skyrocketed, and modems were requested for Commodore, DEC, and Radio Shack computers. A standard interface was required, so they created the Hayes AT command set in June 1981. By 1982, they were selling 140,000 modems annually, with $12 million in revenue.

As companies discovered the benefits of on-line databases, electronic mail, micro-to-mainframe links, and local-area networks (LANs), the appeal of computer communications spread. Competition grew. Novation introduced ''Hayes-compatible'' (a term which stuck) modems; Racal-Vadic, known for industrial modems, jumped in; and U.S. Robotics added memory to its internal modem boards. Others enhanced modems by supporting diagnostics inside to trace bad phone lines and producing encryption and other data security features.

In May 1984, market leader Hayes used its success as a cash cow, expanding into general software with its ''Please'' database-management software, with a menu-based command structure. Dennis Hayes indicated that his company had intended to create software since the start. Hayes bought SoftCom in September. The company automated its Norcross, Georgia factory with six production lines producing over 10,000 finished boards daily, and the product development staff moved into new facilities. By July 1984, Hayes was a leading modem manufacturer, gaining household-name status and holding nearly 60 percent of the 300-baud and 1200-baud markets. Estimates put Hayes's revenue near $25 million, double the 1982 figure, but Hayes announced revenues of $120 million for the year, and Dennis Hayes was already predicting modems would ''get smaller, faster and cheaper.'' By 1985, Hayes held nearly half the PC modem market.

Patent Battles, 1985–91

But troubles were brewing for Hayes. A court battle began in 1985, shortly after the company received the Heatherington U.S. Patent 4,549,302—which, named for its inventor, covered a modem-escape sequence defining how modems switch from interpreting commands to safely sending data over telephone lines—and sent letters to approximately 170 modem makers allegedly using the technology, asking that they license it.

In November 1986, competitors Prometheus Products Inc. and U.S. Robotics filed suit in San Francisco's U.S. District Court of Northern California against Hayes, maintaining escape-sequence technology predated Heatherington's patent, invalidating it and citing another modem-escape patent lawsuit between Business Computer Corp. (Bizcomp) and U.S. Robotics in 1984. Hayes filed a counterclaim against the two and Bizcomp, part of ''The Modem Patent Defense Group,'' beginning a legal offensive in April 1987, claiming they had violated the 302 patent.

The industry watched with interest from the sidelines. Hayes sued Microcom Inc. in December 1987 and Micom Systems Inc. in February 1988. Ven-Tel Inc., in December 1987, joined the group suing Hayes. The industry war began in earnest in mid-1988 when Hayes sued Everex Systems Inc. and OmniTel Inc. Other companies began suing Hayes, including, in December 1988 and February 1991, Multi-Tech Systems Inc., whose president, Raghu Sharma said, ''I know it's an invalid patent so I'm going to fight it to the end . . . We were making Bell 212 modems back in 1978 . . . when Dennis Hayes was fiddling around with 300-baud modem chips at his kitchen table.'' Hayes also sued, in May 1991, Zoom Telephonics Inc., Zenith Data Systems, Cardinal Technologies Inc., Packard Bell, and Ven-Tel again. Because the lawsuits were similar, if not identical, to the first, federal judge Samuel Conti consolidated them into one action.

Most companies settled out of court before the trial began. U.S. Robotics settled in September 1987, agreeing to pay Hayes's attorney fees and to license the patent, for a total nearing $500,000. Bizcomp followed in February 1988, agreeing to pay two percent royalties on sales of modems using the patented sequence and obtaining a licensing contract. That September, Microcom settled, paying a one-time licensing fee for the technology and signing a five-year cross-licensing agreement covering all patents developed by either company. Prometheus admitted infringement against the patent in January 1991, agreeing to pay royalties for the technology. By then, Hayes had dropped to 9.6 percent marketshare behind Codex Corp., Racal-Milgo, and Universal Data Systems Inc.

Some fought on . . . and lost. In February 1991, Hayes won a $3.5 million jury award against Everex, Ven-Tel, and OmniTel, as Conti found them guilty of willfully infringing the Heatherington patent. They appealed, but the court ordered payments of $1.01 million, $1.6 million, and $884,854 plus interest, respectively. OmniTel filed for Chapter 11.

Hayes was back in court in 1992 with Multi-Tech in a dispute over modem reliability, unfair competition, and libel. Hayes claimed the Time Independent Escape Sequence (TIES) coding scheme used by Multi-Tech and others was unreliable and could destroy data. Sierra Semiconductor Corp., which manufactured TIES chipsets, had already won two preliminary injunctions in Minnesota and California U.S. District Courts barring Hayes from running ads titled ''Tick, Tick, Tick. Boom! You're Dead.'' Before it ended, The Federal Trade Commission informally investigated whether Hayes engaged in false and misleading advertising. In May 1994, Hayes, admitting no wrongdoing, agreed to halt escape-sequence advertising unless it was backed up with ''competent and reliable evidence.''

While his company often occupied headlines, Dennis Hayes kept a low profile personally, until he met and married former *Atlanta Journal-Constitution* reporter Melita Easters, who funded the arts, making the two a fixture in Atlanta's society pages. Then the couple underwent a messy, public, and bitter divorce in 1988–89.

Hard Times, 1989–94

Following the divorce, things began going badly for the company. It was not evident initially as Hayes acquired JT Fax and competitor Thousand Oaks, California-based Practical Peripherals Inc. (PPI) in August 1989. But, in October, Hayes cut its workforce nearly 10 percent. Hayes denied allegations of financial woes, releasing the Ultra 9600 modem. Other manufacturers, including Codex, also reduced staff.

In 1990, Hayes began working with AT&T developing boards for integrated services digital networks (ISDN), a communications standard for an entirely digitized telephone system which carried more data than previously was possible. But, in April, Hayes cut staff again by 150, closed sales offices in New York, Los Angeles, Washington, D.C., and Toronto, and moved ISDN development activities to San Francisco. Hayes also accepted resignations from John Reinking, vice-president of sales; Lucy Evans, vice-president of finance; and Neal Coyne, senior vice-president and general manager, and Dennis Hayes's number-two man, who joined Hayes in June 1988.

Business got tighter as over 300 competitors worldwide, including Microcom, U.S. Robotics, Multi-Tech, Motorola, Racal-Milgo, and IBM pressed Hayes for marketshare and Pacific Rim manufacturers flooded the market with lower-priced, cheaper-to-produce clone products.

In January 1991, Hayes, holding approximately 12 percent of the U.S. market, bought the assets of Waterloo Microsystems, a Canadian software firm, and had regional headquarters in London and Hong Kong. The company established a joint venture with Siemens AG for ISDN technology and expanded its authorized distributor network in Australia, Mexico, Sweden, Denmark, Taiwan, and the United Kingdom.

The most ambitious undertaking for 1991 was penetrating the Chinese market. The company opened a technical service station in Beijing in September, supplying modem know-how and technical support to the China National Post and Telecommunications Appliances Corp., an import/export trading arm of the Chinese Ministry of Postal and Telecommunications. The Chinese Ministry of Health in Tienjin, southeast of Beijing, began using Hayes modems to link medical specialists with patients in far-flung facilities, and Hayes modems were also used by the Chinese metallurgy industry, which operated mines, refineries, metal-fabrication factories and plants that made cloisonne.

Hayes entered the operating system (OS) market in June with LANstep, a network OS for small offices, abandoned in 1994 in the face of Novell and other products. In July, Hayes released the V-series Ultra Smartmodem 14400, playing catch-up with competitors like Digicom Systems Inc., who had 14.4Kbps products on the market for over a year.

Although Hayes kept its finances hush-hush, court records showed in 1991 an operating loss of $1.3 million, profits in 1992, and losses of over $47 million the next year. Hayes was not alone though; other manufacturers also felt the pinch: Intel Corp. sold most of its modem business, and Megahertz Corp. reported losses early in 1994, eventually being purchased by U.S. Robotics.

Chapter 11, 1994–96

Although Hayes reportedly had $270 million total sales in 1994, cash-flow problems forced them, with approximately 62 percent of the market, to file for Chapter 11 bankruptcy protection in November 1994 during the industry's largest trade show, COMDEX. The timing was unfortunate and speculation ran rampant as vendors like Digicom and Zoom hoped uneasiness about Hayes's financial situation would have customers switching to their products. Some used Hayes's financial woes to promote their own products. Support came from an unexpected source when one of Hayes's fiercest competitors, U.S. Robotics, publicly hoped Hayes pulled through.

While this gave Hayes breathing room from creditors, it did not spare Dennis Hayes from more turmoil. Boca Research, a smaller modem manufacturer, wanted a merger with Hayes in June 1995, retaining the Hayes name, but putting its own leader in charge. By August, Boca canceled the deal, claiming Dennis Hayes had opposed being second and was negotiating with other investors after they asked him to stop, allegations Hayes denied.

Other investors expressed interest. Hayes presented the court with a plan to emerge as an independent entity, less 49 percent of the company in exchange for a $70-plus million loan from the CIT Group of New York and $17.5 million each from Singapore-based ACMA Ltd. and Canadian telecommunications giant Northern Telecom. The $400-million ACMA, which

rescued Paradigm Technology from 1994 Chapter 11 and nurtured the static-RAM maker to a successful initial public offering (IPO) in June 1995, was considered a good partner. Then Northern backed out in March 1996.

Hayes subsequently lined up ACMA subsidiary Rinzai Ltd.; Kaifa Holdings Ltd.; and Wong's International subsidiary Rolling Profits Holdings Ltd. to replace Northern. The new plan would bring $37.9 million, plus a $6.5 million bridge loan with $7.6 million more available if needed, totaling about $105 million to pay creditors approximately $85 million, buy out minority shareholder Melita, and give Hayes operating cash.

A hostile takeover bid came in October from rival manufacturer Diamond Multimedia Systems and, in May 1995, Belgrave Investment Trust purchased $5 million of unsecured debt from Hayes's creditors in the first step of a hostile takeover. Dennis Hayes admitted making some poor business decisions, saying inventories were badly managed, that products producing no revenue were kept on the books, costing the company money, acknowledged the company had botched some technology transitions and had been out-gunned in some markets, especially by U.S. Robotics, but emphasized the success of his reorganization efforts and attributing the company's failure, in part, to his previous management team.

Belgrave dropped its takeover attempt in July 1995. Diamond was not so easily dissuaded, offering $110 million in January 1996, and $128 million in February. Diamond also offered to pay Dennis Hayes $123 million for his stock. He refused. Diamond's plan suffered when U.S. Bankruptcy Judge Hugh Robinson ruled it would not have the rights to key technology developed by Megahertz (owned by U.S. Robotics), on which Hayes held the only license. Without the patented device, called "The X-Jack," a pop-out plug connecting laptop computers to telephone lines via modems, Hayes, which marketed it as the "Easy Jack," would lose sales and drop in value. Diamond President William Schroder was vocal about keeping the Hayes name, but planned to "tighten up" operations. The judge rejected Diamond's plan in March 1996, not wanting Georgia's economy to suffer by loss of jobs which would result from the Diamond takeover.

U.S. Robotics, second in the market behind GVC Technologies in February 1996, offered $97.5 million to buy third-ranked Hayes, but withdrew its offer. It did issue a legal challenge which would have prevented a post-Chapter 11 Hayes from using the X-Jack technology, claiming Hayes would be a different entity and would need to renegotiate its contract. Robinson rejected the claim. Other proposed plans included a line of credit from GE Capital for $32 million, which would let Hayes pay off $23.6 million owed NationsBank.

If the bankruptcy struggle, running the company, and avoiding hostile takeovers were not enough, the company was torn by internal dissension. Two highly placed Hayes executives, Gary Franza, vice-president of sales and John Stuckey, vice-president of product management, were fired. Mikhail Drabkin, vice-president of corporate engineering, resigned shortly thereafter. The three, called "The Three Amigos," testified in court, praising Dennis Hayes for his vision, but suggesting he withdraw from day-to-day operations, becoming chairman. Hayes filed a lawsuit against the three for "mutiny," and claimed $5 million in damages for insubordination. The three countersued, claiming the company owed them severance pay and performance incentives and that it reneged on promised compensation for working through the bankruptcy proceedings (Hayes had asked the court to approve incentive pay aimed at keeping certain key executives on board, who would have also received bonuses when the reorganization plan was confirmed). Franza and Stuckey also alleged Dennis Hayes damaged their reputation by sending an electronic message to more than 1,000 employees saying the two were terminated "for cause," and asked $5 million each compensation for libel, plus $10 million each in punitive damages.

Part of the emergence plan included downsizing. Hayes tapped Andersen & Co. in February 1995 to oversee restructuring and consolidation of operations. June followed with Hayes closing research and development centers in San Francisco and Waterloo, Ontario, Canada.

Hayes was cleared to emerge from Chapter 11 in March 1996 under its own plan and to remain a privately held company with Dennis Hayes in control. By April, it announced the two best financial quarters in its history and began reporting quarterly earnings like a public company. But Dennis Hayes followed many of his contemporaries out of day-to-day operations. Just as Kenneth Olsen was removed from Digital Equipment Corp., Steve Jobs was forced from Apple (and later rehired), and An Wang had to leave Wang Laboratories, Hayes, at the insistence of "The Three Amigos," agreed to a different role after emerging from bankruptcy.

Dennis Hayes named Joseph Formichelli to run Hayes and, in the nine months following Formichelli's tapping, Hayes cut 25 percent of its costs, which included "tightening up" operations. In September 1996, as prices and profit margins on modems dropped, and U.S. Robotics reportedly dumped months' worth of products into distribution channels, Hayes laid off approximately 400 employees at its California facility. The PPI product line, manufacturing division, and 100 positions were moved to Georgia, where 700 employees already worked, leaving about 50 people in California.

Operations, 1994–Date

The company continued to operate during the bankruptcy proceedings. Following the V.34 transmission protocol ratification, Hayes, in January 1995, released the Accura 28800 V.34/V.FC+Fax and the Optima 28800 V.34/V.FC+Fax (ideal for transferring large files and connecting to LANs). Both supported other protocols, and were bundled with an ESP Communications Accelerator, a 16-bit serial card which enhanced throughput and reduced data loss. The Accura also included Smartcom for Windows LE and Smartcom FAX for Windows LE.

Hayes was in court again in May, attempting to make Rockwell International supply Hayes with data-pump devices used in its 14.4 and 28.8Kbps modems. Rockwell had placed the company on allocation during patent-royalty negotiations. Hayes accused Rockwell of "strongarm" tactics, holding the data-pump devices hostage in an attempt to obtain a paid-up license for patents relating to modem compatibility, which were sup-

posed to be paid for six years. Rockwell had not shipped Hayes parts since early April, and they were unobtainable elsewhere.

In June, PPI released the ProClass 288LCD External Modem and the ProClas 288 with EZ-Port PCMCIA Modem. The Optima 288 V.34+Fax earned top ratings for data-only use, providing the fastest data throughput and handling Telecommunications Industry Association (TIA) compatibility testing better than other modems. The same month, Hayes began manufacturing modems for the Asian market in the Far East to cut freight costs. In July, Hayes cut prices on 144Kbps modems and, in October, began bundling start-up kits for CompuServe, America Online, and its own Smartcom for Windows LE and Smartcom Fax for Windows data and fax communications software, and PPI released the Class 288 MiniTower II V.34.

In November, Hayes announced the Accura 288 DSVD Message Modem, enabling simultaneous voice and data or fax communications over one line. The plug-and-play device featured a full-duplex speakerphone and Radish VoiceView, had data-transmission speeds of up to 28.8Kbps and fax speeds of 14.4Kbps. The external version featured built-in microphone and speakers; the internal product had a microphone integratable with desktop speakers. PPI also released the external Class 288 MiniTower Voice Modem and internal Class 288 Half-Card Voice Modem with external microphone, both of which supported throughput up to 115.2Kbps with compression and 14.4Kbps fax speeds.

In February 1996, Hayes released a 230Kbps Apple Macintosh modem and, in July, joined over 25 other industry leaders from the communications and computer industries, including Ascend Communications Inc., in "The Open 56K Forum," dedicated to implementing 56Kbps analog modem technology by Rockwell and Lucent Technologies Inc.

Hayes entered the RAS market, against vendors like Cisco Systems Inc., Shiva Corp., 3Com Corp., U.S. Robotics, and Ascend, in 1996, shipping the high-end Century 9000 series of modular RASes for Internet service providers (ISPs) in January 1997. Also, late in 1996, Hayes and Go1, which owned the patent for an interface between smart-card (which store information, like network log-in information, vital-health data, cash balances or private encryption codes, in electrically-erasable programmable ROM) readers and modems, released a smart-card modem featuring the Hayes AT command set. Hayes also began working with Schlumberger Electronic Transactions Inc. and GemPlus, the two largest smart-card manufacturers, and began recruiting companies to join the Smart Card International Electronic Transactions Association, an industry group Hayes created.

In March, as Rockwell awaited Federal Communications Commission approval of their requested waiver for power consumption, required to connect at data rates above 53Kbps, they battled (with Cascade Communications Corp., Cisco and 130 others) against Texas Instruments (TI; with U.S. Robotics and Cardinal, among others) over whether TIA would name Rockwell's 56Flex or TI's X2 technology the standard 56Kbps chip. As the titans clashed, Hayes released Accura and Optima PC Card-based 56Kbps modems utilizing Rockwell's technology.

While U.S. Robotics shocked the industry by announcing its acquisition agreement with networking giant 3Com early in

1997, Hayes, faced with possibly missing the lucrative market for 56Kbps modems, hedged its bets and began manufacturing PPI modems using chief competitor U.S. Robotics' X2 technology, and, in March, bought Cardinal. In April, Hayes began manufacturing and marketing cable modems, super-fast devices that delivered Internet connections 20 times faster than 56Kbps modems. Marketed to cable television companies, they were ''one-way,'' designed to have 1Megabps of data coming ''downstream'' from the Net. Analysts estimated demand for the cable modem would reach $4.4 million by 2000 and $19.1 million by 2005.

In June, Micronics Computers discussed acquiring Hayes, but no deal emerged. Access Beyond Inc. agreed in July to a ''reverse acquisition'' in which Access would acquire Hayes and create Hayes Corporation as the new entity. Formichelli stepped down as Hayes CEO and president in September, to be replaced by Vice-President of Operations P. K. Chan. Following the merger, which made Hayes Corporation a publicly traded company, Dennis Hayes became chairman; Ron Howard, Access's chairman and CEO, became vice-chairman and executive vice-president of business development; and Chan became president and chief operating officer.

In October, the new company, facing competitors like Ascend, Compaq, Bay Networks Inc., Efficient Networks Inc., and RAScom, introduced RASes based on standard OSes, designed to streamline wide-area network communications. Hayes also introduced a NetWare version of the Access Hawk 2290 RAS at NetWorld + Interop-Atlanta, which connected 8-72 modem cards, plugged into standard file servers, and offloaded remote-access processing to dedicated CPUs so servers could support other functions. Hayes also debuted two ADSL modem prototypes based on PCI network interface cards from Alcatel Network Systems and asynchronous transfer mode technology from ATML.

In December, Hayes began working with Analog Devices Inc. on chipsets and cable-modem devices complying with the Multimedia Cable Network System consortium's data-over-cable service interface specifications, capable of providing faster data rates over hybrid fiber coaxial cable.

Hayes, in January 1998, debuted an ADSL modem, began looking at wireless technology markets, and planned to acquire other companies dealing with RASes and analog, cable and xDSL modems. Hayes also began working with Alcatel on xDSL technology, building on Access' Hawk RAS, enabling operation as a Windows NT network server and RAS simultaneously.

In February, following long-awaited approval of a 56Kbps modem standard, Hayes joined 3Com, Multi-Tech, and Zoom, releasing the K56flex Optima PC-Card modem, with a more-durable EZjack pop-out connector, sleep/idle mode for lower power consumption, and a cellular phone connector. Hayes embraced the v.90 standard in March with dual-mode internal and external Accura modems, offering software upgrades for modems without enough memory to support both standards. So Hayes, despite enormous challenges during its 20-year history, was still a leader in the modem industry.

Principal Subsidiaries

Cardinal Technologies Inc.; Hayes Microcomputer Products (Canada) Ltd.; Hayes Microcomputer Products Inc.; JT Fax; Practical Peripherals Inc.

Further Reading

''Access Beyond and Hayes Set 'Reverse Acquisition,' '' *New York Times,* July 31, 1997, p. C4(N)/D4(L).

Allison, David, ''Hayes Hopes to Crack Home-Computer Market,'' *Atlanta Business Chronicle,* March 7, 1988, p. 2A.

——, ''Hayes: Staff Cuts Don't Mean Business Is Bad,'' *Atlanta Business Chronicle,* August 13, 1990, p. 2B.

Aragon, Lawrence, ''Menacing Dennis,'' *PC Week,* February 5, 1996, p. A1.

''As Dennis Turns,'' *PC Week,* April 8, 1996, p. A4.

Batterson, David, ''Debate Rages Over Use of 'Hayes-Compatible' Tag,'' *PC Week,* May 22, 1989, p. 127.

Bernard, Viki, ''Hayes Maps Chapter 11 Escape Route,'' *PC Week,* June 5, 1995, p. 49.

Bueno, Jacqueline, ''Hayes' Modem Verdict Sends Signal on Patents,'' *Atlanta Business Chronicle,* February 18, 1991, p. 3B.

——, ''How Sweet a Deal for Hayes CEO: Merger with Boca Research Would Leave Dennis Hayes in Strong Position,'' *Atlanta Business Chronicle,* July 14, 1995, p. 1A.

Gibson, Stan, ''Boca Pulls Hayes Out of Chapter 11: Merged Company to Keep Hayes Name,'' *PC Week,* July 3, 1995, p. 74.

Harris, Nicole, ''The First Name in Modems Gets a Second Chance,'' *Business Week,* December 23, 1996, p. 84.

''Hayes, Boca Merger Called Off,'' *PC Week,* August 28, 1995, p. 3.

''Hayes Breaks a Long Silence,'' *Business Week,* December 5, 1994, p. 46.

''Hayes Comeback Trail,'' *Computerworld,* November 11, 1996, p. 2.

''Hayes Taps Big Six Firm for Restructuring Help,'' *PC Week,* February 20, 1995, p. 107.

''The Humble Modem: Dennis Hayes,'' *Data Communications,* October 21, 1997, p. 80.

Johnston, Christopher, ''Lower Cost Modems Place Price Pressure on Hayes,'' *PC Magazine,* May 13, 1986, p. 41.

Mallory, Maria, ''The King of Modems Has to Hang Up: Dennis Hayes Rode High on the PC Wave—Till Rivals Undercut Him,'' *Business Week,* July 24, 1995, p. 43.

McAleer, Bernard, ''Access Beyond, Hayes Sign Merger Agreement,'' *Electronic News,* August 11, 1997, p. 40.

''Micronics in Talks to Acquire Hayes Microcomputer,'' *New York Times,* June 14, 1997, p. 23(N)/39(L).

Nadile, Lisa, ''Hayes Reorganization Shifts Focus to Four New Product Areas,'' *PC Week,* November 14, 1994, p. 205.

Nobel, Carmen, ''Hayes Looks Ahead,'' *PC Week,* January 12, 1998, p. 114.

——, ''Hayes Loses Its CEO Before Access Merger,'' *PC Week,* September 29, 1997, p. 24.

——, ''Zoom and Hayes Vie for Motorola Division,'' *PC Week,* October 20, 1997, p. 20.

Pickering, Wendy, ''Cash-Flow Problems Force Hayes into Chapter 11,'' *PC Week,* November 21, 1994, p. 138.

Silverthorne, Sean, ''Modem Operandi,'' *PC Week,* August 21, 1995, p. A1.

Verespej, Michael A., ''The Market Uses His Name: Dennis Hayes Wants to Head the Next IBM,'' *Industry Week,* November 10, 1986, p. 133.

—Daryl F. Mallett

Health Risk Management, Inc.

8000 West 78th Street
Minneapolis, Minnesota 55439
U.S.A.
(612) 829-3500
Fax: (612) 829-3578
Web site: http://www.ihqi.com

Public Company
Incorporated: 1977
Employees: 950
Sales: $62.7 million (1997)
Stock Exchanges: NASDAQ
Ticker Symbol: HRMI
SICs: 6324 Hospital & Medical Service Plans

Health Risk Management, Inc. (HRMI) markets integrated healthcare services to both healthcare purchasers and providers. The company distinguishes itself from others in the managed-care field with its emphasis on entering the care management picture during instead of after the diagnostic process. HRMI's range of services include: care review management, case management, price control management, claims administration management, and information services.

The 1970s: Medical Testing Lab Roots

Dr. Gary T. McIlroy, a pathologist who received his medical training at University of California-Los Angeles and the Mayo Clinic, cofounded Midwest Laboratory Associates, a medical testing business, with his wife Marlene O. Travis in 1977. As a provider of services to corporate clients, in addition to hospitals and clinics, McIlroy was approached with concerns about the medical system. Employers were noticing things like rapidly rising costs and inconsistencies in treatment assignments for similar diagnoses.

McIlroy and Travis were well aware of those and other problems, such as duplication of testing caused by coordination of services among different care providers. "Information, and the availability of information at the point where decisions were being made, looked like the solution to us," Travis said in a 1997 *Minnesota Business & Opportunities* article by Anthony F. Giombetti. But the medical community proved to be cool to their idea of using computer-based clinical practice guidelines to guide diagnostic and treatment decisions.

McIlroy and Travis did find that large self-insured corporations and insurance companies were interested in their ideas, so they established a division within the lab business to design and develop an integrated medical information management system to serve that sector. In order to concentrate on developing the new business, McIlroy and Travis sold the medical lab to Damon Corp., a national laboratory firm, in 1980.

The 1980s: A Move from Consultant to Service Provider

First, Health Risk Management, Inc. (HRMI) developed a pilot project with The Gillette Company in St. Paul. HRMI analyzed three years of their healthcare claims and found 40 percent of the services received by Gillette's employees were deemed to be of questionable value based on the most current medical information. HRMI established a medical management program to guide the company's healthcare decision-making and an employee wellness program to improve the general condition of their workers' health.

HRMI was part of a national trend to cut healthcare costs. In the early 1980s, U.S. businesses became painfully aware of the changing marketplace: to compete on a global-level companies had to control costs. Healthcare costs were identified as an important barrier to the United States' success in the world marketplace.

According to an October 1984 *Corporate Report Minnesota* article, HRMI's average client employed 20,000 and spent about $30 million a year on medical payments. Mary Gunderson wrote, "Despite the sharp rise in health-care costs, McIlroy believes most companies can cut 20 to 30 percent from those payments without lowering the quality of care offered to employees." HRMI employed specialists in biostatistics, epidemiology, medicine, benefits design, communications, accounting, computer science, and public health to help clients cut costs without compromising care.

Using the demographic information collected from clinics and hospitals around the country, HRMI was able to compare costs and services within a company's given geographic area. With incidents of excessive payments or unnecessary services identified, HRMI could advise a company regarding its options to reduce costs, such as by setting limits on lab work or hospital stays.

HRMI switched from consultant to service provider during 1984 and 1985, as more clients requested implementation of the plans HRMI devised. The number of their employees jumped from 20 to 120 during the period. An infrastructure to handle healthcare inquiries from clients and their employees, as well as attending physicians, had to be put in place as well. HRMI also began to develop a strategy to electronically integrate four important components of the healthcare system: payments, care management, a national network of care providers and facilities, and information analysis. To finance the rapid growth, HRMI made a private stock placement each year from 1985 to 1989.

Pillsbury Company, Gillette, and Philip Morris were the first to sign on with large contracts. At first HRMI limited its marketing to *Fortune* 1000 companies in order to tap into the health benefits systems already in place and the large number of employees which were necessary for statistical analysis. HRMI sales reached $8.8 million in 1988.

1990s Begin with Public Stock Offering

In 1990, with sales at $12.2 million, HRMI offered stock to the public for the first time. The two million share initial public offering brought in $16.1 million to pay off accumulated debt, continue growth, and further the development of new products. The newly issued stock lost its early momentum when the company announced lower than expected earnings and a slowdown in client base growth a few months later.

Healthcare reform was a hot topic on both a state and federal level in the early 1990s with debates over issues such as "rationed" healthcare and universal coverage. The promotion of Health Maintenance Organizations (HMOs) via federal action in 1973 had changed the way medical services were provided, but the prepaid health plans failed to stop skyrocketing U.S. healthcare costs. Concerns over healthcare costs extended beyond the U.S.: HRMI sold its services to two Canadian provinces in 1991.

In January 1992, HRMI purchased a third party claims administration business, Pension and Group Services Inc., of Kalamazoo, Michigan, for $7 million. Claims administrators process and pay healthcare bills for self-insured clients. The purchase helped boost sales to $27.8 million, but due to a restructuring charge and legal settlement, both one-time charges, the year ended with a net loss.

HRMI began marketing PC-based healthcare management software in conjunction with its practice guidelines, QualityFirst, to large insurance companies, preferred provider organizations (PPOs), HMOs, and hospitals in 1992. In a September 1992 *Star Tribune* article Glenn Howatt noted views regarding computer-based guidelines still remained diverse: supporters saw a useful tool in bringing consistency of treatment to medical practice; detractors called the guidelines "cookbook" medicine.

Regardless of the opinion, the number of managed care providers continued to grow along with the types of services and products offered. Value Health Sciences, Inc. of Santa Monica, California, offered computer-based medical guidelines in direct competition with HRMI's QualityFirst. But according to the Howatt article the Value Health product was based on academic findings, while HRMI guidelines were "designed in an actual user care setting." In the same article analyst Ted Levy said, "From my review, I didn't see any other guidelines as sophisticated, evidenced by the tremendous amount of money they spent."

HRMI was confident in its products and claimed by tracking a sick or injured employee from diagnosis through treatment he or she would receive better care at a lower cost to the employer. In a November 1993 *Twin Cities Business Monthly* article by Phil Bolsta, Travis said, "We impact 23 percent of the cases that we review and can give clients as much as a 10-to-one return on the money they spend with us." According to Bolsta, one HRMI client saved $4.2 million by avoiding duplicate claims processing and another saved $500,000 by monitoring 10 pregnancies at high-risk for premature delivery.

HRMI annual revenue leaped to $40.8 million in fiscal 1993 with net income of $2.3 million. But the rapid growth slowed the following year. HRMI lost some large clients. And across the nation, companies put healthcare service and product purchases on hold as the Clinton administration's pending healthcare reform proposals were being debated. Although revenues for the year increased somewhat, net income fell. HRMI refocused its marketing strategy.

The Mid-to-Late 1990s: Coping with Market Changes

Healthcare reform on a state level was encouraging medium-sized companies to move to self-funded health plans, according to a February 1995 *Minneapolis/St. Paul CityBusiness* article by Carla Solberg. In response to the changes, HRMI trimmed back its utilization review department and bolstered the third-party administration and software development areas. And in an ongoing effort to refine its product and service offerings, HRMI became the first U.S. healthcare company to earn ISO 9000 certification for its claims subsidiary.

The health information market was estimated at $6.5 billion in the mid-1990s and was expected to continue to grow at a rapid pace. But for HRMI, business continued to lag. Fiscal 1996 ended with lower than expected revenues due to a scaled back agreement with a major client and delays in new customer development. Earnings fell for a second year.

In September 1996, HRMI said it had agreed to be acquired by HealthPlan Services Corp. of Tampa. The merger was expected to strengthen HRMI in the areas of distribution, customer base, product development, and capital funding. The $80 million deal was canceled in March 1997, following a sharp decline in HealthPlan stock, a consequence of activity involving two earlier mergers.

HRMI and HealthPlan agreed to continue a joint marketing agreement established at the time of the purchase deal: HealthPlan received managed care tools, and HRMI gained access to HealthPlan's client base. HealthPlan also bought $2.5 million or 4.5 percent of HRMI shares outstanding.

Earnings for fiscal 1997 increased by 12 percent to $2.2 million and revenues climbed 15 percent over 1996 to $62.7 million. Care review and case management services—which included clinical and surgical procedures; mental health and chemical dependency treatment; prenatal care; and disability and workers compensation cases—brought in 41 percent of revenue. The claims administration division accounted for 39 percent of 1997 revenue. HRMI's client list included self-insured employers, insurance companies, unions, government agencies, HMOs, PPOs, and hospitals.

As of September 1997 HRMI employed about 950, including approximately 300 physicians, nurses, and other health professionals. Another 150 physicians served as consultants. In addition to its branch offices around the country, HRMI held four wholly owned subsidiaries in the U.S. and one in Canada. HRMI competed directly with a large number of independent utilization review firms, insurance carriers, third-party administrators, and a small number of software vendors. The company's managed care services competed indirectly with the HMOs and PPOs.

In its 1997 10K report, HRMI said its "principal competitive strengths are its medical expertise, medical and cost databases, QualityFirst healthcare practice guidelines, and proprietary software systems." Of possible future concern to HRMI was its dependence on a small number of clients for a significant percentage of revenues: two clients brought in 33 percent of total revenues in 1997.

Further Reading

Bolsta, Phil, "Corporate Wellness," *Twin Cities Business Monthly,* November 1993, pp. 94–98, 100–01.

Carideo, Anthony, "Stock of Health Risk Management Drops 32 Percent in Heavy Trading," *Star Tribune* (Minneapolis), March 6, 1991, p. 1D.

Child, Elizabeth, "Turning the (Examining) Tables," *Twin Cities Business Monthly,* July 1995, pp. 42–45.

"Corporate Capsule: Health Risk Management Inc.," *Minneapolis/St. Paul CityBusiness,* December 5, 1997, p. 37.

"Flat Revenue Expected by Health Risk," *Star Tribune* (Minneapolis), January 24, 1992, p. 3D.

Giombetti, Anthony F., "Prophetic Entrepreneurs," *Minnesota Business & Opportunities,* August 1997.

Gunderson, Mary, "A Doctor's Advice: Pay Less," *Corporate Report Magazine,* October 1984, pp. 167–68.

Hamburger, Tom, "States Are Leading Way to Innovative Health Care," *Star Tribune* (Minneapolis), October 6, 1991, p. 12A.

"Health Risk Management Inc." *Corporate Report Fact Book 1998,* Minneapolis: Corporate Report, Inc., 1998, pp. 317, 338.

Howatt, Glenn, "Edina Firm to Market Software Aimed at Controlling Costs, Upgrading Quality," *Star Tribune* (Minneapolis), September 10, 1992, p. 1D.

——, "Health Risk Management, HealthPlan Cancel Merger," *Star Tribune* (Minneapolis), March 7, 1997, p. 1D.

——, "Health Risk Management Reports $95,000 Net Loss During 'A Building Year'," *Star Tribune* (Minneapolis), August 28, 1992, p. 4D.

——, "Health Risk Stock Price Falls," *Star Tribune* (Minneapolis), April 10, 1996, p. 1D.

——, "Streetwise," *Star Tribune* (Minneapolis), April 27, 1991, p. 5D.

Lerner, Maura, "Florida Firm Will Acquire HRM," *Star Tribune* (Minneapolis), September 14, 1996, p. 1D.

Lerner, Maura, and Mike Meyers, "'73 'Miracle' Can't Cope with '88 Costs," *Star Tribune* (Minneapolis), June 26, 1988, p. 1A.

"Public Offerings," *Star Tribune* (Minneapolis), December 20, 1990, p. 2D.

Solberg, Carla, "HRM Alters 'Product Mix'," *Minneapolis/St. Paul CityBusiness,* February 10, 1995, p. 2.

—Kathleen Peippo

Hillsdown Holdings plc

Hillsdown House
32 Hampstead High Street
London NW3 1QD
United Kingdom
(0171) 794-0677
Fax: (0171) 433-6409
Web site: http://www.hillsdown.com

Public Company
Incorporated: 1975
Employees: 31,034
Sales:£2.65 billion (1997)
Stock Exchanges: London
SICs: 0251 Broiler, Fryer & Roaster Chickens; 0252
Chicken Egg Production; 0253 Turkeys & Turkey
Eggs Production; 0254 Poultry Hatcheries Production;
1521 General Contractors-Single Family Homes; 2015
Poultry Slaughtering & Processing; 2033 Canned
Fruits, Vegetables, Preserves, Jams & Jellies; 2052
Cookies & Crackers; 2084 Wines, Brandy & Brandy
Spirits; 2086 Bottled & Canned Soft Drinks &
Carbonated Waters; 2098 Macaroni, Spaghetti,
Vermicelli & Noodles; 2099 Food Preparations, Not
Elsewhere Classified; 2519 Household Furniture, Not
Elsewhere Classified; 6719 Offices of Holding
Companies, Not Elsewhere Classified

Hillsdown Holdings plc is a somewhat obscure holding
company for a wide range of food, homebuilding, furniture, and
other subsidiaries—all independently operated—which are organized into six operating divisions. Four are in the area of
European food—Ambient, Chilled, Potatoes, and Poultry—
with the others being Housebuilding and Furniture & Specialist.
Ambient manufactures tea, chocolate beverages, biscuits and
cookies, canned foods, pickles and preserves, and pasta. Chilled
makes salads and a variety of prepared foods. The only subsidiary in the Potatoes division is MBM Produce Limited, which is

a leading U.K. potato processing and packaging concern. Poultry includes chicken and turkey rearing, processing, and breeding, as well as egg producing. Hillsdown's food operations
produce both branded and private-label products and hold a
number of leading positions in the United Kingdom and Europe.
The company's Housebuilding division includes Fairview New
Homes Plc, one of the largest homebuilders in southeast England. The Furniture & Specialist division manufactures furniture for the retail, mail order, and office furniture markets; and
also makes suspended ceilings. Overall, about 70 percent of
Hillsdown's revenues are generated in the United Kingdom,
with about 26.5 percent from continental Europe and the remainder from countries outside of Europe.

Founded in 1975

Established in 1975, Hillsdown's growth has been nothing
short of phenomenal. The company's founders, Harry Solomon
and David Thompson, were a lawyer and a butcher, respectively, when they met in 1964—after their wives had become
friends at a prenatal class. Solomon soon became Thompson's
legal counsel, advising him as he purchased interests in other
companies. In the mid-1970s, they decided to form their own
company to manage their investments in such fields as timber,
stationery, and securities more efficiently. They named their
company Hillsdown, after Thompson's house; rented an office;
hired an accountant; and set out to wring value from businesses
where others saw none. In so doing, Thompson and Solomon
built a company that has had a significant impact on food
production in the United Kingdom.

Hillsdown Holdings' acquisitions began in earnest in 1981,
when the company made its first big purchase, of Lockwoods
Foods Limited, a bankrupt cannery that Hillsdown paid £3.5
million for. By the time Hillsdown purchased the Imperial
Group's poultry, egg, and animal-feed businesses for £39 million the following year, its acquisition strategy was already in
place. In general, Hillsdown shunned hostile takeovers, prefer-
ring instead to make friendly arrangements with the company's
present management. The company was committed to capital
infusion and refused to strip assets from newly acquired properties, believing that adding value to commodities was the key to

success. Rather than attempt to run their properties themselves, Solomon and Thompson from the start appointed independent managers to run Hillsdown's subsidiary companies as if they owned them. The company strived to limit overhead caused by red tape and bureaucracy, and often streamlined management at the firms it bought—Lockwoods' management was reduced to 40 from 120, and a later purchase, Maple Leaf Mills, saw its central staff shrink from 80 to 11. Hillsdown itself maintained a head office of about 20. Control of day-to-day operations remained in the hands of subsidiaries, who reported to directors at economically furnished headquarters in North London. Besides an annual meeting with the Hillsdown director for their industry, subsidiaries were simply required to submit a one- or two-page financial report once a month to Hillsdown.

Hillsdown acquisitions in the same industry were not usually merged, but encouraged to compete—even for the privilege of supplying other Hillsdown subsidiaries with raw materials. In this way, the parent company profited by piecing together its many different companies in the fragmented food-processing field into a vertical whole, allowing it to earn money and control quality at every step. For instance, in the poultry business, Hillsdown companies could provide everything from the breeder hen that lays the egg to the frozen Chicken Kiev dinner it will eventually become.

Despite its dominance in the food industry, Hillsdown eschewed flashiness in both personnel and products. Solomon and Thompson were notoriously publicity shy, and there were few products that bore Hillsdown's name. Instead, each product bore the brand of one of Hillsdown's many subsidiaries, or the mark of one of the leading retailers such as Marks & Spencer, Tesco, and Asda with which Hillsdown has developed close and lucrative ties. The company made a handsome profit on its willingness to work with its customers to provide whatever it was they wanted.

In 1983 Hillsdown continued to grow by purchasing ailing and undervalued food companies such as TKM Foods and Smedley's canning business, both acquired for a token £1, and FMC, Europe's largest slaughterhouse, for a rock-bottom £4.9 million. The next year, Thompson and Solomon picked up Henry Telfer, a manufacturer of meatpies, again for £1. In its first decade, Hillsdown spent about £50 million making bargain-basement purchases of this sort to become the United Kingdom's fourth largest food manufacturer, with sales of £1

billion. But these acquisitions, it soon turned out, were mere warm-up exercises.

Mid-1980s Acquisitions Binge

Hillsdown Holdings went on a marathon buying binge after it put a quarter of its shares on the market in February 1985. The company made 42 acquisitions in 20 months, stunning London's financial community with the pace of its activity. Newspapers reported that Hillsdown bought a new company every six days. Its acquisitions, scattered as they seemed, all fell into one of five major areas: food, timber, furniture, stationery, and property. Skeptics questioned the point of assembling an empire of such disparate parts, and doubted that one company could sensibly manage such far-flung interests. At the end of its spending spree, Hillsdown was the largest British producer of eggs, poultry, meat, and canned goods, and was second in the timber business. Its profits had grown in proportion to its size.

Throughout this period of enormous growth, Hillsdown stuck, for the most part, to a policy of making friendly bids for small companies. London's financial community waited for what rumormongers called the "big one." In spring of 1986, it came. Hillsdown began its first large contested bid for a company by increasing its stake in S. & W. Berisford, a commodities-trading firm that had purchased the British Sugar Corporation in 1982. The company was already conducting talks with an Italian food and agricultural group when Hillsdown came on the scene, and soon Tate & Lyle, another British sugar refiner, entered the fray. In April, Hillsdown made its move, offering to buy Berisford for £486 million with the support of the Italian firm. When both bids were referred to the British Monopolies and Mergers Commission in May, however, Hillsdown withdrew, selling its stake in Berisford back to its Italian partner at a handsome profit.

The following year, Hillsdown strengthened its ability to develop small companies by launching the Hillsdown Investment Trust. HIT was set up to provide money and advice to companies with strong potential that were too small or diverse in activity for Hillsdown to buy outright. That year also saw the company acquire Fairview New Homes, one of the largest homebuilders in southeast England. Also in 1987 Hillsdown began to expand in earnest beyond British shores. In July, it moved into North America with its purchase of Maple Leaf Mills, a Canadian food conglomerate, for £169 million in cash, its largest acquisition yet. At the same time, it launched operations on the European mainland with the formation of Hillsdown International B.V.

Although Maple Leaf Mills (later known as Maple Leaf Foods) appeared to be an excellent match for Hillsdown's interests, the large debt Hillsdown incurred to buy it gave British investors sweaty palms. After making 50 purchases in 1987, Hillsdown found itself with a reputation as a rapacious acquisitor that could only make money through constant buying. To counter this impression, the company began to scale back the pace of its purchases in an attempt to consolidate holdings and reduce its level of debt. Hillsdown restrained itself in 1988, buying only 31 small businesses.

Fighting the perception that the company was "a dead duck in a bear market," as the *Independent* put it, the company strengthened its overseas holdings through further purchases in the Netherlands and North America, and attempted to demonstrate long-term internal growth, rather than short-term acquisitions-fueled growth. Despite lagging performance from its traditionally troubled red-meat companies, Hillsdown largely succeeded in demonstrating that the firm was sound even when it was not buying food companies as often as most people buy food. Attempting to widen the margin of profit on the commodities it produced, Hillsdown concentrated on adding value to its products by processing them as far as possible.

Despite its strong performance, Hillsdown's market value remained stagnant in the year following the 1987 stock market crash, in part, again, because the company's far-flung interests made investors nervous. Moving toward a more unified company profile, in September 1988 Hillsdown sold off a large timber company and purchased Premier Brands Foods—maker of Typhoo and other brands of tea and instant chocolate and malt drinks—for £195 million in May 1989. Shortly thereafter, it sold off stationery and printing businesses, so that more than 80 percent of the company's sales were concentrated in the food industry.

Also in early 1989, David Thompson, Hillsdown's cofounder, sold his final 14.5 percent share in the company for £154 million. Thompson had first stepped down from an active role in the company in April 1987, when he sold half his 30 percent share. The firm's other cofounder, Harry Solomon (who became Sir Harry after being knighted in 1991), was left in charge of Hillsdown following Thompson's retirement.

1990s Restructuring

Solomon faced challenging times in the early 1990s as a recession hurt Hillsdown's commodity-side food businesses—poultry, eggs, and red meat—while the company's processed food companies fared relatively better. By 1992, Solomon had committed to further restructuring of the company's holdings, emphasizing food to an even greater degree. During 1992 Hillsdown closed or sold 17 underperforming and/or noncore businesses, including two property companies. Early the following year, Solomon retired, with David Newton, who had headed the company's North American operations, becoming chief executive and Sir John Nott, a former politician and merchant banker, becoming chairman.

The new leaders continued to restructure Hillsdown's operations, in particular divesting the company's various red-meat businesses over the next few years. First to go in 1993 were several slaughtering facilities. The company's exit from red meat was complete in late 1997 when it sold seven businesses to Cinven for £53.6 million, including its last four remaining meat companies; Strong & Fisher, a leather tanning company; Poupart, a fresh fruit wholesaler; and Firstan, a cardboard packaging concern. Another major divestment during this period was that of Maple Leaf Foods, which Hillsdown sold to the Wallace McCain family and the Ontario Teachers' Pension Plan Board for about C$623 million (£275 million).

Meanwhile, Hillsdown was making very selective acquisitions that built upon its core food businesses, acquisitions funded in part by the company's divestments. In late 1994 the company spent about £20 million for Lyons Biscuits, the U.K. biscuit business of Allied Domecq, which Hillsdown merged into its existing biscuits unit. The first half of 1996 saw two major purchases. Hillsdown paid £121 million for Hobson, a private-label food and drink manufacturer whose tea, biscuits, sauces, and pickles fit in particularly well with Hillsdown's existing product lines. The company also acquired Allied Domecq's Continental Bakeries unit for £49 million, further bolstering its already strong biscuits operations into the number five position in Europe.

In mid-1996 Newton stepped down from his position as chief executive and was replaced by George Greener, who had most recently been chairman of the U.K. financial services businesses of BAT Industries. Under Newton's leadership, Hillsdown had sold businesses that had generated annual revenues of £2 billion while also building the company into leading positions in fresh poultry, canned goods, tea, and chilled salads.

Greener, meanwhile, had a reputation as someone unafraid of making tough decisions. This was perhaps exactly what the company needed as it still in early 1998 held a very unorthodox portfolio of companies, with the homebuilding and furniture operations standing as particular oddballs in a largely food-oriented company. Further dispositions, therefore, seemed likely with equally likely prospects for further food acquisitions.

Principal Subsidiaries

A Krombach & Söhne GmbH (Germany); Chivers Ireland Limited; Chivers Hartley Limited; F.E. Barber Limited; HL Foods Limited; Holco B.V. (Netherlands); Hooimeijer BV (Netherlands); Hubert Hagemann Internationale Gebäckspezialitäten GmbH & CoK.G. (Germany; 60%); Materne SA (France); N.V. Pirou Wafer (Belgium); Picard Holding SA (France); Premier Brands (UK) Limited; Premier Brands France S.A.; Andros Food S.A. (Spain; 80%); Henry Telfer Limited; Johma Holding International B.V. (Netherlands); Kobenhavns Salatfabrik A/S (Denmark); Magdis SA (France); Nadler Werke Holding GmbH (Germany); Pinneys of Scotland Limited; Smedleys Foods Limited; MBM Produce Limited; Buxted Chicken Limited; Buxton Foods Limited; Daylay Foods Limited; Devon Crest Poultry Limited; Hencu Beheer B.V. (Netherlands); Moorland Poultry Limited; Premier Poultry Limited; Ross Breeders Limited; Ross Breeders Inc. (U.S.A.); Ross Poultry Limited; Carleton Furniture Group Limited; Christie-Tyler plc; Fairview New Homes Plc; Formwood Group (UK) Limited; Walker & Homer Group PLC; J.J. Yates & Co., Limited (75%); Riverside Developments (South Bank) Limited (50%).

Principal Divisions

Ambient; Chilled; Potatoes; Poultry; Furniture & Specialist; Housebuilding.

Further Reading

Blackhurst, Chris, "A Meaty Principle," *Management Today,* December 1990, p. 116.

Duval, Brett, "Hillsdown Holdings plc," *Fortune,* January 19, 1987, p. 66.

"Hillsdown Set to Play Role as Premier's Paternal Guardian," *Marketing,* June 1, 1989, p. 4.

Jonquières, Guy de, "The Dilemma Facing Food's Rag and Bone Men," *Financial Times,* September 21, 1992, p. 24.

——, "Hillsdown Seeks to Cure Jitters in the City," *Financial Times,* March 6, 1992, p. 21.

Maitland, Alison, "Hillsdown to Exit Pig Meat Business," *Financial Times,* February 28, 1996, p. 23.

Monopolies and Mergers Commission, *Hillsdown Holdings plc and Pittard Garnar plc: A Report on the Proposed Merger,* London: HMSO, 1989.

Oram, Roderick, "Brands Can Join Forces with Own-Label," *Financial Times,* April 20, 1995, p. 28.

——, "Hillsdown Pays £121M for Hobson," *Financial Times,* December 14, 1995, p. 22.

Urry, Maggie, "A Look at the Life and Times of an Empire Builder," *Financial Times,* December 17, 1992, p. 22.

Warner, Liz, "Solomon's Mind," *Marketing,* September 10, 1987, p. 25.

Willman, John, "Hillsdown Sells Last Red Meat Businesses," *Financial Times,* September 5, 1997, p. 18.

—Elizabeth Rourke
—updated by David E. Salamie

H

Hollinger International Inc.

Hollinger International Inc.

401 N. Wabash Ave., Ste. 740
Chicago, Illinois 60611
U.S.A.
(312) 321-2299
Fax: (312) 321-0629
Web site: http://www.hollinger.com

Public Subsidiary of Hollinger Inc.
Incorporated: 1990
Employees: 17,487
Sales: $2.21 billion (1997)
Stock Exchanges: New York
Ticker Symbol: HLR
SICs: 2711 Newspaper Publishing; 6719 Holding
  Company, Not Elsewhere Classified

Hollinger International Inc. is a publicly traded, American-based company with headquarters in Chicago and investor relations offices in New York City. At the same time, it is also a subsidiary of the publicly traded, Canadian-based Hollinger Inc., headquartered in Vancouver, British Columbia. As of December 31, 1997, Hollinger Inc. directly and indirectly owned 59.9 percent of the combined equity interest in Hollinger International, accounting for 84.3 percent of the voting power of Hollinger International's outstanding common stock. Completing the ownership picture is the figure of The Honorable Conrad M. Black, who maintained control of Hollinger Inc. through his direct and indirect ownership of Hollinger Inc.'s securities. Black was chairman of the board and CEO of both Hollinger Inc. and Hollinger International.

Black Began Building a Global Media Empire in 1985

Conrad Black was born on August 25, 1944, in Montréal, Québec. His father, George Montegu Black, Jr., was a prominent businessman who managed Canadian Breweries, a division of the Argus Corporation, in the 1950s. Conrad Black grew up dreaming of becoming the chairman of Argus Corporation, a dream made remarkable by the fact that he accomplished it in 1978. Conrad and his older brother, Montegu, were able to gain a controlling interest in Argus in July 1978 by combining the block of shares their father had left them upon his death in 1976 with shares purchased from the heirs of the company's founding partners for about $18.4 million. For this remarkable accomplishment, Conrad Black was named "Man of the Year" in 1978 by the *Toronto Globe and Mail,* while *Fortune* magazine called him "the boy wonder of Canadian business."

From 1978 to 1985, Black set about dismantling Argus, which controlled five corporations including farm machinery manufacturer Massey-Ferguson, and selling off its assets. By June 1985 he had bought out his brother's interest and those of other minority shareholders. He then purchased a 14 percent interest in the *Daily Telegraph,* which was England's leading circulation broadsheet newspaper and the newspaper of choice of the country's ruling Conservative party. Black had begun building his global media empire.

By the end of 1985 Black had acquired a 50.1 percent interest in the *Daily Telegraph* for $43 million, a bargain basement price. Later acquisitions would follow a similar model, with Black stepping in and acquiring financially troubled newspapers. He also created Hollinger Inc. as a holding company for his interests. Hollinger was initially headquartered in Toronto, Ontario, but Black moved the company's headquarters to Vancouver, British Columbia, in 1990.

Began Acquiring U.S. Newspapers in 1986

Fearful of the costs associated with big-city newspapers, Black was also interested in small-market newspapers that focused on local news. Through his U.S. subsidiary, American Publishing Co., Black acquired a large number of smaller newspapers in the United States. American Publishing Co. was formed as a privately held, U.S.-based subsidiary of Hollinger Inc. in late 1986. Its first acquisition involved 16 small-town U.S. newspapers. Through a series of acquisitions it grew to rank as the second-largest newspaper publisher in the United States in 1995 by number of titles and the 12th in terms of circulation. It owned 393 newspapers, including 96 dailies, by 1996.

In March 1994 American Publishing completed its acquisition of the *Chicago Sun-Times,* which at the time was the ninth largest circulation metropolitan daily newspaper in the United States. With a daily circulation of 535,000, it was Chicago's number two newspaper. The cost of the *Sun-Times* was approximately $180 million. In April 1994 American Publishing launch an initial public offering (IPO) to raise money to pay for the acquisition. American had reported net losses in 1993 and 1994. At the time of its IPO, it owned 340 newspapers and was the 15th largest U.S. newspaper group based on circulation. The IPO was expected to raise $101 million, and American's shares were traded on the NASDAQ.

Venture into Australian Publishing Eventually Had to Be Abandoned

In late 1991 a group led by Conrad Black's Telegraph plc bought Australia's John Fairfax Holdings Ltd. out of receivership by purchasing a 25 percent interest in the Australian newspaper publisher. Fairfax published the *Sydney Morning Herald, Melbourne's Age,* and the *Australian Financial Review,* among other publications. Australian law prevented Black as a foreigner from owning more than 25 percent of the firm. Although Black's 25 percent interest gave him effective control of Fairfax, he was concerned about the possibility of an Australian media mogul acquiring controlling interest. Black appealed to the Australian government to allow him to increase his ownership to 35 or 50 percent, but permission was never granted. As a result, Black agreed to sell his holdings to a New Zealand investment firm at the end of 1996 for $513 million. Although disappointed, Black's group reportedly made $300 million on its investment. And Black, while happy with his profit, could not resist a parting shot at Australia; he told the *Financial Post,* "It's not a politically mature jurisdiction and foreigners should understand what they're getting into there. . . . [The prime minister] is basically an old-time Australian nationalist." In his letter to shareholders in 1996, he again complained about "Australia's capricious and politicized foreign ownership rules" and complained that foreigners were "treated with official bad faith and insurmountable suspicion."

Acquired Interest in Southam Inc., Canada's Largest Publisher of Daily Newspapers, in 1992

In 1992 Hollinger purchased a 21.5 percent stake in Southam Inc., Canada's leading newspaper publishing company. By 1996 Black was unhappy with the way Southam was being managed, and Hollinger was seeking to boost its ownership of Southam to 41 percent by buying out the co-controlling minority interest of the Power Corporation for $294 million. Black planned to replace most of Southam's independent directors.

Black obtained an advance ruling from Canada's Bureau of Competition Policy, which reviewed the proposed Southam acquisition for any overlap of ownership of newspapers competing for advertising in any one market. The Federal Court of Canada subsequently dismissed a motion by the Council of Canadians opposing Black's acquisition of Southam. During 1996 Hollinger International increased its interest in Southam to 50.7 percent. As

Canada's largest publisher of daily newspapers, Southam published 32 daily newspapers and 58 nondaily newspapers. Its principal publications included the *Gazette* (Montreal), the *Ottawa Citizen,* the *Calgary Herald,* the *Vancouver Sun,* the *Province* (Vancouver), and the *Edmonton Journal.*

Circulation Wars, Weak Capital Markets Force Black to Take Telegraph Private by 1996

In mid-1994 the *Daily Telegraph* was being challenged by Rupert Murdoch's *Times* for market leadership in England. When the *Daily Telegraph* lowered its cover price from 48 pence to 30 pence, the *Times* immediately dropped its cover price from 30 pence to 20 pence. In September 1993, the *Times* had lowered its price from 45 pence to 30 pence. The price cuts had boosted the *Times'* circulation from less than 400,000 copies a day in mid-1993 to average daily sales of 517,000. With its latest price cut, the *Times* expected its daily circulation to climb above 600,000. The price war was having an effect on the *Daily Telegraph*'s readership, the figure that was used to set advertising rates. For the period from December 1993 to May 1994, the *Daily Telegraph*'s readership declined 9.9 percent to 2.49 million, while the *Times'* readership increased 10.6 percent to 1.32 million, according to the National Readership Survey. The *Telegraph*'s CEO Dan Colson told the *Financial Post,* "The *Telegraph* remains the undisputed market leader in the quality segment."

Between October 1995 and August 1996, The Telegraph Group Ltd. became a wholly owned subsidiary of Hollinger International, which paid a total consideration of approximately $455.1 million for all of The Telegraph Group's outstanding shares. By taking The Telegraph Group private, Black was following the advice of investors who warned that it would be difficult to raise equity capital in London markets. Share prices of *The Telegraph* had fallen dramatically in 1994 as a result of the price war with Rupert Murdoch's *Times.* Subject to lingering criticism in the British press and government, Black's comment to the *Financial Post* was, "Never underestimate the conservatism or xenophobic tendencies of the British."

Hollinger International Succeeded American Publishing in 1995–96

In July 1995, Hollinger Inc. announced it would sell its interests in the *Daily Telegraph* and Southam Inc. to its U.S. subsidiary, American Publishing Co. Analysts saw it as a move to strengthen American Publishing's shares, which were traded on the NASDAQ market. American owned the company's U.S. flagship newspaper, the *Chicago Sun-Times,* along with other newspaper chains. The move would also mean a transfer of assets out of Canada and into the United States, where Hollinger felt they would have a higher value.

By September 1995 the plan had changed somewhat. It now involved more of a corporate reorganization of American Publishing and Hollinger Inc., with the Canadian company Hollinger Inc. creating a $1 billion newspaper company with headquarters in Chicago. The Canadian-based Hollinger Inc. would still sell its interests in British Telegraph plc and in the Canadian company Southam Inc. to American Publishing, thereby more than doubling American Publishing's annual revenues of $422 million in 1994.

At the same time, Hollinger International Inc. would be established in Chicago as a new umbrella company over American Publishing Co. F. David Radler, chairman of APC and president and chief operating officer of Hollinger Inc. told *Crain's Chicago Business,* "We're consolidating our assets into one group with greater access to U.S. capital markets, which are the best capital markets in the world. We're de-Canadianizing ourselves and creating an American company."

Conrad Black was named Hollinger International's chairman of the board and CEO. Radler assumed the duties of president and COO. Black's strategy of entering the U.S. capital markets paid off in February 1996, when Hollinger International went public with an IPO that raised $380 million. As described in the company's annual report, "For most of our stockholders, Hollinger International Inc. is a new creation grouping a unique collection of high quality international newspaper assets. For other stockholders, it is a relaunch on a very broad basis of American Publishing Company, which continues as a core asset of Hollinger International."

Corporate Debt an Issue in 1996

As Conrad Black prepared to address shareholders at Hollinger International's annual meeting in May 1996, the company was under two credit reviews for having too much debt. Both the U.S.-based Standard & Poor's Corporation and Canada's Dominion Bond Rating Service put Hollinger International on credit watch. Standard & Poor said that a downgrade was inevitable "in the absence of Hollinger taking significant steps to ease its debt burden." The company had about $445 million of debt outstanding, plus debt it had taken on to increase its stake in Southam and debt it might take on to complete its purchase of the *Telegraph.* Moody's debt-rating service soon followed with an announcement that it, too, was reviewing its rating of Hollinger's debt. At the time, Hollinger International was the third largest newspaper chain in the world behind Gannett Co. Inc. and Rupert Murdoch's News Corp.

In August 1996 Hollinger International completed its acquisition of the minority shares of Telegraph plc, taking the company private and making it a wholly owned subsidiary called Telegraph Group Ltd. In addition to publishing various editions of the *Telegraph,* the Telegraph Group published *Spectator* magazine and owned 24.7 percent of Australia's John Fairfax Holdings Ltd. (which would be sold later in the year for $513 million). As part of the financing of the acquisition, Hollinger International sold 11.5 million shares of its Class A common stock and 20.7 million shares of preferred stock to raise $301.1 million. Those proceeds, together with related bank financing, were used to pay for the acquisition.

Ownership of Newspaper Assets Moved from Canada to United States in 1997

Black began to implement his strategy of moving ownership of his newspaper assets into the United States, where they would be valued higher. In January 1997 Hollinger Inc. announced it would sell almost all of its Canadian publishing assets to its U.S.-based subsidiary Hollinger International for $342 million, excluding working capital of about $181 million. Those assets included Hollinger's interest in Southam and the Sterling Newspapers Company, which owned 26 daily and 49 non-daily newspapers in Canada.

Hollinger Inc.'s other assets included a 20 percent stake in the *Financial Post;* about five percent of Key Publishing, which published *Toronto Life* magazine; an interest in Toronto's Sky-Dome; and part of Gordon Capital Corp., a Toronto securities firm.

In March 1997 Hollinger International's stock hit a two-year low, and the company announced it intended to repurchase up to three million of its Class A common shares as well as some of its preferred stock. Since reaching a high of $13.125 in May 1996, the stock dropped to just under $9 in March 1997 before closing at $9.25.

One analyst explained that the company's complex transactions of 1996 and early 1997 turned off a lot of investors, who wanted companies that were easy to follow. John Reidy of Smith Barney Inc. told the *Financial Post,* "They don't want to talk about EBITDA (earnings before interest, taxes, depreciation, and amortization) or cash flow. Hollinger is an EBITDA and cash flow story, rather than an earnings story." Reidy admitted that Hollinger had a complex capital structure and that the company went through a radical transition in 1996, referring to taking The Telegraph Group private, Hollinger International's IPO, the sale of its interest in Fairfax, and the transfer of assets from its Canadian parent in early 1997.

In April 1997 Hollinger International established a new subsidiary, Hollinger Digital, with offices in the Soho district of New York City. Hollinger Digital would be responsible for managing and making investments in new media properties. One of its management functions would be to coordinate the 90 web sites of Hollinger's more than 350 newspapers. The subsidiary's chairman and CEO was Richard Perle. Perle was also a director of Hollinger International and former assistant secretary of defense for international security during the Reagan administration. He was known as the architect of Reagan's Star Wars defense program.

In November 1997 Hollinger International announced it was selling about 40 percent of its U.S. community newspaper group. These included 160 weekly, small daily, and free circulation newspapers in 11 states with a combined circulation of approximately 900,000. The buyer was the Los Angeles-based Leonard Green and Partners LP, a firm which specialized in leveraged buyouts. The sale price was $310 million, which Hollinger International would use to reduce debt and finance the previously announced purchase of the *Post-Tribune* in Gary, Indiana. The sale was completed on January 27, 1998.

During December 1997 Black also told the *Financial Post* that Hollinger International would probably be cutting back on its acquisitions, because prices were too high. He expected to use the $310 million from the sale of 160 small U.S. newspapers to reduce debt, not make acquisitions. As if to calm investors, he promised a more conservative financial approach in the future. "We will not issue stock at silly prices," he told the *Financial Post.* "We will not issue non-investment grade paper again. It's a much more conservative company.'' In the past, Hollinger had relied on high-yield junk bonds to finance its acquisitions. Hollinger's financial executives never seemed overly concerned about the company's debt level, though, because of the company's strong cash flows.

Black noted that circulations were increasing among the company's Canadian newspaper publishing group. The *Vancouver Sun* was leading with an average weekly increase of 10 percent. ''I think we've earned our spurs,'' he told the *Financial Post.* ''The whole theory of the inexorable decline of newspapers, I still say, is bunk.''

For 1997 Hollinger International reported earnings of $104.5 million. Operating income was up, but overall earnings declined from the previous year's levels due to higher taxes, interest payments, and other expenses not directly related to operations. The company benefited from improved advertising revenues in a good business environment. It also took steps to allay investor fears by reducing costs and making other improvements.

In April 1998 the *Jerusalem Post* announced it would buy 49 percent of the *Jerusalem Report,* its competitor. It was expected that the two English-language publications would merge their administrative, advertising, and circulation departments while remaining independent editorially. The twice-monthly *Jerusalem Report* was established by former *Post* reporters and financed primarily by Canadian businessman Charles Bronfman, chairman of the Seagram Company. It had lost money steadily since it began publishing in 1990.

Hollinger International's History Characterized by Complex Financial Transactions

By the end of 1997 Hollinger International owned or had an interest in 167 paid daily newspapers. Its major newspapers were the *Chicago Sun-Times,* the *Daily Telegraph,* and the *Ottawa Citizen.* It also owned or had an interest in 361 non-daily newspapers as well as other magazines and publications. For the past ten years the company had pursued a strategy of growth through acquisitions. Since 1986, the company had acquired some 400 newspapers and other publications (net of those sold) in the United States, the *Daily Telegraph* in the United Kingdom, the *Jerusalem Post* in Israel, and has made significant investments in newspapers in Canada, including a controlling interest in Southam Inc., Canada's largest newspaper publisher. In 1997 it acquired the Canadian Newspapers division of its parent company, Hollinger, Inc.

Hollinger International's history, including that of its Canadian parent, has been characterized by complex financial transactions and an aggressive acquisitions strategy. Since Conrad Black successfully entered the U.S. capital markets with Hollinger International's IPO in 1996, he has sought to calm

investor fears and simplify the company's financial structure. In 1996 the company divested itself of its 25 percent interest in John Fairfax Holdings Ltd., increased its stake in Southam Inc., and took 100 percent control of The Telegraph Group Ltd. In 1997 it addressed investor concerns by accomplishing three financial goals: 1) it steeply improved operating and net profit; 2) it repurchased some of the company's underpriced stock; and 3) it sold non-strategic assets at advantageous prices. The company also increased its stake in Southam to 58.6 percent. Enjoying a cleaner balance sheet and circulation gains at its major newspapers, Hollinger International appeared ready to consolidate its gains and embark on a more conservative acquisitions and financial program for the future.

Principal Subsidiaries

Hollinger Publishing International Inc.; Hollinger Canadian Publishing Holdings Inc. (includes Southam Inc. and Sterling Newspapers Co.); Chicago Group (includes *Chicago Sun-Times*); Community Newspaper Group; The Telegraph Group Ltd. (United Kingdom); *The Jerusalem Post* (Israel).

Further Reading

Dalglish, Brenda, ''Analysts Support Hollinger Move,'' *Financial Post,* January 9, 1997.
——, ''Black Bites Back,'' *Maclean's,* November 15, 1993, p.24.
——, ''Black Pulls out of Fairfax,'' *Financial Post,* December 17, 1996.
——, ''Black Wants All of Telegraph,'' *Financial Post,* April 25, 1996.
——, ''Debt, Competition Issues Dog Hollinger,'' *Financial Post,* May 29, 1996.
——, ''How Black Plans to Finance Southam Purchase,'' *Financial Post,* May 28, 1996.
Fitzpatrick, Peter, ''Third Debt-Rating Agency Puts Hollinger Under Review,'' *Financial Post,* June 5, 1996.
''Jerusalem Post Buys 49 Percent of Jerusalem Report,'' Reuters Limited, April 6, 1998.
Kirbyson, Geoff, ''TD's US$650M Loan Will Allow Hollinger to Make Telegraph Bid,'' *Financial Post,* July 2, 1996.
Laver, Ross, and David Estok, ''Face to Face with Black,'' *Maclean's,* June 10, 1996, p. 44.
McGugan, Ian, ''Publish and Flourish,'' *Canadian Business,* August 1994, p. 31.
Reguly, Eric, ''Telegraph Faces Long War with Murdoch,'' *Financial Post,* July 6, 1994.
Siklos, Richard, ''Hollinger Takes Telegraph Private,'' *Financial Post,* August 1, 1996.
Sorenson, Jean, ''The Paper Chaser,'' *BC Business,* August 1991.
Theobald, Steven, ''Hollinger Sells Batch of Community Papers, Plans to Use $440 Million to Pay Down Debt,'' *Toronto Star,* November 25, 1997.
''Two Jerusalem Newspapers to Merge,'' Associated Press, April 5, 1998.

—David Bianco

Hubbard Broadcasting Inc.

3415 University Avenue
St. Paul, Minnesota 55114
U.S.A.
(612) 646-5555
Fax: (612) 642-4103

Private Company
Founded: 1923
Employees: 1,450
Sales: $400 million (1997 est.)
SICs: 4833 Television Broadcasting Stations

Hubbard Broadcasting Inc. (HBI) operates one of the few remaining large family-owned television companies in the nation. The value of Twin Cities-based KSTP-TV alone has been estimated at a quarter of a billion dollars. HBI is the majority shareholder of United States Satellite Broadcasting Company Inc. (USSB), a direct broadcast satellite company, and serves as managing general partner of Conus Communications, an innovative satellite-based news gathering organization. The Hubbard family's broadcasting legacy spans three-quarters of a century.

Roots in Local Radio and Television: 1920s to 1960s

Minnesota native Stanley E. Hubbard, a pioneer of commercial radio and television broadcasting, established his first radio station in 1923. "WAMD—Where All Minneapolis Dances—broadcast part-time because Hubbard had to leave the microphone every few hours to go and sell advertising," wrote Kathy Haley in a 1997 *Broadcasting & Cable* article.

Interested in expanding his news coverage, Hubbard started his own news gathering bureau in 1925; Associated Press and United Press International did not yet serve the fledgling radio industry. WAMD merged with KFOY in 1928 to form KSTP. Hubbard broadcast the vaudeville acts of such performers as Jack Benny and the Marx brothers, live sporting events, and educational programs.

Among the first on the scene when television technology was being introduced, Hubbard experimented with closed-circuit broadcasts beginning in 1938 using one of the first RCA cameras. RCA formally presented television to the public during the 1939 New York World's Fair. World War II slowed development of commercial television, but in 1948 KSTP-TV began broadcasting.

KSTP-TV accumulated a series of firsts in the 1950s and early 1960s: the first television station between Chicago and the West Coast; the first independently owned NBC affiliate; the first station to carry a late evening local news program seven nights a week; and the first to do all-color broadcasting. Those early days of television were filled with sensational spot news stories, and Hubbard was known for aggressively seeking them out.

Hubbard expanded beyond the Minnesota borders late in the 1950s when he acquired a radio and television station in Albuquerque, New Mexico. In 1962, Hubbard Broadcasting Inc. was formed with Stanley E. Hubbard as president and general manager and son Stanley S. Hubbard as vice-president. Stanley S. Hubbard, who had been in and around the broadcasting business since his childhood, had come on board full-time in 1951.

Stanley S. Hubbard began making his own mark on the television industry in the 1960s with an operation in St. Petersburg, Florida. "Few independent station owners made money at all in 1968 and none had succeeded in making a go of a UHF in an all-VHF market, but the younger Hubbard had WTOG turning a profit within two and a half years," wrote Haley. Hubbard transformed the station by adding a much larger transmission tower and investing in popular programming.

A Change of Leadership: 1970s

Minneapolis/St. Paul was a competitive market: both radio and television stations fought for the all-important ratings leadership. In the early 1970s, KSTP was losing ground to WCCO on both fronts. Stanley S. Hubbard brought in Marion, Iowa-based media consultant Frank Magid to help turn the tide. The action—initially opposed by founder Stanley E. Hubbard—"ushered in what was perhaps KSTP-TV's most successful era," according to Sandra Earley.

Among significant changes in the TV end of the business, according to Early, were the move to "personality driven newscasts" and the switch from the standard film format to easier to use videotape. The radio station switched to a rock-and-roll format and dropped its lengthy affiliation with NBC. The control of the business had clearly shifted from father to son.

A 1981 *Broadcasting* magazine article estimated Hubbard Broadcasting's worth at $200 million or more. The Hubbards owned three television and five radio stations, a marine radio-supply company, a production company, and a 148-room Miami Beach hotel. While often soundly criticized regarding their treatment of employees, the Hubbards were "held in generally high regard by other station owners," wrote Karl Vick in a March 1981 *Corporate Report Minnesota* article.

In 1984, continuing in their tradition of industry firsts, Hubbard Broadcasting initiated a satellite news gathering organization independent of the big three networks—ABC, CBS, and NBC. Conus (Continental U.S.) Communications bought and leased satellite transponders and then offered satellite access and newsfeeds to member stations. F&F Productions, a Hubbard subsidiary specializing in remote production, built the first satellite news gathering truck using the new Ku-band satellite technology.

Live offsite broadcasts became a practical reality for smaller stations. The C-band satellite systems in use at the time required huge receivers and were tightly regulated by the Federal Communications Commission (FCC) due to their disruptive effect on other signals, and ground-based microwave signals had a limited range and needed a clear pathway. Conus gained 60 member stations within the first few years of operation.

Direct Broadcast Satellite: 1980s-Early 1990s

Stanley S. Hubbard was a true-believer in the efficacy of satellite broadcasting, and his horizons expanded beyond news gathering applications. Back in 1981, when Hubbard Broadcasting was granted one of the first direct broadcast satellite (DBS) licenses, he had begun formulating plans for an advertising-supported home satellite service. The satellite-to-home concept had been tossed around since the early 1960s when Congress created the Communications Satellite Corp. (COMSAT).

The public effort to build a commercial television system around satellite technology failed due to lack of outside support and COMSAT was disbanded in the mid-1980s. Prudential Insurance, General Instrument, and shopping center developer Francesco Galesi formed United Satellite Communications in 1983 but had fewer than 10,000 subscribers when it folded a few years later, according to a 1991 *Forbes* article by Graham Button. SkyCable was scratched in June 1991. But Hughes continued to develop the technology and linked up with Hubbard.

United States Satellite Broadcasting (USSB)—a subsidiary of Hubbard Broadcasting formed in 1981—was also having trouble getting its satellite service off the ground. USSB reformulated its earlier plan to include a mix of advertising, subscription, and pay-per-view programming to be transmitted via two RCA satellites and launched by 1988. But lack of financing foiled the endeavor. Many of the most promising potential investors were already involved in cable—a direct competitor to the satellite service—and others doubted Hubbard could succeed where much larger contenders had failed.

But Hubbard persisted. Nationwide Mutual Insurance, Pittway Corp (a fire alarm maker), and media investor Burt Harris came aboard as investors in the late 1980s. Technological advances improved the odds for success. Digital compression hiked the number of television channels that could be carried by a single transponder, and higher-powered satellites allowed receiver size to be greatly reduced.

In 1991, General Motors' Hughes Aircraft sold five of 16 transponders on its broadcast satellite to Hubbard in a deal valued at more than $100 million. DBS skeptics were quick to point out the market was already largely wired for cable service, and the initial cost to the consumer—about $700 for a receiving dish and signal converter—was much higher than cable. Furthermore, unlike cable, DBS did not transmit local programming.

But Hubbard and other DBS supporters declared the higher capacity digital signals provided far better sound and picture quality than the standard analog signal used by cable and broadcast television. Cable companies themselves were gearing for costly upgrades to fiber optic cable which would carry digital signals and boost channel capacity. Moreover, many cable customers had grown frustrated with persistent service problems.

Thomson Consumer Electronics, a division of France-based Thomson S.A., developed and produced the 18-inch receiver and the converter under the RCA brand name. The consumer-friendly dish could pick up both USSB and Hughes's DirecTV signals. Competitor Primestar, which began service in 1990, required a higher-priced, larger, professionally installed dish and offered fewer channel choices.

Although they shared a satellite and receiving system, USSB and DirecTV were in competition for subscribers. DirecTV had more channels at its disposal than USSB, but Hubbard quickly acquired the right to carry popular premium channels such as Home Box Office (HBO), Showtime, Cimemax, and the Movie Channel. USSB planned to offer the All News Channel, a joint venture between Conus and Viacom International, as well. DirecTV got the jump on rural distribution when the National Rural Telecommunications Cooperative purchased the right to market the service to electric and phone customers. Areas that were not wired for cable were an important source of customers for both companies.

USSB began broadcasting satellite television service in June 1994 aided by funds from Microsoft cofounder Paul Allen, Dow Jones & Company, and Wall Street investor George Soros. More than a half million receiving systems were sold in the first year, making DBS the fastest-selling new consumer electronics product in U.S. history. USSB signed on more than 300,000 subscribers. Hubbard's vision had become a reality. He received further recognition for his accomplishments in 1995, when he and his late father were handed the Distinguished Service Award from the National Association of Broadcasters for their work in radio, television, and DBS.

The once scorned DBS became the darling of investors. In January 1996, AT&T paid $137.5 million for 2.5 percent of

DirecTV, and MCI Communications Corp. and News Corp. paid $682.5 million for a DBS license. The activity boosted the value of satellite broadcasters' stock just as USSB prepared to make an initial public offering. USSB raised $224.1 million in February. The newly public company was valued at more than $3 billion, and the Hubbard family held more than 50 percent of the shares.

Expectations were sky high. But the early phenomenal growth rate cooled. USSB stock price fell steadily from a high of about $37 shortly after the IPO to about $11 per share just over a year after the offering. USSB lost $237 million in its first two and one-half years of operation. "The skeptics are again ascendant. Wall Street analysts, who have recently called for the sale of USSB, say that the company's value lies in the five transponders it owns on a satellite, not in its 1.2 million subscribers," Sandra Earley wrote in a May 1997 article.

Pointed Toward the Future

While new satellite companies geared up—EchoStar Communications (DISH Network) merged with ASkyB and MCI Communications Corporation announced a partnership with News Corp. in 1997—cable remained USSB's main competition. The Digital Satellite Systems (DSS) which USSB shared with DirecTV were found in about 3.3 million U.S. households at the end of 1997 compared with tens of millions of cable subscribers. USSB continued to fine-tune its service in order to place itself in the best possible position in the market and contracted with Lockheed Martin for additional satellites.

A third generation of Hubbards was prepared to lead the family enterprises into the 21st century. Stanley E. Hubbard II served as president and CEO at USSB. Robert W. Hubbard led the television operation. Ginny Hubbard Morris headed the KSTP-FM and AM radio operations. The three were actively involved in the day-to-day affairs of the business and two other siblings all held spots on the HBI board. (Hubbard concerns included KSTP-TV and Conus Communications in Minneapolis/St. Paul; seven television stations located in Minnesota, New Mexico, and New York; a television production company in Florida; and USSB and the radio stations.) Expanding use of digital technology, and the entry of electric utilities and telephone companies into market were among the changes taking place in the industry. But the Hubbard family faced the future with 75 years of experience behind them.

Further Reading

Alexander, Steve, "Hubbard's Satellite TV Subsidiary to Go Public," *Star Tribune* (Minneapolis), December 2, 1995, p. 1D.

Bork, Robert H., Jr., "Conus the Barbarian," *Forbes,* November 4, 1985, p. 111.

Brinkley, Joel, "As Digital TV Arrives, Cable's Picture May Not Be So Clear," *New York Times,* May 5, 1997.

Button, Graham, "Stan Hubbard's Giant Footprint," *Forbes,* November 11, 1991, pp. 344–50.

Chanen, David, "Stan Hubbard, Broadcasting Pioneer, Dies at 95 in Florida," *Star Tribune* (Minneapolis), December 29, 1992, p. 1A.

Covert, Colin, "In Twin Cities, the Digital Picture Is Still Fuzzy Among Broadcasters," *Star Tribune* (Minneapolis), April 4, 1997.

Earley, Sandra, "Stan the Man," *Corporate Report Minnesota,* May 1997, pp. 33–43.

Fiedler, Terry, "They Said Hubbard's Idea Couldn't Fly," *Star Tribune* (Minneapolis), March 12, 1996, p. 1D.

——, "USSB to Drop Lifetime, 6 Other Channels in Favor of More Movies, Pay TV," *Star Tribune* (Minneapolis), January 7, 1998, pp. 1D, 5D.

Fiedler, Terry, and Ann Merrill, "USSB Prepares for Initial Public Stock Offering," *Star Tribune* (Minneapolis), January 30, 1996, p. 1D.

"Fifth Estate," *Broadcasting,* November 23, 1981.

Gross, Steve, "Hubbard's TV Venture Via Satellite," *Star Tribune* (Minneapolis), June 14, 1993, p. 1D.

Haley, Kathy, "The Pioneering Spirit of the Hubbard Family," *Broadcasting & Cable,* March 31, 1997, pp. S1–S15.

"Hubbard Broadcasting Inc.," *Corporate Report Fact Book 1998,* p. 574.

Kearney, Robert P., "Shine On, Stanley Hubbard," *Corporate Report Minnesota,* June 1986, pp. 43–46.

Lambert, Brian, "Family Channels," *St. Paul Pioneer Press,* April 26, 1998, pp. 1E, 4E.

Madison, Cathy, "Launching into National Orbit," *Twin Cities Business Monthly,* April 1994, pp. 27–31.

Merrill, Ann, "Hubbard's Full Cupboard," *Star Tribune* (Minneapolis), April 21, 1995, p. 1D.

Montgomery, Leland, "Cable's Death Star," *Financial World,* May 11, 1993, pp. 32–33.

Schmickle, Sharon, "No Smooth Transition for High Definition TV," *Star Tribune* (Minneapolis), September 22, 1997.

Scully, Sean, "Countdown to DBS," *Broadcasting & Cable,* December 6, 1993, pp. 30, 34.

"United States Satellite Broadcasting Company Inc.," *Corporate Report Fact Book 1998,* p. 498.

Vick, Karl, "The Life and Prime Times of Stanley S. Hubbard," *Corporate Report Minnesota,* March 1981, pp. 85–88, 120–26.

—Kathleen Peippo

Humana Inc.

The Humana Building
500 West Main Street
Louisville, Kentucky 40202
U.S.A.
(502) 580-1000
Fax: (502) 580-3424
Web site: http://www.humana.com

Public Company
Incorporated: 1961 as Heritage House of America Inc.
Employees: 19,500
Sales: $8.04 billion (1997)
Stock Exchanges: New York
Ticker Symbol: HUM
SICs: 6321 Accident & Health Insurance; 6324 Hospital
    & Medical Service Plans; 8741 Management Services

One of the largest publicly traded managed healthcare companies in the United States, Humana Inc. has about 6.2 million people enrolled in its health plans, which are available in 16 states and Puerto Rico. Nearly 45 percent of these customers are in Florida, Illinois, and Texas. Principally offering health maintenance organization (HMO) and preferred provider organization (PPO) plans, Humana also offers Medicare- and Medicaid-related health insurance products; provides managed healthcare services under a contract with the U.S. Department of Defense; and offers such specialty and administrative services as dental plans, group life insurance, and worker's compensation. In late May 1998 Humana agreed to merge with United HealthCare Corporation to create the largest managed-care company in the United States in terms of plan participants (the merged entity would operate under the United HealthCare name).

Began with Nursing Homes in the 1960s

In 1961 two lawyers in Louisville, Kentucky, built a nursing home, pledging $1,000 apiece together with four friends. Wendell Cherry and David Jones—cofounders of that first home, Heritage House—were soon approached with other offers to buy and build nursing homes. Expansion was rapid in the first seven years, and the two men added facilities in Kentucky, Virginia, and Connecticut. With the establishment of Medicare and Medicaid in the mid-1960s, the industry grew quickly. Slightly ahead of the pack in what was to become the most rapidly expanding sector of the nation's economy, Jones and Cherry reincorporated their venture in 1961 and sold stock for seven years to finance further growth. Extendicare Inc., as the group was known, grew to more than 40 facilities, becoming the nation's largest nursing home company.

As Medicare spawned a nursing home glut and stocks suffered, Extendicare experimented with alternatives. There was a brief and unfortunate diversification into mobile home parks between 1969 and 1971, which the company quickly unloaded. Extendicare acquired its first hospital in late 1968, realizing it could apply the same business practices it had developed for operating nursing homes. Within two years, the company had acquired nine more hospitals. The hospitals proved so successful that Extendicare divested all of its nursing homes in 1972.

Hospitals Became Focus in the 1970s

With a focus now entirely on hospitals, the company's name was changed to Humana Inc. in January 1974. Some of the features that distinguished Humana from other hospital chains early on were its nonconforming management decisions, the refusal to overpay in buying hospitals, the refusal to manage hospitals it did not own, and rigid cost-control measures well-enforced through the company's centralized management. These methods became much discussed: first because they seemed remarkable in the industry; later because of complaints by some physicians about overcontrol. For example, Humana's efforts to ensure reimbursement included the insistence on a specific payment-plan agreement before patients were discharged.

The cost controls eventually became one of Humana's greatest assets. Between 1975 and 1980, Humana grew quickly and achieved economies of scale, like other hospital chains, by making bulk purchases of supplies and equipment. Unlike some competitors, however, Humana remained very centralized, operating all patient-billing and data-collection out of its home office in Louisville. Freed from the distraction of managing hospitals it did not own—also unlike most competitors—Humana concentrated on strict productivity and profitability goals.

Doubled Size Through 1978 Acquisition of American Medicorp

As the nation's third largest hospital-management chain in 1978, Humana committed a bold act: it acquired the number two chain, American Medicorp, Inc. This purchase doubled Humana's size and stretched its debt. Having used leveraged debt with confidence for some time during its expansion, Humana was now faced with a debt that one company official claimed was "nearly 90% of capital."

Cofounders Jones and Cherry, chairman and president, respectively, remained untroubled because 45 percent of hospital revenues were coming from government-guaranteed Medicare and Medicaid. The two men also saw the hospital business as recession resistant, even though Humana suffered from low-occupancy rates at some of its facilities during these years.

Meanwhile, Humana unloaded unprofitable hospitals. While the healthcare industry was burgeoning into the second largest industry in the United States, Humana alone was honing its cost controls: between its own growth and government-subsidized medical care, the industry in general had not yet felt the need for cost efficiency.

To build its medical reputation, Humana established a Centers for Excellence program in 1982 for the purpose of specialty care. This included centers for neuroscience, diabetes, spinal injuries, and artificial-heart research and surgery. The artificial-heart projects—which were undertaken partly for the publicity they generated—helped push Humana's name into public view. In 1982 Humana had 90 hospitals, primarily in the sunbelt states. Humana also leased and operated the University of Louisville's teaching hospital, where Jefferson County, Kentucky, citizens without the ability to pay for hospital care received inpatient treatment for no charge—state, city, and county governments covered the costs.

During the following years the healthcare industry's overexpansion and the government and private insurers' cost-containment efforts began to clash. Here, Humana's tradition of tight cost controls helped, but the industry reeled from severe changes: industry-wide hospital occupancy rates dropped below 50 percent from a high of 80 percent just three years earlier. From the onset of federal policies in 1983, with private insurers following suit, the industry changed drastically.

Began to Offer Health Plans in 1984

Early in 1984, Humana launched Humana Health Care Plans, to offer insurance plans with attractively low premiums and punitive deductibles for patients who used rival hospitals. Competitors soon imitated this vertical integration. Humana banked on a 70 percent referral rate from its managed healthcare business, thus ensuring a healthy occupancy rate for its hospi-

tals. Two years into the venture, however, Humana discovered its plan was seriously flawed.

The premiums had been underpriced, missing costs by at least 20 percent. It was assumed policyholders would use Humana hospitals, but in 1986, as losses began to mount, it was found that only 46 percent of Humana's Care Plus group-plan members were using its facilities. The deductibles offered to lure users to their hospitals were not sufficient; independent physicians could recommend any hospital to their patients, and did. Since policyholders were not restricted in their choice of physician, there was no guarantee that they would be referred to Humana facilities by independents. In fact, by this time, a rancor had developed between medical professionals and the business forces behind the cost wars. Humana had incurred further animosity because of its strict business policies. Jones himself contended that in 1986 doctor resentment had resulted not only in patients being steered to other hospitals, but also in strategies to bypass Humana's deductibles for use of other facilities. Doctors would, for instance, claim that a standard admission was an emergency.

Humana addressed these problems by campaigning to change doctors' perceptions of the company, and preventing the use of outside hospitals by enforcing stricter procedures. These procedures included requiring doctors to speak with a health-plan nurse and to accept the Humana hospital recommended for use. Refusal to follow this process would prevent reimbursement. (This type of tightly managed plan would become typical of HMO plans of the 1990s.) Humana also trimmed back the number of policies it offered and avoided cities where the company was not a dominant presence.

In 1987, with founders Jones and Cherry still at the helm, Humana worked to right its insurance plans. Net income had plunged nearly 75 percent between 1985 and 1986. Humana adjusted its insurance plans and underwent restructuring. It closed clinics and purchased several HMOs. That same year, Medicare ceased its practice of prepayment and started requiring bills before all reimbursements. This meant a significant slowing of cash flow for Humana. It was followed by further government cost-reimbursement strictures that directly affected Humana. Public pressure to contain the cost of healthcare was growing.

By 1988, Humana had greatly reduced losses caused by its insurance operations and seemed intent on recovery. By 1989, after five years of losses, Humana's health-plan division made $4 million, its first operating profit. Raising premiums up to 25 percent, reducing its markets from 50 to 17, operating only where it had a strong hospital presence, and ensuring that patients were sent to its hospitals, Humana began to rebound by the end of the 1980s. Humana, continuing to move counter to the industry while competitors increased their debt loads through leveraged buyouts, saw its debt to capital ratio reach an all-time low of 37 percent in 1990.

In October 1990 Humana announced that it had agreed to acquire Chicago-based Michael Reese Health Plan Inc. and Michael Reese Hospital and Medical Center. At the time of the agreement, Michael Reese was one of the largest private academic medical centers in the United States. Michael Reese

Health Plan had 240,000 members; Humana had five times as many members. In 1991 cofounder Cherry died.

Spun Off Its Hospitals in 1993

By the early 1990s Humana's healthcare plans—primarily managed care plans (HMOs and PPOs)—had grown into a $2 billion business with 1.7 million plan participants. Although dogged by a series of charges—overcharging patients for services, using misleading sales tactics, seeking improper Medicare expense reimbursements—that brought ongoing negative publicity, the company's health plan division was much healthier than the hospital side. With its hospitals continuing to post declining profits because of industry-wide cost-containment efforts and falling admissions of full-paying patients (those not covered through government-sponsored plans), Humana decided in 1993 to stake its future on managed healthcare plans. In March of that year, the company spun off the hospital division—including 76 Humana hospitals (most of the company's total)—into a new and separate company called Galen Health Care, Inc. Within six months of the spinoff, Galen merged with Columbia Hospital Corp. (later known as Columbia/HCA after a merger with Hospital Corp. of America).

Humana emerged with $685 million in cash and long-term debt of only $21 million (Galen took on most of Humana's prespinoff debt). The company thus went on a spending spree. In 1994 Humana spent $180 million to acquire Group Health Association, a 125,000-member HMO in Washington, D.C., and CareNetwork, an HMO in Milwaukee. The company in October 1995 acquired EMPHESYS Financial Group, Inc. for $650 million. Green Bay, Wisconsin-based EMPHESYS was a leading provider of health insurance in the small group market, with 1.3 million members, and the tenth largest commercial group health insurer. Thus by the end of 1995 Humana had boosted its overall plan membership to 3.8 million and its revenues to $4.7 billion.

By mid-1996, however, it appeared that Humana had grown too fast. Amid skyrocketing costs, Humana was forced to abandon 13 unprofitable markets. The largest of these was Washington, D.C., and the company sold Group Health Association to Kaiser Permanente in January 1997; in only two years of ownership, Humana had suffered losses of $100 million attempting to turn around the money-losing Group Health HMO. Also sold was Humana's 30,000-member health plan in Alabama. As part of this restructuring, Humana recorded a $200 million pretax charge for the second quarter of 1996, leading to net income for the year of only $12 million, compared to $190 million for the previous year. Also, Jones, still serving as company chairman and CEO, forced out longtime president Wayne T. Smith and CFO W. Roger Drury. Gregory H. Wolf—who had been senior vice-president of sales and marketing and had come to Humana from EMPHESYS, where he had been president and COO—took over as president of Humana in September 1996. He added the CEO title as well in December 1997, with Jones remaining chairman.

Wolf set about resurrecting Humana's image by improving relations with both doctors and patients. He abandoned the use of gag clauses in HMO contracts with doctors, clauses that forbade doctors from discussing the financial arrangements or patient-care policies of the HMO. On the patient side, Humana targeted improvements in basic customer service—answering phone calls faster, mailing out identification cards more quickly, and expediting claims handling.

Humana made two significant acquisitions in late 1997. In September the company acquired Physician Corporation of America (PCA) for $290 million in cash and the assumption of $121 million in debt. PCA had a total of 1.1 million members in its HMOs, with 324,000 in Florida alone where Humana already had 1.1 million members. Humana also gained large plans in Texas and Puerto Rico. In October 1997 Humana bought ChoiceCare Corporation for about $250 million in cash. ChoiceCare managed the largest HMO in the Cincinnati area, which had about 250,000 members.

Meanwhile, Humana continued to restructure its operations by shedding additional noncore operations. During 1997 the company sold its last remaining hospital and its pharmacy benefits management subsidiary. In August 1997 Humana announced it would sell its HMO in California. By early 1998 it had committed to selling all of its Humana health centers. After enjoying an acquisitions-aided increase in revenues to $8.04 billion and a rebound in net income to $173 million in 1997, Humana thus was positioned in mid-1998 as a 6.2-million member group with the number one or number two position in 14 of the major markets in which it operated.

Then, on May 28, 1998, Humana and Minneapolis-based United HealthCare Corporation announced that they intended to merge, creating through a $5.4 billion stock swap what would be the largest managed healthcare company in the United States, with 10.4 million full-paying HMO and PPO members (and overall membership of more than 19 million), exceeding the nine million of Kaiser Permanente. The merged entity would operate under the United HealthCare name in 48 states and Puerto Rico and have annual revenues of about $28 billion. It thus appeared that the history of the acquisitive Humana would itself end through this megamerger.

Principal Subsidiaries

ALABAMA: Humana Health Plan of Alabama, Inc.; QuestCare, Inc. CALIFORNIA: Centerstone Insurance and Financial Services. DELAWARE: EMPHESYS Financial Group, Inc.; Health Value Management, Inc.; Humana Compensation Management Source, Inc.; Humana HealthChicago, Inc.; Humana Military Healthcare Services, Inc.; Humrealty, Inc.; Medstep, Inc.; Physician Corporation of America. FLORIDA: Delray Beach Health Management Associates, Inc.; Family Health Plan Administrators, Inc.; Health Inclusive Plan of Florida, Inc.; Humana Health Care Plans-Davie, Inc.; Humana Health Care Plans-Palm Springs, Inc.; Humana Health Care Plans-Rolling Hills, Inc.; Humana Health Care Plans-South Pembroke Pines, Inc.; Humana Health Care Plans-West Palm Beach, Inc.; Humana Internal Medicine Associates, Inc.; Humana Internal Medicine Associates of the Palm Beaches, Inc.; Humana Health Insurance Company of Florida, Inc.; Humana Medical Plan, Inc.; Humana Workers' Compensation Services, Inc.; Lakeside Medical Center Management, Inc.; PCA Family Health Plan, Inc.; PCA Health Plans of Florida, Inc.; PCA Life Insurance Company; PCA Options, Inc.; PCA Property & Casualty Insurance Co. GEORGIA: Humana Employers Health Plan of Georgia, Inc.; Humana Health Plan of Georgia, Inc. ILLINOIS: Health Direct, Inc.; Humana Health Direct Insurance, Inc.; Humana HealthChicago Insurance Company; The Dental Concern, Ltd. KENTUCKY: ChoiceCare Medical Group, Inc.; HMPK, INC.; HPLAN, INC.; Humana Broadway Corp.; Humana Health Plan, Inc.; Humco, Inc.; The Dental Concern, Inc.; The Dental Concern Insurance Company. LOUISIANA: Humana Health Plan of Louisiana, Inc.; Humana Workers' Compensation Services of Louisiana, Inc. MISSOURI: Humana Kansas City, Inc.; Humana Insurance Company; Humana/MedPay, Inc. NEVADA: Humana Health Insurance of Nevada, Inc. OHIO: ChoiceCare Corporation; ChoiceCare Health Plans, Inc.; Humana Health Plan of Ohio, Inc. OKLAHOMA: Commonwealth Management, Inc. PUERTO RICO: PCA Health Plans of Puerto Rico, Inc.; PCA Insurance Group of Puerto Rico, Inc. TEXAS: Humana HMO Texas, Inc.; Humana Health Plan of Texas, Inc.; PCA Health Plans of Texas, Inc.; PCA Life Insurance Company of Texas, Inc.; PCA Provider Organization, Inc. UTAH: Humana Health Plan of Utah, Inc. VERMONT: Managed Care Indemnity, Inc. WASHINGTON: Humana Health Plan of Washington, Inc. WISCONSIN: CareNetwork, Inc.; EMPHESYS Wisconsin Insurance Company; Employers Health Insurance Company; Humana Wisconsin Health Organization Insurance Corporation; Independent Care, Inc.; Network EPO, Inc.; Wisconsin Employers Group, Inc. BERMUDA: Hallmark Re Ltd.

Further Reading

Benmour, Eric, ''Bullish on Wolf,'' *Business First of Louisville,* September 29, 1997.

——, ''Humana Breakup Leaves Competitors Seeing Double,'' *Business First of Louisville,* September 7, 1992, pp. 1+.

Burton, Thomas M., and Steven Lipin, ''United HealthCare to Acquire Humana,'' *Wall Street Journal,* May 29, 1998, pp. A3, A10.

Freudenheim, Milt, ''Humana Bets All on Managed Care,'' *New York Times,* May 20, 1993, pp. D1, D6.

——, ''Humana Buys Health Plan in Cincinnati,'' *New York Times,* June 6, 1997, p. D3.

Galuszka, Peter, ''Humana, Heal Thyself,'' *Business Week,* October 14, 1996, pp. 73, 76.

Gold, Jacqueline S., ''Humana: Spin Doctors,'' *Financial World,* July 6, 1993, p. 17.

Greene, Jan, ''Humana Gets Happy,'' *Hospitals & Health Networks,* May 5, 1997, pp. 34+.

''History of Humana,'' Louisville, Ky.: Humana Inc., 1997.

Howington, Patrick, ''Young Executive Fuels Turnaround at Humana,'' *Courier Journal,* September 21, 1997.

Johnsson, Julie, ''David Jones: Reinventing Humana for the 1990s,'' *Hospitals,* May 20, 1991, pp. 56+.

Kertesz, Louise, ''Life After Restructuring: Humana Redefines Self After Shedding Hospitals, Clinics,'' *Modern Healthcare,* April 20, 1998, pp. 114+.

Miller, Susan R., ''Humana May Be Just What PCA Needs,'' *South Florida Business Journal,* June 6, 1997, pp. 1+.

Schiller, Zachary, ''Humana May Be Wearing Too Many Hats,'' *Business Week,* June 8, 1992, p. 31.

Schiller, Zachary, Susan Garland, and Julia Flynn Siler, ''The Humana Flap Could Make All Hospitals Feel Sick,'' *Business Week,* November 4, 1991, p. 34.

Shinkman, Ron, ''Humana's Buying Spree: Firm Makes Acquisition Comeback with Three New Deals,'' *Modern Healthcare,* June 9, 1997, p. 12.

Stern, Gabriella, ''Humana Copes with Medicare Probe, Financial Woes,'' *Wall Street Journal,* June 15, 1992, p. B3.

—Carol I. Keeley
—updated by David E. Salamie

Intergraph Corporation

Huntsville, Alabama 35894-0001
U.S.A.
(205) 730-2000
(800) 345-4856
Fax: (205) 730-7898
Web site: http://www.intergraph.com

Public Company
Incorporated: 1969 as M & S Computing
Employees: 8,200
Sales: $1.12 billion (1997)
Stock Exchanges: NASDAQ
Ticker Symbol: INGR
SICs: 3571 Electronic Computers

Intergraph Corporation develops and sells software, hardware, and services for technical professionals, particularly for those customers who are involved in computer-aided design, management, and engineering (CAD/CAM/CAE). Formerly a manufacturer of UNIX-based CAD systems, Intergraph initiated a major transition during the 1990s when it began developing systems based on Microsoft's Windows NT operating system and Intel's Pentium microprocessors, a transition that led to a series of annual financial losses during the decade. During the late 1990s, the company maintained sales and service organizations in 65 countries throughout the world, deriving roughly 45 percent of its revenues from foreign markets.

Late 1960s Origins

In 1969 James Meadlock left his position as an engineer at IBM to found the consulting firm M & S Computing. Meadlock remained in Huntsville, Alabama, not simply because he was a southerner, but because NASA had a flight center there, where Meadlock had helped develop software guiding the Saturn rocket to the moon. Thus, there was engineering talent in the area that Meadlock hoped to tap. Starting up with Meadlock, four engineers, and a secretary, the young company sought to be an innovator in interactive computer graphics, specializing in real-time applications.

As late as 1968, engineers and scientists were communicating with computers in a limited language: the user had to translate graphics for conversion to punch cards, wait for any group of data to be processed, and go to separately situated off-line plotters for the printed output. Real-time application meant the engineer could communicate directly with the computer, describing information in charts or graphs, with the elimination of the delay involved with punch cards and off-line plotters. Real-time graphics let the user maintain what was referred to as "thinking momentum."

Within its first year of operation, M & S Computing developed its first graphics system. The company posted a loss of $64,000 for the year. Given that Meadlock's initial investment had been $39,000 of his own savings, the amount was considerable, but it was the only loss ever posted by the company. By 1972 the company introduced a graphics system to the U.S. Army Missile Command, its first major customer, by creating software for government-supplied hardware. The following year, M & S Computing developed a mapping system for the city of Nashville, Tennessee; on M & S software it was possible for a city planner to call up specific city blocks, together with population and zoning specifics.

The company then worked on three-dimensional mapping, building up its engineering clientele with programs useful for oil exploration. The mapping experience led M & S toward the architectural design industry, a relatively open market at the time. At the time, most other CAD/CAM suppliers were going after the largest market, mechanical design for the aerospace and automobile industries, but this market was beginning to lag behind by the late 1970s.

1980s Expansion

By 1980, what had been known as the "computing industry" was moving forward so fast that a whole new atmosphere with new information technology companies was emerging. In order to compete, the consulting firm M & S Computing felt that it needed a name change. The name Intergraph was chosen and

Company Perspectives:

Intergraph and its business partners work with customers around the world and in virtually every industry to provide the powerful, business-critical solutions they need to succeed. Intergraph believes in providing substantial value for our customers by offering products that have the best technological foundation and are priced to meet today's demanding budgets.

some new strategies were devised. Meadlock decided that with the advent of more powerful 32-bit computers CAD technology would have to be adaptable. While other companies tried to build their own computers, Meadlock went one step further, purchasing a Digital Equipment Corporation (DEC) computer and developing systems around it, a tactic which gave Intergraph a strategic edge. The company's main competitor, Computervision, bogged down in the attempt to create its own computer and fell slightly behind in overall sales, giving Intergraph the chance to move ahead.

Tougher competition lay ahead, however, as Meadlock faced his former employer, IBM, in the mechanical design market. By 1983, Intergraph had a sales force of only 65, while IBM's comprised thousands. Some inroads were made in the mechanical market during this time, however; Intergraph scored a contract with the Xerox Corporation, and one was in the works with Porsche.

Other challenges faced the company at this time, including the problem of rapid growth. With the number of employees proliferating, Intergraph found it necessary to overhaul its training program. The company also implemented a new sales-support group, members of which were called application managers. These specialists concentrated on the needs of individual workers, rather than on an entire industry's needs. The applications managers were assigned different areas, such as architecture, electronics, mapping, and plant design.

As a result of this new approach, Intergraph pulled ahead in several areas. It improved its position in the mechanical design industry, with 20 percent of 1983 company revenues coming from that market. The company also developed new products, including a series of workstations addressing computer-aided design from conceptualization through manufacturing. Devising marketable workstations was a coup for the company, since workstation technology was the wave of the future. Finally, Intergraph entered an entirely new market, marrying graphics to word processing in a technology suitable for the electronic publishing industry.

In an effort to enter the electronic design tool market, in September 1984 Intergraph invested more than $5 million in Tangent Systems, a two-month-old firm specializing in computer-aided engineering (CAE) software. For a 50 percent equity interest in Tangent, Intergraph would use its sales force to market the software in the United States and abroad. At this time the company had some salespeople and distributorships in

place in Canada, but decided that this was not enough. By December 1984 Intergraph acquired the remaining majority ownership of its Canadian affiliates. Industry experts viewed Intergraph's changes favorably, regarding the company's entrance into new markets as good insurance during economic downturns.

A decline did occur, becoming apparent in January 1985, when manufacturers in general began slowing production. Intergraph, likewise, experienced a decrease in equipment orders. The company's stock was temporarily downgraded on Wall Street, but certain analysts believed the slowdown was merely due to Intergraph's emphasis on new product development. While Intergraph's equipment orders were 20 million less than expected in fourth quarter 1984, its long-term growth prospects were still considered excellent. IBM remained number one in the CAD/CAM industry worldwide, with Intergraph and Computervision close behind, vying for second.

By early 1985, industry competitors were taking notice of Intergraph Corporation; Intergraph was the only company to improve its market share against IBM in 1984. Intergraph began designing CAE products compatible with DEC computers; this move, together with the Tangent Systems equity, pushed Intergraph further ahead in its national competition with Computervision. The company also made an aggressive move to establish a Japanese subsidiary in March 1985. With a distributorship in place via Japan's Mutoh Industries, Ltd., Intergraph was now poised to compete in the international CAD/CAM/CAE industry. Other developments at this time included Intergraph's acquisition of The Rand Group, Inc., which agreed to develop engineering design-based software for the company.

With the acquisitions of Tangent and The Rand Group and its production of CAE systems compatible with DEC computers, Intergraph attempted to branch out from its established base of turnkey operations, that is, the provision of an entire CAD/CAM system, including the design, installation, and troubleshooting of all software and hardware. While Intergraph was still viewed as a superior provider of such systems, the company did not want to be left behind as the industry moved toward more flexible PC-based systems. The challenge for Intergraph in the mid-1980s was to maintain its position as the leading turnkey provider while remaining a viable contender as the industry moved from hardware- to software-based systems.

In the area of electronics, Keith Schonrock, executive vice-president, remarked that "Intergraph is firmly committed to not just being a workstation supplier, or a components supplier, or a software-package supplier." Unlike most other competitors, who focused on one or the other categories, Intergraph would not be confined to niche markets. The company got around this problem by using existing technology and finding ways to work it into new markets, rather than simply responding to market demands after the fact.

By 1986 Intergraph branched out once again, acquiring Massachusetts-based Optronics, Inc., a producer of computer peripherals and optical scanning equipment. Intergraph's sales force grew 33 percent in less than a year—by mid-1986 the company employed 5,289 versus 3,483 in November 1984. Once again, the company reorganized its sales staff, dividing into the areas of mapping and energy exploration, mechanical design, and electronics and electronic publishing.

Some Wall Street observers expected the company to do more than refine its sales strategies, however; they called for corporate-wide restructuring. The criticism centered on the fact that Meadlock was still running the company single-handedly. With sales at approximately $500 million and expected to rise, some critics thought that a new level of management was called for as well as the addition of outside advisors to the board of directors.

Setting its sights on new workstation technology, in July 1986 Intergraph introduced new graphics workstations designed with Fairchild Semiconductor Corporation's Clipper 32-bit microprocessor. Key elements of the InterAct and Inter-Pro 32C were their low prices, stand-alone design, and flexible architecture. With three independent subsystems including networking, graphics, and a processor/memory, users could upgrade to new technology without having to change the entire system.

By April 1987 Intergraph had run into trouble when Fairchild failed to provide enough computer chips for the workstation. The company lost approximately $25 million in revenues while waiting for the Fairchild order. This setback, together with the glutted market for Intergraph systems, caused the corporation to lose its status as a growth stock. The next two years proved a challenge, as Intergraph extended itself with a number of acquisitions. In June 1987 the company acquired 50 percent of Pennsylvania's Bentley Systems, MicroStation developer. In September, Intergraph sold Intraph South Africa Ltd. for cash; and in October the corporation acquired the advanced processor division of Fairchild Semiconductor Corporation. In a last attempt to control its investment, in April 1988 Intergraph acquired an additional 32 percent of Tangent Systems for $3.5 million. The deal included the company's additional acquisition of six percent of Tangent's Cadence Design Systems, Inc., a third-party software developer, by December of the same year.

By March 1989 Intergraph changed course entirely, deciding to exchange its 82 percent Tangent ownership for shares in Cadence Design Systems. Tangent, strong in the semiconductor and computer industries, did not give Intergraph entry into the larger range of markets it was looking for. More specifically, Tangent's first software product sold better in conjunction with workstations built by Apollo Computers, DEC, and Sun Microsystems than it did with Intergraph's InterPro workstations.

Although competition was stiff, Intergraph finally outstripped IBM and DEC, moving to number one in CAD/CAM/CAE sales in North America for 1988. While Intergraph ranked second nationally in electronic mapping sales, the company nonetheless finished the first quarter of 1989 falling about 15 percent in overall profits, with revenues down by $15 to $20 million. The last three quarters of 1988 showed marked improvement, however, as Intergraph bounced back with sales for the year up 24.8 percent from 1987.

Intergraph's success just when experts were predicting doom was due in part to the company's founder and chief executive officer, Jim Meadlock. Contending with intense competition and rapid changes in computer technology, Meadlock took an aggressive stance. Technical expertise continued to provide stability for Intergraph in the tumultuous 1980s. While Meadlock admitted in an article in *Industry Week* that he may have "missed the PC boom," Intergraph still had a highly competitive product on the market. MicroStation, only two years old, was the number three PC CAD software shortly after being introduced. Meadlock predicted that hardware would become even cheaper as more and more corporations established a central computer as their own database with individuals working from the desktop.

Fortunately for Intergraph, in August 1989 several major software providers announced they would port packages to the corporation's Clipper workstations, providing Intergraph customers with a number of software options. Within several months the company also decided to offer simplified commands for its UNIX workstations, devised by the Open Software Foundation and based on the icon system developed by Apple Computer. Intergraph increased its holdings in 1989, acquiring Quintus Computer Systems in October for $6.5 million. By November 1990, Intergraph announced its decision to buy Daisy/Cadnetix Inc., a CAD/CAE software producer, for $14 million. Advantages to the acquisition were Daisy/Cadnetix's international marketing stronghold based in Europe, a design center in Israel, and a large customer base. Disadvantages, however, could crop up in the future because Daisy/Cadnetix had been in financial straits for several years and had lost many key employees. When Intergraph sold Tangent Systems in early 1989, the company apparently left the electronic design market; with the Daisy/Cadnetix purchase, the company was once again in the running.

1990s: A Decade of Change

The year 1990 proved a decisive success overall: Intergraph reached $1 billion in revenue, becoming the second-ranked CAD/CAM/CAE vendor in the world and the first in North America. The company also scored a contract with Ameritech, the Midwest regional Bell company, for an estimated $7 million in new revenue over two years, with higher per capita revenue expected in subsequent years. Interestingly, just when Intergraph was riding high, criticism resurfaced. The New York state pension fund implicated Intergraph, as well as four other companies, in a drive to elect more outsiders to corporate boards of directors. Intergraph, however, had already selected a new president, Elliott James. Other criticism came from industry and financial analysts predicting a decline in Intergraph's stature. According to these critics, the corporation, although known for superior customer satisfaction, was not attracting enough new customers. While Intergraph doubled in size between 1985 and 1991, earnings were stagnant. Nevertheless, the company had virtually no long-term debt and continued to grow. Intergraph was second only to IBM in international sales.

Most criticism leveled at Intergraph stemmed from the fact that Jim Meadlock never seemed to do things like anyone else in the CAD/CAM industry, nor like any other hardware/software vendor. At a time when CAD/CAM providers were porting their software to two or more hardware platforms, Meadlock refused to do so. The company lost chances for several multimillion-dollar contracts this way, as Intergraph's Robert Glasier, vice-president of corporate marketing, freely admitted. However, as Glasier stated in *Electronics*: "All the software vendors are trying to get down to one or two platforms because they learned how much it costs to do more than that. We're already there."

Another unique aspect of the company was that while proprietary systems were thought to be dead, Intergraph's were still selling. In fact, in April 1991 the company was awarded a $362 million Navy contract, beating out tough competitors. Finally, Intergraph was involved in both hardware and software when such hopscotching was not deemed feasible or profitable. In spite of such criticism, Intergraph was riding another crest in the spring of 1991. Its stock was in demand, due in large part to the Navy contract that boosted earnings by $15 million that year.

Although Intergraph's success in building proprietary systems belied the prevailing theory that the market had dried up, Meadlock knew he could not expect to buck industry trends forever. A fundamental change in Intergraph's business strategy was needed to ensure financial growth in the long-term—and Meadlock knew it. In 1992, he decided to abandon the proprietary hardware aspect of Intergraph's business and concentrate instead on a standard-platform strategy, a transition harking back to the early years of the company. Meadlock decided the company would write its technical software applications to conform to Microsoft Corp.'s Windows NT operating system and to make Windows NT available on Intergraph workstations. "Windows NT was a defensive decision," Meadlock later remarked. At the same time, Meadlock announced that Intergraph would offer workstations tailored around Intel Corp.'s microprocessor. As the 1990s progressed, Microsoft and Intel achieved a dominant grip on the computer industry, with their software and chips becoming the ubiquitous industry standard.

Meadlock could not have picked two more powerful forces to build Intergraph's systems around than Microsoft and Intel, but the astuteness of his decision did not make the company's transition any easier. The new strategy embraced in 1992 touched off a troubled era in Intergraph's development, in spite of its historic importance. The costs resulting from the company's new product initiative were staggering, resulting in operating losses of $164.6 million in 1993 and $72.6 million in 1994. The downward spiral of Intergraph's operating income was further exacerbated by declining profit margins in the computer industry as a whole, as steadily declining retail prices for all types of computer equipment delivered the second blow of the one-two punch that sent the company reeling during the 1990s. In 1994, for instance, Intergraph sold 41 percent more workstations and servers than it did the previous year, yet workstation and server revenues crept up a mere four percent. For Meadlock, the situation was grave, but there was no turning back. The wrenching transition had to continue forward to ensure the company's long-term future.

Entering the late 1990s, Intergraph continued to struggle from the repercussions of its transition from proprietary, UNIX-based systems to the open environment of Intel and Microsoft.

The company lost money in 1995, 1996, and 1997, while revenues remained virtually static. The answer to whether or not Intergraph's move away from proprietary systems ultimately would pay the dividends expected by Meadlock remained to be determined in the future, but it was clear that the company's previous approach was longer viable in the late 1990s marketplace.

Principal Subsidiaries

Intergraph Computer Systems; International Public Safety; VeriBest Inc.; M & S Computing Investments.

Further Reading

Burrows, Peter, "Intergraph Is Hit Hard As 1985 Starts Poorly," *Wall Street Journal*, January 3, 1985.

"Can Intergraph Catch IBM in CAD/CAM Market?," *Electronics*, May 5, 1986.

"Dazix Deal May Hold Key to Understanding Intergraph," *Electronic Business*, March 4, 1991.

Dumaine, Brian, "A Good Old Boy Scores Big," *Fortune*, July 11, 1983.

"Intergraph Adds to RISC Clipper Line," *Electronic News*, January 20, 1992.

"Intergraph: Back on the Fast Track," *Industry Week*, April 17, 1989.

"Intergraph Closing Tangent Chapter," *Electronic News*, February 27, 1989.

Intergraph: Everywhere You Look, Huntsville, Ala.: Intergraph Corporation, 1991.

"Intergraph Falls 15% on Profit Outlook," *Wall Street Journal*, March 13, 1989.

"Intergraph Invests over $5M in Tangent," *Electronic News*, September 10, 1984.

"Intergraph Only Bidder for Daisy," *Electronic News*, November 26, 1990.

"Intergraph Signs Letter of Intent to Buy Daisy/Cadnetix," *Electronic News*, November 19, 1990.

"Intergraph's Image As a Growth Stock Shrinks," *Wall Street Journal*, April 23, 1987.

"Intergraph Simplifies Workstation Commands," *Design News*, December 4, 1989.

"Intergraph Still Defending Its Contrary Ways," *Electronic Business*, March 4, 1991.

"Intergraph Unit in Japan," *Wall Street Journal*, March 27, 1985.

"Intergraph Wins $362M Navy Pact," *Electronic News*, April 15, 1991.

McHugh, Josh, "Don't Mess with Me," *Forbes*, March 23, 1998, p. 42.

McLeod, Jonah, "Intergraph Returns to Its Roots to Find Its Future," *Industry Week*, May 15, 1995, p. 40.

"More Ports to Clipper Workstations," *Design News*, August 7, 1989.

"PRC Protests Navy Intergraph Pact," *Electronic News*, April 22, 1991.

"Recruit, Interview, Hire, Train," *Inc.*, May 1983.

"These Maps Can Find Oil—or Sell Burgers," *Business Week*, March 13, 1989.

"Three Startups Ride the Boom," *Business Week*, March 25, 1985.

—Frances E. Norton
—updated by Jeffrey L. Covell

Intimate Brands, Inc.

3 Limited Parkway
Columbus, Ohio 43230
U.S.A.
(614) 479-8000
Fax: (614) 479-7079
Web site: http://www.intimatebrands.com

Public Company
Incorporated: 1995
Employees: 43,900
Sales: $3.61 billion (1997)
Stock Exchanges: New York
Ticker Symbol: IBI
SICs: 5632 Women's Accessory & Specialty Stores

Intimate Brands, Inc. is responsible for the operation of numerous retail stores throughout the United States that specialize in lingerie, personal care products, and women's apparel. Intimate Brands is composed of the Victoria's Secret stores and catalogue, Bath & Body Works, Cacique, and Penhaligon's. Gryphon Development is another of the company's holdings, and functions as the division responsible for the creation of many bath and personal care products sold by the company. Most of Intimate Brands' over 1,600 store units are located in shopping malls throughout the United States, although Penhaligon's is based in the United Kingdom. Leading apparel retailer The Limited, Inc. possesses a majority interest in Intimate Brands, Inc. and its holdings.

Intimate Brands' Beginnings

Intimate Brands, Inc. was created in 1995 as the result of a reorganization of corporate holdings initiated by leading retailer The Limited, Inc., who owned Intimate Brands at the time. Despite Intimate Brands' relatively short history as a freestanding entity, however, the different divisions that comprise the company each possess their own history, much of which dates back many years. The company itself was slowly formed throughout the 1980s and 1990s as The Limited acquired different lingerie and personal care product retail operations and added them to its mass of retail holdings.

One of the first acquisitions made by The Limited that later became a member of the Intimate Brands division was that of the Victoria's Secret enterprise in 1982. When The Limited's chairman, Leslie Wexner, initiated the purchase of Victoria's Secret, it was made up of just six struggling lingerie stores and a successful catalogue operation. In fact, 1982 sales figures for the six money losing stores topped off at only around $7 million.

The Victoria's Secret catalogue, however, was enjoying success and achieving earnings in 1982, and Wexner believed that some potential existed for both divisions to grow and prosper if led in the correct direction. In the early years, the catalogue operation catered mainly to often-embarrassed men who were attempting to purchase lingerie as gift items. Catalogue telephone operators would lead its predominately male base of customers through their purchases, patiently helping them figure out bra sizes and the like. Despite its success in that realm, the company was not a big hit with women; Wexner, however, saw potential for a change in focus.

Wexner eventually hired Cynthia Fedus to act as the chief executive officer of the Victoria's Secret Catalogue operation. At that time, it was the company's belief that business would explode if women were targeted as the primary customers, given that women were likely to purchase underwear and lingerie items for themselves on a more regular basis than men. In order to target women, Fedus changed the catalogue's focus, ousting the steamy shots of women with men in the catalogue's photos and replacing them with those of women posing alone in romantic and seductive, yet proper, settings. After the change, catalog sales doubled in one year to more than $100 million.

While the catalogue was busy revamping its image, Grace Nichols had gained control of the Victoria's Secret Stores branch of the business, and was making moves to convince female shoppers that undergarments were actually another part of a well-rounded wardrobe. Management tried to capitalize on what they saw as a woman's desire to indulge, and offered products and marketing strategies that played on this idea.

Other Limited Additions in the Late 1980s

Meanwhile, The Limited had introduced its own private-label intimate apparel business, Lingerie Cacique, and a chain of naturally based toiletries stores called Bath & Body Works. Immediately, The Limited's management experienced a barrage of criticisms by those who felt that chains consisting of such limited product offerings would not fare well. For one thing, the Victoria's Secret store chain was already struggling. Furthermore, many critics felt that women could already purchase underwear, lingerie, soap, and shampoo at department stores, and that there was simply no need for stores specializing in those products.

Despite the doubts expressed by those outside The Limited, the company continued its introduction of new Victoria's Secret, Cacique, and Bath & Body Works store units. Wexner maintained that his new additions were not in the business of selling lingerie or shampoo, but were instead selling indulgences that appealed to its customers' narcissistic tendencies. For example, according to a June 1995 issue of *Forbes* magazine, "the Victoria's Secret customer buys eight to ten bras a year; the typical American woman buys two." The stores were obviously catering to a need that other businesses did not even realize their customer base possessed.

Entering the 1990s, The Limited continued its string of personal care product additions with the purchase of Penhaligon's, a business based in the United Kingdom that had over a century of experience in the marketing of perfume products. The Limited also added Gryphon Development, L.P. to its holdings, which was a producer of personal care products. Gryphon soon became the division responsible for the creation of new products for the Bath & Body Works chain.

Each of The Limited's new holdings slowly grew to become a power in its field. For example, although Bath & Body Works did not experience overwhelming success immediately after its introduction—the business posted sales of only $1.9 million in 1990—it soon grew to become one of the leading natural-based toiletry product store chains in the United States. Within five years, the stores were generating $475 million in annual sales, helping The Limited's lingerie and personal care product division achieve over $2.1 billion in sales for 1994.

The Late 1990s: Intimate Brands, Inc. Is Born

The Limited operated each of its lingerie and personal care products businesses as a portion of its massive retail portfolio until 1995. At that time, the company's holdings had expanded and diversified so much that the decision was made to restructure them into three main operating divisions. Of the three divisions that were created, Intimate Brands came to encompass Victoria's Secret stores and catalogue, Cacique, Bath & Body Works, and Penhaligon's, with Gryphon acting as the research and development arm of the personal care branch.

That same year, Intimate Brands, Inc. was spun off by The Limited, and was listed on the New York Stock Exchange. The Limited maintained a controlling interest in Intimate Brands, but the company began functioning separately on October 23, 1995 and produced its first annual report that year.

At the time of the spinoff, Intimate Brands already possessed an international presence through the existence of its Penhaligon's chain, as well as numerous Victoria's Secret and Bath & Body Works stores, in the United Kingdom. Plans to expand Bath & Body Works on the international level were focused only on further penetrating the U.K. market. Intimate Brands' largest international presence came through its Victoria's Secret Catalogue operation, which distributed intimate apparel, clothing, shoes, and other accessories to shoppers worldwide.

The new company decided against the prospect of franchising any of its businesses, opting instead to maintain corporate ownership of all of its store locations. The company also refrained from selling any of its merchandise at wholesale prices to other vendors who wished to sell Intimate Brands' items in their own retail settings. It would seem that this practice potentially limited the consumer base that Intimate Brands was able to reach, subsequently limiting the company's sales potential as well. But through strict control of the distribution and sales channels used, Intimate Brands instead ensured that its products would not fall into less than high quality retail settings. Thus, the glamorous image of each store chain and its products was maintained.

The company posted sales of $2.5 billion in 1995, marking an increase of over $400 million from the previous year. This financial success was then complemented by the company's involvement in numerous community service organizations and causes. Intimate Brands targeted a portion of its resources toward helping organizations involved in women's and children's issues, education, and community growth. For example, the company offered support to Race for the Cure, the YWCA's Women of Achievement Awards, the Children's Defense Fund, INROADS, the United Negro College Fund, the American Red Cross, and the United Way.

The company's commitment to high moral standards and to providing its employees with opportunities and a pleasant working environment was also apparent in its policies regarding the production and distribution of its products. Intimate Brands refused to do business with suppliers who did not comply with the requirements of the U.S. Customs Service and other government agencies, such as country-of-origin requirements for manufactured goods. The company also mandated that its suppliers and manufacturers provide safe and healthy working conditions, fair wages and benefits, and reasonable working hours to employees.

Intimate Brands soon began to build on the brand recognition it had already earned in the past through the production of new editions of its Victoria's Secret Catalogue. At a steady pace, the company began distributing catalogues which offered new clothing and accessory items in addition to the traditional lingerie products. Very popular were the swimwear, citywear, and country versions of the catalogue. Another marketing trend was the almost yearly introduction of special new lines of Victoria's Secret lingerie, which were accompanied by national-scale television advertisement campaigns. Examples in the late 1990s were the ''Perfect Silhouette'' and ''Angels'' lingerie lines.

As the newly formed Intimate Brands, Inc. approached the end of the century, it was working to position itself for further success. The company was opening new store units for each of its retail operations, and was projecting continued growth throughout its existing markets and in new ones. The increased offerings in the Victoria's Secret Catalogue were also acting to boost sales figures. Intimate Brands' ability to continue increasing the brand recognition of its product lines would determine its potential for further growth and profitability.

Principal Subsidiaries

Victoria's Secret Stores, Inc.; Cacique, Inc.; Victoria's Secret Catalogue, Inc.; Bath & Body Works, Inc.; Penhaligon's Limited (U.K.); Gryphon Development, Inc.; Intimate Brands Service Corporation.

Further Reading

Feldman, Amy, ''Leslie Wexner's Classical Act,'' *Forbes,* December 20, 1993, p. 20.

Machan, Dyan, ''Sharing Victoria's Secrets,'' *Forbes,* June 5, 1995, p. 132.

''That's Entertainment: Fantasy Theme Designs Woo Shoppers,'' *Chain Store Age Executive,* August 1994, p. 62.

Underwood, Elaine, ''Bust-Boosting Bra Battle Begins,'' *Adweek,* September 19, 1994, p. 12.

Wheeler, Claudia D., ''Au Natural,'' *Soap-Cosmetics-Chemical Specialties,* July 1994, p. 36.

—Laura E. Whiteley

J & J Snack Foods Corporation

6000 Central Highway
Pennsauken, New Jersey 08109
U.S.A.
(609) 665-9533
Fax: (609) 6359

Public Company
Incorporated: 1971
Employees: 1,700
Sales: $220.32 million (1997)
Stock Exchanges: NASDAQ
Ticker Symbol: JJSF
SICs: 2052 Cookies & Crackers; 2086 Bottled & Canned
Soft Drinks; 2038 Frozen Specialties

J & J Snack Foods Corporation is a manufacturer and exporter of snack foods, beverages, and frozen specialties. Headquartered in New Jersey, the company considers itself the largest maker of soft pretzels in the United States. The company's hallmark—the SuperPretzel—has changed over time, but remains the foundation of J & J Snack Foods.

In addition to its pretzels, J & J Snack Foods manufacturers a variety of snack foods and drinks, as well as sells frozen carbonated beverages in the United States, Canada, and Mexico. The snack food company markets to the food service industry, retail supermarket customers, and specialty snack food outlets.

The Pretzel Empire Begins in a Waterbed Store

The history of the current J & J Snack Foods begins with Gerald Shreiber, a college dropout whose motto was "Discover, salvage, and build." Shreiber left Rider College in 1960 for work as a machine shop apprentice. By 1967, he was a partner in a metalworking business housed in a garage beneath a pool hall in Philadelphia. Though the company was profitable, Shreiber wanted a product of his own instead of concentrating on the offspring of other companies. Shreiber and his partner sold the business in 1970, with Shreiber taking about a $60,000 share of the profits.

Oddly enough, within a year, Shreiber heard of a foundering pretzel business while shopping in a waterbed store. As the pretzel maker's largest secured creditor, the waterbed store owner—beleaguered by the company's bankrupt owners—complained of the situation to Shreiber. Immediately interested, Shreiber visited the pretzel business and just as quickly recognized its potential. He purchased the waterbed store owner's portion of the company for $30,000 plus a share of its early profits. Then Shreiber obtained the rest of J & J Snack Foods' assets by outbidding the other owners in bankruptcy court. In total, the acquisition cost a little more than $72,000.

By 1972, Shreiber had distributors in Philadelphia and Shrewbury, New Jersey. To expand the business, he looked to innovations. For example, Shreiber developed pre-baked and frozen soft pretzels in response to vendors who disliked baking the snacks. Shreiber also initiated compact pretzel ovens and display cases for the convenience of snack bars. His SuperPretzel business eventually expanded to cities across the United States—in schools, bowling alleys, and sports arenas. "The more business we did," Shreiber told *Forbes*, "the more I thought we could do more."

Growth Through Acquisitions During the 1980s

In 1986 Shreiber made frozen soft pretzels available to consumers through their local supermarkets. He enlisted Michael Karaban, the man who successfully marketed Lender's frozen bagels to the public, to direct the sale of soft pretzels through supermarkets when initial efforts fell short of expectations. Karaban repackaged the J & J Snack Foods' frozen pretzels and re-focused the company's marketing directly to consumers.

J & J Snack Foods acquired ICEE-USA, a semi-frozen carbonated beverage manufacturer, in 1987. A competitor of the Slurpee brand, the slushy ICEE was losing money in a $500 million market when Shreiber bought the company. As a division of J & J Snack Foods, however, ICEE increased its sales and operating income by more than 20 percent annually through the end of 1991. In July 1991, J & J Snack Foods issued a secondary stock offering to expand ICEE from a 15-state market in the western United States, plus Mexico and Canada, to a national brand. The stock offering earned $29 million, which J & J Snack Foods invested in dispensing machines for the frozen beverage. "Having built a successful pretzel business from scrap, can he repeat the trick in frozen drinks?" asked Christopher Palmeri in *Forbes* in 1991. "Chances are he can."

By 1989, J & J Snack Foods controlled 70 percent of the soft pretzel market and enjoyed a 24 percent increase in sales and earnings over the previous five years. The snack food manufacturer produced two million pretzels each day, and its marketing network expanded to include 145 food brokers and 875 independent distributors in all 50 states. Five competitors eventually sold their businesses to Shreiber.

Internal Growth and Strategic Acquisitions in the 1990s

As the market for soft pretzels in the food service industry flattened, Shreiber sought new markets and new products to add to the company's line. He sold soft pretzels to snack bars in warehouse clubs and tested soft pretzel sales at selected McDonald's in the early 1990s. Shreiber also launched a bite-sized soft pretzel—with melted cheese for dipping—for sale in movie theaters.

In 1994, J & J Snack Foods purchased the New Jersey-based Funnel Cake Factory, a supplier to the food service industry and to retail supermarkets. Schreiber explained the rationale for the acquisition to the *Frozen Food Digest:* "Funnel Cake represents another niche product for our distribution channels. We like the product. We like the potential."

J & J Snack Foods was eager to acquire the Funnel Cake Factory for its projected impact on revenue. Conversely, the company also was interested in divesting some of its holdings. So in 1995, J & J Snack Foods offered a subsidiary—Western Syrup Company—for sale. Dispensing with the subsidiary had no adverse effect on the operations or financial situation of J & J Snack Foods.

The following year, J & J Snack Foods expanded its SuperPretzel product line to include Cinnamon Raisin Minis. Made with Sun-Maid brand raisins, Cinnamon Raisin Minis were fully baked and frozen—with packaged squeeze-on icing—for reheating in microwave ovens. J & J Snack Foods also purchased Pretzel Gourmet Corporation, a retailer headquar-

tered in Pennsylvania, in 1996. With outlets in New Jersey, Florida, Nevada, and Washington, D.C., as well as Pennsylvania, Pretzel Gourmet sold $1.5 million in snacks in 1995. "Pretzel Gourmet," Schreiber reported in *Business Wire,* "is known for its superior, freshly baked, hand-rolled soft pretzels and represents an excellent vehicle for us to enter this growing segment." Pretzel Gourmet retained its own identity within J & J Snack Foods after the acquisition. J & J Snack Foods also acquired a manufacturer and distributor of Italian ices and frozen desserts in 1996. Mazzone Enterprises of Cicero, Illinois, earned $4 million annually before its acquisition.

Later in 1996, the company acquired Bakers Best Snack Food Corporation, a Hatfield, Pennsylvania, company also doing $4 million in sales annually. A soft pretzel manufacturer serving supermarkets as well as the food service industry, Bakers Best fit nicely into J & J Snack Foods' product line.

Within one month, J & J Snack Foods purchased the controlling share of common stock in Pretzels Incorporated. Like Bakers Best, this company manufactured soft pretzels for the food service industry and for supermarkets. Pretzels Inc. annually sold $2 million of Texas Twist brand pretzels.

Marketing and Merchandising

By now, J & J Snack Foods established national marketing and merchandising programs for both its food service and supermarket customers. As part of this program, J & J Snack Foods provided food service customers with point-of-sale materials and merchandising equipment such as ovens, warmers, and frozen-beverage dispensers. Through the development of innovative merchandising systems, J & J Snack Foods facilitated adding its soft pretzel systems to existing food service operations or as stand-alone concessions. The SuperPretzel line, for example, gave its customers exclusive mobile merchandising units, display cases, and point-of-sales materials.

J & J Snack Foods' Pretzel Gourmet Express concept was a natural outgrowth of this program. Introduced at the CoreStates Arena in Philadelphia, Pennsylvania, in 1996, Pretzel Gourmet Express provided a complete package to food service customers as a turnkey operation. "Building on the success of SuperPretzel," the company's 1997 annual report revealed, "we . . . launched an upscale branded concept to capitalize on America's growing taste for premium snacks and the evolving trends in the food service industry. It's called Pretzel Gourmet Express." The two Pretzel Gourmet Express concessions that opened at the Philadelphia arena, for example, featured butter-dipped, Parmesan cheese, cinnamon-sugar, and other freshly baked, flavored, and filled soft pretzels sold through a complete food service operation, including proprietary merchandising equipment and promotional programs. J & J Snack Foods developed the Pretzel Gourmet Express concept to solidify its leadership position in the soft pretzel market, as well as to broaden this business category. The concept also responded to identified needs in serving customers on college campuses and in the business dining market segment.

J & J Snack Foods widely promoted its products for retail supermarkets at this time. The company advertised in newspapers and occasionally on television. J & J Snack Foods also offered consumers coupons for its products and conducted in-store demonstrations at supermarkets. "Ask any food company," a J & J Snack Foods annual report revealed. "The world's toughest environment isn't the Amazon, the Sahara, or the North Pole. It's the retail supermarket and, more specifically, the highly competitive freezer case in the supermarket." Nevertheless, J & J Snack Foods' SuperPretzel brand established the company as the leader in retail supermarket soft pretzels.

In 1996, J & J Snack Foods contracted with The Food Group for its advertising and marketing plans for the company's food service division. The Food Group assumed branding development for SuperPretzel, ICEE, Arctic Blast, Luigi's Italian Ices, Shape-ups, Tio Pepe's Churros, and Funnel Cake products manufactured by J & J Snack Foods.

By the end of 1997, J & J Snack Foods expanded its marketing to the global marketplace, establishing distribution of its pretzel products through the United Kingdom, the Pacific Rim, and Israel.

More New Developments

In addition to gains in the soft pretzel market, J & J Snack Foods also made strides in cookies and frozen beverages in 1996. J & J Snack Foods began supplying raw cookie dough to a major national retailer, and the company became the exclusive distributor in both North and South America for frozen carbonated beverages by IMI Cornelius, a beverage equipment supplier.

J & J Snack Foods continued expanding through acquisitions as well. In January 1997, the company purchased Chicago-based Mama Tish's International Foods, a manufacturer and distributor of frozen juice products such as Italian ices and sorbets. Expecting more than $15 million in annual sales from Mama Tish's products, Shreiber noted in a *Business Wire* release that "the combination of increased sales and other synergies should have long-term continued benefits" for J & J Snack Foods.

By the end of the year, J & J Snack Foods acquired the controlling interest in National ICEE Corporation. Headquartered in Philadelphia, National ICEE annually sold $40 million in frozen carbonated beverages to consumers in the eastern United States. The acquisition of National ICEE, Shreiber remarked in *Business Wire,* "represents an excellent opportunity to further develop the frozen beverage category and the ICEE brand on a national basis." "We are embarked on an ambitious program to integrate the National ICEE system into our ICEE-USA subsidiary company," Shreiber explained further. Indeed, this latest acquisition secured J & J Snack Foods' right to sell ICEE frozen beverages throughout the continental United States—to about 17,500 company-owned and customer-owned dispensers.

Future Plans

J & J Snack Foods' plans for the future at the end of 1997 included increased sales of all its product lines. For example, the company tested noncarbonated frozen beverages in an effort to appeal to more mature consumers. The company also changed the image and graphic design for ICEE products. According to an annual report, "this new image is one more example of how J & J Snack Foods is continually evolving to meet the needs of our ever-changing market."

Principal Subsidiaries

Bakers Best Snack Food Corporation; Bavarian Soft Pretzels Inc.; FCB America Corporation; ICEE-USA Corporation; J & J Snack Foods Corporation, Bakery Division (Vernon, California); Pretzels, Inc.

Further Reading

Abelson, Reed, "J & J Snack Foods," *Fortune,* June 19, 1989, p. 148.

"Acquisition," *Frozen Food Digest,* July 1994, p. 44.

"Corporate Profile for J & J Snack Foods Corporation, Dated March 7, 1997," *Business Wire,* March 7, 1997, p. 3070006.

"The Food Group," *ADWEEK* (Eastern edition), July 1, 1996, p. 25.

"J & J Foods Buys Funnel Cake Factory," *Nation's Restaurant News,* June 6, 1994, p. 74.

"J & J Opens Express Concept at Arena," *Nation's Restaurant News,* November 18, 1996, p. 50.

"J & J Snack Foods Acquires Mama Tish's," *Nation's Restaurant News,* March 10, 1997, p. 128.

"J & J Snack Foods Acquires National ICEE," *Business Wire,* December 9, 1997, p. 12090037.

"J & J Snack Foods Announces Major Sales Expansion with National Retailer," *Business Wire,* December 6, 1996, p. 12061020.

"J & J Snack Foods Corporation Acquires Bakers Best," *Business Wire,* October 3, 1996, p. 10030096.

"J & J Snack Foods Corporation Acquires Mama Tish's International Foods," *Business Wire,* January 27, 1997, p. 1271318.

"J & J Snack Foods Corporation Acquires Mazzone Enterprises," *Business Wire,* May 21, 1996, p. 5211016.

"J & J Snack Foods Corporation Acquires Pretzels Inc.," *Business Wire,* November 14, 1996, p. 11141281.

"J & J Snack Foods Corporation Acquires Specialty Pretzel Retailer," *Business Wire,* April 17, 1996, p. 4170048.

"J & J Snack Foods Taps Food Group," *Nation's Restaurant News,* June 10, 1996, p. 112.

"Mergers and Acquisitions: J & J Snack Foods," *Food Institute Report,* June 3, 1996.

"Mergers and Acquisitions: J & J Snack Foods Corporation, Pennsauken, Pennsylvania," *Food Institute Report,* January 27, 1997.

"Mergers and Acquisitions: J & J Snack Foods Corporation, Pennsauken, Pennsylvania, Has Acquired the Assets of Bakers Best," *Food Institute Report,* October 7, 1996.

Palmeri, Christopher, " 'Discover, Salvage, and Build!' " *Forbes,* November 11, 1991, p. 236.

"SuperPretzel Cinnamon Raisin Minis," *Product Alert,* March 25, 1996.

—Charity Anne Dorgan

Jerry's Famous Deli Inc.

12711 Ventura Blvd., Suite 400
Studio City, California 91604
U.S.A.
(818) 766-8311
Fax: (818) 766-8315
Web site: http://www.jerrysdeli.com

Public Company
Founded: 1978
Employees: 1,530
Sales: $56.4 million (1997)
Stock Exchanges: NASDAQ
Ticker Symbol: DELI
SICs: 5812 Eating Places

Jerry's Famous Deli Inc. is known as the number one consolidator of independent delicatessens and restaurants in the United States. In 1998, the company operated ten facilities in the states of California (mostly in southern California) and Florida under the three names of Jerry's Famous Deli, Solley's Delicatessen and Bakery, and Rascal House.

Re-creating the nostalgic ambience of restaurants in Manhattan's theater district, Jerry's Famous Deli, whose motto is "Where food and people mix," has restaurants which operate 24 hours a day, seven days a week. With more than 700 items on their extensive menu, all of which are available for takeout, delivery, and catering, as well as eating in-house, anything one wants to eat can probably be found there.

The company was founded in 1978 with the opening of its Studio City, California, restaurant. Three additional facilities were opened in 1989, 1991, and 1994, with two additional restaurants being opened in February and June 1996. Two more restaurants (Solley's) were acquired as of June 1996, and one additional restaurant (Rascal House) was acquired in September 1996. Another Jerry's Famous Deli restaurant was opened in August 1997.

Guess Who's Coming to Dinner?: The Early Years, 1978–94

The first Jerry's Famous Deli restaurant debuted in Studio City, California, on November 1, 1978, where it has since attracted a wide-ranging loyal customer following of residents and those who work in the nearby area, including the adjoining movie and television studios.

The company's first expansion from its Studio City roots came more than a decade later when, in July 1989, the company acquired a facility in Encino, California. Following one of the company's four strategies for growth, the previously existing eatery was converted into a Jerry's Famous Deli restaurant, and managed to triple its annual revenues very quickly. The Encino restaurant was owned and operated in 1998 through JFD-Encino, a limited partnership of which a wholly owned subsidiary of the company is an 80 percent general partner, with California-based Valley Deli Inc. making up the other 20 percent of the partnership. The general partners receive a management fee equal to three percent of the gross revenues of the Encino restaurant, as well as being allocated 25 percent of net profits, net gains, and distributions of JFD-Encino until such time as the limited partners have received cash distributions equal to 100 percent of their contributed capital plus an amount equal to 10 percent per annum of their capital contribution. Jerry's Famous Deli is also a 7.55 percent limited partner in the agreement. From its inception in April 1981, through December 1994, Isaac Starkman owned Jerry's Famous Deli L.A. Inc., the co-general partner of JFD-Encino. In January of the following year, Starkman contributed the shares of JFD-LA to Jerry's Famous Deli Inc. for no additional consideration.

Two years (almost to the day) later, in July 1991, the company made its first foray outside the San Fernando Valley area, opening a location in Marina del Rey, California. A second high-profile location restaurant opened its doors three years later, in January 1994, when the company set up shop in West Hollywood, near Beverly Hills, across the street from the famous Beverly Center and Cedars-Sinai Hospital. Adjoining, and operated as a part of, the West Hollywood restaurant is a private bar and cigar lounge called Guy's Place, which opened at the end of September 1995.

Company Perspectives:

Jerry's Famous Deli Inc. continues to search for prime locations appropriate for its customer base and to develop them into restaurants, both in the Southern California and Southern Florida areas, as well as new areas, while continuing to provide quality food and service in its existing restaurants.

In 1994, after the company catered a private function for the cast, crew, and guests of the successful "Frasier" television show, several persons complained of food poisoning symptoms and filed claims against the company. Jerry's Famous Deli, believing that the claims made against it were without merit, together with the company's insurance carrier, contested the legal action, which was slated to go to trial in early 1998.

DELI-cious: Going Public, 1995

In January 1995, the company acquired a subsidiary called Pizza by the Pound Inc., owned by Isaac Starkman and one other partner, which operated a 2,300-square-foot pizza restaurant in Sherman Oaks, California, called Jerry's Famous Pizza. But, feeling the restaurant was not in line with the company's growth direction, in June of that same year the company ceased operations at the pizza parlor.

Also that year, in October, Jerry's Famous Deli Inc. became a publicly traded company, listed on the NASDAQ under the symbol "DELI." Total revenue for the company that year reached $28 million, with a net income of $782,234.

On a (Sesame Seed?) Roll, 1996–Date

Proceeds from the successful initial public offering helped the company expand very quickly in 1996, as it more than doubled the number of restaurants it operated. The four original Jerry's Famous Deli restaurants were joined by two new locations in California: in Old Pasadena (opened February 1996) and in Westwood (June 1996) within a matter of a few months. The Westwood restaurant building and adjacent parking spaces and parking lots, were leased from The Starkman Family Partnership, a business entity controlled by Isaac Starkman, who is also the chairman and CEO of Jerry's Famous Deli Inc. His two sons, Guy and Jason, also served as vice-presidents in the company.

The elder Starkman had been involved in the restaurant industry prior to his work with Jerry's Famous Deli. In November 1984, Starkman founded a casual dining establishment called Starky's, which combined a deli operation with a pizza parlor and a video game arcade at the top of The Beverly Center in Beverly Hills, California. Due to the facility's lack of street visibility, its location in an enclosed shopping mall that itself had a limited range of hours of operation, and numerous problems with hygienic conditions at the mall which were outside of Starky's staff's control, the restaurant did not do as well as was expected, and its doors were closed in December 1992.

Also in July 1996, the company acquired two delicatessen restaurants operating under the name "Solley's Delicatessen and Bakery" for approximately $2.3 million. The locations were in southern California, one in Sherman Oaks and one in Woodland Hills. The company, following the growth strategy of buying existing eateries, converted the neighborhood favorite in Sherman Oaks into the Jerry's Famous Deli restaurant concept, and reported annual revenue at that location as having increased from $3.6 million to $5.8 million after its reopening in December 1996. The Woodland Hills location remained a Solley's Delicatessen and Bakery.

In August 1996, the company needed to raise more capital for future growth. Pursuing this, Jerry's Famous Deli entered into an agreement with Waterton Management LLC, Yucaipa Waterton Deli Investors LLC, and Jerry's Investors LLC, eventually raising approximately $5.5 million from the sale of preferred stocks to those entities.

Yet a third strategy employed by the company for growth, acquiring existing restaurants and improving its operations, was put into effect when the company bought the venerable landmark restaurant Wolfie Cohen's Rascal House in September 1996. Jerry's Famous Deli purchased the 42-year-old restaurant following the death of Arthur Goodman, one of the principals of the facility. The 450-seat Miami Beach, Florida-based delicatessen restaurant, which was purchased for nearly $5 million, already was a high-volume restaurant, with well-known brand names and a strong and loyal customer base. The acquisition of the restaurant was the company's first outside of the state of California. With the purchase, the company also acquired the experienced store management and personnel, began accepting credit cards at the facility for the first time in its history, and increased the annual revenue at the location from $7.7 million to $10 million in one year.

In a move to expand revenue, the company in the latter part of 1996 began marketing its expansive menu in a catering business, available via a number of its locations. Following the December 1996 opening of the Woodland Hills restaurant, some customers were drawn away from the nearby Encino and Pasadena facilities. To combat this, the company created a banquet room at the Encino restaurant, and the "Take Out" area was expanded. Marketing efforts were also stepped up at the Old Pasadena restaurant. The company's total revenue for the year reached $40.2 million, with a net income of $578,713.

In March 1997, Kenneth Abdalla, an outside consultant, was given the mantle of president on an interim basis, with the specific objective of assisting in the execution of the company's acquisition and expansion strategy, through December 1998.

Several months later, in June 1997, the company introduced "Early Bird Specials" dinners (offered daily prior to 6:00 p.m. at approximately a 40 percent discount from the normal retail price) to its southern California restaurants, following in the footsteps of the Sherman Oaks facility, which had previously offered them, marginally increasing revenue for the entire restaurant chain.

With Abdalla arriving on the scene to help the company expand, in August 1997 a Jerry's Famous Deli restaurant was opened in Costa Mesa, California. Located in the heart of southern California's posh Orange County area, situated near the megamall complex of The South Coast Plaza, this facility followed the company's first strategy for growth, which was developing "model Jerry's restaurants from scratch."

The fourth part of the company's expansion strategy focuses on clustered growth, exploiting the benefits of its well-known brand names, which is what the company has done with Wolfie Cohen's Rascal House name in south Florida, in addition to expanding the Jerry's Famous Deli name in southern California.

By 1997, Jerry's Famous Deli was following in the footsteps of other successful companies, such as Marina del Rey, California-based Cheesecake Factory Inc. (trading in 1997 at 35 times estimated 1996 earnings), McDonald's Corp. (trading in 1997 at 22 times estimated 1996 earnings), and Wichita, Kansas-based Lone Star Steakhouse & Saloon (trading in 1997 at 25 times estimated 1996 earnings). Total company revenue for 1997 climbed to $56.4 million, with a net income of $563,170.

In January 1998, the company announced the establishment of a wholly owned subsidiary for the company's Florida operations, planning expansion in that state.

The company also announced that month the planned acquisition of a gourmet food store called The Epicure Market Inc., owned by brothers Harry and Mitchell Thal, located in Miami Beach, Florida. The acquisition was completed in April of that year, with the company paying $7.1 million in cash, in addition to nearly a million shares of the company's common stock. The company was planning for The Epicure Market to increase the interior sales area, install additional seating for in-house dining patrons, increase the store's hours of operation, and expand overall operations to include delivery, catering, and home meal replacement. The Epicure Market was owned and operated by the Thal brothers and their family for more than 50 years, and the two brothers agreed to remain on the company's staff as co-managers of The Epicure Market for an initial term of five years under new employment agreements, along with all 150 employees.

Also in January of that year, the company acquired a lease on an 11,000-square-foot restaurant property in Boca Raton, Florida, where the company opened a new Wolfie Cohen's Rascal House in the summer of 1998 after renovations on the existing facility were completed.

By mid-1998, the company was poised for future growth, with the leading industry trade magazine *Restaurant News* noting that, "Jerry's is one of the few deli concepts to grow into a multi-unit operation of any note," and, in its rankings of national restaurant chains in July 1997, Jerry's Famous Deli was ranked as the Number One Deli Growth Chain and the Number Two Unit Growth Chain for 1996. By mid-May 1998, all of the company's facilities, which had been inspected by The Los Angeles County Department of Public Health regarding requirements for food preparation, handling, and storage, had received an "A" rating, the highest rating possible for the restaurant industry.

Knowing that the existing restaurants can not show substantial growth in per-restaurant revenues, the management believes that any significant sales growth will have to come from additional restaurants. Therefore, the company continues to search for prime locations appropriate for its customer base and to develop them into restaurants, both in the southern California and southern Florida areas, as well as new areas such as Las Vegas and New Orleans, while continuing to provide quality food and service in its existing restaurants.

Principal Subsidiaries

JFD-Encino (80%); Pizza by the Pound Inc.

Further Reading

Cole, Mark Benjamin, "Jerry's Deli Stock Does Not Sit Well with Some," *Los Angeles Business Journal*, May 27, 1996, p. 7.

"Jerry's Famous Deli Inc.," *Wall Street Journal*, May 19, 1998, p. B14(W)/B19(E).

"Jerry's Famous Earnings Down 26% for 9 Months," *Nation's Restaurant News*, January 20, 1997, p. 12.

"Jerry's Famous Eyes Rascal House," *Nation's Restaurant News*, August 26, 1996, p. 66.

"Jerry's Famous to Acquire 2 Solley's Restaurants," *Nation's Restaurant News*, May 20, 1996, p. 208.

"Jerry's Plans Changes for Rascal House," *Nation's Restaurant News*, September 30, 1996, p. 22.

"Jerry's Posts Gains in 3rd-Q Profits, Sales," *Nation's Restaurant News*, November 24, 1997, p. 12.

—Daryl F. Mallett

Jervis B. Webb Company

34375 West Twelve Mile Road
Farmington Hills, Michigan 48331-5624
U.S.A.
(248) 553-1220
Fax: (248) 553-1228
Web site: http://www.jervisbwebb.com

Private Company
Incorporated: 1919
Employees: 2,300
Sales: $300 million (1997 est.)
SICs: 3535 Conveyors & Conveying Equipment

Jervis B. Webb Company is the one of the world's leading designers, manufacturers, and installers of custom material handling systems. Founded in 1919, the company has been at the forefront of innovations in material handling since the inception of the industry. Jervis B. Webb's 34 operations worldwide supply integrated material handling systems to a multitude of industries including airline, aluminum, automotive, transportation, warehousing, primary metals, chemicals, publishing, and waste management.

Company Origins in the Early 20th Century

Jervis B. Webb Company was founded in 1919 in Detroit, Michigan, by Jervis Bennett Webb, a young mechanical engineer. While working for the Johns-Manville Company in the Pennsylvania coal fields, Webb had modified a forged chain used in anthracite mining operations for use as a conveyor of industrial equipment. Realizing the potential of this chain for the assembly line production that was beginning to reshape American industry in the early 20th century, Webb set out to reduce the 30 pounds per foot weight of the chain and to adapt it for assembly line use. The resulting rivetless, forged chain, dubbed the ''Keystone'' chain because of its Pennsylvania origins, could go from slack to taut quickly without breaking yet could be taken apart and assembled by hand, making it more versatile than a traditional riveted chain.

It was the automobile industry that led the way in the development of the assembly line method of production and it was to this industry that Webb turned to try to sell his new invention. Although Ford had been using a line process to construct his Model T since 1908, in these early plants men had manually pulled the automobile chassis along the assembly line with a rope while assembly workers had added the necessary parts. Powered by a motor, Webb's Keystone chain, installed on the floor, was attached to four wheeled carts that carried the chassis along the line. In 1920 Webb received his first order for the new conveyor system from the Studebaker Automobile Company. Although the mechanized system increased the speed and efficiency of manufacture, the permanently installed, floor-laid chain impeded movement through the plant and made it difficult to get maximum usage out of the available floor space. Intent on selling his system to the larger automakers like Ford, Webb hit upon the idea of taking the chain off of the floor and mounting it overhead. This would free up valuable floor space, allow greater access to the automobile, and provide more freedom of movement for workers. Webb sold the first version of his overhead conveyor to the Fisher Body Company in Detroit in 1921.

Although Ford expressed interest in Webb's idea, the $14 per foot price tag for installation of the system was prohibitive. Convinced of the value of the overhead conveyor, Webb devised a system of I-beams to carry the Keystone chain. The chain, powered by a caterpillar drive, would pull the automobile chassis along the line by means of simple trolleys which themselves hung on the I-beams by roller skate wheels. The simplicity of this design and its use of readily available, inexpensive hardware reduced the price of the system to $3 per foot, making it economical for use in larger plants. In 1922, Henry Ford agreed to install the new conveyor system in his Walkerville, Ontario, Canada engine and transmission manufacturing plant. Following the success of this trial installation, Ford signed a contract with the Jervis B. Webb Company to supply 30 miles of overhead conveyors to be installed in Ford plants across the

Company Perspectives:

Our company was founded in 1919 by Jervis B. Webb, an engineer who developed the forged rivetless chain conveyor. This invention revolutionized the automotive industry and was the first in a long continuous line of Webb Company innovations. Our mission is to engineer, manufacture, and install material handling systems that increase productivity, improve product quality, and provide production flexibility—all while decreasing lead time and inventory requirements.

United States and Canada. This purchase transformed the company from a small innovative engineering firm to a major manufacturer of material handling systems.

In order to accommodate the demands of the Ford order, Webb purchased land on Alpine Avenue in Detroit where he built a large manufacturing complex. By the end of the decade the Jervis B. Webb Company had established itself as a major force in the growing field of mass production technology. Webb became the holder of a number of patents that were crucial to the development of the material handling industry, including the trolley system for the overhead power conveyor, the caterpillar drive motor for continuous conveyor systems, and the multi-powered equalizing drive that was necessary to maintain smooth flow through in-plant production operations.

Growth and New Applications in the 1930s and 1940s

By the 1930s Webb's overhead conveyor had become the most widely used system in the automobile industry. While the invention had the advantage of freeing up the factory floor, a snafu at one part of the line would cause jamming further along and new production patterns required a major overhaul of the conveyor system. In 1939, in order to solve these problems, Webb introduced the power and free conveyor, a system that was to revolutionize the material handling industry. The power and free conveyor was a dual track system that retained the continuously moving overhead trolley but added a channel track below to carry free trolleys. The powered overhead trolleys pushed the free trolleys by means of downward protruding rods that met upward protruding dogs mounted on the free trolleys. The free trolleys could be easily detached from the overhead powered system, making it possible to divert loads without shutting down the entire system. The floor track was laid flush to allow free movement across the factory floor. The flexibility of the power and free model meant that the system could accommodate unbalanced operations and could allow material to recirculate. In addition the system could be expanded or reworked easily to meet changing production requirements. By the end of the next decade Webb's power and free system was in use in virtually every automotive assembly plant in the United States and Canada.

In 1938 Jervis B. Webb suffered a breakdown in health and his sons Jervis C. and George Webb took on much of the responsibility for management of the company, although Jervis B. retained the title of chairman until his death in 1952. Like most American industry, the Jervis B. Webb Company flourished during World War II. The Webb plants worked 12 hours a day, 7 days a week throughout the war to produce the large number of conveyor systems that were needed to manufacture war-related products.

With the experience gained during the war in the design of conveyor systems for a variety of non-automotive products, the company began after the war to look outside the auto industry for new customers. The company's first major non-automotive project was the design of a material handling system to carry logs from the river to the pulp mill for the Macon Kraft Company's pulp and paper mill in Georgia. This was the forerunner of a number of heavy load, bulk applications designed by the company, most notably the handling of coal in power generation facilities.

In 1948 the Jervis B. Webb Company entered the warehousing/distribution industry with the introduction of the Towveyor floor tow-line conveying system. The Towveyor was used to move individually loaded four wheel carts automatically on a fixed path. Webb's Keystone chain was set into fabricated channels and powered by Webb's caterpillar drive system. The carts were equipped with a steel probe which automatically engaged the moving chain when slipped into the track. The track itself was installed flush with the floor surface to allow free movement of traffic across the warehouse floor. The economical Towveyor system, installed first at the Crown Zellerback Company warehouse in California, was a huge success and became the basis for a line of automatic conveying products that remained one of the mainstays of the company's business for the next half century.

The late 1940s and early 1950s was a period of expansion for the Detroit-based company, now under the management of the second generation of Webbs. In 1949 the growth of industrialization in the western United States spurred the company to form the Jervis B. Webb Company of California, a full service facility that provided engineering, fabrication, installation, and service for Webb's full line of conveyors and material handling systems. In the same year a similar full service facility, Jervis B. Webb Company of Canada, was opened to serve the Canadian market; a southern affiliate, the Jervis B. Webb Company of Georgia, followed in 1955.

With the increasing role of electronic automation used in the Jervis B. Webb conveyor systems, the company decided to form a separate subsidiary to handle the engineering of control systems for industry. The Control Engineering Company, founded in 1949, became the source not only for the controls of Webb conveyor systems but also for a variety of other industrial processing controls. Five years later it became apparent that the electrical engineering on these control systems was a specialized sub-component that merited its own division and the Webb Electric Company was formed.

In 1951 the company made its first venture outside of the materials handling industry with the formation of the Webb Forging Company, a facility that was to provide a consistent source for close tolerance forgings for Webb and other conveyor manufacturers. In a 1985 interview with *Management Review,* Jervis C. Webb reflected on the challenges of this first foray outside of the business he had grown up with. "We bought equipment and buildings and added people. The trouble was that we added *our* people. It took us six months to discover that forging was a business in itself. So we got the people who knew the business—and then we prospered."

It was also in the early 1950s that the Jervis B. Webb Company began to reach out to the international market with the formation of the Jervis B. Webb International Company. Company management made the decision to enter the international arena through 20-year licensing agreements with foreign manufacturers. In a 1985 interview with *Oakland Business Monthly* Jervis C. Webb commented on the company's international strategy: "At the time, when we went into this method [of licensing], rather than trying to build subsidiaries or joint ventures or that sort of thing, the overriding reason we did it was because we didn't have the money to do otherwise. And we were told that they would very easily think that once they got our know-how, why renew for another 20 years or why even continue to the end of 20? But it hasn't happened that way, which I think is a compliment to our showing progress all through this whole period." The company's international operations flourished, with long-term licensing agreements contracted in 18 countries by the 1990s.

Further Diversification in the 1960s and 1970s

Jervis B. Webb Company continued to diversify into nonautomotive applications through the 1960s and 1970s. In the late 1950s the company had engineered an experimental bulk mail sorter for the Detroit Post Office and, following the success of this venture, was awarded the contract for the first fully automated U.S. Post Office in Providence, Rhode Island. Over the next 10 years Webb was responsible for the design of sorting systems for almost half of the major postal facilities in the United States, as well as a substantial number abroad.

In addition to applying the company's conveyor technology to new industries, Webb introduced new product lines. In the early 1960s the company came out with a line of Automatic Guided Vehicles (AGVs) that would eventually be sold to a variety of industries, including storage warehouses, the armed services, airlines, and health care. These AGVs were driverless vehicles that could be guided over relatively long distances by means of low frequency signals transmitted through in-floor guidepath wires. One unconventional application for these vehicles was their use in hospitals where they delivered food and medication to patients' rooms on a set schedule. More typically they were used in industrial applications in which material throughput and distance traveled did not warrant a conveyor or where distances were too long for efficient use of fork trucks.

Another major new arena for the Jervis B. Webb Company in the 1970s was the development of automated storage and retrieval systems. These systems became increasingly desirable through the 1980s and 1990s as just-in-time manufacturing demanded careful control over inventory and storage. The company's presence in this field was augmented in 1977 with the acquisition of the Triax Company of Cleveland, Ohio, the company that pioneered automatic storage and retrieval in the 1950s.

Computerization in the 1980s and 1990s

The most important development in material handling through the last quarter of this century was the advent of computerization. Jervis B. Webb Company entered this field comparatively early with the 1967 purchase of the Ann Arbor Computer Corporation, a company that had been instrumental in Jervis B. Webb's design of the first computerized material handling system some two years earlier. This subsidiary would design computerized control systems for the company's material handling equipment including its storage and retrieval systems and AGVs. In the late 1980s Ann Arbor Computer developed a very successful automatic personal computer-operated inventory management system, called PC AIM, that allowed companies to integrate data management from every level of operation.

Largely in response to the introduction of robotics in automotive assembly, the overhead power and free system that had been the mainstay of the Jervis B. Webb line for decades was literally turned upside down in the mid-1980s. The company's inverted power and free system used a pedestal carrier installed on a floor conveyor, allowing greater access to the vehicle for robotic assembly equipment. Jervis C. Webb commented on the new system in a 1985 interview with *Management Review*: "Dad would turn over in his grave, but I think he would understand the wave of the future and approve of what we were doing."

Jervis B. Webb Company remained a family run company through the late 1990s. As Jervis C. and George Webb reached retirement age, a third generation of Webbs appeared ready to replace them in the top management positions. Out of its new world headquarters in Farmington Hills, Michigan, the company ran 15 operations in the United States and Canada, four international manufacturing operations (in England, Australia, India, and China) and 13 licensees in locations around the world. The annual performance of this intensely private company is difficult to gauge but its leadership position in the American materials handling industry appears solidly entrenched.

Principal Subsidiaries

Jervis B. Webb Company of Georgia; Ann Arbor Computer; Control Engineering Company; Webb-Triax Company; Webb Electric Company; Webb Forging Company; Webb-Materials Handling Equipment; Jervis B. Webb Company of Canada, Ltd.; Jervis B. Webb Company, Ltd. (U.K.); Webb-Conveyor Company of Australia Pty. Ltd.; Europa Engineering Ltd. (U.K.); Webb India Ltd.; Chengde-Webb Conveyors Machinery Company Ltd. (China).

Further Reading

Berry, Bryan H., "IPF Fuels Webb Growth in Detroit," *Iron Age (Manufacturing Management Edition),* July 5, 1985, pp. 50–51.

Delaney, Robert, "Jervis C. Webb: Building Assembly Lines Since the Beginning," *Oakland Business Monthly,* August 1985, pp. 49–57.

Edson, Lee, "Webb's Abstract Style; The Gorey Details," *Management Review,* March 1985, pp. 14–15.

Harvey, Robert E., "Jervis Webb Takes Beachhead in Custom Networking," *Metalworking News,* October 31, 1988, p. 36.

Howard, Lisa S., "Material Handling Industry Optimistic," *Journal of Commerce and Commercial,* February 12, 1982, p. 3A.

Inglesby, Tom, "Material Handling—Present and Future," *Manufacturing Systems,* February 1989, pp. 28–32.

Manji, James F., "Jervis B. Webb Looks Ahead," *Automation,* January 1989, pp. 34–36.

Melloan, George, "Keeping Things Simple in a Big Family Enterprise," *Wall Street Journal,* August 29, 1989, p. 17A.

Moskal, Brian S., "Material Handling Eyes the World," *Industry Week,* November 10, 1980, pp. 60–63.

Pierson, Robert A., "Controls Make the Difference," *Manufacturing Systems,* June 1985, pp. 16–20.

—Hilary Gopnik

John Paul Mitchell Systems

9701 Wilshire Boulevard
Beverly Hills, California 90209
U.S.A.
(310) 276-7957
Fax: (310) 248-2780

Private Company
Incorporated: 1980
Employees: 89
Sales: $165 million (1996)
SICs: 2844 Toilet Preparations

A recognized leader in the beauty industry, John Paul Mitchell Systems markets more than 35 different haircare products in 29 countries, selling its products exclusively at authorized hair salons. John Paul Mitchell, a celebrated hairstylist, and John Paul DeJoria, a struggling salesman, founded John Paul Mitchell Systems in 1980. Together, until Mitchell's death in 1989, the two men shaped their entrepreneurial creation into a market winner, succeeding through Mitchell's haircutting demonstrations, DeJoria's renowned marketing skills, and the company's signature Awapuhi shampoo, made from Hawaiian ginger root. John Paul Mitchell Systems used a three-stage marketing system to drive its sales in the late 1990s. The company shipped its haircare products to distributors who delivered the merchandise to hair salons where consumers purchased the company's products, all packaged in white bottles with black lettering. John Paul Mitchell Systems distributor-to-salon-to-consumer approach has been credited for much of the company's success.

Backgrounds of the Founders

The simple black-and-white packaging of John Paul Mitchell Systems' products reflects the start-up's modest beginnings and the starkness belies the colorful personalities behind the company. From its outset, John Paul Mitchell Systems was a unique enterprise started and stewarded by unconventional corporate leaders, a characterization from which John Paul Mitchell and John Paul Jones DeJoria did not shirk and even embraced. DeJoria and particularly Mitchell had enjoyed success in their careers before starting John Paul Mitchell Systems, but both were, for different reasons, at turning points in their lives, and John Paul Mitchell Systems represented a way forward, a vehicle to disengage them from the past.

Born in Scotland, Mitchell grew up during the 1940s in London, where his father was employed as chief engineer at Buckingham Palace. In London, Mitchell pursued a career decidedly unlike his father's, becoming one of the city's flamboyant hair stylists. Studying under the tutelage of the famed Vidal Sasson, Mitchell became one of the most sought after hair stylists in London during the early 1960s, earning the esteem of the city's "swinging" high society. His rise to the ephemeral top of the salon scene was fueled in large part by the dozens of traveling clinics he conducted. He transformed haircutting presentations into artistic performances, which entertained and attracted clientele and cast Mitchell in the spotlight as an indefatigable showman.

By the mid-1970s, Mitchell was, in his own words, "one of the most recognized hair artists in the world" and profoundly disenchanted by his own success. Life in the limelight had disagreed with him and he was "totally burned out on the whole success trip." To distance himself from the flash and frenetic pace of working as a "hair artist," Mitchell went into seclusion. He decided to live his life according to a new philosophy. The new lifestyle he eagerly embraced would one day underpin the philosophy of John Paul Mitchell Systems itself.

To lose himself from the hair-styling crowd, Mitchell moved to Hawaii in 1975. There, he struggled to find a new perspective on life, a new course for his future. "For nearly a year," Mitchell remembered, "I lived in a one-room beach shack, doing nothing but yoga, meditation, and vegetarianism. Hawaii healed me." On those few occasions when the hairdresser accepted visitors, Swami Muktananda, an Eastern mystic, was his company of choice.

As Mitchell was experiencing life as a tropical-bound, soul-searching recluse, his future business partner was on an entirely different path. His experiences, too, would have considerable influence on the personality of John Paul Mitchell Systems.

Unlike Mitchell's prolific rise to stardom and success during his years before the formation of John Paul Mitchell Systems, John Paul Jones DeJoria spent his years before the company's creation desperately trying to climb the rungs of success—and quite frequently losing his purchase. Ten years Mitchell's junior, DeJoria was a Los Angeles native who left the U.S. Navy in 1964 to enroll in dental school. His plans for dental school were scotched, however, when he was unable to raise the tuition money, forcing him in a different career direction altogether. DeJoria began selling encyclopedias, then he switched to selling copying machines. Insurance became his next focal point as a salesman, a door-to-door job that lasted three months. Next, he sold medical linens, but nothing seemed to work for the young DeJoria. By age 26, he was ready to have a go at the publishing business, and landed a job at Time, Inc. as a sales manager. DeJoria's stay at Time came to an abrupt end when he remarked to his bosses that his office would be more productive if he was permitted to raise commissions and thereby devote less time to supervising his sales force.

Forced to find another job, DeJoria was at a crossroads in his selling career. "I suppose the reason the jobs lasted such a short time," he later mused, "was that I didn't like what I was selling." DeJoria's next job, however, introduced him to products he did enjoy selling. The one constant thread—sales—that ran through an otherwise erratic career life intersected with the world in which Mitchell excelled. DeJoria joined the ranks of the haircare industry.

With the help of a friend who worked at an employment agency, DeJoria secured an interview at Redken Laboratories in 1971. Redken, a pioneer in the distribution of shampoo through hair salons, was a member of a business society tailored to the tastes of DeJoria. "I saw all these salesman in beautiful Italian suits," a friend of DeJoria's remarked, "and I knew it was the place for John." DeJoria quickly affirmed his friend's appraisal, rising in a short time to rank as one of Redken's top salespeople. Generating $1,000 in sales a day, DeJoria leaped up the corporate ladder at Redken, becoming a sales manager within six months, and after 18 months, was appointed national manager of the company's schools and training salons. However, DeJoria then hit a brick wall. "They said I wasn't a businessman," DeJoria later explained, "that I had gone as far as I could." Remaining in the beauty business after his departure from Redken, DeJoria served two more stints as a salesman for beauty products companies, with one job ending when he found himself in the untenable position of "making more money than the guy that owned the company." By 1980, DeJoria was ready for a new challenge and yet in need of constancy, searching for a career opportunity that would enable him to use his talent as a salesman to its full advantage.

Founding and Rapid Growth

In 1980, DeJoria was in Hawaii and there became reacquainted with Mitchell. The two had met for the first time nine years earlier. "It's a show-business industry," DeJoria explained, "and Paul [Mitchell] and I crossed paths often." Each looking to move in a new direction, DeJoria and Mitchell decided to start a business together, with Mitchell cast as the hair-products expert and DeJoria as the marketing expert. The partners pooled their resources and came up with $700—a paltry sum to launch a new enterprise—but neither was disheartened by the modest start. In fact, Mitchell and DeJoria were invigorated by the prospects of a new beginning and hoped to create a business fundamentally different from any other in existence. With the formation of John Paul Mitchell Systems, Mitchell and DeJoria created a business vehicle to express their unique perspectives, a corporate megaphone that each would use to articulate his personal philosophy.

Considering the precarious financial foundation Mitchell and DeJoria stood on when they embarked on their business plan, any means of saving money was searched for and embraced. The need to get the business up and running for under $1,000 led to two money-saving alternatives in particular that would distinguish the company in the years to come. First, the partners decided to use generic white bottles with black lettering as their packaging, a move that saved them a considerable amount of money and, as it turned out, served as an effective marketing tool years later when the company was collecting more than $100 million in sales a year. The second money-saving decision was more ingenious, a move that enabled Mitchell and DeJoria to realize their entrepreneurial dream shortly after they hatched their business plan. Instead of underwriting the cost of a production facility, they convinced a small Los Angeles-based hair- and skincare maker named Star Laboratories Inc. to produce their products for them. By sub-contracting production, Mitchell and DeJoria were able to begin producing and marketing John Paul Mitchell Systems products before the end of 1980, saving much-needed cash for the development of their shampoo and other haircare products.

Every dollar saved by cutting corners wherever possible was invested in developing new products, including shampoo that featured the ginger plant Awapuhi. The investment paid large dividends quickly, as John Paul Mitchell Systems shampoo became a best seller. To market the company's products, DeJoria drew on the approach he had witnessed at Redken, selling John Paul Mitchell Systems products only through professional salons. At first, Mitchell performed haircutting presentations in individual salons, then DeJoria remained behind after the show was finished, vowing not to leave until the last bottle of John Paul Mitchell Systems product was sold. Moving from salon to salon in this way, Mitchell and DeJoria traveled throughout Hawaii, scoring considerable success and creating a stable foundation for their fledgling enterprise. Once the pair had firmly established themselves in Hawaii, they were ready to make the leap to the mainland, where sales of the company's haircare products would flourish.

The overwhelming initial success of the company stood conventional wisdom on its head. Traditional corporate leaders and industry observers may have smirked at the small and lean upstart coming out of Hawaii, but by the early 1980s no one could ignore the explosive growth of the company. This was even more true by the mid-1980s, after expansion had taken the company as far away as China, where John Paul Mitchell Systems products were introduced in late 1986. John Paul Mitchell Systems was a corporate phenomenon, operating with a small staff, little overhead, and capable of generating $5 million in sales a month. In 1986, the company ranked 71st in *Inc.* magazine's top 500 companies, with sales hovering at the $100 million mark. Despite this, there were only 27 employees on the company's corporate payroll. The true personnel strength of the company was elsewhere, vested in the 34 distributors scattered throughout the United States, the seven distributors operating overseas, and primarily in the 350 John Paul Mitchell Systems Associates—the hairstylists who promoted the company's products by giving demonstrations at beauty schools and hair shows. Mitchell, by this point, had settled into semi-retirement on Oahu, conducting the majority of his business from the porch above his hot tub. Although the company bore his name, Mitchell was beginning to recede from the day-to day affairs of the company, leaving DeJoria in full command. A personal tragedy two years later left no doubt as to who was in control of John Paul Mitchell Systems.

DeJoria in the 1990s

Mitchell was diagnosed with pancreatic cancer and died in 1989, stripping the company of one of its integral spiritual leaders. Despite the loss of Mitchell, the performance recorded by John Paul Mitchell Systems hardly missed a beat, as the company entered the 1990s with DeJoria firmly in control. In the early 1990s, DeJoria declared, ''I am the American dream,'' a living testament to the quintessential ''rags-to-riches'' story. Before entering into a partnership with Mitchell, DeJoria had relegated himself to living in a car, yet a decade later he stood atop an exceptionally successful company that was collecting more than $100 million in sales a year. Much of his success during the 1980s was attributable to his partnership with Mitch-

ell, whose marquee name enabled the company to make strides quickly, yet considerable credit went to DeJoria as well. His tireless marketing work created a consistent, long-term money earner, providing the framework that truly supported John Paul Mitchell Systems. As the 1990s progressed, the strength of this framework would be reflected in the continued success of the company.

By the late 1990s, as the company neared its 20th anniversary, John Paul Mitchell Systems continued to distinguish itself as a success story. With sales topping $150 million, the company reigned as a market leader, its 35 different products winning consumers over in 29 countries. The company's three-stage distributor-to-salon-to-consumer marketing system was heralded as the key to its success, convincing DeJoria, who presided as chairman and chief executive officer, that he would never market the company's products at the traditional, retail level. Instead, as the company prepared for the 21st century, it looked to the 700 Paul Mitchell Associate Hairstylists it relied on to fuel the success of the company in the years to come.

Further Reading

''John Paul Mitchell Systems: Teamwork Pays Off,'' *Drug & Cosmetic Industry,* August 1997, p. 22.
Palmeri, Christopher, ''Often Down But Never Out,'' *Forbes,* March 4, 1991, p. 138.

—Jeffrey L. Covell

John Q. Hammons Hotels, Inc.

300 John Q. Hammons Parkway
Suite 900
Springfield, Missouri 65806
U.S.A.
(417) 864-4300
Fax: (417) 864-8900

Public Company
Incorporated: 1969
Employees: 5,200
Sales: $302 million (1997)
Stock Exchanges: New York
Ticker Symbol: JQH
SICs: 7011 Hotels, Motels; 6552 Land Subdividers &
    Developers;
6719 Holding Companies

John Q. Hammons Hotels, Inc. owns and operates 45 full-service, upscale hotels across the United States. The majority of these hotels are franchised under license to Embassy Suites and Holiday Inn, but the company plans to open and manage many more hotels within the next 10 years, some under its own auspices. Designed to appeal to an extremely broad range of customers, including large groups, convention guests, frequent business travelers, leisure travelers, and senior citizens, the company has more than 10,000 rooms for occupancy at any given time. Bucking the trend toward limited service, inexpensive accommodations such as Motel 6, or Days Inn, John Q. Hammons Hotels emphasizes in-house restaurants, room service, and cocktail lounges, and focuses on what is termed secondary or tertiary markets, cities with populations between 100,000 to 300,000 that usually have a university, major airport, or corporate headquarters in them or nearby. In 1995, the company added the Radisson franchise; in 1996, it added the Marriott franchise; and in 1997, the firm developed two first class resorts, World Golf Village, in St. Augustine, Florida, and Chateau on the Lake, in Branson, Missouri.

Early History

The history of John Q. Hammons Hotels is inextricably interwoven with the fortunes and talent of one man, John Quentin Hammons. Hammons was born in 1920 in Fairview, Missouri. His father, an industrious and prosperous dairy farmer during the 1920s, provided his family with all the necessities of life, and then some. As John attended school during the later years of the decade, it appeared as if he were destined to follow in the footsteps of his father and become a dairy farmer.

Yet the stock market crash of 1929 and the coming of the Great Depression changed everything, including the direction of John Hammons's life. Social upheaval and economic chaos characterized the entire decade of the 1930s. Businesses across the United States went bankrupt, and many banks were unable to pay out the money individuals had deposited in their institutions. Suicides were not uncommon, especially among those entrepreneurs who gambled in the stock market and lost their entire holdings. Perhaps the most adversely affected of all the people across the nation, however, were the farmers. Due to an unusual drought across the plains states and the American Southwest, and the lack of proper crop rotating techniques, what was once one of the most fertile growing areas in the world became a dustbowl. Strong winds compounded the problem, eroding the topsoil, and many farmers were faced with both the loss of their farms and malnutrition of their families. Hammons's father was one numbered among these unfortunate people, and lost his dairy farm during the mid-1930s. John watched his father cry at night over the loss of the family farm, and the sight was seared into the young boy's memory.

The decade of the 1940s was no less disappointing to Hammons. Although his family recovered from the loss of the dairy farm, Hammons was determined to make his own fortune, but not in the farming business. In the late 1940s, Hammons started his own concrete concern, providing material to construction companies and development firms located in Missouri. Much to his dismay, the firm never prospered as he expected it would, and the young entrepreneur was forced to close down the operation. Avoiding bankruptcy by the thinnest of margins, Hammons admirably spent two years repaying all his creditors

Company Perspectives:

As always, our mission is to provide outstanding products, reasonable prices, and extra amenities to enrich our customers' experience. Our well-known "signature elements" including larger guest rooms, spectacular atriums, and top quality meeting room space are three additional amenities we offer to add more value to each guest's stay. By stressing superior customer service at every level, we earn the loyalty necessary to keep guests coming back.

and wiping out the remaining debt incurred by his venture into the concrete business.

Rise to Prominence

Determined not to fail again, Hammons carefully considered all his options and finally decided to enter into real estate development. Unlike his foray into the concrete business, however, Hammons approached this new enterprise with a more detailed look at the industry. Convinced that he could find a lucrative niche, Hammons began to study "Highway Houses," a chain of motels developed by one of the most well-known individuals within the real estate development market, Del Webb. Webb, an entrepreneur who focused on the West Coast of the United States, had built a motel chain empire. Webb's strategy was simple. During his era, street corners in both large cities and small towns across the country were occupied by either banking institutions or gas stations. Since these locations were highly visible, and easily located, Webb came up with the idea of purchasing the sites and building motels on them. Not long afterward, many street corners throughout the western part of the nation had inexpensive, budget motels on them. Not only did this idea garner large amounts of money for Webb, but it stimulated a tourist trade that brought additional and unexpected revenue to many of the western states. Soon Webb had numerous competitors, and the budget motel became a piece of western Americana.

With his homework completed, Hammons negotiated a loan from a local investor and entered the real estate development market. Still situated in Missouri, Hammons did not immediately jump into the motel or hotel business, but bided his time and built up his operation by constructing subsidized housing projects and a wide variety of duplex homes in the growing suburbs around Springfield, Missouri. Even though colleagues, financial advisers, friends, and industry analysts tried to convince him to enter the hotel business, he adamantly refused until he was ready. By the end of the 1950s, having built numerous housing projects and constructed duplex houses across the state, Hammons was a millionaire. With a secure financial base, and an astute management team around him, Hammons finally decided it was time to go into the hotel business.

In 1959, Hammons established a partnership with Roy Winegardner, a man who had worked in the building and construction, and real estate development industries for years. Hammons focused on making the financial arrangement for their deals, while Winegardner concentrated on the actual construction of the hotels. From the very beginning of their partnership, the two men worked well together, and their new enterprise grew rapidly. During the early 1960s, the partners purchased 10 Holiday Inn franchises, and built a number of the hotels in secondary or tertiary city markets across the United States. Their strategy was to build a high-quality, full-service hotel in a city which wanted to attract more business, for example. From his study of Del Webb, and the proliferation of too many budget motels on American street corners, Hammons was convinced that the full-service hotel concept was destined to succeed.

Growth and Transition

When Winegardner accepted an offer to become chairman of the Holiday Inn chain of hotels in 1969, Hammons formed his own company and continued in the same tradition. Unfortunately, Hammons hit a brick wall during the early 1970s. Countries that had been producing oil for years at low cost suddenly formed their own umbrella organization and increased the price of oil per barrel. An oil embargo hit the United States and, as a result, many real estate developers halted their planned construction of hotels since they thought there would not be enough money to keep the available rooms occupied. Not one to follow trends, Hammons kept building hotel after hotel. When the effects of the oil embargo ended, and people flocked back to stay at high-quality hotels, the buildings that Hammons had constructed were filled to capacity. By the end of the 1970s, Hammons had earned a reputation as one of the most courageous, determined, and shrewd men in the hotel business.

During the early 1980s, real estate developers gravitated toward building hotels in big cities, such as New York, Chicago, Los Angeles, Boston, and Washington, D.C. Not having done enough market research, however, by the mid-1980s these developers discovered that those cities were overwhelmed with surplus rooms. Consequently, many of them began to lose money, while some were even forced out of the business. In contrast, Hammons was expanding his hotel empire across the United States. By focusing on state capitols and university and college towns, Hammons was building a four or five-star hotel which enjoyed a distinct advantage over budget hotels in the area. Hammons correctly predicted that people would choose to stay at his high-quality hotel rather than a budget hotel, when his hotel was the nicest one in town. Not only statistics, but profits proved him correct. The regionalization of business also aided Hammons. Companies located in smaller cities and towns where a Hammons hotel was operating enabled their business associates to stay in big-city type suites, with all the amenities, at small-town prices. Hammons had found his niche, and developed his company into a multimillion dollar business.

The 1990s and Beyond

When the recession of 1990 hit the real estate development industry, particularly hotel construction, Hammons was well-prepared for the economic downturn. During the mid- and late 1980s, a large number of American cities received federal grants to build convention centers. Due to the recession, however, there was no one to develop and build the hotels that normally adjoined such structures, providing ready access to the convention site for thousands of participants. Hammons was ready and willing to fill the gap, and cities throughout the country were beating down the company's door to build next to the local convention center. By the mid-1990s, Hammons had built the Holiday Inn Pyramid Hotel and Convention Center in Albuquerque, New Mexico, the Capital Plaza Atrium Hotel and Convention Center in Jefferson City, Missouri, and the Embassy Suites Hotel located at the Kansas City International Airport in Kansas City, Missouri. By the end of 1995, Hammons's personal fortune was worth over $400 million, his company owned and operated 42 hotels in 20 states with approximately 10,500 rooms, and employed about 8,000 men and women.

One of the most important reasons that can be provided to explain the company's profitability is the concept of ''bundling.'' During the early and mid-1990s, management made a commitment to revamp its food and drink operation. Previously, many hotels within the industry, including those operated by Hammons, had major lounge facilities with impressive facades and external entrances that focused on alcohol consumption. But as the social climate within the United States changed, and alcohol no longer played the part it previously had in business deals, Hammons changed with it. Rather than focusing on alcohol consumption, the company bought franchises from Damon's, Pizza Hut, and T.G.I. Friday's to operate within Hammons Hotels. By changing its beverage and restaurant orientation from the consumption of alcohol to a family-friendly, major restaurant franchise, the company increased its profits dramatically. In 1994 alone, the food and beverage component accounted for almost 40 percent of the company's profits.

In 1994, Hammons decided to take his hotel company public, and raised over $500 million to continue an aggressive expansion strategy. This strategy included the addition of the Radisson franchise in 1995, and the Marriott franchise in 1996, to enhance the company's position in the upscale, full-service hotel business. The year 1997 was a watershed mark for the company: six new hotels were opened, increasing the firms's overall growth by 15 percent; $302 million in revenues was reported, an increase of 12 percent over the previous year; and two first class resort hotels were added to the list of Hammons Hotels properties, Chateau on the Lake, in Branson, Missouri, and World Golf Village, in St. Augustine, Florida.

Although more rooms are added to the hotel business every year, the average hotel has less than 90 rooms, and the majority of this new space is a result of new construction in the budget, economy, and mid-priced sectors. By maintaining its focus on the upscale, full-service hotel, however, Hammons has been able to take advantage of the lack of new rooms being added to the upscale and luxury sector. Large guest rooms, spacious and high-quality meeting facilities, and amenities such as pools, gyms, and popular franchise food are attractive to both the business traveler and the vacationing family. John Q. Hammons Hotels knows this, and as long as the company remains loyal to its roots, there is no doubt revenues will continue to increase.

Further Reading

Andorka, Frank H., Jr., ''JQH Enjoys Special Focus,'' *Hotel & Motel Management,* March 18, 1996, p. 3.

Bond, Helen, ''Hotel Veterans Build Second Home,'' *Hotel & Motel Management,* December 16, 1996, p. 3.

''Hammons' New Hotel Tries Deskless Check-In,'' *Hotel & Motel Management,* November 6, 1995, p. 50.

Jaeger, Lauren, ''New Summer Spectacular 'Pizazz' Set for Palace Theater in Myrtle Beach,'' *Amusement Business,* November 24, 1997, p. 20.

Palmeri, Christopher, ''Comeback,'' *Forbes,* October 14, 1996, p. 20.

Wolff, Carlo, ''Big Fish in a Small Pond,'' *Lodging Hospitality,* February 1996, p. 34.

——, ''Giving Cities a Leg Up,'' *Lodging Hospitality,* February 1996, p. 39.

''World Golf Village Hotel, Vistana Resort Accepting Bookings,'' *Travel Weekly,* March 23, 1998, p. 83.

—Thomas Derdak

 JONES MEDICAL
INDUSTRIES, INC.

Jones Medical Industries, Inc.

1945 Craig Road
Post Office Box 46903
St. Louis, Missouri 63146
U.S.A.
(314) 576-6100
Fax: (314) 469-5749

Public Company
Incorporated: 1981
Employees: 500
Sales: 125 million (1997 est.)
Stock Exchanges: NASDAQ
Ticker Symbol: JMED
SICs: 2834 Pharmaceutical Preparations; 5122 Drugs,
    Drug Proprietaries, & Druggists' Sundries

Founded in 1981, Jones Medical Industries, Inc. (JMI) is a pharmaceutical manufacturer specializing in nutritional supplements, critical care drugs, and endocrine pharmaceuticals. The company carries out virtually no research and development into its own products. Instead, it acquires from other pharmaceutical companies the rights to manufacture and market existing, underpromoted drugs. This business strategy, which has proved to .be highly effective, allows JMI to save on product development costs and to avoid the drawn-out and expensive approval process of the U.S. Food and Drug Administration.

The Early Years

Dennis Jones, the founder of JMI, was the son of an Illinois farmer. Jones said that he first learned the "art of entrepreneurship—selling, marketing, serving customers—and hard work" while employed at his father's farm equipment business (*St. Louis Business Journal,* June 25, 1996). After completing high school, he served briefly in the Marine Corps and then embarked on his career in the healthcare industry as a pharmaceutical salesman for SIG Laboratories. Though Jones never attended college, he has not regretted his lack of higher educa-

tion. "I'm proud of the fact that I did it without a degree," he asserted to *Investor's Business Daily.* "Not having a college degree was one of the things that got me into my own business." He added that he was pushed to form his own company because the upper echelon of jobs in the corporate world were out of his reach.

Motivated by the desire not to be excluded from the highest rungs of the corporate ladder and by his belief in his own abilities as an entrepreneur, Jones cofounded the company O'Neal, Jones, and Feldman Pharmaceutical in 1969. This small-scale pharmaceutical manufacturer and distributor expanded primarily through acquisitions, and the company eventually rang up sales of nearly $9 million. When the partners sold O'Neal, Jones, and Feldman to the Chromalloy American Corporation in 1978, Jones began to explore the prospect of opening his own business. He told the *St. Louis Commerce* that he founded his own company "because I wanted to see if I could do it as well or better on my own. I guess you could say it's the classic entrepreneurial spirit." Armed with that spirit and $300,000, Jones and his wife, Judy, started Jones Medical Industries in 1981.

JMI initially followed a conservative business strategy. The company did no research and development of its own, instead purchasing a wide variety of drugs and nutritional supplements from other manufacturers and repackaging them under its own trademarks and trade names. Important early products included Duotrate (a medication to relieve angina, or heart, pain), Therevac (a "mini-enema"), and the T-Dry and T-Moist line of cold, cough, and allergy formulations. JMI carefully selected "mature" pharmaceutical products—drugs that had been on the market for a long time—whose profitability was declining. Because JMI recognized that major drug companies could heavily market only a few products at a time, it was able to purchase these mature drugs for about 60 percent of the revenue they generated annually. This focus on already established pharmaceuticals allowed JMI to capitalize on patient and physician familiarity with its products. As a result, JMI could minimize its sales and marketing costs and still make substantial profits. On January 19, 1987, *Barron's* summed up the success of JMI's approach: "By methodically milking his cash cows, Dennis

Jones is showing how well the cautious approach works.'' Sales increased 625 percent from 1982 to 1987.

In 1986, with the goal of retiring an outstanding debt and raising investment capital, JMI made its first public stock offering. The results were positive and helped fund JMI's continued growth.

Product Diversification: 1988–95

JMI took an important step in diversifying its business in 1988, when it acquired the American Vitamin Company's natural vitamin line. JMI marketed these products exclusively to military commissaries throughout the world, and sales of nutritional supplements have remained an important part of JMI's business ever since. With its 1993 purchase of Bronson Pharmaceuticals, a manufacturer of vitamins and dietary supplements, JMI expanded its presence in this field. Using Bronson's staff and sales techniques, JMI was able to develop a new marketing arm to complement its presence in the mature drug market. The nutritional supplement marketing force conducted direct mailings to 400,000 consumers, physicians, pharmacies, and retail outlets in the United States and Canada.

In 1989 the company acquired from the Rorer Group the drug Thrombin, a topical agent used to control bleeding during open-heart surgery and skin grafting. The acquisition of Thrombin (subsequently renamed Thrombin-JMI) was an enormous breakthrough for JMI. Thrombin quickly became JMI's best-selling product, grossing $5 million annually, and a cornerstone of the company's success. In part because of the Thrombin purchase, *Forbes* magazine in 1990 rated JMI one of the 200 best small companies in the United States.

JMI's acquisition of Thrombin represented more than the addition of a highly profitable product. It also marked a major shift in the company's marketing strategy. JMI was able to allow its mature, or long-established, drugs virtually to sell themselves, as the physicians who prescribed them and the patients who took them had a history with those products. Thrombin's purchasers, on the other hand, were primarily hospitals and other institutions. As a result, JMI began to develop a sales force to market the drug more aggressively to these customers in an effort to expand its market share.

In keeping with this more forceful business posture, JMI in 1991 purchased the pharmaceutical company GenTrac, which was the largest domestic manufacturer of Thrombin. JMI was now able to produce its own Thrombin and was no longer reliant on a third party. (Until JMI's acquisition of GenTrac, the Rorer group had continued to produce Thrombin for JMI.) The acquisition was momentous for JMI, which saw its net sales jump to more than $20 million in 1991. In the April 15, 1991, issue of the *St. Louis Business Journal,* Jones said, ''We wanted to control our own destiny and the most efficient way to do it was to acquire the biologically licensed manufacturer of Thrombin.'' Five years later, in the January 28, 1996, issue of the *Wisconsin State Journal,* Jones declared, ''GenTrac has become our single most important operation.''

Following its acquisition of Thrombin and GenTrac, JMI continued to seek out and actively develop other critical care products, such as Brevital Sodium, which JMI purchased in 1995 from Eli Lilly. Brevital was a short-acting, injectable anesthetic used in major surgeries, as well as the primary anesthetic used during dental surgeries. In a story carried on the *Business Wire* on August 31, 1995, Jones explained the purchase. Brevital Sodium, he said, ''competes within the $525 million U.S. anesthetic market [and] enjoys a tremendous loyalty among dental and medical surgeons. We plan to aggressively focus on this market and believe that a tremendous growth opportunity exists.'' Jones's confidence proved correct, as Brevital Sodium, along with Thrombin, led the company's pharmaceutical sales for the year. JMI also continued to produce and develop new forms of its existing critical care and extended care products: Liqui-Char, an antidote used in the treatment of acute toxic digestion; Therevac; the Derma-Scrub line of professional scrub products for surgeons and medical staff; and Panthoderm, an anti-inflammatory skin care product. In 1993 JMI's sales rose to $43.2 million.

Acquisition of Endocrine Drugs: Developments Beginning in 1996

The year 1996 provided new opportunities for JMI and marked a major shift in the company's direction. Although JMI continued to buy existing products from other companies, it chose to focus its acquisitions on endocrine, or hormonal, drugs. In March 1996 JMI purchased from Eli Lilly the drug Tapazole, used in the treatment of hyperthyroidism, a condition in which the thyroid gland is overactive (as in Graves Disease). JMI followed suit by purchasing from SmithKline Beecham two other endocrine drugs—Cytomel, a synthetic form of the thyroid hormone T3, and Triostat, an injectable form of T3–both used as a replacement hormone in patients with hypothyroidism (an underactive thyroid). JMI also acquired Levoxyl, a synthetic form of the thyroid hormone T4 (also used as a hormone replacement), when it purchased Levoxyl's manufacturer, Daniels Pharmaceuticals, Inc., in August 1996.

The takeover of Daniels Pharmaceuticals was a turning point for JMI. In addition to gaining the rights to Levoxyl (another big seller for JMI) and the company's veterinary pharmaceuticals, JMI inherited the entire sales division of Daniels, consisting of 85 marketing representatives. This addition was further enhanced by JMI's purchase, in December 1996, of Abana Pharmaceuticals, a marketing company for generic drugs. The Abana acquisition doubled the size of JMI's sales force, and for the first time JMI had a direct physician sales force. This new marketing arm complemented JMI's two existing sales divisions: its institutional/critical care branch and its direct mail nutritional supplement branch.

JMI profited handily from its product and marketing expansions. Its stock price increased tenfold between 1995 and 1997, trading for as much as $50 per share (JMI's initial stock offering in 1986 was at $6 per share). Sales for 1996 broke the $100 million mark, an increase of nearly $26 million from its 1995 sales and a near tripling of sales since 1992. Net profits for 1996 were $18.2 million, a 46 percent increase over 1995.

The year 1996 was also kind to Jones and his wife, Judy, JMI's executive vice-president and treasurer. Jones was named the 1996 Healthcare Entrepreneur of the Year by Ernst and Young, a national accounting and management consulting firm. As JMI's profits rose, so did the Jones's compensations: Jones earned $477,599 for 1996, and his wife earned $237,518. The couple owned nearly 16 percent of JMI's stock, worth approximately $150 million. Even though Jones was emerging as a major corporate player, he attempted not to forget the lessons of teamwork and hard work he learned earlier in his career. "I demand my managers have an open-door policy," he told *Investor's Business Daily* (June 13, 1996). In JMI's corporate headquarters, private offices were separated by glass walls to create an atmosphere of openness.

In the late 1990s JMI was making plans to acquire additional products and companies that complemented and enlarged its current product portfolio. The company's goal was to reach $250 million in annual sales by the year 2000.

Business analysts concurred with JMI's positive outlook. The company, recognized as one of the "Top 200 Small Companies in the World" by *Forbes* in 1990, 1991, and 1993, was chosen as one of *SmartMoney*'s "Best Investments" of 1998. The December 9, 1996, issue of *Fortune* declared that JMI's "cherry-picking strategy" was "as close to risk free as you can get." Analysts also pointed to the strength of the pharmaceutical industry in general. In the United States the number of elderly people was increasing, and that population group had the greatest need for medications and nutritional supplements.

Principal Subsidiaries

Daniels Pharmaceuticals, Inc.

Further Reading

Cook, Ken, "Jones Medical Plans Public Stock Offering," *St. Louis Business Journal,* May 26, 1986.

"Entrepreneurs of the Year," *St. Louis Commerce,* July 1, 1996.

Galloway, Jennifer, "Medical Alchemy Turns Bovine Plasma into Pharmaceutical Gold," *Wisconsin State Journal,* January 28, 1996.

Gilbert, Jersey, "Where to Invest in 1998," *SmartMoney,* January 1, 1998.

"Healthcare Entrepreneur of the Year," St. Louis Business Journal, June 25, 1996.

"Jones Medical Acquires Thrombinar from Rorer Group," *PR Newswire,* October 4, 1989.

"Jones Medical Completes Acquisition of Daniels Pharmaceuticals," *Business Wire,* August 30, 1996.

"Jones Medical Completes $14 Million Brevital Sodium Acquisition," *Business Wire,* August 31, 1995.

"Jones Medical Reports 33 Percent Increase in Third Quarter EPS," *Business Wire,* October 21, 1997.

"Jones Medical Reports 89 Percent Net Income Increase," *Business Wire,* October 31, 1996.

Mahar, Maggie, "No Thrills Drug Company, " *Barron's,* January 19, 1997.

Miller, Patricia, "Jones Medical Buys Small to Hit $20 Million in Sales," *St. Louis Business Journal,* April 15, 1996.

Murphy, Daniel, "Jones Medical's Dennis Jones: Business Was His College, and He Learned His Lessons Well," *Investor's Business Daily,* June 13, 1996.

Steyer, Robert, "Jones Medical Chairman Gets 23% Increase," *St. Louis Post-Dispatch,* March 20, 1997.

Warner, Melanie, "Jones Medical Catches a Wave," *Fortune,* December 9, 1996, p. 46.

—Rebecca Stanfel

Kanematsu Corporation

2-1, Shibaura 1-chome
Minato-ku
Tokyo 105-05
Japan
(03) 5440-8111
Fax: (03) 5440-6504
Web site: http://www.kanematsu.co.jp

Public Company
Incorporated: 1967 as Kanematsu-Gosho Ltd.
Employees: 2,278
Sales: ¥3.48 trillion (US$28.02 billion) (1997)
Stock Exchanges: Tokyo Osaka Nagoya
SICs: 6799 Investors, Not Elsewhere Classified

Kanematsu Corporation was formed in April 1967 as Kanematsu-Gosho Ltd. in the merger of F. Kanematsu & Co., Ltd. and The Gosho Co., Ltd. Its name was changed to the Kanematsu Corporation on January 1, 1990. Kanematsu Corporation is a *sogo shosha,* a general trading company, which conducts business in diversified import and export markets. Trading companies specialize in bringing together buyers and sellers of a variety of products and handling finance and transport of the resulting transaction. Kanematsu is one of the nine largest trading companies in Japan. In addition to its trading activities, however, Kanematsu is also active in a variety of other areas, including manufacturing, marketing, transportation, construction, and real estate development. Under its umbrella are about 230 subsidiaries and affiliates in more than 50 countries, with these operations organized into the following 13 divisions: machinery, electronics, textiles, foodstuffs/provisions, energy, chemicals/plastics, general merchandise, iron/steel, construction/development, wood products/lumber, transportation, finance, and information systems. In 1997 energy and chemicals/plastics operations represented 32.6 percent of sales; machinery, electronics, and construction/development, 22.2 percent; iron/steel and nonferrous metals, 16.9 percent; textiles,

14 percent; foodstuffs/provisions, 10.9 percent; and general merchandise and wood products/lumber, 3.4 percent.

Early History

F. Kanematsu & Co., Ltd. was established on August 15, 1889, by 44-year-old Fusajiro Kanematsu. With offices in Kobe, Japan, and a staff of seven persons, Kanematsu initially began trading operations in the Australian market. A branch office was set up in Sydney, Australia, in the following year; and a first shipment of 187 bales of Australian wool reached Japan. Trading operations expanded to include wheat, tallow, and other Australian products. In 1918 F. Kanematsu reorganized as a joint-stock company. As Japan's international trade grew dramatically during the early years of the 20th century, F. Kanematsu extended its operations into South Africa and South America. By 1936 it had opened U.S. branch offices in New York and in Seattle, Washington, and a subsidiary in New Zealand. The Kanematsu Trading Corporation, a U.S. subsidiary, was formed in New York in 1941. Much of the trading operations of the company were curtailed during World War II, and as a trading company F. Kanematsu had little to do during the war. Expansion resumed after the war, with Kanematsu New York Inc. being formed in 1951. To adjust itself to postwar economic conditions, F. Kanematsu shifted from its traditional trade in textiles to other areas, including the overseas construction of papermaking plants. In 1961 the shares of F. Kanematsu were sold to the public and the company was listed on the Osaka Stock Exchange.

The Gosho Co., Ltd. was formed by Yohei Kitagawa as Kitagawa & Co. Ltd. in 1891 in Yokohama to engage in the import of cotton yarn. Offices subsequently were moved to Kobe and then to Osaka, where in 1905 it was organized as The Gosho Co., Ltd.; it underwent a reorganization into a joint-stock company in 1917. Direct importing of cotton began from the United States in 1906 and from India in 1907. Crawford Gosho Co., Ltd. and Gosho Corporation, U.S. subsidiaries, were formed in 1912 and 1918, respectively. Until the beginning of World War II, Gosho continued its international trading operations, with cotton as its most important product. From 1935 to 1945, war years for Japan, Gosho withdrew from many interna-

259

tional markets but continued to trade in raw materials. In 1943 it merged with Showa Cotton Co., Ltd. and Pacific Trading Co., Ltd. After World War II it began diversifying its business away from textiles. Gosho Trading Co., Ltd. was formed in Thailand in 1959.

1967 Merger Formed Kanematsu-Gosho

With the 1967 merger of the two companies into Kanematsu-Gosho Ltd., the surviving firm moved into the top ranks of Japanese trading companies. By 1968 the new company had changed its internal organization into the present divisional structure. The head office was moved to Tokyo in 1970. Shares of the company's stock were listed on the Tokyo and Nagoya stock exchanges in 1973. Sales for the fiscal year ended March 31, 1974, reached ¥1 trillion for the first time. Subsidiary companies were formed in Canada in 1972, France in 1973, and Hong Kong in 1975; an office was opened in Beijing in 1979. The oil-price shocks of the 1970s caused difficulties for the company, as they did for much of the Japanese economy. Structural improvements and several long-range plans restored profitability by the end of the 1980s.

As with all Japanese trading companies, Kanematsu-Gosho continued to seek new investment opportunities throughout the world. In 1986, for example, it filled an order with the People's Republic of China for ¥700 million worth of equipment for manufacturing semiconductors; in 1989 it took a 25 percent interest in a joint venture with Nishimbo Industries Inc. in constructing and operating the first cotton textile mill ever in California and also began participation in Kanebo Spinning Inc., a mill in Georgia. The company also became a player in world money markets when, in 1989, US$130 million in dollar-denominated bonds with stock options were sold in the European financial market, and 25 million shares of new stock were issued at prevailing market prices. In 1990, convertible notes worth SFr 200 million were issued. Subsidiaries were formed in the United Kingdom in 1989, in Spain in 1990, and in Italy in 1991, with branch offices being opened in Bucharest, Warsaw, and Berlin in 1990. Also in 1990, Kanematsu-Gosho changed its name to Kanematsu Corporation. In 1991 the Kanematsu (Europe) Corporation was created and given general control over European operations.

As the structure of the world economy continued to evolve, general trading companies such as Kanematsu had to continue to develop new products to trade and new strategies for how to market those products. In particular, they had to adjust their offerings as the Japanese economy became less reliant on exports, with the domestic market becoming increasingly important for total sales. To keep abreast of these changes, in 1987 Kanematsu formed a research-and-development division to investigate new products. In 1990, it established a "Ladies Life and Living" team, an all-woman marketing group with a responsibility for anticipating the product needs of women over the next decade.

The company shifted the emphasis of its operations during the 1980s by importing more products into Japan. In 1982 imports accounted for 24 percent of total sales, compared to 44 percent in 1991. Other categories of operations adjusted accordingly, with exports remaining 15 percent of total sales, domestic sales falling from 51 percent in 1982 to 27 percent in 1991, and overseas sales growing from 10 percent to 14 percent during the period.

Difficult 1990s

The bursting of the late 1980s Japanese economic bubble led to prolonged difficulties for Kanematsu in the 1990s. Nearly all of the *sogo shosha* had diversified aggressively into financial investments during the speculative bubble years, in large part because their traditional activity of marginally profitable commodity trading had been in a deep decline for years; in desperation the companies built large stock portfolios and became hooked on the revenues they could gain through arbitrage (or *zaiteku,* as it is known in Japan). Once the bubble burst, the *sogo shosha* were left with huge portfolios whose worth had plummeted; all of the trading companies were forced to eventually liquidate much of their stock holdings. Unlike some of the larger trading companies, Kanematsu could not afford to quickly liquidate all of the bad investments it had made in the late 1980s; it had to do so gradually, writing some off in 1993 and 1994, the rest in 1997, when the write-offs—and the liquidation of 10 loss-making affiliates—led to an overall net loss of ¥27.53 billion (US$221 million). This poor performance had followed net losses of ¥6.46 billion in 1994 and ¥15.2 billion in 1995. Kanematsu, like all of the *sogo shosha,* also felt a prolonged effect from its involvement in arbitrage in the form of damage to the company's financial credibility, leading to higher borrowing rates.

During the 1990s, with the Japanese economy in a lengthy recession, Kanematsu expanded aggressively in Asia, establishing numerous subsidiaries, affiliates, and joint ventures, particularly in China, Indonesia, Malaysia, Thailand, and Vietnam. By 1997 the company had 44 projects operational in China alone, where it established a Shanghai-based subsidiary in July 1996 to increase its internal trading activities within China. The following year Kanematsu created a Shanghai-based holding company to coordinate and support all of the company's operations in the burgeoning market that China had become.

During this period Kanematsu also placed an increasing emphasis on such high-tech areas as electronics, communications, and information technologies. For example, in December 1996 the company entered into a ¥1.8 billion contract to expand the rural telecommunications network of Nepal Telecommunications Corporation. In April 1996 Kanematsu established with a U.S. partner a U.S.-based joint venture called Extel Semiconductor Corp. to manufacture application-specific integrated circuit chips. In June 1996 Kanematsu acquired the Asia-Pacific operations of Memorex Telex N.V. for US$25 million; Memorex Telex sold automatic tape libraries and network-related equipment and offered systems integration services.

As yet another bubble burst with the outbreak of the Asian financial crisis in 1997, Kanematsu faced the possibility of a repeat of its difficulties stemming from the Japanese economic troubles of the late 1980s and early 1990s since it had grown rapidly in some of the most troubled economies: Indonesia, Korea, and Malaysia. Currency devaluations were already cutting into demand in southeast Asia by late 1997 and in turn hurting the profitability of most Japanese trading companies.

Kanematsu was known for continually restructuring its activities to keep pace with world economic changes and it would have to do so again in order to survive this latest crisis threatening to undermine it.

Principal Subsidiaries

MACHINERY: Guangzhou Showa Shock Absorber Co., Ltd. (China); Hangzhou Kangqiao Automobile Service Co., Ltd. (China); Sanyo Electric Home Appliances (Suzhou) Co., Ltd. (China); Sichuan Ningjiang Showa Shock Absorber Co., Ltd. (China); Suzhou Sanyo Electro-Mechanical Co., Ltd. (China); Tianjin Kaida Transportation Service Co., Ltd. (China); Kanematsu Project Development Co., Ltd. (Hong Kong); Tanashin (Europe) GmbH (Germany); Distribuidora De Vehiculos (Guatamala); P.T. Honda Prospect Engine MFG Inc. (Indonesia); P.T. Imora Honda Inc. (Indonesia); P.T. Metbelosa (Indonesia); ARIES Motor Ltd. (Poland); ARIES Power Equipment Ltd. (Poland); Carpati Motor Ltd. (Romania); Showa Aluminum (Thailand) Co., Ltd.; Thai Refrigeration Components Co., Ltd. (Thailand); FCC (Europe) Ltd. (U.K.); KGK International Corp. (U.S.A.); Transportation Facilities Equipment Engineering Distribution and Leasing Co. (Vietnam); Vietindo Daihatsu Automotive Corp. (Vietnam); Daifuku Co., Ltd.; Kanematsu Industrial Machinery Ltd.; Kanematsu Techno Corporation; Kanematsu-Usic Co.; Kyori Kogyo Co., Ltd.; Nippon Pioneer Co., Ltd.; Nippon Sky Co., Ltd.; Nippon U.S. Machinery Co., Ltd.; Paneltec Corporation; Pioneer Work Co., Ltd.; Tahara Machinery Ltd.; Tokyo Engineering & Manufacturing Co., Ltd. ELECTRONICS: Chu's F.C.C. (Shanghai) Co., Ltd. (China); Glory GmbH (Germany); Yamato Europe GmbH (Germany); KM Aspac Pte. Ltd. (Singapore); Powerchip Semiconductor Corp. (Taiwan); Kanematsu Controls Ltd. (U.K.); Glory (U.S.A.) Inc.; KG Aerospace International, Inc. (U.S.A.); Business Links, Ltd.; Integrated Communication Systems Co., Ltd.; Kanematsu Aerospace Corp.; Kanematsu Design Technology Corporation; Kanematsu Electrical Products Sales Co., Ltd.; Kanematsu Electronic Components Corp.; Kanematsu Electronics Ltd.; Kanematsu Electronics Trading Co., Ltd.; Kanematsu Medical Systems Corporation; Kanematsu Multi-Tech Corporation; Kanematsu-NNK Corporation Duo-Fast Division; Kanematsu Semiconductor Corp.; Memorex Telex Japan Ltd.; Nippon Office Systems Ltd.; Ryosho Electronics Corporation. TEXTILES: Fischer GmbH (Austria); Nantong Sunrise Worsted Spinning Co., Ltd. (China); Shanghai Chugaikunishima Worsted Mills Co., Ltd. (China); Shanghai Jinshan Otsu Woollen Textile Co., Ltd. (China); Shanghai Takaya Fashion Co., Ltd. (China); Zhejiang Zengsong Textile Co., Ltd. (China); Familia Sewing Co., Ltd. (Hong Kong); Fashion Crew (H.K.) Ltd. (Hong Kong); KRK (HK) Ltd. (Hong Kong); P.T. Century Textile Industry (Indonesia); P.T. Flex Indonesia; P.T. Nikawa Textile Industry (Indonesia); Malaysian Topmaking Mills Sdn. Bhd. (Malaysia); Nankai Worsted Spinning (Malaysia) Sdn. Bhd.; Perak Textile Mills Sdn. Bhd. (Malaysia); Toyobo Textile (Malaysia) Sdn. Bhd.; Ascott International Co., Ltd. (Thailand); Artemis Fashion Corp. (U.S.A.); Kanebo Spinning, Inc. (U.S.A.); Nisshinbo California Inc. (U.S.A.); Pan Pacific Yarn, Inc. (U.S.A.); Technical Marketing Associates, Inc. (U.S.A.); Club Monaco Japan Inc.; Fukui Yamamoto Co., Ltd.; Gosen Co., Ltd.; Kamo Trico Co., Ltd.; Kanematsu Apparel Ltd.; Kanematsu Fashion Crew Co., Ltd.;

Kanematsu Lancot Ltd.; Kanematsu Textile Co., Ltd.; Kanematsu Top Co., Ltd.; Kanematsu Woolen Mills, Ltd.; Kanesen Co., Ltd.; Kanewa Apparel Corporation; Kane Wool Corporation; Kaneyoshi Co., Ltd.; KG Garment Supply Co., Ltd.; LB & Co., Ltd.; Masatomo Inc.; Mitsuru Co., Ltd.; Mode Brain Co., Ltd.; Ohno Inc.; Schi Kraft Inc.; Showa Kraft Inc.; Showa Garments Manufacturing Co., Ltd.; Silver Shirts Manufacturing Co., Ltd.; S. Kamei Co., Ltd.; S.T. Studio Co., Ltd.; U Textiles Co., Ltd. FOODSTUFFS & PROVISIONS: Feng Ling Corporation (China); Summit Food Industries Co., Ltd. (Thailand); Hai Viet Company Limited (Vietnam); Akechi Genetics, Inc.; Heisei Feed Manufacturing Co.; Kanematsu Agri-Tech Corporation; Kanematsu Food Corporation; Kanematsu Fruit Corporation; Nippon Liquor Ltd.; Toraube Ltd. ENERGY: Metropolitan Collieries Ltd. (Australia); K.G. International Petroleum Limited (Hong Kong); Greymouth Coal Ltd. (New Zealand); Kanematsu Oil Singapore Pte. Ltd.; Kanematsu Sekiyu Gas Co., Ltd.; Kanematsu Sekiyu Hanbai Co., Ltd.; Kanematsu Yuso Co., Ltd.; KG Babo Petroleum Ltd.; KG Berau Petroleum Ltd.; K.G.I., Limited; KG Kalosi Petroleum Ltd.; KG Wiriagar Petroleum Ltd.; Nisseki Kanematsu Co., Ltd.; Toyo Kokusai Oil Co., Ltd.; UNIX Corporation. CHEMICALS & PLASTICS: Prestige Tyre Center Pty Ltd. (Australia); Yokahama Tyre Australia Pty Ltd.; P.T. Idopherin Jaya (Indonesia); P.T. Java Tohoku Industries (Indonesia); Sanshu-KG (Malaysia) Sdn. Bhd.; Bangkok Polyester Co., Ltd. (Thailand); Gospel Chemical Industry Ltd.; Hanna Plastics Co., Ltd.; Hokuetsu Kasei Co., Ltd.; Kanematsu Chemicals Co., Ltd.; Kanematsu Plastics Company, Ltd.; Kanematsu Wellness Co., Ltd.; Kitaura Plastics Co., Ltd.; Rensoru Co., Ltd. NONFERROUS METALS: Nanjing UBE Magnesium Co., Ltd. (China); P.T. Istana Kanematsu Indonesia; Bangkok Metal Industry Co., Ltd. (Thailand); Hitachi Bangkok Cable Co., Ltd. (Thailand); Thai Kakinuma Co., Ltd. (Thailand); Thai Kikuwa Industry Co., Ltd. (Thailand); Thai Kyowa Engineering & Construction Co., Ltd. (Thailand); Diemakers, Ltd. (U.K.); Diemakers Inc. (U.S.A.); Hibino Corp. of America (U.S.A.); Necoa, Inc. (U.S.A.); Kanematsu Metals Ltd.; Shikoku Cable Co., Ltd.; Technic Japan Inc. GENERAL MERCHANDISE: Chung Chi Leather Co., Ltd. (Taiwan); West Bay Resources Inc. (U.S.A.); Kanematsu Kaneka Co., Ltd.; Kanematsu Rex Corporation. IRON & STEEL: Kanematsu Hoplee Co., Ltd. (Hong Kong); P.T. Emperor Steel Corp. (Indonesia); P.T. Little Giant Steel Corp. (Indonesia); P.T. Maspion Stainless Steel Indonesia; P.T. NAR Stainless Steel Center (Indonesia); Ryoma Steel Sdn. Bhd. (Malaysia); Kobe Mig Wire (Thailand) Co., Ltd.; SKJ Metal Industries Co., Ltd. (Thailand); Thai-Kobe Welding Co., Ltd. (Thailand); KG Specialty Steel, Inc. (U.S.A.); Eiwa Kinzoku Co., Ltd.; Iwaki Steel Center Ltd.; Kanematsu Tekko Hanbai Co., Ltd.; Kanematsu Trading Corporation; Kyowa Steel Co., Ltd.; Kyushu Koki Co., Ltd.; Lanxide K.K.; Nikko Boeki Kaisha Ltd.; World Beam Co., Ltd.; Yachiyo Stainless Center Ltd. CONSTRUCTION & DEVELOPMENT: P.T. Gunung Geulis Sentra Rekreasi (Indonesia); P.T. Mulia Colliman International (Indonesia); Daklak-Japan Properties Ltd. (Vietnam); Aso Country Club; Bizen Country Club; Kanematsu Construction Materials Ltd.; Kanematsu Environment Corporation; Kanematsu E-VALUED Homes Corporation; Kanematsu Housing Ltd.; Kanematsu Toshikaihatsu Co., Ltd.; KR Estate Ltd.; Tsuzuki Concrete Industrial Corp. LUMBER & WOOD PRODUCTS: Forestal

Peteroa Ltda. (Chile); KG-Inversiones (Chile) S.A.; Productos Forestales Kamapu Ltda. (Chile); G.P.K. Wood Products Sdn. Bhd. (Malaysia); Karimoku (M) Sdn. Bhd. (Malaysia); Pana Home Tech (M) Sdn. Bhd. (Malaysia); Hokushin Co., Ltd.; Kanematsu-NNK Corporation; Maruyone Trading Co., Ltd.; Morimoku Kaisha, Ltd. TRANSPORTATION: Dalian Shunda Logistic Services Corporation (China); P.T. Dunia Express Transindo (Indonesia); Pan Pacific Trans-Service Pte. Ltd. (Singapore); Southern Pacific Insurance Pte. Ltd. (Singapore); Mar Bin Trans-Service Co., Ltd. (Thailand); Central Air & Sea Service (U.S.A.) Inc.; Vietnam-Japan International Transport Co., Ltd. (Vietnam); Central Express Ltd.; Indochina Trans-Service Co., Ltd.; Japan Logistics Co., Ltd.; Kanematsu Boeki Service Co., Ltd.; KIT Ltd. FINANCE: KG International Trade & Finance Plc. (U.K.); Kanematsu Finance Corporation. OTHERS: ADEPT Corporation; Kanematsu Computer Systems Ltd.; Kanematsu Kanzai Co., Ltd.; Kanematsu Personnel Service Inc.

Principal Divisions

Machinery; Electronics; Textiles; Foodstuffs & Provisions; Energy; Chemicals & Plastics; General Merchandise; Iron & Steel; Construction & Development; Lumber & Wood Products; Transportation; Finance; Information Systems.

Further Reading

Iwao, Ichiishi, "Sogo Shosha: Meeting New Challenges," *Journal of Japanese Trade & Industry,* January/February 1995, pp. 16–18.

KG Monthly: Special Issue, 100th Anniversary 1989, Tokyo: Kanematsu-Gosho Ltd., 1989.

"March of the Middlemen," *Economist,* September 24, 1988.

Rosario, Louise do, "Lose and Learn: Japan's Firms Pay Price of Financial Speculation," *Far Eastern Economic Review,* June 17, 1993, pp. 60–61.

Terazono, Emiko, "Write-Offs to Put Kanematsu in ¥20bn Loss," *Financial Times,* September 6, 1996, p. 22.

Yonekawa, Shin'ichi, ed., *General Trading Companies: A Comparative and Historical Study,* Tokyo: United Nations University Press, 1990, 229 p.

Yoshihara, Kunio, *Sogo Shosha: The Vanguard of the Japanese Economy,* Tokyo: Oxford University Press, 1982, 358 p.

Young, Alexander, *The Sogo Shosha: Japan's Multinational Trading Companies,* Boulder, Colorado: Westview Press, 1979.

—Donald R. Stabile
—updated by David E. Salamie

Kerr Group Inc.

500 New Holland Avenue
Lancaster, Pennsylvania 17602-2104
U.S.A.
(717) 299-6511
Fax: (717) 299-5844

Private Company
Incorporated: 1903 as Kerr Glass Manufacturing Corp.
Employees: 875
Sales: $104.7 million (1996)
SICs: 2821 Plastics Materials Synthetic Resins; 2891
    Adhesives & Sealants; 3085 Plastics Bottles; 3086
    Plastics Foam Products; 3089 Plastics Products, Not
    Elsewhere Classified; 3221 Glass Containers; 3466
    Crowns & Closures; 5023 Home Furnishings; 5162
    Plastics Materials & Basic Forms; 6719 Holding
    Companies, Not Elsewhere Classified

Kerr Group Inc., formerly Kerr Glass Manufacturing Corp., is a nearly 100-year-old company that is a major producer and distributor of plastic and glass packaging products worldwide. The Lancaster, Pennsylvania-based firm is recognized as a prominent manufacturer and supplier of a full line of plastic packaging products, including child-resistant closures, tamper-evident closures, prescription drug packaging products, as well as glass jars, other closures, containers, and prescription bottles.

Through strong design and process engineering capabilities, Kerr has garnered an impressive customer base, supplying closures to nearly all of the major prescription drug companies in the United States. The company's tamper-evident closures can also be found on most liquor bottles, as well as on many food products. The company also manufactures and supplies prescription packaging products for major drug store chains, including Walgreen's Co. and Eckerd Corporation.

The company is also a market leader in the child-resistant closure (CRC) industry, an industry producing approximately three billion closures per year which are used primarily in the pharmaceutical, automotive, and household chemical markets on products whose safety the U.S. Government regulates. The company is additionally the number two manufacturer of pharmaceutical packaging products (including the amber-colored vials and the associated closure used by pharmacies to package prescriptions filled by pharmacists on site) second only to Owens-Illinois and leading Sunbeam Plastics, a division of Rexham.

The company conducts manufacturing activities at four facilities located in Lancaster, Pennsylvania (plastic closure and container plant and warehouse); Jackson, Tennessee (plastic closure and bottle plant and warehouse); Ahoskie, North Carolina (plastic closure plant and warehouse); and Bowling Green, Kentucky (plastic closure plant and warehouse).

From Kerr Glass Manufacturing Corp. to Kerr Group Inc., 1903–92

Kerr Glass Manufacturing Corp. was first established in 1903 by A. H. Kerr to manufacture home canning supplies for people who canned their own foods, such as preserves, jams, jellies, and the like. The company was incorporated in Delaware that same year.

In 1927, the company was reincorporated with the same name and continued in the same line of work. Nearly 50 years later, in 1974, the company was reincorporated in Delaware, again with the same name (as Kerr Glass Manufacturing Corp.), and was a successor of the 1927 incarnation. The company's present name, Kerr Group Inc., was adopted in May 1992, reflecting the fact that the company had grown to manufacture more than just glass containers.

Acquisitions and Divestitures, 1980–97

In July 1980, the company made one of its first acquisitions, purchasing the Maywood, California-based glass container manufacturing plant of Latchford Glass Co. for approximately $10 million in cash and stock. Acquisitions for Kerr continued when, in May 1981, the company acquired the Chicago Home Canning and Lid facility of the privately held Naperville, Illinois-based Phoenix Closures Inc., a manufacturer of plastic bottle cap lids, with a history dating back to 1890, for approximately $4.7 million in cash and stocks. Several years later, in July 1986, the company purchased a manufacturing facility in Ahoskie, North Carolina, and, in October 1987, the company completed the purchase of SCP Corp., a producer of injected molded plastic jars and closures for $9 million in cash and stock.

But the company's growth was not without problems, and the sporadic acquisitions were interspersed with occasional divestitures. In September 1983, the company sold off four of its glass manufacturing facilities, located at Millville, New Jersey; Maywood, California; Waxahatchie, Texas; and Wilson, North Carolina, to National Can Corp.

Nearly a decade later, in February 1992, the company sold its commercial glass container manufacturing business to Ball Corporation for approximately $68 million. In December of that same year, the company sold its Metal Crown business to Philadelphia-based packaging giant Crown, Cork & Seal Co. Inc. for approximately $7.2 million. The sale included the company's Arlington, Texas, metal crown plant and related machinery, equipment, and inventory. Sales for Kerr in 1992 reached $126.6 million.

Rough Waters, 1980s–90s

The company ended up floundering under the direction of Roger Norian, according to one industry analyst, who said in *Forbes*, "Roger Norian hasn't done much for Kerr Group, but he's done very nicely for himself," and noted that "Kerr had been profitable less than 50 percent of the time from 1982 to 1993, although Norian himself had received over $1.8 million in three years." When Norian was promoted to chief executive officer of Kerr in 1982, he was taking the helm of a basically sound company that faced a strategic dilemma: Should it stay in its old business, making glass bottles and jars, or branch into something new? Norian decided to do a little of both. He concluded that Kerr's big competitors—primarily Owens-Illinois and Ball Corp.—had dominated the market for beer and soft drink bottles with standardized sizes. As a small glass bottle producer in a capital-intensive business, Kerr could not compete. So, in 1983, Norian sold four glass container plants to National Can for between $90 million and $95 million. Norian kept Kerr's business of making glass jars for packaging peanut butter, mayonnaise, and other supermarket staples, plus some small sideline operations that made metal caps for beer bottles and plastic caps for medicine vials. But image problems dogged Kerr's glass jar operations. Early in 1992 Norian threw in the towel and sold the glass jar operations to Ball for approximately $70 million. Eleven months later Norian sold the money-losing bottle cap division. That reduced Kerr to a company with two basic businesses: manufacturing plastic closures for pharmaceuticals, food and spirits, as well as other containers; and consumer goods such as cookbooks and kits for home-preserving fruits and vegetables. Revenues in 1993 reached $127.4 million, but Kerr posted a net loss of $1.6 million.

Early that same year, the industries around Kerr (glass and plastics, container manufacturing, etc.) saw some consolidation, with Ball Corporation completing its merger with Heekin Can, and Crown Cork & Seal's Constar International unit acquiring Wellstar. Airco Coating Technology picked up full responsibility for Eastapac, formerly a joint venture between Airco and Eastman Chemical, and Sun Coast Plastics changed its name to Sun Coast Closures.

At the time, the company was attempting to reinvent itself under Norian's direction. But, the consumer products business division, after posting stellar sales of $34.1 million in 1992, was devastated by numerous inclement weather factors, including the Mississippi River flooding and regional droughts, and sales rapidly fell to $29 million one seemingly endless year later. The plastic products group, however, grew to an estimated $98.3 million from $92.6 million in 1992 without significant price increases but, rather, by increasing market share and shifting product mix to high-value-added products.

In August 1994, Kerr moved its consumer products business operation from its old facility in Chicago to a new low-cost facility in Jackson, Tennessee. The company did a little better, hitting revenues of $139.2 million, and posting a net income of $3.4 million.

In mid-1995, the packaging and container industry began seeing more merger and acquisition activity, such as Crown, Cork & Seal with Carnaud Metalbox, and Ball Corp. with Foster-Forbes. By the end of 1995, though, the rollercoaster ride of Kerr's finances swooped again, with a net loss of $5.3 million on total revenues of $109.2 million.

End of an Era, 1996

Until 1996, the company was a leading manufacturing of home canning supplies, through its consumer products business division, with an estimated 45 percent market share, continuing the work originally started by A. H. Kerr in 1903.

Those operations included the manufacture and sale of caps and lids and the sale of canning jars and lids used by consumers for home canning of fruits, vegetables, jams, jellies, and the like, together with the sale of other related products, including iced tea tumblers and beverage mugs, and plastic dinnerware and drinkware.

Due to a combination of cyclical demand based on annual growing, harvest, and weather conditions; a shift in retail distribution channels for such supplies away from smaller specialty stores and into the larger mass-merchandise retailers such as Wal-Mart and Kmart (with concurrent lower profit margins); and little growth in the unit, operations for the consumer products division were discontinued. Certain assets of the division were sold in March 1996 to Alltrista Corporation for a purchase price of $14.5 million in cash and stocks. Alltrista, parts of which formerly belonged to Ball Corp., was another Muncie, Indiana-based company. The manufacturer of metal stamped jar tops, rubber jar rings, and glass jars for packing, founded in 1991, also produced zinc blanks used to make pennies. Revenues for Kerr hit in the normal range for the struggling company, at $107.4 million, but net losses mounted to $22.3 million.

Through the Looking Glass, 1997–Date

By 1997, Norian was gone, with D. Gordon Strickland taking over as CEO and president. Later that year, Fremont

Acquisition Company LLC and Kerr Acquisition Corporation (KAC) completed their previously announced merger, as the former tendered a cash offer for all of the shares of common stock in the latter. The company remained Kerr Group Inc. but was taken off the New York Stock Exchange and converted into a private company. Fremont Partners also had acquired Global Motorsport (a custom chrome manufacturer for companies such as Harley-Davidson) and Kinetic Concepts Inc. (a manufacturer of medical equipment such as hospital beds).

In March 1998, the company acquired Dallas, Texas-based Sun Coast Industries Inc., a manufacturer of plastic closures, tableware and dinnerware, and melamine and urea resins. The acquisition also included part or all of several Sun Coast subsidiaries, including Plastics Manufacturing Co. (Dallas, Texas); Sun Coast Closures Inc. (Sarasota, Florida), and Custom Laminates Inc. (Dallas, Texas). Most of Plastics Manufacturing Co. (PMC), established in 1946 and which had merged with Sun Coast in 1989, was sold in 1996 to Worthington Custom Plastics, itself a subsidiary of Worthington Industries Inc., for $60 million. Worthington, best-known for its steel-processing business, acquired the group so it could advance its non-automotive plastics sales. The sale included PMC's own subsidiary, IDG Marketing, designer and manufacturer of plastic dinnerware, drinkware, and hardware-related products, which it acquired in June 1993.

Kerr, under new ownership, was looking forward to enjoying more stable waters and continued growth in the future, and was poised to remain a leader in the packaging industry.

Principal Subsidiaries

Santa Fe Plastic Corporation.

Principal Divisions

Plastic Products Division.

Further Reading

Bohner, Kate, "Ask Not What You Can Do for Your Company," *Forbes*, November 22, 1993, p. 120.

"Fremont Partners to Buy Kerr Group for $27 Million," *New York Times*, July 2, 1997, p. C3(N)/D3(L).

"Kerr Group in Talks About Possible Sale of the Company," *New York Times*, June 17, 1997, p. C4(N).

"Kerr Group Inc.," *Wall Street Journal*, August 26, 1997, p. B4(W).

"Kerr Group Inc.—Company Report," Moody's Investors Service, November 11, 1997.

"Kerr Group Inc.—History & Debt," Moody's Investors Service, March 28, 1998.

"Kerr Group Reaches Deal on Pension Plan with Federal Agency," *Wall Street Journal*, August 26, 1997, p. C17(E).

"Separate Talks Are Held on Sale, Unsecured Debt," *Wall Street Journal*, June 17, 1997, p. B4(W)/B8(E).

"Sun Coast Shares Leap on Word It Will Be Acquired," *New York Times*, January 29, 1998, p. C4(N)/D4(L).

—Daryl F. Mallett

KINGFISHER

Kingfisher plc

North West House
119 Marylebone Road
London NW1 5PX
United Kingdom
(0171) 724 7749
Fax: (0171) 724 1160
Web site: http://www.kingfisher.co.uk

Public Company
Incorporated: 1909 as F.W. Woolworth & Co. Ltd.
Employees: 77,436
Sales: £6.41 billion (US $10.73 billion) (1998)
Stock Exchanges: London Paris
Ticker Symbol: KNGFY
SICs: 5251 Hardware Stores; 5261 Retail Nurseries,
   Lawn & Garden Supply Stores; 5331 Variety Stores;
   5712 Furniture Stores; 5722 Household Appliance
   Stores; 5731 Radio, Television & Consumer
   Electronic Stores; 5735 Record & Prerecorded Tape
   Stores; 5912 Drug Stores & Proprietary Stores; 6552
   Land Subdividers & Developers, Except Cemeteries;
   6719 Offices of Holding Companies, Not Elsewhere
   Classified

Based in London, Kingfisher plc is a major European retailing and property group. Its U.K. retail chains include Woolworths, a variety chain of 781 shops; B&Q, a chain of 280 do-it-yourself (DIY) centers; Superdrug, a chain of 705 drug stores; and Comet, a chain of 224 electrical stores. Foreign chains owned by Kingfisher include three retailers of electrical goods: 150-unit Darty, France's leading electrical retailer; New Vanden Borre, with 19 units in Belgium; and BCC, with 17 stores in the Netherlands. Kingfisher also holds a 60 percent stake in Promarkt, an electrical retailer in Germany, and a 26 percent stake in BUT, the fourth largest electrical retailer in France. Two smaller U.K. businesses round out the company's retailing operations: Music and Video Club (MVC), a 34-unit chain selling music CDs and cassettes, pre-recorded videos, and mul-

timedia items; and Entertainment UK, a leading distributor of music CDs and cassettes, pre-recorded videos, video games, CD-ROM computer software, and books. Kingfisher's Chartwell Land plc unit is a property company that started by redeveloping the Woolworth properties and has diversified into redeveloping properties of other companies both in and outside of the group and also manages an investment portfolio.

Woolworth Beginnings

Kingfisher originated as a subsidiary of F.W. Woolworth & Co. of the United States. The American company was founded in 1879. The company's founder, Frank Winfield Woolworth, identified the potential for a walk-around open display type of shop in Britain during his first visit to Europe in 1890. He observed that "the [London] stores . . . are very small and are called 'shops' and not much like our fine stores. I think a good [threepenny and sixpenny] store run by a live Yankee would create a sensation here, but perhaps not." In 1909 he decided to found a subsidiary in Britain even though his chief executives thought that it would be unsuccessful. On July 23, 1909, the subsidiary was incorporated in England as a private limited company, F.W. Woolworth & Co. Ltd., with a share capital of £50,250. In 1912 the share capital was increased to £100,000. After this time the entire increase in assets was built up from earnings and there was no further increase in capitalization. Between 1909 and 1919 the American shareholders received no dividends at all and for the following six years dividends were paltry. This was not for lack of profits but because the shareholders wanted to build up the reserves of the company so that it was always in a position to expand without recourse to borrowing.

The first shop opened at 25 and 25a Church Street, Liverpool, on November 5, 1909. The *Draper* described it as "a penny, threepenny, and sixpenny bazaar on a large scale. In each of the four large salesrooms there are wide counters, extending the full length of the hall, and on these are placed mahogany trays containing the articles for disposal. . . . The public, we are told, are privileged 'to wander round the immense establishment without being importuned to buy.'" During the first two days of business 60,000 people visited the shop.

Company Perspectives:

Our objective is to deliver consistent and superior returns to our shareholders by being one of Europe's most profitable volume retailers.

Our strategy is to achieve this by concentrating on markets centered on the home and family, which we know and understand, and developing strong retail brands with leading positions in our markets. Our growth will be driven by a commitment to continuously evolve the offers we make to meet the changing needs and aspirations of our customers more effectively than our competitors.

Following steady business improvement, Woolworth opened a second shop in Preston and properties were also obtained in Manchester, Leeds, and Hull. In 1910 a third shop was opened, on London Road, Liverpool. The premises were obtained from Owen Owen, a department store owner, who told Woolworth that he had no idea that the "bazaar business could be elevated to such a high standard." On the opening of the third shop there was a riot. The riot made the management wary. When the sixth shop opened in Hull later in 1910, crowd barriers were put in place to stem the anticipated rush of customers. By the end of 1910 the company was operating ten shops, with another two in preparation.

The same business methods that had worked so well in the United States were adopted in Britain. Everything carried a plain price tag, and the prices were one old penny (£0.004), three old pence (£0.0125), and six old pence (£0.025). Supplies were bought directly from manufacturers. As in the United States, Woolworth had difficulty at first in Britain in persuading manufacturers to deal with him directly. Like the U.S. manufacturers, however, the British manufacturers who agreed to supply Woolworth directly soon found they had made the correct decision. Many of these suppliers also grew with Woolworth from small beginnings. A notable example was Duttons Ltd. When the first shop was opened in Liverpool, Duttons received its first Woolworth order. Subsequently, Duttons set out solely to service Woolworth with all types of price tickets, advertising, and printed matter. By the early 1960s Duttons was also responsible for the supply of many items of stationery to the majority of Woolworth's suppliers.

The Woolworth method of retailing moved from strength to strength. By 1912 the chain had expanded to 28 shops, 26 of which were managed by Britons. The year's net profits were more than US $100,000. In 1914 Woolworth opened its 31st shop, in Grafton Street, Dublin. This was the first Woolworth shop in Ireland. After the creation of the Irish Republic, Woolworth established a separate Irish subsidiary, F.W. Woolworth Company of Ireland, Ltd. When World War I began, women store managers took the places of the men who joined the armed forces. When suitable women could not be found, men were drafted from the parent company in the United States. After the war, the British subsidiary was ready for major expansion. The man who was to be principally responsible for the expansion was William L. Stephenson.

Floated As British Public Company in 1931

Frank Woolworth met Stephenson through Edward Owen of Birmingham, a buyer for Wanamaker and other American shops. Stephenson was Owen's assistant. Stephenson started work at the company in September 1909, at the express invitation of Frank Woolworth, even before the first shop had been opened. Stephenson succeeded Fred M. Woolworth, a cousin of Frank, as managing director of the British subsidiary when Fred died in 1923, becoming chairman in 1931 when Woolworth was floated as a British public company and the U.S. parent corporation's interest in its subsidiary was reduced from 62 percent to 52.7 percent of the ordinary shares. Shortly before the flotation, F.W. Woolworth Company of Ireland, Ltd. was voluntarily liquidated and its two shops in Dublin and one each in Cork, Belfast, Limerick, and Kilkenny were incorporated into the British company. The flotation of the chain of 444 shops was underwritten by N.M. Rothschild & Sons. As a result of the company's excellent track record, the Woolworth flotation was a success, despite taking place in the depths of the Great Depression. Since its foundation in 1909 its turnover and profits had never failed to rise from one year to the next, and continued to do so each year until the early part of World War II.

An important change made by Stephenson was to buy properties for his shops instead of taking leases (Stephenson's property investments would later make a major contribution to the revival of Woolworth's successor, Kingfisher, during the 1980s). Under Stephenson's management Woolworth was soon opening shops in Britain at the rate of at least one every fortnight. This remarkable rate of growth was maintained until the early part of World War II. By the late 1930s each shop returned an operating profit two or three times as large as its U.S. counterpart. In 1939, when World War II began, there were 759 British Woolworth shops and nine more under construction.

World War I had brought difficulties to Woolworth but they had been surmounted. From 1914 to 1918 the number of British shops rose from 44 to 81. World War II was different. The expansion program ceased. Furthermore, 23 shops were destroyed and 352 were damaged by enemy action. The company's Channel Island shops in Guernsey and Jersey were placed under German administration from July 1940. In both wars, many of Woolworth's staff joined the armed forces and many did not return. In World War II, however, many who stayed in Woolworth's service were killed by enemy action. In November 1944, a single V2 rocket destroyed the shop at New Cross, London. In this second worst air raid of the war, 160 people in the shop were killed, including the manager and 18 members of her staff, and an additional 108 people were seriously injured.

In 1948 Stephenson retired as chairman of Woolworth. In the early postwar period, it was some time before material losses could be made good. It was not until the latter part of 1956 that the last blitzed shop was reopened. There had been 768 shops in operation in 1940. By 1950 there were still only 762, but from the end of 1951 the expansion program was resumed.

Postwar Expansion at Home and Abroad

In 1954 Woolworth began a new program of expansion into the British Commonwealth with the establishment of a subsidiary in the British West Indies. On November 4, 1954, the company's first store in the West Indies was opened in Kingston, Jamaica. In November 1955 a second West Indian store was opened in Port of Spain, Trinidad. In October 1956 a third shop was opened in Bridgetown, Barbados. Between mid-1958 and the end of 1973 the West Indian subsidiary was expanded to more than a dozen shops located in Jamaica, Trinidad, and Barbados. Woolworth also established a subsidiary in southern Rhodesia, now Zimbabwe, at the end of the 1950s. A shop was opened on March 18, 1959, in the capital, Salisbury. On November 10, 1960, a second shop was opened in Bulawayo. In early 1974 a subsidiary was established in Cyprus and a shop was opened in Nicosia.

Meanwhile, the number of shops in the British Isles also expanded rapidly. The 1,000th shop was opened in Portslade, Hove, Sussex, in May 1958. A peak of 1,141 shops was reached in the late 1960s. With the widening range of merchandise stocked by Woolworth there had to be a wider range of prices. Inflation resulted in the end of the three old pence and six old pence price limits during World War II. In the early postwar period Woolworth pioneered the development of self-service in the variety part of the retail sector. In 1955 Woolworth opened its first British self-service shop in the small village of Cobham, Surrey, modeled on the experience in America. Customers could, if they so desired, collect a wire basket at the shop entrance in which to place their purchases, and payment was made at one of three or four cash desks at the exit, eliminating the need to pay separately at each department visited, as in the traditional shops. The first completely self-service Woolworth shop was opened at Didcot near Oxford in September 1956. By the early 1970s Woolworth had more than 190 purely self-service shops in operation, some of them large by British standards, selling a full variety shop range.

In October 1966 Woolworth founded a new division, the Woolco Department Stores. The division was to oversee the creation of a national chain of up to 20 out-of-town department stores that were to operate independently and in addition to the traditional shops. The stores contained a full range of quality merchandise at competitive prices, including clothes, domestic appliances, toys, groceries, confectionery, car service, and restaurants. The new stores were modeled on the parent company's Woolco stores in U.S. and Canadian suburban shopping centers, which had been in operation since 1962. The first British Woolco was opened in October 1967 at Oadby, Leicester. Oadby provided free parking for about 750 cars away from the congestion of the city center. Between 1969 and 1977 an additional 13 Woolco stores were opened. In 1977, however, Woolworth began to reassess the value of the Woolco division to the company. In December it sold its Woolco store at Kirkby and a hypermarket site with planning permission in Blackpool.

Began Period of Decline in Late 1960s

In the late 1960s profits began to fall at Woolworth. A visible sign of trouble came in 1968, when Woolworth lost its place as Britain's leading retailer and Marks & Spencer overtook it in both sales and profits. Despite a modernization program, Woolworth still possessed a number of small and poorly located branches with an extremely low rate of turnover and profitability. These branches detracted from the improved performance of the larger units. Furthermore, the Woolco stores were still in the development stage. The results announced in January 1970 were the worst since 1962.

During the late 1960s the company's modernization program had been extended to include the enlargement of the company's shops in the major British towns and cities. Two that were opened after extensions in 1968, in Wolverhampton and Ipswich, became the largest in area in Britain. The largest of all, in Wolverhampton, had a shopping area of 70,000 square feet with 1.25 miles of counters. The Aylesbury store, which opened in the jubilee week of the company, on November 7, 1969, became the second largest shop, with an area of 69,000 square feet. In the early 1970s major extensions and modernizations took place at Basingstoke, Brentwood, Hartlepool, Brighton, Leith, Liverpool, Manchester, and Wrexham. These shops included extended male, female, and children's clothing departments; fitting rooms; sports departments; music and record departments; and extended hardware and household departments. They also had extensive food departments and restaurants.

In 1971, with profits still falling, Woolworth began a new cash-and-wrap policy and began to convert 777 shops from conventional behind-the-counter service to a system of centralized payment points in each shop where goods could be paid for and wrapped, thus increasing the speed of service. At the same time the company closed 23 of its unprofitable shops and attempted to trade up and lose its reputation as a purveyor of cheap goods. Nonetheless, the consumer boom of the early 1970s appeared to have passed Woolworth by. Woolworth's profits failed to recover very strongly, in part as a result of the heavy costs of its shop modernization program in the early 1970s and prolonged start-up problems with a new distribution center at Swindon that had been opened in July 1972.

Despite its stated intention to stop selling cheap goods, in 1973 Woolworth decided to open a chain of catalogue discount shops. The new chain, Shoppers World, was launched in Leeds in September 1974 and initially consisted of 15 shops in Birmingham, Liverpool, Manchester, and Leeds. After considerable initial success, the chain also opened an outlet in London in September 1975. Nonetheless, profits continued to stagnate in the mid-1970s. Although the company showed a determination to change with the times, one of its weaknesses was the poor quality of its customer service. Staff turnover was high and this led to consumer dissatisfaction. Another weakness derived from the expansion in the British Isles during the 1950s. Many of the sites chosen were in secondary locations unsuitable for chain stores. An even more serious weakness was that it launched itself into new products in the wrong way. The success of the new products depended on a well-trained staff, first-rate service, and a more polished consumer image than Woolworth had acquired by the mid-1970s. In the late 1970s, however, the performance of the company began to improve. In 1978 the company lifted itself clear of a ten-year profit trough.

Acquired B&Q DIY Chain in 1980

During the late 1970s there was a major change of emphasis in Woolworth away from food into furniture, clothing, do-it-yourself (DIY), and other durable items. In August 1980, in its first ever takeover bid, Woolworth paid £16.7 million for a Southhampton-based chain of more than 40 DIY centers, B&Q (Retail). In October 1981 Woolworth acquired the Dodge City chain of 32 DIY centers for £20.1 million. The centers were complementary to B&Q's 49 existing centers.

Despite the recovery in profits in the late 1970s, Woolworth had still not solved its problems. In 1981, having supposedly repositioned itself upmarket, Woolworth cut prices on 800 of its lines. In addition, Woolworth began to sell off some of its valuable prime town center properties to stem the losses these large shops were making. On balance this made sense, since though these properties were valuable they were also leviathans. The 1981 results, excluding property sales, showed after-tax profits down from £30.3 million to £22.5 million. The company's dividend was cut for the first time in its history. Not only were the shareholders dissatisfied, but also the customers and employees.

Taken Over by Paternoster in 1982

In September 1982 a syndicate of institutional investors led by the merchant bank Charterhouse Japhet launched a £310 million takeover bid for the British Woolworth through the specially created Paternoster Stores plc. Paternoster was led by Wolverhampton-born Chairman John Beckett. By November, more than 90 percent of the shareholders had accepted the syndicate's bid and Paternoster's name was changed to Woolworth Holdings plc. As Paternoster did not have enough money to cover the whole of the bid, U.S. Woolworth temporarily retained a 12.7 percent share in the new company. The holding was sold almost immediately afterward.

Woolworth Holdings began to reorganize by removing the unprofitable parts of the business. Between late 1982 and 1991 the group sold about 200 of its unprofitable Woolworth shops in the United Kingdom, reducing the number to around 790. The group also sold all 18 of its shops in the Irish Republic in 1984. In April 1983 the Shoppers World chain of 45 shops was closed down. Later in 1985 the Woolworth shops in Cyprus were sold and between 1987 and 1990 all of the shops in the West Indies and Zimbabwe were also sold. On the other hand, B&Q, a profitable part of the business, was expanded, mostly through organic growth, with as many as 30 new stores a year. By January 1984 the company's pretax profits had risen from £6.1 million to £29.4 million. To emphasize that the change in the group's Woolworth shops was fundamental, their trading name was changed from F.W. Woolworth to Woolworths in March 1986. In May 1984 the company launched a successful bid for Comet, the electrical goods discount chain, for £128.9 million. During 1984 Woolworths Holdings profits nearly doubled. Profits came from the still-expanding B&Q, now with 153 centers, the newly acquired Comet, and the Woolworth shops disposal program.

In early 1986 Beckett retired as chairman of Woolworths Holdings, having successfully overseen the revival of the group.

During 1986 the company was subject to an unsuccessful £1.75 billion hostile takeover bid from Dixons Group plc, the electronics retailer. During the takeover battle, the group sold its 12 Woolco superstores to Dee Corporation plc for £26 million. The Woolco sale fitted in with the group's "Focus" program—launched in 1985—of concentrating on a narrower range of merchandise: toys, gifts, confectionery, entertainment (including records and cassettes), home and garden accessories, kitchen accessories, kids' clothes, and cosmetics. Food and adult clothing, which contributed 30 percent of sales, were completely abandoned. The Woolco stores, which had specialized in groceries and clothing, had been the first out-of-town food stores and could have become as successful as the Sainsbury superstores later became. The buyers in the old Woolworth were jealous of Woolco's initial success, however, and started cramming them with old-fashioned variety merchandise.

As part of "Focus" the company formed a joint venture with the Rosehaugh property group to redevelop five of its Woolworth shops by reducing the amount of space occupied by the shops. For example, the Wolverhampton shop was shrunk from three floors to one floor. In the opinion of the *Financial Times,* while it made good sense it was a "humiliating climb-down." Also in 1986 came the acquisition of Record Merchandisers, which was later renamed Entertainment UK and which by the mid-1990s was a leading U.K. distributor of pre-recorded music and videos, computer software, and books.

In April 1987 the group was approached by Underwoods, a chain of 40 chemist and consumer goods shops in London. Underwoods suggested the group might like to acquire it, but the chain's profit forecast proved unsatisfactory and the proposal was rejected. The group acquired Charlie Browns, however, a chain of 42 car parts sales and fitting centers in northern England, for £19.2 million. At the end of March the group made a successful bid of £256.9 million for Superdrug plc, a discount chain of 297 drugstores. The company had been established in 1966 by brothers Peter and Ronald Goldstein. In January 1988 the group acquired Ultimate, a chain of 94 electrical retailing outlets, from Harris Queensway for £6.3 million. Ultimate was integrated into Comet. In January 1988 the group launched a successful takeover bid of £13 million for Tip Top Drugstores plc, a chain of 110 drugstores. These were integrated into the 339-store Superdrug chain. Tip Top's strength lay in northern England and Scotland, while Superdrug's lay in southeast England. In February the group launched another successful bid of £32 million for Share Drug plc, a chain of 145 drugstores that was also integrated into Superdrug, strengthening its position in southern England. Also in 1988, Woolworth Properties—the group's property holding and development arm—was renamed Chartwell Land plc.

Renamed Kingfisher plc in 1989

On March 17, 1989, the group was renamed Kingfisher plc. The purpose of the new name was to emphasize how much the group had changed since it was purchased from its U.S. parent in 1982. In October Kingfisher acquired the Laskys chain of 58 electrical goods shops for £3.6 million. Kingfisher claimed that, by taking on £5.3 million of bank debt from Granada PLC, the shops would be integrated with Comet's 308 shops. In fact, most of them were closed after they had been operating under the Comet name for only a few months. In November 1989 Kingfisher acquired the Medicare chain of 86 drug stores from Isosceles for about £5 million. About a third were closed and the remainder was integrated with Superdrug.

In December 1989 Kingfisher launched a hostile £568 million takeover bid for Dixons. In January 1990 the bid was referred by the British government to the Monopolies and Mergers Commission (MMC) because "... there are possible effects on competition in the UK market for the retail of electrical goods." The bid was blocked by the Trade and Industry Secretary at the end of May following the publication of the MMC's report, which had recommended that the merger not be permitted. Also in early 1990, Geoffrey Mulcahy was named chairman of Kingfisher.

Acquisitive 1990s

During the 1990s Kingfisher made a number of acquisitions, in the process becoming a much more diversified retailer and building an enlarged presence in continental Europe. Its first major move of the decade, however, was to grow organically through the launch of a new retail concept, Music and Video Club (MVC), which specialized in such home entertainment staples as music CDs and cassettes, prerecorded videos, and multimedia products; by 1996 there were 34 MVCs in the United Kingdom. Next, Kingfisher made a short-lived move into the office supply superstore arena. In early 1993 Kingfisher entered into a joint venture with Framingham, Massachusetts-based Staples, Inc. to form Staples UK; by late 1996 the venture had opened 34 Staples stores in the United Kingdom. In late 1993 Kingfisher spent £7.9 million to acquire a 33 percent stake in Maxi-Papier-Markt, a German office superstore chain. In late 1996 the company sold its stakes in both Staples UK and Maxi-Papier—both of which were losing money—to Staples, Inc. for £29.4 million, a move designed to enable Kingfisher to concentrate on its core areas.

A successful and burgeoning area for the company in the 1990s was that of electrical goods retailing. With Comet already in the fold, Kingfisher set its sights on the continent. In 1993 the company acquired Le Groupe Darty of France; Darty held the top spot among electrical retailers in France. In 1996 Kingfisher spent £84.2 million to acquire a 26 percent interest in BUT S.A., the fourth largest electrical retailer in France. Discussions in late 1997 regarding a complete takeover of BUT led nowhere. But in the meantime, Kingfisher bolstered its Comet unit through the purchase of NORWEB Retail, a division of NORWEB plc, with about 80 stores subsequently integrated into Comet. The company also gained electrical retail chains in Belgium (New Vanden Borre, with 19 stores) in late 1996 and in the Netherlands (BCC, with 17 stores) in mid-1997. In mid-1998 Kingfisher paid about £50 million (US $83.3 million) for a 60 percent stake in two German retailers—Promarkt Holding GmbH (Holdings) and Wegert Verwaltungs-GmbH and Co. Beteiligungs-KG—whose businesses were then merged. Together, the companies ran 53 Promarkt electrical stores, 108 smaller photographic equipment and film processing services outlets, and 11 units selling CDs and other entertainment items.

In general, the 1990s were a period of increasing sales and profitability. For the 1995 fiscal year, however, Kingfisher's profits dropped significantly, in large part due to sharp falls in profits at both Woolworths and Comet. As a result Alan Smith, who had been brought in as chief executive from Marks & Spencer two years earlier, was ousted in early 1995 and Mulcahy was demoted from chairman to chief executive (Smith and Mulcahy had reportedly clashed over how the company should be managed). By early 1996 John Banham had stepped into the chairmanship, having previously served as director general of the Confederacy of British Industry. Meanwhile, in April 1995 Kingfisher sold the Charlie Browns auto repair and parts chain, now considered "noncore," to Montinex for £19 million.

By fiscal 1998 the company had turned around the Woolworths and Comet chains primarily by restoring their price competitiveness and resolving distribution and systems troubles. For the year, Kingfisher achieved record sales of £6.41 billion (US $10.73 billion), an increase of 10.2 percent over 1997, and profit before tax and exceptional items of £505.5 million (US $846.3 million), an increase of 29.5 percent. B&Q had particularly impressive results, including a same-store sales increase of 12.6 percent.

Around the time that it was announcing these stellar performances, Kingfisher was also denying rumors that it was considering divesting Woolworths and Superdrug to concentrate on B&Q and its electrical retailing units. The company issued a statement saying that "both Woolworths and Superdrug are very much part of Kingfisher's future." It was worth noting, however, that Woolworths, the unit upon which the company was founded, was responsible for only about a quarter of overall sales and less than 20 percent of earnings by the mid-1990s. It appeared likely that at the dawn of a new century, and in the era of European union, the Kingfisher of the future would seek additional opportunities to expand beyond its Woolworths roots and to become even more geographically diverse.

Principal Subsidiaries

B&Q plc; Le Groupe Darty (France); Comet Group PLC; Woolworths plc; Superdrug Stores PLC; Chartwell Land plc; Entertainment UK Ltd.; The Music and Video Club Limited; New Vanden Borre (Belgium); BCC Holding Amstelveen B.V. (Netherlands); BUT S.A. (France; 26%).

Further Reading

Buckley, Neil, "Banham to Head Kingfisher," *Financial Times,* October 16, 1995, p. 24.
——, "Kingfisher Aims to Correct Mistakes," *Financial Times,* March 15, 1995, p. 27.
——, "Kingfisher Moves into Office Supplies Stores," *Financial Times,* December 21, 1993, p. 18.
——, "Kingfisher Sets Out Agenda," *Financial Times,* May 6, 1995, p. 10.
——, "Kingfisher Turns the Corner," *Financial Times,* January 18, 1996, p. 25.
——, "Kingfisher Vows to Set Things Right," *Financial Times,* March 15, 1995, p. 25.
——, "Potential Cost of Selling It Cheap Every Day," *Financial Times,* March 24, 1994, p. 17.
Hollinger, Peggy, and Andrew Jack, "Kingfisher Halts Talks on Bid for Retailer," *Financial Times,* October 13, 1997, p. 27.

Kirkwood, Robert C., *The Woolworth Story at Home and Abroad,* New York: Newcomen Society in North America, 1960.

The Monopolies and Mergers Commission, ''Kingfisher Plc and Dixons Group Plc: A Report on the Proposed Merger,'' London: HMSO, 1990.

Mulcahy, Geoffrey, ''Woolworth Holdings,'' in *Turn-around: How Twenty Well-Known Companies Came Back from the Brink,* edited by Rebecca Nelson and David Clutterbuck, London: Mercury, 1988.

Oram, Roderick, ''Kingfisher Ousts Top Executives,'' *Financial Times,* January 28, 1995, p. 1.

——, ''Kingfisher's Challenge,'' *Financial Times,* February 4, 1995, p. 14.

——, ''Victim in Struggle to Evolve,'' *Financial Times,* January 28, 1995, p. 7.

''Staples Launches British Invasion,'' *Discount Store News,* January 4, 1993, pp. 31+.

Thornhill, John, ''Retailers Must Save Themselves,'' *Financial Times,* October 17, 1992, p. 13.

Urry, Maggie, and Alice Rawsthorn, ''Retail Monarchs in Search of Global Empires,'' *Financial Times,* February 5, 1993, p. 15.

Winkler, John K., *Five and Ten: The Fabulous Life of F.W. Woolworth,* London: Hale, 1941; reprinted, Freeport, N.Y.: Books for Libraries Press, 1970.

''Woolworth: The Story of a Great Achievement,'' *New Bond,* Vol. 18, No. 1, March 1959.

Wright, Robert, ''Kingfisher Surprises with Upturn,'' *Financial Times,* March 19, 1998, p. 26.

—Richard Hawkins
—updated by David E. Salamie

Kohlberg Kravis Roberts & Co.

9 West 57th Street
New York, New York 10019
U.S.A.
(212) 750-8300
Fax: (212) 593-2430

Private Company
Founded: 1976
Sales: $1.2 billion (1996 est.)
SICs: 6211 Security Brokers, Dealers & Flotation
     Companies

Kohlberg Kravis Roberts & Co. (KKR) is one of the largest investment and merchant banking houses in the United States. It was the first to conduct, on a large scale, the leveraged buyouts (LBOs) that privatized many American corporations in the 1980s and, in the biggest LBO ever, purchased RJR Nabisco Inc. for $30.6 billion in 1989. KKR cast a lower profile in the 1990s, but its funds still had $16.4 billion to invest in early 1997—more than any other institutional sponsor of private equity funds. Besides investing on its own account, KKR was trading for such clients as insurance companies, nonprofit organizations, and state pension funds. According to one source, it realized, during its first 20 years of existence, an average annual return of 23.5 percent on its investments, compared with around 15 percent during this period for the Standard & Poor index of 500 stocks.

A Decade of Megabuck Deals: 1976–86

Jerome Kohlberg, Jr., was in charge of the corporate finance department at the Wall Street firm of Bear, Stearns & Co. when he devised or first utilized, in 1965, the technique later to be called the leveraged buyout. Kohlberg believed a company would be better managed if it were owned by a small group of highly motivated investors—often including the top company executives—rather than thousands of shareholders who rarely had the knowledge or time to make sure the business was being run effectively. To raise the money, the investors would borrow heavily—as much as ten times the cash they actually contributed—usually pledging as collateral the assets of the company they intended to acquire. They would reap their profit by later selling the company to new owners or issuing stock to the public.

George Roberts and his cousin Henry Kravis became proteges of Kohlberg at Bear, Stearns, although Roberts relocated to the company's San Francisco office. They conducted 14 buyouts between 1969 and 1975 with generally mediocre results in a time of recession and falling stock prices. One of the companies they bought for $27 million, Cobblers Industries, went bankrupt. However, investors in Vapor Corp., purchased in 1972 for about $37 million, recovered their stake 12-fold when the company was sold in 1978. Industrial Components Groups, a division of Rockwell International purchased in 1975, yielded 22 times the original investment in five years.

Restive at Bear, Stearns, Kohlberg persuaded Kravis and Roberts to join him in the partnership that opened its doors in 1976. KKR created an equity fund which KKR, as general partner, used to purchase companies. Adding to the pool were major lenders entitled to fixed returns and, where law permitted, sweeteners like warrants or common stock free or at bargain prices. A favorite inducement for banks was preferred stock, which offered an 85 percent tax exemption on dividends. Because of the huge debt incurred in LBOs, a prospective target had to be able to generate the high cash flow needed to make interest payments. This excluded high-technology companies with heavy research and development expenditures. The most attractive prospects were businesses like supermarket operators, provided they had little prior debt and a market niche that protected them from severe competitive pressures.

In 1977 KKR bought three companies, but investors were hard to find and the firm made no deals the next year. In 1979, however, KKR bought Houdaille Industries for about $355 million—by far the largest LBO transaction to that time and KKR's first buyout of a major publicly held company. Prior to then no LBO had been for much over $100 million. For investing $12 million of its own money, KKR received 37 percent of the voting common stock. Investors, including big banks, now began to come on board. By the fall of 1980 the firm had paid nearly $800 million to acquire seven companies with combined annual sales totaling about $1.3 billion.

Another breakthrough for KKR came in 1981, when Roberts tapped a conservative investor—Oregon's public employees' pension fund—to contribute $178 million for the leveraged buyout of Fred Meyer Inc., one of the seven companies KKR acquired that year. Soon other state pension funds, looking for a better yield than what they were earning from bonds, were willing to sign on. By 1986 11 state pension funds were partners in KKR equity pools. When KKR initiated a $5.6 billion fund—its largest ever—in 1987, the 11 provided 53 percent of the money.

In addition to pension funds and other limited partners willing to provide equity (about ten percent of an LBO) and banks willing to make loans (60 percent), KKR needed subordinated lenders (30 percent), who earned a higher fixed rate by taking more risk because they were the last to get paid. Historically, insurance companies tended to be the main source of subordinated debt. By the mid-1980s, however, firms such as Drexel Burnham Lambert Inc. had assembled big money by attracting private investors to high-yield junk-bond funds which would assume the necessary risk.

For its own part, KKR collected the standard investment banking fee of around one percent for making a deal, which it usually invested in the stock of the acquired company. It also collected annual consulting fees from the acquired company. KKR partners sat on the boards of these companies and collected directors' fees. KKR also received a 1.5 percent annual management fee on the money in an equity fund not yet invested. But the real payoff for the firm was, as general partner, its 20 percent share of the capital gains from the eventual resale of the acquired company. KKR even took a fee—one percent—when it sold a company at a loss. Everybody in the firm, from the partners to the secretaries, had a stake in the rewards.

By 1983 KKR was claiming an average annual return of 63 percent to its equity partners. That year KKR's fourth equity fund accumulated $1 billion from investors, enabling its roster of companies to reach 18, acquired for a total of $3.5 billion. KKR was using this money for ever-bigger deals. In 1985 the firm acquired Storer Communications for a record $2.5 billion. When Storer was sold in 1988, KKR's partners achieved an annual return of around 50 percent. Also in 1985, KKR conducted its first hostile takeover; previously it had made an acquisition only when management (which got a stake in the deal) agreed.

KKR launched a new, $2 billion fund in 1986. The acquisition of Safeway Stores Inc. that year was the best transaction KKR ever made, according to a *Fortune* article that appeared ten years later. The firm paid $4.3 billion but put down only $130 million itself and reaped more than $5 billion in realized and paper profits. KKR's remaining one-third stake in the company was valued at more than $3.5 billion in early 1997. Even bigger was KKR's 1986 takeover of Beatrice Cos. for about $6.2 billion. The firm put up $402 million in equity capital, while Drexel provided $2.5 billion in junk-bond financing. According to KKR, when the final returns from this deal were realized in 1992, limited partners enjoyed an annual return of 43 percent.

The Going Gets Tougher: 1987–89

By this time, however, Kohlberg was now on his way out. After spending 1984 recovering from a serious illness, he re-turned to find that he was not needed or wanted by his younger partners. Kohlberg was disturbed by KKR's ever more aggressive search for deals that disturbingly echoed the tactics of corporate raiders. He vetoed so many prospective deals that he became known at KKR as "Doctor No." Kohlberg resigned in 1987 to form his own company but remained a limited partner in KKR. In 1990 Kohlberg sued his partners, alleging that they had illegally reduced his ownership stake in several buyout deals. The suit was settled under undisclosed terms.

Of the remaining founders, Kravis was the one who cast the higher profile. While Roberts, in California, avoided the limelight, "King Henry," as the media dubbed Kravis, took fashion designer Carolyne Roehm as his second wife. The couple was prominent on the social scene, contributing heavily to charities and maintaining a Manhattan duplex apartment plus homes in Colorado, Connecticut, and Long Island.

There seemed to be no limit to KKR's dominance at this time. Having raised $5.6 billion for its 1987 fund, the firm bought eight companies in the next two years for $43.9 billion, among them the over $1 billion purchases of Owens-Illinois, Duracell, and Stop & Shop. If ranked as a single industrial company, the businesses KKR controlled would have placed it among the top ten U.S. corporations. When stock prices plunged in October 1987, KKR secretly bought chunks of several top-level U.S. corporations but was unable to sell their chiefs on the LBO idea.

KKR's biggest LBO—indeed the biggest of all time—was its acquisition of RJR Nabisco, Inc. for $30.6 billion. The bidding started with a $17.5 billion offer from Shearson Lehman Hutton. Other interested parties included Merrill Lynch and Forstmann Little, neither of which charged a fee when it sold companies, an annual fee to manage them, or directors' fees for having their executives sit on the boards of the companies they controlled.

KKR topped Shearson, only to have the ante raised in turn by Forstmann Little. In what unsympathetic outsiders described as high-stakes macho posturing and a fitting end to a decade of greed, Kravis won the battle but clearly overpaid for his prize. KKR had to take 58 percent of the company itself. In 1990 it needed to pump in $1.7 billion more for a $6.9 billion recapitalization of RJR, which, after going public in 1991, lost more than $3 billion of its market value in the next two years. In 1995 KKR traded its remaining stake in RJR for ownership of Borden Inc.

KKR made other mistakes during 1987–88. Jim Walter Corp. (later Walter Industries), purchased for about $2.4 billion, later went bankrupt. Seaman Furniture Co., acquired for about $360 million, had to be restructured in 1989 to avoid bankruptcy and was in bankruptcy during 1992–93. Hillsborough Holdings Corp., purchased for $3.3 billion, went bankrupt in 1989. American Forest Products, bought from Bendix Corp. for $425 million, was sold at a loss.

Adapting and Thriving in the 1990s

After the completion of the RJR Nabisco deal in February 1989, KKR did not make another LBO acquisition for three years, not because of any loss of nerve but due to the collapse of the junk-bond market, a growing reluctance of banks to lend for this purpose, and fewer corporate raiders to put companies into play. To some degree, KKR was a victim of its own success, since companies increasingly had put their houses in order before they became vulnerable to a takeover. ''Paying off debt, getting rid of divisions that are not up to snuff—companies can do that for themselves now,'' a University of Chicago professor told a *New York Times* reporter in 1995.

Without lucrative LBOs to put into effect, KKR became less attractive to partners like the state pension funds, which then began complaining about its fees. In 1989 KKR had reported an annualized rate of return of 19.5 percent, well below its average. Investors wanted higher yields to compensate for high risk and the need to keep their money tied up until there was a payoff in the form of a company sale. Bad publicity concerning fired Safeway workers riled some limited partners, especially public pension funds whose constituents included unionized workers.

One alternative KKR tried was ''leveraged buildups.'' The firm bought a piece of Macmillan Inc. in 1989 and turned it into K-III Holdings Inc., a publishing and information-resources conglomerate that had made 52 acquisitions by 1997, when it was renamed Primedia Inc. This venture was unusual in that KKR took and continued to hold most of the equity itself. A similar transaction was KKR's 1991 injection of $283 million into Fleet/Norstar Financial Group for the purchase of the assets of the failed Bank of New England. KKR also took ''toehold'' minority positions in companies such as ConAgra Inc., Texaco Inc., and First Interstate Bancorp, remaining a passive investor.

KKR consoled itself and stilled its critics by taking six prior LBO acquisitions public in 1991 for a combined estimated $6 billion, which meant a sixfold return to the investors in five years, not counting the firm's own fees. In 1992 KKR purchased American Re-Insurance Co. for $1.2 billion, an LBO acquisition at $10 a share. Keeping a one-fourth stake, KKR took the company public only four months later at $31 a share. Also in 1992, the firm raised $1.8 billion for a new fund.

Even so, as the 1990s continued, disillusionment over KKR's performance became more vocal. A *Fortune* article claimed in 1994 that since the early 1980s the firm had barely outpaced the Standard & Poor 500 stock index, at least for its two largest investors, the Oregon and Washington state pension funds. In its 1996 annual report, Oregon's state treasury said it was disappointed with the returns on more than half of its $2.1 billion investment in KKR funds, of which $1.2 billion was in the 1987 fund. Burdened by poor-performing investments in RJR Nabisco and K-III, this fund had an average annual yield of only 12.6 percent through 1996.

As the stock market roared ahead in the mid-1990s, KKR improved its record by cashing in some more of its acquisitions. The sale of Duracell, which had gone public in 1991 as Duracell International Inc., in 1996 to Gillette Co. for stock valued at $7.9 billion brought KKR $3.7 billion for an original investment of $350 million. Between the beginning of 1995 and September 1996 it sold, for $7 billion, stock originally acquired for $1.3 billion. This included American Re for $3.3 billion and Stop & Shop for $1.8 billion. In 1996 alone the firm sold five companies for $5.3 billion.

These gains were counterbalanced by some losers. Flagstar Corp., in which the firm had invested $300 million in 1992, filed for bankruptcy in 1997. KKR put up $250 million for the $1.15 billion LBO in 1995 of the Bruno's Inc. grocery chain but wrote off the entire sum in early 1998, when the company's debt had reached about $1 billion. Spalding & Evenflo Cos., in which KKR had invested $420 million, was barely covering its interest payments in early 1998. Primedia (the former K-III) was still losing money after almost a decade because of the heavy cost of making payments on its acquisition debts.

KKR raised a record $5.7 billion for its 1996 fund. To raise this sum, the firm agreed for the first time to deduct losses from its profits and to reduce its transaction fees. Among the subscribers was the Oregon pension fund, which despite its misgivings committed to $800 million after a sales call by Roberts. For KKR the year was the firm's most lucrative ever, with Kravis and Roberts each believed to have collected $300 million. Kravis's personal fortune was estimated at more than $1 billion.

The following year was a quieter one for KKR, which was reported to be casting its eye on Europe. By early 1998, however, the firm had raised $5.8 billion for its latest equity fund. KKR had 11 partners and 14 associates at the end of 1996. Offices were in New York and Menlo Park, California.

Further Reading

Anreder, Steven S., ''High-Wire Finance,'' *Barron's,* September 24, 1979, pp. 4–6, 8, 20.

Arenson, Karen W., ''Kohlberg's Leveraged Success,'' *New York Times,* September 29, 1980, pp. D1, D5.

Bartlett, Sarah, *The Money Machine,* New York: Warner Books, 1991.

Bianco, Anthony, ''KKR Hears a New Word from Some Backers: 'No','' *Business Week,* April 15, 1991, pp. 80–82.

Burrough, Bryan, and John Helyar, *Barbarians at the Gate,* New York: Harper & Row, 1990.

Eichenwald, Kurt, ''Kohlberg, Kravis Rouses Itself,'' *New York Times,* April 29, 1991, pp. D1, D7.

Farrell, Christopher, ''King Henry,'' *Business Week,* November 14, 1988, pp. 125–127.

Hylton, Richard D., ''How KKR Got Beaten at Its Own Game,'' *Fortune,* May 2, 1994, pp. 104–06.

Jereski, Laura, ''How KKR Recovered from Some Trouble, Chalked Up a Big Year,'' *Wall Street Journal,* December 31, 1996, pp. 1–2.

Kleinfeld, N. R., ''Kohlberg Collects Companies,'' *New York Times,* December 12, 1983, pp. D1, D5.

Lipin, Steven, ''KKR Is Back, and It Boasts Big War Chest,'' *Wall Street Journal,* September 16, 1996, pp. C1, C15.

Loomis, Carol J., ''Ten Years After,'' *Fortune,* February 17, 1997, pp. 114–17.

Nathans, Leah J., ''KKR Is Doing Just Fine—Without LBOs,'' *Business Week,* July 30, 1990, pp. 56–59.

Ross, Irwin, ''How the Champs Do Leveraged Buyouts,'' *Fortune,* January 23, 1984, pp. 70, 72, 74, 78.

Rustin, Richard E., ''Kohlberg Kravis Hones Its Takeover Technique,'' *Wall Street Journal,* September 25, 1980, pp. 35, 38.

Schifrin, Matthew, ''LBO Madness,'' *Forbes,* March 9, 1998, pp. 130–31, 133–34.

Spiro, Leah Nathans, ''KKR Plays a Slower Game,'' *Business Week,* June 29, 1990, pp. 96–97.

Truell, Peter, ''At KKR the Glory Days Are Past,'' *New York Times,* August 10, 1995, pp. D1, D4.

—Robert Halasz

The Learning Company Inc.

1 Athenaeum Pl.
Cambridge, Massachusetts 02142
U.S.A.
(617) 494-1200
(800) 377-6567
Fax: (617) 494-1219
Web Site: http://www.learningco.com

Public Company
Incorporated: 1978 as Micropro International Corp.
Employees: 1,400
Sales: $392.4 million (1997)
Stock Exchanges: New York
Ticker Symbol: TLC
SICs: 7372 Prepackaged Software; 5045 Computers,
   Peripherals & Software; 7373 Computer Integrated
   Systems Design; 8742 Management Consulting
   Services

The Learning Company Inc. develops, publishes, and markets a family of premium software brands that educate across every age and area of interest, from young children to adults. The Learning Company's products are sold in more than 23,000 stores across 40 countries through multiple distribution channels including retail, school, online, and direct marketing.

The Learning Company Inc. is America's premier developer and marketer of educational and reference software for consumers and schools. The company develops and publishes a broad range of high-quality consumer educational software for personal computers (PCs) for all age groups, featuring some of the most well-known brand name products on the market. The company manufactures primarily education and reference software, but also offers materials focusing on lifestyle, productivity, and entertainment.

The company's educational products are generally marketed under The Learning Company and MECC brand names, and include the ''College Prep,'' ''Foreign Languages,'' ''Oregon

Trail,'' ''Reader Rabbit,'' ''Treasure,'' ''Super Solvers,'' and ''Writing and Creativity Tools'' lines. In addition to consumer versions of these products, the company also publishes school editions of a number of them.

The company's reference products include a line of Compton's Home Library brand products, including Compton's Interactive Encyclopedia, as well as the American Heritage Talking Dictionary, Mosby's Medical Encyclopedia, and Body-Works.

The company's premium productivity and lifestyle products are primarily sold under the SoftKey brand name. The company also publishes lower-priced boxed products under the ''Key'' brand name, and a line of budget, jewel-case-only products under the ''Platinum'' brand name. Other lines include products bearing the Sesame Street, Madeline, and School House Rock labels.

From Micropro to WordStar, 1978–93

The company was originally incorporated in California in October 1978 as Micropro International Corp. and then incorporated again in Delaware in November 1986 as a successor to Micropro International Corp.

Based in Novato, California, the company changed its name to WordStar International Inc. in May 1989 due to its focus on developing and distributing the then-popular word processing software of the same name, an early predecessor, and then competitor with Microsoft Word and WordPerfect.

In March 1991, the company acquired Lifetree Software Inc. for $1.9 million in cash, stock, and future payments. Several months later, in July, the company created a foreign subsidiary, WordStar International S.A., France. The company grew a bit in January 1993 when it completed a merger with ZSoft.

SoftKey International Inc., 1994–96

In February 1994, WordStar International Inc. was a fading industry heavyweight whose WordStar word-processing program once dominated the market. With sagging sales, the company gave in to a lucrative three-way merger with Cambridge, Massachusetts-based Spinnaker Software Corp. and Toronto, Ontario-based SoftKey Software Products Inc. Spinnaker brought its "PFS" line of budget personal productivity software and SoftKey brought its budget titles under the "Key" brand name to the deal. The newly formed company was renamed SoftKey International Inc.

Ron Posner, the chairman of WordStar, helped engineer the merger and then stepped aside to become chairman of San Francisco-based Starpress Inc. The top management of the original SoftKey, including President Kevin O'Leary and Chairman Michael Perik, took control, set up headquarters in Cambridge, Massachusetts, and largely dismantled both Spinnaker and WordStar, retaining only a small development team to keep cranking out new products.

The new company's breadth of business included developing personal productivity, educational/entertainment, and personal and office organizational software for home and small business users; developing income tax software and providing comprehensive nationwide tax processing for personal, corporate, and trust tax returns in Canada; and distributing and servicing LANSA software, a family of CASE products for the IBM AS/400 computer. The new company became one of the top U.S. software distributors, and the market leader in the Canadian tax software business.

Acquisitions continued in June as the company acquired Aris Multimedia Entertainment Inc. for an undisclosed amount and, the following month, the company acquired Compact Publishing, Inc. September saw the company acquiring Software Marketing Corporation of Phoenix, Arizona, in exchange for approximately 600,000 shares of common stock and the assumption of $1.6 million in long-term debt.

And, as the company itself grew, so did the industry, with sales of educational software in the United States generating $522 million in 1994.

In 1995, SoftKey went on an acquisition hayride, purchasing numerous companies in an effort to capture more of the market share in educational and entertainment software. In July, the company acquired Tewi Verlag GmbH, a German limited liability company, in exchange for approximately $11.6 million cash paid to Ziff-Davis and approximately $1.5 million cash and 99,045 shares of common stock paid to Kunkel. The following month, SoftKey acquired Future Vision Holding, Inc., a New York multimedia software business.

In December, the company gave itself a Christmas present when it acquired Fremont, California-based The Learning Co. for nearly $606 million in a hostile outbidding of Broderbund Software Inc.'s offer for approximately $552 million. Broderbund—known for its "Where in the World is Carmen Sandiego?" line of products; the math-teaching program The Logical Journey of the Zoombinis; Kid Pix Studio, Math Workshop and Print Shop; and distribution of the hit game Myst—had previously been given the go-ahead for a merger with The Learning Co. in August, but the more lucrative offer from SoftKey caused the latter to give in to the hostile bid. The acquisition gave the company product lines focusing on the kids market, as Learning Co. was best known for its line of educa-

tional children's software, especially the Reader Rabbit (in which children travel with Reader Rabbit, Mat the Mouse, and Sam the Lion through "Letter Lands" containing "Skill Houses" where they learn phonics and words through games and activities, and "Storybooks" where they are taught new words and simple sentences) and Math Rabbit (a similar math adventure) series of learning games, and its Knoxville, Tennessee division's language education software for adults marketed under the "Learn to Speak" brand name.

The Learning Company's products had begun achieving favorable recognition as far back as 1991, when Reader Rabbit 1 won *Technology & Learning* Magazine's Language Arts Program of the Decade. The following year, the company's products continued to gain recognition, with Reader Rabbit 2 winning a Parents' Choice Foundation Award, the Software Publishers Association's Award for Best Elementary Education Product, and *Technology & Learning* Magazine's Award of Excellence. The year 1993 followed with Treasure Cove! and Treasure MathStorm!, both winning Innovations '93 Software Showcase Honors at the Summer Consumer Electronics Show. In 1994, Reader Rabbit 1 won a Gold Medal from The National Association of Parenting Publications Awards (NAPPA); Reader Rabbit 2 won *Technology & Learning* Magazine's Software Award for Excellence—Next in Series; and Treasure MathStorm! received an Honorable Mention—Math from *Practical Homeschooling*'s First Annual Reader Awards and an Award of Excellence from *Technology & Learning* Magazine.

That same month, the company completed a merger with Compton's NewMedia, Inc. from Tribune Company for approximately 4.7 million shares of common stock and Tribune Company made a $150 million strategic investment in the company. The company also acquired EduSoft in late 1995, finishing a $1.2 billion shopping spree for the year and reinventing the company as a category leader in educational software.

But snapping up the competition was not the only thing the company was doing to shake up the industry. With the elimination of elaborate packaging and hard-copy documentation, and the move to jewel-case formats with CD-sized booklets, SoftKey pioneered the budget line of CD-ROM products in 1995, with the company's "Platinum" line titles carrying retail list prices of $12.99 instead of the mid-$30 range most of the premiere products carried. With the new packaging, a new distribution deal was made with SoftKey switching from Stream International to BMG, with the latter company's subsidiary, BMG Distribution, providing fulfillment services for the budget line. The move brought the company's products into a wide range of retail outlets, including Best Buy, Circuit City, Computer City, Egghead Software, Office Depot, Price Club/Costco, Sam's Club, and Staples.

SoftKey's products were well-received in 1995, with Reader Rabbit's Interactive Reading Journey winning a plethora of awards, including *Home PC*'s Award of Excellence, *Parenting* Magazine's Software Magic Award, The Parent Council's Seal for outstanding product, *Technology & Learning* Magazine's Award of Excellence for the School category), an approval from The Parents' Choice Foundation, *Mac Home Journal*'s Reader's Choice Award, *CD-ROM Today* Magazine's Best Children's Program–Reading Award, and *Home Computing &*

Entertainment Magazine's Best Educational Program Award. The Reader Rabbit 1 program also won *Newsweek* Magazine's Editors' Choice Award, and Reader Rabbit 2 and Reader Rabbit 3 both were winners in *Only the Best: The Annual Guide to the Highest-Rated Educational Software/Multimedia, 1994/95.*

With more than 15,000 titles competing for a limited amount of shelf space in a become-a-hit-in-90-days-or-die market, retail prices on software began falling. But the company's revenues for 1995 still grew to $273.6 million, with a net income of $42.1 million.

The Learning Company Inc., 1996–Date

In May 1996, SoftKey, whose products at the time included popular consumer titles like Calendar Creator Plus and The American Heritage Talking Dictionary, acquired Minnesota Educational Computing Corporation (MECC), a publisher and distributor of high-quality educational software for children, in a stock swap worth $361 million, making the company a major force in the education software market. MECC brought to the merger its hit Oregon Trail series of products as well as other educational titles. The acquisition of MECC, combined with the previous acquisitions of The Learning Co. and Compton's New Media, enabled Softkey to capture approximately 16 percent of the educational software market, catapulting the company to the second position behind Microsoft Corp.

The acquisitions of MECC, Compton, and The Learning Company by SoftKey were in keeping with a trend of consolidation in the educational software marketplace. Analysts predicted the hundreds of existing companies in the entertainment and educational software markets would be gobbled up by five or ten larger companies, and the trend appeared to be in fullswing as companies like Starpress Inc. merged with Irvine, California-based Graphix Zone Inc.

Following the MECC acquisition, SoftKey laid off 125 employees of New Media and began aggressively driving the prices of its educational software down to the $20 to $25 range per title, dropping from the usual $40 to $50 at which most such titles were being sold.

The name was changed from SoftKey International to The Learning Company Inc. in October 1996 and the company's Operation Neptune made a splash at COMDEX as an excellent educational tool for children.

Again, in 1996, The Learning Company's products garnered much recognition, with Reader Rabbit's Interactive Reading Journey 2 winning a SuperKids Software Award for Best Reading Software, Reader Rabbit's Interactive Math Journey winning Curriculum Administrator Magazine's Top 100 Districts' Choice Award, and Read, Write & Type! winning Innovations '96's Software Showcase Honors at the Winter Consumer Electronics Show. Revenues for the company in 1996 reached $343.3 million, with net income of $72.3 million.

In June 1997, the company, firmly positioned among the top ten software manufacturers in the United States, signed another deal with BMG Entertainment for the latter company to manufacture and distribute additional CD-ROM products of The Learning Co. BMG's manufacturing division, Sonopress, man-ufactured the actual products, and BMG Distribution handled the fulfillment services. The agreement allowed BMG to diversify beyond its core businesses of music and video and into the CD-ROM market, when many manufacturers of music CDs began devoting much of their production capacity to CD-ROM manufacturing as the floppy disk began losing ground to the CD-ROM, following its music analogs of records and cassette tapes to CD.

A month later, The Learning Co. introduced a double CD-ROM or deluxe edition of their reference software program, Compton's Interactive Encyclopedia, which contained additional multimedia content, enhanced Internet links, and streamlined methods for research. The company, which ranked second in the encyclopedia category behind Microsoft's Encarta and in front of IBM's World Book Multimedia Encyclopedia and Grolier Interactive's Grolier Encyclopedia, respectively, in the retail market worth approximately $45 million in 1996, also added links to Web sites and an "Ask the Librarian" feature that allowed users to e-mail their research topics to Compton's and within 48 hours receive suggested online resources or print materials.

In October, the company acquired Microsystems Software, Inc., the creator of Cyber Patrol, the software which allows parents and teachers to choose what content on the Internet is appropriate for children, letting adults block material organized into different categories, including violence, nudity, explicit sexual material, and hate speech. The program was also customizable for up to ten different children, and contained a list of more than 40,000 inappropriate sites. In addition to blocking unsuitable content, Cyber Patrol also contained a unique ChatGard feature that prevented children from inadvertently divulging personal information, such as age, address, phone number, or school name, to strangers through Web sites and online chatrooms; managed access to chatrooms; and controlled the time that a child spent online.

By the end of December, the company announced that it had acquired all of the equity interest in Redwood City, California-based Creative Wonders LLC from New York City-based ABC Inc., a subsidiary of The Walt Disney Company and Electronic Arts Inc., for approximately $40 million in cash and stock options. The acquisition added a host of popular characters to the company's stables, including those from The Children's Television Workshop's Sesame Street, as well as School House Rock, The Baby Sitters Club, and Madeline.

Growing a bit too fast, The Learning Company suffered a loss of nearly $450 million by the end of 1997. Luckily, The Thomas H. Lee Company, Bain Capital Inc., and Centre Partners Management LLC purchased The Tribune Company's 22 percent stake, approximately 15 million shares of stock, for $123 million, and was awarded several seats on the board of directors. The reinvestment allowed the company to slash its debt by about two-thirds.

Also in December, at The Internet/Online Summit: Focus on Children, as part of a nationwide commitment to ensure that technology solutions would be easy to use and widely available, the company announced it would begin selling its popular Internet filter Cyber Patrol in retail outlets in the United States.

The program, which until then had only been available for purchase via phone; the company's Web site; and through agreements with America Online, CompuServe, Prodigy, Microsoft's Internet Explorer Plus, and other Internet service providers; was the world's most widely used Internet filtering software designed to help protect children in cyberspace.

The company's products continued to achieve recognition, with Reader Rabbit's Interactive Reading Journey 2 picking up a Silver Apple from The National Educational Media Network; and Reader Rabbit's Interactive Math Journey winning kudos by capturing *Home PC*'s Editor's Choice Top 100 Software Award, a Bologna New Media Prize (cosponsored by Children's Software Revue) as Best Math Title, and *Family PC*'s Recommended Software Seal.

As the company entered 1998, four of its titles appeared in *PC Data*'s top ten survey by sales for educational software. American Girls Premiere Special Edition ranked number one (several months in a row), Oregon Trail III came in at number three, Reader Rabbit Kindergarten was number five, and Reader Rabbit Preschool was number seven.

In March, the company acquired Mindscape Inc. from Pearson PLC for approximately $150 million, as the company continued to expand. A mere month later, the Mindscape subsidiary branched out into the genealogy software market as it purchased the "Family Heritage" line of products from IMSI for $2.5 million in cash. The Family Heritage Deluxe product contained a free one-month subscription to the highly regarded Web site for Ancestry, the most comprehensive online genealogy organization whose archives include U.S. census indexes from as far back as 1790, land records, colonial and Quaker family records, early pioneer registers, and selected military records. The Deluxe product also included The Source Research Guide, The Red Book Directory, American Genealogical Gazetteer, and The Social Security Death Index, comprised of more than 52 million death records, as well as Corel PhotoHouse for retouching photographs. The Family Heritage products contain everything needed for researching family lineages, including 160,000 surname histories and coats of arms from the respected genealogy association Swyrich, and a guided tour of more than 23,000 genealogical Web sites.

Also in March, the company's Canadian subsidiary, SoftKey Software Products Inc., sold approximately 6.25 million special warrants to some Canadian institutional investors for approximately $104 million. So, with a strong stable of acquired software, subsidiaries, and personnel, and with its products continuing to sell well, the company appeared well poised to dominate the software market in the 21st century.

Principal Subsidiaries

Compton's Learning Company; Compton's NewMedia Inc.; Future Vision Holding Inc.; HyperGlot Software Company Inc.; Minnesota Educational Computing Corp.; Springboard Software Inc.; WordStar International Inc.; WordStar Atlanta Technology Center; Writing Tools Group Inc.; WordStar USA.

Further Reading

Auerach, Jon G., "Learning Co. Keeps Getting Caught Behind the Curve; Missed Opportunities, Tougher Rivals and a Slumping Market Hurt Results," *Wall Street Journal,* August 4, 1997, p. B4(W)/B4(E).

Baig, Edward, "Parlez-Vous CD-ROM?" *Business Week,* May 29, 1995, p. 99.

"Broderbund Agrees to Buy Learning Co. in Stock Swap," *Wall Street Journal, Europe,* August 2, 1995, p. 4.

Bulkeley, William M., "Learning Co. to Acquire Mindscape from Pearson PLC for $150 Million," *Wall Street Journal,* Europe, March 10, 1998, p. 12.

Christman, Ed, "Learning Co. Links with BMG," *Billboard,* June 28, 1997, p. 59.

Darlin, Damon, "Reaching for the Rabbit," *Forbes,* December 4, 1995, p. 47.

Kerber, Ross, "Investor Group Led by Lee Co. to Pay $123 Million for Stake in Learning Co.," *Wall Street Journal,* August 27, 1997, p. B7(E).

"Learning Company Enters Family Tree Software Category," *PR Newswire,* April 1, 1998, p. 401HSW016.

"Learning Company Rounds Out Its Multi-Subject Product Line with Reader Rabbit's 2nd Grade," *PR Newswire,* February 18, 1998, p. 218SFW013.

"Learning Company Sales Jump," *Television Digest,* February 16, 1998, p. 17.

"Learning Company Sets Deal for Mindscape," *New York Times,* March 7, 1998, p. B3(N)/D3(L).

"Learning Company to Buy Educational Concern in $40 Million Deal," *Wall Street Journal,* October 27, 1997, p. B8(W).

—Daryl F. Mallett

Learning Tree International Inc.

6053 West Century Boulevard
P.O. Box 45028
Los Angeles, California 90045-0028
U.S.A.
(310) 417-9700
(800) THE-TREE (843-8733)
Fax: (800) 709-6405
Web site: http://www.learningtree.com

Public Company
Incorporated: 1974 as Integrated Computer Systems
Employees: 645
Sales: $164.48 million
Stock Exchanges: NASDAQ
Ticker Symbol: LTRE
SICs: 7372 Prepackaged Software; 8243 Data Processing
    Schools; 8299 Schools & Educational Services, Not
    Elsewhere Classified

The brisk advancements in information technology have many corporations worldwide scrambling to catch up with ever-advancing technological capabilities. Learning Tree International Inc. is a key player in the information technology training and education industry, a growing $18 billion field. "The Internet's growth caught many companies off-guard, and they are still struggling to put infrastructure in place to exploit its capabilities. Since there is no slowdown in sight, corporations will find it difficult to find skilled technicians," says industry analyst Doug Rutherford in a 1996 *InfoWorld* article.

Learning Tree has stepped up to the plate to offer corporations personalized training, as well as certification programs to train *and* test the expertise of the technology professionals, engineers, programmers, and systems specialists they target. The demonstration of practical experience provided by these programs helps guard against a corporation hiring what a 1996 *InfoWorld* article by Paul Korzeniowski termed "one-Web-page wonders." In a 1998 study, the Information Technology Association of America in Arlington, Virginia, identified education as crucial to correcting this situation but that, conversely, there are not enough university graduates in this field to fill all the job vacancies.

A purported 10 percent of technical positions in the United States are vacant, and one of the most promising ways corporations are finding to fill the dearth of trained professionals is to retrain workers already employed in the field. According to another 1998 study, by the American Society for Training and Development in Alexandria, Virginia, high-tech companies spend an average of $911 *per employee* on training, more than any other sector. Learning Tree is prepared to take this growing market head-on; in 1998 the company taught 6,300 courses annually. The company has established U.S. education centers in Los Angeles; Boston; Washington, D.C.; and New York City. Additional U.S. course sites include: Atlanta; Chicago; Dallas; San Diego; Irvine, California; and Santa Clara, California. Reston, Virginia, is the site of the Company's U.S. headquarters; worldwide headquarters are located in Los Angeles. Other offices are located in Paris, France; London, England; Toronto, Canada; Ottawa, Canada; Stockholm, Sweden; Hong Kong; and Tokyo, Japan.

1974: Building the Learning Technology

Two engineers, David C. Collins, Ph.D., and Eric R. Garen, developed their common interests in computers and teaching to establish what would become one of the world's largest independent educational resources for information technology professionals. Prior to this collaboration, Dr. Collins earned a Bachelor of Science degree (with distinction) in electrical engineering from Stanford University, and Master's and Ph.D. degrees in the same field from the University of Southern California. Later, he was a University computer science instructor as well as having performed as an advisor to the development of college-level electrical engineering courses. Additionally, Dr. Collins participated in a think tank relating to the advancement of surveillance, communications, and weapons systems. Garen holds a Bachelor's degree in electrical engineering from the California Institute of Technology, and earned a Master's degree in computer science from the University of Southern California, each with honors.

Company Perspectives:

Learning Tree International is dedicated to providing continuing education in information technology in order to accelerate the rate at which industry can absorb new technology and improve the productivity of individuals and the organization.

It was while Garen worked as a design engineer and project manager at Technology Service Corporation, the same organization which employed Dr. Collins, that the two devised an idea for a new business. They realized the great desire and need for engineers in business and government organizations to actively remain on top of their professions and keep up with emerging technologies. Thus, the foundation of their company, then known as Integrated Computer Systems, was established.

Garen was the company's first instructor, as well as author of the first course offering, *Microprocessors and Microcomputers*. He continued teaching on a part-time basis until 1980, when he moved full-time to company management. Garen was elected president of Learning Tree in 1991. Dr. Collins has served as CEO of Learning Tree International since its inception in 1974.

The Late 1970s: Successfully Expanding

In 1975, the "hands-on" courses offered by Learning Tree were the first of their kind in the information technology field. The structure of the class was based on the concept that in order to teach an individual the practical, real-life knowledge of a specific computer operation, it was necessary to provide hands-on experience in the classroom. "They need to be able to apply what they've learned to be successful on a live project. With us, companies get an immediate return on their investment," said Garen in a 1997 *Investor's Business Daily* article. Learning Tree held these course programs in cities across North America and Europe. In addition to the first course offerings in Japan, a new European headquarters debuted in 1975. Much growth occurred in 1976 as the company opened subsidiaries in the United Kingdom, Sweden, and France.

Back in the United States, Learning Tree landed a contract with General Electric, one of the company's first big clients. In addition to training 7,500 General Electric personnel, which included 300 of GM's top 400 line managers, the company also developed a custom course program on the application of microcomputers. Soon thereafter, Learning Tree was hired by IBM to train their top information technology team, who would later use this training to aid in the development of the IBM PC.

The 1980s and the Growing Need for High-Level Education

The technological advances achieved during the 1980s made the shortage of competent professionals in this industry evident. In a 1998 article for *Barron's*, Eric J. Savitz pointed out that

"between 1986 and 1994, the annual number of computer-science graduates dropped 43 percent to 24,200 from 42,195." It was this growing number of vacant positions and lack of new college graduates to fill them that helped renew corporate America's interest in educating their current employees.

Paris, France, was the site of the first "education center," launched in 1983 with classrooms that were fully outfitted for Learning Tree's hands-on training approach. Because of the tremendous success enjoyed by this site, additional centers were opened in Stockholm, London, Los Angeles, and Washington, D.C. Classes could be delivered at such centers, public facilities, or in-house client sites. Course subjects included: Windows 95, Windows NT, and PC Support; Networks, Data Communications, and Telecommunications; Operating Systems and Programming; Software Development and Technical Management; Oracle and RDBMS; and Client/Server Systems.

The 1990s: Expanding to Fulfill the Need

A sixth Learning Tree office and education center was opened in Ottawa in 1989. This same year also brought about the name change from Integrated Computer Systems to Learning Tree International, so that the company was better recognized as a worldwide organization.

With customers such as Sony, Hitachi, and Matsushita, Learning Tree International KK began operations in Japan in 1990. Also in 1990, the company opened a seventh office and education center in Boston. Three years later, in May 1993, a Toronto site was introduced, bringing the total number of Learning Tree education centers to eight.

The company introduced a Professional Certification Program to provide validation of the range of knowledge and capabilities acquired by Learning Tree clients. "The main positive," said Dr. Collins in a 1994 interview with *Computer Reseller News*, "is the value to the customer, and the student in accelerating the completion of their degree program." These classes were recommended for up to ten semester hours of both undergraduate and graduate credit by the American Council on Education. Also granted was credit-transfer approval to more than 1,500 colleges and universities in both the United States and Canada. This credit could also be applied toward the Certified Computing Professional (CCP) and Associate Computing Professional (ACP) from the Institute for Certification of Computing Professionals (ICCP). In a 1994 article in *Computer Reseller News*, Kevin Merrill said that "surveys of companies have found that reviewing training for college credit validates its quality, augments the organization's return on investment and assures cost-effectiveness by reducing tuition-assistance costs," thus bolstering the necessity of this sort of training.

To assist in their efforts to retain and attract clients, Learning Tree introduced the Training Advantage Program in January 1995. With such *Fortune* 1000 corporations as J.P. Morgan, Honeywell, Lockheed-Martin, and Siemens, a partnership was formed which provided such organizations with a substantial discount for their information technology training. The company was hired in March of this same year as designated trainer for Computer Associates International, a $1.2 billion software company, for its CA-Visual Realia and CA-Realia II Workbench. Of the collaboration, CA's vice president of product strategy, Marc Sokol, said in a March 1995 interview with *Computer Reseller News*, "Authorized education is becoming more and more important when delivering training to clients."

New courses continued to be produced in response to the changing field. In March 1995, Learning Tree added a class on Internet-Intranet and Web Site Development, including Web page production training. The addition of this subject proved to be particularly timely for companies which were attempting to establish their business on the Internet. "In many instances, a company building its first Web server does not have the right skills in-house," said Paul Korzeniowski in a 1996 article for *InfoWorld*. Due to the strong response to their Web-related training, Learning Tree added a Hands-On Internet/Intranet for Business Applications, which served to explore Internet connect options, and Internet and Systems Security: Attacks and Countermeasures, which instructed how to safeguard a corporation's internal networks from the Internet. In addition, new certification programs were started: one awarding the title of Internet/Intranet Certified Professional; the second, relating to Java Programming. Learning Tree marked its own place on the Internet as the debut of the company's web site occurred in April 1995. By the end of the year Learning Tree had gone public, trading on the NASDAQ following an initial offer of three million shares at $12 apiece.

In February 1996, Learning Tree introduced a new product line of multimedia interactive computer-based training (CBT). Based on their successful classroom training, the first of the CBTs featured Visual Basic and Local Area Networks. These courses, delivered on CD-ROM, were each six hours in length with four to six lesson modules. A virtual instructor was part of the presentation, and guided the user through the program, complete with quizzes and performance-based testing. LearnTrack management software, included free with each course, assisted in installation and management of the programs, allowing supervisors to check each user's proficiency. These courses were applicable for either stand-alone or server-based systems. At this time Learning Tree projected that an additional 18 courses were to be available by September 1996. Instructor-led training continued to develop as well; by April 1996 the company offered in excess of 100 courses of this type.

Another public offering was made in the fall of 1996, and the amount of shares offered was raised from the proposed 2 million shares to 2.26 million at $30 per share. November 1996 featured another big contract for Learning Tree, when it signed the General Services Administration Schedule contract from the GSA, the government procurement agency. As part of this contract, government-employed information technology professionals received substantial discounts on their tuition.

It was February 1997 when Learning Tree unveiled its newest education center in New York. That year also saw the launch of the Learning Solutions Division of the company, which custom-designed training programs for clients who needed to train large groups of their information technology professionals and/or end-users. General Motors awarded this division's first multimillion-dollar contract in 1997, for the custom training of more than 30,000 employees in 60 cities.

Training went to GM operations across the nation on the new GM Access client server information system.

The Downside of the 1990s

The company hit a sour note with what turned out to be a short-lived new product: the Power Seminar. These one-day high intensity courses failed financially, and were discontinued within the year in November 1997, when stock prices fell 26 percent. From this point the company chose to focus its attention on its more profitable two-, three-, and five-day instructor-led courses. Despite the fact that Power Seminars lost lots of money, sales still grew 59 percent in 1997, according to a 1998 *SmartMoney* article. The company then faced a lawsuit in the spring of 1998 regarding its axed Power Seminar program. Shareholders alleged that Learning Tree officers concealed certain information regarding the performance of this product, enabling them to sell the stock at an inflated price. The suit sought damages for those who bought Learning Tree stock between May 8, 1997, and November 3, 1997.

Learning Tree announced six new Professional Certification programs in October 1997. They included: NT Web Administration; NT Web Development; Lotus Notes/Domino; Oracle 8 Application Development; Cisco Router; and Telecommunications. In 1998, 20,000 information technology professionals participated in the 27 Professional Certification Programs offered by Learning Tree. Furthermore, SkillsTree, a management and assessment program for information technology professionals, was added to the Learning Tree roster in March 1998. It was also at this time that the company had developed more than 100 CBT courses.

Evaluating the Progress

Since its founding in 1974, Learning Tree International has trained over 700,000 information technology professionals (as of March 1998), including employees of Xerox, Intel, IBM, DuPont, GE, Reuters, Sun, Bell Atlantic, and Hewlett-Packard. Courses offered more than just excellent teaching by skilled professionals; according to Robin M. Grugal in a 1997 *Investor's Business Daily* article, "students are even clued in on how to avoid the pitfalls of a technology, something manufacturers (which also offer classes) don't talk about." In addition to the 92 CBT courses marketed in 1998 (with a goal of reaching 200 course titles), Learning Tree has provided services to about 101,000 information technology professionals annually, via some 145 instructor-led courses and 27 Professional Certification Programs. Through the variety and sheer plentitude of course offerings, Learning Tree planned to be a "one-stop" center for information technology training. "Last year alone," stated Eric J. Savitz in a 1998 article in *Barron's*, "companies spent about $18 billion worldwide training their workers in various information technologies .... By 2001 that annual bill should hit $27.9 billion." The company is prepared to continue its role as a major educational resource for this quickly growing field.

Principal Subsidiaries

Learning Tree International USA, Inc.; Learning Tree International, KK (Japan); Learning Tree International Ltd. (U.K.);

Learning Tree International SA (France); Learning Tree International AB (Sweden); Learning Tree Publishing AB (Sweden); Learning Tree International Inc. (Canada); Advanced Technology Marketing, Inc.; Systems for Business and Industry, Inc.; Technology for Business and Industry, Inc.

Further Reading

Barry, Kate, *Dow Jones On-Line News,* December 29, 1997.

Grugal, Robin M., "Cramming," *Investor's Business Daily*, January 29, 1997, p. A4.

Hagy, James R., et al, "To Find the Biggest Values in Today's Market, Think Small," *SmartMoney*, April 21, 1998.

Hibbard, Justin, "The Learning Revolution," *Information Week*, March 9, 1998, p. 44+.

Korzeniowski, Paul, "Mastering the Webmasters," *InfoWorld*, August 5, 1996, pp. 53–54.

"Learning Tree Gets GM Information System Training Pact," *Dow Jones On-Line News*, March 7, 1997.

"Learning Tree Holder Suit," *Dow Jones On-Line News*, April 17, 1998.

Merrill, Kevin, "CA Seeks Out Third Parties for Training," *Computer Reseller News*, June 20, 1994, pp. 115, 121.

——, "Colleges Pass Trainers," *Computer Reseller News*, March 25, 1995, pp. 157–58.

Savitz, Eric J., "For Adults Only: The Business of Training Workers Via Computer Attracts the Interest of Would-Be Visionaries—and Wall Street," *Barron's*, March 2, 1998, p.31.

Scott, Kathy, "Learning Tree Branches Out," *Network World,* February 26, 1996, p. 47.

—Melissa West

Legal & General Group plc

Temple Court
11 Queen Victoria Street
London EC4N 4TP
United Kingdom
(0171) 528 6200
Fax: (0171) 528 6222
Web site: http://www.legal-and-general.co.uk

Public Company
Incorporated: 1920 as The Legal & General Assurance
    Society
Employees: 7,334
Total Assets: £45.88 billion (US$76.16 billion) (1996)
Stock Exchanges: London
Ticker Symbol: LGGNY
SICs: 6082 Foreign Trade & International Banking
    Institutions; 6311 Life Insurance; 6321 Accident &
    Health Insurance; 6324 Hospital & Medical Service
    Plans; 6331 Fire, Marine & Casualty Insurance; 6719
    Offices of Holding Companies, Not Elsewhere Classified

Legal & General Group plc is one of Great Britain's largest insurance concerns. Although it also writes home, auto, health, and other nonlife policies and offers investment-management and banking services, life insurance has always stood at the core of its operations. In fact, it sold nothing but life insurance until after World War I. In the late 1990s, about 90 percent of Legal & General's profits came from its domestic operations, with the remainder generated from subsidiaries in Australia, the United States, France, and the Netherlands.

Founded in 1836 by Six Lawyers

The Legal & General Life Assurance Society was founded in 1836, when British life insurance was just beginning to thrive. At that time, rapid population increases in Great Britain and a surge in real personal income were creating favorable conditions for the life insurance industry. Between 1834 and 1836, 310 joint-stock life insurance companies were created, of which

Legal & General turned out to be one of the most durable. Its founders were six London lawyers—Sergeant John Adams, Basil Montagu, W. C. L. Keene, Kenyon S. Parker, J. H. R. Chichester, and George L. Baker—who convened their first board meeting in a legal office at 18 Lincoln's Inn Fields in June 1836. At that meeting, Adams was elected as chairman and the company's initial capitalization was set at £1 million, a goal it reached through sale of stock in 1839. The first board of directors was set at 24 members, raised to 30 at the next meeting, and shares were limited to members of the legal profession.

In October 1836, Legal & General accepted its first policy, for the solicitor Thomas Smith. Although the society carefully screened each applicant for insurance, Smith proved not to be a good risk—he died four years later and his policy of £1,000 was paid after the society had received only about £177 in premiums. That fall, the firm appointed six provincial agents, including one in Edinburgh, and within its first year of business it accepted more than 100 policies.

Legal & General began to loan money to both corporate and individual customers soon after its founding. In 1841 it loaned £20,000 to the Stockton and Hartlepool Railway, and in 1852 it authorized £60,000 worth of credit to the Regent Canal Company. A request from the Great Western Railway in 1846 for a loan of £65,000 was, however, turned down. A substantial number of London aristocrats also took out loans from the firm at this time, more likely than not to cover gambling debts.

Legal & General expanded throughout the rest of the 19th century. In the 1850s it entered the real estate business, investing heavily in the development of Birkenhead, near London, and the transformation of Belvedere Estate into a residential area in 1860. To serve its growing core life insurance business, Legal & General established its first office outside London, in Manchester, in 1889. At the turn of the century, the firm's total assets exceeded £2 million and it was the second largest insurance company, in terms of capitalization, in Great Britain doing only ordinary life business.

Expansion Overseas Following World War I

Legal & General emerged from World War I intact, despite four years of paying an unusually high number of claims because of war casualties and the influenza epidemic of 1918. In 1920 the society incorporated and dropped the word "Life" from its name. The company began writing fire and accident policies, a business that immediately proved successful; the new popularity of automobile and airplane travel created a huge demand for accident insurance. In 1929 the restriction of society membership to those in the legal profession was lifted. The Great Depression's effect on the world economy in the 1930s was scarcely felt by the British insurance industry. In fact, historian G. Clayton pointed out in his *British Insurance* that, if anything, widespread pessimism in bad times tended to increase the demand for insurance.

Legal & General expanded overseas and by acquiring other companies. In 1931 it opened a life insurance office in Johannesburg. In 1933 it strengthened its pensions operations when it acquired the London office of New York-based Metropolitan Life Insurance, after restrictions placed on U.S. insurance companies in the wake of the 1929 stock market crash made it unprofitable for Met Life to continue its British business. The next year Legal & General further strengthened its position both at home and abroad by acquiring Gresham Life Assurance and Gresham Fire and Accident. The Gresham mergers were particularly important for their long histories of doing business overseas. Gresham's fire insurance business in Australia provided a base from which Legal & General would begin to penetrate the Australian market in 1948.

World War II put a tight squeeze on the British insurance industry. Men and money fueled the war effort; the firms were asked to contribute the former by releasing employees devoted to generating new business and the latter by buying up low-interest government bonds, often selling securities paying higher yields in order to do so. Fire insurance claims skyrocketed as German bombs fell on England. Legal & General was among the many firms forced to relocate offices outside London for the duration because of the bombing. After several temporary relocations, the company ended up at a former school at Kingswood in Surrey. Its head office remained in Kingswood after the return of peace, and later its central computer was located there as well.

Once the war ended, the firm picked up where it had left off in 1939. In 1947 it began writing fire and accident policies in South Africa, as well as life insurance policies. In 1956 the company added life insurance to its nonlife business in Australia. Back home, the firm added marine insurance in 1949, using Andrew Weir & Company as its agent. In 1960 it acquired Andrew Weir's marine subsidiary, British Commonwealth Insurance.

From just after World War II through the late 1960s, Legal & General ranked behind Prudential as Great Britain's second largest life insurance company when measured by total sums insured, maintaining about ten percent of the market. It grew substantially early in the decade, and total assets reached the £1 billion mark by 1970. The 1960s, however, were not without contention for the firm: in 1966 angry shareholders complained when Legal & General failed to raise its dividend and the firm's directors did not adequately explain why. Rumors circulated in the financial press over the next year that Legal & General would "go mutual," with the shareholders selling out to the policyholders, but at its 1967 annual meeting the firm declared that the firm would not change hands.

International Expansion in the 1970s and 1980s

After a reorganization of the executive office in 1970, increasing international expansion of operations marked the decade for Legal & General. In 1972 it entered into cooperation agreements with three European insurance companies: Colonia of West Germany, La Paix of France, and Reale Mutuale of Italy. In 1973 it joined with the West German firm Cologne Reinsurance Company to purchase Victory Insurance, Britain's second-largest reinsurance company. Legal & General took the majority interest and subsequently bought Cologne's minority stake. In the same year, it sold off Gresham Life Assurance but retained most of its overseas businesses. Between 1974 and 1976, it signed cooperation agreements with AGO Holding (later part of AEGON of the Netherlands), Assubel of Belgium, Ireland's Life of Eire, Vadoise Vie of Switzerland, and Nippon Life. In 1976 Legal & General merged its South African general insurance business with that of Norwich Union under the name Aegis Insurance Company. The company also took some domestic actions during the 1970s. In 1971 it introduced a pensions-management subsidiary and set up the Tyndall Fund-Unit Assurance Company to gain a foothold in the unit-trust field. In 1973 Legal & General acquired the real estate developer Cavendish Land.

At the end of the decade, Legal & General underwent a major reorganization. It separated its British insurance operations, its international operations, and its investment-management activities into the three separate subsidiaries. The new parent company, still called Legal & General Group, became a non-insurance company. The move was made to give Legal & General greater financial flexibility and to differentiate its activities more clearly.

After this reorganization, Legal & General ventured into the U.S. market in 1981 when it acquired Government Employees Life Insurance Company for US$140 million. It changed the Washington, D.C.-based company's name to Banner Life the next year. In 1984 it acquired Unilife Netherlands, the Dutch subsidiary of the Unilife Assurance Group, and added it to Legal & General Netherlands. At the same time, however, not all of Legal & General's overseas ventures were working out. The firm decided to terminate its general insurance businesses in France and Australia in 1981. In 1987 Legal & General sold its 45 percent stake in Aegis Insurance, joining the trend among British companies toward divesting South African holdings because of declining profitability, shareholder pressure, and worries over political instability in that country.

The late 1980s were marked by Legal & General's attempt to bolster its U.S. operations amid some difficulty at home. Throughout much of the decade, the performance of Legal & General's pension fund asset management was embarrassingly poor. In 1987 the amount of assets managed by its investment arm shrank from £12.5 billion to £11 billion after the U.S. stock market crash. To remedy the situation, the firm lured David Prosser from his position as chief of the Coal Board's pension fund in January 1988 to head up its investment-management operations. In Prosser's first year, the investment division's asset pool increased to over £14 billion, and in March 1989 Legal & General strengthened its position in the U.S. market when it acquired William Penn Life Insurance Company of New York from Continental Corporation, a U.S. insurance concern, for US$80 million.

Legal & General also expanded in another direction when it reached a cooperative agreement with Kyoei Mutual Fire and Marine Insurance Company of Tokyo in 1989. The agreement gave the company greater access to the Japanese market. At the same time, it provided more business from Kyoei's industrial clients moving into the unified European market.

1990s and Beyond

In the 1990s Legal & General continued to tinker with its various operations, exiting the reinsurance business at the start of the decade by selling off Victory to Nederlandes Reassurantie Group Holding N.V. In 1995 Legal & General entered into a joint venture with Woolwich Building Society to provide Woolwich customers with a variety of general insurance policies, including homeowner's insurance. That same year Legal & General's Australian subsidiary joined with Australian insurer SGIO Insurance to acquire SGIC, the insurance operations of the South Australian government, for A$170 million (£80 million). Through this transaction, Legal & General gained SGIC's life insurance business as well as an investment management contract for the South Australian government's third-party insurance pool. The company sold its commercial general insurance business to Guardian Insurance in 1996 and the following year began offering banking services in the United Kingdom after securing a banking license in June. The first service offered by this new venture was an instant access deposit account service, which was launched in July 1997.

Historically conservative in nature and thus usually capable of avoiding entanglement in scandals, Legal & General nonetheless found itself in the 1990s in the midst of an ongoing pensions misselling scandal. In early 1994 Lautro, an organization that self-regulated the U.K. life insurance industry, fined Legal & General a then-record £400,000 for failing to meet standards set by Lautro. The main charge, which the company did not dispute, was that some of its direct sales agents had convinced thousands of customers to leave lucrative occupational retirement plans and instead purchase personal pensions from Legal & General. Other life insurance companies were also implicated in the scandal, which may have wronged as many as half a million people in the late 1980s and early 1990s. In response, Legal & General established the new post of director of compliance in April 1994. Moreover, in March 1997 the company unveiled a pensions guarantee, which promised to pay individuals the pension they would have received had they retained their occupational retirement scheme. In early 1998, it was estimated that the pensions scandal might cost U.K. life insurance companies as much as £11 billion (US$17.6 billion).

Amid the continuing consolidation of the financial services industry—most notably the purchase of insurance companies by banks—Legal & General became the object of takeover rumors in late 1997 and early 1998, but the company insisted that it was large enough and strong enough to remain independent. In March 1998 Legal & General announced that its new business had increased 40 percent in fiscal 1997 compared to the previous year, while its pretax operating profits had risen 20 percent, to £349.6 million (US$583.8 million). Despite the continuing cloud hanging over it in the form of the pensions scandal, Legal & General appeared determined to stand alone. There was also evidence that the company was seeking to concentrate more intensely on the domestic market as Legal & General announced in late March 1998 that it was considering taking its Australian life insurance subsidiary public.

Principal Subsidiaries

Legal & General Finance plc; Legal & General Assurance Society Limited; Legal & General Insurance Limited; Legal & General Investment Management Limited; Legal & General Assurance (Pensions Management) Limited; Legal & General Mortgages Limited; Legal & General Mortgage Services Limited; Legal & General Property Limited; Legal & General (Unit Trust Managers) Limited; Legal & General Estate Agencies Limited; Legal & General Ventures Limited; Fairmount Group plc; Gresham Insurance Company Limited; Legal & General Life of Australia Limited; SGIC Life Limited (Australia); Legal & General (France) S.A.; Legal & General Bank (France) S.A.; Legal & General Nederland Levensverzekering Maatschappij N.V. (Netherlands); Banner Life Insurance Company (U.S.); William Penn Life Insurance Company of New York (U.S.).

Further Reading

Brown-Humes, Christopher, "L&G Insists on Independence," *Financial Times,* September 12, 1997, p. 23.

——, "L&G May Float Australian Life Side," *Financial Times,* March 31, 1998, p. 28.

——, "L&G Wants to Stay Independent," *Financial Times,* March 13, 1998, p. 27.

——, "Pensions Guarantee Unveiled by L&G," *Financial Times,* March 21, 1997, p. 8.

——, "Legal & General New Business Increases 40%," *Financial Times,* January 16, 1998, p. 22.

Clayton, G., *British Insurance,* London: Elek Books, 1971, 381 p.

Leigh-Bennett, E. P., *On This Evidence,* London: Baynard Press, 1936.

Smith, Alison, "L&G and Woolwich in Insurance Venture," *Financial Times,* July 17, 1995, p. 17.

——, "L&G Looks to Develop Banking Services," *Financial Times,* March 15, 1996, p. 26.

——, "L&G Shake-Up to Benefit Investors," *Financial Times,* November 17, 1995, p. 19.

——, "Record Lautro Fine for Legal & General," *Financial Times,* March 1, 1994, p. 1.

Tait, Nikki, "A $170m Joint Buy for L&G," *Financial Times,* November 21, 1995, p. 23.

Williams, Trevor, "UK's Legal & General Predicts Sour Results," *Journal of Commerce,* February 11, 1991, p. 10A.

—Douglas Sun
—updated by David E. Salamie

Lincoln Snacks Company

4 High Ridge Park
Stamford, Connecticut 06905
U.S.A.
(203) 329-4545
Fax: (203) 329-4555
Web site: http://www.lincolnsnacks.com

Public Subsidiary of Noel Group, Inc.
Incorporated: 1968 as Lincoln Snack Co.
Employees: 73
Sales: $23.1 million (1997)
Stock Exchanges: NASDAQ
Ticker Symbol: SNAX
SICs: 2060 Sugar & Confectionery Products

Lincoln Snacks Company is one of the leading manufacturers and marketers of caramelized pre-popped popcorn in the United States and Canada. The company is a majority-owned subsidiary of Noel Group, Inc. Lincoln's major products include glazed popcorn/nut mixes and sweet glazed popcorn sold under the brand names Poppycock, Fiddle Faddle, and Screaming Yellow Zonkers. Lincoln also processes, markets, and distributes a variety of nuts. The company sells its products to grocery stores, convenience stores, mass merchandise outlets, warehouse clubs, vending channels, military commissaries, and other retailers. Sales are subject to significant seasonal variation, due to buying patterns during traditional holiday seasons. Foreign operations account for less than ten percent of Lincoln's sales. The company plant in Lincoln, Nebraska, makes and packages all Lincoln products.

From Switzerland to Nebraska: 1968–91

Before the Internet, there were roasted peanuts and popcorn. In 1885 Charles Cretor of Chicago developed a gasoline-powered wet corn popping machine, which also had a small peanut roaster. And in 1906 Amedo Obici—an Italian immigrant who, with Mario Piruzzi, cofounded Planters Peanuts—developed a process for commercially roasting shelled peanuts in oil. The snack food industry was on its way. Then came the Information Age and the launch of the official online snack authority: lincolnsnax.com, the web site of Lincoln Snacks Company, advertising its products as "The Official Snack Food of the Internet."

The roots of Lincoln Snacks Company are with a Swiss firm, the Wander Co., founded in Berne in 1865. According to Jeffrey S. Barnes in the *Midlands Business Journal* (MBJ), Wander was best known in the United States for the Ovaltine products manufactured at its Villa Park plant in Illinois and for the Poppycock snack it began producing in 1960. In 1968, another Switzerland-based company, Sandoz Nutrition Corp., bought Wander and moved the Villa Park offices to Lincoln, Nebraska, to create the Lincoln Snack Co. as an operating division. It was there that, by 1986, Lincoln Snack was producing an annual 14 million pounds of Poppycock, Fiddle Faddle, and Screaming Yellow Zonkers, wrote Barnes.

Donovan A. Weddle, former plant manager of the Sandoz division in Nebraska, told *MBJ* that "Americans are becoming 'grazers.' They don't always have three meals a day anymore; they tend to snack more." Weddle's successor, Frank Hudecek, added that "two-income households have done more than anything to fuel the growth [of snacking]. The kids are more active, too, with football, choir and other activities outside the home. . . . It's just too hard for the entire family to sit down together." This growth of snacking also was fueled by the advent of wholesale clubs and discount stores. In 1986, for instance, sales to non-grocery customers (which included companies such as Sam's Wholesale Club, Kmart, and Wal-Mart) accounted for about half of Lincoln Snacks' client base.

While Poppycock was the firm's gourmet product, Fiddle Faddle with peanuts was the top seller; the company sometimes turned out 10,000 to 12,000 cases a day. The most unusual product, as far as name and marketing were concerned, was the Screaming Yellow Zonkers brand, developed in the late 1960s. "We only knew of it as 'S-Y-Z' here at the plant," Weddle commented in an *MBJ* interview. "We had the formula, but not the name. Screaming Yellow Zonkers was put in an almost totally black box; I think [this was] the first food product ever in a black box. It had very funny copy, even for the ingredients, written by people who had been writing for Rowan and Martin's

Company Perspectives:

Lincoln Snacks Company has positioned itself in the fastest-growing segments of the pre-popped popcorn category. The company's strategy for future growth involves continuing to strengthen its existing brand franchise through the addition of new products and through further penetration of existing markets.

Laugh-In,'' said Weddle. The product generated considerable publicity, even to the point of having department stores decorate clothing sections with the name.

To make its products, Lincoln Snack shipped in tons of peanuts, pecans, walnuts, cashews, macadamia nuts, and coconut from California, the southeastern United States, Hawaii, South America, Africa, and India. The company bought corn syrup from Iowa and Illinois, sugar from Minnesota and western Nebraska, and popping corn from nearby producers in Iowa and Nebraska. Crop conditions throughout the world were a constant concern for the company. For instance, a peanut shortage in the late 1970s necessitated new sources for the product and caused the government to relax restrictions on importing peanuts.

Recycling was a major project at the plant. The damaged ends of Poppycock cans, cardboard, and computer paper all were recycled to keep waste from the dumpster. Unpopped kernels of corn were sold to a local farmer as feed. Lincoln Snack held an enviable position in the highly competitive glazed-popcorn industry. "Orville Redenbacher tried to enter it a few years ago and failed, even with a big name like his. Once you get on the shelves in the stores, you have to continue the movement or you'll lose the space. In the non-foods businesses, it's a matter of recognition—people perceive your product as a bargain and buy it on that basis,'' quipped Weddle.

New Parentage in the Mid-1990s

In February 1992 Sandoz announced its intention to sell the Lincoln Snack division. According to Lincoln Snacks' 1994 annual report, the decision to sell the business occasioned a decline in marketing promotion during 1992. In fact, net sales declined to $24.5 million in 1992 from $33.7 million in 1991. However, because Lincoln Snacks' operations were considered product lines within a division, Sandoz did not maintain complete independent financial data for Lincoln Snack. Consequently, limited data are available for periods prior to Lincoln Snacks' becoming the subsidiary of a new parent, New York-based Noel Group, Inc.

It was on August 31, 1992, that Noel Group, Inc. and a management team of former executives of Nestlé Foods Corporation acquired Lincoln Snack Company from Sandoz Nutrition Corporation. Noel changed the name of the Lincoln Snack Company to Lincoln Foods Inc. and located the sales, marketing, and administration headquarters in Stamford, Connecticut. The decline in promotional activity, coupled with the complete turnover of the marketing and sales management of the business, contributed to a decline in net sales during 1992. In a May 19, 1993 interview with the *Lincoln Star Journal,* Scott Kirk—Lincoln Foods' vice-president and general manager—said that the company would come up with new marketing approaches and reach out ''for worldwide sales by pushing Poppycock because there is nothing like it in Europe, the Middle East and other markets.'' He also commented that the manufacturing plant did not always operate at full capacity and that, in order to keep the plant busy all the time, efforts would be made to sell Lincoln products year round. However, according to the 1994 annual report, throughout the first nine months of 1993, net sales continued to be negatively impacted by issues associated with Sandoz's sale of the company.

On March 15, 1993, Lincoln Foods acquired Carousel Nut Products, Inc., an Owensboro, Kentucky-based producer and marketer of roasted, dry roasted, coated, raw, and mixed nuts. For the fiscal year ending December 31, 1993, Lincoln's net sales—excluding those of Carousel—totalled $22.6 million, $1.9 million less than 1992 sales of $24.5 million.

By the first quarter of 1994 Carousel and its operations were integrated into those of Lincoln Snacks' manufacturing facility in Lincoln, Nebraska. On January 14, 1994, Lincoln Snacks Company began trading on the NASDAQ stock exchange under the symbol "SNAX.'' On April 19, 1994, Lincoln Snacks changed its fiscal year-end to June 30.

Initially, Lincoln Snacks marketed its Poppycock and nut products directly through independent brokers. In the United States, sales of Poppycock and nut products were in the hands of four regional business managers working with some 80 brokers located strategically across the country. Lincoln Snacks' personnel saw to orders from large-volume customers and certain exports. In June 1995 Lincoln Snacks agreed to having the Planters Company—a unit of Nabisco, Inc.—be the exclusive distributor of two Lincoln Snacks products: Fiddle Faddle and Screaming Yellow Zonkers. The distribution agreement was limited to an initial term scheduled to expire June 30, 1997, unless renewed for additional one-year periods. By this agreement, Planters was compelled to purchase a minimum number of equivalent cases of Fiddle Faddle and Screaming Yellow Zonkers during the initial term.

On May 9, 1997, Lincoln Snacks and Planters amended the distribution agreement in order to extend Planters' exclusive distribution rights for an additional six months, that is, to December 31, 1997, at which time the distribution arrangement was terminated. As of May 1, 1997, Lincoln Snacks resumed the marketing and distribution of Screaming Yellow Zonkers. However, the amendment required Planters to purchase a specified number of manufactured cases of Fiddle Faddle and to compensate Lincoln for the remaining contract minimums for the 12-month period ending June 30, 1997. Planters purchased 79 percent of the original contract minimum and compensated Lincoln Snacks for the remaining 21 percent. Planters also had to compensate Lincoln Snacks should certain sales levels not be achieved during the calendar year ending December 31, 1997; Planters met this requirement. Sales to Planters represented 47 percent of net sales for the year ending June 30, 1997. On July 11, 1997, Lincoln Snacks entered into a trademark license agreement with Nabisco, Inc. for use of the Planters and Mr. Peanut trademarks on Fiddle Faddle products in the United States for a period of five years, beginning January 1, 1998. A similar agreement was reached with Nabisco Ltd., the holder of the license to distribute Planters' peanut products in Canada, for use of Planters' trademarks on Fiddle Faddle in Canada. Johnvince Foods of Toronto was the distributor of Planters Fiddle Faddle in Canada.

As of June 30, 1997, Lincoln Snacks had 73 full-time employees and no part-time employees. The number of employees varied according to weekly and seasonal production needs, with an average of about 85.

The company's manufacturing facility continued to be located in Lincoln, Nebraska. Here were installed continuous-process equipment for coating popcorn and nuts and four distinct high-speed filling and packing lines for canisters, jars, single-serving packs, and bag-in-box packages. The manufacturing and packaging equipment also allowed for the manufacture of other similar product lines or packaging formats. Depending on the season, the plant operated at an overall rate of from about 40 percent to 75 percent of capacity. The raw materials used for Lincoln Snacks' products were commodity items purchased directly from various suppliers. These items included corn syrup, butter, margarine, brown and granulated sugar, popcorn, nuts, and oils.

Lincoln continued to manufacture and market its three nationally recognized products: Poppycock, Fiddle Faddle, and Screaming Yellow Zonkers. Poppycock was a gourmet treat crackling with "crunchy, toasted nuts in a delicious syrupy glaze" available in three varieties: Butter Almond Pecan Crunch; Maple Walnut Cashew Crunch, and Macadamia Coconut Butter Crunch. The more moderately priced Caramel Fiddle Faddle consisted of popcorn and peanuts coated with caramel, while the butter-toffee variety contained popcorn and peanuts covered with a butter-toffee glaze. Fat Free Fiddle Faddle was made of popcorn in a caramel coating having no fat or cholesterol. Screaming Yellow Zonkers was billed as "the crunchy popcorn you crave, brilliantly lit by a sunny, sweet glaze." Lincoln also processed, marketed, and distributed some ten different kinds of nuts. Poppycock competed with other premium-quality snack products; Fiddle Faddle and Screaming Yellow Zonkers competed directly with other brands, such as American Home Products Corp.'s Crunch 'n Munch, and Borden, Inc.'s Cracker Jack.

Toward the 21st Century

The marketing and distribution agreement with Planters Company ended December 31, 1997; Planters gave Lincoln Snacks a one-time payment amounting to $0.22 per share in compensation for lower than agreed-upon case sales of products for which Planters acted as exclusive distributor. As of January 1, 1998, Lincoln Snacks resumed full responsibility for the marketing and distribution of its entire product line. For the first nine months of Lincoln's 1998 fiscal year, sales decreased five percent to $17.5 million compared to $18.4 million for the same period of 1996. During the third quarter, however, Lincoln sales increased seven percent to $4.6 million, compared to $4.3 million in the third quarter of fiscal 1997. Earnings for the nine months were $2.4 million, or $0.38 per share, versus $0.19 per share in fiscal 1997. The increase in sales was attributable to Lincoln's new copack (packing products manufactured by another company) and private-label business.

As the 21st century drew near, Noel Group, Inc. (Lincoln's parent company) continued to implement the one-to-two-year "plan of complete liquidation and dissolution" that the Noel board of directors had approved in 1997. Noel conducted its principal operations through small and medium-sized companies; it had acquired controlling or major interests in eight companies since 1990. The plan called for distribution of Noel's net assets to shareholders in the form of stock of Noel's holdings or of cash.

Nevertheless, Lincoln Snacks had reason to believe in its future strength and stability. The company committed itself to a three-pronged plan for thriving in the new century: namely, to rebuild sales momentum for core products, capitalize on initial success in the copacking and private-label business, and grow continuously by acquiring other companies.

Further Reading

Barnes, Jeffrey S., "Lincoln Snack Co.," *Midlands Business Journal,* December 5, 1986, pp. 1, 14.
——, "Lincoln Snack Feeds Appetite of Grazers, Wholesalers," *Midlands Business Journal,* February 2–8, 1990, pp. 1, 10.
Barrette, John, "High Hopes Are Poppycock: Sale Brings New Marketing Approach for Ex-Lincoln Snack Co.," Lincoln (Nebraska) Journal, May 19, 1993, p. 26.
Dwight, Donald R., "Noel Group, Inc. Announces [Another Liquidating Distribution]," press release, Noel Group, Inc., April 15, 1998, p. 1.
"Lincoln Foods Acquires Assets of Kentucky Nut Products Plant," *Lincoln (Nebraska) Star,* March 12, 1993, p. 16.
"Lincoln to Tout Planters, Mr. Peanut on Fiddle Faddle," *Brandweek,* August 4, 1997, p. 12.
Switzer, Gerry, "Lincoln Snack Co. Acquired by New York's Noel Group," *Lincoln (Nebraska) Star,* September 1, 1992, p. 8.

—Gloria A. Lemieux

Linens 'n Things, Inc.

6 Brighton Road
Clifton, New Jersey 07015
U.S.A.
(973) 778-1300
Fax: (973) 815-2990
Web site: http://www.lnthings.com

Public Company
Incorporated: 1958 as Great Eastern Linens, Inc.
Employees: 7,700
Sales: $874.22 million (1997)
Stock Exchanges: New York
Ticker Symbol: LIN
SICs: 5714 Drapery, Curtain & Upholstery Stores; 5719
  Miscellaneous Home Furnishings; 5722 Household
  Appliances

Linens 'n Things, Inc. is one of the nation's two largest and most profitable specialty retailers of home textiles, housewares, and decorative home accessories. In 1998 the company was operating 176 stores (153 superstores and 23 smaller, traditional-size stores) in 37 states. The traditional stores averaged approximately 10,000 gross square feet in size while the superstores ranged from 38,000 to 50,000 gross square feet. The stores carry brand name "linens," that is, home textiles—such as bed linens, towels and pillows—and "things," such as housewares and home accessories. The superstores were located predominantly in power-strip centers and, to a lesser extent, in shopping malls. More than 25,000 stock-keeping units (SKUs) supported the company's six product categories: bath, home accessories, housewares, storage, top-of-the-bed, and window treatments. The company bought its inventory from approximately 1,000 suppliers, 95 percent of whom were in the United States. The superstores represented Linens 'n Things' desire to create a compelling one-stop shopping experience for the time-pressed consumer. The company carried many name brands, including Wamsutta, Martex, Fieldcrest, and Waverly in domestics; Libbey, Ravel, Lancaster Colony, Zwiesel Glas, and Luminarc in glassware; Sango, Mikasa, Sakura, Tienshen, and Gibson in stoneware; Calphalon, Circulon, and Farberware in cookware; and Braun and Krups in appliances. Linens 'n Things also sold an increasing amount of merchandise (about ten percent) under its own private label, *LNT,* in order to supplement the offering of brand name products with other high-quality merchandise sold at value pricing below regular department store prices and comparable with, or below, sale prices at department stores.

Creating a Retail Prototype: 1958–83

Eugene Wallace Kalkin laid the initial groundwork for Linens 'n Things, Inc. when he was only 22 years old and began what would be a seven-year stint with Allied Purchasing Corp., the buying office for the second largest department store chain in the United States. In 1958 he entered into a partnership with the retail discount chain known as Great Eastern Mills, Inc.; in that company's stores, called Great Eastern Linens, Inc., Kalkin set up leased-linen departments. Meanwhile, Great Eastern Mills sold its business and its 50 percent share of Great Eastern Linens to Diana Stores Corporation, a ladies' apparel store chain with a strong market position in the southern United States. Thereupon, Diana Stores opened a chain of stores, named Miller's Discount Department Stores, in which Great Eastern Linens operated the linen and curtain department.

Diana Stores later sold its company and its 50 percent interest in Great Eastern Linens to Beverly Hills-based Daylin Inc., a national chain of department stores that leased departments for health and beauty aids. In 1970 Daylin bought Kalkin's share of Great Eastern Linens in exchange for Daylin stock. In 1975, however, Daylin filed for bankruptcy, and Kalkin's stock became almost worthless. During an interview reported in the May 1998 issue of the *UVM Record,* a University of Vermont publication, Kalkin recalled how this bankruptcy affected both his finances and his self-esteem: "It was absolutely a devastating blow to my life. To me, there was no alternative but to go back into business," said Kalkin.

Kalkin did just that. In 1975, from the Daylin bankruptcy court, he bought seven of the leased departments and specialty stores he had started for that company. This seven-unit retail chain with annual sales of $2 million was the beginning of Linens 'n Things, Inc., one of the country's first specialty retail stores dedicated to home furnishings and decorative accessories. Having experienced the unpredictable consequences related to dependency on landlords, Kalkin turned away from the operation of leased departments and applied a novel set of merchandising techniques to the development of Linens 'n Things as a chain of specialty retail stores.

Eugene Kalkin had learned about the European *hypermarchés,* stores in which storage cubes filled with food or general merchandise were piled up to the ceiling, thereby saving space and reducing expenses. This merchandising concept later became popular in the United States in discount chain stores, such as those of Sam's Club, BJ's Wholesale Club, and Home Depot. Influenced by the concept of the *hypermarché* no-frills warehouse environment, Kalkin used his retailing experience to create the retail industry's off-price prototype. He opted for stores with high ceilings in order to save space by installing ten-foot high, warehouse-type shelving for piling up storage cubes. He could then display in 7,000 square feet the quantity of merchandise that previously would have taken 12,000 to 13,000 square feet. In this way, Linens 'n Things cut expenses—especially for rent, lighting, and taxes—and turned a profit while selling quality products at discount prices. "When I went into off-price, the timing was right and we had the right physical format," Kalkin later commented in an interview for a June 1990 story in *Home Fashions Magazine.*

The soft economy of the 1970s did elicit enthusiastic consumer response to Linens 'n Things' off-price stores. Other retailers in the home textiles industry kept an eye on the chain's rapid growth. For instance, Bloomingdales' Norman Axelrod—who would later serve as Linens 'n Things' CEO, president, and chairman—remembered that "Gene [Kalkin] was very dynamic." "Selling brand names in a low-cost environment was a groundbreaking concept," Axelrod commented in a 1995 interview for *Business News New Jersey.*

Transition and Refocus: 1983–95

By 1983 Melville Corporation (later known as CVS Corporation) was also attracted to Linens 'n Things—by then a 55-store chain with sales of over $85 million—and soon acquired the chain. After the sale, Kalkin stayed on to direct the company for two years and was succeeded by his longtime assistant, Robert L. Karan. Sales from 116 stores reached $145.3 million for 1985; $163.4 million from 131 stores for

1986; $175.8 million from 144 stores in 1987; and $180 million for 140 stores by 1988.

Karan's marketing philosophy, however, was very different from that of Kalkin, who was attuned to the volatile, evolutionary nature of the retail industry and had noted an emerging trend to larger stores. In fact, before Kalkin's departure, the company already had experimented with the profitable operation of an 18,000-square-foot store and had begun to increase the "things" side of the business in order to meet customer requests for a larger selection of decorative home accessories. Karan, however, held back on making changes and, according to Lasseter's article, he "scrimped on spending to keep prices low, and sales stagnated." In January 1988, Melville Corporation asked Norman Axelrod—then senior vice-president at Bloomingdales in New York City—if he would run Linens 'n Things. Axelrod reportedly hesitated because the company had "a lot of problems," but Stan Goldstein, Melville's chairman, agreed to invest more money in Linens 'n Things, and in 1988 Axelrod joined the company as chief executive officer.

Axelrod had kept abreast of the radical and dramatic changes taking place in industry and individual lifestyles during the 1980s. Corporate structures were crumbling. Banks, brokerage houses, department stores and specialty stores—to name but a few of the industries needing to change their marketing, distribution and management strategies in order to prosper—were undergoing bankruptcy, acquisitions, and/or consolidation. As for lifestyles, as Barbara Solomon pointed out in an August 1991 article in *Realities of Retailing,* during the 1980s many married people had settled in the suburbs and their discretionary buying power was reduced by mortgages, children, medical bills, and the need to save for the future. Moreover, many women had entered the work force and had less time to visit downtown banks and stores; instead, they went to branch locations in the malls near their homes and increasingly frequented specialty stores. In addition, department stores had become less efficient; more often than not it took several months for new merchandise to reach the shelves. In short, many retailers had lost touch with consumers.

Consequently, Axelrod's initial undertaking was to iron out some of Linens 'n Things' wrinkles and to learn about the needs and spending habits of its "guests," as the company called its customers. With a new management team, Axelrod guided the major part of Melville's first $15 million investment into upgrading the technology in the company's stores; a highly sophisticated point-of-sale system encompassing application of the Universal Product Code (UPC) and electronic data interchange (EDI) was installed. These UPC and EDI systems allowed the stores to track exactly what was selling on a day-to-day basis, thereby making it possible to keep lower levels of inventory and to have a more precise policy of maintaining what people wanted. This line of thinking was underscored by Daniel Raff, an industry analyst quoted in Solomon's 1991 article: "Some of the success of specialty stores has to do with the fact that they have a more sophisticated way of knowing what they're selling. A big part of retailing is having the product in stock and having it out on the floor."

However, maintaining an inventory large enough to meet consumer demand and having products out on the floor required much space. Axelrod recognized that the superstore concept that had inspired Kalkin might solve the space problem. In September 1988 Linens 'n Things opened its first superstore in Rockville, Maryland. In 1989 the company started to convert its store base to superstores ranging in size from to 35,000 to 40,000 gross square feet and began to close all but the most profitable and traditional stores.

The superstore format was meant to save a customer's time by having inventory visible and accessible on the selling floor for immediate purchase. To further enhance customer satisfaction and loyalty, Linens 'n Things strove to provide prompt, knowledgeable sales assistance and enthusiastic customer service. The company offered competitive wages, training, and personnel development in order to attract and retain well-qualified, highly motivated employees dedicated to providing efficient customer service. Recognizing the increasing propensity of consumers to spend more on home decor, Linens 'n Things targeted its product selection to reflect the broadening trends of the 1990s.

The breadth and depth of Linens 'n Things' extensive merchandise offerings enabled guests to select from a wide assortment of styles, name brands, colors, and designs within each of the company's six major product lines. An effort was made to present merchandise in a more visually appealing, customer-friendly manner. The company emphasized its "won't be undersold" policy and explored opportunities to increase sales in its "things" merchandise without sacrificing market share or customer image in the "linens" side of the business. "Linens did not engage in high/low discounting but [held] two clearance events annually, in January and June," noted James Mammarella in *Discount Store News,* an industry publication. He also commented that the company did distribute seasonal fliers containing promotional offers but that "the main message, expressed in the store's slogan, was consistent: 'We give you more for less. Everyday'."

From 1988 through 1995 Linens 'n Things introduced 101 superstores, resulting in the closing of 85 traditional stores. However, although the total number of stores increased only by 15, the company's gross square footage more than tripled, going from 1.4 million square feet on January 1, 1992, to 4.8 million square feet by the end of 1995. Net sales, after slow growth from 1988 to 1992, increased annually with added momentum.

With a view toward maintaining a low-cost operating structure, the company also instituted centralized management and operating programs and also invested significant capital in its infrastructure for distribution and management-information systems. In 1995 the company began full operation of its 275,000-square-foot, state-of-the-art distribution center in Greensboro, North Carolina. The center's EDI capabilities optimized allocation of products to the sites having the highest potential for sales and inventory productivity. Use of this center resulted in lower freight expense averages, more timely control of inventory shipment to stores, improved inventory turnover, better in-stock positions, and improved data flow. Freed from the responsibility of receiving inventory, sales associates had more time to be present on the selling floor to serve the company's guests.

Expanding and Refining: 1996 and Beyond

In October 1995 CVS Corporation, Linens 'n Things' parent company, decided to spin off some of its subsidiaries. On November 26, 1996, Linens 'n Things effected an initial public offering (IPO) of its common stock; CVS retained approximately 32.5 percent of the shares, but sold them during 1997.

In response to consumer demands for one-stop shopping destinations, Linens continued to balance its merchandise by bringing in a fuller assortment of "things." This shift significantly impacted net sales; the "things" side of its business increased from less than ten percent of net sales in 1991 to 35 percent in 1996. The company's long-term goal was to increase the sale of "things" merchandise to approximately 50 percent of net sales. The chain also moved toward more upstairs brands and more elegant presentations of its merchandise.

In a continual effort to offer the best possible customer service, Linens 'n Things also installed satellite transmission for credit card authorizations and upgraded its point-of-sale (POS) system. The company also further refined its planning process through a comprehensive EDI system used for substantially all purchase orders, invoices, and bills of lading. Combined with automatic shipping notice technology used in the distribution systems, the EDI system created additional efficiencies by capturing data through bar codes, thereby reducing clerical errors and inventory shrinkage.

By the end of 1996, net sales increased 25.4 percent to $696.1 million, as compared to $555.1 million in fiscal 1995. The company opened a total of 36 superstores in 1996, increasing gross square footage by 28 percent to approximately 4.6 million gross square feet.

Linens 'n Things superstores continued to grow in size, number, and product line. The operative strategy was to expand market share in new and existing markets, to increase store-productivity levels at existing units, and to penetrate new markets in which the company could become a leading operator of superstores for home furnishings. New markets were located primarily in the western region of the United States, in trading areas of 200,000 persons within a ten-mile radius and having the demographic characteristics that matched the company's target profile. According to Alan M. Rifkin and Kevin M. Hunt's *Home Furnishings Handbook,* Linens 'n Things targeted its product selection "to reflect the broad trends of the 1990s, with an emphasis on consumers' increasing propensity to spend more on home decor." The company succeeded in making "its stores an exciting experience for today's consumer, who continued to prefer home-related goods at the expense of apparel," wrote Rifkin and Hunt.

Linens 'n Things' net sales for fiscal 1997 increased 25.6 percent to $874.22 million, compared with $696.1 million for the same period in 1996. During 1997, the company opened 25 new stores and closed 18 stores. Total square footage of stores increased 16.2 percent to 5.5 million square feet; sales from traditional stores represented less than five percent of total sales. In April 1998 the Linens 'n Things board of directors approved a two-for-one split of the company's common stock to be effected in the form of a stock dividend distributed on May 7, 1998. Commenting on the results of the first quarter of fiscal

1998, Chairman and Chief Executive Officer Axelrod declared that the company began 1998 "with an improved sales and earnings performance, which carried over from a strong 1997 performance. . . . The operating margin for the quarter showed meaningful improvement over the prior year as a result of the increase in comparable store net sales, improved selling mix, and lower markdowns."

The surprise to the bedding industry was that although sales of bedding-specialty chains dropped to 11 percent in 1997 from 13 percent in 1996, "superspecialists Bed Bath & Beyond, Inc. and Linens & Things, Inc. have been growing, both financially and in importance to the whole textiles industry," wrote David Gill in a 1998 issue of *Home Textiles Today*. By way of explanation, Gill quoted Chip Fontenot, president and chief executive officer of New York-based Decorative Home Accents: "You have to understand that there are only two specialty chains that are of any size, [Linens 'n Things and Bed Bath & Beyond] and both of these are emphasizing 'things.' Fewer and fewer customers are running to these stores to buy sheets, while more and more of them are running there to buy kitchen magnets," quipped Fontenot. Linens 'n Things' broad mix of "things" was obviously in sync with the increasing trend of consumer spending for the home.

As the 21st century drew near, the future looked bright for Linens 'n Things. The company planned to open 30 superstores in 1998 while closing 13 traditional stores, thereby expanding its square footage by 17 percent, and to maintain this expansion rate through the next several years by opening 35 to 40 superstores annually. Moreover, the company's ability to keep in step with changing trends and lifestyles, its flexible merchandising strategy, and its continually updated POS and MIS systems all allowed the company to increase market share through expansion and increased productivity. In the late 1990s, the company was within reach of increasing "things" by up to 50 percent and was gradually closing its remaining traditional stores as the annual increase of its superstores kept consumers coming to Linens 'n Things for quality home textiles, housewares and home accessories "at everyday low prices."

Further Reading

Denitto, Emily, "Meeting the Street," *Crain's New York Business,* April 14, 1997, pp. 3–5.

Gill, David, "Specialty Losing Its Steam," *Home Textiles Today,* February 16, 1998, pp. 10, 14.

Hartnett, Michael, "Linens 'n Things Sale Shakes up Home Furnishings Superstores," *Stores,* February 2, 1997, pp. 51–52.

Hogsett, Don, "Fourth Quarter Profits up 38 Percent at Linens 'n Things," *Home Textiles Today,* February 9, 1998, pp. 2, 23.

Lasseter, Diana G., "A Retailer Tries to Blanket Its Market," *Business News New Jersey,* November 15, 1995, pp. 1–2.

Lickteig, Mary Ann, "Kalkins' Service to UVM Knows No Boundaries," *UVM Record,* May 8–21, 1998, p. 7.

Mammarella, James, "Freedom Fuels Linens 'n Things," *Discount Store News,* May 5, 1998, pp. H6–H7.

Rifkin, Alan M., and Kevin M. Hunt, *The Home Furnishings Handbook: A Portfolio Manager's Guide to Understanding and Investing,* Minneapolis: Piper Jaffray Inc., 1998, p. 15.

Solomon, Barbara, "Kalkin's Back," *Home Fashions Magazine,* June 1990, pp. 17–20.

——, "Madness in Store: The New Realities of Retailing," *Management Review,* August 1991, pp. 4–9.

——, "What's Up at Retail," *Home Furnishings Daily: The Weekly Home Furnishings Newspaper,* June 11, 1990, p. 40.

Wright, J. Nils, "Linens 'n Things Likes the Looks of Roseville Power Center," *Business Journal Serving Greater Sacramento,* June 24, 1996, p. 10.

—Gloria A. Lemieux

Little Caesar Enterprises, Inc.

2211 Woodward Avenue
Detroit, Michigan 48201
U.S.A.
(313) 983-6000
Fax: (313) 983-6197

Private Company
Incorporated: 1959
Employees: 90,000
Sales: $1.78 billion
SICs: 5812 Eating Places; 6794 Patent Owners & Lessors

Little Caesar Enterprises, Inc. owns, operates, and franchises Little Caesars Pizza, a predominately carryout chain of pizza and related food products. Best known for its goofy commercials touting two pizzas for the price of one with the tag line "Pizza! Pizza!," Little Caesar's credo is simple: better pizza, and more of it for every dollar spent. With over 4,800 franchises around the globe, Little Caesar vies with competitors Domino's, Pizza Hut, and Papa John's for its slice of the multibillion-dollar pizza marketplace.

Using the same pizza recipe it started with in 1959, this family-run business has grown to become the third largest pizza chain in the United States. Founded by Michael and Marian Ilitch, Little Caesar's interests include its pizza franchises and Blue Line Distributing, a full-service distributor for all units as well as to Kmart's KCafes, which serve Little Caesar products. The Ilitches, well-known sports fans, also own the Detroit Red Wings hockey team, the Detroit Tigers Baseball Club, several sports arenas, the historic Fox Theater in Detroit, and other restaurants. The primary business, a chain of carryout pizza restaurants, has been built on the concept of "two pizzas for the price of one" and other innovative production and marketing techniques. Little Caesar has over 4,825 franchise units in the United States, Canada, Ecuador, Guam, Honduras, Puerto Rico, the Philippines, the Dominican Republic, the Czech Republic, Slovakia, Turkey, and South Korea—and sells over four million pizzas per week.

In the Beginning, 1959–79

The business was established in 1959 in Garden City, Michigan, by Michael and Marian Ilitch. Born during the Great Depression, Michael served in the U.S. Marine Corps from 1947 to 1951 and played on the Detroit Tigers baseball club's farm team from 1951 to 1955; a leg injury cut his professional sports career short. Ilitch sold awnings for the next four years, then founded Little Caesars in 1959.

At the time, the restaurant offered spaghetti, fried chicken, and french fries, as well as pizza. In their first week, the Ilitches sold 296 pizzas and soon realized they had found a niche by offering quality at low prices; they opened a second restaurant in just two years. In 1962 the first franchise was opened in the Detroit metropolitan area. By the end of the 1960s, Little Caesar had built or franchised over 50 restaurants, including one in Canada. During that decade, delivery was a service of most Little Caesars restaurants, but in 1971 the chain moved to carryout only. The restaurant set itself apart from many competitors by using only natural ingredients, including high-gluten flour in the pizza dough, specially grown California tomatoes, and grade A cheese. Little Caesar still prides itself on the use of all-natural spices, as opposed to the synthetic flavorings used throughout the pizza industry.

The 1970s were years of innovation and phenomenal growth for Little Caesar. In 1971 the company began its two-for-one "Pizza! Pizza! Two Great Pizzas! One Low Price!" concept and made it a permanent feature of the company's marketing campaigns in 1975. The marketing strategy has forced competitors in some heavily saturated areas to mimic the two-for-one offer. In 1977 Little Caesar also introduced drive-through windows at its quick-serve locations, and in 1979 developed a pizza conveyor oven that sped up the production of pizza and other baked items.

Building an Empire, the 1980s

During the 1980s Ilitch continued Little Caesar's rapid growth and marketing innovation. In 1980 the chain had 226 units with sales of $63.6 million. By mid-decade annual sales had grown more than fivefold to $340 million. The company achieved successful expansion through an emphasis on several simple concepts: market saturation, two pizzas for the price of one, and carryout only. Approximately 98 percent of Little Caesar units were 1,200- to 1,800-square-foot units offering takeout only—overhead and maintenance on these shops was considerably lower than that of competitors who offered sit-down or even delivery-only service, because the restaurants did not require waiters, waitresses, busboys, dishwashers, or delivery personnel.

In 1984 the company built its 500th restaurant, then saw the 1,000th Little Caesars just two years later. By that time, the company was not only well-established in 38 states and parts of Canada, but had also built an outpost in Great Britain. Marketing innovations included the first college campus restaurant, at the University of Oklahoma, and the first hospital restaurant, in Detroit at Mt. Carmel Mercy Hospital.

The Ilitches also began to develop peripheral interests in the 1980s. They purchased the Detroit Red Wings hockey club in 1982. Then in a slump, the Red Wings club improved markedly after its acquisition by the Ilitch family. The team later captured the Norris Division Championship in the 1986–87, 1987–88, and 1991–92 seasons. In 1992 *Financial World* magazine even reported that the Red Wings were the most valuable franchise in the National Hockey League (NHL). The percent of capacity attendance at Joe Louis Arena (the Red Wings' home ice) was among the highest in the NHL.

The Ilitches also owned the Red Wings' farm team, the Adirondack Red Wings of Glens Falls, New York. The family's sports/entertainment holdings were augmented in 1988 with the purchase of the Detroit Drive arena football team. The team won three out of four Arena Football League championships between 1989 and 1992. The family acquired the Red Wings' home ice as well in 1982. Olympia Arenas, Inc., the management company for Joe Louis, Cobo, and Glens Falls arenas, and Detroit's Fox Theatre have been successful business ventures for the family. In the 1980s Olympia established itself as a trendsetter among arenas when it brought in Little Caesar and Everything Yogurt concessions and separated beer service from all other concessions for speedier service. In 1992 the Meadow Brook Music Festival, an outdoor entertainment center at Oakland University in Rochester Hills, Michigan, was added to the Olympia Arenas group.

The Fox Theatre was a special project of the Ilitch family, who purchased the 5,000-seat historic theater in 1987 and invested $50 million in its restoration. The theater was reopened in November 1988 and was ranked as the nation's top grossing theater—in sales and attendance—by *Performance* magazine that year. The theater's schedule included a variety of concerts, the annual Variety Broadway series, and restored classic films. The Fox was expected to reach the four-million-patron mark during the 1992–93 season. The theater's success was also measured by the other businesses its restoration drew to the formerly declining area of Detroit in which it is located.

Little Caesar moved its corporate headquarters to the Fox Office Centre, adjacent to the Theatre, in 1989. The 10-story office building housed over 500 employees, a child development center, a gift shop, a small convenience shop, and two restaurants. Both restaurants were opened in 1990. America's Pizza Cafe, created by Michael Ilitch, featured thin-crust pizzas baked in a wood-fired oven, gourmet pastas, and desserts. Trés Vite, a bistro-style restaurant, was conceived by Ilitch and nationally known chef Jimmy Schmidt. Ilitch and Schmidt also collaborated on Cocina del Sol, with a Southwestern menu, and Buster's Bay, a seafood restaurant, both in the Detroit metropolitan area. Their fourth restaurant, a northern-Italian eatery called Stelline, was also planned.

Joint Ventures and Advertising, the 1990s

Marketing and promotion efforts for Little Caesar focused on value (''Pizza! Pizza! Two Great Pizzas! One Low Price!'') and quality (''When you make pizza this good, one just isn't enough''). According to Rona Gindin in *Restaurant Business,* the company invested a minimum of five percent of its sales on advertising, and franchises (which constituted 75 percent of all units) spent a comparable percentage on local and corporate promotions. Back in 1986 the company awarded its advertising account to Saatchi & Saatchi's Cliff Freeman & Partners. Freeman had already made a name for himself with Wendy's ''Where's the Beef?'' ads. Freeman's seven 30-second spots constituted the company's first network television campaign. The ads featured comical situations that became the hallmark of Little Caesar promotions.

A spot called ''Yes, But'' employed a carload of non-English-speaking characters who learned the phrase ''Yes, but'' by discovering the hidden costs behind the competition's two-pizza deal. Ads in the early 1990s used outrageously long, rubbery ''cheese pulls'' (melted cheese that stretched between two pieces of pizza) to accentuate the quality and quantity of cheese on a Little Caesar pizza. In one ad, when ''big brother'' hands his high-chair-bound little sister a piece of Little Caesar ''Cheeser! Cheeser!'' pizza that was stretched to its limit, she is yanked from the room, down the hall, around the kitchen table, and out the door into the waiting arms of her grandparents. The ads were credited with doubling Little Caesar sales from 1988 to 1991, to $1.7 billion. Other promotional programs included community services sponsored by the company (the award-winning Little Caesar's Love Kitchen Foundation, two mobile restaurants that served pizza to the needy, had been established in 1985); Ilitch himself volunteered time to such organizations as the Easter Seal Telethon, the Michigan Special Olympics, the NAACP, and a variety of organized children's sports.

Little Caesar also began experimenting with the basic carryout, two-for-one pizza concept. Variations included restaurants with limited seating, drive-through units, and arena concessions. In a joint venture with Kmart Corporation, Little Caesar built over 400 Pizza Stations in Kmart stores and the resulting self-serve restaurants (featuring pasta and vegetable salads, soups, fresh fruits, and the standard pizza, sandwich, and hot pasta) constituted almost half of Little Caesar's 1992 unit growth. The company also introduced such new items as Crazy Bread, Chocolate! Chocolate!, Ravioli! Ravioli!, and Baby Pan! Pan! lunch pizzas. Also during this time, the Ilitches became the sole owners of the Detroit Tigers Baseball Club, the fulfillment of ''a lifelong dream.''

The Little Caesar empire was always a strong family act—Ilitch's wife, Marian, and several of the children were involved with the family business. The Ilitches contended all seven of their children have had a role in the success of the company; and ties extended beyond the immediate family with an estimated 85 percent of Little Caesar franchisees as relatives, with as many as three generations involved in the business. Ilitch also claimed over half of the company's corporate vice-presidents started out at work in the restaurants, crediting this close-knit network with the company's rapid growth.

In the early 1990s, Little Caesar's sales outpaced the industry's growth by 24 percent; yet the company remained locked in a closely fought battle with its two largest competitors, Pizza Hut and Domino's. Moreover, though Little Caesar was named the "Best Value in America" by *Restaurants & Institutions* magazine for the third year running in 1992, trouble was on the horizon as the "Big Three" pizza chains—Domino's, Pizza Hut, and Little Caesar—found themselves in a reluctant expansion to the "Big Four." The new competition came from the rapidly emerging Papa John's chain, gaining ground at every turn. Errors in judgment, like Pizza Hut's disastrous "Triple Decker" pizza, now had more profound repercussions, and Little Caesar suffered its own problems after its nationwide delivery service was not nearly as successful as planned when introduced in the summer of 1995. Yet 1995 was still a decent year for Little Caesar, with the introduction of the enormously popular stuffed crust pizza and revenues of over $1.1 billion.

For Little Caesar, the next few years brought trouble. After leaving the delivery question in the hands of individual franchisees, the company was faced with a series of calamities, large and small, not the least of which was Papa John's lightning-fast growth. Tough times required tough measures and Little Caesar initiated several to bolster its bottom line. Among the trimming was the national advertising budget, slashed by nearly 23 percent from 1994 to 1996, and the layoff of 27 managers at its headquarters in Detroit. The jobs represented one percent of its corporate workforce, and rumors linked the purge to Harsha Agadi's appointment as COO and the company's eight percent decline in domestic sales in 1996. In addition, according to *Nation's Restaurant News,* Little Caesar's market share fell from 14.5 to 13.4 percent for the year, and 184 units closed for a total unit count of 4,004. Meanwhile, over at Papa John's, same-store sales grew by 10 percent and units mushroomed by 32.1 percent to 1,160.

On the positive side, Little Caesar broadened its marketing efforts substantially with three major moves. The first was a joint venture with Holiday Inn in Florida, to put pizza kiosks in two of the chain's biggest-draw hotels. Both hotels were near the state's largest tourist attraction, Walt Disney World, with one in neighboring Kissimmee, and the other located in Disney's Lake Buena Vista resort area. Each location had both a poolside pizza kiosk, another in the lobby, and Little Caesars was also available from room service. The second was the unveiling of a bold new strategy to call attention to its longheld creed—value—with more pizza for every dollar. In a risky move, Little Caesar proudly proclaimed "Bigger is Better" with pizzas 80 percent larger (or four inches in diameter per pie) at the same price. The new, larger pizzas were promoted through Little Caesar's trademark quirky commercials, replac-

ing the "Pizza! Pizza!" with "Bigger! Bigger!" and using a dwarfed Pizza Hut box to show how much bigger the new pizzas actually were. Third, the company's venture with Kmart stores was not only going well, but was expanded into 1,500 of the chain's over 2,000 stores in 1997. There was one slight catch: the stations were renamed KCafe and carried food items from other companies as well—yet Kmart still retained a host of items from Little Caesar and also continued to use the company's Blue Line distribution division.

Outside the pizza business, the Ilitch family was thrilled when the Detroit Red Wings won the Stanley Cup in 1997 and 1998. Yet family ties interfered with business when Little Caesar was sued by a Hollywood movie studio, New Line Cinema, over an endorsement tie-in for the new *Lost in Space* movie. The "deal" was initiated by Mike Ilitch, Jr., who had originally sold the movie rights to New Line and discussed the tie-in with Little Caesar products; however, Ilitch, Sr., and others said Mike Ilitch, Jr., had no power to act on behalf of the Little Caesar organization. The suit also brought Little Caesar's solvency into question, with New Line intimating that the company's cash flow problems were profound and the real reason Little Caesar backed out of the proposed $20.5 million agreement.

In the late 1990s, Little Caesar was still battling its old foes Domino's and Pizza Hut, but Papa John's relentless growth had become a serious threat. According to the *Wall Street Journal,* Papa John's same-store sales were up 12 percent and profits up 66 percent in 1997, and the chain planned to open dozens of new stores each month during 1998. To counter its slipping market share, Little Caesar introduced the use of American Express credit cards at its locations in Utah, and offered pizza at 39 cents a slice on May 7, 1998—to mark its 39th anniversary.

As Little Caesar approached the 21st century, its competition had increased but so had its millions of consumers and admirers. Not only was Little Caesar named the "Best Pizza Value in America" for the 11th year in a row by *Restaurants & Institutions* magazine (Papa John's, however, was chosen as "Best Pizza Chain"), but began opening locations in yet another international venue. Ecuador was the latest to join the ranks, along with locations in Puerto Rico, Guam, Honduras, the Philippines, Korea, the Dominican Republic, the Czech Republic, Slovakia, Turkey, and, of course, the United States and Canada. Although there have been a spate of new products over the years, the company's mission has remained the same—provide more pizza for every dollar than any competitor. With pizza consumption still on the rise in the United States, Little Caesar's niche was a sure thing.

Principal Subsidiaries

Blue Line Distributing.

Further Reading

"American Express Card Now Welcome at Utah Little Caesars Locations," *PR Newswire,* March 13, 1998.

Frank, Robert, "Marketing & Media: Building a Better Pie—Pizza Hut Is Topping Rivals with Cheese . . . ," *Wall Street Journal,* January 18, 1996, p. B14.

Garfield, Bob, "Little Caesar's Cheesy Ad Really Pulls in Audience," *Advertising Age,* November 25, 1991.

Gindin, Rona, "A Fight to Stay on Top," *Restaurant Business,* July 1, 1986.

Howard, Theresa, "Kmart Corp.: Attention Shoppers—Retail Giant Hails 'Caesars' As a Big Guy," *Nation's Restaurant News,* January 1998, p. 84.

——, "Pizza's 'Big Three' Hold the Gimmicks, Serve Simplicity," *Nation's Restaurant News,* January 13, 1997, p. 16.

"Little Caesars Celebrates 39 Years in Business with 39-Cent Slices of Pizza," *Bison Franchise News,* May 6, 1998, http://www.bison1.com/press/pr5-6caesar.html.

"Little Caesars Named Best Pizza Value in America by Consumer Survey," *Bison Franchise News,* March 26, 1998, http://www.bison1.com/press/pr3-26caesar.html.

Maki, Dee Ann, "Ilitch-Lites Is Helping Growth Plans Pan Out for Little Caesar Pizza," *Advertising Age,* May 2, 1988.

McGraw, Bill, "Studio Sues Detroit-Based Little Caesars Over Pizza Commercial," *Knight-Ridder/Tribune Business News,* February 13, 1998, p. 213B1026.

"New Little Caesar Ads Make Pan! Pan! Comical," *Restaurant Business,* June 10, 1988.

Oneal, Michael, " 'Pizza Pizza' and Tigers, Too," *Business Week,* September 14, 1992.

Pittinger, Heather, "Popular and Profitable," *Hotel & Motel Management,* May 6, 1996, p. 49.

Rubenstein, Ed, "Size Matters in New Campaigns Set to Attack the Competition," *Nation's Restaurant News,* September 22, 1997, p. 18.

Walkup, Carolyn, "Little Caesar Cuts 27 Management Posts at Headquarters," *Nation's Restaurant News,* July 14, 1997, p. 27.

Weinstein, Jeff, "Pizza/Italian Shows Strong Growth Curve," *Restaurants & Institutions,* July 8, 1992.

—April Dougal Gasbarre
—updated by Taryn Benbow-Pfalzgraf

LOEHMANN'S
Loehmann's Inc.

2500 Halsey Street
Bronx, New York 10461
U.S.A.
(718) 409-2000
Fax: (718) 518-2766
Web site: http://www.loehmanns.com

Public Company
Incorporated: 1930 as Charles C. Loehmann Corp.
Employees: 3,049
Sales: $417.8 million (1996)
Stock Exchanges: NASDAQ
Ticker Symbol: LOEH
SICs: 5611 Men's & Boys' Clothing & Accessory
Stores; 5621 Women's Clothing Stores; 5632
Women's Accessory & Specialty Stores

Loehmann's Inc. is a retailer of women's clothing, shoes, and accessories, and menswear, and is best known for designer and brand name women's fashion apparel sold at discount prices. In early 1998 the company was operating 86 stores, all of them in the United States.

Family-Run Discounter: 1921–64

The Loehmann's retail chain was founded in 1930 by Charles C. Loehmann. The company's spiritual matriarch, however, was Loehmann's mother, Frieda Loehmann. Mother of three children, she became the family breadwinner in 1916 when her husband, a flutist with a symphony orchestra, developed a paralyzed lip. Mrs. Loehmann was a coat buyer for a fashionable department store until 1921, when, with $800 in cash, she and her son Charles opened, below their Brooklyn apartment, a women's specialty clothing shop named the Original Designer Outlet. "Mama" Loehmann got her merchandise by driving to the garment district on Manhattan's Seventh Avenue in a black limousine and filling it with designers' seasonal overstocks at a fraction of the traditional wholesale price, pay-

ing from a wad of cash she kept in what designer Bill Blass called her "voluminous black bloomers."

Mrs. Loehmann continued to descend daily on the garment district until two weeks before her death in 1962, and the store was doing an estimated $3 million in annual sales at the time. Her one flaw, according to a manufacturer who was one of her suppliers, was that "she thought Brooklyn was the beginning and end of the world." Her son Charles had different ideas. After his mother rejected the notion of expansion, he opened a women's clothing store on Fordham Road in the borough of the Bronx in 1930 and incorporated the enterprise as the Charles C. Loehmann Corp.

Loehmann's gained fame as a discounter, but of high-fashion, first-quality merchandise, made possible by purchasing manufacturer's overruns and "broken lots"—groups of garments in a limited range of sizes and colors. The store also kept its costs down by paying cash for these "odd lots" on the day it ordered them. These were then taken from the manufacturer's plant, processed and ticketed at the company warehouse, and delivered to the store, sometimes all on the same day. As a result, a woman might be able to buy a *couturier*-designed dress for as little as one-third the price at a competing store, with the only difference being that the manufacturer's label had been removed from the garment.

Loehmann's also saved on overhead by hanging most of the clothing on ordinary pipe racks and making women try clothing on in "community" dressing rooms. The mayhem that occurred when a desirable shipment arrived was recalled by one woman as "female bonding" and discussed, more graphically, by Erma Bombeck in her book *Everything I Know About Animal Behavior I Learned at Loehmann's*. The company also saved money by not offering credit, delivery, or alterations, seldom accepting returns, and restricting advertising to the mailing of announcements.

It was not until 1951 that Loehmann's felt ready to open a store outside of New York City. Three such stores were opened during the 1950s, and by 1964, when the company went public, it was operating four stores in New York, one in Connecticut, and one in New Jersey. Specialty stores for women, these establishments sold dresses, coats, suits, sweaters, blouses, skirts, slacks, shorts, separates, raincoats, and bathing suits. Net sales rose from $9 million in 1961 to $15.1 million in 1964; net profit rose from $288,315 in 1961 to $532,712 in 1964. After shares were first offered on the American Stock Exchange in 1964, Charles Loehmann and his wife, Anita, continued to hold a majority of the stock for about a decade. George J. Greenberg succeeded Charles as president of the company, which was renamed Loehmann's Inc.

Under Various Ownership: 1964–88

Before the 1960s ended, Loehmann's had added ten more stores. The company entered Massachusetts in 1965, Maryland in 1967, and Pennsylvania and Virginia in 1968, and it opened a store in Los Angeles in October 1969. The flagship Bronx store remained by far the largest, however, and the company also built a new Bronx corporate headquarters and warehouse in 1968. The new Loehmann's stores were much like the earlier ones, located away from high-rent areas and with furnishings kept to a minimum. Moreover, the company was careful to make sure that the stores were a sizable distance from major fashion retailers normally carrying the same merchandise lines. Net sales passed $37 million in 1970, while net income was reported at $1.1 million.

After the Los Angeles store proved successful, Loehmann's opened its first midwestern outlet in a Chicago suburb and its first southern store in Atlanta. The company also experimented with seven lower-line Charley's Place outlets but converted them into conventional Loehmann's stores in 1972 when the profit margin proved too small. By the spring of that year there were 27 stores in the chain. In 1975, when Loehmann's boasted 31 stores in 12 states, the company broke precedent by beginning to advertise in local newspapers. Still, advertising expenditures in 1976 came to less than one percent of sales.

Five categories of women's sportswear were accounting for 62 percent of Loehmann's sales in 1977. That year Greenberg discussed the company's activities among a group of financial analysts. He noted that Loehmann's blouses could be purchased for as low as $8.98 and that its dresses retailed for as much as $700; the company also carried a wide variety of furs and had sold sables and minks for as much as $12,000. Loehmann's was still striving to process goods in its warehouse and get them to its stores within 48 hours and was turning around its merchandise 12 to 13 times a year, as compared to six to eight for a regular retailer. The company, said Greenberg, was doing "considerable" purchasing outside Seventh Avenue, particularly in Philadelphia, Baltimore, and Los Angeles, but also overseas.

Loehmann's net sales reached a record $159.7 million in fiscal 1980, and its net income came to a record $6.5 million. In April 1980 there were 48 stores (all but two leased) in 21 states. More than half were in shopping centers, including 19 in "Loehmann's Plaza" locations. At the instigation of the Loehmann family, which still held 37 percent of the stock, the company agreed in September 1980 to accept a purchase offer of about $68 million from AEA Investors Inc. Greenberg continued to serve as chairman and president of the company.

Three years later, this investment group sold Loehmann's to Associated Dry Goods Corp., operator of 14 department-store chains, for $96 million. During 1983 the company had posted sales of about $260 to $270 million and extended its operations to 61 stores in 25 states. Along with the rest of Associated Dry Goods, Loehmann's passed in 1986 to May Department Stores Co. By 1988 the number of Loehmann's had grown to 82 in 26 states. That year the original Bronx store was closed, giving way to a 35,000-square-foot outlet—the largest in the chain—in a converted skating rink.

Despite its growth in scale, however, Loehmann's had achieved only modest growth in average sales per store during the mid-1980s and had actually slipped in this category during 1987. A new president and chief executive officer, Allan R. Bogner, closed 13 marginal stores, established a policy of accepting credit cards and personal checks, and hired a trendy New York advertising agency to conduct a $4 million campaign. During 1988 Loehmann's 77 stores had sales of $334 million. In the summer of 1988, however, the chain was sold again—this time to an affiliate of a Spanish firm, Entrecanales y Tavora S.A., and a venture-capital arm of Donaldson, Lufkin & Jenrette Securities Corp.—for a reported $170 million. The new owners took the firm private in a leveraged buyout.

Loehmann's in the 1990s

In its first full year under new management, Loehmann's closed more underperforming stores while expanding rapidly across the nation and achieved an average same-store increase in sales of 18.7 percent. The owners used the profits to buy back about $30 million of the loans they had taken out and the high-yielding "junk" bonds they had issued to pay for the company. Loehmann's lost $4 million in fiscal 1989 (the year ended February 3, 1990). Its sales remained essentially stagnant during the next three years, in which it lost $1.1 million, $6.5 million, and $783,000, respectively. Some sources suggested in 1992 that Loehmann's had sacrificed some of its mystique by venturing into mainstream retailing and stocking many lesser-known brands. By then the 83-store chain was accepting returns as well as credit cards, was leaving the manufacturers' labels in its clothing, and even began offering its own private-label clothing. In March 1992 Bogner was replaced as president by Robert Friedman, a veteran Macy's executive.

Friedman steered Loehmann's toward an even more conventional department store atmosphere, putting up signs in the stores that emphasized manufacturers' names, displaying clothing on mannequins, and even giving customers the option of trying on clothes in private dressing rooms. The company also added shoes, lingerie, hosiery, hats, and accessories such as jewelry, perfume, and sunglasses to its offerings. Loehmann's circulated its own credit card and offered an Insiders Club for special discounts. Still, however, sales continued to drop in 1993. In October of that year the company completed a financial reorganization, repurchasing $30 million of its notes and selling $55.7 million of new bonds, with no repayment of principal required until 1997.

Loehmann's lost a record $12.2 million in fiscal 1993 on net sales of $373.4 million—down by $16 million—and $1.5 million in fiscal 1994 on net sales of $392.6 million. The company was burdened by heavy interest payments—$18.2 million in fiscal 1994—on its considerable debt. During fiscal 1995 net sales dipped to $386.1 million, and the company lost $15 million, after taking a $15.3 million charge to close 11 small, underperforming stores.

Loehmann's went public again in May 1996, raising $60 million after expenses by selling common stock at $17 a share. The proceeds were used to redeem preferred stock held by the investors and to help refinance the company's long-term debt load. Just before going public, the company also sold $100 million worth of junk bonds at 11.875 percent in annual interest, due in 2003, in order to redeem $130 million worth of notes, some of which were at even higher rates. This enabled the company to reduce its interest costs in fiscal 1995 to $13.4 million.

Many analysts agreed with the editor and publisher of a research service who said Loehmann's had lost its way by reducing sales of designer and "bridge" merchandise—apparel just below designer category—to only one-third of overall inventory. Company executives countered that the chain's traditional niche was ill-suited to the expansion they planned—seven new stores in 1996 and seven to ten each in 1997 and 1998. Investors did step up to buy the company's stock, lifting the price of the initial offering to $22.25 by day's end. In October 1996 a secondary stock offering raised $63.8 million for insiders who chose to sell. One month later, Loehmann's common stock reached a peak of $30.25 a share.

On opening day in October 1996, Loehmann's new five story, 60,000-square-foot Manhattan store on 16th Street and Seventh Avenue was mobbed by frenzied shoppers contending for such merchandise as Giorgio Armani bustiers marked down from $2,810 to $750 as well as upscale goods by Jones New York and DKNY in the $100 to $500 range. By August 1997 the number of new Loehmann's stores opened since the beginning of 1996 had reached 13, raising the total to 77. Many, like the Manhattan one, were in high-rent downtown districts where Loehmann's rarely had been located in the past. For fiscal 1996 the company reported record revenues of $417.8 million and net income of $4.5 million after a $7.1 million writeoff on early extinguishment of debt.

During the spring of 1997, however, bad news returned in the form of escalating costs and falling sales. Management attributed the results to its inexperience with large stores in major downtown locations, while observers pointed to the competition Loehmann's faced from the more than 1,900 stores nationwide now competing in the off-price category for designer apparel overruns. Donna Karan International Inc. and Anne Klein & Co., for example, formerly good Loehmann's clients, were now directing their surplus production to their own outlet stores. Some of Loehmann's own employees suggested that as little as two to ten percent of the chain's merchandise on hand was designer clothing, although Friedman maintained that the level remained at 30 percent. At the end of July 1997, shares of Loehmann's common stock were selling for only $6.625. The company's long-term debt was $107.9 million at the end of March 1997.

In October 1997 Loehmann's introduced merchandise for men, including dress shirts, ties, sportswear, and some designer-collection items such as jackets and pants, in 15 of its stores. (Tailored clothing and shoes were not offered.) Design collections included Ralph Lauren, Donna Karan, Calvin Klein, and DKNY. Friedman said the chain's desired merchandise mix was 60 percent women's apparel; 20 percent accessories, intimate apparel, and shoes; and 20 percent menswear, compared to its current merchandise mix of 80 percent women's apparel and 20 percent accessories, intimate apparel, and shoes. Management intended to have menswear in 55 Loehmann's stores by the end of 1998.

Loehmann's announced in February 1998 that, of its existing 86 stores, it was planning to close ten, which combined were losing an estimated $900,000 a year. The company reported a loss of $15.6 million in the fourth quarter of fiscal 1997, including a $9 million restructuring charge to cover closing costs. Still, the company also had plans to open three stores in 1998: in Cincinnati, Cleveland, and Long Beach, California.

Further Reading

Furman, Phyllis, "Loehmann Races Against Time," *Crain's New York Business,* March 30, 1991, pp. 1, 37.

Hemlock, Doreen, "As Retail Rebounds, Investors Snap Up Loehmann's," *New York Times,* May 12, 1996, Sec. 3, p. 3.

"Loehmann's Agrees to Be Purchased; Price Is $68 Million," *Wall Street Journal,* September 26, 1980, p. 7.

"Loehmann's, Inc.," *Wall Street Transcript,* October 6, 1969, pp. 18,132–18,133, and July 11, 1977, pp. 47,588–47,589.

"Loehmann's Styles Smart Advance Selling High Fashion at Low Cost," *Barron's,* January 23, 1967, pp. 22, 28.

Palmieri, Jean E., "Calling All Men to Loehmann's," *DNR/Daily News Record,* October 13, 1997, pp. 12, 16.

Schiro, Anne-Marie, "Tough Balancing Act at Loehmann's," *New York Times,* October 30, 1993, pp. 37, 50.

"A Shopping Cult Goes National," *Business Week,* April 29, 1972, pp. 20–21.

Simmons, Jacqueline, "Loehmann's Plans IPO to Refinance Debt, Redeem Series A Preferred Stock," *Wall Street Journal,* October 3, 1995, p. B10H.

Span, Paula, "A Shrine to Bargains," *Newsweek,* March 21, 1988, p. 81.

Steinhauer, Jennifer, "Bargain Hunting? Keep Looking," *New York Times,* July 30, 1997, pp. D1, D8.

Yaeger, Deborah Sue, "In Women's Clothing, Dean of Discounters Is Still Loehmann's," *Wall Street Journal,* July 6, 1976, pp. 1, 24.

—Robert Halasz

LOT$OFF Corporation

8750 Tesoro Drive
San Antonio, Texas 78217-0555
U.S.A.
(210) 805-9300
Fax: (210) 804-4952

Public Company
Incorporated: 1975 as Shoppers World Stores, Inc.
Employees: 1,200
Sales: $106.19 million (1997)
Stock Exchanges: OTC
Ticker Symbol: LOTS
SICs: 5651 Family Clothing Stores; 5331 Variety Stores

LOT$OFF Corporation, formerly 50-Off Stores, Inc., operates approximately 40 discount stores throughout the United States, all of which offer products at closeout prices. LOT$OFF stores sell clothing for men, women, and children, as well as houseware items, toys, health and beauty aids, stationary, and gift items. LOT$OFF carries name-brand goods that are either surplus or slightly out-of-season, and thus can be marked down in order to sell quickly, as well as private label goods. The chain's store units are located in Texas, Louisiana, Tennessee, Oklahoma, and New Mexico. Under its previous incarnation as 50-Off, the chain operated more than 100 stores and was active in several other states. Following emergence from Chapter 11 bankruptcy protection in 1997, the company adopted the name LOT$OFF and shifted from half-off to deep-discount pricing.

The Early Years

LOT$OFF traces its beginnings to 1975, when a company called Shoppers World Stores, Inc. was formed in New York to manage nine discount department stores in Texas that had just been purchased. The department stores carried merchandise that was also featured by its department store competition at regular high prices, but Shoppers World Stores marketed it instead at discounted prices.

After eight years of decently steady business and marginal success, in 1983 Shoppers World Stores, Inc. was reincorporated in Texas as the successor to the former New York entity. At its head was Charles Siegel, who had already accrued many years of retail experience, after entering the business in 1963 as a department store manager at King Clothing Company. Under his leadership, Shoppers World Stores continued to manage its discount department store chain, while also planning moves to expand.

Two years later, in 1985, the company acquired the inventory and entire holdings of five "Terry Farris" department stores from G.C. Murphy Company. With the acquisition, Shoppers World Stores received not only the stores' inventory, but also their property leases, furniture, display fixtures, and rights to all previous layaway sales. This allowed the new owners to continue business as usual immediately following the transaction.

Just one year later, the company was undergoing drastic changes, making moves to pare down its holdings following a mediocre business year. A recession in Texas was hitting the retail market hard, and Shoppers World Stores was falling as a casualty. Siegel decided to open an outlet store in San Antonio as a means of quickly moving out the company's inventory from the other stores. The new outlet store unit was meant to be temporary, and was only 12,000 square feet. The store was called "50-Off," and was supported by a strong advertising campaign which touted the store's extreme low prices. Inventory was moved into the unit from other stores, and was tagged with both the original price and the discounted 50-percent-off price.

When the 50-Off store opened in January 1986, it was an immediate success. Siegel had done a good job advertising the store, in the hopes that people would stop in to get a last minute bargain before the other stores closed down. Management's expectations were obviously far lower than the store's potential, however, because people flocked to the store and business was great. The television commercials had worked like a charm, as had advertising gained by word-of-mouth after shoppers left the store with goods priced 50 percent below what they would have paid elsewhere. Siegel recognized a new niche with loads of potential, that of the discounted goods retail market. He quickly sold off all existing merchandise through the outlet store, and then made moves to bring in more discount items that would lend themselves well to the 50-Off concept.

Rapid Growth Throughout the 1980s

In September 1987, the company changed its name to 50-Off Stores, Inc. The stores continued the practice of tagging all items at their original "department store" price, totaling this original price at the check-out register, and then pressing a button that slashed the total in half in front of the customer. Customers loved the savings that appeared right before their eyes, and the practice was the store's own method of advertisement. Word of mouth spread quickly, while further television advertisements were also highly effective. After beginning as a "temporary fix" to retail problems during the recession, 50-Off was actually a huge hit.

Most of the 50-Off stores' sales came from women's apparel, followed by children's apparel and then men's, housewares, and other items. The chain found that its typical customer was a female from a two-income family whose annual net earnings were in the category of $25,000 or less. The stores purchased items from vendors that were either suffering from surplus in stock, or who were still holding on to present-season or out-of-season merchandise. In either case, a vendor would be willing to cut 50-Off a good deal in order to rid itself of the merchandise, and 50-Off would then sell the items for just enough to make a profit.

In order to ensure that it would have access to any deals that were available, 50-Off's management hired highly knowledgeable buyers—most of whom had over 20 years of experience in the field—and then authorized each buyer to make any on-the-spot decisions or buys that he or she deemed necessary. This arrangement allowed the company to keep a constant and steady supply of goods in stock that were within the target customer's price range. It also ensured that buyers would not have to pass up on quick deals in order to receive purchasing authorization from their superiors, which gave 50-Off an edge on acquiring merchandise at great prices.

Meanwhile, the store chain was continuing to grow. Management formulated a plan to open new store units near residential areas of low-income customers, or where other demographic information indicated that a deep-discount store would do well. Locations were considered only if and when the real estate costs associated with operating the proposed store totaled four percent or less of the location's anticipated sales potential. All 50-Off stores ranged in size from 10,000 to 50,000 square feet, with the majority averaging 20,000 or above.

The 1990s and Beyond

By the beginning of the 1990s, 50-Off's business was booming and the company was responsible for over 50 stores that were in operation throughout the southern United States. The company decided to list itself as a public company, and offered shares of its stock to the public in July 1991. Management anticipated over $11 million in proceeds from the transac-

tion, which was slated to be used as capital to fund further expansion into new market areas. At that point, the chain was located in Texas, Oklahoma, New Mexico, and Louisiana.

Following the public listing, plans were made to add Georgia to 50-Off's list with a strong entrance into the Atlanta market. In addition, the company was also hoping to open approximately 15 new store units in its present markets by the end of 1991. Sales rose to $130.1 million in 1992, and the company increased its store unit total from 68 at the beginning of the year to almost 100 by December.

Sales jumped to $181 million the following year, and continued to rise each subsequent year through the 1995 sales year, when 50-Off broke the $200 million mark for the first time in the company's history. Celebration of that achievement did not last long, however, as the chain began to experience its first annual sales decline during the decade when 1996 sales dropped by more than $25 million. Apparel sales, which had traditionally been the chain's strongest area, began to slump.

That same year the company filed for Chapter 11 protection and instituted drastic cutbacks, including closing 60 stores in half a dozen states, reducing its corporate staff by 25 percent, and slashing pay to top executives by 20 percent. The company's sales for 1997 fell to $106.2 million. One bright note that year, in addition to the company's eventual emergence from Chapter 11, was a $151 million settlement with Chase Manhattan for mishandling a 1995 company stock transaction two years earlier.

Entering the end of the century under a new name, LOT$OFF Corporation struggled to recover its standing as one of the premier discount retailers in the southern United States. Prior to the decline in earnings that had arisen in 1995, the company had enjoyed steady growth in its market areas and had created a viable niche for itself. Many critics had begun to compare the store chain to such giants in the industry as Wal-Mart, and had actually ranked the company ahead of Kmart in terms of total savings received by the customer. As LOT$OFF approached the end of the 1990s, its management's response to the apparel sales problem and the general financial situation of the company would dictate the store chain's potential for future success and growth.

Principal Subsidiaries

Franklin Stores Corp. of Beaumont.

Further Reading

Arlen, Jeffrey, "Low Prices, Fast Growth," *Discount Store News*, August 3, 1992, p. A14.
"50-Off Offering to Fund Growth," *Discount Store News*, July 22, 1991, p. 4.
"50-Off Set to Buy Back Securities," *Discount Store News*, March 4, 1991, p. 17.
"50-Off Set to Open 6 Units," *Discount Store News*, February 4, 1991, p. 61.
"50-Off Sets Growth Goal," *Discount Store News*, February 18, 1991, p. 4.

—Laura E. Whiteley

The LTV Corporation

200 Public Square
Cleveland, Ohio 44114-2308
U.S.A.
(216) 622-5000
Fax: (216) 622-4610
Web site: http://www.ltvsteel.com

Public Company
Incorporated: 1956 as Ling Electronics, Inc.
Employees: 15,500
Sales: $4.45 billion (1997)
Stock Exchanges: New York Pacific
Ticker Symbol: LTV
SICs: 3312 Steel Works & Blast Furnaces

The LTV Corporation is the third largest steel producer in the United States. As the second largest domestic maker of flat-rolled steel, the company supplies the automotive, appliance, and electrical equipment industries. Other areas in which LTV holds leading positions include carbon electrical steels, electrolytically galvanized steel sheets, ultralow carbon steels, welded steel pipe and tubing products, electrical conduit, and tin mill products. LTV operates two integrated plants in Cleveland and East Chicago, Indiana, for the manufacture of flat-rolled steel, as well as a high-tech minimill in Decatur, Alabama, which is operated under a joint venture—50 percent owned by LTV—with Japan's Sumitomo Metal Industries, Ltd. and the United Kingdom's British Steel plc.

From Electronics Firm to Conglomerate

The man who built LTV from a small electronics firm into one of America's largest corporations was named James J. (Jimmy) Ling. Through a process of acquisition and merger Ling created a modern corporate conglomerate.

In 1947 Jimmy Ling invested $2,000 in order to establish an electrical construction and engineering firm in Dallas. In 1956, after several successful years in business, the Ling Electric

Company merged with L.M. Electronics of California and the name of the company was changed to Ling Electronics. A subsequent merger with Altec Electronics in 1959 changed the name of the company to Ling-Altec. A year later Ling-Altec merged with the Temco Electronics and Missile Company of Dallas. The new company, Ling-Temco, became one of the first major defense companies to be founded after World War II.

In 1961 Ling-Temco merged with the Chance Vought Aircraft Company. Vought was founded in 1917 and became part of the Boeing United Aircraft conglomerate in 1929. After that organization was forced to break up in 1934, Vought became a division of United Aircraft (later United Technologies). A conflict of interest in manufacturing led to United Aircraft's sale of Vought in 1954. Seven years later Ling initiated a difficult takeover of Vought which resulted in his temporary (but voluntary) loss of control over the company and all but 11 shares of company stock. Upon completion of the takeover on August 16, the company's name was again changed to Ling-Temco-Vought.

Ling's notion of what constituted a successful conglomerate was based on the idea that no division should account for more than 30 percent of the company's sales. In addition, concentration of the company's business in related fields was to be avoided at all costs. It was for that reason that Ling-Temco-Vought became interested in Wilson Foods in 1966. Wilson's primary product was fresh meats, but it also operated two other businesses dependent upon animal byproducts: sporting goods and pharmaceuticals. The sporting goods division made (among other things) footballs from pigskin and tennis rackets from animal guts, and the pharmaceuticals division derived hormones, steroids, and other drugs from animal organs. Wilson's president, Roscoe Haynie, knew nothing of Ling's takeover effort until two weeks before it was completed. By January 5, 1967, Ling-Temco-Vought had acquired control of Wilson, and Haynie agreed to move to Dallas and work for Ling. That same year Ling-Temco-Vought was listed number 14 in the *Fortune* 500 ranking with annual sales of over $1 billion.

Ling divided Wilson into three operating divisions: Wilson & Company (meat), Wilson Sporting Goods, and Wilson Pharmaceutical & Chemical, and shares of stock in the three divisions were sold to the public. On Wall Street the share offerings were greeted with some skepticism. Despite this skepticism, Ling believed the parts of the company were worth more separately than together, and in time he was proven correct. Before long Ling-Temco-Vought's remaining share of the three Wilson companies was worth more than its initial investment.

Ling-Temco-Vought's growth in the five years from 1965 to 1969 was impressive. In 1965 the company had total sales of $36 million. In 1969 that figure had grown by more than 100 times to $3.8 billion. This growth was made possible through ''redeployment,'' Ling's term for offering a minority share of a Ling-Temco-Vought division's stock to the public. Under favorable market conditions, private investors would drive up the price of the stock. This provided Ling-Temco-Vought with more collateral to support larger bank loans which were, in turn, used to finance more takeovers.

In 1968 Ling-Temco-Vought acquired the Greatamerica Corporation from Dallas investor Troy Post in return for $95 million in debentures. Greatamerica was the parent company for Braniff Airways, National Car Rental, and a number of insurance companies. Later that same year the company purchased a majority interest in the Jones & Laughlin Steel Corporation of Pittsburgh. Ling-Temco-Vought's numerous acquisitions led the U.S. Justice Department to initiate an antitrust investigation. Ling managed to avoid a federal lawsuit by agreeing to sell Braniff and the Okonite division, which was acquired in 1965. Despite the legal battles, Ling's strategy of redeployment had been successful.

Divestments Began in 1969

Unfortunately, redeployment had an even more serious detrimental effect under unfavorable market conditions. When the economy began to decline in 1969 Ling-Temco-Vought's growth abruptly halted. The company was forced to divest itself of several divisions in order to generate enough cash to compensate for its growing debt. Wilson Sporting Goods was sold for $8.7 million and Wilson Pharmaceuticals was sold to American Can for $16 million. Investors subsequently lost confidence in Ling-Temco-Vought. The same stock that traded for $167 in 1967 was now worth $11.

In May 1970 Ling-Temco-Vought's board of directors voted to remove Ling from the chairmanship. Robert Stewart was named interim chairman until a permanent replacement for Ling could be found. Ling was demoted to president, a position where he had no control over company policy. Six weeks later Ling resigned from the corporation. The board elected W. Paul Thayer of Ling-Temco-Vought's Aerospace division to become the company's new president and, a few months later, its chairman.

Thayer's first objective was to dispose of Ling-Temco-Vought's unprofitable divisions and remove all the others from public trading. Ling-Temco-Vought, which had until this time been more of an investment portfolio than a holding company, was to be converted into an operating company directly involved with its subsidiaries. This reorganization allowed one of the company's divisions to help another financially, something that was not possible under Ling.

Ling-Temco-Vought's debt was restructured and a campaign to acquire the privately held shares of the company's divisions was launched. On May 5, 1971, Ling-Temco-Vought became The LTV Corporation. Later that month the company acquired the remaining shares of Vought Aircraft from private investors. The investors received $3.2 million and two former Ling-Temco-Vought subsidiaries, LTV Ling Altec (the Altec Corporation) and LTV Electrosystems (now called E-Systems). By November 1974 LTV had also acquired the minority interests of Wilson & Company and Jones & Laughlin Steel.

LTV's Vought division was subcontracted to manufacture tail sections for a number of aircraft, including Boeing's 747 and McDonnell Douglas's DC-10 and KC-10. Vought also manufactured the A-7 Corsair II fighter and the S-3A antisubmarine airplane. In the mid-1970s, however, Vought's ability to generate a consistent profit was undermined by the Pentagon when it eliminated Vought from several lucrative defense contracts. Vought then attempted to enter civilian markets when it engineered a $34 million ''Airtrans'' ground transportation system for the Dallas/Ft. Worth Airport. The project was mired in controversy from its inception and a series of problems led Vought to declare a $22.6 million loss on the project. Subsequent orders for the A-7 from the Defense department and the governments of Greece and Pakistan, as well as a contract to produce Lance surface-to-surface missiles, helped to keep Vought in business.

By 1977 LTV was reduced to three principal lines of business: steel (Jones & Laughlin), meatpacking (Wilson), and aerospace (Vought). All three lines of business were cyclical (experiencing alternating periods of good and bad market conditions). In 1977 all three of LTV's divisions were suffering from the adverse conditions in their respective markets. LTV lost $39 million on sales of $4.7 billion.

Acquired Lykes Corporation in 1978

At this time Paul Thayer made a move more characteristic of something Ling would have done. He announced LTV's intention to purchase the Lykes Corporation of New Orleans. Lykes was the parent company of Continental-Emsco, a petroleum equipment supply and service company; the Lykes Brothers Steamship Company, a cargo shipping company; and Youngstown Sheet & Tube, a financially troubled steel finishing plant. As part of the merger agreement LTV (which was already $1 billion in debt) would also become responsible for Lykes's debt of $659 million.

Upon closer inspection, however, the proposed merger was regarded as quite promising. The Youngstown mill could produce steel less expensively with raw steel from the Jones & Laughlin plant in Aliquippa, Pennsylvania. In addition, transportation costs could be reduced and Jones & Laughlin could transfer its backlogged orders to Youngstown's underutilized plants at Indiana Harbor.

The Justice Department had suspected the merger on antitrust grounds until Attorney General Griffin Bell interceded. Bell held a thorough investigation and later declared that Lykes had no chance of surviving without the merger. Despite considerable opposition from Senator Edward Kennedy (who questioned Bell's authority in the matter), Bell overruled the Justice Department and approved the merger, which was completed on December 5, 1978. The new division was renamed J&L Steel.

In 1981 LTV attempted to perform a similar expansion of its aerospace division. This time the takeover target was the Grumman Corporation. However, opposition from Grumman was considerable. The Federal Trade Commission arranged for an injunction on further purchases of Grumman stock by LTV on the grounds that a merger of the two companies would be anticompetitive in the carrier-based aircraft field. In addition, Grumman's pension fund and an employee investment group (who already held 35 percent of the company's stock) began buying large amounts of Grumman stock and refused to tender them for an LTV bid. This invited the interest of the U.S. Labor Department, which was concerned about fiduciary improprieties. Even the company's founder, 86-year-old Leroy Grumman, came out of retirement to campaign for his company's independence. What LTV may have underestimated most was the fierce loyalty of Grumman's employees to their company. Yet it was a U.S. Court of Appeals which prevented LTV's bid from being successful when it ruled against the takeover on antitrust grounds.

Without the additional resources of Grumman, LTV's Vought division was forced to re-equip itself with new equipment in order to meet its 15-year $4 billion contract to produce a Multiple Launch Rocket System for the Defense department. It was a very costly investment which left LTV with liquidity problems at a very bad time.

Sold Wilson in 1981

LTV sold its Wilson subsidiary in June 1981 (before the Grumman bid) in order to generate cash. The Wilson division's share of revenue was quickly replaced, however, by the newly reorganized Continental-Emsco subsidiary. LTV officials claimed to have known in advance that the profitable Continental-Emsco division was about to experience a period of adverse market conditions. According to LTV's president Ray Hay, however, "the business came down so fast we didn't have time to shut off our subcontractors." As a result, Continental-Emsco was left with a year's inventory and was forced to report a substantial operating loss.

Ray Hay came to LTV in 1975 from the Xerox Corporation. He left Xerox out of frustration at being passed over for that company's presidency. At the time, Paul Thayer was looking for a man of Hay's talent and ability to be LTV's next president. Hay accepted Thayer's invitation, and when Thayer left LTV in January 1983 to serve as Deputy Defense Secretary, Hay was elected CEO and chairman of the board.

Thayer's tenure at the Defense Department was shortened in 1985 when he and a Dallas stockbroker named Billy Bob Harris were convicted of obstructing a federal investigation into the illegal use of privileged information. The "insider trading" scheme involved LTV and two other companies on whose boards Thayer served during 1981 and 1982.

In 1983 LTV sold the Lykes Steamship division and reorganized the remaining subsidiaries into three product-oriented divisions. The Vought Corporation was combined with a number of smaller divisions and renamed the LTV Aerospace & Defense Company. In addition, Continental-Emsco became the LTV Energy Products Company.

Acquired Republic Steel in 1984

The following year LTV initiated a takeover of Republic Steel. The company was pleased with the relative success of its Jones & Laughlin/Youngstown merger and believed that by absorbing Republic it could achieve similar results. The Justice Department, however, withheld its approval of the merger because the combined company would control 50 percent of the sheet steel market. In addition, the department was concerned about an impending merger between U.S. Steel and National Steel. If both mergers were allowed the two companies would control nearly half of America's steelmaking capacity. However, a month later U.S. Steel canceled its merger with National and Jones & Laughlin was given permission to merge with Republic on the condition that it sell two of its sheet steel plants. On July 29, 1984, the $770 million takeover was completed with the creation of a new combined subsidiary called the LTV Steel Company.

As a condition to the merger, Republic's chairman Bradley Jones was named CEO of LTV. Furthermore, LTV was forced to offer costly retirement settlements to Republic personnel. The compensation was so attractive that Jones himself decided to take early retirement. He was replaced by LTV's former CEO David Hoag.

Foreign Competition Led to 1986 Bankruptcy

During this time the American steel market was inundated with inexpensive imported steel from modern plants in Japan, Europe, and Canada. In 1985 foreign producers controlled 30 percent of the domestic market. This had the effect of closing American steel plants and reducing production capacity to between 50 and 60 percent.

Attempts to modernize LTV Steel and raise productivity had limited success. At the Aliquippa Works manhours per ton of steel went from eight in 1981 to 3.8 in 1985. And while the company's investments in modernized facilities were generating an annual return of three percent, the debt cost 15 percent per year to service. In effect, the investments were generating a net loss of 12 percent annually. In 1985 steel production at Aliquippa was idled and all but 700 workers (out of 9,700 in 1981) were laid off. In addition, 3,000 white collar jobs were eliminated. For the year, LTV had revenues of $8.2 billion, but posted a net loss of $724 million, the most of any company in that year's *Fortune* 500.

The company's pension fund was turned over to a federal pension insurance agency to which LTV was obligated to make contributions. When LTV requested permission to skip a $175 million payment to the fund, the U.S. government's Pension Benefit Guaranty Corporation (PBGC) asked for and later received a claim on LTV Aerospace for collateral. LTV initiated a $500 million divestiture of most of the nonsteel assets it acquired from Republic. In early 1986 the Gulf States Steel and LTV Specialty Products divisions were sold.

LTV was unable to maintain liquidity and on July 17, 1986, applied for protection under Chapter 11 of the bankruptcy code. According to chairman Ray Hay, "We just could not generate cash flow." Under Chapter 11 LTV was temporarily relieved of its annual $319 million debt service and $350 million pension contributions. LTV began to consider either selling its energy division or closing additional steel plants.

Operations Restructured and Modernized over Seven-Year Bankruptcy Period

LTV remained under Chapter 11 bankruptcy protection for almost seven years—one of the longest, and most complicated, bankruptcy cases in American history. Under Hoag's leadership, the company's steel operations were thoroughly overhauled. LTV closed or sold more than 30 steel plants, and shifted to a concentration on higher-priced flat-rolled steel for automobiles, appliances, and construction, exiting from the bar steel and stainless steel sectors. The company's creditors allowed LTV to invest $2 billion to modernize its remaining steel plants and retrain workers, resulting in productivity improvements of 70 percent, with overall productivity better than the industry average. LTV also sold LTV Aerospace and Defense to Loral and Northrop/Carlyle in 1992. This move led to the relocation of the corporate headquarters from Dallas to Cleveland. Also in 1992, LTV received a crucial infusion of $200 million in cash from Japan's Sumitomo Metal Industries Ltd., a company that already had ties with LTV through two joint ventures.

On June 28, 1993, The LTV Corporation finally emerged from Chapter 11. The firm that emerged was predominantly a steel producer, with a small oil-drilling equipment unit, Continental Emsco Co. It had a workforce with 30,000 fewer employees than in 1986. LTV was able to emerge nearly debt-free by settling with creditors through the issuance of stock. While it was temporarily relieved of making pension contributions during the bankruptcy period, LTV had amassed a $3 billion pension shortfall by the time it emerged from bankruptcy. In an agreement with the PBGC, LTV made a cash payment of $787 million into its pension funds upon its emergence from bankruptcy, and was given 28 years to pay the remainder, amounting to a minimum of $30 million to $50 million annually. In late 1993 LTV received additional funds that it used to further reduce its pension liability when USX Corp. agreed to pay LTV $375 million to settle a lawsuit LTV had filed against Bessemer & Lake Erie Railroad Co., a former unit of USX, for alleged antitrust violations.

Minimills and Value-Added Products Marked Mid-1990s

In 1995 LTV became a steel-only company when it sold Continental Emsco to SCF Partners of Houston, Texas, for nearly $75 million. That same year, construction began on a minimill in Decatur, Alabama, through Trico Steel Company L.L.C., a joint venture 50 percent owned by LTV, with Sumitomo Metal and British Steel each holding 25 percent. LTV contributed $150 million to fund the venture, then borrowed another $300 million to get the minimill into production by early 1997. Minimills, which are typically nonunion, use state-of-the-art equipment and require only a few hundred workers,

resulting in lower costs compared to traditional steel plants. The Trico minimill was designed with a capacity of 2.1 million tons annually, compared to the 8.4 million tons generated each year by LTV's two integrated steel mills in Cleveland and East Chicago, Indiana. LTV said that it planned to consider building minimills in Europe and Asia once the Trico mill reached full capacity. To support Trico and perhaps other minimills, LTV in 1996 formed a joint venture in Trinidad and Tobago with Cleveland-Cliffs Inc. and German engineering firm Lurgi AG to construct a plant to produce iron briquettes used in the minimill steelmaking process. LTV's move into minimills angered the United Steelworkers of America (USWA) union, whose officials considered the Alabama plant a threat to workers at other LTV plants. But many observers noted that LTV's workers faced the larger threat of minimills operated by other steel companies, most notably Nucor Corp., located in competitive proximity to the LTV plants.

In addition to seeking ways of making steel more profitably, Hoag made a number of moves in the mid-1990s to increase LTV's involvement in the production of value-added steel products. In April 1997 LTV and two other integrated steel companies—Bethlehem Steel Corp. and Rouge Steel Co.—each purchased a minority stake in TWB Co., a supplier of laser-welded steel blanks to the automotive industry. That same month, LTV acquired a 25 percent interest in Lagermex S.A. de C.V., which was in the process of building an $18.5 million automotive steel processing operation in Puebla, Mexico. Also in April 1997, LTV paid $187.5 million in cash for the assets of the Varco-Pruden Buildings unit of United Dominion Industries Inc. The Memphis, Tennessee-based Varco-Pruden had eight U.S. factories and joint-venture plants in China, Brazil, and Argentina for the manufacture of low-rise steel building systems for manufacturing, warehousing, school, and commercial applications. In June 1997 J. Peter Kelly, who had been president and COO of LTV Steel since 1991, was named president and COO of The LTV Corporation, with Hoag remaining chairman and CEO.

In July 1997 LTV announced that it would close its 40-year-old, 714-employee coke-making plant in Pittsburgh after the Environmental Protection Agency found the plant in violation of pollution standards. Company officials said that bringing the plant into compliance could cost more than $400 million, an investment they did not wish to make in a facility that was on its last legs. A likely contributing factor in the decision was that minimills—perhaps the key to LTV's future—do not use coke in their steelmaking process. The USWA filed a grievance against the company regarding its decision, but a binding arbitrator ruled in LTV's favor. In February 1998 LTV began the plant-closing process; later that month, LTV and the USWA announced they would work jointly to seek other parties who might be interested in redeveloping the facility.

At the end of the century, LTV had made a rather remarkable comeback from the wreckage of its conglomerate past. And, ironically, it was now a single-industry firm, the very antithesis of the Jimmy Ling business philosophy. Nevertheless, the steel industry was an extraordinarily competitive one, and LTV's future was by no means secure. Under Hoag's steady leadership, however, LTV had returned for the time being to steady profitability through an emphasis on containing costs, using the latest technology, and moving up the steel value chain.

Principal Subsidiaries

Georgia Tubing Corporation; Investment Bankers, Inc.; Jalcite I, Inc.; Jones & Laughlin Steel Incorporated; Kingsley International Insurance Ltd.; LTV Blanking Corporation; LTV/EGL Holding Company; LTV Electro-Galvanizing, Inc.; LTV International, Inc.; LTV International N.V.; LTV Properties, Inc.; LTV Sales Finance Company; LTV Steel Company, Inc.; LTV Steel de Mexico, Ltd.; LTV-Trico, Inc.; RepSteel Overseas Finance N.V.; Trico Steel Company, Inc.; VP Buildings, Inc.

Further Reading

Adams, Chris, "LTV to Close Coke-Making Plant Amid Pressures to Cut Emissions," *Wall Street Journal,* July 15, 1997, p. B4.

Baker, Stephen, "The Bridges Steel Is Building," *Business Week,* June 2, 1997, p. 39.

Baker, Stephen, and Keith L. Alexander, "LTV Is Fixin' to Flatten a Few Minimills," *Business Week,* August 2, 1993, p. 84D.

Byrne, Harlan S., "Tested Mettle," *Barron's,* March 17, 1997, p. 24.

Chakravarty, Subrata N., "Caught in a Steel Maze," *Forbes,* March 14, 1983, pp. 150 + .

Clark, Gordon L., *Pensions and Corporate Restructuring in American Industry: A Crisis of Regulation,* Baltimore: Johns Hopkins University Press, 1993, 305 p.

Dorfman, John R., "More Risk Than Reward: Times Are Tough in the Steel Industry," *Financial World,* August 19, 1986, pp. 44 + .

Holusha, John, "Singing the Steelworker Blues: A Mini-Mill Deal at LTV Leaves Union Feeling Jilted," *New York Times,* December 13, 1995, pp. D1, D4.

Loomis, Carol J., "U.S. Steel and LTV Find Hidden Charms in Losers," *Fortune,* March 5, 1984, pp. 118 + .

LTV Looking Ahead, Dallas: The LTV Corporation, 1980.

Milbank, Dana, "LTV Begins to Emerge from Bankruptcy Proceedings," *Wall Street Journal,* May 26, 1993, p. B4.

Schroeder, Michael, and Aaron Bernstein, "A Brawl with Labor Could Block LTV's Rebirth," *Business Week,* March 16, 1992, p. 40.

Smith, Frank, "Gordon Williams' Best Defense," *Dallas Business Journal,* December 11, 1989, pp. 8–9.

Sobel, Robert, *The Age of Giant Corporations,* Westport, Connecticut: Greenwood, 1972, 257 p.

Thompson, Chris, "LTV Inks Deal for Japanese Cash Infusion," *Crain's Cleveland Business,* September 14, 1992, pp. 1 + .

——, "Timing Crucial for LTV Rebound," *Crain's Cleveland Business,* January 25, 1993, pp. 1 + .

Wagstyl, Stefan, and Richard Waters, "Two Faces of a Changing Steel Industry," *Financial Times,* October 3, 1997, p. 13.

Williams, Scott, "LTV Nears 'Milestone' Sales Deal," *Dallas Business Journal,* January 17, 1992, pp. 1, 21.

—updated by David E. Salamie

Maison Louis Jadot

21, rue Eugène Spuller
B.P. 117
21203 Beaune Cedex
France
(33) 3 80 22 10 57
Fax: 3 80 22 56 03
Web site: http://www.vinternet.fr/LouisJadot

Private Company
Founded: 1859
SICs: 2084 Wines, Brandy & Brandy Spirits

With extensive vineyard holdings throughout France's Burgundy region, Maison Louis Jadot ranks among the premier producers and negociants of the popular Burgundy wine variety. Louis Jadot's list of some 150 labels presents a unique collection of ''premier cru'' and ''grand cru'' appellations (the designations premier and grand cru can refer to both the vineyard as well as the wines produced; grand cru is the highest classification for the Burgundy region, followed by premier cru). The company has long held a reputation for the high quality of its wines. In order to ensure this quality, Louis Jadot has engaged in a string of vineyard acquisitions through the 1980s and 1990s. With more than 300 acres of vines, the company can boast that a large percentage of Louis Jadot wines are made from grapes grown on the company's own vines or in vineyards under the company's management control. The company negotiates its further grape requirements largely through non-binding agreements with primarily Côte d'Or growers. More than a buyer-seller contract, the company's relationship with its outside growers functions as a collaborative partnership, enabling the company to exert a degree of control over the quality of the grape. In exchange, the company has long held a policy of paying finished wine prices for its grape purchases. This enables the company to maintain its supply of grapes as well as a degree of year-to-year consistency among its labels.

Louis Jadot has specialized in Burgundy for nearly 150 years, and the majority of its vineyards are located in the Côte d'Or area of the famous wine-making region of Burgundy. In 1996, however, Louis Jadot took a step towards an expanded portfolio, with the acquisition of the Chateaux St. Jacques label, winemaking facilities, and extensive holdings in Beaujolais vineyards, including some 67 acres of AOC (appelation d'origine controlé) Moulin à Vent vineyards. The company's Côte d'Or holdings represent a collection of prime vineyards that have remained for generations within the founding Jadot family, vineyards owned by the Gagey family, and the company's more recent acquisitions of vineyards and vineyard management contracts. The company's holdings also include a new winemaking facility, completed in August 1997. Since 1996, the company has also operated the cooperative Cadus cooperage to supply the company's wooden casks needs according to its specifications.

While Louis Jadot has adapted modern production techniques, these have remained subservient to the company's insistence on traditional winemaking methods—grapes are harvested and selected by hand, all wines are aged exclusively in wood, and the wines themselves are prepared with only natural ingredients. The company's labels also respect tradition: each label denotes the specific vineyard from which its grapes originated. Louis Jadot wines remain single variety wines in the Burgundian tradition. Nearly half of all Louis Jadot labels are produced from grapes from the company's own vineyards.

In the late 1990s, Louis Jadot was led by President Pierre-Henry Gagey, son of the legendary André Gagey, master oenologist, who guided the company for more than 30 years and continued to serve the company as chairman. While the younger Gagey led the company's management, Louis Jadot's wine production was headed up by technical director Jacques Lardière.

Founding a Legend in the 1850s

Louis Henry Denis Jadot, born in 1821, gave his name to the wine house he founded in 1859. The Jadot family's involvement in winemaking began at the turn of the 19th century. Originally from Belgium, members of the Jadot family emigrated to the area around Beaune, in the central-eastern region of France in the 1790s, purchasing a partnership share in the grand cru vineyard Chevalier-Montrachet Les Demoiselles. Louis Jadot's father expanded the family's vineyard holdings when he purchased the Clos des Ursules, a small, premier cru parcel less than five kilometers from the Chevalier-Montrachet site.

The Jadot family vineyards were transferred to Louis Jadot's uncle after the death of Jadot's father. The young Jadot went to work for his uncle, where he gained a thorough understanding of the art and craft of winemaking, from the cellar to the vine. Part of Jadot's responsibilities entailed selling and distributing the family's wines, often to Belgium—which, formerly a province of the Duchy of Burgogne, remained a principal market for the Jadot and other Burgundy wines—enabling him to build a strong clientele. With this clientele, Jadot went into business for himself. In 1859, Jadot bought a wine negociant house, Lemaire-Fouleux.

Jadot changed the company's name to Maison Louis Jadot and reoriented its sales to the Belgium and northern French markets. Maison Louis Jadot soon came under control of the Jadot family's vineyards. New vineyards, including the Beaune Theurons and Beaune Clos des Couchereaux added their wines to the Jadot list. It was from small parcels such as these—the Theurons vineyard was a mere one hectare; the Couchereaux parcel, slightly larger at 1.3 hectares—that the reputation of the Jadot name and the quality of its wines would grow.

Louis Jadot continued to lead the family operation until his death in 1900. Son Louis Baptiste Jadot, then age 27, inherited not only the Maison Louis Jadot, but his father's gift for wine as well. The younger Jadot would continue building both the winery and its reputation, bringing the Jadot name to new international markets, while expanding its sales throughout France. Jadot also continued to invest in the company and is credited with adding a number of important premier and grand cru vineyards to the family's holdings, including the relatively large, and adjoining, Corton Charlemagne and Corton Pougets vineyards and the Beune Les Boucherottes vineyards.

The third generation of Louis Jadots—Louis Baptiste's son Louis Auguste—joined the family operation in 1931 and took over after his father's death in 1939. Under Louis Auguste Jadot, the company would pursue its strongest international growth, reaching the newly emerging United States market; the company's wines were imported exclusively by the Kobrand Corporation. Other important new markets for the company during this period were the United Kingdom, the Netherlands, and the South American countries. Louis Auguste also expanded the company's vineyard holdings, and its domain labels, with the purchases of Les Chouacheux and Les Bressandes.

New Leadership in the 1960s

The death of Louis Baptiste's son, Louis Alain, who died in an auto accident at the age of 23, left the Jadot's without a natural successor to the line. Future leadership would come from outside the family, in the person of André Gagey, who became Louis Auguste Jadot's assistant in 1954. Gagey, born in 1924 in nearby Dijon, had strong ties to the Burgundy territory. His family had also been involved in winemaking, including the Clos de Malte vineyard in Santenay, purchased—and later sold—by Gagey's grandfather in the mid-1860s. After studying

at the University of Commerce and Administration, Gagey had married Marie-Hélène Tourlière, whose family, like the Jadot's. held a number of important Burgundy vineyards, and had operated a winery and negociant firm in the Beune area since the early 1800s. Gagey went to work for his father-in-law, learning the art of viniculture, winemaking, and cellar operations, as well as gaining experience in the commercial aspects of the negociant business.

Louis Auguste Jadot died in 1962. His widow and daughters retained ownership of the family firm, while placing the management of its operations fully under Gagey, who had become instilled with the Jadot family's commitment to the highest quality wines. Indeed, Gagey himself would become world-renowned as a master oenologist, credited with a gift for selecting grapes and nurturing young wines. Through Gagey, the Maison Jadot would also take over operations of the Gagey/Tourlière vineyards.

Gagey would lead the company for more than 30 years. He would also transform the company from principally a negociant firm, with a minor interest in the production from its own vineyards, into a full-fledged owner-producer. To this end, Gagey hired Jacques Lardière as his assistant in 1970. Lardière, born in 1948 and raised on France's western coast, had studied at the School of Viticulture and Oenology of Alentours, and had continued his research studies at the prestigious Pasteur Institute. Lardière would build a reputation as one of the leading Burgundy winemakers. In 1980, Lardière was named technical director of the Maison Louis Jadot. Gagey and Lardière pursued a policy of expanding the company's vineyard holdings and improving and maintaining the quality of its grapes. By then, the company had determined that its best means of ensuring the consistent quality of its wines was in possessing control of the entire production process, starting with growing the grapes themselves. In 1985, Gagey and Lardière were joined by Gagey's son, Pierre-Henry Gagey, born in 1955, whose educational background included a master's degree in business administration from Paris's Institut des Hautes Etudes Comerciales.

Refocusing Operations in the 1980s

By the 1980s, Maison Louis Jadot possessed more than 45 acres of some of the finest Burgundy vineyards. However, with Gagey approaching 60 years of age in the 1980s, the company faced the problem of succession, as well as the need to ensure the company's future growth. In 1985, the Jadot family, represented by Louis Auguste's widow and his daughters, sold the Jadot operations—excluding the vineyards, which remained the property of the Jadot and Gagey families—to the Kopf family, owners of the company's United States importer, the Kobrand Corporation. The sale was performed as a private transaction, leaving Maison Louis Jadot unaffiliated with Kobrand. Nevertheless, the sale would provide capital for continued expansion.

André Gagey remained as the company's CEO and retained complete control over the house's direction. With the new capital, Maison Louis Jadot intensified the expansion of its vineyard acreage. In 1985, the company purchased the Domaines Clair Dau, an area of 18 hectares (35 acres) which included such distinguished vineyards as Clos St. Jacques, Les

Amoureuses, Chapelle Chambertin, Clos de Bèze, Musigny, Bonnes Mares, and others. This purchase was followed in the 1980s by the acquisition of the ten-acre Domaines Champy, which had been established in 1720. In addition to these purchases, Gagey led Maison Louis Jadot into another direction—that of gaining long-term management contracts for the operation of non-company owned vineyards. A major addition in this way was made in 1986 with the contract to operate the Domaine du Duc de Magenta, which featured 30 acres of premier cru Pinot Noir and Chardonnay grapes.

André Gagey retired to the position of chairman of the company; son Pierre-Henry was named president in his stead, while Jacques Lardière, assisted by Christine Botton, became managing director in charge of all winemaking operations. Gagey's retirement brought the Gagey family holdings definitively onto the Jadot list, with these properties—including the premier crus Nuits-Saint-Georges Les Boudots, Chambolle-Musigny Les Baudes, and Beaune Cent-Vignes, and the grand cru Clos Saint-Denis—added as long-term contracts, their wines labeled as the Domaine André Gagey. The company continued its acquisitions in the first half of the 1990s. In 1993, Jadot purchased the 20-acre Clos de Malte, which had originally been planted by Gagey's grandfather. Two years later, the com-

pany added approximately five acres of premier cru and grand cru vineyards, ranging from the 1.1 acre Les Referts, to the 0.87 acre grand cru Echezeaux. The company also acquired the ten-acre parcel Côte de Nuits Villages, located in the village of Comblanchien, in 1995.

By the mid-1990s, the company's vineyard holdings totaled more than 230 acres of the finest grand cru and premier cru land in the Beaune area. The company would continue to seek new acquisitions—either as outright purchases or in the form of long-term contracts—in its traditional region. However, in February 1997, Maison Louis Jadot ventured outside of the Beaune region for the first time, purchasing the substantial holdings of Chateau des Jacques. Established in the 1700s, and featuring some 98 acres of vineyard, Chateau des Jacques was one of the most important estates of the Moulin-à-Vent appelation. Despite poor weather conditions—resulting principally in lower yields—the first harvest and wines produced from Chateau des Jacques grapes was prepared by Maison Louis Jadot in 1997. Remaining rooted in its Beaune area base, Maison Louis Jadot expected to purchase other properties throughout the region, while keeping true to its Burgundy traditions.

—M. L. Cohen

Malév Plc

1051 Budapest, Roosevelt tér 2.
Hungary
(1) 266 9033, 267 2911
Fax: (1) 266 2685
Web site: http://www.malev.hu

Public Company
Incorporated: 1946 as Maszovlet
Employees: 4,000
Sales: HUF44 billion (1995)
SICs: 4512 Air Transportation, Scheduled

Malév Plc operates one of Eastern Europe's most significant airlines. Its wide-ranging modern fleet of Boeing and Fokker aircraft carries over 1.5 million passengers per year. It is emerging from privatization with the reputation as the most progressive of the former Soviet Bloc carriers, having long embraced Western aircraft and operating standards. As Malév turned 50 in 1996, Hungary celebrated its 1,100-year anniversary. These milestones and the company's investments in long-range Boeing 767 airliners seem to reaffirm its commitment to the long haul.

Postwar Origins Behind the Iron Curtain

Like most of Europe, Hungary was torn to pieces by the hounds of war in the 1940s. Before the war, the country's young aviation industry had been steadily progressing since the Aero Joint Stock Company was formed in 1910. Although this venture was short-lived, military aircraft would be ferrying airmail between Budapest and Vienna within a decade, and these planes and personnel would carry out much the same mission after World War I in the MAEFORT Hungarian Air Transport Joint Stock Company, formed in 1920. Another new airline, the Hungarian Aviation Joint Stock Company, started carrying its own mix of passengers, mail, and cargo on the same route in 1922. Hungarian Aviation took the name Malert in 1928, and leaped into international flights in the 1930s. Much of the talent and material used to form Maszovlet—Malév's precursor—after World War II had been originally employed by Malert.

Maszovlet, the Hungarian-Soviet Civil Air Transport Joint Stock Company, was formed on March 29, 1946, as a joint venture between the Soviet Union and the Hungarian government. Moscow supplied aircraft, parts, other equipment, and training. Li-2 and Po-2 aircraft formed the company's first fleet. Airports and staff were already available in Hungary. Half of these personnel were former Malert employees.

The relatively undamaged Budaörs Airport became the company's base of operations, while comparatively primitive, unlighted airports in outlying areas were rebuilt. Maszovlet took to the skies on October 15, flying to Szombathely and Debrecen.

More regional routes were added at a rapid pace, and in 1947 Maszovlet began service to Prague. The company hired its first flight attendants in the same year. Out of 150 applicants, who were required to be at least bilingual, only four were chosen. The company also started drawing its own pilot trainees from within Hungary.

The company's popular provincial mail deliveries, begun in 1950, were a picture of efficiency. The flight crews simply dropped mail bags out of the plane at designated points. Maszovlet was also able to commence operations from the partially completed Ferihegy Airport in Budapest. Due to regulated airfares, not to exceed first class rail tickets, Maszovlet's domestic passenger operations blossomed in the 1950s. The airline began operating scheduled routes to Warsaw, Berlin, and Bucharest in 1954.

The same year, the Soviet Union withdrew from the cooperative arrangement. The Hungarian state airline, now known as Malév Hungarian Air Transport Company, was able to fly under its own power.

Going West in the 1950s and 1960s

Malév began flying into Western Europe in June 1956 with a new route to Vienna. A short time later, a DC-6 operated by KLM Royal Dutch Airlines touched down in Budapest en route to Cairo. Within a few months, the bloody 1956 Revolution prompted the airline to begin airlifting Red Cross packages from Vienna. However, the Soviet military ended these flights by closing the Ferihegy Airport on November 4.

When operations resumed three months later, the Hungarian government placed a new emphasis on Malév's international routes. This necessitated both airport renovations and the purchase of more capable aircraft. The Ferihegy Airport was fully modernized and several Ilyushin Il-14 airliners were imported from Russia and East Germany. This and the arrival of more Li-2 aircraft from the Hungarian air force (slated for cargo service to Western Europe) gave Malév the largest fleet—28 planes— in its history. By 1961, the company operated routes to about a dozen of continental Europe's greatest cities. At the same time, Western airlines began visiting Budapest in earnest. Hungary became a meeting ground for East and West Germans who could not cross their own partitioned homeland.

Hungary was the first Soviet satellite to operate the Ilyushin Il-18 turboprop, and the big, efficient, and reliable aircraft gave Malév a good tool for expanding its routes across Europe and the Mediterranean. In the 1960s, 28 cities from London and Helsinki to Damascus and Beirut received scheduled service from Malév. Malév Air Tours was opened in 1968 to promote tourism. However, domestic flights proved such a drain on company and government resources that they were discontinued altogether in 1968. The company initiated its charter service with a July 1969 flight to Glasgow.

The Jet Age

The company's first jet airliner, a Tupolev Tu-134, arrived in Budapest in December 1968. The Tu-154 was brought into operations in 1974. These introductions freed the larger Il-18 turboprops to carry the country's produce to the Middle East.

Although the Hungarian Airport Authority (LRI) became independent from Malév in 1973, improvements to the Ferihegy

Airport were not completed until the mid-1980s. A new terminal was part of the renovations. By this time, the carrier, one of Hungary's 10 largest companies, was handling over a million passengers per year and was earning better and better profits year after year. It had given new attention to attracting consumers, opening ticket outlets in a handful of cities and introducing a series of budget fares. In 1983, foreign airlines began competing for Malév's customers. One of Malév's innovations was the offering of 10 nonsmoking flights in the winter of 1986: ''Good air in the air!'' it proclaimed.

Malév acquired a share in the Atrium Hyatt hotel in Budapest in 1982. Other ancillary activities included operating duty free shops and providing airport services for other carriers. A second terminal was built at Ferihegy Airport in 1985.

Post-Perestroika Privatization

By the late 1980s, the company's Tupolev airliners no longer seemed as impressive as when they were first wheeled out. Malév sought the Western-made aircraft it felt it needed to compete effectively, although political pressure to purchase Soviet aircraft delayed these acquisitions for years. A Boeing 737 and a smaller British Aerospace BAe 146, to be used as express freighter in a joint venture with TNT, finally arrived in November 1988. For a short time, it still bought used Russian planes such as the Yak-40 on an opportunistic basis for use on regional routes.

After 50 years as a socialist state airline, Malév was reorganized as a joint stock company in the summer of 1992, after first becoming a public limited company a year earlier. Thomas Deri served as CEO for a year during this transition; he was succeeded by András Pákay. The end of government subsidies meant, for one thing, the airline had to raise fares fivefold on some routes. It also needed support from an outside backer. Although an initial Credit Suisse First Boston attempt to find three minority partners failed, British Airways, KLM, and Lufthansa all expressed interest in the airline. Eventually, Alitalia and the state-owned SIMEST (Societa Italiana per gli Investimenti all'Estero) investment bank bought shares in the company. SIMEST acquired a five percent share; Alitalia's 30 percent share was worth $77 million and gave the company greater access to the East European market. The Hungarian government retained a 51 percent interest, while a small amount of shares were offered to employees and local investors.

Malév and Lockheed cofounded a maintenance company based at Ferihegy, in the hopes that Budapest would emerge as a service hub for the region. The new facility was swiftly certified by both American and European authorities. The airport invested in improvements, expanding its Terminal 2.

Where Soviet experts helped the carrier resume operations after the Great Patriotic War, the West was now called upon to transport Malév into parity with its contemporaries. The International Air Transport Association and Association of European Airlines helped train some of the company's staff. Scandinavian Airlines System helped bring Malév's in-flight service up to standard. A U.S.-based human resources consulting firm helped prepare performance and hiring guidelines and to improve the morale of employees conditioned to apathy by years under an unresponsive bureaucracy.

By 1995, the company was flying 12 737s. The company's two long-range Boeing 767 aircraft (engines supplied by GE) had incurred losses since their introduction (additionally, Pratt & Whitney successfully sued the company for breach of contract related to the use of their engines in a subsequent delivery of 767s). Finally, this operation, which on a scheduled or charter basis, served both New York and Japan, was turned around in 1995. On the whole, Western aircraft, though more expensive to purchase than the Russian Tupolev jets (a remnant of Soviet mercantilism) that had been the company's mainstay, had much lower operating costs. The company brought into operations additional Boeing 737 aircraft and Fokker 70 aircraft, the latter to replace the Tu-134 on regional flights, bringing the carrier towards its goal of an entirely Western-made fleet. Malév posted significant gains in cargo operations in 1995, as it installed a new PC-based system to support this area.

That year, Malév returned to profitability under CEO Sándor Szathmáry, turning a profit of HUF186 million, evidencing the success of its "Recovery Program." The key points of this plan were to reduce costs and to renegotiate certain contracts. The company continued to work with foreign consultants in order to streamline operations further. Factors that worked against the airline were the lifting of the embargo on the former Yugoslavia, which resulted in increased competition from that region's carriers.

Malév continued towards privatization as it approached a new century. Its alliance with Alitalia proved short-lived, as the European Commission ordered the carrier to divest its shares so it could receive an extra $1.6 billion in subsidies from the Italian government. One promising partnership was a joint Budapest-Geneva service operated with SwissAir. An initial public offering was under consideration for 1998.

Principal Subsidiaries

Air Bp. Kft.; Pannon Air Cargo Nemzetközi Szállítmányozó és Szolgáltató Kft.; MALCO Cayman Islands; Malév-Pannónia Hotel Kft. (50%); Aeroplex of Central Europe Kft. (50%); TNT Malév Express Légifuvarozási Kft. (40%); GÉPFET Gépipari Fejlesztõ és Tervezõ Kft. (27.6%).

Further Reading

"Alitalia May Be Eased Out of Malev," *Finance East Europe,* January 10, 1997, p. 12.

Hill, Leonard, "Malév/Alitalia: Synergies for Survival," *Air Transport World,* March 1993, pp. 90–95.

Lenorovitz, Jeffrey M., "Hungarian Carrier Nears Completion of Shift to Western-Style Operations," *Aviation Week and Space Technology,* May 4, 1992.

"Malev Hungarian Looks East," *American Shipper,* January 1997, p. 64.

"Malev Picks Italian Partners," *East European Markets,* January 7, 1993, p. 13.

Malév Plc, "Fifty-One Years of Malév," http://www.malev.hu/aboutmalev/histoc.htm.

"MALÉV-Team /Aerotriga," http://www.elender.hu/aerotriga.

Sparaco, Pierre, "Alitalia, Malev Airlines Enter 'Strategic Alliance,'" *Aviation Week and Space Technology,* January 25, 1993, pp. 60–61.

Wernle, Bradford, "Human-Resource Group Lends Strategy to Hungarian Airline," *Crain's Detroit Business,* International Issue, Fall 1994.

—Frederick C. Ingram

Marks and Spencer p.l.c.

Michael House
37-67 Baker Street
London W1A 1DN
United Kingdom
(0171) 935-4422
Fax: (0171) 487-2679
Web site: http://www.marks-and-spencer.co.uk

Public Company
Incorporated: 1894
Employees: 68,208
Sales: £7.84 billion (US $12.84 billion) (1997)
Stock Exchanges: London
Ticker Symbol: MASPY
SICs: 5311 Department Stores; 5411 Grocery Stores;
5611 Men's & Boys' Clothing & Accessory Stores;
5621 Women's Clothing Stores; 6091 Nondeposit
Trust Facilities; 6159 Miscellaneous Business Credit
Institutions; 6552 Land Subdividers & Developers,
Except Cemeteries

Marks and Spencer p.l.c. is the largest retailer in the United Kingdom, with nearly 300 company-owned Marks & Spencer (M&S) stores in its home market. The stores sell clothing, footwear, gifts, home furnishings, and food, with many of these items sold under M&S's private-label St Michael brand. The company also owns and operates nearly 100 additional Marks & Spencer stores in Europe, Hong Kong, and Canada, and franchises 85 Marks & Spencer stores in Europe, the Far East, Australia, the Middle East, the Bahamas, and Bermuda. Marks and Spencer also owns the Brooks Brothers chain of men's clothing stores, which consists of more than 170 units in the United States and Japan, and the 20-store, New Jersey-based Kings Super Markets grocery store chain. The fast-growing Marks and Spencer Financial Services unit offers its customers credit cards, personal loans, life insurance, and savings, investment, and pension plans. About 17 percent of Marks and Spencer's revenues are generated outside the United States.

Early History

In 1894 Michael Marks, born in 1859 in a Jewish ghetto at Slonim in the Russian Polish province of Grodno, entered into a partnership with Tom Spencer, born in Skipton, Yorkshire, in 1851, with Spencer paying £300 for his half-share. Ten years earlier, Marks, a peddler, had opened his first stall on a trestle table in Leeds market, selling a range of cheap goods all priced at one penny, including hair pins, dolly dyes, and black lead; he is said to have paid 18 pence for the privilege. Tom Spencer, cashier for Leeds textile wholesaler Isaac Jowitt Dewhirst, was an experienced bookkeeper, and Dewhirst had helped Marks by teaching him English and providing him with small loans.

By 1894 Marks had moved house from Leeds and, after living in Wigan, had settled in Manchester, where he acquired a shop and a home. He also had opened market stalls—bazaars, he called them—in several towns, including Warrington, Bolton, and Birkenhead. The new partnership immediately looked further afield to Birmingham and Newcastle and in 1899 to London. Manchester, however, remained the headquarters, and the first Marks and Spencer warehouse was opened there in 1897. In 1903 the partnership was converted into a limited company with £30,000 in £1 ordinary shares of which 14,996 each were allotted to Marks and to Spencer, the latter retiring in 1905. Upon Marks's sudden death in 1907, his executor, William Chapman, a self-made handkerchief manufacturer, became the dominating force in the business.

In each of the first Marks and Spencer bazaars the slogan had been "Don't ask the price, it's a penny," but this selling policy soon changed. It was a landmark date in 1904 when a new store in a shopping arcade was opened in Leeds not far from Marks's first market trestle table. Two years later the most successful store was Liverpool, with yearly receipts of £9,857. Brixton was second with £9,766. Leeds came third with £8,701 and Manchester fourth with £8,459. In 1907 profits reached a new peak of £8,668 and the dividend paid was 20 percent.

Marks's son Simon acquired his first allocation of shares in April 1907, eight months before his father's death, and from the start he was determined to acquire full control over what he conceived of as a family business. It was not until 1916, however, that he ousted Chapman and became chairman. By then the company had expanded significantly; its turnover in 1913 was already £355,000. In addition, it had successfully braved World War I. In 1915, a year of bitter boardroom battles—concerned not with management policy but with financial control—its turnover was more than £400,000, and a dividend of 50 percent was paid. By then there were 145 branch stores, only ten of them in market halls. No fewer than 56 were in the London area. Some of them had been bought in clusters from existing chains.

Simon Marks and Israel Sieff Took Over in the 1910s

Simon Marks, a man of intelligence and drive, in effect entered into his own partnership in 1915 when his close friend Israel Sieff, keenly aware of world trends both in politics and in science, joined the board after having been blocked previously by Chapman. In 1916 Marks won a lawsuit against Chapman, and in June 1917 Chapman resigned. The firm's initials M and S now stood symbolically for Marks and Sieff. The two friends had first met in Manchester, and each was to marry the other's sister. If their talents were complementary, their vision was shared, and it was a vision that extended far beyond the confines of the business. Succession seemed natural in 1964, when on Simon's death, Israel became chairman, to be succeeded in 1967 by his son Marcus, who like Simon Marks and Israel, became a peer.

In 1926 the company, needing an injection of cash, had been converted into a public company to raise new capital, fully supported by the Prudential Assurance Company, which played a key role in the negotiations. The capital consisted initially of one million ordinary shares of ten shillings each, £330,000 of which were issued, and 350,000 cumulative participating preference shares at £1. There were to be further appeals to the public in 1929 and 1934, when the nominal value of the capital of the company was raised to £3.05 million. The new A shares issued then carried no voting rights. Indeed, there was to be a sharp distinction between management and ownership until 1966, when Israel Sieff concluded that the granting of voting rights was by then "in line with the enlightened policy which governs our business."

Marks hoped in 1934 that in the future there would be "an ample margin of working capital" for management to promote a substantial development program that included the purchase of properties as well as store building, and the hope was fulfilled. Already by 1930 approximately four-fifths of the new company's assets consisted of freehold and leasehold proper-

ties, and between 1931—a year of international depression—and 1939 no fewer than 162 new stores were built or rebuilt, all on inner-city sites. On the eve of World War II, Marks placed more emphasis on replacement of old premises by new than on an increase in the number of stores in itself. Store design had been transformed. Customers were to be attracted into them, to look around even when they did not buy.

The business philosophy that Marks and Sieff shared was associated with social change even in years of economic depression. As Marks put it in 1936, "Goods and services once regarded as luxuries have become conventional comforts and are now almost decreed necessities. A fundamental change in people's habits has been brought about. Millions are enjoying a substantially higher standard of living. To this substantial rise in the standard of living our company claims to have made a definite contribution."

"Efficient distribution," he went on, "is not a static conception. It involves constant alertness and study of the changing habits, desires and tastes of the consumer." Sieff, who has given his own account of the ten years from 1926 to 1936, described his "mission" in practical terms. "We saw not through visionary idealists' clouds but from practical results in days of high competition that production and distribution could become a co-operative process making a positive contribution to the common good." Neither he nor Marks wanted to be involved in production, but through bulk buying they were able to influence the policies of those who were producing for them.

In the first postwar year, 1919, turnover had been £550,000; in 1939, when World War II broke out, it was £23.45 million. In the latter year there were 234 stores and more than 17,000 employees. In 1924 the head office of the company moved from Manchester to Friendly House, Chiswell Street, London EC1. In 1928 it was moved to a new building, named Michael House, in the same street. Three years later, there was another move to Baker Street, the present headquarters. Meanwhile, the now-familiar trademark, St Michael, had been applied first in 1928 to products sold in Marks and Spencer stores, and its use was extended gradually until Marks referred to it for the first time in a chairman's speech in 1949.

The Marks and Spencer stores of the interwar years represented a new form of business, challenging the role of older department stores. Yet such interwar stores were simple and unpretentious when compared with the superstores of the late 20th century that were to be visited by prime ministers and royal families. Indeed, the total cost of a new store in the 1920s was exceeded by the costs of electrical installation in the stores of the 1960s.

The prewar stores owed something to American experience, for it was after Marks first visited the United States in 1924 that he decided to follow, if not to copy, American developments. In 1927 a price limit of five shillings per item was set and there was a continuing emphasis on value for money, but there was an increasingly wide range of goods on sale. By 1932 there were more than 20 departments in the biggest stores, including ladies' and children's drapery; men's and boys' wear; footwear; fancy goods; household linens; gramophone records; confectionery; toiletries; lighting; toys; haberdashery; millinery;

china, enamel and aluminum ware; stationery; gifts; and food, recently introduced into a number of stores. Along with textiles, sales of which increased three times between then and 1939, food was to be a Marks and Spencer staple of the future.

Marks was right to emphasize how in relation to textiles, in particular, his business within a changing society was both to respond to consumer tastes and to develop them; in an address to shareholders he stated that "it is the function of the modern distributor to purchase healthier and more attractive clothing." The revolution in food followed a generation later with the introduction of such items as iceberg lettuce, smoked salmon, Indian and Chinese foods, avocados, kiwi fruit, and wine. By then Marks and Spencer stores also were selling toiletries of all kinds, travel and holiday ware, and fashion clothes for men as well as women.

Postwar Boom

Wartime and immediate postwar austerity were bound to influence both consumer tastes and company profits, although even then the company benefited from the standardizing element in the government's Utility Scheme that regulated the design of a range of consumer goods and favored bulk buyers; the scheme remained in operation until 1952 and in modified form until 1955. The company also was well poised to establish an overseas presence. A Marks and Spencer Export Corporation had been founded in 1940, and in 1955 it was exporting goods to the value of £703,000 to other overseas retailers. It was in 1954 that one of the first editions of a new in-house journal, *St Michael's News,* claimed rightly that by then Marks and Spencer was "news to the general public." This was the year when the Chancellor of the Exchequer, R. A. Butler, claimed that the country would double its standard of living during the next quarter of a century, and the company was well-positioned to move into the unprecedented consumer boom of the late 1950s and 1960s.

Turnover rose from £95 million in 1954 to £148 million in 1960, and profit before tax increased from £7.87 million to £12.81 million. It was in 1960, too, that a ten-year progress record became a convenient and impressive feature of the published accounts. The ten-year progress record for the years from fiscal 1973 to fiscal 1984 was to be even more striking in terms of sales and profits, although economic conditions during that period were to be far more difficult. By fiscal 1973 turnover had reached £496 million (excluding new sales taxes); in fiscal 1984 it was £2.9 billion. Meanwhile, profit before tax leapt from £70 million to £265 million. More sophisticated statistics revealed that sales per employee had risen during the same ten years from £18,651 to £73,099 and per square foot of floor space from £96 to £372. Profit per square foot had risen from £14 to £38.

By 1974 there were 17 overseas stores—the first of them opened in Canada in 1972. A Paris store was opened in 1975. Also in the early 1970s came the acquisition of three Canadian chains: Walker's clothing stores, which were eventually converted to Marks and Spencer stores; D'Allaird's women's clothing stores; and Peoples general merchandise stores. Between 1974 and 1977 exports tripled to more than £40 million and the company won the Queen's Award for Export Achievement. It was deeply committed also to another national achievement—

supporting British producers whenever it could and encouraging them to develop efficient new lines of business. In the process it established close connections with a number of suppliers, which placed it in a virtually monopsonistic position. Relationships with the firms from which it was buying were handled as carefully as relationships with customers.

Before 1939 the main emphasis had been on the price-reducing advantages of bulk buying; during the 1960s and 1970s the focus was on quality control, not least in textiles and in food, then the company's two biggest lines of business. There was continuity, however, rather than a basic shift. As early as 1933 a merchandising committee had been formed to coordinate the work of the various buying departments; a small textiles laboratory had been created in 1935, and a merchandising development department had followed a year later. In 1946 a factory organization section, later called the production engineering department, had been opened "to assist manufacturers in the progressive modernization of their plant and to adapt themselves to the latest technical advances," and two years later a food development department was created. The department dealt both with British and with foreign suppliers, including suppliers of Israeli oranges; there were visits to Israel, a country especially favored as a supplier as it was close to the hearts of Marks and Sieff, to deal with storage and packing.

Apart from research development and publicity, the company had devised its own approach to the buying process through the training of specified "selectors," so described for the first time during the 1930s, and merchandisers, who meticulously studied store demand and turnover before placing orders with producers. The system was integrated, and there was feedback from store to factory.

Quality control, encouraging suppliers in the interests of quality to use the most modern and efficient techniques of production provided by the latest discoveries in science and technology, was a "principle" upon which Marks and Sieff insisted. Unlike most retailers, Marks and Spencer had its own laboratories and employed its own scientists. Other "principles"—and they were formulated and listed as such by Israel Sieff in 1967 after Marks's death—were to guarantee customers high quality when they bought products using the St Michael's brand name, "to plan the extension of stores for the better display of a widening range of goods and for the convenience of our customers," "to simplify operating procedures so that the business is carried on in an efficient manner," and "to foster good relations with customers, suppliers and staff." "Operation Simplification," introduced in 1956, led to the saving of huge amounts of paper and electricity. The lessons were never lost.

Staffing matters had been taken seriously even before the 1930s, when a personnel department was set up in 1934, a year when the word "welfare" began to be used inside the business. Thereafter a wide enough range of "welfare activities" was organized to make Marks and Spencer a kind of welfare state in itself. They were appreciated by most employees, although a small minority found them somewhat stifling.

Meanwhile, great attention was paid to breaking down what Marcus Sieff called the "fear, suspicion and insecurity that threatened human relations in industry.'' The familiar term ''industrial relations'' was taboo at Baker Street; it seemed to imply that there were two sides. In consequence, there was some trade-union criticism of the approach. ''We are human beings at work, not industrial beings,'' Sieff emphasized in 1980. In the same year he stressed that training was not mostly a matter for workers on the shop floor whose talents needed to be mobilized. It began at the top. The first task of the chairman was ''to impart the philosophy of our evolving business to our executives.'' The philosophy extended from employees to pensioners and to schemes for neighboring communities as well as for inner-city stores.

In 1965 Israel Sieff became chairman of the company and Marcus, who had joined the company in 1935 and became a director in 1954, was made vice-chairman. He became chairman in 1972 after J. Edward Sieff, Israel's brother, who had joined the company at Simon Marks's invitation in 1933, had had five years in the chair. There was thus a strong family thrust behind the company and Marcus (Lord) Sieff remained chairman until 1984, when a man born outside the family circles, Derek (Lord) Rayner, took over and rigorously developed the group's activities overseas. Spotted by Marcus Sieff as a young manager, he had joined the company in 1953 and became a director in 1967 and joint managing director in 1973. In 1979 he was seconded to Prime Minister Margaret Thatcher's newly elected government in an effort to streamline the civil service, returning to the company in 1982.

Financial Services Introduced in Mid-1980s

Rayner was chairman of the company from 1984 to 1991, and in that time several significant events occurred. In 1985 the Marks & Spencer Chargecard was launched nationwide in the United Kingdom. Although this move came rather late for such a large retailer, Marks and Spencer quickly moved deeper into financial services than other retailers. The company soon introduced personal loans, added unit trusts in 1988, and the following year introduced an investment plan called personal equity plans (PEPs), which were tax-sheltered vehicles for share purchases. These financial offerings eventually would form the nucleus of what became known as Marks and Spencer Financial Services.

In 1986 a line of furniture was introduced into Marks and Spencer stores. Two years later, Rayner began to move more aggressively overseas. In addition to opening the first two M&S stores in Hong Kong that year, the company entered the U.S. market for the first time through two acquisitions: the New Jersey-based Kings Super Markets grocery store chain and the Brooks Brothers chain of men's clothing stores, a £493.4 million (US $750 million) purchase.

Overseas Growth Continued in the 1990s

Rayner retired in 1991 and was succeeded by Richard Greenbury, knighted in the 1992 New Year's Honours List. Keith Oates, who served as deputy chairman and joint managing director under Greenbury, had joined the business at a high level as finance director from outside—a rare kind of appointment—in 1988. Overall, the company continued its foreign expansion under Greenbury, although difficulties with the Ca-

nadian operations led to the 1992 sale of Peoples and the 1996 sale of D'Allaird's, which was purchased by specialty retailer Comark. Brooks Brothers also proved nettlesome, but Marks and Spencer was able, finally, to turn that chain around by the mid-1990s. The company conceded by then that it had paid too much for Brooks Brothers, but was heartened by an 81 percent increase in operating profit in fiscal 1996.

Meanwhile, the Marks and Spencer chain was being expanded both abroad and at home, with both company-owned and franchised units. M&S stores debuted in Greece and Portugal in the early 1990s through franchise agreements, followed by mid-1990s franchise openings in Denmark, Austria, Hungary, Malaysia, Thailand, Turkey, and the Czech Republic. On the company-owned store front, significant funds were committed to expand the chain's presence in two mainstay nations on the continent: France and Spain. In late 1996 the first M&S store in Germany opened in Cologne, with three additional units to open in Germany by late 1998. Two stores opened in Seoul, South Korea, in the spring of 1997. Back in the United Kingdom, the company in July 1997 announced that it would pay Littlewoods Organisation PLC £192.5 million (US $323.1 million) to acquire 19 stores, which would be converted to Marks and Spencer stores. Another franchise agreement was signed late in 1997 toward the opening of the first Australian M&S unit by late 1998. Additional franchised debuts were to take place in Dubai and Poland, with the company also investigating Latin America, China, Japan, and Taiwan.

Also expanded under Greenbury's leadership were the offerings of Marks and Spencer Financial Services. In 1995 the unit entered the life insurance and annuity market by offering five basic products: a protection policy, a critical illness policy, a combination protection and savings policy, and two personal annuity policies. Of further note during this period was the introduction of an M&S mail-order clothing catalog, the company's first foray into home shopping. In addition, Marks and Spencer in March 1998 won a libel suit against Granada Television over a *World in Action* program that had damaged the company's reputation by implying that M&S used child labor and misled customers by labeling clothing made overseas as ''Made in the UK.'' Granada made a public apology and paid M&S an undisclosed sum.

Fiscal 1997 results for Marks and Spencer were impressive, as the company posted a revenue increase of 8.4 percent to £7.84 billion (US $12.84 billion) and an increase in group profits before taxes of 14.1 percent to £1.1 billion (US $1.8 billion). In November 1997 the company announced that it would spend £2.1 billion (US $3.4 billion) in a three-year expansion program, aiming in part to increase the percentage of revenue generated overseas from 17 percent to 25 percent by the early 21st century. A significant portion of the funds were to be spent in Germany, where 20 to 25 additional stores might open. Also to be enlarged was the Brooks Brothers chain, which already had more than 60 stores in Japan, but which now would eventually be extended into the United Kingdom and continental Europe. It seemed as if there was no stopping the Marks and Spencer juggernaut.

Principal Subsidiaries

Marks & Spencer Export Corporation Limited; Marks & Spencer Finance plc; Marks & Spencer Financial Services Limited; Marks & Spencer Property Developments Limited; Marks & Spencer Property Holdings Limited; Marks & Spencer Retail Financial Services Holdings Limited; Marks & Spencer Unit Trust Management Limited; St. Michael Finance Limited; S.A. Marks and Spencer Belgium N.V.; Marks & Spencer Holdings Canada Inc.; Marks & Spencer Canada Inc.; Marks & Spencer (France) S.A.; M&S Export (Ireland) Limited; Marks & Spencer (Ireland) Limited; Marks & Spencer US Holdings Inc.; Brooks Brothers Inc. (U.S.A.); Brooks Brothers (Japan) Limited (51%); Kings Super Markets Inc. (U.S.A.); Marks & Spencer Finance Inc. (U.S.A.); Marks & Spencer Services Inc. (U.S.A.).

Further Reading

Bookbinder, Paul, *Marks & Spencer: The War Years, 1939–1945*, London: Century Benham, 1989.

Briggs, Asa, *Marks and Spencer 1884–1984*, London: Octopus Books, 1984.

Buckley, Neil, "Food for Thought," *Financial Times*, November 10, 1994, p. 20.

——, "Three-P Principles Pull M&S Through," *Financial Times*, June 27, 1994, p. 8.

Fallon, James, "UK-Based Marks & Spencer Says the World's Its Oyster," *Daily News Record*, January 5, 1998, pp. 20+.

Goldenberg, Nathan, *Thought for Food: A Study of the Development of the Food Division of Marks & Spencer: An Autobiography*, Orpington, U.K.: Food Trade Press, 1989.

Hollinger, Peggy, "High Marks and Few Sparks," *Financial Times*, May 24, 1997, p. WFT5.

Lewis, William, and Martin Dickson, "M&S Asks Greenbury to Stay As Chairman," *Financial Times*, December 18, 1995, p. 19.

Marcom, John, Jr., "Blue Blazers and Guacamole," *Forbes*, November 25, 1991, pp. 64+.

Moody, Andrew, "Fighting Force," *Super Marketing*, August 15, 1997, pp. 14+.

"Of Pies and Pensions," *Economist*, April 30, 1994, p. S27.

Oram, Roderick, "Marks and Spencer Sells Canadian Chain," *Financial Times*, March 6, 1996, p. 20.

——, "Marks and Spencer to Open Stores in Germany," *Financial Times*, March 28, 1995, p. 22.

Parker-Pope, Tara, "Brooks Brothers Gets a Boost from New Look," *Wall Street Journal*, May 22, 1996, pp. B1, B4.

——, "Marks & Spencer Takes Its Lumps Abroad," *Wall Street Journal*, May 24, 1995, p. A10.

Rees, Goronwy, *St. Michael: A History of Marks and Spencer*, 1969; rev. ed., London: Pan Books, 1973.

Shenker, Israel, "Marks & Spencer, the 'Uniquely-British Aunty,' " *Smithsonian*, November 1987, pp. 142+.

Sieff, Israel Moses, *Memoirs*, London: Weidenfeld & Nicolson, 1970.

Sieff, Marcus, *Don't Ask the Price: The Memoirs of the President of Marks & Spencer*, London: Weidenfeld & Nicolson, 1986.

——, *Marcus Sieff on Management: The Marks & Spencer Way*, London: Weidenfeld & Nicolson, 1990.

Smith, Alison, "From Pants to Personal Pensions," *Financial Times*, April 22, 1995, p. WFT3.

——, "St. Michael Sees His Future in the Cards," *Financial Times*, February 19, 1994, p. 8.

"Store of Value: British Institutions: Marks & Spencer," *Economist*, June 26, 1993, p. 63.

Terazono, Emiko, "M&S Goes on £192m Spree in Littlewoods," *Financial Times*, July 18, 1997, p. 18.

Thornhill, John, "A European Spark for Marks," *Financial Times*, July 13, 1992, p. 10.

Wahl, Michael, "Pushing Yankee Products in Lord Rayner's Court; Or, How HMG Brokered the Sara Lee-Marks & Spencer Deal," *Brandweek*, July 12, 1993, pp. 26+.

Wentz, Laurel, "Marks & Spencer Eyes Continent," *Advertising Age*, December 2, 1991, pp. 52, 56.

Wright, Robert, "M&S Plans £2bn Expansion," *Financial Times*, November 5, 1997, p. 27.

—Asa Briggs
—updated by David E. Salamie

MARKS BROS. JEWELERS
EST. 1895

Marks Brothers Jewelers, Inc.

155 North Wacker Drive
Chicago, Illinois 60606
U.S.A.
(312) 782-6800
Fax: (312) 782-2367

Public Company
Incorporated: 1895
Employees: 1,000
Sales: $155.5 million (1997)
Stock Exchanges: NASDAQ
Ticker Symbol: MBJI
SICs: 5944 Jewelry Stores; 3911 Jewelry, Precious Metal

Marks Brothers Jewelers, Inc. is a leading American specialty retailer of fine jewelry, primarily gold and diamonds, which owns and operates 188 stores in 24 states across the country. Under the names of Whitehall Company Jewellers, Lundstrom Jewelers, and Marks Brothers Jewelers, the company runs stores in upscale city and suburban shopping malls. From 1992 through the end of fiscal 1997, Marks Brothers Jewelers reported a string of consecutive sales records and earnings. Fiscal 1997 ended with an impressive increase in revenues of almost 20 percent over the previous year, amounting to $155 million. Much of the company's success is due to its ability to take advantage of the highly seasonal aspect of jewelry sales, which occur during the last quarter of the year and usually ends on December 31. The resulting financial success has enabled Marks Brothers to expand rapidly and increase its profile and sales volume. In 1995, the company opened a total of 14 new stores, while in 1996, 19 stores were opened in prime shopping mall locations. This rapid expansion is very unusual in the jewelry retail industry, and provides a good indication of the company's talented and astute management team.

Early History

Marks Brothers Jewelers began its long history in 1895, when a group of brothers from Eastern Europe decided to settle in Chicago and open a retail jewelry store. Pooling their meager resources, the brothers established their family store in the center of downtown Chicago, and welcomed the growing middle and upper classes of the city that were inclined to spend their money on high-quality, elegant diamonds, watches, rings, earrings, and fashionable hat pins. Within a very short time, Marks Brothers Jewelers had garnered a reputation as one of the most reliable and trustworthy jewelers in the city of Chicago, with some of the finest diamonds in the entire Midwest.

During the early years of the 20th century, and through the end of World War I, Marks Brothers Jewelers developed its reputation as a first-rate jeweler. At that time, Chicago was a city that provided ample opportunity to satisfy the ambition of entrepreneurs yearning for success. The railroads had made Chicago hog-butcher to the world, and families such as Kraft and Hormel made their fortunes from the stockyards on the southside of the growing metropolis. The families that managed this new wealth spent their money on items that indicated their status in society, such as diamond-studded tie pins, and gold brooches to highlight the dresses of women attending gala winter balls. But the prosperity of the city was also shared by the growing middle class, who also frequented Marks Brothers Jewelers and purchased items for special occasions, such as diamond engagement rings. By 1919, the company had not only established and solidified its reputation as a jeweler, but had also laid a firm financial foundation for its continuation into the future.

The ''Roaring Twenties,'' as they were called in the United States, had a particularly load roar in Chicago. The Volstead Act, which prohibited the production, sale, and consumption of alcoholic beverages, was a godsend to gangsters who illegally distributed beer, wine, and hard liquor to customers in ''speakeasies'' (private membership clubs). The ownership of these clubs and the territories they were located in generated bitter and violent battles between the gangsters for the large amounts of cash involved. In addition, many individuals in Chicago were making large sums of money speculating on the stock market, and there seemed no end to the growing wealth in the city. Many of these individuals who had made large sums of

318

money legally and illegally bought their diamonds at Marks Brothers Jewelers.

Although the stock market crash of October 1929 sent the entire United States economy into a downward spiral, Marks Brothers Jewelers was able to survive this difficult period. Sales dropped dramatically, of course, and the company was forced to lay off many of its employees, but the brothers were able to gather together their family in order to run and operate the store themselves. As the Great Depression continued throughout the decade of the 1930s, sales at the company remained stagnant. Yet a glimmer of more profitable times was just around the corner.

World War II and the Postwar Period

Even before the beginning of World War II, the country's economy began to improve. President Franklin Delano Roosevelt implemented a comprehensive national program to place the United States on a wartime production schedule, with the manufacture of materials for troops that would be sent overseas to fight the Axis Powers of Germany and Japan. The resurgence of American manufacturing and production stimulated the economy and lifted the country out of the throes of the Depression. As a result, employment rose and people were paid comfortable wages. No longer worried about putting food on the table, people were able to spend more money on luxury items, such as marriage bands and diamond rings. Gradually, with the revitalization of the economy, specialty retailers like Marks Brothers Jewelers benefited from the increase in consumer purchasing power.

By the early 1950s, Marks Brothers Jewelers was riding the wave of American economic prosperity. Employment was high, wages were increasing, and America was the undisputed economic leader of the free world. All of these developments meant that many more American citizens were doing better than they had ever done before, and were able to pursue leisure activities and buy luxury items like no time in the past. This meant higher sales for Marks Brothers Jewelers, especially as more and more young couples decided that expensive diamond rings and gold wedding bans were necessities for their weddings.

Throughout the 1950s and 1960s, Marks Brothers Jewelers prospered, albeit unobtrusively. Still managed and run by family members, the company never valued as a priority the expansion of operations through a strategic acquisitions strategy or, for that matter, any other way. The family was satisfied with running the company as a relatively small but highly regarded operation, with a modest-sized, long-term staff that was knowledgeable about diamonds and fine jewelry. A loyal customer base that grew steadily over the two decades was also a significant factor. By the time the 1960s had come to an end, Marks Brothers Jewelers had increased its revenues dramatically since the end of World War II, but still the family did not want to expand the company's operations.

Growth and Expansion

The jewelry specialty retail business changed significantly during the 1970s, as companies which had traditionally operated as one-store retailers began to expand their business by establishing new stores in different parts of one city or by expanding into different cities altogether. Thus although a well-known company might have its flagship store in downtown New York, it would begin to open stores in Chicago and Los Angeles, for example, and also take advantage of the enormous demographic changes that led to the creation of the suburban "mall." This latter development changed the jewelry retail business forever, since many companies decided at this time to rent mall space in order to attract the growing and affluent middle class that was moving to the suburbs.

Marks Brothers Jewelers did expand its operations during the 1970s, and gradually opened nine additional stores in various sections of downtown Chicago. However, there was no serious consideration of expanding company operations farther than the city limits. This attitude changed in 1979 with the arrival of a new and younger management team. Hugh Patinkin became chairman, president, and CEO, while his brother Matthew Patinkin assumed the position of executive vice-president of store operations, and John Desjardins was brought on board to act as executive vice-president of finance and administration.

Throughout the 1980s, the new management team implemented a comprehensive strategy to expand and improve company operations. Rejecting the trend toward developing high-volume superstores that sold diamonds and jewelry, such as Service Merchandise, Marks Brothers Jewelers remained faithful to its own brand of a unique, small store concept. What this meant was that the size of a Marks Brothers store averaged around 800 square feet, but could be as small as 400 square feet, while the average size of most jewelry stores averaged 1,500 square feet. In addition, management at Marks Brothers decided to locate new company stores in center court locations in malls. The center court location provided the company with a high profile, and the small store concept helped keep rent and operating costs to a minimum. By the beginning of 1990, the new management team had opened 100 new stores in malls across the country.

The 1990s and Beyond

The impressive expansion achievement of Marks Brothers was not done through an acquisition strategy but by a detailed and careful analysis that resulted in choosing prime mall locations one by one. Most of these new stores were opened under the names of either Whitehall Company Jewellers or Lundstrom Jewelers. The modus operandi of the management team was to first open a Whitehall Company Jewellers store, and later open a Lundstrom Jewelers store, an upscale rendition of the Whitehall store in regard to its merchandise, in the same mall. In this way management minimized competition, and customers were not usually aware of the fact that the parent company, Marks Brothers, operated the two stores.

In 1995, the company continued its aggressive growth strategy by opening 14 additional stores, and in 1996 there were 19 new store openings. Most of these stores were located in two new locations, San Diego, California, and Orange County, California. The success of these stores, especially in an extremely competitive environment where upscale merchandise and elegant surroundings were of utmost importance, was largely based on the knowledge and effectiveness of a highly trained sales force.

To make certain these stores were a success, management decided to clean house and rid the company of nearly 10 percent of its sales force that was not meeting company standards. With all the pieces now in place, the company was ready to take the next major step in its expansion strategy, namely, make the change from a private to a public company. In May 1996, Marks Brothers Jewelers went public with a stock offering that garnered over $52 million to fuel its continued expansion.

By the end of fiscal 1997, the company was operating 188 stores in 24 states, all under the names of Whitehall Company Jewellers, Lundstrom Jewelers, and the Marks Brothers Jewelers Company. Traditionally having sold its wares to more affluent customers, management also decided to upgrade merchandise in all of its stores. Diamond jewelry now comprised most of each store's inventory at approximately 60 percent, while gold represented about 20 percent and gemstones about 15 percent of the inventory respectively. The company's focus on selling more diamond jewelry was related to its goal of attracting an aging baby-boomer market that would grow dramatically during the next 10 years. The company had discovered that some of the top items sold to this demographic group included a $7,000 pear-shaped diamond ring, a $3,000 trillion-cut diamond ring, and a $6,000 diamond solitaire ring. Even more exciting for the company was the discovery that items selling at over $1,500 accounted for approximately 25 percent of sales at its Lundstrom and Whitehall stores, while items selling at over $3,000 accounted for 12 percent of sales.

Marks Brothers Jewelers has grown so rapidly in such a short period of time that it is presently the fourth largest mall jeweler in the country, and the sixth largest jewelry retailer overall. Zales, Sterling Jewelry, and Service Merchandise are the company's prime competitors in the malls, while Helzberg Diamond rounds out the general competition. Only two of these companies, Zales and Sterling, continue to expand their operations. Zales, which operates over 1,000 stores, has initiated a major marketing effort to capture new customers and intends to open nearly 200 new stores in the near future, and Sterling, having just gone through a period of consolidation, is also concentrating on opening new stores in malls throughout the United States. Service Merchandise is closing 60 of its stores, and Helzberg Diamond has only opened 10 new stores during fiscal 1997.

With a growing trend toward consolidation in the industry, and the lack of new competitors on the horizon, Marks Brothers Jewelers is well situated to take advantage of the growing market demand from aging and affluent baby boomers for luxury items such as diamonds, jewelry, and gemstones. The family business that once regarded growth with suspicion is now positioned to become one of the most prominent jewelry retailers in America.

Further Reading

Donahue, Peggy Jo, "Teaching a New Generation of Consumers the Value of Quality," *Jewelers Circular Keystone,* March 1997, p. 62.

Elliot, Stuart, "Marks Brothers Jewelers," *New York Times,* June 4, 1997, p. C8(N).

Frischknecht, Donna, "Marks Brothers Jewelers: On Your Mark, Get Set, Grow," *Supersellers,* January 1997, p. 21.

"Quality Diamonds," *Jewelers Circular Keystone,* June 1997, p. 402.

Shor, Russell, "Auction Houses Vs. Luxury Retailers: Myth & Reality," *Jewelers Circular Keystone,* January 1997, p. 134.

Shuster, William George, and Stacy King, "Jewelers As Store Designers," *Jewelers Circular Keystone,* November 1996, p. 86.

Thompson, Michael, "Time Is Money," *Jewelers Circular Keystone,* October 1997, p. 111.

—Thomas Derdak

Martha Stewart Living Omnimedia, L.L.C.

20 West 43rd Street
25th Floor
New York, New York 10036-7400
U.S.A.
(212) 827-8000
Fax: (212) 827-8204
Web site: http://www.marthastewart.com

Private Company
Incorporated: 1997
Employees: 230
Sales: $120 million (1997 est.)
SICs: 2721 Periodicals; 2731 Books; 5961 Catalog &
    Mail-Order Houses; 7812 Motion Picture & Video
    Tape Production

Martha Stewart Living Omnimedia, L.L.C. encompasses the varied publishing, broadcasting, and merchandising enterprises of its founder, Martha Stewart. With products reflecting the personal tastes and style of Stewart, these enterprises make up the Martha Stewart brand, which has been compared to such other brands as Calvin Klein and Ralph Lauren in terms of name recognition and quality. The company is comprised of three main divisions: publishing and online, television, and merchandising. The publishing division is the core of the company. Its magazine *Martha Stewart Living* offers Stewart's decorating ideas, craft projects, instruction in gardening, and recipes. Also overseen by this division is the company's web site, which provides a guide for Stewart's television program, recipes and craft instructions, and opportunities for users to purchase merchandise. The television division produces a daily show also known as ''Martha Stewart Living,'' as well as the weekly appearance of Martha Stewart on the program ''CBS This Morning'' and a weekly 90-second radio feature called ''askMartha.'' The merchandising division handles the company's ''Martha by Mail'' catalogue and its marketing agreements with such retailers as Kmart and Sherwin-Williams paint stores.

1970s Origins As a Caterer

Although Martha Stewart bought the company that bore her name from Time Warner and incorporated it in 1997, the beginnings of the business can be traced to Stewart's activities two decades earlier. Stewart's formal education consisted of a bachelor's degree in history and architecture from Barnard College, and, following limited success as a model and then as a stockbroker, she decided to make a career out of her passion for food preparation and presentation. In 1976, Stewart founded her own business, a catering operation headquartered in the basement of the historic farmhouse she lived in with her husband and daughter in Westport, Connecticut.

By the late 1970s, Stewart was running a successful, upscale catering business on the East Coast and contributing articles to the *New York Times* and *House Beautiful*. She was also hoping to parlay her expertise in party planning into a book on the subject. In 1980 she forged an agreement to write such a book for Crown Publishing, a division of Random House. Stewart reportedly had to fight for the lavish style she envisioned for the book, which included color photographs throughout and the large size and format of a so-called coffee-table book. Published in 1982, Stewart's *Entertaining* helped establish Stewart as an authority on taste; by the mid-1990s the book had sold over half a million copies. The production of that first book also proved to be a blueprint for how Stewart would build her image; she would continue to think big while maintaining her perfectionist's attention to detail.

Stewart authored several more books in the 1980s, including *Martha Stewart's Quick Cook, Martha Stewart's Hors d'Oeuvres, Martha Stewart's Quick Cook Menus,* and *Martha Stewart's Christmas*. Stewart's books proved to have an enduring shelf life, as her backlist generated significant income and all of her books remained in print as of the late 1990s. By 1995, she had more than four million copies of her books in print, and once again, a successful enterprise launched the next phase of Stewart's career. Book tours to promote her work led to paid lecture appearances; the lectures, in turn, helped promote the books and popularize the Martha Stewart style.

Then in the late 1980s came the first step toward making Martha Stewart a nationally known brand name. In 1987 Stewart signed a $5 million, five-year consulting contract with Kmart. Ostensibly, Stewart was to help create products for the retailer to sell, such as a line of Dutch Boy paint colors and a line of bath and bedding products. Stewart's main role, however, was to lend her name to Kmart's products and to make print ad, television, and in-store appearances for the company. "I thought they wanted me to make real decisions for them," Stewart told *Working Woman* in 1995, "but it turns out I was really hired as a personality, not a consultant. So they acted on nothing I proposed." Stewart allowed the contract to lapse in 1992, though Kmart continued to sell Martha Stewart towels, bedding, and paints.

Stewart Starts a Magazine in 1990

Around the same time, Stewart prepared to move in another new direction. In the late 1980s, she pitched an idea for a magazine to the publishing house of Condé Nast. The company's chair, Si Newhouse, was wary of the idea for *Martha Stewart Living,* however, deeming a product dependent on one person as too risky. Stewart's idea was also turned down by Rupert Murdoch's magazine empire. In 1990, however, Time Inc. approved two test issues of *Martha Stewart Living,* with the first one scheduled to come out in November 1990 and the second in March 1991. The public's response was strong enough for Time to commit to six issues a year. Although Stewart had achieved her goal of moving into magazine publishing, the deal with Time was reportedly not very lucrative for her. A writer for *Working Woman,* related that "a very reliable source says Time Inc. agreed only to give her an annual salary of $400,000 or so, with no equity in the magazine until it became profitable." The stingy deal, this unnamed source suggested, stemmed from Stewart's weak bargaining position after being turned down by other publishers.

By 1995, *Martha Stewart Living* was selling 1.2 million copies per issue. The number of advertising pages in the magazine (the major source of revenue for a magazine) rose 76 percent from 1993 to 1994, and ad revenues were up 87 percent in that same period. Despite these promising statistics, the magazine was not yet making a profit. In part, the magazine's rapid growth was to blame for the loss. Time Inc. had upped its commitment by publishing ten regular issues and two special issues in 1995, thus significantly increasing expenses. That same year, *Ad Age* voted *Martha Stewart Living* its "Magazine of the Year."

The magazine spawned several other new enterprises in the early and mid-1990s. Morning television's "Today" show agreed to fund the production costs of an appearance by Stewart every other week on the program. Stewart appeared at no charge and in return received free publicity for her magazine. Time also began publishing books that made use of articles from the magazine, grouped according to theme; the first two were titled *Holidays* and *Special Occasions.*

Once again ready to expand into new areas, Stewart convinced Time to fund a television show based on the magazine, also to be called "Martha Stewart Living." The weekly show covered home decorating, entertaining, gardening, and cooking, and featured Martha Stewart as the host. By 1993 the show was broadcast in 84 percent of the nation's markets.

The Creation of MSL Enterprises in 1995

These new ventures and the continued popularity of her magazine led Stewart to renegotiate her relationship with Time. To help with her negotiations, Stewart gathered a team of lawyers and consultants: Allen Grubman, a prominent entertainment lawyer; Sharon Patrick, strategy consultant; and Charlotte Beers, chair and chief executive of Ogilvy & Mather Worldwide. With these three advisors, Stewart persuaded Time to create a subsidiary of Time Warner called Martha Stewart Living Enterprises and to name Stewart chair and chief executive officer. Time provided all of the funds for the company, and Stewart provided the ideas and her name. The new corporation was jointly owned by Time Inc. Ventures, a division of Time Warner Inc., and Martha Stewart; neither party would reveal the percentage of their ownership. The company encompassed *Martha Stewart Living* magazine, its spinoff books, the new television show, and Stewart's "Today" show appearances. Outside the company's purview were the books Stewart had written between 1982 and 1995 published by Clarkson N. Potter, an imprint of Crown Publishing Group; the royalties from the sales of Kmart bedding, towels, and paints; and Stewart's lecture fees.

Martha Stewart Living Enterprises had a staff of 140 by 1996. Because Time Warner only announced sales figures for its publishing businesses as a whole, not individual units, the value of the company was difficult to ascertain. Some industry analysts placed the value of the company at $70 million and estimated its annual revenues at $200 million.

Stewart began pushing to renegotiate her relationship with Time again just a year after the formation of Martha Stewart Living Enterprises. She wanted a greater equity stake in the company and the power to expand in new directions. In April 1996, she reportedly asked for a 40 percent stake in Martha Stewart Living Enterprises and greater executive control.

MSL Omnimedia Created in 1997

The following year Stewart acquired majority interest in the company and renamed it Martha Stewart Living Omnimedia, L.L.C. With the continued help of Sharon Patrick, Stewart had arranged the purchase of at least 80 percent of the company for about $75 million, although figures vary according to different accounts. Time's remaining stake in the company was generally estimated to be between five and ten percent, with the balance of the stock held by Patrick and staff members. The separation from Time was reportedly a friendly one. Don Logan, chair and CEO of Time Inc., agreed to join the new board for Martha Stewart Living Omnimedia. Stewart initially appointed Patrick president and chief executive officer, but soon took the helm as CEO, while Patrick remained president and COO. The buyout was financed in large part with new contracts from Kmart and Sherwin-Williams. The contracts called for big up-front payments and royalties. ''We did it on cash flow,'' Patrick told the *New York Times,* adding ''We didn't mortgage the company.''

The Kmart deal added to concern among market analysts that Stewart was clouding her image with too many endorsements and target markets that were too varied. One expert in branding and positioning, Clay Timon, speculated to *Advertising Age* that Stewart was in danger of spreading herself across too many categories and images. ''You don't want people asking, 'Who is Martha Stewart? Is [her image] rural, country, city? Williams Sonoma or Kmart?,''' he explained. Stewart defended her move to expand her presence at the discount retailer, remarking in the *New York Times*: ''Why not take good messages to less fortunate people?'' The new Kmart deal was different than the first in that Martha Stewart Living Omnimedia retained control over the entire production process, from design to advertising, of a newly named Martha Stewart Everyday product line. ''Whether it's a hang tag on a dish towel or a label on a paint can, everything has to look as good as the magazine,'' production director Dora Braschi Cardinale explained to the *New York Times.* With such control, the company hoped to maintain a consistent brand image.

The contract with Sherwin-Williams was signed in May 1997 and spelled out an agreement for Stewart to help design a Martha Stewart line of paints. Originally carried exclusively by Kmart, the paint line was offered by Sears beginning in March 1998.

Continued Rapid Expansion in the Late 1990s

Now free to pursue her vision for the company, Stewart led a rapid and varied expansion of Martha Stewart Living Omnimedia in 1997 and early 1998. The ''Martha Stewart Living'' television show moved from a weekly to a weekday schedule. The show was distributed by CBS's Eyemark Entertainment, and Stewart soon left her biweekly appearance schedule on NBC's ''Today'' show to begin appearing weekly on the ''CBS This Morning'' program. In September 1997 the company launched a daily 90-second radio feature known as ''askMartha,'' which was produced in conjunction with a syndicated newspaper column of the same name. In October, the ''Martha by Mail'' insert in the Martha Stewart Living magazine was expanded into a direct mail catalogue. Also in 1997, the company introduced a web site that provided guides for the television show and magazine and published recipes and instructions for the projects presented on the show. The web site also highlighted items from the company's ''Martha by Mail'' catalogue and allowed users to order over the Internet.

Stewart also had plans for the lucrative Kmart partnership. Total Kmart sales from the Martha Stewart Everyday line were up to $500 million a year in 1997, and Stewart hoped to build on

that popularity by introducing new lines of cooking, gardening, and decorating merchandise. According to Steve Riman, a Kmart vice-president, these new products were expected to raise the percentage of Kmart revenues from Martha Stewart products even higher—to 70 percent by the year 2000.

In December 1997 the company completed construction on a new studio in Westport, Connecticut. The $4 million facility was designed for taping Stewart's television and radio shows and included large kitchens for that purpose and state-of-the-art equipment.

Early in 1998, the company's new and established ventures were going strong. The ''askMartha'' newspaper column was syndicated in 212 papers, and the radio feature was being broadcast on 135 stations. The ''Martha Stewart Living'' television program was getting top ratings and was offered on 197 stations across the nation. The 1997 circulation of *Martha Stewart Living* magazine was numbered at 2.3 million, 30 percent higher than in 1996. Kmart bed and bath merchandise sales for 1997 were estimated at $500 to $700 million and sales of Martha Stewart Everyday paint was estimated at $16 million. According to company executives, profits had doubled from 1996 to 1997.

Soon after taking over ownership of the company, Martha Stewart began talking about taking the company public. ''I'd be very keen to do a public offering at some point . . . probably within the next three to five years,'' Stewart told *Advertising Age* in February 1997. Consideration of that possibility continued into early 1998. Debate over the company's ability to stand on its own ensued. ''You have to ask yourself, if Martha Stewart got hit by a cab tomorrow, to what extent is there a viable company there?,'' Linda R. Killian, an analyst and portfolio manager with the Renaissance Capital Corporation, explained to the *New York Times.* She continued, ''Martha Stewart has created brand equity. I think it's completely plausible that she has a viable public company. She's been around for a long time, and she has gone beyond being a one-product company.'' Others, however, questioned whether profits would be hurt by rapid expansion or whether the company could actually go on without Stewart. As for Stewart, she expressed confidence in the independence of her company to the *New York Times:* ''It won't die with me. I think we are now spread very nicely over an area where our information can be trusted.''

Further Reading

Dugan, I. Jeanne, ''Someone's in the Kitchen with Martha,'' *Business Week,* July 28, 1997, pp. 58–59.

Frank, Jackie, ''Martha Stewart May Spin Off Retail Stores,'' *Reuter Business Report,* November 12, 1996.

Kasindorf, Jeanie Russell, ''Martha, Inc.,'' *Working Woman,* June 1995, pp. 26–35.

Kelly, Keith J., ''On Her Own, Martha Stewart Eyes IPO,'' *Advertising Age,* February 10, 1997, pp. 1, 48.

Pogrebin, Robin, ''Master of Her Own Destiny,'' *New York Times,* February 8, 1998, pp. 1C, 14C.

Pollack, Judann, and Alice Z. Cuneo, ''Multitude of Deals Could Hurt Martha,'' *Advertising Age,* November 18, 1996, pp. 26–27.

''Time Warner Says Stewart Talks Continuing,'' *Reuter Business Report,* April 10, 1996.

—Susan Windisch Brown

Marubeni Corporation

Marubeni Corporation

4-2, Ohtemachi 1-chome
Chiyoda-ku
Tokyo 100-88
Japan
(03) 3282-2111
Fax: (03) 3282-7456
Web site: http://www.marubeni.co.jp

Public Company
Incorporated: 1949 as Marubeni Co., Ltd.
Employees: 9,533
Sales: ¥13.97 trillion (US $112.66 billion) (1997)
Stock Exchanges: Sapporo Niigata Tokyo Nagoya Kyoto
    Osaka Hiroshima Fukuoka Düsseldorf Frankfurt
Ticker Symbol: MARUY
SICs: 6799 Investors, Not Elsewhere Classified

Marubeni Corporation is one of the largest of Japan's general trading companies, known as *sogo shosha*. With a global network of almost 200 representative offices and more than 600 affiliated companies in 84 countries, Marubeni is involved in a wide variety of activities, including domestic, import, export, and offshore trade; investment activities; and product development operations—ranging from development of natural resources and raw materials to the marketing of finished products—in a variety of industries. Marubeni is a member of the Fuyo Group, an industrial organization consisting of about 150 companies, including Hitachi (electronics), Nissan (automobiles), Canon (cameras), Showa Denko (chemicals), Kubota (farm machinery), and Nippon Steel; the group is centered around Fuji Bank. The Fuyo Group (*Fuyo* is another way of referring to Mount Fuji) was created by several corporate leaders in the early 1960s and its member companies cooperate through joint ventures and other activities of mutual benefit.

Early History

In 1872 a young merchant named Chubei Itoh established a small store in Osaka to serve as an outlet for his commercial trading business. A symbol for the store was created that placed the word *beni* (Japanese for "red") inside a circle, or *maru*. In 1883, as the Itoh trading company expanded, the Marubeni store was made its head office.

Over the next 20 years, C. Itoh & Company took over an increasing number of duties from foreign trading agents and established its own international trading network. The company experienced particularly strong growth after Japan asserted its military dominance in the region by defeating Chinese armies in 1895 and the Russian navy in 1905. At the outbreak of World War I, C. Itoh & Company took advantage of several opportunities in international trading, created when companies in Europe redirected their energies toward production of war material.

Japan allied itself with the Entente later in the war, and when Germany was defeated in 1919 Japan was awarded German colonies and commercial rights in Asia. Within two years, however, uncontrolled economic expansion caused a serious recession that threatened hundreds of companies with financial collapse. C. Itoh & Company was forced to reorganize in 1921. The company itself was renamed Marubeni Shonten, Ltd., and several divisions belonging to its larger subsidiary C. Itoh Trading became a new company called Daido Trading. Marubeni was mainly involved in textile trading, but expanded over the course of the decade to include a wider variety of industrial and consumer goods.

World War II Years

In the early 1930s a group of right-wing militarists within the Japanese armed forces initiated a rise to political power based on subversion and terrorism. As strong opponents of Communism, these militarists were natural allies of the Nazi and Fascist governments of Germany and Italy. After taking control of the government they declared a "quasi-war economy" in preparation for the Japanese conquest of East Asia and the western Pacific.

Large Japanese conglomerates known as *zaibatsu* (Mitsui, Mitsubishi, and Sumitomo) and companies such as Iwai, C. Itoh, and Marubeni were viewed by the militarists as self-interested institutions of laissez-faire capitalism. One widely recognized goal of the militarists was the nationalization of these companies. At the time, however, nationalization was not possible. These companies were responsible for virtually all of the weapons, machinery, and provisions needed to maintain the Japanese occupation of Korea, Manchuria, and China, and to conduct subsequent military campaigns.

In 1941, as part of an effort to increase the scale and raise the efficiency of Japanese industries, Marubeni was merged with C. Itoh Trading and Kishimoto & Company to form a larger firm called Sanko Kabushiki Kaisha. On December 1 of that year Japanese forces attacked British colonies in Asia, and on December 7 attacked American forces in the Philippines and Hawaii.

Initially, Sanko performed better than most Japanese companies in the war economy. Later in the war, however, Japanese forces failed to consolidate their gains and the war turned in favor of the United States. Additional demands were placed on the economy in general and companies such as Sanko in particular. In 1944, the year the Japanese mainland became exposed to American bombing raids, Sanko was merged forcibly with Daido Boeki and Kureha Spinning to form a new company called the Daiken Company. Chubei Itoh II, the son of Marubeni's founder, was placed in charge of Daiken as its president.

The companies that formed Daiken, indeed even those that formed Sanko, were forced to perform under such extraordinary circumstances that none of them had an opportunity fully to integrate their operations with the other companies. Daiken existed more as an industrial group than a company.

Postwar Reconstruction

When the war ended in the late summer of 1945 most of the country's industrial capacity had been destroyed. An Allied occupation authority under General Douglas MacArthur initiated a plan for reconstruction and the general reorganization of Japanese industry. Large conglomerates, particularly the *zaibatsu,* were divided into hundreds of independent companies in an effort to eliminate monopoly practices and encourage greater competition. In 1949 Daiken, which was not a *zaibatsu,* was redivided into Kureha Spinning, C. Itoh & Company, Marubeni, and a small manufacturer of nails called the Amagasaki Company. Marubeni was given authority to conduct international trade. Under the leadership of President Shinobu Ichikawa, the company utilized its strength in textiles to finance diversification into nontextile items such as food, metals, and machinery.

When the Korean War broke out in June 1950, Marubeni became one of thousands of Japanese companies whose services were urgently needed by the United Nations forces. Marubeni reacted quickly to new opportunities created by the war and, as a result, experienced faster growth than many other companies. The war also transformed Japan's role as a postwar ally of the United States; it was decided that Japan should be developed into an industrial nation.

The Korean War ended in 1953, and many U.N. supply contracts with Japanese companies were terminated. This caused a serious recession in Japan and forced many companies, including Marubeni, to reorganize operations and management. Nonetheless, the company declared itself fully recovered from both World War II and the recession in 1955.

On February 18, 1955, Marubeni merged with Iida & Company, an established name in Japanese business that operated several large department stores under the name Takashimaya. To emphasize its equality with Iida, the Marubeni Company changed its name in September to Marubeni-Iida.

The Ministry for International Trade and Industry (MITI), the Japanese government's coordinating body for the nation's industries, selected Marubeni-Iida to handle trading activities for Yawata Iron & Steel and Fuji Iron & Steel (merged in 1970 to become Nippon Steel). As a result of this decision, Marubeni occupied a leading position in the field of silicon steel and iron sheets, which were being consumed in greater quantities by the growing Japanese appliance and automobile industries.

Marubeni-Iida's newly established machinery trade group was awarded several contracts over a short period during the late 1950s, firmly establishing the company in the area of engineering. These contracts included a nuclear reactor for the Japan Atomic Energy Research Institute, a fleet of aircraft for the Japanese defense agency, and a number of factories that produced components for the electronic industry.

Marubeni-Iida entered the petrochemical industry in 1956 when it helped a leading chemical fertilizer and aluminum company called Showa Denko secure chemical production licenses from American companies. The company fostered relationships with other chemical companies and later became a leading importer of potassium and phosphate rock.

In the ten years from 1949 to 1959 Marubeni had reduced its concentration in textiles from 80 percent of sales to 50 percent. During the 1960s Marubeni-Iida acted as a supplier of materials for Japanese companies as well as a marketing agent for their products. In addition to textiles, metal products, and chemicals, Marubeni-Iida was active in trading light and heavy machinery and rubber products.

Reorganized Twice in the Late 1960s and Early 1970s

In 1965 Marubeni-Iida merged with the Totsu Company, a leading metal and steel trading firm that was closely associated with Nippon Steel. The merger substantially increased the company's size and strengthened its position in metals. With the addition of Totsu's 1,380 employees to Marubeni-Iida's 8,000, the new company became a *sogo shosha,* a large general trading firm like the former *zaibatsu* companies. To cope with its new position as one of Japan's primary instruments for industrialization and growth, the new Marubeni-Iida initiated a general reorganization of its management and planning systems.

When the reorganization was executed in 1968, the company made greater efforts to develop raw material sources overseas, including petroleum products, coal, metal ores, industrial salt, foodstuffs, and lumber. During this time Marubeni-Iida improved its transportation and marketing networks and also improved upon the coordination of its various trading activities.

President Nixon's decision to remove the U.S. dollar from the gold standard in August 1971 resulted in a worldwide disruption of currency values known as the "Nixon shock," or in Japan, *shokku*. The value of the dollar dropped steeply, which made it more difficult for Japanese companies such as Marubeni-Iida to export products to the United States. The company's operations were affected so adversely that it was again forced to reorganize. The company entered promising new lines of business, emphasized its more profitable existing operations, and divested itself of unprofitable slow-growth enterprises. The following January the company's name was changed to the Marubeni Corporation.

In August 1973 Marubeni acquired Nanyo Bussan, a trading firm that handled copper, nickel, chrome, and other metals from the Philippines. The acquisition increased Marubeni's share of the nation's copper imports from 0.8 to seven percent, and refractories (hard to melt metals) from zero to 30 percent. The addition of Nanyo Bussan to Marubeni further diversified the company's operations and strengthened its position in metals.

Rocked by Scandals in the 1970s and 1980s

In February 1976 it was reported that Marubeni illegally diverted commissions from the sale of Lockheed aircraft to officials of the Japanese government. Marubeni was accused of bribing officials for their support of Lockheed sales in Japan. Marubeni, Lockheed's agent in Japan, initially denied any complicity in the scandal. Marubeni Chairman Hiro Hiyama, however, resigned in an effort to preserve the company's integrity. The former vice-chairman of Lockheed, Carl Kotchian, testified that Hiyama advised him to bribe the Japanese officials, in accordance with "Japanese business practices." Hiyama later denied Kotchian's testimony. By July prosecutors arrested nearly 20 officials of Marubeni and All Nippon Airways, including Hiro Hiyama, who was accused of violating Japan's foreign exchange control laws.

The Lockheed scandal came only three years after Marubeni was accused of profiteering in rice by hoarding supplies on the Japanese black market. Marubeni was seriously damaged by its unfavorable public image; more than 40 municipalities canceled contracts with Marubeni, and several international ventures were terminated.

Marubeni's president, Taiichiro Matsuo, who had served in the government's Ministry for International Trade and Industry, assumed the chairman's responsibilities. After declaring that it no longer represented Lockheed, the company implemented a reform of its management structure to improve upon checks and balances at the executive level. In a move toward decentralization, many of the president's administrative responsibilities were redistributed to a board of senior executives.

Marubeni recovered quickly from the Lockheed scandal. In 1977 the company's trading volume was double the figure in 1973. As the third largest of Japan's *sogo shosha*, Marubeni consolidated its international trading network and expanded its business in the United States, Australia, Brazil, Britain, West Germany, and Sweden. Marubeni also opened or expanded

offices in the Soviet Union, the People's Republic of China, the Middle East, and Africa. The company later came to operate offices in more than 100 foreign countries. Through the early 1980s Marubeni was involved in the development of coal mines in the United States and Australia, a copper mine in Papua New Guinea, and nonferrous metal mines in Australia and the Philippines.

When President Ferdinand Marcos of the Philippines was forced into exile in the United States in February 1986, he brought with him 2,300 pages of documents that were seized by the U.S. government. Officials of the U.S. Congress later revealed that some of these documents detailed illegal payments by Japanese companies to President Marcos and several of his friends and associates. Once again, Marubeni was identified as a major participant.

Called into question was the Japanese "aid-for-trade" policy, which promises aid to foreign countries on the condition that Japanese companies perform the work. Whereas the Lockheed scandal brought down the government of Kakuei Tanaka and involved several suicides, however, the Marcos scandal merely damaged Japanese-Philippine relations. For Marubeni it was an unwelcome revelation that further compromised its public image.

In addition, *Diamond's Japan Business Directory* noted in 1986 that Marubeni suffered a ¥900 million appraisal loss due to the company's close association with the financially troubled Sanko Steamship Company. Marubeni also had an outstanding "bad" claim of more than ¥4.3 billion.

1990s Brought Challenges and Opportunities

The bursting of the late 1980s Japanese economic bubble led to prolonged difficulties for Marubeni in the 1990s. Nearly all of the *sogo shosha* had diversified aggressively into financial investments during the speculative bubble years, in large part because their traditional activity of marginally profitable commodity trading had been in a deep decline for years, a development compounded by a trend toward Japanese companies handling their international operations themselves. In desperation the trading companies built up large stock portfolios and became hooked on the revenues they could gain through arbitrage (or *zaiteku*, as it is known in Japan). Once the bubble burst, the *sogo shosha* were left with huge portfolios whose worth had plummeted; all of the trading companies were forced eventually to liquidate much of their stock holdings. Marubeni's troubles were even greater because the company had made large real estate purchases near its Osaka headquarters during the bubble. In 1995 the company wrote off ¥45 billion (US $542 million) from portfolio losses, declines in the value of real estate, and the liquidation and restructuring of both domestic and overseas subsidiaries. Further streamlining moves came in April 1996 when operations were reorganized into 21 divisions within eight business groups, and in April 1997 when the number of divisions was reduced to 19. In late 1997 Marubeni wrote off an additional ¥17.5 billion (US $143.8 million) in portfolio losses.

As Marubeni recovered from the burst bubble, and as it operated within the environment of a prolonged 1990s Japanese recession, it pursued a variety of new revenue streams. In March 1996

Marubeni spent about ¥27 billion (US $230 million) to purchase a 30 percent stake in the U.S.-based Sithe Energies, Inc., the seventh largest independent power producer in the world. In May 1996 Marubeni and Toho-Towa Co., Ltd., Japan's largest film producer, announced that they would invest up to ¥13 billion (US $125 million) over a three-year period in films produced by Paramount Pictures, a subsidiary of Viacom. The consortium's first release was *The Relic,* which opened in the United States in January 1997. In September 1997 Marubeni and France's Cie. Generale des Eaux S.A. announced they would invest ¥100 billion (US $828 million) in a joint venture aiming to develop drainage and sewer infrastructure projects in Asia.

Beginning in late 1996, Marubeni began to investigate ways that it could take advantage of the forthcoming Japanese ''big bang,'' the long-anticipated deregulation of the financial sector, a prime opportunity to secure new revenue sources. Targeting the consumer-financial industry, Marubeni launched its first fund, the MBI Fund, in July 1997 and planned eventually to launch one new fund each quarter. It was likely that the company eventually would acquire a Japanese brokerage house or create an alliance with a foreign brokerage house targeted at the Japanese market.

Marubeni had weathered fairly successfully the variety of challenges it had faced in the 1990s, but confronted additional serious problems thanks to the Asian financial crisis, which began in 1997. The company had numerous operations throughout Asia, including significant activities in the troubled nations of Indonesia and Thailand. The crisis was sure to affect Marubeni for some time to come, but the company had shown on more than one occasion in its history the ability to adapt to the fluctuations of the global economy.

Principal Subsidiaries

Marubeni America Corporation (U.S.A.); Marubeni Canada Ltd.; Marubeni Mexico S.A. de C.V.; Marubeni Brazil S.A.; Marubeni Argentina S.A.; Marubeni Venezuela C.A.; Marubeni U.K. P.L.C.; Marubeni Deutschland GmbH (Germany); Marubeni Benelux S.A. (Belgium); Marubeni France S.A.; Marubeni Italia S.p.A. (Italy); Marubeni Scandinavia AB (Sweden); Marubeni Nigeria Ltd.; Marubeni Bahrain E.C.; Marubeni Saudi Arabia Co., Ltd.; Marubeni Iran Co., Ltd.; Marubeni India Private Ltd.; Marubeni Singapore Pte. Ltd.; Dagangterus Sdn. Bhd. (Malaysia); Marubeni Thailand Co., Ltd.; P.T. Marubeni Indonesia; Marubeni Philippines Corporation; Marubeni China Co., Ltd.; Marubeni Hong Kong Ltd.; Marubeni Taiwan Co., Ltd.; Marubeni Korea Corporation; Marubeni Australia Ltd.; Marubeni New Zealand Ltd.; Marubeni Papua New Guinea Pty., Ltd.

Principal Divisions

Textile Group: Textile Material Division; Apparel Division. Metal Group: Iron & Steel Division; Iron & Steel Material Division; Nonferrous & Light Metals Division. Machinery Group—I: Power Systems Division; Information Business, Telecommunications & Electronics Division; Transportation & Development Machinery Division. Machinery Group—II: Plant & Ship Division; Industrial Machinery & Aerospace Division. Energy Group: Energy Division—I; Energy Division—II. Chemicals Group: Organic & Specialty Chemicals Division; Plastics & Inorganic Chemicals Division. Agri-Marine Products Group: Food Material (Grain & Sugar) Division; Food Division. Construction, Forest Products & General Merchandise Group: Housing Materials & General Merchandise Division; Pulp & Paper Division; Development & Construction Division.

Further Reading

Dawkins, William, and Alice Rawsthorn, ''Japanese Groups Announce Plan to Invest in Paramount,'' *Financial Times,* May 14, 1996, p. 28.

Iwao, Ichiishi, ''Sogo Shosha: Meeting New Challenges,'' *Journal of Japanese Trade & Industry,* January/February 1995, pp. 16–18.

The Japanese Edge: The Real Stories Behind a Sogo Shosha—One of Japan's Unique New Class of Global Corporations, Tokyo: Marubeni Corporation, 1981.

Rosario, Louise do, ''Lose and Learn: Japan's Firms Pay Price of Financial Speculation,'' *Far Eastern Economic Review,* June 17, 1993, pp. 60–61.

Sato, Kazuo, ed., *Industry and Business in Japan,* White Plains, N.Y.: Croom Helm, 1980.

Spindle, Bill, ''Japan's Turmoil Opens Opportunities for Outsiders in Finance,'' *Wall Street Journal,* December 18, 1997, p. A19.

Terazono, Emiko, ''Marubeni Writes Off ¥45bn for Closed Units,'' *Financial Times,* April 12, 1995, p. 29.

The Unique World of the Sogo Shosha, Tokyo: Marubeni Corporation, 1978.

Yonekawa, Shin'ichi, ed., *General Trading Companies: A Comparative and Historical Study,* Tokyo: United Nations University Press, 1990.

Yoshihara, Kunio, *Sogo Shosha: The Vanguard of the Japanese Economy,* Tokyo: Oxford University Press, 1982.

Young, Alexander K., *The Soga Shosha: Japan's Multinational Trading Companies,* Boulder, Colo.: Westview Press, 1979.

—updated by David E. Salamie

Mecklermedia Corporation

20 Ketchum St.
Westport, Connecticut 06880
U.S.A.
(203) 226-6967
(800) 632-5537
Fax: (203) 454-5840
Web site: http://www.mecklermedia.com

Public Company
Incorporated: 1971
Employees: 182
Sales: $55.19 million (1997)
Stock Exchanges: NASDAQ
Ticker Symbol: MECK
SICs: 7375 Information Retrieval Services; 2721 Trade
    Journals: Publishing Only; 7389 Trade Show
    Arrangement

Mecklermedia Corporation is a small but important player in the world of the Internet, with a relatively long history in this young industry. Its business consists of sponsoring trade shows, publishing the weekly *Internet World* magazine, and operating a commercial Web site. Though some of its ventures have failed to pan out, Mecklermedia, led by founder Alan Meckler, has carved out several areas of dominance in the sometimes chaotic business end of the still-maturing online realm. The company's continued success is likely, given the necessary support role that it plays, its experience and established presence in the business, and Mecklermedia's proven ability to roll with the punches.

Early Years: Special Publications for Librarians

Mecklermedia's origins trace to the founding of Meckler Publishing Corporation by Alan Meckler in 1971. Meckler, who had a Ph.D. in American History, initially set out to publish materials for use by librarians. Taking as his example such successful R.R. Bowker publications as *Library Journal, Books in Print, Literary Market Place,* and many others, he concen-trated on servicing the small niche of the library world that consisted of publications done on microfilm. His first venture, launched in 1972, was *Microform Review.* It was followed by other publications targeted to the same niche, including *Micropublishers' Trade List Annual, Micrographics' Equipment Review, Microform Market Place,* and others. Meckler's philosophy was to publish something only if it was not offered elsewhere, or to compete with an existing publication only if he had a distinctly different angle. Over time the company's endeavors expanded to include sponsoring small trade shows geared toward librarians, featuring exhibits of micropublishing vendors' products with informational presentations and speakers. The company would charge vendors' fees to exhibit their wares, as well as charging admission to the library professionals who attended. Occasionally Meckler would publish projects not directly related to microforms, such as a biographical dictionary of the governors of the various states from 1789 to 1978. The company also published several specialized scholarly journals, such as the *International Journal of Oral History.* Meckler himself wrote a book on the history of micropublishing, published by Greenwood Press in 1982.

As the potential applications of computers were becoming apparent in the early 1980s, especially as they related to libraries, Meckler started several publications to cover the emerging technology. *Software Review* and *Videodisc-Videotex,* a quarterly launched in 1981, were two of his earliest moves into this area. Still, the company had only 15 employees by the end of 1983, and was not known outside the world of libraries.

The mid-1980s saw the first commercially available CD-ROMs and other optical disc data storage formats. Librarians were immediately interested in the possibilities they offered for storing vast amounts of information in a small space, and for relatively easy, random access to that information. Meckler had already positioned himself in this area with Videodisc-Videotex, and he sponsored his first trade shows on the subject of optical data discs by the mid-1980s. These annual affairs attracted only a few vendors and attendees at first, but showed substantial growth each year they were repeated. Other Meckler publications, with names like *Small Computers in Libraries* and *CD-ROM Librarian,* which were started during this era, were also inspired by the emerging technology. Meckler continued to publish its microform journals during this time, but the publisher was always game to try something new to see whether it might catch on, abandoning it if there seemed to be no interest. Quoted by *Forbes* in 1994, founder Meckler stated, "I never did market research. My mentality was like a baseball hitter. If you can be successful three times out of ten, you're phenomenal."

The 1990s: Anticipating the Potential of the Internet

By the late 1980s Meckler Publishing was still a fairly small concern. Its publications, tailored mainly to the limited world of technology-minded librarians, were generally successful, but the company was not hugely profitable. In March 1990 Alan Meckler had a conversation with a college librarian which pointed him in a new direction. Having never before heard of the Internet, Meckler was told that it had the potential to be the greatest information-delivery system known to mankind. The publisher decided to start a newsletter called *Research and Education Networking,* and offered a trade show on electronic networking and publishing in 1992. Though the two ventures had lost a combined total of $400,000 by the end of that year, this time Meckler decided to stick with and even expand on the concept. In April 1993, Meckler Publishing launched a monthly magazine called *CD-ROM World* (actually a facelift of *CD-ROM Librarian*), following soon after with *Internet World,* another monthly, and *Virtual Reality World,* a bimonthly magazine. These were no longer publications geared strictly toward the needs of librarians—quite the contrary. All were consumer magazines designed much more for newsstands than the desk of a microform cataloger. Within a year of their launch the two monthlies each had paid circulation of 50,000 issues or more, far higher than any previous Meckler publication.

Continuing its policy of sponsoring trade shows linked thematically to its publications, Mecklermedia soon offered its first consumer trade show, CD-ROM Home and Office World, which debuted in August 1994. Other consumer-focused shows soon followed. The company had for some time been reducing its emphasis on specialized library and scholarly publications, and continued to scale these back until only a handful were left, some being sold and others folded. The last to go was *Computers In Libraries,* sold in 1995, along with its related trade show.

Alan Meckler had sold a third of Meckler Publishing to James Mulholland, Jr., and his son in 1993 for $1.2 million. Desirous of more cash to pay off debts and to further expand

their growing Internet-related business, they decided to take the company public the following year, with an initial public offering of stock on the NASDAQ exchange in February 1994. Despite the fact that Meckler Publishing was cumulatively in debt to the tune of $1.9 million at the time, the offering was a successful one, and the price of the newly christened Mecklermedia Corporation's stock doubled within a few months.

October 1994: Mecklermedia Goes Online

Shortly after its successful stock offering, Mecklermedia took its greatest gamble to date with the creation of MecklerWeb. This was announced in the summer of 1994 as a sort of "Internet Yellow Pages," an "on-ramp" for corporations to present online information centers and offer interactive features that could be used by potential customers. There would be a single Internet address, which, when accessed by a user, would enable him or her to find an individual business of the type they desired through a system of categorization. Some information-only features were also planned, allowing users access to data on related topics. The site would be paid for by the participating businesses, who would be charged an annual flat fee of $25,000 for inclusion in MecklerWeb and $50,000 if Mecklermedia had to put the company's information online. Mecklermedia executive Christopher Locke oversaw the new venture, describing it in *Advertising Age* as ". . . a place in cyberspace where commerce can be conducted both legitimately and effectively, kind of like the old village square in medieval times." An outside firm, Ogilvy and Mather Direct, was retained to design the site's graphic "look and feel." The entire venture was a cooperative effort, with several other companies involved in various ways. The most prominent of these, Digital Equipment, had contributed several hundred thousand dollars worth of computer equipment.

Although the announcement of MecklerWeb attracted a fair amount of attention in the business community, only one company had been signed up by launch time of October 1994. Faced with a potential disaster, CEO Meckler within two weeks decided to pull the plug, leaving Mecklermedia's partners and Christopher Locke shocked and angry. After several heated volleys back and forth in the business press, Locke resigned. Shortly afterwards, however, MecklerWeb was resurrected, albeit in a modified form. The web site was to be more of an information center with paid advertisements, rather than a central location from which other companies' sites could be accessed. Mecklermedia announced it would put *Internet World, CD-ROM World,* and *Virtual Reality World* online as content. The fee for an advertisement was $5,000 for 90 days, actually topping the annual cost of a web site placement in the project's first incarnation by 20 percent. This move was largely seen as an attempt to save face and mollify Digital, which reportedly had an agreement that Mecklermedia would pay it up to several hundred thousand dollars for every quarter that a minimum of 15 new sponsors were not signed up.

The MecklerWeb launch debacle was partially to blame for the company's loss of $1.5 million during the first fiscal year after going public. Some of its endeavors were showing promise, however, with *Internet World* magazine, among the first to cover the territory, growing to 70,000 paid subscriptions by the end of 1994, and attendance at the related *Internet World* trade show hitting a peak of 11,000, up from 4,000 a year earlier.

Mecklermedia continued to try new publications out as well. The year 1995 saw the launch of Web Week, the company's first weekly, a news-oriented offering aimed at Internet professionals. The company also tested a telephone helpline, offering answers to questions about the Internet 24 hours a day over a fee-charging "1-900" phone number. The company's successful trade shows were also being exported by this time, either through licensing agreements or in partnership with companies in the host countries. Within the next several years the phenomenal growth of its trade shows would lead to this line of business becoming Mecklermedia's largest source of revenue.

Streamlining in the Latter Half of the 1990s

Mecklermedia's business was starting to become more focused as the Internet itself began to become more a part of everyday life for many Americans, and the initial speculation and hype surrounding it began to settle down. Sales of the print versions of Mecklermedia's Internet magazines peaked, then stagnated after several years. The company had launched *Internet Shopper* magazine in both print and online versions, but soon found that it was more popular and more appropriate to its subject in its online version, and after several years the print format was discontinued. Mecklermedia also canceled the print version of *Internet World* and another, more technical magazine it had created, *Web Developer*. The company retained the name *Internet World*, however, transferring it to the company's *Web Week* publication in early 1998. Mecklermedia's original consumer-oriented magazine, *CD-ROM World*, had been sold to another company by this time as well.

Mecklermedia continued to beef up its online presence, purchasing the Internet domain name "Internet.com" for a reported $100,000 in May 1997. The company's goal was to offer a web site for Internet professionals with daily news updates, extensive reference sources, and links to businesses. This was an extension and evolution of the MecklerWeb concept (which had later been renamed iWORLD), now a much greater success than that initial disastrous outing had been. The company had been acquiring resources in a variety of ways to add to its web site, with popular features such as SearchEngineWatch.com, Netsearcher.com, Web Developer's Virtual Library, and others added to the site in an ongoing quest to be the largest Internet resource site. The company's efforts bore fruit, as components of the Internet.com web site were honored by both *PC Magazine* and *HomePC Magazine* in annual lists of top sites on the Internet.

Having lost money each of the first two years after going public, Mecklermedia finally showed a profit in the 1997 fiscal year, its gross revenues increasing 80 percent over the total for 1996. The company continued to add services to its web site, and its trade show business also continued to expand. In 1998 Mecklermedia's Internet World trade shows were scheduled for 23 different countries, including Japan, Canada, Brazil, and Australia. After having started as a publishing company in 1971, its sole remaining paper product was the weekly *Internet World*.

Mecklermedia Corporation, much changed from its early years as a publisher of special journals and newsletters for librarians, had grown into an important presence in the world of cyberspace. Its Internet World trade shows were the most prominent in the industry, its Internet.com web site of resources for Internet professionals was popular and award-winning, and its weekly *Internet World* a leading publication of its type. After surviving the early shakedown period of widespread Internet access and growth, the company had settled into a leadership position in its field. It looked certain to remain in that position for some time to come.

Principal Subsidiaries

iWorld Corp.; Mecklermedia Ltd. (U.K.).

Further Reading

Deitch, Joseph, "Portrait" [Alan Meckler], *Wilson Library Bulletin*, December, 1983, pp. 288–89.

Hutheesing, Nikhil, "Internet Inc. (Mecklermedia Online Information Service)," *Forbes*, October 24, 1994, pp. 259–60.

Kelly, Keith J., "MecklerWeb Wants Cyber-Ads Served Sans Flames," *Advertising Age*, May 30, 1994, p. 18.

Manly, Lorne, "Mecklermedia Crests on New-Media Wave," *Folio*, June 15, 1994, pp. 64–65.

——, "More Changes at Mecklermedia," *Folio*, December 15, 1994, p. 32.

Marcial, Gene G., "A Pure Play on the Internet?," *Business Week*, July 4, 1994, p. 80.

Martinez, Andres, "Mecklermedia Sees Earnings Jumping in 1998 on Trade Show Profits," *Dow Jones Online News*, December 5, 1997.

Meeks, Brock N., "MecklerWeb: It's On; It's Off; It's On," *InterActive Week*, November 7, 1994, p. 39.

Parets, Robyn Taylor, "The New America: Mecklermedia Corp.," *Investor's Business Daily*, March 25, 1997, p. A4.

Sandberg, Jared, "Mecklermedia Hopes Fingers Do the Walking on the Info Highway," *Wall Street Journal*, June 1, 1994, p. B5.

——, "Mecklermedia Riding Internet Hype to Profits in FY95," *Dow Jones News Service*, December 9, 1994.

——, "Mecklermedia Zaps New Internet Service Weeks After Launch," *Wall Street Journal*, October 20, 1994, p. B7.

Wingfield, Nick, "Mecklermedia to Halt Print Publication of 2 Magazines Aimed at Internet Users," *Wall Street Journal*, December 17, 1997, p. B6.

—Frank Uhle

Medusa Corporation

3008 Monticello Boulevard
Cleveland Heights, Ohio 44118
U.S.A.
(216) 371-4000
Fax: (216) 371-2912

Public Company
Incorporated: 1892 as Sandusky Portland Cement
    Company
Employees: 1,100
Sales: $376 million (1997)
Stock Exchanges: New York
Ticker Symbol: MSA
SICs: 3421 Cement, Hydraulic; 1423 Crushed & Broken
    Granite

Medusa Corporation is one of the oldest cement companies in the United States, having been in business for over a century. The company is engaged in the production and marketing of portland and masonry cements; mining, processing, and marketing construction aggregates, lawn & garden, and industrial limestone products; and providing construction services for highway safety. Its operations are principally in the eastern half of the United States, with strong market positions in the Great Lakes and Southeast regions.

19th-Century Origins

The company can trace its origins to the founding of Sandusky Portland Cement Company of West Virginia in 1892 by Spencer Newberry and Arthur St. John Newberry. The first cement plant was built at Bay Bridge, Ohio, that year. A second facility was built at Syracuse, Indiana, in 1901, but was later abandoned in 1920. The name was changed to Sandusky Portland Cement Company of Ohio. In 1907, the company opened a plant in Dixon, Illinois, and constructed a white cement plant at York, Pennsylvania. The company was reincorporated in Ohio

in 1916 as Sandusky Cement Co. Founders Arthur and Spencer Newberry died in 1912 and 1922, respectively.

In 1924, the company introduced waterproof nonstaining white cement. New white and gray cement plants were erected at York, Pennsylvania. The company changed names again in April 1929 to Medusa Portland Cement Company. Later that same year, the company acquired Crescent Portland Cement Company in Wampum, Pennsylvania, and Manitowoc Portland Cement and merged with Newaygo Portland Cement Company in September.

In 1938, the company opened a white cement grinding plant in Paris, Ontario, Canada. The western extension of the Pennsylvania Turnpike and the Ohio Turnpike were built with Medusa cement around that time.

Diversification During the 1960s and 1970s

In the mid-1960s, the company committed to build its first greenfield cement plant in four decades and the Charlevoix plant came on-line in 1967. A diversification effort also began in the mid-1960s with several aggregate acquisitions. In September 1966, the company acquired Western Indiana Aggregate Corporation in a stock swap. June of the following year saw the company acquiring Lehigh Stone Company for stock and approximately $121,000 in cash. In June 1968, the company acquired Raid Quarries Corporation in a stock swap. The company acquired The James H. Drew Corporation, based in Indianapolis, Indiana, in a stock swap in April 1970. June 1970 saw the company buying New Hudson Sand & Gravel Inc. In July, the company swapped stock for Bowling Green, Kentucky-based McLellan Stone Company Inc. and paid $425,000 for that company's affiliated McLellan Construction Company Inc. In April 1971, the company acquired Wanatah Trucking Company Inc. in a stock swap. May saw the company acquiring State Contracting and Stone Company Inc. in another stock swap.

Although most of Medusa's acquisitions in the 1960s and 1970s fell outside the cement industry, the Penn Dixie Cement Plant in Clinchfield, Georgia plant was purchased in 1971, marking the company's first move outside its primary marketing area in the Great Lakes region of the United States. The

---

Company Perspectives:

Medusa Corporation produces and sells portland and masonry cements; mines, processes and sells construction aggregates, lawn & garden and industrial limestone products; and provides construction services for highway safety.

---

plant was in poor condition and the company spent $13 million renovating and modernizing the facility. In February 1972, the company acquired Marion Brick Corporation in a stock swap. By the end of March 1972, fully one-third of Medusa Portland's business was in non-cement products. In light of this diversification, the company changed its name to Medusa Corporation.

In January 1974, the company acquired Davis-Snyder Companies, Holston River Quarry, and Holston River Paving Company, and in June acquired Salem Stone Company. That same year, Medusa also acquired Thomasville Stone and Lime Company. In March 1975 the company swapped stock to assume certain liabilities of Woodbridge Clay Products. In May 1977, the company acquired Miller Bros. Company and Geohegan & Mathis Inc. for stock and in June 1977, the company paid approximately $10 million in cash for substantially all the assets of MCQ Inc.

The Crane Years, 1979–88

A takeover battle for Medusa began in 1977, with companies like Moore-McCormack Resources, Ogleby Norton, and Kaiser Cement and Gypsum seeking to purchase the company. It ended in January 1979 with the company's acquisition by Crane Company. Thomas M. Evans, Crane's CEO, completed the modernization and expansion of the Charlevoix plant in December of that same year and took a series of aggressive steps to downsize the company and generate cash. June 1978 saw the sale of Marion Brick for $9 million, a nice profit on the less than 200,000 share stock swap the company made in 1972 to acquire it. In 1979, the Manitowoc cement plant was closed and the Toledo, Ohio cement plant was sold. The Dixon, Illinois cement plant was sold in 1980, together with several aggregate operations. In 1981, the York, Pennsylvania gray cement plant was closed and the York white cement plant was sold the following year.

By 1984, the year Robert S. Evans replaced his father as CEO of Crane, Medusa was a smaller and leaner company that was ready to build on its strengths. Over the next five years, major investments were made to upgrade the Charlevoix, Clinchfield, and Wampum plants. In addition, efforts were made to improve the distribution capability from Charlevoix, including new terminals in Toledo and Owens Sound, Ontario, Canada. By the late 1980s, Medusa had become the low-cost producer of cement and aggregate in most of its major markets.

In an effort to maximize Medusa's value to Crane's shareholders, Medusa was spun off from Crane in October 1988. Immediately prior to the spinoff, Medusa paid an $84.3 million dividend to Crane using borrowed funds, eliminating all but approximately $131,000 of equity from its balance sheet.

Crane's shareholders received $6.88 per share in Medusa's stock, tax-free.

A New Start, Late 1980s–90s

From internally generated cash flow, Medusa reduced the borrowings from the Crane dividend substantially over the next few years. The company had emerged from the Crane years with a lean organization, a tradition of strict financial controls, and excellent operating assets. In May 1990, the company acquired the operating assets and mineral reserves of three aggregate operations in western Pennsylvania for $7.7 million.

With debt down to comfortable levels, Medusa took advantage of the 1991–92 downturn in the cement industry by buying a cement plant in Demopolis, Alabama, related assets, an 814,000-ton, single-kiln plant, and nine cement distribution terminals in the southeastern United States from Lafarge Corporation at a depressed price of $50.5 million in early 1993. In 1996, Thomasville Stone and Lime's name was changed to Medusa Minerals Company.

In 1997, Medusa Minerals tripled in size through the acquisition of Lime Crest Corporation and White Stone Company of Southwest Virginia, establishing a network of industrial limestone and lawn and garden operations along the eastern seaboard. Sparta, New Jersey-based Lime Crest, was acquired in January for $12.8 million. Whitestone, based in Castlewood, Virginia, was a privately owned industrial limestone and aggregate producer, and operated a limestone pelletizing plant in Paradise, Pennsylvania. Whitestone was also a leading producer of home and garden products and other industrial limestone products in certain mid-Atlantic markets and the Southeast, as well as the leading producer of construction aggregates in southwest Virginia. Whitestone's acquisition, combined with Medusa's operations in Thomasville, Pennsylvania, and Sparta, New Jersey, gave the company significant added presence in the lawn and garden industry and with industrial limestone products in the eastern half of the United States.

Also in 1997, Medusa announced the "Clinchfield 2000 Project," a $56 million plant modernization and expansion of its Clinchfield, Georgia cement complex and related distribution facilities. The remodeling promised to boost production of clinker, a cement component, from 175,000 tons per year to approximately 760,000 tons annually.

As the U.S. cement industry's most profitable and longest-lived company, Medusa Corporation seemed well-situated to remain in a leading position.

Further Reading

Akroyd, T. N. W., *Concrete: Properties and Manufacture,* New York: Pergamon, 1962.

Bogue, Robert Herman, *The Chemistry of Portland Cement,* New York: Reinhold, 1955.

A Chronicle of Cleveland, Cleveland: Cleveland Chamber of Commerce, 1940.

Glover, William Bouck, and G. Rowland Cornell, *The Development of American Industries,* New York: Prentice-Hall, 1951.

Lesley, Robert W., *History of the Portland Cement Industry in the United States,* Chicago: International Trade Press, 1924.

Meade, Richard K., "The Manufacture of Portland Cement," *Johns Hopkins Alumni Magazine,* January 1925, pp. 149–78.

——, "The Portland Cement Industry," *Industrial and Engineering Chemistry,* September 1926.

Sedgwick, John, "Strong But Sensitive," *Atlantic,* April 1991, pp. 70–82.

Sobel, Robert, *Centennial in Cement: A History of Medusa Corporation, 1892–1992,* Cambridge, Mass.: The Winthrop Group Inc., 1992, 58 p.

United States Department of Commerce, *Historical Statistics of the United States, Colonial Times to 1970,* Washington, D.C.: U.S.G.P.O., 1975.

Wilcox, John G., *The Portland Cement Industry,* Philadelphia: Robert Morris Associates, 1928.

—Daryl F. Mallett

Michael Anthony Jewelers, Inc.

116 South McQuesten Parkway
Mount Vernon, New York 10550-1724
U.S.A.
(914) 699-0000
Fax: (914) 664-4884
Web site: http://www.michaelanthony.com

Public Company
Incorporated: 1977
Employees: 519
Sales: $129.9 million (1998)
Stock Exchanges: American
Ticker Symbol: MAJ
SICs: 3911 Jewelry & Precious Metal

Michael Anthony Jewelers, Inc. is a leading designer, marketer, and manufacturer of handcrafted jewelry in the United States. Its products, which generally retailed between $20 and $200 in the late 1990s, consist chiefly of 14-karat gold jewelry, including rope chains, bracelets, charms, pendants, earrings, rings, and watches. Most of this jewelry is manufactured at the company's Mount Vernon, New York, facilities. In 1998, Michael Anthony products were available in more than 20,000 retail outlets, as well as through catalogers, wholesalers, and home shopping clubs. The company's two largest customers during this time were Sterling Jewelers and Wal-Mart.

Beginnings: 1977–87

Michael Anthony Jewelers was founded in 1977 by two young men from New York City: Michael Paolercio, the new company's president and chief executive officer, and his younger brother Anthony Paolercio, Jr., chief operating officer. Together, the Paolercios hoped to establish a national jewelry manufacturing concern known for the quality and value of its merchandise.

Success and expansion were quick to find Michael Anthony. The company's net sales grew from $18.8 million in 1983 to $60.6 million in 1986, while net income rose from $985,000 to $5.9 million during this period. The company went public in October 1986, garnering about $10.5 million in proceeds from the sale of more than 30 percent of the outstanding shares of common stock. Michael and Anthony Paolercio remained the major shareholders immediately following this offering, with 37.2 percent and 37 percent of the stock, respectively.

Michael Anthony Jewelers was, in 1987, manufacturing and selling its products to more than 1,200 customers throughout the United States. More than 10,000 retail outlets were carrying its product line, which included a wide variety of handcrafted 14-karat gold jewelry. The chief line of about 2,000 styles of charms and pendants accounted for 58 percent of net sales in fiscal 1987. These charms and pendants included religious symbols; popular sayings (''talking charms''); sports themes and team logos; animal motifs; nautical, seashore, western, musical, zodiac and other thematic figures; initials; and abstract artistic creations. The company's rings were second in terms of percentage of Michael Anthony sales.

During this time, the company strove to become an innovator in its industry. In fiscal 1987 Michael Anthony Jewelers introduced to its manufacturing process a photo-etching technique, enabling the company to fashion simultaneous etching on both jewelry sides that was more finely detailed than possible with the casting, or lost-wax, method. This allowed the company to enter the lower-priced segment of the 14-karat gold jewelry market through production of ultralight jewelry, although less than three percent of the company's sales were derived from such products during the next three years. For casted-product lines, the company began CAD/CAM computer-aided technology to manufacture metal molds that offered important advantages over conventional molding techniques.

Michael Anthony Jewelers also claimed to have pioneered in the diamond-cut process, a technique that produces a sparkling effect on a finished piece of gold jewelry.

Michael Anthony Jewelers acquired Enca Industries Ltd., a manufacturer and marketer of more than 1,200 styles of earrings, in July 1987 at a cost of $925,000. Two months later, the company acquired the operating assets of M.J. Manufacturing

Co., Inc., a manufacturer of rope chain, together with a patent for machinery to make this chain, for about $4 million. A subsidiary (later a division), M.A.J. Manufacturing, using the assets acquired from M.J. Manufacturing, began manufacturing 12 styles of 14-karat gold rope chains, 65 styles of designed gold tubing, and ten styles of bangle blanks used in the production of bangle bracelets. The company also was importing 14-karat gold chains from Italy, and these imported chains accounted for half of net sales in fiscal 1988.

The licensing of popular emblems and characters also became a means for expanding the company's product line. Michael Anthony Jewelers' product line included licensed goods under arrangements with such parties as the National Football League, National Basketball Association, National Hockey League, Major League Baseball, the U.S. Olympic Committee, and Playboy. The company paid a royalty ranging from six to 7.5 percent of sales for the right to depict the popular logos and symbols associated with these licensors on jewelry products, particularly charms, pendants, and pins. Licensed products, introduced in 1985, came to about four percent of the company's net sales in fiscal 1987.

Michael Anthony Jewelers had its executive and manufacturing facilities in Mount Vernon, about 15 miles outside of New York City. The company maintained a showroom and sales offices in a building it owned on West 46th Street in Manhattan and opened a showroom at the Los Angeles International Jewelry Center in fiscal 1987. It was selling to such large retail chains as Sears, Kmart, Wal-Mart, Montgomery Ward, J.C. Penney, and Zale's in 1988. The company's need for gold was being filled through a consignment arrangement with Rhode Island Hospital Trust National Bank that shifted the risk of fluctuations in price to this bank. In subsequent years Michael Anthony made similar arrangements with other banks and with nonbank companies.

Mixed Results: 1988–97

Michael Anthony's growth came to a sudden halt in fiscal 1988, when the company lost $1.1 million despite net sales of $128 million, partly because the imported chains it was selling had a lower margin for profit. As a result the company sold certain operations. Enca, the earring-maker Michael Anthony had acquired in 1987, was sold for $1.7 million. Allcraft Tool & Supply Co., a manufacturer and distributor of jewelry manufacturing equipment and supplies, was sold for $139,000. The Manhattan building was sold for $2.2 million, and the Los Angeles showroom was closed. The number of company customers, which had grown to 1,500 in fiscal 1988, fell to 600 in fiscal 1989. Shares of Michael Anthony stock, which sold for $14 in 1987, were down to $4 in early 1990.

To improve its financial performance, Michael Anthony lessened its reliance on imported chains, slashed its inventory, and installed a new computer system to track its product lines better and respond more quickly to customer demand. It also cut its work force and switched its factory workers to a piecework payment system, thereby improving its productivity level. These measures put the company back into the black, even though net sales dropped to $85.4 million in fiscal 1990.

Michael Anthony Jewelers made some other changes, including a shift in product line to higher-priced jewelry. The company started introducing a more expensive line of sparkle rings and in 1989 acquired Maurice Katz & Co., a high-end line of diamond and gold pendants retailing for as much as $2,000 apiece. This purchase and that of another product line known as 3H added more than 2,000 distinctive jewelry pieces to the company's offerings, most of them high-end designs featuring gold and diamonds.

In 1990 Michael Anthony Jewelers acquired NGI International Precious Metals, Ltd. from a British firm, Beresford International plc, for $1.65 million, a figure not reflecting the $22 million it paid for this company's gold inventory. Following the purchase of this company, which was renamed Jardinay Manufacturing Corp., Michael Anthony introduced a Jardinay line of chains, earrings, and watches, made with diamonds and semi-precious stones as well as 14-karat gold. The company also added jewelry chain stores to its roster of retail customers.

In 1991, Michael Anthony Jewelers entertained an acquisition offer of about $50 million from Jan Bell Marketing Inc., but the deal was not effected. During fiscal 1991 the company earned $2.1 million on sales of $120.2 million, and by 1992 Michael Anthony Jewelers was the largest manufacturer of gold rope chain in the United States.

During fiscal 1992 sales fell to $112.7 million, and Michael Anthony Jewelers lost $369,000. This result was somewhat misleading, however, as the company charged to the fiscal year some $2.9 million it paid in stock to NGI International executives Isaac Nussen and George Weisz in connection with the acquisition. The company had net earnings of $1.6 million on net sales of $119.6 million in fiscal 1993.

Michael Anthony Jewelers' products were being sold in over 20,000 retail outlets in fiscal 1993, including catalogue and discount retailers, as well as in jewelry and department stores. Gold chains accounted for 44 percent of sales that year. The company's 3,700-odd charms and pendants accounted for another 33 percent, with earrings, rings, bangles, bracelets, and other items responsible for the remainder. Licensors now included General Motors, Warner Bros., and United Features Syndicate (licensors of Muppets and Muppet Babies). In early 1994 the company added a full line of "Barbie for Girls" and "Nostalgic Barbie" items under an exclusive licensing agreement with Mattel Inc. By this time Michael Anthony Jewelers claimed to be the premier licensee of precious-metal jewelry in North America.

At the end of 1993 Michael Anthony Jewelers sold a second offering of 1.6 million shares of common stock at $8 a share, raising $11.7 million after expenses. The Paolercio brothers sold another 200,000 shares apiece. The company earned $5 million on record revenues of $142.8 million in fiscal 1994 and, late in the calendar year, purchased the Mount Vernon quarters it had been leasing.

In 1995, however, shares of stock sank to a level of $3 and under, where they generally stayed through 1997. The company announced plans in December 1995 to purchase up to 750,000 of its shares and by November 1997 had bought a total of 638,000 shares at an average of about $3 a share. The drop in the value of Michael Anthony Jewelers shares reflected investor disappointment in its earnings. During fiscal 1996 (the year ended January 31, 1996), the company reported net income of only $728,000 on net sales of $145.3 million. In fiscal 1997 the results were little better: $1.8 million on revenues of $150.6 million. The long-term debt was $12.9 million in November 1997. In fiscal 1998 revenues dipped to $129.9 million. The company lost $2.6 million after taking a pretax charge of $4.5 million from writedown of inventory.

Michael Anthony Jewelers in 1997

In 1997 Michael Anthony Jewelers was offering a broad selection of handcrafted gold and silver jewelry. Many of its products carried the company's "Ma" trademark. The M.A.J. manufacturing division was manufacturing gold rope chain and gold locks used in the production of rope chain. It was also designing gold tubing and bangle blanks used in the production of bangle bracelets. Another manufacturing division, M.A.E., was making gold earrings and certain findings used to assemble jewelry. The company was also manufacturing a line of men's and ladies' 14-karat gold watches, starting at $499, under the "Michael Anthony" brand name. The America Sapphire Collection included a wide selection of rings, earrings, bracelets, pendants, and necklaces in an array of colors. Prices started at $79.95.

In fiscal 1997 the company manufactured about 95 percent of its products from gold bullion and other raw materials and purchased the rest as semi-finished or finished goods. Casted products accounted for about 44 percent of sales; chains for 43 percent; earrings for five percent; and other items for eight percent.

Sales of licensed products accounted for about 11 percent of net sales in fiscal 1997. Michael Anthony's "character" jewelry consisted of the Cathy, Looney Tunes, Peanuts, and Playboy collections; sports jewelry was divided into the Major League Baseball, National Football League, National Hockey League, National Basketball Association, and Collegiate collec-

tions. The company was now paying a royalty ranging from six to 12 percent on sales of licensed products.

Michael Anthony Jewelers was still marketing and selling its jewelry primarily through its in-house sales force. The company maintained a showroom in Mount Vernon, made direct presentations at customers' locations, and promoted its products through the use of catalogues, advertisements in trade publications, trade-show exhibitions, and cooperative advertising allowances with certain customers. It also began a campaign of advertising in consumer magazines and selling to certain retailers a specially selected and packaged line of gold jewelry, including watches, under the "Michael Anthony" name.

Michael Anthony Jewelers was shipping its products in bulk to wholesale distributors. For certain retail chains, such as Sterling Jewelers, Wal-Mart, J.C. Penney, Zale's, Service Merchandise, and Kmart, the company prepackaged and price-tagged most items, then shipped an order of many different items to distribution centers and stores in the chain. Michael Anthony's two largest customers in fiscal 1997, Sterling and Wal-Mart, accounted for 13 and 12 percent of net sales, respectively. In addition to jewelry chain stores, discount stores, department stores, and wholesalers, the company was selling its products primarily to catalogue retailers and television home-shopping networks.

The Paolercio brothers were still Michael Anthony Jewelers' chief stockholders in May 1997. Anthony Paolercio, Jr., held 15.45 percent of the company's common stock, and Michael Paolercio held 13.55 percent.

Principal Subsidiaries

F & F Acquisitions Corp.; Mount Vernon Distributors, Inc.

Principal Divisions

M.A.J. Manufacturing; M.A.E. Manufacturing.

Further Reading

Breznick, Alan, "Jewelry Maker Shines in Rough Market," *Crain's New York Business,* February 19, 1990, p. 7.

Curan, Catherine M., "Michael Anthony Sells 2-Million-Share Offering," *Women's Wear Daily,* January 10, 1994, p. 15.

"Shares Fall on End of Plan to Merge with Jan Bell," *Wall Street Journal,* August 6, 1991, p. C17.

—Robert Halasz

Monro Muffler Brake, Inc.

200 Hollender Parkway
Rochester, New York 14615
U.S.A.
(716) 647-6400
Fax: (716) 647-0945
Web site: http://www.monro.com

Public Company
Incorporated: 1971
Employees: 2,600
Sales: $154.3 million (1998)
Stock Exchanges: NASDAQ
Ticker Symbol: MNRO
SICs: 7533 Auto Exhaust System Repair Shops; 7539
     Automotive Repair Shops, Not Elsewhere Classified

Monro Muffler Brake, Inc. is one of the largest chains of shops offering undercar services in the United States and the only chain whose stores are 100 percent company-owned and operated. Monro stores are part of the "do-it-for-me" segment of the automotive aftermarket and offer a full range of repair services for muffler, exhaust systems, brake systems, steering and suspension systems, and many vehicle maintenance services. As of April 1998, Monro owned and operated 350 outlets in New York, Pennsylvania, Ohio, Connecticut, Massachusetts, West Virginia, Virginia, Maryland, Vermont, New Hampshire, New Jersey, North Carolina, South Carolina, and Indiana. The announced acquisition in 1998 of Speedy Muffler King's U.S. locations would bring that number to 500. The company serviced approximately 1.42 million vehicles during fiscal 1997.

From Franchise to Private Operation: 1957–71

Cars were sporting big tail fins and Dwight D. Eisenhower was president when Charles J. August opened his first store in 1957, a Midas Muffler franchise in Rochester, New York. It was a novel idea, having a shop that did nothing but install and repair exhaust systems, and August's was the only one in the region. Car owners had either done the work themselves or turned to the mechanic at their neighborhood garage or repair shop when they had trouble with a muffler.

But the concept proved popular, as corrosion and rust meant that exhaust systems and pipes had to be replaced frequently, and August began opening more Midas franchises. In 1959, he incorporated his company. By the mid-1960s August was running four Midas franchises and had expanded into the brake business, building and operating four franchised Nationwide Safety Brake Centers. He thought the brake and muffler combination was a winner, particularly as early exhaust emission control systems lengthened the life of a muffler. August wanted to provide both types of undercar service at the same location, but the Midas organization would not let him use the Midas name. In 1966, August decided to end his affiliation with Midas, and he established his own chain of four Monro Muffler stores, naming the company after Rochester's county, Monroe, but leaving off the "e" to save money on his signs. In 1971, he converted his brake franchises to Monro shops as well and renamed the company Monro Muffler Brake, Inc.

Growing Monro Muffler Brake: 1972–84

August expanded his company gradually, opening about three new stores a year, and by 1977 the chain had 20 locations in the Rochester area. That year, August changed his growth strategy and bought two New York chains. The purchase of Kar Service Centers in Buffalo and Barker Service Centers with locations in Albany and the southern part of New York state doubled the size of Monro Muffler Brake, moved the company into new territory in the western and eastern parts of the state, and established Monro as a major player in the region.

To manage the bigger operation, August instituted several organizational changes. He divided the stores into regions and appointed regional supervisors. He bought his own tractor trailers to deliver parts to the stores and created two new departments: a building and maintenance division and an in-house advertising operation.

Over the next several years, August continued to open new stores, but concentrated on keeping his business up-to-date.

Company Perspectives:

Monro Muffler Brake desires to be America's leading chain of company owned and operated undercar care stores, and to be recognized by consumers, employees, vendors and investors as providing: exceptional value and integrity, friendly and professional service, total customer satisfaction, the industry's best trained employees, unparalleled employee opportunity, win/win vendor partnerships, superior investor return. The company further desires to be the number one choice of consumers, employees and investors by consistently exceeding their respective expectations. These objectives will be achieved through innovation, spirited execution and an unwavering employee commitment to excellence.

Stores received state-of-the art equipment and older locations were remodeled. The auto service business was growing and competition was stiff.

The company's beliefs, codified as "The Monro Doctrine," set it apart from its competitors. August established this ten-point company policy early in Monro's history and did not alter it as the years passed. The policy was the company's pledge to provide each of its customers with: a no-obligation inspection of brakes, shocks, front end and exhaust systems; a review of the inspection with the customer; to sell only needed products and repairs; a free written estimate; customer approval before any other work is performed; a written guarantee of the work and parts; no appointments required; fair and reasonable prices; no advertising gimmicks; and work done by professionally trained specialists. With all the stores being company-owned and operated, it was fairly easy to ensure that each conformed to the company policy.

Monro continued to open a few stores each year. By 1984, the company owned and operated 59 stores, mostly in upstate New York, and had recently moved into a new 90,000-square-foot office and distribution center in anticipation of more growth. Sales for the fiscal year ending March 1984 were approximately $21 million. Monro's growth reflected the growth of automotive specialty services as a whole. While specialty service represented only about 14 percent of the $61 billion automotive service market, with sales of about $8.5 million in 1984, the specialty chains were growing faster than the aftermarket segment as a whole, and had higher profits than others (garages, car dealers, or independent shops) providing tune-ups, transmission work, and muffler or brake repairs.

Expansion required money, however. In July 1984, to raise the capital Monro needed, August sold a controlling interest in the company to an investor group led by Peter J. Solomon and Donald Glickman.

Years of Expansion: 1985–89

Specialty repair shops grew significantly during the last half of the decade, gaining a 40 percent share of the car and truck service market by 1989, up from 20 percent in 1986. Such growth could be attributed to several developments. First, cars were becoming more complex. As a result, fewer people had the technical knowledge or equipment to perform the repairs themselves. Garage owners and independent general repair shops had to invest in training their technicians and in buying diagnostic equipment; many did not and lost business.

Second, car parts were lasting longer. This meant that specialists had to expand into other areas if they were to survive. As they did, they took that business from the garages and auto stores. Tire stores, for example, increasingly widened their undercar services.

Finally, convenience had become an important issue. There were more families with both parents working as well as more single-parent families, and they needed their transportation. The logistics of getting repairs done became more complicated, as consumers wondered who would take the car in and how would that person get to work from the garage and then back to pick up the car after work, as well as who would get the kids to school. These customers found specialty outlets, providing a quick turnaround time, evening and weekend hours, and quality work, very attractive. The fastest-growing service between 1985 and 1990 was the quick lube, offering an affordable oil change in ten to 20 minutes.

In 1987, with the company's annual sales nearing $40 million and a chain of some 90 stores in five states, August was ready to retire. Jack M. Gallagher, a seasoned aftermarket executive, was selected to replace him as president and CEO. The company was looking for someone to manage faster growth. Gallagher had done that with Covairs Auto Parts, transforming a ten-store army surplus chain into a 50-store auto parts operation. Prior to that he had worked for Firestone Tire & Rubber Company, moving from store manager to division manager at headquarters before heading up and turning around Firestone's unprofitable Fidesta division.

As Gallagher explained several years later in a 1994 *Rochester Business Journal* article, "What I did was bring system organization. They had no point-of-sale (inventory system) and the warehouse was a sore spot. They had no financial people, and the cash flow was very, very tight." He also saw some problems with the way Monro made its acquisitions, often not giving enough consideration to marketing opportunities. Gallagher got things organized, computerizing the warehouse and initiating the development of a site-selection computer model.

Going Public and Still Growing: 1990–94

By the end of fiscal 1991, the company had grown to 143 outlets in eight states, with sales of over $60 million. Gallagher took Monro public later that year to raise money for more growth. In what was considered an unusual move for Wall Street investors, the Solomon group did not sell its shares. The offering placed about 30 percent of the company in public hands, with the August family, Solomon and his partners, and Monro employees holding the remaining 70 percent.

The typical Monro Muffler Brake store, with its bright yellow and blue signs, was a free-standing building located near a mall or other high-visibility site in a suburban area. Being near a mall helped address the convenience issue; a customer could drop off the car and get in some shopping while the work was being done, accomplishing two things at the same time. A typical shop's 4,500 square feet provided space for a sales area, a parts storage space, six fully equipped service bays, plus parking.

Thirty-five percent of Monro's service sales were for exhaust work. Brake work accounted for 33 percent of sales, and suspension and alignment work for another 21 percent. State inspections, lube, oil and filter work, and similar miscellaneous services made up the remaining 11 percent.

In 1993, the company formed Monro Service Corporation as a wholly owned subsidiary, responsible for warehousing, purchasing, advertising, accounting, office services, payroll, cash management, and semi-truck maintenance wholly performed within New York state. In 1994, Monro opened its 200th store and moved into its 11th state, New Jersey. It also finalized a deal with the city of Rochester to build a new headquarters and warehouse on a 13-acre site in the Hollender Industrial Park.

A large part of its success, according to the company, was due to the fact that all its stores were company-owned. This allowed for better overall control of programs and policies on everything from how customers were treated to running special promotions.

New Leadership/New Initiatives: 1995–97

In April 1995, Jack Gallagher retired as CEO, retaining a seat on the company's board of directors. Under his leadership, the company had grown from 90 to 232 stores, with sales of $109 million and net profits of $9 million. His successor, Lawrence Day, had joined the company in 1993 as chief operating officer, having moved to Monro from the Auto Express division of Montgomery Ward.

Day began a rapid expansion program, adding over 100 stores in three years. During his first year, Monro acquired five auto repair companies for a total of $2.8 million, adding 14 stores to the chain. The largest of these was the seven-store Muffler Xpress division of North Carolina-based Xpress Automotive Group, Inc. That purchase moved Monro into the southeast region of the United States, with stores in North and South Carolina and Virginia.

Day also introduced several initiatives aimed at reaching customers in new areas and increasing brand recognition by linking up with companies offering complimentary services. To reach customers where the only competition came from small independent garages, Day developed his "small town" concept store. Targeted at towns with a population of 15,000 or fewer, the stores had four or five service bays instead of the typical six bays. The first opened in Saranac Lake, New York, in September 1995, and was followed by several more.

Also in 1995, the company reached an agreement with Q-Lube, a division of Quaker State Corp., to jointly develop sites offering both fast lube and undercar services. After some delay, the first four of these joint operations opened in the spring of 1997.

The company also bought three Goodyear Tire dealers in Pennsylvania. Operated as Monro/Goodyear stores, the outlets offered the full complement of both undercar and tire services of both parties. That experience proved successful in attracting brand-loyal tire customers and led Monro to introduce Bridgestone/Firestone tires at most of its outlets, replacing a private label tire. The company instituted promotional offers with national fast-food, video rental, and gas station chains, as well as with regional supermarkets. It also got the Monro name and blue-and-yellow logo onto the NASCAR circuit as a title sponsor for driver Andy Santerre.

In 1997, Monro went after manufacturers' warranty-required maintenance business. Acknowledging that most new-car owners would still go to their dealers for the services, the company still hoped to reach those who tended to ignore manufacturers' recommendations. Outlets were already offering, and the company promoting, more maintenance services, such as flushing radiators, repairing steering systems, and changing oil. According to the company, unperformed maintenance and repairs exceeded $53 billion in 1996.

To reflect its broader offerings, Monro added the words "& Service" to its corporate logo and to the signage at all its new stores as well as some of the existing shops. Throughout the fiscal year, the company's marketing and advertising focused on informing customers of all the services available from Monro.

1998 and Beyond

In February 1998, Day announced his resignation as president and CEO to become chief operating officer of TBC Corporation, a large marketer and distributor of auto replacement products. Jack Gallagher returned as acting CEO while an executive search was undertaken for a new chief.

In April, the company announced an agreement to acquire the U.S. company-owned and franchised shops of Canadian-based Speedy Muffler King, one of Monro's direct competitors. The purchase involved 205 stores in 11 northeastern States and Washington, D.C., with locations concentrated in the metropolitan areas of Boston, Baltimore, Detroit, Cleveland, and the District of Columbia. The company paid $52 million in cash for the operations and assumed about $6 million of liabilities. When completed in the summer of 1998, the purchase would bring Monro's store base to some 550 locations.

In a very competitive business, the leaders of Monro focused on keeping their existing customers (with a 70 percent return rate) by emphasizing customer service and responsiveness, as well as on attracting more customers by providing more services and developing cross-branding programs. Absorbing some 200 stores from the Speedy Muffler King acquisition would be a formidable task for a CEO familiar with the company. Also throwing one of the company's current initiatives into question was the announcement in April 1998 that Pennzoil planned to spin off its Jiffy Lube into a new consumer products company that would acquire Quaker State and its Q-Lube car centers. Whomever was chosen as Monro's new president and CEO faced these immediate challenges as well as a generally soft market in the auto repair industry, as people bought new cars when the economy was going well rather than keep their old ones.

Principal Subsidiaries

Monro Service Corporation.

Further Reading

Astor, Will, "A Firm Hand on Monro Muffler's Wheel," *Rochester Business Journal,* January 28, 1994, p. 10.

——, "City's Monro Deal Hikes Competition," *Rochester Business Journal,* July 22, 1994, p. 1.

——, "Monro Muffler's Stock Action Increases After CEO Resigns," *Rochester Business Journal,* February 20, 1998, p. 16.

——, "Monro to Bid for Warranty-Maintenance Work," *Rochester Business Journal,* September 5, 1997, p. 3.

Aylward, Larry, "Specialty Service Chains; Automobile Service Centers," *Aftermarket Business,* July 1, 1992, p. 34.

Cosgrove, Michael, "NYC Investor Acquires Monro Muffler Shares," *Rochester Business Journal,* December 11, 1992, p. 3.

"Exhaust & Muffler Service . . . Is There Any Profit in It for the Service Dealer?," *Motor Age,* October 1989, p. 22.

Hamilton, Martha M., "Jiffy Lube, Q-Lube to Merge," *Washington Post,* April 16, 1998, p. E3.

"History and Future of Monro Muffler Brake," Monro Muffler Brake, Inc., http://www.monro.com/history.htm.

Katcher, P. R. N., "The Fragmenting Market; Necessity to Design Market Niche," *Automotive Marketing,* August 1989, p. 115.

Kaufman, Edward L., "Competition Hotter Among Service Retailers for Undercar Business," *Automotive Marketing,* June, 1991, p. 15.

——, "Specialty Service: A Fad or Here to Stay? Implications for the Aftermarket Retailer," *Automotive Marketing,* September 1986, p. 24.

——, "Winners and Losers in the Service Market," *Automotive Marketing,* February 1990, p. 18.

"Monro Muffler Brake: The Way to Success," *Automotive Marketing,* November 1992, p. 58.

Monti, Michael A., Jr., "Aftermarket Parts: Those in This Business Face Serious Survival Challenges," *Automotive News,* November 29, 1989, p. 74.

"1993 Entrepreneur of the Year Awards—Jack Gallagher: Monro Muffler Brake Inc.," *Business First-Buffalo,* June 21, 1993, p. 10B.

Serwer, Andrew Evan, "Companies to Watch," *Fortune,* June 29, 1992, p. 87.

"Speedy Muffler Selling U.S. Stores," *Calgary Herald,* April 14, 1998, p. F11.

—Ellen D. Wernick

MONTEDISON

Montedison S.p.A.

Piazzetta Maurilio Bossi, 3
20121 Milan
Italy
(02) 62701
Fax: (02) 62704610
Web site: http://www.montedison.it/indexgb.htm

Public Company
Incorporated: 1966 as Montecatini Edison S.p.A.
Employees: 27,632
Sales: L23.68 trillion (US$13.3 billion) (1997)
Stock Exchanges: Rome Florence Milan Amsterdam
 Brussels Geneva
SICs: 1311 Crude Petroleum & Natural Gas; 1541
 General Contractors-Industrial Buildings &
 Warehouses; 1542 General Contractors-Non-
 Residential Buildings; 1629 Heavy Construction, Not
 Elsewhere Classified; 2035 Pickled Fruits &
 Vegetables, Salad Dressings, Vegetable Sauces &
 Seasonings; 2046 Wet Corn Milling; 2048 Prepared
 Feeds for Livestock; 2062 Cane Sugar Refining; 2075
 Soybean Oil Mills; 2076 Vegetable Oil Mills, Except
 Corn, Cottonseed & Soybean; 2099 Food
 Preparations, Not Elsewhere Classified; 2819
 Industrial Inorganic Chemicals, Not Elsewhere
 Classified; 2821 Plastics Materials, Nonvulcanizable
 Elastomers & Synthetic Resins; 2834 Pharmaceutical
 Preparations; 4619 Pipelines, Not Elsewhere
 Classified; 4911 Electric Services; 6719 Offices of
 Holding Companies, Not Elsewhere Classified; 8711
 Engineering Services

Montedison S.p.A. is one of the largest industrial holding companies in Italy. The group includes five principal activities: agribusiness, through a 50.4 percent stake in France-based Eridania Béghin-Say S.A., generating 79.1 percent of net revenues; energy, through a 61.3 percent interest in Edison S.p.A., generating 11.2 percent; fluorine-based chemicals and peroxides, through wholly owned Ausimont S.p.A., generating 3.8 percent; engineering and heavy construction, through wholly owned Tecnimont S.p.A., generating 3.5 percent; and pharmaceutical intermediates, through wholly owned Antibioticos S.p.A., generating 2.4 percent. With 194 plants in 21 countries, nearly two-thirds of net revenues originate outside Italy. Montedison is affiliated with Compagnia di Participazioni Assicurative ed Industriali S.p.A. (Compart), which holds a controlling 32 percent stake in Montedison. Compart is the name adopted by Ferruzzi Finanziaria S.p.A. (Ferfin) in the summer of 1996. The combined Ferfin-Montedison empire nearly collapsed in the early 1990s under the weight of massive debt brought on by overly acquisitive management.

Montedison was formed on July 7, 1966, through the merger of Montecatini S.p.A. and Edison S.p.A. Edison had been an electric power utility company that had moved into chemicals, while Montecatini had been a chemical company buying and building power plants. The two had had intertwined histories for years, at times with the same man on both boards coordinating their growth, at other times with nothing in common but rivalry.

Early Histories

Edison had been formed as a power utility in 1884 in Milan. Like nearly all the early electrical companies, it grew quickly and steadily. The long strikes by workers in 1913 and the two world wars barely affected its fortunes. In the 1930s, while the rest of the world was in a depression, Edison began to diversify widely and, in the 1950s, began its acquisition of petrochemical companies. By 1960, Edison was Italy's second largest chemical concern.

Montecatini was formed in 1888 as a pyrite mining business in Tuscany. It was run by the Donegani family, in particular by Guido Donegani, who was made director in 1910. Born in Livorno in 1877, he had studied industrial engineering, and was utterly a man of his time. He served in Parliament in 1921, was vice-president of the Banca Commerciale Italiana at the peak of his business career, and soon became the president of his profession's fascist organization.

Within ten years of taking over as Montecatini's director, Donegani had begun to build the small mining company into a much larger enterprise. While he had some domestic backing from the Banca Commerciale and the Credito Italiano, it was mainly through the heavy funding from four Parisian financial and industrial backers that he was able to involve Montecatini in the production of phosphates, fertilizers, and sulfuric acid. The development of all of Italy's chemical industry at the time depended not only on French financing and sales agreements, but on the colonial ventures in phosphate mining in French Tunisia. Montecatini had one of the main mining contracts there, and built much of its later strength on this early cooperation with the French. At the same time, the Banca Commerciale was investing heavily in public utilities, especially the electric ones such as Edison. One of the bank's managers, Guiseppe Toeplitz, worked closely with the Donegani brothers to arrange Montecatini's monopolization of the fertilizer and sulphates production in Italy. With the Banca Commerciale and Donegani directing the growth of both companies, there was no real competition between them, but the ground was obviously prepared for it to begin whenever the leadership of the companies would be different.

After World War I a second phase of growth began for Montecatini. It branched out into aluminum, purchasing its own sulphur phosphate factories, and gradually took over the country's explosives industry. It built the first synthetic ammonia plant in Italy, and then added marble works. Even so, it was a small company by international standards, its 1928 capital being a little over the equivalent of £1 million.

World War II was more drastic, and reduced the company's installations by a third. Reconstruction led to some managerial changes: in 1945, Guido Donegani had been arrested as a collaborator but, like so many, was freed almost immediately, for "negative evidence." His release caused Montecatini's workers to strike in protest. Though he remained free, he disappeared and, in April 1947, died of heart disease.

By 1948, Montecatini had managed to regain its former size, with 57,000 workers, 110,000 shareholders, and a working capital of 18 million lire. It was mining or producing sulphur, bauxite, marble and granite, lead, zinc, and aluminum. The chemical production had expanded from fertilizers to insecticides, pharmaceuticals, and man-made fibers. The company's own electrical production was 1.3 billion kilowatts, from its eight hydroelectrical and one thermoelectrical plants. New ventures included rope making, packaging, and investment in research. It built Europe's first petrochemical plant, at Ferrara. In one of its research facilities, Professor Giulio Natta created the process for manufacturing isotactic polypropylene, of major importance in the production of thermoplastics. (For this work, he was awarded the Nobel Prize in chemistry in 1963.)

1966 Merger Formed Montedison

By this time, the company had overextended itself. Royal Dutch/Shell became a large investor in Montecatini's petrochemical business, while preparation also had to be made for what seemed to be the inevitable nationalization. The 1966 merger with Edison was partly a result of the difficulties brought to Montecatini by overextending and to Edison by

nationalization. Before the merger, Edison had lost its electrical generating interest to nationalization, and was having trouble getting paid for it. Edison's president, Giorgio Valerio, began negotiating the merger of the two companies, which would compensate for Edison's great losses, in such complete secrecy that even Montecatini's president, Carlo Faina, knew nothing about it. When he was ultimately presented with the finalized merger terms, it was something of a fait accompli, though he did try to turn the tables and suggest that Montecatini take over Edison instead. The battle was loud but ineffectual, and the result, Montedison, was a huge conglomerate centered on chemicals and electricity.

Two years later, the Ente Nazionale Idrocarburi (ENI) acquired an interest in Montedison which, combined with that of Istituto per la Riconstruzione Industriale (IRI), gave the state 18.4 percent of the company. Small shareholders were outraged, claiming the move was "surreptitious nationalization." In the riotous annual meeting of 1969, they stood up, shouted, and threw coins and copies of the annual report at the chair. Despite the noise, the state retained its shares.

Disastrous 1970s

The 1970s brought a disastrous period when the company, under Eugenio Cefis, fell to undeclared bankruptcy. While chairman of Montedison, Cefis was called the most powerful man in Italy, but he had studied at the Modena military academy and seemed to have a greater understanding of politics than of industry. As chairman, he operated from within a personal and highly political clique. At the same time, the government thought that the company could come in handy for a massive job creation scheme in the south of the country, and set up businesses through which it had no hope of making a profit. While the government supported the company's debts, Cefis overextended into numerous other industries, and continued to play political games. In 1974 there was a scandal over his receipt of daily reports from military counterintelligence on politicians and industrialists, among them the prime minister. By then, Montedison's losses were averaging 100,000 million lire per year, but Cefis did not resign for another three years. He was followed by another man not up to the job, a former minister of agriculture, Giuseppi Medici, who resigned in 1980.

The hero of Montedison's survival of this crisis was Mario Schimberni, who became chairman in April 1980. Originally a lecturer in industrial technology, he moved into industry and worked his way up the managerial ranks of Montefibre and Montedison. As soon as he took over the latter, he fired seven senior managers and nearly 100 middle managers, in some cases replacing them with younger people having a more internationalist view of business. When ENI sold its shares in 1981, they were bought by Gemina, putting more of Italy's traditionally powerful businessmen among the shareholders, and giving Schimberni a group of people with whom he could work to manipulate the shareholders' decisions about the company. In a major rationalization program, activities in subsidiaries, particularly Montefibre, were cut back. Montedison's 200 or more companies were then divided into groups based on what they produced, and the workforce was cut from 149,000 to 69,000.

Ferfin Purchased Controlling Stake by 1987

Montedison was once again profitable in 1985 and by 1986 Montedison posted sales of US$10 billion and earnings of US$260 million. By that time, however, Schimberni's ambition had gotten the best of him, as he had begun an acquisition drive in 1984 that would eventually lead to his downfall. To raise money for these purchases, Schimberni issued the equivalent of one billion new Montedison shares from 1984 to 1986. This diluted the position of the company's existing shareholders, including the powerful Italian merchant bank Mediobanca. The bank's chairman, Enrico Cuccia, encouraged Raul Gardini, the head of Italy's huge agro-industrial group, Ferruzzi Finanziaria (Ferfin), to build up a significant stake in Montedison. By March 1987 Ferfin had spent US$1.7 billion to gain a 40 percent interest in Montedison. In late 1987 Cuccia and Gardini joined forces to force Schimberni out as Montedison's chairman. Gardini named himself the new chairman, and Ferfin was now firmly in control of Montedison, creating one of the largest agro-industrial groups in the world.

Unfortunately, the strength gained through the group's size was seriously countered by its financial position that was seriously hampered by immense debt—almost US$9 billion in January 1988. Gardini had made numerous other acquisitions besides that of Montedison since taking over as head of the Ferruzzi family-run Ferfin in 1979 following the death of his father-in-law. Ferfin purchased a controlling stake in France-based sugar and paper conglomerate Béghin-Say S.A., which had been founded in 1821, and acquired CPC International Inc.'s European operations, becoming the largest starch producer in Europe. These purchases were at least synergistic and would eventually become part of Montedison. More troubling were such noncore additions as concrete and cement maker Calcestruzzi (later known as Calcemento), insurance group Fondiaria, a national newspaper, and a television station.

Gardini's downfall was nearly as fast as Schimberni's. In a move designed to cut costs for the debt-laden Ferfin-Montedison group, Gardini in early 1989 formed a chemicals joint venture with ENI called Enimont. But Gardini and managers of the state-owned Enimont clashed over how to run Enimont, and Gardini failed in a 1990 attempt to buy out the government's stake in the venture. In November 1990 Gardini accepted an offer from ENI to buy out Montedison's stake in Enimont for L2.8 trillion (US$2.53 billion). He also at the same time resigned from his positions at both Ferfin and Montedison, apparently because of family squabbling. At Montedison, Giuseppe Garofano succeeded Gardini.

Near Collapse in the Early 1990s

Gardini left quite a mess behind him. Debt for Montedison alone stood at L16.5 trillion (US$11.2 billion) in 1992. The company was also losing huge sums of money in the recessionary early 1990s: L1.68 trillion (US$1.14 billion) in 1992 and L1.34 billion (US$801.6 million) in 1993. Some restructuring of operations and divestments occurred in the early 1990s, but not to significant effect. Montedison had combined its paper operations in Europe with those of James River Corporation into a joint venture called Jamont N.V. in late 1989. Montedison, now viewing paper as a noncore area, sold its 50

percent interest in the venture to James River for US$827 million in late 1991. In 1992 Béghin-Say was merged with Eridania Zuccherifici Nazionali S.p.A. to form Eridania Béghin-Say S.A. (EBS). Eridania's history dated back to the late 19th century; it had been purchased by Ferfin in 1978 and was the beet sugar market leader in Italy in the early 1990s. By 1993 Montedison held a 60 percent interest in EBS, whose operations included sugar and derivatives, starch and derivatives, vegetable oils for industry, animal feeds, and consumer food products. In terms of revenues, EBS was by far Montedison's largest business. During 1993, Montedison sold its pharmaceuticals businesses to the Swedish Kabi-Procordia Group for about L1.9 trillion (US$1.12 billion).

Also in 1993, Montedison and Ferfin came extremely close to declaring bankruptcy, with only the intervention of Italian banks preventing this. As part of one of the largest out-of-court financial restructurings ever, the banks pushed for new leadership at the two companies, and Guido Rossi was named chairman of both while Enrico Bondi became managing director. The banks also agreed to a recovery plan in late 1993 involving rights issues to raise money, delayed payments of loan interest, and divestment of noncore assets. Montedison would focus on three main sectors: agribusiness (Eridania Béghin-Say), chemicals (Montecatini), and energy (Edison).

While this plan was being negotiated, Montedison and Ferfin were figuring prominently in a wide-ranging scandal involving fraud, kickbacks, and political payoffs in Italy. Gardini's activities at Ferfin and Montedison faced intense scrutiny, and the former Montedison chairman committed suicide in July 1993 as investigators closed in. One of the principal accusations was that ENI had been persuaded through bribery to pay an inflated amount in the buyout of Montedison's stake in Enimont. In connection with this and other illegalities, Sergio Cusani, a former financial consultant to Ferfin and Montedison, was found guilty of corruption and false accounting and sentenced to eight years in prison in April 1994. He was also ordered to repay L167.8 billion to Montedison. Also in April 1994 Montedison sued Price Waterhouse Italy for breaching accounting standards as the company's auditor from 1983 through 1992. The suit was settled in late 1996 when Price Waterhouse agreed to pay L31 billion (US$20 million) to Montedison. The effects of the scandal were still being felt in the late 1990s as the U.S. Securities and Exchange Commission filed a civil suit against Montedison in November 1996 accusing the company of falsifying its financial records from 1988 to 1993 to conceal hundreds of millions of dollars in bribes. Even Montedison's once-savior, Schimberni, was caught in the web; he was put under house arrest in December 1993, charged with deception and illicit distribution of dividends during the period of his chairmanship of the company.

Montedison slowly struggled to recover from its financial woes and scandalous past in the mid-1990s. The company was back in the black by 1995. Rossi, having succeeded in keeping Montedison afloat, stepped down as chairman in February 1995 and was replaced by Luigi Lucchini, who was also chairman of a privately held Italian steelmaker. Bondi remained managing director. Also in 1995 a long-planned joint venture with Royal Dutch/Shell finally made its debut. The 50–50 venture, called Montell N.V., joined the two companies' polypropylene and polyethylene operations. Two years later, however, Montedison sold its stake in Montell to Shell for L3.59 trillion.

This and other, smaller divestments cut Montedison's total debt to L3.2 trillion by the end of 1997. By that time, Montedison was 32 percent owned by Compagnia di Participazioni Assicurative ed Industriali S.p.A. (Compart), the new name adopted by Ferfin in the summer of 1996 in order to sever its ties with its scandalous Ferruzzi past. As the end of the millennium approached, Montedison was now primarily in the area of agribusiness, through its 50.4 percent holding in Eridania Béghin-Say. The company's Montecatini chemicals business had been reduced, with the disposition of Montell, to Ausimont, a maker of fluorine-based chemicals and peroxides, and Antibioticos, which made chemicals used in the manufacture of pharmaceuticals. Through Edison, 61.3 percent owned by Montedison, the company continued its participation in the energy sector, specifically the production, transport, and marketing of electricity and natural gas. Another significant Montedison company was Tecnimont, an engineering firm and constructor of industrial, environmental, and infrastructure facilities worldwide. It was in these industries that Montedison was staking its future, having twice in the late 20th century neared bankruptcy.

Principal Subsidiaries

Eridania Béghin-Say S.A. (France; 50.41%); Ausimont S.p.A.; Antibioticos S.p.A.; Syremont S.p.A.; Edison S.p.A. (61.33%); Tecnimont S.p.A.; Iniziativa Edilizia S.p.A.

Further Reading

Amatori, Franco, and Bruno Bezza, *Montecatini, 1888–1966: capitoli di storia di una grande impresa,* Bologna: Societa editrice Il Mulino, 1990, 480 p.

Betts, Paul, "Montedison Restructure Begins to Bear Fruit," *Financial Times,* February 5, 1997, p. 24.

——, "Montell Plastics Deal Confirms Montedison's Recovery," *Financial Times,* September 13, 1997, p. 21.

"ENI Buys Out Montedison Stake in Enimont," *Chemical Marketing Reporter,* November 26, 1990, pp. 3, 11.

"Frazzled: Ferruzzi," *Economist,* July 31, 1993, pp. 58+.

Fuhrman, Peter, "Finance, Italian Style," *Forbes,* May 2, 1998, pp. 38+.

Graham, Robert, "Ex-Montedison Chairman Held by Rome Police," *Financial Times,* December 8, 1993, p. 2.

——, "Italian Banks Agree Plans for Ferruzzi Restructuring," *Financial Times,* October 11, 1993, p. 1.

Haber, Ludwig F., *The Chemical Industry, 1900–1930: International Growth and Technical Change,* Oxford: Clarendon Press, 1971, 452 p.

Hill, Andrew, "Bondi Defends Montedison Structure," *Financial Times,* May 14, 1996, p. 26.

——, "Cusani Gets Eight Years in Jail for Corruption," *Financial Times,* April 30, 1994, p. 2.

——, "Ferfin and Montedison Return to Black," *Financial Times,* September 22, 1995, p. 19.

——, "Ferfin Opts for Simplification," *Financial Times,* October 18, 1994, p. 28.

——, "Montedison's Rehabilitation Moves a Step Further," *Financial Times,* December 2, 1994, p. 24.

——, "Montedison Sues Price Waterhouse for L1,000bn," *Financial Times,* April 19, 1994, p. 23.

——, "No Respite for Shareholders in Ferfin Affair," *Financial Times,* December 14, 1995, p. 22.

——, "Price Waterhouse in Settlement Offer," *Financial Times,* September 26, 1996, p. 22.

——, "Rossi Calls It a Day at Montedison and Ferfin," *Financial Times,* February 21, 1995, p. 27.

Maclead, Alison, "Circling Round the Turnarounders," *Euromoney,* September 1987.

Marchi, Alves, and Roberto Marchionatti, *Montedison, 1966–1989: l'evoluzione di una grande impresa al confine tra pubblico e privato,* Milan: F. Angeli, 1992, 573 p.

Miller, James P., and Martin du Bois, "Montedison, Shell Pact Wins U.S. Approval," *Wall Street Journal,* January 12, 1995, p. A5.

Moody, John, "Death Before Disgrace," *Time,* August 9, 1993, p. 39.

Peruzzi, Cesare, *Il caso Ferruzzi: dai primi miliardi di Serafino al blitz di Gardini sulla Montedison: una dinastia padana alla conquista del mondo,* Milan: Edizioni del Sole 24 ore, 1987, 202 p.

Sesit, Michael R., "Montedison Shareholders' Group Seeks to Split Company," *Wall Street Journal,* May 13, 1996, p. A16B.

Simonian, Haig, "Flagship Struggles to Stay Afloat," *Financial Times,* December 22, 1993, p. 18.

——, "Paying the Price for Never Saying 'No,' " *Financial Times,* June 8, 1993, p. 19.

Solomon, Steven, "The Last Emperor," *Euromoney,* October 1988, pp. 42+.

Taylor, Jeffrey, "Italy's Montedison Is Accused by SEC of Hiding Bribes," *Wall Street Journal,* November 22, 1996, p. A4.

Turani, Giuseppe, *Montedison: il grande saccheggio,* Milan: Arnoldo Mondadori, 1977.

Turani, Giuseppe, and Delfina Rattazzi, *Raul Gardini,* Milan: Rizzoli, 1990, 232 p.

Waddington, Richard, "Italy's Ferruzzi Group Tripped Up by Ambition," *Journal of Commerce,* June 22, 1993, p. 7A.

Webster, Richard A., *Industrial Imperialism in Italy 1908–1915,* Berkeley: University of California Press, 1975.

—updated by David E. Salamie

National Picture & Frame Company

702 Highway 82 West
Greenwood, Mississippi 38930-1910
U.S.A.
(601) 451-4800
Fax: (601) 451-4805
Web site: http://www.nationalpicture.com

Wholly Owned Subsidiary of NPF Holding Corporation
Incorporated: 1964
Employees: 639
Sales: $73.4 million (1997)
SICs: 2499 Wood Products, Not Elsewhere Classified;
3231 Products of Purchased Glass; 3499 Fabricated
Metal Products, Not Elsewhere Classified

National Picture & Frame Company is a major designer, manufacturer, and marketer of a wide variety of low-priced picture frames, framed mirrors, framed art, and other home decor items. Its products are sold primarily through 12,000 major stores in North America. Sales are made only to commercial customers in truckload quantities; no sales are made to individuals or small retail stores. The company has about 200 customers; its biggest customer is Wal-Mart, which accounts for more than one-third of National's sales. Other principal customers include discount stores Target, Caldor, and Kmart; warehouse clubs such as Price/Costco and BJ's; variety stores such as Dollar General, Family Dollar, Michael's, and Fred's; and home centers such as Home Base, Builders' Square, Lowes, and Frank's Nursery and Crafts.

Multiple Owners and Corporate Raids, 1960s–80s

During its earliest years, National changed hands frequently. It was founded as a privately held company by Sydney Harris in 1964, sold to Royal Crown Cola in 1969, and then sold again to DWG Corporation in 1984. Unfortunately, Miami-based DWG was one of many companies in the 1980s that were under control of infamous corporate raider Victor Posner. DWG was one of Posner's key holdings and it suffered mightily during his tenure.

A shareholder suit against Posner revealed that, even though federal injunctions were supposed to limit his actions, he had continued to flagrantly misuse DWG's corporate funds. For example, in 1991 he charged $173,000 in meal expenses (about $474 per day) to DWG. In a five-year period, he received salaries and bonuses of $31 million—more than the company's $26 million in earnings for that time period. At the same time, DWG's creditors went unpaid and employees were under a salary freeze. While many of Posner's companies went bankrupt, DWG did manage to survive. Posner and his son were subsequently barred by a federal court in 1993 from ever again acting as officers or directors of any public company.

The Rescue of National Picture, 1992

National's management fortunately stepped in to buy the company back from DWG in 1992, retaining Jesse Luxton as president. During the next year the new owners decided to offer National's stock to the public. National's management and the investment firm Code, Hennessy & Simmons retained about one-third of the stock in the company and began to develop a broader product line, which led to greatly increased sales. After the buyout, National's revenues grew about 15 percent annually, well above the industry average of five percent. Any damage caused by association with DWG and Posner was soon repaired.

Business Strategy

National has a specific target market for its products: large chain operations that attract customers who are seeking low-priced but attractive home decorating items. Traditionally these have been discount stores, warehouse clubs, and home centers. The company's approach has been to provide ''value and fashion,'' as it repeatedly states in its reports and press releases.

National views its business as having two parts: ''continuity business,'' the day-to-day production of photo frames and other core products; and ''promotional business,'' its excursions into developing new product lines and seeking out new customers. A

Company Perspectives:

National is committed to delivering value and fashion in home decor. The company's value orientation is rooted in low-cost production with a fashion focus to bring product to market quickly with attractive margins for retailers at compelling prices.

---

strong emphasis has been placed on the continuity side of the business. Examples of the promotional side of the business are the acquisition of Universal Cork, Inc., whose corkboard products opened the home improvement and hardware store market to National; and innovative products such as the ''windowpane'' mirror, a 1996 addition to the product line that was a great success. To promote its strategy, in the later 1990s National undertook a major regrouping, in which plant facilities were consolidated and several new key management figures were hired.

National has not developed a market for its products outside of the United States, except for limited dealings with companies such as Zellers in Canada. Nor has it developed manufacturing facilities outside of the United States, even though it could most likely reduce its production costs by doing so. National's management consciously projects the image of being proud to produce its goods in this country.

Chief Products

National is one of the largest domestic manufacturers of picture frames. Its 1996 production reflected the size of the company's operations. During that year, National manufactured 22 million plastic frames, 5.2 million metal frames, and 3.6 million wood frames.

In the mid-1990s National offered a variety of major product categories to its commercial customers, all of them moderately priced. EnviroMold photograph frames were the chief product, making up 28 percent of the total 1996 production. Mirrors made up another 19 percent; wood portrait and wall frames 17 percent; EnviroMold document/wall frames 14 percent; wood and EnviroMold art objects 13 percent; metal promotional photograph frames five percent; and wood photograph frames four percent.

In the second half of the 1990s, National began to target the framed mirrors and framed art market, which it estimated would grow at an annual rate of 20 percent. For example, one of its most popular new items in 1996 was a ''windowpane'' mirror, a rectangular mirror with a wooden frame and dividing grids that resembled an old-fashioned windowpane. National's ''Art Fair'' line of framed art in various sizes and colors also was introduced successfully in 1996.

National planned to introduce additional items that had the popular ''country'' look. After its acquisition of Universal Cork in 1996, National also hoped to develop a core product line of framed cork boards and similar items that could expand its market into home improvement and hardware stores. An un-

usual new product introduced in 1996 was the ''Enviro-Pasta'' frame.

Competition Within the Industry

The market for picture frames and framed mirrors and art was highly competitive during the 1990s, dominated by a few large companies, such as Intercraft (a subsidiary of Newell Company) and National itself. National manufactured almost all of its products within the United States, and made a point of prominently displaying ''Made in U.S.A'' on each item (and even on the cover of its annual report). However, many of its competitors moved operations to other countries where labor costs were lower. National, instead, continued to rely on its products' low cost and high quality, plus its reputation for good customer service, to offset its competitors' advantage in labor costs.

Even during the recession of the early 1990s, manufacturers of value-priced frames found a huge market for their products in discount department stores, as well as craft stores, drug stores, and warehouse clubs. The key to success was to produce products with high-fashion appearance, but at budget prices. As National's president Luxton declared in 1991, ''There is no difference in the taste level of a person who shops at Kmart and the person at Macy's. The only difference is the pocketbook.''

Whether or not Luxton's aesthetic judgment was correct, value-priced products continued to be extremely popular. Companies that offered unique but low-priced items, such as ''gold''-embossed frames and National's highly successful windowpane mirrors, continued to grow. Consumers with limited decorating budgets found that they could change a room's look by adding an attractive but inexpensive frame or mirror. In 1995, National also tested Luxton's theory about the taste of Macy's customers, by introducing the Martin Holan line of frames. These items were marketed to a new clientele for National, major department stores. In addition to Macy's, National's initial customers for this product line included other upscale stores such as Eddie Bauer, as well as major moderate-price stores such as Pier 1 and Bed, Bath & Beyond.

Technological Developments

In the mid-1990s National placed an emphasis on manufacturing technology that would allow it to be flexible in addressing customer needs and tapping into new market trends (such as the growth in art print sales). New multi-step ovens were installed that allowed wood frame and mirror moldings to be completed more quickly in one continuous process. National also initiated its own extruding processes for plastic frame production. Management estimated that this inhouse operation saved 40 to 50 percent over the cost of moldings purchased from outside manufacturers. A process also was developed for recycling polystyrene residue that was left over after frame moldings were fit together. This material had been discarded in the past because the residue particles were too small to reprocess. With the new process, almost all of the residue could be recycled.

In 1994 National installed an integrated computerized system, which it used for scheduling, distribution, and purchasing.

Software allowed the company to track orders, to forecast demand for labor and materials, and to manage inventory. Radio frequency was utilized to track the movement of items through the production process, by scanning their bar codes and reporting their location.

Financial Performance in the 1990s

After the leveraged buyout from DWG by management in 1992, National's revenues grew at an average of 15 percent annually, triple the industry average. Its debt level fell from $19.3 million in 1993 to $6.7 million in 1996. Sales rose from $31.3 million in fiscal 1992 (just prior to the buyout) to $60.8 million in fiscal 1995. Fiscal 1996 brought National's best year ever, with sales of almost $67.2 million. During the same five-year period, National's net income more than doubled, from $2.3 million in fiscal 1992 to almost $5.1 million in fiscal 1996.

In comparison, some of National's competitors lost money or barely broke even during the mid-1990s and later 1990s. One industry analyst, George K. Baum & Company, attributed National's success to the cost savings of more than 25 percent in plastic frame production, resulting from its inhouse use of an extrusion process.

Major Acquisitions of the 1990s

In 1996 National acquired Universal Cork, Inc., a 20-year-old company that produced cork boards, dry-erase boards, and blackboards, for $2.4 million. Like National, Universal also was a supplier of low-cost products. This acquisition allowed National to enter the market for a new medium—cork—and to draw on Universal's existing customer base of home improvement and hardware stores, a new customer base for National.

National planned to integrate Universal's operations into its existing wood product facilities in Greenwood, Mississippi. Universal's peak sales periods for bulletin boards and blackboards (the back-to-school months of late summer) were traditionally slow months for National sales; and National's peak months for home decor items (fall and holiday seasons) were slow months for Universal sales. Combining the two operations into one facility, National's management reasoned, would allow it to use its manufacturing facilities much more efficiently.

Management Reconfigured in Mid-1990s

In 1995 and 1996 National made major reconfigurations in its management. While most key officers were retained, including president and CEO Luxton, many new faces appeared. CFO M. Wesley Jordan, Jr., was hired to restructure banking arrangements and save money on workers compensation by improving risk management. The new manager of plastics operations, John Barlow, was an expert in polymers. New materials manager Tom Walburgh's mission was to reduce inventory and also reduce the need for outside financing. And Chuck Polandick was hired as director of marketing and product development, based on his experience in designing mass-market decorator products and his ability to bring them to market quickly.

National Sold Again in 1997

In May 1997 National entered into an agreement to be acquired by Colonnade Capital, a privately held investment firm in Richmond, Virginia. Under the agreement, Colonnade would buy all of National's outstanding stock, at an estimated cost of over $67 million. Colonnade was known as the initiator of friendly buyouts of various manufacturers, consumer product companies, and printing companies. Its policy was to buy companies with growth potential, retain existing management, and provide additional capital and staff. National continued to operate under the Colonnade umbrella as a wholly owned subsidiary of NPF Holding Corporation. For fiscal 1997 it reported net income of $5.7 million on sales topping $73 million. Steady financial growth and continued enhancement of its reputation as a frame manufacturer seemed to be its course for the future.

Further Reading

"Frames Capture High-Ticket, Value Image," *Discount Store News*, March 7, 1994, p. 37.

"Future of Greenwood Company Looks Good Enough to Frame," *Mississippi Business Journal*, December 9, 1996, p. 26.

George K. Baum & Co., "Equity Research Company Report," Kansas City, MO: February 15, 1996.

Goldbogen, Jessica, "Mass Frame Deal; Investment Firm to Buy National Picture," *HFN* [*Home Furnishing Network*], June 9, 1997, p. 51.

"Greenwood Company 'Picture Perfect,' Say Analysts," *Mississippi Business Journal*, June 26, 1995, p. 1.

"National Picture & Frame Reports Fiscal Year Earnings Twelve Percent Above Prior Year," *Business Wire*, June 17, 1997.

"Picture Frame Sales Growing," *Discount Store News*, February 18, 1991, p. 33.

"A Picture Perfect Pact for Zellers," *Discount Store News*, May 2, 1994, p. 41.

"Unchained Company Free to Grow," *Clarion-Ledger* (Jackson, MS), July 24, 1994, p. C1.

Walsh, Sharon, "Posner, Son Barred From Running Firms," *Washington Post*, December 2, 1993, p. B11.

—Gerry Azzata

Navarre Corporation

7900 49th Avenue North
New Hope, Minnesota 55428
U.S.A.
(612) 535-8333
(800) 728-4000
Fax: (612) 533-2156
Web site: http://www.navarre.com

Public Company
Incorporated: 1983
Employees: 239
Sales: $196.65 million (1998)
Stock Exchanges: NASDAQ
Ticker Symbol: NAVR
SICs: 5045 Software, Computer: Wholesale; 5099
    Compact Discs: Wholesale, Tapes & Cassettes,
    Prerecorded: Wholesale; 5734 Computer Software;
    7372 Software, Computer: Prepackaged

Navarre Corporation is one of the largest independent distributors of compact discs, cassettes, and computer software in the United States. Some of the company's business consists of rackjobbing, or placing and maintaining displays of its products in stores, which share in the profits. The company also wholesales directly to retailers. Navarre has exclusive distribution of the music products of more than 30 independent record companies, while it also distributes products from all of the major labels. Navarre subsidiary Digital Entertainment, Inc. produces and markets multimedia CD-ROMs, while the Net Radio Network subsidiary broadcasts more than 150 channels of music and information programming over the Internet, and sells compact discs directly to listeners.

Founded in 1983

Navarre began operations in 1983, when Eric Paulson founded the company. Paulson had worked since the 1960s for Pickwick International and had risen to the position of senior vice-president and general manager. Pickwick was one of the largest rackjobbers and distributors of its time, and also was known for its many "supermarket albums." These widely distributed, budget-priced lps frequently consisted of cheaply licensed early recordings by such then current stars as Simon and Garfunkel or Ray Charles, packaged to suggest that they were actually new releases. Paulson started Navarre with the concept that it would sell both record albums and computer software, because of the two products' complementary sales cycles (record sales peaked before Christmas, while software sales took off after that point), and within two years the company had become the third largest rackjobber of computer software in the United States, and the largest distributor of independent-label records and tapes in its home base of Minneapolis-St. Paul, Minnesota. Paulson took pride in his new company carrying the Pickwick banner, both in its field of rackjobbing and for the fact that Navarre had hired more than half of its workforce from Pickwick, which had fallen on hard times by the early 1980s, when most of its assets were sold to rival Handleman Co. of Troy, Michigan. Paulson also took pride in the company's use of sophisticated computer inventory control and billing systems, which he claimed to be the best in the industry. Because the profit margin on computer software was typically low, such systems were important in helping to contain costs.

During the 1980s the company grew steadily, with annual sales, according to Paulson, rising from about $8 million in the first year to around $40 million by 1989. The company's clients for computer software rackjobbing by this time included the largest chain of computer stores in the U.S., Computerland, as well as the Dayton Hudson department store chain, Best Buy, and others. Typically, Navarre would place software racks in stores which concentrated on sales of other types of products, and had little extra time or energy to manage sales of software. Navarre sent salespeople out to restock and keep track of what was selling, taking care of advertising and other marketing decisions for the retailer. Store managers reported that sales of software often increased dramatically after Navarre took over, and were pleased by the additional foot traffic the displays attracted. While 60 percent of the company's revenues came from its software sales, Navarre also continued to distribute music products on a regional basis.

1990: Navarre Acquired by Lieberman Enterprises

In early 1990, Minneapolis-based Lieberman Enterprises, a recently acquired unit of LIVE Entertainment Inc., completed purchase of Navarre from founder Paulson and several partners, merging Navarre's Computer Products division into Lieberman. Lieberman, the United States' second largest distributor of music products, videocassettes, and software, made Paulson executive vice-president and chief operating officer. Though the purchase looked like a good one for all concerned at the time, following a change of leadership LIVE Entertainment decided to concentrate on the motion picture business, and sold money-losing Lieberman to the Handleman Co. in late 1991, with Paulson and his partners reacquiring Navarre soon after. They had in fact sued Lieberman in 1990 for allegedly breaching "an implied covenant of good faith . . . by taking actions designed to prevent [Navarre] from realizing the benefits of the contract," according to *Billboard* magazine.

Back in control, Paulson immediately began rebuilding Navarre into the company he had originally envisioned. He quickly reestablished relationships with executives of the six major record labels, and opened several regional branch offices to oversee the company's operations in different areas of the country. Navarre reactivated its Computer Products division, which soon began aggressively expanding, with business software and CD-ROMs key new elements of the mix. Strong relationships with such retailers as Best Buy were established, with products coming from such vendors as Sierra On-Line, Broderbund, Warner NewMedia, and Sony Electronic Publishing. Navarre also sought to introduce software products, such as mid-priced CD-ROM computer games, into nonsoftware chains like MusicLand and Kaybee Toy stores. Not unlike predecessor Pickwick, some titles, such as those published by Minneapolis company LaserSoft, were repackaged versions of slightly older releases, sold at a budget price, while others were still cheaper clearance items.

1993: Navarre Begins Publishing, and Goes Public

In late 1993 Navarre announced that it would begin to manufacture software products, typically licensed copies of educational or entertainment programs, and market them alongside the outside vendors' products that it already distributed. Additional software products were to be created in conjunction with other companies, but not published directly by Navarre. This new tack was also being taken by several of Navarre's competitors, such as Handleman and Slash Corp. A major motivating factor was the low profit margin on the products it distributed, which could be increased if Navarre acted as both middleman and originator. By late 1993, the company's soft-

ware business had risen to over 37 percent of total sales, up from 21 percent the year before. Music sales constituted the largest portion of the company's business, with wholesale distribution to the then popular membership warehouse clubs particularly strong at this time. Annual sales for the 1992 fiscal year reportedly had totaled $42.1 million, slightly above the peak of $40 million claimed pre-Lieberman.

In December 1993, the company announced its Initial Public Offering of stock on the NASDAQ exchange. CEO Paulson, the majority owner, sold off a portion of his two-thirds ownership, retaining about 40 percent of the company. The stock offering was not entirely successful, with a fifth of the shares originally offered withdrawn after they went unsold. Six months after going public, Navarre announced the formation of a subsidiary, Digital Entertainment, a joint venture with another Minnesota company, Digital Café. The initial goal of Digital Entertainment was to create multimedia CD-ROMs which integrated music recordings by nationally known artists with video footage and interactive capabilities. Releases would be distributed exclusively by Navarre. The first title to be published was entitled *Backstage with John Tesh,* and featured music, interviews, images of sheet music, and interactive features such as the capability to remix the sound. The disc was made available in both Macintosh and IBM formats, and had a list price of about $40. This release followed shortly on the heels of a successful, exclusive agreement with BMG to distribute a similarly interactive CD, David Bowie's *Jump.* Integrating music and computer software had long been a goal of Navarre founder Eric Paulson, and Digital Entertainment was a culmination of that dream, as well as a new direction for the company, which could augment Navarre's primary business of distribution.

In late 1994 Navarre also consolidated its operations, moving from several different locations to a single facility in New Hope, Minnesota, a suburb of Minneapolis. The new 100,000-square-foot building housed the company's corporate offices, two specialized conference rooms, and the product distribution center. New state-of-the-art computer product movement systems were in place. Annual sales for the fiscal year ending in March 1995 totaled $119.5 million, up 73 percent from the $68.9 million of the previous year, and net income increased over this period by almost 400 percent. During this time the company's sales of music products was still the leading source of revenue, but computer software was gaining. The company continued to sign exclusive distribution contracts with independent record companies, and in September 1995 reached an agreement to market CD-ROMs in selected Blockbuster Music stores. Early 1996 saw similar agreements signed with national music chain Tower Records and The Good Guys!, a West Coast electronics store chain.

1996: Navarre Invests in Net Radio; Stock Frenzy Follows

In May 1996 Navarre announced that it had purchased a 50 percent stake in Net Radio, a small operation which broadcast music and informational audio programming over the Internet, and was considered a "hot" web site, with some 10 million monthly log-ins by users. Navarre planned to sell advertising to record companies and retailers, and presumably take advantage of the opportunity to promote specific artists by programming their recordings, something that was much more difficult to assure on commercial radio stations. Though the operation was not expected to generate any immediate revenue for Navarre, the stock market's fascination with all things Internet at the time caused a surprising amount of attention to be focused on Navarre and Net Radio. Within a few weeks, the price of a share had risen from under $10 to almost $30. Several large Navarre stockholders, including founder and CEO Paulson, made huge profits by selling small chunks of their holdings. Within a short period of time, the price dropped back to under $20. This had all taken place despite the closing figures of the 1996 fiscal year, announced in March, that Navarre's earnings had declined from 1995, with music sales off by 20 percent, although software profits were up, eclipsing music for the first time as the largest revenue source.

Other developments in 1996 included the purchase of Hawaii's largest record distribution company, and the signing of an exclusive distribution agreement with Velvel Records, a new label founded by former CBS Records chief Walter Yetnikoff. Navarre committed itself to provide funding, marketing, promotion, and creative support to the label, the first time it had invested in a record company. Navarre had exclusive distribution agreements with close to 30 other labels at this point as well. The Digital Entertainment subsidiary was also active, releasing several new titles, including interactive sports and educational CD-ROMs.

1997: Restructuring As Music Sales Continue to Slip

Although it had seemingly set its ducks in a row and appeared poised for even greater success than before, another disappointing year in the music industry led Navarre to take a drastic hit in profits for the fiscal year ending in March 1997. Despite an overall sales increase of 26 percent, the company reported losses of $6.2 million, which it blamed on the low margins earned on sales of computer CD-ROMs, and a significant write-down on its investment in Velvel Records. Paulson had earlier stated on several occasions that Navarre would never let either music or software products exceed 60 percent of total revenues, but in fiscal 1997 software accounted for more than 70 percent of sales. Shortly after the unhappy financial report, Navarre announced plans for restructuring, which included a new five-year strategic plan, the departure of the head of the company's Music Products division, a reduction of sales regions from four to three, increased cooperation between sales offices, the company, and retailers, and an increased emphasis on "alternative marketing," including selling through mass merchants and via television shopping channels. At the company's annual employee meeting in July, CEO Paulson took pains to explain the problems Navarre was facing in its Music Products division, and, in a symbolic gesture, issued five shares of stock to each employee to convey to them the stake they had in returning Navarre to profitability.

Apparently, these measures were not deemed strong enough medicine, as the company announced a second restructuring in September. This time, regional distribution territories were reduced from three to two, and additional employees were terminated or moved to different jobs. At the same time that music sales continued to slump, several of Navarre's major retail accounts and music vendors had filed for bankruptcy, further reducing revenues. The company also restructured its lineup of record labels, dropping several lower quality ones, and signing new agreements with others. A lawsuit was initiated in December 1997 against CD-ROM vendor Broderbund, which was refusing to take returns on unsold products. The vendor countersued for payment for the discs. The CD-ROM market had suffered several years earlier from a glut of substandard computer games, and some companies had faced large returns as consumers reacted by keeping their cash in their wallets.

Navarre's efforts to tighten up its operation paid off; year-end results reported in March 1998 showed the company with a loss of only about a million dollars for the period, despite slightly smaller gross revenues, and an improving percentage of sales from music. Although the company was still not realizing a profit from the Net Radio Network, the now wholly owned subsidiary's web site had increased in traffic to over three million monthly "hits," and was now offering over 150 channels of original music, sports, and news programming available in the RealAudio format. The site had won several awards, and Navarre touted it as "the premier provider of real-time digital media on the Internet." Net Radio began selling music directly over the Web beginning in mid-1998, with a catalog of some 250,000 titles advertised. Despite the improving financial outlook, Navarre decided that it still needed an infusion of cash, and in April 1998 was granted the right by NASDAQ to privately sell $20 million worth of stock to a group of investors.

After suffering disappointing results several years running, Navarre appeared to be meeting the challenges posed by the downturn in sales in its Music Products division, and the company's restructuring and other changes were beginning to pay off. The Computer Products division and the Digital Entertainment subsidiary continued on track, although the future of Net Radio was still uncertain. The company had nonetheless shown that it was capable of adapting to the challenges it faced, and continued to stand its ground while others in the sometimes volatile music, software, and Internet businesses gave way.

Principal Subsidiaries

Digital Entertainment, Inc.; Net Radio Network.

Principal Divisions

Music Products; Computer Products.

Further Reading

Alexander, Steve, "Navarre Corp. Plans Overhaul—New Hope Music Distributor Attempts to Reverse Decline," *Minneapolis-St. Paul Star-Tribune*, July 1, 1997, p. 1D.

Apgar, Sally, "Navarre Corp. Stock Takes Wild 10-Day Rollercoaster Ride—Stake in Netradio Leads Swing," *Minneapolis-St. Paul Star-Tribune*, May 25, 1996, p. 1D.

Berry, Kate, "The New America: Navarre Corp. (Looking for a Surge from Internet Wave)," *Investor's Business Daily*, June 12, 1996, p. A4.

Christmann, Ed, "Navarre Restructures Its Music Operations," *Billboard*, July 12, 1997, p. 10.

"C'Land Signs Navarre As Exclusive Rack Jobber for Select Software, Accessories," *Computer Retail Week*, April 10, 1989, p. 62.

"Distributor Dossier: Navarre Corp.," *Computer Retail Week*, April 5, 1993, p. 57.

Fink, Laurie, "Navarre Corp. Racks Up Sales in Computer Software Market," *Minneapolis-St. Paul CityBusiness*, May 15, 1989, p. 14.

Gillen, Marilyn, "Navarre Builds Biz with Sound and Vision: 10-Year Plan Established It As Leader in Multimedia," *Billboard*, November 5, 1994, p. 96.

——, "New Firm Marks Navarre's CD-ROM Bid," *Billboard*, June 25, 1994, p. 90.

Gross, Steve, "Software Distributor's Margins Are Thin As the Disks He Handles," *Minneapolis-St. Paul Star-Tribune*, July 3, 1986, p. 1M.

Hedlund, Kristen, "Navarre Assists Hardware Dealers Recoup Software Sales—Minnesota Distributor Offers Resellers 'Rack-Checking' Services," *Computer Reseller News*, November 7, 1988, p. 98.

Jeffrey, Don, "Navarre Corp. Plans Its Initial Public Offering," *Billboard*, December 11, 1993, p. 110.

Karvetski, Kerstin, "Navarre, Kaybee Toy with Software," *Computer Retail Week*, May 3, 1993, p. 36.

——, "Navarre, the Publisher," *Computer Retail Week*, November 15, 1993, p. 9.

Lewis, Matthew, "Local Distributor May Top the Charts with Polygram Records," *Minneapolis-St. Paul CityBusiness*, July 31, 1985, p. 10.

Morris, Chris, "Navarre Again Reinvents Music Distribution Arm," *Billboard*, September 20, 1997, p. 8.

——, "Navarre Braces Itself for the Future at Sales Meet," *Billboard*, August 9, 1997, p. 45.

"Navarre Adds CD-ROMs to Mix," *Computer Retail Week*, May 3, 1993, p. 52.

"Navarre Files Suit Vs. Broderbund Over Returned Pdts.," *Dow Jones News Service*, December 2, 1997.

Paige, Paul, "Navarre Management Buys Firm Back from Lieberman," *Billboard*, October 19, 1991, p. 5.

Sandler, Adam, "Velvel Sets Distrib," *Daily Variety*, September 4, 1996, p. 7.

Schafer, Lee, "Now Here's a Story (Stock)," *Corporate Report Minnesota*, September 1, 1996, p. 8.

Waters, Jennifer, "Navarre Makes Medley of Music, Computers," *Minneapolis-St. Paul CityBusiness*, November 4, 1994, p. 4.

—Frank Uhle

NFO Worldwide, Inc.

2 Pickwick Plaza
Greenwich, Connecticut 06830
U.S.A.
(203) 629-8888
Fax: (203) 629-8885
Web site: http://www.nfor.com

Public Company
Incorporated: 1991 as NFO Research, Inc.
Employees: 6,000
Sales: $190.2 million (1997)
Stock Exchanges: New York
Ticker Symbol: NFO
SICs: 8732 Commercial Nonphysical Research; 8999
   Services, Not Elsewhere Classified

NFO Worldwide, Inc. is the largest custom market-research firm in the United States and the ninth largest marketing research organization in the world. The company was founded in Toledo, Ohio, by Howard Trumbull in 1946 as National Family Opinion, a private market-research company. Sold to London-based AGB in 1982 and—as part of AGB—to British publishing mogul Robert Maxwell in 1988, the company bought itself back in 1991 and was incorporated as NFO Research, Inc. In 1993 the company went public and was listed on the NASDAQ; in 1997 NFO began trading its shares on the New York Stock Exchange. The company, renamed NFO Worldwide, Inc., premiered panel research and is now the world's largest panel-based research firm. It is a leading provider of custom and syndicated marketing information to the largest companies in the United States and to the international business community. Through its pre-recruited consumer panel and other specialized databases, NFO offers access to more than 550,000 U.S. households (over 1.4 million people) and some 100,000 European households. With operations in 24 countries around the world, NFO uses its market-research expertise, extensive consumer panels, and niche-market knowledge to provide market insight and marketing counsel to over 2,300 clients in key market segments. These clients include 44 of the largest *Fortune* 500 companies, 23 of the top 25 U.S. bankholding companies, 18 of the nation's 20 largest pharmaceutical firms, most of the top U.S. manufacturers of packaged goods, high technology businesses, healthcare companies, leisure and travel firms, and telecommunications companies. In 1997, for the second consecutive year, *Forbes Magazine* named NFO Worldwide to its list of the 200 Best Small Companies in America.

The Early Years: 1946–64

When the austere days of World War II came to an end, Americans began to spend their wartime savings for the new products and conveniences rapidly showing up in a booming economy. Howard Trumbull, a Toledo, Ohio, salesman of assorted glass containers for Owens-Illinois, Inc., realized that consumers had to choose from an increasing variety of brands; furthermore, manufacturers needed to understand consumer needs and preferences. In 1937 Howard tested this insight at Owens-Illinois by introducing a radical method of market research: he organized a panel of 500 families to give their opinions on each of the company's glass products. According to Leil Lowndes's *The NFO Story*, Howard's "Homemakers Guild," as he called the world's first consumer panel, "premiered the concept of 'quota sampling,' by surveying a panel of people demographically matching the U.S. population to forecast the behavior of the population as a whole." Previously, almost all market research had been done by universities that based their results on very expensive samples of probabilities. Howard's research gave the company a marketing tool for convincing customers of the value and use of its products.

Howard, however, envisioned a still more effective application for market research. Convinced that his "quota" concept was more reliable than "random probability" sampling, he thought that consumer panels could help manufacturers not only to sell their products but also to improve them and design new ones in accordance with consumers' expressed wishes. Consequently, in 1946, Howard, Clara (his wife), and Jack (his son) invested their savings to set up a market-research company, National Family Opinion (NFO). An initial background survey was mailed to 18,000 families. An unheard of 40 percent return rate allowed the Trumbulls to set up a panel of 1,000 families representing the nation by geographic division, population density, age, and income.

Howard created benefits, salary guarantees, and hospitalization plans for his employees, and instilled in the company his ethics of complete confidentiality. Furthermore, Howard realized that "the lady of the house" would be the one to answer, or put aside, NFO panel surveys. Using the pseudonym Carol Adams, Clara dealt with panelists, sent out newsletters and "woman-talked" the company into critical mass; astonishingly, returns from surveys often reached 98 percent. While Carol Adams earned the respect and loyalty of panelists, Howard won contracts from some of America's largest businesses. By the late 1950s, NFO had 15 panels of 75,000 families, was billing almost $800,000 a year, and was ready for new ventures. By 1964 NFO had 30 panels consisting of 85,000 families, almost $2 million in billings, and profits of $131,000. Howard retired and son Jack Trumbull took over the presidency of the company.

The Middle Years: 1965–81

To beat the competition for new clients, Jack took to the air. Within a few hours, instead of days, he flew to old and prospective clients to offer first-person service. His tireless investment of energy paid off—major companies joined the roster of loyal NFO clients. Furthermore, a new product developed from a survey conducted for the Conference Board of New York; in the survey NFO panelists gave their opinions about various issues facing the U.S. public. This project evolved into a monthly report called *The Consumer Confidence Survey*. In 1990 the U.S. Department of Commerce referred to the survey as the *Consumer Confidence Index*, a leading economic indicator of the U.S. economy. In 1968 six companies chose NFO to operate the largest job in its history and one of its first syndicated studies, titled the "Consumer Purchase Panel Study."

Over the years NFO moved from recording survey answers on handwritten cards to storing consumer data in a Honeywell computer. In 1970, to avoid the threat caused by the postal workers' strike to its mail-dependent business, NFO used tele-

phone interviewing to stay in contact with its 55 panels. The emergency measure became a permanent feature of the company's operation. In the meantime Jack lured his son-in-law, Bill Lipner—a record-breaking salesman at Honeywell—to join NFO. By 1978 Bill was vice-president of marketing and was leading the company into new technology, including a PBX phone system and the installation of computer terminals.

NFO revenues amounted to $10 million in 1980, $14 million in 1981, and more than $18 million in 1982. The rapid growth of the company, however, had triggered debt. Jack had led NFO for 39 years and thought the time had come for new leadership and new ownership. Sir Bernard Audley, head of London-based AGB, one of the three largest market research companies in the world, had frequently indicated a desire to buy NFO. Jack Trumbull, assured that AGB would provide NFO with the financial expertise and help needed for its development, retired in 1982 after selling the family company to Bernard Audley.

Rise and Fall of Foreign Ownership: 1982–91

The first change that Bernard Audley made was to promote Bill Lipner to president/CEO. From the start, both leaders recognized the complementary strengths of their respective companies. AGB, present in all the major European countries, Australia, and New Zealand, opened up international markets for NFO and brought improvements and substantial financial expertise to the U.S. company. NFO, on the other hand, was a steadily growing business, had the potential to be very profitable, operated with a first-rate professional staff, was relatively free from debt, and had an impressive list of loyal blue-chip clients. NFO exported new research technologies and techniques to AGB. Bill and his team were receptive to AGB's disciplined financial management and streamlined NFO's operations. By 1987 NFO had less than 15 percent of AGB's total employees but produced more than 50 percent of the London company's worldwide operating income.

NFO continued to explore applications of new technology. Substantial enhancements were brought to computer and mail operations, and a computer-assisted telephone interviewing (CATI) system was installed. NFO, one of the first firms to use VCRs for market research, began to test the effectiveness of clients' television commercials by sending videotapes to panelists with VCRs. This experiment evolved into a continuing NFO project later called "Screen-Test." NFO also was the first to develop surveys of telephone Yellow Pages as an advertising medium. Soon after the 1984 deregulation of the telephone industry, the newly formed telephone companies competed aggressively for usage and advertisers. NFO entered the fray by offering the National Yellow Pages Monitor (NYPM), by which the success of the Yellow Pages as an advertising medium was rated from user surveys. NYPM became—and remained—"the leading provider of syndicated audience measurement and information for the entire Yellow Pages $10-billion industry," according to *The NFO Story*. In addition to this NYPM subscription service, NFO inaugurated a service called Active Intermedia Measurement (AIM), which could determine the influence exerted by newspapers, magazines, catalogs, radio, TV—and even coupons—on consumers' decisions.

For a while the partnership was good for both companies. However, AGB's attempt to improve television rating in the

United States slowly clouded the corporate climate. AGB was the premier television-rating service in 14 countries, most of which were in Europe. The British firm wanted to crack the U.S. market for television rating by providing more accurate results than those obtained by the Nielson diary method then in use. AGB distributed ''people meters'' by which individual family members could record the names of the programs they were watching. Telephone lines then brought the information to AGB's central computer bank in Maryland.

AGB, however, had underestimated the difficulty and expense of applying its rating method to U.S. television viewers. For instance, wiring and servicing an adequate number of American households was an appalling task; America had more TV channels than other countries and required more tracking of data over a wide geographic expanse. Soon, AGB was losing over a million dollars a month. Eventually, NFO profits could not make up for AGB's losses and Bernard Audley was forced to sell. In 1988 Robert Maxwell, chairman of London-based Maxwell Communications, bought AGB—and NFO.

Maxwell carefully watched the bottom line. Bill Lipner and his team managed to lead the company through a freeze on hiring and capital resources—without missing a deadline. NFO continued to honor its commitments and even won important new clients. In 1989 the company created ''Nuestra Familia Opina,'' a Hispanic panel designed to reflect the needs, values, attitudes, and past consumer experiences of one of the fastest market segments in the United States. Clients reacted well to marketing research among the Hispanic Panel; each year brought a growing number of studies.

In July 1991, when London's *Financial Times* began to investigate Maxwell's financial position, it became obvious that the whole conglomerate was going downhill. When Maxwell, trying to get out of his financial difficulties, offered Bill Lipner the position of heading the American operation, Bill thanked him for the honor and said ''I want my *family business* back.'' Bill negotiated Maxwell's asking price of $100 million down to $34 million, but the wily British financier stipulated payment in cash within 21 days. Bill and a group of investors met the deadline: on September 21, 1991, NFO was again privately owned and independent.

U.S., Public, Global Company: 1991 and Beyond

After a decade of British ownership, NFO's first full year of operation as an independent American company foreshadowed the worldwide triumphs in store for the once relatively obscure Ohio company. NFO achieved its targets and invested its profits in itself. Bill and his team designed research methods based on new technology, and devised new ways of giving clients better service. The operations department created new graphics and software programs, including a program that reduced a major client's tabulation time from 16 days to three. Spurred by a newfound possibility of unleashing their creativity, a group of euphoric employees began to test more effective methods for recruiting panelists and improving the quality and consistency of questionnaires.

NFO Research, Inc. went public on April 8, 1993, and was listed as NFOR on the NASDAQ. Bill Lipner, according to *The*

NFO Story, said: ''We are now free to pursue our strategic vision independently and to build this business.'' That same year NFO struck a marketing agreement with Connecticut-based ASI, Inc. The blending of ASI's sophisticated copy-testing techniques with NFO's recognized ability to survey targeted samples of consumers gave NFO-ASI clients the best possible assessment of their advertisements in print or on television.

This acquisition was a harbinger of the way Bill and his team would lead NFO into becoming a leading, diversified, marketing information company. NFO evolved by strengthening its core panel-research business with the addition of new clients, products and services; pioneering new advances in technology; acquiring complementary companies in niche markets; and expanding to markets outside the United States. To reinforce relationships with existing and newly contracted clients, NFO opened regional offices in major metropolitan areas close to these clients and dedicated itself to strategic acquisitions that would increase and complement NFO services.

NFO innovations, acquisitions, and alliances dominated the 1990s. NFO had established a HealthMed division in 1992 to survey consumer attitudes. The success of this division led the company to secure a leading position in the healthcare/pharmaceutical business by extending research to doctors and insurance companies through the 1996 purchase of client Migliara/Kaplan Associates, Inc. (M/K), the nation's largest custom pharmaceutical-market researcher. And to secure a place in the financial services niche, in January 1994 NFO acquired Florida-based Payments Systems Inc. (PSI), which specialized in syndicated research for about 100 clients in financial services, 22 of them among the top U.S. banking and holding companies. PSI was already active in international markets and had surveyed European households in 11 countries to assess consumer attitudes toward the use of payment cards and other financial cards. In three years PSI tripled its revenue and brought NFO to the forefront of research in the retail financial industry.

NFO then acquired Advanced Marketing Solutions, Inc. (AMS), a leading provider of expert computer software systems for marketing research. NFO was a leader in gathering data; AMS was a leader in squeezing the data into a valuable sales tool for clients. The combined expertise of the two companies yielded a new product, dubbed SmartSystem, to help NFO clients synthesize data into reports and fact-based sales proposals that made salespeople instant experts in their customers' businesses. Then, during 1995 NFO began to explore and experiment with the interactive technologies, systems, and procedures that became the interactive *NFO//net.source* panel for market research; this panel evolved into the world's largest research panel representative of interactive consumers.

It consisted of more than 75,000 interactive households and over 150,000 interactive consumers. A 1997 alliance with Yahoo!—the acknowledged leader in Internet navigation services—allowed NFO to deliver insight into consumer attitudes, behavior, and preferences on the Internet and the World Wide Web.

In December 1997, NFO Interactive—a division of NFO Worldwide—and Jupiter Communications, LLC—a media research firm specializing in analysis of how the Internet and other technologies were changing traditional consumer industries—formed an alliance to offer clients a range of solutions to business development needs. In a unique product, Jupiter/NFO offered corporations a combination of national sampling of consumer behavior and spending habits, online panel research, and business analyses. The companies scheduled a report for public release in March 1998.

Furthermore, NFO strengthened its presence in the travel and leisure industries through the 1996 acquisition of Los Angeles-based Plog Research, Inc., which conducted custom and syndicated research for major travel and leisure industries. By 1998 Plog operated a fulltime-telephone interviewing facility based on NFO-developed software and was conducting a major study for a sports company. For this study, NFO's research methodology—based on an innovative concept known as "participant observation"—was used in the United States and in five other countries.

In the meantime, many NFO clients had expanded into European markets, and wanted the same kind of panel-based research data about European consumers as NFO gave them about U.S. consumers. To tap the full potential of this continent, NFO searched for a partner that could offer in-depth understanding of European consumers. To this end, NFO entered into a joint venture with Paris-based IPSOS, S.A., the fifth largest marketing research company in Europe and the eighth largest in the world. The partners operated "IPSOS-NFO Select Panels of Europe" in Germany, France, England, and Italy. And in July 1997, the company acquired The MBL Group Plc, a worldwide group of companies providing planning, feasibility studies, research, and consulting in management and marketing. London-based MBL was the parent company of 19 companies in 17 countries located in Europe, the Middle East, Africa, India, Southeast Asia, Australia, and the Americas. This purchase made NFO the largest U.S.-based custom market research firm and the ninth largest market research organization in the world.

To reflect its broadened global reach and the scope of its expanding service offerings, in September 1997 NFO Research, Inc. changed its name to NFO Worldwide, Inc. From then on, the name "NFO Research, Inc." applied only to NFO's original panel-based research business. By year-end 1997 NFO Worldwide had taken major steps toward achieving its goal of being the leading multinational marketing information company. Then, on December 9, 1997, NFO began trading its shares on the New York Stock Exchange under the symbol NFO.

Since becoming an independent company in 1991 and going public in 1993, NFO had built a strong financial foundation. By year-end 1995 revenues topped $73 million, increased 49 percent to $109 million by year-end 1996, and stood above $190 million at the end of 1997. NFO had grown into a world leader in formulating concepts and in gathering and analyzing complex data; the market-research company had become a veritable extension of its clients' organizations.

As 1998 got underway, NFO Worldwide acquired two companies, MarketMind Technologies Pty. Ltd. and Ross/Cooper/Lund, Inc., to accelerate its growth in the $400 million global continuous-tracking market. Australia-based MarketMind's tracking and data-integration system delivered continuous interactive information to help marketers manage their brands more effectively. The MarketMind system was licensed in 20 countries and supported hundreds of brands. The research-based consulting firm of Ross/Cooper/Lund, a U.S. MarketMind licensee, conducted large-scale studies to help clients diagnose brand communications and optimize media budgets. Next came NFO's purchase of Toronto-based CF Group Inc., the largest marketing and research organization in Canada. The Canadian company operated three divisions within Canada: Canadian Facts, Applied Research Consultants and Burke International Research. CF's capabilities for data collection, especially its Canadian Family Opinion panel similar to that of NFO's National Family Opinion US, enabled the companies to offer their respective clients seamless cross-border execution of panel-based research.

In short, at the approach of a new millennium, NFO Worldwide, Inc. continued to acquire companies and to form alliances relevant to its diversification and its global presence, to offer improved and innovative services to clients, to grow as a fiscally sound enterprise, and to remain on the cutting edge of interactive, innovative market research information.

Principal Subsidiaries

Access Research, Inc.; Advanced Marketing Solutions, Inc.; ASI, Inc.; CF Group Inc. (Canada); Chesapeake Surveys; CM Research Ltd (New Zealand); IPSOS-NFO (France); MarketMind Technologies Pty. Ltd. (Australia); The MBL Group Plc (Great Britain); Migliara/Kaplan Associates, Inc.; NFO Research, Inc.; Plog Research, Inc.; Prognostics; PSI Global; Ross/Cooper/Lund; The Spectrum Group.

Principal Divisions

NFO Interactive; InfoCom; NYPM (National Yellow Pages Monitor).

Further Reading

Lorch, Jacqueline, "The History of NFO, and Its Roots in the Panel Business," *WorldOpinion Research Profiles: NFO Worldwide, Inc.*, http://www.worldopinion.com/o/latenews.qry? f=d&news=2186

Lowndes, Leil, *The NFO Story*, Lyme, Conn.: Greenwich Publishing Group, Inc. pp. 10, 54–55, 64–65.

"NFO's Four-Part Plan to Exploit MR Opportunities," *Research Business Special Report*, http://www.nfor.com/newsdoc/nr_ibd0597.htm

—Gloria A. Lemieux

Nichimen Corporation

Mita NN Building
1-23, Shiba 4-chome
Minato-ku
Tokyo 108
Japan
(03) 5446-1111
Fax: (03) 5446-1010
Web site: http://www.nichimen.co.jp

Public Company
Incorporated: 1892 as Nippon Menka Kaisha
Employees: 2,243
Sales: ¥3.89 trillion (US $31.35 billion) (1997)
Stock Exchanges: Tokyo Osaka Nagoya Kyoto
SICs: 6799 Investors, Not Elsewhere Classified

Nichimen Corporation, a member of The Sanwa Bank group, is one of Japan's largest general trading companies, known as *sogo shosha*. The company manages overseas offices in 93 cities worldwide and divides its operations into the following groups: machinery; metals and construction; chemicals, plastics, and energy; textiles; and foodstuffs, lumber, and general merchandise. Nichimen, like other general trading companies, deals globally with a wide variety of product lines, through a large number of domestic and overseas branches concentrating on both import and export. In addition, the company organizes business ventures, often supplying technology and machinery as well as creating markets for the finished products.

First Formation of General Trading Companies in Late 19th Century

General trading companies made their first appearance during the Meiji empire, that lasted from 1868 to 1912. They were formed at the request of the government, which wanted to end the 200-year economic isolation that had characterized the preceding Tokugawa shogunate. Soon after their rise to power, the Meiji rulers noted that their external trade was in the control of foreigners; that international trade regulations, as well as foreigners'

languages and cultural backgrounds were unfamiliar to most of the Japanese business community; and that even domestic documents had to be passed through foreign hands. To eradicate such foreign domination, the government invited a few large, experienced holding companies to organize subsidiaries capable of introducing modern business practices and technology to Japan.

In the World War I years, these holding companies came to be known as *zaibatsu* (wealthy groups). They were family-controlled industrial and financial groups, which were classified as combinations of different companies dealing in goods and services as diverse as banking, shipping, and trading.

By the 1890s, the modernization program had transformed the Japanese economy, and the country's entrepreneurs were ready for international ventures. First to enter the arena was the cotton trade. In earlier times, merchants had sold handspun cotton and hand-woven cloth. In Europe and the United States, machine-made textiles had been produced for some years. At the dawn of the Meiji era, the foreign merchants lost no time in signing commercial treaties with Japan, so that they could export large quantities of textiles and cottons into Japan. This practice soon threatened the domestic cotton industry, which met the challenge in part by establishing its own spinning mills, though supplies of domestic raw cotton were still meager.

Founded to Trade Cotton in 1892

It was in this business climate that Nippon Menka Kaisha (Japan Cotton Company) was established in 1892 by Japanese cotton spinners and merchants. The company's capital in 1892 was ¥100,000, increasing tenfold over the following decade under the directorship of Kita Matazo, a legendary entrepreneur.

Nippon Menka initially imported cotton through exclusive foreign agents. The company gradually started opening its own foreign offices, however. Victory in the Russo-Japanese War in 1905 brought new foreign export markets in Korea and China, and in Manchuria, where the company also started spinning factories and cotton-ginning operations. Nippon Menka opened a Shanghai branch in 1903 and another in Hankow the following year, to export to China the cotton yarn produced by the rapidly expanding Japanese spinning industry. Now a large company with several overseas locations, it also was able to start trading between foreign offices, establishing Menka Gesellschaft in Bremen, Germany, and doing routine business in Liverpool, in London, and in Milan. By 1910 the company even established a U.S. subsidiary called the Japan Cotton Company in Fort Worth, Texas, to give Nippon Menka a gateway to the raw cotton trade.

The World War I years spurred company efforts even further. As European countries with more pressing priorities stopped exporting their wares, Japanese products gained popularity. Seizing the moment, the trading companies began to use their growing expertise to diversify their product lines, increase their markets for raw materials, and invest larger amounts in manufacturing operations.

The company also developed a greater international network by opening more overseas facilities. Following the lucrative wartime growth, Nippon Menka opened its first South Seas office in 1917, with a product line that included cotton cloth, cement, and veneers. It was so successful that more South Seas facilities were opened in 1924.

The company also developed an interest in the South American wool trade during the war years. In 1919 it began to buy wool from Argentina and Uruguay, leading it to open an office in Buenos Aires. The next field of operations was Burma, from where the company began to direct its silk trade operations in 1919, in tandem with other ventures concentrating on cereals, rice, and cotton. Soon, the Burma office expanded its line of interests to include spinning machines, electric fans, beer, and canned goods. Other fields of operation were facilities for rice cleaning and oil manufacturing.

African operations began in 1916, when a representative went to Mombasa, Kenya, from Bombay to trade in raw cotton and cotton cloth. Chinese operations likewise gathered momentum when Nippon Menka started to sell cottons there and to export Manchurian soybeans. Also in China, the company did purchasing for the Nikka Oil Company and acted as a sole agency for a hemp company. Expanding into other activities, the company's India operations started vertical integration. To allow it to complete all operations from buying through the shipping of cotton bales, the Indian office began to operate ginning and compressing factories.

Difficulties in the 1920s

The post-World War I boom collapsed in 1920, and the world slipped into a two-year recession. Although the recession of the early 1920s appeared not to affect Nippon Menka, whose paid-in capital stood at ¥26 million in 1925, with growth largely from the war years, the company was, in fact, losing money.

With the beginning of the Great Depression in 1929, the company problems began to show. Losses were ¥39 million in 1929, ¥2.5 million in 1930, and ¥1.2 million in 1931, for a total nearing ¥43 million. Nippon Menka may have hidden losses from shareholders during the 1920s, but eventually it had to report its financial difficulties.

The company's fortunes declined for two reasons. Competitors, who initially had been loath to brave the heat and uncharted trade routes of cotton-supplying nations such as India, proved to be enthusiastic traders when ways around these inconveniences had been established. Furthermore, during the

1920s, several small spinning companies had merged into larger companies, and these had formed themselves into the Japan Spinners' Association, a production cartel that was capable of gearing production to earn reasonable profits in bad times.

Nippon Menka was a large concern, well able to diversify into fields other than cotton. Along with another general trading company, it organized the production of printed fabric for the Far Eastern markets. Rayon was produced and sold in the same way, and the silk business it had established during World War I was expanded. By the mid-1930s, Nippon Menka was an established textile trader, with overseas offices in several locations.

Despite the heavy losses in the beginning of the Great Depression, the company bounced back quickly. The decline in U.S. and European manufacturing brought opportunity to Japanese traders. One important boost came in 1931, when Japan seized Manchuria from China, establishing the state of Manchukuo in March 1932. Immediately the Japanese government encouraged investment there, as well as the development of heavy industries such as iron and steel, oil, and cement.

For the rest of the 1930s Japan turned more to a wartime economy, expecting war with China. Expectation became fact in 1937, and the government instituted strict control of stocks and import-export prices, especially in the case of war-related products like oil. In other developments, Nippon Menka was assigned by the army to manage factories producing flour, matches, and starch. To show the broadened nature of its business, Nippon Menka Kaisha changed its name in 1943 to Nichimen Jitsugyo (Nichimen Enterprise).

Developed into Top Trading Company Following World War II

When World War II brought defeat to Japan, economic policies were set by the Allied powers, who confiscated all foreign assets and forbade foreign trade. Despite its capital of ¥30 million, the company lost foreign assets worth an estimated ¥36 million during this period. In 1947 the Allied policies gradually began to relax to the point where goods could be sold on the foreign market by correspondence, although Japanese traders were still not permitted to go overseas. By 1949 export price regulations on textiles were removed, and Japanese traders went to all countries open to them.

The Allied occupation also saw the dissolution of the *zaibatsu*. At war's end the four largest *zaibatsu* controlled one-fourth of the Japanese economy. In the interest of economic democracy, these holding companies were broken up to give other businesses foreign trade opportunities. The trading companies still occupied a weak position in relation to manufacturers, who had been in government favor throughout the war years and the inevitable period of shortages that followed.

Nichimen's independence from *zaibatsu* affiliation now paid handsome dividends, for the company became one of the country's top-ten trading companies. In 1951 it captured 4.3 percent of the country's foreign trade. By 1958 its share had grown to six percent.

Along with the other trading companies, Nichimen had difficult postwar problems to face. Goods for foreign trade were in short supply. There was a dearth of export trade itself, for the lucrative China market had been lost to communism. Silk, once a principal export, was being replaced by nylon.

Relationship with Sanwa Bank Began in 1955

Nichimen and other trading companies needed extensive loans to stay afloat. The Ministry of International Trade and Industry decided to help those trading companies that were handling most of the country's international trade. Because these companies also wanted to take advantage of growing domestic opportunities, credit sources able to supply large yen loans became a necessity. Nichimen, previously content with the Bank of Tokyo's international lending ability, now needed another backer. In 1955 Nichimen forged what would become a long-term relationship with Osaka-based Sanwa Bank. Sanwa agreed to finance all of Nichimen's domestic business.

The Sanwa Bank was a non-*zaibatsu* institution that had gained considerable influence during the occupation because it was exempt from the Allies' order to disband. One of the country's largest, it soon became the center of a large conglomerate, gaining further power through the usual banking practice of granting lower-interest loans to selected companies. Nichimen's bond with Sanwa proved both profitable and permanent. Nichimen could not, however, become Sanwa's international general trading arm because that position was already held by Iwai & Co.

To further strengthen domestic ties, Nichimen absorbed two textile dealers, Maruei & Co. in 1954 and Tazuke & Co. in 1960. Nichimen also made efforts to diversify into foodstuffs, wood, pulp, and machinery by networking through its foreign contacts. Extending its interest in industrial equipment, in 1963 the company acquired Takada & Co., a trader in machinery. In 1957 Nichimen Jitsugyo became Nichimen Co., Ltd.

Expanded Well Beyond Textiles by 1970

Between 1955 and 1970 the Japanese economy saw rapid growth. Nichimen enjoyed great export growth, which by 1970 encompassed steel, electronic products, motor vehicles, and fibers—a considerable expansion over the textiles that had formed the nucleus of export operations before 1955. Although the general trading companies still served steelmakers and shipbuilders, most manufacturers began to purchase their own supplies and market their own products.

In 1955 metal sales constituted 15 percent of Nichimen's operations, with textiles making up an additional 57 percent, foods and chemicals 21 percent, and miscellaneous seven percent. By 1965 the balance had changed—metals then constituted 28 percent of sales, textiles 36 percent, foods seven percent, and miscellaneous products 19 percent. Eleven years later, metals and machinery had become the most important group, accounting for 47 percent of operations. Textiles made up 18 percent of the total, with food and chemicals accounting for 26 percent and miscellaneous sales accounting for nine percent.

Nichimen's greatest growth came in steel. Like other general trading companies, Nichimen handled raw materials, purchased fabricated steel products, secured overseas markets for finished products, and handled the details of export. In addition, Nichimen was leasing supermarkets, negotiating agreements with foreign manufacturers looking for Japanese markets, and becoming more involved in farming, poultry, and beef ventures.

As a result of these activities, Nichimen's annual sales rose from ¥305.6 billion in 1960 to ¥777.8 billion by decade's end, rising still higher by 1976 to ¥1.81 trillion. Business activities of the early 1970s included a Japanese joint venture with National Biscuit Company (Nabisco). In 1970 Nabisco took 45 percent ownership, giving ten percent ownership to Nichimen and 45 percent to Yamazaki Baking Company, in exchange for the right to use the Nabisco trademark.

The increase in Nichimen's product lines and its geographical spread was then allowing the general trading companies to organize complex projects cutting across many different industries. Ocean resource development, urban projects, and financial ventures were just three of many areas in which Nichimen first was able to create demands for a widening array of products and then to supply them through different affiliates.

Early 1970s Criticism of Trading Companies

In the early 1970s the Japanese economy began to slow down, and the government started to curb trading companies' stock holdings in response to increasing criticism of the firms. They were accused of stock speculation, of hoarding imported necessities, and of tax evasion. This situation came to a head with the 1973 oil crisis. In self defense, Nichimen and other trading companies decided to shift their emphasis from high-volume sales to social responsibility and efficient management, by adopting codes of behavior that promised ethical conduct in all business dealings.

Nichimen's search for global reach brought the company into many different countries, where they participated in joint ventures. One project, a joint venture between Nichimen and certain other Japanese companies and Deepsea Ventures, Inc., a subsidiary of the U.S. company Tenneco, Inc., mined manganese nodules containing copper, nickel, and cobalt from the Pacific Ocean floor.

By 1976 Nichimen had subsidiaries or branches in London, Hong Kong, Rangoon, Calcutta, Bangkok, Singapore, Kuala Lumpur, and Burma. There also was a vast computerized communications system connecting company offices in most of the world's business centers. These included new additions in Caracas; Lima; Sandakan, Malaysia; and notably, in Warsaw and Moscow, for Nichimen was doing more business in Eastern Europe.

By the late 1970s Nichimen faced harder times. A soaring yen, climbing 25 percent in the year between July 1977 and July 1978, oil price rises in 1973 and 1978, and serious competition from South Korea, Argentina, and other steel- and textile-producing countries with low labor and currency costs brought the accustomed low profit margins even lower.

Undaunted, Nichimen began to look for new avenues, many in developing countries such as China and parts of the Soviet Union. For Nichimen, activities included the construction of a New Zealand sawmill in a joint venture with another Japanese company, a textile-dyeing joint venture in China, and contracts totaling ¥2 billion for the first stages of a water- and sewerage-system modernization program in Giza, Egypt.

New effort also went into third-country trade—overseas business ventures in which the Japanese company sold the products of another country in yet a third country. Vigorous foreign operations did not curb the development of domestic ventures such as condominium and office block construction, jewelry imports, and retailing. Other operations concentrated on importing; lumber came from the Soviet Union and foodstuffs came from Thailand and China.

In 1982 Nichimen Co., Ltd. changed its name to Nichimen Corporation. By the end of the 1980s, the company had opened new offices in Madras, Barcelona, and various cities in the Soviet Union, bringing to 85 its total number of geographical divisions. There were also 129 major subsidiaries and affiliates.

1990s Troubles

The bursting of the late 1980s Japanese economic bubble led to prolonged difficulties for Nichimen in the 1990s. Nearly all of the *sogo shosha* had diversified aggressively into financial investments during the speculative bubble years, in large part because their traditional activity of marginally profitable commodity trading had been in a deep decline for years, a development compounded by a trend toward Japanese companies handling their international operations themselves. In desperation the trading companies built up large stock portfolios and became hooked on the revenues they could gain through arbitrage (or *zaiteku,* as it is known in Japan). Once the bubble burst, the *sogo shosha* were left with huge portfolios whose worth had plummeted; all of the trading companies were forced eventually to liquidate much of their stock holdings.

As it cleaned up its portfolio in the 1990s, Nichimen also sought out ways to become more profitable, leading to the implementation starting in April 1996 of a three-year management plan called CREATE 98. A key aspect of the plan was a shift away from the declining area of what the company called ''soft'' businesses, notably those endeavors that involve logs and lumber, foodstuffs, and chemicals. Nichimen traditionally had achieved much of its profits from these areas. CREATE 98 called for a shift to ''hard'' businesses, that is, those relating to machinery, steel, and construction. Coupled with this shift was a second one in which the company endeavored to move away from projects in which it acted merely as a financial intermediary toward activities where it was much more deeply involved. Another important aim of the plan was to increase the overall level of investments in new businesses to a level more in line with that of other leading *sogo shosha.*

These objectives were evident in a number of initiatives that a more aggressive Nichimen undertook in the mid-1990s. In December 1996 the company announced that it had formed a joint venture with China's largest general trader (China National Cereals, Oils & Foodstuffs Import and Export Corporation) that aimed to achieve US $5 billion in annual sales in food, machinery, and electrical goods. Nichimen in early 1997 joined with AES Corporation, a U.S.-based independent power producer, and Grupo Hermes, a leading Mexican industrial group, in winning a contract to build a 484-megawatt gas-fired combined-cycle power plant on Mexico's Yucatan peninsula. The plant was the first privately run power plant to supply Mexico's

national grid. In June 1997 Nichimen, along with Mitsubishi Corp. and Mitsubishi Heavy Industries Ltd., won a US $300 million contract to build an 830-megawatt thermal power plant northwest of Buenos Aires, Argentina.

In fiscal 1997, the first year of the CREATE 98 plan, Nichimen already was seeing some positive results, notably an 8.7 percent increase in gross trading profit—the main criterion upon which Nichimen planned to measure the success of the plan—to ¥119.31 billion (US $961.4 billion). This increase was the first one in four fiscal years. Unfortunately, the Asian economic crisis, which erupted in 1997, threatened to derail this nascent turnaround, as Nichimen, like nearly all of the *sogo shosha,* was very active throughout Asia, including such trouble spots as Indonesia, Korea, and Thailand.

Principal Subsidiaries

Nichimen America Inc.; Granplex, Inc. (U.S.A.); Nichimen Canada Inc.; Nichimen de Mexico S.A. de C.V.; Nichimen do Brasil Ltda. (Brazil); Nichimen Co. (Argentina) S.A.; Nichimen Europe plc (U.K.); Nichimen Co., (Iran) Ltd.; A.A. Al-Qatami's Sons Trading Co., Ltd. (Kuwait); Nichimen Middle East F.Z.E. (Dubai); Nichimen (China) Co., Ltd.; Nichimen Shanghai Ltd. (China); Nichimen Co. (Hong Kong) Ltd.; Nichimen Orient Wear Ltd. (China); Nichimen Korea Ltd.; Nichimen (Singapore) Pte Ltd.; Nichimen Australia Limited; Nichimen Co. (New Zealand) Ltd.

Principal Divisions

Machinery Group: Plant & Project Division; Electronics Division; Aircraft & Vessels Division; Industrial Machinery Division; Motor Vehicle & Heavy Machinery Division. Metals & Construction Group: Iron & Steel Division; Nonferrous Metals Division; Construction Division. Chemicals, Plastics & Energy Group: Basic Chemicals Division; Fine Chemicals Division; Plastics Division; Energy Division. Textiles Group: Home Furnishing & Industrial Textiles Division; Apparel Division. Foodstuffs, Lumber & General Merchandise Group: Grains & Feeds Division; Foods Division; Lumber Division; General Merchandise Division.

Further Reading

Iwao, Ichiishi, ''Sogo Shosha: Meeting New Challenges,'' *Journal of Japanese Trade & Industry,* January/February 1995, pp. 16–18.

Rosario, Louise do, ''Lose and Learn: Japan's Firms Pay Price of Financial Speculation,'' *Far Eastern Economic Review,* June 17, 1993, pp. 60–61.

Yonekawa, Shin'ichi, ed., *General Trading Companies: A Comparative and Historical Study,* Tokyo: United Nations University Press, 1990.

Yonekawa, Shin'ichi, and Hideki Yoshi Hara, eds., *Business History of General Trading Companies,* Tokyo: University of Tokyo Press, 1987.

Yoshihara, Kunio, *Sogo Shosha: The Vanguard of the Japanese Economy,* Tokyo: Oxford University Press, 1982.

Young, Alexander, *The Sogo Shosha: Japan's Multinational Trading Companies,* Boulder, Colo.: Westview Press, 1979.

—Gillian Wolf
—updated by David E. Salamie

Océ N.V.

St. Urbanusweg 43
P.O. Box 101
5900 MA Venlo
Netherlands
(31) 77 359 2222
Fax: (31) 77 354 4700
Web site: http://www.oce.com

Public Company
Founded: 1877
Employees: 20,000
Sales: NLG 5.4 billion (US$2.74 billion) (1997)
Stock Exchanges: Amsterdam Dusseldorf Frankfurt/Main
  NASDAQ
Ticker Symbol: OCENY
SICs: 3579 Office Machines, Not Elsewhere Classified;
  3577 Computer Peripheral Equipment, Not Elsewhere
  Classified

The Netherlands' Océ N.V. is one of the world's leading developers, manufacturers, and distributors of digital and analog copy and printing systems. With annual sales of more than NLG 5 billion, Océ ranks among the world's top 100 information technology companies. Sales of the company's engineering systems place Océ as the world's top manufacturer and distributor in that market. In addition to the design, manufacture, and distribution of its document reproduction technology—including machines and the software to drive them—Océ supports its sales with a wide range of office and copying supplies, as well as after-sale service. In the mid-1990s, the company also entered the booming facilities management market, providing, or contracting third parties to provide, full-service copying and reprographic services to major corporations. As such, Océ was able to offer its customers a total solution for their document reproduction and distribution needs.

1990s Corporate Structure

Océ is grouped in three principal operating divisions, each governing a specific range of the company's product line and targeting specific market segments. In the late 1990s, the company was the world leader in copy and printing machinery for the engineering systems market. Supporting CAD/CAM applications, among others, Océ's range of products included its flagship digital printers, the 9800 and 9700, introduced in 1997, the 9400, introduced in 1996, and the 9600, expected to be launched in 1998. The extension of this line enabled Océ to offer high-speed digital printing to all volume markets. In addition to the company's digital printers—which already accounted for more than 40 percent of engineering systems and 80 percent of total company sales—Océ also continued to manufacture and sell a popular line of analog and inkjet black-and-white and color copying and printing equipment for the engineering systems market. This division, including sales of supplies and services, accounted for more than NLG 1.6 billion of the company's sales in 1997.

Océ's office systems division represented the largest part of the company's annual sales, posting nearly NLG 2.4 billion in 1997 revenues. The company offered a range of both analog and digital machines, targeted primarily at the medium- through high-volume markets. In the digital printer/copier market, the company's growth was spearheaded by the 3165, introduced in the second half of 1997. The company's model 3100 analog copier, introduced at the beginning of 1998, was capable of producing 100 copies per minute. While most of its sales continued to be supplied by sales of black-and-white copiers and copy/printing systems, Océ also began building a strong presence in the growing color copying market. The Océ 3125C, marketed under a third-party agreement, was expected to add medium-volume color copying capacity in 1998. Included under the office systems division were the company's facilities management operations, which saw its sales double each year in the late 1990s. The company added to its capabilities in this area with the December 1997 acquisition of leading U.S. facilities management provider Archer Management Services.

Company Perspectives:

It's amazing what you can achieve when you focus your energies. And at Océ we're focused like a laser. Every bit of our considerable energy is geared to providing cutting-edge printing and copying solutions for professionals. And with every one of our employees dedicated to that goal, it's no wonder we're always pushing the technological envelope.

The company's printing systems division was given a strong boost in 1996 when it acquired the former printing activities of Siemens Nixdorf International. The acquisition—nearly doubling Océ's printing systems sales—of the SNI division added that company's leading printing products, and manufacturing facilities in Poing, Germany, and Boca Raton, Florida. The expanded division offered both mid-range and high-volume cutsheet printing systems, and related technologies, including toners and print servers, and continuous feed fanfold and roll-based printing systems. In 1997 and 1998, the company introduced its Pagestream 88 (88 pages per minute) low-volume fanfold printer; a cutsheet printer, the Pagestream 158 DC, offering highlight color capacity at 158 pages per minute; and the Twin PS 1000, the fastest machine in the Pagestream family. The company's primary focus remained on the medium-volume market and on the expanding print-on-demand market, for which Océ adapted its Pagestream systems under the name of Demandstream. Printing systems after the SNI acquisition accounted for NLG 1.45 billion of Océ's annual sales.

In the late 1990s Océ N.V. operated more than 30 subsidiary companies in as many countries. The company's Venlo headquarters remained its primary research and development facility, while the company's research and development activities—representing seven percent of annual revenues—were also conducted in Germany, France, and the United States. Océ's manufacturing facilities were located primarily in Venlo, Poing, and France's Guérande. Parts were typically sourced from a network of third-party producers, while the company continued to manufacture certain strategic elements itself, as well as toners and other printing and copying supplies. More than half of the company's 20,000 employees worldwide were engaged in sales and service.

Océ doubled its annual sales between 1993 and 1997 and also posted consistent profits, which topped NLG 236 million for 1997. The company is listed on the Amsterdam, Dusseldorf, Frankfurt/Main, and Electronic Stock Exchange (EBS) in Switzerland, and its shares are also traded as American Depositary Receipts on the NASDAQ exchange.

From Coloring Butter to Color Copies in the 20th Century

The company that would become known as Océ had a quite different focus at its origin. In 1871, Lodewijk van der Grinten, a chemist in Venlo, the Netherlands, began researching ingredients that could be used for coloring butter. By 1877, van der

Grinten had perfected a formula and set up the company, that would later become known as Océ, for manufacturing his coloring agents on a large scale. Van der Grinten was joined by son Frans, who expanded the company to industrial manufacturing of the coloring products, which were used for margarine as well as butter. The company would continue to produce these colorants until 1970, when that division was sold off to Unilever.

By then, the van der Grinten family had developed another specialty. Frans van der Grinten's son, Louis, joined the company in the early part of the 20th century. Louis van der Grinten, who shared his grandfather's background in chemistry, began researching a new area: reprographic materials. In 1920, van der Grinten added the manufacture of blueprint paper to the family concern, overcoming some of the early difficulties of the light-sensitive material, such as a fragile shelf-life and slow development times. During the 1920s, Louis van der Grinten was joined by his brothers, Piet and Karel, who took over the company's butter coloring and production activities, while Louis focused on research and sales. The company's sales were by then already international, developed primarily through local alliances. In the United States, for example, the company's distribution was handled by Charles Bruning, a relationship that would last into the 1990s, when Bruning was acquired by the company.

A German breakthrough in 1923 introduced the van der Grintens' company to a new type of reproduction material: diazo printing. Unlike the negatives developed with blueprint paper, which produced white lines on blue paper, diazo printing offered positive, that is, direct copies, with the added advantage of allowing colored lines on white paper. Louis van der Grinten set to work improving on the diazo process and by 1926 introduced the company's Primulin paper, which would receive international patents and establish the company's international success. Further improvements on the diazo process quickly led to a new name for the company. The new diazo product, dubbed OC from the German *ohne componenten*, or "without components," proved highly successful, and more than becoming a company-owned trademark, it became part of the company's name. (The 'é' was later added to OC for pronunciation reasons.) Until the 1990s, the company would be known as Océ-Van der Grinten, until the name was simplified to Océ.

While blueprint paper and diazo printing materials would continue to form the backbone of the company's sales (blueprint paper production would not be phased out until 1946), Océ continued to seek improved reprographic processes. Blueprint and diazo could be used for reproducing documents created on translucent materials, but documents on non-translucent papers could still be reproduced only by hand or by using photography—the first method being very time-consuming, the second very expensive. Océ became the first manufacturer to solve this problem, introducing, in 1935, its RetOcé process. RetOcé, which continued to utilize the diazo process, enabled the copying of non-translucent documents. This process would remain the sole method of reproducing, quickly and inexpensively, non-translucent documents for several years. The introduction of the electrophotographic copying process in 1940 added a rival technology. Yet RetOcé would continue as the dominant process into the 1950s, when electrophotography came of age with the first copying machines based on this method.

Going Public and International Expansion: 1950s–70s

Océ went public in 1958, listing on the Amsterdam Stock Exchange. The public offering helped the company fuel its international expansion. In the same year, the company launched its first international subsidiary, in Germany. Other subsidiaries followed in the 1960s, including locations in Norway, Italy, and Denmark. At the same time, Océ began expanding into new international territory through acquisitions, notably with the merger of Belgium's Jobé in 1964; with Ingeniörsuntensilor in Sweden in 1966; Photosia, in France, in 1966; and a similar merger that brought the company into Austria. The acquired companies were absorbed into Océ and operated as subsidiaries.

Acquisition would continue to fuel the company's international growth through the 1970s. CIAP of France was acquired in 1969. The company's moves to establish a U.S. presence took on steam with the 1970 acquisition of former Océ licenseholder BK Elliot, based in Pittsburgh, and with the acquisition of another U.S. electrostatic copier and microfilm reader manufacturer, ICP, in 1971. The following year, the company added to its Danish presence with the purchase of Helioprint AS, and entered Brazil with the acquisition of Copirama, while strengthening its Australian position with the majority interest in that country's William Crosby Ltd.

The shift from dedicated document copying firms to inhouse office copying systems began in earnest in the 1960s. New technologies, including "xerography" made famous by Xerox, enabled the use of plain paper for copying, instead of the specialized materials still required for diazo and other printing methods. Océ joined in this revolution, introducing its own plain-paper office copier, the Océ 1700, in 1970. In face of the wide popularity of the Xerox machine for low-volume copying needs, Océ's focus turned especially to the more demanding medium- to very high-volume markets. In the early 1970s, the company introduced several new models, each adapted to specific volume requirements.

Xerography had gained an exclusive share of the market. In 1973, however, Océ introduced a rival reprographic technology, called the Océ Copy Press System, which offered copies and prints with the quality offered by offset printing. During this same period, another new technology was under development—laser printing, introduced by Siemens in 1975. Compatible with the growing computer technology, and able to work with third-party data-processing hardware and software systems, the Siemens ND2 printer, which began shipping in 1977, was capable of outputs of 200 pages per minute, while also capable of respecting the page perforations of the continuous-roll paper used by computer printing systems. Siemens' printing division—which would become part of Océ in 1996—continued to introduce new laser printing technologies, including the first color laser printer in 1984, geared primarily to the medium- to high-volume markets.

New Markets in the 1980s and 1990s

Océ continued its own expansion. In 1977, the company stepped up its U.S. presence with the acquisition of Arkwright Inc. Océ's U.S. activity had focused especially on the engineering systems market, but with the success of the copy press system, the company moved to increase its U.S. office systems activity. In 1983, the company set up a new subsidiary, Océ-Business Systems (renamed Océ-Office Systems in 1987). In the 1990s, the company consolidated its U.S. operations into Océ-USA Inc., based in Chicago. On the international, and especially European front, Océ completed its largest acquisition of the 1970s with its purchase of Ozalid Group Holdings Ltd., Océ's chief competitor, adding that company's network of subsidiaries in 15 countries.

During this time, Océ moved into the new markets offered by the rapid advances in computer technology. The company brought out its own laser printer in 1984; color reproduction technologies, scanners, digital copiers, printers, and plotters were also added to the company's product line. While the company's reprographic activities had long supported the engineering systems market—from its original blueprint papers—the 1980s saw Océ target this arena for further growth. In 1983, Océ launched a wide-format, plain-paper copier adapted to the engineering market. The 1989 acquisition of the plotter division of France's industrial giant Schlumberger gave a further boost to Océ's engineering systems activities, while adding new digital and automation technologies. By the mid-1990s, Océ had established itself as the leading supplier of engineering document reproduction and printing systems, with a 20 percent worldwide share and a 25 percent European share.

In the 1990s, Océ would continue to build on its position as one of the world's top reprographic systems providers. By 1993, the company's revenues had reached NLG 2.6 billion. In the 1990s, the company stepped up its investments in the increasingly dominant digital printing market, while continuing to produce its diazo and analog systems. Nevertheless, these technologies were facing a shrinking market as digital systems became more sophisticated and reliable. A reorganization of the company split its printing and office activities into separate divisions. Océ also began moving into the newly opened Eastern European markets, including the Czech Republic, Poland, Hungary, and Slovakia, while also adding new subsidiaries in the booming Asian market, in China, Hong Kong, Singapore, Malaysia, Taiwan, and Thailand. The company also began building a presence in Japan. In Western Europe, Océ's presence increased with new subsidiaries in Spain, Portugal, Switzerland, and Ireland. In the United States, Océ boosted its market strength with the signing of a distribution agreement with Alco Office Products Inc., the largest independent office systems distributor in the United States.

The mid-1990s for Océ were marked by the successful introduction of new models in both the analog and digital technologies, which also included the growing inkjet market. By 1995, Océ's revenues had neared NLG 5 billion. Yet, the company's biggest score came in 1996, when it agreed to acquire the printing division of Siemens Nixdorf International. The SNI acquisition boosted the company's revenues by more than NLG 1 billion in its first eight months; by 1997, the company's revenues had soared to NLG 5.4 billion.

For the future, Océ remained committed to improving its analog copying and printing systems. However, the company clearly looked to digital systems for its continued growth. By the late 1990s, the company's growing strength in this market, including the development of software systems to drive its machinery, had placed it among the world's top 100 information technology companies. The company expected its future products to emphasize color copying and printing technologies—Océ's mainstay for the 21st century.

Principal Subsidiaries

Océ-Belgium NV/SA; Océ-Czech Republic Sro; Océ-Danmark A/S; Océ-Deutschland GmbH; Océ Printing Systems GmbH (Germany); Océ-Espana S.A.; Océ-France S.A.; Océ-Industries S.A. (France); Océ-Hungária Kft.; Océ-Ireland Ltd.; Océ-Italia SpA (Italy); Océ-Nederland B.V.; Arkwright Europe B.V. (Netherlands); Océ-Norge A.S. (Norway); Océ-Osterreich GmbH (Austria); Océ-Poland Ltd. Sp.z.o.o.; Océ-Lima Mayer S.A. (Portugal); Océ (Schweiz) AG (Switzerland); Océ Svenska AB (Sweden); Océ (U.K.) Limited; Arkwright Inc. (U.S.A.); Océ-USA, Inc.; Océ Printing Systems USA Inc.; Archer Management Services Inc. (U.S.A.); Océ-Australia Limited; Océ-Brasil Comércio e Indústria Ltda. (Brazil); Océ-Canada Inc.; Océ Printing Systems (South Africa) (Pty.) Ltd.; Océ Far East Pte. Ltd. (Singapore); Océ Ltd. (Hong Kong); Océ Ltd. (Thailand); Océ Office Equipment (China).

Principal Divisions

Engineering Systems; Office Systems; Printing Systems.

—M. L. Cohen

Old Spaghetti Factory International Inc.

0715 SW Bancroft
Portland, Oregon 97201
U.S.A.
(503) 225-0433
Fax: (503) 226-6214

Private Company
Incorporated: 1969
Employees: 4,200
Sales: $90 million (1998 est.)
SICs: 5812 Eating Places

Old Spaghetti Factory International Inc. (OSF) was founded in 1969 and has grown into an international restaurant company serving more than 10 million customers annually.

Humble Origins

January 10, 1969 marked the grand opening of the first Old Spaghetti Factory restaurant in Portland, Oregon. Founders Guss and Sally Dussin leased an old warehouse in a run-down part of his hometown of Portland and braved the rain in order to greet the few customers who wandered in that night. The night's receipts totaled $171.80 and many of the Dussins' friends and food-industry colleagues thought their restaurant would never make it. They were wrong. A week later, one night's receipts totaled $900 and by the end of the first year, the restaurant had served over 200,000 people and reached revenue of $400,000. The following year, the Dussins opened two more restaurants and sales jumped to $1.3 million. This promising track record has continued for decades—and in an industry where most companies rarely make it to their seventh anniversary, celebrating nearly 30 years of success is an achievement worth noticing.

The "Old Spaghetti Factory" name was originally trademarked by The Old Spaghetti Factory Cafe and Excelsior Cof-

fee House in the North Beach area of San Francisco. The Dussins purchased the rights to the name, but there has never been a connection between their company, doing business as The Old Spaghetti Factory, and the restaurant in San Francisco, which closed in February 1983.

Prior to founding The Old Spaghetti Factory, Dussin, born in 1925, graduated from the University of Michigan in 1945 with a B.S. in Physics, was commissioned as an ensign in the U.S. Navy Reserve, and saw active duty in the latter part of World War II and in the Korean War. He retired from the Active Naval Reserve in 1965 as a Lieutenant Commander with 22 years of service. He joined his father in the family restaurant business in 1947. Between 1955 and 1970, Dussin added four more restaurants to the family's restaurant group before founding OSF with his wife, Sally. As the OSF chain grew, Dussin sold off the original five restaurants in order to concentrate on the new restaurant company.

Formula for Success

The company's formula for success has been the result of smart thinking, smarter operating instincts, and uncanny devotion to customer value. Dussin, who is known to roll up his sleeves and help out in the kitchen from time-to-time, has been actively involved in the restaurant chain's growth from day one. His belief that a memorable dining experience does not need to cost a lot of money has kept the company growing. The company's principal menu items are spaghetti dinners and other pasta-based specialty items such as spinach and cheese ravioli, spinach tortellini with alfredo sauce, fettucine alfredo, baked lasagna, macaroni and cheese, and penne with fresh vegetables. Other specialty meals include oven baked chicken, breast of chicken fettucine, chicken parmigiana, chicken marsala, shrimp primavera, and seafood fettucine. Each entree comes complete with green salad and a choice of many salad dressings (Italian, creamy pesto, blue cheese, 1,000 Island, or fat-free honey mustard) or soup (minestrone, chicken with orzo, cream of broccoli, chicken mulligatawny, or New England clam chowder), a whole loaf of bread with butter and/or garlic butter, a beverage (freshly ground coffee, hot tea, iced tea, soda, or milk) and a dessert of either spumoni or ice cream, with complimentary refills on the bread and beverages. Other specialty items include Italian cream sodas, mud pie desserts, a wine and beer list, mixed drinks from a full bar, toasted garlic bread parmigiana with three cheeses and marinara sauce. The lunch menu includes sausage sandwiches, meatball sandwiches, turkey & Swiss cheese sandwiches, eggplant parmigiana, and ham and Swiss cheese sandwiches in addition to smaller portions of the dinner menu. The average price of $7.25 per person for dinner and $5.75 for lunch has brought over ten million customers through Old Spaghetti Factory restaurant doors annually. Nearly everything on the menu is made on-site, from scratch, using fresh ingredients. By focusing on the complete meal, OSF has simplified the concept of dining value.

Another factor in the company's success is real estate. Dussin was the pioneer of the concept of developing restaurant properties in places other companies considered unworkable. Old Spaghetti Factory restaurants are usually located in 12,000- to 14,000-square-foot structures which are either historic buildings or unique and distinctive, usually found in older warehouse districts where rent is low. The buildings usually have brick walls and extensive woodwork. One of the Riverside, California restaurants, for example, is located in an old orange packing and loading building situated next to a railroad track. The company did extensive research in the "Citrus Collection" at the University of California, Riverside's Library in the Special Collections Department, studying pictures of the building, reading its history, and consulting with Clifford Wurfel, the collection's curator at that time, prior to beginning restoration on the building to return it to its former glory. One of the San Diego, California restaurants is a restored building in that city's historic gas lamp district. The Phoenix, Arizona-based restaurant was opened in 1971 in the Roosevelt Historic District, which was developed between 1875 to 1930.

In addition to the uniqueness of Old Spaghetti Factory restaurant locations, the restaurants are known for their unusual decor. Each restaurant, which seats approximately 350 to 400 patrons, is filled with antiques from around the world. These antiques surround the centerpiece, a vintage trolley car, which has been refitted for meal seating. The first Old Spaghetti Factory restaurant was furnished by Dussin's wife, Sally, from garage sales and whatever she could find that was inexpensive. In 1997, the company was investing close to $1 million per restaurant in antiques and brass headboards and maintaining a 25,000-square-foot warehouse and crew of craftspeople who restored antiques and created reproductions for the restaurants.

The company is also known for sound financial management and solid cost controls in all of its operations, especially food. The company trains its employees to be very efficient in the kitchen, wasting as little food as possible. The less waste, the less overhead, the lower the price of a meal for its customers. The Old Spaghetti Factory management team has remained steady as well. Most of the core management team has been with the company since its inception, adding to the company's continuity and consistency. The company does actively recruit on college campuses for new managers and puts recruits through an intensive 14-week training program. Each restaurant employs between 90 and 180 employees and three to six managers.

Franchise Expansion During the 1990s

Dussin has acted as an advisor to some of his in-laws in opening Old Spaghetti Factories in Canada, but there is no business connection between Dussin's Old Spaghetti Factory International Inc. and the Canadian restaurants. However, knowing that a company's consistency must be mixed with dynamics to stay afloat, the company allowed franchises to be opened up. Franchises were granted to Guss Dussin's sister Georgia Dariotis, who, with her husband Mike, owns the California restaurants located in Sacramento, Rancho Cordova, Concord, and Roseville; to another Dussin family member, Alice Pulos, who owns the Phoenix, Arizona restaurant and to son Chris Dussin, who owns the Fullerton, California restaurant. Alice Pulos and her ex-husband Mike opened a second restaurant near Arizona State University in Tempe, Arizona, and a third in Scottsdale, Arizona, but after their divorce in the late 1990s, they split the difference: she kept the Phoenix unit and remained part of the OSF International company, the Tempe unit was given to her ex-husband and the name was changed to The Spaghetti Company, and the Scottsdale restaurant was closed. Chitaka Foods International was granted a franchise in 1980 to open and operate an Old Spaghetti Factory restaurant in Nagoya, Japan, the first of ten total to be opened in that country. The other nine are from a similar agreement in force with OSF Japan Ltd., which by 1997 owned and operated seven OSF restaurants and sub-franchised two more and which would be OSF International's primary franchisee in Japan in the future. OSF International was studying other countries for possible expansion. The U.S. portion of the restaurant chain, meanwhile, grew to 35 restaurants by 1997, located in Washington, Oregon, California, Hawaii, Arizona, Utah, Colorado, Missouri, Indiana, Ohio, Kentucky, Tennessee, Virginia, and Georgia.

In 1997, Dussin turned over day-to-day operations to his son Chris Dussin and son-in-law David Cook, both of whom have been active in management for many years. True to OSF's beginnings, new menu items were carefully being added and food preparation was always being studied for ways to improve the speed of service without compromising quality. New locations continued to be developed in suburban markets, with a distinctive building design that reflected the company's penchant for downtown warehouse restaurants.

Further Reading

Liddle, Alan, "OSF's Dussin Hands Daily Duties to Son, Son-in-Law," *Nation's Restaurant News,* January 20, 1997, p. 3.
Slater, Pam, "Tried and True: Old Spaghetti Factory Sticks to Basics—For 20 Years," *Sacramento Bee,* January 31, 1998.

—Daryl F. Mallett

Oracle Corporation

500 Oracle Parkway
Redwood Shores, California 94065
U.S.A.
(650) 506-7000
Fax: (650) 506-7200
Web site: http://www.oracle.com

Public Company
Incorporated: 1977
Employees: 34,000
Sales: $5.68 billion (1997)
Stock Exchanges: NASDAQ
Ticker Symbol: ORCL
SICs: 7372 Computer Software Manufacturers; 5731
Television & Radio Dealers; 5734 Computer
Software; 7371 Computer Services

Oracle Corporation is the largest supplier of database management systems software and the second largest independent software and services company in the world. The company's principal business activities include the development and marketing of an integrated line of computer software products used for database management, computer-aided systems engineering, applications development, and decision support, as well as families of software products used for financial, human resource, and manufacturing applications (known as enterprise resource planning—or ERP—software). Through its subsidiaries, Oracle markets its products along with related consulting, educational, support, and systems integration services in more than 140 countries.

Databases for the CIA: 1977–81

Oracle Corporation traces its roots to 1977 when two computer programmers, Lawrence J. Ellison and Robert N. Miner, teamed up to start a new software firm. Ellison had been a vice-president of systems development at Omex Corporation and a member of a pioneering team at Amdahl Corporation, which developed the first IBM-compatible mainframe computer, while Miner had served as Ellison's former supervisor at another computer company, Ampex Corporation. Both men had significant experience designing customized database programs for government agencies, and the pair persuaded the Central Intelligence Agency (CIA) to let them pick up a lapsed, $50,000 contract to build a special database program. Ellison and Miner then pooled $1,500 in savings to rent office space in Belmont, California, and start Oracle for the purpose of developing and marketing database management systems (DBMS) software. Ellison became president and chief executive and took charge of sales and marketing for the new company, while Miner supervised software development. The pair of entrepreneurs sought out well-known private venture capitalist Donald L. Lucas to become chairman of the board.

While working on the CIA project, Ellison continued monitoring technical documents published by IBM, a practice he had established while working as a programmer at Amdahl. Ellison noticed that the computer giant was interested in new types of speedy, efficient, and versatile database programs, called relational databases, that were projected to one day allow computer users to retrieve corporate data from almost any form. What was expected to make this possible was the IBM innovation called the Structured Query Language (SQL), a computer language that would tell a relational database what to retrieve and how to display it.

Banking on what later proved to be a correct hunch—that IBM would incorporate the new relational database and SQL into future computers—Ellison and Miner set out to provide a similar program for Digital minicomputers and other types of machines. In 1978 Miner developed the Oracle RDBMS (relational database management system), the world's first relational database using SQL, which would allow organizations to use different-sized computers from different manufacturers but still standardize on software. A year after its pioneering development, Oracle became the first company to commercially offer a relational database management system, two years before IBM debuted its own RDBMS system.

After its initial innovation, Oracle quickly became profitable, and by 1982 the company, then with 24 employees and a mainframe and minicomputer customer base of 75, reported annual revenues of nearly $2.5 million. That same year the company began its international expansion with the creation of Oracle Denmark. About one-fourth of 1982 revenues were poured back into research and development, leading to a 1983 Oracle innovation, the first commercially available portable RDBMS. The portable RDBMS enabled companies to run their DBMS on a range of hardware and operating systems—including mainframes, minicomputers, workstations, and personal computers—and helped Oracle to double revenues that year to over $5 million.

Expansion, Competition, Going Public: 1982–86

By the early 1980s Oracle began jousting with new entrants in the DBMS market. But the company's reputation for innovations and its aggressive style of advertising, which mentioned competitors' products by name, helped to push Oracle's sales upward, and by 1985 the company logged better than $23 million in revenues. The following year annual sales more than doubled to a record $55.4 million.

The year 1986 proved to be transitional and historical for Oracle in a number of respects. In March, Oracle made its first public offering of stock, selling one million common shares. That same year Oracle lauded itself as the fastest-growing software company in the world, having recorded 100 percent-or-better growth in revenues in eight of its first nine years. Much of that growth came from Oracle's targeted end users—multinational companies with a variety of what had previously been incompatible computer systems. By 1986 Oracle's customer base had grown to include 2,000 mainframe and minicomputer users represented by major international firms operating in such fields as the aerospace, automotive, pharmaceutical, and computer manufacturing industries, as well as a variety of government organizations.

To serve those customers, by 1986 Oracle had established 17 international marketing subsidiaries based in Australia, Canada, China, Europe, and the United Kingdom to market Oracle products in a total of 39 countries. By the same time, Oracle had also expanded the scope of its business operations to include related customer support, education, and consulting services.

One of the principal reasons for Oracle's success during the mid-1980s was the 1986 emergence of SQL as the industry standard language for relational database management systems, which in turn led to increased market acceptance of Oracle's SQL-compatible RDBMS. In 1986 Oracle expanded its RDBMS product line and debuted another industry first, a distributed DBMS based on the company's SQL*Star software. Under the distributed system, computer users could access data stored on a network of computers in the same way and with the same ease as if all a network's information were stored on one computer. Although initially limited to operating principally on IBM and IBM-compatible computers, the Oracle SQL*Star software was the first commercially available software of its kind and was soon expanded to include dozens of additional computer brands and models.

Setting the Standard: 1987–90

By 1987 Oracle had emerged as the relational DBMS choice of most major computer manufacturers, allowing the company to expand the scope of hardware brands on which Oracle's products could operate. Largely as a result of such acceptance, in 1987 Oracle achieved two major milestones by topping $100 million in sales and becoming the world's largest database management software company with more than 4,500 end users in 55 countries.

During the late 1980s Oracle's growth had a spiraling and enticing effect within the computer industry, allowing the company to further expand its development, sales, and support partnerships with computer hardware manufacturers. Oracle's partnerships with software manufacturers also began to blossom, and in 1987 the number of software companies using Oracle products as a foundation for their software applications grew fivefold. In order to maximize the benefits of these partnerships, in 1987 Oracle established its VAR (Value-Added Reseller) Alliance Program, aimed at building cooperative selling and product-planning alliances with other software manufacturers.

Oracle continued its tradition of innovation and firsts in 1988 when it introduced a line of accounting programs for corporate bookkeeping, including a version of a database for personal computers to work in conjunction with the Lotus Development Corporation's top-selling Lotus 1-2-3 spreadsheet program. That same year the company introduced its Oracle Transaction Process Subsystem (TPS), a software package designed to speed processing of financial transactions. Oracle's TPS opened a new market niche for the company, targeting customers such as banks that needed software to process large numbers of financial transactions in a short period of time.

In 1988 Oracle unveiled its initial family of computer-aided systems engineering (CASE) application development tools, including its CASE Dictionary, a multi-user, shared repository for items pertaining to a computer application development project; and CASE Designer products, a graphical "workbench" of computer tools that enabled computer application analysts and designers to develop diagrams directly on a computer screen and automatically update the CASE Dictionary.

During Oracle's first decade of operations its relational database system was expanded to operate on about 80 different hardware systems. Extending its alliances with hardware manufacturers, in 1988 Oracle introduced its first version of a database management system program to run on Macintosh personal computers. Also in that year Oracle formed the subsidiary Oracle Complex Systems Corporation (OCSC), adding systems-integration services to its line of customer services. Shortly after the subsidiary was formed, OCSC purchased Falcon Systems, Inc., a systems integrator company.

In 1989 Oracle's emergence as a major player in the software industry was recognized by Standard & Poor Corporation, which added Oracle to its index of 500 stocks. That same year the company relocated its corporate headquarters from Belmont to a new, larger office complex in nearby Redwood Shores, California. Seeking to break into new markets, Oracle formed the wholly owned subsidiary Oracle Data Publishing in December 1989 to develop and sell reference material and other information via electronic form. Oracle closed its books on the 1980s posting annual revenues of $584 million while netting $82 million.

Oracle Stumbles: 1990–92

Oracle entered the 1990s anticipating continued high growth, and in January 1990 the company decided to seek $100 million in public financing to support its expansion. But the company's expectations were misplaced and its image as a darling of Wall Street soon began to tarnish. In March 1990 Oracle announced a record 54 percent jump in quarterly revenues but only a one percent rise in net earnings. The company's first flat earnings quarter, attributed to an accounting glitch, shook Wall Street out of a long love affair with Oracle; the day after the earnings announcement the company's stock plummeted $7.88 to $17.50 in record one-day volume with nearly 21 million of the company's 129 million shares changing hands.

In April 1990 a dozen shareholders brought suit against Oracle, charging the company had made false and misleading forecasts of earnings. On the heels of that suit, Oracle announced in May that it would conduct an internal audit and immediately restructure its management team with Lawrence Ellison assuming the additional post of chairman, while Lucas remained a director. Oracle also formed a separate domestic operating subsidiary, Oracle USA, aimed at addressing management and financial control problems of domestic operations, which the company attributed to poor earnings. Gary D. Kennedy was named president of the new subsidiary.

For the fiscal year ending May 31, 1990, Oracle initially posted record sales of $970.8 million and a net of $117.4 million. But those results were below Oracle's own estimates and the company's stock price responded by falling $2.50 to $19.88. Oracle's stock plunged deeper in August to $11.62 after

the results of an internal audit were released and Oracle restated earnings for three of its four fiscal 1990 quarters, although initially the restatement did not affect annual sales and earnings.

Late in August 1990 Oracle negotiated a $250 million revolving line of credit from a bank syndicate. A few weeks later Oracle reported the company's first-ever quarterly loss, posting a net loss of nearly $36 million with expenses outpacing revenues by 20 percent. Stockholders suffered a quarterly loss of 27 cents a share and Oracle's stock tumbled to $6.25 a share on the announcement, with the stock having lost more than $2.7 billion in market value in six months.

In response to widespread criticism concerning overzealous sales techniques, revenue recognition methods, poor management controls, and miscalculations of market strength, another management shakeup followed. After less than four months on the job, Kennedy was replaced as president of Oracle USA by Michael S. Fields, a company vice-president. Oracle also moved to reduce its annual growth rate goals from 50 to 25 percent, then laid off 10 percent of its domestic workforce of 4,000, cut two levels of its five-tier sales hierarchy, consolidated Oracle USA's financial and administrative operations to come under corporate management control, and folded various international organizations into a single division.

With Oracle's stock tumbling, the company's board approved an anti-takeover stockholder rights plan in December 1990, making any hostile attempt to acquire the firm more expensive and more difficult. Despite Oracle's most turbulent year in its history, 1990 was not without its firsts. With communism bowing out in Eastern Europe, the subsidiary Oracle Eastern Europe was formed to serve Oracle's first customer sites in Bulgaria, Czechoslovakia, Hungary, Poland, Romania, and what was then the Soviet Union.

Oracle began 1991 on a sour note, however, reporting in early January quarterly losses of $6.7 million despite a 29 percent increase in revenue. The report again sent shock waves rippling through Wall Street, and Oracle's stock fell to $6.62. By the middle of January 1991 Oracle's bankers had cut the company's line of credit from $170 million to $80 million while granting the company much-relaxed loan covenants.

Oracle announced in March 1991 that it would restate prior financial results because of accounting errors and name a new chief financial officer, Jeffrey Henley. As part of its restatement, Oracle adopted a change in accounting methods requiring that sales be booked when software was delivered, not when a contract was signed as previously allowed. Oracle's restatement of 1990 figures lowered annual revenue more than $50 million to $916 million and decreased earnings about $25 million to $80 million. The increased need to use reserve funds for accounts receivable put Oracle in violation of its loan covenants and for the second time in as many fiscal quarters the company sought a waiver of loan requirements.

Oracle's sales growth continued to decline from previous years and the company was forced to admit it had overexpanded. For fiscal 1991 Oracle topped the $1 billion sales plateau for the first time in history and at the same time posted its first annual loss in history, of $12.4 million. In October of that year Oracle secured a new $100 million revolving line of credit from another bank syndicate. Two months later Oracle negotiated an agreement for $80 million in financing from Nippon Steel Corporation, which also agreed to sell Oracle products in Japan. In return, Nippon was given rights to purchase as much as 25 percent of Oracle Japan, Oracle's marketing subsidiary in Japan.

By the end of its 1992 fiscal year, Oracle's balance sheet had improved as sales inched modestly upward and earnings rebounded, with the company logging $1.18 billion in sales while netting $61.5 million. Oracle entered 1993 with no bank debt, solid long-term financing in place, and in an improved financial position controlled by a revamped management team. As Oracle's chief executive Ellison told *Forbes* magazine in 1991: ''You pay a price for growing too rapidly.''

Oracle7 and the Promise of Interactive TV: 1993–95

The release of Oracle7 in 1992–93 seemed to signal the end of Oracle's brief taste of corporate mortality. The program supported a larger number of users than previous versions, handled more transactions, allowed data to be shared between multiple computers across a network, and improved application development features. It won industry praise, and in 1993 Ellison began talking up Oracle's role in a new technology that would expand the role of (Oracle) databases even further. In a partnership with British Telecom and Apple Computer, Oracle used its software to deliver video on demand to a test group of interactive TV users in Great Britain.

By early 1994 Ellison's new push to develop a consumer market for Oracle's databases had evolved into the ''media server alliance,'' in which Oracle's Oracle Media Server would be the database engine supplying interactive TV viewers with, for example, movies ordered through a ''digital multimedia library.'' The hardware motor for this future super media service would be massively parallel computers made by nCube, a company in which Ellison was the principal shareholder. With his typical ebullience, Ellison declared, ''I believe the sheer impact of the interactive network into the home will rival that of the electric light, the telephone and the television.''

By mid-1994, Oracle's sales had reached $2 billion, its consulting services were accounting for a healthy 20 percent of sales, and it continued its strategy of internationalizing its franchise and fueling corporate America's switch from the mainframe to the client/server computing model. The year 1994 also saw the release of Oracle7, version 7.1, an improved release that supported slow, expensive, or unreliable network environments; the copying of data between different locations; and the processing of data on multiple processors—an application increasingly favored in the so-called ''data warehouses'' used by large corporations. To serve the data warehouse market better, in 1995 Oracle acquired a product line of Information Resources, Inc. (IRI), whose online analytical processing (or OLAP) software enabled users to perform sophisticated analyses of business data in data warehouses. IRI's products also enabled users to incorporate video into their data warehouses, and when Oracle released version 3 of Oracle7 in late 1995, these new video and data-crunching capabilities enhanced its claim of having the most powerful and most multimedia-ready database product on the market.

With its share of the data management market now at 40 percent, Oracle unveiled Oracle Workgroup/2000, a forerunner of Oracle8 that would enable users to run and access databases on laptops as well as larger computers. By thus retooling its products to work with smaller computers, Oracle hoped to exploit the transition underway to more localized client/server computing environments: because these client and server computers were by definition more numerous than the huge and expensive mainframe computer, Oracle stood ready to enjoy a potentially vast increase in sales. Meanwhile, Oracle's traditional rivals, Sybase and Informix, were dropping back in market share, and Microsoft—whose enormous resources enabled it to absorb the cost of pricing its own database programs below its competitors—was positioning its SQL Server database to eventually compete head on with Oracle.

The Network Computer and Oracle8: 1996–97

As Oracle readied Oracle8 for release, it introduced its WebSystem software in late 1995 to take advantage of the growing popularity of the Internet and its small-scale in-house cousins, the corporate intranet. WebSystem promised to enable corporations to organize and distribute their data over the Internet. With Oracle's revenues topping $4 billion, in May 1996 Ellison took on the ''Wintel'' (Microsoft Windows software plus Intel's processing hardware) monolith by unveiling the ''Network Computer'' (NC). Joining with such partners as Sun Microsystems and Netscape, Ellison offered to free corporations from the costly upgrades Intel and Microsoft forced on them with every new release of Windows and the x86 family of processors. Using Ellison's $500 NC—a kind of stripped-down PC with no hard drive and therefore no applications—data and applications could be stored and accessed as needed via the World Wide Web or remote server computers, equipped, naturally, with Oracle's databases. Since corporations would no longer have to buy storage and applications for each computer, they could save millions with no loss in functionality, and Oracle would have a vast new market for its database products.

By late 1996, this strategy had evolved into the ''Network Computing Architecture,'' a new three-tier world for corporate computing that replaced the client computer-plus-server computer model with a client computer (the computer accessed by the user), an applications (such as word processing software) server, and a database server. Gone, Oracle hoped, was the expensive, fully loaded client computer, and in its place was a virtually hollow interface computer with enough power to access the servers that held its software and all its data. The virtue of this new ''open standard'' model, Ellison believed, was that it was independent of any proprietary program like Windows: the Network Computer would run any maker's applications, which would be shuttled between the three tiers—or across the Internet—in self-contained ''objects'' using cross-platform programming languages like Java or ActiveX.

Launched with much fanfare in June 1997, Oracle8 combined Oracle's longtime relational database features with the new object-based technology that Ellison's Network Computer was designed to promote. With annual sales of $5.7 billion, a ten-year annual growth rate of 30 percent, and fully 50 percent of the world's relational database market, Ellison seemed to be in a position to confidently believe what he said—Oracle8 and the NC heralded ''nothing less than a new era in computing.'' Since Ellison's announcement of the inexpensive NC a year before, however, rivals Microsoft and Intel had reacted quickly and effectively to the Oracle/Sun/Netscape threat. Microsoft had purchased WebTV, a manufacturer of an NC-like computer-television hybrid that had actually come to market, and Intel had slashed processor prices to bring powerful full-featured personal computers below the $1,000 price mark. Since NC computers were not scheduled to reach users until late summer 1997 at the earliest, to some Ellison's multimillion-dollar NC marketing campaign seemed premature at best.

Because the Asian and Pacific Rim countries accounted for 15 percent of Oracle's sales and were its fastest-growing market, when their economies began to collapse in late 1997 Oracle felt the brunt. In December 1997 Ellison announced that Oracle's earnings, though still expanding at a 35 percent annual rate, would be lower than projected. A record 172 million Oracle shares changed hands on the news, sending Oracle's stock price down 30 percent and wiping out more than $9 billion in equity.

Speaking Softer: 1998

Ellison took a conciliatory tone in a press conference in early 1998 when he admitted that Oracle had erred in talking up the Network Computer before the product had been realized. ''We just couldn't deliver network computing,'' he admitted. Oracle's public statements began to focus less on the NC and more on Oracle8, which was experiencing increasing competition from Microsoft's SQL Server database product. In mid-1998 Oracle released an updated Oracle8 to meet the Microsoft challenge head on. At the close of its 1998 fiscal year in May, Oracle could take solace in quarterly sales of $2.4 billion—a 26 percent increase over the previous year.

Principal Subsidiaries

Network Computer, Inc.; Datalogix International, Inc.; Intercom Global Corporation; Intercom Software Corporation; Intercom Network Corporation; Oracle Credit Corporation; Oracle China, Inc.; Oracle Complex Systems Corporation; Oracle Corporation Japan; Oracle Deutschland GmbH (Germany); Oracle Europe Manufacturing Limited (Ireland); Oracle Corporation United Kingdom Limited (U.K.); Oracle Corporation Canada, Inc.; Oracle Mexico S.A. de C.V.; Oracle Systems China (Hong Kong) Limited.

Further Reading

Brandt, Richard, and Evan I. Schwartz, ''The Selling Frenzy That Nearly Undid Oracle,'' *Business Week,* December 3, 1990.

Cook, William J., ''Shifting into the Fast Lane,'' *U.S. News & World Report,* January 23, 1995, p. 52.

Hatlestad, Luc, ''The Greatest Show on Earth,'' *Red Herring,* August 1997.

Maloney, Janice, ''Larry Ellison Is Captain Ahab and Bill Gates Is Moby Dick,'' *Fortune,* October 28, 1996.

Perkins, Anthony, ''Oracle CEO Larry Ellison on Building the Multimedia Library,'' *Red Herring,* May 1994.

Pita, Julia, ''The Arrogance Was Unnecessary,'' *Forbes,* September 2, 1991.

''Return of the Prophet,'' *Economist,* June 28, 1997, p. 66.

Schlender, Brenton R., ''Software Tiger: Oracle Spurs Its Fast Growth with Aggressive Style,'' *Wall Street Journal,* May 31, 1989.

—Roger W. Rouland
—updated by Paul S. Bodine

Panavision Inc.

6219 De Soto Avenue
Woodland Hills, California 91367-2602
U.S.A.
(818) 316-1000
(800) FOR-PANA (367-7262)
Fax: (818) 316-1111

Public Company
Founded: 1954
Employees: 805
Sales: $124.64 million (1996)
Stock Exchanges: New York
Ticker Symbol: PVI
SICs: 3861 Photographic Equipment & Supplies; 5946
   Camera Equipment & Photographic Supply Stores;
   7819 Services to Motion Pictures

Panavision Inc. is the foremost designer and manufacturer of cameras and lenses for the motion picture and television industries. Its products are considered by many to be the finest in cinematography. In fact, many cinematographers, directors, and producers hold Panavision's equipment as the industry standard, particularly the company's high-precision film camera systems, comprising cameras, lenses, and other accessories. As an integral provider of equipment to the motion picture and television industries, Panavision is a well-recognized brand name among professionals and the general public.

A Prominent Place in the Industry

Most motion pictures are filmed using Panavision cameras and lenses. Approximately 90 percent of all Hollywood productions utilize the company's cameras. Each of the top ten motion pictures of 1995—including *Batman Forever, Apollo 13, Die Hard with a Vengeance,* and *Ace Ventura: When Nature Calls*—were filmed using Panavision systems. In 1996, nine of the ten leading box-office successes utilized Panavision cameras and equipment, notably *Independence Day, Mission: Impossible, Twister, Ransom, The Rock,* and *A Time to Kill.*

In addition to financial success, motion pictures filmed with Panavision systems also earn acclaim for cinematography within the industry. From 1954 through 1995, the company won 14 awards from the Academy of Motion Picture Arts and Sciences. Since 1990, the Academy recognized Panavision with two Oscars and 17 awards for scientific and technical achievement. In fact, two of every three Oscar nominees for best cinematography since 1990 filmed their works with Panavision systems. Since the decade began, five of every six Oscar-winning cinematographers filmed their productions with Panavision cameras.

Panavision has been equally successful on the small screen, providing cameras and equipment for the most watched television series of the 1990s. "Friends," "Seinfeld," "Fraser," and "ER" were all filmed with Panavision equipment. "There is no question that Panavision has a dominant place in the industry," noted Christopher Dixon, an analyst with PaineWebber, in *Going Public: The IPO Reporter.*

Equipment for Rent

Panavision leases its cameras and equipment to clients through owned and operated facilities throughout the world and through a network of agents. Panavision was among the first companies in Hollywood to adopt a rental-only system for its equipment. Unlike its competitors who sell their cameras to non-affiliated rental agents, Panavision maintains ten owned and operated rental facilities in the United States, Canada, and the United Kingdom. In addition, the company has established a network of agents throughout the United States, Europe, Asia, Australia, South Africa, and Mexico.

Panavision was renowned for the level of customer service it provided through its rental facilities and agent network. The company also offered its customers 140 technicians and 160,000 square feet of factory space in which to develop new equipment. For the 1997 Hollywood blockbuster *Titanic,* for example, Panavision designed a special camera for filming underwater. Similarly, for the movie *JFK* the company engineered cameras that mounted on the hoods of cars and trucks.

Two Major Subsidiaries

Lee Lighting Ltd., a Panavision subsidiary, rents lighting, lighting grips, power distribution, power generation, and transportation equipment. One of the larger lighting rental companies in the United Kingdom, Lee Lighting also maintains two owned and operated facilities in North America: one in Orlando, Florida, and the other in Toronto, Canada. Panavision also manufactures and markets lighting filters, color correction filters, and diffusion filters through Lee Filters.

Humble Beginnings in a Los Angeles Camera Store

Panavision started in Los Angeles in 1954 in a camera store owned and operated by Robert Gottschalk. Besides being a camera retailer, Gottschalk also was an inventor of photography-related innovations. His first major breakthrough was his design and perfection of a camera lens that did not distort images in wide-screen motion pictures. He officially introduced the first Panavision lens in 1957.

Ten years later Gottschalk sold Panavision to Kinney Corporation, a predecessor company of Time Warner. Despite the sale, Gottschalk remained active in Panavision. He went on to invent the Panaflex camera, a mobile unit that was lighter and more portable than earlier camera models.

Panavision After Gottschalk

After Gottschalk died in 1982, a variety of owners bought and sold Panavision—notably Ted Field, the grandson of Marshall Field, founder of the large U.S. retail chain. Field bought Panavision in 1985 from Warner Communications for $52 million. Shortly after purchasing the company, Field bought out his investment partners, giving him total control of the enterprise. Under his direction, Panavision played a role in the production of many successful motion pictures, including *Outrageous Fortune, Critical Condition,* and *Revenge of the Nerds.* Field sold the company in September 1987 to Britain's Lee International for $142 million.

In 1988, Warburg Pincus Capital Company assumed control of Panavision. The capital company invested $60 million to keep Panavision solvent. Yet the company struggled financially when camera production dropped from 25 in 1988 to a mere 15. Panavision spent the next five years securing its place in the industry, returning to profitability in 1993.

Going to New Places in the 1990s

In 1994, Panavision led the investment group that established Panavision New York, a dealership with the right to inventory and rental of the company's cameras and lenses in the northeastern United States. The new company's president, Peter Schnitzler, CFO, Ira Goodman, and general counsel, Charles Hopfl, comprised the remainder of the investment group. Goodman explained the significance of Panavision's role in the New York-based company to *SHOOT:* "Besides Panavision actually being a minority owner of Panavision New York, they actually enter into a franchise/leased agreement . . . which gives us the right to rent Panavision cameras to production companies."

Panavision relocated its headquarters from Tarzana, California, to the Warner Center in Woodland Hills, California, in 1995. Relocation "was necessitated by our company's continued success and growth," President John S. Farrand told the *Los Angeles Business Journal.* "This new facility will allow us to bring our manufacturing, rental, and administrative operations under one roof."

Modern Innovations

In the spirit of Gottschalk, Panavision introduced a new camera system in 1995. The system was the company's enhanced version of an innovative lens created by Jim Frazier, an Australian camera operator. Frustrated by conventional lenses, Frazier developed a Deep Focus Lens System that had an almost infinite depth of field. The camera operator's system then kept objects in the foreground and background in focus. The Panavision/Frazier Lens System, however, augmented the original design. Panavision's system focused images in the same way as Frazier's, but also included a swivel tip to allow filming at various angles and the ability to rotate images in the lens. Observers considered the Deep Focus systems to be one of the foremost optical innovations since the zoom lens.

The next year, Panavision's small optics shop launched another innovation that greatly pleased cinematographers. In 1996 Panavision utilized the Tecnara MST modular RAA head to manufacture lens barrels to the exact specifications of professional camera operators.

Panavision As a Public Company in 1996

In total, Panavision manufactured 35 camera systems in 1996. With strong sales that year, the company initiated a recapitalization and its initial public offering of stock. In November 1996, Panavision offered 2.8 million shares of stock at

$17 per share. The stock sales brought the company $47.6 million for the repayment of debt and the generation of working capital, and the company decreased its annual interest expenses to $3.9 million. Within seven days of the initial public offering, Panavision stock jumped to $22.25 per share.

Panavision manufactured no less than 80 cameras in 1997. Owing to this increase in sales and the successful initial public offering, Panavision's earnings rose from $13 million in 1996 to $18 million. This new climate prompted the company to seek out acquisitions, as well as to continue the development of new photographic innovations.

In June 1997, Panavision acquired the Film Services Group of Visual Action Holdings PLC, a London-based company, for $61 million in cash. The purchase of this enterprise solidified Panavision's foothold in camera rental operations throughout the world, including the United Kingdom, France, Australia, New Zealand, Singapore, Malaysia, and Indonesia. Panavision also expanded its U.S. camera rental operations when it assumed Visual Action operations in Atlanta, Georgia; Chicago, Illinois; and Dallas, Texas.

New Technologies in the Mid-1990s

In 1997, Panavision introduced the Panavision Take 1—Digital Video Assist, which combined digital and optical technologies for quick editing, optical effects, and bridging special effects and post-production operations. Other features of the new system included multi-camera recording, random access searching, and instant playback.

Panavision released a second innovation in 1997 as well. Its Millennium camera system launched a new generation of Panaflex camera systems. This 35 mm sync-sound film camera system used optical and electronic technologies, materials, and coatings. With optical and video view finders, the system featured custom-designed and manufactured optics with advanced coatings, in addition to a full-field view finding system. The camera's enhanced light path created brighter, clearer images, and its light weight made the system versatile. For example, the studio quiet camera operated as a Steadicam and converted quickly to a handheld camera.

Into the Future

In 1997, Panavision faced the future prepared to manufacture additional camera systems and accessories in response to the growing feature film and television commercial markets in North America, the United Kingdom, and Europe. From 1992 until 1996, feature film production in North America grew from 104 to 124 films, more than a 19 percent increase. Likewise,

independent filmmaking on this continent increased from 246 in 1992 to 367 films in 1996. Europe produced 500 feature films in 1996 alone. The growth in feature film production offered many opportunities for Panavision's future prosperity, since each motion picture could require as many as ten cameras, 40 lenses, and a variety of video cameras and focusing devices—as much as $600,000 in equipment.

Similarly, Panavision expected television production to increase beyond 1997. The company prepared for greater opportunities in television as more cable channels, new networks, and increased video distribution took hold in North America. The privatization of network channels in Europe, as well as the growth of satellite networks there, also pointed to an increase in television production abroad. In 1997, Panavision estimated that revenues from commercial television production grew 61 percent since 1992, while episodic television production-related revenues increased 75 percent in those five years.

Panavision's plan was to capitalize on this growth-oriented environment. As Farrand and William C. Scott, chairman and chief executive officer of the company, wrote in Panavision's 1996 annual report: "In 1997 and beyond, we intend to take advantage of this growth in worldwide demand for filmed entertainment by leveraging our superior brand name, extensive distribution network, increased design and manufacturing capacity, and strategic financial position."

Principal Subsidiaries

Panavision International L.P.; Lee Lighting (United Kingdom); Lee Filters; Visual Action Holdings (United Kingdom).

Further Reading

Berton, Brad, "Panavision Signs $20 Million Long-Term Lease," *Los Angeles Business Journal,* July 10, 1995, p. 11.

"Creative Optics Shop Takes Aim at Tough Problems," *Modern Machine Shop,* January 1996, p. 134.

"Firm Commitment IPOs Issued in November: Panavision Inc.," *Going Public: The IPO Reporter,* December 16, 1996.

Giardina, Carolyn, "Panavision N.Y. Obtains General Camera Corporation," *SHOOT,* June 17, 1994, p. 1.

Gubernick, Lisa, "Behind the Scenes," *Forbes,* June 2, 1997, p. 108.

Newcomb, Peter, "Divided We Stand: At Thirty-two, Ted Field Has $260 Million and a Burning Ambition to Emerge from the Shadow of Older Half-Brother Marshall V," *Forbes,* October 26, 1987, p. 68.

"Panavision Inc.," *Venture Capital Journal,* January 1, 1997.

"Panavision Records Public Offering," *Going Public: The IPO Reporter,* December 2, 1996.

Soter, Tom, "Depth of Field," *SHOOT,* October 6, 1995, p. 36.

—Charity Anne Dorgan

Parker-Hannifin Corporation

6035 Parkland Boulevard
Cleveland, Ohio 44124-4141
U.S.A.
(216) 896-3000
Fax: (216) 896-4000
Web site: http://www.parker.com

Public Company
Incorporated: 1918 as Parker Appliance Company
Employees: 33,289
Sales: $4.09 billion (1997)
Stock Exchanges: New York
Ticker Symbol: PH
SICs: 3593 Fluid Power Cylinders & Actuators; 3594
   Fluid Power Pumps & Motors; 3728 Aircraft
   Equipment, Not Elsewhere Classified; 3714 Motor
   Vehicle Parts & Accessories

Motion control through the use of air, liquid, and gas is the principal concern of Parker-Hannifin Corporation. Operating internationally through numerous subsidiaries, the company manufactures fluid power systems and components for use in industrial machinery, military equipment, air, sea, and space craft, and automobiles.

Beginnings in Brakes

Parker-Hannifin started as an automobile brake company. The automotive market has been a lucrative one since its early 20th-century infancy. Thought of at first as a rich man's toy, private transportation was within the reach of the middle class well before 1911, when Henry Ford sold 78,000 Tin Lizzies. By 1918, the first year of the Parker Appliance Company's existence, there were more than one million cars a year coming out of factories in Detroit, Michigan; Cleveland, Ohio; and other centers.

Engineer-inventor Art Parker entered this profitable field modestly, with a pneumatic brake booster designed to make stopping easier for trucks and buses. This initial effort was doomed; the company's first promotional tour came to an abrupt end when an ice patch on a Pennsylvania hill sent Parker's only truck careening over a cliff. This catastrophe sank his bank balance but did not douse his dream of heading a motion control manufacturing business.

In 1924 he tried again, offering new flared-tube fitting components to expand his one-product line. Useful for many purposes, these attracted a wide variety of industrial manufacturers. The successful new start encouraged Parker to broaden his horizons. Noting opportunities in the fledgling aviation industry, he made lifelong customers of such pioneers as Donald Douglas of Douglas Aircraft Company and Robert Gross of Lockheed, who soon learned to rely on him as much for his knowledge of hydraulics as for dependable parts. Parker accepted their challenges willingly, helping them to design a hydraulic successor for the heavy gear-and-chain-driven parts then being used to move all airplane control surfaces. This cooperation was so valuable that neither Parker nor the flight industry suffered during the Depression. Instead, all parties flourished, aided by the growing military importance and commercial potential of their products.

Like the aviation section, the automotive division of the Parker Appliance Company grew during the Great Depression years. Though there was a drop of almost 500,000 in privately owned vehicles between 1930 and 1935, this decline did not affect Parker's profits. Travelers without their own cars simply used buses, which always need parts for maintenance and repair.

Now indispensable to two transport industries, the company achieved $2 million in sales in 1934. Other businesses were not so lucky: although almost four million cars rolled off assembly lines in 1935, many smaller factories had to close their doors. A victim of the Depression, the bankrupt Hupp Motor Car Corporation sold its Cleveland building to Parker.

World War II Era

By 1938 the company was ready to look for international markets for its aircraft components. Technologically advanced in both the automotive and the aviation fields, Germany seemed

Company Perspectives:

To be a leading worldwide manufacturer of components and systems for the builders and users of durable goods. More specifically, we will design, market and manufacture products controlling motion, flow and pressure. We will achieve profitable growth through premier customer service.

to be a good prospect. Parker and his wife, Helen, changed their minds after a three-month tour of German aircraft factories, because the activity they saw there convinced them that Adolf Hitler was arming for war.

Once back in Cleveland, Art Parker took immediate action. First, he licensed several patents for military aircraft parts that would broaden his previously patented product lines. His next step was to concentrate his energies on the aircraft market, shifting his focus from the automotive side of the business. Then, he placed an order for lathes—the largest that his manufacturer had ever filled.

Equipping his business for the demands of war took huge amounts of money. No longer able to channel capital from his recently abandoned commercial and industrial base, Parker insured himself against a cash-flow shortage by selling 10,000 shares of stock. During the final days of 1938, Art Parker saw his business become a public company.

By the time President Franklin Roosevelt declared war on Japan and its allies in December 1941, patents held by the Parker Appliance Company were setting standards for such components of military aircraft as hydraulic tube couplings, fuel system valves, and pumps. Two years later, there were 5,000 employees working three shifts seven days a week to produce these parts.

Though urgent at the time, this focus on purely military equipment to the exclusion of other business proved costly after the war. Art Parker, who died eight months before hostilities ended, however, was spared the sight of idle factory floors and the employment roll that had shrunk to 200 people as soon as the company's lone customer, the U.S. government, turned its attention back to peacetime pursuits. Although the prospect of bankruptcy now faced Helen Parker, she chose to keep the business running and to recruit new management.

With the help of the company's banker, Charles Sigmier, S. Blackwell Taylor was persuaded to assume the presidency of Parker and to bring his business associate Robert Cornell with him. The two men set to work immediately, selling off surplus inventory and machinery before they did anything else.

Setting long term goals to provide direction was their second task. The strategic operations plan they formulated, quickly dubbed the Corporate Creed, emphatically stated that the company was not for sale. It also stressed that management would now strive to reduce the percentage of government business, while still increasing sales to government customers; a wise precaution that would stand the company in good stead during

the Korean War. Other proposals declared that growth would henceforth take place both internally, through research and development, and externally, through friendly acquisitions. Parker, however, had to be the dominant party in all acquisitions, which would be undertaken to expand the company's product lines and keep it on the cutting edge in the field of fluid power. Targets would be profitable family-owned businesses wherever possible, and each new subsidiary would enjoy considerable autonomy. Along with these decisions came the resolve to supply only top quality products and service.

The postwar era also brought increasing interest in automation, much of which relied on fluid power to control motion through pneumatics and hydraulics. Making every effort to meet these needs by developing the range of their products, Parker also began to experiment with synthetic rubber to be used for more effective seals. The demand for these seals soon became so universal that the company became a leader in the worldwide standards that were benefiting original-equipment industries as well as many other engineering concerns. Another innovation was the decision to emphasize the production of replacement parts for those components whose constant motion caused them to wear out.

Acquisition of Hannifin, 1957

In 1957, a year that showed sales totaling $28.5 million, the Parker Appliance Company acquired the Hannifin Corporation of Des Plaines, Illinois. A manufacturer of hydraulic and air-power cylinders and of presses and other essential products used in liquid, gas, or air pressure systems, Hannifin was not a small company itself. Its $7.5 million price brought Parker two Illinois plants and one in Ohio, plus an employee roll of 600. It also brought a name change, for the Parker Appliance Company now became the Parker-Hannifin Corporation. In line with company policy, the former Hannifin customers now became customers of the entire corporation. Also in line with company policy, the new acquisition was assured that there would be no competition for the original equipment manufactured by clients.

In 1960 Parker-Hannifin organized an international division to market its products worldwide. Situated in Amsterdam, it was followed in June 1962 by Parker-Hannifin NMF GmbH in Cologne, West Germany, a subsidiary gained by the purchase of Niehler Maschinenfabrik, a manufacturer of hydraulic components. These two new channels brought the company a stronger market for valves, pumps, hoses, air filters, and regulators, as well as for the industrial products of its other ten semi-autonomous subsidiaries.

Also burgeoning at this time was the aircraft division, which had entered the specialized field of cryogenics. Joining the product line of tube fittings, missiles, space vehicles, and systems for the control of wing flaps and landing gear was a ball valve handling liquid oxygen for the *Saturn* space booster. Other components for both commercial and military use included hydraulic torpedo parts and ground support equipment. Important for military action, these items played a significant strategic role when the United States entered the Vietnam War in 1965. Later this division would produce another important device; a special assembly for the main flight control of the

Sikorsky Black Hawk helicopter. Consisting of only five pounds of bulletproof steel, it continued to function if damaged.

Keeping ahead of the competition in these ways had taken a great deal of prior planning. Mindful of the need for ultra-modern manufacturing plants, in 1961 the company had made a heavy investment in equipment to increase capacity and improve operating efficiency. This paid off handsomely the following year, with year-end sales of more than $61 million.

This modernizing, plus the strategic acquisition of profitable foreign companies that continued throughout the 1960s, added a line of refrigeration components and expanded the range of other Parker-Hannifin products now being made in Canada, Italy, France, and South Africa. Like domestic plants, overseas plants manufactured standardized components that were easily replaceable. The wisdom of this practice was reflected in 1967 sales, which totaled more than $152 million.

In 1968, outgoing President Robert Cornell was succeeded by the founder's son, Patrick Parker. Parker had spent three years running the seals division after gaining experience in various departments in Cleveland. Parker introduced new training for machine operators to ensure skilled technical labor for affiliates and subsidiaries. Next came two 1973 courses for distributors and customers. Designed to explain the increasingly complex range of Parker-Hannifin products, the first course covered basic industrial hydraulic technology; the second, advanced circuit analysis.

Growth During the 1970s and 1980s

To reduce Parker-Hannifin's vulnerability to the cyclical swings of the capital goods field, the new CEO focused on the lucrative automotive aftermarket. Reasoning that wear on cars always makes replacement parts necessary, he set his sights on the Plews Manufacturing Company, a maker of quick-disconnect couplings, acquiring this concern in 1968. A 1971 newcomer was the Ideal Corporation, which manufactured hose clamps and turn indicators. Following shortly afterwards were the Roberk Company, which made windshield wipers and rear view mirrors, and in 1978, EIS Automotive Corporation, manufacturers of hydraulic replacement parts for drum- and disc-brake systems.

The automotive section was not the only business segment receiving company attention at this time. The aerospace division, although offering a profit potential of 14 percent—compared to 12 percent apiece from the other two units—was not growing fast enough. In 1978 Parker-Hannifin remedied this situation by broadening both its customer base and its product line. Parker-Hannifin acquired two new subsidiaries: Vansickle Industries, a maker of replacement wheels and brakes for light-weight private aircraft, and Bertea Corporation, providing electro-hydraulic flight controls for commercial airliners. Both companies had previously been leaders in their fields, Bertea showing a 12-month backlog of orders as well as a $19 million contract on primary flight-control actuators for new Boeing 767 airliners.

Internal efforts were also needed to pull the company successfully through business cycle troughs. A recession in 1971, causing profits to tumble, prompted a new strategic plan called cycle forecasting. The brainchild of Tommy McCuiston, vice-president of corporate planning, the forecasting plan is based on the premise that each industry follows its own cyclical rhythm for a period normally lasting three to four years. Six phases are apparent during this time span: growth, prosperity, warning, recession, depression, and recovery. Each phase demands planning providing for the next. During the growth phase, the company anticipates prosperity by expanding the work force and speeding up its training programs. In line with its acquisition philosophy, it also looks for new manufacturing sources. The prosperity phase finds Parker-Hannifin executives planning for the months of warning ahead. Expansion is curbed and superfluous companies are sold at this period of peak earning power. The kingpin of the strategy is strict inventory control, allowing for heavy manufacturing activity during depression periods, before growth phase demand makes production expensive because of overtime wages.

Proof of the strategy's success came with the year-end sales figures for 1980, which passed $1 billion for the first time. Another benefit of the planning came to the fore in the research field, allowing the company to move actively into the field of biomedical engineering. Here, long-used principles of hydraulics were applied to the development of life-enhancing equipment like the implantable insulin dispenser for diabetics, made by the aerospace division.

In 1984, Paul Schloemer succeeded Patrick Parker as CEO and president. Adding 14 acquisitions to Parker's previous 50, Schloemer guided the corporation into the untapped areas of industrial filters and pneumatics, with the addition of Schrader Bellows, in 1984; and electromagnetic motion control, with the acquisition of Compumotor in 1986.

The 1980s brought other significant changes. A weaker dollar against the Japanese yen and the West German mark lost a considerable amount of value between 1984 and 1987. This brought down the price of U.S. technology and products to a level competitive with those of Japan and Europe, making it cheaper to produce components for foreign machinery in the United States than to import them for later assembly.

The automotive market scored heavily here. Quoted in a 1987 article in *Fortune*, investment strategist John Connolly noted that between 1986 and 1987, Honda had scaled down from one-half to one-quarter the number of parts it planned to import for cars assembled in the United States. This trend, plus joint product ventures like the Mazda/Ford Probe alliance assured a market for automotive components that helped Parker-Hannifin achieve more than $2 billion in sales in 1988, its 70th anniversary.

Other promising trends for growth came from the aerospace division. Several air disasters and near misses brought commercial airlines and air safety associations to the conclusion that tighter maintenance procedures and more frequent replacement of aircraft were necessary. This meant a greater need for complete hydraulic systems and parts for aircraft in frequent service.

In November 1989 Parker-Hannifin sold its three automotive aftermarket components divisions to an investor group headed by the president of the Parker automotive group. The company received about $80 million in exchange for its automotive parts business, and continued to manufacture original equipment for the automotive market. Parker-Hannifin also divested its small biomedical group in January 1990. The biomedical group had 1989 sales of about $4 million. These sectors were sold to allow Parker-Hannifin to concentrate on its core motion control markets—both industrial and aerospace.

Further Expansion During the 1990s

Nevertheless, growth by acquisition continued into the 1990s under the leadership of CEO Duane E. Collins, driving sales above the $3 billion mark by 1995. The 1996 purchase of Swedish-based VOAC Hydraulics fortified the company's product line with hydraulic systems for mobile heavy equipment. The Abex/NWL division of Pneumo Abex, also acquired in 1996, supplied aerospace hydraulic actuation gear. Parker-Hannifin bought New Jersey-based EWAL Manufacturing, a maker of fittings and valves, in 1997.

After 60 years, Parker-Hannifin moved into a new, 125,000-square-foot headquarters in August 1997. It donated the old headquarters building at 17325 Euclid Ave. to the Cleveland Clinic Foundation, an institution promoting medical research.

Parker-Hannifin's sales had grown vigorously, due to the earning power of its acquisitions, success in new markets abroad, and to sheer good fortune. Many plants had to run at full capacity in order to keep up with orders. It seemed Parker-Hannifin's investments in superior technology, commitment to customer service, and attention to timing and the business cycle were paying off.

Principal Subsidiaries

iPower Distribution Group Inc.; Parker de Puerto Rico, Inc.; Parker-Hannifin International Corp.; Parker Intangibles Inc.; Parker Properties Inc.; Parker Services Inc.; Abex Industries GmbH (Germany); Acadia International Insurance Limited (Ireland); Alenco (Holdings) Limited (United Kingdom); Brownsville Rubber Co., S.A. de C.V. (Mexico); Ermeto Productie Maatschappij B.V. (Netherlands); Parker Automotive de Mexico S.A. de C.V.; Parker Enzed (N.Z.) Limited (New Zealand); Parker Seal de Baja S.A. de C.V. (Mexico); Parker Seals S.p.A. (Italy); Parker Sistemas de Automatization S.A. de C.V. (Mexico); Parker Zenith S.A. de C.V. (Mexico); Parker Hannifin (Africa) Pty. Ltd. (South Africa); Parker Hannifin Argentina SAIC; Parker Hannifin A/S (Norway); Parker Hannifin (Australia) Pty. Ltd.; Parker Hannifin B.V. (Netherlands); Parker Hannifin (Canada) Inc.; Parker Hannifin Danmark A/S; Parker Hannifin de Venezuela, C.A.; Parker Hannifin (Espana) SA; Parker Hannifin GmbH (Germany); Parker Hannifin Hong Kong Limited; Parker Hannifin Industria e Comercial Ltda. (Brazil); Parker Hannifin Japan Ltd.; Parker Hannifin NMF AG (Switzerland); Parker Hannifin Oy (Norway); Parker Hannifin plc (United Kingdom); Parker Hannifin RAK, S.A. (France); Parker Hannifin S.p.A. (Italy); Parker Hannifin Sp. z.o.o. (Poland); Parker Hannifin S.r.o. (Czech Republic); Parker Hannifin Singapore Pte. Ltd.; Parker Hannifin Sweden AB; Parker Hannifin Taiwan Ltd.; Polar Seals ApS (Denmark); VOAC Hydraulics AB (Germany).

Principal Divisions

Atlas Cylinder; Daedel Division; Fluidex Division; Parker Compumotor Division; Air and Fuel Division; Airborne Division; Aircraft Wheel and Brake Division; Automotive Connectors Division; Brass Division; Commercial Filters Division; Control Systems Division; Cylinder Division; Finite Filter Division; Fluidpower Pump Division; Fluidpower Sales Division; Hose Products Division; Hydraulic Filter Division; Hydraulic Valve Division; Instrumentation Connectors Division; Instrumentation Valve Division; JBL Division; Pneumatic Division; Quick Coupling Division; Refrigeration and Air Conditioning Division; Schrader Bellows Division; Tube Fittings Division; Startoflex Aerospace/Military Division; United Aircraft Products Division.

Principal Operating Units

Fluid Connectors; Instrumentation; Filtration; Hydraulics; Automation; Climate & Industrial Controls; Seal; Aerospace; Asia Pacific; Latin America.

Further Reading

Byrne, Harlan S., "High Stepper," *Barron's,* February 12, 1996, p. 18.
Ozanian, Michael K., "17325 Euclid Avenue," *FW,* November 8, 1994, pp. 50–53.
Parker-Hannifin Corporation, "Targets: A Decade of Prodigious Employee Achievement," http://www.parker.com/corp/annualreport/targets.html.
Parker, Patrick, *Parker-Hannifin Corporation,* New York, The Newcomen Society in North America, 1980.
Wrubel, Robert, "Sum of the Parts," *Financial World,* February 23, 1988, pp. 24–25.

—Gillian Wolf
—updated by Frederick C. Ingram

Patina Oil & Gas Corporation

1625 Broadway, Suite 2000
Denver, Colorado 80202
U.S.A.
(303) 389-3600
Fax: (303) 389-3680

Public Company
Incorporated: 1996
Employees: 163
Sales: $100.3 million (1997)
Stock Exchanges: New York
Ticker Symbol: POG
SICs: 1311 Crude Petroleum & Natural Gas

A company looking to grow through acquisitions, Patina Oil & Gas Corporation is an independent energy company engaged in the acquisition, development, exploitation, and production of oil and gas properties. Patina was formed in 1996 to facilitate the consolidation of oil and gas properties owned by Snyder Oil Corporation and Gerrity Oil & Gas Corporation. All of Patina's assets were located at the Wattenberg Field in Colorado. During the late 1990s, the company held interests in 3,500 producing wells and 775 development projects. Approximately three-fourths of Patina's reserves were related to natural gas. The company's biggest customer during the late 1990s was Duke Energy Field Services, Inc., which accounted for 41 percent of the revenues collected by Patina in 1997.

Patina's Formation in 1996

Patina's sole asset at its inception were interests in oil and gas properties in the Denver-Julesberg Basin, a territory whose outer boundaries encompassed greater than a quarter of north-eastern Colorado and small parts of the border territory separating Colorado from Wyoming and Nebraska. All of Patina's properties were in Colorado, specifically at the Wattenberg Field, located approximately 35 miles northeast of Denver. Discovered in 1970, the Wattenberg Field stretched across the counties of Adams, Boulder, and Weld and was regarded as a major producing field. When Patina inherited the properties at Wattenberg in 1996, the field had produced in excess of three trillion cubic feet of natural gas equivalents during its 26-year existence as an oil and gas development property. Patina, from its inaugural day, became the largest operator in Wattenberg, responsible for producing more than 30 percent of the field's production. Within a 40-mile radius, Patina held financial stakes in 3,550 producing wells and, perhaps more impressive, maintained operational control over 95 percent of the wells in which it retained an interest. This enviable level of ownership gave the company control over all operating procedures, an advantage that enabled company executives to implement decisions that best helped Patina without deference to external decision making. Patina officials decided when and where to invest capital, they decided when developmental drilling was appropriate, and they determined how best to optimize the production from the field to secure the best pricing for Patina and its shareholders.

To the other companies operating in Wattenberg, Patina appeared overnight as their biggest rival, assuming a stalwart position in the highly regarded Wattenberg Field that must have drawn covetous eyes. For its part, Patina was indebted to its predecessors for its vaunted debut as a corporation. The circumstances surrounding the company's formation and its bountiful inheritance were directly related to the reaction of Patina's predecessors to the forces at work in Wattenberg. Wattenberg was not the place for oil and gas drillers to chance upon one great producing well and collect their riches. Wattenberg was a field pocked with myriad wells, each containing relatively small amounts of oil and gas reserves. The strategy at Wattenberg revolved around drilling a large number of wells and drawing a relatively small amount of reserves from each drilling. Whereas this strategy would not strike outside observers at first blush as a lucrative business undertaking, Wattenberg offered oil and gas operators an inviting alternative to wells with massive returns on investment. The characteristic that made Wattenberg economically attractive was that nearly every drilling realized a producing well. Better than 95 percent of the wells drilled at Wattenberg became producers, a success rate that made drilling at Wattenberg a low-risk venture in a high-risk industry.

Company Perspectives:

Patina plans to increase its reserves, production and cash flow in a cost-efficient manner primarily through: selectively pursuing consolidation and acquisition opportunities; efficiently controlling operating and overhead costs; operating its properties in order to enhance production through well workovers, development activity and operational improvements; and utilizing improved exploitation and development techniques to maximize the value of its properties. The company intends to pursue further consolidation and exploitation opportunities in Wattenberg while simultaneously focusing on acquisitions in other basins where Patina's economies of scale and operating expertise give it a competitive advantage.

With much of the risk removed from oil and gas exploration, success at Wattenberg hinged on factors other than discovering the mother lode. To realize profits, companies were dependent on the reservoir characteristics of the specific area where they drilled and their ability to astutely manage the drilling. Success, accordingly, was linked to decidedly corporate functions and capabilities, that is, keeping capital and operating costs at a level that generated the greatest profits. There was, however, one other factor that dictated success at Wattenberg, and its influence led to the formation of Patina.

No matter how well managed a company was, its executives could not control the fluctuations in the price of gas. In an oil and gas field where the corporate capabilities of a company came to the fore, the price of gas meant much when financial totals were tallied. Patina's predecessors—the companies who owned the oil and gas properties at Wattenberg prior to Patina's formation—stood as a prime example of the effects gas price fluctuation could deliver at Wattenberg. When gas prices soared to $2.08 per Mcf in 1993, Snyder Oil Corporation and Gerrity Oil & Gas Corporation, both of whom maintained a presence at Wattenberg, moved to take advantage of the price upswing. Each company launched large-scale drilling programs, but gas prices began to slip precipitously shortly thereafter. In 1994 the price dropped to $1.70 per Mcf. In 1995 the price of Rocky Mountain natural gas continued its collapse, plunging to $1.34 per Mcf. Snyder Oil and Gerrity Oil found themselves in a potentially threatening bind. With gas prices down to their 1995 level, neither could earn a reasonable return on its production from Wattenberg. To resolve their dilemma, the two companies decided to consolidate their Wattenberg interests in a publicly traded company. That company became Patina Oil & Gas Corporation, the new, dominant presence at the Wattenberg Field.

1997 Independence

The merger of the two companies' Wattenberg assets into a publicly traded company, which, for reporting purposes, was majority-owned and consolidated into Snyder Oil, made the most sense economically. Patina, therefore, was formed in January 1996, a separate entity 74 percent owned by Snyder Oil,

with Gerrity Oil shareholders owning the balance. In May 1996, Gerrity Oil was acquired by Patina. Although the arrangement struck Snyder Oil executives as the best response to the collapse of Rocky Mountain gas prices, the spinoff reportedly confused investors in Snyder Oil shares. Consequently, Snyder Oil executives made a strategic decision to sell its ownership in Patina and to plow the funds gained from the sale into the company's core operations. Snyder Oil's decision left Patina as a truly independent company able to pursue its own destiny without the influence of its majority owner, Snyder Oil. The decision to cut loose Patina from Snyder Oil caught the imagination of Snyder Oil's president and the architect behind Patina's creation, Thomas J. Edelman. Edelman saw the opportunity to use Patina's assets as a foundation for building Patina through acquisitions. It was a strategy Edelman possessed considerable experience in employing.

As Edelman weighed the opportunity available to him, he looked from a vantage point supported by a career in the oil and gas business that spanned nearly two decades. Edelman had built two oil and gas companies from the ground up during his years in the petroleum industry, creating Lomak Petroleum, Inc. and the company he presided over during the mid-1990s, Snyder Oil. With each company, his formula for success had been predicated on the gains to be realized through acquisitions. In the process of building Lomak and Snyder, Edelman had completed more than 200 acquisitions with an aggregate worth of more than $1 billion. He was a respected, seasoned veteran in the art of acquisition, demonstrating negotiating skills that made his experience nearly as valuable to Patina's regard on Wall Street as the company's assets at Wattenberg.

Edelman resolved to embark on a new era in his career, with Patina as his vehicle for achieving growth. To execute the severance of Patina from Snyder Oil, Edelman completed a series of transactions that eliminated Snyder Oil's majority ownership in Patina. Of the nearly 14 million shares of Patina stock owned by Snyder Oil, 10.9 million shares were sold to the public in a secondary offering at $9.87 per share, while the balance was purchased by Patina itself using the proceeds raised from a $40 million private placement to institutional investors. In addition, Patina sold $3 million of unregistered common shares to a group of its key managers. Of these shares sold to Patina executives, Edelman purchased $2 million. The whole series of transactions was completed in October 1997.

Expectations for the Future

Against this backdrop, Edelman had at his disposal a larger asset base than he enjoyed when he began shaping Lomak Petroleum and Snyder Oil into powerful petroleum forces. This was one of several factors that pointed to a promising future for Patina. The company's presence at Wattenberg was another factor, a valuable asset considering the low risk involved in finding reserves and because of the distinctive attractive features of Wattenberg. There were as many as eight productive formations, or "zones," beneath the field, ranging in depths from 3,600 feet to 8,000 feet. Each zone was given a name; in descending order they were Parkman, Sussex, Shannon, Niobrara, Codell, D-Sand, J-Sand, and Dakota. As Patina set out on its own in 1997, the primary drilling objectives were within the Codell and Niobrara formations, but other zones had yielded reserves. Between 1992 and 1997, Patina and its predecessors had invested roughly $350 million on development projects in the eight layers of Wattenberg, drilling 1,400 wells during the period. Development expenditures attributed exclusively to Patina totaled $8.3 million in 1996 and more than doubled the following year as the company became more aggressive, rising to $17 million.

Although Patina's presence at Wattenberg represented a promising starting point in the minds of Edelman and Wall Street analysts alike, that was all it represented—a starting point. For the company to grow, suitable acquisitions needed to be completed, which put the burden of responsibility directly on Edelman's shoulders. In late 1997 and early 1998, Edelman marshaled his forces to begin the expected acquisition campaign that would determine the worth of the company and the prudence of his decision to leave Snyder Oil. Edelman reduced Patina's debt by $51 million in 1997 to enhance the company's ability to acquire and he announced two corporate appointments that augured an imminent move on the acquisition front. In March 1998, Jay W. Decker was appointed president of Patina, freeing Edelman from one of the three top executive titles he had held since Patina's formation. Continuing to serve as chief executive officer and chairman of Patina, Edelman offered a strong reference to the company's imminent plans for expansion when he announced Decker's appointment, saying, "his [Decker's] addition will greatly strengthen our management team and broaden our exposure to acquisitions as we seek to substantially expand the company." Acquisition was the keyword as well when the company appointed another individual to its management team. In May 1998, James A. Lillo was hired as vice-president of acquisitions. Edelman noted the addition of Lillo to Patina's management team and reiterated the company's focus on acquiring oil and gas properties, saying, "We are delighted that Jim has elected to join Patina. He brings strong technical and operational skills to the management team and will be instrumental in identifying and evaluating acquisition opportunities for us as we expand our operations into other areas."

With its management team in place, Patina readied itself for the acquisitions that, to a large degree, would determine its fate. Analysts expected the company to identify acquisition candidates in the Rocky Mountain region. Their beliefs were based on conversations with Edelman, who reportedly perceived oil and gas properties in the Rockies to be undervalued in comparison with the Gulf Coast and Gulf of Mexico regions, and on the existence of other basins in the Rockies that shared characteristics with the company's Wattenberg Field. As the company moved forward in the late 1990s, however, theories concerning its future acquisition targets were pure speculation. Patina was a work in progress, yet to make its first defining move.

—Jeffrey L. Covell

Phillips-Van Heusen Corporation

1290 Avenue of the Americas
New York, New York 10104-0101
U.S.A.
(212) 541-5200
Fax: (212) 468-7064

Public Company
Incorporated: 1914 as Phillips-Jones Co., Inc.
Employees: 11,850
Sales: $1.35 billion (1997)
Stock Exchanges: New York
Ticker Symbol: PVH
SICs: 2321 Men & Boys' Shirts; 3143 Men's Footwear,
Except Athletic; 5136 Men's & Boys' Clothing; 5137
Women's, Children's & Infants' Clothing &
Accessories; 5611 Men's & Boys' Clothing &
Accessory Stores; 5699 Miscellaneous Apparel &
Accessory Stores

Phillips-Van Heusen Corporation (PVH) is a leading marketer of dress shirts, sportswear, sweaters, underwear and outerwear, and other casual clothing and accessories under the Van Heusen, Gant, Izod, and Geoffrey Beene names and footwear and related products under the Bass name. The company also markets its own private-label dress shirts and those of a few outside brands. PVH manufactures some lines of dress shirts and footwear, wholesaling its products to major retailers, chain stores, and catalog merchants, and retailing them through its own stores, generally located in factory-outlet malls.

Origins as Phillips-Jones: 1907–57

PVH's roots may be traced to the late 19th century. In 1881 Moses Phillips, a Polish-born pushcart peddler, began selling flannel shirts sewn by his wife, Ida, to coal miners in Pottsville, Pennsylvania. His business grew, and by 1887 it was known as M. Phillips & Son. Twenty years later Phillips merged his business with D. Jones & Sons, an operator of a chain of factories in Lebanon County, Pennsylvania.

The merged company was incorporated in New York in 1914 as Phillips-Jones Co., Inc. and was renamed Phillips-Jones Corp. in 1919. The following year the company revolutionized its industry by turning out the first collar-attached dress shirt. Phillips-Jones also began manufacturing men's underwear. With Moses Phillips's son Isaac as company president during this time, Phillips-Jones marketed its garments to retailers, including the Chain Shirt Shops, in which it held an interest. The company's main plants at this time were in New York City, and Albany, New York, as well as in five Pennsylvania municipalities, including Pottsville, which would by the 1940s become its main facility. Corporate headquarters were located in New York City.

Phillips-Jones's sales came to $7.2 million in 1919 and net income was reported at $1.1 million. Profits, on $11.1 million of sales in 1922, reached $1.4 million—a peak not surpassed until 1947. Although Chain Shirt Shops was dissolved in 1926, the company's retail client base continued to increase, and by the end of the decade Phillips-Jones was producing 335,000 dozen shirts a year and quantities of pajamas, underwear, nightshirts, collars, silk cloth, and piece goods.

Sales took a dip of almost $2 million in 1930, the first full year of the Great Depression. Phillips-Jones lost money in this year, as well as in the next two years, and discontinued paying dividends, a practice not resumed until 1947. Operations then became profitable again, with the exception of the recession year of 1938, when the company's sales dropped by about one-third and led to a loss of $1.7 million.

Isaac Phillips's son Seymour became president of Phillips-Jones in 1939. He revamped the styling of shirts to improve their quality and durability, expanded the company's research and development facilities, and halved its 2,000 retail accounts to a profitable 1,000 while increasing the advertising budget from less than $10,000 a year. By 1940 the company had closed its Albany plant and opened one in Geneva, Alabama.

During the 1940s Phillips-Jones added neckwear to its product line and opened two more Alabama plants. Sales and profits increased rapidly after World War II. In 1949 the company introduced its Century collar-attached shirt; with heavy promotion, some 12.5 million of these shirts were sold in the next five years.

By 1950 the company had combined annual production of 550,000 dozen dress shirts, 250,000 dozen sports shirts, 200,000 dozen neckties, 450,000 collars, and 40,000 dozen pajamas. Phillips-Jones was operating 12 plants in 1954 and serving some 6,000 department stores and haberdashers. It also had added swimwear to its 2,000 different styles of garments.

Acquisitions and Divestitures: 1957–87

Phillips-Jones changed its name to Phillips-Van Heusen in 1957 in honor of one of its well-known shirt brands. The company also reentered the retail business by purchasing Kennedy's, Inc., a chain of 15 New England menswear stores, in 1958. The company introduced Lady Van Heusen shirts and blouses in 1962, when shirts accounted for 80 percent of its sales (excluding Kennedy's). In 1964 the company acquired 11 Florida outlets, which continued operations under the Kennedy name.

By 1964 PVH had 7,000 accounts. It was offering liberal credit to these customers and also assisting them with advice on fixturing, stock, promotion, display, and turnover. The company was spending more than $2.5 million a year on advertising. About two-thirds of all men's dress shirts were wash-and-wear by 1965, when PVH introduced its Vanopress permanent-press model, available in Dacron and cotton and offered for the company's sports shirts and pajamas as well. Developing the industry's first all-cotton permanent-press shirt, PVH bet on the popularity of the new permanent-press models and announced that it would discontinue all its wash-and-wear shirts, including Century Vanaplus, the nation's largest-selling $5 wash-and-wear brand.

By this time the Lady Van Heusen line was offering a full line of sportswear, with slacks and coordinates as well as shirts and blouses. Kennedy's was selling women's and children's wear as well as men's clothing and furnishings. The company now had 16 plants, situated in Arkansas and Puerto Rico as well as in Alabama and Pennsylvania. PVH's acquisition program continued. In 1966, for example, it entered the tailored-clothing field by purchasing Joseph & Feiss Co. of Cleveland, and then outerwear with the purchase of Wind Breaker Inc. of Danville, Illinois. The company also established a men's toiletries division in 1965. Sales took a big leap in 1966, to $143.3 million, and the firm's net income reached $4.3 million, more than triple the level in the late 1950s. Seymour Phillips moved up to board chairman in 1967 and was succeeded as president by his son Lawrence in 1967.

With the February 1968 acquisition of Hamburger's & Sons, PVH was operating 39 stores, in Baltimore as well as in Florida and New England. Its retail division grew to 69 stores later in the year with the addition of four chains, including 12-store Redwood & Ross, which was part of the acquisition of Kalamazoo Pants Co., a manufacturer of slacks for teenagers. Also in 1968, PVH purchased Somerset Knitting Mills, Inc., a manufacturer of men's sweaters, and Brookfield Industries, a manufacturer of men's suits, Moyer tailored slacks, and walking shorts.

PVH liquidated Kennedy's Florida stores and the Lady Van Heusen line in 1969 but added three more retail businesses with six stores. That year the men's and boys' furnishings and outerwear division accounted for 41 percent of sales, the men's tailored-clothing division for 26 percent, and the retail division for 33 percent. With the purchase of Harris & Frank's 32 West Coast stores in 1971 from Botany Industries, the number of retail stores reached 109, accounting for 41 percent of the company's revenues. That year PVH had record net income of $7.1 million on record net sales of $253.8 million.

The economically troubled decade of the 1970s saw a number of divestitures rather than acquisitions. During this period the Van Heusen division began to lose sales to retailers' own private-label shirt offerings. The company responded by initiating its own private-label operations, closing its Pennsylvania factories, and relocating in cheaper-labor venues in the South and the Caribbean. PVH liquidated the unprofitable Wind Breaker division, with its four manufacturing plants, in 1977, and the 21-store Redwood & Ross retail chain was sold in 1979 to its former owner. Efficiency of operation enabled the company to achieve record net income of $8.9 million in the fiscal year ended February 3, 1979, on net sales and revenue of nearly $327 million.

PVH's Joseph & Feiss operation, which included the Cricketeer and Tempo labels, became more designer-oriented with the addition (under license) of a Geoffrey Beene division in 1976 and a Cricketeer Tailored Women collection in 1981. Van Heusen introduced a Halston collection in 1981. The parent company's chain of factory outlet stores, first introduced in 1976, reached 36 in 1984, while its retail division fell to 53 stores in 1984 with the sale of eight Rices Nachmans units to Hess's Department Stores. In 1987 PVH sold Joseph & Feiss and its 45 remaining specialty clothing stores to managers of these divisions for a total of $41.4 million.

These divestitures were prompted by Phillips's struggle to avoid a takeover by Dallas-based investment concern Rosewood Financial, Inc., which acquired almost one-fifth of the common stock and made a $22-per-share offer for the rest of the company. PVH's president later told a *Fortune* reporter, ''A couple of arrogant Texans came in here and said they were going to take over and run this company. They didn't know their ass from their elbow about running this or any other corporation.'' Armed with $73 million from Prudential Insurance Co. of America for convertible preferred stock and $210 million in bank loans to finance a $146 million stock buyback (at $28 a share) and the purchase of a footwear company, PVH also borrowed $77 million from Prudential by issuing high-yield notes. Rosewood admitted defeat, selling almost all of its stake for about $61 million.

PVH's management had preserved its independence at the cost of raising its long-term debt from $7 million to $121 million and seeing its common stock plunge. Essential to a corporate turnaround was the rehabilitation of footwear manufacturer and retailer G.H. Bass & Co., which PVH purchased in 1987 from Chesebrough-Pond's Inc. for $79 million, in spite of its loss of $47 million the previous year. Phillips offered his top 11 officers a $1 million bonus each if PVH's earnings per share rose at a compound annual rate of 35 percent during the four fiscal years ending in January 1992. PVH turned around Bass's losses, liquidating obsolete inventory, upgrading the product line, narrowing the range of sizes, raising prices, and increasing advertising for the Weejun and Bass trade names, the nation's predominant brands of casual shoes.

Resurgence in the 1990s

Essential to the corporate strategy was creating new markets for Van Heusen shirts, Bass shoes, and private-label shirts (made by Van Heusen) and sweaters (made by Somerset). Accordingly, at the end of 1989 the parent company purchased Windsor Shirt Co., a 39-store men's-furnishings group. By the fall of 1991 the company was fielding more than 600 tastefully designed stores in the outlet malls rapidly being erected around the country, under the names of Van Heusen, Bass, Cape Isle Knitters (sweaters), Geoffrey Beene (designer's shirts), and Windsor Shirts (private-label men's furnishings). These outlet stores proved to be the key to PVH's turnaround in the early 1990s.

By late 1990 PVH had passed Arrow Shirt Co. to become the nation's largest shirt manufacturer, having gained market share with stylish features such as spread collars, bright stripes, chambrays, and denims. One division was selling the Van Heusen brand for about $25, another was making private-label shirts for retailers like Bloomingdale's and Lands' End, and the third was selling Geoffrey Beene designer-label shirts for about $32. Also available were the Hennessy, Cezani, and Etienne Aigner labels, at prices up to $45. One key to sales success was PVH's heavy advertising in women's magazines, as studies indicated that women were purchasing at least 60 percent of all men's shirts. PVH announced in 1992 that Van Heusen had become the top-selling shirt brand in the United States, having grown 20 percent in the previous year. In 1994 Van Heusen introduced a line of wrinkle-free shirts, which it publicized as "The shirt that irons itself."

By mid-1993 PVH's outlet stores, which reached a peak of about 1,000, were accounting for half the company's revenues and even more of its earnings, according to analysts. At the same time, since the company could ill-afford to alienate the department stores it was also supplying, it situated the outlet stores in such locations as vacation resorts and small towns lacking department stores. During this time, in the midst of a national economic recession, PVH's stock price soared to nearly $40 a share, prompting a two-for-one stock split.

PVH made news in May 1993 when Bruce J. Klatsky, the company's president since 1987, was appointed company chairperson, the first chief executive not a member of the founder's family. Lawrence Phillips, who yielded the chairman's post to Klatsky in 1994 and sold the family's remaining 11 percent stake in the company in 1995, had, in 1972, given his employees the power, based on pension fund shares, to scrutinize and vote on decisions about the stock PVH held in other corporations. Klatsky, likewise, had a reputation as a champion of human rights for overseas workers and served on a White House committee to eliminate sweatshops. Consequently PVH was more than a little embarrassed by allegations in 1992 that the company had made a concerted effort to block the unionization of its workers in Guatemala. In rebuttal, Klatsky pointed out

that PVH's 650 Guatemalan employees received free on-site health care and subsidized lunches.

Although PVH fell about one-third short of its goal of a 35 percent annual compound gain in earnings per share during 1988–92, the company continued to profit through fiscal 1993 (the year ended January 31, 1994), recording its sixth consecutive year of double-digit earnings and sales growth, with net income of $43.3 million on sales of $1.15 billion. In early 1995 PVH purchased Crystal Brands Inc.'s apparel group for $114.7 million, adding the Gant, Izod, and Salty Dog brands to its apparel but also raising its long-term debt to $230 million.

In 1994, PVH's fiscal results showed a dip in profits to $30 million despite sales growth to $1.26 billion. The company closed three U.S. shirt factories in 1995 and, on revenues of $1.46 billion, reported annual net income of only $294,000 after taking a charge of $17.3 million for closing the plants. In fiscal 1996 PVH earned $18.5 million on net sales of $1.36 billion. By the fall of 1997 about 75 percent of PVH's products were being made in less-expensive overseas factories. PVH announced in August 1997 that it would close 150 of its more than 750 remaining outlet stores over a two-year period and stop manufacturing sweaters, a segment of its business that had been losing money.

At the end of fiscal 1997 (the year ended February 1, 1998) PVH disclosed that it would move Bass's shoemaking operations from Wilton, Maine, to Puerto Rico, the Dominican Republic, and other places where labor and manufacturing costs were cheaper. Footwear sales had declined following an attempt to raise Bass's moderately priced shoes to a higher price bracket. PVH announced a net loss of $66.6 million for the fiscal year after taking $85.5 million in charges for closing the Maine plant and 150 outlet stores.

PVH in the Late 1990s

About 23 percent of PVH's net sales in fiscal 1997 came from dress shirts. In the United States, Van Heusen was the best-selling men's dress shirt brand and Geoffrey Beene the best-selling men's designer dress shirt brand. Sales of other apparel, primarily branded sportswear, accounted for about 44 percent of company sales. Van Heusen was the best-selling woven sport shirt brand in the United States. Izod products included the best-selling men's sweater brand, the top-ranked golf apparel brand in pro shops and resorts, and one of the best-selling basic knit shirts. Gant represented the largest collection brand in several European countries. Footwear and related products accounted for about 33 percent of PVH's sales. Bass was the leading brand of moderately priced casual shoes in the United States.

PVH was manufacturing dress shirts in Alabama, Arkansas, Costa Rica, Guatemala, and Honduras, but most of its dress shirts and substantially all of its sportswear were being made by independent manufacturers in the Far East, Middle East, and Caribbean. About 80 percent of its footwear was also being manufactured independently, chiefly in Brazil and the Far East. Most of PVH's products were being wholesaled to major department stores and men's specialty stores nationwide, but the Gant brand was available in some 35 countries. The more than

50 Gant stores (all but one, ironically, on foreign soil) included a flagship unit that opened on Fifth Avenue in New York City in 1997. These stores were being run by Pyramid Sportswear, in which PVH held a quarter-interest. Gant planned to open an additional 10 stores in the United States by the year 2000. PVH also had about 695 company-owned stores at the end of the fiscal year, primarily in factory-outlet retail malls.

Principal Subsidiaries

Bass Net, Inc.; Camisas Modernas, S.A. (Guatemala); Caribe M&I Ltd. (Cayman Islands); Confeciones Imperio, S.A. (Costa Rica); GHB (Far East) Limited (Hong Kong); G.H. Bass Caribbean Inc.; G.H. Bass Comercio Exportacacao Ltda. (Brazil); G.H. Bass Franchises Inc.; Phillips-Van Heusen (Far East) Ltd. (Hong Kong); Phillips-Van Heusen Puerto Rico LLC; PVH Retail Corp.; The IZOD Gant Corporation.

Further Reading

Agins, Teri, "Women Help Van Heusen Collar Arrow," *Wall Street Journal,* May 22, 1992, pp. B1, B5.

Bounds, Wendy, "Critics Confront a CEO Dedicated to Human Rights," *Wall Street Journal,* February 24, 1997, pp. B1–B2.

——, "Phillips-Van Heusen Has Plans to Close Outlet Stores, Stop Making Sweaters," *Wall Street Journal,* August 1, 1997, p. A9A.

Davis, Peter, "Phillips-Van Heusen Styles Smart Advance," *Barron's,* December 25, 1972, p. 20.

Dolan, John K., "Phillips-Van Heusen," *Wall Street Transcript,* July 13, 1970, pp. 21,134–21,135.

Freeman, William M., "News of the Advertising and Marketing Fields," *New York Times,* September 5, 1954, Sec. 3, p. 8.

Furman, Phyllis, "Trying to Collar a Niche," *Crain's New York Business,* November 26, 1990, pp. 3, 42.

Kamen, Robin, "Phillips Buttons Market for Shirts," *Crain's New York Business,* June 14, 1993, pp. 1, 43.

Knowlton, Christopher, "11 Men's Million-Dollar Motivator," *Fortune,* April 9, 1990, pp. 65–67.

Morgenson, Gretchen, " 'We're Still Hungry'," *Forbes,* October 14, 1991, pp. 60, 62.

"P-VH Stacks Deck Against Rosewood," *Daily News Record,* July 31, 1987, pp. 1, 5.

Reidy, Chris, and Richard Kindleberger, "Maine Town Stunned," *Boston Globe,* February 2, 1998, pp. A1, A9.

Sloane, Leonard, "Clothier Marks Quarter Century," *New York Times,* March 7, 1964, pp. 27, 29.

"Stylish Gains Seem Set for Phillips-Van Heusen," *Barron's,* April 12, 1965, p. 25.

—Robert Halasz

PIC International Group PLC

100 George Street
London W1H 5RH
United Kingdom
(0171) 486-0200
Fax: (0171) 935-3120
Web site: http://www.pic.com

Public Company
Incorporated: 1884 as Dalgety and Company, Ltd.
Sales:£215 million (US$358 million) (1997)
Stock Exchanges: London
SICs: 0751 Livestock Services, Except Veterinary

PIC International Group PLC is the world's leading supplier of genetically improved breeding stock to the pig industry. It sells pigs as breeding stock to farmers, who raise the offspring for sale to the market. With activities in more than 30 countries, PIC leads the market in North America with a share in excess of 30 percent and the market in Western Europe with about ten percent. The company has also established a presence in such emerging markets as Central Europe, Asia, and South America. PIC is the successor company to Dalgety PLC, which, prior to its transformation into PIC in mid-1998, had a number of interests in addition to pig breeding: agricultural supplies, food ingredients, consumer food, pet food, and food distribution.

Origins As a Wool Trading Firm in the 19th Century

Dalgety was founded by Frederick Dalgety, a Scotsman who emigrated to Australia in 1833 at the age of 16. Dalgety apprenticed with a Sydney merchant until 1840, when he moved to Melbourne and found a job as the manager of a wool trading firm. Dalgety soon secured a partnership in the business, and, when his partners left the firm, he formed his own company in 1846. Dalgety and Company outfitted sheep ranchers with supplies and financed them in anticipation of yearly wool sales. The firm then shipped wool to England, where it was sold to the textile industry.

The Australian wool market collapsed in the late 1840s, and Dalgety would have been hard-pressed to continue had it not been for the discovery of gold in Australia in 1851. Dalgety and Company made a fortune supplying prospectors with food and digging equipment. The company also bought gold from the miners and then sold it abroad for a substantial profit. Although the gold rush brought Frederick Dalgety sudden wealth, he did not abandon his original business. The wool market recovered from its slump and Dalgety expanded his firm's activities throughout the continent and to New Zealand. Dalgety's connections with the wool trade became so pervasive that sheep farmers nicknamed the company and its representatives "Uncle Dal."

In 1854 Dalgety established an office in London to expedite his overseas transactions and thereafter managed his business from England. As Dalgety's firm came to dominate the Australian and New Zealand wool market, it became apparent that incorporation was necessary to supply the needed capital. Thus, in 1884 the business was floated as a public limited company—Dalgety and Company, Ltd.—with a capital of £4 million. The share issue was a great success, and Frederick Dalgety acted as the company's first chairman until his death in 1894.

First Diversification Moves in the 1890s

The new company experienced a number of hardships in its early years. In 1893 an Australian banking crisis led to financial contraction on that continent. Then, Australia's agrarian economy was devastated by the Great Drought, from 1895 to 1902. Dalgety's new chairman, Edmund Doxat, saw fit to charter a new course for the company. Dependence on wool had left Dalgety vulnerable to the drought, so Doxat began a policy of diversification.

The new process of refrigeration allowed Dalgety to tap into New Zealand's farming communities. Lamb and mutton as well as butter and cheese could now be transported safely to European markets. Refrigeration gave rise to a New Zealand dairy industry which eventually rivaled Europe's. Entry into the food business helped Dalgety weather the Great Drought, and the company began the 20th century with newfound strengths.

The early years of the new century were a prosperous time for Dalgety. World War I later stimulated wool production, for uniforms, and the postwar economic boom increased the demand for Australian and New Zealand food products. Dalgety benefited greatly from the prosperity of the 1920s, but, like many other businesses, was caught unawares by the stock market crash of 1929. The Great Depression was a lean time for the company, marked by losses and employee pay cuts. Although the outbreak of World War II in 1939 ended the Depression, wartime price controls and regulations prevented Dalgety from reaping the full benefits of the economic upswing.

The Allied victory in 1945 inaugurated a period of unprecedented growth for Western business generally, but not for Dalgety and the wool trade. In the decade following World War II, the advent of synthetic fibers such as rayon and orlon greatly undermined the wool industry. Because of falling profits during the 1950s, Dalgety attempted to narrow its field of competition by acquiring rival wool firms. The company's amalgamation policy culminated in the 1962 merger with the New Zealand Loan and Mercantile Agency, making Dalgety the largest wool broker in the world. Near monopoly status, however, could not protect the company from seasonal swings in the wool market or fluctuations in the Australian climate.

Wide-Ranging Diversification: 1960s–80s

During the 1960s drought once more wreaked havoc on the Australian wool industry. Dalgety had survived drought in the 1890s through diversification, and the company's management again decided to expand into other fields. From the late 1960s through the late 1980s, a series of acquisitions brought Dalgety into a vast range of agricultural and food businesses that eventually resulted in the multinational conglomerate of the early 1990s.

In 1966 Dalgety bought the two Balfour Guthrie companies of North America. This acquisition consisted of a Canadian trading company, with a major interest in western Canada's lumber industry, and a poultry business in the United States. Dalgety next acquired two British firms: the feed company, Grossmith Agricultural Industries, in 1969, and a pig-breeding concern called the Pig Improvement Company (the company that would become the core of PIC International Group), in 1970. In 1972 Dalgety purchased Associated British Maltsters, Britain's largest malting firm, for £19 million. With these acquisitions, the company moved away from its original base in Australia and New Zealand so that by 1976, the vast majority of Dalgety's profits came from activities in England, Canada, and the United States.

Dalgety underwent a marked shift of direction into the food business during the 1970s and 1980s. In 1977, food processing and distribution accounted for only 16 percent of Dalgety's product sales, but by 1981 this sector had risen to 45 percent, while the company's agribusiness sector became less important. The shift toward food began in 1977, when Dalgety initiated a hostile takeover of Spillers, the British flour milling, pet food, and grocery giant. There was a fierce battle between the two companies, both of which waged heated press campaigns to win the support of Spillers' shareholders. Dalgety finally acquired Spillers in 1979 for £76.5 million, giving the company a leading role in grocery product manufacture. That same year Dalgety purchased the American company Martin-Brower, one of the world's largest distributors of fast food and supplier to McDonald's restaurants in the United States and Canada. Dalgety once again increased its food product holdings in 1985 with the acquisition of the Anglo-American firm Gill & Duffus, the world's largest trader of cocoa.

During the 1980s Dalgety became a major supplier of ingredients to food manufacturers. In addition to its flour, malt, and cocoa businesses, Dalgety acquired the ingredients firms James Fleming of England and Modern Maid Food Products of America. These companies produced flavorings, coatings, and glazes for baked goods and frozen foods.

In 1987 Dalgety initiated a vigorous rationalization program to reduce company debt from previous acquisitions and concentrate on its core food business. Dalgety therefore sold a number of subsidiaries, including Balfour Guthrie and Associated British Maltsters. By late 1987 the company's asset disposal had raised some £150 million for continued expansion into the food industry.

Dalgety next moved into the lucrative snack food business, purchasing in 1987 the four Golden Wonder companies of England and Holland, producers of a popular line of potato chips and processed snacks. The following year Dalgety acquired Continental Savouries, a British company that manufactured frozen pizza. The addition of Hunters' Foods in 1989 gave Dalgety the leading role in British snack foods.

In 1989, under the leadership of Chairman Peter Carey and new Chief Executive Maurice Warren, Dalgety conducted a major review of its businesses and strategy. Seeking to reduce debt and focus on its core businesses in the United Kingdom and continental Europe in the value-added areas of food and agribusiness, the company sold Gill & Duffus in October 1989. Dalgety also substantially reduced its holdings in Australia and sold its business in Zimbabwe.

Major Changes in 1990s: From Dalgety to PIC

In 1992 John West was appointed chairman but had to resign in February 1993 due to sudden illness. Maurice Warren was appointed his replacement, with Richard Clothier taking over as chief executive. During 1993 Dalgety purchased two companies from Unigate that bolstered its food ingredients and agribusiness sectors. Morton Foods, a supplier of batter and crumb coatings to the food industry, was added in the food ingredients area, while Oldacre, which managed eight animal feed mills, joined the agribusiness sector. Also in 1993 the company spent

£42 million to buy Paragon Petcare from British Petroleum, giving Dalgety about 12 percent of the European pet food market.

By 1995 Dalgety had decided to trim its activities somewhat by focusing on pet food, food ingredients, agribusiness, and food distribution. That year the company sold its consumer food operations, Golden Wonder and Homepride Foods (cooking sauces and baking mixes). Dalgety added further strength to its pet food business in 1995 by acquiring the European pet food business of Quaker Oats for £442 million (US$700 million). The purchase increased Dalgety's share of the European pet food market to 21 percent. Integrating this acquisition led to special charges of £33.4 million (US$52.9 million) for fiscal 1995, cutting into the company's profits. Meanwhile in April 1995 Dalgety's Pig Improvement Company (abbreviated as PIC) acquired the National Pig Development Company, increasing its dominance of the industry. For the year, PIC sold more than one million breeding pigs to farmers.

Dalgety was seriously thrown off course in 1996 and 1997, in part by the crisis in British agriculture stemming from worries over Bovine Spongiform Encephalopathy (BSE) in cattle and its link to so-called "mad cow disease" in humans who eat beef from infected cows. The BSE crisis affected Dalgety's agribusiness sector as well as its pet food area. Writeoffs associated with BSE and the continuing reorganization in the pet food area were largely responsible for a steep drop in net profits in fiscal 1996 to £59.2 million and for a net loss of £89.3 million in fiscal 1997. In the midst of these troubles, Warren retired from his position as chairman in July 1996 and was replaced by Denys Henderson, former chairman of Imperial Chemical Industries. In September 1997 Clothier resigned as chief executive, succeeded by Ken Hanna, who had only joined Dalgety in May 1997 as finance director, having come to Dalgety from United Distillers.

Within a matter of months, all that would remain of Dalgety would be the Pig Improvement Company, as Dalgety management determined that making significant divestments would be worth more to shareholders than attempting to right the current ship. In early 1998 the company sold the bulk of its food ingredients business to Kerry Group PLC of Ireland for £335 million (US$560 million), with the unit's research activities and intellectual property related to wheat-based food ingredients going to E. I. DuPont de Nemours & Co. for £24.5 million (US$41 million). Next to go were the pet food business, sold to Nestlé S.A. for £715 million (US$1.2 billion), and Martin-Brower, which was bought by Illinois-based McDonald's supplier Reyes Holdings, Inc. for £120 million (US$200 million). Dalgety had initially intended to remain in the pet food business, but essentially received an offer from Nestlé that it felt it could not refuse. Finally, on May 1, 1998, Dalgety announced that it had agreed to sell its agricultural supply business through a management-led buyout for £50 million (US$84 million). Out

of the more than £1 billion pounds raised through these divestments, Dalgety planned to return about £675 million (US$1.13 billion) to shareholders in late June 1998, use about £300 million (US$500 million) to repay debt, and retain the balance.

Also in June 1998 the name of the company was changed to PIC International Group PLC, reflecting its position solely in pig breeding. PIC was increasingly active outside of Europe, initiating operations in China and Vietnam in 1997, and acquiring Pig Improvement Canada Ltd. (renamed PIC—Canada Ltd.) in April 1998. In May 1998 PIC increased its share of a joint venture in Brazil called Agroceres PIC from 12.3 percent to 49 percent. PIC had activities in more than 30 countries—15 of them through partnerships—and appeared to have a bright future as the world's undisputed market leader.

Principal Subsidiaries

The Pig Improvement Company Inc. (U.S.A.); PIC—Canada Ltd.; Agroceres PIC (Brazil; 49%).

Further Reading

Gibson, Richard, "Quaker to Sell European Pet-Food Line to Dalgety of U.K. in $700 Million Pact," *Wall Street Journal*, February 6, 1995, p. A7E.

Gresser, Charis, "Dalgety Chief Resigns Amid Restructuring Programme," *Financial Times*, September 16, 1997, pp. 1, 24.

——, "Dalgety Gets Head Down over Petfood," *Financial Times*, September 16, 1997, p. 26.

——, "When Pet Food Proves Hard to Stomach," *Financial Times*, August 12, 1997, p. 22.

Oram, Roderick, "Dalgety Hit by BSE and Warns," *Financial Times*, September 17, 1996, p. 21.

——, "Dalgety in £442m Pet Food Purchase," *Financial Times*, February 4, 1995, p. 20.

——, "Petfood Integration Hits Dalgety," *Financial Times*, September 12, 1995, p. 26.

——, "Pet Foods Problems Undermine Dalgety," *Financial Times*, February 6, 1996, p. 18.

——, "Well Balanced on Three Legs?," *Financial Times*, February 4, 1995, p. 10.

Rich, Motoko, "Dalgety Sells Pot Noodles," *Financial Times*, July 5, 1995, p. 22.

Urry, Maggie, "Charged with Making Pigs and Petfoods Fly," *Financial Times*, September 27, 1997, p. 18.

——, "Dalgety Sells Agricultural Division to Buy-Out Team," *Financial Times*, May 2, 1998, p. 21.

——, "Dalgety Transformation Proves Just the Job for the CV," *Financial Times*, February 7, 1998, p. 16.

——, "Slimmer Dalgety Starts to Shape-Up," *Financial Times*, February 5, 1998, p. 23.

Vaughan-Thomas, Wynford, *Dalgety: The Romance of a Business*, London: Henry Melland, 1984, 96 p.

Willman, John, "Kerry Pays £335m for Dalgety Food Arm," *Financial Times*, January 27, 1998, p. 23.

—updated by David E. Salamie

PIERCE LEAHY

Pierce Leahy Corporation

631 Park Avenue
King of Prussia, Pennsylvania 19406
U.S.A.
(610) 992-8200
Fax: (610) 992-8324
Web site: http://www.pierceleahy.com

Public Company
Incorporated: 1948 as Leahy & Co.
Employees: 2,500
Sales: $183.5 million (1997)
Stock Exchanges: New York
Ticker Symbol: PLH
SICs: 4225 General Warehousing & Storage

Pierce Leahy Corporation, which calls itself ''North America's Filing Cabinet,'' is a full-service provider of records management and related services and the largest such company in North America, based on the volume of records under management. The company helps clients determine what records they need to keep, and then stores those using whatever type of media clients want to use, including paper, computer tapes, optical disks, microfilm, video tapes, and x-rays. To give customers prompt access to all this material, the company also retrieves and delivers records and offers imaging, facilities management, and consulting services. As of May 1998, Pierce Leahy managed more than 65 million cubic feet of records in its some 200 facilities in the United States and Canada for over 30,000 customers.

The Beginnings of Records Management: 1930–50

President Franklin D. Roosevelt helped create the need for the records management industry by dramatically increasing the size of the federal government, first with his New Deal programs and then with the defense bureaucracy related to World War II. Roosevelt recognized the problems he was creating and wanted to use the Pentagon, which he hated architecturally, to store records after the war. But Roosevelt's interest was primarily archival; in 1934 he signed the legislation establishing the U.S. National Archives.

It was a contemporary of Roosevelt's, Emmett J. (Ed) Leahy, who first began thinking about the economic consequences of all these government records and investigating ways to manage the whole records process. Leahy started testing his ideas, first while working at the U.S. Archives, and then as director of records coordination for the Navy Department during the war.

Looking for ways to make records work more cost-efficiently, Leahy introduced the concept of high-density storage in records centers, thus reducing the amount of floor space needed for inactive records. Other initiatives included management of active files, guide and form paragraphs and letters (called correspondence management), and microfilming important and voluminous records as well as those needed for security reasons. During his four years at the Department of the Navy, Leahy's innovations saved the Navy $21 million and earned him the Navy Commendation Ribbon.

After the war, Leahy continued to work in the field as a consultant with a private company, developing the concept of a life cycle for records and producing statistics on the costs of recordkeeping. While assisting the first Commission on the Organization of the Executive Branch of Government from 1947 through 1949, Leahy pushed for the separation of records management, which he viewed as concerned with economics, effectiveness, and efficiency, from historical archiving. His efforts in this area resulted in the establishment of a new agency, the Federal Records Administration as part of the General Services Administration, not the National Archives.

In 1948, Leahy formed his own business, Leahy & Co., to advise local governments, including New York City, how to keep their records from ballooning. The following year, when he showed Eastern Airlines president Eddie Rickenbacker how that company was wasting money on inefficient recordkeeping, Eastern become Leahy's first corporate client. Other companies followed, and Leahy's client list soon included du Pont, Bethlehem Steel, and the Aluminum Company of America (Alcoa).

From Consulting to Storage: 1951–70

In 1951, with his consulting business reporting profits of $100,000, Leahy started Leahy Business Archives, a records storage business. This was the first company in the industry offering private companies a means to store their inactive records. Leahy considered records storage an economic issue, and he established his new company in New York City, where space was at a premium. Leahy served as president of his two companies and continued to promote records management until his death in 1964 at age 54.

The cost of space was not the only consideration driving companies to store their records during the early years of the Cold War. Iron Mountain Atomic Storage used the possibility of a nuclear conflict in the marketing of its bomb-proof storage facilities, located in an abandoned iron mine near Hudson, New York. Western States Underground Storage Vaults offered storage space in an old Southern Pacific railroad tunnel south of San Francisco and had a picture of a mushroom-shaped cloud over the city on its first brochure.

As new records storage companies were opening, Leo W. Pierce, Sr., founded L.W. Pierce Co., Inc. in 1957, to supply filing systems and related equipment to businesses in and around Philadelphia. In 1969, he established a subsidiary, Pierce Business Archives, when Scott Paper Co. asked him to help sort out and organize "the mess in the basement," according to a 1984 article in *Dun's Business Month*. Once the records had been organized, Scott Paper asked Pierce to store them. The company began as a $9,000 operation in, logically, the basement of Pierce's home.

Over the next two decades, Pierce's businesses expanded primarily through internal growth. During this period, Leahy Business Archives was bought by the Britannia Security Group plc of London and served as its U.S. data management division.

Expansion of Off-Site Recordkeeping: 1970s–80s

Through the early 1970s, companies (and their legal departments), considered records management simply a way to keep important papers organized. But as government agencies, both federal and state, wrote more regulations, as employee benefits expanded, and as the fear of litigation grew, companies found it was not enough to store records for their own protection. Now a company needed to store its records to protect the company itself against lawsuits and to comply with government regula-

tions. The demand for storage increased dramatically. In 1982, Pierce had revenues of over $4 million.

Leahy Business Archives and Pierce Business Archives were among a handful of large companies in the records storage business; most were small, local operations. By 1984, Leahy had 11 facilities in the Northeast, Texas, and Illinois, and was storing four billion pieces of paper for 1,200 clients. Storage costs ranged from $2 to $4 per cubic foot a year. Pierce had 1,100 clients for whom they stored 4.2 billion pieces of paper in ten facilities throughout Pennsylvania, New York, New Jersey, and Connecticut. Clients paid $2.28 to $2.40 per cubic foot annually. Both companies offered same-day retrieval to stored records, which were now keyed by computer.

"Each document is indexed and its description and location stored in a Sperry Univac 90/30 mainframe computer. With the computer indexing and records storage, a document can be located in five minutes or less," Leo Pierce explained to *Modern Office Technology* in 1985. Companies made some 1,500 requests for stored documents each day, and if received before 3:30 p.m., Pierce would deliver it the morning of the next business day. Emergency requests were filled in three hours or less.

In marketing their services, both Pierce and Leahy focused on the cost savings of a storage company over in-house, off-site storage managed by the client. With companies increasingly needing to cut costs, this approach helped convince clients to contract out their records storage activities. "Microfilm is a wonderful product, especially when used to store active records," Pierce said in the *Modern Office Technology* article. However, he estimated that for what a company paid to microfilm the contents of a four-drawer file cabinet they could store the same amount of paper for 30 years. Thus, since most records were kept for only five years, the company was wasting money microfilming.

One other factor also contributed to the increased demand for records storage: the computer. Although early in the 1980s, magazine articles were predicting that computers would herald the "paperless office," desktop publishing and other software programs actually made it easier for companies to generate even more paper.

In 1988, Britannia Security acquired Instar, Inc., a records storage company based in Massachusetts, and merged it with Leahy Business Archives. The new subsidiary was named Leahy-Instar Inc.

Growing the Company: 1989–96

By the end of the 1980s, Leo Pierce had started planning for his retirement. L.W. Pierce & Co. and the archives storage subsidiary were in good financial shape, and Pierce had designated his son Peter, one of eight children, as his successor, naming him president of the company in 1984. But Leo Pierce saw changes coming in the business as liability insurance costs soared and customers began demanding more services. It was evident to him that small operations would have a hard time making it in the coming years and that the records storage business was ripe for consolidation. Pierce Archives had become one of the industry's larger firms by concentrating on adding new customers and increasing the storage capacity of existing clients. Leo and Peter Pierce agreed that the time had come to add acquisitions to their growth strategy.

In 1989, Britannia Security decided to concentrate on its security operations, to get out of the data management business, and to put Leahy Business Archives on the market. The following year, Britannia sold Leahy Business Archives to Pierce for nearly $39 million, most of which was in cash. The acquisition doubled the size of Pierce, which was reincorporated as Pierce Leahy Corporation. The company now had branches in Connecticut, New Jersey, Maryland, Massachusetts, Rhode Island, Florida, Texas, California, and Illinois.

Pierce Leahy waited two years before making another acquisition, and then, in April 1992, the company bought Muhlenhaupt Records Management and proceeded to go on a spending spree. Between 1992 and the end of 1996, Pierce Leahy bought and integrated 25 more companies, adding some 12.4 million cubic feet of records. Among the purchases, in 1995, was Command Records Services, Ltd., Canada's leading records management company, for approximately $25 million. The new acquisition became Pierce Leahy Command. In January 1995, Leo Pierce retired as chief executive officer, although he remained chairman of the board. Peter Pierce assumed the CEO responsibilities.

The acquisitions placed a great deal of debt on the company, beginning with $30 to $40 million in financing for the Leahy Business Archives purchase. In 1996, Pierce Leahy issued $200 million in notes and arranged for $110 million in bank credit. That year, Pierce Leahy had revenues over $100 million for the first time and a net loss of $1 million.

From Storage to Records Management: The 1990s

The company's name change in 1990 to Pierce Leahy Corporation reflected more than the combining of two businesses. By eliminating the reference to business archives, the change acknowledged the desire by the industry, at least for the larger companies, to be perceived as offering more than just storage facilities for corporate records.

In 1991, the company began a two and one-half year, $8 million development project, and two years later introduced its core management information system, Pierce Leahy User Solution (PLUS). The PLUS computer system offered the only centralized system for records management in North America. Using PLUS, the company was able to locate, on a real-time basis, each unit of a customer's records, no matter where they were stored. Customers could also use a common, centralized database to access their records and information about those records, on-line. The company found PLUS reduced costs through centralization, improved customer service levels, and made it easier and less expensive to integrate the companies it acquired.

During the decade, the term ''records management'' became more prevalent in magazine articles and marketing materials, and ''document retention,'' one step in the process of records management, replaced ''records storage.'' The entire process, originally described by Ed Leahy, included six steps: creation, indexing, filing, retrieval, retention, and destruction.

To help clients, the company offered a series of services. As company President Peter Pierce explained it, ''We begin at the beginning, looking at how and why documents, records and files are created. We examine the procedures and systems in an effort to streamline, and where appropriate, eliminate record-keeping burdens for our clients.''

Following that, the company might install an active records management system to monitor every step in the life of the document and track paper, microfilm, microfiche, and any other type of storage media. Or, through its facility management division, Pierce Leahy might operate a customer's file room or storage facility. It also offered imaging and micrographic services and would even sell a customer storage containers. Still, the management of inactive records remained the largest segment of the company's business.

In 1996, to help pay down some of the debt from its purchases, the company issued $200 million in public notes without offering stock to the public. Revenues for the year passed the $100 million level, reaching $129.7 million, but the company had a net loss of over $1 million.

The Race for Number One: 1997 and Beyond

Pierce Leahy continued its three-prong growth strategy: new sales; increased use by current customers by selling additional services; and acquisitions. Companies continued to cut costs by outsourcing functions, including records management, and Pierce Leahy went after that business. The company estimated that, in 1997, only 25 percent of the records management market had been outsourced. Pierce Leahy's primary growth target, however, remained acquisitions. In the first six months of 1997, the company bought eight more records management companies, adding some 7.2 million cubic feet of records.

With the company owing more than $250 million in long-term debt, the family took Pierce Leahy public in July, offering $110 million in stock (about one-third of the company) and $120 million in notes. Of the proceeds from the stock offering, $70 million went to pay off the notes issued in 1996. The rest went to the family for its shares. The money from the new notes was used to pay off the company's big bank debt.

The year saw records under storage increase by 45 percent to 58.8 million cubic feet, with 5.2 million from new customers, 2.9 million added by existing customers, and 10.3 million from 17 acquisitions. Revenues for the year reached $183.5 million, with a net loss of $15.1 million.

Acquisitions, including that of a Canadian competitor, continued in 1998. As it approached the 21st century, Pierce Leahy had a diverse client base, annual and multiyear contracts, and a customer retention rate of 98 percent. Its reputation and low-cost service made it a strong candidate to attract a good portion of the 75 percent of all records management in North America currently being done in-house.

Principal Subsidiaries

Pierce Leahy Command Company (Canada); Monarch Box, Inc.; Advanced Box, Inc.

Further Reading

Brickley, Peg, ''Montco Records Firm Grows with Acquisitions and IPO,'' *Philadelphia Business Journal,* March 31, 1997.

——, ''Pierce Leahy Scores with Its IPO,'' *Philadelphia Business Journal,* July 11, 1997, p. 3.

''Filing: Cheaper by the Billion,'' *Modern Office Technology,* February 1985, p. 70.

Gray, Patricia Bellew, ''Howard Ross Wants You,'' *Money,* February 12, 1998.

Hill, Andrew, ''Britannia Security Sells US Data Division for 39 Million Dollars,'' *Financial Times (London),* November 28, 1989, p. 32.

''Instar to Be Acquired by Leahy in Records Storage Deal,'' *PR Newswire,* March 9, 1988.

''The Money Trail,'' *Barron's,* June 30, 1997.

''Moore Sells Records Management Subsidiary,'' *Business Wire,* November 2, 1995.

Narod, Susan, ''Cutting the Cost of Keeping Paper,'' *Dun's Business Month,* August 1984, p. 64.

Nickolaison, Ray, ''Retaining Records Is Costly, But Needed,'' *Office,* March 1993, p. 14.

Pemberton, J. Michael, ''Emmett Leahy: Patron Saint of Records Management?,'' *Records Management Quarterly,* Association of Records Managers and Administrators, April 1993, p. 56.

Pollack, Andrew, ''Computer Disaster: Business Seeks Antidote,'' *New York Times,* August 24, 1983, p. A1.

Polzer, Karl, ''Would Your Company's Records Survive Disaster?,'' *Boston Business Journal,* June 13, 1988, p. 8B.

Roberts, Jamie Cohen, ''Archive Strikes Gold in Basements of Business,'' *Philadelphia Business Journal,* June 25, 1990, p. 6B.

''Seeking Security Underground,'' *Business Week,* December 4, 1978, p. 2B

Shepherd, Ritchenya A., ''Deal Makers: Pierce Leahy Corp. Goes Public with $230 Million, Stock and Note Offering,'' *Legal Intelligencer,* August 22, 1997, p. 1.

''Solutions Today,'' King of Prussia, Penn.: Pierce Leahy Corp., 1997.

''We Set New Records for Service Every Day,'' King of Prussia, Penn.: Pierce Leahy Corp., 1996.

—Ellen D. Wernick

PMT Services, Inc.

3841 Green Hills Village Drive
Nashville, Tennessee 37215
U.S.A.
(615) 254-1539
Fax: (615) 254-1548

Public Company
Incorporated: 1994
Employees: 330
Sales: $284.2 million (1997)
Stock Exchanges: NASDAQ
Ticker Symbol: PMTS
SICs: 7389 Business Services, Not Elsewhere Classified

PMT Services, Inc. is one of the largest independent service organizations in the United States that markets and services electronic credit card authorization and payment systems to merchants, including sale and leasing of related equipment, catering primarily to small retail, wholesale and professional businesses located throughout the United States. The company provides services to merchants pursuant to contracts between the company and various processing banks.

Industry Overview

In 1997, transactions by cash or check made up approximately 75 percent of the volume of all sales at the point of sale, leaving 25 percent for credit cards, debit cards, and other electronic commerce. Since 1994, the number of debit-capable terminals shipped has exceeded the number shipped in the 15 years previous to that time. As the labor-intensive costs of processing paper checks and physical money transactions grows, analysts predict the electronic transaction processing industry will grow an average of 15 percent annually through the year 2005 as banks issue more and more credit and debit cards.

Private Company, 1984–93

The company was founded in 1984 by Richardson M. Roberts and Gregory S. Daily, current chairman and president, respectively. The two met when both had previously worked at Comdata Holdings Corporation in 1982, a fleet management company located in Brentwood, Tennessee. They both also went to work at Concord EFS, an independent service organization in Memphis, where they learned how to do credit card authorizations. Together, the two started a company that assisted truck drivers in securing money transfers while they were out on the road. Working with companies that had fleets of five trucks or less, the two were successful in not competing with their previous employer, Comdata, who serviced large-fleet companies. The company, in 1997, was a major competitor of Concord.

In 1986, PMT became an independent service organization for Rocky Mountain Bankcard, a bank credit card company which was eventually purchased by First Bank System, Inc. From 1987 to 1990, the company was financed with venture capital from Nashville, Tennessee-based Massey Burch, which provided $3.5 million. The company also began a business relationship with Omaha, Nebraska-based First National Bank, which eventually went on to handle over 50,000 of the company's accounts by 1996.

Through a fortuitous connection Roberts made at a cocktail party with George M. Miller, president and CEO of Sirrom Capital, the company received $2 million in venture capital from Sirrom. With the money, the company purchased its first portfolio from South Street Bank of Boston, Massachusetts, receiving half of the bank's accounts. The other half went to Nabanco, another independent service organization.

The company was running among the most competitive merchant acquirers in the credit card industry including megacorporations such as First Data Corporation, Nova Information Systems, National Data Corporation, and First USA Paymentech. The bigger companies service ''Tier 1'' companies, large corporations doing more than $100,000 per year on credit and debit cards; companies such as Sears, Mervyn's, Robinsons May, and The Broadway. PMT Services contracts with "Tier 2" and "Tier 3" companies, smaller merchants doing less than $100,000 per year in electronic transactions. Every time a card is swiped through one of PMT Services' terminals, the company makes 34 cents. With the company processing somewhere between 125 million and 135 million transactions a month, and with charge or debit volume totaling nearly $14 billion per year, revenues in 1993 reached $62 million, with a net income of $1.8 million.

Going Public, 1994–Date

The company went public in 1994 when, in August of that year, an initial public offering of approximately 3.5 million shares at $8 per share was completed, which generated an income of approximately $15.9 million. Revenues reached $97.2 million and net income hit $3.2 million.

In 1995, the company began purchasing merchant portfolios which gave the company the right to service specific merchants under contract to processing banks for electronic authorization and payment processing. Nine of these merchant portfolios were purchased in 1995. The first, acquired from Chicago, Illinois-based BankCard America, Inc., was purchased in April for approximately $7.7 million. Two more portfolios were purchased several months later, in July; these were from TermNet Merchant Services, Inc. and Clearwater, Florida-based Consumer Payment Services, Inc. The former, which brought the company approximately 4,000 merchant accounts at a $500 million annual charge volume, was paid approximately $6.2 million and the latter, which brought the company nearly 5,600 merchant accounts at a $350 million annual charge volume, close to $6 million.

A third portfolio was acquired in October of that year. Imperial Bank sold the company the portfolio for approximately $8.7 million. That same month, the company also underwent a second public offering of over 2.2 million shares, bringing in income of nearly $40.8 million. In mid-December of that year, the company split its stock in a two-for-one transaction. Revenues reached $139.6 million and net income of $5.5 million.

In March 1996, with some of the proceeds from its successful second public offering earlier in the year, the company purchased a merchant portfolio from Kansas City, Missouri-based United Missouri Bank, N.A. (UMB) for $13.5 million. The portfolio also serviced approximately 15,000 accounts. A strategic alliance was also set up with UMB Financial Corporation, a $6.3 billion holding company, in which the bank would

continue to service those accounts generated at its banking locations through its own alliance with Hackensack, New Jersey-based First Data Corp.

The following month, in April, the company made a third public offering, with over 3.9 million shares of stock being sold and generating income of approximately $100 million. That same month, the company purchased a second merchant portfolio from Bankcard America for approximately $6.3 million. In mid-May, the company's stock split again, but this time three-for-two. The company also purchased four merchant portfolios in 1996.

During fiscal 1996, the company began issuing common stock to acquire operating businesses with both existing merchant portfolios and sales organizations capable of generating new accounts. In July, the company acquired Martin Howe Associates, Inc. in exchange for approximately 594,000 shares of common stock. The acquisition of Martin Howe, under the direction of Jack Martin, gave the company an additional annualized charge volume of $1 billion, a sales force with an established presence in the professional sports market, and wireless radio technology for applications in the National Football League, the National Hockey League, the National Basketball Association, the Professional Golfers' Association, major league baseball, and automotive racing. The following month, in August, the company issued more stock to acquire all the outstanding stock of Chicago, Illinois-based Data Transfer Associates, Inc. Data Transfer CEO John Rante brought a Midwestern U.S. sales force that produced 175 new accounts monthly and a merchant portfolio worth approximately $400 million.

In September 1996, the company entered into an agreement with Kentucky-based National Processing Co., the operating company of National Processing, Inc., the second largest merchant processing company of MasterCard and Visa transactions in the United States at the time, in which National would provide the company with merchant card authorization and back-end processing services. National serviced "Tier 1" merchants such as Kmart Corporation and Wal-Mart, and had over 125,000 accounts and $80 billion in sales at the time of the agreement.

December saw the company issue another 424,000 shares of stock to acquire Tampa, Florida-based Fairway Marketing Group, Inc. Under the direction of CEO Eugene "Skip" Barker, Fairway brought the company a $700 million merchant portfolio and approximately 200 new accounts per month. Revenues for the year reached $214.9 million and net income was $10.3 million. According to the *Nilson Report,* the company jumped from 17 to 12 on the list of merchant-acquiring companies in 1996 and stayed firmly in the top five for non-bank acquirers. The other four were First Data Corp., National Data Corp., First USA Paymentech, and Nova Information Systems.

From 1995 to 1997, the company grew faster than any other company in its market, reaching an unprecedented 200 million transactions per year with approximately $12 billion in annualized charge volume (up 70 percent from 1996). The company quadrupled internal account generation in 1997 and enlarged its direct sales staff—through the strategically targeted acquisitions of Martin Howe, Data Transfer Associates, and Fairway Marketing in 1996, as well as four other companies by mid-1997—from approximately 100 people at the end of 1996 to over 300 by the end of the following year. The acquisitions also gave the company an entry into every major market in the United States.

The company made a total of 11 acquisitions in fiscal 1997, two of them in late January. The first acquisition was Bancard Systems, Inc., under the leadership of Michael M. McCormick, in a 3.1 million share transaction. The second came three days later when Retail Payment Services, Inc. was acquired for another 567,000 shares of common stock. Irvine, California-based Bancard Systems brought an annualized charge volume of nearly $1 billion to the company, with approximately 11,000 merchant accounts, and was producing approximately 500 new accounts per month, significantly expanding the company's presence on the West Coast. McCormick also joined the company's board of directors.

IMA Bancard, Inc., under the direction of president Joyce Cook, was acquired in March, followed by CVE Corporation, Inc. in April. IMA brought the company a southeastern U.S. sales force, a merchant portfolio worth approximately $300 million in annualized charge volume, and approximately 2,000 new merchant accounts. The acquisition of the Omaha, Nebraska-based CVE Corp., under the direction of CEO Mike Schneider, brought the company a $400 million merchant portfolio, with close to 4,000 merchant accounts, and was generating approximately 125 new accounts per month. CVE Corp. brought the additional benefit of enabling the company to become a full-service provider of check verification services, with over 3,500 accounts in that market alone.

Also in April, the company began a new marketing alliance with Salt Lake City, Utah-based Zions First National Bank, a subsidiary of Zions Bancorporation, purchasing an account portfolio from the banking giant which generated an annualized charge volume of $1 billion in 1996. By the end of the first quarter of 1997, the company had added over 11,000 merchant accounts to its portfolio for a total reaching over 105,000 accounts. The acquisition of the Zions portfolio gave the company an entrance into the bank portfolio acquisition market. The banking giant would also service the company's accounts through its 145 branches throughout Arizona, Nevada, and Utah.

In June the company acquired Eric Krueger, Inc. in exchange for approximately 579,000 shares of the company's common stock, and a month later acquired LADCO Financial Group, Inc., a leader in leasing credit card terminals to small businesses, for approximately 1.5 million shares in a $22.5 million stock swap. Traditionally, the company had sold the leases on the approximately one-third of the accounts it serviced to companies like LADCO. The acquisition of LADCO would allow the company to improve its ability to provide direct service to its accounts and to capture additional leasing revenues. The combined acquisitions of IMA Bancard, CVE, and the one other operating business which was acquired during the year, came to the company in exchange for nearly three million shares of stock. In addition to the acquisitions of seven companies in fiscal 1997, PMT Services also purchased nine merchant

portfolios, moved from Brentwood, Tennessee, to new headquarters in Nashville, and grew to approximately 140,000 merchant accounts. Revenues for the year reached $284.2 million, a 32.3 percent increase over 1996, and net income reached $16.4 million, up 92.6 percent.

Early in fiscal 1997, the company acquired Boulder, Colorado-based Bancard Inc. and Youngstown, Ohio-based Retail Systems Consulting, Inc. Bancard added to the company a $2.2 billion annual volume in sales and 70 new employees, while Retail Systems added an income volume of $300 million per year.

In October of the same year, the company purchased Chatsworth, California-based American Heritage Bankcard, one of the largest remaining independent sales organizations in the merchant processing business. Nicholas Ferrante, president of American Heritage, brought with him an annual sales volume of $800 million, a merchant base of approximately 17,000 accounts, and 20 staffers.

Looking Ahead

In June 1998, PMT announced plans to merge with Atlanta-based NOVA Corporation, becoming a wholly owned subsidiary of the latter company. The $1.3 billion pooling of interests would create the fourth largest provider of merchant bankcard processing services in the United States, with a combined portfolio of 350,000 accounts worth $40 billion annually.

Further Reading

Jennings, Robert, "PMT Services Buys 5,600 Merchant Accounts," *American Banker*, July 21, 1995, p. 12.

——, "PMT Services in Deal to Buy BankCard America Portfolio," *American Banker*, April 5, 1995, p. 12.

Piskora, Beth, "PMT Services Buys Merchant Portfolio," *American Banker*, November 6, 1995, p. 17.

"PMT Reports Earnings Leapt 92.5% in Quarter," *American Banker*, July 29, 1997, p. 28.

"PMT Services Buys TermNet Portfolio," *American Banker*, July 17, 1995, p. 13.

"PMT Services Inc.," *New York Times*, January 28, 1997, p. C4(N)/D4(L).

"PMT to Buy Bancard Systems," *Wall Street Journal*, January 28, 1997, p. B9(W).

Quittner, Jeremy, "Deal for Merchant Accounts Puts PMT at Growth Goal," *American Banker*, January 30, 1997, p. 15.

——, "Hungry PMT Buys Another Independent Sales Firm," *American Banker*, April 9, 1997, p. 15.

——, "Little PMT Thrives Among Merchant-Acquiring Giants," *American Banker*, April 3, 1997, p. 1.

——, "Merchant Acquirer, Bulking Up, Buys UMB's Portfolio," *American Banker*, March 15, 1996, p. 11.

——, "National Processing in Deal with Small Vendor to Diversify Market," *American Banker*, September 13, 1996, p. 11.

——, "PMT Buying American Heritage, a Calif. ISO," *American Banker*, October 16, 1997, p. 16.

——, "PMT Buying Another Merchant Portfolio," *American Banker*, April 3, 1996, p. 15.

——, "PMT Buys Zions' Merchant Portfolio," *American Banker*, April 25, 1997, p. 15.

Waxler, Caroline, "Credit Crunch," *Forbes*, February 10, 1997, p. 202.

—Daryl F. Mallett

QANTAS

Qantas Airways Limited

Qantas Centre
Level Nine, Building A
203 Coward Street
Mascot
New South Wales 2020
Australia
(02) 9691 3636
Fax: (02) 9691 3277
Web site: http://www.qantas.com.au

Public Company
Incorporated: 1920 as Queensland and Northern
    Territory Aerial Services Limited
Employees: 30,080
Sales: A$7.83 billion (US$5.89 billion) (1997)
Stock Exchanges: Australia
SICs: 4512 Air Transportation, Scheduled

Qantas Airways Limited, Australia's number one domestic airline, is one of the major international airlines based in the Asia-Pacific region. It is the second oldest airline in the world, after KLM of the Netherlands. Qantas serves 105 cities in 29 countries worldwide: 52 in Australia, 28 in the Asia-Pacific region (excluding Australia), 11 in Europe, 11 in North America, two in southern Africa, and one in the Middle East. In addition to its flagship Qantas line, the company also operates several regional airlines in Australia: Eastern Australia Airlines, Southern Australia Airlines, Sunstate, and Airlink. Qantas and its regional subsidiaries carry more than 18.5 million passengers a year. Qantas has a fleet of 99 Boeing jet aircraft, while the regional subsidiary lines use a mix of 49 de Havilland, Shorts, British Aerospace, and Cessna aircraft. Qantas maintains a number of alliances with British Airways PLC, which holds a 25 percent interest in Qantas; the company itself owns 17.5 percent of Air Pacific.

Early History

Qantas was founded by two World War I veterans, William Hudson Fysh and Paul McGuiness, who had served with the Australian Flying Corps. In March 1919 they gained the support of a millionaire industrialist to enter a competition for a prize of A$20,000 offered by the Australian government for the first Australians to fly from Britain to Australia within 20 days. Unfortunately, their patron died before the arrangements for their flight had been made. They accepted a related task from the Australian Chief of General Staff to survey the air race route from Longreach in Queensland to Katherine in the Northern Territory and to lay down supplies along the route for the competitors.

After the completion of their overland survey in August 1919, Fysh and McGuiness were convinced that aircraft could play an important role in transporting passengers and freight over the sparsely populated areas of western and northern Queensland and northern Australia, and they decided to form an airline. The pair had insufficient capital to launch their new venture, but a chance meeting between McGuiness and Fergus McMaster, a prominent Queensland grazier, led to the latter's involvement in the project. McMaster, together with his fellow grazier Ainslie Templeton, agreed to provide financial backing for Fysh and McGuiness's proposed air service for western Queensland.

On November 16, 1920, Queensland and Northern Territory Aerial Services Limited (Qantas) was registered in Brisbane with an initial paid-up capital of A$12,074. McMaster became the first chairman of the airline; he was to prove anything but a silent partner. Without his constant efforts on behalf of Qantas, it is doubtful whether the airline would have survived.

In 1921 the airline's head office was moved from Winton to Longreach, another small Queensland outback town. During its early years, the airline encountered serious problems in obtaining suitable aircraft, as most of the British-manufactured aircraft were inappropriate for the Australian outback and the country's hot climate. Eventually, in 1924, the company found an aircraft up to the challenge: the de Havilland DH50. In the early days, passengers were few in number and most of the airline's revenue came from joyriders and air taxi work.

It soon became clear that Qantas would need a government subsidy to survive. In late 1921 Qantas won the contract for a weekly subsidized mail service between Charleville and

Cloncurry in Queensland, and the airline's first scheduled service was inaugurated on November 2, 1922. Later in that year, Mc-Guiness left the company, leaving Fysh as the sole employee from what John Gunn described in *The Defeat of Distance: Qantas 1919–1939* as the airline's "dreamtime days." In February 1923, Marcus Griffin, the airline's first professional manager, resigned. With McMaster's support, he was replaced by Fysh.

In 1924 the subsidized mail service was extended from Cloncurry to Camooweal, and three years later another subsidized mail service was started from Cloncurry to Normanton. The following year the Australian Medical Service—renamed the Flying Doctor Service in 1942—was formed, and Qantas was contracted to operate medical flights on demand. On April 17, 1929, Qantas inaugurated the 710-kilometer Charleville-Brisbane service on the first direct link to the coast, bringing its total route network to nearly 2,380 kilometers. In 1930 the airline's headquarters were moved to Brisbane, the capital of Queensland.

QEA Formed in 1934

The original link with Britain's Imperial Airways took place in 1931, when Qantas assisted in carrying the first official airmail as part of an experimental Australia-Britain route. Qantas carried the airmail between Darwin, the capital of the Northern Territory, and Brisbane. On January 18, 1934, Qantas Empire Airways Limited (QEA) was formed as a 50-50 joint venture between Imperial Airways and Qantas to enable the Australian airline to participate in the new airmail service. QEA secured subsidized airmail contracts for the Brisbane-Singapore via Darwin and also Cloncurry-Normanton services. The new weekly transcontinental service began on December 10, 1934. In 1936 a second weekly service was begun between Brisbane and Singapore.

On June 10, 1938, the route between Australia and Britain was upgraded to a thrice-weekly subsidized service with the introduction of Short Brothers Empire Flying Boats, extending the route to Sydney. Imperial Airways and QEA's flying boats were flown directly across the whole route, with the British crews taking over the aircraft in Singapore. During the same year, QEA's headquarters were moved to Sydney.

During the 1930s KLM emerged as a major competitor with its Amsterdam-Batavia (Jakarta) service. In July 1938 its partner airline, KNILM, started a service between Batavia and Sydney. QEA regarded KLM's service as superior to that of Imperial Airways, partly because of KLM's use of American aircraft. In the earliest days of air travel, British aircraft had been superior to those built in the United States, but with the development of a major commercial airline industry in the 1930s American planes gained dominance. Pan American Airways (Pan-Am) also emerged as a strong competitor to the Imperial Airways-QEA Sydney-London service with the inauguration of a United States West Coast-Honolulu-Auckland service in 1940 after an abortive start in 1938.

World War II Efforts

After the outbreak of World War II, the Sydney-London route over which the flying boats operated became a vital line of communication. QEA continued to fly to Singapore. After the occupation of Singapore by Japan, however, all QEA aircraft eventually were recalled to Broome in Western Australia as Japanese forces advanced ever closer to Australia. QEA continued a token domestic service, but it ceased to be an overseas commercial passenger airline until the end of the war. More than half of the QEA fleet was commissioned for war service by the Australian government. Later in the war, QEA crews served alongside the Royal Australian Air Force in the battle zones of New Guinea.

In 1943 an agreement was signed between QEA, the British Air Ministry, and British Overseas Airways Corporation (BOAC—formerly Imperial Airways) to reestablish an air link between Britain and Australia. Using Catalina flying boats—obtained from the United States and leased from the Australian government—regular flights were carried out between Perth, the capital of Western Australia, and Ceylon. The single ocean route of 5,600 kilometers was the longest ever undertaken. Between July 10, 1943, and July 18, 1945, 271 flights were completed.

Postwar Rebuilding and Expansion

Having survived World War II, QEA was left with virtually no aircraft. Hence it immediately began the task of rebuilding and modernizing its fleet. Against bitter opposition from the British government, BOAC, and their friends in Australia, QEA refused to consider seriously the purchase of what it regarded, correctly as it later transpired, as inferior and unairworthy British aircraft not even off the drawing board. Instead, in October 1946 an order worth A$5.5 million was placed with Lockheed for four Constellation aircraft. The DC3 aircraft also was introduced by QEA for use on the Australia-New Guinea and on internal New Guinea and Queensland routes.

QEA had been the national overseas airline of Australia since 1934. The nationalization of Imperial Airways in 1940 by the British government, however, had led to pressure in Australia for the nationalization of QEA. In 1947 the Australian ALP government purchased BOAC's 50 percent share of QEA and later in the year also purchased Qantas's 50 percent share as well. In October McMaster retired as the result of persistent ill health, and Fysh became chairman of the newly nationalized QEA in addition to his role as managing director.

The first L749 Constellation arrived in October 1947, and on December 1 QEA began its first regular weekly service right through to London via Singapore on the famous "Kangaroo

Route." The Douglas DC4 Skymaster was introduced to the fleet in June 1949 on the new Hong Kong service. In 1949 Qantas handed over its services in Queensland and the Northern Territory and the Flying Doctor Service to Trans-Australia Airlines (TAA). TAA had been formed in December 1945 as a state-owned domestic airline. It was government policy that TAA should operate only domestic routes and that Qantas should confine itself to overseas routes. In 1950 a commercial service to Japan was inaugurated, followed in 1952 by a fortnightly service to Johannesburg, South Africa. In October 1953 QEA received permission to operate its first scheduled service to North America with the transfer of this service from the previous operator, British Commonwealth Pacific Airways (BCPA). QEA eventually took over BCPA.

In 1954 QEA began taking delivery of Lockheed Super Constellation aircraft and was able to inaugurate its new twice weekly transpacific service to North America on May 15. One service flew on to San Francisco, and the other to Vancouver. During 1957 Qantas moved to new headquarters in Sydney. The following year QEA inaugurated its first round-the-world service with the establishment of the "Southern Cross Route" via San Francisco and New York. An agreement had been signed in 1957 for QEA to operate between Britain and Australia via the United States. In mid-1958, despite Qantas's weak financial position, the government decided that both its internal operations in New Guinea and Sydney were domestic in nature. Hence it decided that Qantas's New Guinea services would be taken over by TAA, which was done in 1960.

Entered Jet Age in 1959

In 1959, ahead of all of its non-U.S. competitors, QEA took delivery of seven Boeing 707-138 jet aircraft. These were introduced in turn on both the Southern Cross and Kangaroo Routes during the same year. The Boeing 707 fleet was expanded rapidly and frequencies increased. By 1964, 13 707 jetliners were operating on most of the Qantas routes, and the airline had begun selling off its aging propeller-driven aircraft. By March 1966 Qantas's Boeing fleet had reached 19 jets, six of which were the larger 707-338C series, with five more on order.

In June 1966 Sir Hudson Fysh retired as chairman of Qantas because of his ill health. His retirement was soon followed by that of the man most responsible for the postwar Qantas expansion, Sir Cedric Turner, who had been general manager since 1951 and chief executive since 1955. Captain R. J. Richie, who had taken a leading role in building up the company's fleet and airline network after World War II, was appointed general manager; Sir Roland Wilson, a Qantas Board member, was appointed as the new chairman.

The same year Qantas made the decision to standardize its fleet with the larger Boeing 338C series and to dispose of its 138B aircraft. It also considered purchasing an even larger, innovative aircraft: the Boeing 747. As a result of the high costs involved, it was decided that Qantas would hold on to its 21-strong 707 fleet to protect its immediate position and would wait for the more advanced "B" series of the 747. An initial order for four Boeing 747Bs was placed in August 1967. Although this meant that Qantas's competitors would have been operating the wide-bodied jet for nearly two years before it took

delivery, the B series had features and refinements particularly suited to long-haul operations. The airline also changed its name on August 1, 1967, to Qantas Airways Limited. At the end of the 1960s Qantas came under government pressure to cut its airfares because the Australian Tourist Commission and some government ministers felt that lower fares were essential for the development of the Australian tourist industry. Qantas, which was facing rising costs and falling revenue yields, did not want to cut its fares.

In 1970 Qantas again decided to standardize its fleet with Boeing aircraft when it rejected the option of purchasing cheaper DC10s in favor of 747s. In the early 1970s, the airline was facing strong competition, particularly on the Pacific, where it had excess capacity and one of its principal rivals, Pan-Am, was already using 747s. Qantas was forced to eliminate some of its air crew. Qantas also experienced problems with the United States Civil Aeronautics Board (CAB), which banned its 747 operations even though Pan-Am used 747s on its flights to Australia. As a result Qantas introduced its 747s on routes to Singapore and London instead of on transpacific services to the United States West Coast. The Australian government was forced to allow more American airline services between the United States and Australia. In return the CAB allowed Qantas to begin 747 services to the United States in January 1972.

Low Fare Policy Debuted in Early 1970s

In the early 1970s, Qantas formed a charter subsidiary, Qantair Limited, with the strong support of the Australian government and with the intention of recovering the traffic it had lost to charter services on the Europe-Far East part of the journey to Australia. At the same time, Qantas decided to embark upon a low fares initiative in late 1971. On April 1, 1972, subject to British government approval, it cut the one-way fare between London and Sydney from £276 to £169. Single fares between Australia and four other European cities were cut similarly. The British government deferred approval for the new fare, but Qantas sold unapproved tickets in the face of bitter opposition to the new low fare from its rivals. In late May Britain approved the new fare. Britain's liberal line earned it a good deal of anger from other countries and non-British airlines. Qantas offered travelers charter-level fares while still retaining the benefits of scheduled services. As a result, the airline's passenger traffic and revenue grew dramatically, despite the huge increase in the price of aviation fuel.

In August 1972 the Australian government authorized Qantas to go ahead with the construction of the International Centre, the new headquarters located in downtown Sydney. In December the ALP replaced the Liberals as Australia's governing party. The new government confirmed its predecessor's decision that Qantas would replace the two domestic airlines Ansett and TAA on the highly profitable route between Port Morseby and Australia after Papua New Guinea (PNG) became independent on December 1, 1973. Qantas had been forced to surrender this route to TAA in 1960.

After the introduction of its low fare policy in 1972, Qantas embarked upon a major rationalization of its route network. Margins were extremely tight and the airline could not afford to spread its operations over wide areas of the world for reasons of prestige alone. Hence Qantas decided to discontinue its "Southern Cross Route" to London as it had done earlier in the case of operations between Hong Kong and London.

During the late 1970s, Qantas readopted its policy of offering bargain fares between Britain and Australia, beginning with fare cuts of up to £79 in 1977. Further fare cuts of up to one third were made in February 1979 as a means of meeting the potential threat of cheap advance booking charter fares proposed by Laker Airways of Britain. Qantas's policy was opposed by members of the Association of South East Asian Nations (ASEAN). Singapore especially opposed it because the policy excluded stopovers in their countries, cutting tourism and airline profits. At a meeting in Kuala Lumpur in May 1979, however, Australia succeeded in forcing ASEAN to accept its new policy.

With the sale of its last Boeing 707 in 1979, Qantas became the world's first airline to operate a fleet composed entirely of Boeing 747s. The final roundtrip 707 flight operated between Sydney and Auckland at the end of March. Over the next few years, Qantas took delivery of several 747 variations. In 1980 the chairman since 1975, Sir Lenox Hewitt, retired. He was replaced by Jim Leslie, who was initially only a part-time chairman as well as continuing temporarily to be chairman and managing director of Mobil Oil Australia.

Fleet Modernized in Early 1980s

In the early 1980s, Qantas suffered from large operating losses. After the election of the new Labor (ALP) government in 1983, one of its first actions was to increase Qantas's capital base from A$89.4 million to A$149.4 million. The airline had been denied adequate capital by the previous government and had been obliged to borrow heavily to maintain its aircraft fleet in a modern, efficient,. and competitive form. The government hoped that the injection of new capital would assure the future of Qantas as a wholly owned government enterprise.

The new government approved Qantas's largest-ever aircraft order, an A$860 million fleet modernization program involving the purchase of three stretched upper-deck Boeing 747s and six of the Extended Range Boeing 767 twin-engined jets. The latter would help service airports such as Adelaide, which joined the Qantas network in November 1982, and Cairns, Darwin, and Townsville. The twin-engined jets also were to be used on the New Zealand routes and expanded to Asian and Pacific destinations. Qantas was to sell its six oldest 747s progressively as the new aircraft were delivered.

Qantas returned to profitability in 1984, making a record pretax profit from airline operations of A$58 million in the year to March 31. This was a particularly strong performance given the depressed state of world aviation at that time. Qantas was able to sustain its strong recovery throughout the mid-1980s. Leslie felt that there was now more optimism because of depressed fuel prices and cost-cutting by airlines; he felt the main opportunity in Australia lay with tourism. Although the introduction of large, long-range aircraft could affect Australia's neighbors, Leslie reasoned, tourist traffic from the Asian region itself could be increased.

In 1987 Qantas embarked upon the next stage of its fleet modernization program with an order for four fuel-efficient Boeing 747-400s, which the company hoped would keep it competitive with British Airways (the successor to BOAC) and Singapore Airlines on its Britain-Australia and transpacific routes. The record profits made in 1986–87 of A$63.4 million showed that the airline had become one of Australia's top export earners.

In 1988 the governments of Australia and New Zealand decided to merge and partially privatize their state-owned airlines, Qantas, Australian Airlines (formerly TAA), and Air New Zealand. This plan was abandoned after it met with strong opposition in New Zealand. The New Zealand government decided to privatize Air New Zealand in its existing form. In December Qantas was part of a consortium led by Brierley Investments of New Zealand (BIL) that purchased Air New Zealand, defeating a consortium led by British Airways. As a result Qantas acquired a 19.9 percent stake in the airline. The following year it was revealed that Qantas had reached a secret financial agreement with its partners in the consortium consisting of BIL, American Airlines, and Japan Air Lines to prevent control of Air New Zealand going to British Airways. The subsequent disclosure of this agreement damaged the reputation of Qantas.

At the same time, it was revealed that A$5.4 billion was to be spent on aircraft by 1992 and that the company would need a capital injection of A$600 million by the Australian government unless shares were sold to private investors. In 1989 the Australian government proposed the complete privatization of Qantas because it needed substantial capital injections to remain competitive, which the government was unable to fund. This new proposal led to a bitter argument in the ALP. During the year Qantas took delivery of the first of its ten long-haul Boeing 747-400s and flew it nonstop from London to Sydney. It was the first airline to do so and, at 17,850 kilometers, it was the longest single distance any commercial aircraft had ever flown.

Transformative 1990s

In 1990 Qantas reported a loss as a result of its fleet expansion program and the five-month-long domestic pilots' dispute. These losses increased during 1990 as a result of the Persian Gulf crisis, and by early 1991 the airline was facing its worst financial situation since its foundation, including the Great Depression. It was decided to lay off 5,000 employees, sell nine Boeing 747s earlier than planned, and cut flying hours by 14 percent in the year to June 30, 1991.

In early 1990 Leslie was succeeded as chairman by Bill Dix, with John Ward continuing as chief executive, a position he attained in the late 1980s. In September 1990 the ALP had been persuaded to support the privatization of 49 percent of Qantas. The Australian government abandoned plans to float the airline in early 1991, however, and decided on a trade sale instead.

Change came swiftly and dramatically for Qantas in the mid-1990s. In June 1992 the Australian government approved Qantas's purchase of 100 percent of Australian Airlines' shares for A$400 million; in October 1993 the operations of Qantas and Australian Airlines were merged under a single brand:

"Qantas—The Australian Airline." It was also announced in June 1992 that later that year 49 percent of Qantas would be sold through a trade sale, and the remaining 51 percent would be floated publicly during the first half of 1993. Foreign interests were to be allowed to invest up to 35 percent, with the Australian government retaining a "golden share." These plans were soon altered, however, when British Airways in late 1992 stepped in with an offer that was accepted—and completed in March 1993—to buy a 25 percent stake in Qantas for A$665 million (US$470 million). The move was part of British Airways' push to create a global airline through the creation of a series of alliances, and it followed previous British Airways deals for 49 percent of TAT of France, 49 percent of Deutsche BA, and 31 percent of Air Russia. British Airways soon added a 25 percent stake in American carrier USAir. Meanwhile, in March 1993 the Australian government pumped A$1.35 billion into Qantas to enhance the company's competitive position ahead of privatization.

For Qantas, the deal with British Airways created management turmoil, as it was reported that both Dix and Ward opposed the alliance. By mid-1993 both had departed the company, replaced by Gary Pemberton, former chief executive of Brambles Ltd., a transport and industrial services group, in the chairman's slot and James Strong, who had previously served as chief executive of Australian Airlines, in the chief executive's chair.

The new management team immediately faced the challenge of completing the privatization, as well as improving upon the dismal results of fiscal 1993—an after-tax loss of A$376.8 million (US$250 million) incurred in part as a result of difficulties encountered integrating the operations of Australian Airlines. A plan for a September 1993 public offering of the remaining 75 percent of Qantas still owned by the government was pushed back because a spate of privatizations were hitting the Australian market at about the same time. The long-anticipated initial public offering (IPO) finally took place in July 1995, and the company's shares were listed on the Australian Stock Exchange; the foreign ownership limit was set at 49 percent. Qantas thus celebrated its 75th anniversary in 1995 as a public company.

From 1993 through 1997 the alliance between Qantas and British Airways evolved into a comprehensive collection of code-sharing arrangements, reciprocal frequent flyer programs, reciprocal lounge access agreements, and scheduling and pricing coordination efforts. The core of this alliance—and most airline alliances—was the code-sharing, whereby a passenger's trip involves two legs, one a Qantas flight and one a British Airways flight, but the entire trip is booked as either entirely Qantas or entirely British Airways. During this period, Qantas developed or enhanced several other alliances, including ones with American Airlines, Canadian Airlines International, Air Pacific, Asiana, Japan Airlines, Emirates, and Reno Air.

In March 1997 Qantas sold its 19.9 percent stake in Air New Zealand to ANZ Securities for NZ $425 million (US$295 million), using the after-tax profits of A$66.8 million to reduce debt. This move was made in anticipation of Air New Zealand's purchase of an equity stake in Qantas's Australian rival, Ansett Australia. Later that year Qantas began a A$560 million

(US$430 million), three-year fleet modernization program, including the refurbishment of all of its international 747s and 767-300ERs with new seats featuring seat-back personal video screens.

By fiscal 1997 Qantas was solidly in the black, achieving net profits of A$252.7 million (US$190.1 million) on revenues of A$7.83 billion (US$5.89 billion). In early 1998, however, the Asian financial crisis forced the company to cut back on some of its Asian service, including destinations in Indonesia, Malaysia, and Thailand. The crisis threatened to derail, at least temporarily, what had been a fairly successful start to Qantas's public company era.

Principal Subsidiaries

Eastern Australia Airlines; Southern Australia Airlines; Sunstate Airlines; Airlink; Qantas Flight Catering Limited.

Further Reading

"AAL Sets Melbourne Date," *Flight International,* October 28, 1971.
"Action Pending?," *Flight International,* June 3, 1971.
"Aircraft Sale Underlines Qantas Rise," *Financial Times,* December 13, 1991.
"Airfares Pacific Punch-up," *Economist,* March 31, 1979.
"Air Transport," *Flight International,* May 18, 1972.
"Australia Accounts," *Flight International,* January 27, 1972.
"Australia and ASEAN Agree to Be Dissatisfied in Air Fares War, But Canberra Comes Out on Top," *Far Eastern Economic Review,* May 18, 1979.
"Australian Airlines Joins the Rat Race," *Financial Times,* April 26, 1991.
"Australian Charter Activity," *Flight International,* August 12, 1971.
"Australian Labor Party Reopens Row over Privatisation," *Financial Times,* June 9, 1989.
"Australian Party Backs Airline and Telecom Selloff," *Financial Times,* September 25, 1990.
"Australian Sector," *Financial Times,* February 5, 1990.
"An Australian View," *Flight International,* February 22, 1973.
"Australia Set for Airline Shake-up," *Flight International,* June 10, 1992.
"BA Defeated in Bid for Air New Zealand," *Financial Times,* December 22, 1988.
Ballantyne, Tom, "Flying Doctor," *Airline Business,* December 1993, pp. 30+.
——, "Global Horizons: The Linkage with British Airways Should Open Up New Opportunities for Qantas," *Airline Business,* April 1993, pp. 32+.
——, "Qantas: Hard Times," *Airline Business,* May 1991, pp. 16+.
——, "A Step in the Dark: Australia's New Aviation Policy Is a Gamble Designed to Help Smooth the Privatization of Qantas and Australian Airlines," *Airline Business,* May 1992, pp. 44+.
Beyond the Dawn: A Brief History of Qantas Airways, Sydney: Qantas Public Affairs, 1997.
"CAA Approves £196 Sydney Fare," *Flight International,* June 1, 1992.
"Canvassing for Qantas," *Flight International,* August 28, 1971.
Deans, Alan, "Flight to a Merger: Australia's Main Airlines to Form Mega-Carrier," *Far Eastern Economic Review,* June 25, 1992, pp. 51+.
Donoghue, J. A., "Approaching Privatization," *Air Transport World,* July 1995, pp. 54+.
"Flying in Formation: Airline Alliances," *Economist,* July 22, 1995, pp. 59+.
Fysh, Hudson, *Qantas at War,* Sydney: Angus & Robertson, 1968.

——, *Qantas Rising: The Autobiography of the Flying Fysh*, London: Angus & Robertson, 1966.

——, *Wings to the World: The Story of Qantas 1945–1966*, [Sydney]: Angus and Robertson, [1970].

Gallagher, Jackie, "The World's Favourite Jigsaw?," *Airline Business*, December 1993, pp. 50+.

"Government Support for Qantas," *Flight International*, August 24, 1972.

Gunn, John, *Challenging Horizons: Qantas 1939–1954*, St. Lucia: University of Queensland Press, 1987.

——, *The Defeat of Distance: Qantas 1919–1939*, St. Lucia: University of Queensland Press, 1985.

——, *High Corridors: Qantas 1954–1970*, St. Lucia: University of Queensland Press, 1988.

——, *Pioneers of Flight: An Abridged History of Qantas Airways Limited*, The Company, c. 1987.

Hall, Timothy, *Flying High: The Story of Hudson Fysh, Qantas, and the Trail-Blazing Days of Aviation*, Sydney: Methuen of Australia, 1979.

"Hard Time for Qantas Too," *Flight International*, April 22, 1971.

Hill, Leonard, "Re-Creating Qantas," *Air Transport World*, May 1994, pp. 74+.

Leonard, Bruce, *A Tradition of Integrity: The Story of Qantas Engineering and Maintenance*, Sydney: UNSW Press, 1994.

"Lower Fares Predicted to Australia," *Times* (London), June 20, 1978.

"Many Happy Returns," *Airline Business*, September 1995, pp. 84+.

"Month's Delay on New Australia Fare," *Flight International*, April 27, 1972.

"National Carrier Gets Boost," *Financial Times*, January 10, 1984.

"New Zealand May Slow Pace of State Asset Sales," *Far Eastern Economic Review*, January 26, 1989.

"NZ Backs Qantas Bid for Stake in Airline," *Financial Times*, September 20, 1988.

"130,000 in Rush for Cheap Flights to Australia," *Daily Telegraph*, February 2, 1979.

"Pacific Brinkmanship," *Flight International*, July 29, 1971.

Phelan, Paul, "Adventurous Analyst," *Flight International*, August 12, 1992, p. 36.

"Profitable Outlook Forecast for Airlines," *Financial Times*, January 14, 1986.

"Progress in Pacific Dispute," *Flight International*, September 16, 1971.

"Qantair Deferred," *Flight International*, December 30, 1971.

"Qantas' Airline Loss Doubles," *Financial Times*, December 2, 1983.

"Qantas: Airline of the Year," *Air Transport World*, February 1996, pp. 30+.

"Qantas and Australian to Merge," *Financial Times*, June 3, 1992.

"Qantas Blames Losses on Fleet Expansion and Pilots Dispute," *Financial Times*, June 30, 1990.

"Qantas Cutback," *Flight International*, April 29, 1971.

"Qantas Cuts Fares," *Flight International*, April 13, 1972.

Qantas Empire Airways and Q.A.N.T.A.S.: Chronological History, Sydney: Qantas Empire Airways, 1946.

"Qantas Faces Financial Crisis," *Financial Times*, March 18, 1991.

"Qantas First All-747 Carrier," *Flight International*, April 7, 1979.

"Qantas Gains in New Guinea," *Flight International*, September 28, 1972.

"Qantas Is Confident in Its Pacific Role," *Travel Weekly*, December 16, 1985, pp. 1+.

"Qantas May Still Merge with Air NZ," *Financial Times*, April 2, 1988.

"Qantas Merger with Air NZ Ruled Out," *Financial Times*, April 21, 1988.

"Qantas-NZ Merger Plan Wins Cool Reception," *Financial Times*, April 5, 1988.

"Qantas on the Move," *Interavia Aerospace World*, September 1993, pp. 44–46.

"Qantas Profit Soars," *Financial Times*, June 5, 1986.

"Qantas Renews Drive for Airline Link-up," *Financial Times*, June 29, 1988.

"Qantas Sees Lower Profits After Posting Record Year," *Financial Times*, October 13, 1989.

"Qantas Soars to Record Results," *Financial Times*, July 28, 1987.

"Qantas Switches 747s," *Flight International*, August 26, 1971.

"Qantas to Buy Four Boeings," *Financial Times*, March 3, 1987.

"Qantas Trijet Choice," *Flight International*, August 27, 1970.

"Secret Formation for Air NZ Deal," *Financial Times*, March 28, 1991.

"Shake-up in Australia," *Flight International*, December 21, 1972.

"Sir Lenox Hewitt Leaves Qantas," *Flight International*, July 5, 1980.

Skapinker, Michael, "UK Stays Qantas 'Flagship' Route," *Financial Times*, July 18, 1997, p. 23.

". . . So Does Qantas," *Flight International*, December 9, 1971.

Stackhouse, John, *From the Dawn of Aviation: The Qantas Story, 1920–1995*, Double Bay, New South Wales: Focus Pub., 1995.

"State-owned Australian Airlines to Get More Cash," *Financial Times*, May 4, 1983.

"Strong Return to Black for Qantas," *Financial Times*, June 1, 1984.

Tait, Nikki, "Qantas Finds Privatisation Route Far from Smooth," *Financial Times*, April 28, 1995, p. 26.

——, "Qantas Set to Alter Its Share Structure," *Financial Times*, November 23, 1995, p. 31.

Thomas, Geoffrey, "Asian Competition Prompts Qantas to Modernize Fleet," *Aviation Week & Space Technology*, June 9, 1997, pp. 40–41.

——, "Asian Downturn Expected to Hit Qantas, Ansett, Air NZ," *Aviation Week & Space Technology*, March 2, 1998, p. 51.

"Threat to Airline," *Daily Telegraph*, January 12, 1979.

"Unapproved Fares Offered," *Flight International*, May 11, 1972.

"USAir: BA's American Dream," *Observer*, July 12, 1992.

Westlake, Michael, and Jacqueline Rees, "Birds of a Feather," *Far Eastern Economic Review*, July 6, 1995, pp. 69–70.

Woolsey, James P., "Qantas Changing Course to Capture New Growth Possibilities," *Air Transport World*, May 1986, pp. 24+.

——, "Qantas Is Trying to Rise from 1989 Turmoil," *Air Transport World*, June 1990, pp. 32+.

—Richard Hawkins
—updated by David E. Salamie

Rawlings Sporting Goods Co., Inc.

1859 Intertech Drive
Fenton, Missouri 63026-1926
U.S.A.
(314) 349-3500
Fax: (314) 349-3588

Public Company
Founded: 1887
Employees: 1,420
Sales: $147.6 million (1997)
Stock Exchanges: NASDAQ
Ticker Symbol: RAWL
SICs: 3949 Sporting Athletic Goods, Not Elsewhere
    Classified; 5091 Sporting & Recreational Goods &
    Supplies; 5941 Sporting Goods Stores & Bicycle Stores

Rawlings Sporting Goods Co., Inc. is a leading supplier of baseball, basketball, and football equipment and team uniforms in North America and, through a licensee, of baseball equipment and uniforms in Japan. The company also was, in 1997, manufacturing and distributing hockey equipment, volleyballs, and soccer balls, and various sports accessories, and licensing its name for numerous products, including golf equipment, athletic shoes, activewear apparel, socks, and sports drinks. Rawlings' own manufactured products accounted for about one-quarter of its net revenues in fiscal 1997. The company also owned four factory outlet stores stocked with its own products and those of other parties.

Sporting Goods Pioneer, 1887–1967

The company was founded in 1887 by George and Alfred Rawlings, brothers who opened a small store in St. Louis. Its first catalogue characterized the company as "Dealers in Fishing Tackle, Guns, Baseball, Football, Golf, Polo, Tennis, Athletic and General Sporting Goods." The store soon went up in flames, so the Rawlings brothers got into manufacturing in 1898 in partnership with Charles W. Scudder, who put up the money.

Rawlings Manufacturing Co. introduced the first shoulder pads for football players in 1902, a fiber-and-felt model it

named, for an executive, "Whitley's Armor Clothing." It designed the first all-weather football, began outfitting baseball's St. Louis Cardinals with team uniforms in 1906, and first provided baseballs to a professional league in 1907.

Bill Doak, a Cardinals pitcher, designed the first modern baseball glove in 1919, when he separated the thumb and forefinger with a few strands of rawhide to form a deep pocket. Doak took the idea to Rawlings, which manufactured it and made it a bestseller for more than 25 years. Harry Latina, who joined the company in 1922, was dubbed the "Glove Doctor," for devising such models as the Deep Well Pocket (1930), Trapper (1940), and V-Anchored Web (1950). He took out some 30 patents for features such as adjustable thumb and pinky loops, the V-anchored web, and the "Edge-u-cated" heel. Latina's son Rollie assumed his father's job in 1961 and retained it until 1984.

Rawlings was the fourth largest sporting goods concern in the United States in 1954, with sales of about $12 million. The following year it was sold for $5.7 million in stock to A.G. Spalding & Bros., Inc., the second largest sporting goods company in the nation. At this time Rawlings was producing—aside from baseball gloves, balls, and shoes, and protective football equipment—equipment and supplies for badminton, basketball, bowling, boxing, golf, softball, tennis, track, volleyball, and wrestling.

In 1957 the company introduced the prestigious Rawlings Golden Glove Award to recognize fielding excellence for the best major league baseball players at each position.

Following a review of the Spalding acquisition, the Federal Trade Commission charged that the deal represented a violation of antitrust laws and in 1960 ordered Spalding to divest itself of Rawlings. Spalding took the case to court but lost and in 1963 sold the firm—which had been renamed Rawlings Sporting Goods Co.—to a group of private investors for about $10.3 million in cash and notes. John L. Burns, the new chairman and chief executive officer, said Rawlings' sales had exceeded $20 million in 1962 and that the company had not lost money in any year of its existence.

Now renamed Rawlings Corp., the company was the only privately owned sporting goods manufacturer in the United States. It retained headquarters in St. Louis and had eight factories, including three in Puerto Rico. Most had been built within

---

Company Perspectives:

To produce high quality, innovative products that enhance the performance of athletes around the world. Rawlings' "The Mark of the Pro" represents our commitment to customer satisfaction for all ages and levels of play.

---

the last decade. Rawlings discontinued athletic footwear in 1967 after losing business to more advanced German molded-shoe models. Also a factor was a ban placed on the importation of kangaroo hide, which the company had been using to produce cleated athletic footwear. Rawlings had been making cleated shoes since the 1890s.

A-T-O/Figgie Unit, 1967–94

Rawlings had annual sales of about $20 million and six manufacturing plants—four in Missouri and two in Puerto Rico—when it was sold in 1967 to Automatic Sprinkler Corp. of America, which changed its name to A-T-O Inc. in 1969. This conglomerate made the company a division under its prior Rawlings Sporting Goods name. In 1970 12 major league teams were wearing Rawlings-made uniforms, including the Pittsburgh Pirates, clad in the division's newly introduced doubleknit nylon and cotton uniforms. The American Basketball Association was using Rawlings' red-white-and-blue ball. A-T-O said that in just one year Rawlings had become the largest manufacturer of quality hockey equipment in the United States. Rawlings also was making golf and tennis equipment.

Early in 1971, A-T-O acquired Adirondack Industries, best known for its baseball bats but also an important producer of toboggans and winter toys as well as archery bows and hockey sticks. The Adirondack operation was combined administratively with the Rawlings division. Rawlings' earnings slumped in the early 1970s but recovered following a restructuring in the middle of the decade that stressed advertising and marketing. The company claimed to have achieved 20 percent annual sales growth between 1975 and 1978. Rawlings Golf was established in 1976 as a separate A-T-O division. Its products consisted of clubs, balls, shoes, bags, gloves, and Toney Penna custom equipment.

Rawlings raised its baseball profile in 1977, when it replaced Spalding as the supplier of baseballs to the major leagues. This contract amounted to 30,000 dozen Haitian-produced balls a year, not counting additional special ones for the World Series and the All-Star Game. In addition, Rawlings was, in 1979, the chief source of baseballs for the amateur market, accounting for about one-third of the annual sale of some 1.2 million dozen baseballs. Rawlings also had taken the lead from Wilson Sporting Goods Co. in the baseball glove business, with a market share between 28 and 30 percent and more than 50 percent of the gloves sold to professional players. Adirondack bats were less prominent, because of the longtime dominance of Hillerich & Bradsby Co.'s Louisville Sluggers. Nevertheless, Adirondack bats held 15 to 20 percent of the (strictly wooden bat) professional market and 25 percent of the amateur market.

A-T-O was renamed Figgie International, Inc. in 1981. By 1983 Adirondack was no longer making toboggans. The Rawlings Sporting Goods division had added soccer balls to its line of products. Rawlings Golf was manufacturing and distributing clubs under both the Toney Penna and Rawlings brand names, and it was also distributing balls, bags, shoes, and gloves. This division had been discontinued, however, by 1986.

Baseball equipment was accounting for half of Rawlings' sales in 1985. It was still the sole supplier of major league baseballs, which were still being hand-stitched in Haiti. The bats (now renamed AdirondackRawlings bats) were being made (as well as Sherwood hockey sticks) in Dolgeville, New York, from timber in the Adirondack Mountains, with the plant heated from wood shavings. Most U.S.-sold baseball gloves were now being manufactured in the Far East, but Rawlings maintained three plants in Missouri, plus a Tennessee facility that produced leather for some of the gloves and covers for the baseballs.

By 1990 Rawlings was one of only two companies manufacturing baseball gloves in the United States. Hides from steers raised in Missouri were taken to a Chicago leather company, where they were tanned and sorted. Each animal yielded two hides, one from each side, with each hide providing enough material for almost four gloves. From Chicago the hides were being shipped to a Rawlings plant in Ava, Missouri, where all of the company's professional baseball gloves, most of its baseball helmets, and most of its footballs were produced.

Rawlings resumed manufacturing athletic footwear in 1989, with made-in-Taiwan baseball, softball, and football shoes featuring both metal and rubber cleats for natural and artificial surfaces. The top-of-the-line series came in kangaroo hide—again legal for some species—while two lower-priced series came in leather and synthetic material. Rawlings dropped the football shoes in 1991, however, because of poor sales. The company opened a baseball manufacturing plant in Costa Rica in 1987 and closed its Haitian factory in 1990 because of political instability. It had discontinued Haitian-based production of baseball gloves in 1986 and clothing in 1989.

In 1987 Rawlings was designated the "Official Uniform and Protective Equipment Supplier to Major League Baseball," the first company to earn that recognition. Its five-year contract as the supplier of team uniforms for major league baseball and licensed apparel such as replica jerseys and T-shirts was not a success for the company, however, and was not renewed. Also in 1987, Rawlings balls were selected as the "Official Basketball and Football for NCAA Championships," and the company became the exclusive licensee for a complete line of NCAA retail basketballs, footballs, and accessories.

Rawlings' net revenues dropped from $145 million in 1991 to $135.8 million in 1992. Although the company had record net income of $7.1 million in the latter year, industry observers said it was experiencing manufacturing and distribution problems that made it unable to develop and market goods to sports retailers on a timely basis. The end of the major league baseball licensed apparel contract was a blow to Rawlings' clothing division, which accounted for about one-fourth of company sales and had been targeted for growth to offset the flat sales of hard goods. In an effort to turn things around, the company appointed its fifth president in the last six years—and the ninth in the last 11 years—in 1992.

Public Company, 1994–97

Sales remained stagnant and profits dropped in the next two years. Rawlings executives later blamed a lack of investment by parent Figgie International, Inc., forcing the firm to limit production of certain products and to cancel certain customer orders. In 1994 Figgie put Rawlings up for sale to the public, collecting $127 million, including a one-time cash dividend. The newly independent company assumed debt equivalent to 60 percent of its capital. Another new chief executive officer, Carl Shields, assumed the helm that year and vowed to make changes. Figgie, he said in the March 1995 issue of *Bobbin*, had been "a metal-bending, heavy manufacturing-type company that never did understand how to operate in a consumer goods industry."

Accordingly, Rawlings fielded a new management team whose objective was to emphasize apparel, tripling sales in this category during the next three years without investing in new facilities. During this period the company began selling "hotel wear"—spruced-up sweatsuits and similar items that athletes might wear hanging around a hotel or traveling to a game. Rawlings did not neglect its traditional baseball market, however, renewing its contract to make major league baseballs through the year 2000 and, in 1994, becoming the exclusive supplier of baseballs to the 18 minor leagues through 2000.

To increase sales in Canada, its largest foreign market, Rawlings in 1997 purchased Daignault Rolland, primarily a manufacturer of hockey equipment, although it also made baseball equipment for Canada only. Later in the year Rawlings also purchased the Victoriaville line of hockey equipment, used by more than 150 professional hockey players, from California Pro Sports Inc. for $14 million. Rawlings had reentered the hockey business previously by contracting with other companies to make pads and some kinds of gloves endorsed by St. Louis Blues star Brett Hull. The company also announced that it would soon resume offering products for volleyball and soccer.

In 1998 Rawlings started production, in Taiwan, on Radar Ball, a baseball with a built-in microchip and display unit for measuring the speed of a pitch. It also introduced a new aluminum bat less prone to dents and cracking and had developed one that could be customized by adding up to eight ounces of weights and counterweights. Some analysts, however, contended that the company remained overdependent on baseball, a stagnating source of revenue whose sales in fiscal 1997 (the year ended August 31, 1997) came to $80.8 million—$7.5 million less than the previous year. Annual net revenues for the company as a whole during fiscal years 1995 through 1997 ranged between $144.1 million and $149.7 million, while net earnings ranged between $4.6 million and $5.5 million. The company's long-term debt was $32.6 million at the end of fiscal 1997.

Perhaps most important for Rawlings' future was a five-year contract it signed in 1997 with Host Communications Inc., the nation's leading sports marketer. Host vowed to raise the company's visibility in the marketplace by such comparatively inexpensive means as working its contacts with coaches' orga-

nizations and the amateur sports contests that Host was sponsoring around the world. Bull Run Corp., a holding company that owned 30 percent of Host, had acquired ten percent of Rawlings' stock and had purchased warrants to buy an even larger share of the company.

In 1997 Rawlings believed itself to be the leading supplier of baseballs, baseball gloves, and baseball protective equipment in North America. It was offering 14 types of baseballs and more than 125 styles of gloves, ranging in retail price from $5.99 to $159.99 for the Heart of the Hide series. Rawlings also was selling 20 different types of basketballs, 22 types of footballs, and football shoulder pads, other protective gear, and accessories. The acquisition of the Victoriaville hockey business added hockey sticks and protective equipment to supplement the full line of protective hockey equipment the company had developed in 1996. Rawlings also had licensing agreements with 16 companies in the United States to use the brand name on various products and with the ASICS Corp. in Japan for use of the Rawlings name on all types of baseball equipment, team uniforms, and practice clothing.

Rawlings was manufacturing, in 1997, baseball gloves, batting helmets, footballs, and injection-molded accessories in Ava, Missouri; wooden baseball bats in Dolgeville; apparel in Licking, Missouri; tanned leather in Tullahoma, Tennessee; hockey sticks in Daveluyville, Quebec; hockey protective equipment in Montreal; and hockey goaltender equipment in London, Ontario. The balance of its products (accounting for three-quarters of net revenues) was being manufactured by third parties in various Asian countries and Mexico.

Of Rawlings' net revenues in fiscal 1997, baseball equipment accounted for 55 percent; basketball, football, and volleyball equipment for 19 percent; apparel, 11 percent; international, five percent; licensing, four percent; and miscellaneous, six percent.

Principal Subsidiaries

Rawlings Canada, Inc.; Rawlings de Costa Rica; Rawlings Sporting Goods Company of Missouri.

Further Reading

Cedrone, Lisa, "Rawlings Scores with New Lineup," *Bobbin*, March 1995, pp. 42, 44, 46–49.

LaMarre, Thomas E., "Squeeze Play," *Nation's Business*, November 1985, p. 87R.

Marshall, Christy, "Rawlings' Baseball Line Hits Grand Slam," *Advertising Age*, April 16, 1979, pp. 22, 62.

"Playing to Win," *St. Louis Commerce*, September 1991, p. 6.

Sanford, Robert, "Glove Affair," *St. Louis Post-Dispatch*, May 8, 1994, pp. E1, E5.

Stamborski, Al, "Challenges Force Rawlings To Learn How To Innovate," *St. Louis Post-Dispatch*, February 22, 1998, pp. E1, E8.

Stichnoth, Matthew M., "Baseball and Beyond," *New York Times*, March 15, 1998, Sec. 3, p. 4.

Wessling, Jack, "Rawlings Re-Enters Athletic Footwear After 22 Years," *Footwear News*, September 4, 1989, p. 26.

Wulf, Steve, and Kaplan, Jim, "Glove Story," *Sports Illustrated*, May 7, 1990, pp. 73–76.

—Robert Halasz

Rayonier Inc.

1177 Summer Street
Stamford, Connecticut 06905-5529
U.S.A.
(203) 348-7000
Fax: (203) 964-4528
Web site: http://www.rayonier.com

Public Company
Incorporated: 1926 as Rainier Pulp and Paper Company
Employees: 2,500
Sales: $1.1 billion (1997)
Stock Exchanges: New York
Ticker Symbol: RYN
SICs: 0811 Timber Tracts; 2411 Logging; 2421 Sawmills
& Planing Mills; 2426 Hardwood Dimension &
Flooring Mills; 2611 Pulp Mills

Rayonier Inc. is an international leader in the forest products industry, operating in more than 70 countries. The company manages 1.5 million acres of timberland in the United States and New Zealand, which provide the raw material for its products. It also operates two pulp mills and three lumber manufacturing facilities in the United States, plus a fiberboard plant in New Zealand that was acquired in 1997. Over two-thirds of Rayonier's income is derived from sales of timber and wood products; its remaining income comes from sales of specialty pulp products, such as cellulose pulp used in photographic film. Rayonier focuses heavily on the international market; about half of its sales in 1997 were made outside of the United States. During the late 1990s, along with many other companies in this industry, Rayonier experienced a drop in sales and income. In 1997 it was forced to close a third pulp mill in Washington, and its sales reflected a six percent decrease from the previous year. Rayonier's operations also were greatly affected by environmental regulations, especially in the Pacific Northwest.

A New Use for a Weed

In the mid-1920s, the aptly named Edward M. Mills (formerly a Chicago banker) began to seek investors to develop pulp and paper mills in the largely untapped forests of the Pacific Northwest. The result was the Rainier Pulp and Paper Company, founded in Shelton, Washington, in 1926. The company's first product was pulp produced from hemlock, which grew so plentifully on the Olympic Peninsula that it was considered a weed and so was very cheap. Unfortunately for the new company, the Great Depression threatened its early success. Mills turned to a new market, convincing the Dupont Company to use hemlock instead of cotton to manufacture rayon, which was just beginning to be popular.

This strategy proved immensely successful. By 1937, the Rainier Company merged with two other mills in Washington, to form Rayonier Incorporated. This name was a combination of "rayon" and "Rainier," the mountain visible from the original Shelton mill. Rayonier immediately became the largest rayon pulp manufacturer in the world, and was listed as a publicly traded company on the New York Stock Exchange.

Becomes Part of ITT Takeover Saga

In 1968, Rayonier was acquired by the ITT Corporation (originally the International Telephone and Telegraph Corporation), and became part of ITT's steady growth into a conglomerate. The new entity, ITT Rayonier, became a wholly owned subsidiary of ITT, and the 1980s found Rayonier immersed in the world of hostile corporate takeovers. In 1979 ITT had hired a new CEO, Rand Araskog, a West Point graduate and an interrogator of Soviet defectors for the National Security Agency in the 1950s. An aggressive investor, he fought off three takeover attempts of ITT in the 1980s, later chronicling these events in a book whose title illustrated his approach to business, *The ITT Wars*. At the same time, his salary of $8.5 million (high even in the late 1980s) was questioned by numerous investors in ITT, including the California Public Employees' Retirement System, especially given ITT's mediocre performance. Facing growing criticism, Araskog split ITT into three separate corporations, and several subsidiaries were spun off as independent corporations, including Rayonier. As of February 28, 1994, Rayonier once again was an independent company, and it took back its original name. Its president through the ITT years, Ronald Gross, shortly afterward became chair-

---

Company Perspectives:

Our commitment is to provide long term value to shareholders. We won't be satisfied with anything less than financial performance consistently within the top quartile of our industry. We will achieve these business objectives while maintaining high ethical standards and meeting our responsibilities to our communities, the environment and our employees. We're a company built on a solid foundation, whose strong roots and global reach shape us unlike any other in the forest industry.

---

man and CEO, a position he still held in 1998. Araskog continued to serve on the Rayonier board of directors as well.

Focus on International Operations

Rayonier had long been active in the international arena, having marketed its pulp products in Japan since the 1930s and in Korea and China since the early 1980s. The newly independent Rayonier also placed a great deal of attention on operating as a multinational company, targeting Europe, Asia, and Latin America. In 1995, sales outside of the United States made up 59 percent of Rayonier's total sales of $1.26 billion. Rayonier managed timber holdings in New Zealand (almost 220,000 acres) that supplied much of the Asian market, and it also purchased lumber from Chile and Russia. There was a significant difference in the "rotation age" of timberland in the United States and elsewhere. Timber in the southeastern United States (primarily softwoods such as Southern pine) would mature in only 20–25 years; but in the northwestern United States (home to Douglas fir and hemlock), the cycle was 45–50 years. In New Zealand, the average rotation period was 25–28 years. Thus the New Zealand timber holdings became more desirable. More than half of Rayonier's specialty pulp products also were sold to foreign countries.

In the later 1990s, however, Rayonier's international operations became less profitable, particularly as the Asian economies became less stable. In 1996, the share of sales outside of the United States dropped to 55 percent; in 1997 they decreased even more, to only 49 percent. Nevertheless, Rayonier had great hopes for expanding its business in the two most populous countries in Asia, China, and India. These developing markets carried unique challenges, with delivery technology often not matching the demand for products. As described by Dennis Snyder, a Rayonier vice-president, in the *Journal of Commerce*, when Rayonier began to ship fluff pulp to China in the late 1980s, Chinese ports lacked the equipment needed to handle the packages of this product. It had to be broken into individual rolls that could be handled manually.

As of 1997, the geographic distribution of Rayonier's two key product lines (timber and wood products, and specialty pulp products) broke down as follows: timber and wood (United States, 62 percent; Japan, 18 percent; South Korea, nine percent; New Zealand, seven percent; other, four percent), specialty pulp (United States, 41 percent; Europe, 23 percent; Japan, 14 percent; Latin America, ten percent; other Asian countries, nine percent; other, three percent).

Plagued by Environmental and Legal Concerns

Rayonier is subject to many state and federal environmental laws and regulations, affecting its handling of air emissions, water discharges, and waste disposal. Its operations also have been greatly influenced by federal laws governing the cutting of timber, particularly the Endangered Species Act. Rayonier claims to have spent over $100 million in the 1990s for voluntary and required environmental measures. Much of Rayonier's timberland in Washington is home to presently endangered species such as the northern spotted owl and the marbled murrelet, as well as several varieties of salmon. As a result, there have been ongoing negotiations and more heated interactions involving Rayonier, the Environmental Protection Agency (EPA) and state agencies, and environmental groups.

A graphic example of this clash was seen in the fate that befell the Rayonier pulp plant in Port Angeles, Washington. Throughout the 1990s, the company had to reduce the amount of timber harvested from private land that was the home of endangered species. As a result, the Washington hemlock that was used at the Port Angeles mill became more expensive, and the mill lost money almost every year. Also, the plant facility itself was considered an environmental problem, and required numerous expensive upgrades. (As described in a *Seattle Times* article, "For nearly 70 years, the smokestacks of the Rayonier mill have scented the air . . . with a faint, sulphur-like smell.") However, the mill provided jobs for several hundred workers, and paid taxes that amounted to ten percent of the city's budget. When it appeared inevitable that the plant would close, workers began to display bumper stickers saying, "Millworkers are an endangered species, too!" Rayonier closed the mill permanently in February 1997, citing its inability to continue competing with plants in lower-cost areas such as the southeastern United States, South Africa, and Asia.

The issue of environmental measures taken against companies such as Rayonier was a heated political topic in the late 1990s. Controversial measures that were satisfactory to neither enviromentalists nor timber companies were taken in the areas of clear-cutting timber, air emissions, and water discharges. Notably, a growing number of companies were allowed to adopt "Habitat Conservation Plans" (HCPs). In exchange for the right to do commercial logging on private property, the companies were required to adopt voluntary conservation plans that exempted them from some other environmental regulations. Many environmental organizations, such as the National Wildlife Federation, were greatly concerned that the voluntary plans would not adequately protect plant and animal life. For instance, the Washington state office of the National Audubon Society found that the vast majority of the proposed HCPs in that state involved the cutting of older (and hence more commercially valuable) trees on private land, and relied on using adjacent federal forestland as a refuge for the displaced endangered species. The federal approval process for new plans, including Rayonier's, was temporarily suspended in December 1997 as the result of a lawsuit.

Other environmental problems also faced Rayonier in the 1990s. For example, in 1994 its former wholly owned subsidiary, Southern Wood Piedmont Company (SWP), was named as a Potentially Responsible Party (PRP) under the EPA's Comprehensive Environmental Response Compensation and Liability Act

(CERCLA), based on coal tar derivative deposits found in Tennessee's Chattanooga Creek. SWP had ceased operations in 1986, but Rayonier would remain liable for its actions. According to Rayonier's 1997 annual report, it was designated as a PRP or the state equivalent in eight separate federal and state actions.

In addition to the numerous environmental concerns facing Rayonier, it also was named as a defendant in a 1997 Georgia lawsuit brought by Powell-Duffryn Terminals. Rayonier had stored a pulp manufacturing byproduct (crude sulfate turpentine) at one of Powell-Duffryn's marine terminals and storage facilities, and a major fire and explosion caused extensive damage. As a result, damages of $57 million were being sought against Rayonier and the other defendant.

Products, Prospects, and Strategy in the Late 1990s

As of 1998, Rayonier's products fell into two categories: timber and wood products; and specialty pulp products. It managed almost 1.5 million acres of standing timber in the United States (1.23 million acres) and New Zealand (219,000 acres), much of it fast-growing softwood. A specialized market was logs and wood products sent to Pacific Rim countries, made with wood obtained from its own acreage, as well as from timber stands in Chile and Russia. Its U.S.-based lumber mills (two in Georgia and one in Idaho) produced boards and assorted lumber products for both domestic sale and export. A newly opened plant in New Zealand produced medium-density-fiberboard (MDF), which was used in place of solid wood in furniture, cabinets, and paneling. Its specialty pulp products were of three varieties, produced in two mills located in Georgia and Florida. Chemical cellulose was used to produce a wide variety of common products (including cigarette filters, photographic film, cellophane, paint, cement, printing ink, explosives, and textile fibers). Fluff pulps found their way into disposable products, such as diapers and personal hygiene products. Specialty paper pulps were the primary material used in filter papers, decorative laminate papers, and special printing and writing papers.

In the mid- and late 1990s, the timber and pulp industries both were experiencing hard times, a fate shared by Rayonier. Its 1992 sales (while owned by ITT) stood at $974 million, with a $103 million loss in the income column; 1993 saw sales drop to $936 million. After Rayonier became an independent company again, its sales rose gradually at first ($1.07 billion in 1994 and $1.26 billion in 1995), but then began to decline again. For 1996, sales totalled $1.18 billion (with a loss of $98 million); 1997 sales dropped again, to $1.1 billion. Although the U.S. timber market was relatively strong in the late 1990s, there was a sharp decline in the demand for timber from New Zealand, and pulp prices were also dropping. For example, a grade of pulp that sold for $975 a ton in mid-1995 brought only $500 a ton in early 1997. In a January 1998 press release, CEO Gross attributed this problem to developing economies in Asia, which had been a key market for these products: "The turmoil in Asia has clouded the near-term outlook." In early 1998, there was some hope that at least the pulp market was recovering, as the rating firm Goldman Sachs raised its ratings on a number of pulp-related companies, including Rayonier.

In its 1997 annual report, the management of Rayonier set out a detailed strategy for its coming years. Aware of the possibility that Asian economies might continue to falter, Rayonier anticipated another "challenging year." In a belt-tightening mode (adopting cost controls and reducing discretionary spending), the company planned to adopt a four-pronged strategy: (1) to manage its U.S. and New Zealand timber acreage for strong cash flow; (2) to enhance its position as the world's leading supplier of specialty pulp, an already highly profitable segment; (3) to pursue strategic opportunities in its timber and wood product operations; and (4) to remain in the top quartile of company financial results in the industry. Two early results of this strategy were a cut of $15 million in operating costs in 1997, plus the announcement of a worldwide timberland alliance with Grantham, Mayo, Van Otterloo & Co. LLC (GMO), a global investment management firm based in Boston. GMO chose Rayonier in early 1998 to manage its forest and timber operations, in return for an option to co-invest in the GMO properties.

Principal Subsidiaries

Rayonier Timberlands, L.P. (RTLP); Rayonier Forest Resources Company; Southern Wood Piedmont Company (SWP).

Principal Operating Units

Timber and Wood Products; Specialty Pulp Products.

Further Reading

Araskog, Rand V., *The ITT Wars*, New York: Holt, 1989, 241 p.

Armbruster, William, "Rayonier Inc.; Producer of Paper Products Finds Ways to Push Its Way Overseas," *Journal of Commerce Online*, May 21, 1997, http://www.joc.com.

Brown, Leslie, "Cutting a Clear, New Path," *Morning News-Tribune* (Tacoma), November 2, 1997, p. G2, http://archive.tribnet.com.

Erb, George, "Volatile Pulp-and-Paper Industry Slowly Rebounds," *Puget Sound Business Journal*, July 28, 1997, http://www.amcity.com/seattle.

"50th Annual Report on American Industry, 1998," *Forbes Online*, January 1, 1998, http://www.forbes.com.

"Focus on: Rayonier Inc.," *Hartford Courant*, April 10, 1998, p. D2.

Greenwald, John, "ITT's Strip Show," *Time Online*, June 23, 1997, http://www.pathfinder.com.

Lipske, Michael, "Giving Rare Creatures a Fighting Chance," *National Wildlife*, February/March 1998, http://www.nwf.org.

"Paper Companies Up on Earnings, Ratings Upgrades," *Motley Fool*, April 14, 1998, http://www.newsalert.com.

"Rayonier Pulp Mill in Port Angeles Closes After 67 Years; 365 to Lose Jobs," *Morning News-Tribune* (Tacoma, WA), March 2, 1997, p. B2, http://archive.tribnet.com.

Solomon, Christopher, "Facing the Inevitable," *Seattle Times*, November 5, 1996, http://www.seattletimes.com.

Sonner, Scott, "Administration Halts Habitat Plans," *Morning News-Tribune* (Tacoma), December 31, 1997, p. A8, http://archive.tribnet.com.

—Gerry Azzata

Ryder System, Inc.

3600 Northwest 82nd Avenue
Miami, Florida 33166
U.S.A.
(305) 500-3726
Fax: (305) 500-4129
Web site: http://www.ryder.com

Public Company
Incorporated: 1934 as Ryder Truck Rental System, Inc.
Employees: 42,000
Sales: $4.89 billion (1997)
Stock Exchanges: New York Chicago Pacific Berlin
Ticker Symbol: R
SICs: 7510 Automotive Rentals, No Drivers

The largest provider of transportation services in the world, Ryder System, Inc. designs and manages logistics and transportation solutions, focusing on three service areas: global logistics, truck leasing, and public transportation services. After restructuring in the mid-1990s, Ryder stood poised as a market leader in several business areas. The company provided full-service commercial leasing and short-term rental of trucks, tractors, and trailers to clients such as Domino's Pizza, Home Depot, and Sprint. It managed inbound and outbound logistics for major manufacturers, retailers, and other businesses. Also, the company transported students by school buses in 21 states and managed more than 80 public transit systems. During the late 1990s, Ryder maintained operations in the United States, Canada, the United Kingdom, Argentina, Brazil, Germany, The Netherlands, and Poland. Its stock was a component of the Dow Jones Transportation Average and the Standard & Poor's 500 Index.

1930s Origins of an Industry Pioneer

In 1932 James A. Ryder gave up his job as a straw boss in a construction firm and bought a Model A pickup truck with a down payment of $125. Ryder hauled trash from Miami beaches and delivered construction materials to Palm Beach. In 1934 he entered the truck-leasing business through a contract with a local beer distributor. At the age of 21, Ryder was the owner of the first truck-leasing firm in the United States, Ryder Truck Rental System, Inc.

In 1939 Ryder took on a partner, Roy N. Reedy, and the two men set out to build a trucking empire. Truck leasing was novel, and the company broke new ground. Highway trucking began to rival rail as a means of overland shipping, based partly on the vast network of better highways constructed during the 1930s. World War II boosted demand for trucking as the war economy stretched the existing transportation system to capacity, and Ryder's trucking and leasing operations grew.

The postwar era brought continued growth to the trucking industry as the interstate highway program further improved the efficiency of trucking. By 1952 Ryder was bringing in $3 million annually by renting 1,300 trucks. In the summer of that year news came that the Southeast's largest, most profitable trucking outfit, the Great Southern Trucking Company, was up for sale. Ryder was familiar with Great Southern; his company leased its pickup and delivery trucks. Founded in 1933 by L. A. Raulerson, it had grown into the Southeast's largest freight carrier with some routes as long as 1,100 miles. Ryder raised the $2 million asking price by December 1952. His company's revenues were then quadruple what they had been, and Ryder was a huge motor carrier, as well as a major truck-leasing concern.

The Great Southern acquisition put Ryder on the map. Ryder System, Inc. was created in 1955 to absorb Ryder Truck Rental and Great Southern, and the new company offered shares to the public. Shortly thereafter Ryder System bought more than 25 companies in five years. The larger companies included Baker Truck Rental, Inc., of Denver, Colorado; Barrett Truck Leasing Co., of Detroit; T.S.C. Motor Freight Lines, Inc.; the truck leasing business of Columbia Terminals Co.; Dixie Drive-It-Yourself System, of Alabama; the truck leasing business of Barrett Garages, Inc., of San Francisco; Morrison International Corporation; and International Railway Car Leasing Corporation.

This growth resulted in certain problems, however, since the company had neglected proper financial controls. By 1960 Ryder

Company Perspectives:

Ryder is the world's largest provider of integrated logistics and transportation solutions. As businesses exhaust cost-cutting measures in the traditional areas of price and quality, the ability to reduce costs in the delivery of products, warehousing and other transportation and logistics areas is becoming increasingly important. Ryder's transportation solutions are custom-designed to help businesses improve customer service, reduce inventory and speed products to market.

System was forced to write off $2 million in bad debt, and profits dipped from $2.7 million in 1959 to about $1 million in 1960. A central accounting system was implemented to remedy the problems, and steady growth returned in the early 1960s.

In 1965 Ryder System sold its motor carrier division to International Utilities (IU), a diversified holding company. The trucking division grew under IU's direction until its spinoff in 1982, keeping the Ryder name. Ryder System focused on the fast-growing truck-leasing business and, despite common misconceptions, had not operated as a freight carrier since 1965.

The late 1960s saw the development of new services in truck leasing and rental. In 1967 Ryder began offering one-way truck rental service. This service had been introduced and popularized by the U-Haul Company several years earlier. Ryder started with 1,000 trucks and expanded the one-way fleet to 7,630 the first year. Competition in this field grew rapidly; Hertz Corporation and E-Z Haul, a division of National Car Rental System, Inc., entered the field at the same time. As a result, the one-way market was oversupplied, and Ryder's one-way unit got off to a slow start. Ryder was intent on capturing this market, however. In 1968 the company offered to buy U-Haul International Co., a subsidiary of Americo, Inc., but no deal was ever worked out. Ryder expanded its one-way dealership network through an agreement with Budget Rent-A-Car. While many competitors dropped out in the early 1970s, Ryder did not, selling surplus vehicles when necessary, and eventually surpassed U-Haul's one-way rental in 1987.

In 1968 Ryder entered the new-automotive carriage business when it acquired M & G Convoy, Inc., and expanded it with the purchase of Complete Auto Transit, Inc., in January 1970. Ryder's automotive carriage services were used by General Motors Corporation and Chrysler Corporation for the transport of new automobiles to dealerships. Also around this time, Ryder entered the dedicated contract carriage business, in which it provided transportation and distribution services customized for its clients.

Late 1960s Diversification Breeds Problems

In the late 1960s Ryder System also diversified into services unrelated to transport leasing. In late 1969 Ryder made a foray into the growing temporary help industry, initially placing office and industrial personnel, and later placing technical help. Ryder also acquired several trade schools in 1969 and 1970, offering courses in auto mechanics, truck driving, and a number of other technical fields. In 1970 Ryder purchased Mobile World Inc., a distributor of mobile homes and a mobile-home-park operator and franchiser. Also that year an insurance firm, Southern Underwriters, Inc., was acquired and a joint venture, Ryd-Air Inc., was formed to provide pickup and delivery service for 27 airlines in New York.

Although Ryder's main line—full service truck leasing—remained strong in the early 1970s, the company's management was spread thin over a growing number of new service fields. The oil crisis of 1973 prompted Ryder to purchase Toro Petroleum Corporation of Louisiana to ensure a steady fuel supply for its trucks, but the acquisition proved rash. The value of Toro's oil reserves dropped as oil prices fell a few months after the purchase. Ryder had bought high and ended up with a $7 million operating loss.

Other problems—adjustments in the calculation of receivables from the education unit, tax assessments on the mobile home subsidiary, and reserve assessments on the insurance subsidiary—resulted in a 13 cents per share adjustment to Ryder stock following the company's 1973 audit. The truck leasing and rental businesses continued to borrow in order to finance an expanded fleet. Ryder's debts were more than $400 million, four times shareholders' equity. Thus, Moody's Investors Service downgraded Ryder's rating on commercial paper in late 1974. Ryder System lost $20 million, and the company's investors were deeply concerned. The board of directors began to question James Ryder's ability to guide the future of the growing concern.

The recession of 1973–74 had taken a heavy toll on Ryder's vast contract carriage and automotive carriage operations, which were heavily dependent upon the welfare of the automotive industry. Although Ryder's core business of truck leasing and rental was holding its own despite the hard times, company borrowing had gotten out of control. Stockholders, displeased with the company's troublesome acquisitions from the early 1970s, demanded a refocusing of attention back on Ryder's basic businesses. In 1975 James Ryder, under pressure from the boardroom and his bankers, announced that he was seeking a "more professional manager" to run the still growing company. In the summer of 1975, after disposing of such unprofitable subsidiaries as Toro Petroleum and Miller Trailers, Inc., as well as the major portion of the technical schools, James Ryder stepped down as head of the company he had founded.

Ryder's successor was Leslie O. Barnes, former head of Allegheny Airlines. Barnes inherited a company that was tattered after weathering a great storm, and the 59-year-old CEO was intent on whipping Ryder System back into shape. The debt-to-equity ratio was quickly pared from four-to-one to three-to-one. Ryder Liftlease Inc., a small but troublesome subsidiary, was sold, as were the remainder of the technical schools. Refocused on its primary businesses, Ryder rebounded. In 1977 the company acquired a major automobile carrier, Janesville Auto Transport Company, for $10 million in common stock. Ryder's automotive carriage operations were profitable as a result of the industry's rebound and tighter financial controls. During the 1979 downturn in the automotive markets, Ryder's automotive contract carriage unit, representing 16 percent of Ryder System's turnover, made a profit.

In the late 1970s Ryder continued to grow internally and through acquisitions in the full-service truck-leasing business, in which the company continued to lead the continually expanding market. According to Barnes, only 38 percent of the U.S. private truck fleets were wholly owned by 1980, down from 60 percent in 1970. The vast majority of fleets were at least partially leased. Encouraged by the basic business's performance during the latter half of the 1970s, Ryder System once again began to seek acquisitions in new areas. Barnes, however, unlike James Ryder, was inclined to test out new ventures on a small scale before fully committing to them. In 1978 a parcel delivery service, Jack Rabbit Express, was acquired. Moreover, a small property and casualty reinsurance company, Federal Assurance Co., was added to existing insurance operations.

By the late 1970s the one-way rental market was well-established. Ryder trailed U-Haul in this field, and in 1978, a third major competitor, Jartran Inc., joined the field. Jartran was an acronym for James A. Ryder Transportation. Giving up a $100,000 annual stipend to get out of his noncompetition agreement with Ryder System, James Ryder founded Jartran, which made a smashing entry into the field, building a 30,000 vehicle fleet in less than 18 months. James Ryder's new company became a thorn in the side of his former company. The feisty Ryder appeared in Jartran ads as "the man who invented truck rental," and his new vehicles resembled Ryder System's enough to spark a lawsuit.

Nevertheless, Jartran had trouble making a profit. Once again, it appeared that James Ryder had grown the company too big too fast. As a downturn in the economy in 1979 killed the short-term rental market, Jartran cumulatively lost $30 million in 1979 and 1980. By July 1981 Jartran had dumped its commercial leasing division, and the company was foundering.

Ryder System, on the other hand, grew under the balanced leadership of Barnes and his new executive vice-president, M. Anthony Burns. In the early 1980s, new tax laws encouraged diversification into new areas. Ryder began shopping for a financial services company in order to take full advantage of available tax credits. Insurance was the obvious choice because of Ryder's existing insurance business. In September 1981 Ryder System announced its desire to purchase the third largest insurance broker in the United States, Frank B. Hall and Co. Hall, however, was not interested in being acquired and maneuvered to avert a takeover. In October 1981 Hall announced its intentions to purchase Jartran, Ryder System's troubled competitor, opening up potential antitrust obstacles for a takeover. Hall also filed a number of suits against Ryder.

Ryder System's pursuit of Hall continued through 1982, and by August of that year Ryder System had boosted its holdings in Hall to 9.5 percent. Jartran was on its way to bankruptcy, but Hall had bought enough time to discourage Ryder System from acquiring any more Hall stock. In 1983 Ryder sold its interest in the insurance broker for $33 million.

In 1982 a severe recession shook the North American economy. Ryder System was well-prepared, however, with a $70 million cash surplus and a very low debt-to-equity ratio. While the majority of transportation companies were devastated, Ryder System's profits increased. Burns moved up to CEO, and

soon proclaimed Ryder's intention to "be more forward-thinking, more risk-taking." By slashing prices in half on one-way rentals, Ryder usurped a huge chunk of the market. By acquiring two new strategically located automobile carriage firms, Ryder improved its efficiency, reducing the number of trailers sent back empty.

1980s Acquisitions

Ryder System's longstanding desire to enter financial services was satisfied in 1983 when the company became an 80 percent partner in a pension fund specialist, Forstmann, Leff, Kimberly. The joint venture set up long term trusts for pension fund investors. Ryder also decided to revise its in-house business information systems and offer them for sale to other transportation companies.

In its core transportation businesses, Ryder continued to make strides. Deregulation had been the industry trend since 1980. In 1983 new rules concerning single-source leasing allowed private fleet operators to secure drivers through Ryder as a part of the leasing agreement. Private shippers were also allowed to solicit outside freight business, effectively allowing direct competition with independent truckers. Ryder set up a new division to handle single-source leasing and bought three new freight packaging companies to book return loads for private shippers leasing from Ryder. In 1984, Ryder sold its Truckstops Corporation of America unit for $85 million to free managerial resources for more profitable businesses.

In the early 1980s Ryder System began to delve into another expanding transportation field—aviation leasing. In 1983 the Aviation Sales Co. Inc. and its subsidiary General Hydraulics Corporation, of Florida, an aircraft leasing firm and spare parts firm, respectively, were acquired. In 1985 Ryder bought Aviall, Inc., a turbine engine repair and overhaul firm located in Dallas. Aviall was also a parts distributor. A number of smaller leasing and repair companies were acquired. By late 1986 aviation services made up about one-fifth of Ryder System's revenues, and in 1987 the division branched out overseas with the purchase of Caledonian Airmotive, Ltd. The Scottish subsidiary serviced the big engines on British Caledonian Airways' DC-10s and 747s, among others. Caledonian Airmotive complemented Aviall's operation both geographically and in services offered.

By 1988 just six years after entering the field, Ryder System was the world's largest jet engine overhaul and rebuilding company, the largest aviation parts distributor, and one of the largest aircraft and jet-engine leasing companies. Ryder's aviation division counted 300 commercial airlines among its clients, as well as dozens of private operators. In 1988 revenues from aviation neared $1 billion.

Ryder's truck leasing continued to surge ahead. In 1986 a major federal tax law revision made it desirable for private fleet operators to lease their fleets rather than buy. Ryder had been determinedly expanding its truck fleet; between 1984 and 1988 it nearly doubled its fleet. More and more fleet operators turned over the hassles of fleet purchase, maintenance, and insurance to Ryder, allowing them to concentrate on manufacture and sale of their products.

In one-way rental, Ryder excelled. The longtime leader in the field—U-Haul—was distracted as family members battled amongst themselves for control of the business. U-Haul started renting all kinds of equipment, from rototillers to hoists, and its truck fleet quietly grew old. In 1987 the average age of a U-Haul truck was ten years. Ryder's, on the other hand, averaged two years, and boasted all sorts of features not found at U-Haul, such as power steering, air-conditioning, AM-FM radios, fuel efficient engines, and radial tires. Ryder's market share was 45 percent, equal to U-Haul's in 1987, and surging forward.

Between 1983 and 1987 Ryder System spent $1.1 billion on 65 acquisitions. This time the company's rapid expansion was readily digested. In 1985 Ryder entered the school-bus leasing business and quickly grew to be the second-largest private student transport company in the United States. Ryder also entered into public transportation system consulting and leasing at about the same time. Dedicated contract carriage received greater attention in the late 1980s. Ryder provided trucks, drivers, and management system design to such specialty freight companies as Emery Air Freight, such retailers as Montgomery Ward, Sears, and J.C. Penney, and such newspaper publishers as Dow Jones and the *Miami Herald*.

In 1989 Ryder's growth flattened out, but its potential in its existing areas of operation remained strong. Late in the year the company sold its insurance operations, and, anticipating the coming recession, trimmed its fleet to better match demand. Ryder had proven its ability to manage well in tough times during the 1982 recession. As the automotive carriage and commercial truck operations were in the downside of the cycle, Ryder focused on improving market share while awaiting a general economic recovery. Its success was demonstrated in 1990 when Ryder moved 39 percent of the automobiles shipped in the United States and Canada.

Burns and the 1990s

As Ryder System entered the 1990s, its full-service truck leasing, contract carriage, jet turbine aircraft overhaul and maintenance, and new aviation parts-distribution units were performing well; other units would eventually rebound alongside the manufacturing economy. As the 1990s progressed, however, it became clear to company leader Burns that fundamental changes were needed to properly position the company for long-term growth and profitability. Burns—who had completed his ascent of the company's management ranks to preside as president, chief executive officer, and chairman—wanted to lessen the company's interests and sharpen its focus, a desire reminiscent of Ryder's mid-1970s restructuring. His intent was to adapt to changing market conditions before the trends of the future passed Ryder by. His vision was forward-looking, a perspective that he hoped would prevent Ryder from falling victim to the cyclicality of its business.

As the "new Ryder" took shape during the mid-1990s, both recent and age-old components of the company were shed. No divestment was larger than the October 1996 sale of the company's consumer truck rental business, its famed yellow Ryder rental truck fleet. The sale of the consumer truck rental business represented a $574 million deal, stripping the company of more than $400 million in annual revenue. Less than a year later, Burns also sold Ryder's automotive carrier business, reaching an agreement with Allied Holdings, Inc. for a $111 million sale price. With the divestiture of the consumer truck rental business and the automotive carrier business, Burns felt his company was "leaner, more focused, more disciplined, more profit-minded," and less vulnerable to the vagaries of capricious market conditions, ridding Ryder of businesses that were "seasonal, transactional, highly volatile, and in difficult markets." With these two business segments gone, along with others, Burns pinned the company's hopes for the future on three main business areas: logistics, corporate truck leasing and rental, and public transportation services.

As Ryder entered the late 1990s, the company could not point to strong, tangible evidence that its "new" operating structure would provide all the answers for the new century ahead—and it did not expect to. At work were sweeping, fundamental changes that would take more than several years before a proper, accurate evaluation could take place. What Burns did achieve, however, was a measurable increase in contractual business and a growing position in logistical services. Although the company was heavily dependent on its truck leasing and rental business—the largest Ryder enterprise and a consistent, stable contributor to its bottom line—there were great expectations for the future of its logistical services business, the smallest Ryder enterprise. Whether or not expectations would develop into reality remained unanswered as the 21st century neared, but at Ryder's corporate headquarters there was confidence that the near future would provide an answer welcomed by all, especially Burns.

Principal Subsidiaries

Ryder Integrated Logistics, Inc.; Ryder Transportation Services; Ryder Public Transportation Services, Inc.; Ryder Integrated Logistics—Canada; LogiCorp; Ryder Plc (U.K.); Ryder Deutschland GmbH (Germany); Ryder de Mexico, S.A. de C.V.; Ryder Polska Sp.z.o.o. (Poland); Ryder Argentina, S.A.; Ryder do Brasil, Ltda. (Brazil); Ryder Netherlands, B.V.; Ryder Truck Rental Canada Ltd.

Further Reading

Cook, James, "Repetition Compulsion," *Forbes*, March 21, 1988.
Engardio, Pete, "Tony Burns Has Ryder's Rivals Eating Dust," *Business Week*, April 6, 1987.
"From Wings to Wheels," *Forbes*, September 18, 1978.
Ryder, James A., "Shooting for the Big Time—and Making It," *Nation's Business*, January 1970.
Wax, Alan, "Institutions Grill Ryder over Earnings Change," *Commercial and Financial Chronicle*, April 8, 1974.

—Thomas M. Tucker
—updated by Jeffrey L. Covell

Safety 1st®

Safety 1st, Inc.

---

210 Boylston Street
Chestnut Hill, Massachusetts 02167
U.S.A.
(617) 964-7744
Fax: (617) 928-3205

Public Company
Incorporated: 1984
Employees: 203
Sales: $104.97 million (1997)
Stock Exchanges: NASDAQ
Ticker Symbol: SAFT
SICs: 3089 Plastic Products, Not Elsewhere Classified

First known for its "Baby on Board" signs, Safety 1st, Inc. is an industry leader in the development, marketing, and distribution of childcare products. In the late 1990s it sold more than 300 safety, convenience, feeding, teething, and health and hygiene items in more than 60 countries. Among these products was a complete line of home security devices. Safety 1st's business strategy has focused on developing strong brand recognition and loyalty. It has improved and repackaged products already marketed by other companies and developed new offerings of its own, always emphasizing the quality of the items sold under the Safety 1st label. Safety 1st has come to dominate the childcare products market in part because of its success in developing relationships with such large retailers as Wal-Mart, Kmart, and Toys "R" Us, which have chosen to carry the company's products to the exclusion of most of its competitors.

Founding a Business: 1984

Safety 1st was founded in 1984 by Michael Lerner. The 30-year-old was running an executive search firm with his father when he encountered a couple who had recently returned from Europe with an unusual idea. The two had noticed drivers in Germany who had hung safety signs from their car windows in hopes of encouraging others to be cautious behind the wheel. The couple had sought to market similar signs in the United States but had so far been unsuccessful. Lerner purchased the rights to the concept and,with $30,000 of his own money, began to produce and package bright yellow "Baby on Board" signs. Lerner had not anticipated that he would spark a national phenomenon and was astounded by his success. He sold 10,000 of the signs in September 1984 and by the end of the following year was selling half a million of them each month.

As the "Baby on Board" craze waned, Lerner plotted his next move. "I suppose I could have just gone with the fad and taken the profits," he told *Inc.* in December 1992. "But I wanted to be more than a flash in the pan." After reading children's magazines, he realized that child safety issues were a growing concern among parents. But stores only offered a handful of generic and drearily packaged child-proofing devices. Lerner recognized the potential in the untapped market of child safety products. He recruited Michael Bernstein, an experienced baby-products marketer, to assist him in leading Safety 1st beyond the novelty sign business. Using the profits netted from the "Baby on Board" venture, Lerner and Bernstein extended Safety 1st's product line to 20 child safety items, such as outlet plugs and drawer and cabinet locks. The two did not focus on inventing new child safety products. Instead, their strategy was to improve upon existing products by adding innovative features and wrapping the products in colorful and eye-catching packages. Lerner also capitalized on the national distribution network he had established with his "Baby on Board" signs to make Safety 1st's products widely available.

Safety 1st's big break came in 1987, when Toys "R" Us, the nationwide chain of children's merchandise stores, selected Safety 1st as its sole supplier of child safety products. Lerner recognized the importance of this opportunity and continued to improve the appearance of his merchandise. Commonplace child safety items were dressed up in four-color packages with images of the product in use. Consumers loved what they saw. Martin Fogelman, vice-president of Toys "R" Us, explained Lerner's insight in the April 1, 1995 issue of *Nation's Business.* "There were people in the safety business way before Michael. But he was the one who made the product appealing."

Diversification in the Late 1980s

As Safety 1st's brand name became synonymous with basic child safety products, the company sought to broaden its line to include larger items. Safety seats, balcony guards, and safety gates were some of the new offerings. Lerner and Bernstein's next step was to continue Safety 1st's growth by expanding beyond the narrow niche of child safety products and into the broader market of childcare convenience and activity items. In 1987 Safety 1st released an assortment of new products, such as baby monitors, bath seats, toddler cups, pacifiers, and teethers. The company did not alter its proven strategy of updating and refining drab items already found in stores. For example, Safety 1st's baby bath seat came in a vibrant blue instead of the standard, functional white. Moreover, unlike other models of bath seats, Safety 1st's featured a swivel seat, which made a parent's task easier. After it was released in 1990, the seat quickly became the best-selling version in the nation. A spokesperson for Safety 1st's top competitor, Kiddie Products, Inc., summed up Lerner's success for the October 25, 1993 issue of *Forbes*. "Today novelty sells. It's gone from basics to fashion business."

A key to Safety 1st's increasing profitability at this time was its relationship with Wal-Mart, Kmart, and the Home Depot. When these three retail giants joined Toys "R" Us in carrying Safety 1st's juvenile merchandise line, Lerner's enterprise flourished. In a July 1993 press release, Lerner credited his company's "strong performance" to "the strength of our distribution network, which included such mass merchants as Wal-Mart, Toys "R" Us, and K-Mart." Sales to these three retailers soon accounted for 44 percent of the company's revenues. Lerner noted in the same article that "our ability to provide a full line of products appeals to merchants that increasingly want to utilize fewer suppliers." Safety 1st's goods sold well in these retail behemoths. Toys "R" Us named the company its "Vendor of the Year" in 1990, and Wal-Mart followed suit a year later, awarding the company "Vendor of the Quarter."

Growth and Development in the Early 1990s

Safety 1st grew at a meteoric rate. Sales jumped from $7.7 million in 1989 to $43 million in 1993. By that year the company's original product line of 20 items had burgeoned to 175, and it distributed its merchandise to 3,700 retailers. With plans to introduce another 50 new products in 1994, Safety 1st wanted to raise revenue and repay its accumulated debt. In an effort to do so, the company made its first public stock offering of two million shares in April 1993. The stock sale was a

success, and Safety 1st's expansion continued to exceed expectations. Product sales in 1993 increased more than 50 percent from the year before, while profits for the year nearly doubled to reach $4.2 million. Delighted with his young company's success, Lerner pushed for more growth. He recruited new executives from much larger corporations in hopes of spurring his company to mature quickly. "That overqualified individual allows me to grow faster," he told *Nation's Business* in April 1995. "The company develops to the executive's level."

Nineteen ninety-four was a banner year for Safety 1st. Net sales for the year were up 63 percent and reached $70 million. In an April 1994 press release, Lerner attributed his company's strong sales to the new product offerings, particularly larger "bulk" goods. The company introduced such items as the "Turn 'N Seal Diaper Pail," "The Night Light Bed Rail," and the "Step Stool and Scale." An extremely profitable product that year was a baby monitor that went beyond merely broadcasting the baby's cries. Safety 1st's model automatically played a Brahms lullaby every time the baby made noise. At the close of 1994, the company's product line topped 300 items.

Safety 1st scored an impressive triumph in March 1994, when it reached a licensing agreement with Walt Disney Co. to produce a new line of infant care products under the "Disney Babies" brand name. According to Safety 1st's 1995 annual report, this was quite an achievement, as Disney was "one of the most coveted licenses in the juvenile industry." At the same time, the company ventured in a different direction by expanding outside juvenile products altogether. Safety 1st launched a line of home security products, such as deadbolts and carbon monoxide monitors. Lerner hoped that recognition of the Safety 1st brand name would lead to the new line's success in hardware store chains. Lerner's efforts were rewarded with national recognition. *Forbes* ranked Safety 1st second in its annual "Emerging Growth Companies in the United States."

Many analysts believed Safety 1st's stunning success was achieved on the coattails of a growing juvenile products industry, which had seen its sales balloon to $3.5 billion in 1993. The April 17, 1994 edition of the *Boston Globe* correlated this industry-wide growth to the baby boom, or so-called boomlet, of the 1980s. At the same time that more babies were being born, the average mother's age increased. In 1993 women over 30 accounted for almost 40 percent of all births. With their higher earnings, these women had more to spend on their children. In fact, birthrates in households earning more than $25,000 a year jumped 50 percent between 1985 and 1990.

On many fronts 1995 appeared to be yet another year of progress for Safety 1st. Once again sales soared, reaching $103 million, and net income increased to $3 million. Safety 1st continued to emphasize expansion and introduced 100 new products accordingly. Lerner also positioned the company for international growth by initiating two acquisitions in 1995. Safety 1st announced its intentions to acquire EEZI, Ltd., as well as Orleans Juvenile Products, Inc. EEZI, a British developer and marketer of home safety products and juvenile accessories, offered Safety 1st the potential to expand its international customer base. Orleans, originally Safety 1st's Canadian distributor, was one of the largest distributors of juvenile products in Canada. These transactions underscored Safety 1st's "commitment to broadening [its] international presence," Lerner said in a March 1996 press release. International sales rose 58 percent in 1995 and accounted for almost 15 percent of the company's total sales.

Structural Difficulties in the Mid-1990s

While Safety 1st continued to expand in a variety of directions, organizational and structural problems emerged in 1995. Ironically these difficulties were created by Safety 1st's dynamic growth and the unstinting demand for its wares. In April 1995 production problems forced the company to delay the release of some new items, causing Safety 1st's share price to drop from $25 to $16.75. A woeful Lerner told the *Boston Business Journal* in April 1995, "We thought we would have products sooner than we did; we just failed to take into account time to debug production of new products." A September 1995 *Forbes* article chalked up Safety 1st's troubles to "a case of growing pains." In December of that year, the company experienced an inventory shortfall that cost it $4.5 million. Safety 1st's computer system had been unable to accurately keep track of its inventory, which caused the company to accept orders for products it could not ship. In response, the company's share price dropped 21.4 percent in one day.

Lerner did not wait passively for the situation to improve. In 1996 Safety 1st began aggressively to address many of the growth-related, structural impediments it faced. The company continued to expand internationally, especially when it finalized its acquisition of EEZI and Orleans that year. (These wholly owned subsidiaries were renamed Safety 1st Europe and Safety 1st Canada, respectively.) But, as Lerner stated in the company's 1997 annual report, the difficulties of 1995 helped him realize that Safety 1st's product offerings "had exceeded a manageable level." Moreover, the company had moved too far from its core competency of juvenile products. Safety 1st had been "carried away by its early success," *Forbes* declared on November 3, 1997. "Many of the new items, like deadbolt locks and door peepholes, were not strictly child-related, and ran against stiff competition from hardware makers." The continual expansion had complicated all its operational aspects and had led to substantial increases in expenses.

In response, Safety 1st sought to improve the infrastructure of its management team by hiring a slew of talented executives. To oversee revised fiscal policies, Lerner recruited Richard Wenz to the newly created position of president and chief operating officer. (Lerner remained chairman and chief executive officer). In addition, Lerner ensured that the company installed an enterprise-wide business management computer system to aid inventory control and fiscal management.

Safety 1st also reexamined its overall business strategy. In 1996 Lerner initiated a lengthy and costly product realignment to refine the company's sales and marketing objectives. Every Safety 1st product was evaluated in terms of profitability, inventory turnover, and rate of customer return. Those that did not meet the standard were discontinued. Eventually the company reduced its product offerings by 350 items, a cut of nearly 54 percent. But the product realignment took a toll on net profitability in 1996. The total cost of the process, mostly in inventory write-offs from discontinued products, was estimated to be between $24 million and $26 million. Although sales for the year were up, the company's net loss was over $44 million. Lerner explained in the November 3, 1997 issue of *Forbes,* "We're focusing on our core strengths. I wish we had done this three or four years ago. We have learned a lot." He added that after the crisis of 1995 and 1996, he considered more moderate growth of 15 percent a year to be ideal. Left with its 300 best-selling, highest-margin juvenile and home security products, the company hoped to return to profitability in 1997.

Successful Reemergence in the Late 1990s

Throughout 1997 Lerner and Safety 1st continued to apply their newfound principles of managed growth. Although the company recognized that new product development was a core strength, it remained committed to maintaining a more balanced approach. Greater emphasis was placed on preproduction market research and cost analysis prior to the development of a product line. Safety 1st also began to experiment with business strategies other than simply releasing more items. One such approach was to license the Safety 1st name to other companies, such as Delta Enterprise, which produced a line of baby strollers bearing Safety 1st's logo. Shored up by this sort of venture, Safety 1st's sales remained stable in 1997, even though its product lines had been dramatically reduced. Moreover, Safety 1st returned to profitability with a net income of $10.5 million. The company held a 50 percent share in the safety category and held more top-ranking category positions than did any other manufacturer in the juvenile industry.

Sales outside the United States flourished in 1997, demonstrating the company's commitment to international expansion. During the year Safety 1st formed a global team to research and develop international markets in order to guarantee that any new products would meet world standards. Safety 1st maintained an extensive global distribution network in 60 countries worldwide.

After weathering the storms of overexpansion, Safety 1st reemerged as a force in the juvenile products industry. With its program of managed growth in place, Safety 1st's outlook was positive. The company also intended to capitalize on anticipated beneficial demographics. The U.S. birthrate, after remaining stable to the turn of the century, was expected to escalate early in the 21st century to surpass the birthrate of the baby boom years of the 1950s and 1960s. Safety 1st, along with the juvenile products industry as a whole, predicted only steady growth.

Principal Subsidiaries

Safety 1st Europe, Ltd.; Safety 1st Canada.

Further Reading

Barrett, William, "The Perils of Success," *Forbes,* November 3, 1997.

Gold, Donald, "Investor's Corner: Kiddie Stocks Continue to Toddle Ahead," *Investor's Business Daily,* October 14, 1994.

Hyten, Todd, "Safety 1st at a Loss on Drop of Stock Price," *Boston Business Journal,* April 14, 1995.

Mangelsdorf, Margaret, "The Hottest Entrepreneurs in America: The Finalists," *Inc.,* December 1, 1992.

Novack, Janet, "Entrepreneur on Board," *Forbes,* October 25, 1993.

Reynes, Roberta, "Profits on Board," *Nation's Business,* April 1, 1995.

Rosenberg, Ronald, "This Baby Is Big on the Board. Michael Lerner Has Parlayed a Clever Idea into a Successful Firm, " *Boston Globe,* April 17, 1994.

Schifrin, Matthew, "Safety 1st Suffers Lower Than Expected Earnings," *Forbes,* September 11, 1995.

"Safety 1st Announces First Quarter Results," *Business Wire,* April 29, 1994.

"Safety 1st Announces Second Quarter, Six Months Results," *Business Wire,* July 28, 1993.

"Safety 1st Completes Acquisition of Orleans Juvenile Products," *Business Wire,* March 18, 1996.

—Rebecca Stanfel

Safeway Inc.

5918 Stoneridge Mill Road
Pleasanton, California 94588-3229
U.S.A.
(510) 467-3000
Fax: (510) 467-3321
Web site: http://www.safeway.com

Public Company
Incorporated: 1926
Employees: 147,000
Sales: $22.48 billion (1997)
Stock Exchanges: New York Pacific
Ticker Symbol: SWY
SICs: 5411 Grocery Stores

With 1,368 stores in the United States and Canada, Safeway Inc. is the second largest food and drug retailer in the United States, trailing only The Kroger Company. About a dozen major Safeway distribution centers deliver thousands of food and nonfood items, both national and private-label brands, to the company's retail outlets, which are located in the western United States, Alaska and Hawaii, the mid-Atlantic region, and western Canada. The company also holds a 49 percent stake in Casa Ley, S.A. de C.V., which operates 74 food and general merchandise stores in western Mexico. Kohlberg, Kravis & Roberts Company acquired Safeway and took it private in 1986, after which the company radically downsized itself in the following two years. Safeway's streamlining efforts were so successful at reducing the debt incurred during the leveraged buyout that the company went public again in 1990.

Early History

In the early days of this century S. M. Skaggs saw that the grain farmers in his community of American Falls, Idaho, were poorly served by their local grocery stores. Without money except at harvest time, their buying power was considerably reduced by the heavy credit charges that store owners levied. Also, the variety and quality of goods was poor, causing much customer dissatisfaction. As a minister, Skaggs was interested in solving these problems. He talked a local bank president, D. W. Davis (later the governor of Idaho), into a loan, and then set himself up in an 18-by-32-foot store and opened for business.

Despite his zeal, Skaggs could not make his store particularly profitable, so in 1915 he sold it to his son, M. B. Skaggs, who at age 27 had already been involved in business for years. The younger Skaggs added energy and sound business sense to his father's sense of mission, and by 1926 he was running a chain of 428 grocery stores throughout California and the Pacific Northwest. People flocked to Skaggs's stores, not only for the cash-and-carry plan which his father helped to create, but because Skaggs used every inch of store space to stock a large variety of goods and worked hard to get quality meat and other perishables.

In 1926 Charles Merrill, one of the founders of Merrill Lynch, was looking to expand his investment firm's involvement in the retail chain store business. Seeing a huge potential for growth in the West, he purchased Safeway Stores, Inc., a chain of some 240 stores founded by Sam Seelig in 1914 that covered most of the West Coast. Merrill had the capital and the stores to do business; all he needed was experienced management. Merrill asked the president of Safeway, James Weldon, who the best man to run the new venture was. Weldon named M. B. Skaggs as his only choice, and soon Skaggs had been persuaded to add his chain of 428 stores to Safeway's 240. The newly expanded venture kept the Safeway name and Skaggs was made president of Safeway's operating subsidiaries in California and Nevada in addition to retaining control over his own stores.

Merrill had insisted his deal with Skaggs be profitable, so Skaggs expanded the business at a tremendous pace during its early years. By 1928 Safeway had expanded to 2,020 stores and its stock was listed on the New York Stock Exchange. All of this pleased Merrill so much that he made Skaggs president of the entire company. The following year Safeway even ventured into international expansion, establishing Canada Safeway Ltd. in Winnipeg. Noting the different distribution system used in Canada, Safeway acquired a Canadian wholesaling business to eliminate the usual high price markup there.

The Great Depression years decreased consumers' food budgets dramatically, creating difficulty in the low-profit-margin grocery industry, but Safeway was able to survive, thanks once again to Charles Merrill. In 1928 Merrill had sent Lingan A. Warren to run a string of about 1,400 grocery stores in the Pacific Northwest known as the MacMarr Stores. Warren had earned Merrill's confidence through his insight into the mechanics of store management. In 1931, with both the MacMarr and Safeway chains hurt by sliding profits, a deal was brokered to unite the two chains, and Lingan Warren became a part of Safeway; the merger helped Safeway Stores reach an all-time high of 3,257 stores that same year (this number would decline substantially over the succeeding decades as the company concentrated on larger stores, closing many smaller ones). Assuming the presidency of the company in 1934 and holding it until 1955 (Skaggs became chairman of the board), Warren exerted a huge influence on Safeway throughout his tenure with the firm. He helped to innovate policies that educated consumers about what they were getting, such as supplying scales to price fruits and vegetables by the pound rather than the piece. Warren pushed the idea of allowing customers to serve themselves whenever possible, cutting overhead costs, and he also involved the company in special merchandising campaigns that served more individual grocery needs. Together Skaggs's energy as chairman of the board and Warren's nuts-and-bolts insight gave Safeway the strength to weather the Great Depression.

Rapid Growth Following World War II

World War II brought much needed relief to the grocery business, as the general economic turnaround created by huge government spending put money back into consumers' hands. After the war, Safeway shared in the economic explosion that the United States, and particularly the West, experienced. Soldiers returning from the Pacific theater liked what they saw of the West Coast, and by 1947 they made up a third of Safeway's workforce and helped the firm reach $1 billion in sales. In 1949 Safeway launched a massive building campaign to replace more than 1,000 old stores with newer, larger models. The $200 million project brought many conveniences such as dairy sections, self-help meat stands, and frozen food cases into the Safeway mainstream.

Despite the Korean War, when wage and price controls as well as material rationing were still in effect, Safeway prospered enough to improve and expand its warehousing and distribution operations. The famous "S" insignia, adopted in 1952, could be seen on vast new warehouses in most western states. This extensive warehousing system quickly gave it a reputation for stocking high-quality meats, which meant that many consumers felt that Safeway was the only major grocery chain that could offer them the chance to fill all their food needs under one roof.

In 1954 Safeway joined the list of firms that offered their employees major medical coverage, a move that helped cement good labor relations. In 1955 an era ended at Safeway when Lingan Warren retired from his posts as president, general manager, and director of the company. The slight, bespectacled, reedy-voiced superclerk had been one of the driving forces in the firm for almost a quarter century. Warren was succeeded as president by Milton A. Selby, a longtime member of Safeway

management. Robert A. Magowan, Charles Merrill's son-in-law, was named company director and chairman of the board, leaving his post as securities and marketing services director at Merrill Lynch.

Magowan took over Safeway completely when he was named president of the firm in 1957. That same year the company reached $2 billion in sales, a doubling of total volume in only ten years. Safeway was the only firm west of the Mississippi selling at that volume. Under Magowan, Safeway would expand at an even faster rate than ever before, becoming the first retail food chain to sell more than $10 billion worth of merchandise. Magowan's aggressive marketing strategy and hunger for expansion attracted national attention and greatly enhanced the public profile of the company. By 1959, under Magowan's leadership, Safeway had moved into Alaska and Iowa.

Overseas Expansion in the 1960s

At the beginning of the 1960s, Safeway's construction program had ensured that almost half of the firm's retail outlets were less than five years old and close to two-thirds were less than a decade old. In 1960 the company opened operations in Louisiana. Safeway's first overseas expansion campaign came in 1962, when the company bought a string of 11 stores in England. The following year Safeway crossed the Pacific to open stores in Australia—through the purchase of three Pratt Supermarkets in the Melbourne area—and Hawaii, and strengthened its presence in Alaska. In 1964 Safeway moved into West Germany—with the acquisition of several Big Bear Basar stores—and opened the first "international" supermarket in Washington, D.C. Stocking food products from all of the world's major cuisines, this store was built to be a kind of United Nations of food, offering Washington's shoppers everything they needed to prepare native dishes from around the world.

In 1965 the Amalgamated Meat Cutters and Butchers Workmen's Local 576 picketed Safeway's Kansas City stores. Most stores in the area were able to operate, but some were shut down and business was hurt at almost all local stores. This was one of several labor disputes that occurred in the 1960s and 1970s.

When the company reached its 40th anniversary in 1966 it proudly announced that it had achieved $3 billion a year in sales—and had paid a dividend through the Great Depression, World War II, and ten years of material shortages and price controls. During the same year, Quentin Reynolds succeeded Robert Magowan as president of the company.

In 1969 Robert Magowan resigned as CEO of the firm, phasing out his active involvement in the company. This created some uncertainty since his tenure as Safeway's lead manager had been spectacularly successful.

In 1970 Quentin Reynolds became Safeway's CEO and William Mitchell succeeded Reynolds as president; Robert Magowan kept only his post as chairman of the executive committee. Mitchell would lead the firm to yet more expansion—in 1972 Safeway surpassed the Great Atlantic & Pacific Tea Company (A&P) as the world's largest food retailing chain. In 1971 Safeway was among the first to adopt the now common practice of labeling ground beef by fat content rather than by weight alone, continuing the firm's tradition of supplying consumers with all the facts they needed to make a purchasing decision.

In the mid-1970s several legal issues surrounding the company came to a head. In 1973 a suit filed against Safeway by the United Farm Workers (UFW), led by Cesar Chavez, was denied class action status, a major victory for Safeway. The UFW, along with other groups, had wanted Safeway to pressure lettuce and grape growers to accept the UFW as the employees' collective bargaining agent. Safeway claimed that when it refused, the UFW undertook a campaign of harassment and sabotage, and countersued the UFW for $150 million.

Then in 1974 Safeway was named with most of its competitors in a $1.5 billion suit brought by a group of cattlemen for allegedly fixing prices in the purchase of dressed beef. Although Safeway only paid the cattlemen $150,000, in making the payment the firm agreed "to continue to comply with the antitrust laws."

Dale L. Lynch was named president of Safeway in 1977, taking William Mitchell's place. Lynch thought that Safeway needed to offer a greater variety of goods and services to maintain its position as the leading food retailer. Eventually Lynch's idea led to the execution of the one-stop-shopping concept.

Robert Magowan officially ended his active role in Safeway in 1979, serving only as honorary director of the firm after this time. He had resigned his post as a company director and chairman of the executive committee in the previous year. That year Safeway was involved in another legal case. A young shelf-stocker challenged his dismissal by the firm for violating a "no beard" policy and took his case all the way to the Supreme Court. The Court upheld Safeway's position, setting an important precedent regarding a company's right to regulate workers' appearances.

KKR Takeover and Streamlinings Marked 1980s

In 1980 Peter A. Magowan, Robert Magowan's son, succeeded William Mitchell as chairman and CEO of the firm. Peter Magowan's corporate strategy stressed state-of-the-art technology in retailing and merchandising, aggressive marketing campaigns, and incentive programs for employees.

Magowan, as part of his expansion plans, reached agreements to buy a chain of stores in Australia. In 1981 the company entered into a joint venture with Casa Ley, S.A. de C.V., after which Safeway held a 49 percent interest in the 13-store chain in western Mexico. This heightened internationalism helped to compensate for price wars with A&P and Giant Food Inc. Even though Safeway was selling about $16 billion worth of goods each year, any dip in consumer interest hurt profits because the profit margin in the retail food business is only about one percent.

In 1982 Safeway increased its appeal to customers by beginning to sell many health-oriented products, implementing Dale Lynch's concept of one-stop shopping. The firm also formed a joint venture with the Knapp Communications Corporation to create a string of gourmet food stores called Bon Appetit. Two

such stores in the San Francisco Bay area offered such delicacies as truffles and rare cheeses in a supermarket setting.

James A. Rowland replaced Lynch as president and CEO in 1983. Rowland was known for his sensitive management style; his appointment heralded a new era of improved employee relations. One innovation Rowland introduced was the PAYSOP program, which linked employees' success to Safeway's by granting most workers stock in the company as part of their pay. At this time Safeway also began offering bulk food items and installed salad bars to keep pace with its customers' desires.

In 1985 Safeway merged its Australian operations with Woolworth's Ltd. amid increasing speculation that the chain would be the victim of a takeover bid. The merger between Safeway and Woolworth's gave Safeway a large pretax cash bonanza, leading to speculation that the firm might be trying to liquidate some of its assets to slim down and create a cash pool to buy its own stock and thwart any unfriendly bids (Safeway also gained a 20 percent stake in Woolworth's). Also in 1985 the company sold its operations in West Germany.

In June 1986 all speculation ended when the Dart Group Corporation, led by the Haft family, announced that it had acquired about six percent of Safeway's stock and would try to gain a controlling interest. Since the Hafts were known raiders and had no food retail experience, Safeway never believed that the takeover would be anything but unfriendly. Dart ultimately offered $64 a share for Safeway. Safeway management rebuffed the takeover bid with talk of breaking up the company. The matter was finally resolved in August 1986 when Safeway was acquired and taken private by Kohlberg, Kravis, Roberts & Company (KKR) for $69 a share or $4.3 billion. The Hafts ended their hostile takeover bid for an option to buy 20 percent of the holding company that was founded to buy Safeway.

Saddled with enormous debt after the buyout—$5.7 billion worth—Safeway was forced to streamline its operations and sell a large number of its stores to reduce the crushing interest burden it had assumed. In 1987 Safeway sold its Liquor Barn retail outlets to Majestic Wine Warehouses Ltd., its 59 grocery stores in Texas and New Mexico, and its entire Oklahoma division. The biggest sale of all—in a deal valued at close to $1 billion—was that of Safeway's British operations to the Argyll Group PLC (which in 1996 changed its name to Safeway PLC, a company with no relation to Safeway Inc.).

The streamlining of Safeway ended in 1988 when the firm divested its Kansas City and Little Rock divisions and part of its Richmond division; sold its 99 Houston-area stores to an investment group led by local Safeway management; and sold its 162-store southern California division to The Vons Companies, Inc., in exchange for a 30 percent stake in Vons, plus cash. The sale and trimming of unprofitable operations reduced Safeway's debt and increased its profitability so much that KKR announced in 1988 that Safeway might go public again within a year or two. Chairman and CEO Magowan claimed that the leveraged buyout of Safeway forced it to become more competitive than it had been, so much so that in 1988 the firm made a greater operating profit on $14 billion in sales than it did on $20 billion in sales in 1985. By selling a total of around 1,100 stores for about $2.4 billion, Safeway was able to slash its debts while losing assets that only created $50 million in profits a year after taxes.

1990s Brought New Era As Public Company

Safeway Stores, Inc. did in fact go public again, with the company emerging as Safeway Inc. in 1990 through a public offering, after which KKR still held much more than a majority stake in Safeway. Proceeds from the offering were earmarked toward a $3.2 billion capital improvement program that aimed to renovate existing stores and open new ones. Safeway, however, was still saddled with a fairly high debt load of $3.1 billion, and had to face a most difficult competitive environment in the early 1990s: an economic downturn and increasing pricing pressures from burgeoning discounters and warehouse clubs. Net income for 1992 was a minuscule $43.5 million on sales of $15.15 billion. In October of that year, Steve Burd—a longtime consultant to Safeway with experience at two other food chains with connections to KKR, The Stop & Shop Companies, Inc., and Fred Meyer, Inc.—was named president, then in April of the following year was named CEO as well. Magowan, who relinquished day-to-day control of Safeway in order to become president and managing general partner of the San Francisco Giants baseball team, remained chairman.

Over the next several years, Burd concentrated on three main priorities: slashing costs, increasing sales, and reducing debt. Costs were cut in part by taking a hard line with the employee's unions, which led to a number of protracted strikes and lockouts in the 1990s. Cost savings were used to lower prices in a successful attempt to increase sales. Same-store sales, which had fallen 1.6 percent in 1992, increased 5.1 percent in 1996. Sales hit $17.27 billion by 1996, a total achieved from 1,052 Safeway stores, 51 fewer than the 1,103 stores in the chain in 1992. Safeway was also significantly more profitable as well, as 1996 net income reached $460.6 million. Burd also succeeded in cutting debt by retiring some and restructuring some; the company's total debt had been reduced to $1.98 billion by 1996.

During this turnaround period, Safeway consolidated its private-label brands under the Safeway brand and a new Safeway SELECT brand; the latter was used for premium products, more than 650 of which were introduced from 1993 through 1996, from soft drinks to laundry detergent. At the same time, the company concentrated much of its capital expenses on modernizing numerous stores, with 320 stores receiving makeovers from 1994 through 1996 alone. In early 1996, KKR sold about 14 percent of its stake in Safeway through a secondary offering; following the offering, KKR held about 50 percent of Safeway stock.

Operating in an industry that had seen its share of marriages in the merger-crazed world of the mid-1990s, Safeway was now in a strong enough position to consider growing through acquisition itself. Its first target was Vons, already 34 percent owned by Safeway. In April 1997, in a $1.376 billion deal, the company completed the purchase of the rest of Vons and its 325 stores in southern California. As part of the deal, Safeway also

repurchased 32 million KKR-controlled shares, leaving KKR with a stake of about 38 percent. With the acquisition—which made Safeway second only to Kroger in the U.S. grocery industry—sales increased 30 percent in 1997 to $22.48 billion, while net income increased 21 percent to $557.4 million. For the year, Safeway and Vons combined to invest $829 million in capital expenditures, including opening 37 new stores, remodeling 181 stores, and starting construction of a new distribution center in Maryland.

In May 1998 Magowan retired and Burd took on the additional title of chairman. As a new century loomed, Burd seemed likely to continue to concentrate on containing costs, growing sales, and spending capital wisely. Additional acquisitions also seemed certain to figure significantly in the company's future, with moves into new territory—or the reclamation of territory once held—very possible.

Principal Subsidiaries

Safeway Canada Holdings, Inc.; Safeway Australia Holdings, Inc.; Safeway Leasing, Inc.; Oakland Property Brokerage, Inc.; Glencourt, Inc.; Milford Insurance Ltd.; Pak 'N Save, Inc.; Safeway Trucking, Inc.; Photo Acquisition I, Inc.; Photo Acquisition II, Inc.; Safeway Southern California, Inc.; Safeway Denver, Inc.; Safeway Richmond, Inc.; Safeway Dallas, Inc.; Safeway Supply, Inc.; Safeway Corporate, Inc.; Safeway Stores 42, Inc.; Safeway Stores 43, Inc.; Safeway Stores 64, Inc.; Safeway Claim Services, Inc.; Safeway Stores, Incorporated; Safeway Warehouse, Inc.; Casa Ley, S.A. de C.V. (Mexico; 49%).

Further Reading

Bank, David, "Safeway to Buy Vons for Stock Valued at $1.57 Billion," *Wall Street Journal,* December 17, 1996, p. B4.

Bole, Kristen, "Safeway Initiates Food Exports to Japan," *San Francisco Business Times,* May 17, 1996, pp. 1+.

Hector, Gary, "How Safeway Coped with the Quake," *Fortune,* November 20, 1989, p. 101.

Milligan, John W., "Peter Magowan of Safeway Stores: An LBO That Works," *Institutional Investor,* October 1990, pp. 49+.

Mitchell, Russell, "Safeway Faces Brawls in Every Aisle," *Business Week,* September 7, 1992, p. 78.

——, "Safeway's Low-Fat Diet," *Business Week,* October 18, 1993, pp. 60–61.

Morgenson, Gretchen, "The Buyout That Saved Safeway," *Forbes,* November 12, 1990, pp. 88–90, 92.

Tosh, Mark, "Changing Safeway," *Supermarket News,* October 19, 1992, pp. 1+.

Weinstein, Steve, "The Resurrection at Safeway," *Progressive Grocer,* January 1997, pp. 17+.

Zwiebach, Elliot, "Burd Named President at Safeway," *Supermarket News,* November 2, 1992, pp. 1+.

——, "Safeway, Vons Are Poised to Benefit from Tie's Synergy," *Supermarket News,* December 23, 1996, pp. 1+.

——, "Turnaround at Safeway: CEO Steven Burd Has the Debt-Laden Giant Well on the Road to Recovery," *Supermarket News,* April 25, 1994, pp. 1+.

—Wallace Ross
—updated by David E. Salamie

Saks Holdings, Inc.

12 East 49th Street
New York, New York 10017
U.S.A.
(212) 940-4048
Fax: (212) 940-4299

Public Company
Incorporated: 1902 as Saks and Co.
Employees: 15,636
Sales: $2.19 billion (1998)
Stock Exchanges: New York
Ticker Symbol: SKS
SICs: 5311 Department Stores; 5651 Family Clothing
Stores; 6719 Holding Companies, Not Elsewhere
Classified

The name ''Saks'' is known throughout the retail world, synonymous with luxurious haute couture. Saks Holdings, Inc. is the holding company for the famous Saks Fifth Avenue retail chain which includes over 56 traditional full-line, resort-area, and Main Street stores, over three dozen OFF 5TH stores (a bargain-priced outlet chain), and its high-gloss direct mail service, called Folio. Saks, along with other tony retailers like Neiman Marcus, Barneys, and more recently Nordstrom, rule the fashion empire with beautifully outfitted stores from coast to coast, with an elite global clientele. With roots dating back to just after the Civil War, the company has undergone several ownership changes, including that by the Bahrain-based Investcorp International in 1990. Investcorp took Saks public in 1996, yet retained a 50 percent stake, which was then put up for sale in early 1998. In July Proffitt's, Inc. announced that it would purchase Saks; the news was largely heralded by industry analysts, who saw a rosier future for the classic chain under new ownership.

The Earliest Saks Stores, Late 1800s to 1925

Andrew Saks was born in Baltimore, Maryland, and moved to Washington, D.C., to make his fortune. He established a successful clothing business in 1867, and opened a store in New York on 34th Street in 1902 as Saks and Co. Andrew Saks ran the New York store as a family affair with his brother Isadore, and his sons Horace and William. Young Horace, who had been privately schooled and attended Princeton University, became the driving force of the family enterprise after Andrew died in 1912. With a keen eye and good business sense, Horace pushed to open a new store on Fifth Avenue, to appeal to a higher-class clientele. At the same time Horace Saks was exploring his options in the New York retail world, another young man, Bernard Gimbel, was considering the attributes of a merger between the two families.

The Gimbels were well-known in the retail business, their empire begun in Vincennes, Indiana, in 1842 by Adam Gimbel. After successfully opening stores in Milwaukee and Philadelphia, Gimbel Brothers, Inc. (made up of Adam's eight sons, including Bernard's father, Isaac) opened a store in New York at Bernard's urging. The resulting Gimbels built in 1910 at Broadway, between 32nd and 33rd Streets, was just a stone's throw from Saks. After going public in 1922, Gimbel Bros. approached the Saks family, and the two joined forces. Although the Gimbel family ultimately secured ownership of the Saks stores, each continued to operate under the Saks name and Horace Saks oversaw operations.

In 1924, the first joint effort of the Saks and Gimbel families was to create an upscale ''specialty'' store on Fifth Avenue, between 49th and 50th streets. The proposed site of the Saks/Gimbel store was in a mostly residential area, occupied by the Buckingham Hotel and the Democratic Club—both of which were demolished to make way for the store of the future. Saks and Gimbel envisioned an elegant high-fashion mecca of excellent fabrics and styles for men and women, with customer services to match.

The new Saks Fifth Avenue opened on September 15, 1924—a year in which Ford produced its 10-millionth car, Calvin Coolidge won the presidential election, and Knute Rockne's Fighting Irish were undefeated. The store's debut proved historic, as a monument to both architecture (the building won a gold medal from the Fifth Avenue Association for the best structure) and merchandising. In the midst of all the hoopla, Bernard Gimbel's cousin, Adam, became Horace Saks's right-hand man. It was a serendipitous move; for upon Horace's

Company Perspectives:

Saks Fifth Avenue's customers are changing—and Saks Fifth Avenue is changing with them. Month by month, we are rolling out new initiatives focused to reach and satisfy this affluent and selective group. They are younger in spirit, increasingly discerning, career—and family—driven. They want quality, value and service. With our merchandising experience, we have the intuition to SENSE what these customers want—in fashion, cosmetics, fragrance, accessories and shoes—for their changing lifestyles. Our business, marketing and financial acumen gives us the ABILITY to deliver what they need, when and where they need it—in new and rewarding ways—at home, at work, at vacation resorts. Our innovative SENSE/ABILITY is propelling the continued growth of Saks Fifth Avenue as we move into a changing retail world.

untimely death from septic poisoning in 1925, Adam Gimbel succeeded him as president of Saks Fifth Avenue and was credited with not only keeping the Saks vision alive, but turning an extraordinary store into a national chain. In the years that followed, Saks Fifth Avenue garnered a global reputation, one that would eclipse even the Gimbel name.

High Times and Higher Sales, 1926–69

After Horace's passing, Adam Gimbel initiated a series of progressive changes with long-ranging implications. As the permanent wave, invented by Antonio Buzzacchino, gave men and women a variety of hair fashions, Adam decided to give them a refashioned Saks. He turned the store into a modern art masterpiece à la Paris Exposition, and broke up the huge department-store floor into specialty salons for the discriminating tastes of his clients. While few stores measured up to Saks for many years, competitors emerged from time to time, some with far greater staying power than others. Among these was Neiman Marcus, a similarly elegant store founded in Texas in 1907 by Herbert Marcus, his sister Carrie Marcus Neiman, and her husband A. L. Neiman. The rivalry between Saks and Neiman Marcus kept both retailers on their toes into the next century.

Meanwhile, Gimbels had become the largest department store chain in the world, with some 20,000 employees and net sales of $123 million in 1930, a year in which the U.S. population had grown to 122 million, and New Yorkers could not stop talking about the Max Schmeling-Jack Sharkey fight. Bernard became president of Gimbels Bros. Inc. as cousin Adam made his name and reputation at Saks. As a purveyor of the finest in fashion and taste, Adam sought to distinguish Saks Fifth Avenue from its competitors and from Gimbels; the latter was not difficult since Gimbels catered to consumers of virtually all income levels and Saks dealt exclusively with wealthy shoppers who were enamored of Greta Garbo in *Anna Christie* and Marlene Dietrich in *Blue Angel*. To keep Saks head-and-shoulders above its competitors, Adam sought not just to meet his clients' needs but to exceed them and predict them.

Saks and Gimbels remained intricately connected through the years, the former often mirroring the successes of the latter. In the 1950s, a time when 30 percent of the United States' workforce worked in commerce and industry, retailing began moving out of the cities and into suburban areas. Gimbels was reluctant to jump on the suburban mall bandwagon, even as competitors built store after store in non-metro malls. Saks, too, was a city establishment and few could imagine a store of Saks's reputation in a mall. Yet as more and more shoppers frequented outlying department stores, buoyed by the musical hit "Baubles, Bangles, and Beads," Gimbels established its first in 1953. Like Gimbels, Saks eventually moved to suburbia as well, and even took another cue from the venerable chain—entering the bargain-priced merchandise arena as well.

By the mid-1960s as teens mooned over the Beatles and their folks crooned Sinatra's "It Was A Very Good Year," there were over two dozen Saks stores, many of them gracing the new suburban shopping malls. Gimbels, too, had grown to 27 stores, though the company's fortunes were destined to slow down as Saks's heated up. At the end of the decade, in 1969 when Adam Gimbel retired from Saks, Richard Nixon had become the 37th president of the United States, Apollo 11 landed on the moon, and the world's population had grown to 3.5 billion people. It was a year in which inflation reared its head, though not so much so to Saks's wealthy clientele. As Gimbel stepped down, ending an era of close association with both the Gimbel name and its retailing enterprises, he had managed not only to make Saks Fifth Avenue a jewel of Manhattan, but had placed similar gems in major metropolitan areas throughout the United States.

New Frontiers, 1970–90

Over the next two decades, Saks's expansion plans branched into the direct-mail marketplace. Its first mail-order catalogue, Folio, was produced in the early 1970s, and sought to entice customers who could not get to a Saks store to order its merchandise. The catalogue also provided national exposure for the company, at a time when Saks was opening stores in the Midwest, Texas (Neiman Marcus's stronghold), and elsewhere in the United States as older stores were remodeled and updated to maintain the high standards associated with the Saks name.

Towards the end of the decade, Saks began a construction project to renovate its New York flagship store (including the installation of escalators, an innovation widely used after Ellis Gimbel put one in the family's Philadelphia store), heightening not only its look and feel but square-footage by building a 36-floor office and retail complex behind it. The massive undertaking, which took years to complete, gave Saks almost 30 percent more selling space, and a more spectacular landmark as well.

By the 1990s, change was imminent. Saks was bought by the Bahrain-based Investcorp International for $1.6 billion, stunning the retail industry with a price said to be over $300 million more than the company was worth at the time. While analysts scratched their heads, Investcorp's principals had long-range goals in mind—to trim expenses, expand sales, and add more luxurious stores in strategic locations. Nonetheless, Investcorp was known for buying well-branded companies and spinning them off (such as Tiffany & Company and later Gucci) and many wondered whether Investcorp would be true to form with Saks as well. Philip B. Miller was named vice-chairman in

1990, and Brian Kendrick was appointed senior vice-president and CFO the following year. At the close of 1991, Saks generated $1.25 billion in sales, though suffered an operating loss of over $40 million.

Public and Private Woes and Triumphs, 1995 and Beyond

In the early 1990s Saks, which previously sold "residue" merchandise to stores like Filene's Basement, decided to try its hand in the burgeoning outlet market with a store called Saks Clearinghouse, in Franklin Mills, Pennsylvania. Though the move raised eyebrows and was decidedly unglamorous, the outlet store held its own with pricing from 25 to 75 percent lower than traditional Saks stores. The chain (later rechristened OFF 5TH in 1995) even produced a 64-page catalogue mailed to 750,000 Saks clients. While outlet sales in the industry remained strong, Saks planned to open as many as 20 new outlet stores, including one in downtown New York, not far from its flagship Saks Fifth Avenue store, over the next few years.

While some of the competition turned up their noses at the OFF 5TH gambit as beneath the status of a high-end retailer like Saks, others applauded the company's initiative. Such initiative was Saks's way of preparing for the future amidst ever-growing competition and a fluctuating marketplace. In 1993, Miller was named chairman and CEO, and the next year Kendrick became vice-chairman as Saks moved west in a big way, buying up former rival I. Magnin's stores in Beverly Hills, Carmel, San Diego, and Phoenix. By the next year, when Saks West debuted on Rodeo drive, it was the largest retailer in the area with 260,000 square feet, including the space occupied by its sibling Saks East, which had been remodeled and expanded. For 1994, Saks's sales were $1.42 billion with an operating income of $66.1 million.

Though Saks had dabbled in several retail areas to accommodate shoppers, like its mail-order business and OFF 5TH, less productive areas like home furnishings and children's apparel were phased out of its stores in 1995 to concentrate on its core business in women's sportswear and designer labels, accessories (including shoes and jewelry), cosmetics, and fragrance. In the case of home furnishings, however, what was taken out of the stores went into a new catalogue, set to mail in the fall to over a million of Saks's clients. Saks also prepared to toss its hat into another fashion arena, an underserved and not always popular market segment—larger-sized women's clothing. Seemingly on the right track, year-end total sales had climbed to $1.69 billion, with an operating income of $79.7 million—an increase of 17 percent over 1994's—then reduced to $36.3 million after deducting special charges (including a new, state-of-the-art distribution facility in Aberdeen, Maryland; the integration of the four I. Magnin stores; and higher management fees for the fiscal year).

Saks reached an important and expected milestone in 1996 by becoming a publicly traded company. The company's IPO sold nearly 18.1 million common shares at $25 each, raising $418 million. Shares peaked at just over $41 in the third quarter, but closed the year back at the IPO level. Some analysts were less than enthusiastic about Saks's share data, such as *Money* magazine's Junius Ellis, who declared Neiman Marcus's stock a

far more stable buy in the winter of 1996, and stating "Saks is destined to disappoint." Others speculated Saks was spreading itself too thin, and many times the numbers seemed to bear this out. Year-end net sales, however, proved Saks was holding on by topping $1.95 billion, an increase of 15.3 percent over 1995, and an impressive 37 percent from 1994. Comparable sales grew by 10.3 percent, which contributed to a surge in operating income to $109.4 million, and the $418 million raised through the IPO helped decrease debt to $708 million (down from the previous year's $976 million). Division-wise, the primary stores (full-line, resort, and Main Street) brought in the lion's share of sales (86 percent) at $1.67 billion, to OFF 5TH's 10 percent or $200.1 million (up from six percent in 1995 and four percent in 1994), while Folio maintained a four percent share or nearly $80 million.

Saks took the bull by the horns in Texas in 1997, going head-to-head with rival Neiman Marcus on the latter's home territory. By opening two new stores within a week in Houston, the first in the legendary Galleria, a stronghold of Neiman Marcus, and another at the Town and Country Center, Saks turned up the heat in Houston's tony retail market. Was the market big enough for both Saks and Neiman Marcus? Chairman and CEO Miller thought so (and he was a former Neiman Marcus executive from 1977 to 1983)—and the Galleria store brought in over $2 million in sales in its first three days. Well-heeled shoppers seemed to think there was room enough for both as well, flocking from one store to the other.

Saks continued its Texas invasion with another new store in Austin, and additional stores in San Antonio and the Dallas-Ft. Worth area. Meanwhile, back on the West Coast, the battle between Neiman Marcus and Saks became even more heated with the appearance of a new Barneys New York in Beverly Hills. As was the case in Houston, shoppers found the competition invigorating, and analysts believed the stores complemented one another. Whether each could maintain profits in such hothouse conditions, however, remained to be seen.

Despite some shaky quarters, and the closing of several underperforming stores, Saks had plans for further expansion in California, Florida, and New York. Yet as the Saks stock price dipped to all-time lows and its credit rating was downgraded, Investcorp, which still owned 50 percent of Saks, opened its doors to suitors in early 1998. The news of either a merger or selling the retailer outright brought share prices up to a 52-week high, with analysts speculating about old rivals Neiman Marcus, Macy's, or Nordstrom as buyers, or even Hong Kong's Dickson Poo or London's Harrods coming to the rescue. Although the *New York Times* reported that would-be suitors might be kept at bay by an asking price of as much as $2.5 billion, Birmingham, Alabama-based Proffitt's secured Saks in early July for a price of $2.1 billion [for the history of Proffitt's, please see *IDCH* 19]. The all-stock deal, expected to be finalized by October 31, 1998, would create a $6 billion retailing company with 330 stores in 38 states. In addition, the Saks name would be assumed by the larger Proffitt's, which held the number four position among the nation's department store chains. In a *St. Cloud Times* article, industry forecaster Kurt Barnard called the merger "a very good deal for Saks, Proffitt's and the investment community. Referring to Investcorp's sale of its stake, Barnard added, "Under the new management of Proffitt's, Saks will find a far more sympathetic ear for its needs and potential.'' Whatever the future held, one thing remained unchanged: that Saks was far more than a retailer or chain of stores, it was an establishment whose name would forever signify the very embodiment of style and elegance.

Further Reading

Bird, Laura, ''Investcorp's Saks to Add Its Catalogues with September Home-Furnishings Book,'' *Wall Street Journal,* August 18, 1995, p. B10.
——, ''Retailing: Department Stores Target Top Customers,'' *Wall Street Journal,* March 8, 1995.
——, ''Saks, in Fifth Year Under Bahrain Firm, Is Scrutinized . . . ,'' *Wall Street Journal,* July 28, 1995, p. B4.
Ellis, Junius, Why You Can Make 36% with Neiman Marcus but Strike Out with Saks,'' *Money,* Winter 1996, p. 35.
''Focus—Saks Mulls Sale, Stock Rallies,'' Reuters News Service, June 25, 1998.
Hollandsworth, Skip, ''Store Wars,'' *Texas Monthly,* August 1997.
''Moody's Affirms Saks Holdings Inc.,'' Reuters News Service, June 26, 1998.
''Profitts Soars with Saks Purchase,'' *St. Cloud Times,* July 6, 1998, p. 1A.
Sparks, Debra, ''Skin Deep,'' *Financial World,* June 17, 1996, p. 22.
Tannen, Mary, ''Lone-Star Wars,'' *Vogue,* December 1997.
Williamson, Rusty, and David Molin, ''Saks Houston: Ready to Duke It Out,'' *Women's Wear Daily,* October 7, 1997.

—Taryn Benbow-Pfalzgraf

Schawk, Inc.

1695 River Rd.
Des Plaines, Illinois 60018-3013
U.S.A.
(847) 827-9494
Fax: (847) 827-1264
Web site: http://www.schawk.com

Public Company
Incorporated: 1953
Employees: 890
Sales: $116.1 million (1997)
Stock Exchanges: New York
Ticker Symbol: SGK
SICs: 2796 Platemaking & Related Services; 2752
    Commercial Printing Lithographic

Schawk, Inc. is one of the leading graphics arts services companies in the United States and Canada, providing prepress imaging and information technology services for consumer products packaging, advertising, and promotion markets—primarily for the food and beverage industry. Schawk's clients include *Fortune* 1000 accounts such as Bayer, Campbell Soup, ConAgra, General Mills, Hershey, Keebler, Leo Burnett, Nestlé, Pepsico, Pillsbury, Publisher's Clearing House, and Quaker Oats. Services include digital artwork, image capture and manipulation, direct digital printing, and computer-to-plate technology for the three main processes used in the graphic arts industry: lithography, flexography, and gravure. The company operates or has business alliances with 26 business divisions spanning seven countries, including prepress service providers in the Far East, Europe, and Australia.

Founded in 1953

The company was founded in Chicago, Illinois, in 1953 by Clarence W. Schawk. At that time Schawk, Inc. functioned as a small, single-location platemaking company. Within a few years, however, the company began to expand rapidly, with a strategy of acquiring companies in niche markets with *Fortune* 1000 client lists. Other attributes considered before the selection of additional businesses included evidence of excellent client service or proprietary products and solid management in companies with revenues ranging from $2 million to $20 million. Start-up operations were added when client servicing requirements or market conditions warranted. Clarence's son, David Schawk, began by serving as a Schawk director prior to serving as company president beginning in 1985. Clarence Schawk's commitment to the industry was attested to by his work as president and director of the International prepress Association. Between 1965 and 1985 Schawk acquired Process Color Plate (PCP), Kalacraft, and Molded Rubber Printing Plate, which was merged with PCP. Next, the company acquired Litho Services and merged it with Kalacraft to form LSI/Kala. Crown Rubber Plate Company, North American Flexo Company Progressive Litho, and Fotographics, Inc. were also merged into PCP, among numerous other acquisitions and new client locations.

Schawk, Inc. was structured into two primary operating divisions, the Imaging and Information Technologies Group and the Plastics Group. The Imaging Group concentrated on prepress industry services, art design, and products for consumer products packaging and related marketing and advertising materials in the United States. The division grew through a combination of internal growth, new products and services, and an ongoing series of acquisitions. The role of prepress services involved encompassing tasks for preparation of an image for reproduction by any of several types of printing processes. The prepress services did not actually encompass the printing or production of packaging materials, only the various steps such as electronic and digital art production design, color separation, and other photoplatemaking services prior to printing. Product cartons, boxes, trays, cans, containers, packaging labels, and related point-of-sale and promotional materials were developed by the creative designers in cooperation with consumer products manufacturers. Traditionally, prepress services were performed by skilled craftsmen almost entirely by hand. The Imaging Group, along with its competitors, became increasingly computerized. Artwork that was once created directly by hand was now manipulated by computers using scanning devices and laser optics, then digitized and output to film, tape, or disc.

Company Perspectives:

From our beginnings as a producer of printing plates, we have developed into a multinational group of premier, quality-oriented companies serving the industries in which we participate.

Our growth has occurred in two ways. One, an aggressive strategy of acquisition has provided the strength that comes with diversity.

Two, we adhere to sound management principles that have guided us from the start: fiscal responsibility, the latest training and most appropriate technology for our employees, and a commitment to our customers that no competitor can match.

Increasingly, material supplied by clients to Schawk was presented on digitized format on a variety of removable media, including tape, floppy disk, and CD-ROM.

1984: Entering the Plastics Business

In 1984 Schawk acquired Robinson Industries, a supplier of visual packaging products, in a move that cast Schawk into the plastics business. Robinson's visual or blister packaging operation was a natural extension for Schawk, expanding the company's expertise in production package design by increasing packaging capabilities. The Plastics Group became a leader in the manufacture of injection molded plastic filtration, custom specialty plastic, and thermoformed products. That group was partially comprised of Filtertek, Plastic Molded Concepts, Inc. (PMC), Tek Packaging Group, Inc. (formerly known as Robinson Industries, Inc.), Fuzere Manufacturing Company, Inc., and the Fuzere Midwest division. Schawk continued to acquire as well as launch various plastics companies, and was introduced to major producer Filtertek, Inc. via its association with Robinson, a supplier to that company. In 1992, Schawk acquired a controlling interest in Filtertek. Two years later, the corporation known as Schawk, Inc. (''Old Schawk'') was merged into Filtertek. The surviving corporation in the merger was Filtertek, which then changed its name to Schawk, Inc., according to company reports. The Plastics Group was comprised primarily of what had been the business of Filtertek prior to the merger and the Imaging Group was comprised primarily of what had been the business of the ''Old Schawk'' companies.

An emerging industry trend of establishing on-site services was adopted by Schawk. The company developed a strategy of implementing conveniently located services, providing clients with less costly prepress management, and offering exceptional technological advantages and speedier turnaround time. The company placed an emphasis on investment in state-of-the-art systems and equipment, plus continual training and development of its employees through company-sponsored programs, on- and off-site. Schawk's on-site locations included those at Brach and Brock Confections, Inc., Campbell Soup Company, International Home Foods, The Keebler Company, Nabisco Foods Group, Pepsico, Inc., Pillsbury, Inc., The Quaker Oats Company, and Stouffer Foods Corporation. The company also

expanded south of the border with a start-up operation for a client in Queretaro, Mexico.

Further Expansion in the 1990s

Three significant acquisitions were added in 1996: Converterscan, StanMont, Inc., and Stebbins Photography. Converterscan had a reputation for expertise in digital imaging, previously based in Stamford, Connecticut, and Atlanta, Georgia. The company was consolidated with Schawk's LSI/Atlanta operation in Georgia. Based in Montreal, Quebec, StanMont, Inc. had five operating divisions spanning locations throughout Toronto and Montreal, serving a strong client base and operations intended to serve the imaging needs of Schawk's consumer products clients in Canada. StanMont also added a strong base of advertising and catalog clients in addition to growth opportunities in the packaging market. Stebbins Photography, based in Minneapolis, Minnesota, added a strong presence in the emerging digital photography area. In 1998, Schawk completed the acquisition of S&M Rotogravure Service, Inc. of Milwaukee, Wisconsin. That company specialized in products and services for the packaging segment of the imaging industry and had 1997 revenues in excess of $6 million.

Recognizing the importance of establishing global brand imagery as consistently as possible, Schawk worked to identify market trends. Researchers determined that shoppers were spending less time shopping, and were looking for ways to make purchasing decisions simpler. They learned that consumers make up to 70 percent of their grocery food purchase decisions in-store. The importance of ''brand'' remained closely tied to packaging. The goal for businesses was to find what commanded shoppers' attention, what could be communicated quickly, and what could persuade powerfully. Brand imagery, logos, and brand colors required consideration. In addition, special attention was required in order to ensure accurately produced imagery on materials as diverse as plastic, glass, metal, cardboard, colored stock, and other substrates. Finally, competition for in-store shelf space created intense pressure to create bold, informative packaging. The utilization of special promotions as a marketing tool also affected decisions in terms of speed-to-market time.

In 1996, the company announced the sale of its Plastics Business Segment after determining that its managerial and financial resources should be more focused on its primary area of competency in imaging technologies. In December of that year, Schawk sold the remaining Plastics Business Segment to the ESCO Electronics Corporation of St. Louis, Missouri.

Net sales from continuing operations for 1997 increased 27.9 percent to $116.1 million from $90.8 million for 1996. A substantial growth in operating income—an increase 48.5 percent—was also reported for that period, largely due to increased sales volume and increased operating efficiency. The sale of the plastics business segment resulted in repayment of the entire revolving credit facility of $22.5 million. In February 1998 the company completed a public offering of 3,450 shares of common stock, raising $16.5 million.

A trade advertising campaign was initiated in 1997, supported by targeted direct-mail and public relations. Following events of 1997 which included the addition of nine more client locations, Schawk executives reported with glowing optimism that ''Our existing client base is strong. We enjoy a client list of nearly all the major food and beverage producers in the U.S. Our 10 largest clients accounted for approximately 36 percent of the Company's revenues in 1997. Approximately seven percent of the total revenues came from the Company's largest single client.'' Efforts were made over time to enter key North American markets including New York, Los Angeles, Chicago, Philadelphia, Atlanta, Cincinnati, Minneapolis, Kalamazoo, Toronto, Montreal, and Mexico—positions close to clients' bases of operations. By the end of 1998, Schawk planned to be on-site at 30 client locations, following growth of 68 percent in that area of operations over the previous year. The company considered itself well-positioned to meet future challenges in the fast-paced products packaging, advertising, and promotion environment. Schawk management predicted that the packaging segment of the industry was particularly centered around speed-to-market issues, an area where Schawk officials felt confident that efforts would pay off.

Principal Divisions

Amber Design; Batten Graphics (Canada); Color Data East, Inc.; Cyberimages (Canada); Dimension Imaging; LSI/ Atlanta; LSI Kala; Process Color Plate; Schawk Cinci; Schawkgraphics/ Total Reproductions; Lincoln Graphics; Litho Colorplate; StanMont, Inc. (Canada); Weston Engraving; Xzact (Canada).

Further Reading

''Filtertek Will Merge with Majority Holder,'' *Wall Street Journal,* October, 17, 1994, p. B4.

Jorgensen, Dennis, ''Corporate Sponsors Enhance AMA Mission,'' *Marketing News*, March 17, 1997, p. E13.

''Schawk Unit to Be Bought in $92 Million Agreement,'' *Wall Street Journal*, December 20, 1996, p. B6.

—Terri Mozzone

Scitex Corporation Ltd.

P.O. Box 330/Hamada Street, Industrial Park
46103 Herzlia B
Israel
972-9-959-7222
Fax: 972-9-950-2922
Web Site: http://www.scitex.com

Public Company
Founded: 1968
Employees: 3,400
Sales: $676 million (1997)
Stock Exchanges: NASDAQ
Ticker Symbol: SCIXF
SICs: 3577 Computer Peripheral Equipment, Not
 Elsewhere Classified; 7812 Motion Picture, Video
 Tape Production

Herzlia, Israel-based Scitex Corporation Ltd. is known worldwide as a leading developer, manufacturer, marketer, and servicer of interactive computerized prepress systems primarily for the graphic design, printing, and publishing markets. The company is a pioneer of Israeli high-tech, and a prototype for other Israeli electronics firms.

Scitex's graphic arts group, the largest component of Scitex and a major supplier of electronic prepress and short-run digital printing systems, specializes in digital cameras and scanners, color workstations for page assembly and retouching, client-server systems, professional inkjet color printers, and image-setters and platesetters.

Scitex's digital printing division manufactures high-speed inkjet printers enabling document personalization for invoicing, business forms, and mail-order applications. Scitex's digital video division manufactures video post-production and on-line systems for non-linear editing and special effects creation.

The company's Scitex America Corp. subsidiary, headquartered in Bedford, Massachusetts, manufactures products in its Response line for page make-up, designed for specific operations, and modular, for custom configuration.

The company started out developing pioneering technology for high-quality color prepress equipment used by newspapers and magazines throughout the world, but Scitex also produces output devices, including the Raystar flatbed laser plotter, introduced in 1985; the Eray laser plotter; and the ELP electronic laser plotter.

Other Scitex systems serve applications in mapmaking, interpretation of seismic data, and the design and preparation of printed circuit boards.

From Start to Trouble and Back Again, 1979–92

Scitex was founded in 1968. Arie Rosenfeld joined the company at that time, established Scitex's European subsidiary headquarters in Brussels in 1974, and went on to become COO (1987) and CEO (1988).

Scitex stunned the printing industry in 1979 by introducing the minicomputer-based turnkey Response 300 color prepress system, instantly outselling its two main competitors, Hell Graphic Systems and Crosfield Composition Systems Inc. (first to bring out automated input/output devices for color digital prepress systems), filling an enormous need, and serving a labor-intensive, costly niche—gathering graphic elements, correcting color separations, then preparing photographic film of the resulting page to be run on a press. The company's sales increased and technology improved every year for the next eight and, by 1984, sales reached $104 million.

In 1983, Scitex entered the printed circuit board (PCB) manufacturing industry with its Insight system, hoping to cash in on the computer market. But management was disappointed—expecting 1985 sales of nearly $18 million—when the computer industry sagged and manufacture of PCBs concurrently dropped. When the industry recovered several years later, PCBs were being designed by CAD/CAM systems, which designed entire engineering structures on a computer screen, technology Scitex did not have. In addition, while the market for prepress equipment in the U.S.—Scitex's core business—was

---

Company Perspectives:

Scitex is a world leader in Visual Information Communication. We design, develop, manufacture, market and support products, systems and devices, primarily for the industries that parallel our three business units: Graphic Arts Group (color electronic prepress and short-run, color digital printing), Scitex Digital Printing Division (variable data high-speed digital printing), and Scitex Digital Video Division (non-linear video editing and special effects generation).

---

far from exhausted, profits sagged from high product costs (Scitex's top-of-the-line Response system carried a pricetag of $1.5 million, out of reach for all but the largest publishing houses). Scitex did introduce a scaled-down Response system for $300,000, opening up the market for smaller graphics shops and publishing houses.

In 1985, Scitex America created HANDSHAKE, a proprietary program which was the first in the industry to establish standards for data transfer and multivendor system integration in page makeup and design layout. HANDSHAKE was a standardized software package allowing a wide variety of devices to pass information to, or receive information from, a Scitex Response color electronic prepress system. That same year, Crosfield, D.S. America, Eikonix, Hell, Scitex, and 3M met to establish a set of Digital Data Exchange Standards for the data imaging industry so varied systems would be compatible.

In September, Efraim Arazi, Scitex's founder, president, and CEO, passed the mantle to executive vice-president Arthur Low. By October, Scitex was leading the $3 billion computerized printing industry, with such clients as *Time*, *Newsweek*, the *Chicago Tribune*, and *U.S. News & World Report*.

A year later, in August 1986, Scitex America entered a joint venture with Contex Graphics Systems Inc. and Continental Can Company Inc. to market a packaging design system allowing designers to create three-dimensional packaging and label designs without preparing mock-ups or prototypes for each design.

By April 1987, Scitex America, with the Response system, was among the four top manufacturers of such equipment, with Crosfield (Studio), D.S. America (Sigmagraph), and Hell (Chromacom). Royal Zenith Company's scanner division and 3M were minor competitors.

Also that year, N.V. Phillips and DuPont Optical undertook to market and install optical disk storage—a 12-tape lookalike, write-once, optical disk, featuring two gigabytes (GB) in single-drive or jukebox (16–20 disk) format—on pagination systems, replacing magnetic tape storage. The four major companies in the industry began working with Phillips and DuPont on the project.

In 1988, Scitex America began working with *Sports Illustrated* as a technology provider. That March, Quark Technologies Inc., which made high-end Macintosh desktop-publishing

software, announced an alliance with Scitex, allowing users of *QuarkXPress 2.0* to generate compound documents containing text, color graphics, and photographs.

In July, Scitex America released a full-color, PC-based page design/layout system for direct access to electronic prepress operations called Visionary, combining concept-to-proof design functionality linked directly to a Response system for final production work. Visionary consisted of a Mac II platform, Sharp color scanner, Mitsubishi color thermal proofing printer, and Scitex's software/hardware interfacing package, *Gateway*, utilizing *HandshakeXPress*, providing users with an interface enabling their design workstations to communicate with and transfer text, graphics, and page geometry to a Scitex system.

By early 1989, the system had caught on in the magazine publishing industry, with many design departments, including those at *Victoria* and *Modern Bride*, using the system, getting linked by high-speed modems to Scitex prepress systems at service bureaus. Visionary allowed multiple four-color images on a page to be resized, moved, rotated, color corrected, or airbrushed in minutes, sometimes seconds, working with low-resolution scanned images of actual artwork, with flow-around type. Proofs could be pulled at the designer's workstation, with low-resolution color reasonably representative of the finished four-color pages.

By this time, though, Scitex was hurting financially, posting net losses for three years averaging $17.2 million annually. Scitex wrestled with transitioning its main product line from programs run on proprietary Hewlett-Packard based minicomputers to proprietary Intel chip-based workstations, while simultaneously selling off side businesses to finance the changeover. At the time, Israel's inflation rate was over 100 percent.

However, after the industry crises of the mid-1980s, Scitex continued introducing workstations, laser plotters, and powerful software as its competitors struggled under new corporate parents. Crosfield, formerly owned by DeLaRue, a Swiss holding company, chafed under joint ownership by DuPont and Fuji in 1989, and Hell floundered under the management of Linotype after being sold by Siemens in 1990. By February 1992, Scitex held 45 percent of the worldwide color prepress market and, within the printing industry, had become as recognized as Xerox Corporation.

Interesting Side Notes, 1991

Two instances of unusual and unexpected publicity arrived at Scitex's doorstep in 1991. The first occurred amidst the Gulf War, when schools shut down throughout Israel. Although a Scud missile landed 1,000 yards from company headquarters, Scitex continued business as usual, and hired 150 teachers to set up makeshift classrooms in a sealed bomb shelter on corporate grounds so parents could still come to work. The second surfaced near the end of the year, in November, when British tycoon Robert Maxwell died mysteriously at sea. His holdings in Scitex were considerable, amounting to some 27 percent of the company stock.

Acquisitions and Growth, 1991–Date

In April 1991, Scitex signed a 10-year agreement with Quark to develop custom extensions to *QuarkXPress* software under the Visionary page design/layout system. In October, Scitex and Optrotech agreed to cooperate on computerized retouching for the printing industry.

In March 1992, Scitex bought Leaf Systems, a highly regarded American manufacturer of desktop and portable scanners, filmless cameras, and preprint systems, for $35 million.

That June, International Paper, the largest paper product company in the world, acquired 11 percent of Scitex for $209 million; Scitex acquired RICOH Corporation's Telepress TP15 and TP25 product lines of compression and communication technologies, used to link prepress with remote proofing, plotting, and printing devices via satellite; and Scitex's research and development staff received the Rothschild Prize for excellence in the field of advanced technology.

In January 1993, Scitex, with Britain's DSP Group Ltd. (a major supplier of Application-Specific Digital Signal Processing chipset solutions to original equipment manufacturers (OEMs) for speech processing, speech-and-data compression, noise suppression, and image processing), formed a joint venture company—Nogatech Inc.—to develop, market, and sell chipsets and electronic components for a number of applications, including enhanced CD video and audio recordings, and digital cameras and camcorders for capturing visual images.

The business climate for publishing industry technology suppliers slumped, and Scitex, Apple Computer Inc., and International Business Machines Corp. suffered falling stock prices and huge losses ($8.04 billion for IBM in one quarter). But Scitex bounced back. In June, Eastman Kodak's Dayton, Ohio-based inkjet operations was acquired for approximately $70 million, following Scitex's general strategy to meet multiple applications, and achieving direct-to-paper color digital printing. Scitex also allied itself with RasterOps Corporation (merged with Truevision in 1992, creating an industry leader in the development of color transformation, calibration technology, and Postscript raster image processors for printers and imagesetters), investing $10 million in the high-quality monitor maker for 13 percent of the stock, and giving Scitex entry into the video world.

In July, three major shareholders (Clal Electronic Industries Ltd., Discount Investment Corporation Ltd., and P.E.C. Israel Economic Corporation) bought $15 million worth of Scitex shares. In August, the Scitex Graphic Arts Users Association—the largest graphic arts users group in the industry—celebrated its 25th anniversary. At the conference, Scitex America exhibited new products, including four scanners, two workstations, connectivity programs, communication and network innovations, direct-to-plate and press development projects, an advanced workstation for packaging professionals, Dolev imagesetters, management tracking and production files, and screening technology called Scitex Class Screening. Scitex also continued development in *PostScript* and began exploring video post-production products, picture databases, and pushing digital signal processing technology for voice recognition. Additionally, an agreement was signed with Kodak and three other prepress vendors (competitors Dainippon Screen Manufacturing Ltd., Linotype-Hell Ltd., and Crosfield) to work with a Kodak PrintPhoto CD product, allowing the input capabilities provided by Photo CD and ProPhoto CD Master discs, as well as scanned input to be stored in prepress systems. In October, Scitex developed a device turning Xerox photocopiers into color laser printers, entering competition with E.F.I. Electronics For Imaging.

In May 1994, Scitex America introduced two new Mac-based scanners—the Smart 340L, to scan reflective art and transparencies (color and black-and-white) directly into the computer; and the Smart 730PS, to scan and edit multiple images simultaneously—and ResoLUT PS, a NuBus card, to convert YCC and RGB file formats into CMYK, and perform color correction and transformation on the Mac.

In its pursuit of prepress systems, Scitex in September purchased Iris Graphics Inc., a leading manufacturer of equipment for the digital printing industry that made the first direct digital color-proofing continuous-tone system, for $24 million. Also that month, Scitex entered the broadcast market, acquiring ImMIX from Carlton Communications PLC for $21 million, including ImMIX's *VideoCube* digital video editing system used by studios and independent producers. ImMIX, established by Carlton in 1990, began selling its editing systems in July 1993, reaching $19 million in sales the first year. Scitex also allied with International Paper, and sold its 50 percent of Nogatech to DSP Group Ltd. The following month, Scitex introduced the Savanna color workstation for large magazine publishers.

In December, Scitex America and Leaf introduced the Leaf CatchLight, a charge-coupled device (CCD) camera at the VISCOMM '94 conference. The single-exposure digital camera had the highest-quality photographs of moving subjects at the time, applying microscopic filters to the pixels on the CCD to capture color photographs, and could postprocess images as RGB files on the PowerMac 8100.

By 1995, with widespread acceptance of personal computers and the advent of desktop publishing, Scitex workstations—selling for $1.5 million each and making up nearly 70 percent of the company's income—became too expensive for most publishers and Scitex's earnings plummeted nearly 85 percent. The company boosted its digital printing division, selling machines which printed up to 6,000 black-and-white pages a minute, and its digital video business, with equipment that converted video and film footage so it could be edited on a computer.

Also in 1995, Kobi Bendel approached Scitex in a last-ditch effort to create a virtual advertising technology company which would place computer-generated corporate logos on playing surfaces, such as the center court of Wimbledon, visible only to television audiences. By June 1997, when Scitex announced the creation of SciDel Technologies Ltd., the venture was a $10 million company with offices in three countries. The technology premiered commercially in August 1996 at the Toshiba Tennis Classic in San Diego.

That September, the company acquired Abekas Video Systems from Carlton for $52 million, integrating the major digital video production equipment manufacturer (of special effects devices, digital disc recorders, switchers, and character generators) with ImMIX to create the Scitex Digital Video Division, giving the company a broader reach in the digital video market.

In November, Scitex expanded its repertoire with packaged software for diverse applications, including database management; created Scitex America Publishing, a division devoted to the publishing industry; and acquired 100 percent of P.Ink Press, a software publisher developing applications for structured query language databases, which Scitex had purchased 25 percent of and controlled since 1987. The P.Ink Publishing System brought competition from Quark, Atex Publishing Systems' *Press2Go*, and North Atlantic Publishing Systems Inc.'s *Workflow Administrator*. But in 1995, the company suffered net losses of $34.5 million on total revenue of $730.3 million. In early 1996, Scitex extended its strategic OEM program with Xerox.

In 1990, newspapers were produced on-demand via fax machines, but were gray, curly editions with limited success. Six years later, in March 1996, at The Newspaper Association of America's inaugural Operations SuperConference, Scitex's PressPoint system was released, using satellite transmission technology to make remote, multicolor printing on tabloid-plus page size and full-color printing on sturdy, white stock paper possible to deliver newspapers on-demand.

In April, American-Israeli businessman Davidi Gilo attempted a hostile takeover, but the four largest Scitex shareholders—Clal, Discount, P.E.C., and International Paper—purchased $7 million worth of shares. A month later, Rosenfeld left and was replaced by Yoav Chelouche. In July, Patrick Kareiva became president and CEO of Scitex America.

During the 1996 Summer Olympic Games in Atlanta, Scitex America provided *Sports Illustrated* with nearly $1 million in high-end imaging equipment to help the magazine produce more than 250,000 copies per day of the *SI Olympic Daily*. Scitex built an entire imaging department in the Olympic Press Center, providing hardware and software required to scan, proof, store, and transmit text and image files; color corrections and page layouts; and store, locate, and retrieve files; altogether processing some nine GB of information daily, sending it via T1 line to an off-site press imagesetter, producing 300,000 copies of the daily 40-page magazine. Scitex America also provided its PressPoint system, from which fans could print their hometown newspapers, including the *Daily Telegraph* and the *Daily Mirror* from the U.K., South Africa's the *Star*, Germany's *Bild* and *Die Welt*, and France's *Liberation*.

Also that summer, Scitex released a line of advanced digital front-end output devices called Brisque, providing unique integration and automation facilities of prepress production output operations and compatible with Mac, PC, and Unix computers.

In August, Scitex signed an agreement with Imation Corp., an imaging and information company spun off from 3M, to integrate with the Realist print engine developed by Iris, as a component in one of Imation's digital proofing systems.

Although Scitex underwent large-scale restructuring, laying off 20 percent of the company's largest division, the company still posted an overall net loss of $178.3 million in 1996 on

revenues of $695 million. But by August 1997, Scitex was in the black again, recording its first positive income figure in four quarters, with net income of $157,000 in the second quarter on $167 million in revenues.

In 1997, the graphic arts industry experienced negative growth, and Scitex faced fierce competition from giants Kodak, DuPont, and Agfa. In February, Scitex released an enhanced Ripro data-management system, incorporating Informix's database technology, enabling the automatic routing and storage of documents without user intervention.

In April, Scitex and Xerox ended their joint marketing of the Spontane digital printing system. But, a month later, a separate agreement continued as Scitex and Xerox released the SX3000 Digital Front-End (DFE) for the DocuColor 70 color digital production system and the SX3000 DFE second-generation model for the DocuColor 40 system. Also in May, Scitex and Indigo integrated the Indigo E-Print digital printer into the Brisque DFE workflow.

Scitex also allied with British Telecom (BT) and MCI Corp. to develop and test advanced network-based applications for the graphic arts and printing industries, including a secure, high-capacity, managed-communications platform called The Digital Graphic Network (DGN), supporting a range of specialized applications for various stages of the graphic arts digital workflow, from image capture to printing. DGN also provided the graphic arts industry with a global ''community-of-interest network,'' linking service providers for all stages in the production process, including corporate marketing, departments, designers, advertising agencies, picture libraries, digital trade shops, printers, and publishers and covered applications like remote file transfer, advertisement delivery, remote proofing, distributed printing, and high-resolution image access and transfer. DGN began in the U.K., France, Germany, and the U.S. and spread worldwide. The agreement came after BT and MCI agreed to merge, and provided one of the first network-based industry-specific applications in the world. In September, Scitex and Komori, one of the world's largest manufacturers of printing machines, agreed to jointly develop and market new technologies. The company continues to develop new technologies and set the standard for digital video and on-line video editing.

Principal Subsidiaries

Karat Digital Press Israel; Scitex America Corp. (U.S.); Scitex Digital Printing Inc. (U.S.); Scitex Europe (Belgium); Scitex Israel.

Further Reading

''Acquisitions and Product Announcements,'' *Graphic Arts Monthly*, April 1990, p. 88.
Appleton, Elaine, ''Desktop Solutions,'' *Folio: The Magazine for Magazine Management, Annual*, 1995, p. 206.
Atlas, Riva, ''Taking Advice,'' *Forbes*, June 17, 1996, p. 228.
Bainerman, Joel, ''Scitex's Successful Acquisition Strategy,'' *Israel Business Today*, September 16, 1994, p. 18.
''Better Late Than Never,'' *ICEN*, May 10, 1991, p. 10.
Brown, Elicia, ''The Manipulator at Bay,'' *Financial World*, February 4, 1992, p. 30.

——, "When the Scuds Fly. . ." *Financial World*, February 4, 1992, p. 32.

"California Executive Offers $856 Million to Buy Scitex," *Wall Street Journal, Europe*, April 2, 1996, p. 6.

"Call Options on Five Israeli Companies," *Israel Business Today*, March 25, 1994, p. 3.

"Carlton Comms in $21M Sale," *Financial Times*, September 30, 1994, p. 22.

"Carlton Communications PLC," *Wall Street Journal, Europe*, September 19, 1995, p. 12.

"Carlton Communications PLC Last Week Sold Its ImMIX Unit to Israel's Scitex Corp. Ltd. for $21 Million in Cash," *Broadcasting & Cable*, October 3, 1994, p. 64.

Carnoy, David, "Bolder Is Better: Investors Buy into a Dream, Not Just a Concept," *Success*, June 1997, p. 20.

Carroll, Paul B., "Scitex's Pursuer Is an Enigma and Bid Outcome Is Cloudy," *Wall Street Journal, Europe*, April 3, 1996, p. 8.

"CCD Camera Aims at Moving Models," *Graphic Arts Monthly*, December 1994, p. 80.

Churbuck, David, "Desktop Color," *Forbes*, October 1, 1990, p. 238.

"A Class Action Has Been Filed Against Scitex in New York," *Israel Business Today*, January 15, 1996, p. 3.

Cross, Lisa, "The Key to CTP," *Graphic Arts Monthly*, April 1996, p. 15S.

——, "Serious Publishing for the '96 Games," *Graphic Arts Monthly*, August 1996, p. 56.

Dempsey, Judy, "Losses at Scitex Deepen to $178M," *Financial Times*, February 14, 1997, p. 22.

——, "Scitex Slips Further into Deficit," *Financial Times*, November 18, 1996, p. 25.

Dickson, Glen, "Abekas," *Broadcasting & Cable*, August 4, 1997, p. 51.

——, "Scitex Acquires Abekas for $52 Million," *Broadcasting & Cable*, September 25, 1995, p. 54.

——, "Scitex Digital Video (SDV)," *Broadcasting & Cable*, October 20, 1997, p. 64.

"Discount Provident Fund Buys Scitex," *ICEN*, October 25, 1991, p. 6.

"Dovrat Picks Israeli Winners," *Israel Business Today*, January 17, 1992, p. 3.

"Exciting New Scitex Venture," *ICEN*, April 26, 1991, p. 13.

"$15 Million of Scitex Shares Bought," *Israel Business Today*, July 30, 1993, p. 6.

Fitzgerald, Mark, "The Changing Role of Scitex," *Editor & Publisher*, November 11, 1995, p. 36.

——, "Suite Judy Cyan Eyes," *Editor & Publisher*, September 30, 1995, p. 12C.

Flax, Steven, "Like Edwin Land—But Better at Business," *Forbes*, April 13, 1981, p. 109.

Forbes, Jim, "Quark Leads Parade of New Publishing Products," *PC Week*, March 1, 1988, p. 18.

Frichtl, Paul, "A Giant Step for Desktop: Scitex Link with Adobe Combines Top-Quality Color with Page Layout Software," *Folio: The Magazine for Magazine Management*, June 1988, p. 39.

Giardina, Carolyn, "Scitex Acquires Abekas, Forms Scitex Digital," *SHOOT*, October 20, 1995, p. 1.

"The Global View of Scitex," *Israel Business Today*, April 24, 1992, p. 19.

"Indigo and Scitex Make Chicago Announcements," *Israel Business Today*, September 15, 1997, p. 21.

"International Paper Seeks Scitex Share Buyer," *Israel Business Today*, March 31, 1997, p. 19.

"Int'l Paper Puts $209M into Scitex," *Israel Business Today*, March 6, 1992, p. 3.

"Israeli Stocks Headed for Berlin," *Israel Business Today*, January 28, 1994, p. 9.

"Israel Shares in Maxwell Trial," *Israel Business Today*, June 16, 1995, p. 17.

"Israel's Scitex," *Television Digest*, September 25, 1995, p. 5.

Jaben, Jan, "Scitex Sets First Image Ads," *Business Marketing*, April 1994, p. 4.

Johnston, Peter, "Prepress for Printers," *Graphic Arts Monthly*, April 1996, p. 3S.

"Kareiva Takes Scitex U.S. Top Spot," *Israel Business Today*, July 31, 1996, p. 22.

Landau, Pinchas, "Tapping Our Markets: More Israeli Firms Sell Shares in the U.S.," *Barron's*, October 28, 1991, p. 18.

Love, Barbara, "Scitex at Drupa," *Folio: The Magazine for Magazine Management*, May 1990, p. 88.

——, "Scitex Introduces Mid-Range Color Pre-Press System," *Folio: The Magazine for Magazine Management*, April 1990, p. 89.

Lunzer, Francesca, "None But the Brave Deserve the Fair," *Forbes*, October 21, 1985, p. 64.

Machlis, Avi, "Scitex Back in the Black," *Financial Times*, February 13, 1998, p. 29.

Marcial, Gene G., "Why the Slide in High Tech Hasn't Touched Scitex," *Business Week*, July 8, 1991, p. 80.

Martin, Teresa A., "The Digital Proof: A New Approach," *Graphic Arts Monthly*, July 1991, p. 74.

"Maxwell Cashes in His Chips," *ICEN*, August 2, 1991, p. 1.

"Maxwell Reaps the Maximum," *ICEN*, April 19, 1991, p. 4.

"Maxwell Sells More Scitex," *ICEN*, July 26, 1991, p. 3.

"Maxwell Unloads Scitex and Teva," *ICEN*, October 18, 1991, p. 3.

Mayer, John, "Scitex Opens Door to Lawsuits: Investors Encouraged by Scitex Class Action Suit Have Targeted Other Israeli Companies for Court Battles," *Israel Business Today*, December 9, 1994, p. 1.

McDougall, Paul, "Publishers Benefit from Technology Turmoil," *Folio: The Magazine for Magazine Management*, September 1, 1993, p. 18.

——, "Scitex Seeks to Smooth Infopike," *Folio: The Magazine for Magazine Management*, October 1, 1994, p. 26.

——, "A Slumping Scitex Restructures," *Folio: The Magazine for Magazine Management*, February 1, 1994, p. 21.

McLymont, Rosalind, "Ending Dependence on Home Market Key to Global Endurance," *Journal of Commerce and Commercial*, January 18, 1994, p. 3A.

Mehlman, William, "Scitex Corp.," *Insiders' Chronicle*, February 27, 1989, p. 2.

"More Sales of Scitex Shares," *ICEN*, June 14, 1991, p. 11.

"More Scitex Acquisitions in the Video Field?" *Israel Business Today*, October 28, 1994, p.11.

"New Tool Smooths Output Operations," *Graphic Arts Monthly*, September 1996, p. 110.

"Partners Increase Interest in Scitex War," *Israel Business Today*, April 30, 1996, p. 22.

"Scitex and Indigo Unite Brisque Work," *Israel Business Today*, May 15, 1997, p. 16.

"Scitex and KBA-Planeta Unveil 74 Karat Press," *Israel Business Today*, June 15, 1997, p. 17.

"Scitex and Xerox Halt Joint Marketing," *Israel Business Today*, April 15, 1997, p. 17.

"Scitex Announces Xerox DocuColor 70," *Israel Business Today*, May 31, 1997, p. 20.

"Scitex at Winter Olympics," *Israel Business Today*, January 31, 1992, p. 4.

"Scitex Back to Black," *Israel Business Today*, May 10, 1996, p. 1.

"Scitex, BT and MCI Join Forces," *Israel Business Today*, May 15, 1997, p. 17.

"Scitex Buys P.Ink," *Folio: The Magazine for Magazine Management*, March 15, 1994, p. 29.

"Scitex Buys RasterOps Shares," *Israel Business Today*, July 9, 1993, p. 5.

"Scitex Buys U.S. Digital Video Firm for $21M," *Israel Business Today*, October 14, 1994, p. 5.

"Scitex Clinches OEM Deal with 3M Spin-Off," *Israel Business Today*, August 31, 1996, p. 21.

"Scitex Corporation Back on Profit Track," *Israel Business Today*, February 28, 1998, p. 23.

"Scitex Finally Reaches Black Spot," *Israel Business Today*, August 31, 1997, p. 21.

"Scitex 4th Quarter Profits Up 14%," *Israel Business Today*, March 4, 1994, p. 3.

"Scitex Returns to Losing Ways," *Israel Business Today*, August 15, 1996, p. 22.

"Scitex to Help Turn Olympics into Global Village," *Israel Business Today*, July 15, 1996, p. 21.

Silber, Tony, "Scitex Shake-Up Mirrors Shifting Industry," *Folio: The Magazine for Magazine Management*, March 1, 1996, p. 39.

—Daryl F. Mallett

Scovill Fasteners Inc.

1802 Scovill Drive
Clarkesville, Georgia 30523
U.S.A.
(706) 754-4181
(888) SCOVILL
Fax: (706) 754-2826
Web site: http://www.scovill.com

Private Company
Incorporated: 1850 as Scovill Manufacturing Company
Employees: 700
Sales: $300 million (1997 est.)
SICs: 3965 Fasteners, Buttons, Needles & Pins; 3714
   Motor Vehicle Parts & Accessories; 3812 Search &
   Navigation Equipment

One of the oldest manufacturing concerns in the United States, Scovill Fasteners Inc. is a leading designer, manufacturer, and distributor of apparel fasteners and specialty industrial fasteners, supported by production and distribution facilities in the United States, Canada, Mexico, Belgium, and throughout Asia. Scovill was founded in 1802 in Waterbury, Connecticut, where the company began making pewter buttons. During the course of the company's business life, Scovill was involved in an assortment of businesses that centered around its metal casting and rolling operations, including the production of lamp burners, hinges, wire, artillery cartridge cases, and a number of other products. Buttons, however, represented the common thread connecting the modern Scovill to its early 19th-century roots. Scovill buttons were worn on U.S. military uniforms in every war during both the 19th and 20th centuries, beginning with the pewter buttons worn by military personnel in the War of 1812. During the late 1990s, the company was divided into two divisions: apparel and industrial. The apparel division manufactured fasteners for basic garments such as jeans, infantswear, childrenswear, and outerwear. On the industrial side, Scovill manufactured fasteners for a broad array of customers, including manufacturers of marine textiles, sporting and recreational products, electronics, and footwear. In 1997, Scovill moved its headquarters from Waterbury, where it had been based for the previous 195 years, to Clarksville, Georgia. After the move, management acquired the company from Kohlberg & Company, a Mt. Kisco, New York-based merchant banking firm.

The Early Years

From the founding date recognized by the company, Scovill began business in 1802 in what was most likely a small wooden shed hidden behind a house in Waterbury, Connecticut. Its origins were steeped in the much-vaunted tradition of New England entrepreneurship, although the exact details of its first decade of business were murky at best, clouded by the passage of time and the modest origins from which it sprang. A handful of businessmen were affiliated with the company at its outset, when the business was known as Abel Porter & Company, including its namesake, the self-proclaimed "first Gilt Button Maker in the United States." Abel Porter, whose tenure with the company lasted less than a decade, was joined in 1808 by David Hayden, a button maker from Attleborough, Massachusetts, who stayed with the company through its first meaningful transition in 1811. In 1811, the cadre of Abel Porter & Company directors went their separate ways to pursue other interests, giving way to a new triumvirate of leaders. Hayden was one of the trio, a "second partner," whose prominence on some undetermined level fell short of a new arrival in 1811, Dr. Frederick Leavenworth. Leavenworth, who according to contemporary reports was "possessed of a quick insight into men and things," breathed new life into the company and offered himself as its leader. Although Leavenworth asserted his seniority in both the name of the new business and his rank within it, the true leader of the company was its third partner, James Mitchell Lamson Scovill. Together, the three formed Leavenworth, Hayden & Scovill, the successor to Abel Porter & Company.

Prior to the arrival of new blood in 1811, the company made buttons with pewter, a material most likely obtained by melting down old kitchen utensils, but soon the switch was made to buttons made out of brass. Waterbury, the company's home town for nearly two centuries, was regarded as the brass center of the United States, and Scovill, as one of the primary brass producers in the region. With the metal, Scovill manufactured a wide range of products, including buttons, hinges, and many other commodities at its metal castings operation. In the beginning, however, the company's production capabilities were decidedly meager. For nearly a decade, the company used horses to power its small "flatting" rolls, but when Leavenworth and Scovill arrived they invested several thousand dollars in a new production facility to manufacture one of the commodities the company made from brass. The new button shop, built in 1812, helped accommodate the surge in demand for buttons ushered in by the War of 1812. Leavenworth, Hayden & Scovill supplied pewter shank buttons for naval forces during the war, as well as buttons for the U.S. Army, Artillery, and Rifleman, beginning a long tradition of supplying the federal government with military buttons for every war from 1812 to the end of the 20th century.

Although Leavenworth appeared at first blush to be the leader of the company, closer scrutiny suggested otherwise. Leavenworth assumed the role of traveling representative, shuttling from market to market to sell the company's variegated list of products, while Scovill, third in line in the partnership's hierarchy, assumed the mantle of leadership. His ancestral roots in Waterbury stretched back to the mid-17th century, when his great-great-great-grandfather, John Scovill, left Shapwick, Dorset, England, and settled in what would become the state of Connecticut. The younger Scovill, referred to as Lamson Scovill in the company's historical accounts, went into business for himself at age 19, although there is no historical record to suggest what type of business endeavor he undertook. Lamson Scovill was 22 years old when he joined the three-man partnership, and with Leavenworth frequently on the road representing the company and Hayden naturally inclined toward the technical management of the firm, Scovill blossomed into the partnership's leader. According to the best estimate, Leavenworth, Hayden & Scovill was earning $5,000 a year when the three-man partnership was dissolved in 1827. To fill its place, a new partnership was formed between Lamson Scovill and his younger brother, William Henry (W. H.) Scovill. Operating under the name J.M.L. and W.H. Scovill, the partnership comprised two individuals with distinctly different yet complementary personalities. Lamson Scovill emerged as the salesman, traveling the circuit as Leavenworth had done, while W.H. Scovill was described as "the planner, the organizer, the man-at-home."

Under the stewardship of the Scovill brothers, the company made a name for itself as a producer of buttons, hinges, and other goods, some of which were sold in the company's general store in New York. Their business interests were diverse and loosely organized, but the heart of their interests—the business that would survive and thrive for two centuries—received a new button factory shortly after a fire destroyed the original structure in 1830. A second manufacturing facility was constructed in Oakville, Connecticut, in 1833, leading up to major investments in capital improvements midway through the century. In 1850, when the company was averaging $300,000 in sales per year, the Scovill brothers incorporated the core of their business pursuits as Scovill Manufacturing Company, which was 60 percent owned by the pair, and kept J. M. L and W. H. Scovill as a partnership to handle their other business activities.

When the brothers died in the mid-1850s, neither left any direct descendants able or willing to take over the business. Consequently, their shares were distributed to others, but control of the company was restricted to a limited group of individuals predominated by members of the two branches of the Scovill families. A nephew of the brothers, Scovill Merrill Buckingham, succeeded W. H. Scovill as treasurer, while Samuel William Southmayd Hall replaced Lamson Scovill as president, but their influence over the company's progress was widely considered ineffective. During their era of control, Buckingham and Hall did little to move the company forward, despite the energetic growth of the brass industry in Waterbury during the time. Consequently, the company did not enjoy the dynamic leadership it had enjoyed under the hands of the two Scovill brothers until the Kingsbury, Goss, and Sperry era began in 1868. For nearly a half-century, Chauncey Porter Goss and Mark Leavenworth Sperry exerted considerable influence over the direction of Scovill Manufacturing, but for nearly three decades of their tenure they held junior offices under F. J. Kingsbury, Buckingham's cousin and the son-in-law of Frederick Leavenworth, Lamson Scovill's partner from 1811 to 1827.

Late 19th-Century Growth

Kingsbury became president of Scovill Manufacturing beginning in 1868, but his true position at the company, despite its length, was largely ceremonial. Kingsbury was a figurehead, never closely in tune with the day-to-day activities at Scovill Manufacturing. His business interests were too scattered, according to a company historian, "to permit of his leading (Scovill) anywhere, except into a merger with its rivals and to the loss of its individuality." With the roving Kingsbury attending to his variegated endeavors, direction of the company's development fell to his two underlings, Chauncey Porter Goss and Mark Leavenworth Sperry, who represented "the drive, the true entrepreneurship" of Scovill Manufacturing, according to a company historian. Goss and Sperry joined the company as clerks and forged a business relationship that was reminiscent of the complementary style of Lamson Scovill and his brother W. H. Scovill. Goss was like Lamson, while Sperry, the "stay at home in Waterbury," was similar in personality to W. H; one the outside promoter, "a keen buyer and seller, and the other the ''patient administrator.'' Under their command, which lasted until 1918, Scovill Manufacturing achieved great strides, growing and expanding during the last quarter of the 19th century and gaining great financial gains during the first decades of the 20th century.

Goss and Sperry invested heavily in capital improvements during their decades of control, following the trend toward mechanized industrial development that characterized the late 19th century and early 20th century in the United States. During this era of industrial progress, Scovill exceeded the pace of growth recorded by both the copper industry and the United States as a whole, outstripping the increase in production output registered by both broadly defined sectors. The company entered new business areas, including the production of electrically-conductive wire, the rolling of aluminum sheet, and the production of lamb burners, adding to the already diverse metal manufacturing talents of the company. By the beginning of World War I, after decades of dynamic growth under the tutelage of Goss and Sperry, Scovill Manufacturing was generating annual sales of between $7 million and $8 million and averaging 15 million pounds of output per year at its mill. Although these figures represented meaningful growth in comparison to the company's financial stature before the arrival of Goss and Sperry, Scovill Manufacturing was still a relatively small organization when compared to others in its industry. The war years, however, proved to be a financial boon, lifting the company's financial totals in great, unprecedented leaps. By 1915, Scovill Manufacturing's annual sales total had jumped to $34 million. Two years later, as the Goss and Sperry era was coming to an end, annual sales towered at $58 million, more than eight times the total collected in the decade before World War I.

By virtue of the lucrative war years and the strong business foundation entrenched by Goss and Sperry, Scovill Manufacturing entered the 1920s on solid financial footing and in a position to strengthen its market position by inaugurating an acquisition campaign. During the decade, the company embarked on its first large-scale expansion program by purchasing several of the firms that used the products manufactured at its brass mills. Scovill Manufacturing, in short, began acquiring its customers. The strategy bred vertical integration, giving the company a number of brass-using subsidiaries that heightened its control over the otherwise capricious nature of its business. In 1923, Scovill Manufacturing acquired American Pin Company and the Oakville Company, purchasing the two companies in a transfer of Scovill stock. Both American Pin and Oakville had contributed meaningfully to the development of Waterbury as the brass center of the United States; their inclusion as subsidiaries within Scovill's fold bolstered the might of an already formidable competitor. Also in 1923, the company acquired Racine, Wisconsin-based Hamilton Beach Company, a producer of domestic appliance and small electric motors. Two years later, Scovill Manufacturing acquired Gilchrist and Company, a maker of soda fountain equipment and another heavy brass user.

Thanks to the company's aggressive progress during the 1920s, it entered the Great Depression in a financially strong position, enabling it to parry many of the blows delivered by the decade-long economic turmoil touched off in 1929. Although the company suffered its share of the devastation wrought by a moribund economy, Scovill Manufacturing emerged from the 1930s with its physical assets intact and its organization, seasoned by more than a century of business, relatively unscathed. During World War II, the raw materials Scovill Manufacturing used fell under wartime restrictions, which forced the company into new business areas. It began manufacturing fuses and cartridge cases for artillery shells during the war years, and continued to record meaningful growth as a result. By the time the postwar economic boom period began, the company occupied an enviable market position, holding sway as a fastener manufacturer able to reap the full rewards generated by a national economy on the rise. In the decades to follow, the company never relinquished its lead over other competitors. The latter half of the 20th century witnessed the venerable leader solidify its position and sharpen its business focus.

Late 20th Century

The wide-ranging, multifarious business interests that had occupied the company's attention throughout its history were stripped away during the second half of the 20th century. What remained was the company's fastener business, its sole business area during the 1990s. During the 1990s, much was done to strengthen and to organize its fastener business, including the addition of an industrial fastener manufacturer early in the decade. In 1991, Scovill acquired the DOT line of industrial fasteners from Cambridge, Massachusetts-based TRW, Inc. and consolidated all of DOT's manufacturing operations into the Scovill plant in Clarkesville, Georgia, established during the 1950s. A series of acquisitions followed five years later, but first the company sold its Clarkesville-based zipper division to Ideal Fastener Corp. After this 1996 divestiture, Scovill acquired Daudé of Paris, France, which manufactured eyelets and grommets. Daudé's manufacturing operations were subsequently moved to Braine-le-Comte, Belgium, where Scovill had previously established manufacturing facilities. Further acquisitions followed in 1996, including the purchase of New Bedford, Massachusetts-based PCI Group, a manufacturer of eyelets, grommets, and automatic insertion machinery. As with the DOT acquisition, PCI's manufacturing operations were relocated to Scovill's Clarkesville plant. Next, the company acquired RAU Fasteners, makers of Klikit brand snaps.

With these additions, Scovill was positioned in two sectors of the fastener industry through its two divisions: apparel and industrial. Its apparel division manufactured ''Gripper,'' ''Maxi Snap,'' and ''Mighty Snap'' snap fasteners, which were used in more than 80 percent of the garments produced by the 14 largest sleepwear manufacturers, and ''Duramark'' tack buttons, rivets, and burrs, which were metal reinforcements used in denim apparel. The company's industrial division comprised the DOT and PCI product lines, which were sold in a variety of market segments, including marine, luggage/leather, footwear, automotive, safety, and medical.

In 1997, two important developments changed the face of Scovill as it prepared for its third century of business. First, in July, the company moved its corporate headquarters, leaving its nearly two-century-old base in Waterbury and relocating in

Clarkesville. Next, in November, company management effected a buyout of Scovill, acquiring the company with the help of a private investment group named Saratoga Partners, based in New York City. Scovill managers and Saratoga acquired the company from Kohlberg & Company, a merchant banking firm based in Mt. Kisco, New York. Following the announcement of the deal, Scovill's president and chief executive officer, Dave Barrett, proclaimed, "Scovill is a classic American company with a proud heritage of service excellence that has been honed over nearly two centuries. With the financial expertise and consistent strategic view of Saratoga, we look forward to capitalizing on the initiatives that we have worked hard to put in place over the last two years." On this note, Scovill entered the late 1990s and prepared for the century ahead, confident that two centuries of stability would provide firm footing for the company's future course.

Principal Divisions

Industrial Division; Apparel Division.

Further Reading

Clune, Ray, "Scovill Fasteners Inc.," *Daily News Record,* November 26, 1997, p. 9.
"Scovill in Deal to Purchase Dot from TRW," *Daily News Record,* July 31, 1991, p. 8.

—Jeffrey L. Covell

Shubert Organization Inc.

234 West 44th Street
New York, New York 10036
U.S.A.
(212) 944-3700
Fax: (212) 944-3755
Web site: http://www.shubert.com

Wholly Owned Subsidiary of Shubert Foundation
Incorporated: 1904 as Sam S. and Lee Shubert, Inc.
Employees: 1,600
Sales: $290 million (1997 est.)
SICs: 6513 Operators of Nonresidential Buildings; 7922
    Theatrical Producers (Except Motion Picture) &
    Miscellaneous Theatrical Services

Shubert Organization Inc. is the successor to the firm, established by the Shubert brothers early in the 20th century, that grew to became the most successful business enterprise in the history of the American theater. In the late 1990s this enterprise owned and operated, as it had for at least 50 years, about half of the theaters on Broadway. It also was producing or co-producing some of Broadway's biggest hits, including the musical *Cats,* which in 1997 became Broadway's longest-running play ever. The Shubert Organization also owned valuable nontheatrical real estate in New York City and a few theaters in other cities.

Rise to Theatrical Dominance, 1894–1924

Levi (Lee), Samuel (Sam), and Jacob (J. J.) Shubert were born in eastern Europe, probably in East Prussia or Lithuania, and grew up in poverty, with a brother and four sisters, in Syracuse, New York. Sam, the natural leader of the three, became a theatrical producer in 1894, while still in his teens. By the turn of the century the three were leasing five theaters in upstate New York and managing several stock companies. The Shuberts leased their first New York City theater in 1900, at Broadway and 35th Street. Of their first production, a *New York Times* reviewer declared, "Nothing nearly as awful has been seen in 20 years."

At this time an enterprise called the Theatrical Syndicate owned, leased, or controlled the booking of more than 700 theaters across the United States, virtually excluding competition. Sensing a growing threat from the Shuberts, the Syndicate decided in 1903 to break them by denying them theaters and performers. Nevertheless, by the summer of 1904 they owned, leased, or booked the acts of some 50 theaters. In the fall of 1905 they presented Sarah Bernhardt in a tour that barnstormed the country. Barred from Syndicate-controlled theaters, they put on the show in rented circus tents, which held three times as many customers as the typical theater. Sam Shubert was killed in a train crash in 1905. J. J., who had been managing the firm's interests out of town, now came to Broadway. The junior partner, he was generally responsible for musicals and for the construction and maintenance of the theaters. Lee usually handled straight plays, finances, publicity and advertising, and nontheatrical real estate.

By the fall of 1910 the Shuberts owned 73 theaters outright, held booking contracts with many more, and possessed at least 50 dramatic and musical companies. They were fully as despotic as the Syndicate and banned a number of critics from their premises for less than enthusiastic reviews. The brothers favored musical material, such as revues similar in concept to (but much less lavish than) the Ziegfeld Follies, and operettas, especially those composed by Sigmund Romberg. Operettas were favored in particular because they required neither expensive stars nor, as "costumers," even shapely chorines. Sometimes as many as 20 Shubert operettas would be touring on the road. Of the straight plays, the brothers had a firm rule: "All plays have to have love interest. If you have no love interest, you have no play."

The brightest of Shubert stars was Al Jolson, who made millions for the brothers, as well as for himself. Between 1911 and 1918 six Jolson-starring shows played at the Shuberts' commodious Winter Garden Theater, a converted stable at Broadway and 50th Street—far uptown at this time. The brothers also organized an unprofitable vaudeville circuit in 1921 and backed a venture that made some 350 movies between 1914 and 1919, usually under the World Film Studio name.

The Shuberts also were major owners of nontheatrical real estate, including a number of office buildings, hotels, and shops in New York, Boston, and Chicago. Between 1913 and 1917 they leased four theaters between Broadway and Eighth Avenue and 44th and 45th Streets—still the heart of New York City's theater district. Shubert Alley was constructed west of Broadway as a private street to connect the Shubert Theatre on 44th Street to the Booth Theatre on 45th Street. The Shuberts bought the four theaters and the land under the alley in 1948 for between $3.5 million and $4 million, thereby taking full possession of the entire city block except for hotels at either end.

Zenith and Decline, 1924–72

The Shubert Theatrical Corp. was founded in 1924 as a public company taking over the business of earlier Shubert enterprises. At this time it was operating 86 theaters in 31 cities, including 30 in New York City alone, collecting 30 to 50 percent of the box office receipts as rental. The company's United Booking Office was placing shows for some 750 more theaters. In all, the Shuberts were producing one-fourth of the nation's plays and controlled three-fourths of all theatrical ticket sales. The company also claimed to hold the largest scenery, costume, and equipment inventories in the world. It even owned a shoe factory and compelled all of its dancers to buy their dancing shoes from the company.

The Shuberts were, in their heyday, heartily despised for their hammerlock on the American theater. Shrewd dealmakers, contentious litigators, tight-fisted producers, they raised intimidation to an art form and, despite acts of charity, kept their benevolent impulses as private as possible. Their wariness even extended to each other; although Lee lived above the Shubert Theatre and J. J. in a penthouse apartment facing the theater, they rarely met and conducted necessary business through separate staffs. (Only two photos exist showing the brothers together.) Besieged by thousands of women and girls seeking careers on stage, both Shuberts behaved like the proverbial kids locked in a candy store. According to their biographer, "Although they did not invent the casting couch, it is believed that the Shuberts developed its functions."

The number of Shubert theaters reached 101 in 1928, but the corporation's net profit peaked at $3 million in 1926. Partly because of the advent of talking pictures and the growing popularity of radio programs, the American theater was beginning to pass its prime about this time. After the 1929 Wall Street crash, the value of the Shubert properties fell drastically. The brothers found it necessary to sell some of their theaters—including their half-interest in five London ones acquired in 1925—and to reduce substantially the number of shows they produced. In 1931 the Shubert Theatrical Corp. and eight other Shubert companies in one way or another affiliated with the parent—including script, music publishing, scenery, and costume companies—fell into bankruptcy.

Lee Shubert, however, was named co-receiver, and in 1933 he bought back the company's assets for $400,000—some ten cents on the dollar—renaming it Select Theatres Corp. After paying off bondholders, stockholders, and creditors of the old corporation, the Shuberts held more than 60 percent of the successor company, which included scenery, equipment, and 27

theaters. The brothers also retained many of their theaters and other real estate independent of this corporation, through their Trebuhs (Shubert spelled backwards) Realty Co.

Although the Shuberts' career as producers virtually came to an end in the 1940s, they remained active as ticket brokers, bookers, investors in shows, and operators of theatrical real estate. Tired scripts and worn sets and costumes were resurrected and recycled for touring shows and summer stock. In 1950 the Shuberts moved some 9,000 pieces of furniture, 40,000 square feet of draperies and flats, and numberless theatrical odd lots—all from the more than 1,000 shows produced, controlled, or purchased since 1900—across the Hudson River to Fort Lee, New Jersey.

In 1948 the Shuberts still owned 16 theaters in New York City and 21 elsewhere—about half of all the legitimate theaters in the United States—including all the Philadelphia theaters and all the Boston theaters but one. Through their United Booking Office, they were able to make producers book their shows exclusively in Shubert theaters around the country as a condition for renting a Shubert theater on Broadway. In a 1955 U.S. Supreme Court decision, however, the Shubert interests were found to be in violation of antitrust laws. As a result, in a 1956 consent agreement Select Theatres agreed to halt its booking activities for 25 years. It also was required to sell about a dozen theaters in six cities, including four in New York. United Booking Office was dissolved and Select Theatres ceased to exist, at least as a public company.

Lee Shubert died in 1953 and J. J. in 1963. The latter's son, John, had in 1956 taken over day-to-day operation of the business, assisted by Lawrence Shubert Lawrence, Jr., a grandnephew of the brothers who assumed management of the Shubert interests on John's death in 1962. The worth of the brothers' holdings was estimated in 1963 at $50 million and included 17 theaters in New York, two each in Chicago, Cincinnati, and Philadelphia, and one in Boston.

The Shubert Resurgence, 1972–97

The Shubert Organization was a cluster of 23 corporations when its board fired Lawrence in 1972 and hired company executives Gerald Schoenfeld and Bernard Jacobs—who were serving on the board—to run the enterprise. The two later said they found the Shubert operations in more disarray than they had suspected, and Jacobs claimed the business was losing about $2 million a year. The Broadway houses—half of them vacant—were run-down. To fill these theaters they returned the enterprise to producing plays in 1974. They met with instant success in the form of the hits *Pippin, Grease,* and *Equus.* The most successful was *A Chorus Line,* which debuted in 1975 and ran at the Shubert Theatre for 15 years. The Shubert Organization, which had been the first theatrical business to accept personal checks, telephone reservations, and credit cards, launched its own computerized system for selling theater tickets in 1979. The company also linked its box offices to Ticketron outlets.

Lee and J. J. Shubert had established the Shubert Foundation in 1945 to lighten their income tax load and, eventually, their estate taxes. The bulk of both men's estates passed to the

Foundation, which in 1972 became owner of the for-profit companies that the Shuberts had controlled. Most of the real estate continued to be held by the Shubert Organization, but certain key properties were deeded to the foundation so that rent and lease income on which the organization was paying taxes could become tax-exempt. Some of that property was sold later at substantial profit and was likewise exempt from capital gains taxes. In 1974 the state of New York charged the executors of J. J.'s estate—Lawrence, Schoenfeld, and Jacobs—with conflicts of interest depriving the foundation of millions of dollars due to "grossly excessive, unjustified and unreasonable" claims. The suit was withdrawn later when the charged parties agreed to reduce their claims on the foundation by $2 million.

In 1979 the Shubert Foundation won a ruling from the Internal Revenue Service allowing revenue from the Shubert Organization, after taxes, to flow to the foundation and be invested to produce tax-free income for the foundation. This was an exemption to federal tax laws that generally bar private charities from owning a controlling interest in a profit-making business. Otherwise, the foundation argued, it would have to sell the Broadway theaters, and as a result "the legitimate theater will be destroyed" and the new owners, most likely, would exploit the theaters for such purposes as "the showing of pornographic films" or would raze them for parking lots. (The Shubert brothers had used the same or similar arguments over the years in combating the threat of antitrust litigation.)

The rival Nederlander and Jujamycn theater chains were most unhappy about this ruling, pointing out that the foundation gave some of the tax-exempt money to performing arts groups that used it to generate plays that then appeared in Shubert theaters. The argument that New York's theater district might cease to exist unless the Shubert Organization received favorable tax treatment seemed to lose its force when all but one of the enterprise's Broadway theaters were declared landmarks by the city in the 1980s, making them difficult to convert to any alternative use.

The Shubert Organization continued to score a number of big successes on Broadway with its own productions, including *Ain't Misbehavin'* and *Dancin'* in 1978, *Amadeus* and *Children of a Lesser God* in 1980, and *Dreamgirls* in 1981. Its biggest hit of the decade was *Cats,* which made its U.S. debut in 1982. Co-produced with Andrew Lloyd Webber's company, *Cats,* which played at the Winter Garden, broke the record previously set by *A Chorus Line* when it gave its 6,138th consecutive performance on Broadway in 1997. Shubert's drama productions of the 1980s included Pulitzer Prize winners *Glengarry Glen Ross* and *The Heidi Chronicles.*

The Shubert Organization, in 1994, had recorded a profit in every year since 1976. That year it owned 16 Broadway theaters and the land beneath them. It also owned another one (the Music Box) jointly with the estate of Irving Berlin. In addition, it owned the Sardi Building (1501 Broadway) and the land beneath it, the land beneath the office building at 1675 Broadway, and air rights leased to the Tower 45 (120 West 45th Street) and Bertelsmann (1540 Broadway) buildings. Outside of New York City, the Shubert Organization owned Boston's Shubert Theater (which it leased to the Wang Center for the Performing Arts in 1996) and Philadelphia's Forrest Theater. It also was leasing the Shubert Theater in Los Angeles and managing the National Theatre in Washington, D.C. The Shubert Theater in Chicago was sold to the Nederlander Organization in 1991. The Shubert Organization's real estate holdings were free and clear, with no remaining mortgages.

Jacobs, president of the Shubert Organization, died in 1996 and was succeeded by Philip J. Smith, who had been executive vice-president. Schoenfeld continued to serve as chairman.

Further Reading

"The Boys from Syracuse," *Time,* November 22, 1948, pp. 89–90.

Gussow, Mel, "Bernard E. Jacobs, a Pillar of American Theater As Shubert Executive, Dies at 80," *New York Times,* August 28, 1996, p. D18.

Hector, Robert, "Tyrants of Thespis," *Saturday Review,* December 14, 1968, pp. 29–31.

"J. J. Shubert Dies; Last of 3 Brothers," *New York Times,* December 27, 1963, pp. 1, 23.

Kleinfield, N. R., "How Shubert Fund Produces and Directs," *New York Times,* July 10, 1994, pp. A1, A22.

——, "I.R.S. Ruling Wrote Script for the Shubert Tax Break," *New York Times,* July 11, 1994, pp. A1, B6.

Liebling, A. J., "The Boys from Syracuse," *New Yorker,* November 18, 1939, pp. 26–30; November 25, 1939, pp. 23–27; December 2, 1939, pp. 33–37.

Marks, Peter, "2 Presidents at Shubert, But Just One Chairman," *New York Times,* September 18, 1996, pp. C13, C19.

——, "Who Will Fill the Void on Shubert Alley?," *New York Times,* August 30, 1996, p. C3.

McNamara, Brooks, *The Shuberts of Broadway,* New York: Oxford University Press, 1990.

Nadel, Norman, "When the Shuberts Fit," *Horizon,* October 1981, pp. 54, 56–58.

Richards, David, "The Shuberts, Kingpins of Broadway," *Washington Post,* September 22, 1985, pp. H1, H9–H10.

Schumach, Murray, "Shubert No Longer a Family Affair," *New York Times,* July 11, 1972, p. 24.

Stagg, Jerry, *The Brothers Shubert,* New York: Random House, 1968.

Taylor, Markland, "Shubert Domain Cut; Wang Takes Over Hub," *Variety,* March 18, 1996, pp. 55, 58.

—Robert Halasz

Sikorsky Aircraft Corporation

6900 Main Street
P.O. Box 9729
Stratford, Connecticut 06497-9129
U.S.A.
(203) 386-6086
Fax: (203) 386-7300
Web site: http://www.sikorsky.com

Wholly Owned Subsidiary of United Technologies Corporation
Incorporated: 1923 as the Sikorsky Aero Engineering Corporation
Employees: 9,000
Sales: $1.6 billion (1997)
SICs: 3720 Aircraft & Parts

For much of the time since its founder first tinkered with helicopter design, the Sikorsky Aircraft Corporation has stood for the leading technology in vertical flight. The company's advanced, intermediate to heavy helicopters set standards in the world market, and its swift H-60 series of Blackhawk and Seahawk helicopters has long been the staple of military rotary wing fleets. Sikorsky made the helicopter practical—it also made it fast and, in some cases, downright huge.

A Pioneering Heritage

Igor Sikorsky was in a sense born to a pioneering family. His father, Ivan, was a researcher in the infant field of psychiatry during the late 19th century. As a boy, Sikorsky's interest in aviation was propelled by reading Jules Verne, particularly his *Clipper of the Clouds,* which described a hypothetical vertical flight machine.

Leonardo Da Vinci had also conceptualized such a machine, whose corkscrew would pull it straight up into the air. But imaginative horsepower was not enough; as with the history of powered fixed-wing flight that the Wright brothers first mas-

tered, the limiting factor would be finding engines both strong enough and light enough to fly.

In 1908, Sikorsky's imagination was further stoked by seeing the Zeppelin dirigible in Germany and by hearing accounts of the Wright brothers' heavier-than-air flying machine, which was then touring Europe. Sikorsky had meanwhile studied at the Naval Academy in Saint Petersburg and Polytechnic Institute of Kiev, and had attended lectures in France as well. He returned to Russia in 1909, entering the passionate center of the nascent aviation community, where he was inspired by meeting legendary aviators Louis Bleriot and Ferdinand Ferber, who told Sikorsky his idea for a flight machine was unattainable.

Sikorsky's sister purchased for him the same type of engine that had powered Bleriot's channel-crossing flight, and Sikorsky returned to Kiev the next spring to build a helicopter. His first two attempts failed, however, and he turned to designing conventional aircraft. Sikorsky's fifth plane, appropriately dubbed the S-5, actually flew, though poorly. His next three designs, comprising the S-6 series, would both cement his reputation and attract a patron.

M.V. Shidlovskiy, impressed with the potential of both the airplane and Sikorsky himself, placed him in charge of the St. Petersburg aviation factory of the Russ-Baltic Wagon Company. There, in addition to building airsleds, Sikorsky built two streamlined aircraft that won competitions against France's most advanced military planes.

His next project was truly a gargantuan undertaking. The idea of multiple engines was viewed with some suspicion at the time, but Sikorsky began building a giant, four-engined flying machine which received several appellations. First called the *Ruskii vityaz* (Russian knight) by its designer, the aircraft picked up the tag the "Petersburg Duck" from skeptics before it had flown and eventually became known as the *Grand.* The stable craft proved multi-engined flight was viable, even with the loss of one or more engines.

The *Grand* was damaged while parked when a lesser aircraft's engine fell out of the sky and through its wing. Its successor, the *Il'ya Muromets,* succeeded on an even grander

Company Perspectives:

Welcome aboard the fastest way to the future of vertical flight. Sikorsky. Designers and builders of the world's most advanced helicopters for commercial, industrial and military use. Our mission is to put our customers at the forefront of vertical flight. And we accomplish that mission, every day, through the extraordinary efforts of the world's finest engineers and manufacturing personnel. Their unmatched experience and legendary craftsmanship enable our people to take full advantage of Sikorsky's major investment in leading edge design and production techniques. Results. Aircraft that perform like nothing else in the sky today.

scale and brought Sikorsky worldwide acclaim. In 1914, one of its most memorable achievements was to fly, in stages, a 1,600-mile roundtrip between St. Petersburg and Kiev. Eventually 70 of these aircraft were built for use as bombers in World War I, bringing in the age of the heavy bomber. As would become a tradition for aircraft designers in Russia, Sikorsky was given the rank of General during the conflict.

Revolution in Russia and a Move to America

Sikorsky fled the Bolsheviks in February 1918; his patron, Shidlovskiy, was captured and executed. The impoverished Sikorsky soon made his way to France, where he won a contract to build military bombers. When the Great War soon came to an end, Sikorsky sailed for America.

Despite an unsuccessful venture with other émigrés in New York, in 1919 Sikorsky won a contract with the U.S. Army Air Service and moved to Washington, D.C. However, the plan was soon dropped for lack of funding, and Sikorsky returned to New York with a new focus on commercial aviation. A second attempt to form a partnership in 1920 also failed, and Sikorsky began teaching night classes to Russian immigrants to supplement his income. On March 5, 1923, Sikorsky formed the Sikorsky Aero Engineering Corporation with help from his predominantly Russian expatriate supporters. Most of the shares were worth $100, but the esteemed composer Sergei Rachmaninoff gave Sikorsky $5,000, allowing him to rent hangar space at Roosevelt Field.

A chicken farm housed the company's first workshop, where Sikorsky's motivated team transformed a piece of junk—actually many pieces of salvaged materials such as hospital beds—into an aircraft dubbed the S-29-A. Despite such inauspicious beginnings, the craft did get off the ground, though it quickly proved underpowered and its first attempt resulted in a crash landing. With new engines, the 14-passenger S-29-A finally overcame gravity on September, 25, 1924. A tour and numerous publicity stunts ensued, earning the fledgling company a place in the American imagination. Four years later the S-29-A (A for ''America'') ended its service life in the hands of another eminent aviation enthusiast, Howard Hughes, who destroyed it for a film stunt in the picture *Hell's Angels*.

Aviation dominated the American imagination in the Jazz Age. Airplanes became a popular art deco design motif and the airways became a stylish way to travel. The Sikorsky firm produced several designs for air races, including one for the Orteig transatlantic crossing prize that Lindberg eventually claimed. However, this plane, the S-35, was destroyed in a disastrous accident.

In spite of this setback, the company moved to a better equipped facility in College Point, New York. It settled in to producing clippers—the long-range amphibious aircraft that became a staple of international airlines such as Pan American. The fact that they were essentially flying boats naturally made them popular with aviators flying overseas routes concerned about safety. The S-38, the most successful of the lot, also appeared in corporate and military roles.

The company had become the Sikorsky Manufacturing Corporation in 1925, now led by Massachusetts businessman Arnold Dickinson as president. The company expanded quickly, relocating to Stratford, Connecticut, and reorganizing as the Sikorsky Aviation Company in 1929. It was promptly taken into the folds of the United Aircraft and Transport Corporation, which would be reorganized as the United Technologies Corporation in 1975.

The Whirling 1930s

The refined S-42 outclassed all of its clipper competitors upon its appearance in 1934. However, the heyday of the flying boat was rapidly coming to an end, and the company would have to scramble to stay in business.

Sikorsky persuaded United Aircraft management to let him revisit his old studies on developing a practical vertical flight apparatus. Some headway had been made since Sikorsky abandoned his projects. Engines and building materials had become lighter and stronger and the autogiro, essentially a conventional aircraft with a large free-rotating propeller on top instead of a fixed wing, first flew in the 1920s. So, in 1939, Sikorsky began to work on the project again at the Vought-Sikorsky plant in Stratford, Connecticut.

Although Sikorsky had patented in 1931 a design for a single-rotor helicopter, others had outpaced him by the time he reentered the field. The World War I aviator Henrich Focke had built a twin-rotor helicopter in 1936, and others in Germany and France were also producing working models. In fact, Anton Flettner's Fl-282 Kolibri (Hummingbird) became operational in the German military in 1940.

As a helicopter's rotor turns one way, opposite forces swing the body the other. Some balance is needed in order to keep the machine stable—usually either another, counter-rotating rotor or a small vertically-mounted tail rotor. Sikorsky was unique in devoting his efforts to the single-rotor philosophy, which he erroneously believed he had originated. (His countryman Boris Yuriev had developed such a design in 1912.)

Sikorsky borrowed the main rotor design from the autogiro developed by Juan de la Cierva, which was by then being made in America. The first models of the VS-300 actually had three tail rotors; a number of different configurations were tried.

The VS-300 first flew on September 14, 1939, the dawn of World War II. It was just a short, tethered flight, but it confirmed the viability of the craft. After a change of engines and other adjustments over the next several months, it became capable of extended flights, although controllability in forward flight remained a problem.

Nevertheless, the progress of the VS-300 earned Sikorsky Aircraft a contract to build a model for the U.S. Army in January 1941, to be dubbed the XR-4. In May, the refined VS-300-A set a stunning endurance record, hovering for one hour and 30 minutes. Sikorsky, and the United States, stood at the forefront of vertical flight.

Military Helicopters' Heyday: 1940s–60s

Sikorsky built 131 of the R-4 series during World War II; over 200 other models were also built. The British firm Westland built a version of its successor, the R-5, under license, dubbing it the Dragonfly. The helicopters were used for reconnaissance and rescue missions right away. In 1944, an R-4 flying in Burma made the first combat aerial rescue. Soon these types of missions were being flown routinely, since the helicopter could reach places that no fixed-wing aircraft could, and its hovering ability made it practical to pluck people from harm's way. R-4s were used extensively in the Korean War.

The R-4 spawned the company's first civil helicopter, known as the S-51. In spite of its unparalleled military and civil applications, the helicopter never became the consumer item that Sikorsky envisioned after the war. Every man, it turned out, would not one day have a helicopter in his backyard, as illustrated in one of the company's wartime promotional films.

Postwar Prosperity

For a time in the 1950s and 1960s, three commuter airlines, serving New York, Chicago, and Los Angeles, operated aircraft such as the large S-61 twin-rotor helicopter to ferry passengers from the outlying airports of the jet age to urban centers. Due to the high cost of flying the helicopters ($3.68 per seat per mile in 1954), these operations were heavily subsidized (half the average fare, or a total of $4.3 million in 1965). The flights were consigned to history after the subsidies were eliminated in 1970, though the popularity of the flights had grown and the per-seat cost had fallen to only $.32 per mile by 1964.

The S-64 "flying crane," a huge, powerful helicopter specifically designed to carry large loads, created its own unique heavy-lifting niche. The copter was unique in that it did away with the cargo compartment that would otherwise limit its lifting capacity, instead latching onto containers. It first flew in 1962, but never developed into the modular commuter vehicle Sikorsky had envisioned. Of 98 aircraft made, 88 were used in military applications. Among the few commercial customers, U.S. Steel tested the concept of lifting manufactured houses to remote locations with these aircraft.

Sales of helicopters to the U.S. military during the Vietnam War peaked in the mid-1960s, when corporate orders were also rising. Between 1953 and 1996, Sikorsky sold 1,444 of its S-58 models to the U.S. government. The commercial sector was dominated by competitor Bell Aerospace, which also sold thousands of its military UH-1 series. Sikorsky introduced its CH-53, designed to carry troops for the Marine Corps and at the time the largest helicopter in the world, in 1962. Sikorsky faced some Soviet competition in South America for military and oil industry clients.

Passing of a Legend

Sikorsky, who had retired in 1957, died on October 26, 1972. By the time of Sikorsky's death, the helicopter had become well established in the civilian world. By 1970, almost 300 hospitals in the United States relied on helicopters for ambulance duties, and the number of heliports had grown within a decade from about 360 to more than 2,300.

Passenger helicopters were still being used by some commuter carriers, and the industry as a whole (including entrants such as Bell, Hughes, and Boeing's Vertol division) shipped more than 500 units per year to the commercial sector. Growth was expected in several areas, such as servicing offshore oil platforms, which remained a viable area, as well as serving in corporate fleets. Sikorsky sought to increase its exports.

In the mid-1970s the company promoted its S-67 Blackhawk attack helicopter as a replacement for the Vietnam era Bell AH-1 Cobra. Although its testing program suffered a lethal crash in 1974, the machine eventually became a favorite of the U.S. armed forces. Sikorsky continued to dominate the military marketplace throughout the 1970s.

Military contracts kept coming during the Reagan years, including a $950 million contract for 294 UH-60 helicopters. By 1982 Sikorsky had grown into a military giant, with total sales of $1 billion and 12,000 employees.

In the mid-1980s, Boeing and Sikorsky entered into a joint venture to develop the $22 billion LHX program of light helicopters. They were awarded the military contract in 1991, assuring both companies a place in attack helicopter niches as well as the prospect of future international sales. At the time, the company was producing only four models: the Black Hawk, Seahawk, S-76, and CH-53. However, its research interests were diverse, including studying materials for a hypersonic aircraft.

Sikorsky sought international manufacturing partners throughout the 1980s. In 1984, the company succeeded in selling two dozen commercial helicopters to China. Nevertheless, only a fraction of sales, which totaled $1.5 billion in 1987, came from foreign sources.

New Horizons in the 1990s

The company remained dependent on military contracts, a liability in the 1990s. It laid off nearly 2,000 workers in the first two years of the decade. The S-92 carried Sikorsky's hopes for the future in the commercial medium helicopter segment, where the company expected the most growth.

In July 1997, Sikorsky announced an agreement to supply the U.S. Army, Navy, and Air Force with helicopters for five more years. The Army ordered 58 UH-60L Black Hawks, while the Navy ordered 42 CH-60 assault helicopters, and the Air Force ordered eight HH-60G Pave Hawk helicopters for search and rescue.

In 1994, international clients accounted for one-third of the company's $2.1 billion in sales. It produced 18 different models in order to satisfy the divergent demands of the international marketplace. The company also looked abroad, specifically in Turkey, to develop relationships with foreign suppliers.

In 1997, Korean Air Lines Co. joined Sikorsky in a six-year, $400 million agreement to develop general purpose helicopters. Sikorsky also shared technology with De Bono Industries of Malacca as part of a $20 million helicopter sale to the Malaysian government.

Further Reading

Bartlett, Robert M., *Sky Pioneer: The Story of Igor I. Sikorsky,* New York: Charles Scribner's Sons, 1947.

Brown, David A., "US Helicopter Lead Threatened," *Aviation Week and Space Technology,* May 28, 1973, pp. 179–81.

Cochrane, Dorothy, Von Hardesty, and Russell Lee, *The Aviation Careers of Igor Sikorsky,* Seattle: University of Washington Press for the National Air and Space Museum, 1989.

DeLear, Frank J., *Igor Sikorsky: His Three Careers in Aviation,* New York: Dodd, Mead and Company, 1969.

Driscoll, Lisa, "It'll Take More Than Saddam for Sikorsky to Soar Again," *Business Week,* October 1, 1990, p. 37.

Finne, K. N., *Igor Sikorsky: The Russian Years,* edited by Carl J. Bobrow and Von Hardesty, translated and adapted by Von Hardesty, Washington: Smithsonian Institution Press, 1987.

Hughes, David, "Boeing Sikorsky Fantail Demonstrates Unprecedented Maneuverability," *Aviation Week and Space Technology,* July 8, 1991, pp. 45–49.

Kandebo, Stanley W., "Sikorsky Boosts Quality, Cuts Costs with Kaizen," *Aviation Week and Space Technology,* May 1, 1995, pp. 39–40.

Kastner, J. "Sikorsky's Helicopter: A Flying Machine Which May Some Day Be Everyman's Airplane," *Life,* June 21, 1943, pp. 80–84.

"Military Helicopter Production Reaches Peak," *American Aviation,* May 1967, p. 139.

"New Markets Give Helicopter Industry a Whirling Future," *Industry Week,* February 22, 1971, pp. 18–20.

Phillips, Edward H., "Sikorsky Forging Ahead with S-92 Program," *Aviation Week and Space Technology,* January 5, 1998, pp, 48–49.

Ropelewski, Robert R., "Blackhawk Future Pondered After Crash," *Aviation Week and Space Technology,* September 9, 1974.

Sikorsky, Igor I., *The Invisible Encounter,* New York: Charles Scribner's Sons, 1947.

——, *The Message of the Lord's Prayer,* New York: Charles Scribner's Sons, 1942.

——, *The Story of the Winged-S: An Autobiography,* New York: Dodd, Mead and Company, 1938 (rev. ed. 1958).

Siuru, Bill, "Igor Sikorsky: Aviation Pioneer and Engineering Entrepreneur," *Mechanical Engineering,* August 1990, pp. 60–63.

Smart, Tim, and Stan Crock, "Choppy Winds at Sikorsky," *Business Week,* May 27, 1996, p. 40.

Velocci, Anthony L., Jr., "Boeing Sikorsky Could Reap Bonanza in Foreign Military Sales After LH Win," *Aviation Week and Space Technology,* April 15, 1991, pp. 72–73.

Wetmore, Warren C., "Sikorsky Pushes Export of S-67 Gunships," *Aviation Week and Space Technology,* July 29, 1974, pp. 39, 42, 47.

Wright, Robert A., "Helicopter Firms to Seek Big Commercial Market," *New York Times,* October 22, 1967, p. F1.

—Frederick C. Ingram

Sorrento

Sorrento, Inc.

2375 South Park Avenue
Buffalo, New York 14220-2653
U.S.A.
(716) 823-6262
Fax: (716) 823-6454

Wholly Owned Subsidiary of Besnier S.A.
Incorporated: 1947 as Sorrento Cheese Co.
Employees: 1,000
Sales: $400 million (1996 est.)
SICs: 2022 Natural Processed & Imitation Cheese

Based in Buffalo, New York, Sorrento, Inc. is a producer of Italian-style cheeses. On its 50th anniversary, in 1997, Sorrento ranked sixth in cheese production in the United States and was the nation's leader in sales of Italian cheeses. This product was available in 75 percent of U.S. markets through a well-developed network distributing the company's Sorrento and Precious brands.

Sorrento was acquired in 1989 by Source Perrier S.A. and in 1992 by another French food firm, Besnier S.A.

The First 40 Years, 1947–87

Sorrento was founded in 1947 by Louis Russo, an immigrant from Sorrento, Italy, who brought with him a family tradition of making soft Italian cheese. Russo made cheese the old-fashioned way for his Sorrento Cheese Co., established in Blasdell, New York, a suburb of Buffalo. He bought fresh cans of milk every morning and spent the early hours making ricotta and mozzarella. Afternoons were devoted to traveling throughout western New York, selling the products of the morning's labors. In 1960 Sorrento's 18 employees moved to the location on South Park Avenue in Buffalo that was still the company home in the late 1990s.

Louis's son Joseph became president and chief executive officer of Sorrento Cheese in 1978. The company had estimated sales of $32 million in 1980. Sorrento Food Service, Inc. was founded in 1986 to distribute food products to restaurants, institutions, and other clients. Sorrento, Inc., the parent firm, was the Buffalo area's fifth largest private company in 1988, having recorded sales volume of $175 million in 1986 and $215.6 million in 1987, when it acquired California Cheese, a San Jose, California, cheesemaker. That year Sorrento also purchased J. Beres & Son, a milk processor that, in addition, made juices and fruit drinks and produced private-label goods for national companies selling to schools and the government. Sorrento, Inc. also had another subsidiary, Sorrento Express, Inc., functioning as a common-carrier trucking company.

Sorrento's facilities were capable at this time of producing 150,000 pounds of cheese per day, most of it mozzarella, ricotta, and provolone. The company had benefited from the rise of popularity in such cheeses. According to the U.S. Department of Agriculture, U.S. consumption of cheese per person rose from 13 to 25.3 pounds between 1971 and 1988 and consumption of Italian varieties increased from 2.3 to 8.1 pounds over the same period.

Acquisitions, Expansion, and Divestitures, 1988–97

Société des Caves de Roquefort, a subsidiary of the French firm Source Perrier S.A., purchased a majority interest in Sorrento in 1988. This gave Sorrento the backing to pursue other acquisitions. The company acquired the former Joseph Malecki Corp. sausage-making plant in Cheektowaga, New York, a Buffalo suburb, in 1988. The following year it purchased Hickman Coward & Wattles, a $70-million-a-year food service division of Peter J. Schmitt Co. that was supplying 2,000 restaurants and other institutions in three states from a facility of 70,000 to 80,000 square feet in an industrial park in West Seneca, another suburb of Buffalo.

Sorrento decided in 1989 to add 72,000 square feet to its Buffalo cheesemaking plant on South Park Avenue, where it also maintained company headquarters; to add 36,000 square feet to the former Malecki manufacturing and warehousing facility; to add 46,000 square feet to the former Schmitt-owned West Seneca facility; and to construct an office, repair facility, and distribution center in Blasdell. Sorrento also was selling its Walden Avenue plant in Buffalo to Wegmans Food Markets, Inc. and was shifting freezer space from this plant to the former Malecki facility. Sorrento Food Service, the distribution subsidiary, was to move into this building.

The Erie County Industrial Development Agency approved $26 million in bonds for the expansions and renovations. This agency had worked with Sorrento when it acquired the former Malecki and Schmitt facilities. ''Any time a locally owned and managed company is acquired by out-of-town interests, there has to be some concern,'' an agency official explained to a Buffalo-area reporter. ''Being part of the Perrier family gives Sorrento the opportunity to make these new investments and commitments.'' In 1992 Besnier S.A., a French company with worldwide dairy holdings, acquired Caves de Roquefort, Sorrento's immediate parent.

Sorrento Cheese Co. completed a three-year, $15 million renovation program in 1994. This effort included an upgrade of its refrigeration and electrical service and an 8,700-square-foot addition to a packaging area for cheese products. In 1996 the company began preparing a 53,000-square-foot expansion of the South Park Avenue manufacturing plant to add production capacity. Sorrento Cheese recently had added automated equipment as part of an automation upgrade of its ricotta unit. It also had a manufacturing plant in Goshen, New York.

This expansion, it was soon revealed, was for a building that would house Sorrento Cheese's research and development units. Most manufacturers—including Sorrento—were converting milk into cheese through a time-honored process in which enzymes separate partially skimmed milk into curds and whey. The curds are then pressed into cheese, with the type of enzymes determining the ultimate flavor or type of the cheese. The new facility was to include a pilot plant where company research engineers would modify and test various layouts, equipment, and processes.

The new building was completed in the late summer of 1997 with the aid of the Erie County Industrial Development Agency, which had promised to issue bonds valued at $4.28 million to finance its construction. The company also was granted about $600,000 in tax breaks over 15 years. The agency said these incentives were justified because Sorrento was a company that did not have to be in Erie County.

The South Park Avenue expansion also meant an end to the Cheektowaga plant, which was put up for sale in 1997. Two product lines were being made there: a string cheese snack and a prepackaged topping made by taking excess cheese from large molds at the South Park plant and shredding it. This plant was employing about 200 workers, of which 80 were transferred to the South Park operation.

Also closed in 1997 was Sorrento Express's refrigerated trucking operation in Blasdell. This subsidiary was then phased out, with some 50 employees cut from the company payroll. The 21,000-square-foot property was sold to Penske Truck

Rental by means of a three-way deal in which Sorrento received a combination of cash and trade credits—in this case commodities that middleman Icon International had purchased from vendors at a discount because of their volatile shelf life. Another Sorrento business, J. Beres & Son, was sold in 1995.

Sorrento Food Service was sold to JP Foodservice Inc. in early 1998 for an undisclosed sum. Sorrento's wholesale food distribution subsidiary was serving about 7,200 accounts in western New York, western Pennsylvania, and Ohio and had sales volume of $108 million in 1997.

Sorrento Cheeses in the 1990s

Sorrento Cheese was producing a complete retail line of mozzarella, ricotta, string, and shredded cheeses in the 1990s. It also added a line of Mascarpone Italian cream cheese in 1993 for specialty pastry and dessert recipes. By the end of 1996 the Buffalo plant was taking in more than 1.5 million gallons of milk on any given day for processing into cheese, making it far and away the largest user of milk in western New York. This plant was producing 100 million pounds of cheese a year, almost half the company's total of 210 million pounds. Sorrento Cheese was accounting for about three-fourths of company revenue, with Sorrento Food Service accounting for the remainder.

Dairy Foods, a trade magazine, named Sorrento's International Shredded Cheese line as one of the top new dairy foods of 1997. Varieties consisted of English Country (a blend of Cheshire, farmer, Gloucester, and sharp cheddar), Mediterranean (Asiago, fontina, kasseri, mozzarella, and provolone), and Old European (emmental Swiss, farmer, Gouda, and muenster). Also available in shredded form were ''Mexican combo'' (a combination of mozzarella and cheddar with added spices), ''pizza cheese'' (a blend of mozzarella, romano, and parmesan), and stand-alone sharp and mild cheddars and mozzarella (in whole-milk, part-skim, low-fat, and fat-free options).

Sorrento's nonshredded mozzarella was available in whole-milk, whole-milk low-moisture, part-skim, low-fat, and fat-free options and also in string form. Its ricotta was available in all of these options except low-moisture. Sorrento Food Service also offered whole-milk diced mozzarella, provolone in block and sliced form, and ricotta colored green and red as well as white. The company completed an update for its retail packaging of ricotta, mozzarella, and shredded cheese, with a new logo unveiled to commemorate its 50th anniversary. In early 1998 Sorrento Cheese Co. launched a new television advertising campaign featuring both 10- and 30-second spots in major U.S. markets and starring Father Guido Sarducci of ''Saturday Night Live'' fame.

Principal Subsidiaries

Sorrento Cheese Co., Inc.

Further Reading

Baker, M. Sharon, ''In Mini-Mart Age, Milk Machines Remain Uncowed,'' *Business First-Buffalo,* July 13, 1992, p. 1.

Debo, David, ''Buffalo Cheese Producer Selling Packaging Plant,'' *Business First-Buffalo,* January 20, 1997, p. 4.

——, "Cheese Producer Wheys Expansion," *Business First-Buffalo,* October 21, 1996, p. 1.

Fink, James, "Sorrento Grabs Growing Market," *Business First-Buffalo,* December 25, 1989, p. 1.

Odato, James M., "Sorrento to Expand Plant in City, Shut One in Suburb," *Buffalo News,* February 15, 1997, p. B11.

"Schmitt Sells Food Service Division," *Supermarket News,* April 3. 1989, p. 4.

"Sorrento Cheese Co. International Shredded Blends," *Dairy Foods,* November 1997, p. 76.

"Sorrento Comes Back—New," *SN/Supermarket News,* February 9, 1998, p. 12.

Stouffer, Rick, "Sorrento Gets Cash, 'Trade Credits' in Exchange for Trucking Facility," *Buffalo News,* May 3, 1997, p. B13.

—Robert Halasz

The South African Breweries Limited

2 Jan Smuts Avenue
Johannesburg 2001
South Africa
(011) 407-1700
Fax: (011) 339-1830
Web site: http://www.sab.co.za

Public Company
Incorporated: 1895
Employees: 105,000
Sales: R 32.40 billion (1998)
Stock Exchanges: Johannesburg
Ticker Symbol: SBWRY
SICs: 2082 Malt Beverages; 2083 Malt; 2084 Wines,
Brandy & Brandy Spirits; 2085 Distilled & Blended
Liquors; 2086 Bottled & Canned Soft Drinks &
Carbonated Waters; 3211 Flat Glass; 3229 Pressed &
Blown Glass & Glassware, Not Elsewhere Classified;
5661 Shoe Stores; 5699 Miscellaneous Apparel &
Accessory Stores; 5712 Furniture Stores; 7011 Hotels
& Motels

The South African Breweries Limited (SAB) is a holding company whose principal line of business is brewing. The company holds an impressive 98 percent share of the beer market in its home country of South Africa, where it sells 14 brands of beer, including local lagers Castle and Lion as well as foreign brands brewed under license—Heineken, Guinness, Amstel, and Carling Black Label. Aggressive overseas expansion following the end of apartheid, however, has also given SAB ownership of, or stakes in, more than 25 breweries in the emerging markets of central Europe, China, and sub-Saharan Africa. Overall, in terms of volume, South African Breweries is the world's fourth largest brewer. SAB also has a variety of nonbrewing operations, such as carbonated and natural fruit drinks and other beverages, retailing, hotels and gaming, and manufacturing of safety matches and glass. The company has been divesting many of these noncore assets in the late 1990s.

SAB's history is in many ways the history of the South African brewing industry, most notably through the government-ordered merger of the largest breweries in 1956. The company's history was also greatly influenced by the apartheid system and its effect on the domestic economy, on domestic firms, and on foreign investment in South Africa.

Early History

The discovery of gold on the Witwatersrand (a region encompassing Johannesburg) in 1875 brought large numbers of prospectors to South Africa. Small outposts for white settlers were transformed into busy cities with new industries. Several brewmasters, most with little experience, began to produce a variety of beers which immediately gained popularity with the settlers.

In 1889 a British sailor named Frederick Mead left his ship in Durban and took a job working in the canteen of a local army garrison at Fort Napier. While there, Mead, who was only 20, became acquainted with a businessman in Pietermaritzburg named George Raw. Neither of them knew anything about brewing, but they persuaded the local residents to help establish the Natal Brewery Syndicate. After purchasing a factory site, Frederick Mead returned to England to procure machinery and raise capital. In need of brewing expertise, Mead approached W. H. Hackblock, head of Morgan's Brewery in Norwich. The two men became friends and Hackblock agreed to serve as chairman of Mead's company, which was registered in 1890 as the Natal Brewery Syndicate (South East Africa) Limited. The company brewed its first beer in July 1891.

Mead remained interested in establishing a brewery in the rapidly growing Witwatersrand. In 1892 he purchased the Castle Brewery in Johannesburg from its proprietor Charles Glass. The expansion of this facility, however, was beyond the means of the Natal Brewery Syndicate, and Mead returned to England to attract new investors. In the final arrangement, Mead formed another larger company based in London called The South African United Breweries. This company took over the operations of both the Natal Brewery Syndicate and the Castle Brewery.

After construction of the new Castle Brewery, South African United Breweries made additional share offerings which were purchased by South Africa's largest investment houses. Subsequent growth precipitated a restructuring of the company and reincorporation in London on May 15, 1895, as The South African Breweries Limited.

In 1896 South African Breweries purchased its first boarding houses. That same year, Frederick Mead moved to England for health reasons but continued to occupy a seat on the board of directors and frequently returned to South Africa. From London, Mead directed the purchase of machinery for brewing lager beer from the Pfaudler Vacuum Company in the United States. Patent restrictions and mechanical difficulties delayed production of Castle lager until 1898. The beer gained such widespread popularity that competing breweries rushed to introduce their own lagers.

South African Breweries, or SAB, was listed on the London Stock Exchange in 1895 and two years later became the first industrial company to be listed on the Johannesburg Stock Exchange. Through these listings SAB had greater access to additional investor capital.

On October 11, 1899, a war broke out between British colonial forces and Dutch and Huguenot settlers known as Boers. The war drove residents of Johannesburg out of the city and forced the Castle Brewery to close for almost a year. When British troops recovered the area, the brewery had sustained little or no damage. British authorities regarded the plant as an essential industry, and encouraged the company to resume production in August 1900. Disrupted supply lines caused shortages of yeast and other raw materials, but within a year production had returned to full capacity.

The Boer War ended in 1902 but was followed by a severe economic depression. The brewing industry was not as adversely affected as others, however, and SAB was able to continue its expansion across southern Africa. The company acquired the Durban Breweries and Distillers company, and established a new plant at Bloemfontein. SAB purchased Morgan's Brewery in Port Elizabeth in 1906 and, five years later, acquired another brewery in Salisbury, Rhodesia (now Harare, Zimbabwe). At its northernmost point, SAB established a brewery at Ndola, Northern Rhodesia (now Zambia).

W. H. Hackblock died in 1907 and was succeeded as chairman by Sydney Chambers. In 1912 Chambers led the company into an innovative arrangement with its competitor, Ohlsson's Brewery, to cultivate hops jointly at a site near the city of George, midway between Port Elizabeth and Cape Town. A joint subsidiary called Union Hop Growers spent many years developing new hybrids, which delayed the first commercial use of South African-grown hops until 1920.

Diversified into Bottles, Lodging, and Mineral Water in Early 20th Century

After Frederick Mead died in August 1915, John Stroyan, who succeeded Sydney Chambers a few months earlier, became the most important figure in SAB management. Stroyan faced a serious challenge the following year when hostilities during World War I interrupted the supply of bottles to South Africa. SAB decided to establish its own bottle-making plants in 1917. Actual production, however, did not begin until 1919, the year the war ended.

Another economic depression beset South Africa after World War I, but steady growth in the demand for beer reduced many of the detrimental effects of the depression. SAB was financially strong enough in 1921 to purchase the Grand Hotel in Cape Town, an important addition to the company's lodging business. SAB gained an interest in the mineral water business in 1925, when it purchased a substantial interest in the Schweppes Company.

The Great Depression of the early 1930s had little effect on the South African brewing industry; SAB continued to expand its operations and improve its facilities. The company's biggest problems were shortages of labor and capital. The Spanish Civil War and rising political tensions in Europe during the mid- and late 1930s caused a disruption in the supply of cork to South Africa. Faced with a severe shortage of cork seals for its beer, SAB developed a method of recycling old cork until a new supplier of cork could be found.

Castle Beer accompanied South African soldiers to the East African and Mediterranean theaters of World War II, but apart from its involvement in Europe, South Africa was relatively unaffected by World War II. When hostilities ended in 1945, SAB turned its attention to further modernization and expansion. Arthur Griffith-Boscawen, who had succeeded John Stroyan as chairman in 1940, died in 1946, and was replaced by John Stroyan's son, Captain John R. A. Stroyan. Under the leadership of the younger Stroyan, SAB concentrated on the establishment of a South African barley industry as an extension of the joint agricultural project it operated with Ohlsson's.

Takeover of Ohlsson's and United Breweries in 1956

South African Breweries entered a new stage of its development in 1950. That year, in the midst of a large corporate modernization program, SAB decided to move its head office from London to Johannesburg. In 1951 the company acquired the Hotel Victoria in Johannesburg, and a second brewery in Salisbury. Captain Stroyan retired the following year and returned to England. His successor, a talented barrister named

J. K. Cockburn Millar, died after only four months in office, and was replaced by a solicitor, S. J. Constance.

After producing nothing but beer for more than 60 years, SAB began to introduce a range of liquor products. The incentive to diversify was provided by increased taxes on beer. Consumption of beer in South Africa fell for the first time on record and showed every indication of further decline.

Officials of the three largest brewing companies in South Africa, SAB, Ohlsson's Cape Breweries, and United Breweries, met on several occasions in London and Johannesburg to discuss the viability of competition under deteriorating market conditions. In 1956 these officials decided that the three companies should merge their operations into one large brewing concern. SAB acquired all the shares of Ohlsson's and United Breweries, thus retaining the South African Breweries name. B. C. Smither of Ohlsson's and M. W. J. Bull of United Breweries joined the SAB board of directors.

Although the new company controlled 90 percent of the market for beer in South Africa, antiquated production facilities narrowed profit margins. In response, company activities were centralized in the Transvaal and the Western Province, areas where the three companies had previously competed. In addition, the old Castle Brewery in Johannesburg was closed in 1958. After succeeding Constance as chairman in 1959, M. W. J. Bull initiated a further diversification into wines and spirits. In 1960 SAB acquired the Stellenbosch Farmers Winery and later added Monis Wineries. Bull retired at the end of 1964 and was replaced by Dr. Frans J. C. Cronje, an economist and lawyer with substantial experience in government.

The company encountered a severe financial crisis in 1966 when Whitbread and Heineken entered the South African beer market. The most damaging market developments, however, came from government quarters as successive increases in excise duties made beer the most heavily taxed beverage per serving. Consumers began to abandon beer for wine and sorghum beer. SAB was able to reduce the effect of this crisis by increased sales of products from the Stellenbosch winery.

South African Breweries CEO Ted Sceales was instrumental in the creation of a new subsidiary called Barsab Investment Trust, jointly held by SAB and Thomas Barlow & Sons Ltd. (later Barlow Rand), the rapidly expanding mining services group. Barsab permitted SAB and Barlow to invest in each other and pool their managerial and administrative resources. It also provided SAB with the resources needed to adapt to rapidly changing market conditions. Sceales died following an auto accident in 1967, but the success of Barsab continued under the new chief executive, Dick Goss.

South African Breweries first attempted to move its legal domicile from Britain to South Africa in 1950, but was prevented from doing so by complex tax obligations to the British government. Consequently, SAB, which still derived about one-third of its income from investments in Rhodesia and Zambia, was bound to observe the British trade embargo against Rhodesia in 1967.

Reincorporated in South Africa in 1970

Parliamentary motions to permit the reincorporation of SAB in South Africa were initiated in 1968. These motions, however, did not gain approval until March 17, 1970. On May 26, 1970, after 75 years as an English company, SAB became a de jure South African company.

During the late 1960s SAB began brewing a number of new beers—some under license from foreign brewers—including Guinness, Amstel, Carling Black Label, and Rogue. The company also acquired the Old Dutch and Stag brands, as well as Whitbread in South Africa. While sales of wine and spirits continued to rise, SAB sold a number of its liquor-oriented hotels, and reorganized those that remained under a new subsidiary called the Southern Sun Hotel Corporation. Southern Sun, which operated 50 hotels in South Africa, was formed by the merger in 1969 of the existing SAB hotel interests with those of the Sol Kerzner family.

The South African government barred SAB from further investment in the liquor industry and limited its ability to invest overseas. The company then made several attempts to diversify its operations. In 1972 SAB and Barlow Rand decided to alter their collaboration and dissolve Barsab. As a result, two former Barsab holdings, the Shoe Corporation, and Afcol, South Africa's largest furniture manufacturer, came under SAB control. The following year, SAB acquired OK Bazaars, a large discount department store chain. Certain other investments were disposed of, however, including ventures in banking and food products.

Several brewing interests attempted to challenge SAB's dominant position in the South African market. Various German interests set up breweries in Botswana and Swaziland in a failed attempt to gain a foothold in South Africa. Louis Luyt, a South African entrepreneur, also failed, and sold his breweries to the Rembrandt Group in 1973. The Luyt breweries, which formed the core of Rembrandt's alcoholic beverage group, were later incorporated as the Intercontinental Breweries. Determined to succeed, Rembrandt's chairman, Dr. Anton Rupert, committed his company to a scheme of competition based on control of liquor retail outlets. In 1978 Rembrandt acquired a 49 percent share of Gilbey's, the third largest liquor group in South Africa. The addition of Gilbey's 100 retail outlets gave Rembrandt access to a total of 450 stores. South African Breweries responded by acquiring Union Wine, an independent liquor retailer with 24 hotels and over 50 retail outlets.

Once again, market conditions were not conducive to competition. The government, therefore, proposed a rationalization program in which SAB would take over Rembrandt's brewing interests and turn over its wine and spirits operations to an independent subsidiary called Cape Wine and Distillers. The program, executed in November 1979, also called for Rembrandt to turn over its Oude Meester wine and spirits operations to Cape Wines, in which SAB, Rembrandt, and the KWV wine growers cooperative each owned a 30 percent interest. The remaining 10 percent interest was sold to private investors.

Government Restrictions Led to More Diversification in the 1980s and Early 1990s

By the early 1980s the South African government's system of racial separation (apartheid) and deteriorating social conditions for blacks had become international issues. Many business leaders openly called for change, but the government still prevented companies such as SAB from transferring capital out of South Africa through foreign investments. Often these companies had little choice but to reinvest their surplus capital in South African ventures, which in turn gave them a more crucial interest in the resolution of social and human rights problems within South Africa.

Many foreign-owned companies, which faced fewer restrictions on divestment, sold their South African subsidiaries and closed their offices in South Africa. This trend made acquisitions by South African companies easier. SAB took over control of the ABI soft drink concern from Coca-Cola, and later added several clothing retailers, including Scotts Stores (acquired in 1981) and the Edgars chain (added in 1982). A government order in 1979 for SAB to sell its Solly Kramer retail liquor stores was completed in 1986, five years before its deadline. Also in 1986 SAB established a joint venture with Ceres Fruit Juices to sell leading noncarbonated juice brands Ceres, Liquifruit, and Fruitee.

In 1987 Murray B. Hofmeyer succeeded Cronje as chairman. Hofmeyer and his successor, Meyer Kahn, continued to diversify through acquisition, adding Lion Match Company, the leading manufacturer of safety matches in Africa, in 1987; Da Gama Textiles Company, a leading South African textile manufacturer, in 1989; and the Plate Glass Group, a manufacturer of glass and board products, in 1992.

End of Apartheid Fueled Major Changes in the 1990s

The dismantling of apartheid finally began in 1990, with the unbanning of opposition political parties, including the African National Congress, and the release of political prisoners, including Nelson Mandela. Major political changes rapidly followed. In 1991 the remaining apartheid laws were repealed. In 1992, an all-white referendum approved a new constitution that would lead to eventual free elections. Finally, in 1994, the first nationwide free elections were held and were won by the ANC, with Mandela elected president.

SAB—acting largely out of self-interest since 85 percent of the beer in South Africa was purchased by blacks—was well out in front of the political changes as it had begun to hire blacks in the early 1980s. By 1985 28 percent of salaried employees were black, a figure that rose to 48 percent by 1994. Nevertheless, the threat of a government-forced breakup of SAB's beer monopoly hung over the company following the end of apartheid.

Partly in response to this threat, and partly in response to the loosening of laws regarding foreign investment, the Kahn-led South African Breweries aggressively expanded outside its home country starting in 1993. That year, SAB spent US$50 million for an 80 percent stake in Hungary's largest brewer, Dreher Breweries, the first of a series of moves into the emerging markets of central Europe. In 1996 the company gained joint control of two of the largest breweries in Poland, Lech Brewery and Tyskie Brewery, as well as three breweries in Romania and one in Slovakia. In 1994 SAB created a joint venture with Hong Kong-based China Resources Enterprise Limited; by early 1998 this joint venture had gained majority control of five breweries in China. A third area of foreign growth for SAB was in sub-Saharan Africa, where management control was gained of breweries in Botswana, Swaziland, Lesotho, Zambia, Tanzania, Mozambique, Ghana, Kenya, Ethiopia, Zimbabwe, and Uganda during this period.

In August 1997 Kahn was appointed chief executive of the South African police service, becoming the first civilian to hold the post. The outspoken Kahn, who had been vocal in calling for the rapid liberalization of the economy and for a restoration of law and order, was made responsible for cracking down on a national crime epidemic. Taking over as acting chairman of SAB was Cyril Ramaphosa, South Africa's most prominent black capitalist and a former militant trade unionist.

By this time, South African Breweries was the world's fourth largest brewer and had a rapidly expanding international brewing empire. The company was now free to unload its noncore businesses in order to concentrate more closely on brewing and its other beverage operations. Under Ramaphosa, it did just that. In late 1997 and early 1998 SAB divested its holdings in OK Bazaars, Afcol, and Da Gama Textiles, and announced that Lion Match and Conshu Holdings, a footwear maker, were also likely to be jettisoned. These divestments were not proceeding quickly enough for some observers, but SAB had already managed to strengthen its overall position in the face of the continued threat of the breakup of its domestic beer monopoly. Selling off noncore assets was freeing up capital for additional investment in foreign breweries, which would further mitigate the impact of any government intervention.

Principal Subsidiaries

Southern Associated Maltsters (Pty.) Ltd.; SAB Hop Farms (Pty.) Ltd.; SAB International Holdings Inc.; SAB International (Africa) B.V. (Netherlands); Botswana Breweries (Pty.) Ltd. (40%); Kgalagadi Breweries (Pty.) Ltd. (Botswana; 40%); Swaziland Brewers (Pty.) Ltd. (60%); Lesotho Brewing Company (Pty.) Ltd. (39%); Tanzania Breweries Ltd. (46%); Cervejas de Mozambique Limitada (65%); Zambian Breweries Plc (45%); Nile Breweries Limited (Uganda; 40%); SAB International (Europe) B.V. (Netherlands); Dreher Breweries (Hungary; 85%); Lech Browary Wielkopolski S.A. (Poland; 32%); SC Vulturul S.A. (Romania; 70%); Compañía Cervecera de Canarias S.A. (Spain; 51%); SC Pitber S.A. (Romania; 81%); SC Ursus S.A. (Romania; 73%); Browary Tyskie Górny Slask S.A. (Poland; 45%); SAB International (Asia) B.V. (Netherlands); China Resources Enterprise Beverages Ltd. (49%); China Resources Shenyang; Snowflake Beer Co. Ltd. (China; 44%); China Resources Dalian Brewery Co. Ltd. (49%); Shenzhen C'est Bon Food and Drink Co. Ltd. (China; 33%); China Resources (Jilin) Brewery Co. Ltd. (90%); Delta Corporation Ltd. (Zimbabwe; 23%); Seychelles Breweries Ltd. (20%); Accra Breweries Limited (Ghana; 50.5%); Amalgamated Beverage Industries Ltd. (68%); Coca-Cola Canners (Pty.) Ltd. (24%); Can Vendors (Pty.) Ltd.; Appletiser South Africa (Pty.) Ltd.; Appletiser Pure Fruit Juices (Pty.) Ltd.; Ceres Fruit Juices (Pty.)

Ltd. (35%); Valaqua (Pty.) Ltd.; Associated Fruit Processors (Pty.) Ltd. (50%); Traditional Beer Investments (Pty.) Ltd.; Distillers Corporation (SA) Ltd. (30%); Stellenbosch Farmers' Winery Group Ltd. (30%); Edgars Stores Ltd. (65%); Amalgamated Retail Ltd. (''Amrel'') (68%); Southern Sun Holdings Ltd.; Plate Glass and Shatterprufe Industries Ltd. (68%); Da Gama Textile Company Ltd. (61%); The Lion Match Company Ltd. (71%); Conshu Holdings Ltd. (67%).

Further Reading

Ashurst, Mark, ''Breweries Chief to Head SA Crackdown on Crime,'' *Financial Times,* May 26, 1997, p. 22.

Bobinski, Christopher, and Roderick Oram, ''South African Breweries in Polish Acquisition,'' *Financial Times,* October 2, 1996, p. 24.

Fridjhon, Michael, and Andy Murray, *Conspiracy of Giants: The South African Liquor Industry,* Johannesburg: D. Stein, 1986.

Grey, Sarah, ''No Small Beer from This SA Giant,'' *Accountancy,* November 1997, pp. 26–27.

la Hausse, Paul, *Brewers, Beerhalls, and Boycotts: A History of Liquor in South Africa,* Johannesburg: Ravan Press, 1988.

Lenzner, Robert, ''Empowerment: South Africa's Most Visible Black Capitalist Was Formerly Its Most Militant Union Leader,'' *Forbes,* August 25, 1997, p. 47.

''Lion of Africa, Brewer to the People,'' *Economist,* September 9, 1995, p. 72.

Mallet, Victor, ''SA Breweries Set to Unbundle Non-Core Assets,'' *Financial Times,* March 25, 1998, p. 44.

McNeil, Donald G., Jr., ''In South African Beer, Forget Market 'Share,' '' *New York Times,* August 27, 1997, pp. D1, D4.

Ross, Priscella, ''SA Breweries Moves into Ethiopia, Uganda,'' *African Business,* December 1997, p. 28.

The South African Breweries Limited: 100 Year Commemorative Brochure, Johannesburg: South African Breweries Limited, [1995?].

''Trouble Brewing for the ANC,'' *Economist,* May 21, 1994, pp. 70, 73.

''Under the Froth: South Africa's Beer Wars,'' *Economist,* February 8, 1997, p. 73.

—updated by David E. Salamie

Southwest Airlines Co.

2702 Love Field Drive
P.O. Box 36611
Dallas, Texas 75235
U.S.A.
(214) 904-4000
Fax: (214) 904-4022
Web sites: http://www.iflyswa.com
http://www.southwest.com

Public Company
Incorporated: 1967 as Air Southwest Co.
Employees: 25,175
Sales: $3.82 billion (1997)
Stock Exchanges: New York
Ticker Symbol: LUV
SICs: 4512 Air Transportation, Scheduled

If there is a model for success in budget air transportation, it is Southwest Airlines Co. Others have been more profitable—ValuJet, for example, but they have failed to match Southwest's record over time; most budget start-up airlines have the life span of fruit flies, try as they might to emulate Southwest, where the average fare costs about $75 and covers 400 miles.

The company flies only Boeing 737s, to simplify maintenance, and employee productivity is high: planes are turned around for their next flight in just 15 minutes, one-third the industry average. Despite complaints from travel agents, the airline eschews the use of a reservation system to avoid paying the required fees. With its unique operating philosophy, Southwest is a maverick in the airline industry.

Passengers in half of the United States have found that Southwest's rock bottom pricing creates almost a new form of transportation, more in competition with the automobile than other airlines. They are willing to forsake in-flight meals, baggage transfers, and other traditional frills for economically amenable wings.

Beginning a Labor of Love

Southwest Air was founded in 1966 when a group of Texas investors, including Rollin King, M. Lamar Muse, and Herbert D. Kelleher, pooled $560,000 to form the Air Southwest Company. Incorporated in 1967, the company was envisioned as a commuter airline serving three cities within Texas: Dallas, Houston, and San Antonio. Although the Texas Aeronautics Commission (TAC), the regulatory body responsible for overseeing aviation within the state, granted the company permission to fly the routes it had requested in February 1968, three competing airlines filed suit to prevent the airline from getting off the ground. Kelleher, an attorney whose stake in the airline was a mere $20,000, took the case all the way to the U.S. Supreme Court, and in December 1970 this court ruled in favor of Air Southwest.

Six months later, after fighting numerous legal battles, changing its name to Southwest Air, and selling stock in the company, the fledgling airline began operations on June 18, 1971. Under the stewardship of President M. Lamar Muse, the airline offered six daily roundtrip flights between Dallas and San Antonio, and 12 daily roundtrip flights between Dallas and Houston. One-way tickets cost $20.

Courting the commuter, the company stressed "no-frills" convenience and, in reference to Love Field in Dallas, its home base, made "love" its promotional theme. Flight attendants were dressed in hot pants and go-go boots to serve "love potions" and "love bites" (also known as drinks and peanuts) to the company's clientele of mostly male business fliers. Southwest made much of its scantily-clad women, whose pin-up-like images would eventually appear widely, including the cover of *Esquire* magazine.

By the end of 1971, Southwest owned four aircraft, offered hourly flights between Dallas and Houston, and had inaugurated service between San Antonio and Houston, completing the last leg of a triangular route. In the following year, the company transferred its Houston service from Houston Intercontinental Airport to William P. Hobby Airport, located much closer to the city's downtown, in an effort to become more convenient to commuters. In 1973, Braniff Airlines began a fare war with

452

Company Perspectives:

Southwest Airlines is a symbol of freedom. Since 1971, our low fares have given millions of Americans the freedom to fly. From our flag to our open seating, from our all-jet fleet to our declaration of freedom, our Southwest Spirit illuminates our past, guides our present, and forges our future.

Southwest Airlines Co. is the nation's low fare, high Customer Satisfaction airline. We primarily serve shorthaul city pairs, providing single class air transportation, which targets the business commuter as well as leisure travelers. The Company, incorporated in Texas, commenced Customer Service on June 18, 1971, with three Boeing 737 aircraft serving three Texas cities—Dallas, Houston, and San Antonio. At year-end 1997, Southwest operated 261 Boeing 737 aircraft and provided service to 52 airports in 51 cities throughout the United States. Southwest has the lowest operating cost structure in the domestic airline industry and consistently offers the lowest and simplest fares. Southwest also has one of the best overall Customer Service records. LUV is our stock exchange symbol, selected to represent our home at Dallas Love Field, as well as the theme of our Employee and Customer relationships.

Southwest over service from this airport to Dallas; Southwest resorted to giveaways of liquor, leather ice buckets, and 50 percent discounts on fares. The company also introduced cargo service between the airports it served and by the end of 1973 had notched its first profitable year, carrying over half a million passengers.

Still More Controversy in the 1970s

Southwest again found itself involved in legal controversy in 1972, when the cities of Dallas and Fort Worth and their Regional Airport Board filed suit to force the airline to move from Love Field to the newly constructed Dallas-Fort Worth regional airport, hoping that by charging higher landing fees and rent there, they could help offset the cost of the expensive project. While all the other airlines had signed a contract to move to the new airport in 1968, Southwest had not done so because it was not in existence at that time. In a big break for Southwest, a federal judge ruled in 1973 that the airline could continue to operate at Love Field in Dallas as long as the airport remained open. Thwarted, the Dallas City Council subsequently passed a law closing the airport to all scheduled airlines, but this law was thrown out in court.

In 1974, Southwest's competitors began moving out to the Dallas-Fort Worth Airport, leaving the airline with a monopoly on service from the cheaper, more convenient airport. After defeating yet another legal challenge, this one from the other carriers, Southwest was able to solidify its presence at Love Field and its newly renovated facilities at Houston's Hobby Airport, making its strong commuter service the basis for broader operations.

This expansion began in 1975, when the airline inaugurated service to the Rio Grande Valley, with four roundtrip flights each day to Harlingen. By the end of that year, the company had acquired a fifth plane, and its stock was listed on the American Stock Exchange under the ticker symbol "LUV." In the following year, Southwest laid plans to extend service to five other Texas cities and again found itself the object of hostile litigation by competitors.

In 1977, the airline put into effect its plan to offer service from Corpus Christi, Lubbock, Midland/Odessa, El Paso, and Austin. Its stock was transferred to the New York Stock Exchange, and the company issued its second and third quarterly dividends, the latter totaling seven cents per share. In May of that year, the airline exceeded the five-million passenger mark.

Deregulated at Last

In 1978, Congress passed the Airline Deregulation Act, fundamentally altering the nature of the airline industry. Although Southwest was now legally free to greatly expand its operations, the company planned conservative growth to avoid the perils of taking on large debts.

In early 1978, the airline applied for permission to purchase a wholly owned subsidiary, Midway (Southwest) Airway Company, in order to inaugurate service from Chicago's Midway Airport to six Midwestern destinations. Although it received tentative approval to do so, Southwest abandoned this ambitious attempt at expansion in August. Instead, the company added service to the mid-sized Texas city of Amarillo and the Jefferson County Airport. In July 1978, the company implemented its first fare increase since 1972, adding three dollars to the cost of a one-way ticket, and five dollars for a roundtrip fare. By the end of the year, the airline's fleet had grown to 13 Boeing 737 planes.

In March 1978, significant changes were made in Southwest's upper-level management. After a dispute with the airline's governing board, President M. Lamar Muse, who had largely shaped the company during its early years, was deposed by the board and replaced by lawyer Kelleher, who became chairman of the board. In August, Howard D. Putnam, a United Airlines executive, became president and chief executive officer.

In 1979, Southwest introduced self-ticketing machines in many of its airports to speed up and simplify passenger ticketing, and the airline introduced service to New Orleans, its first destination outside Texas. In late December 1979, earlier opponents of Southwest's continuing use of Love Field won a partial victory in Congress. Speaker of the House Jim Wright, a Congressman from Texas, attached a rider to a federal trade law which forbade traffic between Love Field and any states other than Louisiana, Arkansas, Oklahoma, and New Mexico, the four states surrounding Texas. This severe limitation of Southwest's interstate flights from its hub forced the airline to conform to its established role as a commuter service for the energy belt, now in a severe depression. The airline inaugurated service to Oklahoma City, Tulsa, and Albuquerque in April 1980.

Earlier that year, Southwest was hit by a machinists' strike, which curtailed operations for several weeks. The company brought in temporary workers to keep 12 of its 18 planes flying, and the union eventually settled for what the airline had initially offered.

In 1981, celebrating its tenth year of operation, the airline introduced a multimedia advertising campaign featuring the theme, "Loving you is what we do," and produced an ad picturing six Southwest flight attendants, all purportedly "physical 10s," grouped around a birthday cake, promising, "You ain't seen nothin' yet." In June 1981, the airline was found guilty of sex discrimination in a class action suit filed by a man seeking a job as a ticket agent and ordered to cease its discriminatory hiring practices. Also in 1981, after a series of petition drives, stewardesses won the right in their new contract not to wear hot pants on the job.

In September 1981, President Howard Putnam resigned to become the head of Braniff International Airlines, and was succeeded as president and chief executive officer by Chairman Kelleher, who brought his flamboyant personal style to the job of running the airline. With Kelleher at the helm, the airline's pace of expansion picked up markedly, despite the nationwide recession and difficulties arising from an air traffic controllers' strike. In early 1982, Southwest introduced service from Kansas City, Missouri, to seven destinations. Just a few weeks later, the airline made its entry into the western air travel market when it began flights from San Diego, Las Vegas, and Phoenix. Additional California service was inaugurated that fall, when Los Angeles and San Francisco came on line.

The airline's steady growth continued in 1983, as it added customers, flights, and airplanes. The company ratified a two-tier wage system, secured a one-year pay freeze from its pilots' association, and signed contracts with several of its unions, including its mechanics and flight attendants. Service from Denver began in May 1983.

Stretching Out in the 1980s

In a departure from its previous policy of sticking to short-haul flights, Southwest inaugurated two routes between Texas and California—El Paso to Los Angeles and San Antonio to Los Angeles—as well as a major north-south California route from San Diego to San Francisco. Entry into these long-haul markets, coupled with bad weather throughout the Southwest region, curtailed profits somewhat during this period.

In 1984, helped by ongoing peace with its labor unions, Southwest continued to increase capacity and rack up steady profits, despite growing competition from Continental, Braniff, and Muse Air, founded by the former president of Southwest. In July 1984, the company implemented limited cost-cutting measures, paring back unprofitable flights and limiting hiring. The company took delivery on the first of a new generation of planes, the Boeing 737-300, and introduced service from another Midwestern city, Little Rock, Arkansas.

The following year, Southwest further expanded its Midwestern network of routes, adding flights to St. Louis and Chicago's Midway airport. The company unveiled its "Just Say When" promotion, touting itself as the most convenient way to travel. The airline also made its first big acquisition when it paid $60 million for Muse Air Corporation, a Houston-based competitor, to prevent another competitor, Continental Airlines,

from snatching it up. Unlike Southwest, Muse Air offered longer flights and full service to its customers. Kelleher kept the full-service frills and renamed the airline Transtar. In its first year, the money-losing company was able to turn a small profit.

By 1986, Southwest had scheduled flights from 25 cities. The airline introduced a number of fare-cutting measures in efforts to maintain its market share in the heavily competitive post-deregulation airline industry. "Incredible Pair Fares," "Fly Now, Pay Less," programs, $25 tickets for senior citizens, and finally "Fun Fares" became part of the strategy to lure more fliers to the skies. In addition, the airline was waging a fare war at its Phoenix hub against America West Airlines, offering flights between California and Arizona for $25.

During the summer of 1986, the airline stepped up the hoopla surrounding its low fares, making "fun" its new corporate byword and implementing a "fun" uniform of golf shirts, surfer shorts, and tennis shoes, along with in-flight games and giveaways. In July, the golf shirts were replaced by red Southwest T-shirts asserting that "Southwest Fliers Have More Fun." In an effort to simplify ticketing, a drive-through ticket window was installed near the airline's Dallas hub in August 1986, and in October tickets became available through automatic teller machines at 7-Eleven stores in Corpus Christi, Texas.

By 1987, Southwest's full-service subsidiary Transtar was locked in head-to-head combat with Continental for service out of Houston's Hobby Airport. The competing airline hit Transtar with cheaper flights scheduled 15 minutes before and after every Transtar departure, and the Southwest subsidiary was soon draining off $2 million in losses every month. In August 1987, after suffering a net loss for the first quarter of the year, Southwest shut down Transtar. The Transtar debacle cut the company's year-end earnings by 60 percent.

Despite aggressive pricing, Southwest found its rapid expansion thwarted in some markets, as full-service rivals drove the airline out of Denver, hampered its ambitious plans for operations in Nashville, and continued to put up stiff resistance in Phoenix. In addition, the airline was fined $402,000 by the Federal Aviation Authority in 1987. Faced with the demands of business fliers, the company introduced its first frequent flier program. Unlike the programs of other airlines, which award prizes based on mileage accrued, Southwest's program was designed to reward the short-haul flier, allotting prizes on the basis of number of trips taken.

In 1988, Southwest president Kelleher announced plans to double the airline's size by 1994. His strategy for accomplishing this was to increase the frequency of flights between cities already on the Southwest route map and to open up new routes in California and the Midwest. In keeping with the airline's policy of flying out of airports that are close to urban centers, Southwest also switched its Detroit flights to Detroit City Airport from the more remote Metro Airport.

Also in 1988, as a sign of the ever-growing airline's commitment to lightheartedness, Southwest painted one of its 737s to resemble a killer whale to celebrate the company's agreement to become the official airline of Sea World of Texas. Shamu One, named after Sea World's mascot killer whale, was eventually joined by Shamu Two and Shamu Three. When Federal anti-smoking regulations went into effect on all domestic flights, Southwest offered its passengers lollipops as a substitute for the now-banned cigarettes. Passengers on flights during the winter holiday season of 1988 reported that flight attendants were dressed as elves and reindeer, and that the pilot sang Christmas carols over the public address system while gently rocking the plane from side to side.

In the spring of 1989, Southwest began its planned assault on the California market and touched off a fare war with much larger carriers, such as American Airlines and United Airlines, when it introduced $19 fares from Oakland International Airport, in the San Francisco Area, to Ontario, a suburb of Los Angeles. Aiming to reach $1 billion in revenues for the year, Southwest planned continued expansion of its fleet of planes and added Indianapolis to its route map. In a novel pairing of businesses, the company offered, for a limited time, a free companion ticket to anyone buying a holiday meal at Kentucky Fried Chicken.

Prudence Prevails in the 1990s

As a result of its steady growth, Southwest entered the 1990s as a major airline, with a fleet of 94 planes serving 27 cities. Relying on conservative financial management, the company was able to avoid the pitfalls of debt that crippled many other carriers in the early 1990s, and despite suffering a loss in its fourth quarter, turned an overall profit in 1990.

Southwest took advantage of the misfortunes of its competitors in 1991, scooping up market share abandoned by ailing US Air in California and by bankrupt America West in Phoenix, and buying gates at Midway Airport from its defunct Chicago competitor, Midway Airlines. By year's end, Southwest had 124 jets flying to 32 cities.

By 1992, the company's concerted push into the California market had begun to become profitable, and Southwest became the second largest carrier in the state. The company looked to the Midwest as its next largest site of expansion. When the Department of Transportation began ranking airlines based upon baggage handling, customer satisfaction, and on-time performance, Southwest outpaced its larger, more expensive colleagues to win the first "Triple Crown" in 1992. And it kept winning them year after year. In 1993, when Southwest was expanding to the East Coast via Baltimore/Washington International Airport, Southwest was the only major carrier to take home a profit.

Southwest aggressively pursued non-traditional means of ticketing passengers. It sidestepped Apollo and other established reservation networks in lieu of more direct contact with travel agents. It dubbed its own network SWAT, for Southwest Air Travel.

Takeovers of Morris Air and Arizona One in 1994 expanded the company's network still further; the company continued to add routes to the Midwest and California. Southwest followed suit with its low-budget peers by eliminating paper tickets.

In 1995, the company reached $2.8 billion in operating revenues. Within five years, Southwest had added more than 10,000 employees to its roster. Southwest commemorated its 1996 silver anniversary with a special plane called *Silver One*. Internet ticket sales debuted along with new Florida service, which added the carrier's 50th city in 1997.

For the 25th consecutive year, the carrier posted a profit—$317.7 million—in 1997. Due to its low fares, the carrier's entering a market could increase the volume of passenger traffic fourfold, and some businesses used the availability of Southwest service as a prime criterion in choosing new locations. The airline's 2300 flights per day, impressive safety record, and status as a much-admired corporate citizen suggested it would long remain one of the industry's legendary survivors.

Further Reading

Brown, David A., "Southwest Airlines Gains Major Carrier Status by Using Go-It-Alone Strategy," *Aviation Week & Space Technology,* March 5, 1990.
Chakravarty, Subrata N., "Hit 'Em Hardest with the Mostest," *Forbes,* September 16, 1991.
Freiberg, Kevin, and Jackie Freiberg, *Nuts! Southwest Airlines' Crazy Recipe for Business and Personal Success,* Austin, Bard, 1996.
Gibney, Frank, Jr., "Southwest's Friendly Skies," *Newsweek,* May 30, 1988.
Keating, Peter, "Rating the Airlines: The Best Airlines to Fly Today," *Money,* November 1, 1997.
Kelly, Kevin, "Southwest Airlines: Flying High with "Uncle Herb'," *Business Week,* July 3, 1989.
Labich, Kenneth, and Ani Hadjian, "Is Herb Kelleher America's Best CEO?" *Fortune,* May 2, 1994.
Levering, Robert, and Milton Moskowitz, *The 100 Best Companies to Work for in America,* New York: Doubleday, 1993.
——, "The 100 Best Companies to Work for in America," *Fortune,* January 12, 1998.
Loeffelholz, Suzanne, "The Love Line," *Financial World,* March 21, 1989.
Maglitta, Joseph, "Lean, Mean Flying Machines," *Computerworld,* July 11, 1994.
Putnam, Howard D., *The Winds of Turbulence,* Harper Business, 1991.
"Southwest Airlines—A Brief History," http://www.iflyswa.com/info/airborne.html.
Southwest Airlines History, Dallas: Southwest Airlines, 1991.
Taylor, John H., "Risk Taker," *Forbes,* November 14, 1988.
Troxell, Thomas N., Jr., "Deregulation in Stride," *Barton's,* January 23, 1984.
Weber, Joseph, "These Two Airlines Are Doing It Their Way," *Business Week,* September 21, 1987.
"Why Herb Kelleher Gets So Much Respect from Labor," *Business Week,* September 24, 1984.
Zellner, Wendy, "Striking Gold in the California Skies," *Business Week,* March 30, 1992.

—Elizabeth Rourke
—updated by Frederick C. Ingram

STAGE STORES INC.
BEALLS · PALAIS ROYAL · STAGE

Stage Stores, Inc.

10201 Main Street
Houston, Texas 77025
U.S.A.
(713) 667-5601
(800) 579-2302
Fax: (713) 660-3342
Web site: http://www.stagestoresinc.com

Public Company
Incorporated: 1988 as Specialty Retailers, Inc.
Employees: 14,069
Sales: $1.07 billion (1997, fiscal year ended January 31, 1998)
Stock Exchanges: New York
Ticker Symbol: SGE
SICs: 5600 Apparel & Accessory Stores

Houston-based Stage Stores, Inc. (Stage) was founded in 1988 as a private company and went public in 1996. The company is an apparel-retail chain operating mainly in over 600 small towns and communities in the United States. The retail chain, through its wholly owned subsidiary—Specialty Retailers, Inc.—operates primarily under the Stage, Bealls, and Palais Royal trade names to offer nationally recognized, moderately priced brand-name apparel, accessories, fragrances, cosmetics, and footwear for the entire family. Indeed, Stage is America's leading small-town retailer geared to the needs of women, men, and children. By following a strategy based on "thinking big in small-town America," the company enjoys one of the highest operating margins in the apparel-retailing industry.

Stage operates 660 stores in 35 states. More than 85 percent of these stores are located in small towns and communities with populations below 30,000 people and generally range in size from 12,000 to 30,000 selling square feet. The remainder of the company's stores operate in outlying metropolitan areas, mainly in the suburban Houston and Galveston areas. As the only retailer focused on consolidating the fragmented, small-

market retailing of branded products, Stage faces limited competition and enjoys favorable store economics, thrives on economies of scale resulting from an expanding store base, commands strong vendor relationships, maintains state-of-the art operating systems, and exercises innovative merchandising and marketing strategies. Stage buys merchandise from a base of over 2,000 vendors. More than 85 percent of fiscal 1997 sales consisted of branded merchandise, including nationally recognized brands such as Levi Strauss, Liz Claiborne, Chaps/Ralph Lauren, Calvin Klein, Guess?, Hanes, Nike, Reebok, and Haggar Apparel. The company's private-label merchandise makes up for the difference. Sales for fiscal 1997 increased 38.2 percent to $1.07 billion from $776.55 million in fiscal 1996.

Beginnings of a New Retail Concept: 1988–92

Stage Stores' operating history dates back to late 1988 when, through a leveraged buyout, the former management team of Palais Royal, Inc., Bain Capital Funds, and Acadia Entities formed a separate company—named Specialty Retailers, Inc. (SRI)—to acquire Palais Royal, a retail chain of 28 stores. Concurrently, SRI acquired Bealls Brothers, Inc. which operated 126 stores. Both Palais Royal and Bealls were family-owned, Houston-based apparel retailers that since the 1920s had built strong regional franchises in the central and southwestern United States. Palais Royal focused mainly on the operation of large stores in metropolitan markets while Bealls's business consisted primarily of smaller stores in rural markets. SRI's management team focused on integrating Palais Royal and Bealls and refined the retail concept that would differentiate the company from both department stores and specialty stores: SRI stores offered more convenience and customer service than were usually found in department stores, provided leading brand names of apparel, and made available a broader assortment of merchandise than could be found in specialty stores.

Palais Royal had relied on automation to improve operating efficiency, as evidenced by its early implementation of an automated personnel scheduling system, electronic point-of-sale cash registers, and a credit-application and behavioral-scoring system. SRI recognized the advances Palais Royal had made in automation and developed a retail concept that relied on efficient operating systems, advanced technology, centralized decision-making, and tight control of operating expenses. In about 18 months SRI substantially completed the consolidation of Bealls's general and administrative functions into those of Palais Royal. Within three years, under-performing Bealls stores had been closed and the financial performance of the remaining Bealls stores had significantly improved.

Expenses of acquisition and consolidation notwithstanding, SRI's net sales increased at a 3.5 percent compound annual rate to $447.14 million in 1991, from $403.9 million in 1988.

According to Kenneth R. Pybus's story in the *Houston Business Journal,* in 1992 SRI wanted to go public and "sought to raise $192 million in a dual debt and equity offering, but pulled back when the response was less enthusiastic than expected." Jim Marcum, vice-chairman and chief financial officer for Stage Stores, later commented that the filing was made "in anticipation of future growth. Because the future growth really hadn't been executed yet, they just felt you couldn't get the best valuation for the company," so they withdrew the filing. Undaunted, SRI focused on growth through additional acquisitions and consolidations of complementary apparel retailers, improved sales performance of acquired stores, and opened new stores, especially in small rural markets. In June 1992 the company acquired Colorado-based Fashion Bar, Inc., a family-owned business having 71 stores of which approximately 75 percent were comparable to Palais Royal and Bealls stores while the remainder were small specialty stores. Including Fashion Bar, as of June 26, 1992, SRI operated 230 stores in Texas (141 stores), Colorado (66 stores), Oklahoma (nine stores), New Mexico (six stores), Alabama (three stores), California (three stores), and Wyoming (two stores).

When SRI reviewed its operations for the 1988–92 period, it could pinpoint the special features that distinguished Palais Royal and Bealls from other apparel retailers: namely, store size, layout, and location; merchandising strategy; customer service; operating systems and technology; and growth strategy.

The format and locations of the Palais Royal and Bealls stores offered a convenient and efficient shopping experience to customers. These stores, smaller than typical department stores yet larger than most specialty stores, accommodated apparel and accessories for an entire family. The stores were small enough for strategic locations in rural markets—where the company faced limited competition—or in convenient locations in outlying metropolitan areas. The company used a multimedia advertising approach to position its stores as the local

destination for fashionable, brand-name merchandise. In the early 1990s consumers in small markets usually had been able to shop for branded merchandise only in distant regional malls. Consequently, SRI's merchandising strategy focused on the traditionally higher-margin merchandise categories of family apparel and accessories.

The company emphasized excellent customer service and promoted its private-label, credit-card program, which in 1991 included over one million active accounts and contributed approximately 60 percent of net sales. Early in its history, Palais Royal had applied highly automated, integrated systems to reduce operating costs in labor-intensive areas, such as, merchandising, credit, personnel management, accounting, and distribution. These proprietary systems increased sales per square foot, reduced markdowns, lowered overhead, increased efficiency, and allowed store personnel to focus on customer service and selling. Furthermore, automation allowed buyers to select and allocate merchandise according to the local demographics and sales trends of the various stores.

The company's successful experience in choosing complementary acquisitions and the timely consolidation of Bealls brought out several facts. Firstly, many family-operated apparel retailers had healthy customer franchises but were under-performing due to lack of advanced systems and buying economies; secondly, gaining market share through acquisitions was generally more economical and offered greater opportunity for rapid growth than opening new stores.

Extending the Small-Market Franchise: 1993–96

In order to eliminate the possibility of having Specialty Retailers, Inc. be identified as only a specialty retail chain, in 1993 SRI's board of directors formed Apparel Retailers, Inc. (ARI), which concurrently became the parent company of SRI. Management recognized the potential of a unique franchise in small markets and committed the company to several initiatives for bringing about the full realization of this potential. These initiatives included: recruitment of a new senior management team; expansion in new markets through store openings and strategic acquisitions; emphasis on customer service and aggressive promotion of ARI's proprietary card; continuing refinement of ARI's concept; and closure of unprofitable stores.

On July 1, 1993, Carl Tooker—who had 25 years of administrative experience in the retail industry—was chosen as ARI president to lead the company's growth; a year later he became chairman and chief executive officer. Tooker succeeded 70-year-old founding President Bernard Fuchs, who retired after having been in the retail industry since 1944.

During 1994, ARI approved The Store Closure Plan that provided for the closure of the 40 under-performing Fashion Bar stores that were part of a 1992 acquisition and did not seem good candidates for consolidation into ARI's evolving small-market strategy. The ARI Board believed that the merchandising strategy and market positions of these stores—located in major regional malls within the Denver area—were not compatible with its overall strategy. Then in late 1994 ARI initiated the series of acquisitions that became the backbone of its expansion into the small-market niche. The company purchased the

45 stores of Beall-Ladymon, Inc. and reopened the stores in the first quarter of 1995 under the Stage name. Where did that name come from? Fashion Bar had operated a small group of stores known as Stage Stores, which already had become part of ARI's operation. In 1996 ARI completed the closure of the other Fashion Bar Stores but kept the Stage name.

The results of the Beall-Ladymon acquisition confirmed the value of ARI's strategy for growth. The acquired stores posted an annual sales increase of 78 percent and a store-contribution margin more than twice that of the previous year. The company also opened 23 new stores. Total ARI sales increased 17.4 percent to $682.62 million in 1995, compared to $581.46 million in 1994. This increase was due in part to increased sales from 23 stores opened during 1994–95. The increase, however, was partially offset by the effects of the Store Closure Plan and the 1995 devaluation of the Mexican peso, which negatively impacted sales at the six Bealls stores located on the Texas/Mexico border.

In keeping with its strategy of controlled geographic growth, ARI completed its second major entry into small markets with the June 1996 purchase of Uhlmans Inc., a privately held retailer with 34 locations in Ohio, Indiana, and Michigan—states where the company previously had no stores. These stores were similar in size and content to ARI's existing stores and were compatible with the company's retail concept. The company opened 35 new stores in the central United States and reported record sales of $776.55 million for 1996.

On October 25, 1996, more than four years after filing—and then withdrawing—an initial public offering (IPO) with the U.S. Securities and Exchange Commission, Apparel Retailers, Inc. changed its name to Stage Stores Inc., completed another IPO by selling 11 million shares of common stock at $16½ per share, and began to trade on the NASDAQ. In conjunction with its stepped-up expansion strategy, Stage Stores applied its small-market retail concept to micromarkets in communities with populations of from 4,000 to 12,000. The company capitalized on its favorable operating experience in scaling its store concept to an appropriate size of less than 12,000 square feet to operate in these small markets that generally had lower levels of competition as well as low labor and occupancy costs.

According to industry analysts David M. Mann and Ethan J. Meyers's December 1997 report on Stage Stores and the retail industry, during the last two decades, many small towns were experiencing ''a resurgence as computer and communications technologies allowed professionals to live/work in small towns and improve their quality of life.'' Furthermore—due to the proliferation of electronic, computer, and print media—customers in small markets were generally as aware of current fashion trends and were as sophisticated as consumers in larger urban centers. National retailers, such as J.C. Penney and Sears, Roebuck & Co., had abandoned small towns in favor of locations in cities and large suburban malls; the majority of independent apparel retailers had been put out of business by the national discount retailers that still operated in small towns, but these discounters did not carry the depth of family-oriented, fashionable brand-name merchandise offered by Stage.

Mann and Meyers's analysis of the regional family apparel sector found that there were 22 companies operating more than 850 stores generating $2.3 billion. Within the relatively short span of less than 10 years, Stage had recognized the latent opportunities in this market, noted the emergence of new lifestyles (for example, career women did not spend as much time shopping for the family as did the women of earlier decades), and developed a retail strategy based on convenient locations where all the family members of small communities could find nationally advertised, branded apparel.

Toward a New Millennium: 1997 and Beyond

With the June 1997 purchase of C.R. Anthony Company (Anthony's), Stage Stores strengthened its position as the dominant branded-apparel retailer in small-town America. Anthony's consisted of 246 family-apparel stores located in small markets in 16 states; the largest concentration of stores was in Texas, Oklahoma, Kansas, and New Mexico. Approximately 87 percent of Anthony's stores were located in small markets and communities having populations generally below 30,000. During the 1997 calendar year, Stage converted 130 of the acquired locations to its format, primarily under the Stage and Bealls trade names; the final group of the other 105 stores were converted and included in Stage's operation by the summer of 1998. The 11 Anthony's stores that were located in overlapping markets were closed.

Acquisition of the Anthony's stores gave Stage the opportunity to accelerate its expansion program in existing markets and to extend its presence in new markets. Both companies benefitted from synergizing their administrative infrastructures, leading, for example, to cost savings on overhead and enhanced opportunities for increased revenue and gross margins. Sales for 1997 increased 38.2 percent to $1.07 billion from $776.55 million in 1996.

As mentioned above, Stage Stores operated under three different store nameplates: Palais Royal, Bealls, and Stage. Both the Stage and the Bealls nameplates identified the company's small-market stores. The company kept the two nameplates because Bealls was so well known in its home states. The Palais Royal nameplate identified the company's larger-market stores located in suburban neighborhoods and high-traffic strip centers, mainly in the Houston and Galveston areas. Although these large stores generated a significant amount of cash, which the company applied mainly to continue expanding into small-market stores, their profit margins were lower than those of the smaller stores. Stage continued to focus its growth primarily on small markets and did not plan significant expansion of the Palais Royal stores.

On March 25, 1998, Stage Stores announced that the Office of the Comptroller of the Currency had granted the company preliminary approval of an application for a credit-card bank charter. Pending further approval by the FDIC and the completion of all remaining conditions, Chief Financial Officer James Marcum stated that the company felt ''confident that we will begin to see the economic benefits of the bank by the end of the third quarter.'' At this period in its history, the company had more than 2 million active credit accounts and proprietary credit-card purchases accounted for approximately 51 percent of the company's sales. Final approval of the bank charter allowed Stage to maximize fees and rates, the majority of which were subject to limits set by each state.

In April 1998 Stage began trading on the New York Stock Exchange. Sales for the first quarter of fiscal 1998 (ending May 2) peaked at a record $272.2 million, a 42.1 percent increase from 1997 first quarter sales of $191.5 million. Shares of stock rose to the $44-$52 price range, compared to the $16½ price per share when the company went public in October 1996.

During fiscal 1997 the company's store count almost doubled, going from 315 stores in 19 states to 606 stores in 24 states as of January 1998. Furthermore, Stage clearly demonstrated that it had the ability and wherewithal to successfully open and convert a significant number of stores. As the 21st century drew near, Stage Stores continued to implement its aggressive small-market growth strategy through organic store openings, strategic acquisitions, and efficient consolidations. In June 1998 the company gained a foothold in the Pacific Northwest through the acquisition of 15 Tri-North Department Stores in Montana, Nevada, Oregon, and Washington. Upon completion of the acquisition, Stage completely remodeled and re-merchandized the stores; they were opened under the Stage name and format in the early fall of 1998. For the near future, Stage identified six viable acquisitions of privately held companies having a total store count of 425. The company's total vision, however, encompassed 1,200 potential U.S. markets that met its criteria for remaining the store of choice for well known, national brand-name family apparel throughout America's small towns and communities.

Principal Subsidiaries

Specialty Retailers, Inc.

Further Reading

Mann, David M., and Ethan J. Meyers, ''Stage Stores, Inc.,'' New Orleans: Johnson Rice & Company L.L.C., pp. 1–4.

Palmeri, Christopher, ''Stage Stores: Smelling Nice for Choir Practice,'' *Forbes,* August 25, 1997, p. 64.

Pybus, Kenneth R. , ''Retail Firm Ready to Go Public Again,'' *Houston Business Journal,* June 21, 1996, pp. 1–2.

''Stage Stores Inc.: Initiating Coverage of Niche Retailer Thriving in Small-Town America,'' Chicago: EVEREN Securities, Inc. Equity Research, pp. 1, 3–8.

—Gloria A. Lemieux

The Stop & Shop Companies, Inc.

1385 Hancock Street
Quincy, Massachusetts 02169
U.S.A.
(781) 380-8000
Fax: (617) 770-6033

Wholly Owned Subsidiary of Royal Ahold N.V.
Incorporated: 1925 as Economy Grocery Stores
    Corporation
Employees: 30,000
Sales: $4.12 billion (1996)
SICs: 5311 Department Stores; 5411 Grocery Stores

The Stop & Shop Companies, Inc. runs the largest grocery chain in New England, with about 200 supermarkets and combination supermarket-general merchandise stores in Connecticut, Massachusetts, New York, and Rhode Island. Stop & Shop is a wholly owned subsidiary of Dutch international food retailer Royal Ahold N.V., the number four supermarket company in the United States. Ahold is the largest grocery concern on the East Coast of the United States, a position gained through the acquisition of several major chains starting in 1977. Stop & Shop, acquired by Ahold in 1996, is one of the Dutch firm's largest subsidiary operations.

Started As Economy Grocery Stores

When Sidney R. Rabb went into his uncle Julius's business, it was a small chain of stores known as the Economy Grocery Stores Company specializing in the sale of grocery products. Such specialization was hardly new—the Great American Tea Company (later A & P) had begun to modify the traditional general store as early as 1859, and even the practice of chain store ownership dated back into the 19th century. The chains did not formally begin until after 1912, however, when A & P introduced the "economy store," using efficient management and smaller store size to offer lower prices on a cash-and-carry basis—no credit, and no home delivery. The idea rapidly caught on across the country, and it was this merchandising

trend that Julius Robbins, his brother Joseph, and his nephew Sidney Rabb followed after the war. Following a period of instability, their chain, Economy, righted itself and, buoyed by the surging economy of the 1920s, began a program of rapid growth through acquisition in Massachusetts.

As chain store operators gained in strength they were soon able to convince manufacturers to sell to them directly instead of through the usual wholesalers, thus vastly reducing their costs and increasing the competitive advantage they already enjoyed over the traditional independent owner. Consumers preferred the lower prices of the chains; by the mid-1920s, Economy had expanded to 262 stores. In 1925 Sidney Rabb was named chairman, a post he would hold for the next 60 years. In the same year, Economy issued its first shares of public stock, and Norman S. Rabb joined his brother Sidney in the business. Ten years later, Irving Rabb, youngest of the brothers, also joined the company. Economy's operations continued to gain momentum; the brothers bought a chain of meat retailers and gave them space in each of their grocery stores.

Although the Great Depression brought many industries to a standstill, the resulting need for tight household budgeting was in many respects a boon to the Economy chain stores. The Rabbs continued to expand with the purchase in 1932 of 106 Grey United Stores located throughout northern New England. The supermarket, a concept that had originated in southern California, based its customer appeal on rock-bottom prices, increased product selection, self-service (the customer roamed about the store while the clerk remained at a cash register), and intensive advertising. To the store owner, the new format promised streamlined operation and excellent overall profit. In 1935 the Rabbs opened New England's first supermarket in Cambridge, Massachusetts, in a converted automobile assembly plant. First-year sales were nearly $2 million, equivalent to the revenue of 45 conventional stores.

Converted Fully to Supermarkets Following World War II

The Rabbs built more of the new stores as fast as they could, calling them Stop & Shop Supermarkets. The program continued to do well until the onset of World War II in 1941, when the food industry was swept up in the war effort and had little money or manpower with which to expand. The labor shortage during the war years, however, proved to be an unexpected boon to the supermarket business, as customers grew accustomed to serving themselves in all departments of the store, including the meat section. Such total self-service created lower labor costs and an increased number of purchases per customer. When the war ended, Economy was well-positioned to proceed with the conversion of its entire chain to the supermarket format, effectively reducing its number of stores while increasing total sales and profits. By 1947 annual sales topped $47 million and the company had changed its name to Stop & Shop, Inc., signaling its total commitment to the supermarket concept.

The postwar boom years saw another period of tremendous growth for Stop & Shop. In order to distribute products more efficiently, between 1948 and 1960 the company built a central bakery, a perishable goods distribution warehouse, and a grocery distribution center, all in strategic Massachusetts locations. Stop & Shop also quickly established itself in Rhode Island and Connecticut, and by the end of the 1950s the company was nearing $200 million in sales. The company made an important decision in 1961 to diversify outside the food business with its purchase of Bradlees, a small chain of discount department stores operating largely in shopping centers that already featured a Stop & Shop supermarket. The Rabbs saw in Bradlees a company based on the same high-volume, low-margin marketing used in the food industry. Their expertise soon turned a few moribund stores into a thriving chain. With the addition of new outlets each year, Bradlees' sales increased from $5 million to $107 million between 1962 and 1968.

Over the years Stop & Shop tried to develop and maintain excellent relations with the communities in which it did business. The company was one of the first to unionize in the 1930s; it created the Stop & Shop Foundation in 1951 to support various civic and cultural projects; and in 1967 it initiated its Consumer Board Program in response to growing public concern about health and environmental issues. In a further move to accommodate changing customer demands, in 1971 the company gave far greater autonomy to each of its store managers, freeing them to respond more directly to the needs of local customers. On the other hand, the company was twice sued for allegedly conspiring to fix the prices of certain grocery, meat, and dairy products. Both suits were settled.

Both Stop & Shop and Bradlees continued their robust growth into the mid-1980s. Building on an ever more sophisticated network of warehouse distribution centers, the two chains expanded their geographic range, their total number of stores, and their total sales. In addition, in 1968 and 1969, respectively, the company established the Medi Mart Drug Store Company and acquired the Charles B. Perkins Company, a 21-unit New England retailer of tobacco and sundries. A year later all four retailing chains were brought together as divisions of a newly renamed The Stop & Shop Companies, Inc., which at that point included 150 supermarkets, 52 Bradlees Department Stores, 10 Medi Marts, and 25 Perkins Tobacco Shops, together totaling about $750 million in sales. Four years later the company celebrated its first $1 billion year; it had doubled that figure by 1980.

Other acquisitions were not as successful. In 1978 Stop & Shop bought Off the Rax, a discount women's clothing store chain, but sold it after six less than spectacular years. Similarly, a venture into a more upscale segment of the department store world ended in 1987 with the sale of Almys, a 19-store chain the company had purchased just two years before. Despite a history of steady growth and good profits, Medi Mart and Perkins were also put on the block in the mid-1980s as Stop & Shop decided to concentrate its resources on its two biggest and most lucrative divisions, supermarkets and Bradlees. Bradlees reached a high of 169 units in 1987, combining with the 113 supermarkets to bring in $4.34 billion in sales.

In 1985 Sidney R. Rabb died and was succeeded as chairman by his son-in-law, Avram J. Goldberg. Goldberg and his wife Carol, who became president of the company, moved decisively to keep pace with the trend toward the "superstore," a greatly enlarged and further diversified model of the traditional supermarket. Superstores typically combined a grocery store with a general merchandise store. Stop & Shop's superstores—known as Super Stop & Shops—were immense, averaging 55,000 to 60,000 square feet in size, and were planned around a "street of shops" concept in which each class of product received its own well-defined and suitably decorated segment of the store and was offered to the consumer in an ever-larger variety of brands and packaging. In 1982 Stop & Shop completed its first superstore—considered to be the first superstore in New England. In certain respects this development brought shopping full circle back to the pattern of 100 years ago, when families made their progress through a series of neighborhood stores, each specializing in a different product line. The "street of shops" had simply moved indoors.

Taken Private in 1988

Stop & Shop took another step reminiscent of its past when, for the first time since 1924, it once again became a privately owned corporation. Responding to a hostile 1988 takeover bid by corporate raider Herbert Haft, Stop & Shop's board of directors enlisted the aid of Kohlberg Kravis Roberts & Company (KKR) in forming a privately held acquisition company to buy all outstanding shares for approximately $1.23 billion. The acquisition company merged with Stop & Shop, whose top management was largely unaffected. To pay down some of its hefty debt, Stop & Shop sold 70 Bradlees stores and eliminated 450 positions. In November 1989 the Goldbergs suddenly quit their jobs, reportedly because of differences between them and KKR officials, ending more than 70 years of family management. Lewis Schaeneman took over as chairman and CEO.

Stop & Shop became a public company once again in late 1991 through a public offering that sold 41 percent of the company for $212.5 million, the bulk of which was used to reduce debt at the still highly leveraged company. KKR retained control of the business following the offering. At the time of the offering Stop & Shop operated 117 stores in Massachusetts, Connecticut, Rhode Island, and New York, 62 of which were Super Stop & Shop combination stores. The company also owned the 130-unit Bradlees chain, but it was spun off to the public in the summer of 1992 in order to further focus on the core supermarkets and to further reduce Stop & Shop's $1.1 billion debt load.

Robert G. Tobin, who had become president of Stop & Shop in March 1993, added the title of CEO in May 1994 and the title of chairman in January 1995, as Schaeneman gradually retired. One day before Schaeneman's last day in office, around 60 FBI agents raided the company headquarters as an outgrowth of an investigation of possible mishandling of merchandise incentive funds paid by manufacturers through brokers to retailers. In June 1997 Stop & Shop—without acknowledging guilt—agreed to pay $700,000 to settle allegations over vendor promotions and temporary price reductions.

As Stop & Shop continued to improve its financial health in the mid-1990s, expansion once again became the watchword. In mid-1995 the company made plans to enter the highly competitive, highly fragmented greater New York City area through the opening of superstores. In November 1995 Stop & Shop acquired Purity Supreme, a chain based in North Billerica, Massachusetts, for about $255 million. To satisfy regulators, the company had to divest 17 overlapping stores, meaning that it gained a net 38 stores through the deal. The purchase also temporarily extended Stop & Shop's territory into New Hampshire, but the units in that state were soon sold off. Also gained with Purity was a 64-unit chain of Li'l Peach convenience stores, but this noncore operation was quickly divested, in mid-1996, to Tedeschi Food Shops Inc. of Rockland, Massachusetts. In December 1995 Stop & Shop spent $87 million for Melmarkets, which ran a Foodtown chain with 17 units on Long Island, thereby gaining its first foothold in the New York region.

Acquired by Royal Ahold in Mid-1996

By this time the expanding Stop & Shop had caught the eye of the highly acquisitive Dutch global food retailing giant Royal Ahold N.V., which acquired Stop & Shop in its entirety, including the KKR stake, in July 1996 for $2.9 billion. Stop & Shop thus became another in a string of eastern U.S. grocery subsidiaries of Ahold. The Dutch company had first gained a foothold in the United States in 1977 when it bought the Bi-Lo chain in North and South Carolina and Georgia. Ahold then purchased the Pennsylvania-based Giant Food Stores, which operated under the Giant, Edwards, and Martin's brands, in 1981. Finast Supermarkets, of Ohio, Connecticut, New York, and Massachusetts, was bought in 1988. To gain regulatory approval of its purchase of Stop & Shop, Ahold agreed to sell 29 stores in Massachusetts, Connecticut, and Rhode Island, states in which Stop & Shop and Edwards had overlapping operations. Also in July 1996, William J. Grize, who had joined the company in 1967, was named president of Stop & Shop; he added the CEO title as well in December 1997, with Tobin remaining chairman.

Within days of closing the Stop & Shop deal, Ahold reorganized its U.S. operations. The reorganization gave Stop & Shop 35 Edwards stores in Massachusetts, Connecticut, Rhode Island, and New York. The New York stores, however, were located in counties north of the New York City region, as Ahold had decided to halt Stop & Shop's expansion there, turning the Long Island locations acquired in the Melmarkets deal over to Edwards. As a result, Stop & Shop solidified its position as the largest supermarket chain in New England, with nearly 200 units by the end of 1996. The additional stores were expected to push the company's annual revenue to more than $5.3 billion, making Stop & Shop Ahold's largest unit worldwide.

In May 1998 Ahold agreed to acquire Landover, Maryland-based Giant Food Inc. for about $2.7 billion. The purchase of Giant Food—which operated 173 stores in Washington, D.C., Maryland, Virginia, Delaware, New Jersey, and Pennsylvania—made Ahold the fourth largest supermarket company in the United States and solidified its number one position on the East Coast. Stop & Shop, meanwhile, was concentrating on its core New England market and was expanding geographically only in three counties north of New York City: Westchester, Dutchess, and Putnam.

Further Reading

Alaimo, Dan, ''Stop & Shop to Open Separate Video Store,'' *Supermarket News*, July 19, 1993, p. 27.

Baljko, Jennifer L., ''Ahold Closes Stop & Shop Deal,'' *Supermarket News*, July 29, 1996, p. 1.

——, ''Ahold Realigning Stores, Officials,'' *Supermarket News*, August 5, 1996, p. 4.

Collins, Glenn, ''Circling the Grocery Carts: Stop & Shop Plans a Foothold in the New York Region,'' *New York Times*, August 5, 1995, pp. 31, 33.

Emert, Carol, ''Stop & Shop Completes Purity Deal by Agreeing to Sell Off 17 Stores,'' *Supermarket News*, November 6, 1995, p. 4.

Farnsworth, Steve, ''Stop & Shop Going Public Again,'' *Supermarket News*, October 14, 1991, p. 1.

Fox, Bruce, ''Stop & Shop Gets Stronger,'' *Chain Store Age Executive*, June 1992, p. 23.

Gold, Howard, ''Learning the Hard Way,'' *Forbes*, May 19, 1986, p. 80.

Goldberg, Avram J., ''Stop & Shop Chief Talks Business,'' *Progressive Grocer*, April 1984, p. 25.

Hirsch, James S., and Charles Goldsmith, ''KKR's Dutch Treat: Stop & Shop Sold to Ahold NV for $1.8 Billion,'' *Wall Street Journal*, March 29, 1996, pp. A3, A8.

Peak, Hugh S., and Ellen F. Peak, *Supermarket Merchandising and Management*, Englewood Cliffs, New Jersey: Prentice-Hall, 1977.

Petreycik, Richard M., ''Stop & Shop Comes Back in a Big Way,'' *Progressive Grocer*, March 1991, p. 104.

Schaeffer, Larry, ''Tobin's Turn,'' *Progressive Grocer*, September 1994, p. 28.

''Stop & Shop Plans $176M Bradlees Public Offer,'' *Discount Store News*, May 18, 1992, p. 1.

''Stop & Shop Settles Billback, TPR Dispute,'' *Supermarket News*, June 16, 1997, p. 1.

Zimmerman, M. A., *The Super Market: A Revolution in Distribution*, New York: McGraw Hill, 1955.

Zwiebach, Elliot, ''FBI Raids Stop & Shop Main Office, Data Center,'' *Supermarket News*, February 6, 1995, p. 1.

——, ''Stop & Shop's New Properties,'' *Supermarket News*, March 25, 1996, p. 1.

——, ''Stop & Shop Starts Internal Probe,'' *Supermarket News*, February 20, 1995, p. 42.

——, ''Stop & Shop to Buy Purity Supreme Chain,'' *Supermarket News*, May 1, 1995, p. 1.

—Jonathan Martin
—updated by David E. Salamie

Sukhoi Design Bureau Aviation Scientific-Industrial Complex

125284 Moscow
Ulitsa Polikarpov, 23 A
Russia
7-095-945-65-25
Fax: 7-095-200-42-43

State-Owned Company
Incorporated: 1939 as Sukhoi Design Bureau
Employees: 17,000
SICs: 3721 Aircraft

Sukhoi Design Bureau Aviation Scientific-Industrial Complex has earned a reputation for quality and originality, although against great odds. Its founder, Pavel Sukhoi, was no favorite of Stalin and the firm itself was disbanded for a time before a glorious rebirth in the 1950s. Since then, many of its products have been widely used by the former Soviet Union and its allies. World class designs such as the Su-27 interceptor and the Su-26 aerobatic plane dominate the record books, and present a rare bright spot in Russia's international trade potential.

Starting with Tupolev in Tsarist Russia

Pavel Osipovich Sukhoi was born in 1895 in a small village in Byelorussia. He eventually made it to the illustrious Imperial Moscow Higher Technical Institute. Due to the ongoing war with Germany, he entered the army in 1916, but returned home in 1920 due to failing health. Once again at the Institute, he wrote a thesis on fighter design under his mentor, Andrei Tupolev, who had already established a name for himself at the center of Russian aviation circles.

Upon graduation in 1925, Sukhoi joined the Central Aero-Hydronamics Institute (TsAGI), a forerunner of the Tupolev Design Bureau. Sukhoi subsequently played a significant role in some of the firm's designs—torpedo boats as well as aircraft. His career progressed rapidly; in 1938 he was named design department deputy chief. His work on the record-setting ANT-25, which flew across the North Pole to the United States,

earned him worldwide attention and decorations from the Soviet government.

World War I convinced the world's leaders that air would be the key to the next conflict. All the major powers raced to develop the next generation of military aircraft to dominate the skies. Sukhoi led the Tupolev bureau's entrant in a contest to develop a light bomber for the Soviet military. This entrant, designated the Su-2, was chosen over designs from the Polikarpov, Nyeman, and Grigorovich firms in 1938. The next year, a new design bureau, led by Sukhoi, was created at an aircraft factory in Kharkov.

Stalling Under Stalin

Sukhoi disliked the factory's intellectually isolated location and it was moved to Moscow (Podmoskovye airfield) by 1940. Sukhoi named an invaluable associate, Evgenii Alekseyevich Ivanov, chief engineer after the move to Moscow. He was instrumental in arranging the evacuation to Perm to avoid the advancing Nazi forces in October 1941. While Sukhoi liked to concern himself with prototypes, Ivanov had a flair for organizing production on a large scale. "I'm a designer—not a production controller, not an organizer, and not a fixer," said Sukhoi, quoted in the underground account *Tupolevskaya sharaga* (reprinted as *Stalin's Aviation Gulag*). Ivanov was all of these, and the two reportedly shared a wonderfully complementary relationship.

Like his comrade, Andrei Tupolev, Sukhoi fell under the suspicion of Stalin. However, he did not suffer incarceration, like Tupolev. Although Sukhoi was decorated for his work on certain designs, he was omitted from honors typically given to other general designers. While his peers were made generals in the military during World War II, Sukhoi retained the rank of ensign that he had earned in World War I.

In 1942, Stalin asked Sukhoi to oversee development of the Pe-2 aircraft after its designer, Vladimir Petlyakov, died. Sukhoi, immersed in the development of the Su-6 ground attack aircraft, hesitated to accept, and Vladimir Myasischev took his place instead. Although test models of the Su-6 proved capable and the design earned Sukhoi an award, Stalin did not want to reduce total aircraft output by converting production to the new design. The engines used by the plane never reached production either. Throughout this time, Sukhoi lacked a devoted production facility.

After the war's end, the Sukhoi OKB returned to Moscow and developed their first jet aircraft, the Su-9. It brought to the Soviet Union such innovations as an ejection seat, hydraulic controls, booster rockets for takeoff, and a braking parachute—all features that would remain standard on jet fighters for the next 20 years. However, Stalin felt the Su-9 looked too similar to the Messerschmitt 262, the Luftwaffe's supreme fighter, and preference was given to the jets of Artem Mikoyan's design bureau, such as the MiG-9, MiG-15, and MiG-17. Furthermore, the Sukhoi OKB was effectively liquidated in December 1949. Sukhoi again found himself at the Tupolev OKB, this time as deputy chief designer. Ivanov joined him, assuming leadership of Tupolev's flight testing.

Catching Up in the Cold War

After the death of Stalin in 1953, the Sukhoi OKB was revived (this time near Khodynskoye field in central Moscow) and Sukhoi rejoined the game with gusto. He submitted proposals for four supersonic aircraft, two with delta wings and two with swept wings. The novelty of the proposal—both the wing shapes were relatively untried—prompted some derision from other designers, such as Aleksandr Yakovlev, who had long had a habit of criticizing his competitors even since Tupolev first jockeyed with him for support under Stalin. One of the new swept-wing planes called the S-1 was the first to bring Mach 2 (twice the speed of sound) sonic booms to the Soviet Union in 1955. It spawned the Su-7 family of fighter-bombers. Likewise, the delta-winged T-3 spawned the Su-9, Su-11, and Su-15 interceptors.

The T-4 was unique, however. Although only one was ever built, it remained a highlight of the firm's history. This time it was Tupolev rather than Yakovlev who gave Sukhoi flak. "Sukhoi will never be able to manage such a vehicle," he said, according to *OKB Sukhoi: A History of the Design Bureau and Its Aircraft.* "I assert this because he is my disciple." Sukhoi parried that that was the very reason he *would* be able to pull it off.

Similar in appearance to the American XB-70 Valkyrie, the T-4 was created to give the Soviet Union high-speed, high-altitude bombing or reconnaissance capabilities. It was made of titanium and designed to reach speeds of Mach 3. It incorporated several features which put it well ahead of its time when it first flew in 1972. The most striking was the nose, which dropped to allow the pilot forward vision during takeoffs and landings. In cruising flight, there was no forward vision at all and the crew relied entirely on instruments (a periscope was installed in the prototype, however). The fly-by-wire control system and canards also seemed advanced. On top of all that, the plane was huge and was powered by four massive one-of-a-kind Kolesov jet engines.

Pavel Sukhoi died in 1975. After some delay, Evgenii Ivanov was designated his successor in 1977. Since the 1960s, he had handled the necessary reporting to the Communist Party,

freeing Sukhoi from this administrative burden. He had also taken on more management duties as Sukhoi's health worsened.

In 1969, Sukhoi competed with Ilyushin Yakovlev for a Ministry of Aircraft Industry contract for a new ground attack aircraft. Sukhoi's entry, the winner, became the Su-25 and a mainstay in the Soviet military. Around the same time, Mikhail Petrovich Simonov joined the company. He had previously headed his own design bureau specializing in gliders. Simonov earned a Lenin Prize for his work on the Su-24 fighter-bomber in the 1970s. This aircraft employed a variable-sweep wing (swing-wing) inspired by the successful American F-111.

The fighter aircraft of the Vietnam War period generally had been conceived as capable of two roles: ground attack and interception. Experience proved the interception role required a specialized machine, however. The United States developed the F-14 Tomcat and F-15 Eagle, two very fast, high-altitude aircraft that excelled at air combat. It was against this backdrop that Sukhoi began work on what would become the Su-27, one of its most successful products.

The competition for this project began in 1971 and included the Mikoyan and Yakovlev design bureaus. Sukhoi's entry was chosen and reportedly subjected to more wind tunnel tests than any other Soviet aircraft except the Tu-144 supersonic transport.

Unfortunately, the T-10 ultimately failed to meet its design objectives, chiefly due to avionics (electronic equipment) that were much heavier than anticipated and Lyulka engines that burned more fuel than had been promised. Simonov, who had become general director in 1983, anguished with his staff for a solution. Production was canceled in order to refine the aircraft's aerodynamics.

The new version, known as the T-10S, was a winner. The type began mass production in the late 1980s and numerous variants, including carrier-based ones, were developed. It stocked the air forces of satellite countries, as well as India, before the collapse of the Soviet Union. Syria and China later began flying the Su-27, the latter country acquiring production rights worth $2 billion.

In 1988, Viktor Pugachev piloted a stripped-down version to break several climbing records set by F-15 pilots. During further testing, the famous "Pugachev cobra" maneuver, in which the aircraft pitches nose-up but continues level flight, was developed. The only plane in the world capable of such "dynamic braking," it proved a natural choice for the Russian Knights demonstration team.

The torch passed from the Su-27 to a derivative, the Su-35, as the most advanced Russian fighter. The plane, under production in the mid-1990s, incorporated state-of-the-art advances such as thrust-vectoring nozzles on the engines and advanced composites in the airframe.

After the Cold War

Besides heading the Sukhoi Design Bureau, Simonov has also served as Russia's Deputy Minister of Aircraft Industry. He was called on in this capacity to develop a new aerobatic plane, as Russian stunt pilots had suffered a plague of accidents due to in-flight breakups in aircraft such as the Yak-50. Sukhoi's resulting design, the Su-26, was made to handle the stresses of virtually any maneuver. A huge piston engine and extensive use of composite materials gave the plane superior lightness and power as well as strength. Thanks to the new aircraft, Soviet aerobatic pilots began to dominate the world championships by the late 1980s. It also proved a striking success for Soviet trade. The Pompano Air Center began distributing it in America, making the first U.S. purchase of a production aircraft from the Soviet Union. The $200,000 aircraft also proved popular in newly affluent southeast Asia, and a Singapore investor bought 31 percent of the subsidiary manufacturing these planes, Sukhoi PTS.

Simonov and his staff began working on a supersonic business jet (SSBJ) in 1988 in order to meet a perceived need among international business travelers. Gulfstream Aerospace Corporation, a well-established American producer of business jets, signed on to the project the next year. However, in spite of extensive design work on numerous possible configurations, the S-21 was grounded after Gulfstream abandoned the project in 1992.

Sukhoi also began work on a larger supersonic transport known as the S-51. The company planned to complete a prototype by 2005. Plans to develop the Su-37, a follow-up to the successful Su-27 fighter, were canceled in 1992 amid a lack of interest among domestic customers and foreign investors. Other projects in the works at the end of the century included an advanced military trainer (S-54), a utility aircraft to be powered by General Electric engines (S-80), a light plane (S-84), and a crop duster (Su-38). At this time, Sukhoi was devoting half of its attention to commercial projects.

Wing-in-ground-effect (WIG) vehicles formed a final group of advanced studies. WIG seaplanes, besides being able to take off and land in water, were designed to specifically exploit the reduced drag and increased lift found when flying just above the surface of the water.

Russia's armament sales increased to about $3.5 billion per year in the late-1990s. Sukhoi aircraft made up a significant portion. India ordered 40 Su-30 fighters worth $1.8 billion, and Indonesia also bought a dozen. Poland planned to manufacture Su-39 aircraft, a derivative of the Su-25, to contribute towards repayment of $2 billion of Russian debt.

Principal Subsidiaries

Sukhoi PTS.

Further Reading

Anoshkin, Viktor, ''Russia to Make New 'Concordsky' Executive Jets,'' *Reuters,* November 13, 1995.

Antonov, Vladimir, et al, *OKB Sukhoi: A History of the Design Bureau and Its Aircraft,* Leicester, England: Midland Publishing, Aerofax, 1996.

Covault, Craig, and Boris Rybak, ''Sukhoi May Seek US Partner for New Fighter,'' *Aviation Week and Space Technology,* September 27, 1993.

Fink, Donald E., ''New Su-35 Boasts Greater Agility,'' *Aviation Week and Space Technology,* December 6, 1993, pp. 44–46.

Gustafson, David A., ''Russian Sukhoi for America,'' *Air Progress,* August 1988.

Kerber, L. L. [A. Sharagin, pseud.], *Stalin's Aviation Gulag: A Memoir of Andrei Tupolev and the Purge Era,* edited by Von Hardesty, Washington and London: Smithsonian Institution Press, 1996. Originally published as *Tupolevskaya sharaga* (Tupolev's special prison workshop), Druck: Possev-Verlag, V. Gorachek KG, Frankfurt/M., 1971.

Mehta, Ashok K., ''A Whiff of Corruption to the Sukhoi-30 Deal,'' *Rediff on the Net,* http://www.rediff.co.in./news/may/14sukhoi.htm.

Novichkov, Nickolay, ''Desperate for Sales, Moscow Courts Seoul,'' *Aviation Week and Space Technology,* November 18, 1996, p. 31.

——, ''Sukhoi Set to Exploit Thrust Vector Control,'' *Aviation Week and Space Technology,* August 26, 1996.

''Russian Aircraft May Be Assembled in Poland,'' *ITAR-TASS,* December 12, 1997.

''Russian Jets Fly Asian Skies,'' *The Jakarta Post,* August 11, 1997.

''Russian 'Sukhoi' Fighter-Maker Plans to Feed Itself,'' *ITAR-TASS,* September 3, 1996.

Rybak, Boris, ''Russians Advance Privatization Plans,'' *Aviation Week and Space Technology,* March 29, 1993, p. 60.

Smith, Gene, ''Socialist Tool,'' *Air Progress,* June 1990.

Strokan, Sergei, ''India-Russia: New Delhi's Arms Buying Spree Gets Moscow Excited,'' *Inter Press Service English News Wire,* March 26, 1997.

''Sukhoi Design Bureau Expands Civil Aircraft Development Efforts,'' *Aviation Week and Space Technology,* June 5, 1989.

—Frederick C. Ingram

Sundt Corp.

4101 East Irvington Road
Tucson, Arizona 85714
U.S.A.
(520) 748-7555
Fax: (520) 747-9673
Web site: http://www.sundt.com

Private Company
Incorporated: 1946 as M.M. Sundt Construction Co.
Employees: 1,375
Sales: $436 million (1997 est.)
SICs: 1541 Industrial Buildings & Warehouses; 1542
  Nonresidential Construction, Not Elsewhere
  Classified; 1611 Highway & Street Construction;
  1623 Water, Sewer & Utility Lines; 1629 Heavy
  Construction, Not Elsewhere Classified; 1522
  Residential Construction, Not Elsewhere Classified

A major general contractor in the United States and abroad, Tucson-based Sundt Corp. provides a full range of construction services to commercial, industrial, and government clients worldwide, concentrating on large-scale projects that cost between $250,000 and $100 million. In the construction business for more than a century, Sundt boasted a diverse resume of completed construction projects, starting from its first big project, a 55-foot dam built for the Agua Pura Water Company in 1910. In the decades to follow, the company's operations diversified both geographically and across the spectrum of public- and private-sector commercial and industrial construction work. Sundt was the general contractor for the nuclear research facilities at Los Alamos, the company called upon to build the underground launching sites for intercontinental ballistic missiles, and the general contractor for various residential housing projects, utility plants, and numerous highways in its home state of Arizona. During the 1990s, the company, through its subsidiaries, was involved in industrial construction, heavy construction, military housing construction, and a host of commercial and residential construction projects through its building division. Internationally, Sundt had built projects in Asia, Europe, South America, Central America, the Middle East, and Australia.

19th-Century Roots

Mauritz Martinsen Sundt, the patriarch of the Sundt family, was born in a small town north of Oslo in Gjovik, Norway, in 1863. Independent and industrious, Sundt decided to strike out on his own at age 12 and opted for a life on the sea. He joined Norway's merchant marine and spent the bulk of his teenage years sailing the Baltic and Atlantic waters, earning his keep by honing his skills with the tools of a ship's carpenter. After sailing aboard old windjammers for four years, Sundt settled in the United States, where his last voyage as a merchant marine had taken him. He moved to Wisconsin and spent several years working as a carpenter on houses and farms before his penchant for living life on the move returned and prodded him west. Sundt was not alone in his desire to travel toward the Pacific Coast; wave after wave of settlers were migrating west in search of the rumored riches to be found in the Western Territories, but Sundt's trek was cut short when his wife died at the couple's first stop in Colorado. From Colorado, Sundt set out on his own again and moved to Las Vegas, then part of New Mexico Territory. At the time, Las Vegas had recently made the transition from a fractured community comprising scattered tent camps into a bustling town boasting the stereotypical flavor of the Wild West. The presence of the Santa Fe Railroad line running through the town had guaranteed its survival, and also brought the unseemly, attendant trappings of a boom town in the American frontier. Sundt was a devout Methodist who did not smoke, drink alcohol, dance, or work on Sundays, but in Las Vegas, where lawlessness and drunkenness held sway, he had found his permanent home.

Although his travels had spanned more than a decade, Sundt was only 27 years old when he settled in Las Vegas and started a business with another carpenter named V. A. Henry. The pair purchased a local construction company that included a planing mill and a cabinet shop and renamed the enterprise Henry & Sundt, Contractors and Builders. With a new business and a permanent residence to call his own, Sundt remarried and fathered nine children, adding to the three his first wife had given birth to. From this amply-sized family, the future generations of Sundt management were drawn—the foundation upon which a family dynasty was created—but for Mauritz Sundt the idea of a long string of Sundt descendants in the construction business was far from his most pressing concern. Sundt's primary goal as the 19th century ended was keeping his fledgling construction firm in business. To his descendants would fall the responsibility of perpetuating the family name in the business world; Sundt had to establish the business in the first place.

Toward this end, one of the first contracts Henry & Sundt, Contractors and Builders received was for the construction and remodeling of hospital facilities at Fort Stanton, located in southern New Mexico. Sundt took an active role in the completion of the project, moving his family in a covered wagon to Fort Stanton to personally supervise the work. His attention to detail and his desire for control eventually led to sole command over the construction business. Several years after the Fort Stanton project, Sundt bought out Henry and renamed the company, M.M. Sundt, Builder. It was a straightforward name, without pretensions, which matched the reserved personality of the conservative Methodist who headed the company, but the scale of the construction projects undertaken by M.M. Sundt belied the unassuming nature characterizing both the man and the company. Early in its history, M.M. Sundt established its future as a contractor for large construction projects.

M.M. Sundt began work on the project that would establish the company's forte in 1910. It was Mauritz Sundt's first major construction project, the construction of a large dam in Peterson Canyon for the Agua Pura Water Company. Using mules and wagonloads of laborers, carpenters, and mule skinners, Sundt built the 55-foot-tall structure for a total cost of $21,843. The dam, which was still in use when M.M. Sundt's successor celebrated its 100th anniversary, did much to establish Sundt's reputation as a reliable and skillful contractor for the large-scale construction projects that would proliferate in a burgeoning country. Buoyed by its newly established prominence, M.M. Sundt was awarded contracts for the construction of homes, schools, government buildings, and business establishments, making a name for itself as one of the prominent general

contractors in the region. Among the buildings constructed by M.M. Sundt during its formative years were the Las Vegas Y.M.C.A., built in 1905; the company's first shopping center, completed in 1919; The Meadows Hotel, built in 1923; and the Johnson Mortuary, designed by Mauritz's son, Thoralf, completed in 1926.

The Great Depression and World War II

By the end of the 1920s, Mauritz's sons were beginning to exert a greater influence over the family business. Thoralf had distinguished himself as an architect, serving for many years as the Chief Architect for the Bureau of Architecture of the Methodist Church while he worked for his firm, Sundt & Wenner of Philadelphia. In 1929, he designed a new Methodist church to be built in Tucson, Arizona, which drew the attention of his brother John, who had been assisting Mauritz Sundt for a number of years. Mauritz sent his son John to Tucson to bid on the job, which the Sundt's won. To complete the job, John moved to Tucson and after the church was completed he remained in Tucson, establishing the first branch office of his family's business. For the next several years, the two offices of the company operated separately, with one compensating for slow construction periods experienced by the other, but before long the Arizona office demonstrated a more vibrant vitality than the Las Vegas office. Before the end of the 1930s, the hierarchical order of the two offices was reversed, with the Tucson office becoming the company's headquarters and the Las Vegas office relegated to a divisional office for New Mexico. The transfer of authority between the two offices mirrored an identical transfer of power between father and son. Midway through the decade, John Sundt acquired his father's interest in the company and became the new leader of M.M. Sundt Construction Co. (The new name, a slight variation on the original, was taken from the name John Sundt used when he had applied for an Arizona contractor's license for the Methodist church project.)

John Sundt took over the family business at an inauspicious time in American history. The nation was mired in an economic depression of an unprecedented magnitude when he bought out his father, but M.M. Sundt Construction managed to stay in business during the harsh economic times by completing work ordered by the Public Works Administration. In 1936, the company was awarded a contract for six projects included in the expansion of the University of Arizona's Tucson campus. The projects, constructed simultaneously, included the erection of six separate buildings that kept M.M. Sundt financially afloat during the latter half of the 1930s.

The lingering effects of the Great Depression were wiped away by the early 1940s, as the United States prepared to enter World War II. By this time, as the nation geared itself for war and the voracious demand for materials of all sorts, M.M. Sundt was regarded as one of the leading general contractors in the southwestern United States, a vaunted position that directed a considerable amount of construction work into John Sundt's lap. In 1942, the company's New Mexico Division—its former Las Vegas headquarters—built a railroad battalion camp at Clovis and a mobile air training depot station at Oxnard, while the Tucson office busied itself with the construction of an aircraft modification center that later served as an early home for the Tucson International Airport. The company also served as the contractor for the Naval Air Station at El Centro, California, but by far the biggest and most noteworthy construction project undertaken by M.M. Sundt during the war years was located on a remote site in the mountains northwest of Santa Fe. The facilities built by the company would later be known to the world as Los Alamos, where scientists involved in the Manhattan Project created the first atomic bomb.

Initially, the secret project totaled $300,000 of work for the company's New Mexico Division, but by November 1943, the contract's value had ballooned to more than $7 million. The work completed at Los Alamos, which remained a secret to all those at M.M. Sundt until the atomic bomb was dropped on Hiroshima on August 6, 1945, provided the company with money it would sorely need in the years immediately following the conclusion of World War II, when construction activity in the country slowed to a crawl. During this lull in business, John Sundt organized the company as an Arizona corporation, naming himself president and conferring upon himself the authority accorded to the company's principal shareholder. Next, he decided to shutter the company's New Mexico Division and replace it with a new company called Albuquerque Gravel Products, Inc., which supplied ready-mixed concrete and construction aggregates throughout New Mexico.

Postwar Expansion and Diversification

The postwar economic boom period swept up M.M. Sundt by 1948, when the company once again enjoyed a steady stream of business. In 1948, expansion at the University of Arizona was underway and M.M. Sundt figured as one of the prime contractors presiding over the construction of new buildings for the university. In subsequent expansion efforts, M.M. Sundt was frequently employed as a contractor. The company built an addition to the chemistry and physics building in 1948 and built the university's new aeronautical engineering building in 1949. By the time M.M. Sundt was building its first two postwar buildings at the University of Arizona, one of the university's students had joined the company's fold, Thoralf's son, Robert S. Sundt. Robert Sundt graduated in 1950 and quickly rose through the company's ranks to become one of the key figures responsible for shaping the family business's future. In 1957, he was joined by his brother, H. Wilson Sundt; together the two brothers directed their family business during the latter half of the 20th century.

Against the backdrop of a new generation of Sundts taking their place in the family business, the construction activity at M.M. Sundt occurred at a decidedly animated pace. The company entrenched its position and began to move far afield, developing into a powerful, multifaceted contractor. In 1952, the company made its foray into the heavy construction business when it entered a joint-venture project to build a new, 14,000-foot runway at Davis Monthan Air Force Base near Tucson. M.M. Sundt also resumed its work for the University of Arizona by constructing the university's student union building, library, music building, and several dormitories. M.M. Sundt was called upon to install sewers, water lines, and other utilities around the Tucson area to accommodate the city's rapid growth. The company also renewed its business relationship with the

U.S. military, drawing upon its experience with the construction of Los Alamos to earn contracts for other massive construction projects. During the 1950s, M.M. Sundt constructed the first underground ballistic missile launching facility, erecting its pioneering structure at Vandenberg Air Force Base in California. The underground structure at Vandenberg became the prototype for all Titan I Missile installations subsequently built in the United States.

M.M. Sundt's stature as a general contractor, which had risen to regional awareness by the beginning of the 1940s, increased to a national and international level by the beginning of the 1960s, thanks in large part to the much-publicized military work the company had completed. During the 1960s, the company's work at Los Alamos and at Vandenberg paved the way for additional construction projects, including the Atlas "F" complex of 12 missile silos at Schilling Air Force Base in Salina, Kansas, built with two other partners for a total cost of $51 million, and the first launch facilities for the Titan II intercontinental ballistic missiles at Vandenberg. M.M. Sundt also contributed to another chapter in American history by building Launch Pad 39-A at Cape Canaveral, Florida, which was the site of many Apollo missions, including Apollo 11, the flight that put man on the moon for the first time, and the site used to launch the space shuttle Columbia. In Arizona, the company constructed many of the highways in its home state and continued to construct new buildings for the University of Arizona.

The 1960s proved to be a decade of remarkable achievement for M.M. Sundt, establishing it as a contractor with a roster of talents. The company built its first high-rise office building in 1966, the 21-story Tucson Federal Savings Tower. It ventured into the international market for the first time in 1962 by constructing sewage treatment facilities in Trinidad, West Indies. M.M. Sundt joined the expansion of southern Arizona's mining and utility concerns, constructing an addition to the Cochise Power Plant, a research laboratory for The Anaconda Company, and an expansion of ASARCO's copper smelter in Hayden, Arizona. As these projects were underway, the company also moved into the construction of prefabricated housing, forming its Dyna-Strux division in 1968 to manufacture and market a patented modular wall and roof system for homes and schools. Unlike the hundreds of projects carried out by the company, the attempt to build a profitable prefabricated housing business failed. Only 100 homes and several portable school buildings were constructed with Dyna-Strux components, but despite the division's failure the foray into prefabricated housing paved the way for a huge contract the company was awarded in the 1970s. As in the 1960s, M.M. Sundt was active on all construction fronts during the 1970s. The company's 80th anniversary marked the beginning of a decade of profound growth and meaningful internal changes.

During the 1970s, M.M. Sundt completed more than 700 projects, ranging from commercial and government buildings in Arizona, to $200 million worth of highway projects, to condominiums in Saudi Arabia. The 1975 labor and management contract to build 485 condominiums in Saudi Arabia's Eastern Province for the Arabian American Oil Company was an indirect offshoot of the company's failed attempt at prefabricated housing, helping to assuage the sting suffered from the formation of Dyna-Strux. M.M. Sundt's work in Saudi Arabia extended to 1986, by which time the value of the work completed by the company exceeded $750 million. At home, management decided to convert M.M. Sundt into an employee-owned corporation, which eventually led to the formation of Sundt Corp. at the end of the decade as a holding company, under which M.M. Sundt became a wholly owned subsidiary.

1970s: The Modern Sundt Takes Shape

Several new subsidiaries made their debut under the unfurling Sundt corporate umbrella during the 1970s and 1980s, defining the parameters of the company's widening operational scope. In 1972, the company acquired Novato, California-based C.R. Fedrick, Inc., a contractor for water resource projects that included dams, pipelines, water transmission and distribution lines, pumping stations, and canals. The company's corporate structure was fleshed out further with the establishment of a military housing division in 1984, which was formed to meet the demand ushered in by the Department of Defense Design/Build program. In 1989, as the company's centennial approached, Sundt acquired San Diego, California-based Ninteman Construction Co., which had played a leading role in the construction of commercial, industrial, and institutional projects throughout southern California since 1947.

As centennial celebrations were underway, Sundt entered a decade that would bring the final additions to its corporate structure for the new century ahead. During the 1990s, Sundt withstood the pernicious effects of a severe economic recession thanks to its diverse range of capabilities and an expansive geographic presence, which insulated the company from declining business tied to one particular type of construction in one particular market. When the economy turned considerably more robust, Sundt returned to its acquisitive approach to growth by purchasing CRF Integrated Solutions through its C.R. Fedrick subsidiary. Organized as a subsidiary of C.R. Fedrick, CRF Integrated Solutions was a provider of telecommunications facilities throughout California. The company's next acquisition followed in 1996, when it acquired Sacramento, California-based Earl Construction Company. For more than a decade prior to the acquisition, Sundt had engaged in business with Earl Construction through various joint-venture projects. Earl Construction's addition to Sundt's stable of operating companies added a general contractor with strong market presence in northern California.

Supported by five divisions whose work was conducted by four subsidiary companies, Sundt entered the late 1990s on strong financial footing with numerous construction projects underway to fuel the company's growth as it prepared for the dawn of the new century ahead. In the 21st century, the era of Sundt management (the family owned 30 percent of the company, with employees owning the balance) was expected to come to an end, but the diversified expertise developed by three generations of the family augured well for its future. Certainly well beyond what Mauritz Sundt had envisioned when he started his own company in 1890, the Sundt Corp. of the late 1990s represented a strong regional force with international connections that could draw on a legacy of past achievements to guide its future growth. With its range of construction skills supporting it, the company braced itself for the construction projects of the future, continuing to build on the work of an industrious Norwegian carpenter whose 19th-century influences were still evident a century later.

Principal Subsidiaries

C.R. Fedrick, Inc.; CRF Integrated Solutions; Earl Construction Company; Ninteman Construction Company.

Principal Divisions

Building Division; Industrial Division; Heavy Construction Division; Military Housing Division; International Division.

Further Reading

Conroy, Bill, ''J. Doug Pruitt: Sundt Exec Build Reputation for Ethics, Commitment to Construction Industry,'' *Business Journal— Serving Phoenix & the Valley of the Sun,* January 14, 1991, p. 12.

Reinke, Martha, ''Arizona Firms Target Business Opportunities in the Middle East,'' *Business Journal—Serving Phoenix & the Valley of the Sun,* March 11, 1991, p. 8.

Sevilla, Graciela, ''Arizona Contractor Sees Wisdom of Plunge into Mexico,'' *Knight-Ridder/Tribune Business News,* August 2, 1996, p. 8.

''Sundt Builds on 100-Year Tradition of Quality Work,'' *Business Journal—Serving Phoenix & the Valley of the Sun,* March 19, 1990, p. 21.

Sundt Corp. *1890–1990: The First 100 Years.* Tucson, Ariz.: Sundt Corp., 1990.

—Jeffrey L. Covell

SYSCO.

SYSCO Corporation

1390 Enclave Parkway
Houston, Texas 77077-2099
U.S.A.
(281) 584-1390
Fax: (281) 584-2880
Web site: http://www.sysco.com

Public Company
Incorporated: 1969
Employees: 32,000
Sales: $14.45 billion (1997)
Stock Exchanges: New York
Ticker Symbol: SYY
SICs: 5141 Groceries, General Line; 5149 Grocers &
    Related Products, Not Elsewhere Classified

SYSCO Corporation (an acronym for Systems and Services Company) is the largest marketer and distributor of foodservice products in North America. With 70 distribution facilities serving more than 150 of the largest cities in the continental United States and parts of Alaska and Canada, SYSCO provides food and related products and services to approximately 270,000 restaurants, schools, hospitals, nursing homes, hotels, businesses, and other organizations. The company's line of products includes about 200,000 items, including fresh and frozen meats, seafood, poultry, fruits and vegetables, baked goods, paper and disposable items, chemical and janitorial products, beverages, dairy foods, and medical supplies. Founded in 1969, SYSCO has grown steadily ever since—mainly through dozens of acquisitions of smaller distributors—with annual increases in sales and earnings of 20 percent almost every year.

Founded Through Combination of Ten Distributors

John Baugh was the guiding force behind the founding of SYSCO. Baugh had grown up on a ranch near Waco, Texas, and got his start in the food business through a part-time job at a local A&P grocery store when he was in high school. He eventually founded Zero Foods Company of Houston, a Houston-based food distributor. In 1969 Baugh convinced the owners of eight other small food distributors to combine the nine companies, forming what he hoped to mold into a national foodservice distribution organization, one that would be able to distribute any food despite its regional availability. The other eight original companies were: Frost-Pack Distributing Company (Grand Rapids, Michigan); Global Frozen Foods, Inc. (New York); Houston's Food Service Company (Houston); Louisville Grocery Company (Louisville, Kentucky); Plantation Foods (Miami, Florida); Texas Wholesale Grocery Corporation (Dallas); Thomas Foods, Inc. and its Justrite Food Service, Inc. subsidiary (Cincinnati); and Wicker, Inc. (Dallas). The combined 1969 sales for the nine founding companies were $115 million.

SYSCO went public in 1970 and that year made its first acquisition, of Arrow Food Distributor. In its early years the company grew by acquiring a number of small foodservice distribution companies, carefully chosen for their geographic regions. These acquisitions helped to realize Baugh's early goal of providing uniform service to customers across the country. Throughout the 1970s SYSCO Corporation built many new warehouses to deal with this rapid expansion, later incorporating freezers into its warehouses and adding multi-temperature refrigerated trucks to transport produce and frozen foods.

During the 1970s SYSCO grew steadily except for a brief earnings drop in 1976 caused by a canned food glut and excessive start-up costs due to increasing capacity. One reason for such rapid recovery and regular growth was SYSCO's continuing diversification into new products, such as fish, meat, and fresh produce. In 1976 SYSCO acquired Mid-Central Fish and Frozen Foods Inc., expanding the company's distribution capabilities around the nation. In 1979 SYSCO's sales passed the $1 billion mark for the first time; by 1981 the company was rated as the largest U.S. foodservice distribution company. That year SYSCO set up Compton Foods in Kansas City to purchase meat, and began to supply supermarkets and other institutions with meat and frozen entrees.

Company Perspectives:

As the leading foodservice supplier in North America, SYSCO is well-positioned to anticipate and respond rapidly to customers' menu requirements. This may be arranging for products to be custom-tailored to meet an emerging trend in a certain market segment or bringing to market new products that will benefit a broad customer base. Perhaps it is developing easier food preparation methods or creating initiatives and having products developed to address customer concerns. For all of these and more—SYSCO is the leading source.

1980s—Rapid Growth Through Acquisitions

In 1983 John E. Woodhouse, whom Baugh had hired as chief financial officer in September 1969, became CEO of SYSCO, with Baugh remaining chairman. The following year SYSCO continued its strategy of acquiring its competitors when it purchased three operations of PYA Monarch, then a division of Sara Lee. SYSCO's largest acquisition to date occurred in 1988, when the company paid $750 million for CFS Continental, at that time the third largest food distributor in the country, which added 4,500 employees and increased the number of markets SYSCO served to 148 out of the top 150 markets. Although much of the United States and especially Texas experienced hard financial times during the 1980s, as a national company in a relatively recession-proof industry, SYSCO Corporation was not adversely affected.

SYSCO also made several smaller acquisitions of foodservice distributors in the late 1980s, including Olewine's Inc. (Harrisburg, Pennsylvania), which was renamed Sysco Food Services of Central Pennsylvania, Inc.; Lipsey Fish Company, Inc. (Memphis, Tennessee); Hall One Chinese Imports, Inc. (Cleveland); and Fulton Prime Foods, Inc. (Albany, New York). By the end of the decade, sales had reached $6.85 billion, making SYSCO twice as large as its closest competitor in foodservice distribution and second only to McDonald's in the overall foodservice industry. Despite its size and growth (through some 43 acquisitions since its founding), SYSCO accounted for less than eight percent of overall foodservice distributor volume, a testament to the continuingly fragmented nature of the foodservice distribution industry—and evidence that SYSCO had plenty of room for future growth.

1990s and Beyond

During the early 1990s, SYSCO made several additional acquisitions, increasing the company's geographic spread still further. Among the more important purchases were the 1990 acquisition of the Oklahoma City-based foodservice distribution business of Scrivner, Inc., which became Sysco Food Service of Oklahoma, Inc.; the 1991 acquisition of four of Scrivner's northeastern U.S. distribution businesses, including that of Jamestown, New York, which became Sysco Food Services-Jamestown; the 1992 acquisition of Philadelphia-based Perloff Brothers, Inc., which operated as Tartan Foods;

and the 1993 acquisitions of the St. Louis Division of Clark Foodservice, Inc. (which became Sysco Food Service of St. Louis, Inc.) and of Ritter Food Corporation of Elizabeth, New Jersey (which was renamed Ritter Sysco Food Services, Inc.).

In 1991 SYSCO created a subsidiary called The SYGMA Network, Inc. to consolidate its chain restaurant distribution systems and improve its service to chain restaurants. By 1997 SYGMA consisted of 11 distribution centers serving customers in 37 states, and posted sales of $1.3 billion.

By 1995 Baugh had assumed the title of senior chairman (he retired in late 1997), Woodhouse was chairman, and Bill M. Lindig, who had joined the company in 1970, had become CEO. SYSCO revenues had grown to $12.12 billion, but the company still held less than 10 percent of the foodservice distribution market. That year, Lindig told the *Houston Business Journal:* ''We could grow at 20 percent a year for the next five years and we'd still have only 20 percent of the market.'' (From 1978 to 1997, the company's compound growth rate was 16.4 percent.)

Also by this time, the company's management structure had grown somewhat unwieldy. SYSCO's operating companies, which by 1995 numbered 58, had always been allowed to function in a largely autonomous manner. This decentralized structure, however, meant that 58 operating company presidents were reporting directly to the corporate staff. With SYSCO expecting to soon have about 75 operating companies, corporate management decided to add four senior vice-presidents of operations, each of whom would have full responsibility for about 10 SYSCO operating companies. Nineteen companies would still report directly to corporate.

In the later 1990s SYSCO slowed its pace of acquisition, although acquisitions were still seen as important for growth in selected new markets, particularly such far-flung areas as Alaska and Canada. In mid-1996 the company purchased Strano Foodservice of Peterborough, Ontario, which gave SYSCO a presence in the Toronto market, while Alaska Fish and Farm, Inc. was bought in early 1997. Beginning in 1995, however, SYSCO added a ''fold-out'' expansion strategy as an additional method of growth. This strategy involved developing a sales base in markets distant from an existing operation, then building a new distribution center, staffing it with transferred staff, and thereby creating a new stand-alone operating company serving a new market. In 1995 SYSCO opened its first-ever brand-new distribution center in Connecticut through this program. Over the next four years, ''fold-out'' operating companies were added in Tampa, Florida; Wisconsin; North Carolina; Riviera Beach, Florida; Birmingham, Alabama; and San Diego.

SYSCO posted record sales of $14.45 billion in fiscal 1997, along with record net earnings of $302.5 million. Although the company's growth had slowed somewhat in the 1990s as fewer acquisitions were made, the ''fold-out'' expansion strategy was still keeping SYSCO growing much faster than the foodservice industry as a whole. With its attention to customer service and it strong management team—a team that had been strengthened over the years by a company policy of retaining the managers of acquired firms—SYSCO was well-positioned to continue into the new millennium with a steady increase in market share, which stood at about nine percent for the 1996 calendar year.

Principal Subsidiaries

Arrow-Sysco Food Services, Inc.; Baraboo-Sysco Food Services; Cochran/Sysco Food Services; Deaktor/Sysco Food Services; Hallsmith-Sysco Food Services; Hardin's-Sysco Food Services, Inc.; Lankford-Sysco Food Services, Inc.; Maine/Sysco, Inc.; Major-Sysco Food Services, Inc.; Mid-Central/Sysco Food Services, Inc.; Miesel/Sysco Food Service Company; Nobel/Sysco Food Services Co. Albuquerque; Nobel/Sysco Food Services Co. Denver; Robert Orr-Sysco Food Services Co.; Pegler-Sysco Food Services Company; Ritter Sysco Food Services, Inc.; Smelkinson Sysco Food Services, Inc.; Strano Sysco Foodservice Limited (Canada); The SYGMA Network, Inc.; Sysco Food Services-Albany; Sysco Food Services of Arizona, Inc.; Sysco Food Services of Arkansas, Inc.; Sysco Food Services of Atlanta, Inc.; Sysco Food Services of Austin, Inc.; Sysco Food Services of Beaumont, Inc.; Sysco Food Services of Central Alabama, Inc.; Sysco Food Services of Central Florida, Inc.; Sysco Food Services of Central Pennsylvania, Inc.; Sysco Food Services of Charlotte, Inc.; Sysco Food Services-Chicago, Inc.; Sysco Food Services/Cincinnati; Sysco Food Services of Cleveland, Inc.; Sysco Food Services of Connecticut; Sysco Food Services of Dallas, Inc.; Sysco Food Services of Eastern Wisconsin; Sysco Food Services of Grand Rapids, Inc.; Sysco Food Services-Horseheads; Sysco Food Services of Houston, Inc.; Sysco Food Services of Idaho, Inc.; Sysco Food Services of Indianapolis, Inc.; Sysco Food Services of Iowa, Inc.; Sysco Food Services-Jacksonville, Inc.; Sysco Food Services-Jamestown; Sysco Food Services of Los Angeles, Inc.; Sysco Food Services of Minnesota, Inc.; Sysco Food Services of Montana, Inc.; Sysco Food Services of Oklahoma, Inc.; Sysco Food Services of Philadelphia, Inc.; Sysco Food Services of Portland, Inc.; Sysco Food Services of St. Louis, Inc.; Sysco Food Services of San Antonio, Inc.; Sysco Food Services of San Diego, Inc.; Sysco Food Services of San Francisco, Inc.; Sysco Food Services of Seattle, Inc.; Sysco Food Services of South Florida, Inc.; Sysco Food Services of Southeast Florida, Inc.; Sysco Food Services-Syracuse; Sysco Food Services of Virginia, Inc.; Sysco Food Services-West Coast Florida, Inc.; Sysco Intermountain Food Services, Inc.; Sysco/Konings Wholesale (Canada); Sysco/Louisville Food Services Co.

Further Reading

Bagamery, Anne, " 'Don't Sell Food, Sell Peace of Mind,' " *Forbes,* October 11, 1982, p. 58.

Civin, Robert, "Sysco: Distribution's $7-Billion Entrepreneur," *Institutional Distribution,* April 1990.

"Distribution's Multi-Branch Giants," *Institutional Distribution,* October 1985, p. 169.

Fisher, Daniel, "Little Things Mean a Lot for Giant Sysco," *Houston Business Journal,* August 18, 1995, p. 24.

Geelhoed, E. Bruce, *The Thrill of Success: The Story of SYSCO/Frost-Pack Food Services, Incorporated,* Muncie, Ind.: Bureau of Business Research, College of Business and Department of History, Ball State University, 1983.

"Great Distributor Organization Study: SYSCO Corporation," *Institutional Distribution,* June 1980.

Harrison, Dan, "Sysco Eyes $10 Billion," *Institutional Distribution,* April 1989, p. 52.

Jones, Jeanne Lang, "Keeping Sysco on Course," *Houston Post,* January 8, 1995.

Lawn, John, "Sysco's Strategy: 'Divide and Multiply,' " *Foodservice Distributor,* January 1995, p. 32.

Loeffelholz, Suzanne, "Voracious Appetite: Sysco's Ability to Digest Its Acquisitions Can Only Mean More Deals Ahead," *Financial World,* April 18, 1989, p. 72.

Mack, Toni, "V.P.s of Planning Need Not Apply," *Forbes,* October 25, 1993, p. 84.

Reiter, Jeff, "Sysco and Dairy," *Dairy Foods,* October 1995, p. 113.

Ruggless, Ron, "John F. Woodhouse," *Nation's Restaurant News,* January 1995.

"Sysco Corporation: Since 1980," *Institutional Distribution,* September 15, 1986, p. 60.

—updated by David E. Salamie

Tesco PLC

Tesco House, Delamare Road
Cheshunt, Hertfordshire EN8 9SL
United Kingdom
44-1-992-632-222
Fax: 44-1-992-630-794
Web site: http://www.tesco.co.uk

Public Company
Incorporated: 1932 as Tesco Stores Limited
Employees: 181,000
Sales: £17.78 billion (US$29.92 billion) (fiscal year ended
    February 28, 1998)
Stock Exchanges: London
Ticker Symbol: TSCDY
SICs: 5331 Variety Stores; 5411 Grocery Stores; 5541
    Gasoline Service Stations; 5921 Liquor Stores

Tesco PLC holds the leading position among food retailers in Great Britain, with a market share that exceeds 15 percent. In England, Scotland, and Wales, the company runs 588 supermarkets, 257 of which are superstores—stores that sell food items in addition to a variety of other products, including gasoline, clothing, housewares, and alcoholic beverages. Tesco also operates 32 stores in Northern Ireland and 77 in the Republic of Ireland under various brands, 43 in Hungary under the Global and Tesco names, 31 in Poland under the Savia name, and 13 in the Czech Republic and Slovakia under the Tesco brand. In Northern Ireland, the company also runs 52 Wine Barrel off-license outlets. Tesco is the largest independent gasoline retailer in Britain; its 288 gas stations sell 12.5 percent of the gasoline sold in the United Kingdom. Recent company innovations include the Clubcard loyalty card as well as offerings from Tesco Personal Finance, which include a grocery budgeting account called Clubcard Plus, a Tesco Visa Card, and a Tesco savings account.

Early History

In John Edward (Jack) Cohen's day, a retailer's product line was comprised of whatever could be housed in a tiny stall. Cohen in 1919 invested his £30 stipend from his World War I service in the Royal Flying Corps in stock for his small grocery stall in the East End of London and began his career as a market trader. He soon became a successful trader in other London markets outside of the East End and also branched out into wholesaling for other market traders. In 1932 Cohen officially founded Tesco Stores Limited. The name was originally that of a private-label brand of tea Cohen sold, created from the initials of T. E. Stockwell, a merchant from whom he bought tea, and the first two letters of his last name.

Over the next eight years, the company grew rapidly, as Cohen opened more than 100 small stores, mainly in the London area. In 1935 Cohen was invited to the United States by several major American suppliers and became an eager student of the American food retailing system. His vision of taking the American self-service supermarket concept back to the United Kingdom was thwarted temporarily by World War II. But Cohen's dream became a reality in 1947 when Tesco opened its first self-service store, in St. Albans, Hertfordshire, the same year that shares in Tesco Stores (Holdings) Limited were first offered for sale to the public. Although the St. Albans store closed in 1948 after failing to capture the interest of British shoppers, it reopened one year later to a much warmer reception.

Over the next two decades, Tesco expanded quickly across the United Kingdom. This growth was accomplished almost exclusively by the acquisition of smaller grocery chains, including the 19-store Burnards chain in 1955, the 70-store Williamsons Ltd. in 1957, the 200-branch Harrow Stores Ltd. in 1959, the 97-unit Charles Phillips & Company Ltd. in 1964, and the 47-store Adsega chain in 1965. In 1956 the company opened its first supermarket, in Maldon, Essex, to carry fresh foods in addition to its traditional dry goods.

In 1960 Tesco established a special department in its larger stores called Home 'n' Wear to carry higher-margin, nonfood merchandise, including apparel and household items. Seven years later, the company completed construction on a 90,000-square-foot warehouse in Westbury, Wiltshire. The following year, Tesco opened its first 40,000-square-foot "superstore" at Crawley, Sussex. The term superstore referred not only to the store's size but also to its vast selection of inexpensive food and nonfood items.

By 1976 Tesco operated nearly 900 supermarkets and superstores on the ''pile it high, sell it cheap'' formula that Cohen
had imported from America. The firm's management found that
the effectiveness of this strategy had deteriorated over time,
however, leaving the company with uncomfortably slim margins and a serious image problem among consumers. While
Tesco had been preoccupied with opening as many stores as
possible and loading them with merchandise, the company had
missed important signs that its market was changing, and had
come to value merchandise quality over quantity.

Turnaround Began in the Later 1970s

The task of turning the company around fell on the shoulders
of Ian MacLaurin, who had risen through the Tesco ranks to
become managing director in 1973. In the first phase of his
rescue plan Tesco discontinued the use of Green Shield trading
stamps (which had been introduced in 1963), an action that
major stores in the United States had also taken recently. This
was followed in 1977 by a controversial tactic dubbed Operation Checkout, in which Tesco cut prices across the board in an
attempt to increase sales and market share during a period when
consumers were spending less money on food purchases. Although the company accomplished these original objectives—
market share rose from 7 to 12 percent in the span of a year—
Operation Checkout did little to improve Tesco's sagging image among consumers. Most of Tesco's stores were cramped,
difficult to operate, and even harder to staff. Customer service
was poor and merchandise selection in many outlets was limited. Tesco also touched off a price war with J. Sainsbury PLC,
one of its major rivals, which ended up driving a number of
smaller retailers and independent grocers out of business or into
the arms of larger companies when they found themselves unable to compete with the prices offered by the two warring
retailers.

Next, in order to reposition itself, Tesco embarked upon a
massive modernization program, intended in part to take the
chain upmarket. It closed 500 unprofitable stores, and extensively upgraded and enlarged others, including the upgrading of
lighting and use of wider aisles. Tesco pursued the superstore
concept much more aggressively than it had in the past in order

to compete more successfully with other major retailers and be
more responsive to consumers who preferred to shop where
parking was convenient and the selection of goods was broad.
The company made a significant investment not only in improving the physical appearance of its stores but also in providing
the higher-quality merchandise consumers wanted. Superstores
were also seen as a way to generate a higher volume of business
at increased margins while reducing overhead.

The superstores averaged 25,000 square feet to begin with,
but eventually grew as large as 65,000 square feet. Each superstore functioned as a self-service department store coupled
with a supermarket. The company placed a heavy emphasis on
having a varied selection of fresh, high-quality foods available,
as well as a wide range of general merchandise such as household items and clothing designed to appeal to more sophisticated tastes.

To support these stores and its new high-quality, service-
oriented image, Tesco introduced its own private-label product
lines, developed through an extensive research-and-development program. Tesco also restructured and computerized its
distribution system, opening its own centralized warehouses for
storing inventory which could then be supplied to its stores as
needed, instead of having to rely on manufacturers' delivery
schedules.

In 1979, in an attempt to increase its overall sales volume
through larger stores, Tesco acquired 17 outlets affiliated with
Cartiers Superfoods. This acquisition and another involving
Ireland's Three Guys store chain, together with lower sales in
nonfood merchandise than the company had expected, drained
Tesco's profits the following year.

Continued to Battle for Market Share in the 1980s

By late 1981, food sales also appeared to be settling into
another slump, placing additional pressure on Tesco's bottom
line. In an effort to rekindle activity, MacLaurin initiated
Checkout '82, cutting prices between three and 26 percent on
approximately 1,500 food items. Like the strategy employed in
1977—but operating in an environment of smaller net profit
margins—Checkout '82 touched off renewed price wars between Tesco and J. Sainsbury, in which each chain devoted all
of its energies to outdoing the other to win customer loyalty.

In the midst of this ongoing battle, Tesco also established its
Victor Value chain of discount stores. Growing over the next
four years to a total of 45 outlets, the stores were sold to the
Bejam Group PLC in 1986, the same year in which the Three
Guys chain, renamed Tesco Stores Ireland Ltd., was sold to H.
Williams and Company, Ltd., a Dublin-based supermarket
chain. This divestiture resulted primarily from the company's
inability to operate effectively in Ireland from its home base in
England.

In 1983 the company changed its name to Tesco PLC. The
following year, it joined forces with Marks & Spencer, the
upscale British variety store, to develop shopping centers in
areas outside the country's major cities. Their first venture,
which became a model for subsequent centers, was established
at Brookfield Centre, near Cheshunt, and placed a 65,000-
square-foot Tesco superstore next to a 69,000-square-foot
Marks & Spencer department store. Supported by 42 computer-

ized checkout counters and 900 employees, the Tesco store offered a variety of food and nonfood departments, in addition to services ranging from a bank to a gas station to baby-care facilities to a consumer advisory kitchen staffed by home economists. The Marks & Spencer store featured mostly nonfood merchandise, though it devoted a small amount of space to the popular specialty food items it marketed under its own St. Michael label.

In 1985 Ian MacLaurin became chairman of Tesco, the same year that Tesco opened its 100th superstore in the United Kingdom. The construction of this outlet, located in Brent Park, Neasden, was a source of controversy between the company and the local governing council from the date Tesco first acquired the 43-acre site in 1978. The council made a number of objections to the proposed development, maintaining that the store did not fit the planning needs of the area and did not make adequate allowances for future warehousing requirements. The council's greatest concern was the threat the Tesco store would pose to existing shopping centers and local merchants. Once Tesco's store finally opened for business it became London's largest food store.

Also in 1985, Tesco launched a major capital spending program for aggressive store and warehouse expansion and for more efficient technology in existing stores, both at the checkout counters and behind the scenes. Tesco's investment in the development of a sophisticated distribution system, together with other facility improvements, enabled the company to incorporate its 1987 acquisition of the 40-store Hillards PLC chain easily. This expansion also gave Tesco increased visibility in Yorkshire. In 1988 and 1989 the company spent £500 million to build 29 new stores. In the late 1980s Tesco also introduced a composite six-warehouse distribution system to serve its stores, resulting in increased efficiency and improved service.

Expansion Outside Great Britain Marked 1990s

By the beginning of the 1990s, Tesco had 371 stores in England, Scotland, and Wales—150 of which were superstores—and the company had become one of the United Kingdom's top three food retailers. The early 1990s saw the culmination of Tesco's fight for market share fueled in part by a two-year £1 billion development program launched in 1990 which added about 60 new stores and more than 2.3 billion square feet of store space. By 1991 Tesco had become the largest independent gasoline retailer in Great Britain. Four years later the company reached the number one spot among food retailers in terms of market share. This achievement was due in part to the 1992 introduction of the Tesco Metro format, which debuted at Covent Garden, London. The Metro stores were smaller outlets—10,000 square feet or so—designed for urban areas and offering a few thousand product lines tailored specifically for the local market. Whereas Tesco had typically concentrated its stores in suburbia, the Tesco Metro stores were slated for city neighborhoods and were intended to compete directly with Marks & Spencer's successful urban food-only stores. By 1997 Tesco had opened 40 Tesco Metro units.

Perhaps more important longer term for Tesco, however, was the company's aggressive 1990s push outside of Great Britain. In 1993 Tesco paid £175 million (US$282 million) to purchase Catteau S.A., a 92-store grocery chain in northern France. This first foray onto continental Europe proved ill-founded, however, as Catteau struggled to compete against discounters and larger chains such as Promodes and Carrefour. Lacking the critical mass needed to compete successfully, Tesco decided to exit from France four years after it had entered the country, selling Catteau to Promodes in December 1997 for £250 million (US$416.9 million).

Other Tesco expansion moves in the 1990s were more successful. In August 1994 the company acquired William Low, gaining 57 stores in Scotland and northern England for £247 million. Also in 1994 Tesco moved into the burgeoning central European market for the first time through the £15 million purchase of a 51 percent stake in Global, a supermarket chain with 43 stores in northwest Hungary. The following year Tesco acquired the 31-store Savia chain in Poland for £8 million. And in 1996 the company spent £79 million for 13 Kmart stores in the Czech Republic and Slovakia, which it soon converted to the Tesco name. Initially, Tesco's central European operations suffered operating losses in large part because of hefty development costs, but the company announced in early 1998 that it aimed to be a major food retailer in the region, that it would spend £350 million through the year 2000 to expand its base, and that it expected to be making a profit there by the turn of the century. In 1997 Tesco acquired the Irish food retailing businesses of Associated British Food PLC for £630 million (US$1 billion), thereby gaining leading market share positions in both the Republic of Ireland (through 75 stores) and Northern Ireland (through 34 stores).

Meanwhile, back in Britain, Tesco was experimenting with additional new formats and introducing innovative new services. The year 1994 saw the opening of the first two Tesco Express gasoline stations, both located in London. The Express format was a combination filling station and convenience store; by late 1997, 15 of them had opened. In 1997 Tesco opened the first Tesco Extra unit in Pitsea, Essex. This store covered 102,000 square feet, with one-quarter of the sales area consisting of expanded nonfood departments. It soon became the company's number one store in terms of sales.

In February 1995 Tesco became the first British retailer with a loyalty card when it introduced the Tesco Clubcard. In 1997 Tesco created a new unit called Tesco Personal Finance in order to provide its customers with a wide array of financial services, including a Tesco Visa Card, a Tesco savings account, in-store bank branches, Tesco Travel Money and Insurance, and Clubcard Plus, a combination loyalty card and savings account.

The year 1997 also marked the end of an era for Tesco as MacLaurin retired, with John Gardiner taking over as chairman; Gardiner had been appointed deputy chairman of Tesco in 1993 and also served as chairman of Larid Group PLC. That same year Terry Leahy was appointed chief executive; Leahy, who joined Tesco in 1979, had played a key role in Tesco's rise to the top of U.K. food retailing as the company's first marketing director. With a new management team in place, Tesco aimed to build upon its multiformat empire in the United Kingdom, to continue to develop innovative products and services (particularly financial services), to turn its central European operations into profitable ones, and to seek other overseas expansion opportunities, such as in the emerging markets of Asia.

Principal Subsidiaries

Tesco Capital Limited; Tesco Insurance Limited; Tesco Property Holdings Limited; Tesco Stores Hong Kong Limited; Tesco Stores Limited; Global TH (Hungary); Savia S.A. (Poland).

Further Reading

Church, Chris, "How Tesco Took the Low Road to Scotland," *Grocer,* September 30, 1995, p. 14.

Corina, Maurice, *Pile It High, Sell It Cheap: The Authorized Biography of Sir John Cohen,* London: Weidenfeld & Nicolson, 1971, 204 p.

Fallon, James, "Tesco Grows Restless," *Supermarket News,* August 10, 1992, pp. 1+.

"The Grocer Focus on Tesco Supplement," *Grocer,* September 20, 1997.

Hollinger, Peggy, "A French Blot on Tesco's Copybook," *Financial Times,* December 10, 1997, p. 30.

——, "The Skier Keeping Tesco Away from Slippery Slopes," *Financial Times,* February 28, 1997, p. 25.

——, "Tesco Considers Expanding into South-East Asia," *Financial Times,* August 4, 1997, p. 1.

O'Connor, Robert, "Tesco, Safeway, Sainsbury Target Ireland," *Chain Store Age Executive,* December 1997, pp. 134+.

Powell, David, *Counter Revolution: The Tesco Story,* London: Grafton, 1991.

Price, Chris, "Tesco Checks Out As Leader," *Financial Times,* September 21, 1996, p. WFT5.

Reier, Sharon, "Branding the Company," *Financial World,* November 26, 1991, pp. 32+.

"Tesco's New Tricks: British Supermarkets," *Economist,* April 15, 1995, pp. 61+.

Wilsher, Peter, "Housekeeping?," *Management Today,* December 1993, pp. 38+.

—updated by David E. Salamie

Thermo Fibertek, Inc.

81 Wyman Street
P.O. Box 9046
Waltham, Massachusetts 02254-9046
U.S.A.
(617) 622-1000
Fax: (617) 622-1102
Web site: http://www.thermofibertek.com

Public Subsidiary of Thermo Electron Corporation
Incorporated: 1992
Employees: 1,100
Sales: $192.2 million (1996)
Stock Exchanges: American
Ticker Symbol: TFT
SICs: 3554 Paper Industries Machinery; 3567 Industrial
Process Furnaces & Ovens; 3569 General Industrial
Machinery & Equipment, Not Elsewhere Classified;
3823 Industrial Instruments for Measurement, Display,
& Control of Process Variables, & Related Products;
8711 Engineering Services; 8731 Commercial,
Physical, & Biological Research; 8742 Management
Consulting Services

Thermo Fibertek, Inc. is an international developer, manufacturer, and marketer of a wide range of equipment, products, process equipment, and accessories for the domestic and international papermaking and paper recycling industries. Its systems are designed to convert wastepaper into usable fiber, enhance the efficiency of papermaking machinery, and reclaim wastewater for reuse in the recycling process. Some of the products manufactured by the company include de-inking systems, stock preparation equipment, water management systems, and spare parts and accessories.

Spinout Vs. Spinoff

Thermo Fibertek is a "spinout" of Thermo Electron Corporation, as opposed to a "spinoff." George Hatsopoulos, CEO of

Therm Electron, the parent company, differentiates the two, since his subsidiaries are created to stand on their own but are not cast off by the parent. Of the ten or so first-generation spinouts from Thermo Electron, all are still partially owned by the parent company, itself a leading manufacturer of environmental monitoring equipment, biomedical, and health equipment. Other first-generation spinouts include Thermedics, Thermo Instrument, Thermo Power, Thermo TerraTech, and Thermo Trex. Each of the first-generation spinouts has second-generation spinouts orbiting it, and some even have third- and fourth-generation spinouts.

George Hatsopoulos, whose uncles and cousins were successful in technical fields but failures in business, vowed to succeed in both. He received degrees in both engineering and thermodynamics from Massachusetts Institute of Technology, and then founded Thermo Electron in 1956. The company made its initial public offering in October 1967 at 68 cents per share. In March 1996, the stock was valued at $61.25 per share. Thermo Fibertek made its initial public offering in November 1992 at $5.33 per share. Its value in March 1996 was $23.38 per share.

That same year a down cycle in the pulp and paper industry adversely affected Thermo Fibertek. Revenues reached $192.2 million, compared with $206.7 million in 1995 and net income reached $19.9 million, down from $20.2 million the previous year, though the stock share remained the same at $0.33 per share. However, that year the company bolstered its position as the technological leader in white paper de-inking as their facility in Menominee, Michigan, started up operations, recycling approximately 570 tons of mixed office waste into 400 tons of high-grade, de-inked pulp per day.

Second-Generation Spinout—Thermo Fibergen, Inc.

Increasing demand for environmentally safe industrial waste disposal methods has opened new opportunities for the application of Thermo Fibertek's advanced technologies. In February 1996, Thermo Fibertek incorporated a Delaware corporation spinout company called Thermo Fibergen, Inc.

Company Perspectives:

We have maintained our position as a leader in the pulp and paper industry because each of our business units works hard to solve today's problems—while anticipating tomorrow's.

Located in newly built headquarters in Bedford, Massachusetts, Thermo Fibergen was created to address the problems of papermaking waste, called sludge, from paper mills. Each year, the pulp and paper industry worldwide produces 25 million tons of waste material—enough, according to company literature, ''to cover the entire borough of Manhattan with a layer 30 feet deep!''—that must be disposed of in landfills and incinerators, and the industry spent nearly $2.5 billion in 1996 to get rid of its sludge, a figure projected to rise as landfills close and incinerators become more difficult to site. The move toward recycled paper, which saves both trees and energy, actually intensifies the waste problem, since recycling mills produce eight times more sludge than virgin-pulp mills. A typical recycling mill converts 600 tons of wastepaper per day into 450 tons of recycled pulp, leaving 150 tons of sludge solids, made up of long and short fiber, minerals, and ''fines'' (fiber fragments too small for papermaking). Since disposal of sludge waste is complicated—mills must purchase and use expensive polymers to make the solids clump so the water can be pressed out; the sludge must be transported to disposal facilities, and disposal providers must be paid tipping fees to bury sludge in landfills—costly, and an increasingly larger headache for papermakers, Thermo Fibertek saw an opportunity.

Thermo Fibergen, under the direction of Chief Executive Officer Yiannis A. Monovoukas, was created to develop proprietary technology to recover the long fibers (approximately 15 percent of the sludge solids) and short fibers (approximately 35 percent) and clarify water so that both can be reused in papermaking. Thermo Fibergen plans to finance, build, own, and operate sludge-processing facilities at or near the site of pulp and paper mills, and sign contracts to take responsibility, for a fee, for the sludge generated by these mills. Each of the facilities will be able to process more than 30,000 tons of wastewater per day.

During the summer of 1996, Thermo Fibergen built a portable version of its proprietary fiber-recovery technology and demonstrated its effectiveness at paper mills around the country. Thermo Fibergen offered its initial public offering in September of that year, raising approximately $54 million to fund research and development and the commercialization of its fiber-recovery technology, and becoming one of 12 second-generation ''grandchildren'' companies spun out by Thermo Electron.

But what to do with the remaining minerals and chemicals created as sludge byproducts? Since approximately 50 percent of the sludge solids are made up of minerals and chemicals such as calcium carbonate, kaolin clay, and titanium dioxide, Thermo Fibergen acquired a subsidiary in July 1996 called GranTek, Inc. to turn the problem into yet another opportunity.

Creating new markets for itself by doing so, GranTek was acquired in order to convert the minerals and chemicals into a product line called Biodac—virtually dust-free, organic-based granules which will be sold commercially for use as carriers of agricultural chemicals in the 160,000 tons-per-year professional turf, home lawn and garden, and mosquito-control markets; for use in the 240,000 tons-per-year agricultural row-crop market (approximately $50 million in the U.S. alone in 1996); for the 575,000 tons-per-year market for absorbents for oil spill and grease clean-up (approximately $35 million in wholesale revenue in 1996), with the added advantage that the used granules can be burned to generate energy since the absorbent product is made from paper waste; and for the 1.5 million tons-per-year kitty litter market (a market worth approximately $400 million per year). Thermo Fibergen expected to begin marketing these products in 1998 and revenues for the spinout company reached $2.2 million in its first year, with a net loss of $367,000.

Black Clawson Acquisition, 1997

In February 1997, Thermo Fibertek signed a letter of intent to acquire the assets of the Middletown, Ohio-based Black Clawson Company, a privately held, multinational company with manufacturing facilities, technical centers, and sales and engineering offices in strategic places throughout the world including Canada, the People's Republic of China, Singapore, France, England, and the United States, with a network of agents in Latin America, and its world headquarters in New York City. The company is a leading supplier of recycling equipment used in processing fiber for the manufacture of brown paper, such as that used for corrugated boxes.

Black Clawson began as a small machine shop in Hamilton, Ohio, whose work was limited to roll grinding and repair work for paper mills in Ohio's Miami Valley. To broaden the scope of their business, the company began building paper machinery, and the first Fourdrinier was built in 1881. Based on the success of the paper machinery business, the company expanded rapidly. By 1900, it was exporting Fourdriniers to Great Britain, Europe, and Japan. Other successes included the development of a cylinder machine, seamless dryer, and triple deck dryer arrangement.

Just north of Hamilton, in Middletown, Ohio, another machine shop, Shartle Brothers, was internationally recognized as the major builder of stock pumps, beaters, and refiners. Black Clawson purchased Shartle in 1926. The two product lines complemented each other such that the company offered a wider range of equipment to paper and board mills than any competitor.

The merger of Dilts Machine Works of Fulton, New York, Shartle's main competitor, into the Shartle organization led to the development of new screens for old mixed stock, the first pressure screen, and the ''Hydrapulper'' pulping machine that revolutionized the way wastepaper was processed.

In 1946, Shartle took on sole responsibility for all stock preparation equipment. Its growth over the years has led to world leadership in pulp mill systems, stock preparation equipment, and recycling equipment. Black Clawson designed and manufactured recycling systems even before it became a critical issue in the 1990s. By 1997, more than 80 percent of America's recycled paper was produced on Black Clawson equipment.

Black Clawson also manufactures process and equipment capabilities in virgin fiber processing; horizontal belt washers and a complete product line of equipment used exclusively in the production of virgin pulps; all of the major components that follow the digesters, including knotters, cleaners, screens, and non-chlorine bleaching technology; and the "Liqui-Filter," a specially designed pressure filter for removing fiber from the liquor recovery systems.

Black Clawson's Fulton, New York-based Black Clawson Converting Machinery Corporation is a leading supplier of web handling machinery, engineering and manufacturing machine lines for converting paper, paperboard, plastic film and sheeting, foil, and non-woven materials, as well as application-engineered complete machine lines including unwind/splicing equipment, universal coating, air flotation and web-supported dryers, continuous winder/roll changing equipment, and slitter/rewinders.

The acquisition of Black Clawson afforded the company access to the Pacific Rim markets, where the paper recycling industry was expected to grow significantly in the 21st century.

More Second-Generation Spinouts, and a Look to the Future

In addition to Thermo Fibergen, other spinouts of Thermo Fibertek have included Auburn, Massachusetts-based Thermo Web Systems, which designs and develops paper machine doctoring systems and doctor blades for efficient roll cleaning and sheet peeling; Thermo Wisconsin, Inc., based in Kaukauna, Wisconsin, specializing in drying technologies used in both the paper and printing industries; and Lamort, the largest subsidiary of Thermo Fibertek, located in Vitry-le-Francois, France, serving as a center for technological development of recycling products.

Thermo Fibertek, along with its parent company and subsidiaries, shows no sign of slowing down. As the realization of recycled paper and products grows, Thermo Fibertek, which, through its Black Clawson subsidiary was manufacturing products for the industry long before it was "politically correct," will continue to grow and dominate that marketplace.

Principal Subsidiaries

AES Engineered Systems; AES Equipos y Sistema (Mexico); Thermo AES Canada; E & M Lamort (France); Thermo Black Clawson, Inc.; Thermo Black Clawson China; Thermo Black Clawson Ltd. (U.K.); Thermo Black Clawson SA (France); Thermo Fibergen, Inc.; GranTek, Inc.; Thermo Fiberprep, Inc.; Thermo Fibertek UK; Thermo Web Systems, Inc.; Thermo Wisconsin, Inc.

Further Reading

Brickates, Evanthia V., "Deal Puts Thermo in Asian Recycling Market," *Boston Business Journal*, March 7, 1997, p. 4.
"Buffalo Paperboard Co.," *Pulp & Paper*, January 1996, p. 25.
"Divestment to Fund Black Clawson Plan," *Plastics News*, April 7, 1997, p. 16.
Gerena, Charles, "Meter Maid," *Equities*, October 1996, p. 44.
"Industry News," *BioCycle*, March 1997, p. 87.
"Mill Operations," *Pulp & Paper*, February 1995, p. 27.
"News from Suppliers," *Textile World*, March 1994, p. 82.
"Scott Paper Co.," *Pulp & Paper*, January 1996, p. 25.
"Thermo Electron Acquisition," *Wall Street Journal*, May 23, 1997, p. B9B(E).
"Thermo Fibertek Acquisition," *Wall Street Journal*, February 28, 1997, p. A6(E)/B5(W).
"Thermo Fibertek to Buy Black Clawson for $110 Million," *New York Times*, February 28, 1997, p. D3.

—Daryl F. Mallett

Thomas H. Lee Co.

75 State Street
Boston, Massachusetts 02109
U.S.A.
(617) 227-1050
Fax: (617) 227-3514

Private Company
Founded: 1974
Employees: 100
Sales: $1.5 billion (1995 est.)
SICs: 6799 Investors, Not Elsewhere Classified

Thomas H. Lee Co. is one of the oldest and most successful private equity investment firms in the United States, identifying and acquiring substantial ownership positions in middle market growth companies through leveraged acquisitions, recapitalizations, and direct investments. Since its founding, the company has invested over $2.5 billion in more than 100 businesses, building companies of lasting value and generating attractive returns for its investors and operating managers.

Thomas H. Lee may not be a household name, but many of the companies he has owned are. The "Lee" list has included all or part of such companies as General Nutrition (GNC), Ghiradelli Chocolates, The Learning Company, Playtex Home Products, Rayovac Corp., TRW Information Systems & Securities, Sun Pharmaceuticals, and Snapple Beverage Company, just to name a very few.

Getting Started, 1974–91

The company was founded in 1974 as a private investment firm by Harvard University graduate and former First National Bank of Boston employee Thomas H. Lee. The Boston-based company manages $3 billion in capital, focusing on acquisitions of middle-market growth companies and known for acquiring equity in established companies, often through leveraged buyouts.

In 1982, Lee paid $15.5 million for a controlling interest in Guilford Industries, a $41 million manufacturer of office furniture fabric, putting up $2.5 million in equity cash and raising another $6 million in financing and $7 million in bank debt. In 1987, he sold out, making nearly $35 million.

One of Lee's best early deals happened in 1985 when he bought Akron, Ohio-based Sterling Jewelers for $28 million, 90 percent of which he had to borrow. He turned around and sold Sterling in 1987 for $210 million to what is now Signet, one of Europe's largest jewelry retail chains.

But success has not made Lee blind. He is very quick to point out his own mistakes. And he made one in 1985. That year Lee's uncle, Herbert Schiff, was nearing retirement as CEO of $1.3 billion SCOA Industries, a regional discount retailer based in Columbus, Ohio, a company Lee's grandfather founded as The Shoe Corp. of America in 1905.

SCOA's largest and most profitable subsidiary was Hills Department Stores. Still managed by founder Herbert Goldberger and his son, Stephen, Hills could boast 125 stores, 29 consecutive years of increasing sales and operating profits, an earnings growth rate of 23 percent over the previous 10 years, and an average return on equity of 24 percent. Hills, quite literally, was floating the entire SCOA enterprise.

Lee spun off Hills and sold the rest of SCOA for $55 million. The company then invested $11 million of stock in Hills, and obtained nearly $110 million more from four classes of preferred stock; $270 million worth of junk securities in three separate debt issues placed by Drexel to the likes of Columbia Savings & Loan, First Executive and Equitable Life; and $252 million more from banks.

Eighteen months later, in July 1987, Lee took the company public under the old Hills Department Stores name, bringing in nearly $40 million. Lee himself owned some 48 percent of the company. But then, purportedly blinded by family ties and dreams of making the company profitable again, Lee did not cash out. With the retail industry in the Northeast already going sour while Stephen Goldberger aggressively pursued expansion plans for some 89 new store openings, including 33 Gold Circle outlets picked up from the struggling Federated Department Stores, the company unraveled. Hills filed for Chapter 11 in 1991. Lee, his company, Merrill Lynch, and Westinghouse Credit all tried to save Hills with money, but that, too, failed. Lee took over as CEO, reportedly booting Goldberger, and closed stores determinedly. Chemical Bank entered the picture with a $250 million debtor-in-possession loan and Hills continued operating its remaining 154 stores.

In January 1991, Thomas H. Lee Co. acquired part of a supermarket chain when it bought Florida, New York-based Big V Supermarkets from affiliates of First Boston Corp. and Metropolitan Life Insurance Co. of New York for $212 million. The acquisition brought Lee Co. 27 Big V ''ShopRite'' stores in New York for $212 million. Additional partners in the venture included three other investment affiliates, members of Big V's senior management, and some outside investors.

It was the company's first full-scale investment in the retail food industry. The supermarket chain, founded in 1942 by William Rosenberg, had struggled, being purchased by First Boston for nearly $170 million from a retiring 79-year-old Rosenberg in 1987. J. Arthur Rosenberg, the 62-year-old son of the founder, stepped down as chairman. The company had revenues of $630 million in 27 stores at the time of the sale. David G. Bronstein became the new chairman and retained the titles of president and chief executive. Seven stores in Albany were sold, and several new stores were opened after the sale to Lee Co.

Business Is a Snap-ple, 1992–94

Although in business for nearly 20 years, Thomas Lee worked behind the scenes, quietly making deals and money (his personal net worth on the *Forbes* Four Hundred was listed at some $420 million in 1994, jumping to nearly $600 million in 1995 and $750 million by 1997).

That all changed in 1992, when he became a legend in investment circles. His firm purchased 63 million shares of Snapple Beverage Company in April. Eight months later, Lee took Snapple public, and a short two years later, in 1994, he leveraged the sale of Snapple to Quaker Oats Co. for $1.7 billion, making approximately $900 million from the sale. Unfortunately, Quaker Oats did not fare so well, buying Snapple when its popularity was peaking, tinkering with the company's distribution system, and ending up selling the struggling beverage company in 1997 for $300 million, $1.4 billion less than it paid, leading to Quaker Chairman William Smithburg's ouster.

In July 1992, Lee Co. bought 83⅓ percent of First Alert and BRK Electronics from Chicago-based Pittway Corp. for $92.5 million. The acquisition was especially notable since it garnered Lee the two leading manufacturers and distributors of smoke detectors, fire extinguishers, rechargeable flashlights and lanterns, timers, and other home security products. Pittway retained 16-⅔ percent of the companies. That December, Lee Co. purchased Pompano Beach, Florida-based Sun Pharmaceuticals, the third largest manufacturer of sun and skin care products in the United States.

In June 1994, Restaurants Unlimited Inc. (RUI) executives, Thomas H. Lee Co., and Union Bank of Switzerland bought out

RUI's majority shareholder, New York investor Eli S. Jacobs, who acquired control of then-privately owned RUI when he restructured the company in 1990, leaving RUI manager-stockholders with cash but little stake in the company. The deal followed Jacobs's forced bankruptcy in 1993 by a group of international banks claiming the formerly wide-ranging investor, with ownership in Memorex and the Baltimore Orioles, among other things, owed them nearly $60 million.

The acquisition brought Lee Co. partial ownership of the Cinnabon ''gourmet'' cinnamon roll bakery chain, with 255 company-owned or franchised locations in 33 states, Canada, and Mexico; four Palomino ''Euro-Bistro'' dinner houses, in Seattle, Minneapolis, San Francisco, and Palm Desert, California; one Zoopa all-you-can-eat ''international marketplace'' buffet restaurant in Tukwila, Washington; and full-service concepts like Cutters, Stepps, and Simon & Seafort's spread across six states.

The Late 1990s

In January 1995, Garth Drabinsky, owner of Livent, sold 13 percent of that company to Lee. The entertainment firm, suffering from a shortfall of cash from its purchase in 1993, released such films as *Kiss of the Spider Woman*. Also in 1995, Thomas H. Lee Co. formed a venture with BancBoston to buy the mortgage operations of Prudential Insurance Companies of America, but lost the deal to Norwest Corp., who eventually bought Prudential Home Mortgage. Lee Co. also sold subprime lender Equicredit to Barnett Banks Inc. that year, creating another long-lasting relationship.

In October 1995, the Gillette Co., parent company of Braun, agreed to acquire Thermoscan Inc., the leading manufacturer of infrared ear thermometers from Thermoscan's founders and Thomas H. Lee Co. for $105 million. Thermoscan would be operated by Braun, who marketed the leading electric dental unit, the Braun Oral-B, in the U.S. and Europe. That month was marred by Lee's highly publicized divorce from first wife, Barbara Fish Lee.

The following month, however, Playtex Home Products, itself substantially owned by Lee Co., bought the latter's 78 percent ownership of Banana Boat Holdings (BBH), a sun and skin care line, for $40.4 million, increasing the feminine hygiene company's stake in BBH to a full 100 percent.

In January 1996, Lee Co. purchased almost 25 percent of New York Restaurant Group (NYRG), owner of several prestigious restaurants in New York City and Chicago, including Smith Wollensky steak house, contemporary American cuisine-based Park Avenue Cafe, a seafood unit called The Manhattan Ocean Club, and Mrs. Parks Cafe, from NYRG founder and President Alan Stillman. Stillman, who once sold oils to perfume manufacturers, created T.G.I. Friday's in 1965 on Manhattan's Upper East Side as a way to supplement his income. His moonlighting excursion changed the course of the casual-theme dining industry, spawning a restaurant chain that would become one of the most imitated concepts in that market. Stillman planned to use the investment to finance national expansion into such cities as New Orleans, Philadelphia, and Washington, D.C.

A bit of Thomas Lee's success was due to the quality of business partners he surrounds himself with. In February 1996, the company, in its first co-investment with Bain Capital Inc. (whose managing director was Mitt Romney, son of former Michigan Governor George Romney), acquired 84 percent ownership of TRW Information Systems & Services Inc. of Orange, California, for $1 billion from Cleveland-based TRW's much larger manufacturing businesses that make such products as automobile air bags and missile tracking systems.

The deal for one of the most prominent names in the information business, best known for its reports on Americans' credit histories, as well as being one of the nation's largest providers of real estate information and direct marketing services, was financed by Chemical Banking Corp. and Bankers Trust. The acquisition gave TRW—with consumer credit reporting services in Mexico and Japan, online business credit reports worldwide, a reciprocal partnership with a consortium of European countries and Canada to offer business credit information on European, Canadian, and U.S. companies—the muscle it needed to compete with market leader Atlanta-based Equifax Inc. and third-place Trans Union Corp. of Chicago. A public bond sale was held that June, raising approximately $300 million to help pay for the acquisition. The company's name was changed to Experian Information Solutions.

Experian was sold in November to Great Universal Stores PLC, a Manchester, United Kingdom-based mail-order giant that also owned the Burberry clothing retailer, for $1.7 billion. The British company, chaired by Lord Wolfson of Sunningdale (chief of staff under British Prime Minister Margaret Thatcher), merged Experian into its much smaller credit-reporting business, CCN Group in Nottingham, U.K. and ran it under a holding company, CCN Experian Ltd.

In March 1996, Thomas H. Lee Co. and Madison Dearborn Partners, another venture capital firm, paid $135 million to Bank of Boston Corp. for 55 percent of its BancBoston Mortgage division, creating HomeSide Inc. Bank of Boston Corp. retained a 45 percent stake in the new company, seen as a groundbreaking way to capitalize on economies of scale by combining mortgage systems and servicing, and industry analysts praised the merger, which turned two mid-size mortgage lending operations into one of the largest and most efficient mortgage servicers in the United States.

Two months later, HomeSide bought Barnett Banks Inc.'s mortgage servicing operations, bringing $33 billion in servicing finance to the $42 billion already in place from BancBoston. Barnett obtained a one-third stake in HomeSide, reducing the other two investors also to 33⅓ percent ownership. HomeSide went public in January 1997 at $15 a share. After the offering, Thomas H. Lee Co. owned about 20 percent of the Jacksonville, Florida-based mortgage lender, Madison Dearborn six percent, and the two banks 26 percent each. In October 1997, HomeSide was sold to National Australia Bank for $1.23 billion, bringing Thomas H. Lee Co.'s stake up to nearly $250 million, $160 million more than its initial investment.

In September 1996, Donaldson, Lufkin and Jenrette Inc. financed Lee Co.'s $200 million recapitalization of battery-maker Rayovac Corp., with BankAmerica Corp. acting as the administrative agent. Lee Co. picked up an 80 percent ownership in the third largest battery manufacturing company in the United States, behind Duracell and Energizer, selling to such major customers as Sears and Wal-Mart. The battery maker was taken public in November 1997. In December 1997, Rayovac purchased BRISCO G.M.B.H. in Germany and BRISCO B.V. in Holland, distributors and assemblers of customized hearing aid battery packages in Europe and, in March 1998, expanded into the rechargeable battery market with the acquisition of the retail business of Direct Power Plus (DPP) of New York, a full line marketer of rechargeable batteries and accessories for cellular phones and video camcorders, for around $7.4 million.

In October 1996, Syratech Corp., Leonard Florence's tabletop and giftware company, reached a merger agreement with Lee Co. in a $288 million transaction, giving the latter a nearly 75 percent ownership in the former. The acquisition also brought ownership in Syratech's core silver brands, Towle, Wallace, and International Silver, which together held nearly 45 percent of the silver flatware market. Florence headed Towle in the late 1970s and early 1980s and acquired 14 companies before resigning in 1985. The company twice thereafter filed for bankruptcy. Florence went on to found Syratech Corp. in 1986, buying Wallace, International Silver, and Syroco that year and Towle in 1990 before going public in 1992. Syroco, a supplier of plastic outdoor furniture, was sold for $140 million, and Florence purchased Silvestri, Carvel Hall, Elements, Rauch Industries, C.J. Vander, and Farberware—for nearly $42 million—a leading manufacturer of cookware and small electric appliances in February 1996, shortly before selling to Lee Co., and then licensed the name out to Meyer Corp. for some $25 million.

In August 1997, Lee Co., backed by a $900 million loan from Chase Manhattan Corp. and Merrill Lynch & Co., leveraged a $1.06 billion buyout of Hampton, New Hampshire-based Fisher Scientific International, maker of scientific equipment, outbidding hostile Bass Group of Fort Worth, who held 10 percent of the company. Chase Securities Inc., Chase Capital Partners, Merrill Lynch, and Donaldson, Lufkin & Jenrette's DLJ Merchant Banking Partners also invested equity in the deal.

Also in August, following $1.2 billion in acquisitions in a short period of time, Cambridge, Massachusetts-based computer software firm The Learning Company issued $150 million in preferred stock to Lee Co., Bain Capital Inc., and Centre Partners Management LLC of New York, who bought out The Tribune Co.'s share of The Learning Company, to cut its debt. Lee and the other investors received roughly 25 percent of the company. The Learning Company, itself purchased in 1995 by SoftKey International Inc., which took the former's name, was responsible for such hit programs as the award-winning Reader Rabbit and Oregon Trail.

In September 1997, CIBC Wood Gundy Securities Corp.'s New York unit, along with First Union Corp., contributed a $115 million bank loan and a $75 bridge loan to help with the financing for Thomas H. Lee Equity Fund III's $300 million recapitalization of Transwestern Publishing Co. LP, a San Diego-based publisher of telephone directories, until the latter company could complete a high-yield bond offering later that year. The Fund itself closed in 1995 with a value of $1.5 billion.

Continental Illinois Venture Corp., a subsidiary of BankAmerica Corp. and Transwestern's largest shareholder, also contributed to the investment. CIBC and First Union had originally made a loan in 1993 which financed Continental Illinois' management buyout of Transwestern.

As the company entered 1998, it showed no sign of slowing down, acquiring a stake in an eye care center chain, among other investments. If Lee's history is any indication, he will remain personally on the *Forbes* 400 list, and drive his company to further success.

Further Reading

Berman, Phyllis, "Tom Lee Is on a Roll," *Forbes,* November 17, 1997, p. 126.

Bernard, Sharyn, "Syratech Opts for Buyout: OKs $32 a Share from Equity Firm," *HFN: The Weekly Newspaper for the Home Furnishing Network,* October 28, 1996, p. 1.

"Braun Parent Okays Thermoscan Buyout," *HFN: The Weekly Newspaper for the Home Furnishing Network,* October 23, 1995, p. 6.

Bulkeley, William M., "Buyout Firm Cuts Fisher Scientific Bid Due to UPS Strike," *Wall Street Journal,* September 15, 1997, p. B11A(W)/B12A(E).

——, "Thomas H. Lee Co. Agrees to Buy Fisher Scientific for $1.06 Billion," *Wall Street Journal,* August 8, 1997, p. B4(W)/B4(E).

——, "Thomas H. Lee Outbids 2 to Buy Fisher Scientific," *Wall Street Journal, Europe,* August 8, 1997, p. 3.

Dunaief, Daniel, "Donaldson Acts As Lead Bank in Rayovac Buyout Loan," *American Banker,* September 5, 1996, p. 1.

Fickenscher, Lisa, "Sale Seen Reviving TRW Credit Reporting Unit: Market Share Had Dwindled Under Preoccupied Parent," *American Banker,* February 14, 1996, p. 12.

"First Alert, BRK Sold to Investment Group," *Chilton's Hardware Age,* August 1992, p. 30.

"Fisher Scientific International Inc.," *Wall Street Journal,* January 20, 1998, p. B4(W)/C10(E).

"Fisher Scientific Reaches Revised Deal with Lee," *New York Times,* September 13, 1997, p.25(N)/37(L).

Gerard, Jeremy, "Livent Sells 20% Stake: Drabinsky Writes Off 'Kiss of the Spider Woman,' " *Variety,* January 23, 1995, p. 75.

Goldblatt, Jennifer, "Chase, Merrill to Market $900M Loan in Fisher LBO," *American Banker,* August 11, 1997, p. 16.

——, "CIBC, 1st Union Co-Lead $300M Recapitalization Deal for Thomas H. Lee," *American Banker,* September 29, 1997, p. 19.

Goodwin, William, "$140 Million Deal Proves Tough Sell for 1st Chicago," *American Banker,* September 5, 1991, p. 1.

"Harvard in Group Buying Oxford Clothes," *Crain's Chicago Business,* February 5, 1990, p. 46.

"Investment Firm to Acquire Stake in Eye Care Centers," *New York Times,* March 10, 1998, p. C3(N)/D3(L).

"Investor Group Offers $1.4 Billion for Fisher," *New York Times,* August 8, 1997, p. C3(N)/D3(L).

Kehoe, Ann-Margaret, "Syratech Merger Complete," *HFN: The Weekly Newspaper for the Home Furnishing Network,* April 21, 1997, p. 47.

Kerber, Ross, "Investor Group Led by Lee Co. to Pay $123 Million for Stake in Learning Co.," *Wall Street Journal,* August 27, 1997, p. B7(E).

La Monica, Paul R., "Buyout Artist Scores Again with HomeSide Sale," *American Banker,* October 30, 1997, p. 13.

"Learning Co. Stake Will Be Purchased by Investment Group," *Wall Street Journal,* August 27, 1997, p. B6(W).

"Lee Buyout Firm to Raise $2.5 Billion for New Fund," *Wall Street Journal,* September 11, 1997, p. C22(W)/B2(E).

"Lee Buys Sun Pharmaceuticals," *Supermarket News,* December 21, 1992, p. 28.

Liddle, Alan, "Restaurants Unltd. Execs, Partners Buy Out Jacobs," *Nation's Restaurant News,* June 13, 1994, p. 1.

Marsh, Ann, "Lee's New Deal," *Forbes,* November 20, 1995, p. 14.

Mehlman, William, "Hills Department Stores, Inc.," *Insiders' Chronicle,* October 26, 1987, p. 3.

Ourusoff, Alexandra, "Obsession: How Hills Department Stores Became Tom Lee's Waterloo," *Financial World,* September 3, 1991, p. 32.

"Pittway to Sell First Alert/BRK Electronics Unit," *HFD: The Weekly Home Furnishings Newspaper,* July 6, 1992, p. 6.

Prewitt, Milford, "Investment Firm Buys 25% of NY Restaurant Group," *Nation's Restaurant News,* January 8, 1996, p. 1.

"Syratech to Be Acquired by a Boston Financier for $300 Million in Cash," *Wall Street Journal, Europe,* October 25, 1996, p. 3.

Talley, Karen, "Bank of Boston Sells Part of Unit in Step Toward Link with Barnett," *American Banker,* March 20, 1996, p. 12.

Tau, Stephen, "Toting Up Tom Lee's Snapple Gains," *Financial World,* December 6, 1994, p. 14.

Zwiebach, Elliot, "Big V Supermarkets Is Sold in Second LBO," *Supermarket News,* January 14, 1991, p. 1.

—Daryl F. Mallett

Thorn plc

Thorn House
124 Bridge Road
Chertsey, Surrey KT16 8LZ
United Kingdom
(01932) 573 700
Fax: (01932) 573 782

Public Company
Incorporated: 1996
Employees: 18,183
Sales:£1.25 billion (US$2.04 billion) (1998)
Stock Exchanges: London NASDAQ
Ticker Symbol: THRNY
SICs: 6719 Offices of Holding Companies, Not
  Elsewhere Classified; 7299 Miscellaneous Personal
  Services, Not Elsewhere Classified; 7389 Business
  Services, Not Elsewhere Classified

Thorn plc is an international rental and rent-to-own group whose various chains rent electronics, personal computers, appliances, telephones, furniture, and jewelry. Thorn's customers are predominantly individual consumers but also include hotels and educational institutions. In the United Kingdom, Thorn runs four primary chains: Radio Rentals, Easiview, DER Direct, and Crazy George. Thorn's overseas operations were put up for sale in mid-1998 and include the Rent-A-Center and other chains in the United States, as well as operations elsewhere in Europe and in the Asia-Pacific region. In its present form, Thorn plc was incorporated in 1996 when Thorn EMI plc "demerged," becoming Thorn plc and EMI Group plc, nearly 17 years after they had merged.

Roots in Electrical and Electronics Businesses

Jules Thorn was born in Austria in 1899, and as a young man attended the University of Vienna, where he completed a degree in business management. During the 1920s Thorn traveled to England on several occasions as a sales representative for an Austrian gas mantle firm. In 1928, shortly after he moved to England, Thorn established the Electrical Lamp Service Company, which imported light bulbs and radio components from the continent. In 1932 he purchased a controlling share of the Chorlton Metal Company. Thorn operated a radio rental shop, which was established as Lotus Radio in 1933. That same year he purchased Atlas Works, manufacturer of an electric lamp known as the Atlas Lamp. With the profits from these operations, Thorn acquired the Ferguson Radio Corporation in 1936, enabling him to manufacture as well as sell radio sets. The company's operations were subsequently merged that year under the name Thorn Electrical Industries.

Thorn's electronic businesses prospered until 1940 when Britain declared war on Germany. As a result of the war, the British economy was severely affected. Virtually all products, including those manufactured by Thorn, fell under a tightly controlled government rationing program.

When the war ended in 1945, Jules Thorn initiated an ambitious expansion of his company's interests through acquisition. Ecko-Ensign Design and Tricity Cookers, both electrical engineering firms, were purchased in 1950 and 1951, respectively. Throughout the 1950s Thorn Electrical Industries consolidated a firm position in the field of electronics and electrical appliances. Thorn personally supervised every aspect of his company's activities, gaining a reputation for hard work and tireless enthusiasm for profit.

By the end of 1961, Thorn had acquired Philco and Pilot, in addition to Ultra Radio & Television and interests in HMV and Marconiphone. Through its acquisitions that year, Thorn Electrical Industries had become the largest producer of radio and television sets in Britain. In recognition for his contributions to the British electronics industry Jules Thorn was knighted Sir Jules in 1964.

The transmission of television programs in color did not begin in Britain until December 1967. Jules Thorn recognized that this development would drastically increase demand for color television sets, the technology and patents of which were difficult to acquire in Britain. Thorn arranged for blank tubes to be imported from the United States and coated with the necessary color-sensitive chemicals in his factories. Because of Thorn's imaginative and timely solution, Thorn Electrical Industries was able to further consolidate its position in the British television market.

As a result of the merger of Robinson Radio Rentals and Thorn interests, the combined Thorn/Radio Rentals group became the world's largest television rental company, controlling just under one-third of the 7.5 million televisions in Britain. Other acquisitions during this period reflected the company's continued diversification. Metal Industries was acquired in 1967, KMT Holdings in 1968, Parkinson Cowan in 1971, Clarkson International Tools in 1974, and Cleveland Twist Drill in 1976.

Thorn EMI Forms in 1979

Thorn's largest takeover bid by far came in 1979 when an opportunity arose to purchase the financially ailing EMI Ltd., a diversified entertainment and electronic instruments conglomerate. Jules Thorn had retired earlier in 1979; his domineering personality had squelched a proposed merger between the two firms a few years earlier. (Thorn died on December 12, 1980, at the age of 81.)

Institutional investors, who held a three-fourths voting majority in Thorn, expressed concern that a merger of the two companies would be problematic because Thorn and EMI were very different companies. In the event of a merger, Thorn would have to let EMI management run itself, at least for a few years, because Thorn knew so little about EMI's businesses. Another cause for concern was that EMI's new management team, led by the very capable Lord Delfont, had to prove itself under difficult circumstances.

At the end of October 1979 EMI rejected a £145 million bid by Thorn. The offer was resubmitted the following week for £165 million and accepted. The new company's name was changed to Thorn EMI plc on March 3, 1980.

The various divisions within the old Thorn and EMI organizations continued to operate independently of each other and, to some extent, of the central management group. Management implemented a planning model developed by the Boston Consulting Group which provided for the development of new enterprises by channeling funds from profitable operations. This had the effect of starving the successful enterprises within the company of funds needed to maintain competitive product lines. Just as the model failed in the early 1970s, it was failing again a decade later. Thorn EMI was less like a successful operating company and more like a weak investment portfolio. In an attempt to raise money and reduce losses during 1980 and 1981, the company sold its medical electronics business, its hotels and restaurant division, and parts of the leisure and entertainment division.

Peter Laister, chairman of Thorn and later Thorn EMI, attempted to create a more efficient operation out of the fragmented organization by acquiring new divisions. Laister wanted to develop an integrated communications and entertainment business with particular emphasis on advanced electronics. Inmos, a microchip manufacturer, was acquired in 1984, but an attempt to purchase British Aerospace plc that same year failed.

Unable to fulfill his plan or shake Thorn EMI out of stagnation, Laister was removed from the board of directors in what was described as a boardroom "coup" in July 1985.

Thorn EMI Restructures in 1985

Thorn EMI's new chairman, Graham Wilkins, handed Laister's managing director position over to Colin Southgate, who had been in charge of the company's information technology division. Southgate advocated a much different approach than Laister's, emphasizing a return to the basic industries upon which Thorn and EMI had been separately built: lighting, rental, and retail as overseen by Radio Rentals, Rumbelows electronics stores, and HMV music stores; technology, including computer software, defense electronics, and security businesses; and music.

Southgate quickly initiated a dramatic program of rationalization, divesting—by the end of the decade—more than 50 noncore operations, bringing in more than US$700 million. The divestment of these unpromising operations began in earnest during the 1985–86 fiscal year with the disposal of Thorn EMI Screen Entertainment (the expensive films and cinema division), Thorn EMI Heating Ltd., divisions of Metal Industries that had not already been sold, cable television interests, and a portion of its interest in Thames Television Ltd. Southgate took the cash generated from these sales and plowed them back into the company's core areas. The first major purchase for Thorn EMI in the Southgate era came in late 1987 when Wichita, Kansas-based, 700-store Rent-A-Center, Inc. was acquired for £371 million (US$594 million). The purchase gave Thorn EMI 50 percent of the rental market in the United States and made the company the largest rental company in the world. Acquisitions of lighting fixture makers in France and Sweden made Thorn EMI the leader in lighting in Europe. Additional acquisitions bolstered the music operations, most notably the 1989 acquisition of SBK Entertainment World, Inc. for £165 million (US$337 million), which added the 250,000-song catalog of CBS Records to EMI Music Publishing. In July 1988 Southgate became CEO of the company upon Wilkins retirement.

In the early to mid-1990s Southgate further focused the company's interests until there were only two: the rental business and music. The software business was disposed of in 1991, and two years later Thorn EMI sold its lighting division, the business upon which the Thorn side had been founded. Over the course of several years and several transactions, the company's defense businesses had been divested by 1996. In 1994 Thorn Security was jettisoned. (In each of these cases, Thorn EMI at least initially kept a minority stake in the disposed unit.) Also divested was the troubled Rumbelows chain, which was closed down in February 1995; one month later, 231 of the former Rumbelows were sold to Escom, a German computer manufacturer and retailer.

During this time, an article in the September 22, 1993 *Wall Street Journal* accused the Rent-A-Center chain of a variety of improprieties, most notably claims of questionable sales practices and of strong-arm tactics used to deal with customers who were late in making rental payments. Thorn EMI quickly set up an independent investigation headed by former U.S. senator Warren Rudman. In February 1994 the investigation issued a report that largely cleared the Rent-A-Center name. Despite this publicity setback, Thorn EMI continued to invest in its U.S. rental operation, acquiring U-Can-Rent Inc. and its chain of 83 rental stores in small cities of the southeastern United States in August 1995.

Thorn EMI also poured money into its music operations in the early to mid-1990s. In 1990, 50 percent of Chrysalis Records was purchased, with the other half acquired two years later. Virgin Music Group Ltd. was bought for £510 million (US$957 million) in 1992, a deal that included both record labels and publishing catalogs. Sparrow Records, the largest Christian music label in the United States, was added in 1992, while Intercord, a leading independent record company in Germany, was acquired in 1994. Thorn EMI also entered into joint ventures that launched the VIVA and VIVA2 music television channels in Germany, as well as the Channel V music channel in Asia. In 1995 a U.K. bookstore chain called Dillons was acquired and was added to the HMV division.

1996 Demerger of Thorn EMI

By mid-1996 Thorn EMI essentially consisted of two strong divisions—music and rental—both world leaders. They had little in common, however, leading to the long-anticipated August 29, 1996, demerger of Thorn EMI, out of which arose Thorn plc and EMI Group plc, both initially headed by Southgate as chairman. EMI Group included all of Thorn EMI's music-related operations: music recording, publishing, and retailing, as well as investments in the music channels. It also included the Dillons bookstores, which continued as part of the HMV Division. Several noncore businesses—Central Research Laboratories, Thorn Secure Science International, Thorn Transit Systems International, and a holding in Thorn Security—that EMI retained after the demerger were divested less than a year later.

Thorn plc, meanwhile, debuted as an almost exclusively rental company (a consumer electronics and music retailing subsidiary in Denmark was sold for £76 million [US$122 million] in November 1997). In the United Kingdom it had several chains, including Radio Rentals, Crazy George, Easiview, and DER Direct, which rented telephones. U.S. operations included the Rent-A-Center, U-Can-Rent, and Remco chains. Thorn also ran additional rental businesses on continental Europe and in Australia.

Unfortunately, Thorn almost immediately ran into serious troubles in its newly independent guise. At home the rental business was experiencing a sharp downturn, leading to the February 1997 announcement that 90 Radio Rentals shops would be closed. The company's European chains were losing money, too, resulting in the closure of rental operations in France, the Benelux countries, and Finland, a move announced in July 1997. In the United States, Thorn faced the prospect of losing several class-action lawsuits brought against Rent-A-Center, lawsuits that accused the chain of employing rental contracts that charged more interest than allowed by law. In September 1997 a court in New Jersey ruled against Rent-A-Center in a class-action suit that Thorn estimated could cost it £75 million (US$120 million). Similar suits were pending in

Minnesota, Texas, Pennsylvania, and Wisconsin. Thorn announced it would appeal the New Jersey judgment.

For the fiscal year ending March 31, 1998, Thorn saw its revenues fall two percent to £1.25 billion (US$2.04 billion), while profits fell 30.9 percent to £118.2 million (US$193.3 million). The month prior to making these dismal results known, Thorn announced that it had been approached by an unnamed suitor about a takeover. Then, after the 1998 results were announced, Thorn in late May 1998 put up for sale all of its non-U.K. businesses: Thorn Americas (Rent-A-Center and the other U.S. chains), Thorn Nordic, Thorn Asia Pacific, and a business-to-business rental operation in Europe. Provided that a buyer or buyers could be found for all the units—and Thorn Americas was going to be a tough sale because of the pending litigation—Thorn plc would be left with its four U.K. chains, which it could focus on for a possible turnaround. After 70 years that encompassed an amazing variety of businesses in numerous countries, it appeared that Thorn's immediate future—as an independent company or not—would focus on a single type of business in a single country.

Principal Subsidiaries

Thorn Business Communications Ltd.; Thorn Nordic; Thorn Americas Inc. (U.S.); Rent-A-Center, Inc. (U.S.); Thorn Asia Pacific.

Further Reading

Blackwell, David, "US Court Ruling Impales Thorn," *Financial Times,* September 17, 1997, p. 33.
Bonte-Friedheim, Robert, "Thorn Shares Fall After Court Ruling in Class-Action Suit," *Wall Street Journal,* September 16, 1997, p. A16.
Clark-Meads, Jeff, Adam White, and Don Jeffrey, "Thorn EMI Demerger Proceeding Smoothly," *Billboard,* August 31, 1996, pp. 1, 127.
"Duet for One: Thorn EMI," *Economist,* November 27, 1993, p. 71.
Foster, Anna, "Leading Light at Thorn," *Management Today,* August 1988, p. 46.
Foster, Geoffrey, "Three over Thirty," *Management Today,* May 1996, pp. 64–66.
Freedman, Alix M., "Peddling Dreams: A Marketing Giant Uses Its Sales Prowess to Profit on Poverty," *Wall Street Journal,* September 22, 1993, pp. A1, A10.
Gubernick, Lisa, "Don't Worry, He's Happy," *Forbes,* April 17, 1989, p. 154.
Hollinger, Peggy, "Thorn Sells Majority Stake in Security Arm," *Financial Times,* May 28, 1994, p. 10.
——, "Thorn Shares Tumble on Warning," *Financial Times,* January 21, 1997, p. 21.
Iliot, Terry, "EMI Faces Thorny Dilemma," *Variety,* September 14, 1992, p. 32.
Jarvis, Paul, "Thorn's '98 Net Will Be at Low End of Forecasts," *Wall Street Journal,* February 17, 1998, p. B19B.
Midgley, Dominic, "Thorn EMI's Fissile Future," *Management Today,* August 1994, pp. 24–28.
Pandit, S. A., *From Making to Music: The History of Thorn EMI,* London: Hodder & Stoughton, 1996.
Price, Christopher, "Thorn Runs into Prickly Problems," *Financial Times,* November 23, 1996, p. 5.
Rawsthorn, Alice, "A Musical Spin-Off," *Financial Times,* July 22, 1995, p. 7.

——, "Thorn and EMI Prepare to Dance to Different Tunes," *Financial Times,* July 22, 1996, p. 23.

Rose, Matthew, "Thorn Shares Rise 38% After U.K. Firm Says It Is in Discussions with a Bidder," *Wall Street Journal,* April 8, 1998, p. A18.

Skapinker, Michael, "Thorn Chairman Answers Rent-A-Center Critics," *Financial Times,* September 25, 1993, p. 12.

Snoddy, Raymond, "New Chapter for Thorn EMI," *Financial Times,* March 3, 1995, p. 20.

Wright, Robert, "Mystery Suitor Stalks Thorn," *Financial Times,* April 8, 1998, p. 24.

——, "Thorn Looks for Disposal Opportunities," *Financial Times,* November 16, 1997, p. 26.

—updated by David E. Salamie

TOMEN

Tomen Corporation

6–7, Kawaramachi 1-chome
Chuo-ku
Osaka 530-91
Japan
(06) 208-2211
Fax: (06) 3588-9980
Web site: http://www.tomen.co.jp

Public Company
Incorporated: 1920 as Toyo Menka Kaisha Ltd.
Employees: 2,795
Sales: ¥5.4 trillion (US $41.9 billion) (1998)
Stock Exchanges: Tokyo Osaka Nagoya
SICs: 6799 Investors, Not Elsewhere Classified

Tomen Corporation is Japan's seventh largest general trading company (or *sogo shosha*), Japan's 17th largest company overall, and the world's 40th largest firm in terms of sales volume. Tomen is an international power concentrating on four main areas: independent power production, agricultural chemicals, food processing, and telecommunications. The company, which began as an importer of raw cotton, has a global network of more than 100 branches and offices in more than 60 countries.

Early History

During the 1920s, as Japan became increasingly industrialized, spinning and weaving arose as an important industry in Japan. Among the most prosperous of Japan's industrial groups was Mitsui & Company. Tomen established itself as Toyo Menka Kaisha Ltd., or Oriental Cotton Trading, in April 1920, with capital of ¥25 million. It was formed to import raw cotton and sell textiles both domestically and abroad when Mitsui & Company spun off its cotton department. Mitsui did so because the cotton trade became very risky during the post-World War I era. Raw cotton is an internationally traded commodity, and the global postwar recession of this period made trading in such a market highly speculative.

The company's first years were troubled, especially during Japan's financial panics of 1922 and 1927. Nonetheless, the company captured ten percent of the Japanese cotton market within a few years. Before 1920 Mitsui & Company had served 30 percent of the market. By 1924 Toyo Menka had founded its first overseas arm, the Southern Cotton Company in Dallas, Texas. During the early 1930s Toyo Menka and Mitsui & Company had sufficient confidence in the textile market to offer to buy Brazil's entire cotton crop. The companies encouraged Japanese immigrants to Brazil to grow cotton, and the São Paulo cotton crop was nearly doubled by Japanese farmers. Despite the unstable economic climate and Japan's involvement in the Sino-Japanese War, Toyo Menka expanded quickly, increasing its capital to ¥35 million by 1940. By 1935 it imported nearly 20 percent of Japan's raw cotton and provided more than 20 percent of the country's cotton-textile exports to India. Indonesia and India were a strong market for Toyo Menka, which was able to import Indian raw cotton, process it, and sell the cotton textiles in India more cheaply than the Indians. The demand for processed cotton fabrics increased in the mid-1930s. Toyo Menka then gained markets in Europe and became Japan's largest importer of raw cotton. The company owed part of its success to its ability to exploit cheap labor in its colonies and in Manchukuo and China. Toyo Menka wielded considerable influence in China before and during World War II.

The outbreak of World War II had a severe impact on trading companies in Japan as distribution of their commodities was limited to the Greater East Asia Co-Prosperity Sphere, those areas in East Asia over which Japan exercised at least some control. Toyo Menka's exports were limited to cotton-textile shipments to Manchuria and China, and even these were virtually suspended eventually. Toyo Menka was able to take over large cotton-textile operations in Shanghai and other occupied cities, however, and it thrived domestically. Trading activities were controlled further by the government's Trade Control Committee, established in 1942, which essentially made a government subcontractor of Toyo Menka. Toyo Menka worked closely with the Japanese government during the war and enjoyed a great deal of political influence. Some of Toyo Menka's Chinese branch offices were used by an undercover agency known as the Kodama Machine, for its leader, Yoshi Kodama.

488

The Kodama Machine acted as a clearinghouse for looted valuables leaving China and black market goods entering China.

Postwar Recovery and Expansion

After the war business activities in Japan were regulated by the Allied occupation authorities. This period was marked by the dissolution of *zaibatsu*, business conglomerates, including Mitsui, of which Toyo Menka had remained a member. Between 1945 and 1949, Toyo Menka's operations were curtailed by its classification by authorities as a restricted company, but it began handling metals, machinery, and food products in 1947. Business dealings were eased when most of the responsibility for self-government was given back to Japan in 1949. Toyo Menka began to rebuild, with its staff halved.

In 1950 Toyo Menka turned the corner into real growth, aided by postwar economic stability and especially by the Korean War, begun in June 1950. The war stimulated rapid economic recovery in Japan. Industrial plants and the textile industry thrived. Toyo Menka's capital increased to ¥150 million, and the company was listed on the Osaka and Tokyo stock exchanges in 1950.

As world trade volume soared during the 1950s Toyo Menka expanded its overseas network, beginning with the establishment of Toyomenka (America) Inc. in 1951. Toyo Cotton Company opened in Dallas, Texas, in 1952. A Bangkok branch was opened in 1954—the first Japanese trading company posted there—followed by a London branch in 1956. Toyo Menka had 33 branches and offices internationally by 1955. Toyomenka (Australia) Pty., Ltd. was founded in 1957. Japan was working toward integration in the international community at this time; it joined the United Nations in 1957 and established the Japan External Trade Organization in 1958.

Concurrent with its international expansions, Toyo Menka sought to increase its offerings by merging with specialized trading companies. In 1955 it absorbed Kanegafuchi Shoji and increased its textile activities. Toyo Menka acquired Honcho Real Estate in 1956. Toyo Menka's real estate division eventu-

ally grew into an international urban development group, emphasizing residential developments, with more than 20 affiliated companies. Activities included urban renewal projects and recreational facilities. The division oversaw the development of residential subdivisions, shopping centers, condominiums, and golf courses.

With the sustained economic boom of the 1960s, Japan became a world power, exporting in enormous quantities and widening its product range. Toyo Menka's merger with Taiyo Bussan in 1961 expanded its food products divisions. The absorption of Nankai Kogyo in 1963 brought Toyo Menka increased iron and steel activities. Toyo Menka was importing about 70 percent of Japan's machine tools. This merger boosted Toyo Menka's exports of steel and iron to the United States, and exports of plant, machinery, and ships to Asia. In the early 1990s, Toyo Menka's iron and steel division handled products that ranged from iron ore and other raw materials to finished products. Company capital more than doubled between 1960 and 1973. Toyo Menka also began importing hard coking coal from Australia. Other ventures begun in overseas subsidiaries in the 1960s included a fabric processing mill in Thailand, a cottonseed oil manufacturer in Brazil, and a manufacturer of synthetic textiles in Indonesia. Toyo Menka celebrated its 50th anniversary in 1970 and changed its Japanese name from Toyo Menka to Tomen, although its English name remained Toyo Menka Kaisha, Ltd.

As the oil crisis of the mid-1970s spawned recession in the United States and Europe, Toyo Menka reviewed its internal organization and expanded its product line. In the late 1970s, Toyo Menka began issuing a variety of bonds in Europe and the United States to strengthen its financial and capital structure. Bond issuance continued through the 1980s. The recession stalled Toyo Menka's growth; sales only inched up between 1973 and 1978. The company worked on establishing joint overseas ventures and projects. These included forklift trucks in West Germany and sheet glass production in Malaysia. The 1973 oil crisis prompted Toyo Menka to establish new ties to petroleum at home.

Just as the economic climate began to improve, the 1979 oil crisis occurred. During the late 1970s, Toyo Menka continued its overseas activities, establishing more companies in Thailand, Indonesia, and Australia. In 1979 Toyo Menka was active with orders for construction machinery, desalination projects, ships, and offshore drilling equipment.

Diversification Continued in the 1980s

Toyo Menka's energy division separated from the chemicals and fuels division in 1981, as the company's energy-related transactions escalated. This division's main activities were the import of crude oil and liquefied gas as well as offshore dealings, the import and export of petroleum products, and uranium imports. It also supplied lubricating oils and fuels to vessels in major ports around the world. Domestic affiliates within this division included many gasoline stations. Toyo Menka also expanded into fields of electronics and data technology in the early 1980s. Tomen Information Systems Corporation was established in 1982, and Tomen Electronics Corporation was founded the following year. Company sales went from US $18 billion in 1980 to US $25 billion in 1984. Another diversification at this time included apparel retailing.

With attention being drawn to the trade imbalances favoring Japan in the mid-1980s, Toyo Menka focused on expanding its domestic activities, and by 1989, domestic transactions had increased dramatically. Toyo Menka became Japan's leading importer of wine, taking advantage of that fast-expanding market. In the fall of 1990, Toyo Menka Kaisha, Ltd. changed its name to Tomen Corporation. Tomen had been Toyo Menka's nickname since its founding. That spring, it spun off its own cotton department as Toyo Cotton (Japan) Company.

1990s Difficulties Led to Radical Restructuring

The bursting of the late 1980s Japanese economic bubble led to prolonged difficulties for Tomen in the 1990s. Nearly all of the *sogo shosha* had diversified aggressively into financial investments during the speculative bubble years, in large part because their traditional activity of marginally profitable commodity trading had been in a deep decline for years, a development compounded by a trend toward Japanese companies handling their international operations themselves. In desperation the trading companies built up large stock portfolios and became hooked on the revenues they could gain through arbitrage (or *zaiteku,* as it is known in Japan). Once the bubble burst, the *sogo shosha* were left with huge portfolios whose worth had plummeted; all of the trading companies were forced eventually to liquidate much of their stock holdings.

Tomen waited until fiscal 1998 before making its largest write-down of portfolio losses, ¥25 billion (US $194 million). The write-down led to a net loss of ¥19 billion (US $147 million)—the first in more than 40 years—and to the company not paying a dividend, again for the first time in more than 40 years.

Simultaneous with the March 1998 announcement of this dismal news, Tomen said that it would begin a radical restructuring (at least by Japanese standards), which had at its heart three main components. First, Tomen would abandon the soup to nuts approach that has been traditional for all *sogo shosha* in favor of a concentration on four main areas, from which the company hoped to generate 80 percent of its profits: independent power production, agricultural chemicals, food processing, and telecommunications. Managing director Takeshige Yuzo told the *Financial Times:* "The era in which trading companies handle everything from ramen [noodles] to rockets is over." As part of this major change, Tomen planned to divest or integrate up to 50 affiliated companies over a two-year period, as well as streamline its sales and administrative departments with a concomitant reduction in staff by 400. Second, Tomen aimed to reduce its liabilities by ¥200 billion (US $1.55 billion) through liquidating securities, real estate, and other investments. Third, to improve and speed up the company's decision-making process, Tomen's entire organizational structure was to be streamlined, by cutting the number of directors in half, by forming a management committee with fewer than ten members, and by using locally hired experts to run overseas offices rather than Japanese managers.

All told, these changes represented a significant departure from tradition for a Japanese company. Much of the plan was designed to turn Tomen into more of an Anglo-American-style company, where shareholder value is the prime measure of success. Tomen picked a particularly challenging time to take this type of large risk, as the Japanese economy continued in stagnation, and as the Asian financial crisis had seemingly only just begun. It was quite possible that if Tomen succeeded in its efforts to reshape itself, many other Japanese firms would follow its lead.

Principal Subsidiaries

NORTH AMERICA: Tomen America Inc. (U.S.A.); Chickasha Cotton Oil Co. (U.S.A.); Toyo Cotton Co. (U.S.A.); Casio, Inc. (U.S.A.); Goldtex, Inc. (U.S.A.); Tomen Power Corp. (U.S.A.); Techno Steel Corp. (U.S.A.); Trans-Aqua International Inc. (U.S.A.); Tomen Agro Inc. (U.S.A.); Tomen Canada Inc. CENTRAL AND SOUTH AMERICA: Tomen de Mexico, S.A. de C.V.; Tomen Corporation do Brasil Ltda. (Brazil); Oleos ''MENU'' Industria e Comercio Ltda. (Brazil); Hokko do Brasil Industria Quimica e Agro Pecuaria Ltda. (Brazil); Kanebo Silk do Brasil S.A. Industria de Seda (Brazil); Superfine Industria e Comercio Ltda. (Brazil); Tomen Panama, S.A.; Tomen Latin America, S.A. (Panama); Ecuatoyo Cia, Ltda. (Ecuador); Centragas-Transportadora de la Region Central de Enron Development & Cia, S.C.A. (Colombia). EUROPE: Tomen Deutschland G.m.b.H. (Germany); Tomen Textilmaschinen G.m.b.H. (Germany); Casio Computer Co., G.m.b.H. Deutschland (Germany); Tomen France S.A.; Nutri-Tomen S.A. (France); Yangtzekiang-Tomen S.A. (France); Tomen Europe Ltd. (U.K.); Tomen (U.K.) PLC; Tomen Power Corporation (U.K.) Ltd.; Tomen Netherlands B.V.; Tomen Finance Nederland B.V. (Netherlands); Feedadex B.V. (Netherlands); Tomen Corporation Espana S.A. (Spain); Tomen Italia S.p.A. (Italy); Budapesti Eromu Rt. (Hungary); Salgotarjan Glass Wool Ltd. (Hungary); Agroferm Hungarian-Japanese Fermentation Industry Ltd. (Hungary). NEAR AND MIDDLE EAST: Tomen Iran Ltd.; Alexandria National Iron and Steel Co., S.A.E. (Egypt). ASIA: Sheng Yu Steel Co., Ltd. (Taiwan); Grand Biotechnology Co., Ltd. (Taiwan); Taiwan Chao Yang Chemical Co., Ltd.; Ton Yi Industrial Corp. (Taiwan); Toyo Cosmos Enterprise Co., Ltd. (Taiwan); Young Sun Chemtrading Co., Ltd. (Taiwan); Tomen Korea Corp.; Korea Fine Chemical Co., Ltd.; Korea Polyol Co., Ltd.; Tomen (Thailand), Ltd.; Tomen Enterprise (Bangkok) Ltd. (Thailand); Eastern Chemical Co., Ltd. (Thailand); Lohakit Steel Service Center Co., Ltd. (Thailand); Sukosol & Mazda Co., Ltd. (Thailand); Sukosol & Mazda Motor Industry Co., Ltd. (Thailand); Thai Chemical Terminal Co., Ltd. (Thailand); Tovecan Factory (Vietnam); Quang Ninh-Tomen Gum Rosin Industry (Vietnam); LMG-Chemicals Co. (Philippines); Norgate Apparel Manufacturing, Inc. (Philippines); Sakamoto Orient Chemicals Corp. (Philippines); Northern Mindanao Power Corp. (Philippines); Growchem Trading (Singapore) Pte. Ltd.; Tomen Petroleum (Singapore) Pte. Ltd.; Tomen Construction & Leasing (Singapore) Pte. Ltd.; Tomen International (Malaysia) Sdn. Bhd.; Alpha Industries Sdn. Bhd. (Malaysia); Hino Motors (Malaysia) Sdn. Bhd.; Kohno Plastic (Malaysia) Sdn. Bhd.; Toyo Plastic (Malaysia) Sdn. Bhd.; P.T. Tomenindo Lestari (Indonesia); P.T. Canvas Industry Indonesia; P.T. Indonesia Petroleum Industries; P.T. Kanebo Tomen

Sandang Synthetic Mills (Indonesia); P.T. Karka Nutri Industri (Indonesia); P.T. Styrindo Mono Indonesia; P.T. Teijin Indonesia Fiber Corp.; P.T. Tembaga Mulia Semanan (Indonesia); P.T. Tomenbo Indonesia; P.T. N.G.K. Busi Indonesia; TDT Copper Ltd. (India); Ghandhara Nissan Ltd. (Pakistan); Kohinoor Energy Ltd. (Pakistan); Dalian Huaqi Fashion Co., Ltd. (China); Huaxing Stone Industry Co., Ltd. (China); Tianjin KDS Corp. (China); Dalian Advanced Chemical Co., Ltd. (China); Nantong Hui Shou Di Fashion (China); Shanghai Kunimi Fashion Co., Ltd. (China); Zhong Shan Zhonglong Aguatic Co., Ltd. (China); Tomen (H.K.) Co., Ltd. (Hong Kong); K&T Foods Co., Ltd. (Hong Kong); Tomen Finance (H.K.) Ltd. (Hong Kong); Tomen (Asia) Hong Kong Ltd.; Tomen Hot-Line (Hong Kong) Ltd.; Yuen Long Textile Co., Ltd. (Hong Kong). OCEANIA: Tomen Australia Ltd.; Oakbridge Ltd. (Australia); Dyechem Industries Pty. Ltd. (Australia); Tomen (N.Z.) Ltd. (New Zealand); Polymers International Ltd. (New Zealand).

Principal Divisions

Steel Products & Raw Materials Division; Nonferrous Metals Division; Housing & General Merchandises Division; Power & Utility Projects Division; Information & Communications Division; Industrial Project Division; Electronics & Automobile Division; Produce Division; Foodstuff Division; Organic Chemicals Division; Specialty & Inorganic Chemicals Division; Plastics Division; Energy Department; Textile Materials & Fabrics Division; Industrial Textiles Division; Apparel Division; Media & Telecommunication Business Office.

Further Reading

"Continental Cable Plans Joint Venture with Tomen in Japan," *Wall Street Journal,* March 15, 1995, p. C10.
Harbrect, Douglas, and Hiromi Uchida, "For Japan Inc., a Kentucky Whipping," *Business Week,* November 8, 1993, pp. 56–57.
Iwao, Ichiishi, "Sogo Shosha: Meeting New Challenges," *Journal of Japanese Trade & Industry,* January/February 1995, pp. 16–18.
Nakamoto, Michiyo, "Directors Cut in Tomen Shake-Up," *Financial Times,* March 16, 1998, p. 26.
——, "From Noodles and Rockets to Shareholder Value," *Financial Times,* March 20, 1998, p. 30.
Roberts, John G., *Mitsui: Three Centuries of Japanese Business,* 2nd ed., New York: Weatherhill, 1989.
Rosario, Louise do, "Lose and Learn: Japan's Firms Pay Price of Financial Speculation," *Far Eastern Economic Review,* June 17, 1993, pp. 60–61.
Toyo Menka Kaisha, Ltd., Osaka: Toyo Menka Kaisha, Ltd., [1988].
Yonekawa, Shin'ichi, ed., *General Trading Companies: A Comparative and Historical Study,* Tokyo: United Nations University Press, 1990.
Yoshihara, Kunio, *Sogo Shosha: The Vanguard of the Japanese Economy,* Tokyo: Oxford University Press, 1982.
Young, Alexander K., *The Soga Shosha: Japan's Multinational Trading Companies,* Boulder, Colo.: Westview Press, 1979.

—Carol I. Keeley
—updated by David E. Salamie

TOTAL S.A.

24, cours Michelet
92800 Puteaux
France
33-1-41-35-52-29
Fax: 33-1-41-35-52-20
Web site: http://www.total.com

Public Company
Incorporated: 1924 as Compagnie Française des Pétroles
Employees: 57,555
Sales: FFr191.09 billion (US$31.75 billion) (1997)
Stock Exchanges: Paris London New York
Ticker Symbol: TOT
SICs: 1221 Surface Mining-Bituminous Coal & Lignite;
1231 Anthracite Mining; 1311 Crude Petroleum &
Natural Gas; 1321 Natural Gas Liquids; 1381 Drilling
Oil & Gas Wells; 1382 Oil & Gas Field Exploration
Services; 2851 Paints, Varnishes, Lacquers, Enamels
& Allied Products; 2891 Adhesives & Sealants; 2893
Printing Ink; 2899 Chemicals & Chemical
Preparations, Not Elsewhere Classified; 2911
Petroleum Refining; 3052 Rubber & Plastics Hose &
Belting; 3053 Gaskets, Packing & Sealing Devices;
3089 Fabricated Rubber Products, Not Elsewhere
Classified; 5172 Petroleum & Petroleum Products,
Not Elsewhere Classified—Except Bulk Stations &
Terminals—Wholesale

TOTAL S.A. is one of the largest oil, natural gas, and specialty chemicals companies in the world. Its activities are organized into three main areas: upstream, downstream, and chemicals. TOTAL's upstream sector consists of the exploration for and production of crude oil and natural gas, along with development activities in gas and electricity and operations in coal mining; its downstream unit focuses on refining, marketing, and trading of petroleum products; while the chemicals sector includes rubber products made by its Hutchinson subsid-

iary (the bulk of which are products for the automotive industry), resins, paints, inks, and adhesives. The French state held a more than one-third stake in TOTAL for much of the company's history, but by 1996 France owned less than one percent.

Roots in World War I French Oil Crisis

The motto of the Compagnie Française des Pétroles (as TOTAL was first named)—France's oldest and, for most of its life, largest oil company—at its foundation in 1924 might well have been "never again." World War I had brought home to the French the need for secure energy supplies. In late 1917 France had come within three months of running out of fuel and seeing its war effort grind to a halt. President Georges Clemenceau addressed a desperate appeal to U.S. President Woodrow Wilson, asking him to resume American oil shipments across the Atlantic. The U.S. oil companies had concluded that the German navy had made the North Atlantic trade too hazardous. Wilson persuaded them to think again.

The French were latecomers to the oil business. At the turn of the century the Americans and the Russians, with their huge domestic resources, had supplied 90 percent of the world's oil needs. Since then, the British had developed a powerful presence through the activities of the Anglo-Persian Oil Company—today's British Petroleum—and Royal Dutch/Shell.

If the war engendered among the French an awareness of their desperate need for oil, it also created the opportunity for them to acquire it. The key was the 25 percent stake in the fledgling Turkish Petroleum Company (TPC) held by Germany's Deutsche Bank.

The TPC had been founded in 1911 to exploit the oil fields of Mesopotamia on either side of the German-built railway to Baghdad. The British-owned National Bank of Turkey had originally been TPC's major shareholder with 50 percent, but in 1914 the British government persuaded the bank to sell out to Anglo-Persian. A further 25 percent was held by Royal Dutch/Shell.

In 1915 the 25 percent stake in TPC still held by Deutsche Bank was sequestered by the British. Two years later, letters were exchanged between the British Foreign Office and the

Quai d'Orsay in Paris, committing the British government to hand over Deutsche Bank's shares in TPC to the French after the war.

The go-between had been the Armenian businessman Calouste Gulbenkian, an early minority shareholder in TPC. Royal Dutch/Shell was won over to the idea on the understanding that it would have the right to get France's share of the oil out of the ground.

To this end, the Société Française pour l'Exploitation du Pétrole was founded in 1920, owned 51 percent by Royal Dutch/Shell and 49 percent by the Banque de l'Union Parisienne. Deutsche Bank's 25 percent share in TPC had been formally transferred to the French under the Treaty of San Remo earlier that year.

CFP Founded in 1924

Four years later a new French government under Raymond Poincaré concluded that it was unacceptable that a foreign company should control the exploitation of France's oil rights in Mesopotamia, and the Compagnie Française des Pétroles (CFP) was established.

CFP's purpose was spelled out by Prime Minister Poincaré in a letter to the company's first chairman, Ernest Mercier. The new company's function was wide-ranging and not limited to Mesopotamia. In the interests of developing an oil producing capacity "under French control," Mercier was charged with acquiring stakes in "any enterprise active in whatsoever oil producing region" of the world. Central and South America were mentioned specifically. CFP was also to "co-operate, with the support of the Government, in . . . exploiting such oil wealth as may be discovered in France, her colonies and her protectorates."

Notwithstanding its close government tutelage, the Compagnie Française des Pétroles was set up as a private, not a state-owned, firm. Mercier, who had formerly been chairman of the Franco-British oil company Steaua-Romana, showed great energy in drumming up shareholders from a nation which had hitherto shown little enthusiasm for investing in the high-risk oil business.

He found backers among the French banks and also among the oil distributing companies, which had to this time been dependent on the foreign companies for their supplies. Although the support of powerful distributors such as Desmarais Frères was a boon at the outset, it later came to restrain CFP's freedom of action. Before World War II the company was effectively blocked from retailing oil that it had produced, transported, and refined, because of the powerful vested interests of its own shareholders.

On October 15, 1927, the Turkish Petroleum Company struck oil—a large find—at Baba Gurghur in the Mosal field just to the north of Kirkouk in Iraq. The discovery at Baba Gurghur ended a debate among the TPC shareholders, some of whom wanted to receive dividends on their investments, others of whom wanted to be remunerated in crude oil. The French had favored crude, having no oil fields of their own; after Baba Gurghur they received it.

Another result of the strike was the 1928 restructuring of the TPC. The Americans had been clamoring for admittance for years. In 1928 Anglo-Persian, acting on a deal hammered out between the British and American governments in 1923, ceded half its stake to a consortium of five U.S. oil companies. The return of Calouste Gulbenkian as "Mr. Five Percent" left the Compagnie Française des Pétroles holding 23.75 percent, on a par with Anglo-Persian, Royal Dutch/Shell, and the American consortium.

The shareholders in the TPC signed a nonaggression pact known as the Red Line Agreement after Gulbenkian's gesture in ringing a large area of the map of the Near and Middle East with red crayon. The area within the red line corresponded to the old Ottoman Empire at the end of World War I. It encompassed Turkey, Syria, Saudi Arabia, Lebanon, Iraq, and Palestine. Within that region the TPC shareholders, now including the American giants Standard Oil of New York and Standard Oil of New Jersey, undertook not to compete with one another.

Entered Refining in 1929

Meanwhile in France CFP was undergoing restructuring of its own. Mercier was coming up against opposition from some of the company's shareholders to his cherished plans to launch CFP into refining. Certain of the oil distributors backing CFP objected. They had built up close relationships with foreign refiners and they did not want these disrupted.

Mercier turned to his friend Raymond Poincaré, once again prime minister. Together they elaborated a plan for the French state to acquire a 25 percent stake in CFP and a 10 percent stake in a new refining subsidiary to be created by CFP, the Compagnie Française de Raffinage.

The official convention between the government and CFP which enshrined this new shareholding relationship was signed on March 19, 1929. It provoked a great political hue and cry, with the socialists under Léon Blum clamoring for greater state involvement and the right complaining that Poincaré's *dirigisme*—or interventionism—already went too far.

In the end it was the dirigistes who won. On July 8, 1931, the French parliament ratified an increase in the state's stake in CFP from 25 percent to 35 percent—the level at which it stayed until the early 1990s. The state also acquired 40 percent of the voting rights at CFP assemblies and the French government was authorized to nominate two commissioners for the company's board to safeguard the state's interest.

From Ernest Mercier's point of view it was a satisfactory outcome. He had won political support for his refining project and translated that support into boardroom control. However, the government's increased participation in CFP fell very far short of thoroughgoing nationalization. The risk of politically motivated interference in the day-to-day running of the company was averted.

The Compagnie Française de Raffinage (CFR) was founded in April 1929. Its first refinery was opened at Gonfreville near Le Havre in Normandy in the summer of 1933. It had to wait until the next year for the first shipment of CFP's own oil from

Iraq; the necessary pipeline from the wells to the Lebanese port of Tripoli was not in operation until July 1934.

In the years up to World War II CFR's refining capacity grew steadily, outstripping CFP's ability to supply it with crude. Further crude shipments came from Venezuela and the United States. By 1936 CFR was supplying nearly 20 percent of French demand for refined oil from two plants located at either end of the country, one in Normandy and the other at La Mède in Provence.

By 1929 the Turkish Petroleum Company had long since ceased to have anything to do with Turkey. Its oil came from Iraq under a concession awarded by the Iraqi monarch, King Feizal, installed by the British in 1921. Appropriately enough, TPC changed its name to the Iraq Petroleum Company in June 1929.

The renamed company's major task in the early 1930s was to transport its recently discovered oil from Iraq to the Mediterranean. Plans for a single pipeline were scuttled by French insistence that the oil should pass through the French protectorates of Syria and Lebanon, and Britain's determination that it should cross Jordan and Palestine, territories then under the protection of his majesty's government. These opinions proved irreconcilable, and two pipelines were laid, one to Tripoli in Lebanon and the other to Haifa in Palestine. The oil came on stream at both ports in 1934.

Another link in the chain between the extraction of CFP's share of the Iraqi oil and its distribution to French consumers was forged in 1931. CFP set up the Compagnie Navale Des Pétroles to ship its own oil to its own refineries. In the prewar years it shared this task with the Compagnie Auxiliaire de Navigation, one of CFP's founding shareholders. Much later, in the 1970s, CFP was to take control of the Compagnie Auxiliaire.

Vertically Integrated Oil Company by World War II

By the outbreak of World War II, the Compagnie Française des Pétroles had become a vertically integrated oil company, extracting, transporting, and refining oil. It had two weaknesses. One, the lack of any meaningful distribution capacity, was remedied in the 1950s with the creation of the TOTAL brand name and the gradual absorption of the independent distributors. The other was the company's heavy reliance on Middle Eastern oil. The balanced supply from around the world which Raymond Poincaré had hoped for in 1924 had not been achieved.

Far more worrying for the French during the war were the designs of CFP's fellow shareholders in the Iraq Petroleum Company (IPC) regarding the French 23.75 percent stake. CFP's stake in the IPC was put under the control of the official Custodian of Enemy Property in London after the French capitulation. The risk for CFP was that its participation in IPC could be reduced by new share issues to which it was powerless to subscribe.

Fortunately—and fortuitously—this change did not occur. CFP had a "war chest" of US$20 million held by its American bankers which enabled it to keep pace with the wartime recapitalization of IPC. The bulk of this money—US$15 million—had been borrowed from the Mannheimer Bank in the Nether-

lands just before the war to fund two new pipelines to Tripoli. The remaining US$5 million belonged to the Compagnie Française de Raffinage.

The French interests in IPC were tended to by Harold Sheets, the chairman of Standard Oil of New York, to whom they were entrusted by CFP's new chairman, Jules Mény, in 1940. Ernest Mercier had resigned that year, being out of favor with Vichy. Calouste Gulbenkian also remained a good friend of France, refusing—together with the Americans—to take any of CFP's share of IPC's oil. The British, with tanks and planes to fuel, were less scrupulous: not until 1950 did they grant the French modest compensation.

The rapid succession of chairmen at CFP during the war reflected the instability of those times. At least Vichy allowed Mercier to depart peacefully. The same could not be said of Jules Mény who, in 1943, was taken hostage by the Nazis and deported to Dachau. He never returned. Mény's successor, Marcel Champin, died in 1945, leaving the task of determining CFP's postwar strategy to his deputy, Victor de Metz, who was to serve as chairman for 25 years.

Rapid Postwar Expansion at Home and Abroad

The nationalization drive that affected so many French companies after the war did not engulf CFP: its private shareholders were powerful and not worth alienating. More threatening for CFP in the long run was President Charles de Gaulle's creation in 1945 of the Bureau de Recherches de Pétrole (BRP), which was much later to form one of the constituent parts of Elf Aquitaine. At its creation, however, BRP was charged exclusively with searching for oil in France, its colonies, and protectorates. This mandate did not constitute an immediate threat to CFP and de Metz gave the new state-backed venture his support.

In the late 1940s and early 1950s CFP expanded rapidly both at home and abroad. The company's annual supply of oil from the Middle East increased from 806,000 tons in 1945, to 1.61 million tons in 1950, to 8.824 million tons in 1953. This was made possible partly by the collapse of the restrictive Red Line Agreement under heavy American pressure. Oil began to flow from new IPC installations at Qatar in 1949: by 1953 production had reached 3.5 million tons per year.

Another major boost to CFP's supplies resulted from the opening of a new 30-inch pipeline from Kirkouk in Iraq to the Syrian port of Banias in November 1952. The original pipelines from Kirkouk to Tripoli and Haifa were only 16 inches in diameter.

The security of these supplies depended on the continuing stability of the region and its rulers' continuing respect for the oil companies' prewar concessions. The fragility of CFP's position was perceived by Victor de Metz. He recognized that CFP needed to diversify its sources of supply.

An agreement signed with the Venezuelan oil company Pantepec in 1947 did not bear fruit in the long term. It did ensure deliveries of Venezuelan crude amounting to some 600,000 tons per year through the late 1940s; but a technical agreement between the Venezuelan firm and CFP over the development of new fields in Venezuela broke down amid acrimonious exchanges in 1950.

A purely French venture to develop the oil wealth of Algeria fared better. In 1946 the state-owned Bureau de Recherches des Pétroles had established, jointly with the French colonial government in Algeria, an oil exploration company, the Société Nationale de Recherche de Pétrole en Algérie (SN Repal). In 1947 CNP sent a geologist, Willy Bruederer, to Algeria to evaluate the region's prospects. In the early 1950s SN Repal and CFP teamed up to explore a huge region designated promising by Bruederer, some 250,000 square kilometers in size. These joint efforts yielded their reward in 1956. A huge oil field was discovered at Hassi-Messaoud in June and an equally impressive gas field at Hassi R'Mel in November.

Notwithstanding its expansion, the Compagnie Française des Pétroles remained far from being a household name in France. CFP petrol stations did not cover the land, even though a large proportion of the fuel that the independent distributors sold had been refined at the plants of a CFP subsidiary.

Distribution was not a particularly profitable activity but a major oil producer without distribution facilities of its own risked being held for ransom by its distributors with the threat of losing their business. From 1946 Victor de Metz worked to remove this risk. His first step was the creation in that year of the Compagnie Française de Distribution en Afrique to sell CFP's refined oil products in francophone Africa.

TOTAL Brand Debuted in 1954

The move into distribution was made possible by the unveiling of the TOTAL brand name in 1954. The distributors of oil refined by CFR were now entitled to deck out their service stations in the TOTAL colors and logo, giving them a stronger market identity. The plan was first tested in Africa and then brought to France in 1957. It worked. In 1961 refineries belonging to CFP or working on its behalf treated 12 million tons of oil. Seven million tons of these treated products went on to be distributed under the TOTAL brand name. Notwithstanding the eyecatching new livery and brand name, France's independent fuel distributors were experiencing hard times. Tougher competition from the big foreign oil companies was pushing them towards bankruptcy. One by one they sold out—usually to CFP.

CFP's original shareholders, companies that had frequently exerted a powerful influence over CFP before the war, now found themselves being swallowed up by their own creation. In 1960 CFP took over Omnium Français de Pétroles, acquiring valuable distribution outlets in north Africa. In 1966 CFP acquired the largest independent distributor, Desmarais Frères, with a 10 percent share of the French market to CFP.

While CFP was making strides in refining and selling its oil, the process of extracting it was becoming increasingly difficult. The model for a new relationship with the Middle Eastern governments was the 50-50 profit-sharing agreement signed by the Saudi government and the U.S. oil producers' consortium Aramco in 1950. In the same year IPC struck a similar profit-sharing deal with the Iraqi government.

The risks posed by nascent nationalism in the Middle East were made clear in 1951 when Muhammad Mussadegh came to power in Iran. He nationalized the assets of the Anglo-Iranian Oil Company—formerly the Anglo-Persian Oil Company and forerunner of British Petroleum—and an international embargo of Iranian crude failed to change his attitude. More effective was a revolt linked to the British and American intelligence services, which led to the restoration of the shah and Mussadegh's imprisonment in 1953.

A year later the oil companies and the Iranian government came to terms. An international consortium of oil companies was created, led by Anglo-Iranian with a 40 percent share. CFP took a modest six percent stake in the venture.

Increased Reliance on Algerian Oil in the 1960s

Upheavals such as the one in Iran spurred the French effort to develop oil production in its Algerian colony. However, there was another reason for heavy investment in Algeria, both from CFP and from the state-controlled BRP. This was the fact that any oil or gas discovered in Algeria would lie within the franc zone. The IPC installations in Iraq did not fall into this category and CFP had to fund its share of investment in the Iraq Petroleum Company in pounds sterling. In the late 1940s and early 1950s, when the franc was fast losing its purchasing power, this arrangement was not very satisfactory.

To help balance its currency exposures CFP endeavored during the 1950s to increase its sales abroad, notably to countries within the sterling zone. During the late 1950s a potentially greater threat emerged to CFP's historic position as cornerstone of France's energy policy. Immediately after the war the French government had endowed BRP with plentiful resources to carry out one of the tasks originally assigned by Poincaré to CFP—to search for oil in France, her colonies, and protectorates. In Algeria BRP had found oil in abundance. By 1959 it was looking at ways of refining and selling it.

April 1960 saw the creation of l'Union Générale des Pétroles (UGP) to refine and distribute oil from the Hassi Messaoud field in Algeria. UGP rapidly acquired existing refineries and started to build others. It bought a refinery and a major distribution network from Caltex, a joint venture between U.S. oil majors Texaco and Standard Oil (California). UGP's expansion was supervised by Pierre Guillaumat, the first chairman of BRP immediately after the war. Within five years Guillaumat had created a French rival to CFP.

Particularly irksome to de Metz and CRP was the government's imposition of a so-called *devoir national*, or national obligation on oil refiners to take a certain proportion of their crude from the franc zone. In practice this meant Algeria and BRP and the other French state-controlled operations in that country. Most of CFP's oil still came from the Middle East. The reason for this discriminatory measure was that Algerian crude was more expensive than Middle Eastern crude. Demand had to be encouraged.

Just over a decade later the tables were turned. In 1971 the Algerians nationalized the assets of both CFP and Entreprise de Recherches et d'Activités Pétrolières as it had now become. The younger company was hit far harder than CFP: it relied on

Algeria for 80 percent of its oil supplies. CFP took only a fifth of its production from that country.

A deal with the Algerians was finally struck in June 1971. The newly appointed chairman of CFP, René Granier de Lilliac, informed shareholders that "over a five year period, once renewable, the group is . . . assured of annual production in the order of seven million tons." This was less than half the production of CFP (Algérie) before nationalization. De Lilliac took over from Victor de Metz in 1971. In his last years at the helm of CFP, de Metz had been encouraging the diversification of the group's sources of supply. In the late 1960s discoveries were made at Bekapai and Handil in Indonesia and, at the start of the 1970s, in the North Sea.

Despite the Iraqi nationalization of the assets of the Iraq Petroleum Company in 1971, in its 1971 annual report CFP was able to announce that "the rights of [the company in Iraq] will be maintained as before." On de Metz's retirement in 1971 the Compagnie Française des Pétroles was one of the largest oil companies in the world. During the 1960s the company's oil production had risen at a rate 30 percent faster than global oil production.

Diversified in the Difficult 1970s

The 1970s proved tougher. The new chairman, Granier de Lilliac, had headed the Compagnie Française de Raffinage for five years before taking charge of the group as a whole. In the 1970s CFP's refining activities faced the greatest difficulties. The group's refining capacity was still concentrated in France, although in 1975 sales abroad outstripped sales in France for the first time. The oil price rise of 1971 prompted by the OPEC cartel also led to a sharp reduction in world demand over the level anticipated. In 1975 CFR's refineries were working at only 67 percent capacity. At the same time exploration costs, particularly in the North Sea, were rising steeply. In France, price controls prevented CFP from passing on the full rise in crude prices to the consumer. As at Elf, diversification appeared to be the answer. In 1974 a major step was taken with the purchase of France's largest manufacturer of industrial rubber products, Hutchinson-Mapa. In the petrochemicals field, ATO Chimie was set up as a joint venture with Elf-ERAP in 1973: ten years later CFP's share was to be taken over by Elf.

CFP also moved into developing other energy sources. In uranium mining, CFP created in 1975 a joint subsidiary, Minatome, with Pechiney-Ugine-Kuhlmann. This venture was the core of today's TOTAL Compagnie Minière which in 1989 mined 711 tons of uranium in France and the United States. The same company sold 5.2 million tons of coal in 1989; again, the first steps were taken in the mid-1970s. Nevertheless, TOTAL has never diversified from its original core business as heavily as Elf.

During the 1980s unprofitable refineries in France, West Germany, and Italy were closed: the group's capacity in this area was in excess of demand. TOTAL's remaining refineries reported improved operating margins. Refining and distribution accounted for almost half the group's cash flow by 1989.

In 1985 the name by which CFP had come to be known universally was incorporated in its official title: CFP became TOTAL CFP. At the same time the Compagnie Française de Raffinage and its distribution subsidiary, TOTAL CFD, merged to become CRD TOTAL France.

Serge Tchuruk Led a More Aggressive Company in the Early 1990s

At the beginning of 1990 René Granier de Lilliac stood down as chairman, and was succeeded by Serge Tchuruk, an engineer by training, who had served as manager of strategic planning for Mobil Oil Corp. in the 1970s, and who had managed in the 1980s to turn around two other French firms—the chemical giant Rhone Poulenc and French state chemicals group Orkem—prior to being hired by TOTAL. One of Tchuruk's first tasks was to incorporate part of Orkem into TOTAL's chemical operations. Under a restructuring of the industry superintended by the French government, TOTAL acquired Orkem's specialty chemicals businesses, producing inks, adhesives, paints, and resins.

Tchuruk also moved quickly to transform TOTAL—which had by the early 1990s ceded its position as France's largest oil company to Elf Aquitaine—from a bureaucratic, complexly organized, rather sleepy firm into a sleeker, more modern, and more aggressive company. Two hundred subsidiaries were abolished, saving hundreds of millions of francs in expenses, and were replaced by a mere six profit centers; one-seventh of TOTAL's service stations network was closed in 1991; and about 6,500 jobs were eliminated. At the same time, Tchuruk aggressively expanded the company's marketing operations into new, potentially more lucrative markets, with TOTAL purchasing interests in service station chains in Spain, Portugal, Czechoslovakia, Hungary, and Turkey.

On the production side, Tchuruk sought to lessen TOTAL's reliance on the unstable Middle East, aiming to increase oil and gas production outside the Middle East by 50 percent by 1995. In 1991 a joint venture—40 percent owned by TOTAL—with British Petroleum and Triton Energy discovered an oil field at Cusiana in Colombia, while TOTAL on its own discovered a significant gas field at Peciko in Indonesia. In 1993 production began at a gas field in Thailand at Bongkot. By 1995 Tchuruk's emphasis on beefing up the company's gas business had made TOTAL the world's third largest gas producer, trailing only Royal Dutch/Shell and Mobil.

In June 1991 the company changed its name to TOTAL S.A. Soon thereafter, TOTAL began trading on the New York Stock Exchange for the first time. The following year, Tchuruk convinced the French government to reduce its direct share holding in the company to 5.4 percent. This development increased TOTAL's independence and its ability to act quickly and aggressively.

Thierry Desmarest Headed a Controversial Firm in the Later 1990s

In 1995 Tchuruk left TOTAL to attempt yet another turnaround, this time at Alcatel Alsthom. Replacing him was 15-year company veteran Thierry Desmarest, who almost immediately closed a US$610 million deal to develop two offshore oil fields in Iran; TOTAL thus became the first foreign oil company allowed back in Iran since the overthrow of the Shah in 1979. These Iranian fields were the very ones that Conoco Inc. had been forced to abandon under pressure from the U.S. government. TOTAL already had stakes in two oil fields in Libya, another country subject to U.S. sanctions. The company was also a partner in a consortium formed in 1992 to build a US$1.2 billion offshore gas pipeline in Burma (Myanmar) to carry gas from the Gulf of Martaban to Thailand. Despite Burma's being subject to sanctions starting in the mid-1990s because of its repressive military regime, TOTAL stuck with the project. Through its willingness to operate in such controversial countries, TOTAL had fewer competitors for its projects and was able to make better deals; in part, this led the company's exploration and development costs to be among the lowest in the industry. In turn, lower exploration costs contributed to steadily increasing profits; net income rose from FFr2.85 billion (US$600 million) in 1992 to FFr7.61 billion (US$1.26 billion) in 1997.

In 1996 the French state divested another four percent of its TOTAL stake, leaving its stake at only 0.97 percent. The following year, the company entered into another controversial project when it announced in September that it would invest $2 billion to develop an Iranian gas field. Prior to signing the deal, however, Desmarest got advance backing from the French government and the European Union, lessening the possibility that U.S.-sponsored sanctions would threaten it. Furthermore, TOTAL had just days before signing this Iranian deal completed its sale of TOTAL Petroleum (North America) Ltd.—its North American refining and marketing arm—to Ultramar Diamond Shamrock Corp. for an approximate eight percent stake in Ultramar, with the additional proviso that Ultramar would assume around $435 million in TOTAL Petroleum debt. Desmarest told *Business Week* that "having only a small part of our activities in the U.S. leaves us more comfortable with the U.S. reaction [to TOTAL's Iranian venture]."

In November 1997 the company continued to beef up its upstream activities with the formation of a consortium 40 percent owned by TOTAL to extract and develop a 175,000-barrels-a-day find in Venezuela. The following month it paid £86 million for the adhesives and textile coatings division of BTP, a U.K.-based specialty chemicals manufacturer.

Despite quite a large exposure to the Asian financial crisis that arose in 1997, TOTAL's results for that year were extremely healthy: a 7.9 percent increase in sales to FFr191.09 billion (US$31.75 billion) and a 35 percent increase in profits to FFr7.61 billion (US$1.26 billion). TOTAL's aggressive approach in the 1990s had turned the company into one of the most profitable in the industry as well as one of the most fearless in terms of controversial dealmaking. As the century was coming to a close, Desmarest announced that TOTAL would aim to make more deals with Iran; meanwhile, the company had already agreed to develop the huge Nahr Umar oil field in Iraq, although in that case TOTAL had to wait until U.N. sanctions were lifted. Clearly, the era of TOTAL as (profitable) maverick was only beginning.

Principal Subsidiaries

Bostik AB (Sweden); Bostik S.A.; CFP Algérie; Cray Valley S.A.; Finalens (90.4%); Hutchinson (62.1%); Norsokappa; Omnium Insurance Reinsurance Cy (99.9%); Omnium de Participations S.A. (99.9%); Polichem S.A.; Société Financière d'Auteuil (99.9%); TOTAL America, Inc.; TOTAL Australia Ltd.; TOTAL Chimie; TOTAL Deutschland GmbH; TOTAL Empresa Portuguesa; TOTAL España; TOTAL Hungaria (91.5%); TOTAL Inchiostri S.p.A.; TOTAL International Ltd.; TOTAL Oil Holdings Ltd.; TOTAL Outre Mer; TOTAL Raffinage Distribution S.A. (98.9%); TOTAL Transport Maritime; Tüpgaz (99.8%).

Principal Divisions

Exploration & Production; Middle East; Gas, Electricity & Coal; Trading & Shipping; Refining & Marketing; Chemicals Hutchinson.

Further Reading

Avati, Helen, "Total Wants to Be the Best of the Rest," *Petroleum Economist,* January 1993, pp. 4+.

Bahree, Bhushan, and Thomas Kamm, "Total Seeks More Pacts with Iran, Despite U.S.," *Wall Street Journal,* March 17, 1998, p. A13.

Beckman, Jeremy, "Total Beginning Program of Global Expansion," *Offshore,* August 1993, pp. 126+.

Catta, Emmanuel, *Victor de Metz: de la CFP au Groupe Total,* Paris: Total Edition Presse, 1990.

Corzine, Robert, "Maverick Total Stays Relaxed Under Fire," *Financial Times,* February 12, 1997, p. 32.

Dawkins, William, "Shaping Up for Competition," *Financial Times,* November 12, 1990.

Fleming, Charles, and Bhushan Bahree, "France's Total Dismisses U.S.-Sanctions Threat," *Wall Street Journal,* September 30, 1997, pp. A18, A19.

George, Dev, "Total Focuses on Offshore and Gas," *Offshore,* August 1994, pp. 80+.

Giraud, André, and Xavier Boy de la Tour, *Géopolitique du Pétrole et du Gaz,* Paris: Editions Technip, 1987, 418 p.

Grayson, Leslie E., *National Oil Companies,* New York: John Wiley, 1981, 269 p.

Guillon, Eric, and Gérard Pruneau, *Total Votre Groupe,* Paris: Total CFP, 1988.

Reed, Stanley, and Stan Crock, "Total Loves to Go Where Others Fear to Tread," *Business Week,* October 13, 1997, p. 52.

Reier, Sharon, "State of Grace," *Financial World,* October 13, 1992, pp. 34–37.

Rondot, Jean, *La Compagnie Française des Pétroles—du Franc-Or au Petrole-Franc,* Paris: Librairie Plon, 1962; reprinted, New York: Arno Press, 1977.

"Sprint Start: France's Total," *Economist,* August 8, 1992, pp. 60–61.

Toy, Stewart, "Total May Pull Off a Total Turnaround," *Business Week,* September 25, 1995, pp. 114F, 114H.

"Trouble in the Pipeline," *Economist,* January 18, 1997, p. 39.

Vielvoye, Roger, "Modern Management Style Brings New Look to Total," *Oil and Gas Journal,* February 25, 1991, pp. 15+.

—William Pitt
—updated by David E. Salamie

Tower Automotive, Inc.

4508 IDS Center
Minneapolis, Minnesota 55402
U.S.A.
(612) 342-2310
Fax: (612) 332-2012

Public Company
Incorporated: 1993 as Tower Automotive, Inc.
Employees: 8,750
Sales: $1.23 billion (1997)
Stock Exchanges: New York
Ticker Symbol: TWR
SICs: 3714 Motor Vehicle Parts & Accessories; 3444
  Sheet Metal Work; 3334 Primary Aluminum

A leading supplier of automotive components to U.S. and foreign carmakers, Tower Automotive, Inc. makes metal stampings, metal assemblies, and other products for the automotive industry. Tower recorded explosive growth during the 1990s, as it embarked on an acquisition campaign that transformed it from a small metal stamping company into a full-service giant capable of supplying automotive manufacturers with the components used to make their products. At production facilities in the United States, Canada, Japan, Brazil, Mexico, and Italy, the company produced car hood hinges, brake components, car and truck frames, axles, and a bevy of other products that carmakers purchased from outside vendors. The company's most important acquisition during the 1990s was its 1997 purchase of the automotive products unit belonging to A.O. Smith, which tripled the size of Tower. During the late 1990s, Tower derived the bulk of its sales from three domestic customers—Ford, Chrysler, and General Motors—but was making a concerted move into international markets.

1993 Formation

In the 1990s, there were two closely allied trends in the automotive industry that supported Tower's meteoric rise in the automotive components industry. First, car manufacturers increasingly were turning to outside manufacturing sources for a sizeable number of the components used to make their products. It was a trend borne out of the need to reduce costs, enabling car manufacturers to avoid high wages and benefits they otherwise would have had to pay to their union workers. As carmakers increased their reliance on outside vendors, they demonstrated a desire to limit their contracts to outside sources to an exclusive few. Rather than subcontracting their components-manufacturing business to hundreds of outside sources, car manufacturers preferred to deal with only a handful of vendors. This was the second trend, which, when combined with the first, caused the automotive components industry to grow and consolidate at the same time. The production of components such as car hood hinges, brake components, fenders, frames, and a host of other assemblies and parts became big business, and that business would only be won by automotive component companies large and technologically sophisticated enough to earn the esteem of the giant car manufacturers. Against this backdrop, Tower flourished in the foreground, mirroring the industry trends swirling around it. The company awoke from its sleepy origins to record animated growth during the 1990s. It grew by taking actions that caused the general trend toward consolidation: Tower rose to the top of its industry by swallowing up competitors, acquiring one company after another until it had seized a leading market position. Starting from the less than $100 million in sales it generated in 1993, Tower embarked on a period of prodigious financial growth, creating an industry giant four years later, when the company's revenues eclipsed $1 billion. From there, the company set its sights on global dominance.

Behind Tower's remarkable ascent were forces other than the two industry trends that supported the company's growth. When Tower began its prolific rise in the automotive industry in 1993, it was an $85-million-in-sales company known as R.J. Tower Corporation. The company was a small yet respected steel stamping concern with two production facilities, one in Greenville, Michigan, and another in Auburn, Indiana. R.J. Tower was preparing to establish another facility in Bardstown, Kentucky, when its destiny was altered significantly by the entrance of an industrial management firm based in Minneapolis, Minnesota, named Hidden Creek Industries. At first blush, Hidden Creek, with a total payroll of eight people, would not strike outsiders as a company capable of changing the face of R. J. Tower forever, but behind Hidden Creek was Onex Corp., a large Toronto-based holding company that ranked as one of the 25 largest companies in Canada. With the financial help of Onex, Hidden Creek was formed in June 1989 with the primary objective of acquiring automotive-related manufacturing companies. The new, privately held partnership was given $23 million to carry out its objective. When the paths of Hidden Creek and R.J. Tower crossed, the result was Tower Automotive Inc., a small sheet metal parts-fabricating company that was about to begin its new life and reshape the automotive components industry.

Hidden Creek, led by S. A. "Tony" Johnson, bought R.J. Tower in April 1993 and emplaced Dugald "Dug" K. Campbell as its president and chief executive officer. Campbell, who was in charge of Tower's day-to-day operation while Johnson presided as chairman of the board, was the individual chiefly responsible for leading Tower Automotive Inc. to new heights. Although Campbell acquired rival companies at a pace that bespoke industry domination, his management style was far from that of a typical corporate autocrat. Abhorring the classic "top-down" management structure that prevailed throughout the country, Campbell instilled a business culture that focused on team leadership and eschewed corporate titles. Employees, from janitors up to Campbell's position, were never referred to by job titles. They were all "colleagues," working in "teams" for an organization without traditional hierarchies. "Team leader" was as prestigious a job title as anyone at Tower could earn, and that designation was only applied if other team members agreed.

This new, iconoclastic Tower began to take shape in 1993 shortly after Campbell moved into the company's operating headquarters in Grand Rapids, Michigan. There, where a total of 11 employees worked in conjunction with financial headquarters staff in downtown Minneapolis, the process of developing Tower into an industry leader got underway. In 1994, the company acquired Edgewood Tool & Manufacturing, based in Romulus, Michigan, and officially became Tower Automotive. Other acquisitions quickly followed, as the company moved forward with its agenda to develop a dominant automotive components manufacturer predicated on the principle of employee empowerment. The old R. J. Tower Corp. was replaced with the Tower Automotive of the 1990s through the acquisitive bent of Campbell and his loosely

organized "team leaders." Following the purchase of Edgewood Tool & Manufacturing, Tower acquired Kalamazoo, Michigan-based Kalamazoo Stamping & Die Co. in June 1994. In August 1994, the company completed its initial public offering of stock. Next, in January 1996, the company acquired Trylon Corporation from MasoTech Inc. and four months later purchased another company from MasoTech Inc. called MasoTech Stamping Technologies Inc., based in Rochester Hills, Michigan. As the new companies were absorbed into Tower's operations, the company's revenue volume swelled, rising from $85 million to $220 million by the end of 1994, and up to $400 million by the end of 1996.

1997 A.O. Smith Acquisition

Less than three years after new owners and new management took over, Tower was a vastly different company than the small stamping manufacturer that had operated as R.J. Tower Corp. The new version of the Tower name was registering $20 million in operating earnings from the production output at its 11 manufacturing facilities and deriving the bulk of its sales from Ford Motor Co. Specializing in producing body structure chassis and suspension components, Tower also supplied Chrysler Corp., Mazda, Honda of America Manufacturing, Toyota Motor Manufacturing, and Nissan Motor Manufacturing, quickly making a name for itself among the elite cadre of car manufacturers as a well-equipped, well-managed supplier. With nearly 3,000 employees, Tower was on the verge of breaking into the upper tier of its industry segment, but the company needed one large acquisition to push it over the edge separating industry stalwarts and runners-up. That decisive push arrived in early 1997, when Tower announced a pending acquisition that would serve as a catapult to launch the company toward the top of its industry. The acquisition reflected the times: The automotive components industry was consolidating in a rush; it was either acquire or be acquired for some the seasoned veterans of the business.

In early January 1997, Tower announced it had struck a deal to acquire the automotive products unit of A.O. Smith Corp., one of the oldest and largest manufacturers of automotive components in the United States. A.O. Smith had built the first pressed steel car frame in the country, making its pioneering part in 1899. The company had manufactured frames for the Ford Model N in 1906, and subsequently had developed intimate ties with all the largest car manufacturers during a nearly century-long legacy in the automotive parts business. The $625 million acquisition was a telling example of the forces at work in the automotive components industry; an age-old legend was about to be acquired by a burgeoning upstart, the old was giving way to the new. Executives at A.O. Smith were unable to rationalize the expenditure required for the capital improvements needed to keep their automotive components unit competitive, and had decided to fold their hand. Tower, surging forward with a resolute conviction to climb the industry's rungs, stood to benefit handsomely from the deal. The purchase price was hefty, but the company's stature as an automotive components manufacturer able to garner the business of car manufacturers would increase dramatically once A.O. Smith's business was absorbed.

The acquisition, completed in April 1997, tripled the size of Tower, lifting its revenue volume to $1.3 billion. Prior to the acquisition, A.O. Smith's automotive products unit had generated $860 million in sales and produced operating earnings of $110 million, financial figures that overshadowed Tower's $400 million in revenues and $20 million in operating earnings. Tower's payroll, totaling 2,900 employees, ballooned to more than 8,000, once the 5,200 former A.O. Smith employees were assimilated into Campbell's egalitarian organization. In terms of manufacturing might, the acquisition more than doubled Towers' production operations, adding 14 plants in the U.S., Canada, and Japan to the 11 facilities the company owned before grabbing its much larger rival.

Aside from the numerical gains, the acquisition engendered other advantages, namely, the addition of A.O. Smith's leadership in the car frame business, which complemented Tower's strength in the chassis, suspension, and body structure business. The combination of the two business areas created unmatched system capabilities that Tower could use to lure business away from competitors. The capability to provide a full-range of automotive components to original equipment manufacturers such as Ford and General Motors was becoming a necessity for survival as the 1990s progressed, and the addition of A.O. Smith's talents did much to improve Tower's appeal to its clientele. The acquisition also broadened Tower's customer base, particularly its relations with General Motors. Before the absorption of A.O. Smith, Tower drew two-thirds of its business from Ford, 10 percent from Chrysler, 9.2 percent from Honda, but only a negligible 3.5 percent from General Motors. After Tower and A.O. Smith were fully integrated, however, industry pundits were projecting that nearly a fifth of the company's business would be derived from General Motors, the same percentage it was expected to draw from Chrysler. Further, the addition of A.O. Smith established stronger links with large Japanese manufacturers Nissan and Isuzu.

By all accounts—as one industry analyst chimed in after another—the acquisition of A.O. Smith was heralded as an astute move on Campbell's part, strengthening the company across all fronts and thrusting it into an enviable market position as the dollar value of its industry increased. "Whereas everyone knows that systems integration is the wave of the future with interiors," one analyst pointed out, "most suppliers in the stamping business have been slow to respond to the need for modularity. That's where Tower has been ahead of its competitors." Another analyst noted the behind-the-scenes presence of Hidden Creek, saying, "Hidden Creek has become a big player in this industry; a lot of people assume they are just financial types, but they are very operationally and strategically focused. And that shines through in a company like Tower." Campbell was pleased, but by no means ready to sit back and forego further growth through acquisitions. In a letter to Tower shareholders, he demonstrated a flair for the dramatic, writing, "We know the plot and a bit about all the characters, but the story is incomplete. As we go into 1997 with the (A.O. Smith) acquisition, the curtain is coming up on the crucial second act. . . ." One outside observer suggested he knew what that second act would be when he remarked to *Automotive Industries,* "I'm sure that (Onex and Hidden Creek, Tower's corporate parents) are on the acquisition trail now, especially in Europe. The fundamental challenge to maximizing this business is taking it global. That will be the next step."

Late 1990s International Expansion

Indeed, international expansion was the next step taken by Tower, as the company pushed its presence overseas with the purchase of a Turin, Italy-based stamping company named Societa Industria Meccanica Stampaggio S.p.A. On the heels of this acquisition in May 1997, the company announced in August 1997 that it was purchasing a 40 percent interest (held by A.O. Smith) in automotive steel frame-maker Metalsa SA de CV, Mexico's largest supplier of auto frames and structures. Next, in February 1998, Tower agreed to acquire a 40 percent interest in Metalurgica Caterina S.A., a supplier of structural stampings and assemblies to the Brazilian automotive market. When the deal was announced, Campbell expressed his pleasure about the equity stake, remarking confidently, "Brazil represents one of the fastest growing automotive markets in the world and presents a substantial opportunity for Tower Automotive's growth over the long-term."

As Tower prepared for the beginning of the 21st century, it was clearly a company to watch in the years ahead. There was no evidence to suggest that the company's strident rise in the automotive components industry would come to a halt. Further acquisitions, particularly those that bolstered Tower's presence in international markets, were in the offing as the company prepared for the future. The company was financially sound and led by a management team that had given it an early lead over competitors in the race to become full-service suppliers to original equipment manufacturers. The only nagging question clouding the company's future was how its laissez-faire management approach would translate in foreign markets, but with Campbell at the helm Tower's global expansion was moving briskly forward, mindful of the concern. The day when the Tower name would be recognized as a global leader hung like a carrot in front of the chief executive's eyes, prodding the company forward toward worldwide dominance.

Further Reading

Hawkins, Lee, Jr., "Minneapolis-Based Tower Automotive to Grow Through Acquisition," *Knight-Ridder/Tribune Business News,* January 29, 1997, p. 12.

Keenan, Tim, "Tower Makes Strategic Leap," *Ward's Auto World,* March 1997, p. 125.

Lowell, Jon, "Follow the Leader: Tower's Unconventional Management Approach," *Ward's Auto World,* July 1997, p. 48.

McCartney, Jim, "Tower Automotive to Acquire Automotive Products Unit of A.O. Smith Corp.," *Knight-Ridder/Tribune Business News,* January 28, 1997, p. 12.

Mullins, Robert, "Tower: Team Approach to Boosting Milwaukee," *Business Journal-Milwaukee,* September 19, 1997, p. 23.

Phelan, Mark, "Tower Becomes a Global Player," *Automotive Industries,* March 1997, p. 96.

"Tower Automotive Agrees to Acquire 40 Percent Interest in Metalurgica Caterina S.A.," *PR Newswire,* February 6, 1998, p. 2.

Wrigley, Al, "Mergers Build a Bigger Tower," *American Metal Market,* February 17, 1997, p. 4.

——, "Tower Deal: Mexican Steel Boon," *American Metal Market,* August 20, 1997, p. 2.

—Jeffrey L. Covell

TRANS WORLD ENTERTAINMENT

Trans World Entertainment Corporation

38 Corporate Circle
Albany, New York 12203
U.S.A.
(518) 452-1242
Fax: (518) 452-3547

Public Company
Incorporated: 1972 as Trans World Music Corporation
Employees: 4,100
Sales: $571.3 million (1997)
Stock Exchanges: NASDAQ
Ticker Symbol: TWMC
SICs: 5735 Record & Prerecorded Tape Stores

Trans World Entertainment Corporation is one of the largest specialty music and video-store chains in the United States. It sells compact discs, prerecorded audio cassettes, prerecorded videocassettes, and related merchandise in both mall outlets and stand-alone stores. Trans World operates primarily under the names Record Town, Coconuts Music & Movies, and Saturday Matinee. It also owns stores under the name F.Y.E. (For Your Entertainment). Originally incorporated as Trans World Music Corporation, the company in 1994 changed its name to Trans World Entertainment Corporation to more adequately reflect the various markets in which it participates.

The Great Expansion of the Early Years: 1972–88

Prior to founding Trans World Music Corporation, Robert J. Higgins worked as the Eastern divisional sales manager for Trans Continental Music Corporation. There he gained important experience, and in 1972 he opened his own company, Trans World Music Corporation, with a $30,000 personal investment. Originally a wholesale music distributor, Trans World was headquartered in Albany primarily because Higgins, a native of Albany, recognized the city's advantage of having easy access to both the Northeast and Mid-Atlantic markets.

Although Trans World initially entered the profitable wholesale prerecorded music business, it did not take long for the company to take advantage of Higgins's experience and knowledge of the industry as a whole, and in 1973 it opened its first retail operation under the name Record Town. By the end of 1974, Trans World was a $5.5 million company. The following year Higgins and Trans World made another important foray into the retail field: recognizing that Americans were spending a great deal of time and money in malls, Trans World opened the first of many Record Town mall locations. Then, in 1979, the company made a further commitment to the malls, opening its first specialty mall store under the name Tape World, selling prerecorded music tapes rather than records. One of the presiding factors in the decision to open the Tape World stores—and in its eventual success—was that tapes were much smaller than records, allowing Tape World to fit more music titles into a smaller, less-expensive space.

By 1982 Trans World had sales of $25 million and was operating 38 retail units. That year the success of Record Town and Tape World encouraged Trans World to sell its wholesale business and to begin an aggressive expansion of its retail stores. At the time, most of Trans World's stores were clustered on the East Coast, but the expansion would eventually spread the company's stores throughout the United States.

Trans World made its initial public offering in 1986, trading shares on the NASDAQ exchange with the ticker symbol TWMC. (The ticker symbol remained TWMC even after the name change to Trans World Entertainment Corporation in 1994). Higgins, president and chief executive officer, retained the majority of Trans World shares and also served as chairman of the board of directors. Trans World continued rapid expansion throughout the 1980s and early 1990s, mostly by opening stand-alone and mall stores associated with the company but also through acquisition of retail outlets. On June 1, 1985, Trans World acquired all outstanding stock of the B&B Record Corporation, and in 1988 the company acquired the 14 Great American Music Stores located primarily in the Minneapolis-St. Paul area. Trans World's rapid expansion eventually contributed to an oversaturation of the music and video retail market, and by 1990 company profits began to erode.

Company Perspectives:

Generating a competitive return on investment for shareholders is Trans World Entertainment's foremost responsibility, and this is the principal goal that guides the board of directors and the entire management team.

Legal and Financial Trouble in the Late 1980s and Early 1990s

In 1989 a judge ruled that Trans World had to pay $2.5 million in damages to Peaches Entertainment Corporation. Peaches had given Trans World a license to use its trademark, but when the license expired in August 1986, Trans World continued to use the trademark in three states. The charge put a dent in profits for 1989, but Higgins said of the award: "We are happy to get this non-operating issue behind us so that we can turn our management focus back to . . . operating the business."

In part because of the costs of its continued rapid expansion, the early 1990s saw declining profits for Trans World. In the third quarter of 1990, for example, the company's net income of $992,000 represented a drop of 47 percent compared with that in the same period of 1989. Though revenue was up 11 percent in the third quarter of 1990 to $74.4 million, costs associated with the opening of 40 new stores devoured Trans World's profits. These problems were reflected in the company's stock. Trans World had announced a plan in July 1990 to make a public offering of one million shares, 750,000 of which were owned by Higgins and 250,000 by the company. The offering was to be made at approximately the market value—at the time about $31.50 per share—but by November 1990 the price of Trans World stock had fallen to $14.00 per share, and the company withdrew its public offering registration, citing poor stock market conditions as the reason for withdrawal. By 1993 net income was $9.8 million, down from $14.5 million in 1990, and in 1994 Trans World operated at a net loss of $6.3 million.

Part of the reason for the company's poor returns was the increasing competition from stores such as Best Buy Co., Inc., and Circuit City Stores Inc., which would often sell its music recordings at or below cost in an effort to attract customers into their stores (customers who might then buy other items). In 1996 music companies attempted to discourage stores from this practice by establishing the Minimum Advertised Pricing (MAP) policies, which threatened to withhold marketing allowances to retailers that sold their product below MAP prices. But retailers seemed to ignore the MAP policies until it became apparent that their loss-leader practices were not helping their sales.

In May 1994 Higgins purchased 10,000 shares of Trans World stock at $11 per share. The price might have seemed like a bargain (down from $31.50 in July 1990), but Trans World shares would eventually trade at a low of $1.75 during the fourth quarter of 1995. Recognizing that the market was probably oversaturated with retail music and video stores and that something drastic had to be done to turn Trans World around, Higgins announced on February 2, 1995, that Trans World would close 143 stores. The move was to eliminate poor-performing stores and concentrate on a core group of productive stores. Though Trans World closed 180 outlets during the year (more than the 143 initially announced), sales declined only 3.7 percent. The company also reduced its inventory by $28 million while increasing the product mix available to stores. Trans World took a net loss for 1995 of $25.4 million, due in large part to the $35 million charge for restructuring and closing.

By 1996 the store closings were beginning to pay off, and net income had risen to $7.1 million. Trans World operated a total of 479 stores at the year's end, and by the third quarter of 1996, the share price had returned to $9.50. The positive income figure included a record single-quarter net income of $14.7 million for the fiscal 1996 fourth quarter, which meant fourth-quarter earnings of $1.51 per share.

Growth and Reorganization in the 1990s

On December 10, 1993, Trans World Music opened its first F.Y.E. (For Your Entertainment) store in Trumbull, Connecticut. F.Y.E. was to be Trans World's highest-volume mall operation. Billed in company literature as "larger than life, bigger than anyone had imagined, with more store, more product, more of everything the customer wants," F.Y.E. was Trans World's prototype of a multimedia superstore where there is something to see, do, and ultimately buy for everyone in the family. "This amazing superstore is about having a great time in the family game center, pulling up a chair in a reading nook, or celebrating a child's birthday or other event with an F.Y.E. party." Trans World was hoping to distinguish F.Y.E. from its competition by being one of the few family-oriented, multimedia retail superstores designed to fit in a mall environment.

Also important to the success of F.Y.E. and other Trans World retail outlets was the fact that by 1993 children ages four to 12 controlled or influenced as much as $132 billion a year in spending. The influence of children was particularly strong in the sales of movie videos. For example, the Walt Disney Company's *Beauty and the Beast* was not only the best-selling video of 1992 but the best-selling video ever. In 1993 *Aladdin,* also by the Walt Disney Company, outperformed *Beauty and the Beast,* becoming the best-selling video ever. Following *Aladdin* as top sellers for 1993 were *Pinocchio, Free Willy,* and *Homeward Bound,* all movies with children as the targeted audience. Recognizing this trend, Trans World Music made several moves in 1993 to take advantage of this huge source of sales. In their new F.Y.E. stores, a special department was set aside with children's music, books, and videos. Within the Saturday Matinee stores, a special section called Kids' Matinee was designed; called a "store within a store" by Trans World, Kids' Matinee offered similar merchandise as that found in their F.Y.E. children's section.

In 1992, when the Tandy Corporation was packaging its Incredible Universe electronic superstores, it turned to Trans World to supply the "soft" goods, such as compact discs and prerecorded videotapes, to accompany Tandy's electronic "hard" goods, such as compact discs and VCRs. Trans World agreed to supply the music and video products to the giant stores, some of which occupied nearly 200,000 square feet of retail space, of which 10,000 square feet on average was devoted to the music and video departments. At the launch of Incredible Universe in the fall of 1992, Tandy chairman John Roach predicted that the United States could accommodate up to 50 of these "gigastores," with a total sales of $3 billion. Trans World hoped that the joint venture with Incredible Universe would provide a broader customer base with a lower capital investment, thus lowering overhead and start-up costs and increasing profitability.

Though initial response to the Incredible Universe stores had been positive, performance over a longer period was lackluster. In 1996, in an effort to increase plunging profits, Incredible Universe announced plans to promote Coconuts, Record Town, or F.Y.E.—depending upon the popularity and market recognition of the Trans World stores in the various Incredible Universe markets—as retail outlets inside the superstores. But it was already too late. In late 1996 Tandy Corporation announced that all its Incredible Universe stores were to be closed or sold. Retail analyst Lynn Detrick, of Williams MacKay Jordan & Co. in Houston, told *Time* magazine that "maybe this does suggest that you can take it too far, that stores can be too big and inconvenient." Though not especially good news for Trans World, the closing losses were primarily Tandy's.

Once Trans World began to see consistently positive results from its restructuring, Higgins began again to turn his sights toward growth and expanding market share. Though Trans World was to close another 37 stores in 1997, it was also planning to open 70 new stores, 40 of which would be relocations.

Meanwhile, Higgins and John Sullivan, the chief financial officer, began to talk publicly about acquiring another company. A few companies that did not respond well to sluggish sales and market oversaturation in the 1990s—especially those that had filed for bankruptcy—seemed ripe for takeover. "Due to the financial difficulties of our competitors," said Higgins, "our acquisitions in real estate will be opportunistic. We will only acquire profitable stores and save them [with] economies of distribution." The reduction in the total number of music and video stores nationwide made it possible for Trans World to pursue exclusive operating agreements with shopping malls so that a Trans World retailer would be the only music and video store in the mall. The closing of hundreds of stores across the industry also made it possible for Trans World to expand again without falling into the same trap it had in the early 1990s. The company could rapidly pick up market share with relatively slow openings of new stores in strong sales areas and by making a few strategic acquisitions.

Adding to Trans World's good news, the company announced a new debt agreement to shareholders on June 5, 1997. The new refinancing agreement was reached with Congress Financial Corporation, a CoreStates Company, at interest rates averaging below the prime rate. "This new debt agreement finalizes our successful restructuring efforts," said Higgins in a press statement. "By offering such favorable rates, our lenders clearly recognize that we have effectively repositioned our company. Based on current borrowing levels, the company will save up to $2.5 million per year in interest charges alone." The company had previously obtained waivers from lenders to keep from being in default of two provisions of its loan agreements. The loans were initially made to finance store openings and relocations. The waivers had included agreements to pay higher interest rates.

Much of Trans World Entertainment Corporation's turnaround has been credited to Higgins. A majority shareholder with slightly more than 50 percent of shares, he continued to have a vested interest in the company performing well. In 1997, as a testament to Trans World's turnaround, Higgins received *Billboard* magazine's Video Person of the Year award.

Further Reading

Christman, Ed, "Trans World Losses Down; MCA Golden in 4th Quarter," *Billboard,* November 30, 1996, p. 68.

——, "Trans World Unwraps Plan for 'Comeback' 4th Quarter," *Billboard,* October 7, 1995, pp. 83–84.

Fitzpatrick, Eileen, "Trans World at 25," *Billboard,* July 5, 1997, pp. 68–75.

Frank, Stephen E., "Insiders at Specialty Retailers Purchase Shares in Their Own Troubled Businesses," *Wall Street Journal,* August 3, 1994, pp. C23–24.

Goldstein, Seth, "Q&A: Bob Higgins," *Billboard,* July 5, 1997, pp. 65–72.

Jeffrey, Don, "Falling Stocks Zap Retail; Ongoing Price War Hobbles Chains," *Billboard,* February 18, 1995, pp. 1–3.

Lanctot, Roger C., "Data Points," *Computer Retail Week 1996,* April 15, 1996, p. 15.

"The Perils of Having Way More Than Enough," *Time,* January 13, 1997, p. 58.

Reilly, Patrick M., "Music Retailer Trans World Reports Narrowed Loss for Fiscal Third Period," *Wall Street Journal,* November 19, 1996, p. B13.

Scally, Robert, "Incredible Universe Comes to an End; Final Sales Over by Mid-March," *Discount Store News,* March 3, 1997, pp. 1–2.

"Trans World Music Plans Public Offering," *Wall Street Journal,* July 24, 1990, p. C21.

"Trans World Music's 1st-Period Net Slashed by Damages Liability," *Wall Street Journal,* May 9, 1989, p. C22.

—Terry Bain

TRU★SERV™

TruServ Corporation

8600 West Bryn Mawr Avenue
Chicago, Illinois 60631-3505
U.S.A.
(773) 695-5000
Fax: (773) 695-6558
(800) 621-6025
Web site: http://www.truserv.com

Cooperative Company
Founded: 1997
Employees: 6,000
Sales: $4.5 billion (1998 est.)
SICs: 5100 Wholesale Trade Nondurable Goods; 5251
    Hardware Stores; 5261 Retail Nurseries & Garden
    Stores; 5531 Auto & Home Supply Stores; 5211
    Lumber & Other Building Materials; 7350 Misc.
    Equipment Rental & Leasing

TruServ Corporation is the largest 100 percent member-owned cooperative in the $145 billion do-it-yourself industry, with its members operating hardware stores, lumber yards, home centers, and equipment rental stores. Formed on July 1, 1997, by the merger of Cotter & Company and ServiStar Coast to Coast Corporation, TruServ supports more than 10,500 independent retailers in the United States and 65 other countries. The retail names making up the TruServ cooperative are: True Value; ServiStar Hardware, Lumber Yards and Home Centers; Coast to Coast Hardware; Coast to Coast Home & Auto; Grand Rental Station; Taylor Rental Center; Home & Garden Showplace; and Induserve Supply. TruServ also manufactures exclusive brands for its retail identities, including paints, brushes and rollers, spray paint, and cleaning supplies.

Company Roots 1855–1910

The companies that combined to form TruServ Corporation were deeply rooted in the wholesale hardware business. Hibbard Spencer Bartlett & Co., a hardware wholesaler that eventu-

ally developed the True Value name, was founded in 1855. American Hardware & Supply Company, the precursor of ServiStar Corporation and the first wholesale hardware cooperative in the United States, was established in 1910, and Coast to Coast Corporation grew from a wholesale hardware cooperative formed in 1928.

In 1910, harness was a big hardware seller and there were only 46 states in the Union when 20 hardware store owners from western Pennsylvania, West Virginia, and Virginia came together. The hardware industry was made up of hundreds of small independent stores whose owners bought their merchandise from various wholesalers, such as Hibbard's.

The men who met in Pittsburgh that day were looking for a way to cut their costs and keep their prices competitive. They decided to form a nonprofit cooperative that would serve as their own wholesaler and distributor. As members of a co-op, they could pool their buying power to negotiate better prices for hardware from manufacturers and then sell the merchandise with a small markup to themselves and other hardware dealers who owned the shares of the co-op. The annual profits that were not invested in the company would be returned to the dealer-owners at the end of the year. And they could reduce costs by consolidating their distribution, operating, and promotional activities into one company.

The company's charter was approved and the first stockholders' meeting of American Hardware & Supply Company was held on October 25, 1910. The company began operating out of a warehouse in Pittsburgh.

Company Building: 1911–48

Over the next 20 years, American Hardware demonstrated that a low-cost cooperative wholesaler made sense in the hardware business, and by 1929 sales were just over $1 million. Others liked the concept and followed American's lead. In 1928, the Melamed brothers of Minneapolis, Minnesota, established a franchise-store cooperative that would become the Coast to Coast Corporation.

504

Company Perspectives:

Our Goal is Simple. To help customers improve, beautify and repair their #1 investment—their home. And to maximize our Member stores' profitability and growth by aggressively providing cost-effective, innovative products, programs and services.

Meanwhile, Hibbard Spencer Bartlett & Co., which was not a cooperative, was increasing its marketing activities throughout the Midwest. In 1928, the company published its first "Toy Parade" consumer catalog and invited dealers to its first Toy Show, and in 1932, Hibbard's introduced a new private-brand line of hand tools under the True Value label. To help dealers increase sales, Hibbard's developed a kit of marketing aids, introduced a Dealers' Service Department, and set up a model store at its headquarters where dealers could get marketing suggestions.

During World War II, Hibbard's tried a new approach by opening nine company-owned stores using the True Value name. The company's regular customers did not like the competition, and Hibbard's closed the test stores after the war.

The fourth company in the TruServ history, Cotter & Co., came on the scene in 1948. The company's founder, John M. Cotter, started in the hardware business a few years after American Hardware & Supply Co. was incorporated when, at the age of 12, he went to work in a neighborhood hardware store in St. Paul, Minnesota. After high school Cotter worked as a salesman for a regional hardware wholesaler, then in his own hardware store, in Eau Claire, Wisconsin. In his mid-20s, Cotter went back on the road, eventually working for a Chicago-based merchandising group.

In the late 1940s, competition from discount stores and other chain operations caused independent dealers to increasingly turn to low-cost distributors. In his review of Edward R. Kantowicz's biography of John Cotter in *Chilton's Hardware Age*, Jim Cory explained that Cotter "stumbled on dealer-ownership by accident." He had noticed, as a young salesman, that "the best, the busiest, the cleanest hardware store in every town ... belonged to Our Own Hardware Co.," a Minnesota-based dealer-owned cooperative.

At a convention of Our Own early in 1947, Cotter began chatting with Bill Stout, the general manager of American Hardware. Wrote Kantowicz, "Cotter and Stout, talking long into the night, looked up the *Hardware Age* dealer listing for Illinois, Michigan, Iowa, and Indiana and determined that there was room for a dealer-owned wholesaler in Chicago." By that time, there were some dozen hardware cooperatives around the country, serving small and widely separated regions, and their share of the market was tiny. Ace Hardware, the largest of the cooperatives, had sales in 1948 of $10 million. Hibbard's, in contrast, dominated the Midwest with sales of over $28 million.

A few months after his talk with Stout, John Cotter and 12 hardware dealers founded Cotter & Company in Sycamore,

Illinois, and the new wholesale cooperative opened for business in January 1948. Operating out of a rented warehouse in Chicago, Cotter & Co. offered "... hardware merchandise at attractive prices, a barebones warehouse operation, semi-annual dealer markets, consumer advertising, and merchandising help for the retailer ...," according to Kantowicz. Cotter went back out on the road, spending six months visiting Midwestern dealers to convince them to put up the $1,500 it would cost to buy shares in his co-op.

The Hibbard's Takeover: 1950–62

From its experience with the True Value test stores during World War II, Hibbard's had learned the value of having stores buy everything from one wholesaler with a complete merchandising and operating plan. In the 1950s, Hibbard's acquired several smaller wholesalers around the Midwest and started a voluntary chain of franchise dealers who bought most of their merchandise from Hibbard's and used the company's True Value ads and promotions. In 1956, the company reached record sales volume of $33 million.

Deciding to concentrate on the True Value franchise, Hibbard's stopped selling to thousands of small accounts and laid off many of its salesmen. The company ended the decade with a chain of nearly 1,000 dealers and four distribution centers, with stores from the Appalachian Mountains to the Rockies, and sales of $19 million.

But Hibbard's underwent another change as well during the 1950s. As it bought up rival wholesalers, the company went after their real estate, not their hardware business. Eventually it reached a point where all its net income was coming from real estate and other investments, with the hardware business some years actually operating at a loss. In 1962 the board of directors decided to liquidate the hardware business, which had been around for more than 100 years, and establish the company instead as a real estate investment firm.

John Cotter had been busy acquiring and raiding smaller rivals in the Midwest and outside the region, and Cotter & Co. had surpassed Hibbard's in sales volume in 1960. Cotter had also been keeping a close eye on happenings at Hibbard's, and had figured out what was happening with the company's hardware business. In 1961 he secretly indicated that he was interested in buying Hibbard's assets. Although nothing came of that approach, when the Hibbard board decided to sell, Cotter & Co. was their first choice.

Cotter wanted access to the True Value dealers before other wholesalers recruited them. According to Kantowicz, the Hibbard's takeover was one of the best-kept secrets in business history. During the summer and fall of 1962 John Cotter and a small number of his top people met secretly with Hibbard's directors and a handful of senior-level employees to hammer out the deal, using code names throughout the process.

The final price for all of Hibbard's assets was $2.5 million, including $2,500 for the True Value trademark. Cotter and Hibbard's announced the sale the day after Thanksgiving, and most of the 400 Hibbard's dealers agreed to become shareholders in the Cotter & Co. co-op. Not only were dealers allowed to continue to use the True Value name, Cotter & Co.

members decided to add that name to all their stores. Cotter's acquisition of Hibbard's increased the company's sales 56 percent and, for what was certainly one of the true values in business history, gave Cotter a brand name that would become its national identity.

Fine Tuning Store Programs: 1960s–80s

Cotter & Co. honed its True Value advertising and store programs, setting a model for low-cost distributors and helping to keep independent hardware retailers competitive with discount and chain stores. In 1966, the company's sales topped $100 million and it was the largest hardware distributor in the country. Cotter's success and the company's methods were felt beyond the Midwest.

In Pennsylvania, American Hardware moved into a new facility in rural East Butler, a town north of Pittsburgh, in 1960, and expanded its inventory, hired new personnel, and implemented new procedures. In 1965, the company, with 450 members and sales of around $18 million, began to expand through a series of acquisitions. In 1977, the company instituted its ServiStar advertising program, planning to create a voluntary chain of owner-dealers. By the end of the 1970s, after 15 years of expansion, American had increased the number of members to 3,500 and had sales of slightly over $300 million. Sales volume at Cotter and Co. topped $1 billion in 1979.

American's ServiStar program was completely voluntary. When American introduced the ServiStar concept, the approach was simply to get the ServiStar sign in the window. As American president Larry Zehfuss explained in an article in the October 1983 issues of *Chilton's Hardware Age,* ''We'd go in, sign the store, show the dealer how the program worked, and tell him to call us if he had any problems.''

But following a share-of-market analysis that showed the company was getting only a small percentage of the ServiStar dealers' purchases, American increased its sales staff and went after those purchases, implementing an array of marketing and merchandising services and expanding the ServiStar private label program to include plumbing and electrical departments, even brooms and garbage cans, along with the more familiar paint and paint sundries. In the process, American became the first hardware cooperative to establish a customer service department.

Over the next several years, dealers' average purchases increased substantially, and by 1983, some 2,100 of American's owner-dealers displayed the ServiStar sign and accounted for 70 percent of the company's sales. That same year, consumer recognition of the ServiStar name topped 50 percent. Aiming to increase that recognition to 90 percent by the end of the 1980s, the company began making large advertising investments ($10 million in 1985), using magazines, newspapers, circulars, and television ads to actually sell the product. In 1987, the company had sales of $1.1 billion, and nearly 4,000 hardware, lumber, rental, and home and garden centers across the country. In 1988, in recognition of the growing diversity of its business, American changed its corporate name to ServiStar Corporation.

John M. Cotter died in 1989, at age 85, having built Cotter & Co. into a $2.1 billion company with over 8,000 members. A

wheeler-dealer, a master politician, a born manager, and a champion of dealer-ownership, Cotter witnessed and contributed to a major transformation of the hardware industry during his 73 years in the business. But another transformation was occurring in the industry as independent, neighborhood dealers began losing customers to giant home improvement chains such as Lowe's and Home Depot, and Sears began opening free-standing hardware and paint stores that were smaller than the superstores but larger than most independents and offered well-known brand names.

Competing with the ''Big Box'' Chains: 1990–95

The introduction of the giant chains combined with a recession in the housing market sent the independent dealers and their wholesalers scrambling. Trying to preserve membership as well as gain new members, the cooperatives focused on new services and leaner operations.

Cotter & Co., where John's son Daniel was president and CEO, stressed regionalization, adding thousands of items to their merchandise offerings to meet the needs of different geographic markets. The company, along with other hardware wholesalers, also targeted the home remodeling market.

ServiStar expanded westward, gaining members in the Northwest and Rocky Mountain states, and strengthened services for its different niche markets. Some 200 of the co-op's members who operated garden centers as well as the many hardware and lumber center dealers who sold lawn and garden merchandise had been complaining that the company was not meeting their needs in terms of products, especially plants, or advertising. After looking at their complaints, ServiStar developed a complete marketing campaign called Home & Garden Showplace geared to retailers who operated garden centers. In 1990, the company opened the prototype Home & Garden Showplace store, in Amherst, New York, near Buffalo.

In July 1990, ServiStar merged with Denver-based Coast to Coast to form a $1.8 billion international co-op. Coast to Coast, the company founded by the Melamed brothers in 1928, and its parent company, Amdura, had been in bankruptcy proceedings and had lost about 200 of its 1,000 stores when ServiStar bought it for $25 million. The company, with dealer owners primarily in the Midwest and West, operated two types of stores: Coast to Coast Total Hardware and Coast to Coast Home and Auto, selling automotive merchandise from mufflers to waxes to tires. The merger was a boost to both companies; after one year, sales rose 16 percent and profits rose 46 percent.

In 1993, ServiStar Coast to Coast added to its rental business with the purchase of the 288 franchise units of Taylor Rental Corp., a subsidiary of The Stanley Works. Each qualified franchisee was offered a licensing agreement from the co-op, with a reduction in pricing averaging 12 percent. The Taylor stores and the company's 260 Grand Rental Station locations made ServiStar the largest general rental chain in the United States.

As the superstore home center chains continued to grow, the presidents of the four largest hardware co-ops met ''to help members fight the chain stores,'' Dan Cotter explained to *National Home Center News.* Presidents from ServiStar Coast to Coast, Ace Hardware, and Hardware Wholesalers, Inc. joined

Cotter. To avoid antitrust accusations, the presidents did not discuss pricing or a "co-op of co-ops," but as a result of the sessions, both Cotter & Co. and ServiStar Coast to Coast individually began exploring merger opportunities. Each independently identified the other as the best match.

But merger was not the only route for expansion. Both companies were also moving into other countries. In 1994, Cotter established True Value International, an independently-operated division based in Georgia, to serve stores outside the United States. ServiStar, which had opened its first store outside the U.S. in 1971, in Bermuda as an executive perk, also had numerous members in other countries.

A New Company: 1996 and Beyond

In July 1996, Dan Cotter and Paul Pentz met privately to discuss the possibility of merging the two co-ops. In December, the joint boards unanimously approved the merger and proposed it to their membership. In January 1997, the two presidents addressed the companies' conventions, and beginning in February, more than 6,000 retailers attended a series of over 500 town hall meetings across the country to answer questions and address concerns.

In March, Cotter's Tru-Test facilities produced their first batch of ServiStar paint, and in April, the merger received 95 percent approval from the memberships. The new corporation, headquartered in Chicago, was officially created on July 1, 1997. Dan Cotter was named chairman and CEO, and ServiStar's president Paul Pentz delayed his retirement to become president, COO, and a director.

The history of TruServ has been the history of the hardware industry over the past 150 years. It included distribution innovations, bitter rivalries, novel marketing and sales techniques, community involvement, and retailer raids. But primarily it was the story of independent hardware retailers joining together to be more successful at selling while maintaining their service, product knowledge, and personal involvement in the community—the traditional strengths of the hardware retailer. The creation of TruServ was the most recent step in this long history, and whether it would withstand the competition of the "big box" stores remained unknown. But based on past experience, the odds looked good.

Principal Divisions

True Value; ServiStar Hardware, Lumber Yards and Home Centers; Coast to Coast Hardware; Coast to Coast Home & Auto; Grand Rental Station; Taylor Rental Center; Home & Garden Showplace; and Induserve Supply.

Further Reading

"A Day in the Life of Cooperative America: Become Better Operators," National Co-op Bank, http://www.ncb.com/day/a6d.htm.

"American Hardware Supply Company," [advertisement], *Chilton's Hardware Age*, April 1985, p. 58.

"American Hardware Supply: Style Is the Difference," *Chilton's Hardware Age*, October 1983, p. 64.

Bamford, Jan, "SERVISTAR Has Home Town Flavor," *Pittsburgh Business Times & Journal*, September 26, 1988, p. 9S.

"Co-op Presidents Join Together to Fight Chains," *National Home Center News*, May 24, 1993, p. 5.

Cory, Jim, "Book Reviews—John Cotter: 70 Years of Hardware," *Chilton's Hardware Age*, March, 1987, p. 108.

Feder, Barnaby J., "Independents Have a Weapon Against the 'Big Boxes,'" *New York Times on the Web*, June 11, 1997, http://archives.nytimes.com/archives/

Frieswick, Kris, "Of Mergers and Margins: How the True Value/ServiStar Merger Will Impact the Hardware Manufacturing World," *Manufacturing Marketplace*, December 1996, http://www.manufacturing.net/closeup/margin.htm.

Hoover, Jon, "ServiStar Adds Garden Center to Its Program Line-up," *Chilton's Hardware Age*, February 1990, p. 59.

"Introducing a Retail Co-op as Unique as You Are," Chicago: TruServ Corporation, 1997.

Jackson, Susan, and Tim Smart, "Mom and Pop Fight Back," *Business Week*, April 14, 1997, p. 46.

Kantowicz, Edward R., "Hardware Hardball: The Building of True Value," *Crain's Chicago Business*, January 12, 1987, p. 41

——, *John Cotter: 70 Years of Hardware*, Chicago: Cotter & Company, 1987.

Murphy, H. Lee, "A Wrenching Time: Cotter Tries to Hammer Out Hardware Combo," *Crain's Chicago Business*, Mary 5, 1997, p. 4.

"No Longer Just Coasting Along," *Do-It-Yourself Retailing*, May 1991, p. 85.

Rouvalis, Christina, "Smitty's: Where Muscovites Come to Shop," *Pittsburgh Post-Gazette*, October 16, 1991, p. 23.

"ServiStar and Coast to Coast Mark 1st Merger Anniversary," *Aftermarket Business*, October 1, 1991, p. 17.

"Servistar to Acquire Taylor Rental Franchise," *Chilton's Hardware Age*, July 1993, p. 28.

Sutton, Rodney K., and Carollyn Schierhorn, "Co-ops and Buying Clubs Plot New Strategies," *Building Supply Home Centers*, August 1990, p. 90.

"TruServ At-A-Glance," TruServ Corporation, http://www.truserv.com/about/background.asp.

"TruServ: Short History," TruServ Corporation, http://www.truserv.com/home/history.asp.

"TruServ: The Making of a Merger," TruServ Corporation, http://www.truserv.com/about/merger.asp.

—Ellen D. Wernick

Ultrak Inc.

1301 Waters Ridge Drive
Lewisville, Texas 75057
U.S.A.
(972) 353-6500
Fax: (972) 353-6679
Web site: http://www.ultrak.com

Public Company
Incorporated: 1980
Employees: 672
Sales: $188.7 million (1997)
Stock Exchanges: NASDAQ
Ticker Symbol: ULTK
SICs: 3663 Radio & Television Broadcasting &
    Communications Equipment; 3669 Communications
    Equipment, Not Elsewhere Classified

Ultrak Inc. is a worldwide leader in the design, manufacture, marketing, selling, and servicing of innovative electronic products and systems for the security and surveillance; industrial, dental, and medical video; professional audio; traffic management; and manufacturing markets.

Some of the company's products include a broad line of cameras, lenses, high-speed dome systems, monitors, switchers, quad processors, time-lapse recorders, multiplexers, wireless video transmission systems, access control systems, computerized observation and security systems, audio equipment, video closed-circuit television systems, and accessories.

The company's closed-circuit television (CCTV) management systems are used to control hundreds and even thousands of cameras, monitors, and recorders in the gaming marketplace, one of the most complex CCTV applications. Ultrak's MAXPRO CCTV management system, which allows a virtually unlimited number of output devices to work seamlessly together, is ideal for casinos and offers powerful synergies with the company's Diamond Electronics' dome systems. To effectively cater to this market, the company set up an office in Las Vegas, Nevada, and installations have been made at Harrah's, Desert Inn, and The MGM Grand in Las Vegas, as well as at many other casinos around the world.

Ultrak markets its products under its proprietary brand names (Ultrak, Exxis, Smart Choice, Beck, Mobile Video, and UltraCam, to name a few), but also markets products under licenses from Dedicated Micros, Mitsubishi, Panasonic, and Sony. The company markets to wholesale distributors, installing dealers, large end users, mass merchants, and manufacturing companies.

Private Patrols, 1969–87

In 1969, George K. Broady, a former military policeman as well as a stock analyst in the trust department of First National Bank in Dallas, invested $80,000 in building a wireless home security system before realizing the project was a dead-end.

One year later, inspired by a television news show about how few police cars were available for neighborhood patrol, Broady was convinced there was a future in home security. Confident that he could figure out how to take advantage of the opportunity, Broady invested $10,000 of his own money, bought a police car, hired a retired police officer, and entered the private patrol business with Network Security Corp. Broady went door-to-door in affluent Dallas neighborhoods, offering to provide more patrol hours as more residents joined. By 1986, the company he founded posted net income of $5.3 million on revenues of $59 million. In 1987, Broady sold Network Security to Switzerland-based conglomerate Inspectorate International for $165 million, putting over a million dollars in his own pocket and planning to go back into merchant banking.

But Inspectorate International wanted to divest themselves of the Ultrak division of Network Security, which imported alarm equipment components. They offered Ultrak to Broady for book value, $662,000, saying that otherwise the division would be shut down. Feeling a sense of loyalty to the employees he had hired, Broady took the offer, and Ultrak Inc. was created.

Surveillance Systems, 1987–96

Broady quickly narrowed the company's focus to closed-circuit television surveillance systems. Huge Japanese corporations such as Mitsubishi, Sony, and Toshiba dominated this industry. In order to compete with these giants, Broady traveled to Korea where small companies were manufacturing essentially the same products that the Japanese corporations were selling. Soon Ultrak had a system on the market which was big enough to cover a grocery store for approximately $24,000, 20 percent less than the competition.

During the next three years, Broady put up $2.5 million of his own cash and raised $1.2 million from a 1990 stock offering, putting the money into expanding Ultrak's distribution to wholesalers such as Arius and King Alarm, security companies like ADT and Brink's, and installers like Wells Fargo and Mosler.

In September 1990, the company expanded by acquiring a Mancos, Colorado-based software development company, Loronix Inc., in exchange for 10 million shares of Ultrak stock. The acquisition enabled Ultrak to move quickly into the growing commercial/industrial identification badge security market. Loronix's software program translated data from an ID badge into a photograph. The system allowed a security guard to scan the badge and see a photograph of the badge holder displayed on a computer terminal, making forgery of ID badges much more difficult. The acquisition was timely since in 1991 the Federal Aviation Administration began requiring major airports to have a badge identification system to positively identify all airline and airport personnel. Other uses included management of prisoner records, identification for check cashing, and security in hospitals. The acquisition brought 85 employees, including 22 in Denver, and another subsidiary called Loss Prevention Inc. in Maryland.

Business took off in 1991 when retail giant Wal-Mart, a large account for Ultrak, began looking for a video surveillance system to retail to homes and small businesses. Broady found a Korean manufacturer who could turn out a home system that could sell for under $300. Shortly before Christmas that year, Ultrak began shipping to Sam's Club a video camera and monitor that hooked to a VCR and began recording if a motion detector was triggered. The system retailed for just under $300,

and included an add-on feature for another $180 that would automatically dial an emergency number and play a prerecorded break-in message. Broady marketed a similar line to discounters Target and Kmart in 1992.

In 1992, Ultrak tried to repeat its success with inexpensive surveillance outfits by selling cheap PCs into the warehouse club market. The timing was abysmal at best since bigger names in the computer industry such as Compaq, Dell, and Gateway were beginning to cut prices in order to sell to discounters. The following year, Ultrak took a $1.5 million hit as it closed its computer manufacturing operations, but the company still managed to post 1993 revenues of $80 million and net income of $804,000, down from $838,000 in 1992.

In 1994, net income was $2.5 million on revenues of $79.1 million. Sales remained steady through 1995 with net income of $2.6 million on revenues of $101.2 million.

Shopping Spree, Mid-1990s

The year 1996 was a breakthrough year for Ultrak, with a number of developments and acquisitions broadening the company's product line and geographic distribution. Ultrak's products successfully made inroads into the Asian market, including China where the company's Diamond Electronics products were being used in a number of large projects such as airports. The company also began distribution in Japan, as well as in India, Indonesia, Malaysia, the Philippines, Singapore, and Thailand, where the company's MAXPRO products were being used primarily for casino applications, airports, and prisons. The South American market, including Argentina, Brazil, Chile, Honduras, Mexico, Paraguay, Peru, and Venezuela, was also developed in 1996. South Africa, where Diamond Electronics and Maxpro each secured a significant presence, became another market for Ultrak's products.

In 1996, the company continued to develop its UltraCam subsidiary, which designed multimedia dental systems, creating the OpNet system, a dental operatory network system that worked with the intraoral camera already marketed by the firm.

In August of that year, the company's CCTV Management & Digital Recording Systems division was strengthened by the acquisition of an Australian CCTV management system leader called Maxpro Systems, which brought to Ultrak one of the most sophisticated computer-controlled matrix video switching systems on the market. The powerful MAX-1000 incorporated advanced VCR management functions necessary for continuous surveillance using video or alarm monitoring. The MAX-1000 was successfully installed in London's Heathrow Airport, the Ellington and Martindale Military Airports in the United States, and various prisons in Australia and Singapore in addition to traffic and public safety application installations in Perth, Australia, and various other locations. The acquisition also strengthened the company's access to the Australian, New Zealand, and Asian markets.

The December 1996 acquisition of VideV, a prominent German designer, manufacturer, and marketer of CCTV systems, components, and products, added to Ultrak's stable of products a sophisticated digital video recording system, designed to be one of the most advanced bank automatic teller machine security systems available on the German market, and the EuroLine brand name of products.

February 1997 brought the company U.K.-based Intervision Express, a young and aggressive marketer of products in the British CCTV market, one of the largest and most advanced in Europe. The following month, Ultrak acquired Casarotto Security, a prominent and respected player in the Italian CCTV market, which, through its exceptional purchasing skill, was able to bring the most advanced CCTV products to the Italian market at very competitive prices under the Videosys brand name. These three acquisitions immediately gave Ultrak a powerful position in three of Europe's CCTV markets.

A new black-and-white camera with back-light compensation was released by the company in 1996 to complement Ultrak's color, $\frac{1}{3}$-inch CCD camera with back-light compensation. The company also designed and developed a unique digital color camera using solid-state digital signal processing technology to consistently produce the sharpest images possible at a cost close to that of conventional analog color cameras, which can be used for both conventional video and Duplex Analog Video Encoder (DAVE) applications. The acquisition of Diamond Electronics also added product innovations to the company's product line, particularly with the SmartScan III top-of-the-line, high-speed pan/tilt dome system. Diamond successfully installed its systems in traffic and public safety applications in Montgomery County, Maryland, and the Olympic Village in Atlanta, Georgia.

In March, the company released three new real-time quad systems, making Ultrak America's largest supplier of such systems, which allow the simultaneous viewing of up to four cameras on a single monitor. The company also introduced two quad observation systems aimed at the do-it-yourself market, and ideal for residential and small commercial applications, in addition to CCTV Designer, a proprietary software package that was the first to automate the design of CCTV systems through an on-screen user questionnaire.

In September of that year, the company made a minority investment in Lenel Systems International Inc., a New York-based software company, giving it access to the latter's flagship product, Lenel OnGuard Plus, which offered multimedia ID management, access control, and alarm monitoring using Windows 95- and Windows NT-based platforms. Lenel's integrated multimedia systems are used to protect Microsoft's headquarters in Washington state, as well as Yale University's campus.

Also that month, the company acquired Paris-based Groupe Bisset, making its first entry into the European CCTV market, estimated to be at least as large as the U.S. market. The French company brought its position as a leading marketer of CCTV products, as well as experience in successfully designing and marketing its own line of audio and public address equipment, marketed under the BST brand name.

Other new products in 1996 included the UltraDur camera housings, made of a special polymer compound, offering both style and strength; a real-time event recorder for continuous or event recording; and a line of CCTV camera power supplies using fuseless technology to eliminate the risk of blown fuses due to surges or shorted cables.

By the end of 1996, the company was debt-free, with $72 million in cash and cash equivalents, even after purchasing and making investments in four companies; early in 1997, the company made three more acquisitions. Added to the roster of Ultrak companies were: Maxpro Systems, a manufacturer of a powerful CCTV management system; Monitor Dynamics, a creator of high-end access control systems; Veravision, a designer of intraoral cameras for dental applications; as well as Groupe Bisset in France, VideV in Germany, Intervision Express in England, and Casarotto Security in Italy, giving the company a strong international marketing and sales presence. Revenues for the year reached $136.6 million, with total net income jumping to $7.5 million.

The company began working on access control systems, often the heart of an integrated security system, in 1996. In February 1997, the acquisition of California-based Monitor Dynamics Inc. (MDI), the leading designer, manufacturer, marketer, and seller of very high-end security and access control systems added to the company's progress in this field. MDI developed the SAFEnet system for OS/2 Warp-, Pentium-, and Windows NT-based computing, which was one of the most powerful systems of its kind on the market at the time. The SAFEnet system's redundancy and reliability made it especially suitable for high-security applications where downtime is unacceptable. MDI's high-end security and access control systems have been installed at BankOne, Caterpillar, General Motors, Honda, John Deere, MBNA, Motorola, NationsBank, Texas Instruments, and Toyota facilities, as well as at a number of U.S. government installations.

In March 1997 Ultrak entered negotiations with Checkpoint Systems Inc. about a possible merger between the two companies but, in the following month, Checkpoint retreated from the deal. Also early in 1997, Ultrak introduced its own line of camera lenses and recorders as well as released PointGuard, the company's first access control system, which included Windows 95- and Windows NT-based software, control hardware, and card readers designed to manage small- to mid-sized systems. PointGuard was easier and faster to install and set up than any other system on the market at that time.

By the end of 1997, the company's core business experienced a slight pickup. The Sam's Club chain, which carried the company's consumer do-it-yourself products, began selling a new Ultrak dental camera called Ultracam, and the company's DAVE system had already been installed in six locations, with an additional 15 installations in the works, including Superfresh and Publix supermarkets. Sales in the CCTV market in the United States were slow, but overall revenue for the year reached $188.7 million, with a net income of $2.4 million.

In June 1998, the company introduced the System 2000, using Ultrak's DAVE Technology. Awarded the Security Industry Association New Product Showcase's coveted Practitioner's Choice Award, the system was being touted as the most exciting product in the security industry. This system, which was ideal for multi-camera settings like retail stores, reduced installation and capital costs by 25 percent or more over traditional systems.

In mid-1998, the company formed a new operating unit, Ultrak Europe. With headquarters located in Antwerp, Belgium, Ultrak Europe was to be responsible for managing the company's business interests in Europe, the Middle East, and South Africa, thus poising Ultrak for future international growth.

Principal Subsidiaries

Diamond Electronics Inc.; Exxis Securities.

Principal Operating Units

Ultrak Europe.

Further Reading

Bounds, Jeff, "Ultrak Struggles to Overcome Wall Street's Expectations," *Dallas Business Journal*, September 26, 1997, p. 4.

"Checkpoint Pulls Out of Ultrak Takeover, Issues Profit Warning," *Wall Street Journal*, April 4, 1997, p. C13.

"Checkpoint Systems Inc.," *Wall Street Journal*, March 12, 1997, p. C22.

Dowling, Mark, "Ultrak Inc. Secures Growth in Merger with Software Firm," *Denver Business Journal*, October 19, 1990, p. 11.

"Pact Is Set to Buy Ultrak for $340 Million in Stock," *Wall Street Journal*, March 13, 1997, p. B5.

"Shares Fall As Checkpoint and Ultrak End Talks," *New York Times*, April 5, 1997, p. 23.

Sullivan, R. Lee, "Expensive Lessons," *Forbes*, January 30, 1995, p. 92.

"$364 Million Security-Surveillance Merger Set," *New York Times*, March 12, 1997, p. C4.

"Ultrak Inc.," *Wall Street Journal*, June 25, 1997, p. B4.

"Ultrak Inc.," *Wall Street Journal*, August 12, 1997, p. B7.

"Ultrak to Buy Back Shares," *Wall Street Journal*, April 9, 1997, p. B12.

—Daryl F. Mallett

Ultra Pac, Inc.

21925 Industrial Boulevard
Rogers, Minnesota 55374-9575
U.S.A.
(612) 428-8340
(800) 999-9001
Fax: (612) 428-2754

Public Company
Incorporated: 1987
Employees: 362
Sales: $61.71 million (1997)
Stock Exchanges: NASDAQ
Ticker Symbol: UPAC
SICs: 3089 Plastics Products, Not Elsewhere Classified

Ultra Pac, Inc. ranked 12th among 48 U.S. thermoform manufacturers in the $1 billion plastic food packaging industry according to 1997 estimates. The majority of Ultra Pac sales were to bakery customers; a second sizeable market was among produce distributors. Ultra Pac also manufactured bakeable plastic products for the baking, home meal replacement, and delicatessen segments of the food industry.

Entry into the Plastics Industry: 1970s–80s

Calvin S. Krupa's entrepreneurial spirit led him to the plastics manufacturing business. ''It happened in the process of trying to sell a little chemically activated hand-warmer he'd started manufacturing in the early 1970s while working as a traffic manager at Pillsbury,'' wrote Dick Youngblood. Krupa purchased equipment to make plastic packaging for the product but later expanded the enterprise.

Through his company Custom Thermoform, Krupa produced rigid plastic containers for products such as fishing tackle, cosmetics, and hardware from 1973 through 1984—the thermoforming process uses heat and pressure to mold plastic sheets into containers. But undercapitalization and the recession of the early 1980s compelled him to merge the business with

Innovative Plastics, where as vice-president of marketing Krupa developed 25 packaging products for bakery supermarkets.

Innovative Plastics, like Krupa's earlier venture, was plagued by lack of capital funds which ultimately hampered the company's ability to bring new products to the marketplace. Krupa moved on and established Ultra Pac in February 1987 with Twin Cities businessman James A. Thole. Funds from two other investors and a public offering of $150,000 helped get the business off the ground.

Ultra Pac began production in an 8,000-square-foot facility in the Minneapolis suburb of Plymouth. The first product was packaging for compact disc (CD) recordings. Krupa had developed the 6x12 CD Blister Pack in 1983 for RCA Records; it became widely used by the industry. The company added a line of food packaging for bakery and delicatessen products toward the end of the year.

Expanded Food Packaging Operations: The Early 1990s

In 1989, CD packaging brought in 57 percent of Ultra Pac's $2.8 million in revenues. But by 1991 only about 10 percent of sales came from the CD package production. Food packaging had become the company's primary product. Ultra Pac produced about 80 different designs and held about five percent of the national plastic food packaging market. The company now operated out of a 60,000-square-foot facility in Rogers, Minnesota, northwest of Minneapolis.

In a January 1991 *Corporate Report Minnesota* article, Krupa attributed his company's early success in the food packaging market to the recyclability and durability of the product as well as Ultra Pac's rapid response to customers' requests for new designs. To ensure continued growth, Ultra Pac invested nearly $1 million in sheet extrusion equipment. The company expected to save up to $400,000 per year, by producing their own plastic sheets instead of buying them ready-made.

Ultra Pac placed 37th on *Business Week*'s 1991 list of the top 100 small U.S. corporations based on sales growth, earnings growth, and return on investment capital. Fiscal 1991 revenues were $11.6 million, more than double the 1990 figure. Wall Street took note, and Ultra Pac's stock price began rising.

With the recording industry moving away from oversized CD packaging, Ultra Pac phased out its first product: CD packaging had contributed just 6.4 percent of fiscal 1992 net sales. In line with environmental concerns of the time, Ultra Pac actively promoted the recycling of its food packaging products. The polyethylene terephthalate (PETE) used in production was a high-quality material which was the most widely recycled plastic in the world. Ultra Pac also used post-consumer PETE in the production of some of its containers—federal government regulated the use of recycled plastic for food items.

Plastic packaging companies used generally the same technology, so companies attempted to distinguish themselves from competitors with product design which was granted some limited patent protection. According to Youngblood, "Thus, the Ultra Pac line now includes some 300 items ranging from party platters for supermarket delis, buckets for McGlynn's cookies and hinged clamshells for berries to compartmentalized tubs for candy, casserole lookalikes for carryout chicken, even a platter molded in the shape of a sombrero for nachos and salsa." In addition to the bakery, supermarket, and deli products, Ultra Pac was expanding their product line to include packaging for fruit and produce distributors and florists.

According to Youngblood, Ultra Pac had 18 production lines mid-year 1992 and was adding two more. The equipment cost about $300,000 per line. Molds were $50,000 to $100,000, and mold inserts used to vary designs could run up to $10,000. Three private placements and a secondary offering, all made during the previous five years, raised $7 million to help finance the growth.

Krupa received recognition for his entrepreneurship in 1992, and Ultra Pac was ranked 23rd among the 100 best small companies in the nation by *Business Week*. Richard S. Teitelbaum wrote in an August 1992 *Fortune* article, "When its competitors are the mammoth plastic container units of Mobil and Tenneco, a bantamweight like Ultra Pac (fiscal 1992 sales: $18.3 million) had better bring something special to the deli counter." Teitelbaum said Ultra Pac set themselves apart with their PETE products which kept foods fresher than the less flexible oriented polystyrene (OPS) typically used by the big plastic container makers. In addition, the big manufacturers offered pre-made packaging while Ultra Pac emphasized its custom-made capabilities and customer service.

But the banner year ended with a big drop in earnings: $270,000 in 1993 versus $1.3 million in 1992. The drop was due to costs related to the new packaging lines and a second plastic extruder, plus the introduction of new products. Net sales, on the other hand, continued to rise. For a second year in a row, Ultra Pac exceeded a 50 percent growth rate. Fiscal year 1993 revenues reached $27.6 million.

Ultra Pac entered the international marketplace through a joint venture with Minneapolis-based floral retailer Bachman's Inc. to sell and market plastic containers in 17 countries in the Middle East. In a November 1993 Twin Cities Business Monthly article by Kane Webb, Krupa said the company was "laying the ground work for the future." He went on to say, "We're growing like crazy, and I don't refuse many offers." Although sales continued to grow, earnings fell again in fiscal 1994.

Ultra Pac introduced products made from oven and microwave tolerant plastic, cellular PETE or C-PET, in fiscal 1995. The company also entered into a licensing agreement with a New Zealand company for the manufacturing and marketing of PETE packaging. Net earnings for the year rebounded back above the million mark.

Increased Competition and Costs: Mid-1990s

Fiscal 1996 marked Ultra Pac's first unprofitable year since 1987. Losses were $3.2 million. The company said significantly higher raw material costs, higher fixed overhead costs, and higher labor costs were major contributors to the deficit. Prices on PETE resin, which accounted for about 50 percent of total manufacturing costs, were driven up by increased demand in the market. New sales did not keep pace with Ultra Pac's expanded production capacity; increased competition, especially from companies making lower cost non-PETE products, hurt the important bakery and deli sales. Other factors such as the trend toward low-fat food items and adverse weather conditions in California's berry producing region added to the pressure on the company. Ultra Pac responded by trimming its 600-person work force and strengthening the management team. The company moved to improve efficiencies and reduce costs in the thermoforming and extrusion operations and in distribution. Long-term debt that had been in default during the year was restructured. Aided by lower raw material costs, reduced labor costs, and improved manufacturing efficiencies, Ultra Pac returned to profitability in fiscal 1997. Capital expenditures had been cut to about $500,000, down from about $9 million the previous year. The number of stock products was trimmed to 230 from more than 600. Net earnings were $1.8 million, but net sales for the year declined due to the emphasis on margin improvements rather than growth and the continuing pressure from competition. Ultra Pac introduced a dual-ovenable product line named the RESERVATIONS Series for the home meal replacement and kitchen-ready food segments of the market in February 1997. With Americans spending more and more money on take-home prepared food, grocers began offering products in direct competition with chains such as Boston Market. Ultra Pac tapped into the trend with sturdy, attractive packaging which could also be used to reheat food in the microwave or oven. According to the *Wall Street Transcript* interview with Krupa in April 1997, in addition to developing products for the home meal replacement market, the company planned to concentrate more on bakeable type containers for bakery and deli use. Ultra Pac said the baking industry was demanding more bakeable plastic trays which they used in place of aluminum or solid metal baking pans. In September 1997, Ultra Pac announced plans for distribution facilities in California and Florida in order to serve the produce markets there more efficiently. Third quarter earnings, announced in November, were at a record pace for the first nine months of fiscal 1998; analysts expressed optimism about the company's short-term future. But when the company announced fiscal year figures were to be moderately below estimates, Ultra Pac's stock price dropped 20 percent.

Future Plans for Plastic Packaging

The huge U.S. market produced most of Ultra Pac's sales, but the company continued to develop its international market. Ultra Pac held a 49 percent interest in a produce container manufacturing operation in Chile in addition to licensing and distribution agreements in New Zealand and Australia. The company wanted to expand its southern hemisphere markets to help balance out the seasonality of fruit and produce production. A European market was also being developed. Future capital expenditures over the next year or two were expected to be $1 million or less and earmarked for introducing new products and improving manufacturing efficiencies. Ultra Pac's aggressive expansion had allowed the company to produce all of its PETE plastic sheets, despite periodically operating the extrusion equipment at less than full capacity. Krupa and Ultra Pac were banking on greater use of plastic food packaging due to advantages in presentation, sanitation, and labor saving when compared to other containers on the market.

Further Reading

Carideo, Anthony, "Growing Pains," *Star Tribune,* November 17, 1992, p. 2D.

——, "Rogers Firm Wraps Its Plastic Packaging Around Most Anything," *Star Tribune,* September 2, 1991, p. 1D.

"CEO Interviews," *Wall Street Transcript,* April 14, 1997.

"Corporate Capsule," *Minneapolis/St. Paul CityBusiness,* September 12, 1997, p. 44.

Egerstrom, Lee, "Climbing the Food Packaging Chain," *Pioneer Press Dispatch,* September 16, 1997, pp. 1E-2E.

Foster, Jim, "Seven Small State Firms Among Top 100," *Star Tribune* (Minneapolis), May 18, 1991, p. 1D.

"In Brief," *Star Tribune* (Minneapolis), August 2, 1994, p. 3D.

Merrill, Ann, "Focusing on Future," *Star Tribune* (Minneapolis), February 26, 1997, p. 1D.

"Minnesota's Best Entrepreneurs," *Minnesota Ventures,* July/August 1991, p. 56–57 and July/August 1992, p. 36.

Schafer, Lee, editor, "Analyst's Views," *Corporate Report Minnesota,* August 1991, pp. 98–99.

Teitelbaum, Richard S., "Companies to Watch,"*Fortune,* August 24, 1992, p. 133.

"Ultra Pac's Fresh Success," *Corporate Report Minnesota,* January 1991, p. 21.

"Ultra Pac Stock Tumbles 20 Percent," *Star Tribune* (Minneapolis), January 16, 1998, p. D3.

Webb, Kane, "Green Pastures," *Twin Cities Business Monthly,* November 1993, pp. 82–87.

Youngblood, Dick, "Customer Service Is Part of Ultra Pac's Package for Plastic Industry Success," *Star Tribune* (Minneapolis), July 8, 1992, p. 2D.

—Kathleen Peippo

Univision Communications Inc.

1999 Avenue of the Stars
Suite 3050
Los Angeles, California 90067
U.S.A.
(310) 556-7676
Fax: (310) 556-7697
Web site: http://www.kmex.com/information/univision

Public Company
Incorporated: 1961 as Spanish International
    Communications Corp.
Employees: 1,500
Sales: $459.7 million (1997)
Stock Exchanges: New York
Ticker Symbol: UVN
SICs: 4833 Television Broadcasting Stations; 4841 Cable
    & Other Pay Television Services; 7812 Motion
    Picture & Video Tape Production

Univision Communications Inc. owns and operates Univision, the leading Spanish-language television network in the United States, and Galavision, a Spanish-language cable television network. The company, in 1997, also owned and operated 21 television stations. The Univision network was providing, in addition to the company's own stations, 27 over-the-air and 835 cable affiliates with 24-hour-a-day programming.

Spanish-Language Pioneer, 1961–87

Univision began in 1961 as the Spanish International Communications Corp. (SICC), which was founded by Rene Anselmo, with the purchase of KWEX-TV in San Antonio, Texas. The Massachusetts-born Anselmo had worked in Mexico for Emilio Azcarraga Milmo, president of Telesistema Mexico (later Grupo Televisa), which indirectly provided SICC with 20 percent of its financing—the legal limit on foreign control of a television station—and all of its programming. Anselmo also became head of the Spanish International Network (SIN), established to handle advertising sales for the stations but eventually becoming a full-fledged network with more than 350 affiliated stations. Telesistema Mexico was able to hold 75 percent of SIN (with Anselmo holding the other 25 percent) because limits on foreign ownership of television stations did not extend to television networks.

SICC and SIN almost singlehandedly established Spanish-language television in the United States. By the autumn of 1968 SIN had added KMEX-TV in Los Angeles, WXTV in New York City, and KPAZ-TV in Phoenix to its holdings. All of these were UHF stations. Along with a non-SIN UHF station in Chicago, they constituted the only television stations in the United States broadcasting exclusively in Spanish. Five Mexican stations also belonged to the network.

During the 1970s the Spanish-speaking population of the United States increased seven times faster than the population at large.

SIN, in 1976, became the first network to deliver its signal by earth satellite. By paying $1.5 million for a transponder on Western Union's Westar II satellite, SIN was able to increase its potential outlets and pick up direct transmissions from abroad, while bringing its transmission costs down markedly.

Communications satellites greatly enhanced SIN's capabilities, enabling it to reach about two-thirds of all Hispanics in the United States by 1980, beaming 100 hours of weekly programming to ten over-the-air stations, 21 cable systems, and hundreds of CATV systems. By 1982 all but two of the 35 all-Spanish television stations in the United States were receiving programming from SIN. About 55 percent of the programming came from Televisa, with the other 45 percent produced in the United States. The fare included news, variety shows, World Cup soccer, and the wildly popular soap opera series known in Latin America as *telenovelas*. SIN's revenues were estimated at $10 million for 1978, $20 million for 1980, and $45 million for 1984. SICC, whose revenues came to about $90 million in 1985, also owned a string of Spanish-language radio stations.

In 1979 SIN also launched Galavision, a commercial-free pay cable television service in Spanish with programming beamed by satellite. First offered in Arizona, Colorado, New Mexico, and Florida, the Los Angeles-based network had 60,000 subscribers in early 1981 and more than 100,000 in early 1984. Featuring films, sports, and *telenovelas,* it was offering 14 hours a day of programming in early 1984. Galavision became a basic cable network in 1987 and in 1989 was on some 300 cable systems in 12 states and the District of Columbia. Its 24-hour-a-day fare of news, entertainment, and variety shows was supplied by Televisa and appeared to be aimed primarily at Mexican-Americans. Like SIN, Galavision was 75 percent owned by Azcarraga and other principals of Televisa and 25 percent owned by Anselmo. Galavision and a dozen other companies operated under a U.S. subsidiary of Televisa called Univisa.

Under Subsequent Ownership, 1987–95

In 1986 a Federal Communications Commission administrative law judge refused to renew the licenses of the SICC stations, ruling that they were under the control of Azcarraga and his relatives in violation of the 20 percent legal limit on ownership by foreigners. As a result, in 1987 SICC sold its ten TV stations for roughly $300 million to Hallmark Cards Inc. and its minority partner, First Chicago Venture Capital, who established Univision Holdings Inc. By the terms of the sale, SIN, which was renamed the Univision Network, was to provide all of the programming. In 1988 Hallmark purchased a majority stake in the Univision Network for $265 million. Revenues of Univision Holdings, including its network subsidiary, came to about $150 million that year.

Under the direction of William Grimes, formerly chief executive of ESPN Inc., Univision launched Spanish-language clones of such English-language shows as "Saturday Night Live," "Entertainment Tonight," "The People's Court," the Oprah Winfrey and Phil Donahue talk shows, and the "20/20" celebrity magazine-format program. It hired 16 more news correspondents and became noted for its coverage of Latin American hot spots, including the wars in El Salvador and Nicaragua. Its most popular offering, however, remained, "Sabado Gigante" ("Giant Saturday"), a three-hour-long combination variety-game-talk show, and the new programs it introduced were not as popular as the Televisa-made *telenovelas* they supplanted.

Univision and rival network Telemundo suffered from low advertising bookings; although Hispanics made up eight percent of U.S. residents in 1989, the Spanish-language networks received only about two percent of the $11 billion the Big Three—CBS, NBC, and ABC—collected in revenue from commercials. Univision reportedly lost about $50 million that year. Hallmark had taken on $555 million in debt to buy the stations and network, nearly half of it in the form of high-yielding junk bonds issued by Univision Holdings. When this subsidiary missed interest payments on the bonds in early 1990, Hallmark bought them back from the holders, but at a deep discount, paying only about 49 cents on the dollar. In 1992 Hallmark sold Univision Holdings to A. Jerrold Perenchio for $550 million.

Univision at this time had annual revenues of more than $200 million, 13 Spanish-language television stations, and a potential audience of 90 percent of the nation's Hispanic households. Perenchio, a non-Hispanic producer of TV shows who had owned and operated Spanish-language television stations, made his purchase in partnership with Grupo Televisa and Venevision, Venezuela's largest broadcasting company. Perenchio received 75 percent of the station group and 50 percent of the network, with the foreign companies splitting the remainder of each. They also received warrants enabling them to acquire 50 percent of the station group if U.S. laws were changed to permit greater foreign ownership of broadcast outlets.

This sale was approved by the FCC despite protests by Telemundo and three Hispanic groups who feared Univision would end production in the United States (where it was producing, in Miami, 41 percent of its programming) and farm all of its programming out to Televisa and Venevision. When Univision dropped three U.S.-made shows in 1993 (replacing two of them with Mexican programs) and fired 70 people who worked on them, critics of the network felt their misgivings were confirmed. By the end of 1997 Televisa and Venevision were providing Univision with 92 percent of its programming.

Some Hispanics of Caribbean background were already angry at the company because Galavision was being aimed at the growing Mexican and Central American population. And in late 1990 Puerto Ricans demonstrated in front of Univision's New York City metropolitan-area station to protest remarks during a program about Puerto Rican "welfare mothers." As a result of the controversy Coca-Cola and Goya Foods withdrew advertising from the network. At nearly the same time Mexican-Americans in Los Angeles were protesting what they perceived as the "Cubanization" of both Univision and Telemundo in hiring and programming. The protests against Univision in Los Angeles began in May 1989, after the network announced it was consolidating its operations in Miami, where Cuban-Americans had a large presence and there were few Mexican-Americans.

Univision won some praise from Hispanics (as well as some criticism by non-Hispanics) for donating $100,000 in 1994 to a group fighting the ballot initiative known as Proposition 187, which sought to deny government benefits to illegal immigrants in California. Ironically, at the same time Perenchio was making huge donations to Governor Pete Wilson of California and the Republican Party, whose policies—including support for Proposition 187—were unpopular with many Hispanics.

Univision in the Middle and Late 1990s

Between 1992 and 1997, Univision's share of Spanish-language television viewing in the United States grew from 57 to 83 percent. With the acquisition of Chicago and Houston stations in 1994 and a Sacramento station in 1997, Univision was operating 13 full-power over-the-air UHF stations, including 12 in the top 15 metropolitan areas in terms of numbers of Hispanic households. Each ranked first in Spanish-language television viewership in its metropolitan area, as did all of Univision's ten full-power affiliated stations.

Much of Univision's fare was similar to that offered by the U.S. English-language networks, starting with "Despierta America," a "Today"-type early morning program, and continuing with a morning talk show, "Maite," another talk show, "Cristina," the popular magazine show "Primer Impacto," and, of course, the telenovelas.

Cuban-born Cristina Seralegui claimed to be the most watched talk show host on earth, seen by 100 million people from Boston to Chile. In 1997 the network added a late night variety show, "Al Ritmo de la Noche." Of the 20 top prime-time Spanish-language programs in the United States in that year, the first 14 all belonged to Univision.

"Noticiero Univision" was the most influential and highest-rated Spanish-language news program in the United States. WLTV, the Univision affiliate in Miami, led the CBS, NBC, and Fox stations in news ratings, and KMEX, in Los Angeles, led all of the network newscasts. According to a 1994 study, 45 percent of a typical "Noticiero Univision" broadcast dealt with Latin American events, compared with less than two percent of the main nightly ABC newscast. A 1996 poll found that Univision was the second most trusted institution among the nation's Hispanics, trailing only the Roman Catholic Church. In smaller, poorer Latin American countries, television stations often simply taped Univision stories for their own use.

As a subsidiary of Univisa, Galavision had not been included in the sale of SIN to Hallmark, but it was acquired by Univision in July 1996. This cable network was offering such attractions as classic movies, original series, and exclusive rights to sporting events, including baseball's Caribbean World Series and Mexican League soccer championship games. Galavision, in 1997, was reaching about 2.5 million of the 4.4 million Hispanic households wired for cable service on more than 370 U.S. cable systems. After the parent company joined with Home Shopping Network to form Spanish Shopping Network in 1997, Galavision began carrying its offerings.

Galavision was also being used by the parent company to connect with younger, bilingual, or English-dominant Hispanics in the United States reported to be turning away or turned off by Univision's programming. A Hispanic producer told a *Los Angeles Times* reporter, "In a lot of Latino households, mom and pop are at one TV set watching *telenovelas* and the kids are at another set watching 'Moesha' or 'Friends.'" Galavision began targeting this segment of the market in 1997 with two English-language shows aimed at Hispanics: "Cafe Ole with Giselle Fernandez," including crossover Latino actors as celebrity guests, and "Funny Is Funny," an all-comedy half-hour series hosted by comedian Carlos Mencias.

The station group, Univision Communications, made its initial public offering in September 1996, selling 19 percent of its common stock at $23 a share. In early 1998 Perenchio held 26.5 percent of the Class A common stock, while Grupo Televisa and Venevision each held 10.3 percent, plus warrants that if exercised would nearly double their stakes. Because of his full ownership of Class P stock, however, Perenchio held 78.5 percent of the voting power.

Curiously, Perenchio's partners also were potential threats to Univision's future. Televisa, for example, had agreed with several partners to develop and operate a direct broadcast satellite venture that would use Televisa programming. Univision was threatening legal action, contending that it had exclusive rights to any such venture. Similarly, Univision said it was considering action against Venevision, claiming that the Venezuelan network had not made available the nine hours per day of programming required by an agreement that locked in Univision's rights to Televisa's and Venevision's *telenovela* output through 2017.

Univision's net revenues grew from $104.7 million in 1993 to $459.7 million in 1997. After losing money in 1993, 1994, and 1995, the company had net income of $10.4 million in 1996 and $82.6 million in 1997, including $19.5 million as a carryover for earlier losses. Univision's 1997 revenues were almost double the previous year's, primarily reflecting the acquisition of Univision Network L.P. in October 1996. Interest expenses in 1997 came to $40.1 million. The company's long-term debt was $481.3 million in September 1997.

Principal Subsidiaries

Galavision, Inc.; PTI Holdings, Inc.; Sunshine Acquisition Corp.; Sunshine Acquisition, L.P.; and California general partnerships for each of Univision's 13 full-power stations.

Further Reading

Arrarte, Anne Moncreiff, "And Galavision Makes Three," *Advertising Age,* February 12, 1990, p. S-2.
Bagamery, Anne, "SIN, the Original," *Forbes,* November 22, 1982, pp. 96–97, 99.
Barnes, Peter W., "Spanish-Language TV Faces Big Changes," *Wall Street Journal,* April 24, 1986, p. 6.
Dolan, Kerry A., "Muchas Gracias, Congress," *Business Week,* October 7, 1996, pp. 46–47.
"Hispanic TV Is Beaming in on the Big Time," *Business Week,* March 23, 1981, p. 122.
Kurtz, Howard, "Hispanic TV, Not Just Fun & Games," *Washington Post,* March 2, 1991, pp. D1, D9.
Landro, Laura, "Univision Expansion Plan Is Under Way," *Wall Street Journal,* January 23, 1989, p. B9.
McDougal, Dennis, "Univision May Face Ad Boycott," *Los Angeles Times,* January 1, 1991, p. F3.
Moffett, Matt, and Johnnie L. Roberts, "Mexican Media Empire, Grupo Televisa, Casts an Eye on U.S. Market," *Wall Street Journal,* July 30, 1992, pp. A1, A9.
Murray, Kathleen, "Banging the Drums As Spanish TV Comes of Age," *New York Times,* April 10, 1994, Sec. 3, p. 10.
Mydans, Seth, "Spanish-Language TV Called Biased," *New York Times,* July 24, 1989, p. C16.
Pollack, Andrew, "The Fight for Hispanic Viewers," *New York Times,* January 19, 1998, pp. D1, D6.
Puig, Claudia, "Univision Sale Raises Concerns," *Los Angeles Times,* April 27, 1992, pp. F1, F11.
Rohter, Larry, "In Spanish, It's Another Story," *New York Times,* December 15, 1996, Sec. 4, pp. 1, 6.
Shiver, Jube, Jr., "Keeping Univision Alive," *Los Angeles Times,* February 19, 1990, pp. D1, D4.
"Spanish TV Network Traces Growth to Satellite Usage," *Communications News,* February 1980, pp. 68–69.

Stevenson, Richard W., "Hallmark to Sell Its Univision TV Group," *New York Times,* April 9, 1992, pp. D1, D4.

Tebbel, John, "Newest TV Boom: Spanish-Language Stations," *SR/Saturday Review,* June 8, 1968, pp. 70–71.

Tobenkin, David, "Univision Vs. Telemundo," *Broadcasting & Cable,* October 6, 1997, pp. 40, 42.

"Univision Staves Off Chapter 11," *Chicago Tribune,* April 14, 1990, Sec. 2, p. 2.

Volsky, George, "Spanish-Language Cable Network Gaining," *New York Times,* May 1, 1989, p. D10.

——, "3d Hispanic Network Seeks Viewers," *New York Times,* April 10, 1990, p. D17.

Waters, Harry F., "The New Voice of America," *Newsweek,* June 12, 1989, pp. 54–55.

Wylie, Kenneth, "Hispanic Cable TV Strives to Reach Its Potential," *Advertising Age,* March 19, 1984, pp. M36–M37, M40.

—Robert Halasz

Unocal Corporation

2141 Rosecrans Avenue, Suite 4000
El Segundo, California 90245
U.S.A.
(310) 726-7600
Fax: (310) 726-7817
Web site: http://www.unocal.com

Public Company
Incorporated: 1890 as Union Oil Company of California
Employees: 8,394
Sales: $6.06 billion (1997)
Stock Exchanges: New York Pacific Midwest Singapore Basel Geneva Zurich
Ticker Symbol: UCL
SICs: 1061 Ferroalloy Ores, Except Vanadium; 1099 Miscellaneous Metal Ores Mining, Not Elsewhere Classified; 1311 Crude Petroleum & Natural Gas; 1321 Natural Gas Liquids; 2873 Nitrogenous Fertilizers; 3339 Primary Smelting & Refining of Nonferrous Metals, Except Copper & Aluminum; 4612 Crude Petroleum Pipe Lines; 4911 Electric Services

Unocal Corporation is the largest U.S.-based independent energy exploration and production company. Its principal oil and gas exploration and production sites are in Asia, Latin America, and the Gulf of Mexico. Unocal, which has survived three major hostile takeover battles in its history, was a fully integrated oil company—with a major presence in oil refining, marketing, and transportation on the U.S. West Coast—until the mid-1990s, when it shed most of its downstream operations. In addition to its leading upstream position, Unocal is the leading producer of geothermal energy in the world, and it constructs and operates electrical power generation plants. The company's Diversified Business Group makes and markets nitrogen-based fertilizers, petroleum coke, graphites, and specialty minerals and has various petroleum pipeline activities.

Formed Through Three-Way 1890 Merger

Unocal was founded in 1890 as Union Oil Company of California from the merger of three California oil companies: Sespe Oil and Torrey Canyon Oil, both of which were owned by oil and land baron Thomas Bard of Ventura County, and Hardison & Stewart Oil. Hardison & Stewart began as a "gentlemen's agreement" partnership between Lyman Stewart and Wallace Hardison in 1883 and incorporated later that year. In constant need of cash to finance exploration, Hardison and Stewart were referred to Bard by their bankers in 1885. Bard became their partner and operated his companies in an informal alliance with theirs. Hardison & Stewart frequently ran short of cash, however, and Bard finally proposed that they merge their companies. Hardison and Stewart consented, and Union incorporated in Santa Paula, California, as a mining company, with Bard as president, Stewart as vice-president, and Hardison as treasurer. The Santa Paula plant was, in 1891, the site of the first petroleum research facility in the western United States.

The merger proved to be anything but stable. Hardison, who had been gradually losing enthusiasm for the oil business, sold out his interest in 1892 and left Union to engage in fruit growing. His shares found their way into the possession of Stewart's family. This, in turn, bred in Stewart a conviction that the company was his by rights and led to a conflict with Bard. Although both were Pennsylvania-born wildcatters who had been drawn to California by geologist Benjamin Silliman's predictions of vast oil deposits there, Lyman Stewart and Thomas Bard differed in temperament. Stewart had lost his savings in a youthful oil venture in his native state; despite this early failure, he flung himself into the oil business with the zeal of one who believed that worldly success was a sign of God's salvation. Bard was a calm and shrewd negotiator who would later become a U.S. senator. Stewart wanted Union to put more effort into marketing petroleum products; Bard wanted it to remain a producer and wholesaler of crude.

In 1894 Bard resigned as president to protest an expansion of Union's refining capacity that Stewart initiated and that was approved by other directors. Bard was succeeded by D. T. Perkins, his hand-picked successor. Stewart, however, faced Perkins down at an annual meeting several months later, and

Company Perspectives:

Unocal: Making the Right Connections.

Linking markets to resources: Unocal targets growth opportunities in emerging energy markets, primarily in Asia and Latin America.

Taking an integrated approach: Unocal focuses on regional energy solutions, entering the value chain upstream or downstream to develop resources, pipeline systems, power generation plants, or related projects.

Meeting the competition: Unocal's fast-acting business units—guided by a corporate focus on solid value creation—have the flexibility and autonomy to be the best in their businesses.

Building relationships as the "partner of choice": Unocal's track record as a loyal, low-cost, reliable supplier opens doors to building our businesses in both developed and frontier areas.

Stewart assumed the presidency himself. Bard, still a director, continued to object to Stewart's free-spending expansion schemes but was outvoted time after time. Finally, he sold out his interest in Union in 1900 and began his political career. In 1901 Union moved to Los Angeles.

With Stewart as president, his son Will Stewart, a former University of California football star, became general manager. Under the Stewarts, Union continued to expand both its production and retailing operations. Union spent much money on technological advances, organizing the first petroleum-geology department in the U.S. west in 1900, launching a prototypical tanker in 1903, and completing the first successful cemented oil well in 1905. In 1913 the company opened its first service station, at the corner of Sixth and Mateo Streets in Los Angeles. In time, Union came to miss Thomas Bard's fiscal sobriety. As Lyman Stewart continued to buy up real estate with alarming aggressiveness, the company remained poor in cash. To keep up bond payments Union had to borrow ever-larger sums from local banks and financiers. As the situation worsened, creditors forced the elder Stewart to resign in 1914, and the board of directors elected his more conservative son to succeed him.

Survived First Takeover Attempt in Early 1920s

Under Will Stewart, Union continued to expand. In 1917 it acquired Pinal-Dome Oil, a local company that added 20 service stations in Los Angeles and Orange County to its retail network. Union also opened a refinery in Wilmington, California, near Long Beach Harbor, in 1917, just as U.S. involvement in World War I increased the demand for fuels. The company emerged from the war still in vulnerable financial condition. A speculative scramble for Union shares in 1920 generated takeover rumors, and the next year a foreign syndicate headed by what later became Royal Dutch/Shell Group formally launched an acquisition attempt. In response, Lyman Stewart and two other directors, banker Henry Robinson and retired Borden executive Isaac Milbank, organized Union Oil Associates, the sole purpose of which was to accumulate Union shares and prevent

them from falling into Shell's grasp. The contest took on jingoistic overtones and came down to a proxy vote at a stockholders meeting in March 1922. When the votes were counted, Union Oil Associates won. Union Oil Associates began to merge with Union itself, and two years later, Shell dumped its Union shares on the open market.

The last great battle of his life over, Lyman Stewart died in 1923. Winning that same fight had left Union in stronger financial condition than ever, and the company continued to prosper. In 1928 it joined with Atlantic Refining to form Atlantic-Union Oil, a marketing venture in Australia and New Zealand. By the end of the decade, Union's annual sales had reached $90 million, and it was pumping more than 18 million barrels of oil per year. The Great Depression abruptly ended the good times for Union. Will Stewart died suddenly in 1930. He was succeeded as president by Vice-President Press St. Clair, who pursued a cautious strategy in response to the worsened business climate. In 1931 Union sold its interest in Pantepec Oil, which held leases for exploration in Venezuela. Two years later, the company sold its share of Atlantic-Union.

Union emerged from the Great Depression with an advertising motif that stood the test of time. In 1932 the company was looking for a distinctive brand name for its gasoline. Robert Matthews, a director and British national who was studying U.S. history to qualify for citizenship, suggested "Union '76," as in "The Spirit of '76" for its patriotic connotations. The octane rating of Union's most potent gasoline also happened to be 76, and the marketing department adopted Matthews's idea.

Provincialism Prevailed from 1938 to 1964

Press St. Clair retired in 1938 and was succeeded by Reese Taylor, president of Consolidated Steel and a Union director. Taylor, who was something of a regional chauvinist, would run Union with an iron hand for 24 years. Under his direction, the company would take St. Clair's caution to an extreme and remain tucked into its geographical niche, rejecting expansion. It would eventually pay for this provincialism, falling behind in the game when other major oil companies embarked on worldwide expansion. First, however, World War II broke out, and Union boosted its crude production in response to increased demand for petroleum products. The production of aviation fuels was increased to seven times prewar levels. The company was well located to keep U.S. Navy ships operating in the Pacific Ocean supplied with fuel.

It was after the war that most of the U.S. oil giants began to develop overseas sources of crude, while Union concentrated its operations in North America. In 1949 Union acquired Los Nietos Company, an oil and gas concern the holdings of which were concentrated in California. It also discovered and began exploiting substantial fields in Louisiana. Nevertheless, Union could not find enough crude to keep up with increasing demand for petroleum products, and it had to dip into its reserves to keep customers happy.

Union made some sporadic attempts to find oil in Latin America, North Africa, and Australia. It got nothing but dry holes for its trouble. Injecting steam into abandoned California wells added 70 million barrels to its reserves, but by 1956 the company was strapped for both oil and cash. That year, Taylor turned to a friend, Gulf Oil President William Whiteford, and swung a deal to acquire Gulf's surplus crude in exchange for convertible debt securities. Those debentures, however, could be exchanged for enough Union stock for Gulf to control Union. Gulf, cash and oil rich, sought entry into the western market and Union once more became a takeover target, all the more so because it accounted for more than ten percent of gasoline sales in the Pacific Coast market. As Gulf mulled over the possibilities, in 1959 Oklahoma-based Phillips Petroleum began acquiring Union stock and became Union's largest shareholder the next year with 15 percent. Union bought back the Gulf debentures for $120 million—$50 per share—and got a federal court to bar Phillips from acquiring any more of its stock, ending the second major threat to Union's independence.

None of this, however, addressed the problem of expanding the company's oil reserves and marketing presence. At the end of the 1950s, two-thirds of Union's production was still coming from California, including the Torrey Canyon field discovered by Lyman Stewart in 1889, but a prolonged management shuffle prompted by Reese Taylor's sudden death in 1962 distracted the company from finding a solution. Union's board brought back Albert C. Rubel, who had retired as president in 1960 (Taylor had become chairman in 1956), to take over until a permanent successor could be found. Under Rubel, Union entered into merger talks with Atlantic Refining in 1963, but Atlantic called off the deal because it did not want Union to be the surviving company, losing as it would then its own identity in its East Coast markets. Finally, in 1964, Rubel appointed Senior Vice-President Fred Hartley to take over as CEO.

Stepped-Up Exploration Efforts in the Late 1960s and 1970s

Blunt and outspoken, Hartley was a chemical engineer by training but had shown good business instincts as head of the marketing division. His first actions as CEO were to improve Union's bottom line through layoffs and closing unprofitable service stations. The company also broke out of its provincialism in 1965 by acquiring Pure Oil Company, a struggling oil concern that nonetheless had an extensive distribution network in the Midwest and Southeast. Hartley concluded the deal over the objections of shipping magnate Daniel Ludwig, who had become a Union director when he bought Phillips' 15 percent stake in 1963. The company quickly raised $146 million and bought up all of Ludwig's shares at $36.50 per share.

Hartley saw the need for increased exploration. "If we don't explore we'll go backward and if we don't explore with success we'll go backward and broke," he was fond of saying at the time, as quoted in *Fortune* in April 1967. Union cast a wide exploration net, but it mostly dredged up dry holes. In 1969 the company suffered a public relations disaster when one of its drilling platforms off the coast of California leaked hundreds of thousands of gallons of oil into the water and onto the beaches of Santa Barbara. It took months for Union to get the seepage down to a manageable level. The company maintained that it responded to the leak promptly and had minimized environmental damage, but the incident helped turn public and political opinion against offshore drilling. Various governmental authorities sued Union, Mobil, Gulf, Texaco, and Peter Bawden Drill-

ing, and in an out-of-court settlement reached in 1974, the defendants agreed to pay a total of $9.7 million in damages to the state of California, Santa Barbara County, and the cities of Santa Barbara and Carpinteria.

The Santa Barbara spill and Union's peppery response to criticisms stemming from it gained the company a bad reputation among environmentalists. Throughout the 1970s, even before oil prices began to skyrocket, Union had charted an aggressive course in research and development of alternative energy sources. Union spent substantial sums on developing geothermal power and liquefied natural gas as an automotive fuel. Hartley stopped using a Cadillac as his company car in favor of an Audi, complaining about U.S. automakers' unwillingness to build cars with better gas mileage. In 1974 Union began building an experimental oil shale processing plant in Colorado. Many oil companies turned to shale in the 1970s as a potential source of crude. It was an old enthusiasm of Hartley's; he had written a thesis on it while a student at the University of British Columbia. In 1980, while others were still marking time, Union announced that it would begin constructing a commercial-scale oil shale plant in Parachute Creek, Colorado.

In the 1970s Union joined with Standard Oil of New Jersey, Atlantic Richfield, Standard Oil of Ohio, Mobil, Phillips, and Amerada Hess to form Alyeska Pipeline Service, which would build the TransAlaska pipeline. Union, which was already drilling in Alaska's Cook Inlet, would thus participate in the exploitation of the immense deposits lying under Prudhoe Bay. Union entered a niche of the metals industry in 1977 when it acquired Molycorp, Inc., a producer of rare-earth metals used in high-tech applications.

1980s Brought Third Takeover Attempt

After 15 years under the guidance of Fred Hartley, Union approached the 1980s in a state of financial strength, giving its shareholders a higher-than-average return on assets. Its exploration efforts had begun to pay off, making it rich in oil and gas reserves. At the same time, Hartley's age—he turned 65 in 1980—and the lack of an heir apparent made Union the subject of takeover speculation on Wall Street. To thwart any such attempts, it reorganized in 1983, creating Unocal Corporation as a holding company and reincorporating in Delaware, where incorporation laws made it harder for outsiders to gain control of a company without approval by its directors.

None of this, however, deterred Mesa Petroleum Chairman and corporate raider T. Boone Pickens, Jr., who launched the third major threat to Unocal's independence. Pickens began acquiring Unocal shares in late 1984, even as he was beginning a separate takeover bid for Phillips Petroleum, and eventually accumulated a 13.6 percent stake of Unocal. The Phillips bid failed, but when Pickens walked away from it in January 1985 he did so with a hefty greenmail payment and more than $1 billion in unused credit lines and potential margin loans on his Unocal stock. In the meantime, Hartley refused to sacrifice the money Unocal was pumping into exploration to initiate a stock buyback and inflate its price, although institutional shareholders were clamoring for such a move. Observers speculated that it was only a matter of time before Pickens and Mesa pounced.

Hartley knew that something was up. In early April, the two met by chance as they waited to testify in congressional hearings on the recent spate of hostile takeover bids for major oil companies. *Business Week,* April 15, 1985, reported that Pickens extended his hand in greeting but Hartley refused it, growling, "Go away." "Fred, you're talkin' to your largest stockholder," Pickens said. "Isn't that a shame," Hartley shot back.

Later that month, Mesa announced that it was offering $54 per share in cash for the 37 percent of Unocal stock that it would need for a controlling interest and the same amount in debt securities for the remaining shares. Unocal responded with an offer to buy back 49 percent of its stock for $72 worth of debt per share, but only if Mesa reached its target of 37 million shares. Any shares in Mesa's possession were excluded from this deal, meaning that Pickens could not sell them back to Unocal at a hefty profit. Pickens challenged this last provision in court and initiated a proxy battle to delay the company's annual meeting until he could field his own slate of candidates for the board of directors. Loyal shareholders, however, voted Pickens down in May and reelected Hartley as chairman.

Several days later, the Delaware Supreme Court ruled that Unocal had no legal obligation to include Mesa's holdings in its partial buyback offer. Unocal had stalemated Pickens. To get rid of him, the company agreed to buy back one-third of Mesa's shares at $72 per share; other stockholders would be allowed to sell back some of their holdings as well. Pickens admitted that he would do well to break even on the deal. The most ambitious attempt in his campaign to restructure the oil business—and his first genuine failure—had ended. For its part, Unocal was anything but triumphant in victory. To finance the stock buyback, it had increased its debt load from $1.2 billion to $5.3 billion. Cuts in capital outlays would be necessary.

Fred Hartley was forced to retire in 1988 (he died in October 1990). He had built Unocal into the 14th largest oil company in the United States, but it was left to his successor, CEO Richard Stegemeier, to cope with the bulk of the debt load incurred in the battle against Pickens. Under Stegemeier, Unocal closed unprofitable production and refining facilities and sold off real estate that did not hold oil or gas, including its headquarters building in downtown Los Angeles. Unocal also exited from the no longer promising oil shale business, having spent nearly $1 billion since the mid-1990s and seeing little in return. By the end of the decade, the company was ready for further expansion. In 1989 Unocal joined with Petróleos de Venezuela to form Uno-Ven, a marketing and refining partnership in the midwestern United States. In May 1990 Unocal added to its gas reserves by acquiring Prairie Holding Company from gold mining concern Placer Dome.

Transformative 1990s

Overall, however, Unocal continued to be haunted by the Pickens takeover attempt well into the 1990s. At the end of 1991 long-term debt stood at a still-high $4.54 billion, resulting in annual interest expenses of about $300 million, which led to a lack of cash for capital projects. For example, the company's California gas stations were long neglected, leading to a market share drop from 13 percent in 1985 to 11 percent in 1993. Stegemeier thus was forced to sell additional assets, $527 mil-

lion worth in 1993 alone. But these moves were not nearly the dramatic steps needed to turn the company's fortunes around, and at the end of 1993 debt had been reduced only to $3.45 billion.

It was under Roger C. Beach, who took over as CEO in May 1994, that Unocal finally found the strong leadership needed to extricate itself—in dramatic fashion—from its troubled past. Although longtime employee Beach had headed the company's domestic gasoline refining and marketing unit from 1986 to 1992, overseas was where he saw Unocal's future. He began to aggressively expand the company's oil and gas exploration and production outside of the United States, particularly in Asia and Latin America, while concentrating domestic efforts offshore, in the Gulf of Mexico. The quintessential California oil company cut its California production roots in late 1996 when it sold the last of its Golden State fields. Even more dramatic was Beach's rapid divestment of the company's domestic downstream operations. In March 1997 Unocal sold virtually all of its West Coast refining, marketing, and transportation assets to Tosco Corporation for $1.4 billion in cash. Later that year, Unocal sold off its interest in Uno-Ven, the Midwest refiner and marketer. Then, in another move aiming to refocus the company's exploration and production activities, Unocal sold the bulk of its Canadian oil and gas production assets to Tarragon Oil and Gas Ltd. in exchange for a 28.7 percent stake in Tarragon.

While he was leading the company through this amazing transformation, Beach also was stepping up Unocal's presence in such high-growth, high-yield areas as geothermal energy, electrical power plants, and pipelines, often through international joint ventures. In October 1997, for example, a Unocal-led consortium, called Central Asia Gas Pipeline Ltd, was formed to build a $1.9 billion, 790-mile gas pipeline from a field in Turkmenistan to Multan, Pakistan, crossing Afghanistan in the process. With these projects, Unocal faced the challenge of gaining approval from politically unstable governments, such as that of Afghanistan. Even more troubling in the case of the Central Asia Gas Pipeline was that Unocal immediately was slapped with a $15 billion lawsuit from the Argentina-based Bridas S.A., which had plans for a natural gas pipeline of its own and alleged that Unocal had interfered with its Turkmen operations.

Unocal also had to contend with challenges from human rights advocates when it proposed projects for nations with repressive governments, most notably that of Myanmar (Burma). That nation's military regime had led the U.S. government to impose sanctions on it in April 1997. Unocal had a 28 percent interest in an international consortium—led by TOTAL S.A. of France—which was developing a natural gas field in the Andaman Sea off the coast of Myanmar and was constructing a pipeline from this field to Rathaburi, Thailand. In response to political pressure and in a possible first step toward "de-Americanization," Unocal in April 1997 opened a "twin corporate headquarters" in Kuala Lumpur, Malaysia, where company President John F. Imle, Jr., and several other senior executives would be based, with Beach remaining at the El Segundo, California, headquarters.

By the turn of the millennium, Unocal had certainly left the provincialism of its past far behind. If the company's future lay in Asia—where it was doing two-thirds of its capital spending in the late 1990s—then new challenges were in store, most notably the Asian economic crisis that unexpectedly erupted in 1997. With major operations in two of the hardest hit nations—Thailand and Indonesia—Unocal faced possible setbacks and delays in some of its projects. At the same time, the company was contending with a fall in revenue thanks to a drop in oil prices, which had fallen below $15 a barrel by early 1998. In response Unocal announced in April 1998 that it would cut its 1998 capital-spending budget by about $175 million, or 11.5 percent. After more than a century in which its existence had often been precarious, Unocal once again would need to prove itself tough enough to survive.

Principal Subsidiaries

Union Oil Company of California; Philippine Geothermal, Inc.; Unocal Geothermal of Indonesia, Ltd. (Bermuda); Unocal International Corporation; Unocal Canada Limited; Unocal Canada Resources; Unocal Canada Exploration Limited; Unocal Canada International Company; Unocal Canada Management Limited; Unocal Indonesia, Ltd. (Bermuda); Unocal Indonesia Company (Bermuda); Unocal Myanmar Offshore Co., Ltd. (Bermuda); Unocal Netherlands B.V.; Unocal Thailand, Ltd. (Bermuda); Unocal Capital Trust.

Principal Operating Units

Spirit Energy 76; Diversified Business Group; Asia Operations; International Operations/Geothermal; Unocal Global Trade.

Further Reading

Abramson, David, "Unocal Nears U.S. Downstream Exit with Deal to Sell Uno-Ven to PDVSA," *Oil Daily*, December 30, 1996, pp. 1+.
Bancroft, Thomas, "Playing It Safe," *Forbes*, January 20, 1992, p. 101.
Byrnes, Nanette, "Scorched Earth," *Financial World*, August 2, 1994, pp. 32+.
Collin, Jane, "Unocal Sets Preparation for Dividing Headquarters Between Malaysia, L.A.," *Oil Daily*, April 10, 1997, pp. 3+.
Culbertson, Katherine, "Unocal Heads Overseas, But Plans to Keep Home Fires Burning," *Oil Daily*, January 13, 1997, pp. 1+.
Darlin, Damon, "Getting the Lead Out," *Forbes*, July 17, 1995, pp. 106+.
Eisen, Peter, "Unocal, Bridas Set for Battle in Houston Court over Turkmen Project," *Oil Daily*, November 5, 1997, p. 4.
Ewing, Terzah, "Unocal to Slice Capital Spending As Oil Prices Sag," *Wall Street Journal*, March 20, 1998, p. A4.
Fairclough, Gordon, "Troubled Waters: International Oil Firms in Middle of Burma Battle," *Far Eastern Economic Review*, August 15, 1996, p. 66.
Fan, Aliza, "Unocal Realigns Operations to Focus on Growth in Its Overseas Business," *Oil Daily*, August 19, 1996, pp. 1+.
——, "Unocal's Shift Toward High-Growth Projects to Include Sale of Dutch North Sea Assets," *Oil Daily*, March 7, 1996, pp. 1+.
Fine, Howard, "Unocal's Boss Takes Off the Gloves: Stegemeier Sheds Units, Refocuses, Spars with Critics," *Orange County Business Journal*, March 2, 1992, pp. 1+.
George, Dev, "Unocal Becoming Largest Gas Producer in the Growing Asian Market," *Offshore*, November 1994, pp. 34+.
Holloway, Nigel, "Long Arm of the Law: Unocal Faces Novel Suit over Its Burma Activities," *Far Eastern Economic Review*, September 19, 1996, p. 61.
Hutchinson, W. H., *Oil, Land and Politics: The California Career of Thomas Robert Bard*, Norman: University of Oklahoma Press, 1965.
Kovski, Alan, "Tosco to Acquire West Coast Refining, Marketing, Shipping Assets from Unocal," *Oil Daily*, November 19, 1996, pp. 1+.
Kravetz, Stacy, "Unocal Receives $70 Million Award in Gasoline Suit," *Wall Street Journal*, November 4, 1997, p. B5.
"The Luck of the Drill Bit," *Forbes*, January 15, 1970.
Mack, Toni, "Wildcat Drilling," *Forbes*, June 16, 1997, p. 52.
MacSearraigh, Stephen, "Unocal, Total Actions Prepare Them for World of Sanctions," *Oil Daily*, March 4, 1997, pp. 2+.
O'Hanlon, Thomas, "Fred Hartley and His Well-Oiled Multiplying Machine," *Fortune*, April 1967.
Pasztor, Andy, and Stacy Kravetz, "Unocal Is Shifting Strategy to International Operations," *Wall Street Journal*, November 20, 1996, p. B4.
Pederson, Barbara L., *A Century of Spirit: Unocal, 1890–1990*, Los Angeles: Unocal Corporation, 1990.
Pope, Hugh, "Unocal Group Plans Central Asia Pipeline," *Wall Street Journal*, October 27, 1997, p. A17.
Prasso, Sheri, and Larry Armstrong, "A Company Without a Country?: Unocal Says It Won't Leave Burma, But It May De-Americanize," *Business Week*, May 5, 1997, p. 40.
Rose, Frederick, and Pauline Yoshihashi, "Unocal Plans Another Round of Asset Sales, Job Cuts," *Wall Street Journal*, April 28, 1992, p. B4.
Sanger, David E., "Unocal Signs Burmese Gas Deal; U.S. May Ban Such Accords," *New York Times*, February 1, 1997, p. 4.
"Trouble in the Pipeline," *Economist*, January 18, 1997, p. 39.
"Unocal Pursues Plans to Shed Refining Unit," *Wall Street Journal*, October 30, 1996, p. A6.
Welty, Earl M., and Frank J. Taylor, *The 76 Bonanza*, Menlo Park, Calif.: Lane Magazine and Book Company, 1966.

—Douglas Sun
—updated by David E. Salamie

Vastar Resources, Inc.

15375 Memorial Dr.
Houston, Texas 77079
(281) 584-6000
Fax: (281) 584-3268
Web site: http://www.vastar.com

Public Subsidiary of ARCO (Atlantic Richfield Company)
Incorporated: 1993 as Vastar Resources, Inc.
Employees: 1,100
Sales: $1.01 billion (1997)
Stock Exchanges: New York
Ticker Symbol: VRI
SICs: 1311 Crude Petroleum & Natural Gas

Vastar Resources, Inc. was created out of the interests of the ARCO Corporation in 1993. The company develops petroleum and natural gas reserves within the United States, producing more than a billion cubic feet of natural gas per day. Approximately 60 percent of its more than 1,000 employees work at its Houston headquarters. The firm, which prides itself on low-cost production, is valued at approximately $4 billion and remains 82.6 percent owned by ARCO. Vastar is regionally focused and emphasizes internally generated growth.

An Early 1990s Spinoff

Vastar Resources, Inc. was created in October 1993 as the Atlantic Richfield Company (ARCO) reorganized its exploration and production interests in the contiguous United States. The move created Vastar out of the Dallas-based ARCO Oil and Gas Co.'s Natural Gas Growth unit, which had a net income of $32 million in 1992 and $1.13 billion in revenue. The new company was headquartered in Houston. Three smaller oil companies (Arco-Permina, Arco-Bakersfield, and Arco-Long Beach) were formed at the same time. ARCO eliminated 1,300 jobs through the restructuring.

Vastar's assets, 65 of ARCO's best properties, were grouped into four main regions: the (offshore) Gulf of Mexico, the Gulf

Coast (of Texas and Louisiana), San Juan Basin (New Mexico, Colorado, and Wyoming), and Mid-Continent (Oklahoma, Arkansas, and Kansas). Proved reserves totaled 2.1 trillion cubic feet of natural gas and 99 million barrels of crude oil, natural gas condensates, and other liquid byproducts of natural gas production.

Vastar also inherited, among other subsidiaries, ARCO Natural Gas Marketing, Inc., which became Vastar Gas Marketing, Inc. In addition, it retained access to ARCO's sophisticated research center in Plano, Texas.

The company wasted little time in commencing its aggressive development efforts. In 1993, Vastar drilled in the Gulf using 3D seismic data combined with direct hydrocarbon indicators. This would prove the company's most effective technology, achieving a better than 60 percent success rate. The Gulf would remain the object of much of Vastar's attention for years to come.

Vastar produced the equivalent of 963 million cubic feet per day in 1993 and posted profits right out of the gate. Net revenues were $797 million, with net income of $117 million.

Going Public in 1994

Vastar announced its initial public offering in February 1994. The event raised $453 million in cash. When it was completed on June 27, ARCO owned 82.3 percent of the company and retained control of its board. ARCO's large stake in the company seemed to make investors wary in spite of Vastar's respectable performance.

In an interview with *Oil and Gas Investor,* CEO Michael Wiley (who first joined Arco in 1972), president of Arco Gas and Oil Co. until the restructuring in 1993, recalled that the change in the company's culture was swift, as the unit shifted from being part of an established major player to a progressive, independent, more entrepreneurial one. In particular, Vastar reduced its cost structure surprisingly quickly. It changed its compensation program and empowered workers at lower levels with more control over decisions.

Cash from the IPO, one of the year's largest, allowed Vastar to increase its drilling budget, which soon resulted in impressive results. In its first year as an independent, Vastar replaced all of its reserves and increased production at half of its fields. It quickly established a reputation for making impressive finds at low cost.

Although commodity prices fell in 1994, Vastar's results improved thanks to increased production and unit production costs which fell by more than 25 percent. The company posted a $149 million profit on $817 million in net revenues while producing the equivalent of 1.04 billion cubic feet of natural gas per day.

The company started new drilling in 60 percent of its fields in 1995 as development continued in earnest. It would again replenish its reserves, adding 146 percent of proved reserves. Vastar produced 810 million cubic feet of gas per day in 1995.

In September 1995 Vastar increased its holdings in the San Juan Basin area, its most productive area by volume. Although ostensibly mature, Vastar's technologies managed to spur growth there. In November, the company made a significant new discovery in the Gulf's South Pass 60 field unit, which would become its second largest producing area. Another area that attracted attention was the Lodgepole trend in Montana and North Dakota. Vastar bought a 55 percent interest in 150,000 acres there in the fall of 1995. Three-D seismography was again responsible for the sizeable find.

In 1995, Vastar began operating the Grand Chenier gas processing plant. In spite of increased production, the company's sales fell to $739.5 million, earning a profit of $103 million. The equivalent of 1.08 billion cubic feet per day was produced.

In June 1996, the company signed a three-year contract for the use of Diamond Offshore Drilling Inc.'s Ocean Victory semi-submersible drilling rig. This gave it capability in deepwater exploration to begin in November 1997. By 1996, about 80 percent of Vastar's offshore drilling was based on 3D DHI surveys. In August 1996, the company drilled a record 10,000 feet in 10 days at its South Pass 60 field. That year, development capital amounted to $260 million.

While it had previously sold all of its natural gas liquids to ARCO, in April 1996 it began marketing them independently. Vastar sold about three billion cubic feet equivalent of natural gas per day in 1996, most of it from other producers. This made it the 11th largest natural gas marketer in the United States, capturing $30 million in profits. Vastar Power Marketing, Inc. began trading in the middle of 1996, with hopes of becoming a major player with the coming of deregulation in the electricity market.

The company posted a greater than 100 percent return on equity in 1996. It was simply a great year for Vastar. Commodity prices were their highest in years, while the company's costs continued to fall. On sales of $966.6 million, the company posted a profit of $220 million. It produced the equivalent of 1.17 billion cubic feet per day and replaced 144 percent of its reserves. Capital expenditures continued to increase, to $585 million.

New Plays in the Late 1990s

In March 1997, Charles Davidson succeeded Michael Wiley as president and CEO. Wiley returned to ARCO. Otherwise, the company seemed to progress as usual. Vastar received its first U.S. patent, for ''Chemically Induced Stimulation of Coal Cleat Formation'' in September.

In September 1997, Southern Company Energy Marketing (SCEM), a joint venture with giant $10-billion-a-year electric utility Southern Co., began its bid to be one of the country's top electricity and natural gas marketers with the coming of deregulation. Vastar initially held a 40 percent share in the project. Southern paid Vastar $40 million and planned to own three-quarters of the venture by century's end, when SCEM was expected to be producing $40 million in profits per year. SCEM was headquartered in Atlanta instead of energy industry center Houston, though natural gas was sold at Vastar's Houston trading floor. SCEM expected to add 100 employees per year to its initial workforce of 250. Vastar agreed to sell SCEM all natural gas produced for ten years.

Vastar suffered a 9,400-gallon oil spill off the coast of Louisiana in December 1997. The mile-long slick, which came from an oil platform, was classified as minor, however, and no wildlife was reported to be harmed.

On revenues of $1.014 billion, the company saw $240 million in net income. It produced 1.19 billion cubic feet equivalent per day and reached a record reserve replacement level of 154 percent.

A Strong Fin de Siècle

Production reached record levels (1.21 billion cubic feet equivalent per day) in early 1998 as recent offshore discoveries were brought on-line. However, declining commodity prices pushed the company's first quarter profits down to $48 million from $63 million a year before. Crude oil and natural gas averaged $17 and $11 per barrel, respectively, down from $24 and $16 the year before.

Several discoveries in the Gulf of Mexico fostered optimism; the company announced 12 favorables out of 16 attempts, including the "King" prospect being drilled by the leased Ocean Victory drilling rig (this news was tempered by an engine room fire which forced the rig to be taken off-site for repairs). Shell and BP were minority partners in this effort. By contrast, Vastar's properties on the Gulf Coast, many of which had been producing for 50 years, were described as mature. In April 1998, Vastar Resources traded some deepwater properties in the Gulf of Mexico south of New Orleans to obtain a 25 percent interest in a well being drilled for Shell Deepwater Development Inc. The company planned to participate in four or five deepwater wells in 1998.

In May 1998, the company announced plans to invest at least $700 million to support its growth, a record level of investment. The company had spent $672 in capital expenditures in 1997. Development of 80 fields accounted for little more than half the 1998 budget. Given Vastar's historically impressive return on investment, it would seem to be money well spent.

Principal Subsidiaries

Southern Company Energy Marketing L.P. (40%).

Further Reading

ARCO Environment, Health, and Safety Department, "Wetlands," *1995 ARCO Environment, Health, and Safety Report,* Los Angeles: Atlantic Richfield Company, 1996.

"The Chronicle 100," *Houston Chronicle,* May 18, 1997, http://www. chron.com/content/chronicle/business/97/05/18/chron100/index.html.

Davis, Michael, "Vastar Seeks to Establish Own Identity," *Houston Chronicle,* January 8, 1997.

De Rouffingnac, Ann, "Vastar Will Hold 40 Percent Interest in Energy Marketing Joint Venture," *Houston Business Journal,* August 11, 1997.

Haines, Leslie, "From the Driver's Seat," *Oil and Gas Investor,* January 1996, pp. S2–S5.

Healy, Meg, "Downstream from Here," *Oil and Gas Investor,* January 1996, pp. S11–S12.

Jones, Gregg, "Oil Fields of Dreams: New Finds May Lift Arco's Prudhoe Bay Curse," *The Dallas Morning News,* June 25, 1996.

Koprowski, Gene, "Data Mining, Meet Oil Drilling," *Wired,* February 17, 1997, http://www.wired.com/news/topframe/2101.html.

Pybus, Kenneth R., "Vastar Resources Will Go Public with $500 Million Stock Offering," *Houston Business Journal,* February 14, 1994, pp. 1, 17.

Quinn, Matthew C., "Southern's Natural Gas Marketing in the Pipeline: Joint Venture Set to Begin Operations Next Week," *Atlanta Journal and Constitution,* August 29, 1997.

"Vastar Cites Ship Shoal Gas Finds," *Natural Gas Week,* March 31, 1997.

"Vastar Joins Gulf Kings," *Upstream,* July 18, 1997.

—Frederick C. Ingram

White Rose, Inc.

380 Middlesex Avenue
Carteret, New Jersey 07008
U.S.A.
(732) 541-5555
Fax: (732) 541-5710
Web site: http://www.whiterose.com

Wholly Owned Subsidiary of Di Giorgio Corp.
Incorporated: 1920 as Seeman Brothers, Inc.
Employees: 1,135
Sales: $1.07 billion (1997)
SICs: 5141 Groceries, General Line; 5142 Packaged
    Frozen Foods; 5143 Dairy Products, Except Dried or
    Canned

White Rose, Inc. is the largest independent wholesale food distributor in the New York City metropolitan area. In 1997 it was supplying more than 18,000 food and nonfood items to more than 1,600 stores from Maryland to New England, especially supermarkets and chains in New York City, Long Island, and northern New Jersey. About 850 grocery, frozen food, and dairy items were being offered with the White Rose label.

Seeman Brothers Business, 1886–1965

Joseph and Sigel Seeman were among five Seeman brothers who founded Seeman Brothers & Doremus in New York City in 1886 with capital of $4,500. The two had decided to start their own business after failing to persuade their uncle to switch his wholesale grocery from cash-and-carry to delivery. When Doremus dropped out shortly after, the name became Seeman Brothers. Delivery was by horse and carriage, and the Seemans' matched teams were renowned. Gas-powered trucks began replacing them in 1905, but the last company horse-drawn wagon did not disappear until 1930.

When branded goods became popular, the Seemans gave the White Rose name to their entire line, which originally consisted of just three canned products: corn, tomatoes, and peas. But it was tea that made White Rose a household name. Since black fermented tea was popular at the turn of the century, in 1901 Seeman Brothers introduced a potent variety grown in Ceylon to wean coffee drinkers from their traditional brew. Every conceivable promotional technique of the time was used to establish White Rose Tea, from flyers to attractive young girls dispensing free tea by the potful. Seeman also pioneered in canned fish. The company reportedly bought the entire U.S. production of canned tuna in 1911 to offer it exclusively to White Rose customers.

Seeman Brothers converted from a partnership to a corporation in 1920 and became a public corporation in 1926. Net sales grew from $10.8 million in 1921 to $15.6 million in 1925, and net profits increased from $210,564 to $532,441 in 1922. Net profits came to $344,033 in 1925. Even during the Depression, the company made a profit and paid a dividend in each year. In 1943 it acquired Wilkinson, Gaddis & Co.'s wholesale grocery business in Newark, New Jersey, and added its warehouse to the one Seeman maintained in New York City. Net sales reached a postwar peak, not surpassed until 1955, of $33 million in 1948; net income, however, slumped after a peak of $775,530 in 1950 and came to only $115,353 in 1955.

Seeman Brothers became a very different company under John B. Fowler, Jr., who, with a group of associates, acquired control in 1959 and took the position of chairman and chief executive officer. He acquired, at very little cost, Francis H. Leggett & Co., an unprofitable wholesale grocer with distribution in Pittsburgh and Cincinnati, to add its Premium brand name to White Rose's own. He then acquired control of Seabrook Farms Co. to put Seeman into the frozen food business, along with three other quick-freezing operations and a wholesale food distributor in Hagerstown, Maryland. In fiscal 1960 (the year ended February 27, 1960), the company passed $1 million in earnings for the first time, although most of the gain came from Leggett's tax-loss carryover.

Fowler then organized, through Seeman's Leggett subsidiary, a voluntary association of independent food stores that by June 1962 had enrolled at least 56 stores with sales exceeding $40 million a year. In return for a pledge to buy nearly all of their inventories from Seeman, the members received price advantages and services such as advertising and merchandising advice to help them compete more successfully with big supermarket chains. Seeman's sales rose from $85 million in fiscal 1960 to $125 million in fiscal 1961.

But excess supplies of frozen vegetables forced Seeman to dump its products, sometimes below cost, thereby sustaining a deficit for fiscal 1962, despite a rise in sales to $135 million. Results continued to worsen because Seeman's voluntary cooperative of small stores was no substitute for a hookup with large chains, severe labor troubles, and Seabrook's problems as a relatively high-cost packer. Between 1962 and 1965 Seeman Brothers lost $9.1 million. To reduce a debt of more than $19 million, the company sold its wholesale business, including the White Rose and Premier labels, in 1965 to Di Giorgio Corp. for more than $3 million. This operation had lost $4.3 million on net sales of $34.8 million in fiscal 1965.

Di Giorgio Business, 1965–90

Di Giorgio also was taking control of another New York-area wholesale food distributor, Met Food Corp. Founded in 1941, Met Food had its headquarters in Syosset, Long Island, in 1963, when it earned $104,459 on sales of $45.5 million. The company also was sponsoring a small retail chain under the Met banner. Di Giorgio acquired a 34 percent interest in the company for cash in August 1964 and increased its stake to 97 percent in March 1965. Met Food became a subsidiary that included the former Seeman wholesale operation. In 1970 Met Food was distributing to retail stores dry groceries, frozen foods, dairy products, and other items, principally from a leased, 15-acre, enclosed modern warehouse in Farmingdale, Long Island, opened in 1967. About ten percent of its sales were under its own brands, the most important of which was the White Rose brand. That year it became the first U.S. company to make freeze-dried tea.

By 1973 Met Food was the largest wholesale grocer in the New York metropolitan area. It changed its name to White Rose Food Corp. in 1974. This operation was distributing about 7,000 products in 1979, about 500 of which were under the White Rose label, including frozen as well as canned fruits and vegetables and delicatessen items, which were introduced when the dairy operation moved to Carlstadt, New Jersey, in 1976. White Rose Food accounted for about $400 million of Di Giorgio's $897 million in sales in 1978. The subsidiary introduced its first television campaign in 1982, airing 50 30-second commercials a week for seven weeks on five local stations to publicize White Rose products. In 1983 White Rose became the leading distributor of ice cream in the New York area. It added fresh meat to its line by acquiring Schnoll Foods in 1984. By 1988 it was the largest wholesale distributor of fresh meat in the metropolitan area.

In 1987 White Rose was handling more than a million cases of groceries per week, 15 percent under its own private labels. It was sponsoring voluntary groups under the Met Food and Super Food names and was a supplemental source of supply to the King Kullen, Gristede's, Red Apple, Sloan's, and Waldbaum chains and the ShopRite and Foodtown co-op members. Supermarket chains carrying the White Rose private labels included Royal Farms, Scaturro Supermarkets, Dan's Supreme, Domino Supermarkets, and Kings—in all, more than 1,800 stores. Aside

from airing TV commercials, White Rose was advertising its private-label line heavily on radio, buses, newspapers, and point-of-sale material. Its significant amount of Spanish-language advertising included commercials broadcast in the Dominican Republic, even though White Rose did not distribute there. (It was selling, however, to Puerto Rico and the Virgin Islands, as well as to Bermuda.)

Except for its huge, 615,000-square-foot grocery warehouse in Farmingdale, White Rose had its operations in New Jersey: dairy in Carlstadt (but moved to Kearny in 1989), frozen foods in Secaucus, and meat in Newark. Its distribution now included candy, house chemicals, poultry, paper products, and soft drinks. In 1989 White Rose acquired Pioneer Food Stores Co-op for an undisclosed sum, adding the company's New Jersey grocery warehouse to its facilities. Founded in 1944, Pioneer, at the time of its purchase, was serving 51 Pioneer stores, 50 of them in New York City and one in Westchester County, New York.

In 1989 Arthur M. Goldberg, a former trial lawyer and an active investor, made a successful tender offer for the company's outstanding shares that cost him and his backers about $166 million. Armed with $175 million in bank loans, he took control of the company in 1990, converted it to a private firm, and began selling all of its five divisions except White Rose, a process completed in 1994, when Di Giorgio and White Rose became, in effect, synonymous.

White Rose in the 1990s

Di Giorgio was losing money when the company changed hands, and its expenses mounted as interest payments on its debt—more than half of which had been incurred for the acquisition—came due. Goldberg started a cost-cutting campaign almost immediately, offering White Rose drivers and warehouse workers a new three-year contract in 1990 with no increase in wages and elimination of overtime, which had allowed many of them to earn $900 to $1,000 a week for a 50- to 60-hour workweek. The contract also contained a clause shifting 20 percent of health insurance premiums to employees and, according to an International Brotherhood of Teamsters official, another clause effectively eliminating seniority and allowing the company to hire nonunion subcontractors.

Although members of Teamster locals representing the frozen food and dairy divisions signed the contract, workers in the Farmingdale local went out on strike in February 1991. Goldberg closed this warehouse in July, shifting the operation to Elizabeth, New Jersey. He fired the 425 strikers in August, replacing the truck drivers with nonunion personnel and the warehouse workers with lower-paid Teamsters hired by a New Jersey subcontractor. In July 1992 the Farmingdale local agreed to end the strike in return for its members sharing in a $1.5 million settlement and being placed on preferential hiring lists for jobs that would pay them less money than previously.

Di Giorgio sold White Rose's meat division in 1991. In 1992 the company acquired the Global division of Sysco Corp. for $11.75 million and moved White Rose's frozen food division from Secaucus to Global's facility in Garden City, Long Island. Two years later Di Giorgio purchased Royal Foods from Fleming Cos. for $17.2 million and moved White Rose's dairy and deli operations from Kearny to Royal's plant in Woodbridge, New Jersey. In early 1995 the grocery and dry goods division moved from Elizabeth to a new 645,000-square-foot distribution center in Carteret, New Jersey. Soon after, White Rose and Di Giorgio moved to this location from Somerset, where Goldberg had established executive quarters on acquiring the company. The Farmingdale facility was sold in 1997 for $12.5 million.

White Rose gained more business in 1993, when Red Apple Group, owner of the Gristede's and Sloan's supermarket chains, dropped the Krasdale Foods private-label brand from Sloan's and began offering White Rose goods instead. Sloan's even bought a full-page *New York Times* advertisement promoting White Rose products. In 1994 White Rose made the first major redesign to its product label in several decades in connection with an advertising campaign that was carried on coupons, newsprint, more than 250 billboards, and 180 bus routes throughout the New York metropolitan area.

Despite Goldberg's crackdown on labor costs and year-to-year gains in revenue, Di Giorgio lost money in every year of the 1990s through 1997 except for 1996, when it reported net income of $2.1 million. The annual interest expense rose as high as $24.9 million in 1995. Di Giorgio earned $5.7 million on operating income in 1997 but lost almost $3 million after taking an extraordinary charge of $8.7 million for early extinguishment of debt. Its long-term debt was $159.3 million at the end of 1997.

Further Reading

"Bad Dream," *Forbes,* March 15, 1966, p. 58.
Crowe, Kenneth C., "Dark Days at White Rose: Teamsters Strike Enters 13th Week," *New York Newsday,* April 28, 1991, pp. 66–67.
——, "Union Ends Strike at White Rose," *Newsday,* July 24, 1992, pp. 47–48.
"Di Giorgio Cites Buyer Interest in White Rose," *Supermarket News,* September 25, 1989, p. 4.
Fox, Bruce, "White Rose Label Continues Blooming After 100 Years," *Supermarket News,* March 9, 1987, pp. 10, 12.
Freeman, William M., "Wall St. View Boon to Executive," *New York Times,* September 1, 1961, pp. 37, 39.
Hammer, Alexander R., "56-Store Voluntary Food Group Is Formed by Seeman Brothers," *New York Times,* April 3, 1962, p. 51.
Maier, Thomas J., "White Rose Fires Strikers," *New York Newsday,* August 2, 1991, pp. 35–36.
Turcsik, Richard, "Pioneer Food Stores Agrees to Be Bought by White Rose," *Supermarket News,* March 6, 1989, p. 6.
——, "White Rose Is Advertising Revised Label," *Supermarket News,* April 4, 1997, p. 17.
Weinstein, Steve, "101 Years New," *Progressive Grocer,* February 1987, pp. 41–42, 44, 46, 48, 50.

—Robert Halasz

Wilson

Wilson Sporting Goods Company

8700 W. Bryn Mawr
Chicago, Illinois 60631
U.S.A.
(773) 714-6400
Fax: (773) 708-3178
Web site: http://www.wilsonsports.com

Wholly Owned Subsidiary of Amer Group Ltd.
Incorporated: 1913 as Ashland Manufacturing Company
Employees: 3,062
Sales: $300 million (1997 est.)
SICs: 3949 Sporting & Athletic Goods

Wilson Sporting Goods Company has the largest market share in the sporting and athletic goods industry, with its strongest competitors such as Anthony Industries, Inc., Johnson Worldwide Associates, and Spalding & Evenflo far behind. Wilson Sporting Goods has maintained the lion's share of the market throughout its history primarily because of its focus on manufacturing high-quality products in the categories of basketball, football, volleyball, golf, baseball, soccer, racquetball, squash, footwear, team uniforms, and an extensive line of sports apparel. Of all the company's products, it was the sale of golf equipment that catapulted Wilson Sporting Goods into a place of prominence within the industry during the 1980s and 1990s. The company's plant in Humbolt, Tennessee, was manufacturing more than 45,000 golf balls on a daily basis, and had grown to become the third largest golf ball plant in the world. Due to its position in the marketplace, and its growing presence overseas, Wilson Sporting Goods was purchased by WSGC Holdings, Inc. in 1985. A 1989 merger between WSGC Holdings and Bogey Acquisition Company, an affiliate of the Amer Group Ltd., resulted in Wilson Sporting Goods becoming a wholly owned subsidiary of the Amer Group, located in Helsinki, Finland.

Early History

Wilson Sporting Goods was incorporated in 1913 as the Ashland Manufacturing Company, and was originally established to find unique ways of using slaughterhouse byproducts of a nearby meat-packing firm, its parent company owned by Sulzberger and Schwarzchild. By 1914, the company was producing such items as tennis racket strings, violin strings, and surgical sutures, and had expanded into baseball shoes and tennis racquets. In 1915, the company appointed Thomas E. Wilson as president, and from that moment onward nothing was the same. Wilson, a hard-headed businessman who saw the potential of a sporting goods company, broke away from the parent firm of Sulzberger and Schwarzchild, began to focus exclusively on the manufacture of sporting and athletic equipment, and then named the company after himself in 1916.

Thomas Wilson immediately started to expand the operations of his company by acquiring the Hetzinger Knitting Mills and a small caddie bag company. Hetzinger was purchased for the purpose of producing high-quality athletic uniforms, while the caddie bag company's extensive line of luggage products was reduced to the manufacture of golf bags alone. Basketballs and footballs were also added to the company's rapidly growing list of items for sale. In 1917, the company was so confident in the quality of its product line that it announced a two-year unconditional guarantee on all of its products. During the same year, the company began manufacturing golf clubs and football helmets. Although Thomas E. Wilson left the company in 1918, no interruption occurred in either the manufacture of its products or the growth of its revenues. By the end of the year, sales reached the $1 million mark, an enormous amount of money for a company that had been in existence for only a short time. The company closed out the decade by acquiring Chicago Sporting Goods Company, a manufacturer of uniforms, by reaching an agreement to supply all the equipment for the Chicago Cubs baseball team, and by hiring Arch Turner, one of the prominent craftsmen in the leather industry. Hiring Turner was prophetic since his innovative designs for the leather football had a profound influence on the development of the game.

The decade of the 1920s was one of the most successful and most innovative periods for the company. In 1922, Wilson introduced the Ray Schalk catcher's mitt, which from that time onward set the standard for design, comfort, and padding within the baseball industry. During the same year, the company established its advisory staff of athletes, with the famous golfer Gene Sarazen as its first member. The most influential member of the advisory staff, however, was the football coach of Notre Dame, Knute Rockne. Rockne worked with Wilson to develop a new double-lined leather football, and the first football that was valve inflated. These two developments were instrumental in helping Rockne to develop the modern passing game in college football. In addition, Rockne and Wilson developed the first waist-line football pants with pads that could be removed, thus providing the player with the ability to move more freely. Wilson was also making a major impact in other areas of sports as well, such as the cardboard tube containers for tennis balls that soon became the standard packaging for the industry.

When Knute Rockne died in a plane crash in 1931, Wilson was able to form a close collaboration with Dana X. Bible, the football coach at the University of Nebraska, in an attempt to continue its development of innovative football products. And, although Bible was able to help Wilson develop helmets and shoulder pads, the company was unable to match the degree of influence on the game achieved with Rockne during the 1920s. As a result, company management decided to focus on the game of golf.

In 1932, the company developed the R-90, a sand wedge golf club inspired by Gene Sarazen's victory in the 1932 British Open. That year alone, Wilson sold over 50,000 of the sand wedge clubs. One year later, the company introduced a design that distributed the weight of the club in the toe of the club's head, anticipating the future design of what was to be termed "perimeter weighting." In 1937, Wilson signed the soon-to-be-famous Sam Sneed as a member of the firm's advisory committee, and introduced the Blue Ridge Golf Clubs, named after the region in Virginia where Sneed was born. In 1939, Wilson achieved a major innovation in the design and manufacture of golf clubs with its ability to bond different layers and types of wood together to produce a criss-cross pattern that resulted in more power, better direction, and a longer period of use than previous designs which employed other wood. By the end of the decade, it was evident Wilson had managed its product development so well, and had marketed its items so successfully, that even through the worst years of the Great Depression the company not only survived but prospered.

World War II and the Postwar Era

Wilson continued its focus on the development of innovative products during the war years, including the introduction of the Wilson Duke football, featuring the best leather, ends that were hand-sewn, lock-stitch seams, and triple lining. Soon after its entry on the market, the Wilson Duke football was adopted by the National Football League as the official ball. Yet the war effort seriously affected Wilson's manufacture of athletic equipment and uniforms, since almost all of the company's production facilities were retooled to make war material such as duffel bags, tents, and helmets to be used by American soldiers fighting overseas. As a result, management at Wilson decided to concentrate on fostering an increased participation of the nation's youth in sports, and through a rather sophisticated marketing campaign the company continued its high profile in the sporting goods industry.

Having remained at the forefront of sports equipment and uniform manufacturers, after the war ended in 1945 the company began to expand and grow dramatically. Ted Williams became a member of the company's advisory staff, and brought an inestimable value to the reputation of Wilson's line of baseball products. Jack Kramer, regarded as the "Father of Modern Tennis," also became a member of the company's advisory board and a close collaborator with Wilson in the design of innovative tennis equipment. More than 10 million autographed Jack Kramer tennis racquets would be sold during the next 30 years. As the 1940s drew to a close, the company owned 15 factories, and 31 sales offices and warehouses throughout the United States.

Not only were the 1950s years of continued technological innovation and high-quality product introduction for the company, but administrative changes and new organizational developments also marked the decade. L. B. Icely, who replaced Thomas E. Wilson in 1918, and had guided the company through what many business historians regard as its most creative period, died in 1950. His tenure was distinguished by one achievement after another, one of the most important (and perhaps the most overlooked) being the introduction—the first such in the sporting goods industry—of the computer for inventory control. Icely had organized the company in such an efficient manner that, upon his death, there was no interruption in product introduction. Sales continued to increase, and revenues for the company reached an all-time high during the late 1950s. In 1957, the company constructed its own administrative office facility in River Grove, Illinois, a short distance from Chicago's downtown area.

During the 1960s Wilson continued its strategy, originally conceived and formulated in the 1930s, of vertical integration through the acquisition of highly specialized firms. Following up on its acquisition in 1955 of the Ohio-Kentucky Manufacturing plant located in Ada, Ohio, one of the most innovative design firms for footballs in the United States, in 1963 the company purchased Masters Golf Bag Company in Collierville, Tennessee, a firm that focused exclusively on the manufacture of golf bags, and Cortland Tennis Company, a firm specializing in the manufacture of tennis racquets in Cortland, New York. In 1964, Wilson purchased Wonder Products Company, a firm with a seemingly unrelated product line of toys and custom-molded items. But soon the purchase of this company was made evident when management began to use its facility to custom-mold parts for protective equipment in football and baseball, such as face masks for football helmets and leg guards for baseball catchers. International expansion also figured into management's strategy at this time. Wilson not only established its first plant overseas, a baseball manufacturing facility in Aguadilla, Puerto Rico, but also opened sales and marketing offices in Wimbledon, Wiesbaden, Tokyo, and Hong Kong. In 1967, however, a major change occurred when Wilson Sporting Goods was purchase by the aerospace conglomerate Ling-Temco-Vought (LTV Corporation), located in Dallas, Texas.

The 1970s and 1980s

In 1970, the company was acquired by PepsiCo, Inc., who wanted to take advantage of Wilson's high profile and leadership role in the industry in order to enhance its own image. In return, PepsiCo provided Wilson with the financial base that was needed for the company to expand into the international market. By 1976, Wilson opened a manufacturing plant in Galway, Ireland, to enter the rapidly growing market for tennis products. But the company's most important growth opportunities were still in the United States. During the decade, the Wilson brands were chosen as the official basketball of the National Basketball Association, and the official football of the National Football League. Wilson provided almost all of the uniforms for teams in Major League Baseball, and the company also provided the United States Summer Olympic team with all of its official uniforms and clothing. The publicity garnered from these agreements was unprecedented—the Wilson brand name was not only known throughout the United States but around the world. With growth opportunities seemingly endless, PepsiCo management decided to divide the company into three divisions: Golf, Racquet Sports, and Team Sports, each with its own marketing and sales teams.

One of the strategies Wilson employed over the years to increase sales and enhance its product image was to pursue the endorsement of professional athletes. During the 1980s, Wilson products were endorsed by over 100 of America's most famous and well-respected athletes, including Sam Sneed in golf, Walter Payton in football, Michael Jordan in basketball, and Roger Clemens in baseball. This strategy paid off handsomely in sales as golf club professionals and tennis club professionals used and promoted Wilson products. At the same time, Wilson entered into contractual agreements with national and regional retailers across the United States to sell its products. Among the major retail chain customers were Target Stores, Sportmart, Kmart, Herman's Sporting Goods, and Sears, Roebuck & Company.

In September 1985, Wilson Sporting Goods was acquired by Westray Capital Corporation through one of its affiliates, WSGC Holdings, Inc. As a result of the purchase, Wilson became a wholly owned subsidiary of WSGC Holdings. In March 1989, WSGC Holdings merged with Bogey Acquisitions Company. Since Bogey was affiliated with the Amer Group Ltd., a multinational corporation located in Helsinki, Finland, Wilson ultimately was owned and operated by the management team at Amer Group. Wilson's new parent company took immediate advantage of its international presence and began to build on the foundation that had already been laid. Under Amer Group's direction, Wilson opened subsidiaries in Japan, the United Kingdom, Germany, France, and Canada. Through a comprehensive marketing and distribution network Wilson was soon able to sell sporting equipment and uniforms in over 100 countries worldwide. In Japan, golf balls and clubs accounted for the majority of sales, while in the United Kingdom tennis rackets and balls sold as briskly as golf balls and clubs. As the decade drew to a close, Wilson was also expanding its production facilities overseas, including new plants in Haiti, St. Vincent, Canada, and Scotland.

The 1990s and Beyond

During the 1990s, Wilson renewed its commitment to manufacture innovative designs for sporting equipment. The revolutionary Hammer 2.7si tennis racquet, introduced in 1990, soon became one of the industry's top-selling racquets. The new Conform baseball glove was brought out in 1993, which allowed ballplayers to customize a glove to the contours of their hand. In 1994, the company introduced the Jet basketball, a leather version made specifically for the outdoor market. In the field of golf, in 1995 Wilson introduced the Invex driver, a uniquely designed head made from stainless steel and titanium, which almost overnight became the largest selling of all the firm's golf clubs to date.

During the early 1990s, Wilson had the largest market share of all the sporting goods companies around the world, with total sales amounting to 8.5 percent of the market. Its closest competitors, Anthony Industries, Inc., Johnson Worldwide Associates, and Spalding & Evenflo Co., Inc., had achieved seven percent, 4.9 percent, and 4.6 percent shares of the market, respectively. Clearly, the international manufacturing and distribution network Wilson was building owed much of its success to the contacts and resources provided by its parent company, the Amer Group. In the mid-1990s, a strategic plan was in its initial implementation phase to increase the company's profile and, in turn, its sales in high-growth areas such as Hong Kong, Korea, Taiwan, Italy, Australia, and Singapore.

The name Wilson has remained synonymous with sporting equipment: from young boys who play basketball on asphalt courts in the inner city of Chicago to professional athletes who play baseball in enormous stadiums with manicured fields across the United States, the product of choice is a Wilson basketball, baseball, glove, or uniform. And few other sporting goods companies in the world have garnered high-powered endorsements as Wilson has. Perhaps the greatest basketball player of all time, Michael Jordan, continued to promote his own line of Wilson signature basketballs, selling over one million annually for nearly 14 consecutive years. With this kind of savvy marketing behind its high-quality products, Wilson Sporting Goods could be expected to retain the largest share of the sporting goods market for years to come.

Further Reading

Agoglia, John, and Mark Tedeshi, ''The Outdoor Industry's Excellent Adventure,'' *Sporting Goods Business,* August 7, 1997, p. 58.

Gallagher, Leigh, ''Balance of Powder,'' *Sporting Goods Business,* February 24, 1997, p. 26.

King, Daniel E., ''Wilson,'' *Encyclopedia Of Consumer Brands,* Detroit, Mich.: St. James Press, 1995, p. 622.

Losee, Stephanie, ''Wilson's Hammer System Racket,'' *Fortune,* November 19, 1990, p. 138.

McEvoy, Christopher, ''Acquiring Minds,'' *Sporting Goods Business,* August 1995, p. 44.

''Outdoors '95,'' *Sporting Goods Business,* August 1995, p. 72.

''Showscope '96,'' *Sporting Goods Business,* March 1996, p. 32.

Young, Kevin, ''Standard Operation,'' *Sporting Goods Business,* August 1995, p. 48.

—Thomas Derdak

Wisconsin Central Transportation Corporation

One O'Hare Centre
Suite 9000
6250 N. River Road
Rosemont, Illinois 60017-5062
U.S.A.
(847) 318-4600
Fax: (847) 318-4618
Web site: http://www.wclx.com

Public Company
Incorporated: 1987
Sales: $333.5 million (1997)
Employees: 2,254
Stock Exchanges: NASDAQ
Ticker Symbol: WCLX
SICs: 4011 Railroads, Line Haul Operating

Wisconsin Central Ltd., the core railroad of the holding company Wisconsin Central Transportation Corporation, was the brainchild of Edward Burkhardt, a 27-year career railroad industry veteran for the Chicago & Northwestern (C&NW). During his quarter century in the business, Burkhardt—like other railroad lifers—had watched with dismay as an industry once synonymous with the technological achievements of the American economy lost large swaths of the transportation market to the trucking sector. However, Burkhardt believed railroads were still an intrinsically competitive freight shipping option and was convinced their market share losses were due as much to crippling labor regulations and outmoded operating practices as to their rigid and unimaginative approaches to the competition offered by the trucking industry. Joining forces with Milwaukee Road executive Thomas F. Powers, Jr., former Illinois governor Richard Ogilvie, and two other investors, Burkhardt mortgaged his home and raided his savings to create a new "entrepreneurial railroad" that would steal back business lost to trucking through efficiency, faster service, lower charges, and responsive customer service.

Deep Roots: 1871–1987

Most of the trackage the new Wisconsin Central acquired in 1987 was descended from lines laid by the original Wisconsin Central beginning in the 19th century. That first Wisconsin Central had been formed in 1871 to haul pulpwood, iron ore, and grain between central Wisconsin and Lake Superior, and by 1884 it had expanded to service St. Paul and by 1886 Chicago. Always financially shaky, in 1909 the original Wisconsin Central formed an alliance with the Soo Line (i.e., the Minneapolis, St. Paul & Sault Ste. Marie, which had been owned by the Canadian Pacific since 1888). The Soo Line bought a majority stock interest in Wisconsin Central but allowed it to retain its operational independence. For the next 32 years the original Wisconsin Central remained a subsidiary of the Soo Line, although following Wisconsin Central's bankruptcy in 1932 the Soo Line became its operating agent as well. Between 1945 and 1960 the original Wisconsin Central made the transition from steam to diesel power and upgraded its passenger service.

In 1960 the original Wisconsin Central and the Soo Line merged with the Duluth, South Shore & Atlantic to form the so-called "New Soo." Between 1968 and 1970 the last dedicated passenger service on both the New Soo and the Wisconsin Central was discontinued. Although the New Soo was a profitable railroad in the 1960s and 1970s, it failed to raise its operating speeds (kept to a noncompetitive 40 miles per hour) or renegotiate tougher labor contracts with unions to enable to run with more efficient crew sizes. To expand its network to compensate for the decline in heavy industry on its traditional routes, the New Soo bought the Milwaukee Road in 1985 for $575 million, thereby expanding its trackage from 4,400 to 7,500 miles and widening its network to cover the Canadian border to the north and Louisville and Kansas City to the south. Although it was suddenly the nation's tenth largest railroad, the purchase entailed the assumption of Milwaukee Road's staggering debt and substandard equipment and infrastructure. The Soo's history of profitability was threatened.

Rechristened "The Soo/Milwaukee System," the Soo attempted to create a new internal "railroad within a railroad"—dubbed the Lake States Transportation Division—to regain its profitability. Under the Staggers Rail Act of 1980 smaller regional railroads were exempt from the regulations that hampered so-called Class I railroads, which allowed them to operate trains with smaller crews, adjust their shipping rates, and negotiate long-term contracts. The new separately managed Lake States railroad would operate within the bounds of St. Paul to the west, Lake Superior to the north, Lake Michigan to the east, and Chicago to the South—virtually the same territory as the original Wisconsin Central. Some railroad unions refused to allow Lake States to negotiate less costly work rules, however, and the Soo's management concluded that servicing "light-density" markets with the costs of a Class 1 carrier was a losing proposition. To reduce its still large debt levels, in April 1987 it decided to sell the Lake States operation to Burkhardt's newly formed Wisconsin Central Ltd. company.

"Retailing Transportation Services": 1987–90

Burkhardt established the new Wisconsin Central's operations and customer service headquarters in Stevens Point, Wisconsin, and the corporate headquarters in the Chicago suburb of Rosemont. A holding company structure—Wisconsin Central Transportation Corporation—was created under which Wisconsin Central Ltd. (WCL) would operate the rail service; WCL Railcars, Inc. would own the locomotives and cars (leasing them to WCL); and Wisconsin Bridges Inc. held the stock of the bridge operation company Sault Ste. Marie Bridge Co., an essential component in a territory dotted by valleys, rolling terrain, and waterways. By the end of the summer of 1987 four hundred new railroad workers had been recruited to run the railroad.

On the eve of the September 1987 date set for the railroad's launch, however, the Interstate Commerce Commission (ICC)—the government body that regulates interstate transportation—shocked Burkhardt's team by announcing that it needed 45 more days to evaluate its approval of the startup. As the locomotives lined up for the September launch date were leased away to other companies, a deluge of protests by Wisconsin Central's industry and community supporters convinced the ICC to change its mind and, a month late, Wisconsin Central's 85 locomotives and 2,900 freight cars were finally permitted to roll. Already $8 million behind because of the ICC's delay, the Wisconsin Central was further hampered by a computer glitch that caused some 3,000 trains to suddenly disappear from its tracking system, and in its first few months train schedules had to be improvised on the fly. Order was finally achieved by the end of the year, however, and in the words of the railroad's historian (*Wisconsin Central: Railroad Success Story*) "shipper complaints [began] turning into compliments."

By March 1988 Wisconsin Central was turning its first profit, and by the end of the year revenues stood at $94 million. Relying primarily on contracts to ship materials for Wisconsin's paper, pulp, and converting mills to and from Chicago, Wisconsin Central soon began to vindicate Burkhardt's vision of a marketing-savvy, customer-driven, cost-efficient railroad that could beat the trucking industry at its own game. Its marketing plan focused on getting more business from existing customers, regaining former Soo customers who had shifted to trucks, and finding new shippers by offering competitive freight rates. It began to go after the more profitable Canadian and iron ore traffic, and by 1996 iron ore had replaced paper industry products as Wisconsin Central's largest type of traffic (in terms of carloads shipped). As early as December 1989, Wisconsin Central was also reporting a 60 percent increase in its "intermodal" traffic (in which railroads "piggyback" the containers or trailers hauled by trucks over part of the shipping route). Flexible work rules allowed Wisconsin Central to use an average crew size of two, and because they had been cross-trained in various aspects of rail duty its crews could be called upon to perform tasks as required without raising a labor representative's ire. As a result, Wisconsin Central's labor expense as a percentage of revenue was soon at 30 percent—versus the national rail industry's 45 percent.

Other innovations included the first use by a regional U.S. railroad of a computer program called the Transportation Control System (originated by Union Pacific), which enabled Wisconsin Central to compute trip schedules, process work orders, generate waybills, and crunch shipment data. Moreover, Wisconsin Central began upgrading the aging rail infrastructure—installing welded rails, replacing ties, applying gravel ballast—it had inherited from the Soo Line and created its own state-of-the-art rail vehicle maintenance and upgrade facility so it could turn cheaply purchased used freight cars and engines into modern equipment. By the end of 1988 Wisconsin Central had also secured more track rights for direct connections to Chicago's railroads, and its four main "gateways" enabled it to escape overdependence on any single connector railroad to keep its freight moving.

Expansion in Wisconsin and New Zealand: 1991–93

By the early 1990s Wisconsin Central had already caught the eye of the national business press and, more importantly, the accolades of its customers and industry trade magazines, who began citing it with quality awards. Wisconsin Central's ore shipping traffic began to rise substantially in 1990, and by 1994 it was shipping more than 32,000 carloads of ore a year. Its intermodal traffic also increased, from 28,300 units in 1991 to more than 42,000 units in 1994. As early as 1991 Wisconsin Central had met the ICC's technical definition for a Class 1 railroad (revenues exceeding $90 million for three straight years), but it successfully petitioned to retain its Class 2 status—thus evading the burdensome regulations that hampered the nation's largest railroads. In May 1991, Burkhardt decided to take Wisconsin Central public, raising $36.2 million in an initial public stock offering (IPO), which he used to pay down the high debt taken on at the Soo/Lake States acquisition in

1987 (by 1994 Wisconsin Central had lowered its debt-to-capital ratio to 35 percent).

Nevertheless, by 1991 Wisconsin Central, for all its success, was still not generating enough revenue to assure the regular upkeep of its infrastructure, and Burkhardt decided that revenue could only be had through expansion. In January 1992 he therefore created a new subsidiary, Fox Valley and Western Ltd., to acquire two smaller Wisconsin railroads: the century-old Green Bay & Western (GB&W) and the Fox River Valley (FRV), a spinoff of the Chicago & Northwestern (C&NW) that serviced the eastern central portion of Wisconsin. Burkhardt's former employer, CN&W, attacked the proposed purchase from the start, claiming it established "monopolistic" conditions—despite the fact that the trucking industry had long ago crushed any rail industry dreams of a transportation monopoly. The deal was finally closed for $61 million in September 1992, giving Wisconsin Central 479 miles of track, 53 locomotives, 1,275 freight cars, and 100 new customers in the Fox River Valley alone.

Burkhardt's expansion strategy continued. Shortly before beginning a new intermodal service with trucking giant J. B. Hunt in August 1992, Wisconsin Central signed a deal with C&NW that gave it the shortest direct line to the crucial Lake Superior shipping ports of Duluth, Minnesota, and Superior, Wisconsin—and thus access to the lucrative Canadian haulage business bound for Chicago. This new link to the Canadian market eventually evolved into a new intermodal agreement, in April 1996, between Wisconsin Central, CSX Intermodal, and Canadian National.

As Burkhardt was completing negotiations for the Green Bay & Western and the Fox River Valley acquisition, he was approached by New Zealand investment bankers who were helping their government privatize the island's only rail service, the state-run New Zealand Rail Ltd. Regional carriers like Wisconsin Central and RailTex were regarded as experts at running the new-style "entrepreneurial" American railroad, and Burkhardt's company in particular had earned a reputation as a "well-run, high-quality customer-service" railroad (as Burkhardt himself later recalled). Because New Zealand Rail's $400 million, 2,500-mile system was almost twice as large as Wisconsin Central's, Burkhardt knew he would need help in closing the $222 million acquisition. He therefore turned to Berkshire Partners, his partners in buying Wisconsin Central's lines from the Soo Line, and created a new subsidiary, Wisconsin Central International, to run the new unit. When the deal was closed in July 1993, Wisconsin Central had added 5,300 employees, 269 locomotives, and 6,000 freight cars. Burkhardt decided that three full-time executives in New Zealand would be sufficient to manage New Zealand Rail's (renamed Tranz Rail in 1995) transition to an American-style private carrier. Among their first acts was the downsizing of New Zealand Rail's bloated workforce. In June 1993, as Wisconsin Central was transforming itself into a player in the international transportation market, a Wisconsin Central locomotive was hauling the railroad's one millionth rail shipment.

Into Canada and Great Britain: 1994–95

In 1994 Wisconsin Central placed the largest single order—for over 1,000 hoppers, gondolas, and boxcars—for new cars in the history of modern regional railroads. It was also continuing its successful campaign to keep unions out of its workforce. In the fall, employees of the Fox River Valley failed to meet the 50 percent vote threshold needed to win union representation. Although Wisconsin Central declared the vote an endorsement of the railroad's profit sharing and 401(k) benefits packages, they were no doubt privately concerned that each successive union vote won greater worker support for the Brotherhood of Locomotive Engineers.

In January 1995, Wisconsin Central acquired Algoma Central Railway, a 321-mile regional Canadian line operating between Sault Ste. Marie and Hearst, Ontario. For a price of $24.4 million, the purchase added 23 locomotives and 866 freight cars to Wisconsin Central's stable, bolstering its access to the important Canadian freight market. The addition also gave Wisconsin Central its first fully unionized operation—a development that prefigured the decision by Wisconsin Central's engineers and conductors in July 1997 to accept representation by the railworkers' union.

In 1995, Wisconsin Central began adopting Tranz Rail's policy of using one-man crews, an innovation made possible by technology that enabled the caboose to be controlled remotely from the locomotive cabin. The Tranz Rail purchase was also bearing fruit of a different kind. The New Zealand firm that had helped Burkhardt buy New Zealand Rail Ltd. teamed with him and Berkshire Partners again in December 1995 to acquire ownership of Great Britain's Rail Express Systems Limited (RES), the letter-carrying rail service for the Royal Mail, a division of Britain's Post Office. A month later Burkhardt led another consortium of investors—North & South Railways Limited—to buy 90 percent of Britain's freight rail service from British Rail. The addition of these three companies—Loadhaul, Mainline, and Transrail—immediately added 7,000 workers, 910 locomotives, and 19,300 freight cars to Wisconsin Central's fleet. Rechristened the English Welsh & Scottish Railway Ltd. (EWSR), the new company was in desperate need of Burkhardt's entrepreneurial talents. Its locomotives leaked, its infrastructure cried out for modernization, and its workforce suffered from the same redundant crew bloat as the U.S. railroads Burkhardt sought to replace. Burkhardt immediately cut 1,800 jobs and twisted the arm of Railtrack, the British firm leasing it the rights to use the rails, convincing them to agree to a more reasonable flat rail-use fee in place of the exorbitant 50 percent-of-revenues Railtrack had initially levied. The remaining EWSR workforce was offered profit-sharing and incentive plans, and within months Burkhardt had reduced EWSR's shipping rates between 30 and 50 percent. The profit potential of Burkhardt's latest international foray looked better than ever. While 40 percent of U.S. freight was shipped by rail, British freight carriers moved only six percent, offering substantial room for growth.

At the end of 1995, Wisconsin Central could look back at annual growth of 22 percent or higher since 1993, a 69 percent increase in carloads, and annual operating revenues approaching $265 million.

Weyauwega and After: 1996–97

On March 4, 1996, a one-crew Wisconsin Central locomotive entering the center of Weyauwega, Wisconsin (midway between Appleton and Stevens Point, Wisconsin) derailed, sending 34 cars off the tracks, 14 of which were loaded with propane or liquefied petroleum. An explosive fire erupted, forcing 1,700 Weyauwega residents to flee (there were no fatalities), and continued to burn for two weeks. Wisconsin Central immediately offered to lodge the town in nearby hotels and motels at its own expense, paid for inspection teams to analyze the wreckage and certify the safety of all the homes and businesses in the area, underwrote all the repair costs, and donated $400,000 to the Red Cross and Salvation Army for their aid expenses. The $27 million accident was nevertheless a public relations disaster, and news cameras beamed images of the burning wreckage across the country. Worse, less than a month before the *Milwaukee Journal Sentinel* had run an article citing "safety concerns" over Wisconsin Central's rapid growth. As investigations into the incident continued an internal Wisconsin Central memo surfaced demonstrating that three months before the accident the company had warned its crews that "switching errors" were causing an inordinate number of derailings and sideswiped trains.

Public officials soon began questioning Wisconsin Central's decision to embrace the one-man crew work format, and newspapers ran articles complaining that Wisconsin Central was permitting insufficiently trained engineers to run its fleet. In February 1997 federal rail safety officials announced that Wisconsin Central would be the subject of a thorough safety inspection because its accident rate was two to three times above the industry norm. Wisconsin Central responded by agreeing to spend 30 percent more on improvements to its tracks (bad track as a result of improper employee maintenance training had been identified as the cause of the Weyauwega accident) and pointed to "dramatic" reductions in its accident rates during the first nine months of 1996.

However, Wisconsin Central's safety record came under renewed scrutiny in November 1997 when a derailing train plowed into a factory in Fond du Lac, causing the first fatality as a result of a Wisconsin Central derailment and the first such death in Wisconsin in 11 years. This time, Wisconsin Senator Russ Feingold and Governor Tommy Thompson publicly expressed concern over the railroad's efforts to bring its safety performance up to speed. The federal government's safety investigation into Wisconsin Central was given a one-year extension.

Safety Concerns and Tasmania: 1997–98

As Wisconsin Central's earnings suffered the multiple blows of these public relations setbacks and revenue downturns caused by weather and changing business conditions, Burkhardt led the company forward. By 1996 its stock had appreciated 800 percent since the company's IPO in 1991, and in ten years it had become the largest regional railroad in the United States, with a five-year average sales growth of 24 percent. In January 1997

Wisconsin Central added 216 miles of trackage through acquisitions of small lines in northeastern Wisconsin, the upper peninsula of Michigan, and Hayward and Wausau, Wisconsin. It also entered into a safety compliance agreement with the Federal Railroad Administration to create and evaluate new programs for improving railroad safety. As part of this effort increased capital costs were set aside for new cross ties, ballast, and welded rails.

With Wisconsin Central's newly unionized workforce now forcing the railroad to face some of the same labor costs as the Class 1 railroads, Burkhardt's international strategy grew in importance. In late 1997 Wisconsin Central thus acquired Railfreight Distribution Limited from the British government, giving it a share of the freight business traveling through the Channel Tunnel and potential access to the continental European market. It also created a new subsidiary, Australian Transport Network Limited, to acquire one-third of Tasrail, the commercial rail freight service on the Australian island of Tasmania. Although Wisconsin Central was a minority owner of all three of its overseas operations, it was the controlling party, and its international operations now surpassed its domestic operations in locomotives in service, route miles operated, employees, and revenues generated. By 1997–98 its traffic volume has risen 169 percent over the past seven years and its freight car fleet had tripled in size.

Principal Subsidiaries

Wisconsin Central Ltd.; WCL Railcars, Inc.; Sault Ste. Marie Bridge Company; Fox Valley & Western Ltd.; Wisconsin Central International, Inc.; WC Canada Holdings, Inc.; Algoma Central Railway Inc. (Canada); Wisconsin Central International, B.V. (Netherlands).

Further Reading

Burke, Jack, "Wisconsin Central's Intermodal Overcoming Obstacles," *Traffic World,* April 28, 1997.

Carey, Susan, "Wisconsin Central Becomes Little Railroad That Could," *Wall Street Journal,* April 8, 1996, p. B4.

Dobnick, Otto P., and Steve Glischinski, *Wisconsin Central: Railroad Success Story,* Waukesha, Wis.: Kalmbach Books, 1997.

"Long Haul," *Investor's Business Daily,* March 27, 1997.

Martin, Chuck. "Wisconsin Central Railroad Picks Up Steam and Profits," *Milwaukee Journal,* May 3, 1992, p. 1D.

"The New America: Rolling On," *Investor's Business Daily,* January 19, 1996.

Sansoni, Silvia, "They're Really Working on This Railroad," *Forbes,* November 3, 1997, pp. 160–61.

"Wisconsin Central Anniversary Issue," *Soo* (magazine of the Soo Line Historical and Technical Society), Fall 1997.

"Wisconsin Central History: Introduction," The Unofficial Wisconsin Central Homepage, http://pages.prodigy.com/Wisconsin Central/about.html.

"Wisconsin Central Makes the Most of a Bad Situation," *Trains Magazine,* June 1, 1996.

"Wisconsin Central Reports Record Financial Results," press release, Rosemont, Ill.: Wisconsin Central Transportation Corporation, January 28, 1998.

Young, David, "Tracks Stretch Around the World," *Chicago Tribune,* October 11, 1997, (business), pp. 1–2.

—Paul S. Bodine

Wizards of the Coast Inc.

1801 Lind Avenue SW
Renton, Washington 98055
U.S.A.
(425) 226-6500
Fax: (425) 271 5215
Web sites: http://www.wizards.com
http://www.tsr.com

Private Company
Incorporated: 1990
Employees: 500
Sales: $150 million (1997 est.)
SICs: 3944 Games, Toys, & Children's Vehicles

Wizards of the Coast Inc. is an international leader in the adventure game industry and is perhaps best known as the publisher of the world's best-selling trading card game, *Magic: The Gathering*.

Wizards of the What?: Starting, 1991

Wizards of the Coast was founded in 1990 by Peter Adkison, a systems analyst at Boeing. With a dream of establishing a career in the adventure gaming business, Adkison and six other young visionaries began creating and developing role-playing games in their spare time.

Adkison asked game aficionado Richard Garfield—who, with a B.S. in Computer Mathematics and a Ph.D. in Combinational Mathematics, was teaching at Whitman College in Walla Walla, Washington, at the time—to design a card game that was fun, portable, and could be played in under an hour. Garfield, who had been designing his own games since age 15, and George Skaff Elias, another graduate student in mathematics, went away and worked on it.

Gathering the Magic, 1993

Two years later, in August 1993, WotC (rhymes with Yahtzee), with a staff of eight, operating out of the basement of Adkison's home, released that trading card game created by Garfield and Skaff, called *Magic: The Gathering*.

The game, set in the imaginary realm of Dominia, featured wizards challenging one another for control of the land. Players used cards representing fantastic creatures and spells to reduce their opponents' score from 20 to 0 and win the game.

Magic: The Gathering—both a game *and* a collectible item—was the first product of its kind to be released and it surprised the gaming industry, becoming one of the most popular games in history, outselling *Monopoly* and *Trivial Pursuit*, and spawning an entire new sub-industry within the gaming industry, based on trading cards. Each deck of 40 or so cards is different from every other deck, giving players/collectors no lack of items to buy. The Black Lotus card, which is extremely rare, has sold for over $1,000 in a flourishing ''black market'' for cards. Over 10 million cards were sold in six weeks in more than 10,000 book, music, and comic book stores, including Barnes & Noble, Tower Records, Babbages/Software Etc., and Borders Books. More than five million players throughout the world would go on to play it, and it would be published in nine languages and in over 65 countries. A bimonthly magazine called the *Duelist*, which offers rules, strategy tips, and tournament news, was also created.

Due to the success of *Magic*, Garfield, whose influences included Lewis Carroll and J. R. R. Tolkien, was able to quit teaching and pursue his true passion of game design, coming on board with WotC full-time in June 1994. Several months later, in October, WotC released Garfield's *RoboRally*, the company's first major board game, designed by Garfield while he was still a graduate student at the University of Pennsylvania. In the fast-paced, futuristic game, players attempt to be the first to maneuver their robots across a wild and treacherous factory floor.

The company's skyrocket to the top allowed it that year to relocate to an office in Renton, Washington, and open international offices in Milan, Paris, and Antwerp. Trading card collecting in general surged in popularity from 1992 to 1995, losing a bit of momentum in the wake of 1994's Major League Baseball strike.

In 1995, Garfield created a card game called *The Great Dalmuti*, which was WotC's first game to be distributed through retail channels. The game is based on a medieval theme, and players are either kings, peons, or merchants.

That year the company also purchased Ohio-based Andon Unlimited, a company which ran trade shows. But, suffering from growing pains, WotC eliminated its *Everway*, *Ars Magica*, and *Slay Industries* games.

In 1996, telecommunications giant MCI entered into a partnership with WotC, with an estimated $750,000 three-year sponsorship of the latter's *Magic: The Gathering* U.S. Tournament, and releasing prepaid phone cards featuring *Magic* artwork—a perfect premium for a collectible-friendly market and a hotline number for fans wanting up-to-the-minute tournament information, including tour dates, individual player rankings, and game strategy.

In November of that year, WotC released a *BattleTech* trading card game, based on FASA Corporation's popular board game of the same name. The WotC strategic card game transports players into the 31st century, where they assume the role of commanders and control armies of 30-foot-tall walking tanks known as "BattleMechs." The game would go on to become the second best-selling trading card game in the United States, behind *Magic: The Gathering*.

David Buys Goliath: Wizards of the Coast Buys Struggling TSR, 1997

By February 1997, in order to not dilute *Magic*'s pure gamer image, WotC had only teamed with eight licensees, including software developers Acclaim Entertainment Inc. and Microprose Inc. (who released two CD-ROMs: *Magic: The Gathering*, a PC version of the game, and *Magic: The Gathering Desktop Themes*, images from the game), book publishers Workman and Carlton Books Limited, and apparel manufacturer Nice Man, to generate approximately $1 million in licensed *Magic* business. The company had also already received movie and television offers, but was holding off for the time being. Acclaim's comics division began publishing a *Magic* comic book series and publisher HarperCollins released 12 paperback science fiction and fantasy novels based on the game under the HarperPrism imprint, featuring such authors as William R. Forstchen.

In April, in a move that stunned the gaming world, WotC, still considered an upstart by many analysts despite the staggering success of its *Magic: The Gathering* card game, announced its intent to acquire struggling veteran gaming company TSR Inc. for an undisclosed amount.

TSR, founded in 1973, in its 25 years in business, had created hundreds of games, including children's board games, adult strategy games, dice games, card games, war games, and, of course, numerous role-playing games, translated into more than a dozen languages and sold in over 50 countries.

TSR was best known for its publication of former insurance underwriter E. Gary Gygax's highly successful fantasy/adventure role-playing games *Dungeons & Dragons* (debuting in 1974), followed by *Advanced Dungeons & Dragons*, which went on to be played by millions of gamers throughout the world, singlehandedly creating the billion-dollar role-playing game industry. The *D&D* concept went on to expand into supporting settings such as *Greyhawk Adventures*, the *Forgotten Realms* classic sword-and-sorcery campaign set in a medieval world, the *Planescape* campaign in alternate realities and different planes of existence, and the *Ravenloft* classic gothic horror campaign in the haunted lands of the vampire Strahd and the archlich Azalin.

A second gaming system, called *Saga*, concentrates more on roles than rules, in an easy-to-use role-playing system that revolves around drama and storytelling, featuring the wildly successful *DragonLance* saga, set on the world of Krynn and brought to life in novels by authors Margaret Weis and Tracy Hickman, and the *Marvel Super Heroes Adventure Game*, which lets players role-play in one of the most popular universes in the world, featuring Spider-Man, The X-Men, The Avengers, and The Fantastic Four.

TSR also ranked as one of the world's top fantasy and science fiction book publishers. Since first publishing in the early 1980s, the company had sold millions of copies of its novels, most derived from its gaming series, some of which would reach *New York Times* best-selling status, and featuring authors such as Simon Hawke, Rose Estes, Christie Golden, James Lowder, and Gygax himself, as well as launching the careers of R. A. Salvatore, Troy Denning, and Douglas Niles, among others.

In addition to book publishing, TSR also published two successful gaming periodicals, *Dragon Magazine* and *Dungeon Adventures Magazine*, both of which focused on the role-playing game industry, specifically TSR's games. TSR also licensed its properties to other media, including television (Total Entertainment Network) and electronic games (Interplay Inc. and Sierra On-Line). Former TSR president Lorraine Williams assumed majority control of the firm from Gygax in the mid-1980s after a hotly contested stock sale to Williams by two other shareholders.

Speculation ran rampant as to what would happen to the gaming giant under its new ownership by WotC. TSR headquarters and most of the staff (including *Amazing Stories* editor Kim Mohan, but notably excluding TSR book editor Brian Thomsen) were moved from their longtime home of Lake Geneva, Wisconsin, to WotC's facility in Washington state. WotC announced its intention to continue running the world's largest gaming convention, with attendance at over 25,000 annually, GenCon in Lake Geneva.

One of the major issues to be resolved in the purchase was the payment of royalties owed to a number of TSR authors. TSR was publishing nearly 60 books per year at the time of its purchase, all of which were distributed by Random House Inc. The Science Fiction and Fantasy Writers of America Inc. (SFWA) led a vocal group of writers into negotiations, which finally resulted in WotC agreeing to cover TSR's debts.

Not content with just one acquisition, WotC also purchased Five Rings Publishing Group Inc. in 1997, best known for its *Legends of the Five Rings* trading card game, the *Star Trek: The Next Generation* collectible dice game, and the *Dune: Eye of the Storm* trading card game.

WotC also released two new games designed by WotC wizard Richard Garfield. *Corporate Shuffle*, a card game based on the United Features Syndicate *Dilbert* comic strip by Scott Adams, was released in May 1997. The game, featuring full-color cartoons of Dilbert, his ignorant superiors, his clueless coworkers (including the delightful Ratbert and evil Human Resources Director Catbert), and his cynical dog, Dogbert, appealed to gamers of all ages, satirizing the chaos and quirks of 1990s corporate life as players compete in a mad dash to climb the corporate ladder and assume the title of ''Big Boss,'' with all its perks.

By then the fervor for *Magic* cards had sparked criminal acts, with dealers reporting theft of the cards from their stores. A *BRANDWEEK* article entitled ''The Gathering Storm'' highlighted a report that ''four street toughs mugged a trio of gamers at knifepoint for their collection of *Magic* cards valued at nearly $2,400.'' Other stories surfaced about riots in Japan, precipitated by dwindling supply. WotC insisted such stories were exaggerated, but the company took tighter rein of its image in June 1997, launching its first national ad campaign via Moffatt Rosenthal, San Francisco.

Hoping to extend the popularity of its highly successful *Magic: The Gathering* game beyond a young, male demographic, WotC released an introductory version of the game called *Portal*, which introduced new players to the same sophisticated game mechanics, portability, and professional artwork that made *Magic: The Gathering* an international success. The national cable-television ad campaign, which accounted for 62 percent of WotC's entire advertising budget was supplemented by ads appearing in *Rolling Stone*, *Spin*, and *Swing*, among others, and demos appearing at state fairs, the H.O.R.D.E. music tour, in-line skating and mountain biking events, military bases, and Miller Lite's Dog Days of Summer Concert Series featuring acts like Patty Loveless and Ted Nugent. *Portal Second Age* would quickly follow, as well as the advanced-level *Fifth Edition* game of *Magic*, and expert-level products like the *Tempest* and *Stronghold* expansion decks.

Also in 1997, WotC opened The Wizards of the Coast Game Center in Seattle, the first gaming environment and entertainment center for adventure gaming enthusiasts in the world. The facility featured more than 250 games, including the *BattleTech* virtual reality center, with a dozen interactive simulator pods; 3,800 square feet of state-of-the-art video game and pinball machines; 1,800 square feet of retail store; a selection of computer network games; a 5,000-square-foot tournament center for organized game playing; and multiple players' lounges. The center became a testing site for other top gaming manufacturers such as Atari and Williams/Bally, and also the headquarters for the official *Magic: The Gathering* World Tournament,

featuring more than $1 million in prize money. WotC also received a patent on The Trading Card Game Method of Play by the U.S. Patent Office.

WotC started 1998 with a bang, releasing four games (*Twitch*, *Pivot*, *AlphaBlitz*, and *Go Wild!*) in February. The *Twitch* card game is all about quick reflexes, speed, and accuracy. Three-to-six players quickly flip colored cards into a bowl. If players are slow or make mistakes, others may challenge and penalize them. Like *Go Fish* or *Uno*, the first one to run out of cards wins.

In the *Pivot* card game, a dynamic game of ups and downs, two to eight players must turn on a dime. Rules change, directions switch, and play shifts, adding to the excitement of the game. Again, the first player to run out of cards wins.

The *AlphaBlitz* game introduced an innovative approach to word games. Created by one of the world's leading word-puzzle designers, the card game pits two to six players against each other in a race to unscramble words and stump their opponents. *AlphaBlitz* can be played either for speed or strategy, making it two word-making games in one product.

In the *Go Wild!* game of wild cards, two to six players play sets of matching colored cards to win tricks and points. The first player to win the first of three tricks becomes ''The Wild One''—the only player who can use wild cards—until another player seizes the title. The balance of power shifts quickly in the strategic card game, making it uncertain who will score 20 points first and win.

Several months later, in April, WotC teamed with WildStorm Productions to release *C-23*. The science fiction trading card game, part of WotC's new ARC System of games (which eventually would feature games based on *Xena: Warrior Princess* and *Hercules: The Legendary Journeys*), featured story and art by famed comic artist Jim Lee (best known as co-creator of Image Comics and WildStorm Productions) and writer Brandon Choi (the team responsible for creating such major comic properties as *Gen13* and *WildC.A.T.S.: Covert Action Teams*), blending the fundamentals of a traditional trading card game with comic-style art.

The post-apocalyptic Earth setting featured cybernetically enhanced humans and genetically altered humans battling for control of the planet's surface. Players compete by using resource, character, action, and combat cards to discard cards from their opponents' decks. The first player to empty his or her opponent's deck of cards wins. The release was accompanied by a *C-23* comic book series, the first issue of which was written by Jeff Mariotte (also writer for *Desperadoes*, *Hazard*, and *DefCon 4*, among others), and featured painted covers by Travis Charest, and was drawn by Alexander Lozano.

In May, WotC announced an agreement with Viacom Consumer Products, the licensing division of Paramount Pictures, for the premiere issue of the relaunch of *Amazing Stories*, the world's oldest science fiction magazine (founded in 1926 by Hugo Gernsback, the father of modern science fiction), to feature cover art and original short stories from the legendary *Star Trek: The Next Generation* television show.

Also in 1998, TSR released *Alternity*, a science fiction role-playing game which furnishes rules for all science fiction, from contemporary Earth settings to far-future space epics. *The Star*Drive Campaign* features a universe of star-spanning adventures set in the distant future in The Verge, a region of space on the frontier of human exploration. So the upstarts on the West Coast continued into the end of the 20th century with nothing but growth in sight.

Principal Subsidiaries

Five Rings Publishing Group Inc.; TSR Inc.

Further Reading

Adler, Jerry, ''Magic's Kingdom,'' *Newsweek*, May 26, 1997, p. 68.

Angel, Karen, ''Harper Titles with a Magic Touch,'' *Publishers Weekly*, February 3, 1997, p. 31.

Baker, M. Sharon, ''Wizards' Magic Is Powerful, But Other Games Falter,'' *Puget Sound Business Journal*, December 15, 1995, p. 3.

——, ''Wizards of the Coast Seeks to Extend Magic's Powerful Spell,'' *Puget Sound Business Journal*, January 27, 1995, p. 1.

Benezra, Karen, ''Richard Garfield; George Skaff Elias,'' *BRANDWEEK*, November 13, 1995, p. 46.

——, ''Wizards Conjure $4-5M Gameplan,'' *BRANDWEEK*, June 23, 1997.

Engle, Tim, ''Try to Understand . . . the Magic Man,'' *Starmagazine*, March 15, 1998.

Miller, Brian, ''Playing the Corporate Game,'' *South County Journal*, February 14, 1997, p. B1.

Milliot, Jim, ''Wizards, New TSR Owner, Will Make Good on Debts,'' *Publishers Weekly*, June 23, 1997, p. 20.

——, ''Wizards to Discuss TSR Issues After Merger,'' *Publishers Weekly*, April 21, 1997, p. 16.

Romell, Rick, ''Lake Geneva, Wis.-Based TSR Inc. to Be Bought By West Coast Rival,'' *Knight-Ridder/Tribune Business News*, April 11, 1997, p. 411B1254.

Rose, Cynthia, ''It's Magic,'' *Seattle Times*, August 14, 1997, p. E1.

''Total Fusion,'' *Comics Buyers Guide*, April 3, 1998, p. 30.

''TSR to Be Sold,'' *Publishers Weekly*, April 14, 1997, p. 12.

Warner, Bernhard, ''The 'Gathering' Storm,'' *BRANDWEEK*, February 17, 1997, p. 20.

''Wizards of the Coast Conjures Up a Higher Profile,'' *BRANDWEEK*, April 13, 1998, p. S12.

—Daryl F. Mallett

THE ZIEGLER COMPANIES, INC.

The Ziegler Companies, Inc.

215 North Main Street
West Bend, Wisconsin 53095-3348
U.S.A.
(414) 334-5521
Fax: (414) 334-3433
Web site: http://www.ziegler.com

Public Company
Incorporated: 1920 as B.C. Ziegler and Co.
Employees: 634
Total Assets: $167.47 million (1997)
Stock Exchanges: American
Ticker Symbol: ZCO
SICs: 6153 Short-Term Business Credit Institutions
(Except Agriculture); 6211 Security Brokers &
Dealers

The Ziegler Companies, Inc. provides a complete range of investment services and is widely regarded as the largest institutional bond underwriter in the United States, not to mention the largest investment banking firm for healthcare finance outside Wall Street.

In 1902, West Bend, Wisconsin, was a small bustling mill town famous for the hotels it had built to put up travelers making the two-day trip between Milwaukee and Fond du Lac. The son of a hotelier and county treasurer, 18-year-old Ben Ziegler had been selling fire insurance policies to area farmers and merchants to supplement his income as an assistant for the county's treasurer and register of deeds. In 1902 an insurance agency owned by a friend of Ziegler's father ran into financial trouble; as the agency's co-signer, Ziegler's father assumed its debt and the responsibility for finding a new agent for the business. Despite Ben's young age, Ziegler's father made Ben that new agent, and the young entrepreneur promptly began selling insurance policies to area businesses out of a room in his father's hotel. By 1905 Ben had saved up $6,500, which he used to pay off his father's farm and saloon, and a home for him two

years later. By 1906 Ziegler and his former employer in the insurance business, Henry Opgenorth, formed a new agency, Opgenorth and Ziegler, which fell apart only 18 months later after disagreements over the business. Opgenorth and Ziegler split the territories and went their separate ways.

''The Real Beginning'': 1906–29

Still only 22, Ziegler had built a reputation as an enterprising, sharp-witted businessman, and in 1906 he was elected a director of the West Bend Mutual Fire Insurance Co. To drum up business, he began bicycling to the nearby Wisconsin communities of Grafton, Two Rivers, Manitowoc, and Sheboygan to sell fire insurance and farm mortgages to anyone who wanted them. In 1902 representatives of a land company convinced Ziegler to recruit West Bend home seekers to buy property in South Dakota. When Ziegler himself visited the South Dakota lands, however, he learned that the sellers were peddling $300 dollar properties for a grossly inflated $1,600. Burned by the boondoggle, Ziegler vowed that any loan he made in the future would have to be secured by an owner who was ''known to be responsible'' in the West Bend area. Rather than offer the six or seven percent return investors were promised in South Dakota, Ziegler's four to 4.5 percent return was smaller but far more secure. His reputation for conservatism was established.

As the radius of his insurance territory grew in the early 1900s Ziegler traded in his bicycle for a horse and buggy so he could still make it back to West Bend every night to help his mother at the family's boarding house. By 1907, Ziegler's insurance business had grown to encompass virtually all of southeastern Wisconsin and its three largest cities, Milwaukee, Racine, and Kenosha. In the years that followed Ziegler's business steadily expanded northward and westward. The so-called Roosevelt Panic of 1907 ironically turned out to be one of the biggest blessings of Ziegler's young career. The bank panic had caused depositors around the country to pull their savings from their neighborhood banks, and Ziegler was no exception. When the crisis passed and depositors began returning their savings to the nation's bank vaults, however, Ziegler decided to keep his, using the money instead to make loans to local businesspeople. ''The net result,'' Ziegler later recalled, ''was that I

Company Perspectives:

We believe in the American free enterprise system. We shall consistently treat our clients, employees, shareholders and community with honesty, dignity, fairness and respect. We will conduct our business with the highest ethical standards.

---

did more business in 60 days than I had done in the four years previous. This was the real beginning of the investment business for B.C. Ziegler and Co.''

Ziegler also capitalized on his readiness to service his territory personally to learn more about the insurance needs of his far-flung customers. He soon counted among his customers such typical of the time Wisconsin businesses as elevator makers, gas engine plants, saloons, breweries, and malt houses. In 1911, two West Bend businessmen approached Ziegler for his advice on potentially profitable new businesses for the West Bend area. Having recently visited an aluminum manufacturing plant in Two Rivers, Ziegler recommended they start an aluminum plant, and in September 1911 Ziegler and his new associates formed the West Bend Aluminum Company, which was soon making pie plates, pudding pans, and dish pans. The company, with Ziegler at the helm, became the largest manufacturer of aluminum cooking utensils in the United States by the 1920s. Ziegler also helped establish the first national bank of West Bend and by 1917 had become its president as well.

But Ziegler's core business remained insurance and loans. By 1913 B.C. Ziegler and Co. was one of the largest insurance agencies and farm mortgage companies in eastern Wisconsin. The business that would eventually become Ziegler and Co.'s stock in trade—institutional lending—began modestly in 1913 when the pastor of West Bend's Church of the Holy Angels asked Ziegler's father if his son would loan him the money to build a new church. Ziegler deemed the risk a reasonable one, and the pastor walked away with a $30,000 bond issue. Next, the pastor of Sacred Heart Church of Racine requested and received a $13,000 loan from Ziegler as well. Within a few years Ziegler was also doing business with the so-called ''building pastors'' of Milwaukee, and in 1922 Ziegler made his first major bond issue with a $100,000 offering for St. Sebastian's church. In 1928 Ziegler arranged its first institutional loan outside Wisconsin, extending a $485,000, five percent bond to the Missionary Sisters, Servants of the Holy Ghost, of Techny, Illinois, so they could erect a hospital in Waukegan. Without planning on it, Ziegler had initiated the business that would soon make his company the largest church bond issuer in the country's history.

While attending the Republican Party's national convention in Chicago in 1916 Ziegler ran into Delbert J. Kenny, the assistant principal back at West Bend High School. Ziegler and Kenny struck up a conversation and, impressed by Kenny's personality, Ziegler offered him a place with his firm on the spot. Kenny would eventually rise to become Ziegler and Co.'s third president. When the United States entered World War I in 1917 most of Ziegler's male employees left to join the fight in

Europe. Business stagnated, but when Ziegler's men demobilized in 1919 Ziegler's firm began a renewed period of growth. In 1920 Ziegler incorporated B.C. Ziegler and Co. and by the early 1920s the firm had become one of the state's leading farm financing companies, prudently extending loans only to the most stable dairy farmers of southern Wisconsin. As the U.S. economy boomed in the 1920s Ziegler expanded his company's bond business by charging a fair rate of interest on bonds, never offering ''speculative'' securities, paying investors their interest and principal on time, and willingly lending moneys to home and farm owners who could establish their ''good reputations and good security.'' By the late 1920s Ziegler's customers numbered more than 5,000, and Ziegler was one of the 10 or 12 largest insurance agencies in Wisconsin, issuing primarily fire and tornado (though not life) insurance policies through the Mutual and Old Line insurance companies.

Growth Through Church Bonds: 1929–59

If Ziegler sought a new opportunity to demonstrate his business acumen, the great crash of 1929 gave it to him. While traveling in Kansas in early 1929, Ziegler saw firsthand the financial problems facing Kansas farmers. Figuring that if the country's farmers were facing difficulties, the national economy as a whole might not be as healthy as Wall Street wanted to believe, Ziegler concluded, he later recalled, ''that business had just about reached its high point, and that we might be looking forward to a recession.'' He therefore sold all his stock and instructed his partner at West Bend Aluminum to commit to no new production and to cancel as many of his current commitments as he could. Moreover, he told his vice-president at Ziegler and Co. to pay off the company's $300,000 in debt within 60 days. By October 1929, when ''the stock crash came,'' Ziegler recalled, ''we had practically no commitments, no debts, and a nice cash position.''

Ziegler also proved clairvoyant about the severity of the Depression. While attending a Rotary convention in Vienna, Austria, in mid-1931, Ziegler was struck by Europe's desperate economic conditions and on his return readied his company for the worst. By October 1931, when the post-crash downturn bottomed out into full-fledged depression Ziegler had liquidated $2.5 million in debts, and could confront the worst economic period in U.S. history with a war chest of cash. As the Depression staggered on, Ziegler managed to *increase* the size of its workforce, prevent its investors from losing money on their institutional bonds, and boast the best ratio of losses on farm loans of any lender in Wisconsin. In the last quarter of 1931, in fact, Ziegler issued more institutional bonds than in all of 1930. Ziegler's willingness to lend money to finance-strapped churches turned into a shrewdly conservative investment in the speculation-shy climate of the 1930s, for as one of Ziegler's lieutenants later recalled, ''people were afraid of everything—except church bonds.''

In 1936 Ziegler made the largest institutional bond issue in its history, a $3.1 million issue to St. Mary's College and Academy and Marygrove College, both of Michigan. In the same decade, Ziegler established a subsidiary, Home Builder's Inc., to build about three to six homes a year in the West Bend area, and began acquiring farms that had gone bankrupt as the economy spoiled. Ziegler's Real Estate Department then began to sell the properties, adding another income stream to Ziegler's machine. Ziegler also established The Security Company, which in the 1940s and 1950s bought up land in the West Bend area and subdivided it into housing properties. In 1942, Ziegler's West Bend Aluminum Company was awarded Navy "E" for excellence awards for its munitions manufacturing achievements, and in 1944, with the war's end in sight, Ziegler and Co. made its first institutional underwriting on the West Coast—a $900,000 loan for the Lutheran Hospital Society of Southern California. By the time of founder Ben Ziegler's untimely death at age 62 in May 1946, his company's thriving institutional bond business was expanding nationwide through ongoing college and church loans (its two biggest categories) to communities in the Midwest and South. (Ziegler's partner, Delbert Kenny, who had assumed the firm's reins in 1942, continued on as president until 1965.)

As millions of U.S. servicemen began streaming home in 1945 and 1946, Ziegler and Co. had used its property purchases to create new parcels of home-sized lots ready for sale to them. In the postwar years, Ziegler's' foray into the housing industry continued when the company became a distributor and builder for National Homes, a maker of $10,000-plus prefab homes for the booming residential housing market. With its bond and mortgage business expanding, Ziegler and Co. was forced to update its correspondence-based marketing network, and in 1949 opened its first sales office in Milwaukee, which was followed by offices in Fort Atkinson, Appleton, and Minneapolis by 1952. By the early 1960s, Ziegler's sales office network had grown to 12, extending from Toledo, Ohio, and St. Louis to as far west as San Francisco.

From Church to Hospital Bonds: 1961–77

Ziegler sold more church bonds between 1945 and 1965 than at any previous period in its history—most for the construction and modernization of church-owned schools and retirement homes. The early 1960s were a particularly active period for Ziegler's church bonds, and the period was quickly dubbed "the diocese financing." The diocese of Buffalo, New York, raised $16 million through Ziegler in 1960, for example, and between 1962 and 1964 the Archbishop of Boston raised $35 million with Ziegler bonds. In 1964, Ziegler was a pioneer of a new type of institutional financing instrument known as the collateral trust bond. Through its new subsidiary, First Church Financing Corporation of America (FCFCA), Ziegler acquired loans made to churches and other institutions that, because they were too small to justify issuing as individual bonds, were merged and marketed as collateral trust bonds. Between 1964 and 1967 alone, FCFCA issued and marketed $23.8 million of these bonds. Following founder Ben Ziegler's penchant for diversification, in the early 1960s Ziegler and Co. became the underwriter for the first institutional bond offering insured by the Federal Housing Authority, for a retirement home in Seattle.

By the time the son of Ben Ziegler's longtime partner Delbert Kenny assumed Ziegler's presidency in 1965, the construction boom in church and church-related educational facilities had topped out. Thomas Kenny thus began to focus the firm's energies on the still-growing niche of bond underwritings for the construction, enlargement, and modernization of hospitals. Despite the sophistication of the instruments Ziegler's sales force was selling, their methods were straightforward enough. A salesman would be assigned to a new hospital and set up camp in a hospital office for a few days, counting on the kind of local interest a large newly expanded facility attracts to bring customers to his door. As a Ziegler sales manager would later tell *Bond Buyer* magazine: "At that time [i.e., when a hospital has been enlarged or modernized] everybody had such a great feeling about their local hospital that we would get tons of people coming in. They wanted to buy it; they wanted to support it."

One instrument Ziegler used to finance its new hospital bond business was the short-term (three- to nine-month) construction note, which was sold to corporations across the country to fund the period early in a hospital's construction or modernization program before a bond sale or other form of "permanent" financing secured the project's capitalization. Stemming from this innovation, in 1969 Ziegler and Co. formed the Ziegler Financing Corporation (ZFC) as an operating company to provide similar short-term construction loans for commercial and industrial projects. In the years that followed, ZFC would underwrite short-term notes for the construction of nursing homes, condominiums, industrial buildings, retirement homes, mobile home parks, hotels, and housing projects authorized by the federal government's Housing and Urban Development (HUD) agency.

In 1971 another child of Ziegler's hospital underwriting business emerged, when the Ziegler Leasing Corporation (ZLC) was formed to design customized leases for hospitals seeking to lease medical equipment such as X-ray machines, intensive care equipment, nuclear medicine devices, and other hospital technologies. This in turn led in 1972 to a new department within ZLC created specifically to handle leases for commercial and industrial equipment. With its stable of operating companies proliferating, Ziegler decided to create a new holding company structure to give its individual units free rein. The Ziegler Company, Inc. was thus formed in December 1971 and its stock issued to the over-the-counter market.

In June 1972 President Thomas J. Kenny, his wife, and four of his children were killed when their jetliner crashed in South Vietnam on a flight from Thailand to Hong Kong. The tragedy (which was apparently accidental and unconnected to the fighting on the ground) shocked the close-knit West Bend business community. Longtime Ziegler veteran Ken Marsden assumed the firm's presidency, and a year later founder Ben Ziegler's two sons, Bernard and R.D.—who had not planned to join their father's business—were named chairman of the board and president/CEO, respectively. Ziegler and Co.'s business was meanwhile showing no interruption. New branch sales offices had been opened in Kenosha and La Crosse, Wisconsin, and Springfield, Illinois, in 1967; Sheboygan, Wisconsin, in 1969; Green Bay, Wisconsin, and East Lansing, Michigan, in 1970; and Orlando, Florida, in 1971.

The firm also continued its historical penchant for scouting out new business opportunities by becoming the sole distributor of a mutual fund based in Milwaukee in 1967 and then three years later unveiling its own family of mutual funds. Taxable hospital bonds remained Ziegler's largest investment product in the late 1970s, but it also expanded into more conservative investment instruments during the period. In 1973, for example, it acquired a Chicago firm that specialized in originating and underwriting municipal and nonprofit revenue tax-exempt bonds. The addition, renamed Ziegler Securities in 1976, expanded still further Ziegler's portfolio in the management of tax exempt financing in the healthcare industry. In 1974, Ziegler had also introduced its American Tax-Exempt Bond Trust and in the late 1970s unveiled the American Income Trust, a portfolio of corporate bonds designed to throw off high income while preserving the investor's principal.

Steady Growth: 1978–93

By the late 1970s, Ziegler remained the largest institutional bond underwriter in the United States (some 2,600 bond issues valued at almost $4 billion by 1977) and had solidified its claim to truly national status by opening branch sales offices in Denver and Portland in 1975 and Indianapolis and Grand Rapids in 1976. It had sold more hospital bonds than any other firm in U.S. history, and 625 of the nation's 3,364 private-sector, not-for-profit general hospitals had used Ziegler as the underwriter of their bond issues by 1977. Ziegler continued to underwrite major bond issues for prominent U.S. institutions and corporations in the 1980s, including a $12 million mortgage bond issue for Associated Doctors Hospital and a $20 million notes issue for American Family Financial Services, both in 1980, and in 1982 a $10 million underwriting of senior notes for Northwestern Mutual Insurance. In the early 1980s, Ziegler Securities became a separately named division of the B.C. Ziegler and Company, and in 1984 the firm launched a ''fully hedged'' tax exempt bond fund to broaden its offerings of high-yield but capital-preserving investment vehicles. Similarly, in 1987 Ziegler and Co. teamed up with Wisconsin banking giant M & I bank to serve as ''co-advisers'' of a new mutual fund. In April 1986, a third generation of Zieglers assumed command of the firm when Peter D. Ziegler (a first cousin of founder Ben Ziegler's grandson) was elected president of the holding company and all its subsidiaries, and in December 1989 Ben Ziegler's son R. D. finally stepped down as CEO after 16 years at the helm. Within a month Peter Ziegler was the new CEO.

In 1990 Ziegler's collateral trust bond subsidiary was newly incorporated as First Church Financing Corporation (FCFC) to issue, like its predecessor, mortgage-backed bonds collateralized by pools of notes secured by the first mortgages on church buildings and properties. That same year, Ziegler Securities marketed 47 healthcare financings—the most of any firm in the nation. In 1991, Ziegler's annual revenues, which had seesawed back and forth between $34 and $40 million a year since 1986 finally reached the $40 million plateau for good and by 1993 were breaking the $50 million mark. In 1991 Ziegler began listing its stock on the American Stock Exchange and established two new subsidiaries: Ziegler Asset Management, Inc. (ZAM) and Ziegler Collateralized Securities, Inc. (ZCS). ZAM provided money management services (such as pension planning) in stocks and bonds to individual customers, institutions, and the parent firm's Principal Preservation Portfolio family of mutual funds. By late 1997 ZAM was managing some $1 billion in assets. ZCS was formed to issue bonds that were collateralized by pools or leases and other types of debt instruments packaged and sold to it by Ziegler Leasing Corporation, the firm's equipment leasing business.

By 1993, two new subsidiaries had also joined the Ziegler stable. Ziegler Thrift Trading (ZTT) was created to offer discount brokerage services to the booming stock, bond, mutual fund, and options market without the advice and research services that characterize full service brokerage houses. Waste Research and Reclamation (WRR) reflected Ziegler's willingness—first reflected in Ben Ziegler's participation in the creation of West Bend Aluminum in 1911—to diversify into nontraditional areas of business. WRR (founded in 1970) operated hazardous waste treatment and waste solvent recycling facilities for industrial chemicals and solvents in Eau Claire, Wisconsin, and by 1995 was generating revenues of $3.8 million—or almost nine percent of Ziegler's total 1995 revenues. Two of Ziegler's diversifying ventures were short-lived. Beginning in 1994, Ziegler held a one-third interest in Heartland Capital Company, a loan originator for the construction of affordable housing projects, and the same year it began purchasing automobile installment loans to be held until they could be pooled together and sold as securities. By 1997, however, Heartland had gone under and Ziegler had uncovered unpromising information about the quality of the auto loans it had purchased and began retreating from that line of business.

''Senior Living Debt'' and Stocks: 1994–98

In 1993 Ziegler underwrote the largest church bond issue of its history, a $14 million issue for the Germantown Baptist Church of Memphis, Tennessee. By then the firm was also widely regarded as the largest investment banking firm for healthcare finance outside Wall Street. Just as Ziegler had seen the writing on the wall in the 1960s and switched its emphasis from church to hospital bonds, so too in the consolidating and chaotic healthcare climate of the early 1990s it looked for new, still-growing bond markets. ''Senior-living debt'' was the answer. As the population aged, the demand for retirement facilities snowballed and Ziegler and its Senior Living Finance Group rushed in. As John Wagner, Ziegler's retail sales manager, told *Bond Buyer* in 1996, ''maybe 10 years ago, we did very few issues in senior-care living, and the majority of our underwritings were in health care and hospitals. We've totally flip-flopped that now.... How many hospitals in your area do you see expanding anymore?'' By the end of 1995, Ziegler's shift into senior living bonds was a fait accompli: it underwrote more than $450 million in retirement facility construction bonds versus only $220 million for its onetime meal ticket, healthcare. But its sales strategies remained the same: send a sales rep to the retirement center and attract the interest of local investors—including the often affluent residents of the retirement centers themselves. In 1997 Ziegler's Senior Living Finance Group completed 41 financings worth $175 million—making Ziegler the largest senior living facility bond underwriter in the United States.

Ziegler was also undertaking another even more fundamental shift in its business model—stepping gradually but firmly away from its historical image as a ''bonds only'' house. When some its clients began to take their equity (or stock) investments elsewhere and the stock market boom of the 1990s began generating fortunes for equity brokerages, Ziegler decided to recast its image into a ''full-service brokerage.'' As John Wagner told *Bond Buyer* magazine, ''We also realized that to bring the younger client in, you've got to do more of the equity side of it and the mutual funds side. You still get their fixed-income business as they mature and age.'' In 1994 Ziegler began offering its customers stocks as well as bonds, and in 1997 Ziegler's Thrift Trading was set to launch the single feature perhaps most emblematic of the democratization of the U.S. stock market in the 1990s: low-commission online trading via the World Wide Web. Reflecting its decision to embrace the equity markets, in July 1997 Ziegler acquired Glaisner, Schiffarth, Grande & Schnoll and its GS;s2 subsidiary, a Milwaukee-based institutional equity sales, trading, and research firm with more than $1 billion in managed assets. Dick Glaisner, the acquired firm's CEO, became the director of Ziegler's newly organized financial services division with responsibility for its money management and equity sales operations. A newly reconstituted Ziegler securities division would handle the firm's ''capital formation, investment banking and institutional fixed-income [i.e., bond] sales and trading.'' In an indication of the early success of Ziegler's strategy to cover all the investment industry bases, sales of its mutual funds totaled $100 million in 1997.

Principal Subsidiaries

B.C. Ziegler and Company; GS;s2 Securities, Inc.; Ziegler Assets Management, Inc.; Ziegler Capital Company LLC; Ziegler Financing Corporation; Ziegler Collateralized Securities, Inc.; First Church Financing Corporation; Ziegler Thrift Trading, Inc.; WRR Environmental Services.

Further Reading

''B.C. Ziegler Co.: A 75-Year Niche in the World of Finance,'' *West Bend News,* October 15, 1977, p. 1.

''B.C. Ziegler Company Opens New Office,'' *West Bend News,* April 4, 1928, p. 1.

''B.C. Ziegler's Unfinished Autobiography Outlines Earliest Days,' *West Bend News,* October 15. 1977, p. 6.

''Bernhard C. Ziegler: 1884–1946,'' West Bend, Wis.: B.C. Ziegler and Company, n.d.

Dymale, Nan, ''Bernard C. Ziegler,'' West Bend, Wis.: B.C. Ziegler and Company, May 1988.

''Firm Expanding, Creating New Opportunities,'' *Main Street Journal,* West Bend, Wis.: B.C. Ziegler and Company, December 3–5, 1993.

Roberto, Sondra, ''Midwestern Firm Banks Its Future on Senior-Living Centers,'' *Bond Buyer,* July 2, 1996.

''Two Ziegler Brothers Leave Dart to Join Father's Firm,'' *West Bend News,* October 2, 1972, p. 1.

The Ziegler Story: 1902–1977, West Bend, Wis.: B.C. Ziegler and Company, 1977.

—Paul S. Bodine

Zondervan Publishing House

5300 Patterson Avenue, S.E.
Grand Rapids, Michigan 49530
U.S.A.
(616) 698-6900
Fax: (616) 698-3223
Web site: http://www.zondervan.com

Wholly Owned Subsidiary of HarperCollins Publishers Inc.
Incorporated: 1931
Employees: 350
Sales: $50 million (1997 est.)
SICs: 2731 Books, Publishing Only; Textbooks,
Publishing Only; 2741 Miscellaneous Publishing;
7372 Prepackaged Software

Zondervan Publishing House (ZPH), a wholly owned subsidiary of HarperCollins Publishers, is one of the largest Christian publishing companies in the world. Its products range from the best-selling New International Version of the Bible, to inspirational fiction, self-help, reference, biography, history, and textbooks, to gift products, audio- and videotapes, and multimedia software programs. Since becoming a subsidiary of HarperCollins in 1988, Zondervan has concentrated its energies on its traditional focus of religious book publishing, while extending its reach beyond the evangelical market with best-selling memoirs of Christian celebrities such as Oliver North, Colin Powell, and Dan Quayle. With problems involving hostile takeover attempts and financial improprieties now well in the past, and having divested itself of a chain of bookstores and a music company, Zondervan appears to have properly found its niche and is again doing what it does best.

Founded in 1931

Zondervan was started in 1931 by brothers Pat and Bernard Zondervan, in their mother's Grandville, Michigan farmhouse as a religious book-selling company. In 1932 the brothers opened their first bookstore in neighboring Grand Rapids. The following year saw the first two books published under the Zondervan imprint. The company's home base of West Michigan was a particularly religious, conservative area, and was a perfect locale for such a business. Grand Rapids, known as the city with the most churches per capita in the United States, was home to a number of seminaries and church-affiliated colleges, and was the headquarters of The Reformed Church in America, the Dutch Protestant sect founded on the principles of John Calvin.

From the 1930s through the 1950s, the company continued to expand. In 1959 Zondervan bought a religious music company, Singspiration. The following year the company took over publication of *Halley's Bible Handbook* from a private concern, eventually selling over four million copies of the title. Zondervan's bookstore operation had over the years expanded to a number of locations, and in the early 1960s the first outlet was opened in a shopping mall. The success of this store led the company to open in other malls, eventually placing all new outlets in such locations. In 1966 Zondervan purchased the Bible department from the larger Harper & Row publishing company, which brought to Zondervan a number of specialized Bible textbooks and Bibles, including the popular *Harper Study Bible*. That same year cofounder Bernie Zondervan died, but brother Pat continued to lead the company. Zondervan's publishing efforts included a somewhat broad range of material, not always books with a strictly conservative, religious bent. Titles such as *The Act of Marriage* by Tim and Beverly LaHaye from 1959 and *Sexual Happiness in Marriage* by Herbert Miles from 1967 were published alongside more typical fare such as biographies of missionaries, discussions of theological issues, Bible encyclopedias and concordances, and tracts on the evils of tobacco or communism. Zondervan also occasionally published religious titles with mass appeal, such as Hal Lindsey's *The Late Great Planet Earth* from 1970, which eventually sold some 10 million copies.

In 1971, Zondervan made an investment in the financially ailing International Bible Society's translation of the New International Version of the Bible, a move that would later repay itself many times over. The New Testament of the New Interna-

Company Perspectives:

ZPH publishes general and academic books, with the intent to meet the spiritual needs of people at all ages and all intellectual and interest levels. ZPH seeks to express its commitment to God's truth with a philosophy of acquisitions, writing, editing, producing, marketing, and selling that is consistent with biblical faith, practice, and ethics. ZPH determines a book's worth by its content and contribution, the goal being not only to confirm readers' faith and understanding, but also to challenge and stretch their thinking.

While ZPH publishes books within the historic evangelical mainstream of Christian faith and practice, it does not hesitate to publish books that represent the various currents within that mainstream.

tional Version was published in 1973, with Zondervan given exclusive rights in the United States. The entire Bible was ready in 1978, and it was a sensation, quickly rising on the best-seller lists to second place behind the King James Version. Zondervan was suddenly vaulted to the front ranks of religious publishing houses. The NIV, as it was known, was a scrupulous translation from the original languages into contemporary English, and it appealed to many Christians of different branches of the faith. Within a few years it had been adopted as the Bible of choice by a wide range of churches, from Baptists to Episcopalians. With the NIV also came the opportunity to create many derivative works such as concordances and study materials, all of which found a ready market.

Further Expansion in the Late 1970s and 1980s

Zondervan had gone public in 1976, issuing stock on the NASDAQ exchange. Following the success of the NIV Bible, the company began to acquire other businesses. In 1980 the John T. Benson company, a religious music publisher, was purchased, making Zondervan the second largest producer of religious recordings in the United States. In the early 1980s other acquisitions included religious publishers Chosen Books, Francis Asbury Press, and Fleming H. Revell Co., as well as Zondervan's first foreign subsidiary, Marshall Pickering Holdings Ltd., a United Kingdom-based religious publishing, printing, and music company. A specialty bindery, Tapley-Rutter Co., was also purchased at this time.

Zondervan's business, while based on the apparently steady and predictable religious book market, was actually more tenuous than appeared on the surface. In 1979 there had been difficulties related to the bookstore chain, resulting in unexpected losses. Though sales and profits had more than doubled within the next five years, with annual revenues in 1983 of $93 million, in 1984 it was discovered that the company's books had been incorrectly kept for several years running, with previously unreported losses of several million dollars. These were ultimately attributed to poor inventory control and unanticipated expenses such as unrecoverable publishing advances, but the company's chief financial officer was dismissed, and

Zondervan was sanctioned by the Securities and Exchange Commission. A lawsuit from a disgruntled New Jersey investor followed, eventually being settled out of court in 1989 for $3.6 million.

Just before the discovery of its financial problems, Zondervan had chosen James Buick as Chief Executive Officer, replacing Pat Zondervan's successor Peter Kladder, who had been with the company since 1956. Buick, previously an executive at bowling and marine equipment company Brunswick Corp., immediately had his hands full, and things continued to get worse. Zondervan posted losses for the next several years following the bookkeeping debacle, and in 1986 a hostile takeover attempt was organized by British investor Christopher Moran. After some months of wheeling and dealing, including a visit from Moran to Pat Zondervan and an emergency prayer session held by employees, the company's board reached an agreement with its stockholders to seek a third-party buyer. Not long afterwards, Moran began quietly selling off his shares. The stock price, which had been driven up by the takeover attempt, plummeted when Moran's sell-off was discovered. Many investors were angry, and when the company was finally sold over a year later for $56.7 million to Harper & Row, other lawsuits were initiated on behalf of investors who felt the board had accepted an unfairly low price. During the course of the takeover attempt, Zondervan had also sold off its Revell and Chosen Books subsidiaries, and had closed a Grand Rapids-based printing operation.

Smoother Waters Follow Purchase by Harper & Row in 1988

Harper & Row (which soon merged with Collins Publishing, a British religious book company, to form HarperCollins) was owned by The News Corporation Ltd., a conglomerate headed by Rupert Murdoch. Murdoch's other interests included the Fox film and television studios, and several tabloid-style news publications. Zondervan employees and the company's chairman emeritus expressed concerns that the publisher's traditional religious, evangelic focus would be changed as part of a more aggressive pursuit of profits, much as they had also worried about Chris Moran's intentions several years earlier. Fortunately for Zondervan, there was no apparent downside to the change of ownership, as the company's editorial policy was not altered. In fact, there was an enhancement of Zondervan's ability to cross-market titles into the mainstream. Successful books such as the memoirs of Dave Dravecky (a baseball pitcher who had lost his pitching arm), Oliver North, Colin Powell, and Dan Quayle were co-marketed or co-published with HarperCollins, enabling them to reach a larger audience. In some cases, they were from authors that Zondervan might not have been able to attract on its own, but were brought in due to the association with the larger HarperCollins. By 1991 the company's estimated annual sales were $175 million, up from $106 million just four years earlier. The publishing division was issuing an average of 130 new titles a year, with 1,000 titles in the back list.

Though its business had been on a much more even keel since the sale to HarperCollins, Zondervan management still seemed to have its doubts about the relationship remaining amicable. In mid-1992, the company's management announced it was seeking investors to help it buy the company back from HarperCollins. At around this time the rival Word publishing company came up for sale. Zondervan soon began to court Word and put the buyout plans on hold, but after Word was sold to America's top religious publisher Thomas Nelson, the company announced that the buyout plan had been abandoned. Apparently satisfied that it could remain editorially independent, Zondervan now concentrated on streamlining operations and developing new products. Sales had slumped early in 1992, with layoffs in February, and in November the company sold its Benson Music subsidiary and left the music business completely. A more major change came almost a year later. In September 1993, the company split in two, with the publishing operations retaining the name of Zondervan Publishing House, and the Family Bookstores chain becoming a separate entity (though still owned by HarperCollins, and with its offices in the same building as Zondervan). CEO James Buick, who had directed the company for almost ten years and had been instrumental in the breakup, had reorganized himself out of a job, retiring and leaving the management of Zondervan to publishing division chief Bruce Ryskamp.

With sales of personal computers beginning to surge in the late 1980s, the company had created a software division, marketing computer-formatted Bibles and study aids. Other divisions had been founded to create video and audio products, and these operations were merged in early 1995 to form ZPH New Media. Products included BibleSource for Windows, macBible, several series of religious studies and children's videos, and audio versions of some of the company's books. The products were primarily distributed to Christian bookstores.

The Mid-1990s: Bible Sales Hit Peak, Then Stagnate

The NIV Bible, which had been Zondervan's crown jewel since 1978, had remained a consistent best-seller and in 1986 had eclipsed the King James Version as the top-selling Bible. The company continued to capitalize on its success, issuing many derivative works and variant versions. Increasingly, Bible sales were being targeted to specific niche groups. One method of repackaging the NIV was to create a ''Devotional Bible,'' which added numerous prayers and commentaries directed toward a specific audience, such as mothers with young children or retirees. In late 1994, the Christian Booksellers Association's sales chart of best-selling Bibles, which had already for some years been topped by the NIV, saw Zondervan products holding down all 10 slots. It was estimated that 45 percent of all Bibles sold were NIVs. The company continued to seek new markets, purchasing in August 1995 Editorial Vida (known in the United States as Vida Publishers), a distributor of Bibles in French, Spanish, and Portuguese. Zondervan also announced a new version of the NIV called the New International Reader's Bible (or NIrV), which was written at a third grade reading level. The audience for this version was people with poor reading skills and new immigrants with a limited command of English. It was an instant success.

With so many different niche Bibles on the market (from Zondervan as well as its rivals), it was hardly surprising that Bible sales had begun to slump by 1996. Several newly published translations did poorly, and Zondervan's former chain of bookstores (now owned by its management following a 1995

buyout) reported shipping more than $200,000 worth of King James Bibles back to their publishers. Despite the industry-wide sales slowdown, Zondervan was only slightly affected, and unveiled plans for Devotional Bibles targeted at college students and African-Americans. Another Bible project embroiled the company in controversy, however.

In the years since it had been introduced, the NIV had been subject to occasional revisions, as new discoveries of ancient sources were made, or new Bible scholarship was published. In the spring of 1997 a committee of scholars was looking at making changes to a number of gender-specific terms in the translation, removing references to ''man'' and substituting gender-neutral language when a particular passage actually referred to all of humankind. This was not an especially radical move, as the committee was composed of respected, conservative scholars, and changes of this type had already been incorporated into several Bible translations including the recently published NIrV and the United Kingdom version of the NIV. However, a report in a Christian publication that implied the changes were being made as a sop to feminist radicals stirred up a great deal of anger among fundamentalists, and Zondervan decided to cancel the revision. The International Bible Society, which was responsible for the NIV and NIrV, also announced that it would revise the NIrV back to the older NIV language standards.

Despite this setback, Zondervan's business continued to do well, with the successful publication of The African-American Devotional Bible in the fall of 1997, and the scheduled rollout of The Collegiate Devotional Bible in mid-1998. The company was releasing 150 books, 80 gift products, 50 Bible products, and 50 new media products per year, with a total of 2,000 publications and other goods available. Zondervan had also, in 1995, renewed its contract with the International Bible Society to continue to publish the NIV through the year 2023, giving it almost certain continued dominance in that market. As the millennium approached, the future looked bright for the company's continued prosperity.

Principal Operating Units

Bibles, Books; New Media, Gifts; Vida Publishers.

Further Reading

''Baptists Irate Over Zondervan Plan for New Bible,'' *Grand Rapids Press*, May 14, 1997, p. A1.

''Bible Bust: Publishers Are Making Too Many Bibles for Too Few Christians,'' *Grand Rapids Press*, November 9, 1996, p. B1.

Buss, Dale, ''Fight to Take Over a Religious Publisher Becomes a Holy War,'' *Wall Street Journal*, August 14, 1986.

Calabrese, Dan, ''Family Bookstores Gets New Ownership in Zondervan Break,'' *Grand Rapids Business Journal*, December 12, 1994, p. 3.

''Captures 30% of Market—New International Version of Bible a Big Seller,'' *Los Angeles Times*, September 19, 1987, p. 4.

Couretas, John, ''Zondervan Cuts 49 From Work Force,'' *Grand Rapids Press*, February 11, 1992, p. B6.

Crossen, Cynthia, ''Harper & Row Says It Will Acquire Zondervan, Expand Religious Line,'' *Wall Street Journal*, July 14, 1988.

Grenier Guiles, Melinda, ''Zondervan Says Financial Chief Relieved of Job,'' *Wall Street Journal*, December 17, 1984.

Harger, Jim, ''Turning the Page: Zondervan's Breakup into Publishing, Bookstore Firms Is Success Story,'' *Grand Rapids Press*, May 10, 1994, p. E1.

——, ''Zondervan Gets 28 Year Contract to Publish Bible,'' *Grand Rapids Press*, June 13, 1995, p. B8.

——, ''Zondervan Splitting into Two Companies,'' *Grand Rapids Press*, September 3, 1993.

Knorr, David, ''Litigation Fails to Block Zondervan Merger,'' *Grand Rapids Business Journal*, August 15, 1988, p. 1.

LeBlanc, Doug, ''Hands Off My NIV!'', *Christianity Today*, June 16, 1997, pp. 52–53.

Luymes, Robin, ''High-Profile Books Boost Local Outlet,'' *Grand Rapids Business Journal*, November 18, 1991, p. 3.

Meehan, Chris, ''Selling the Word,'' *Grand Rapids Press*, December 28, 1997, p. G1.

——, ''Zondervan's Mission and Marketing Goals Translate into Retail Expansion,'' *Publishers Weekly*, March 9, 1984, pp. 90–93.

Perlman, Lisa, ''Christian Publisher Says Chapter on Its Woes Is Closed,'' *Los Angeles Times*, September 11, 1988, p. 7.

Ruark, James E., and Theodore W. Engstrom, ''The House of Zondervan,'' Grand Rapids, Mich.: Zondervan Publishing House, 1981.

Rublin, Lauren R., ''Do Zondervan Shareholders Have a Prayer? The Unorthodox Behavior of a Bible Publisher's Stock,'' *Barron's*, October 19, 1987, p. 18.

Schifrin, Matthew, ''Bible Bungle,'' *Forbes*, March 11, 1985, p. 123.

Simmons, Rebecca, ''Diversity—New Bible Aimed at Blacks,'' *Dayton Daily News*, October 4, 1997, p. 6C.

Steel, Johannes, ''Zondervan May Prove an Investment Made in Heaven,'' *Oklahoma City Times*, November 11, 1983, p. O.

Terbel, John, ''A History of Book Publishing in the United States,'' New York: R.R. Bowker, 1981.

Veverka, Amber, ''James G. Buick: Inside Track,'' *Grand Rapids Business Journal*, May 28, 1991, p. 5.

——, ''Zondervan Nixes Plan for Management Buyout,'' *Grand Rapids Business Journal*, October 5, 1992, p. 3.

''Zondervan Corp. Finally Finds Suitable Suitor,'' *Grand Rapids Business Journal*, July 18, 1988, p. 1.

''Zondervan Corp. Says It Expects to Post Loss of $3.5 Million for 1984,'' *Wall Street Journal*, April 17, 1985.

''Zondervan Ready to Sell Its Benson Music Business,'' *Grand Rapids Press*, November 17, 1992, p. A7.

''Zondervan's $3.5 Million Settlement Approved by Judge,'' *Associated Press*, February 27, 1989.

—Frank Uhle

INDEX TO COMPANIES

Index to Companies

Listings in this index are arranged in alphabetical order under the company name. Company names beginning with a letter or proper name such as Eli Lilly & Co. will be found under the first letter of the company name. Definite articles (The, Le, La) are ignored for alphabetical purposes as are forms of incorporation that precede the company name (AB, NV). Company names printed in bold type have full, historical essays on the page numbers appearing in bold. Updates to entries that appeared in earlier volumes are signified by the notation (upd.). Company names in light type are references within an essay to that company, not full historical essays. This index is cumulative with volume numbers printed in bold type.

United Aircraft and Transportation Co., **I**
48, 76, 78, 85–86, 96, 441, 489; **9** 416,
418; **10** 162, 260; **12** 289; **21** 140
United Airlines, I 23, 47, 71, 84, 90, 97,
113, 116, 118, 124, **128–30**; **II** 142,
419, 680; **III** 225; **6** 71, 75–77, 104,
121, 123, **128–30 (upd.)**, 131, 388–89;
9 271–72, 283, 416, 549; **10** 162, 199,
301, 561; **11** 299; **12** 192, 381; **14** 73;
21 141; **22** 199, 220; **24** 21, 22
United Alaska Drilling, Inc., **7** 558
United Alkalai Co., **I** 351
United American Insurance Company of
Dallas, **9** 508
United American Lines, **6** 398
United Arab Airlines. *See* AirEgypt.
United Artists Corp., **I** 537; **II** 135,
146–48, 149, 157–58, 160, 167, 169; **III**
721; **IV** 676; **6** 167; **9** 74; **12** 13, 73; **13**
529; **14** 87, 399; **21** 362; **23** 389. *See
also* MGM/UA Communications
Company.
United Bank of Arizona, **II** 358
United Biscuits (Holdings) PLC, II 466,
540, **592–94**; **III** 503
United Brands Company, II 595–97; **III**
28; **7** 84–85; **12** 215; **21** 110, 112
United Breweries Ltd. **I** 221, 223, 288; **24**
449. *See also* Carlsberg A/S.
United Cable Television Corporation, **II**
160; **9** 74; **18** 65
United California Bank, **II** 289
United Car, **I** 540; **14** 511
United Carbon Co., **IV** 373
United Central Oil Corporation, **7** 101
United Cigar Manufacturers Company, **II**
414. *See also* Culbro Corporation.
United City Property Trust, **IV** 705
United Co., **I** 70
United Communications Systems, Inc. **V**
346
United Computer Services, Inc., **11** 111
United Consolidated Industries, **24** 204
United Corp., **10** 44
United County Banks, **II** 235
United Dairies, **II** 586–87
United Dairy Farmers, **III** 190
United Distillers & Vintners. *See* Diageo
plc.
United Dominion Corp., **III** 200
United Dominion Industries Limited, IV
288; **8 544–46**; **16 499–502 (upd.)**
United Drapery Stores, **III** 502; **7** 208
United Drug Co., **II** 533
United Electric Light and Water Co., **13**
182
United Engineering Steels, **III** 495
United Engineers & Constructors, **II** 86; **11**
413
United Express, **11** 299
United Factors Corp., **13** 534–35
United Features Syndicate, Inc., **IV** 607–08
United Federal Savings and Loan of
Waycross, **10** 92
United Financial Corporation, **12** 353
United Financial Group, Inc., **8** 349
United 5 and 10 Cent Stores, **13** 444
United Foods, Inc., 21 508–11
United Fruit Co., **I** 529, 566; **II** 120, 595;
IV 308; **7** 84–85; **21** 110–11
United Funds, Inc., **22** 540–41
United Gas and Electric Company of New
Albany, **6** 555
United Gas and Improvement Co., **13** 182

United Gas Corp., **IV** 488–90
United Gas Improvement Co., **IV** 549; **V**
696; **6** 446, 523; **11** 388
United Gas Industries, **III** 502; **7** 208
United Gas Pipe Line Co., **IV** 489–90
United Geophysical Corp., **I** 142
United Graphics, **12** 25
United Grocers, **II** 625
United Guaranty Corp., **III** 197
United Health Maintenance, Inc., **6** 181–82
**United HealthCare Corporation, 9
524–26**; **24** 229, 231. *See also* Humana
Inc.
**The United Illuminating Company, 21
512–14**
United Image Entertainment, **18** 64, 66
United Independent Broadcasters, Inc., **II**
132
United Industrial Syndicate, **8** 545
United Information Systems, Inc., **V** 346
United Insurance Co., **I** 523
Oy United International, **IV** 349
United International Pictures, **II** 155
United Investors Life, **22** 540
United Iron & Metal Co., **14** 156
United Kent Fire, **III** 350
United Kingdom Atomic Energy Authority,
6 451–52
United Knitting, Inc., **21** 192, 194
United Liberty Life Insurance Co., **III**
190–92
United Life & Accident Insurance Co., **III**
220–21; **14** 109
United Life Insurance Company, **12** 541
United Light & Railway Co., **V** 609
United Light and Power, **6** 511
United Machinery Co., **15** 127
United Match Factories, **12** 462
United Media, **22** 442
United Medical Service, Inc., **III** 245–46
United Merchandising Corp., **12** 477
**United Merchants & Manufacturers,
Inc., 13 534–37**
United Meridian Corporation, **8** 350
United Metals Selling Co., **IV** 31
United Microelectronics Corporation, **22**
197
United Micronesian, **I** 97; **21** 142
United Molasses, **II** 582
United Mortgage Servicing, **16** 133
United Natural Gas Company, **6** 526
United Netherlands Navigation Company.
See Vereenigde Nederlandsche
Scheepvaartmaatschappij.
United Newspapers plc, IV 685–87
United of Omaha, **III** 365
United Office Products, **11** 64
United Oil Co., **IV** 399
United Optical, **10** 151
United Pacific Financial Services, **III** 344
United Pacific Insurance Co., **III** 343
United Pacific Life Insurance Co., **III**
343–44
United Pacific Reliance Life Insurance Co.
of New York, **III** 343
United Packages, **IV** 249
United Paper Mills Ltd., II 302; **IV** 316,
347–50
United Paramount Theatres, **II** 129
**United Parcel Service of America Inc., V
533–35**; **6** 345–46, 385–86, 390; **11** 11;
12 309, 334; **13** 19, 416; **14** 517; **17
503–06 (upd.)**; **18** 82, 177, 315–17; **24**
22, 133

United Pipeline Co., **IV** 394
United Power and Light Corporation, **6**
473; **12** 541
United Presidential Life Insurance
Company, **12** 524, 526
United Press Assoc., **IV** 607, 627, 669; **7**
158
United Press International, **IV** 670; **7**
158–59; **16** 166; **19** 203; **22** 453
United Refining Co., **23** 406, 408
United Resources, Inc., **21** 514
United Retail Merchants Stores Inc., **9** 39
United Roasters, **III** 24; **14** 121
United Satellite Television, **10** 320
United Savings of Texas, **8** 349
United Servomation, **7** 471–72
United Shirt Shops, Inc. *See* Aris
Industries, Inc.
United Skates of America, **8** 303
United Software Consultants Inc., **11** 65
United States Aluminum Co., **17** 213
United States Aviation Underwriters, Inc.,
24 176
United States Baking Co., **II** 542
United States Can Co., **15** 127, 129
United States Cellular Corporation, 9
494–96, **527–29**
United States Department of Defense, **6**
327
United States Distributing Corp., **IV**
180–82
United States Electric and Gas Company, **6**
447
The United States Electric Lighting
Company, **11** 387
United States Export-Import Bank, **IV** 55
United States Express Co., **II** 381, 395–96;
10 59–60; **12** 534
United States Fidelity and Guaranty Co.,
III 395
United States Filter Corporation, I 429;
IV 374; **20 501–04**
United States Foil Co., **IV** 186; **19** 346
United States Glucose Co., **II** 496
United States Graphite Company, **V**
221–22
United States Gypsum Co., **III** 762–64
United States Health Care Systems, Inc.
See U.S. Healthcare, Inc.
United States Independent Telephone
Company, **6** 332
United States Leasing Corp., **II** 442
United States Mail Steamship Co., **23** 160
United States Medical Finance Corp., **18**
516, 518
United States Mortgage & Trust Company,
II 251; **14** 102
United States National Bank of Oregon, **14**
527
The United States National Bank of
Portland, **14** 527–28
United States National Bank of San Diego,
II 355
United States Pipe and Foundry Co., **III**
766; **22** 544–45
United States Plywood Corp., **IV** 264, 282,
341; **9** 260; **13** 100; **20** 128
United States Postal Service, 10 60; **14**
517–20
United States Realty-Sheraton Corp., **III** 98
United States Satellite Broadcasting
Company Inc., **24** 226
United States Security Trust Co., **13** 466

INDEX TO INDUSTRIES

Index to Industries

IMC Fertilizer Group, Inc., 8
Imperial Chemical Industries PLC, I
International Flavors & Fragrances Inc., 9
Koppers Inc., I
L'air Liquide, I
Lawter International Inc., 14
LeaRonal, Inc., 23
Lubrizol Corporation, I
M.A. Hanna Company, 8
Mallinckrodt Group Inc., 19
Mitsubishi Chemical Industries, Ltd., I
Mitsui Petrochemical Industries, Ltd., 9
Monsanto Company, I; 9 (upd.)
Montedison SpA, I
Morton International Inc., 9 (upd.)
Morton Thiokol, Inc., I
Nagase & Company, Ltd., 8
Nalco Chemical Corporation, I; 12 (upd.)
National Distillers and Chemical
  Corporation, I
National Sanitary Supply Co., 16
NCH Corporation, 8
NL Industries, Inc., 10
Nobel Industries AB, 9
Novacor Chemicals Ltd., 12
NutraSweet Company, 8
Olin Corporation, I; 13 (upd.)
OM Group, Inc., 17
Pennwalt Corporation, I
Perstorp A.B., I
Petrolite Corporation, 15
Praxair, Inc., 11
Quantum Chemical Corporation, 8
Reichhold Chemicals, Inc., 10
Rhône-Poulenc S.A., I; 10 (upd.)
Rohm and Haas, I
Roussel Uclaf, I; 8 (upd.)
The Scotts Company, 22
Sequa Corp., 13
Shanghai Petrochemical Co., Ltd., 18
Solvay & Cie S.A., I; 21 (upd.)
Sterling Chemicals, Inc., 16
Sumitomo Chemical Company Ltd., I
Terra Industries, Inc., 13
Teva Pharmaceutical Industries Ltd., 22
TOTAL S.A., 24 (upd.)
Union Carbide Corporation, I; 9 (upd.)
Univar Corporation, 9
Vista Chemical Company, I
Witco Corporation, I; 16 (upd.)
Zeneca Group PLC, 21

CONGLOMERATES

Accor SA, 10
AEG A.G., I
Alcatel Alsthom Compagnie Générale
  d'Electricité, 9
Alco Standard Corporation, I
Alfa, S.A. de C.V., 19
Allied-Signal Inc., I
AMFAC Inc., I
Aramark Corporation, 13
Archer-Daniels-Midland Company, I; 11
  (upd.)
Arkansas Best Corporation, 16
Barlow Rand Ltd., I
Bat Industries PLC, I
Bond Corporation Holdings Limited, 10
BTR PLC, I
C. Itoh & Company Ltd., I
Cargill Inc., 13 (upd.)
CBI Industries, Inc., 7
Chemed Corporation, 13
Chesebrough-Pond's USA, Inc., 8
CITIC Pacific Ltd., 18
Colt Industries Inc., I
Daewoo Group, 18 (upd.)

Deere & Company, 21 (upd.)
Delaware North Companies Incorporated, 7
Desc, S.A. de C.V., 23
The Dial Corp., 8
Elders IXL Ltd., I
Engelhard Corporation, 21 (upd.)
Farley Northwest Industries, Inc., I
First Pacific Company Limited, 18
Fisher Companies, Inc., 15
Fletcher Challenge Ltd., 19 (upd.)
FMC Corporation, I; 11 (upd.)
Fuqua Industries, Inc., I
Gillett Holdings, Inc., 7
Grand Metropolitan PLC, 14 (upd.)
Great American Management and
  Investment, Inc., 8
Greyhound Corporation, I
Grupo Carso, S.A. de C.V., 21
Grupo Industrial Bimbo, 19
Gulf & Western Inc., I
Hankyu Corporation, 23 (upd.)
Hanson PLC, III; 7 (upd.)
Hitachi Ltd., I; 12 (upd.)
Hutchison Whampoa Ltd., 18
IC Industries, Inc., I
Inchcape plc, 16 (upd.)
Ingram Industries, Inc., 11
Instituto Nacional de Industria, I
International Controls Corporation, 10
International Telephone & Telegraph
  Corporation, I; 11 (upd.)
Istituto per la Ricostruzione Industriale, I
Jardine Matheson Holdings Limited, I; 20
  (upd.)
Jason Incorporated, 23
Jefferson Smurfit Group plc, 19 (upd.)
Justin Industries, Inc., 19
Kanematsu Corporation, 24 (upd.)
Kao Corporation, 20 (upd.)
Katy Industries, Inc., I
Kesko Ltd (Kesko Oy), 8
Kidde, Inc., I
KOC Holding A.S., I
K2 Inc., 16
Lancaster Colony Corporation, 8
Lear Siegler, Inc., I
Leucadia National Corporation, 11
Litton Industries, Inc., I; 11 (upd.)
Loews Corporation, I; 12 (upd.)
Loral Corporation, 8
LTV Corporation, I
Marubeni Corporation, 24 (upd.)
Marubeni K.K., I
MAXXAM Inc., 8
McKesson Corporation, I
Menasha Corporation, 8
Metallgesellschaft AG, 16 (upd.)
Metromedia Co., 7
Minnesota Mining & Manufacturing
  Company, I; 8 (upd.)
Mitsubishi Corporation, I; 12 (upd.)
Mitsui Bussan K.K., I
Montedison S.p.A., 24 (upd.)
NACCO Industries, Inc., 7
National Service Industries, Inc., 11
Nichimen Corporation, 24 (upd.)
Nissho Iwai K.K., I
Norsk Hydro A.S., 10
Ogden Corporation, I
Onex Corporation, 16
Orkla A/S, 18
Park-Ohio Industries Inc., 17
Pentair, Inc., 7
Preussag AG, 17
Pubco Corporation, 17
Pulsar Internacional S.A., 21
The Rank Organisation Plc, 14 (upd.)
Red Apple Group, Inc., 23

Rubbermaid Incorporated, 20 (upd.)
Samsung Group, I
San Miguel Corporation, 15
Sara Lee Corporation, 15 (upd.)
ServiceMaster Inc., 23 (upd.)
Sime Darby Berhad, 14
Standex International Corporation, 17
Stinnes AG, 23 (upd.)
Sudbury Inc., 16
Sumitomo Corporation, I; 11 (upd.)
Swire Pacific Ltd., I; 16 (upd.)
Talley Industries, Inc., 16
Teledyne, Inc., I; 10 (upd.)
Tenneco Inc., I; 10 (upd.)
Textron Inc., I
Thomas H. Lee Co., 24
Thorn Emi PLC, I
Thorn plc, 24
TI Group plc, 17
Time Warner Inc., IV; 7 (upd.)
Tomen Corporation, 24 (upd.)
Tomkins plc, 11
Toshiba Corporation, I; 12 (upd.)
Tractebel S.A., 20
Transamerica Corporation, I; 13 (upd.)
The Tranzonic Cos., 15
Triarc Companies, Inc., 8
TRW Inc., I; 11 (upd.)
Unilever PLC, II; 7 (upd.)
Valhi, Inc., 19
Valores Industriales S.A., 19
Veba A.G., I; 15 (upd.)
Viacom Inc., 23 (upd.)
Virgin Group PLC, 12
W.R. Grace & Company, I
Wheaton Industries, 8
Whitbread PLC, 20 (upd.)
Whitman Corporation, 10 (upd.)
Whittaker Corporation, I
WorldCorp, Inc., 10

CONSTRUCTION

A. Johnson & Company H.B., I
ABC Supply Co., Inc., 22
Abrams Industries Inc., 23
AMREP Corporation, 21
The Austin Company, 8
Baratt Developments PLC, I
Beazer Homes USA, Inc., 17
Bechtel Group, Inc., I; 24 (upd.)
Bilfinger & Berger Bau A.G., I
Bird Corporation, 19
Black & Veatch LLP, 22
Bouygues S.A., I; 24 (upd.)
Brown & Root, Inc., 13
CalMat Co., 19
Centex Corporation, 8
Cianbro Corporation, 14
The Clark Construction Group, Inc., 8
Dillingham Corporation, I
Dominion Homes, Inc., 19
Eurotunnel PLC, 13
Fairclough Construction Group PLC, I
Fleetwood Enterprises, Inc., 22 (upd.)
Fluor Corporation, I; 8 (upd.)
George Wimpey PLC, 12
Hillsdown Holdings plc, 24 (upd.)
J.A. Jones, Inc., 16
John Brown PLC, I
John Laing PLC, I
Kajima Corporation, I
Kaufman and Broad Home Corporation, 8
Kitchell Corporation, 14
The Koll Company, 8
Komatsu Ltd., 16 (upd.)
Kumagai Gumi Company, Ltd., I
L'Entreprise Jean Lefebvre, 23

ENGINEERING & MANAGEMENT SERVICES

ENTERTAINMENT & LEISURE

Istituto per la Ricostruzione Industriale
S.p.A., 11
The John Nuveen Company, 21
Kleinwort Benson Group PLC, II
Kohlberg Kravis Roberts & Co., 24
KPMG Worldwide, 10
MasterCard International, Inc., 9
Merrill Lynch & Co., Inc., II; 13 (upd.)
Morgan Grenfell Group PLC, II
Morgan Stanley Group Inc., II; 16 (upd.)
National Association of Securities Dealers,
Inc., 10
National Auto Credit, Inc., 16
New Street Capital Inc., 8
New York Stock Exchange, Inc., 9
The Nikko Securities Company Limited, II;
9 (upd.)
Nippon Shinpan Company, Ltd., II
Nomura Securities Company, Limited, II; 9
(upd.)
Orix Corporation, II
PaineWebber Group Inc., II; 22 (upd.)
Piper Jaffray Companies Inc., 22
The Quick & Reilly Group, Inc., 20
Safeguard Scientifics, Inc., 10
Salomon Inc., II; 13 (upd.)
SBC Warburg, 14
Shearson Lehman Brothers Holdings Inc.,
II; 9 (upd.)
Smith Barney Inc., 15
State Street Boston Corporation, 8
Student Loan Marketing Association, II
T. Rowe Price Associates, Inc., 11
Total System Services, Inc., 18
Trilon Financial Corporation, II
The Vanguard Group of Investment
Companies, 14
VeriFone, Inc., 18
Visa International, 9
Waddell & Reed, Inc., 22
Washington Federal, Inc., 17
Waterhouse Investor Services, Inc., 18
Yamaichi Securities Company, Limited, II
The Ziegler Companies, Inc., 24

FOOD PRODUCTS

Agway, Inc., 7
Ajinomoto Co., Inc., II
Alberto-Culver Company, 8
Aldi Group, 13
Alpine Lace Brands, Inc., 18
American Crystal Sugar Company, 11
American Maize-Products Co., 14
Amfac/JMB Hawaii L.L.C., 24 (upd.)
Associated British Foods PLC, II; 13
(upd.)
Associated Milk Producers, Inc., 11
Barilla G. e R. Fratelli S.p.A., 17
Beatrice Company, II
Beech-Nut Nutrition Corporation, 21
Ben & Jerry's Homemade, Inc., 10
Besnier SA, 19
Bestfoods, 22 (upd.)
Booker PLC, 13
Borden, Inc., II; 22 (upd.)
Brach and Brock Confections, Inc., 15
Brothers Gourmet Coffees, Inc., 20
Broughton Foods Co., 17
Brown & Haley, 23
BSN Groupe S.A., II
Burger King Corporation, 17 (upd.)
Cadbury Schweppes PLC, II
Cagle's, Inc., 20
Campbell Soup Company, II; 7 (upd.)
Canada Packers Inc., II
Cargill Inc., 13 (upd.)
Carnation Company, II

Castle & Cooke, Inc., II; 20 (upd.)
Cattleman's, Inc., 20
Celestial Seasonings, Inc., 16
Central Soya Company, Inc., 7
Chicken of the Sea International, 24 (upd.)
Chiquita Brands International, Inc., 7; 21
(upd.)
Chock Full o'Nuts Corp., 17
The Clorox Company, 22 (upd.)
Coca-Cola Enterprises, Inc., 13
Conagra, Inc., II; 12 (upd.)
Continental Grain Company, 10; 13 (upd.)
CPC International Inc., II
Curtice-Burns Foods, Inc., 7; 21 (upd.)
Dalgety, PLC, II
Dannon Co., Inc., 14
Darigold, Inc., 9
Dawn Food Products, Inc., 17
Dean Foods Company, 7; 21 (upd.)
DeKalb Genetics Corporation, 17
Del Monte Corporation, 7
Del Monte Foods Company, 23 (upd.)
Di Giorgio Corp., 12
Diageo plc, 24 (upd.)
Dole Food Company, Inc., 9
Doskocil Companies, Inc., 12
Dreyer's Grand Ice Cream, Inc., 17
Emge Packing Co., Inc., 11
ERLY Industries Inc., 17
Eskimo Pie Corporation, 21
Farmland Foods, Inc., 7
Fieldale Farms Corporation, 23
Fleer Corporation, 15
Flowers Industries, Inc., 12
FoodBrands America, Inc., 23
Fresh America Corporation, 20
Fromageries Bel, 23
General Mills, Inc., II; 10 (upd.)
George A. Hormel and Company, II
Gerber Products Company, 7; 21 (upd.)
Gold Kist Inc., 17
Good Humor-Breyers Ice Cream Company,
14
Gorton's, 13
Goya Foods Inc., 22
Grist Mill Company, 15
H.J. Heinz Company, II; 11 (upd.)
The Hartz Mountain Corporation, 12
Hershey Foods Corporation, II; 15 (upd.)
Hillsdown Holdings plc, II; 24 (upd.)
Hormel Foods Corporation, 18 (upd.)
Hudson Foods Inc., 13
Hunt-Wesson, Inc., 17
IBP, Inc., II; 21 (upd.)
Imperial Holly Corporation, 12
International Multifoods Corporation, 7
Interstate Bakeries Corporation, 12
Itoham Foods Inc., II
J & J Snack Foods Corporation, 24
The J.M. Smucker Company, 11
J.R. Simplot Company, 16
Jacobs Suchard A.G., II
Jim Beam Brands Co., 14
John B. Sanfilippo & Son, Inc., 14
Kal Kan Foods, Inc., 22
Kellogg Company, II; 13 (upd.)
Kikkoman Corporation, 14
King Ranch, Inc., 14
Koninklijke Wessanen N.V., II
Kraft General Foods Inc., II; 7 (upd.)
Krispy Kreme Doughnut Corporation, 21
Lamb Weston, Inc., 23
Lance, Inc., 14
Land O'Lakes, Inc., II; 21 (upd.)
Lincoln Snacks Company, 24
Malt-O-Meal Company, 22
Mars, Inc., 7
McCormick & Company, Incorporated, 7

McIlhenny Company, 20
McKee Foods Corporation, 7
Meiji Milk Products Company, Limited, II
Meiji Seika Kaisha, Ltd., II
Mid-America Dairymen, Inc., 7
Mike-Sell's Inc., 15
Monfort, Inc., 13
Murphy Family Farms Inc., 22
Nabisco Foods Group, II; 7 (upd.)
Nantucket Allserve, Inc., 22
National Sea Products Ltd., 14
Nestlé S.A., II; 7 (upd.)
New England Confectionery Co., 15
Newhall Land and Farming Company, 14
Nippon Meat Packers, Inc., II
Nippon Suisan Kaisha, Limited, II
Nisshin Flour Milling Company, Ltd., II
Northern Foods PLC, 10
NutraSweet Company, 8
Ocean Spray Cranberries, Inc., 7
Ore-Ida Foods Incorporated, 13
Oscar Mayer Foods Corp., 12
Perdue Farms Inc., 7; 23 (upd.)
Pet Incorporated, 7
Philip Morris Companies Inc., 18 (upd.)
PIC International Group PLC, 24 (upd.)
Pilgrim's Pride Corporation, 7; 23 (upd.)
Pillsbury Company, II; 13 (upd.)
Pioneer Hi-Bred International, Inc., 9
The Procter & Gamble Company, III; 8
(upd.)
Quaker Oats Company, II; 12 (upd.)
Ralston Purina Company, II; 13 (upd.)
Ranks Hovis McDougall PLC, II
Reckitt & Colman PLC, II
Rich Products Corporation, 7
Roland Murten A.G., 7
Rowntree Mackintosh, II
Russell Stover Candies Inc., 12
Sanderson Farms, Inc., 15
Sara Lee Corporation, II; 15 (upd.)
Savannah Foods & Industries, Inc., 7
Schwan's Sales Enterprises, Inc., 7
Smithfield Foods, Inc., 7
Snow Brand Milk Products Company,
Limited, II
SODIMA, II
Sorrento, Inc., 24
Stouffer Corp., 8
Sun-Diamond Growers of California, 7
Supervalu Inc., 18 (upd.)
Sylvan, Inc., 22
Taiyo Fishery Company, Limited, II
Tasty Baking Co., 14
Tate & Lyle PLC, II
TCBY Enterprises Inc., 17
Thomas J. Lipton Company, 14
Thorn Apple Valley, Inc., 7; 22 (upd.)
TLC Beatrice International Holdings, Inc.,
22
Tombstone Pizza Corporation, 13
Tone Brothers, Inc., 21
Tootsie Roll Industries Inc., 12
Tyson Foods, Incorporated, II; 14 (upd.)
Uncle Ben's Inc., 22
Unigate PLC, II
United Biscuits (Holdings) PLC, II
United Brands Company, II
United Foods, Inc., 21
Universal Foods Corporation, 7
Van Camp Seafood Company, Inc., 7
Vienna Sausage Manufacturing Co., 14
Wattie's Ltd., 7
Wisconsin Dairies, 7
WLR Foods, Inc., 21
Wm. Wrigley Jr. Company, 7
Worthington Foods, Inc., 14

Helen of Troy Corporation, 18
Helene Curtis Industries, Inc., 8
Henkel KGaA, III
Herbalife International, Inc., 17
Invacare Corporation, 11
IVAX Corporation, 11
John Paul Mitchell Systems, 24
Johnson & Johnson, III; 8 (upd.)
Kao Corporation, III
Kendall International, Inc., 11
Kimberly-Clark Corporation, III; 16 (upd.)
Kyowa Hakko Kogyo Co., Ltd., III
L'Oreal, III; 8 (upd.)
Lever Brothers Company, 9
Lion Corporation, III
Luxottica SpA, 17
Mary Kay Corporation, 9
Maxxim Medical Inc., 12
Medco Containment Services Inc., 9
Medtronic, Inc., 8
Nature's Sunshine Products, Inc., 15
Neutrogena Corporation, 17
Nutrition for Life International Inc., 22
Patterson Dental Co., 19
Perrigo Company, 12
Physician Sales & Service, Inc., 14
Playtex Products, Inc., 15
The Procter & Gamble Company, III; 8 (upd.)
Revlon Group Inc., III
Revlon Inc., 17 (upd.)
Roche Biomedical Laboratories, Inc., 11
S.C. Johnson & Son, Inc., III
Safety 1st, Inc., 24
Schering-Plough Corporation, 14 (upd.)
Shionogi & Co., Ltd., III
Shiseido Company, Limited, III; 22 (upd.)
Slim-Fast Nutritional Foods International, Inc., 18
Smith & Nephew plc, 17
SmithKline Beecham PLC, III
Sunrise Medical Inc., 11
Tambrands Inc., 8
Turtle Wax, Inc., 15
United States Surgical Corporation, 10
Wella Group, III

HEALTH CARE SERVICES

The American Cancer Society, 24
American Medical International, Inc., III
Applied Bioscience International, Inc., 10
Beverly Enterprises, Inc., III; 16 (upd.)
Bon Secours Health System, Inc., 24
Caremark International Inc., 10
COBE Laboratories, Inc., 13
Columbia/HCA Healthcare Corporation, 15
Community Psychiatric Centers, 15
CompDent Corporation, 22
Comprehensive Care Corporation, 15
Continental Medical Systems, Inc., 10
Express Scripts Incorporated, 17
Extendicare Health Services, Inc., 6
FHP International Corporation, 6
Genesis Health Ventures, Inc., 18
GranCare, Inc., 14
Health Care & Retirement Corporation, 22
Health Risk Management, Inc., 24
Health Systems International, Inc., 11
HealthSouth Rehabilitation Corporation, 14
The Hillhaven Corporation, 14
Hooper Holmes, Inc., 22
Hospital Corporation of America, III
Humana Inc., III; 24 (upd.)
Jenny Craig, Inc., 10
Kinetic Concepts, Inc. (KCI), 20
Manor Care, Inc., 6
Matria Healthcare, Inc., 17

Maxicare Health Plans, Inc., III
Mayo Foundation, 9
National Health Laboratories Incorporated, 11
National Medical Enterprises, Inc., III
NovaCare, Inc., 11
Oxford Health Plans, Inc., 16
PacifiCare Health Systems, Inc., 11
Palomar Medical Technologies, Inc., 22
PHP Healthcare Corporation, 22
St. Jude Medical, Inc., 11
Sierra Health Services, Inc., 15
U.S. Healthcare, Inc., 6
United HealthCare Corporation, 9
Universal Health Services, Inc., 6
Vencor, Inc., 16
Vivra, Inc., 18

HOTELS

Aztar Corporation, 13
Bristol Hotel Company, 23
Caesars World, Inc., 6
Carlson Companies, Inc., 22 (upd.)
Castle & Cooke, Inc., 20 (upd.)
Cedar Fair, L.P., 22
Choice Hotels International Inc., 14
Circus Circus Enterprises, Inc., 6
Club Mediterranée S.A., 6; 21 (upd.)
Doubletree Corporation, 21
Fibreboard Corporation, 16
Four Seasons Hotels Inc., 9
Granada Group PLC, 24 (upd.)
Grand Casinos, Inc., 20
Grand Hotel Krasnapolsky N.V., 23
Helmsley Enterprises, Inc., 9
Hilton Hotels Corporation, III; 19 (upd.)
Holiday Inns, Inc., III
Hospitality Franchise Systems, Inc., 11
Howard Johnson International, Inc., 17
Hyatt Corporation, III; 16 (upd.)
ITT Sheraton Corporation, III
John Q. Hammons Hotels, Inc., 24
La Quinta Inns, Inc., 11
Ladbroke Group PLC, 21 (upd.)
The Marcus Corporation, 21
Marriott International, Inc., III; 21 (upd.)
Mirage Resorts, Inc., 6
Motel 6 Corporation, 13
Omni Hotels Corp., 12
Park Corp., 22
Players International, Inc., 22
Promus Companies, Inc., 9
Red Roof Inns, Inc., 18
Resorts International, Inc., 12
Ritz-Carlton Hotel Company, 9
Santa Fe Gaming Corporation, 19
Showboat, Inc., 19
Trusthouse Forte PLC, III
Westin Hotel Co., 9

INFORMATION TECHNOLOGY

Adobe Systems Incorporated, 10
Advanced Micro Devices, Inc., 6
Aldus Corporation, 10
Amdahl Corporation, III; 14 (upd.)
America Online, Inc., 10
American Business Information, Inc., 18
American Management Systems, Inc., 11
Amstrad PLC, III
Analytic Sciences Corporation, 10
Apollo Group, Inc., 24
Apple Computer, Inc., III; 6 (upd.)
Asanté Technologies, Inc., 20
ASK Group, Inc., 9
AST Research Inc., 9
AT&T Bell Laboratories, Inc., 13
AT&T Istel Ltd., 14

Autologic Information International, Inc., 20
Automatic Data Processing, Inc., III; 9 (upd.)
Autotote Corporation, 20
Aydin Corp., 19
Battelle Memorial Institute, Inc., 10
BBN Corp., 19
Bell and Howell Company, 9
Bloomberg L.P., 21
Booz Allen & Hamilton Inc., 10
Borland International, Inc., 9
Bowne & Co., Inc., 23
Brite Voice Systems, Inc., 20
Broderbund Software, Inc., 13
CACI International Inc., 21
Cadence Design Systems, Inc., 11
Caere Corporation, 20
CalComp Inc., 13
Canon Inc., III
Caribiner International, Inc., 24
Catalina Marketing Corporation, 18
CDW Computer Centers, Inc., 16
Cerner Corporation, 16
Cheyenne Software, Inc., 12
CHIPS and Technologies, Inc., 9
Ciber, Inc., 18
Cincom Systems Inc., 15
Cirrus Logic, Incorporated, 11
Cisco Systems, Inc., 11
Citizen Watch Co., Ltd., 21 (upd.)
Commodore International Ltd., 7
Compagnie des Machines Bull S.A., III
Compaq Computer Corporation, III; 6 (upd.)
CompuAdd Computer Corporation, 11
CompuCom Systems, Inc., 10
CompuServe Incorporated, 10
Computer Associates International, Inc., 6
Computer Data Systems, Inc., 14
Computer Sciences Corporation, 6
Computervision Corporation, 10
Compuware Corporation, 10
Comshare Inc., 23
Conner Peripherals, Inc., 6
Control Data Corporation, III
Control Data Systems, Inc., 10
Corel Corporation, 15
Corporate Software Inc., 9
Cray Research, Inc., III
CTG, Inc., 11
Data General Corporation, 8
Datapoint Corporation, 11
Dell Computer Corp., 9
Dialogic Corporation, 18
Digital Equipment Corporation, III; 6 (upd.)
The Dun & Bradstreet Corporation, IV; 19 (upd.)
Dun & Bradstreet Software Services Inc., 11
ECS S.A, 12
Edmark Corporation, 14
Egghead Inc., 9
El Camino Resources International, Inc., 11
Electronic Arts Inc., 10
Electronic Data Systems Corporation, III
EMC Corporation, 12
Encore Computer Corporation, 13
Evans & Sutherland Computer Corporation, 19
Exabyte Corporation, 12
First Financial Management Corporation, 11
Fiserv Inc., 11
FlightSafety International, Inc., 9
Franklin Electronic Publishers, Inc., 23
FTP Software, Inc., 20

INSURANCE

RETAIL & WHOLESALE

TEXTILES & APPAREL

TOBACCO

TRANSPORT SERVICES

UTILITIES

WASTE SERVICES

NOTES ON CONTRIBUTORS

Notes on Contributors

AZZATA, Geraldine. Freelance writer, researcher, and editor based in Medford, Massachusetts; former academic reference librarian with graduate degrees in law and library science. She has published numerous materials in the areas of law, business, health, and online research.

BAIN, Terry. Freelance writer living in Spokane, Washington.

BIANCO, David. Freelance writer.

BODINE, Paul S. Freelance writer, editor, and researcher in Milwaukee, specializing in business subjects; contributor to the *Encyclopedia of American Industries, Encyclopedia of Global Industries, DISCovering Authors, Contemporary Popular Writers,* the *Milwaukee Journal Sentinel,* and the *Baltimore Sun.*

BROWN, Susan Windisch. Freelance writer and editor.

COHEN, M. L. Novelist and freelance writer living in Paris.

COVELL, Jeffrey L. Freelance writer and corporate history contractor.

DERDAK, Thomas. Freelance writer and adjunct professor of philosophy at Loyola University of Chicago.

DORGAN, Charity Anne. Detroit-based freelance writer.

GOPNIK, Hilary. Ann Arbor-based freelance writer.

HALASZ, Robert. Former editor in chief of *World Progress* and *Funk & Wagnalls New Encyclopedia Yearbook;* author, *The U.S. Marines* (Millbrook Press, 1993).

INGRAM, Frederick C. South Carolina-based business writer who has contributed to *GSA Business, Appalachian Trailway News,* the *Encyclopedia of Business,* the *Encyclopedia of Global Industries,* the *Encyclopedia of Consumer Brands,* and other regional and trade publications.

LEMIEUX, Gloria A. Freelance writer and editor living in Nashua, New Hampshire.

MALLETT, Daryl F. Freelance writer and editor; actor; contributing editor and series editor at The Borgo Press; series editor of SFRA Press's *Studies in Science Fiction, Fantasy and Horror;* associate editor of Gryphon Publications and for *Other Worlds Magazine;* founder and owner of Angel Enterprises, Jacob's Ladder Books, and Dustbunny Productions.

MOZZONE, Terri. Iowa-based freelance writer specializing in corporate profiles.

PEIPPO, Kathleen. Minneapolis-based freelance writer.

PFALZGRAF, Taryn Benbow. Freelance editor, writer, and consultant in the Chicago area.

SALAMIE, David E. Part-owner of InfoWorks Development Group, a reference publication development and editorial services company.

SKOLNIK, Leslie-Anne. Freelance writer living in Mount Vernon, New York.

STANFEL, Rebecca. Freelance writer living in Alberton, Montana.

UHLE, Frank. Ann Arbor-based freelance writer; movie projectionist, disc jockey, and staff member of *Psychotronic Video* magazine.

WERNICK, Ellen D. Freelance writer and editor.

WEST, Melissa. Freelance writer.

WHITELEY, Laura E. Freelance writer based in Kalamazoo, Michigan.